The American Way of Government

NEW YORK · JOHN WILEY & SONS, INC.

London · Chapman & Hall, Limited

The
American
Way
of
Government

by

ALFRED DE GRAZIA

Stanford University

NATIONAL, STATE,

AND LOCAL EDITION

Copyright © 1957 by John Wiley & Sons, Inc.

Library of Congress Catalog Card Number: 57–5911

Printed in the United States of America

Foreword

IN THIS WORK I have aimed at describing the principles and operations of the American national government in simple, clear, and direct language. I have also tried to observe certain rules that, to my mind, are of importance in introducing students to the subject. One rule is that the American way of government should not be made to appear divorced from the universal problems of government in history and in other parts of the world; the work makes numerous comparisons among nations, and contains some systematic discussion of the nature of government, of the limits on government, and of other world-wide questions.

A second rule is that, especially in the early portions of the work, *realistic* materials should be given precedence over *legalistic* materials. I do not mean to imply that no legalistic materials are realistic, for some kinds certainly are; I have tried to deal with them at length. Rather, I hoped to avoid conveying the notion that American government is a simple deduction from court decisions and statutes. The structure of every important organization is sketched; however, where the structure points to no significant discovery about the operations of government, it is relegated to a secondary and abbreviated treatment.

A third rule is that detail should be subordinated to meaning. This rule has two aspects: first, the avoidance of unnecessary description of trifles; and, second, the use of *denotative* in preference to *connotative* language, by which in part I mean talking to the subject rather than around it. Terms are defined as sharply as possible. Circuitous references to plain concepts are avoided, so that a post office is a post office and not "the home of the men in gray who carry our letters."

A fourth rule was that historical data should be rationally employed to advance the text, not utilized so as to convert it into a course in American history. I have used historical materials extensively, but I have tried to select that portion of American and world history that leads directly to an understanding of the major structural and behavioral features of American government today.

A fifth rule was to reduce the volume of argumentation and quotation throughout, so that the line of progression would not be lost amidst special disputes and redundant expressions of points of view.

Finally, I sought to treat the subjects of American government objectively, without fear or favor. The essence of politics is human conflict over ends and means; however, I have tried to reserve my own preferences regarding these subjects, conceding to professors and students their right and necessity to make their choices freely. My guiding ambition was to help students to think clearly and energetically about their government, to hold realistic expectations about its activities, and to form practical demands regarding politics and government.

Two minor rules may be mentioned. Colleagues who have experienced my addiction to footnotes in other writings may wonder at their almost complete absence in these pages; the explanation is that I thought it best to present students with as simple a format as possible. For the same reason, the bibliography, which I have found to be little used by the student save for occasionally selecting an outside reading, is placed in an appendix to the book. Perhaps it is pertinent also at this point to suggest to that rare student who may read a preface that he will find the extensive index useful in providing cross references for topics in the text; the events and principles in American government are so interconnected that many statements can be fully appreciated only in the context of related statements made under a different chapter heading.

I do not know whether to classify the fact that the book has many more illustrations than almost any other text in the field as a major or a minor feature. For those who learn easily from graphic material, it may be a major boon. For the others, my defense is that many of the charts and figures are synopses of information that would require several pages of text to relate; often the long history of an institution or trait is depicted in a simple measured line.

Another feature of the book that requires explanation concerns its treatment of rights and liberties. Often, in other textbooks, a distinct chapter surveys the whole field of rights and liberties. I believe that three types of rights and liberties may be well separated for purposes of exposition: political rights and liberties, which properly fall in the section of the book that describes political activity; judicial rights, which are best dealt with in discussion of the judicial process and the rule of law; and economic rights and liberties, whose analysis occurs appropriately in the chapter that treats of the scope and limits of governmental activity. By this arrangement, rights and liberties are explained closer to their context of thought and action. Furthermore, their different origins and the distinctive forces that enliven them may be more readily separated.

An early reader of the book questioned its emphasis upon various ideas of an economic or social nature. Thus such concepts as "authority," "parity," "law," "money," and "birth rates," and such institutions as "banks," "corporations," and "unions" are explained in detail. Although it may be asserted that these discussions reduce somewhat the attention given to the formal detail of government, I doubt that students in courses in American Government would know of such matters beforehand or could hold up their end of a hundred conversations about American government without understanding them. Therefore, if a student should know a little more political economy and political sociology for reading this text, and a little less of the details of administrative structure, he would still be more liberally educated in the balance.

A final unique element warrants explanation. Chapter 5 contains the text of the Constitution, with certain annotations. Whatever the good intentions of students, they rarely, in my experience, read the Constitution thoroughly without being coaxed or coerced into it. Its present location is designed to promote the reading of the Constitution at the proper time and with the required stress. The annotations are of a special kind; they are intended to highlight the reading of the Constitution as a document rather than to explain what it means; a number of facts that can best be learned in the process of its reading are tied directly to its text.

My thanks extend to a number of friends who have assisted me in the present work. Foremost among them is Mr. Thomas H. Stevenson, who worked side by side with me from the beginning, contributing greatly to the content and style of the text and reacting vigorously and informatively to my ideas. The book owes a great deal to him. Mrs. Jacqueline Medway solved various troublesome secretarial problems. Mrs. Irma Goldner, Documents Librarian of Stanford University, graciously lent her efficient energies to many inquiries. Others of the Stanford University Libraries were helpful, especially Mr. Joseph Belloli, the Chief Reference and Humanities Librarian. My colleagues, Professors Thomas S. Barclay, Hubert R. Marshall, Robert A. Horn, and Neal Cotter, made useful suggestions, and Professor Donald Castleberry of San Francisco State College allowed me to expound the text to a class at his institution. The names of officials of the government who responded quickly and capably to my requests for information are too many to repeat here, so that a mere salute to them must suffice. Such too must be my greeting and thanks to the colleagues and students of the past for their help—from the present moment back to the time of my first teaching assignment, at Indiana University in East Chicago, Indiana, where, at the age of twenty-one, I was told that I was old enough to teach courses in American government. When it turned out that I was also old enough to fight, I entered the Army one cold morning, fittingly enough with one of my students, who seemed pleased at this chance to discuss the place of buck privates in American government.

Many teachers who may find use for this study know more about American government than I do; wise students may take this as a hint not to set up this text against instructors, but I say it in order to invite comments from my colleagues regarding errors of fact, interpretation, omission, and balance.

ALFRED DE GRAZIA

Los Altos, California
January, 1957

NATIONAL GOVERNMENT

STATE AND LOCAL GOVERNMENT

PART I

The Roots
of American Government

Reproduced through the courtesy of the Connecticut State Library.

Government has two beginnings and no end. It began somewhere in the dawn of mankind and it begins anew in the life of each person. It has no end because no one can dispense with government, although some have tried, and because no one has proved that a future without it is possible. That government is inevitable is fairly certain. No more monumental error in the history of political theory can be recorded than the assertion of Karl Marx that communism would bring about a "withering away of the state." The triumph of communism, first in Russia and since then in other areas, has proved to be a direct route to totalitarian government, which is the exact opposite of no government at all. There is probably more truth than the average man realizes in the popular saying that "only two things are certain: death and taxes," taxes being the life companion of government. Particular governments can end. Government can change, of course, as character and

3

customs can change. But government itself is endless, save with the end of man.

Government a part of human nature

Government begins and ends with man—such a sweeping fact can be accepted only if one understands that government is part of human nature. The nature of government is the nature of man. Government is as personal to man as his appearance, his character, his religion, his friends, or his enemies. It is part of his own troubles and reflects his own genius. He can neither manage it to his entire satisfaction nor separate himself from it. He may stop reading newspapers; he may score zero on a quiz about the facts of his government; he may denounce all politics as useless or down-right evil; but he need only see a policeman, hear the national anthem, go to school, or pay a tax, in order to be embraced by attitudes, ideas, fears, hopes, or some other actual or imagined experience having to do with government. Robinson Crusoe, as soon as another man joined him on his island, faced major problems of government: he sought means of winning the respect of his Good Man Friday, of gaining power, of avoiding revolt, and of planning for education, defense, collective production, and social security. In brief, he entered inevitably into government.

Government defined

If government must exist and is part of man's nature, it is important enough to be clearly defined. Therefore let the term "government" refer to *men acting in the name of the people of a land.* The definition is simple and disarming; it makes government seem insignificant and transient. All that is needed to have government is that in any group some members act in the name of all the members. But it is not so simple to say what the definition implies. Millions of men have died under the banner of a gov-ernment; peoples have drifted apart in language and culture because they lived under different governments; one out of every seven employed Amer-icans is on a government payroll.

In truth the definition gives little inkling of the enormity of the problem of government. The larger meaning of those bland words, "men acting in the name of the people of a land," opens up a world of infinite causes and effects, loves and hates, laws and rulelessness. Perhaps the best way to understand the phrase and its consequences is to look out upon government as it began to develop with mankind and as it comes into the ken of the child.

THE ORIGINS OF GOVERNMENT

The historical development

No one knows when government began; but most scholars believe that in a real sense it began with man himself. Probably man has always lived

---

"Adoption of the Connecticut 'Fundamental Orders,' January, 1639." A mural painting by Albert Herter serves to show the strong original attachment of the New England colonists to the doctrine of the social compact.

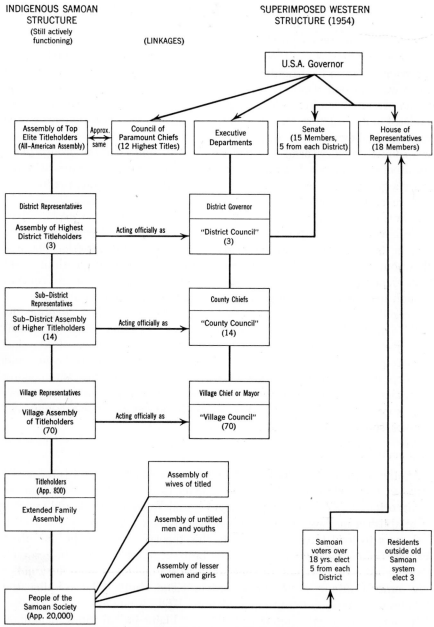

INDIGENOUS SAMOAN STRUCTURE
(Still actively functioning)

(LINKAGES)

SUPERIMPOSED WESTERN STRUCTURE (1954)

U.S.A. Governor

Assembly of Top Elite Titleholders (All–American Assembly)

Approx. same

Council of Paramount Chiefs (12 Highest Titles)

Executive Departments

Senate (15 Members, 5 from each District)

House of Representatives (18 Members)

District Representatives
Assembly of Highest District Titleholders (3)

Acting officially as

District Governor
"District Council" (3)

Sub–District Representatives
Sub–District Assembly of Higher Titleholders (14)

Acting officially as

County Chiefs
"County Council" (14)

Village Representatives
Village Assembly of Titleholders (70)

Acting officially as

Village Chief or Mayor
"Village Council" (70)

Titleholders (App. 800)
Extended Family Assembly

Assembly of wives of titled

Assembly of untitled men and youths

Assembly of lesser women and girls

People of the Samoan Society (App. 20,000)

Samoan voters over 18 yrs. elect 5 from each District

Residents outside old Samoan system elect 3

Keesing, Felix M. and Marie M., "Elite Communication in a non-Western Society: A Study of Leadership in Samoa" (unpublished manuscript).

Figure 1. The Original and Imposed Governments of American Samoa. The ancient government is still functioning and a second government has been placed alongside it. The new one is a copy of the American government in many ways whereas the old one has the strong emphasis on family organization and village assemblies that is found in a great many simple communities.

in some kind of family life. The family in turn has the fundamental traits of government, for a parent acts in the name of the other members. The usual notion of government draws rapidly closer with the form of society known as the *extended family*. In this arrangement grandparents, uncles, relatives by marriage, and cousins reside together or near one another. It is a common form of primitive society, and sometimes the form even lasts into a well-developed culture. The Scottish clan is a widely known example of the extended family. The American Indian tribe is based upon an extended family structure. So, too, is the Samoan native government, whose structure is shown in Figure 1. Frequently the oldest man rules the group, or a council of elders or of warriors decides the policies of the group. This primitive state already has the major features of the colossal states to come. It has a government, laws, a sense of owning territory, and interests in social welfare and religion.

How the family expands into the larger society has been explained in several ways by different scholars. More than one of these explanations may be true of some times and places. A series of favorable events may allow one patriarch with one or more wives, many sons, daughters, and other dependents, and great ingenuity, to gather enough property, inspire enough fear, and garner enough allies so as to establish a durable nomadic or agricultural community. Certain peoples have traced their governments back to an original lawgiver—a Hebrew Moses, a Cretan Minos, a Spartan Lycurgus, or a Roman Numa. The half-forgotten memory of a grand patriarch is suggested in the beliefs. Probably such men were leaders and codifiers of law (bringing together older laws and customs, and making them clear and consistent), rather than founders of larger societies. Americans speak of the Founding Fathers in much the same way as these ancient peoples spoke of their patriarchs centuries later.

The social compact

Another important theory to explain the source of government is the *social compact* (or contract). The social compact theory holds that government has its origins in a convenient agreement among free individuals and families to establish a method of ruling among themselves. There are few historical cases to lend forceful support to this theory. Perhaps the numerous instances of confederations provide the best examples of a kind of contract. Confederation is a voluntary and cooperative merger of various smaller governments into a larger organization. The United States under the Articles of Confederation (from 1781 until 1788) is one example. Another is the temporary combining of several Great Plains Indian tribes for buffalo hunts, after which the compounded society would disband. Also some Teutonic tribes formed temporary unions for marauding the Roman Empire in its declining years. Even the United Nations organization (UN) is a kind of confederation based on a contractual agreement among free national groups. (See Figure 123, Chapter 48.)

However, in all these cases, groups larger than individuals or families were "contracting." Only when men have been thrown together under extraordinary circumstances have examples of individual or familial contracting occurred. During the chaotic centuries following the end of the Roman Empire in western Europe, many such contracts were negotiated between the great landed nobles and lesser men, to gain servants for the former and protection for the latter; these agreements fixed mutual rights and obligations. More nearly the perfect type of the social contract was

MEMORANDUM OF AGREEMENT

WE, the undersigned, are desirous of engaging in an enterprise on the golden shores of CALIFORNIA, the paradise of America, where Summer reigns perpetually, while the fertile soil is yielding its increase abundantly, fruits growing spontaneously, fishes sporting most plentifully, and where wild game is most prolific, on the shores of the Pacific. Our object is to settle a Township, and effect a permanent settlement on the Coast of CALIFORNIA, at some central point, in some capacious and commodious harbor, where the salubrity of the climate, the fertility of the soil, mill privileges, timber for ship building and other purposes, conveniences for the fisheries, for coasting, and other natural advantages, shall warrant a healthy and rapid settlement.

For the accomplishment of the above-mentioned object, we appoint GEORGE KIMBALL, of Frankfort, county of Waldo, and State of Maine, as our lawful Agent, to purchase or build, man and equip a ship suitable to perform said voyage to CALIFORNIA ; said ship to be ready for sea by the tenth day of October, 1849. And said ship is to be considered as divided into Shares of $101 each ; and we severally agree to take as many Shares and pay as many Dollars as are set against our names below ; no one to own more than five shares in said ship. The payment of said Shares to be made as follows, viz : $10 per Share to be paid to GEORGE KIMBALL, our Agent, by the tenth day of April, 1849 ; $41 July 15, and $50 per Share to be paid to the Agent, owner or builder, September 15, and said ship is to be ready to launch by the last day of September, 1849, at which time bills of sale are to pass from the lawful owner to the several Sharesmen, who shall have made payment according to the above agreement.

Among our reasons for leaving our native shores, are the following, viz : 1st, the land has nearly all passed from government, into the hands of speculators, who exact more for the soil than we are able to pay ; 2d, the lumber is nearly gone, and the fishing business is very uncertain ; 3d, the land fails to yield its usual increase, the potatoe and some other crops being almost an entire failure ; 4th, the summers are so short, and the winters so long, that we have to become the humble servants of our cattle about eight months of the year ; 5th, the despotism of fashion is so oppressive, and its exactions so insupportable, that like our Puritan Fathers, in order to preserve our integrity, we flee into the wilds of the far distant west ; 6th, at this trying moment, Providence has opened to us a door of mercy and hope, and we gladly accept the proffered favor ; 7th, we go because a continual summer, a salubrious climate, a fertile soil, and other natural advantages, open to us an unbounded field for industry and enterprise in that region.

From two to three hundred of us will build and own a fine Packet of 600 tons, by paying $101 each ; this Packet will make one voyage per annum from MAINE to CALIFORNIA, taking out passengers, produce, &c., and return with the exports of the Pacific. We take our Families, Farming Utensils, Tools for the Mechanic, apparatus for a Saw-Mill. On our arrival the first object will be to select our Township ; 2d, build a Saw-Mill ; 3d, erect a public depot for our families and baggage until private dwellings can be built. When the Packet sails, a school will commence for all on board, where the art of Reading, Writing, Arithmetic, Navigation, Surveying, and such other branches of Natural Science will be taught as will be most needed in the new settlement.

Below is a plan of our intended village.

Central Wharf.

1	2	3	4	5	6	7	8	9	10
11	12	13	14	15	16	17	18	19	20
21	22	23	School House.				24	25	26
27	28	29	Meeting House.				30	31	32
33	34	35	Town House.				36	37	38
39	40	41	42	43	44	45	46	47	48
49	50	51	52	53	54	55	56	57	58

Each man draws by lot one block or house lot in each tier, and each lot to contain about one half an acre ; all are to settle as near together as convenient, for mutual aid and protection.

This " California Packet" is now lying at Central Wharf, Boston, February 4, 1850.

Figure 2. The Social Compact in Western Settlement. Facsimile of an agreement among pioneers to found a colony in California. Note how the plan for a new home calls for the establishment of old and familiar institutions such as the New England Town Square. No reference to the gold rush is made; perhaps to search for gold was not a respectable ideal in their society.

the Mayflower Compact, signed aboard ship by the Pilgrim men before landing and establishing Plymouth colony. The Fundamental Orders of the elders of the Connecticut Colony, drafted somewhat later, furnish another analogue. The picture that introduces this chapter shows that scene as a painter has imagined it. Even more close to the ideal was the formation of wagon trains or ships' companies to move West in pioneer days, when temporary governments had to be established for the long journey and the new settlement. Even here people were moving only from one government to another which was closer to their own ideas and interests; often the new resembled the old almost to the smallest detail. Figure 2 shows a reproduction of a contract made prior to the voyage of a ship to California.

Expansion by conquest

It is unlikely that the social compact theory, with its benign accent on the growth of government through cooperative endeavor, explains as much history as the development of government through conquest of one people by another. Probably more multi-family groups and permanent unions of peoples have occurred through the use of force than through any other means. Man may be ultimately destined to a government by cooperation of individuals or small villages, but history has given few previews of this blessed condition. On the other hand, to retrace the history of many governments is to recall, one after another, with monotonous frequency, their various conquerors, until finally the government is lost to recorded history or archeology.

UNIVERSAL BELIEFS ABOUT GOVERNMENT

The feeling of belonging

Governments during history have arisen in connection with several fundamental ideas held by men. Wherever one finds government, one finds these attitudes as well. Among them is the feeling of belonging together: men believe that they belong willingly, by their own consent, to their country and people, and that they are among those in whose name the government speaks. The illusion of free choice can become so strong as to let one pridefully sing, like the Englishman in Gilbert and Sullivan's operetta *H.M.S. Pinafore:*

> For he might have been a Roosian,
> A French or Turk or Proosian,
> Or perhaps Itali-an
> But in spite of all temptations
> To belong to other nations
> He remains an Englishman.

Comic though excesses of egotism may be, loss of a feeling of belonging would be tragic for most people. Most children and adults are deeply touched by the story of "The Man without a Country," doomed to a life in accord with his own wish that he might never see or hear the name of America again, a wish that to many hearers would be blasphemous. Feeling at one with the people and the government is akin to feeling oneself part of a family; a person is inclined to believe that both groups are right in disputes over any subject unless proved indubitably wrong. Although "my country, may she always be right, but my country, right or wrong," is a toast to a nation and not to a government, whatever government is in office benefits by the halo of near-sacredness encircling the sense of patriotism.

Respect for authority

Beside the sentiment that government exists by consent of the people stands the notion that the government demands respect. The government "is usually right" and "should be obeyed." Pronouncements of government are more respected than are those of private citizens, no matter how brilliant the men may be, nor how great their prestige. Perhaps respect for power goes back to the innumerable conquests men have made of one another. The repressive features of government have always been noteworthy; rarely has the whip or the chain been far from the hand that rules. Wanting to belong to the group they are inalterably part of, men change their attitude toward sheer power. Instead of reluctantly conceding that the government in fact has, or ought to have, naked power—the ability to bend others to its will—they assign to government a rightful power that is called *authority*.

Civic training

In its turn the government, to make its work easier and its acceptance among the people greater, trains each generation in citizenship. Primitive headmen or elders may not call it by name, but they will faithfully attend to the civic training of their population. In both the simplest and the most complex societies, citizens learn those political beliefs that people must hold and those government symbols that must be admired or adored. The flag, the national anthem, patriotic holidays, and other such institutions are the modern counterparts of the age-old training of men to fit well the role they must play in government. A thoroughly trained population is likely to feel at one with the government—superior to other peoples, respectful of the government's authority, and eager to assist it in its operations and endeavors.

Sovereignty and law

In fact, the belief in authority often reaches such an intensity that people hold their government to be all-powerful; it has to account to no one; it is a free agent in the world. Many people will become quite angry when this belief about their government is disputed, either by insiders or by foreigners; indeed, the defense of national sovereignty (a term which, though it has several meanings, is often used to describe this belief) has been a major justification for at least one side in most of the international wars that have occurred in the past three centuries.

From its august and austere throne of sovereignty, authority, and power, the government makes rules known as laws. Laws direct people to behave

or not to behave in certain ways; there is an excellent chance that their
violation will result in the arrest, conviction, and punishment of the cul-
prit. Laws are obeyed for one or more of the following reasons: people
believe that the government should be obeyed; they are habituated to obeying laws; they realize that other people cherish the laws; and they are
directly afraid of the penalties or sanctions of the law.

THE WEAKNESS OF GOVERNMENT

Despite all its sources of support, government is never immune to change
by the people in whose name it rules. It must constantly recruit new
officials; being itself composed of people, it must have some contact with
other people who are not government officials; there may be disgruntled
elements in the government; and outside factions and critics abound. All
of these forces play a part in bringing change to government. A political
process ensues—politics more or less as Americans know it—that consists
of the varied efforts of men and women to achieve different goals under the
umbrella of government. Sometimes they try to hold the umbrella themselves. On occasion the political process becomes so chaotic that the sovereignty and authority of the government vanish. A revolution follows. Then
power, stripped of authority, has to be constantly proved before its orders
are carried out; manipulation, violence, and propaganda flourish. People
feel insecure, unloved, suspicious, and some even become neurotic, until
political order is reborn.

The average life of states

Some government must exist; however, particular governments are far
from permanent. To begin with, the classic political unit is the *state* (not
to be confused with an American State, which is not a *state* in the accepted
sense). A state may be defined as a group of people inhabiting a definite
territory under a relatively stable government which possesses sovereignty.
(The American States do not possess full sovereignty.) Figure 3 demonstrates how in the Chinese language these elements are combined to form
the single ideogram for "state." Following this definition, the average life
of states through history is shorter than 300 years, far shorter than that of
a good olive grove or a clump of California redwood trees. About two-
thirds of the states of the present world did not exist at the time of the
American Revolution. One-third did not exist before World War I.

But states last longer than kinds of governments. If one noted changes
from monarchies to republics, republics to dictatorships, and so on, one
would find that even among the old states there are very few old governments. Of the ninety-odd states in the world, barely a half-dozen have a
general frame of government as old as that of the United States.

Particular governments fall into the shadows of history at an even faster
rate than general frames of government. A particular government may be
regarded as the rule of any one individual or group within a general frame
of government. One speaks of the "government" of the Conservative Party

Figure 3.   An Ancient Chinese Idea of the "State."   The Chinese ideograph for "state," in modern script, is:

Perhaps for 2000 years, Chinese lexicographers, in analyzing this symbol, have given to it a meaning remarkably similar to that used by modern political science. A traditional analysis of the graph maintains the following:

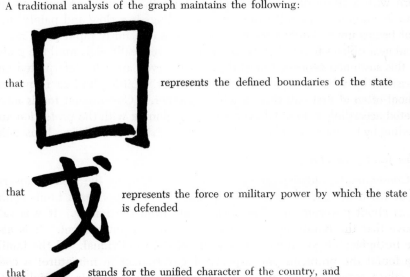

that   represents the defined boundaries of the state

that   represents the force or military power by which the state is defended

that   stands for the unified character of the country, and

that   signifies the ruler or his capital

in Great Britain, and of the "government" of Marshal Bulganin in the Soviet Union. American constitutions prescribe a rapid rate of turnover for the particular governments. The turnover is periodic (for example, two years for the House of Representatives) and fixed. Other governments turn over quite rapidly but erratically; for instance, the French government, composed of the Premier and his cabinet, changed twenty times between 1945 and 1955 alone, at irregular intervals.

Durability of cultures

The state, or the nation, as it is sometimes called, exists longer than kinds of governments or particular governments, as can be seen from the definition above. Cultures and civilizations, such as the Greco-Roman and the Arabic, are the most long-lived of all great communities, for they may include one after another several great states which possess the same cultural characteristics. For evident reasons, they are also fewest in number: Oswald Spengler, in his *Decline of the West,* unearthed only eight major cultural cycles; and Arnold Toynbee, using in his *Study of History* somewhat different grounds of choice from those of Spengler, discovered only twenty-one of what he considered to be authentic civilizations in the history of mankind.

DEVELOPMENT OF THE IDEA OF GOVERNMENT IN THE CHILD

The infant obviously is not born with a sense of government. He is not born with a sense of anything outside himself. He has no outer world. The separation of himself from his surroundings is a slow and painful task that begins immediately after birth, continues at a fairly rapid pace, moves from near objects to far objects, and in fact never really ends until the grave. In this sustained process, things that are observed are later interpreted and classified by what is seen and learned earlier. Little children in nursery school often at first call their teachers "mother." Government too is interpreted according to familial experiences, beginning with the protection and feeding by the mother and extending to the activities of the larger household.

The family as state

Consequently, although the child may be baffled by the idea of government when he first encounters it, he already possesses some fundamental ideas about government. The ideas come from the family. It was said above that the family was probably the primeval government. It is also the birthplace of government in the life of each individual. In the family are found the problems and aspects of government in miniature: a code of ethics regarding sex, manners, and property; economic specialization between the wage-earner (or hunter) and the kitchen supervisor; the ruling and education of the young; laws regarding the creation, use, and transfer of property; sanctions for violations of ethics and rules that include force, deprivation of food, and ostracism or milder psychological penalties; feelings that the parents are all-powerful, right, and authorized to penalize offenders; and the opposing rebellious feelings that come from parental inconsistency, outsiders' "subversive" comments, and the frustrating of strong desires of all kinds.

The parents as governors

The infant is born helpless and utterly dependent upon his attendants. Not until puberty do most children lose their need for immediate attention; not until passing through adolescence are most of them freed completely of physical dependence. During all of this time, they learn of the "superpower" of their parents to love and to punish. Wherever they may go, and however independent they may feel, people as adults are likely to expect, to some degree, a similar kind of super-power in the government. The place of the parents is assumed by the rulers of the motherland or fatherland. Government is expected to rule as parents do—with laws, sanctions, mercy, and competence. Government is expected to help one, as parents do. It is more remote and indirect than parents; but that distance is well adapted to one who has passed into adulthood.

Earliest impressions of political government

The child learns in his first few years of life that the government is an unusual "they." "They" are protectors; the police, the army, and the firemen are common visitors to the child's mind. "They" are also punitive; police can arrest speeders and soldiers can kill "bad" enemies. "They" are inclusive: those that belong with them have a warming comradeship, with flags, songs, holidays, processions, and heroic stories; the belongers, their land, and the government are all together part of the political community known as the state. "They" are also restrictive; those that do not belong with "them" are different, suspect, perhaps to be feared or admired at a distance. "They" are demanding; they ask for taxes or service, so that at times it seems a rather exacting family to belong to.

Thus goes the process of learning about government as a child: ideas that are first acquired in the family are transferred to new conditions and underlie the child's notions of government. Lest the picture be painted too sharply, it is well to realize that, as families vary greatly, so likewise do children's and adults' relations with the government. These are the differences that make politics. The point to be made is that certain experiences are sufficiently widespread among families and cultures to have influence upon the organization and operations of government, in America as well as in the rest of the world.

QUESTIONS AND PROBLEMS

1. What is meant by the statement that government is part of human nature?

2. In what ways does the foundation of a club, sorority, fraternity, association, or another group on campus resemble the theory of the social compact? How may it be different?

3. Write a 300-word essay on what you can recall as your first impressions of government.

4. Using the *Statesman's Year-Book*, the *Encyclopedia Americana*, or the *Encyclopedia Britannica*, find one case of a state that has existed for more than 500 years, one state with a form of government that has lasted for over 200 years, and one particular government that has held office for twenty-five years. Avoid examples given in the text.

5. Write a 300-word essay comparing your family "government" when you were a child with the general psychological characteristics of government as outlined in the text.

6. In what ways do the following organizations possess one or more of the four cardinal elements of the state? Canada; Illinois; Hong Kong; the Communist Party of the Soviet Union; the American Navy; the Congress of Industrial Organizations; the United Automobile Workers; the American Medical Association; the Episcopal Church; the Roman Catholic Church; the Democratic

Party; the National Association of Manufacturers; and, finally, your own family structure.

7. Name two states whose citizens speak more than one language; name two states whose territory is little more than that of one city; name one state in which the tribal pattern of constantly changing residence is still quite noticeable; name three states whose existence may be questioned because it is difficult to decide whether or not they are independent. Explain your answers.

Reproduced through the courtesy of the Historical Society of Pennsylvania, Philadelphia.

"SURELY," someone will say, "a government is more than a mental complex." It is indeed. Be it American or Japanese, it is also made up of ideas, people, tasks, and tools. This chapter will introduce these four elements of government and show how the American way of government shares them in an essential manner with the governments of other peoples but puts them together in a different fashion.

POLITICAL DOCTRINES

Political doctrines are the beliefs that men hold about the nature and the goals of the state. What is the aim of government? Who should be helped

15

or harmed by government? What persons make the best leaders and how should they be chosen? What are the limits to the things that governments should do and to the ways in which they are done? These are questions that one poses to the political philosophers because the political philosophers are, in a way, specialists in advising people what is good for them. However, often the philosophers do not agree in their prescriptions, so that one must choose from among them. Furthermore, for better or worse, most people—both the ordinary sort and the highly placed—have never adopted the habit of consulting philosophers. But two other classes of moral advisers are available—public opinion and politicians. All three groups yield political doctrines in abundance; that is, they give many and conflicting answers to the questions set forth above.

Merely knowing this fact is useful. When the question is asked: "What is American political doctrine?" or "What are the American ideals?," a preliminary (and sometimes annoying) logical response can be made, as follows:

American political doctrines or ideals (and those of any other nation, for that matter) consist of:

1. *The doctrines of political philosophers,* who (*a*) when they are alive, are usually to be found in universities, writing, conferring, and lecturing; and who (*b*) when they are dead, give the present generation ideas in broad forms: as written works, exemplary lives, and living laws and institutions founded in part upon their beliefs.

2. *The doctrines of politicians,* who (*a*) may be alive and able to apply their beliefs to current issues or (*b*) may be dead and afford the present their writings and deeds, and the laws and institutions descended from them.

3. *The doctrines of the public,* which (*a*) may be the present public, whose habits and beliefs weigh heavily in the reckonings of philosophers and politicians as to what should be done and what can be done by the government, and (*b*) may have been another generation or a series of generations and whose ideas have affected the present as popular beliefs, myths, folk tales, practices, and customs—many of them incorporated into the present institutions of government.

The response to the question, "What is American political doctrine?" should also point out that none of the groups mentioned is or has been unanimous in its conclusions. Most of the time the groups have been split. The philosophers argue amongst themselves and with dead philosophers; they argue with living and dead politicians; they argue before a living audience; and so on. Whether or not their human occupants are aware of it, the dining halls, barber shops, newspaper offices, and workshops of the land play their part. The debate is complicated and endless. It is bewildering, fascinating, and, of course, crucial in the lives of all Americans.

"Congress Voting Independence," July 4, 1776, painting by R. E. Pine and Edward Savage. The Declaration of Independence was a document and an event with many meanings. It is particularly important to this chapter inasmuch as it presented to the world a clear and complete set of political doctrines to which a group of political leaders subscribed their lives and fortunes.

Some leading American doctrines

Some of the leading American doctrines may be mentioned here; others may be noted elsewhere in the book. The Declaration of Independence and the Preamble to the Constitution come close to being authoritative doctrine

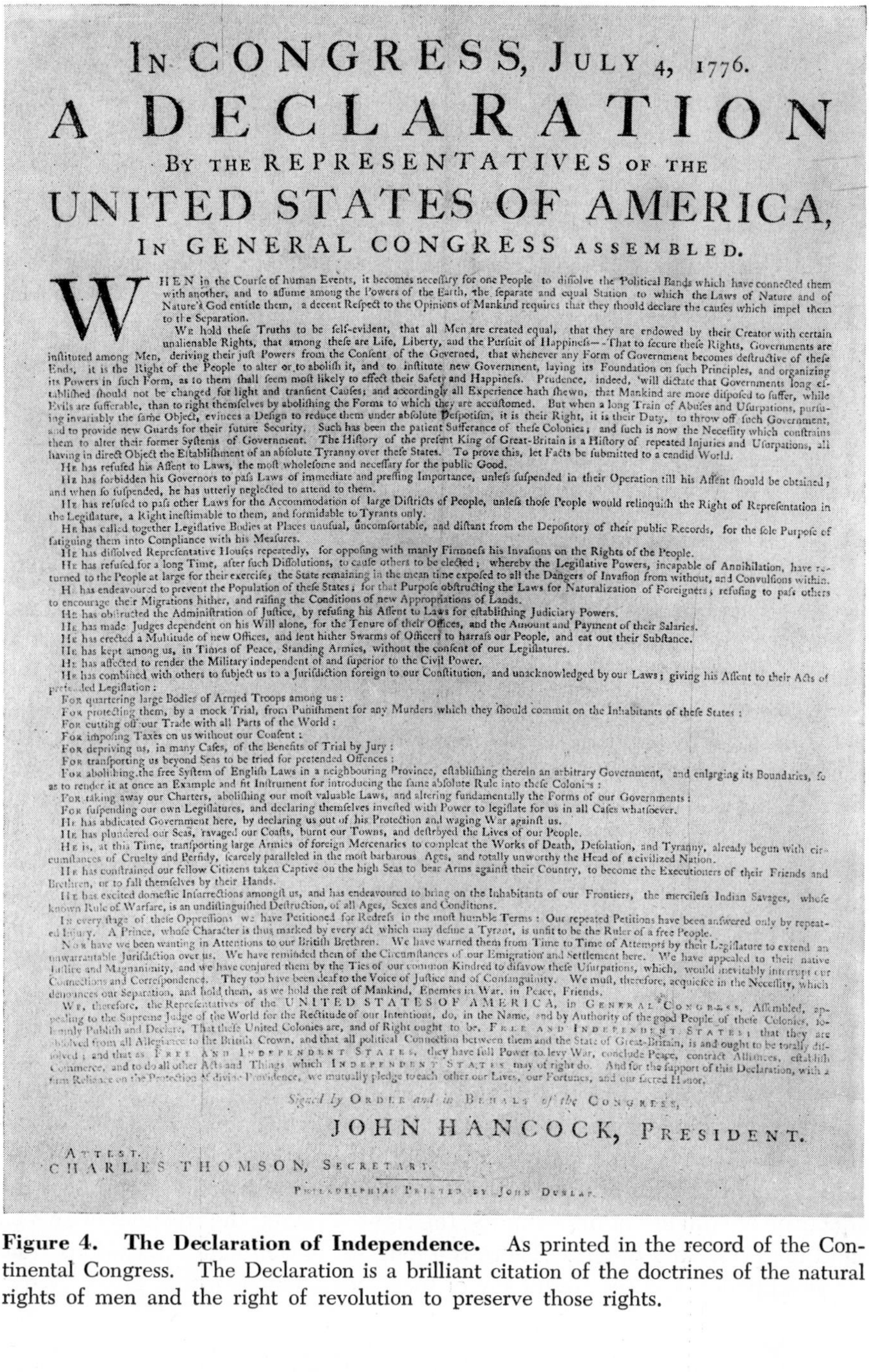

IN CONGRESS, JULY 4, 1776.

A DECLARATION

BY THE REPRESENTATIVES OF THE

UNITED STATES OF AMERICA,

IN GENERAL CONGRESS ASSEMBLED.

WHEN in the Course of human Events, it becomes necessary for one People to dissolve the Political Bands which have connected them with another, and to assume among the Powers of the Earth, the separate and equal Station to which the Laws of Nature and of Nature's God entitle them, a decent Respect to the Opinions of Mankind requires that they should declare the causes which impel them to the Separation.

WE hold these Truths to be self-evident, that all Men are created equal, that they are endowed by their Creator with certain unalienable Rights, that among these are Life, Liberty, and the Pursuit of Happiness—That to secure these Rights, Governments are instituted among Men, deriving their just Powers from the Consent of the Governed, that whenever any Form of Government becomes destructive of these Ends, it is the Right of the People to alter or to abolish it, and to institute new Government, laying its Foundation on such Principles, and organizing its Powers in such Form, as to them shall seem most likely to effect their Safety and Happiness. Prudence, indeed, will dictate that Governments long established should not be changed for light and transient Causes; and accordingly all Experience hath shewn, that Mankind are more disposed to suffer, while Evils are sufferable, than to right themselves by abolishing the Forms to which they are accustomed. But when a long Train of Abuses and Usurpations, pursuing invariably the same Object, evinces a Design to reduce them under absolute Despotism, it is their Right, it is their Duty, to throw off such Government, and to provide new Guards for their future Security. Such has been the patient Sufferance of these Colonies; and such is now the Necessity which constrains them to alter their former Systems of Government. The History of the present King of Great-Britain is a History of repeated Injuries and Usurpations, all having in direct Object the Establishment of an absolute Tyranny over these States. To prove this, let Facts be submitted to a candid World.

HE has refused his Assent to Laws, the most wholesome and necessary for the public Good.

HE has forbidden his Governors to pass Laws of immediate and pressing Importance, unless suspended in their Operation till his Assent should be obtained; and when so suspended, he has utterly neglected to attend to them.

HE has refused to pass other Laws for the Accommodation of large Districts of People, unless those People would relinquish the Right of Representation in the Legislature, a Right inestimable to them, and formidable to Tyrants only.

HE has called together Legislative Bodies at Places unusual, uncomfortable, and distant from the Depository of their public Records, for the sole Purpose of fatiguing them into Compliance with his Measures.

HE has dissolved Representative Houses repeatedly, for opposing with manly Firmness his Invasions on the Rights of the People.

HE has refused for a long Time, after such Dissolutions, to cause others to be elected; whereby the Legislative Powers, incapable of Annihilation, have returned to the People at large for their exercise; the State remaining in the mean time exposed to all the Dangers of Invasion from without, and Convulsions within.

HE has endeavoured to prevent the Population of these States; for that Purpose obstructing the Laws for Naturalization of Foreigners; refusing to pass others to encourage their Migrations hither, and raising the Conditions of new Appropriations of Lands.

HE has obstructed the Administration of Justice, by refusing his Assent to Laws for establishing Judiciary Powers.

HE has made Judges dependent on his Will alone, for the Tenure of their Offices, and the Amount and Payment of their Salaries.

HE has erected a Multitude of new Offices, and sent hither Swarms of Officers to harrass our People, and eat out their Substance.

HE has kept among us, in Times of Peace, Standing Armies, without the consent of our Legislatures.

HE has affected to render the Military independent of and superior to the Civil Power.

HE has combined with others to subject us to a Jurisdiction foreign to our Constitution, and unacknowledged by our Laws; giving his Assent to their Acts of pretended Legislation:

FOR quartering large Bodies of Armed Troops among us:

FOR protecting them, by a mock Trial, from Punishment for any Murders which they should commit on the Inhabitants of these States:

FOR cutting off our Trade with all Parts of the World:

FOR imposing Taxes on us without our Consent:

FOR depriving us, in many Cases, of the Benefits of Trial by Jury:

FOR transporting us beyond Seas to be tried for pretended Offences:

FOR abolishing the free System of English Laws in a neighbouring Province, establishing therein an arbitrary Government, and enlarging its Boundaries, so as to render it at once an Example and fit Instrument for introducing the same absolute Rule into these Colonies:

FOR taking away our Charters, abolishing our most valuable Laws, and altering fundamentally the Forms of our Governments:

FOR suspending our own Legislatures, and declaring themselves invested with Power to legislate for us in all Cases whatsoever.

HE has abdicated Government here, by declaring us out of his Protection and waging War against us.

HE has plundered our Seas, ravaged our Coasts, burnt our Towns, and destroyed the Lives of our People.

HE is, at this Time, transporting large Armies of foreign Mercenaries to compleat the Works of Death, Desolation, and Tyranny, already begun with circumstances of Cruelty and Perfidy, scarcely paralleled in the most barbarous Ages, and totally unworthy the Head of a civilized Nation.

HE has constrained our fellow Citizens taken Captive on the high Seas to bear Arms against their Country, to become the Executioners of their Friends and Brethren, or to fall themselves by their Hands.

HE has excited domestic Insurrections amongst us, and has endeavoured to bring on the Inhabitants of our Frontiers, the merciless Indian Savages, whose known Rule of Warfare, is an undistinguished Destruction, of all Ages, Sexes and Conditions.

IN every stage of these Oppressions we have Petitioned for Redress in the most humble Terms: Our repeated Petitions have been answered only by repeated Injury. A Prince, whose Character is thus marked by every act which may define a Tyrant, is unfit to be the Ruler of a free People.

NOR have we been wanting in Attentions to our British Brethren. We have warned them from Time to Time of Attempts by their Legislature to extend an unwarrantable Jurisdiction over us. We have reminded them of the Circumstances of our Emigration and Settlement here. We have appealed to their native Justice and Magnanimity, and we have conjured them by the Ties of our common Kindred to disavow these Usurpations, which, would inevitably interrupt our Connections and Correspondence. They too have been deaf to the Voice of Justice and of Consanguinity. We must, therefore, acquiesce in the Necessity, which denounces our Separation, and hold them, as we hold the rest of Mankind, Enemies in War, in Peace, Friends.

WE, therefore, the Representatives of the UNITED STATES OF AMERICA, in GENERAL CONGRESS, Assembled, appealing to the Supreme Judge of the World for the Rectitude of our Intentions, do, in the Name, and by Authority of the good People of these Colonies, solemnly Publish and Declare, That these United Colonies are, and of Right ought to be, FREE AND INDEPENDENT STATES; that they are absolved from all Allegiance to the British Crown, and that all political Connection between them and the State of Great-Britain, is and ought to be totally dissolved; and that as FREE AND INDEPENDENT STATES, they have full Power to levy War, conclude Peace, contract Alliances, establish Commerce, and to do all other Acts and Things which INDEPENDENT STATES may of right do. And for the support of this Declaration, with a firm Reliance on the Protection of divine Providence, we mutually pledge to each other our Lives, our Fortunes, and our sacred Honor.

Signed by ORDER *and in* BEHALF *of the* CONGRESS,

JOHN HANCOCK, PRESIDENT.

ATTEST.
CHARLES THOMSON, SECRETARY.

PHILADELPHIA: PRINTED BY JOHN DUNLAP.

Figure 4. The Declaration of Independence. As printed in the record of the Continental Congress. The Declaration is a brilliant citation of the doctrines of the natural rights of men and the right of revolution to preserve those rights.

for both people and leaders. The Declaration, whose text appears in Figure 4, describes the conditions under which revolution is morally permissible; both proclaim the sovereignty of the people; and the Preamble asserts that the ends of the government are to "form a more perfect union, establish justice, insure domestic tranquillity, provide for the common defense, promote the general welfare, and secure the blessings of liberty to ourselves and our posterity." All of these doctrines have long histories in political philosophy and political activity; the Declaration, for example, takes almost verbatim phrases from the writings of a philosopher dead nearly three-quarters of a century in 1776, John Locke (1632–1704); and Locke himself had imbibed from Aristotle and the heady draughts of rebellion in seventeenth-century England. Other principles of the Constitution, such as the right to own property, the freedom of religion, and the like, are discussed more fully in later chapters, as a glance at the Index will show.

The Constitution does not clearly emphasize the belief in equality; but anyone with a slight knowledge of Americans will adduce the belief as perhaps the most prominent of all. Alexis de Tocqueville (1805–1859), the famous early French writer on American government, and Gunnar Myrdal, a present-day Swedish sociologist who came to the United States a century after de Tocqueville, are expert foreign witnesses to the preeminence of the belief in equality. The list presented in Table 1 contains some of the other attitudes of Americans and the behavior associated with these attitudes.

Differences between doctrine and behavior

These are some of the important fundamental political beliefs of large numbers of Americans. They lack concreteness, of course. They do not describe at all accurately the moral or ethical *conduct* of American politicians and the American public. They are ideals separated from the institutions that are set up to carry them out. One cannot judge their full meaning, nor their effectiveness as ideals, unless one follows them into the everyday thinking of Americans. One would not say that a man who cheats his neighbor six days a week and on the seventh worships a God of charity who taught, "And as ye would that men should do to you, do ye also to them likewise," could be described as one who *practiced* Christian doctrine. One would not say so even if the man held this belief to be a cardinal truth.

The behavior of Americans deviates to a considerable extent from the fundamental doctrines they profess. For instance, some of the belief in equality is withdrawn by some Americans in special ways. Thus, American Negroes are sometimes not treated as equals, even by persons who believe in equality for everyone else. Also, part of the belief in equality holds that every man is entitled to occupy public office; yet many believe that government offices should be manned by those especially trained for careers in government. That is, Americans display the lapses from the state of grace that are typical of mankind. Also, they frequently deny specific portions of the doctrine of equality of opportunity, the right of revolt, the freedom of speech and the press, and others. There is a long list of deliberate deviations from avowed belief, and the frequency of these deviations is rather great. How-

TABLE 1.   TRAITS THAT WRITERS HAVE AGREED ARE TYPICALLY AMERICAN[1]

Despite opposing evidence and diverging opinion, it was possible for Mr. Coleman to compile a list of traits which were so often mentioned by writers on Americanism that they may well have a strong basis in fact.

Sovereignty of the people, characteristically exercised through *public opinion* (a manifestation of democracy that receives such emphasis as to necessitate separate mention).

Equality of all, a fundamental belief and in large degree a fact.

Individualism, rugged or otherwise, in all realms of life, but especially in the economic.

Worship of schooling, and universal public education—this whether the motivation be materialistic or idealistic, and despite superficiality of the schooling and a distrust of academic theory in practical life.

Distrust of strong government, especially as expressed in an overemphasis on division of responsibility and "checks and balances."

Love of size and bigness, based on an actual fact of bigness everywhere.

Adaptability and freedom from the past; openness to change, and fact of constant change and revolution.

Associational activity, an aptitude for organization that makes Americans the world's greatest organizers and joiners, and the doing by means of such voluntary organizations of many things that elsewhere would be done by governmental action or not at all.

Optimism, especially as expressed in a belief in progress and a faith in the perfectability [*sic*] of man.

Opportunity, especially the belief in equal opportunity for all and the fact of much greater opportunity than in most other countries.

Constitutional government and the great power of the judiciary—limitation on the immediate will of the majority and the presence of a power higher than the legislature, plus the position of the judges as arbiters of the validity of laws.

"Localism"—local government, local patriotism, local initiative and responsibility.

"Missionary spirit"—reforming others, interfering with their lives, making over the world.

Humanitarianism and philanthropy, sympathy for the "under-dog"—this more than in any other country in the world.

Spirit of the pioneer and tradition of the frontier—the strong influence of the "great open spaces" and the pioneer way.

National self-consciousness and conceit, incessant bragging and boasting, sensitiveness to criticism.

Mobility, migration, restlessness—the world's most mobile people.

Liberty, freedom, independence—all-important ideals and to a large extent actualities, except for some notable exceptions.

Emphasis on money-making, and belief that it is duty and virtue—but not money-making to the exclusion of idealism, philanthropy, and "service."

Desire for peace and disbelief in war, especially as expressed in pacifism, and a belief in arbitration and the rights of neutrals.

Political isolationism, "freedom from entangling alliances."

Practicality, absence of theories and philosophizing, and disbelief in them.

Dominance of women, their freedom and high status.

Party government and party loyalty, straight-party voting.

Widespread popular knowledge and education—this despite credulousness and a "passion for humbug."

Glorification of the "common man" at the expense of the "expert" and the intellectual.

Ingenuity and invention, high level of initiative and research.

[1] From "What is American," Coleman, Lee, *Social Forces*, 19 (1940–1941), 496–497.

ever, for all human beings there is a gap between fundamental doctrine and actual behavior. Still, it is most questionable whether Americans tend, more than most Europeans, South Americans, or Asiatics, to violate their protestations of doctrine.

POLITICAL LEADERS

Doctrine helps to establish, and then permeates, the governmental structure. The doctrines of the Founding Fathers live today in the structure of government that issues from the Constitution. Leaders direct institutions, and, to a greater or lesser extent, accomplish changes in them. Leaders are, particularly in America, in close contact with the public, so that the behavior of both contributes to the structure of government.

Traditional classification of leaders

The question of what types of political leaders dominate a government was one that greatly concerned the ancient Greeks. The most famous of all classifications came from them; it is still very widely used. It distinguishes three types of governments, according to the number of their political leaders: governments directed by one man, by the few, and by the many. The first was called a tyranny (a word which for the Greeks did not have the exclusively bad sense that it has today); the second, an oligarchy; and the third, a democracy. Sometimes the first form was termed a monarchy; and sometimes the second, an aristocracy.

Confusion in classification

These categories have been useful, but they have also caused much confusion. For example, the British government has the form of a monarchy, since it has a single hereditary ruler. Yet it has also been called a democracy, for all the people vote for and elect Parliament, which is the source of the active power of the government. Moreover, England was for many years an obvious aristocracy, since power was concentrated in the grasp of a few wealthy, landed nobles and businessmen. There have been other governments which have shared traits of more than one type of government, according to the Greek system of classification.

Indeed, it is noteworthy that there have been and are many governments that were or are democracies in form but oligarchies in fact. Some of the most evident instances today include the Soviet Union, Poland, Czechoslovakia, Hungary, Romania, Eastern Germany, China, and so on; many Latin American countries also fit this pattern. In fact, when the government of any country is closely inspected, it reveals some degree of concentration of power in a few hands. Even a country as near to an absolute tyranny as that which exists in Yugoslavia under Marshal Tito, for example, exhibits traces of oligarchy; for the leader depends heavily upon the men about him, and they exercise great powers in their own right.

Consequently the ancient classification has been to some degree supplanted in modern times by the theory that all governments, whatever their form, are ruled more or less by a few leaders. They are all oligarchies of some kind. The important phrase here is "more or less." How exclusive are the few? How powerful are they? How do they become powerful? What are their policies? In other words, the formal name of the kind of government is an important fact; but to appreciate who actually runs the government, one must discover the answers to the above questions.

Much will be said later of the situation of the American government with respect to the concentration of power or the filtering down of power into the public; this latter, of course, is a trend toward democracy. At the moment, it is well to declare merely that the size of the effective ruling group in America is very large by standards of past and present governments. The form of American government is not fully democratic; that is, there is some ambiguity about its being in form a democracy, because there are limitations in its structure on the rule of the majority of the people. Examples are the non-elected federal judges, and equal representation of the States in the Senate.

Governments are also often classified as either hereditary or republican. Here again there is confusion. A hereditary government is usually, but not always, a monarchy; and a republican government is frequently, but not necessarily, a democracy. For instance, the powerful, wealthy, and long-lived Venetian Republic actually became a hereditary oligarchy. The Roman Republic was long ruled by a hereditary Senate. The French Senate in 1804 put forward the remarkable proposition that "The government of the Republic is entrusted to an emperor," and a popular vote approved making Napoleon the hereditary ruler of the French "Republic." But today at least, no one would term a government with hereditary leaders a republic. Too, it is certain that the United States is a republic without formal hereditary offices. The whole distinction between republican and hereditary forms achieved renown in those particular eras in history when certain secondary hereditary leaders—the landed noblemen—fought for power under the banners of kings or of commoners.

Centralized and decentralized leadership

One other important way of classifying leading groups or institutions is according to whether they are centralized or decentralized. Centralized leadership generally comprises a pyramid capped by one or a few preeminent individuals (see Figure 5A); decentralized leadership more nearly resembles a truncated pyramid, with a plane at the top made up of a fairly large number of comparatively equal persons (see Figure 5B). The leaderships of the executive and of the legislative branches of the American national government provide illustrations, respectively, of centralized and decentralized leadership. In the executive branch, the President is supreme over all other officials; he alone must bear the responsibility for the actions of the presidency. In Congress, on the other hand, leadership is divided first by the fact of two houses; then it is subdivided in each house among

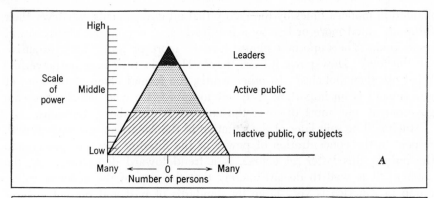

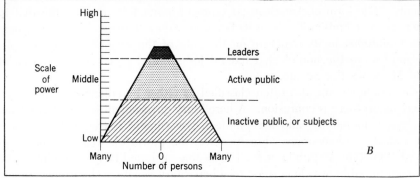

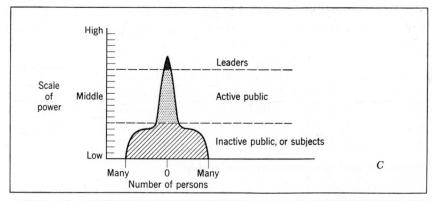

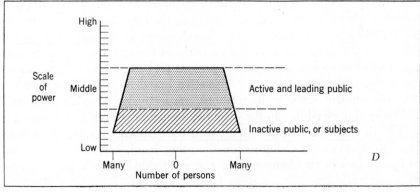

the outstanding Representatives and Senators, each of whom is the legal and constitutional equal of each of the others. The very fact, of course, that the American national government is composed of several independent organs—the President, Congress, and the Supreme Court—makes it as a whole a decentralized government. The federal system, admitting additional independent authority to the State governments, makes the total governmental picture even more decentralized. Foreign contrasts are provided by England, where the sum of powers given the Prime Minister and his cabinet is very large, and by the Soviet Union, where despite all doctrine the Presidium of the Central Committee of the Communist Party centralizes all power.

THE PUBLIC

The *public* comprises that part of the population that has influential and active connections with the leaders. Thus, the American public elects its officials, may criticize them, may run for offices, and may engage in a general political activity that is denied many populations of the world. Those populations that have no active connections with their leaders, in either fact or doctrine, may be termed *subject populations* or *masses*.

The modern public

In most modern industrial nations the population is divided into political leaders, a larger group of active citizens, and a very large number of persons who are inactive and uninfluential, as shown in Figure 5C. However, these latter groups are not often legally barred from political activity. The formal organization of both the Soviet Union and the United States provides for officials and a public which embraces all the remaining adult population; in neither are there subject masses (see Figure 5D). Certainly, in Soviet Russia, power is concentrated in very few hands; but everyone theoretically has equal formal rights under the constitution of the USSR; and, in fact, there is a large amount of participation, though not influence, among the general population. In the United States, more of the public becomes part of the leading groups, and, as in the Soviet Union, there are no subject population or masses.

On the other hand, in societies where the caste, status, or feudal system

---

Figure 5. Four Types of Power-Pyramids. *A.* The ideally proportioned pyramid: In this pyramid, the greater the amount of power, the smaller the number of people possessing it. Available evidence suggests that this chart greatly overestimates the number of people who are active. Therefore this pyramid does not resemble any known real distribution of power. It reflects an ideally centralized structure with one man, or a few men, having the greatest power. *B.* The truncated pyramid: In this pyramid, there are numerous leaders possessing approximately equal power. This chart portrays an ideally decentralized leadership. *C.* Probably the typical distribution of power resembles this chart, which has the contours of an upside-down mushroom. *D.* Distribution with an active and leading public. This situation has been found among only a few small tribes, or cities, or non-governmental organizations such as the Society of Friends (Quakers).

prevails, there is a large mass of people without the vote, without political influence or power, and a small ruling nobility or special caste group that is charged with political affairs. Similarly, the peoples of the medieval and early modern kingdoms in Europe and England could only be called the ruled masses, for they lived at the base of a pyramid, the top of which was occupied by the king and the nobles. As recently as 1830, only 220,000 Englishmen had the right to vote for the 656 members of the House of Commons. Not until the end of the eighteenth century was it generally advocated that whole nations should constitute publics; previous examples of such publics were to be found only among smaller territories, such as the Greek cities of ancient times, the Italian cities of the Middle Ages and early modern era, and the Swiss cantons. But since the American and French Revolutions, the public has come to be deemed an essential part of the leading group in democratic countries. Hence a great deal of attention has been devoted to the problem of relating this public to the leading group in such a way as to maximize the power of individual citizens without destroying the order, stability, and prudence of the government.

One after another of the modern states has faced crises in dealing with the enormous present-day publics, trained by universal education and vested with the power of the vote. Russia, after various revolts brought on by pressures from the peasants and factory workers, led by intellectuals, had only a few months of constitutional government in 1917; then a tiny Bolshevik faction overthrew this regime and installed a communist dictatorship. Italy and Germany could not cope, either, with the problem of gearing a large active public into the government; they succumbed to Fascism and Nazism. Other countries have likewise yielded; still others have managed to beat off recurrent threats to constitutional government from the extremists.

The United States has, on the whole, successfully coped with the pressures generated by movements of extremists within the public. Yet it has had such extreme movements as Shays' Rebellion in Massachusetts in 1786; the Jacobin panic in the 1790's about the immigration of French revolutionaries; civil war in Rhode Island in 1842 over the right to vote; the Know-Nothing movement of the 1850's; the Greenbackers and the Populists after the Civil War; the anarchist rebels against all government, especially after 1900; Nazi imitators; and a small communist organization. The chief problem aroused by the massive publics of the twentieth century lies in the different interests, values, and doctrines that exist among various parts of the population. When one moves up and down the ladder of occupations, one acquires different political views; conservatism increases as one moves from the less wealthy and less skilled occupations to the better-paid and more skilled ones.

How to adjust these differences peaceably is a critical problem of government. They put a constant strain upon the relations between leaders and the public; and any upsetting conditions, such as war or economic depression, are likely to bring disaster to the structure of government. Obviously one of the most important concerns in the study of American government is to learn how the American structure is built to resist such strains.

THE TASKS OF GOVERNMENT

What is usually thought to be the "structure" of the government comprises the offices, departments, bureaus, and their various subdivisions that conduct public business. But a moment's thought will persuade one that these are only the most visible and tangible evidences of structure. Ideals and men, too, are essential to offices and tasks; for the structure of human action requires goals and leaders.

If the doctrines of the leaders are known, their tasks become fairly plain to the observer. If rulers are dedicated to religion, churches will be many; it took a long time for thousands of workers to build the great pyramids of Egypt, and another long period for hosts of artisans to erect the cathedral at Rheims. If the rulers are devoted to commerce, the nation will have myriad counting-houses and an ample shipping fleet. Conversely, the tasks being performed are evidence of the intent. When one tours a country, he judges the ambition of the people by what they are doing and what they have done. Although there may be a gap between doctrine and behavior, the leading doctrines are discernible in behavior, and the most important activities can be anticipated from the major doctrines.

However, a complication interferes with the easy transition from doctrine to activity, or from activity to doctrine. The subject here is *governmental* tasks or activity; but tasks which are governmental in one place are executed by private individuals in another place. Consequently, unless one knows that a leading doctrine calls upon the government itself to perform certain publicly desired tasks, one cannot be sure who will be managing a given activity.

Certain elemental tasks are performed by all governments. Some governments do them well; others do them poorly. Such tasks include the maintenance of law and order, and protection of the citizens against foreign enemies. Other tasks are carried out only by some governments; such a task is the management of government-owned commercial farms, which do not even exist in the United States. Literally hundreds of different tasks are performed by most governments, each task of course representing some doctrine or belief of the leading individuals in the community. Chapter 30 will explain in detail the extent to which governments are devoted to these tasks. At the moment, it is enough to consider that the size and shape of government—its contents that must be understood—are given it by the number and kinds of tasks it performs.

THE TOOLS OF GOVERNMENT

Whatever the state may want to do at a particular time demands some method of implementation. A decision or policy must be carried out; the whole community, or a great part of it, must move in accord. The major forms of getting the desired activity under way and of preventing or meeting opposition to it are: domination, education, force, and economic pressure.

Most states use all these means. Different states are apt to use one method more frequently than others, depending upon what sort of treatment their populations are accustomed to. For instance, to enforce the laws, the Russians usually prefer force where the Americans would prefer economic pressure. But new situations may require new means. Violent death in the arena could rarely shake the Christian martyrs. Imprisonment never abated Ghandi's resolve. Reductions in wages will not destroy labor unions.

Domination is the determining of men's wills and actions through sheer commands. The commands depend upon the strength of fundamental loyalties to the government for their effect. Thus, when a policeman tells a crowd to move along, most people simply move without question. Of all these means, education is the most subtle and demands the longest time to instill, but is perhaps most durable in its power to impose conformity upon men's wills. Force is least subtle, can be applied immediately, and often loses its effectiveness once it is removed. Napoleon once said that man can do anything with bayonets except sit on them; but it is notable that he did not rule long enough to test the truth of his witticism. Economic pressure is the management of wealth and of means of production, especially by various taxes, to obtain conformity. For example, when the federal government during the last generation has wanted to restrict the production of certain crops, it has paid for their non-production instead of resorting to simple command.

Such are the general tools of government. In any given government—such as the American—specific kinds of political organization or structure are set up to manage the instruments of control. A glance at the table of contents for this book will show that a general organization of this type is present in the United States, and what is true here is also true abroad. Governments have organs of command in the form of councils or legislative bodies, executive or administrative establishments, and judiciaries. They further provide agencies for dealing with internal order (police), with external order (armed forces), with education (school systems and information offices), and with economic measures (the treasury and budget offices). Since these highly important agencies are discussed in detail as the book proceeds, they need not be considered further here.

QUESTIONS AND PROBLEMS

1. Besides those named in the text, suggest other political doctrines that are prevalent among the American public; use your own beliefs and those you have observed that many other people possess.

2. Recite as many instances as you can of differences between American doctrine and American behavior.

3. Realizing that a great variety of opinions exist regarding what the goals of government should be, what do you personally believe the goals of the American government should be?

4. From any two issues of the *New York Times* make a list of all actions mentioned as having been performed by officials at any level of American government, national, State, or local. In each case determine whether the official employed force, economic management, or education.

3. Early American Governments and the Confederation

Photo courtesy George S. Flohn.

THE next task in understanding the American way of government is to discover how the American government has achieved its particular structure of the moment. Granted its inheritance of the universal sentiments and shape of government, what accounts for its numerous special traits? Much of the governmental system of the United States stems from the early colonial times of the seventeenth century. The traditions and beliefs underlying the system date from many centuries before then. The present federal Constitution, which is the oldest document of its sort in the world that is still in effect, was adopted in 1788. It was based to a considerable degree upon the revolutionary State constitutions and the Articles of Confederation. The first State constitutions, in turn, were quite similar to the charters of colonial government which they supplanted. The colonial governments themselves rested upon those political doctrines with which the colonial ruling groups were best acquainted and to which they were most accustomed—the doctrines of seventeenth-century English parliamentarism. The English government itself had evolved its peculiar character from long years of domestic struggle, which had reached a peak in that century, and from numerous influences and sources in Anglo-Saxon, Norman, and church culture and law.

British parliamentarism was then in a critical stage. Hundreds of years of English governing experience had laid a road toward parliamentarism, but it was an unpaved road. The Great Charter (Magna Carta) of 1215 had only partially defined the relationship of political authority to individual freedom in England. During the 1600's alone three revolutions in England contributed to a further clarification of this relationship.

Thus, a full analysis of the ancient sources of American government merits not merely a chapter but a volume or series of volumes on western civilization. At the moment, a cursory presentation of early American governments and the Confederation will suffice to offer at least some notion of the original character of government in the United States and simultaneously to indicate the remarkable stability of some fundamental American political institutions and issues of today.

COLONIAL GOVERNMENTS

Types

There were three general types of government in the British colonies in North America. They were the charter colony, the proprietary colony, and the royal colony. Their typical forms are drawn in Figure 6. These types could be distinguished from one another chiefly by the relationship that each had with the British king. Whatever the relationship, it is well to note that all three types reacted strongly against the king, and, later on, pursuing the logic of that hatred, against all executive power.

Charter: The charter or corporate colony was farthest removed from the king's control. Initially a charter colony was a joint-stock company—a type of business organization akin to a modern corporation—whose intended function was to make profits for the company owners. After the owners had secured their charter from the king, they determined what sort of government their colony should have. In general the inhabitants of charter colonies showed the greatest resistance toward British rule, in part because the structure of their government gave them liberty to do so. Consequently one after another of these colonies lost their charters, so that at the time of the American Revolution there remained only two—Connecticut and Rhode Island.

Proprietary: The proprietary colony was somewhat more easily disciplined by the king. It comprised a tract of land which the king had awarded to an individual, or to a group of individuals whose interrelationships more nearly resembled those of a partnership than those of a corporation. Along with the tract of land the proprietor or proprietors acquired the power of establishing a government for the colony. Since the settlers of some proprietary colonies also became rebellious, their lands were taken away from the original owners; by 1775 there were but three—Pennsylvania, Delaware, and Maryland.

Replica of the Capitol of Virginia as it Stood in Colonial Times, at Williamsburg.

Royal: The royal colony was the type immediately under the governance of the king; he and his ministers, especially the Board of Trade and Plantations, directly supervised their rule. Charter and proprietary colonies, such as, respectively, Virginia and the Carolinas, were converted into royal colonies when they became unmanageable. At the outbreak of the Revolution there were eight of them—all but the two charter and three proprietary colonies noted above.

Structure

The governments of the different colonies, whether charter, proprietary, or royal, bore great structural similarity to one another; all, too, came to resemble the British government. This similarity is quite understandable; for the British colonists, like most colonists in history, established the type of governmental structure most familiar to them. All colonial governments thus possessed three somewhat distinct branches, the executive, legislative, and judicial, a division that later Americans made permanent in both philos-

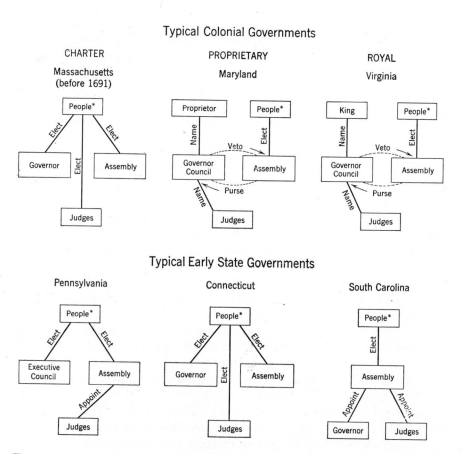

Figure 6. Organization of Early American Governments. *The term "people" here refers particularly to those men, often a small number, who had the right to vote.

ophy and practice. There was considerable overlapping of function among the branches, however.

The Executive Branch: The chief of the executive branch in each colony was the governor. He was appointed by the king in the royal colonies, named by the proprietor in the proprietary colonies, and chosen by the voters in the charter colonies. (Note the origins of later practice here.) Associated with the governor was a council, usually appointed by the agent that chose the governor. Together the governor and his council administered the affairs of the colony. Moreover, during the eighteenth century the executive was under increasing pressure to emphasize the colonial policy of the British crown. The fact that governors named by the voters or the proprietor might be unreliable in carrying out this latter task, especially if they were native colonists, justified, in the eyes of the crown, the transformation of some settlements into royal colonies, in which the governor would be more obedient to the king and to British direction.

As executive chiefs of the colonies, the governors of the royal and proprietary colonies enjoyed, at least on paper, large powers. For example, they were authorized to exercise a suspensive (that is, temporary) veto, or a full veto, upon acts of the colonial legislatures. Thus was the now familiar veto originated in America. Moreover, governors could woo and win supporters through their appointive power (a device termed *patronage*, still an important function). But ultimately how much of their power they could utilize depended upon many factors, the most important of which was the vigor of the colonial legislature.

The Legislative Branch: The legislative branch of the colonial government, after it had undergone a process of development, finally consisted of a two-chambered, or bicameral, body whose principal task was the enactment of laws. Colonial governments at the outset were not equipped with legislatures; legislation as well as administration was confided to the governor and his council. The first colonial popular assembly was established in Virginia in 1619, twelve years after the colony was founded. Popular assemblies emerged partly because of the demands of the colonists, and partly because of the wish of some of the charter companies to win the support of the people in their occasional contests with the British government. At first the legislature consisted of the governor, his council, and a popular assembly seated together. Subsequently the council tended to join with the elective body as its upper house. The union of an erstwhile executive council with a popular assembly set the pattern for Congress and the State legislatures after the Revolution; the upper house usually had longer terms, more exacting qualifications for both members and electors, and certain vestiges of executive functions, such as confirming the President's and the Governors' appointments.

The degree of power available to the legislature grew steadily during the eighteenth century. A main source of power lay in the control which the legislatures secured over the voting of taxes and appropriations; once this power of the purse was won, a colonial legislature could defy the governor. Eventually, in some colonies the governor was obliged to petition the legislature for payment of his salary. Generally it was the popular assembly, or lower house, which acquired this monetary ascendancy; here it only adopted the means exploited centuries before by the British House of Commons in its struggle with the king. At the same time it founded an American tradition which the Founding Fathers accepted when they gave the House of Representatives exclusive power to initiate bills levying taxes.

Colonial legislatures also won the right to be sole judges of their membership, thus forbidding governors to arbitrarily unseat a duly elected representative. Furthermore, they wrested the choice of the presiding officer, the Speaker, from the governor; and this official soon became the leading spokesman for the colonial cause. Indeed, the legislatures of some colonies effected deep invasions of the executive power; for instance, they secured the right to appoint several administrative officials, beginning with the colonial treasurer. In most respects, the practices described here have descended to the legislatures of the present.

The Judicial Branch: The judicial branch of the colonial government, which was the last to emerge, included finally courts of first instance (that is, where cases might be first brought to trial) and courts of appeal. Initially the governor and his council dealt with all cases. As the population increased and the judiciary assumed greater burdens, lower courts were instituted; the governor and his council remained essentially the supreme court of the colony. Many cases, especially those involving British officials, could be further appealed to the king in England. Colonial judges were named by the king or governor, or even elected by the people, according to the type of colony. (Both the gubernatorial and the popular means for selecting judges are used widely in America today.) In their courts the colonists were eventually guaranteed those judicial rights that protected Englishmen at home.

Competing colonial interest groupings

From the founding of the Jamestown settlement, colonial society and politics displayed the competing interest groupings that can be discerned in every large-scale human organization. [Sometimes the poor were ranged against the rich, the coastal dwellers against the frontiersmen, and the newcomers against the established settlers.] As shall be shown in later pages of this book, the American government is colored throughout by the activities of myriad such groupings. Moreover, to the quarrels among these colonial groupings were added disputes between the partisans of the colonies and those of the mother country. These external groupings sometimes coincided with, and sometimes cut across, the several internal groupings. That is, Americans who were opposed to the crown could be either rich or poor, or might be old settlers or immigrants.

EARLY STATE GOVERNMENTS

One of the first results of the American Revolution was the conversion of the colonies into thirteen independent States. Indeed, each of the States had an organized legal government before they were united under the Articles of Confederation into the first American national state. The new State governments were quite similar to the previous colonial governments; in fact, the constitutions which the State leaders eventually framed often did little more than establish a new legal basis for the regimes which developed after the British officials had fled. A new authority and sovereignty were claimed. Hence, just as the former colonial governments had resembled one another, so did the new State governments. However, certain major changes were instituted, partly in reaction to the governing principles of King George III.

The State constitutions

Each of the new State governments quickly adopted a written constitution. One of the most important aims of American leaders was the securing of written constitutions. These men were imbued with the compact theory of government, which held that governments arise through contracts between rulers and ruled, stating mutual rights and duties; they believed that a constitution was such a compact. Hence they argued that these documents would offer greater protection from an arbitrary ruler, since the ruler or government would feel bound by their provisions; if the ruler or government did not abide by these documents, the people could withdraw their part of the bargain. The colonists had experienced such documents, in the form of charters. Now, as citizens of independent States, they demanded constitutions that would establish representative, republican governments controlled by contracts with the people.

This doctrine was stated explicitly in some constitutions; thus Article I of the North Carolina constitution of 1776 asserted, "That all political power is vested in and derived from the people only." Additional guarantees that the sphere of government action was limited were afforded by clauses assuring the exercise of rights and liberties traditional in British political theory, such as freedom of speech and of assembly. In some instances, beginning with Virginia, these rights were embraced in a single section and placed at the first of the constitution as a Bill or Declaration of Rights. The Virginia Bill of Rights probably influenced all other State constitutions, the Federal Bill of Rights, and even the French Declaration of the Rights of Man and the Citizen. Like the Declaration of Independence, it bespoke the prevalent theory that men are by nature politically equal and possessed of natural rights which the state was created to safeguard.

The structure of government

The structure of the new State governments, like that of the earlier colonial regimes, comprised an executive, a legislative, and a judicial branch. Figure 6 shows three forms that they took. Mindful of the turmoil of colonial politics, the authors of the new constitutions aimed at preventing conflicts among the three branches by making the separation of powers explicit and emphatic, so that no one branch would encroach upon the scope of any other. For example, Article I of the Georgia Constitution of 1777 provided that "The legislative, executive, and judiciary departments shall be separate and distinct, so that neither exercise the powers properly belonging to the other."

However, despite these earnest professions, actual power in the governments was entrusted chiefly to the legislative branch. The creators of these new regimes were reacting to their experiences with colonial governors who had sought to restrain the colonial assemblies. In one sense they were conservatives or even reactionaries; for to them the dangerous revolutionary was King George III, whom they charged with attempting to overthrow the results of the Glorious Revolution of 1688, which supposedly had established the supremacy of Parliament. They believed that a legislature was less capable than an executive of building a tyranny, for they viewed it as a representative body which could be checked by the people who had elected it and whom it represented. They could not foresee the benign despotism which the British Parliament was even then fashioning; nor could they predict the Terror soon to reign under the French National Convention of 1792–1795. Finally, they neglected the fact that the colonial governors just prior to the Revolution had been effectively reined by the power which the assemblies possessed over finances; only intervention from overseas kept the governors strong.

The Executive Branch: In every State except Pennsylvania the executive branch consisted of a Governor and a council. Pennsylvania at first experimented with a collegiate executive of thirteen members. Only in the five northern States of New Hampshire, Massachusetts, Rhode Island, Connecticut, and New Jersey was the Governor chosen by the people; elsewhere he was named by the legislature, a method that completely disappeared early in the nineteenth century. Generally his functions were restricted, even where he was popularly elected, by a council appointed by the legislature. His term was one year, save in New York, Delaware, and South Carolina; and all the States south of Pennsylvania limited his reeligibility as fifteen States, most of them southern, do today. The powers of the Governor were confined to such tasks as the execution of the laws, commanding the state militia, and pardoning and reprieving convicted persons. He could make appointments only in conjunction with his council or with the legislature; and his veto power had all but vanished.

The Legislative Branch: In each State save Pennsylvania and Georgia the legislature was bicameral; the two exceptions maintained unicameral legislatures for a few years only. The bicameral form imitated the colonial institutions, in which the governor's council formed the upper house and the popular assembly the lower. Now the upper house became likewise an elective body; however, qualifications for its voters and its members were sometimes higher, and in some States its members served longer terms. In the lower houses short terms were common, one year being the usual duration. The belief was that short terms discouraged the rise of despotism. These legislatures exercised vast powers; as noted above, they took part directly or indirectly even in the appointive function, which is normally viewed as proper to the executive. In keeping with colonial practice, the initiation of money bills was confided to the lower house.

The Judicial Branch: The judicial branch in the early State governments was quite similar to that under British rule. In every State there arose the two customary levels of jurisdiction, the courts of first instance and the courts of appeal. Generally the lowest courts were those of the justices of the peace. In some States judges were named by the Governor; in others they were appointed by the legislature. The maintenance of traditional juridical procedure was guaranteed by the statements of rights which appeared in all State constitutions, either in the Bills and Declarations of Rights or in the body of the constitution. At the outset these courts did not possess the power of judicial review, that is, of declaring a State law unconstitutional.[1] Since this power comprises a major check upon the legislative function, its absence partially accounts for the political supremacy of the legislatures in these governments.

THE CONFEDERATION (1781–1788)

The Confederation, which was the first American national government, sprang directly from the political needs of the Revolution; as institutionalized by the Articles of Confederation, it reflected American distaste for the principles of British rule. The Confederation was the offshoot of the Continental Congress, which itself had been sired by the intercolonial Committees of Correspondence. These Committees, which have been called the first American political party, comprised groups of antagonists of what were deemed the tyrannical aspects of British colonial policy. In 1774 the First Continental Congress, which had been summoned by the Committees, convened at Philadelphia to consult together regarding colonial resistance to the British. After adopting a series of resolutions, the members of the Congress called for a similar gathering in the following year. This Second Continental Congress, meeting at Philadelphia in May, 1775, was confronted by the Revolution, which had erupted the previous month at Lexington and Concord. The Congress secured control of the revolutionary army and henceforth was the government of the united colonies. Soon it urged the colonies to draft constitutions as independent political units; and committees of the Congress wrote the Declaration of Independence and the Articles of Confederation.

Political structure of the Confederation

The Articles of Confederation provided a constitutional basis for the government under the Continental Congress. The new edifice was described as a "perpetual Union." The supreme organ was the unicameral Congress. Each State was to elect a delegation of from two to seven members, who served annual terms but no more than three years out of any six. Each

---

[1] Cf. Chapter 29, "Judicial Review."

State was to pay the salaries of its delegation. Regardless of its size, every State had but one vote, based upon a majority decision of its delegation; should the latter divide evenly, the State lost its vote. Any legislative proposition required the votes of nine States for passage. No executive or judicial branch was created. As needs developed, the Congress established committees to manage certain executive tasks; later it created executive departments to handle foreign affairs, finance, and military concerns. Under the Articles, the national government relied almost entirely upon State courts; Congress itself was to adjudicate disputes between States, and provisions were made for erecting a system of admiralty courts to hear cases involving sea-borne vessels and commerce.

National powers under the Articles of Confederation

Under the Articles of Confederation the national government ostensibly had rather broad powers. However, these were largely the powers which the British government had exercised prior to the Revolution, so that in establishing the national government the States yielded little or nothing. Most of these powers were delegated to the Congress; however, they were not so much legislative as they were executive, managerial, or supervisory. They included the conduct of foreign relations; the declaration of war and the negotiation of peace; the exchange of ambassadors; the establishment of standards for weights, measures, and the coinage; the creation of a postal system; the borrowing of money and the contracting of debt; and the regulation of the armed forces. Actually the Continental Congress had enjoyed most of these functions before the Articles were ratified, in 1781.

Weaknesses of the Confederation

Structural Weaknesses: To those accustomed to the arrangements under the present Constitution, the outstanding structural weakness of the Confederation lay in the absence of an independent executive and an independent judiciary; inasmuch as these functions were subordinate to the legislature, there was no separation of powers nor system of checks and balances. However, Great Britain flourished for many decades under a legislature as powerful as that of the United States under the Articles. Possibly the heads of the departments which Congress had already created, along with those which it might establish in the future, might have combined to form a parliamentary-cabinet type of government. Perhaps the true weakness of the Confederation structure lay in its inability to satisfy an influential and determined group of men who wanted a strong executive to check the legislature and provide the government with a unifying and conservative force. It must be remembered that the Articles of Confederation, like some of the early State constitutions, were drafted by a radical group, or coalition of radical groups, which owing to the Revolution had won temporary preeminence in American life. New groups, accepting independence wholeheartedly, yet taking a favorable view of the merits of business and other moneyed interests and an unfriendly view of "instable and reckless populism," came forward with their program for the nation.

Functional Weaknesses: In analyzing the functional weaknesses of the Confederation, one must keep in mind the distribution of powers under the Articles. Just as under the present Constitution, the national government had only delegated powers, whereas the states had reserved powers. However, under the Confederation, the States were sovereign; the national government had no real control over the States or over the citizens. In other words, today theoretically both the national and the State governments exercise powers delegated to them by the people; but under the Articles of Confederation, according to the same type of reasoning, the State governments exercised powers derived from the people whereas the national government held only such powers as had been granted by the States. These latter powers were scanty, so much so, in fact, that although the Confederation was termed a perpetual union it is difficult to see what might have been attempted had a State seceded. The needs of the Revolution had brought a temporary and perhaps illusory union which tended to dissolve once the Revolution had ended.

The Articles, then, were more nearly a treaty of alliance than a constitution; and the structure and functioning of the Congress intimates that it was to operate as a convention of ambassadors from the States, not as a lawmaking organ. It will readily be seen that the powers denied the national government were those which the colonies had resisted when the powers had been administered by Great Britain. The Revolution itself was directed against a central authority. Actually, in light of the jealousy in which the States held their hard-won sovereign rights, it is evident that the framers of the Articles had achieved as much unity as was possible under the circumstances.

The chief powers *forbidden* the national government under the Articles were: (1) *The levying of taxes.* Congress could collect no taxes from the people; it could only requisition money from the States. Moreover, it had no means for compelling the States to pay. Hence it was impotent; for without money it had no funds to support armed forces. The problem could have been resolved only if the States abandoned their disinclination to provide the money; and they never viewed the national government as important enough to do so. (2) *The regulation of commerce.* Congress had no power over interstate commerce; and it could regulate foreign commerce only through treaties. Only the States could impose tariffs; and during the Confederation period some States waged persistent trade wars with their neighbors. (3) *The exclusive control over money.* The Articles granted the national government the power to establish standards of coinage; however, they permitted the States to issue paper money. Since during the Revolution the Congress had printed large amounts of currency to finance the war, national paper money was so inflated as to be almost worthless. Hence the States circulated paper money to the extent demanded by the dominant groups. Since the debtor interests controlled the Rhode Island government, that State issued huge sums of paper money to help them pay their debts. In Massachusetts, on the other hand, where the creditor interests were supreme, the refusal of the State government to inflate the currency led in 1786 to a movement of armed resistance by the debtors known as Shays' Rebellion. The fact that the Massachusetts militia had to quell the uprising, since the Confederation had no troops for the task, contributed greatly to the movement for revising the Articles.

The denial of these three powers to the national government probably added to the economic difficulties that the United States was suffering in the 1780's. However, the Articles were not solely responsible for these difficulties, because the country was undergoing the inflation that usually follows a war. Moreover, it was now denied the economic protection it had enjoyed under British rule; and the British were flooding American markets with cheap manufactured goods, possibly in a deliberate effort to crush the infant American industries. At the same time the British were seeking to expel American shipping from the oceans. Actually the financial distress was much more serious in the realm of public funds than it was in the field of private enterprise.

Finally, the Confederation was unable to conduct a strong foreign policy, almost certainly because of its internal weaknesses. The two nations with which the United States had its principal dealings in the Confederation era were Great Britain and Spain, whose colonial properties bounded the United States on the north, west, and south. Each of these great powers aimed at restraining any further territorial expansion by the United States. Great Britain still occupied several outposts in the Great Lakes region; and Spain commanded the mouth of the Mississippi by its possession of New Orleans. Certain leaders among British ruling circles were convinced that a large portion of the United States wished a return to colonial status under the British flag. Both the Spanish and the British were aware of American political and economic impotence. Hence American emissaries could not negotiate treaties with them to relax border tension, or, in the case of Great Britain, restrict British competition with American trade and industry.

Inflexibility of the Articles: Many of the shortcomings of the Articles might have been remedied by agreement of the constituent States had it not been for the requirement that an amendment to the Articles must be ratified by all of the States.

This requirement was simply further testimony to the nature of the Confederation; it expressed the unwillingness of any one State to permit interference by the other States in what it considered its sovereign realm. Once Congress proposed an amendment that would have authorized the national government to levy a tariff; but Rhode Island refused to ratify it. When the same amendment was proposed a second time, Rhode Island overcame its reluctance, but New York interposed its veto. This inflexibility almost guaranteed the failure of all attempts to expand the authority of the national government.

Steps toward a new government

Within a few years of the adoption of the Articles, the first steps were taken toward the creation of a new government. These steps signalized the revival of the groups that favored a strong central authority and an executive sufficiently weighty to provide an effective balance and check to the legislature. Leadership in the movement was taken primarily by men concerned with the safety of property, the increase of trade, the stability of money, and the prestige of the United States abroad. In 1785 a group of such men, delegates from Maryland and Virginia, convened, upon George Washington's invitation, at Mount Vernon for the purpose of reaching agreements respecting commerce on the Potomac River and in Chesapeake Bay. Although they partially achieved their aims, they urged the summoning of another convention the next year at Annapolis to deal with problems of broader application, which would have delegates from all the States.

However, only Virginia, Pennsylvania, New York, New Jersey, and Delaware were represented at the Annapolis Convention of 1786; hence that body could not speak for the majority of the States. But it did accept the recommendation of Alexander Hamilton that another convention assemble at Philadelphia in the following year; and it applauded his proposal that this convention discuss fundamental changes in the Articles. The Annapolis delegates thereupon urged the legislatures of their States to prepare for such a convention and to counsel the States not represented at Annapolis to do likewise. Shortly afterward Virginia named its deputies for the Philadelphia Convention; and soon New Jersey, Pennsylvania, Delaware, North Carolina, and Georgia also chose representatives. Now Congress formally approved the convention, thereby giving the movement a legal basis. Later every State but Rhode Island sent representatives to the convention, which opened at Philadelphia in May, 1787, with the goal of amending the Articles of Confederation.

QUESTIONS AND PROBLEMS

1. Describe the actual conditions of the separation of powers in the American colonies.

2. What changes in State government were wrought by the Revolution before 1789?

3. Summarize the conditions favoring an attempt to reorganize the government under the Articles of Confederation.

4. Trace the attitudes of American colonists and revolutionaries toward executive authority, as contrasted to the authority of legislatures.

5. Which, if any, of the several kinds of colonial, State, and confederational governments would you prefer to have lived under? Why?

Philadelphia Convention and Visitors Bureau, Chamber of Commerce.

THE Constitution that was prepared at Philadelphia in 1787 and approved by most of the States in the following year has been regarded by many statesmen and scholars, as well as by common people, as one of the greatest works that has come from the mind of man. Its solutions were ingenious and many times of lofty imagination. Its foresight was great, greater than those who participated ever dreamt. But, like many great works of the human mind, it had a social explanation; it fitted together past, present, and future social forces into an enduring pattern. In social terms, the drafting and ratifying of the Constitution consummated a process that had been going on since the end of the Revolution. This process may be described as one in which one group of leaders superseded another, adding its political ideals and institutions to those of its predecessors.

Transition from Revolution to Constitution

Many of the first band of American leaders, the men who fought the Revolution, signed the Declaration of Independence, and wrote the Articles of Confederation, were in terms of their own era radicals. They were perhaps most highly concerned with liberty, not only of the American colonies from Great Britain but also of the individual from the government. Partly because they believed, like the French democratic theorist Jean-Jacques Rousseau (1712–1778), that human freedom can be safe only in small political units, and partly because they were compelled by circumstances, they granted the national government under the Articles very few effective powers.

However, a few years' experience with this regime demonstrated that an excess of liberty in certain spheres of society was leading to the absence of political order. The growing turbulence of the 1780's at the same time diminished the prestige of the revolutionary leaders and stimulated the public demand for leadership that would restore order.

A loose grouping of such men made its appearance early in the 1780's. It was composed mainly of those who had been discontented with the Articles from the time of their adoption. With the passage of years this group continued to attract recruits; however, not until Shays' Rebellion, which shocked men of property in every State, did it win a considerable body of adherents throughout the nation. It was this group which stepped forward in 1787 to revive the balance between liberty and order.

DRAFTING THE CONSTITUTION

Membership of the Philadelphia Convention

The members of the Philadelphia Convention had much in common economically, socially, politically, and intellectually. They came almost exclusively from the prosperous and well-educated professional, mercantile, and financial groups of the coastal cities, and the landed interests. There was no member from the ranks of shopkeepers, city laborers, or small farmers. Among the fifty-five who actually attended the Convention (seventy-four altogether were chosen, but nineteen refused to take part), more than half had been to college. A similar fraction were lawyers; and there was a scattering of doctors and teachers. About two-thirds owned national or State bonds, giving them considerable interest in the stability of money and credit. Nearly one-half had lent money at interest; any cheapening of money would enable their debtors to pay them back in money that would be worth less. Approximately one-fourth were engaged in manufacturing or merchandising; a slightly greater fraction owned slaves.

Furthermore, the Convention included many members schooled in poli-

Independence Hall, Where the Constitutional Convention Met.

tics; more than two-thirds had been delegates to Congress; more than half had sat in State legislatures; and a few had been representatives in colonial assemblies. A few were then, or had been, State Governors or State judges. About one-fifth had participated in State constitutional conventions. Therefore this body consisted of many of the wealthiest and most influential men in the country. A large proportion of these leaders were tied together, directly and indirectly, by bonds of family, finance, and office. For example, Alexander Hamilton was the son-in-law of Major-General and Senator Philip Schuyler, whose nephew, Walter Livingston, had been a member of the Board of the Treasury under the Articles.

That the Philadelphia Convention was made up of different elements from those that led the Revolution is shown by the fact that among the thirty-nine signers of the Constitution were to be found only six of the forty-three surviving signers of the Declaration of Independence. Another signer of the Declaration, Elbridge Gerry, took part in the Convention but refused to endorse the Constitution. Several other signatories of the Declaration, such as Richard Henry Lee, were appointed to the Convention but declined to attend, and subsequently opposed ratification in their States. Patrick Henry, the firebrand of the Revolution, refused to go because he "smelt a rat." If he and others had gone, they might have caused the Convention leaders much trouble. Moreover, two of the most notable signers of the Declaration, John Adams and Thomas Jefferson, were unable to take part because they were abroad on diplomatic missions.

Organization and functioning of the Convention

The Philadelphia Convention was organized much like a legislature. However, at the first meeting two special rules were adopted. The first was that, as in the Congress of the day, each State was to have but one vote, cast according to the desires of the majority of its delegation. Hence the small States had as great a voice as the large States. The second important rule was that the sessions were to be conducted in secrecy; it was hoped that with no public audience the members would be able to complete their work more quickly and with less fear of criticism.

Also at their first meeting, the members chose George Washington as presiding officer. By parliamentary rule, the chairman cannot take part in debate and must be impartial; hence his great influence favoring strong and conservative federalism was exercised behind the scenes and in pushing the order of business to a successful conclusion. The members appointed a secretary as well, to keep the minutes of their doings. However, this journal later turned out to be a mere skeletal description of the actions of the Convention. The most nearly complete record of this gathering lies in the notes written daily by James Madison, perhaps the outstanding member.

In its functioning also, the Convention resembled a typical formal assembly. Much of its work was accomplished while the Convention operated as a committee of the whole, to facilitate its work. Although fifty-five delegates at one time or another attended meetings, usually only about thirty members were present. With so few listeners, speakers had little cause for engaging in lengthy oratory. Instead, much of the time was passed in quiet discussion and debate. Moreover, like a legislative body, the Convention more than once referred a knotty question to a specially-chosen committee ("select committee") for deliberation and resolution.

Work of the Convention

The work of the Convention, which was of course the framing of a new Constitution, consisted primarily of adjusting differences among a number of interests. It must at the outset be stressed that the delegates were united in their sentiment that there must be a more powerful central government. This unity was, as noted above, largely the result of the process by which the delegates were chosen. At the same time there were significant differences, based on political ideals, economic attachments, sectional feelings, and other grounds. The principal task of the Convention was to achieve greater federated strength by means most pleasing to the strongest combination of interests, without driving any important group into enraged opposition. Hence no one interest group saw all of its desires fulfilled.

The Chief Issue: The chief issue before the Convention was that of determining the relationship of the national government to the States. The assemblage at Philadelphia might do no more than confer additional specific tasks upon the national government while reaffirming the sovereignty of the States. On the other hand, it might erect a strong central authority that would possess control over the States. The State legislatures would probably oppose the latter plan, for such a national government would greatly diminish the State powers; they visualized only the former project.

It should be noted that of the two possibilities, the former entailed merely amending the Articles; the latter implied drafting an entirely new Constitution. The will of the States can be seen from the authority that the Virginia legislature, the first to respond to the recommendations of the Annapolis Convention, gave its delegates: they were to unite with the representatives from the other States "in devising and discussing all such Alterations and farther Provisions as may be necessary to render the Foederal Constitution adequate to the Exigencies of the Union and in reporting such an Act for that purpose to the United States in Congress as when agreed to by them and duly confirmed by the several States will effectually provide for the same." This commission, which was copied or paraphrased by several other States, clearly authorized the members solely to amend the Articles. Indeed, the Delaware representatives were given the added instructions "that such Alterations or further Provisions, or any of them, do not extend to that part of the Fifth Article of the Confederation . . . which declares that 'in determining Questions in the United States in Congress Assembled each State shall have one Vote.' " This injunction revealed the essential position of the small States, which feared lest any amendment be adopted that would deny them equality in the legislative branch. Hence the delegates were also forced to decide whether or not to exceed the powers granted them by their legislatures.

Competing Interest Groups about the Chief Issue: The Convention quickly divided on the question of what powers the national government should possess; indeed, this rift had been evident even before the delegates assembled at Philadelphia, in the assertions emanating from the different States. One group at Philadelphia wished to establish a strong central authority. The other wished only to endow the existing central structure with a few added powers, so as to increase its efficiency in dealing with matters of interstate and foreign concern. In the main, the large States tended to favor the first plan; the small States, the second. That division probably arose from the fact that the large States expected to dominate any strong central government, whereas the small States feared to be so dominated.

However, at the end, a number of delegates did not permit the size of their States to determine their position; rather, they seem to have espoused one or the other plan according to their beliefs with respect to a strong central authority. For example, Alexander Hamilton, a delegate from New York, the fifth most populous State, urged the creation of an all-powerful central regime. On the other hand, George Mason, a representative from Virginia, the most populous State, refused to sign the Constitution since he felt that it made the national government too strong. In fact, the only question over which States chose sides on the basis of size was that of representation in the legislature. Therefore, with this one exception, one might best view the terms "large-State position" and "small-State position" as symbols, respectively, of proposals for a strong central government and for a weak central government. One should not expect those terms to mean a clear division of the big and the small States on votes, or a solidarity among the delegates from each type of State.

Proposals of the Two Groups: At one of the first meetings of the Convention, just after it had been organized, John Randolph of Virginia presented what has come to be called the Virginia Plan. This plan called for a strong central government, and it was endorsed by the large States. According to its preamble, "Resolved, that the Articles of Confederation ought to be so corrected and enlarged so as to accomplish the objects proposed by their institution; namely, 'common defense, security of liberty and general welfare.'" The plan recommended a bicameral or two-chambered legislature whose membership should be distributed among the States according to either the population or the amount of taxes paid by the State. The first house should be elected by the people, and the second house by the first but from a list of candidates nominated by the State legislatures. Each branch should be allowed to propose laws, for action by both branches. There should be a national executive and a national judiciary, to be named by the legislature. To checkrein the sovereignty of the States, it was urged that the national legislature be given the power to veto all State laws running counter to the national constitution, and that the national government be authorized to summon its armed forces against any State which did not perform its duties under the constitution. The Virginia Plan was debated for about two weeks after its introduction; and a large part of its recommendations were accepted by the majority at the Convention.

In reaction to the Virginia Plan, William Paterson of New Jersey offered a proposition for a national government of little more power than it possessed under the Articles; the New Jersey Plan is viewed as reflecting the wishes of the small States. This plan proclaimed, "Resolved that the Articles of Confederation ought to be so revised, corrected, and enlarged, as to render the federal Constitution adequate to the exigencies of Government, and the preservation of the Union." The Plan provided that the national government be empowered to levy a tariff on imported goods, and to regulate commerce. Furthermore, whereas the national authorities should continue to make requisitions upon the States, they should do so in proportion to the population of the States; and in the event of non-payment, these authorities might "direct the collection thereof." There should be a plural federal executive of several men appointed by Congress, and a federal court system whose judges would be chosen by the executive. If any State should oppose the enforcement of federal laws or treaties, "the federal Executive shall be authorized to call forth the power of the Confederated States, or so much thereof as may be necessary" to force compliance with the laws or treaties. The New Jersey Plan also provided that all laws and treaties made under the authority of the United States "shall be the supreme law of the respective States . . . any thing in the respective laws of the Individual States to the contrary notwithstanding." Although it was not recognized as uniquely significant at the time, this last clause came to be the keystone of the present Constitution.

There followed several days of debate in the Convention over the comparative merits of the Virginia and the New Jersey Plans, which are diagrammed in Figure 7. It is interesting to speculate what might have happened had the two plans been submitted at the same time; for when the Convention first gathered, the New Jersey Plan probably more closely mirrored what most delegates thought they were expected to produce. However, by the time the New Jersey Plan was offered, the spokesmen for the Virginia Plan appear to have convinced the majority of the need for a strong central government. Hence, when the debates were concluded, the Convention supported the Virginia Plan by a vote of seven States to three, the vote of Maryland being divided and New Hampshire and Rhode Island being unrepresented.

Consequently the delegates henceforth used the Virginia Plan as the basis for their deliberations. On the surface, the Plan did not really provide for more than a greatly strengthened confederative government. The provisions that the national government might veto acts of the States, and that it might coerce the States to perform their duties, show that the authors of this plan had as yet been unable to discard the practice of regarding the national government as primarily an agency of the States, dealing with States. It was only in the deliberations that followed that the adherents of the Plan asserted their intention of establishing a national government which dealt directly with the citizens.

The Connecticut Compromise: The Connecticut Compromise, sometimes termed the Great Compromise because of its importance, resolved the prob-

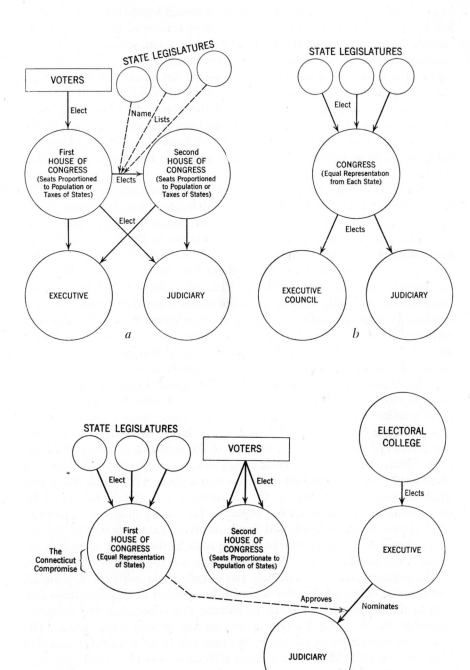

Figure 7. The Virginia (*a*), New Jersey (*b*), and Final Plans (*c*).

lem of apportioning representation in the national legislature. Although it had been hinted at in the recommendations of several of the States, it was brought forth officially by the Connecticut delegation, which had shown a tendency to side with the large States in erecting a strong central government. The Convention had voted to supplant the unicameral Congress of the Confederation with a bicameral legislature; the chief aim probably was to introduce internal checks into the legislative branch by letting one house review the work of the other. Then it had been provided, pursuant to the Virginia Plan, that membership in the lower house be distributed according to population; hence the large States might be thought to control this house.

Next the Convention turned to the question of representation in the upper house. It was now that the Connecticut delegates offered a proposal for equal representation in the second house, to placate the small States that were dissatisfied with proportional representation in the lower body. On the Connecticut suggestion the Convention at first divided evenly, five States to five. Now the members agreed to submit the issue to a committee having one representative from each State. Through some manipulations which can probably never be known, the large States were represented by such conciliatory men as Franklin of Pennsylvania, whereas the small States sent such unyielding deputies as Paterson of New Jersey. The result was a triumph for the small States; the committee urged that each State have an equal voice in the upper house, and the Convention so voted.

Sectional Interests and Compromises: Two general conflicts of sectional interests were carried before the Convention, the North-South and the East-West conflicts. Usually the former receives more notice; yet both were important. One must realize that in 1787 the slavery issue was not outstanding; slaves did not become a vital part of the southern economy until the United States had become a great cotton-producing country, which did not occur until after the introduction of the cotton gin in 1792. It is likely that whatever dispute there was at the Convention was greatly magnified by later historians writing under the impact of the slavery question. The principal dispute between North and South revolved about whether or not the slaves should be counted in apportioning seats in the House; including the slaves in the population would, of course, increase the number of seats held by the southern States. Ultimately the so-called "three-fifths compromise" was adopted, whereby five slaves should be counted as equal to three free men in the distribution of seats; to balance this concession, the delegates agreed to use the same fraction in levying any federal direct taxes. The relative unimportance of slavery at this time can be seen from the fact that only Georgia and South Carolina raised difficulties about this issue.

Another North-South compromise involved the federal regulation of commerce. At this time many governments financed themselves largely through taxes on both imports and exports. The southern States, which exported large amounts of raw materials and imported most of their finished goods, feared that they might contribute disproportionately to the support of the federal government, especially if the North should have a congressional majority. Some southern States also were disturbed lest the national government ban the slave trade. Hence the southern States demanded that export taxes be prohibited, and that navigation acts require a two-thirds congressional majority. The northern States, on the other hand, wished the central government to have full powers over foreign trade. The issue was compromised when the southern States yielded their demand for an extraordinary majority in voting on navigation acts, in exchange for a constitutional guarantee that the slave trade would not be halted for twenty years and that no export taxes would be levied. Again, Maryland and Virginia agreed, not with Georgia and the Carolinas, but with those who denounced slavery.

The split between East and West, although less apparent at the Convention, was probably even more significant; for it involved the ultimate political disposition of the western regions. There was no compromise here; the West was not represented at the Convention, and in any case would have had little if any bargaining power. The decision marked rather the triumph of one eastern attitude over another. Many at the Convention wished that the West should never attain political equality with the coastal States; they argued that the territory would never be sufficiently civilized for such privileges. As Gouverneur Morris said, "The busy haunts of men, not the remote wilderness, was [sic] the proper school of political talents." Their chief concern, of course, was to assure eastern control of the national government. However, other delegates, perhaps mindful of the fact that the whole country had once been a wilderness, persuaded the majority to accept a provision for admitting new States on a par with the old. The final action guaranteed that the United States would be a republic of continental dimensions, not an Atlantic seaboard commonwealth with a vast interior colonial dependency.

Other Settlements and Conclusions: In completing its work the Convention had to settle many more problems, often by means of compromise. One of the most important concerned the election of the chief executive. The delegates in general hesitated to entrust the choice of this officer to the public; on the other hand, they sensed that election by the legislature would tend to subordinate the executive branch to the legislative. Hence the delegates proposed a system of indirect election through a special body to be termed the Electoral College. The Convention also had to agree on methods for choosing congressmen and federal judges. It assigned various powers among the different organs of the government, and it established means for amending the Constitution.

Sources and Authorship of the Constitution: As Figure 8 shows, the delegates were acutely aware of the many historical struggles between liberty and despotism. Yet the sources for much of the work of the Convention were quite American; many of them were part of the daily life of the delegates. One important source was the Articles of Confederation, particularly for the statements of congressional power. Even State constitutions, especially that of New York, afforded materials for the Constitution. The simple fact that the Constitution included a large element of the familiar doubtless eased the transition from the old government to the new, and hastened its acceptance by the general public. Many Americans of that generation lived

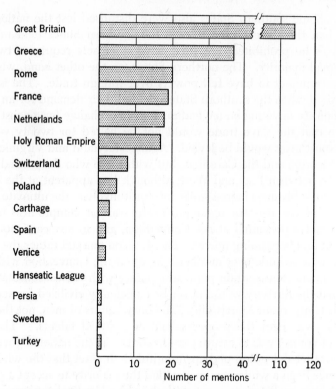

Figure 8.   References to the Experiences of Other Nations During the Constitutional Convention.   (As mentioned in the notes of James Madison.)

their lives out without fully realizing what great changes the Constitution had wrought.

The Constitution was the product of extensive rewriting.   Once the Great Compromise had been adopted, the Virginia Plan was converted into a series of resolutions.   These were then referred to a five-member committee on detail for expansion into a frame of government.   After some days this committee reported to the Convention; the whole body then deliberated the work of the committee for about five weeks.   A five-member committee on style now undertook to rephrase the work of the Convention in a single draft; this was chiefly the work of one committee member, Gouverneur Morris.   The Convention made a few changes in the draft presented by the committee on style, then prepared to submit the document to the public.

At the end, it seemed desirable that the Convention appear to be unanimous; however, some of the delegates refused to sign the Constitution.   Now Franklin, at the behest of Morris, suggested that the form be: "Done in Convention, by the unanimous consent of the States present. . . ."   All but three of the forty-two members then present signed the Constitution; the document was released to the press; and the Convention adjourned for the last time.

RATIFYING THE CONSTITUTION

The method of ratifying

It was provided in Article VII of the new Constitution that ratification was to be effected by a favorable vote in conventions in nine States. This clause demonstrates how far the delegates at Philadelphia had veered from their instructions to draft a group of amendments to the Articles; for, according to the Articles, this procedure was not only irregular but actually illegal. In the first place, Congress alone was authorized to propose amendments to the Articles. Furthermore, any amendments must be ratified by the State legislatures. Finally, an amendment, to become active, must secure the votes of all the States. However, the delegates realized that the State legislatures would be loath to ratify an instrument that would reduce their powers; and they could not see their way to obtaining ratification from all the States, especially since Rhode Island had not even sent delegates to Philadelphia. Furthermore, they felt that all the forces behind the new Constitution could be mustered for a supreme effort in electing friendly delegates to the special ratifying conventions.

Therefore, with some trepidation, they decided to send their work to the Confederation Congress, for approval of the ratifying procedure. A letter from George Washington, urging Congress to make haste, accompanied the Constitution. Already some opposition had arisen in Congress, led by Richard Henry Lee and by certain delegates at Philadelphia who had rejected the Constitution. Nevertheless, after some debate, Congress voted unanimously to submit the document to the State legislatures with instructions to refer it to the State conventions.

Public debate over ratification

Once the Constitution was made public, it became the subject of widespread debate. Soon the debaters split into contending groups of supporters and antagonists known respectively as Federalists and Antifederalists, which later became the first two political parties under the Constitution. The split had political, economic, and sectional aspects. Federalists insisted on the need for strengthening the central authority; Antifederalists argued that the new central government could not fail to become a tyranny (see Figure 9). Federalists found recruits especially from among the prosperous groups, the creditors, the hard-money proponents; they supported the constitutional clauses guaranteeing payment of the national debt and forbidding the States to emit bills of credit, which are a form of paper money backed by the credit of the State. (Art. VI, cl. 1; Art. I, sec. 10, cl. 1.) Antifederalists were more numerous among the small farmers and workingmen, the debtors, the paper-money advocates—those, in short, who had not been speculating in government securities or who wanted the States to issue inflated paper currency.

Federalists were concentrated along the coast, where the wealth and political influence of America then lay. Antifederalists included most of

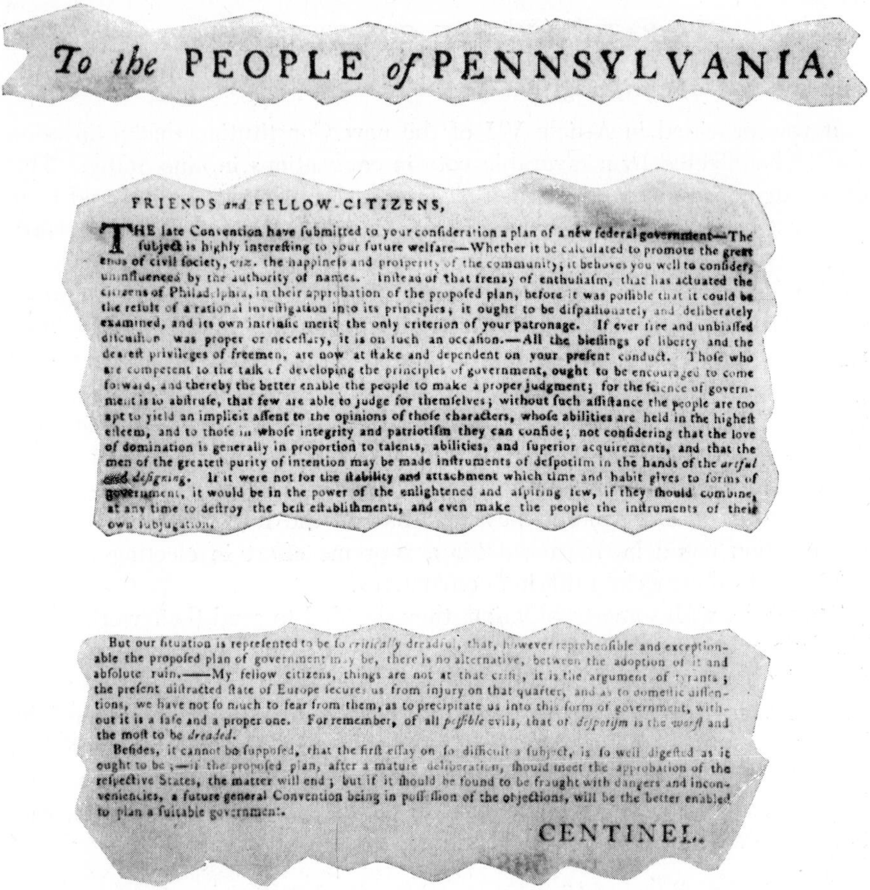

To the PEOPLE *of* PENNSYLVANIA.

FRIENDS *and* FELLOW-CITIZENS,

THE late Convention have ſubmitted to your conſideration a plan of a new federal government—The ſubject is highly intereſting to your future welfare—Whether it be calculated to promote the great ends of civil ſociety, viz. the happineſs and proſperity of the community; it behoves you well to conſider, uninfluenced by the authority of names. Inſtead of that frenzy of enthuſiaſm, that has actuated the citizens of Philadelphia, in their approbation of the propoſed plan, before it was poſſible that it could be the reſult of a rational inveſtigation into its principles, it ought to be diſpaſſionately and deliberately examined, and its own intrinſic merit the only criterion of your patronage. If ever free and unbiaſſed diſcuſſion was proper or neceſſary, it is on ſuch an occaſion.—All the bleſſings of liberty and the deareſt privileges of freemen, are now at ſtake and dependent on your preſent conduct. Thoſe who are competent to the taſk of developing the principles of government, ought to be encouraged to come forward, and thereby the better enable the people to make a proper judgment; for the ſcience of government is ſo abſtruſe, that few are able to judge for themſelves; without ſuch aſſiſtance the people are too apt to yield an implicit aſſent to the opinions of thoſe characters, whoſe abilities are held in the higheſt eſteem, and to thoſe in whoſe integrity and patriotiſm they can confide; not conſidering that the love of domination is generally in proportion to talents, abilities, and ſuperior acquirements, and that the men of the greateſt purity of intention may be made inſtruments of deſpotiſm in the hands of the *artful and deſigning*. If it were not for the ſtability and attachment which time and habit gives to forms of government, it would be in the power of the enlightened and aſpiring few, if they ſhould combine, at any time to deſtroy the beſt eſtabliſhments, and even make the people the inſtruments of their own ſubjugation.

But our ſituation is repreſented to be ſo *critically* dreadful, that, however reprehenſible and exceptionable the propoſed plan of government may be, there is no alternative, between the adoption of it and abſolute ruin.——My fellow citizens, things are not at that criſis, it is the argument of tyrants; the preſent diſtracted ſtate of Europe ſecures us from injury on that quarter, and as to domeſtic diſſentions, we have not ſo much to fear from them, as to precipitate us into this form of government, without it is a ſafe and a proper one. For remember, of all *poſſible* evils, that of *deſpotiſm* is the *worſt* and the moſt to be *dreaded*.

Beſides, it cannot be ſuppoſed, that the firſt eſſay on ſo difficult a ſubject, is ſo well digeſted as it ought to be;—if the propoſed plan, after a mature deliberation, ſhould meet the approbation of the reſpective States, the matter will end; but if it ſhould be found to be fraught with dangers and inconveniencies, a future general Convention being in poſſeſſion of the objections, will be the better enabled to plan a ſuitable government.

CENTINEL.

Library of Congress.

Figure 9. A Broadside Against the Constitution. "To the People of Pennsylvania" from "Centinel" was one of numerous propaganda leaflets and commentaries attacking the proposed Constitution and urging that it not be ratified.

the people of the interior, save the Germans and Scots-Irish of the Shenandoah valley; the interior folk not only were debtors but also feared lest the new government barter away the mouth of the Mississippi, which was necessary to them if they hoped to export their surplus grain. The residents of the Shenandoah valley were drawn perhaps because the commercial power of the new central government could assist their trade with Baltimore and Philadelphia, which, rather than the mouth of the Mississippi, were the terminal cities for their shipments of grain. A great many Americans, it is also proper to recall, had no sense of the defects of the Articles and no desire to see them changed.

Federalist advantages in the debates

The Federalists had certain notable advantages in the contest over ratification. In their ranks were some of the best minds and most facile pens of the nation. This was best illustrated in New York, where the two parties were nearly equal in strength. To win public support for the Constitution, Alexander Hamilton, James Madison, and John Jay wrote a series of essays defending the Federalist cause and expounding the principles of the new Constitution. Although a contemporary French observer derided them as " . . . no use to the educated . . . too learned and too long for the ignorant," these brief essays, first published in a newspaper (see Figure 10) under the title of *The Federalist,* gained increasing respect with the passage of time. They are among the most important American contributions to political theory. It should not be thought that the Antifederalists were mute, however; Richard Henry Lee's *Letters of the Federalist Farmer* were an able defense of the Antifederalist position. Actually one of the cleverest acts of the supporters of the Constitution was the adoption of the name Federalist; for this name, to many people, connoted an attachment to the confederative form of government. Another Federalist advantage emerged from the unity that bound them through the mere fact of their having written the Constitution. Even before they submitted their work to the people, the authors of the Constitution had elaborated arguments on their own behalf. Hence from the beginning the Antifederalists had to assault a well-constructed fortress.

State adoptions

The First States: States began ratifying the Constitution in 1787, within three months of its being tendered to them. Among the first five States to ratify, four—Delaware, New Jersey, Georgia, and Connecticut—were small States. Evidently the granting of equal representation in the upper house had removed small-State fears that they would be dominated by the large States. After the first five States had adopted the Constitution, a brief period elapsed before the necessary four additional States acted. In Massachusetts the Antifederalists, led by John Hancock and Samuel Adams, offered determined resistance. Federalist leaders appear to have won Hancock by intimating that he would be supported for governor, that he might be named Vice President, and that if Virginia failed to ratify he would be in a good position to become the first President. Samuel Adams evidently convinced himself of the likelihood of adoption and of the resultant political dangers inherent in opposition. Hence after considerable discussion in the convention, Massachusetts voted to adopt the Constitution.

At the same time the convention offered a group of amendments to the Constitution, in the form of a Bill of Rights, which it proposed as a first order of business after ratification had been completed. Opponents of the Constitution had insisted all along that it created a potentially tyrannical central authority; the Federalists had repeatedly argued, however, that no tyranny was possible, since the national government had only certain delegated powers. Why, asked the Federalists, should the Constitution be amended to deny certain acts to the government when the Constitution did not authorize these acts in the first place? The Antifederalists were no more impressed with this argument now than they had been earlier. They

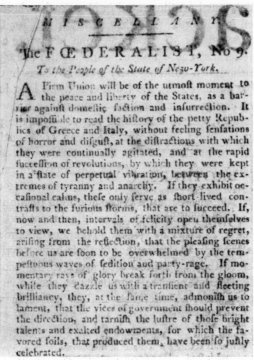

Figure 10.   A Portion of One of the *Federalist* Papers.

consequently obliged the convention to submit amendments designed to erect barriers against the power of the federal government. Subsequently nearly every State ratifying after Massachusetts likewise presented desired amendments.

Now Maryland, South Carolina, and New Hampshire all ratified the Constitution. In the case of the last-named State, the Federalists had to resort to delaying tactics in order to win adoption. When the New Hampshire convention first assembled, it had an obvious Antifederalist majority. Supporters of the Constitution were able to procure an adjournment until certain members of the convention could change their stand. When the convention again met, eight States had now voted for ratification, a fact that probably served to convince some waverers. After a few days of deliberation, the New Hampshire convention voted for ratification. The requisite nine States had now endorsed the Constitution, so that on paper, at least, the new government could come into being.

Adoption by the Remaining States: Although nine States had now ratified the Constitution, the government could not hope to be effective without the adherence of Virginia and New York. Each of these States was peculiarly significant. At this time Virginia was the most populous State in the Union; and New York, although not one of the largest States, separated New England from the rest of the country. Hence winning their ratification was essential to making the national government workable.

In Virginia the Antifederalists, under such leaders as Patrick Henry, were especially critical of the vast domestic powers of the new central government. Moreover, western Virginians feared lest the national government arrange a pact with Spain whereby the Spanish would receive the mouth of the Mississippi in exchange for a commercial treaty favorable to New England. However, under James Madison the Federalists won the day; the Virginia convention ratified the Constitution.

In New York a major objection was brought against the national power to levy tariffs. Americans had just waged a revolution partly to expel the cus-

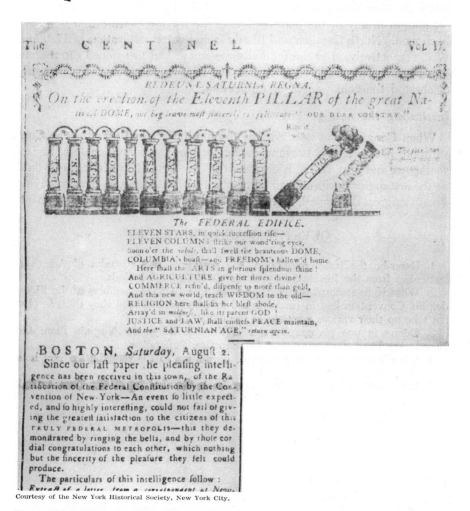

Figure 11. Wavering Pillars of the Temple. An early cartoonist is moved to poetry by New York's ratification of the Constitution, and points also to the two reluctant states that had not yet acted.

tomsmen of a central authority; they did not now wish to admit others. Furthermore, since much of the seaborne trade of New Jersey, Connecticut, Massachusetts, and Vermont came through the port of New York City, the State had amassed a large portion of its revenue through State tariffs; the great landowners of the Hudson valley would have to assume a larger fraction of the burden of State financing if the federal government abolished the State customs. It was specifically in an effort to sway the voters of New York that Hamilton, Madison, and Jay wrote *The Federalist*, a fragment of which is reproduced as Figure 10. Certainly their work was influential; but another fact motivating the New York convention to ratify the Constitution was that, since Virginia had ratified, New York would stand with only North Carolina and Rhode Island outside the Union. Confronted by this possibility, the New York convention voted for adoption, although by the narrowest margin in any of the States. The battle for the Constitution now had been won. North Carolina and Rhode Island voted ratification in 1789 and 1790, respectively, after the federal government had threatened discrimination against their trade. Figure 11 shows how one cartoonist of the day celebrated the achievement of ratification.

Instituting the new government

When Congress was notified that the ninth State had adopted the Constitution, it directed that arrangements be made to name Senators, Representatives, and presidential Electors. It declared that New York City would be the first national capital, and that Congress should meet on March 4, 1789. Then Congress disbanded, leaving the United States to its new government.

QUESTIONS AND PROBLEMS

1. Describe the transformation of the personnel and attitudes of American leadership from the Revolutionary to the Constitutional Periods.

2. What were some of the traits and attitudes that the members of the Philadelphia Convention had in common and in what respects did they differ? (Do not take up their various positions in the debates.)

3. Define in one paragraph each of the following: the Virginia Plan; the New Jersey Plan; the Connecticut Compromise; Federalists.

4. What were the various sources of opposition to the Constitution and how were they effectively blocked?

5. What sectional interests were at stake in the drafting of the Constitution?

PART II

The Federal System

5. The Text
of the Constitution

THE text of the Constitution is the fundamental law under which the government of the United States operates. Yet the vast majority of the American people seem to know very little about the federal Constitution. A few years ago, a public opinion poll showed that thirty-one per cent of American adults had never heard of the Bill of Rights; that another thirty-six per cent had heard of it but could not identify it; and that twelve per cent more gave incorrect versions of what it is. Thus seventy-nine per cent, or almost four out of five, of American adults were unable to identify the Bill of Rights correctly. When, in a later poll in Madison, Wisconsin, some Amer-

icans were asked to sign the Bill of Rights as evidence of subscribing to
its principles, practically all refused, suspecting a subversive plot. The
most charitable interpretation of these occurrences would be that people
could not see the forest for the trees; in other words, they could not recognize as parts of the Constitution a few sentences whose import was technical.

The aim of this chapter is to familiarize the student with the text of the
Constitution. Like other great works of the mind and spirit, the Constitution should be read like a love letter. It deserves a careful reading as
it stands; all too many students have read *about* the Constitution without
having had the experience of reading the document itself. As it is read, a
number of its interesting features can be noted that would be puzzling if
explained apart from the text. The facts noted are not necessarily the
most important elements of the Constitution; they are simply those that
highlight the form and exemplify the meanings and development of the
Constitution.

In the following presentation, the text of the Constitution appears in the
left-hand column, and observations about certain points in the text appear
in the right-hand column. The left-hand column includes only those parts
of the Constitution that are used today or that might, under changed conditions, be used in the future. The parts that have been invalidated by later
Amendments have been placed in the right-hand column; for they no longer
comprise elements in the fundamental law of the American national government. Certain other passages in the Constitution have become obsolete;
these have been placed in the left-hand column, but the fact that they are
inactive today has been noted in the right-hand column.

CONSTITUTION OF THE UNITED STATES

We the people of the United
States, in order to form a more perfect union, establish justice, insure
domestic tranquility, provide for the
common defense, promote the general welfare, and secure the blessings of liberty to ourselves and our
posterity, do ordain and establish
this Constitution for the United
States of America.[1]

Article I[2]

Section 1

All legislative powers herein
granted shall be vested in a Congress of the United States, which
shall consist of a Senate and House
of Representatives.[3]

1. Introductory doctrine: *This introductory sentence is termed the* Preamble. *It is not strictly necessary to
the Constitution. It comprises not law
but doctrine. For example, it is never
cited as authorization for a power exercised by any branch of the government.
The ideas stated in the Preamble are
consonant with the "enlightened" beliefs of the eighteenth century. Note
the doctrine of the social compact in
"We the people . . . do ordain and
establish. . . ."*

2. How the Constitution is subdivided: *The principal divisions of the
Constitutions are the* Articles, *of which
there are seven.* Articles *are subdivided into* Sections, *and* Sections *into*
clauses.

3. Origins of law in the legislature:
Article I, it can be seen, is devoted to

The Beginning Passages of the Original Copy of the Constitution.

Section 2

1. The House of Representatives shall be composed of members chosen every second year by the people of the several States, and the electors in each State shall have the qualifications requisite for electors of the most numerous branch of the State legislature.

2. No person shall be a representative who shall not have attained to the age of twenty-five years, and been seven years a citizen of the United States, and who shall not, when elected, be an inhabitant of that State in which he shall be chosen.

3. Representatives and direct taxes[4] shall be apportioned among the several States which may be included within this Union, according to their respective numbers. . . .[5] The actual enumeration shall be made within three years after the first meeting of the Congress of the United States, and within every subsequent term of ten years, in such manner as they shall by law direct. The number of representatives shall not exceed one for every thirty thousand, but each State shall have at least one representative; and until such enumeration shall be made, the States of New Hampshire shall be entitled to choose three, Massachusetts eight, Rhode Island and Providence Plantations one, Connecticut five, New York six, New Jersey four, Pennsylvania eight, Delaware one, Maryland six, Virginia ten, North Carolina five, South Carolina five, and Georgia three.[6]

4. When vacancies happen in the representation from any State, the executive authority thereof shall issue writs of election to fill such vacancies.

5. The House of Representatives shall choose their Speaker and other officers; and shall have the sole power of impeachment.

the legislative power. This arrangement reflects the belief of the time that policy-making is prior to policy-executing, and that policy is initiated by legislative bodies. *Note that Article I is as long as the remaining six Articles combined.*

4. A provision inoperative since the Civil War: *The provision regarding direct taxes is more or less inoperative, since the national government does not levy direct taxes. See the Sixteenth Amendment.*

5. A clause eliminated: *Originally, ". . . which shall be determined by adding to the whole number of free persons, including those bound to service for a term of years, and excluding Indians not taxed, three fifths of all other persons." This is the famous "three-fifths compromise." It lapsed with the emancipation of the slaves, and was in part formally superseded by the Fourteenth Amendment.*

6. An example of legislative matter in the Constitution: *This provision for the size of the State delegations to the House is actually legislative rather than constitutional. That is, it is matter which, if only because it is not expected to be enduring, might be better fixed by a law passed by Congress than by a constitutional provision. However, it was essential for getting the new regime into motion.*

Section 3

1. The Senate of the United States shall be composed of two senators from each State . . . ;[7] and each Senator shall have one vote.[8]

2. Immediately after they shall be assembled in consequence of the first election, they shall be divided as equally as may be into three classes. The seats of the senators of the first class shall be vacated at the expiration of the second year, of the second class at the expiration of the fourth year, and of the third class at the expiration of the sixth year, so that one third may be chosen every second year; . . .[9]

3. No person shall be a Senator who shall not have attained to the age of thirty years, and been nine years a citizen of the United States, and who shall not, when elected, be an inhabitant of that State for which he shall be chosen.

4. The Vice President of the United States shall be President of the Senate, but shall have no vote, unless they be equally divided.

5. The Senate shall choose their other officers, and also a president *pro tempore*, in the absence of the Vice President, or when he shall exercise the office of President of the United States.[10]

6. The Senate shall have the sole power to try all impeachments. When sitting for that purpose, they shall be on oath or affirmation.[11] When the President of the United States is tried, the Chief Justice shall preside: and no person shall be convicted without the concurrence of two-thirds of the members present.

7. Judgment in cases of impeachment shall not extend further than to removal from office, and disqualification to hold and enjoy any office of honor, trust or profit under the United States: but the party convicted shall nevertheless be liable and subject to indictment, trial,

7. A changed phrase: *Originally, ". . . chosen by the legislature thereof for six years. . . ." This phrase was superseded by the Seventeenth Amendment, which instituted direct popular election of Senators.*

8. A confederative idea with a national bent: *That each State should have two Senators elected by the State legislature was an important concession to the principle of federalism. However, that each Senator should have one vote, rather than that each State should have one vote in the Senate, reveals the intention of the Founding Fathers that the Senate should be a truly national legislature and not a conclave of ambassadors from the States.*

9. *Originally, ". . . and if vacancies happen by resignation, or otherwise, during the recess of the legislature of any State, the executive thereof may make temporary appointments until the next meeting of the legislature, which shall then fill such vacancies." This clause was also superseded by the Seventeenth Amendment.*

10. The interlocking of parts: *Naturally, here, the authors had to recall that elsewhere they had provided for the Vice President's succession to the presidency, which would then leave a vacancy in the presidency of the Senate.*

11. Added procedure for unusual functions: *When acting as a court, the Senate adds new solemnity to its proceedings. Note elsewhere that when an organ does "double duty," it is somewhat changed. For instance, according to the Twelfth Amendment, the House, if it must choose the President, votes not as individuals but as States; another instance is the requirement that a congressional rejection of a veto must have a two-thirds majority* (Art. I, sec. 7, cl. 2).

judgment and punishment, according to law.

Section 4

1. The times, places and manner of holding elections for Senators and Representatives, shall be prescribed in each State by the legislature thereof; but the Congress may at any time by law make or alter such regulations, except as to the places of choosing senators.[12]

2. . . .[13]

Section 5

1. Each House shall be the judge of the elections, returns and qualifications of its own members, and a majority of each shall constitute a quorum to do business; but a smaller number may adjourn from day to day, and may be authorized to compel the attendance of absent members, in such manner, and under such penalties as each House may provide.

2. Each House may determine the rules of its proceedings, punish its members for disorderly behavior, and, with the concurrence of two-thirds, expel a member.

3. Each House shall keep a Journal of its proceedings, and from time to time publish the same, excepting such parts as may in their judgment require secrecy; and the yeas and nays of the members of either House on any question shall, at the desire of one-fifth of those present, be entered on the Journal.

4. Neither House, during the session of Congress, shall, without the consent of the other, adjourn for more than three days, nor to any other place than that in which the two Houses shall be sitting.

Section 6

1. The Senators and Representatives shall receive a compensation for their services, to be ascertained

12. A fine point for State independence: *The phrase, "except as to the places of choosing Senators," was inserted to prevent Congress from influencing the sites of State capitals, or perhaps from making the electors go to the national capital. This provision is meaningless today since the people, and not the State legislatures, elect Senators.*

A missing "ghost" clause: *In an early draft of the Constitution this clause was to be followed by one stating that "The legislature of the United States shall have authority to establish such uniform qualifications of the members of each House, with regard to property, as to the said legislature shall seem expedient." Since the delegates to the Convention could not agree on this question, the clause was omitted entirely from the final draft of the Constitution. Several other such "ghost" clauses prowl the pages of the Constitution.*

13. An amendment produces an excision: *Originally, "The Congress shall assemble at least once in every year, and such meeting shall be on the first Monday in December, unless they shall by law appoint a different day." This clause was replaced by the Twentieth Amendment, section 2.*

by law, and paid out of the Treasury of the United States.[14] They shall in all cases, except treason, felony and breach of the peace, be privileged from arrest during their attendance at the session of their respective Houses, and in going to and returning from the same; and for any speech or debate in either House, they shall not be questioned in any other place.

2. No Senator or Representative shall, during the time for which he is elected, be appointed to any civil office under the authority of the United States, which shall have been created, or the emoluments whereof shall have been increased during such time, and no person holding any office under the United States shall be a member of either House during his continuance in office.[15]

Section 7

1. All bills for raising revenue shall originate in the House of Representatives; but the Senate may propose or concur with amendments as on other bills.[16]

2. Every bill which shall have passed the House of Representatives and the Senate, shall, before it become a law, be presented to the President of the United States; if he approve he shall sign it, but if not he shall return it, with his objections to that House in which it shall have originated, who shall enter the objections at large on their Journal, and proceed to reconsider it. If after such reconsideration two-thirds of that House shall agree to pass the bill, it shall be sent, together with the objections, to the other House, by which it shall likewise be reconsidered, and if approved by two-thirds of that House, it shall become a law. But in all such cases the votes of both Houses shall be determined by yeas and nays, and the names of the persons

14. A fine point for nationalism: The provision that the congressmen should be paid by the national government instead of by the States, as under the Articles of Confederation, indicated how the members of the Convention aimed at strengthening the power of the central government.

15. A detail of the separation of powers: The principle of the separation of powers is nowhere mentioned in the Constitution. However, the provisions of this clause definitely separate the personnel of the legislative branch from those of the other two branches.

16. Altered meaning through practice: The power to amend is almost as strong as the power to originate. But the colonial tradition made the authors desirous of putting money bills into the hands of the "popular" chamber, even though times were already changing the original reasons for the doctrine.

voting for and against the bill shall be entered on the Journal of each House respectively. If any bill shall not be returned by the President within ten days (Sundays excepted) after it shall have been presented to him, the same shall be a law, in like manner as if he had signed it, unless the Congress by their adjournment prevent its return, in which case it shall not be a law.[17]

3. Every order, resolution, or vote to which the concurrence of the Senate and the House of Representatives may be necessary (except on a question of adjournment) shall be presented to the President of the United States; and before the same shall take effect, shall be approved by him, or being disapproved by him, shall be repassed by two-thirds of the Senate and House of Representatives, according to the rules and limitations prescribed in the case of a bill.[18]

Section 8 Art. I

1. The Congress shall have the power to lay and collect taxes, duties, imposts, and excises, to pay the debts and provide for the common defense and general welfare of the United States; but all duties, imposts, and excises shall be uniform throughout the United States;

2. To borrow money on the credit of the United States;

3. To regulate commerce with foreign nations, and among the several States, and with the Indian tribes;[19]

4. To establish a uniform rule of naturalization, and uniform laws on the subject of bankruptcies throughout the United States;

5. To coin money, regulate the value thereof,[20] and of foreign coin, and fix the standard of weights and measures;

6. To provide for the punishment of counterfeiting the securities and current coin of the United States;

17. Omission of a famous word: This lengthy clause describes the veto process, without once employing the word "veto."

18. An omission of a form of law: Although apparently intended to be comprehensive, this clause does not apply to concurrent resolutions, as opposed to joint resolutions (on pages 385 and 388).

19. A vastly altered meaning: This power was desired by the North and opposed by the South. The South permitted it only after securing the guarantees of its own interests found in Art. I, sec. 9, cl. 1 and 5. The meaning of "commerce" has greatly evolved since 1788. For more than a century most lawyers thought it meant "trade" and nothing more. Today it embraces "manufacturing" as well, thanks to Supreme Court decisions.

20. A source of implied power: Alexander Hamilton argued that from this authorization the power to establish a Bank of the United States could be implied. This was the first claim of an implied power.

7. To establish post offices and post roads;

8. To promote the progress of science and useful arts, by securing for limited times to authors and inventors the exclusive rights to their respective writings and discoveries;

9. To constitute tribunals inferior to the Supreme Court;

10. To define and punish piracies and felonies committed on the high seas, and offenses against the law of nations;

11. To declare war, grant letters of marque and reprisal,[21] and make rules concerning captures on land and water;

12. To raise and support armies, but no appropriation shall be for a longer term than two years;

13. To provide and maintain a navy;

14. To make rules for the government and regulation of the land and naval forces;

15. To provide for calling forth the militia to execute the laws of the Union, suppress insurrection and repel invasions;

16. To provide for organizing, arming, and disciplining the militia, and for governing such part of them as may be employed in the service of the United States, reserving to the States respectively the appointment of the officers, and the authority of training the militia according to the discipline prescribed by Congress;[22]

17. To exercise exclusive legislation in all cases whatsoever, over such district (not exceeding ten miles square) as may, by cession of particular States, and the acceptance of Congress, become the seat of the government of the United States, and to exercise like authority over all places purchased by the consent of the legislature of the State in which the same shall be, for the erection of forts, magazines, arse-

21. An obsolete authority: *Letters of marque and reprisal are a commission given by a government to a private citizen to operate a merchant ship as a warship, or privateer, and to capture enemy property. Letters of marque and reprisal were renounced by the countries signing the Declaration of Paris of 1856. Although the United States was not a signatory of the Declaration, it has honored this prohibition. Hence this power is obsolete. In any event, modern technology has made warships so greatly different from merchant vessels that fitting out a privateer to compete with present-day warships would be a rather vain effort (see Figure 12).*

22. A joint national-State function: *The small amount of power left to the States with respect to the militia shows the influence of Federalist theory.*

Transmitter photo by courtesy of Radio Free Europe

Figure 12. Privateers, Ancient and Contemporary. Battle between the Schooner *Dolphin,* **the British Ship** *Hebe,* **and a Brig, off Cape Vincent, Jan. 25, 1813; Radio Free Europe 135 Kilowatt Medium-Wave Transmitter in Holzkirchen, Germany.** When America had a small navy and warships were not costly, the government issued licenses (called letters of marque and reprisal) to private ships to wage war on the high seas. The Constitution authorizes the power. Today a new form of private cold war is possible; private groups, with government blessing, attack Communism by radio and other means of communication. The Constitution did not foresee this modern mode of international conflict, but authority for the activity has not been questioned.

nals, dockyards, and other needful buildings;[23] and

18. To make all laws which shall be necessary and proper for carrying into execution the foregoing powers and all other powers vested by this Constitution in the government of the United States, or in any department or officer thereof.[24]

Section 9[25]

1. . . .[26]

2. The privilege of the writ of *habeas corpus* shall not be suspended, unless when in cases of rebellion or invasion the public safety may require it.

3. No bill of attainder or *ex post facto* law shall be passed.

4. No capitation, or other direct, tax shall be laid, unless in proportion to the census or enumeration hereinbefore directed to be taken.[27]

5. No tax or duty shall be laid on articles exported from any State.

6. No preference shall be given by any regulation of commerce or revenue to the ports of one State over those of another: nor shall vessels bound to, or from, one State be obliged to enter, clear, or pay duties in another.

7. No money shall be drawn from the Treasury, but in consequence of appropriations, made by law; and a regular statement and account of the receipts and expenditures of all public money shall be published from time to time.

8. No title of nobility shall be granted by the United States: and no person holding any office or profit under them, shall, without the consent of the Congress, accept of any present, emolument, office, or title, of any kind whatever, from any king, prince, or foreign State.

Section 10[28]

1. No State shall enter into any treaty, alliance, or confederation;

23. *This clause simply empowers Congress to govern the capital city of the United States. It should be noted that no precise location is given here. The various sections of the country all sought to have the capital; Hamilton finally arranged to situate it on a tract of one hundred square miles, of which about thirty were ceded by Virginia and seventy by Maryland, in exchange for which those States would support his plan to have the national government assume the State debts. The District of Columbia today contains only about seventy square miles; for the Virginia part of the District was retroceded in 1846.*

24. A clause enlarging the previously-enumerated powers: *This is the "necessary and proper" clause, which is the basis for the implied powers of Congress, and for many of the great debates following ratification of the Constitution.*

25. Guards against old abuses: *Section 9 includes several important limitations on the powers of Congress. Some of these limitations show what the Founding Fathers thought had been abuses in English rule; others are associated with some of the compromises necessary to secure acceptance of the Constitution at the Philadelphia Convention.*

26. A self-terminating clause: *Originally, "The migration or importation of such persons as any of the States now existing shall think proper to admit, shall not be prohibited by the Congress prior to the year one thousand eight hundred and eight, but a tax or duty may be imposed on such importation, not exceeding ten dollars for each person." This clause merely forbids Congress to prohibit the slave trade until 1808. Obviously, the clause is self-repealing.*

27. A clause modified by amendment: *This clause has been modified, although not repealed, by the Sixteenth Amendment.*

28. Some reactions against Confederation experience: *Section 10 includes a number of prohibitions on the States. These prohibitions show what the Founding Fathers believed were the*

grant letters of marque and reprisal; coin money; emit bills of credit; make anything but gold and silver coin a tender in payment of debts; pass any bill of attainder, *ex post facto* law, or law impairing the obligation of contracts, or grant any title of nobility.

2. No State shall, without the consent of the Congress, lay any imposts or duties on imports or exports, except what may be absolutely necessary for executing its inspection laws: and the net produce of all duties and imposts laid by any State on imports or exports, shall be for the use of the Treasury of the United States; and all such laws shall be subject to the revision and control of the Congress.

3. No State shall, without the consent of Congress, lay any duty of tonnage, keep troops, or ships of war in time of peace, enter into any agreement or compact with another State, or with a foreign power, or engage in war, unless actually invaded, or in such imminent danger as will not admit of delay.

Article II[29]

Section 1

1. The executive power shall be vested in a President of the United States of America. He shall hold his office during the term of four years, and, together with the Vice President, chosen for the same term, be elected, as follows:

2. Each State shall appoint, in such manner as the legislature thereof may direct, a number of Electors, equal to the whole number of Senators and Representatives to which the State may be entitled in the Congress: but no Senator or Representative, or person holding an office of trust or profit under the United States, shall be appointed an Elector. . . .[30]

weaknesses of the government under the Articles of Confederation. These prohibitions are clearly associated with the powers extended to Congress; hence they were placed in Article I.

29. The logic of Articles I, II and III: *Article II describes the executive branch of the government. The logic here was that the executive branch did not frame policy and that its work followed that of Congress. Note that Article III then fittingly treats of the judiciary, which comes into action only after a law has been enacted and enforced.*

30. The first mode of presidential election: *Originally, "The Electors shall meet in their respective States, and vote by ballot for two persons, of whom one at least shall not be an inhabitant of the same State with themselves. And they shall make a list of all the persons voted for, and of the number of votes for each; which list they shall sign and certify, and transmit sealed to the seat of the government of the United States, directed to the President of the Senate. The President of the Senate shall, in*

3. The Congress may determine the time of choosing the Electors, and the day on which they shall give their votes; which day shall be the same throughout the United States.

4. No person except a natural-born citizen, or a citizen of the United States, at the time of the adoption of this Constitution,[31] shall be eligible to the office of President; neither shall any person be eligible who shall not have attained to the age of thirty-five years, and been fourteen years a resident within the United States.

5. In case of removal of the President from office, or of his death, resignation, or inability to discharge the powers and duties of the said office, the same shall devolve on the Vice President, and the Congress may by law provide for the case of removal, death, resignation, or inability, both of the President and the Vice President, and such officer shall act accordingly, until the disability be removed, or a President shall be elected.[32]

6. The President shall, at stated times, receive for his services a compensation, which shall neither be increased nor diminished during the period for which he shall have been elected, and he shall not receive within that period any other emolument from the United States, or any of them.

7. Before he enter on the execution of his office, he shall take the following oath or affirmation:—"I do solemnly swear (or affirm) that I will faithfully execute the office of President of the United States, and will to the best of my ability, preserve, protect, and defend the Constitution of the United States."

Section 2

1. The President shall be Commander-in-Chief of the army and navy of the United States, and of

the presence of the Senate and the House of Representatives, open all certificates, and the votes shall then be counted. The person having the greatest number of votes shall be the President, if such number be a majority of the whole number of Electors appointed; and if there be more than one who have such majority, and have an equal number of votes, then the House of Representatives shall immediately choose by ballot one of them for President; and if no person have a majority, then from the five highest on the list the said House shall in like manner choose the President. But in choosing the President, the votes shall be taken by States, the representation from each State having one vote; a quorum for this purpose shall consist of a member or members from two-thirds of the States, and a majority of all the States shall be necessary to a choice. In every case, after the choice of the President, the person having the greatest number of votes of the Electors shall be the Vice President. But if there should remain two or more who have equal votes, the Senate shall choose from them by ballot the Vice President." This passage was superseded by the Twelfth Amendment, which gave the Electors separate votes for the President and the Vice President. That the House should choose the President in case the Electoral College was unable to do so was another concession to the notion of federalism; it was perpetuated, in somewhat altered form, in the Twelfth Amendment.

31. An interim provision: *It has been many years since there was any living person who was a citizen in 1788; hence this provision is obsolete.*

32. A murky clause, clarified by amendment: *The succession to the presidency has been clarified by the Twentieth Amendment.*

the militia of the several States, when called into the actual service of the United States; he may require the opinion, in writing, of the principal officer in each of the executive Departments, upon any subject relating to the duties of their respective offices, and he shall have power to grant reprieves and pardons for offenses against the United States, except in cases of impeachment.

2. He shall have power, by and with the advice and consent of the Senate, to make treaties, provided two-thirds of the Senators present concur; and he shall nominate, and by and with the advice and consent of the Senate, shall appoint ambassadors, other public ministers and consuls, judges of the Supreme Court, and all other officers of the United States, whose appointments are not herein otherwise provided for, and which shall be established by law; but the Congress may by law vest the appointment of such inferior officers, as they think proper, in the President alone, in the courts of law, or in the heads of departments.

3. The President shall have power to fill up all vacancies that may happen during the recess of the Senate, by granting commissions which shall expire at the end of their next session.

Section 3[33]

He shall from time to time give to the Congress information of the state of the Union, and recommend to their consideration such measures as he shall judge necessary and expedient;[34] he may, on extraordinary occasions, convene both Houses, or either of them, and in case of disagreement between them with respect to the time of adjournment, he may adjourn them to such time as he shall think proper;[35] he shall receive ambassadors and other public

33. A catch-all section: Section 3 contains a hodge-podge of presidential powers, dealing with his legislative functions, his executive duties, and his role in the conduct of foreign relations. Oddly enough, the greatest of all presidential legislative powers—the veto— is described in Section 7 of Article I, which is supposedly devoted to Congress.

34. Source of an annual practice: This clause authorizes the "State of the Union" message delivered at the opening of a congressional session each January.

35. An unused power: This authority has never been used because the House and Senate have always agreed on a date for adjournment.

ministers; he shall take care that the laws be faithfully executed, and shall commission all the officers of the United States.[36]

Section 4

The President, Vice President, and all civil officers of the United States, shall be removed from office on impeachment for, and conviction of, treason, bribery, or other high crimes and misdemeanors.

Article III

Section 1

1. The judicial power of the United States shall be vested in one Supreme Court, and in such inferior courts as the Congress may from time to time ordain and establish. The judges, both of the Supreme and inferior courts, shall hold their offices during good behavior, and shall, at stated times, receive for their services, a compensation, which shall not be diminished during their continuance in office.

Section 2

1. The judicial power shall extend to all cases, in law and equity, arising under this Constitution, the laws of the United States, and treaties made, or which shall be made, under their authority:—to all cases affecting ambassadors, other public ministers and consuls;—to all cases of admiralty and maritime jurisdiction;—to controversies to which the United States shall be a party;—to controversies between two or more States;—between a State and citizens of another State;[37]—between citizens of different States—between citizens of the same State claiming lands under grants of different States, and between a State, or the citizens thereof, and foreign States, citizens or subjects.

2. In all cases affecting ambassa-

36. Imitation of State constitutions: *For example, the New York Constitution of 1777 declared "that it shall be the duty of the governor to inform the legislature, at every session, of the condition of the state, so far as may respect his department; to recommend such matters to their consideration as shall appear to him to concern its good government, welfare, and prosperity; . . . to take care that the laws are faithfully executed to the best of his ability; . . ."*

37. A limiting of meaning by amendment: *This power is limited by the Eleventh Amendment, which denies the federal courts jurisdiction in cases in which a citizen of one State sues another State.*

dors, other public ministers and consuls, and those in which a State shall be party, the Supreme Court shall have original jurisdiction.[38] In all the other cases before mentioned, the Supreme Court shall have appellate jurisdiction, both as to law and to fact, with such exceptions, and under such regulations as the Congress shall make.

3. The trial of all crimes, except in cases of impeachment, shall be by jury; and such trial shall be held in the State where the said crimes shall have been committed; but when not committed within any State, the trial shall be at such place or places as the Congress may by law have directed.

Section 3

1. Treason against the United States, shall consist only in levying war against them, or in adhering to their enemies, giving them aid and comfort. No person shall be convicted of treason unless on the testimony of two witnesses to the same overt act, or on confession in open court.

2. The Congress shall have power to declare the punishment of treason, but no attainder of treason shall work corruption of blood, or forfeiture except during the life of the person attainted.[39]

Article IV

Section 1

Full faith and credit shall be given in each State to the public acts, records, and judicial proceedings of every other State.[40] And the Congress may by general law prescribe the manner in which such acts, records and proceedings shall be proved, and the effect thereof.

Section 2

1. The citizens of each State shall be entitled to all privileges and im-

38. Origins of judicial review: *This "original jurisdiction" provision was the basis for Chief Justice John Marshall's finding in the celebrated case of* Marbury *versus* Madison, *that laid the foundation for judicial review.*

39. A special doctrine for a special crime: *This clause imposes a ban on Congress, yet is in the judiciary Article, presumably because of the judicial procedure described in the preceding clause.*

40. An imitation of the Articles of Confederation: *A near copy of a clause in the Articles which states:* "Full faith and credit shall be given in each of these States to the records, acts and judicial proceedings of the courts and magistrates of every other State." *Under this clause, a corporation chartered in one State may conduct business in any other State.*

munities of citizens in the several States.

2. A person charged in any State with treason, felony, or other crime, who shall flee from justice, and be found in another State, shall on demand of the executive authority of the State from which he fled, be delivered up to be removed to the State having jurisdiction of the crime.[41]

3. No person held to service or labor in one State under the laws thereof, escaping into another, shall, in consequence of any law or regulation therein, be discharged from such service or labor, but shall be delivered up on claim of the party to whom such service or labor may be due.[42]

Section 3

1. New States may be admitted by the Congress into this Union;[43] but no new State shall be formed or erected within the jurisdiction of any other State; nor any State be formed by the junction of two or more States, or parts of States, without the consent of the legislatures of the States concerned as well as of the Congress.

2. The Congress shall have power to dispose of and make all needful rules and regulations respecting the territory or other property belonging to the United States; and nothing in this Constitution shall be so construed as to prejudice any claims of the United States, or of any particular State.[44]

Section 4

The United States shall guarantee to every State in this Union a republican form of government, and shall protect each of them against invasion; and on application of the legislature, or of the executive (when the legislature cannot be convened) against domestic violence.

41. A clause interpreted in favor of State authority: *This clause, which deals with the practice known as* rendition *or* extradition, *does not have compulsory power over State governors.*

42. A special, detailed guarantee to the slave-owners: *This clause was designed for the benefit of the slave-owning interests. It authorizes the owner of a fugitive slave to procure, in his home State, a warrant for the arrest of the slave, then pursue him into a free State where police officers according to the "full faith and credit" clause must respect the warrant and assist in capturing the fugitive. Of course, the clause became obsolete with the end of slavery.*

43. A deliberate vagueness: *This clause was written so as to be deliberately vague; for it says nothing as to whether the new States shall be constitutionally and legally the equals of the original States. This ambiguity was introduced primarily at the urging of Gouverneur Morris, who feared lest the West secure political equality with the East.*

44. An evasion of an existing feud between the national government and the States: *Some States still claimed lands in the West.*

Article V

The Congress, whenever two-thirds of both Houses shall deem it necessary, shall propose amendments to this Constitution, or, on the application of the legislatures of two-thirds of the several States, shall call a convention for proposing amendments, which, in either case, shall be valid to all intents and purposes, as part of this Constitution when ratified by the legislatures of three-fourths of the several States, or by conventions in three-fourths thereof, as the one or the other mode of ratification may be proposed by the Congress; Provided that no amendment which may be made prior to the year one thousand eight hundred and eight shall in any manner affect the first and fourth clauses in the ninth section of the first article;[45] and that no State, without its consent, shall be deprived of its equal suffrage in the Senate.[46]

Article VI

1. All debts contracted and engagements entered into, before the adoption of this Constitution, shall be as valid against the United States under this Constitution, as under the Confederation.[47]

2. This Constitution, and the laws of the United States which shall be made in pursuance thereof; and all treaties made, or which shall be made, under the authority of the United States, shall be the supreme law of the land; and the judges in every State shall be bound thereby, anything in the Constitution or laws of any State to the contrary notwithstanding.[48]

3. The Senators and Representatives before mentioned, and the members of the several State legislatures, and all executive and judicial officers, both of the United States and the several States, shall be

45. Another obsolete clause: *This proviso is an additional safeguard for the South that there would be no interference with the slave trade. It is, of course, inoperative now.*

46. A case of absolute State veto power: *This is an exceptional guarantee for the small States.*

47. A reassurance to financial interests: *This clause is an assurance to the holders of bonds issued by the Confederation.*

48. The federal supremacy clause: *This clause, which was borrowed from the New Jersey Plan, is sometimes called "the keystone of the Constitution," since it establishes the supremacy of the federal government over the States.*

bound by oath or affirmation to support this Constitution; but no religious test shall ever be required as a qualification to any office or public trust under the United States.

Article VII

The ratification of the conventions of nine States shall be sufficient for the establishment of this Constitution between the States so ratifying the same.[49]

Done in Convention by the unanimous consent of the States present the seventeenth day of September in the year of our Lord one thousand seven hundred and eighty-seven, and of the independence of the United States of America the twelfth. In witness whereof we have hereunto subscribed our names.

AMENDMENTS[50]

First Amendment[51]

Congress shall make no law respecting an establishment of religion, or prohibiting the free exercise thereof; or abridging the freedom of speech, or of the press; or the right of the people peaceably to assemble, and to petition the government for a redress of grievances.

Second Amendment

A well regulated militia, being necessary to the security of a free State, the right of the people to keep and bear arms shall not be infringed.[52]

Third Amendment

No soldier shall, in time of peace, be quartered in any house, without the consent of the owner, nor in time

49. A daring violation of instructions: *This was a revolutionary Article; for amendment of the Articles of Confederation—presumably the task of the Philadelphia Convention—required unanimous consent of the States.*

50. Amendments properly termed Articles: *Officially the Amendments are termed "Articles" and are numbered as Article I, Article II, and so on. Since this procedure leads to duplication with the body of the Constitution, this text will employ the term "amendment."*

51. The Bill of Rights: *The first ten Amendments are known as the Bill of Rights. They were adopted on December 15, 1791. They were designed to prevent arbitrary actions of the government, some of which had been experienced under British rule. It should be noted that apart from the guarantees of judicial rights these Amendments are negative, as contrasted with the United Nations Declaration of Human Rights.*

52. A diminished popular power: *This Amendment has lost its original significance. It was adopted by a nation that abhorred professional, mercenary armies and held up the citizen-soldier as the military ideal. In this respect, Americans of this era sought to emulate what they believed were the antique virtues of the Roman Republic. George Washington was compared with the Roman Cincinnatus, who according to tradition left his plow to command an army.*

of war, but in a manner to be prescribed by law.[53]

Fourth Amendment

The right of the people to be secure in their persons, houses, papers and effects against unreasonable searches and seizures, shall not be violated, and no warrants shall issue, but upon probable cause, supported by oath or affirmation, and particularly describing the place to be searched, and the persons or things to be seized.[54]

Fifth Amendment

No person shall be held to answer for a capital, or otherwise infamous crime, unless on a presentment or indictment of a grand jury, except in cases arising in the land or naval forces, or in the militia, when in actual service in time of war or public danger; nor shall any person be subject for the same offense to be twice put in jeopardy of life or limb; nor shall be compelled in any criminal case to be a witness against himself, nor be deprived of life, liberty, or property, without due process of law;[55] nor shall private property be taken for public use without just compensation.

Sixth Amendment

In all criminal prosecutions, the accused shall enjoy the right to a speedy and public trial, by an impartial jury of the State and district wherein the crime shall have been committed, which district shall have been previously ascertained by law, and to be informed of the nature and cause of the accusation; to be confronted with the witnesses against him; to have compulsory process for obtaining witnesses in his favor, and to have the assistance of counsel for his defense.

53. The banning, perhaps unnecessary, of an old abuse: *Colonial Americans had been enraged by the English habit of quartering soldiers in their homes without previous consultation. Since troops have their own billets today, this protection is unused.*

54. Imitation by a would-be State: *The Hawaiian territory in its proposed State constitution copies this Amendment word for word, with minor changes in punctuation, but places it in the first article with most other parts of the federal Bill of Rights.*

55. Due process, number I: *The due process guarantee is repeated in the Fourteenth Amendment, which enforces it upon State courts.*

Seventh Amendment

In suits at common law, where the value in controversy shall exceed twenty dollars, the right of trial by jury shall be preserved, and no fact tried by a jury shall be otherwise reexamined in any court of the United States, than according to the rules of common law.

Eighth Amendment

Excessive bail shall not be required, nor excessive fines imposed, nor cruel and unusual punishments inflicted.

Ninth Amendment

The enumeration in the Constitution of certain rights shall not be construed to deny or disparage others retained by the people.[56]

56. Preventing unforeseen oppression: *This Amendment means that there may be or are other rights that are not named in the Constitution.*

Tenth Amendment

The powers not delegated to the United States by the Constitution, nor prohibited by it to the States, are reserved to the States respectively, or to the people.[57]

57. An attempt to restrict the national government: *This Amendment is important in that it distinguishes between the delegated powers of the national government and the reserved powers of the State governments.*

Eleventh Amendment

The judicial power of the United States shall not be construed to extend to any suit in law or equity, commenced or prosecuted against one of the United States by citizens of another State, or by citizens or subjects of any foreign State.[58]

58. An uprising by States-rightists: *This Amendment was adopted on January 8, 1798. It shows the will of the States to retain as much as possible of their sovereignty.*

Twelfth Amendment

The Electors shall meet in their respective States, and vote by ballot for President and Vice President, one of whom, at least, shall not be an inhabitant of the same State with themselves; they shall name in their ballots the person voted for as President, and in distinct ballots, the person voted for as Vice President, and they shall make distinct lists of all persons voted for as President and of all persons voted for as Vice President, and of the number of votes for each, which lists they shall sign and certify, and transmit sealed to the seat of the government of the United States, directed to the President of the Senate;—the President of the Senate shall, in the presence of the Senate and the House of Representatives, open all the certificates and the votes shall be counted;—The person having the greatest number of votes for President, shall be the President, if such number be a majority of the whole number of Electors appointed; and if no person have such majority, then from the persons having the highest number not exceeding three on the list of those voted for as President, the House of Representatives shall choose, immediately, by ballot, the President. But in choosing the President, the votes shall be taken by States, the representation from each State having one vote; a quorum for this purpose shall consist of a member or members from two-thirds of the States, and a majority of all the States shall be necessary to a choice. And if the House of Representatives shall not choose a President whenever the right of choice shall devolve upon them . . .[59] then the Vice President shall act as President, as in the case of the death or other constitutional disability of the President. The person having the greatest number of votes as Vice President shall be the Vice President, if such number be a majority of the whole number of Electors appointed, and if no person have a majority, then from the two highest on the list, the Senate shall choose the Vice President; a quorum for the purpose shall consist of two-

59. An amended Amendment: *Originally, "before the fourth day of March next following. . . ."* This phrase has been superseded by the Twentieth Amendment.

thirds of the whole number of Senators, and a majority of the whole number shall be necessary to a choice. But no person constitutionally ineligible to the office of President shall be eligible to that of Vice President of the United States.[60]

Thirteenth Amendment

1. Neither slavery nor involuntary servitude, except as punishment for crime whereof the party shall have been duly convicted, shall exist within the United States, or any place subject to their jurisdiction.

2. Congress shall have power to enforce this article by appropriate legislation.[61]

Fourteenth Amendment

All persons born or naturalized in the United States, and subject to the jurisdiction thereof, are citizens of the United States and of the State wherein they reside. No State shall make or enforce any law which shall abridge the privileges or immunities of citizens of the United States; nor shall any State deprive any person of life, liberty, or property, without due process of law; nor deny to any person within its jurisdiction equal protection of the laws.[62]

2. Representation shall be apportioned among the several States according to their respective numbers, counting the whole number of persons in each State, excluding Indians not taxed. But when the right to vote at any election for the choice of Electors for President and Vice President of the United States, Representatives in Congress, the executive and judicial officers of a State, or the members of the legislature thereof, is denied to any of the male inhabitants of such State, being twenty-one years of age, and citizens of the United States, or in any

60. Qualifications of the Vice President: *This Amendment was adopted on September 25, 1804. It was aimed at preventing another situation akin to that which arose in 1800, when Thomas Jefferson and Aaron Burr received equal numbers of votes from the Electoral College. This Amendment also filled a gap in the Constitution by fixing the qualifications for the Vice President.*

61. A need for enforcement realized: *This Amendment was adopted on December 18, 1865. The second clause is noteworthy; it shows the recognition of the fact that an Amendment standing by itself has no force, and that it can be executed only by the normal processes of law.*

62. Due process, number II: *These provisions were intended to override the Dred Scott decision of the Supreme Court, in which it was held that a slave could not be a citizen and was not authorized to sue any other person in court, i.e., was not entitled to equal protection of the laws. The new "due process" usage has become of great importance in many ways.*

way abridged, except for participation in rebellion, or other crime, the basis of representation therein shall be reduced in the proportion which the number of such male citizens shall bear to the whole number of male citizens twenty-one years of age in such State.[63]

3. No person shall be a Senator or Representative in Congress, or Elector of President and Vice President, or hold any office, civil or military, under the United States, or under any State, who, having previously taken an oath, as a member of Congress, or as an officer of the United States, or as a member of any State legislature, or as an executive or judicial officer of any State, to support the Constitution of the United States, shall have engaged in insurrection or rebellion against the same, or given aid or comfort to the enemies thereof. But Congress may by a vote of two-thirds of each House, remove such disability.[64]

4. The validity of the public debt of the United States, authorized by law, including debts incurred for payment of pensions and bounties for services in suppressing insurrection or rebellion, shall not be questioned. But neither the United States nor any State shall assume or pay any debt or obligation incurred in aid of insurrection or rebellion against the United States, or any claim for the loss or emancipation of any slaves; but all such debts, obligations, and claims shall be held illegal and void.[65]

5. The Congress shall have power to enforce, by appropriate legislation, the provisions of this article.[66]

Fifteenth Amendment

Section 1

The right of citizens of the United States to vote shall not be denied or abridged by the United States or by

63. An unenforced clause: *This clause has never been enforced, since it would outrage many interests and also prevent literacy tests for voting. It should be noted that it assumes the popular election of the Electoral College. This provision is a sizable interference with the powers of the States, for it (a) sets the highest minimum age that any state may require of voters, and (b) concerns itself with State elections.*

64. Retaliation against Confederate leaders: *This provision was intended to disqualify leaders of the Confederacy from holding political office.*

65. More retaliation: *The first clause of this provision was an assurance to the financial interests holding bonds of the national government that the government would honor its obligations. The second clause annulled the bonds of the Confederacy. The latter clause also admitted that liberation of the slaves had its monetary side; in fact, emancipation cost southern slave-owners about four billion dollars—the market value of their slaves.*

66. The Union centralized: *The Fourteenth Amendment was adopted on July 28, 1868. It breathed the spirit of northern revenge toward the South; in fact, southern States had to ratify this Amendment before they could be readmitted to the Union. It also shows the trend toward strengthening the national government with respect to the States.*

any State on account of race, color, or previous condition of servitude.

Section 2

The Congress shall have power to enforce this article by appropriate legislation.[67]

Sixteenth Amendment

The Congress shall have power to lay and collect taxes on incomes, from whatever source derived, without apportionment among the several States, and without regard to any census or enumeration.[68]

Seventeenth Amendment

The Senate of the United States shall be composed of two Senators from each State, elected by the people thereof, for six years; and each Senator shall have one vote. The electors in each State shall have the qualifications requisite for electors of the most numerous branch of the State legislature.

When vacancies happen in the representation of any State in the Senate, the executive authority of such State shall issue writs of election to fill such vacancies: *Provided,* That the legislature of any State may empower the executive thereof to make temporary appointments until the people fill the vacancies by election as the legislature may direct.

This Amendment shall not be so construed as to affect the election or term of any senator chosen before it becomes valid as part of the Constitution.[69]

Eighteenth Amendment

. . .[70]

Nineteenth Amendment

The right of citizens of the United States to vote shall not be denied

67. A limit on State controls over the right to vote: *This Amendment as adopted on March 30, 1870. Southern States were also required to ratify it. Presumably it only empowered the Negroes to vote. It also was one phase of a Republican Party plan to secure dominance over the whole country: for Republican leaders expected that the Negroes would vote Republican, giving that party control in the South.*

68. A reversal of a Supreme Court decision by amendment: *This Amendment was adopted on February 25, 1913. It was designed to override a Supreme Court decision which had held that an income tax was a direct tax and must therefore be apportioned among the States according to population.*

69. An endorsement of a growing State practice: *This Amendment was adopted on May 31, 1913. It simply arranged for the direct, popular election of United States Senators. This practice existed in effect in many States; more than half the State legislatures had to choose a Senator from among candidates who had been named by the people in primary elections.*

70. The Prohibition Amendment, since repealed: *Originally, "After one year from the ratification of this article, the manufacture, sale, or transportation of intoxicating liquors within, the importation thereof into, or the exportation thereof from the United States and all territory subject to the jurisdiction thereof for beverage purposes is hereby prohibited. The Congress and the several States shall have concurrent power to enforce this article by appropriate legislation. This article shall be inoperative unless it shall have been ratified as an amendment to the Constitution by the legislatures of the several States, as provided in the Constitution, within seven years from the date of the submission hereof to the states by Congress." The Eighteenth Amendment was adopted on January 29, 1919. It was repealed in 1933 by the Twenty-first Amendment. This was the first Amendment to include a time limit for ratification.*

or abridged by the United States or by any State on account of sex.

The Congress shall have power by appropriate legislation to enforce the provisions of this article.[71]

71. The women's suffrage Amendment: *This Amendment was adopted on August 26, 1920.*

Twentieth Amendment

Section 1

The terms of the President and Vice President shall end at noon on the 20th day of January, and the terms of Senators and Representatives at noon on the 3rd day of January, of the years in which such terms would have ended if this article had not been ratified; and the terms of their successors shall then begin.[72]

72. The "Lame Duck" Amendment: *The purpose of this section was to end the so-called "lame duck" sessions of Congress, i.e., those sessions that met after a November election and contained numerous members who had been voted out of office. The section also had the aim of shortening the interval between elections and the seating of federal officers.*

Section 2

The Congress shall assemble at least once in every year, and such meeting shall begin at noon on the 3rd day of January, unless they shall by law appoint a different day.

Section 3

If, at the time fixed for the beginning of the term of the President, the President-elect shall have died,[73] the Vice President-elect shall become President.[74] If a President shall not have been chosen before the time fixed for the beginning of his term, or if the President-elect shall have failed to qualify, then the Vice President-elect shall act as President until a President shall have qualified; and the Congress may by law provide for the case wherein neither a President-elect nor a Vice President-elect shall have qualified, declaring who shall then act as President, or the manner in which one who is to act shall be selected, and such person shall act accordingly until a President or Vice President shall have qualified.

73. Adherence to the original literary style: *Note the persistent use of the future perfect tense, probably in imitation of the earlier parts of the Constitution since this tense is archaic today.*

74. A formal designation of the succession: *This section provides that the Vice President shall, under certain conditions, "become" President. It is nowhere stated in the Constitution that if a President dies in office, the Vice President shall "become" President; it is provided only that the powers and duties of the office shall "devolve" upon the Vice President. However, the Vice President does function as President, whatever his constitutional status.*

Section 4

The Congress may by law provide for the case of the death of any of the persons from whom the House of Representatives may choose a President whenever the right of choice may have devolved upon them, and for the case of the death of any of the persons from whom the Senate may choose a Vice President whenever the right of choice shall have devolved upon them.

Section 5

Sections 1 and 2 shall take effect on the 15th day of October following the ratification of this article.

Section 6

This article shall be inoperative unless it shall have been ratified as an amendment to the Constitution by the legislatures of three-fourths of the several States within seven years from the date of its submission.[75]

75. *This Amendment was adopted on February 6, 1933.*

Twenty-first Amendment

Section 1

The eighteenth article of amendment to the Constitution of the United States is hereby repealed.

Section 2

The transportation or importation into any State, territory, or possession of the United States for delivery or use therein of intoxicating liquors, in violation of the laws thereof, is hereby prohibited.[76]

Section 3

This article shall be inoperative unless it shall have been ratified as an amendment to the Constitution by conventions in the several States, as provided in the Constitution, within seven years from the date of the submission hereof to the States by the Congress.[77]

76. Federal aid in enforcing State criminal law: *In other words, the federal government uses its powers over interstate commerce to assist States with local prohibition laws.*

77. Ratification by conventions: *This Amendment was adopted on December 5, 1933. It is the only Amendment to be ratified by conventions rather than State legislatures.*

Twenty-second Amendment

Section 1

No person shall be elected to the office of the President more than twice, and no person who has held the office of President, or acted as President, for more than two years of a term to which some other person was elected President shall be elected to the office of President more than once. But this article shall not apply to any person holding the office of President when this article was proposed by Congress, and shall not prevent any person who may be holding the office of President, or acting as President, during the term within which this article becomes operative from holding the office of President or acting as President during the remainder of such term.[78]

Section 2

This article shall be inoperative unless it shall have been ratified as an amendment to the Constitution by the legislatures of three-fourths of the several States within seven years from the date of its submission to the States by the Congress.[79]

78. A courtesy to the incumbent: *The second sentence of this Section is probably already obsolete, with the decision of Harry Truman not to be a candidate in 1952 or 1956 and with the speedy adoption of the Amendment.*

79. *This Amendment was adopted on February 27, 1951.*

QUESTIONS AND PROBLEMS

1. Where is the doctrine of the social compact to be noticed in the Constitution? Can you explain its presence and its position?

2. Outline in topical form the general structure of the Constitution.

3. Cite two examples of obsolete statements in the Constitution.

4. Cite an example from the Constitution of matter that is ordinarily regarded as "legislative" in character.

5. Cite and describe each place in the Constitution that sets up or presumes the equality of the States.

6. Cite three provisions of the Constitution that change the nature or mode of operation of an office or an agency when a special task is placed upon it.

7. Cite a "ghost clause" of the Constitution and two examples of deliberate vagueness. Explain each instance.

8. It is often stated that the Constitution must be understood to be a "political" document, as well as a "philosophical" document. Cite examples of provisions supporting each view.

9. Name three famous terms used to describe the structure and operation of government that are not mentioned in the Constitution.

10. What specific abuses of power seemed to trouble the Philadelphia conven-

tion; which others seemed to trouble the ratifying conventions and First Congress? Do the differences between the two types have any philosophical meaning?

11. Cite an instance in which the Constitution imitates a State constitution.

12. The Constitution gives guarantees to property in general. Does it guarantee any specific property from confiscation or damage?

13. Where does the term "due process" occur in the Constitution?

14. Name an unenforced clause of the Constitution.

15. What was the first amendment to include a time limit on its ratification?

16. Cite two instances in which the federal government is charged by the Constitution with assisting State governments or helping them enforce their laws.

6. Principles of the Constitution

Bettman Archive (Engraving by Theo. L. Davis, 1868)

THE Constitution provides the fundamental law under which the national government operates. It establishes the several branches of the government. It confers certain powers upon the government, and denies it others. It outlines the relationships between the national government and the States, and the national government and the citizens. It sets forth means for amending the national law.

The major principles

At the time of its adoption the Constitution was unique. It possessed certain salient principles: the rule of law, or constitutionalism; popular sovereignty; the republican form of government; a federal system; the separation of powers, coupled with checks and balances; and the protection and extension of free enterprise. Each and every one of these principles helped to produce a "limited government." Alone, each of these principles was

85

known at least in theory, if not in practice. The uniqueness of the American Constitution lay in their combination in a single document proposing to organize a government for a country of continental dimensions. Subsequently the American Constitution has been imitated often in form but never in spirit nor in operation.

THE RULE OF LAW, OR CONSTITUTIONALISM

The Fathers of the Constitution sought to create a government based on the rule of law, or constitutionalism. This latter term must be carefully distinguished from *constitution,* for there is no necessary correlation. A *constitution* is the organic or fundamental law of a state. Every country with an established government has a constitution; Soviet Russia has, and Nazi Germany had, a constitution no less than the United States. Even having a written constitution does not confer constitutionalism upon a nation. Many countries, such as the Soviet Union, that have written constitutions do not possess constitutionalism. *Constitutionalism,* or its virtual equivalent, the rule of law, may be defined as a legal order in which the laws are stable, can be known to all, and cannot be subverted by the caprice of a ruler or official. For instance, constitutionalism is the trait of a government in which every person charged with the same crime will be tried in the same fashion and, if convicted, will receive the same sentence regardless of his economic status, political attitudes, or any other ground for personal distinction.

The Founding Fathers, along with many other contemporary political theorists, drew a sharp line between the rule of law and its opposite, the rule of men. The numerous tyrannies of George III alleged in the Declaration of Independence typified for them the spirit of the rule of men. They felt that a government should be based on a rule of law which could prevent despotic behavior by their governors. The social compact, incarnated in a written constitution, seemed to be the best mode of irrevocably guaranteeing the rule of law. It should be borne in mind that for this period law had a much greater dignity, a more impressive source, than it has today. Numerous modern legists hold that law is but the expression of the moral and ethical code of the community. To the Founding Fathers, law comprised a universal code bequeathed by the Creator. This notion had been expounded by Aristotle in ancient times and by St. Thomas Aquinas in the medieval era. It had been widely accepted throughout Western Civilization by political philosophers; it reached America primarily by means of such writings as those of John Locke in England and François Voltaire in France. American leaders were imbued with this belief not merely because they were conversant with the writings of Locke and Voltaire but also, perhaps more important, because the principle of natural

---

The Senate as a Court of Impeachment of Andrew Johnson. So marked is the physical separation of the branches of government in the Constitution that the impeachment and trial of the President is the only occasion that formally assembles the three branches together, and then, of course, the President is an unhappy party.

law had permeated American intellectual life. The Declaration of Independence is an outstanding statement based upon a doctrine of natural law. The Constitution was an effort to actualize a doctrine of natural law.

POPULAR SOVEREIGNTY

The Constitution envisions a government based upon the active consent of the people. This is the doctrine of popular sovereignty; the people are deemed the fountainhead of political authority. It should at once be pointed out that the term "people" had a rather restricted sense in the eighteenth century. The Federalists confined the term to the well-to-do; even Thomas Jefferson perhaps would have excluded the urban workers. Within these limitations, the idea of popular sovereignty was current and enjoyed the respectability of tradition; it was derived not only from John Locke but also from as ancient a document as the Magna Carta. Its premise was that political authority, descending from the Creator, was conferred upon the people, who in turn granted a portion of it to their rulers. It was to be contrasted with the belief, then still prevailing on the European continent, that authority was extended by the Creator to the king or emperor, to be exercised at his discretion subject only to divine restraint. The principle of popular sovereignty in those days was the instrument for limiting the powers of government. Since all power was held to be inherent in the people, and since only a portion of this power was transferred to the rulers, the authority of the rulers was limited to that delegated part. The other powers still resided in the people. Whereas this doctrine was only implicit in the original Constitution, it was more clearly declared in the Tenth Amendment.

The Constitution itself simply erected a government in which more or less democratic rule was possible. It has been noted above that popular sovereignty did not in the eighteenth century mean universal adult suffrage, or rule by all the people. The conventions which ratified the Constitution were elected by fewer than ten per cent of the population. The authors of the Constitution feared an extensive electorate; and they established numerous safeguards against it in the Constitution itself. Only the House of Representatives was to be directly elected; the President and the Senate were to be indirectly elected, and the judiciary appointed and confirmed by indirectly elected officers. Even the electors of the House of Representatives were subject to limitations by State laws and constitutions, which often set property-owning, taxpaying, or religious qualifications for the suffrage. Quite probably this use of varying means for choosing public officials in part comprised another effort to achieve a balance among interests, in this instance between the economically prosperous and those who were not so fortunate.

The full emergence of the democratic creed in the nineteenth century did not upset the general functioning of the American government, nor did it require lengthy formal amendment of the Constitution. Beginning first at the level of the State governments, and later in the national government, the people won an increasingly greater political power within constitutional bounds. For example, one important formal constitutional change was the adoption of the Seventeenth Amendment, providing for the popular election of the Senate; and in practice, through their power to nominate candidates for the Senate, the voters of more than half of the States already had some voice in senatorial elections. Thus a constitution drafted with the ideals of an enlightened eighteenth-century aristocratic group was readily adapted to the principles and behavior of a twentieth-century democratic people.

A REPUBLICAN FORM OF GOVERNMENT

The Constitution creates a republican form of government. The Founding Fathers thought such a form necessary in order to insure the principle of popular sovereignty. In the twentieth century several monarchies, such as those of Great Britain, Holland, Belgium, and Sweden, have acknowledged the ultimate authority of the people. Two centuries ago, however, monarchic government was closely associated with the principle of rule by divine right. As the Declaration of Independence attests, George III's ministers were held to be responsible to him, and equally reprehensible in their actions toward the colonies. Hence it was felt that only a republican government, in which public officials are subject to frequent change, or at least criticism, through direct or indirect election, could safeguard the rule of law. Denied permanent tenure, officials could not lay claim to ruling by divine right.

A FEDERAL SYSTEM

The Constitution establishes a federal system of government, based on the two levels of State and nation. Figure 13 presents the contrast between the new federal and old confederative systems. This system affords a geographical distribution of powers, some being entrusted to the federal government, a second group to the States, and a third group to both the federal government and the States. In a purely practical sense this form of government was almost inevitable at the time the Constitution was drafted, since the thirteen States had become accustomed to viewing themselves as sovereign nations. Their people and their governments could not be expected to surrender voluntarily all their powers to the new central regime. Furthermore, considering the speed of transportation and communication at the time—European travelers often complained about the poor condition of American roads—it would have been well-nigh impossible for the central government at New York to have supervised matters of sheerly local importance.

Hence the national government was granted only such powers as were thought to be of national interest, those of conducting war and peace, managing foreign relations, regulating interstate and foreign commerce, coining money, and the like. The remaining powers were left to the States, or to the people. The federal system allows representation to local, State, and regional claims that could be stifled in a centralized, unitary state. The American federal system should be compared with the unitary framework in Great Britain, France, and the American States themselves, where the central government creates all local governments and endows them with their powers.

THE SEPARATION OF POWERS; CHECKS AND BALANCES

The Constitution provides a government in which the different powers of ruling are separated among various governing organs. Following Locke and the Baron Charles de Montesquieu, author of the influential work, *Spirit of the Laws* (1748), it creates a functional distribution of powers. In this way the Founding Fathers discerned three principal powers: legislative, executive, and judicial. To implement these powers they established three branches of government: Congress, the presidency, and the federal

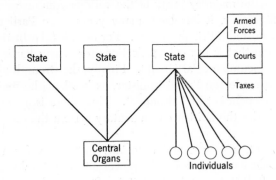

Confederative Government

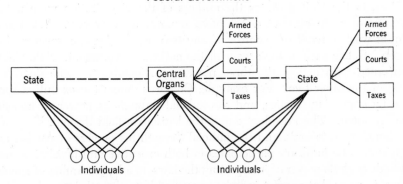

Federal Government

Figure 13. Confederative and Federal Government.

judiciary. It was held to be a great peril to the rule of law that any two of these powers be conferred primarily upon the same organ. Therefore each of the three organs was entrusted chiefly with one of the three powers.

This type of government, the *presidential republic*, which is commonest among the nations of the Americas, is often contrasted with the *parliamentary* system that characterizes the representative governments of Europe. In the parliamentary system political power appears to be concentrated in the legislative assembly; the legislature names as an executive a cabinet whose members are drawn from the majority party or coalition of the legislature; and it dismisses the cabinet by registering an adverse vote on a measure proposed by the cabinet. Under this system, it is argued, there is no separation of powers; all power belongs to the legislative branch.

This is an erroneous view so far as the British government is concerned. Whereas no constitutional separation of powers exists, there does occur a functional division. Members of the cabinet perform three quite distinct functions: (1) as members of Parliament, they vote to enact laws; (2) as members of the executive, they carry out the laws; and (3) unless they are ministers without portfolio, as heads of government departments they convey the policy of the majority party to the various administrative agencies of the state. Moreover, it has been many years since Parliament by an adverse vote has ousted a British cabinet. For decades the British executive has been so strong that it has called elections for a new Parliament rather than yield to the incumbent Parliament. Finally, the strength of the British party system has made the Prime Minister, as head of the majority party, comparatively independent of Parliament. Thus there is a greater separation of powers under the British parliamentary system than appears on the surface.

On the continent, however, and especially in France, for a number of reasons the cabinet has never won the power and quasi-independence that it enjoys in Great Britain; as a result it is often overthrown by a parliamentary vote. Consequently the chief executive is often at the mercy of the legislature. On the other hand, precisely because the executive is so weak, the permanent high officials of the bureaucracy gain everyday powers of great importance; this process creates in effect an unofficial separation of powers.

Even in the United States the authors of the Constitution were not so doctrinaire as to attempt a complete separation of powers. What they sought was to avoid the control of any two powers by one governmental organ. Hence each of the organs of the national government, while chiefly concerned with one of the three powers, participates to some degree in each of the other two. For example, Congress enters the executive function by approving treaties, and the judicial through its power to impeach the President. The President enters the legislative field through his power to sign or to veto laws, and the judicial through his powers of pardon and reprieve. The judiciary participates in both executive and legislative functions through its power of interpreting the laws, in a large number of specific cases, in ways that are not invariably agreeable to the other two branches.

(The Index to this book under "checks and balances" points to a number of additional illustrations.)

Thus the separation of powers is spanned by the checks and balances which each branch of the government offers the other two, so that no one branch possesses a monopoly of even one of the governing powers. By refusing to sign a law the President may bar legislation which he considers unjust. Through particular interpretations of the laws, the federal courts may on occasion alter the will of the President and Congress. By refusing to approve a treaty the Senate may impair the President's power to conduct foreign affairs in a way congressmen think improper. In theory the principle of the separation of powers coupled with the system of checks and balances makes each organ of the government a perpetual sentinel over the other two.

Figure 14 depicts the separation of powers and the system of checks and balances in the American government.

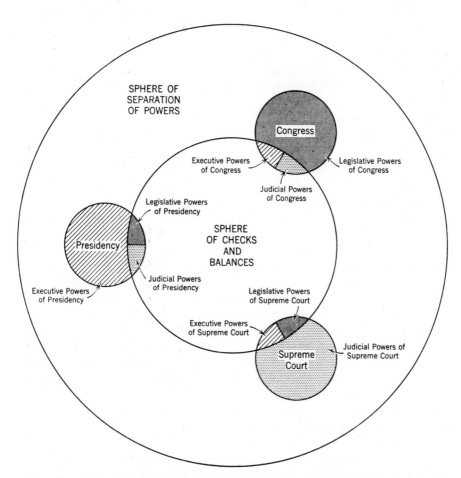

Figure 14. The Separation of Powers and Checks and Balances. Each major branch of the government has a large sphere of powers clearly its own, plus some powers of the type possessed by the other two branches.

THE PROTECTION AND EXTENSION OF FREE ENTERPRISE

The five principles just described are mainly political: they determine the kind of government machinery and how the machinery will work. But they also are very important to the economic order of society. Thus constitutionalism gives hospitable surroundings to businessmen because they can know the rules under which they may operate. The rules are stable, and will not be twisted to the desires of the government. Popular sovereignty, especially as it was first conceived, gave to the middle classes the justification for insisting that the government follow their wishes. A republican form of government guaranteed bankers, merchants, and manufacturers freedom from hereditary discrimination and relief from the unsympathetic dominion of a nobility.

The system of the separation of powers and of checks and balances gave the businessman (1) a free judiciary that decided cases without political abuse; (2) a legislature springing only partially from the mass of people that might become unfriendly to business; and (3) an executive who could check the legislature by his veto, who had no powers to hamper business, and who was efficiently set up to protect business and commerce in ways prescribed by the Constitution. The federal system, insofar as it was State-controlled, limited the scope of operations of those men interested in national and international business; however, insofar as it was nationally-controlled, and thus a great step away from the Confederation, it promoted those same interests.

This inviting political home for free enterprise was then fitted out with substantial economic furniture. Some major clauses and many minor ones demonstrate the concern of the Constitution with protecting and expanding free enterprise. A guiding principle of most of its authors and of the provisions themselves was, "What is good for business is good for the country." Examine the Constitution: patents are protected; copyrights are protected; contracts are protected; property is protected; payment of the national government debt is guaranteed; a uniform monetary system is provided, and the States are restrained from the coinage of money; standards of weights and measures are provided for; even the slave trade is protected for a certain period of time despite the humanitarian feelings that were shocked by the idea of "human chattels." The national government is granted the great power to regulate interstate and foreign commerce; it is allowed to levy customs and excise taxes. In sum, the Constitution was not only a pioneering venture into the mechanics of government; it was also a deep expression of faith in the good of economic free enterprise.

In recent years some restraints have been placed upon the complete freedom of private business, and the government itself has become active in some economic undertakings. Yet, too, much of the later development of the Constitution redefined and strengthened the principle of free enterprise as well as the other principles heretofore described. A description of this later evolution is the task of the next chapter.

QUESTIONS AND PROBLEMS

1. Which is more important to a nation, according to your set of values, a written constitution or constitutionalism? Explain your answer.

2. Discuss the differences between the principle of *popular sovereignty* as found in the Constitution, and *democracy*, defined formally as "rule by the many" in Chapter 2.

3. Do you believe that any one of the several principles underlying the Constitution could be dispensed with without destroying constitutionalism? Explain your answer.

4. Discuss the differences between the separation of powers as it is known in the United States and as it functions to a greater or lesser degree elsewhere.

5. Reread the Constitution. Are there any other principles similar to those outlined in this chapter, perhaps not quite so important, that should be emphasized?

ALTHOUGH the general principles of the Constitution are more or less fixed, their interpretation and application are constantly changing. The Constitution may be the final authority with regard to the seating of power in the various branches of the federal government. That is a stable principle. However, the way that real power settles among the different interest groups that take part in government is not exactly determined. The true location of political power is set by a variety of factors such as military force, personal prestige, public opinion, economic influence, religious justification, ideals, and customs. Because these factors and their comparative weight are always changing, the arrangement of political power derived from them is likewise ever shifting. Hence the Constitution, which sets forth the rules defining the relationships among these political powers, must undergo constant change; it is interpreted and applied in keeping with the altered power situations.

Since the American Constitution appears to be embraced in a single document, and also because it is rather difficult to amend, it is sometimes described as being fairly rigid. On that ground it is often contrasted, favorably or unfavorably—depending upon the critic's viewpoint—with the British Constitution, which, being "unwritten," is held to be more flexible. Actually, although the British Constitution does not appear in a single document, it does consist mainly of a few great documents whose principles the British government would not lightly discard. Moreover, the American Constitution is far more than a single document. It includes innumerable laws, administrative and judicial decisions, and customs and habits. The whole Constitution is as broad as the political life of the American people. Hence it is both as rigid and as flexible as that political life.

FORMAL AMENDMENT

The process of formal amendment

The process of formal amendment of the Constitution includes two principal steps: proposition and ratification. The Constitution provides two ways for accomplishing each of these steps (Art. V).

Proposition: An amendment may be proposed either by a two-thirds majority vote of those present and voting in each house of Congress, provided a quorum is present, or by a convention which Congress shall summon when so directed by the legislatures of two-thirds of the States. All present Amendments have been proposed by congressional vote; indeed, no amending convention has ever been summoned. On many occasions one or more of the State legislatures have petitioned for such a convention. However, it is difficult to know just how long such petitions remain active. Almost certainly if a considerable number of State legislatures should call for a convention, the public opinion that stimulated this action would also have brought the election of congressmen who themselves would undertake to propose the amendment. Congress in any event would be loath to surrender its initiative to a convention. Finally, there is no means for controlling the extent of power inherent in such a convention; as matters stand, it could draft an entirely new constitution to be submitted to the people. In essence this was the action of the Philadelphia Convention of 1787.

Ratification: An amendment may be ratified either by the legislatures of three-fourths of the States, or by conventions in three-fourths of the States. Congress is to decide which ratifying method shall be used. There are two matters which, if dealt with by amendment, would require even more than a three-fourths majority. The Constitution provides that the boundaries of a State may be changed only with the consent of the State or States involved (Art. IV, sec. 3, cl. 1), and that a State may be denied

---

Convention to Ratify the 21st Amendment in the State of Utah, December 5, 1933. Utah was the thirty-sixth and conclusive State to approve the only amendment submitted to State conventions rather than State legislatures.

equal suffrage in the Senate only with its own consent (Art. V). Any amendment related to either of these matters would presumably need not only a three-fourths majority but also the ratifying vote of the State or States concerned. Figure 15 illustrates the possible combinations of proposition and ratification, and the frequency of their use.

The first twenty Amendments were all ratified by State legislatures. Congress provided, however, that the Twenty-first must be ratified by conventions. One explanation for the procedure adopted with respect to the Twenty-first Amendment is based on the intent of the Amendment, which was to repeal the Eighteenth Amendment and legalize the manufacture and sale of alcoholic beverages. Congress, it is assumed, feared lest State legislatures, dominated as they were, and are, by rural, "dry" groups, would reject the Amendment; and it chose to have the Amendment put before conventions, which could give larger representation to the urban, "wet" influence.

Technicalities of the Amending Process: Numerous technicalities have arisen in conjunction with the amending process. For example, a State may vote *against* ratifying a projected amendment, then later reverse itself and ratify the amendment. (The Supreme Court established this principle in 1939 in the case of *Coleman* versus *Miller.* This principle is consonant with the doctrine that no one session of a legislature may bind the action of any succeeding session. Moreover, should a legislature want to reverse itself in this manner, it would show that the electorate which chose it had probably reversed its opinion about ratification. It would be difficult to forbid a legislature to respond to a change of opinion among its con-

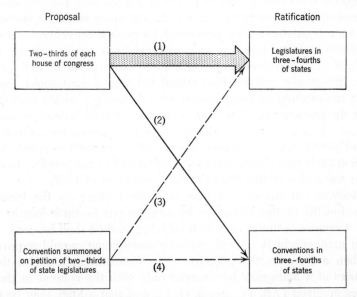

Figure 15. Four Methods of Formal Amendment of the Constitution. The thickness of the arrows signifies the frequency with which a method has been used. Note that two methods have not been used at all, one method only once, and the fourth on twenty-one occasions.

stituents. However, a State may not withdraw its ratification once it has ratified an amendment. This was decided by Secretary of State Seward and Congress in 1868 when Ohio and New Jersey sought to withdraw their ratifications of the Fourteenth Amendment. The complications which would flow from such a power would be enormous. Certainly this power could not be used once an amendment had the approval of enough States to ratify it; but even at an earlier stage, the whole process would be thrown into confusion by the retraction of a positive approval.

It has never been established how long a proposed amendment is active after Congress has submitted it to the States. Conceivably the amendment to regulate child labor, which was proposed by Congress in 1924, is still subject to ratification. To avert problems that might develop over this question, Congress provided a seven-year limit in the text of the Eighteenth, Twentieth, Twenty-first, and Twenty-second Amendments. The probabilities are that the Supreme Court would maintain that any proposed amendment is active unless the Congress has specifically withdrawn the amendment from circulation.

The President has no formal role in the proposing or ratifying of an amendment. In 1798 the validity of the Eleventh Amendment was disputed on the ground that it had not been signed by the President. However, the Supreme Court refused to hear the case (*Hollingsworth et al.* versus *Virginia*); and Associate Justice Samuel Chase commented that the constitutional provision relative to presidential approval of congressional acts did not apply to an amendment since it was not ordinary legislation. Had the Court sustained the position that the President should sign an amendment, it would have cast a shadow over the validity of the Bill of Rights. But if the President has no formal role in the amending process, he is restrained by little more than political considerations from using his influence, especially with Congress, for or against an amendment. The latest example of such presidential action was the adamant position that President Eisenhower adopted against the proposed Bricker amendment, and that he communicated to Congress.

Nature of the Amendments

Considering the amount of change that has taken place in the American government since 1787, it is rather surprising that there have been very few Amendments. It might be held that there have been only twelve, since of the entire twenty-two the first ten, or Bill of Rights, were adopted so quickly after the ratification of the Constitution that they might almost be considered integral with the original Constitution. These twenty-two Amendments have had considerable influence upon the American government. In general, they have had one or more of the following purposes: (1) to limit the power of the federal government; (2) to limit the power of the State governments; (3) to increase the power of the federal government; or (4) to change the structure or machinery of the government.

Limits on National Power: The first eight Amendments set limits such as guarantees of freedom of religion and the press, and the assurance of trial by jury and the due process of law in federal courts. The Ninth Amendment answered those who argued that a list such as the first eight Amendments would suggest that *only* those rights were to be guaranteed; it declared that other rights may also be possessed by the people. The Tenth Amendment confines the powers of the national government to those enumerated in the Constitution. The Eleventh Amendment takes away from the federal courts all cases begun by a citizen of one State against another State. This additional guarantee of State sovereignty was demanded by those who feared lest the States might be brought before the bar of federal justice in numerous suits over debts they had not paid. The Thirteenth Amendment, which prohibits slavery, implicitly denies the federal government the power to protect slavery in the territories, and removes its indirect power to protect slavery in the States by enacting a fugitive slave law. The Amendment is also a limit on State powers as well, forbidding State governments to uphold slavery. The Twenty-first Amendment, by repealing the Eighteenth, bars the federal government from outlawing the manufacture and sale of alcoholic beverages.

Limits on State Power: The Thirteenth Amendment forbids the States to allow slavery. The Fourteenth Amendment contains several limitations on State power, designed to control legislation in the southern States after the Civil War. It guarantees all persons due process of law, that is, a fair and objective trial, in State courts, and forbids States to take away any person's vote save for participation in rebellion or other crime. Subsequently the due process clause of this Amendment was applied by courts to business corporations as well as to individuals so as to restrict the ability of the States to regulate business practices. The Fifteenth Amendment forbids the States to deny any person the suffrage on the ground of race or previous condition of servitude; this Amendment aimed at enfranchising the southern Negroes. The Nineteenth Amendment makes a similar prohibition with regard to sex; it was intended to guarantee woman suffrage.

Increases in Federal Power: In a sense each of the three Amendments curtailing State power actually increased the power of the federal government, since the federal courts became umpires in cases involving alleged infractions of the Amendments. The Sixteenth Amendment, which empowers the federal government to levy an income tax without regard to the population of the several States, vastly increased the federal taxing powers and tax resources. However, it must be stressed that in itself the Amendment did not add a new formal power to the federal government, because the government always had the power to levy an income tax. What the Amendment did was to change the method of collecting the tax, so that the tax could be easily and practicably levied. In consequence, it allowed the federal government to increase its functions greatly, for it now could afford to pay for more functions. The Eighteenth Amendment, prohibiting the sale and manufacture of alcoholic beverages, authorized the federal government to control the dietary habits of many people.

Changes in the Structure and Machinery of the Government: The Twelfth Amendment greatly altered the means of electing the President and Vice

President.   Formerly each member of the Electoral College had cast two votes; the candidate securing the largest number, provided it was a majority, was declared President; the candidate winning the second largest number became Vice President.   The Amendment provides that each Elector shall cast one vote for President and one for Vice President.   It was adopted after the election of 1800, in which the same number of Electors had chosen both Jefferson and Burr, so that Burr, who had been thought of as Vice President, almost became President.   As noted above, the Sixteenth Amendment formally changes the machinery for collecting a federal income tax. The Seventeenth Amendment provided for the popular election of the Senate.   Inasmuch as Senators beforehand were elected by State legislatures, this Amendment lessened the power of the States.   The Twentieth Amendment advanced the inauguration of the President from March until January after his election.   It also advanced the first meeting of Congress from December thirteen months after an election to January immediately after the election, thereby eradicating the "lame duck" session (as was termed the meeting of Congress attended by "lame ducks" who had been voted out of office in November but held their seats until the next March). This Amendment was designed to bring the schedule of the government into step with present transportation speeds.   The Twenty-second Amendment bans the election of any person to more than two terms as President. It was proposed and ratified after Franklin D. Roosevelt had been elected to the presidency four times; it made law of the maxim set by Washington and Jefferson that no man should be President for more than two terms. The graph in Figure 16 shows the various functions for which the Amendments were designed, or which they serve; note that some Amendments fill more than one function.

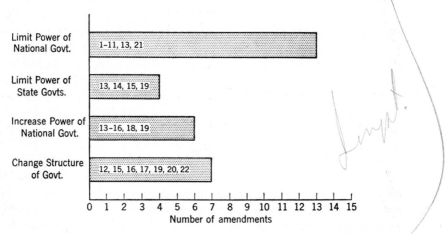

Figure 16.   Functions of the Amendments.   This bar chart shows how many, and which, of the Amendments to the Constitution have been designed to limit or increase the powers of the state and federal governments.   Observe that some of the Amendments perform more than one function, and that the Thirteenth Amendment both limits and increases the power of the National government as well as limits the power of the States.

Some proposed amendments

According to one authority, between 1789 and 1953 there were 4,484 proposals for amendments to the Constitution laid before Congress.[1] It is noteworthy, however, that very few have attained the required two-thirds majority in the House and Senate. Fewer than ten proposed amendments that Congress has supported since 1800 have failed of ratification by the States. This is not difficult to understand; when two-thirds of the Congress approves an idea, the idea is sure to have considerable popular and legislative support across the nation as a whole. At present only one proposed amendment is in the ratification stage: that empowering Congress to legislate concerning child labor, which has been ratified by the legislatures of twenty-eight States. It appears unlikely to secure a favorable vote from the eight more States needed to add it to the Constitution. Actually the federal government today, thanks to Supreme Court decisions, has the power to regulate child labor that is connected with interstate commerce. It exercises this power through provisions of the Fair Labor Standards Act of 1938 and its amendments. Here was an occasion in which the Constitution evolved not through formal amendments but by means of a court decision (see below, page 103). Currently other proposals that have some support are: (1) a definite mention of the principle that treaties which conflict with, or go beyond, the Constitution are not permissible; (2) a guarantee of equal rights to women; (3) the abolition of the Electoral College, or at least some alteration in the method of electing the President; (4) a ban on the payment of a poll tax as a qualification for voting in federal elections; (5) removal of exemption from federal taxation now enjoyed by State and local bonds; (6) authorization for federal marriage and divorce legislation; (7) empowering State governors to appoint Representatives in the event of vacancies; (8) empowering the President to veto items in general appropriation bills; (9) limiting the income tax to no more than twenty-five per cent of personal income; (10) increasing the term of Representatives from two years to four; (11) extending the vote in federal elections to those eighteen years of age and older; and (12) a revision of the process of amending the federal Constitution, making it easier or more difficult, depending upon the position assumed by the supporter of the amendment.

Criticism of the amending process

Some critics have charged that it is too easy to amend the Constitution. By elaborate mathematical calculations they have shown that cooperation among the Representatives and Senators of the thirty-two least heavily populated States might propose an amendment desired by fewer than half the people of the United States. They have also shown how it would be possible for State legislators from thinly settled constituencies to ratify an amendment despite a national popular majority opposing it. Other critics have

[1] Brown, Everett S., *Proposed Amendments to the Constitution of the United States* (Ann Arbor: George Wahr, 1953), p. 1.

asserted that the amending process is too difficult, showing how legislatures in thirteen States could thwart ratification although an enormous popular majority might be supporting it. Both arguments may have force in some future cases, but they have not come into play thus far.

More important to the question of how rigid is the Constitution is the fact that formal amendment is not the sole means of changing it. Tremendous change has been effected by new ideas and practices not described in the Constitution and by divers informal means of amendment. To say this in the language adopted at the start of this chapter, the American Constitution (the basic organization of the government) contains the Constitution itself, with its Amendments; developments in directions foreseen by the Constitution; and a number of alterations in what was expected or planned by the authors of the Constitution.

INFORMAL GROWTH AND AMENDMENT

Legislation

Legislation enacted by Congress and by State legislatures has added emphasis to certain features of the Constitution. For instance, in 1788 the Constitution afforded but a skeleton for the federal government, which must be fleshed by congressional and State legislative enactments. For the federal judiciary the Constitution supplied only the Supreme Court; it empowered Congress to "from time to time ordain and establish" other courts (Art. III, sec. 1). Congress might have delegated all inferior federal jurisdiction to the State courts; instead, beginning with the Judiciary Act of 1789, it laid the basis for a system of federal district courts of first instance. The Constitution says little about the executive Departments; it merely authorizes the President to "require the opinion . . . of the principal officer in each of the executive Departments. . . ." (Art. II, sec. 2, cl. 1.) The First Congress created several Departments and provided for the appointment of their principal officers by the President with the advice and consent of the Senate.

With respect to State legislatures, they were obliged at the outset to determine the qualifications of the electors of the House of Representatives, which were to be "the qualifications requisite for electors of the most numerous branch of the State legislature" (Art. I, sec. 2, cl. 1). State legislatures participated in the election of George Washington, because the Constitution asserts that "Each State shall appoint, in such manner as the legislature thereof may direct, a number of Electors. . . ." (Art. II, sec. 1, cl. 2.) To take another example of the States' participation in molding the Constitution, they developed the election laws under which federal officers are chosen, including the forty-eight elaborate systems for nominating candidates for federal office.

Executive and administrative actions

Legislation is but one step in governing; it must be followed by execution and administration of the laws. By his interpretation and subsequent application of a law, often drawn from his partisan political convictions, an executive or administrative officer can bring about major revisions in the sense of the Constitution. As chief of an administrative body of more than two million civil servants, the President can and does affect the meaning of the Constitution through the directives he issues to his subordinates. In a lesser fashion, Department heads and other administrative policy-making officials influence constitutional development. For example, the impeachment of President Johnson revolved about the President's interpretation of his constitutional power to remove officers he had appointed, without the permission of the Senate—as required by the Tenure of Office Act. According to Johnson's views, therefore, the Tenure of Office Act was unconstitutional—a belief which the Supreme Court supported some years later when it ruled the law in violation of the Constitution.

Similarly, the President may alter the emphasis of a law through his interpretation of the law and his subsequent procedure in executing and enforcing the law. The implementation of the Sherman Antitrust Act of 1890 offers one illustration of how different Presidents give different operational meaning to an act of Congress. Following passage of the Sherman Act, Presidents Benjamin Harrison, Cleveland, and McKinley rarely invoked it, since they believed that the federal government should not try to regulate business practices. But their successors, Theodore Roosevelt and Taft, together applied the Act more than one hundred times; for they held that the federal government should police interstate commerce.

The President influences constitutional evolution also through the legislative powers vested in him by the Constitution. Presidents from Washington to John Quincy Adams rarely used the veto power; it was their contention that it was designed solely to prevent unconstitutional legislation. President Jackson, on the contrary, employed the veto against laws running counter to his political philosophy. His immediate successors did not follow his example; but Jackson had set the precedent for the huge number of vetoes cast by Cleveland, F. D. Roosevelt, Truman, and the many vetoes of other Presidents. This "positive" veto has helped to increase the President's legislative power.

Judicial decisions

Judicial decisions have effected many significant changes in the Constitution. The Constitution ordains that the federal judicial power "shall extend to all cases, in law and equity, arising under this Constitution, the laws of the United States, and the treaties made, or which shall be made, under their authority. . . ." (Art. III, sec. 2, cl. 1). Hence any law, once executed, is subject to being challenged and brought to court for interpretation in connection with a case at law. Each judgment so rendered will comprise a step in constitutional development.

The courts draw additional force from the power of judicial review of the constitutionality of federal and State laws. This power enables courts to declare whether a federal or State law conflicts with the Constitution; in so doing, of course, the courts must establish first the meaning of the Constitution for this particular matter. Federal judicial review is itself a product of constitutional interpretation, firmly settled by 1803 in the case of Marbury *versus* Madison. That is, in order to begin the career of judicial review, the Supreme Court had first to declare in a case that it had the power of judicial review. By means of such review, the federal Supreme Court has brought about major alterations in the Constitution.

For instance, the Constitution is not clear as to the relationship between manufacturing and commerce. It gives Congress the power to regulate interstate commerce, but says nothing of manufacturing. Until 1937 the federal courts consistently ruled that manufacturing is only incidental to commerce; on that ground they struck down as unconstitutional federal laws governing manufacturing. But in 1937, the Supreme Court held that manufacturing is closely enough related to interstate commerce to permit congressional supervision, and upheld the National Labor Relations (Wagner) Act (*National Labor Relations Board* versus *Jones and Laughlin Steel Corp.*). From this decision Congress drew vast powers over the national economy, working a fundamental change in the Constitution. Through its power of judicial review the Supreme Court may be described as a permanent constitutional convention.

Custom and habit

American society has experienced great changes since the adoption of the Constitution, giving birth to new political forces and altering the alignments among the original forces. International and interstate trade have strengthened the mercantile groups. Manufacturing and finance, which were of comparatively modest stature in 1787, in the twentieth century exercise great power. Moreover, new interests have won substantial influence in certain regions of the country. New England, a mercantile area in 1787, has become a great workshop. The Midwest and Far West, once primarily agricultural, have become—especially in the States of Ohio, Michigan, Illinois, and California—highly urbanized. In the South, industry is acquiring political strength equal to that of farming. Finally, universal suffrage has authorized over half the population to take a direct part in the governing process, whereas at the time the Constitution was ratified no more than one person in ten could participate in government.

Many of these social and economic changes, with the corresponding shifts in political power they have occasioned, have occurred so rapidly, or have created so many complications, that no new formal political institutions have been erected to deal with them. There has been a considerable lag between the emergence of economic and social institutions on the one hand, and governing bodies on the other. Hence the people involved in these new forces and alignments have frequently improvised extraconstitutional political forms to manage them. Continued reliance upon these forms has won public acceptance for them. The mass of the people have gotten the habit of using them, and have incorporated them into the body of public custom.

There are many instances of this mode of constitutional change. The

Some men look at constitutions with sanctimonious reverence, & deem them, like the ark of the covenant, too sacred to be touched. they ascribe to the men of the preceding age a wisdom more than human, and suppose what they did to be beyond amendment. I knew that age well: I belonged to it, and labored with it. it deserved well of it's country. it was very like the present, but without the experience of the present: and 40. years of experience in government is worth a century of book-reading: and this they would say themselves, were they to rise from the dead. I am certainly not an advocate for frequent & untried changes in laws and constitutions. I think moderate imperfections had better be borne with; because when once known, we accomodate ourselves to them, and find practical means of correcting their ill effects. but I know also that laws and institutions must go hand in hand with the progress of the human mind. as that becomes more developed, more enlightened, as new discoveries are made, new truths disclosed, and manners and opinions change with the change of circumstances, institutions must advance also, and keep pace..

I tolerate with the utmost latitude the right of others to differ from me in opinion without imputing to them criminality. I know too well the weakness & uncertainty of human reason to wonder at it's different results. both of our political parties at least the honest portion of them agree conscientiously in the same object.

Another most condemnable practice of the supreme court to be corrected is that of cooking up a decision in caucus, & delivering it by one of their members as the opinion of the court, without the possibility of our knowing how many, who, and for what reasons each member concurred. this compleatly defeats the possibility of impeachment by smothering evidence. a regard for character in each being now the only hold we can have of them, we should hold fast to it. they would, were they to give their opinions seriatim and publicly, endeavor to justify themselves to the world by explaining the reasons which led to their opinion.

Genl. Washington set the example of voluntary retirement after 8 years. I shall follow it, and a few more precedents will oppose the obstacle of habit to any one after a while who shall endeavor to extend his term. perhaps it may beget a disposition to establish it by an amendment of the constitution.

Constitution provides that a member of the House must be a resident of the State from which he is elected (Art. I, sec. 2, cl. 2); custom and habit have dictated that, with rare exceptions, he must also be a resident of the district he represents. The Constitution authorizes the choice of a Speaker by the House (Art. I, sec. 2, cl. 5); custom has made him a member of the majority party, and consequently a figure of great strength (as distinct from the Speaker of the British House of Commons, who is nonpartisan and relatively unimportant). The Constitution established an indirect means for electing the President (Art. II, sec. 1, cl. 3); habit instructs the members of the Electoral College to act as directed by the plurality vote in their State. Among extraconstitutional bodies, political parties and pressure groups have become indispensable to the functioning of the federal government; yet the Constitution does not mention them. The British Constitution is often held to be the creature of custom; the American Constitution, like any other constitution that is mature, is hardly less the result of custom.

Public opinion

Ultimately every constitution must settle with public opinion. The group originally drafting the constitution must attune it to important public wants; at the same time the group must endeavor to mold opinion favorably toward the constitution. Figure 17 presents several excerpts from the letters of Thomas Jefferson; through hundreds of such letters, Jefferson established his leading role in the definition of the spirit of the Constitution and of American government. A constitution that does not mesh with the opinions of strong sections of public opinion cannot succeed. The modern world, which has placed great faith in written constitutions, has seen the failure of large numbers of them, notably in eastern and southern Europe and in Latin America; for these constitutions were not consonant with the opinions of the publics that they were designed to organize and rule. In the same way, constitutional change and interpretations must be supported by public opinion.

The way in which the federal government initiated first the adoption, then the rejection, of the prohibition of the manufacture and sale of alcoholic beverages affords an unusual illustration of the effect of public opinion upon the Constitution. During the so-called prohibition era, millions of people violated the law consciously and often. The transformation in public opinion compelled Congress to propose an amndment repealing the Prohibition Amendment; and this, the Twenty-first Amendment, was ratified in record time. A constitutional change, whatever its form, is usually first manifest in public opinion.

Figure 17.   Some Important American Doctrines of Politics and the Constitution, as Stated by Jefferson. These facsimiles, excerpted from four of his handwritten letters, show the type of sharp and vibrant argument that influenced his own and all succeeding American generations.

QUESTIONS AND PROBLEMS

1. Can any threats to the continuation or peaceful change of the Constitution, similar to that posed by the Civil War, be foreseen at this time? What might they be?

2. Are you satisfied that the Constitution provides adequate means for formal amendment? Explain why or why not. If not, can you suggest a supplemental or amended method that would better suit your preference?

3. Which Amendment of the twenty-two do you regard as most important in its consequences? Explain your answer. Do you think it is logically or ethically necessary that other persons agree with your choice? Explain why so or why not.

4. Which of the twelve current proposals to amend the Constitution that are mentioned seems to you to be the most important and desirable? Why?

5. Which of the informal "amendments" to the Constitution do you regard as having been the most important in its consequences? Why do you select that particular transformation?

6. Of the Congress, the Supreme Court, and the presidency, which in your opinion is most likely to bring the greatest change to the Constitution in the next twenty-five years? Explain your answer.

7. Is it more important, in your opinion, that a constitution be acceptable to the leaders, or to the public, or to some combination of elements, in order to be enduring and applicable? Explain your answer.

Virginia Department of Conservation and Development, Richmond

THE GOVERNMENT of the United States is a federal union. That is to say, it consists of a central authority endowed with great yet limited powers to enact and execute laws regulating matters of general interest throughout its whole area; then, this area is made up of forty-eight States, each of which is in a sense subordinate to the central authority but possesses important powers of its own right. A federal union in terms of the relationship between the central authority and the State or provincial governments contrasts on the one hand with a unitary government, such as that of Great Britain or of an American State, and on the other hand with a confederation, such as the government of the United States under the Articles. In a unitary government the central authorities may have only limited powers; but the subordinate governing units, such as the British counties and the American cities, have no powers of their own right, but only those conferred upon them by the central government. In a confederation the central authority has only those powers with which the smaller units invest it; the smaller units alone have power of their own right.

DISTRIBUTION OF FEDERAL POWERS

Exclusive and concurrent powers

The distribution of powers in the federal union, as devised in 1787, has undergone great modification. Under the Constitution the national government alone enjoys certain powers, such as those of declaring war and negotiating peace; the States alone enjoy certain other powers, such as creating local governments and enacting codes of criminal law. These powers are termed *exclusive.* At the same time the national and State governments together share certain powers. Each level may assess taxes; each may support a police force; each may create a judicial system. These powers are called *concurrent.* Questions regarding the exercise of concurrent powers are so important that the same political party may be divided on the national and the State levels over them. The concurrent powers have contributed much to that distinctive American situation that finds party organizations of the same "national" party working not only independently of one another but even for opposing ends. For example, the national party organization may work for the construction of a federal dam across a river to produce hydroelectric power; at the same time the party organization of the State concerned may urge State or even private exploitation of these water resources.

The Constitution draws no sharp line between the national and the State exercise of the concurrent powers. In fact, since it would be impossible to enumerate all political powers, it would also be impossible to draw a strict boundary between the areas of national and State jurisdiction. Hence there is a wide belt of political territory that is in dispute between national and State authorities. The contests over this disputed territory provide the chief material for the constitutional history of the United States.

Supremacy of national law

It must be noted, however, that in the area of concurrent power, federal legislation always takes precedence over State legislation. That is, once federal action is taken, a State law may not overturn the federal law, or lessen its effectiveness. Moreover, the federal government is ultimately supreme over State governments. This federal supremacy is established by the Constitution, which states that "The Constitution, and the laws of the United States, which shall be made in pursuance thereof, and all

---

Capitol of the State of Virginia, at Richmond. The Maison Carrée, a little Roman temple at Nîmes, France, was Thomas Jefferson's inspiration for the central section of the Virginia Capitol, begun in 1785 and completed in 1788. Here meets the oldest representative legislative assembly in the new world.

treaties made, or which shall be made, under the authority of the United States, shall be the supreme law of the land. . . ." (Art. VI, cl. 2).

Tools of national supremacy

The Supreme Court is the umpire in any instance in which it is alleged that a State law contravenes a federal law or the Constitution: the Judiciary Act of 1789 established the procedures whereby it should hear any case of this nature. In these hearings the federal Supreme Court has tended to favor the national government, an understandable tendency when one reflects that the Supreme Court is an arm of the national government. Actually, as will be seen below, there have been tremendous pressures upon the national government to exploit this supremacy. In fact, granted the taxing powers that the federal government has under the Constitution as amended, it is difficult to see how with its great financial resources it could be other than supreme over the States. At the same time this constitutional clause legalizes the supremacy and sets aside any need for national compulsion of the States.

Inherent and delegated powers

Before advancing toward an analysis of how the federal structure of the American government has developed, it would be well to note another means of classifying the types of political power under the national Constitution. According to this scheme of classification, powers are either *inherent* or *delegated*. An inherent power may be defined as a power which a government is authorized to employ simply because the power rightfully belongs to that government, and because the government concerned has the strength to exercise that power. Thus the presence or absence of inherent powers depends upon an accepted doctrine about the sources of a specific government's authority, and upon that government's aggressiveness in seeking powers.

In the United States, the State governments possess inherent powers, by general consent of scholars, judges, and leaders. These powers are, according to their doctrine, subject to the limitations imposed by the national Constitution and the constitution of the given State. In other terms, a State government may enact and carry out laws in any field not barred to it by the federal Constitution or its own constitution. The inherent powers of the States are sometimes called *reserved* powers, for the Tenth Amendment to the Constitution asserts that "The powers not delegated to the United States by the Constitution, nor prohibited by it to the States, are reserved to the States respectively, or to the people."

Meanwhile the federal government possesses the inherent power of conducting its relations with foreign governments. That is, in declaring war, making peace, or negotiating treaties, the national government need seek no constitutional authorization for its activity; for it is held that the conduct of foreign affairs is an inherent power of any national government. The only constitutional questions that arise concern the problem of which branch of the government is empowered to act. However, it should be noted that this is practically the only sphere of action in which there is general consent to the doctrine that the national government has inherent powers.

A delegated power, by contrast, is a named power that has been conferred upon a government from some external source, which, following various political concepts, may be another government, one or more non-governmental institutions, the people as a whole, or God. For example, under the Articles of Confederation the national government possessed delegated powers which had been conferred by the States. Under the present Constitution, modern American doctrine holds that the national government has delegated powers which were conferred by the people. In other words, the national government may do only what is authorized by the Constitution and its Amendments, so far as domestic affairs are concerned. Hence the national government is also said to have _enumerated_ powers, that is, powers that are enumerated in the Constitution.

To sum up, acts justified in the name of inherent powers come almost entirely from the State governments; the national government almost always resorts to acts justified by delegated powers. A reading of the national and the State constitutions will highlight the difference. The national Constitution is composed largely of affirmative statements declaring the various powers of the national government. State constitutions, on the other hand, contain many negative statements, the prohibitions on the exercise of powers that the State governments might otherwise enjoy as inherent powers. In any event, the powers of both the national and the State governments are limited by accepted doctrine—all by the national Constitution, and those of the State governments by their own constitutions as well. The adjoining diagram (Figure 18) points out the principal parts of the doctrine of American federal powers.

THE DEVELOPMENT OF NATIONAL POWER

The doctrines of the sources of power of the nation and States have not changed much in an absolute sense. Through later Amendments (from the Thirteenth to the Twenty-first) and some new ideas (for example, the inherent powers of the nation in foreign affairs), some reallocation of powers has occurred within the framework of the delegated and inherent powers doctrine. But the powers themselves have been increasingly used. Since the adoption of the national Constitution, the powers-in-use of the national government have greatly expanded. During the same era the powers-in-use of the State governments have not diminished; rather, they too have greatly expanded, but not to the degree that the national powers have. It is essential to investigate why and how this expansion in national power has taken place, and what its effects have been upon federal-State relations.

Causes for the expansion

The principal material causes for the expansion in the powers of the federal government appear to be economic and technological. In addition, there were psychological causes as well—the mushrooming of nationalism in America as in the rest of the world, and the idea of collective responsibility for problems that were once considered personal or local, to name only two. At the time the Constitution was adopted, businesses in the main were so small that they could be policed by local authorities; hence there were few significant pressures upon the national government to undertake their supervision. (But recall that just such exceptional pressures were

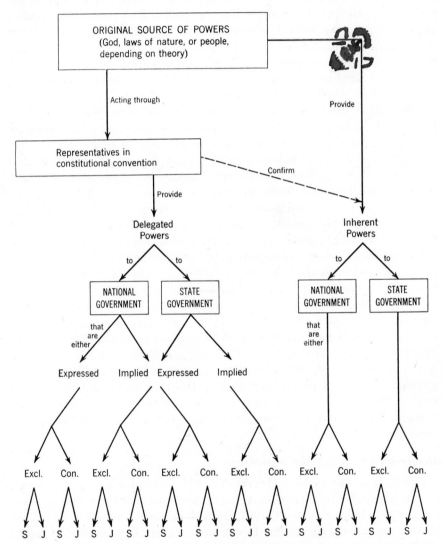

Figure 18. The Doctrine of the Powers of American Government. American constitutional and legal doctrine maintains that every act of the government can and must be justified as to its *source*, its *original form* (delegated or inherent), its *principal* (national or state government), its *form of expression* (expressed or implied), its *exclusiveness* or *concurrency* to the federal or state government or both, and its *mode of administration* (separate or joint). In the diagram, Excl. means exclusive; Con. means concurrent; S means separately administered; and J means jointly administered.

behind the drive for the Constitution.) On the other hand, since the War between the States there has emerged an economy based on aggregations of industry, commerce, and finance, whose operations extend across the borders of several States or even across the nation, and whose resources, annual budgets, and payrolls in some cases surpass those of any State in the country. Later there developed nation-wide unions of workingmen to deal with these business aggregations. Soon various interests were calling for governmental regulation or governmental promotion of these aggregations and unions. It was impossible for the States to control such bodies, especially since the federal government has exclusive power to legislate with regard to interstate commerce. Indeed, more than a suspicion arose that some large corporations and syndicates controlled several States. Hence the federal government alone could shoulder the burden of regulation and promotion which was demanded.

Other important factors leading to the expansion of national power have been the depression of the 1930's and the two world wars of the twentieth century. During the depression the responsibility of caring for the unemployed and the aged was frequently greater than many States could or would assume. Two world wars exacted an amount of unity and direction unknown in peacetime. Only the federal government could impose that unity. Hence the national government has overseen the distribution of raw materials, the maintenance of production levels, the allocation of manpower, and a host of other activities relative to the production of armaments and the other necessities of war. These national powers are not "emergency powers"; they are based upon the authority given Congress by the Constitution "To raise and support armies, . . ." "To provide and maintain a navy," and "To make rules for the government and regulation of the land and naval forces" (Art. I, sec. 8, cls. 12–14). Often at the end of a war the statutes are not repealed; they are simply no longer administered. Hence World War II was fought to a considerable degree on World War I laws, and the Korean conflict on statutes of both world wars. Moreover, some of these wartime laws could be invoked even if no war existed, providing there was no clause in them confining their validity to wartime; however, the Supreme Court may then reexamine them for their constitutionality in peacetime.

Means of achieving the expansion

The Principle of Implied Powers: The chief means whereby the powers of the national government have been expanded has been through constitutionally *implied* powers. An implied power is a power which, although not expressly conferred by the Constitution, is so closely related to, or similar to, one or more of the delegated powers that its constitutionality may be assumed. The first use of implied powers came shortly after the adoption of the Constitution, when Secretary of the Treasury Alexander Hamilton sought to have Congress charter a Bank of the United States. Hamilton held that the national government was empowered to charter a bank because of its delegated authority to regulate currency and because of the power conferred upon Congress "To make all laws which shall be necessary and proper for carrying into execution the foregoing powers, and all other powers vested by this Constitution in the Government of the United States, or in any department or officer thereof" (Art. I, sec. 8, cl. 18). In spite of the opposition of Secretary of State Thomas Jefferson, who maintained that the "necessary and proper" clause was not sufficient authorization, Congress chartered the bank.

The federal Supreme Court is the final arbiter as to the constitutionality of an implied power. In the case of McCulloch *versus* Maryland (1819), a case in which the constitutionality of the Bank of the United States was challenged, Chief Justice John Marshall gave general authorization to the principle of implied powers in his ruling that ". . . Let the end be legitimate, let it be within the scope of the constitution, and all means which are appropriate, which are plainly adapted toward that end, which are not prohibited but consist with the letter and spirit of the constitution, are constitutional." Marshall himself was an advocate of a strong central government; and the Supreme Court under his leadership laid the foundation for a powerful national authority. The expansion of this national authority has been based primarily upon new implied powers; and the Supreme Court has more often upheld than overthrown these novel assumptions of power.

Strict Constructionists versus *Broad Constructionists:* The dispute between those who make a strict construction of the Constitution and those who make a broad construction is the dispute between those who would limit the powers of the national government and those who would expand them. The strict constructionists are mostly also supporters of States' rights; the broad constructionists are the proponents of a strong central government. The first great instance of such a dispute after the adoption of the Constitution was the contest between Jefferson and Hamilton respecting the establishment of the Bank of the United States. Since that time similar disputes have arisen virtually every time that the national government has assumed some new power. The position of the strict constructionists is simply that the national government may do no more than is specifically provided in the Constitution. The position of the broad constructionists is paraphrased in John Marshall's ruling in the case of McCulloch *versus* Maryland.

In general it may also be said that the proponents of a broad construction are those who at the moment are in command of the national government; and that those who uphold a strict construction are those who are out of power. Hamilton was a Federalist, one of the group that was in power from 1789 until 1801; Jefferson was an Antifederalist, or a Republican, one of the group then out of power. When the Antifederalists came to power in 1801 with the election of Jefferson to the presidency, they soon adopted a broad construction of the Constitution; they were compelled to in order to justify such an act as the Louisiana Purchase, which is certainly not referred to in any way in the Constitution. Their opponents, the Federalists, who were now out of power, soon expressed the strict-constructionist point of view, carrying it to the extreme of threatening secession during the War of 1812; for they felt that the war was being fought for the benefit of the Republican West at the expense of Federalist New England.

Another illustration of the connection between political control and the attitude toward the construction of the Constitution occurred when Abraham Lincoln was elected President in 1860. His party, the Republican—not to be confused with Jefferson's group—revealed itself to be a partisan of a strong central government; and elements of the Democratic Party—the successor to Jefferson's group—as adherents of States' rights, went to the point of leading the South, which they controlled, into secession from the Union. Later, after Franklin D. Roosevelt was elected as Democratic candidate for the presidency in 1932, the national Democratic Party urged the need for a strong central regime whereas the Republicans argued in behalf of States' rights.

These seeming contradictions concerning a broad or a strict construction among proponents of a strong central government and supporters of States' rights have an explanation. A partial solution concerns interest groups. Behind every major party candidate for the presidency stands a combination of interests that want something from the government. After his election, the successful candidate normally will attempt to satisfy at least some of the wants of his supporters. Often in his attempt he will take recourse to certain new implied powers; this is especially true of those Presidents who have been backed by groups that before his election were not in power, as in the cases of Jefferson, Lincoln, and F. D. Roosevelt. The Louisiana Purchase aided the agrarian groups behind Jefferson; the National Bank Act of 1862, the financial groups behind Lincoln; and the Social Security Act of 1935, the labor organizations behind Roosevelt.

At the same time, in satisfying the wants of his supporters, the President, along with Congress, almost inevitably wreaks some injury upon those interest groups out of power; for example, the Louisiana Purchase, by increasing the size of the United States and thereby making possible the future election of agrarian-minded congressmen from the new States of the area, menaced the power of the New England financial and commercial interests in Congress. Hence the groups that are out of power will tend to support a strict-construction, States'-rights point of view, in which they will argue that the actions taken by the national government have been unconstitutional, since beyond the proper scope of its authority. Thus these groups are acting in defense of their interests, which they feel are being injured by the measures of the national government.

COOPERATIVE FEDERALISM

As the national powers have expanded, more of them have been administered in conjunction with the State governments. For more than a century after the adoption of the Constitution, the State and national governments were assumed to be solely competitors. The then popular theory of the relationship between the two levels of government may be termed *separatist federalism*. This position is illustrated by a portion of the Supreme Court ruling in *Tarble's Case* in 1871: ". . . there are within the territorial limits of each State two governments, restricted in their spheres of action, but independent of each other, and supreme within their respective sphere. Each has its separate departments; each has its distinct laws, and each has its own tribunals for their enforcement. Neither government can intrude within the jurisdiction, or authorize any inter-ference therein by its judicial officers with the action of the other."

However, about the time of World War I this position came to be sup-planted by one that may be called *cooperative federalism*. Under coopera-tive federalism the State and national governments began consciously collaborating toward certain ends. Rather than remaining as separate as possible, they began to consider the potentialities of mutual aid. Some of the new cooperation occurred in the area of concurrent powers (for in-stance, highways) and some in areas reserved to the States, especially among the so-called *police powers*—that is, the power to legislate with respect to public health, morals, welfare, and safety. In reference to the police powers, the workings of cooperative federalism brought about a considerable extension in the powers and functioning of the national government.

The system of grants-in-aid

Probably the chief instrument whereby the national government has pene-trated fields once limited to the States has been the grant-in-aid. The system of grants-in-aid has been especially prominent since 1933; however, it existed on a narrower basis for many years before. The provision of the Land Ordinance of 1785 that in the new western States the federal gov-ernment should give each State government one section out of every town-ship for the maintenance of public schools was one of the first grants-in-aid. Today, however, the principal form of such grants is money, for such broad purposes as social welfare, education, veterans' services, agriculture, public works, natural resources conservation, public housing, and the National Guard. Table 2 presents a chart showing the total sums of these grants expended on different functions in 1955.

Conditions for Grants: Today these grants are usually made on a con-ditional basis alone, by which the national government fixes a number of standards which the State governments must meet in order to qualify for the grants. Normally the State governments must themselves appropriate money for the undertaking, up to an amount equal to the contribution of the national government. The projects must use bookkeeping and account-ing methods prescribed by the national government. Workers on the projects ordinarily must be employed according to some measure of ability, without partisan considerations—a requirement that has stimulated the rise of State civil service systems based upon merit. The funds must be expended only for specified activities that have been planned in collabora-

TABLE 2. FEDERAL GRANTS TO THE STATES FOR VARIOUS FUNCTIONS[1]

(Figures in millions of dollars)

State	ALL GRANTS	Old-age Assistance	Aid to Dependent Children	Education	Highways	Health, Hospitals
All States	2,762.4	921.5	376.2	299.2	592.5	80.1
Alabama	59.2	17.5	6.7	5.9	16.9	3.2
Arizona	22.0	5.6	3.6	1.7	7.0	0.4
Arkansas	45.5	15.9	4.2	4.8	11.1	2.3
California	317.8	112.7	42.8	76.3	38.2	4.3
Colorado	46.9	19.4	4.2	3.3	9.1	0.6
Connecticut	20.8	7.0	3.5	1.8	2.6	0.6
Delaware	7.7	0.5	0.7	0.9	3.8	0.5
Florida	63.6	25.5	11.2	5.3	12.7	2.5
Georgia	80.4	32.0	9.5	7.6	14.5	4.9
Idaho	20.8	3.2	1.3	1.1	10.8	0.6
Illinois	114.3	39.2	16.8	12.3	27.0	3.0
Indiana	43.9	12.6	6.4	7.7	9.9	1.2
Iowa	48.6	16.0	4.7	7.6	14.5	1.1
Kansas	42.2	13.9	3.3	3.5	16.1	0.7
Kentucky	50.7	17.2	11.0	3.9	9.2	2.4
Louisiana	89.0	48.0	11.3	5.4	9.6	2.8
Maine	17.0	4.8	3.0	0.9	4.4	0.5
Maryland	25.0	3.9	5.0	3.9	4.2	1.1
Massachusetts	82.4	38.9	10.2	3.7	10.9	1.2
Michigan	99.1	29.1	14.2	15.3	22.0	2.0
Minnesota	56.3	19.3	5.5	8.2	14.6	1.5
Mississippi	49.3	18.2	4.2	6.0	10.3	3.2
Missouri	102.6	52.7	13.3	5.0	17.1	1.3
Montana	21.6	3.5	1.5	1.9	9.7	0.3
Nebraska	23.1	6.3	1.7	2.4	9.6	0.6
Nevada	9.8	1.1	. . .	0.6	5.0	0.5
New Hampshire	8.8	2.4	0.8	0.7	2.8	0.2
New Jersey	37.6	8.2	4.0	4.1	6.6	1.9
New Mexico	29.5	4.2	4.5	3.6	8.9	1.0
New York	210.2	47.0	45.2	10.6	45.8	3.2
North Carolina	65.8	14.8	11.3	8.5	13.4	3.4
North Dakota	14.0	3.1	1.1	1.1	5.9	0.3
Ohio	105.4	42.3	11.3	6.5	24.8	2.0
Oklahoma	72.0	37.6	9.5	3.8	11.4	1.6
Oregon	35.5	7.8	3.1	2.7	9.3	0.5
Pennsylvania	117.7	19.0	20.6	12.5	32.0	2.1
Rhode Island	13.6	3.3	2.6	1.0	2.2	0.4
South Carolina	39.4	12.7	4.0	3.4	7.7	3.1
South Dakota	17.1	4.0	2.0	1.4	7.1	0.4
Tennessee	63.7	20.8	12.9	5.0	11.8	3.4
Texas	149.5	73.0	11.8	12.4	30.7	6.0
Utah	20.5	3.7	2.3	3.1	6.0	0.9
Vermont	8.2	2.5	0.8	0.6	2.4	0.2
Virginia	33.2	4.4	5.1	5.2	10.9	1.4
Washington	59.0	23.2	6.3	6.0	9.2	1.2
West Virginia	35.6	6.7	11.3	2.9	6.0	1.6
Wisconsin	47.3	15.2	5.7	6.4	11.6	1.2
Wyoming	19.4	1.6	0.4	1.0	5.1	0.7

[1] U.S. Department of Commerce, Bureau of the Census, *Compendium of State Government Finances in 1955* (Washington, D.C.: United States Government Printing Office, 1955), 14–15.

tion with federal authorities. Finally, the federal government is free to withdraw the grant whenever it discovers that a State is not complying with the stipulated conditions.

Cooperation without grants

The national and State governments cooperate in numerous other ways which do not involve the transfer of funds. Some of the more important include collaboration among national, State, and local officials, and the exchange of information among different levels of government. For example, in criminal investigations, State and local police officers often work with agents of the Federal Bureau of Investigation and the Treasury Department. Data from the criminal files of the FBI are available to all cooperating law agencies. At one time law enforcement officials of the States were greatly hampered by their inability to cross State lines to arrest criminals who had moved out of the State, sometimes taking their loot with them. Today, however, drawing authority from its warrant to regulate interstate commerce, the national government has made it a federal offense to cross a State line in an effort to evade prosecution for crime, or to transport stolen goods across a State line.

THE STATES UNDER THE CONSTITUTION

However limited the relations between the States and the national government may have once been, the Constitution from the outset provided certain major bonds between the two. The national government plays an important part in the creation of new States; it has certain fundamental obligations to the States; and at the same time the Constitution prohibits certain actions to the States.

Creation of new States

The chief task of Congress in the creation of new States is that of admitting them to the Union; for presumably the residents of the area themselves create the State and its governing machinery. When the people of a given area seek admission as a State they petition Congress to declare under what conditions they may be admitted. If Congress is willing that the area enter the Union, it passes an enabling act, under which the people of the area summon a convention to draft a constitution. If Congress finds the proposed constitution satisfactory, it may then by joint resolution admit the State. Congress may establish requirements that must be satisfied in the constitution; for example, it demanded that Oklahoma include a pledge to keep the State capital at Guthrie until 1913. However, Oklahoma promptly violated this provision after being admitted; and in 1911 the Supreme Court held this violation justifiable, inasmuch as by requiring such a pledge the national government might make some States unequal to others (*Coyle* versus *Smith*).

The admission of States may be complicated by political considerations. Serious consideration has been given in the 1950's to the admission of

Hawaii as a State. However, the project has been blocked in part by some southern Democrats who profess to fear the racial admixture of the Hawaiian people, in part by other Democrats who feel certain that Hawaii will elect two Republican Senators, and in part by congressmen of both parties who suspect that the Communist Party dominates the Hawaiian waterfront. Some Democrats have insisted that in spite of its slender population Alaska should be admitted to the Union at the same time; for it appears that Alaska will elect two Democratic Senators, so that neither party will gain an advantage from these admissions.

Duties of the national government to the States

The national government has several important duties with respect to the States. The most notable of these duties are: the guarantee of a republican form of government in the States; the assurance of the territorial integrity of the States; and the protection of the States from foreign invasion and domestic disorder. All these duties are prescribed by the Constitution. However, even if the Constitution had not provided them, the first and last would probably have been assumed by the national government for its own security.

Guarantee of a Republican Form of Government: According to the Constitution, "The United States shall guarantee to every State . . . a republican form of government. . . ." (Art. IV, sec. 4.) However, the Constitution does not define "republican form of government," nor does it indicate which branch of the national government shall judge when a State does not have such a government. In the terminology of 1787, "republican" was probably construed to mean that the government should be composed of elected officials, with great leeway as to form. The term does not mean exclusively "representative"; in 1912, certain citizens of Oregon asserted in court that the direct initiative and referendum in their State deprived them of a republican form of government; the Supreme Court ruled that the matter was beyond its jurisdiction; Congress meanwhile continued to seat Representatives and Senators from Oregon. Hence it may be assumed that the national government has found direct public participation in the legislative process to be consonant with a republican form of government.

The Oregon dispute followed the usual pattern in the determination of whether a State has a republican form of government. The federal Supreme Court has refused to rule in such cases, holding that they are political rather than legal matters. Hence the onus of decision has fallen upon the President and Congress. The prime criterion lies in the position adopted by Congress with respect to Senators and Representatives from the State or States concerned. After the Civil War, for example, Congress while controlled by the extremist Republicans refused to accept members from the southern States until those States had ratified the Fourteenth and Fifteenth Amendments and had made certain changes in their political structures; otherwise, it was alleged, those States would not have a republican form of government. Considering the general powers of Congress, such as the one permitting it to withhold federal funds from a State, it appears that the judgment of Congress can be final and compulsory.

The Assurance of Territorial Integrity: The Constitution provides that ". . . no new States shall be formed or erected within the jurisdiction of any other State; nor shall any State be formed by the junction of two or more States or parts of States, without the consent of the legislatures of the States concerned as well as of Congress" (Art. IV, sec. 3, cl. 1). Part of the logic underlying this provision has been suggested above. It should also be noted that if there were no obligation to consult the State legislatures before redrawing the boundaries of a State, the party in power in the national government might change these boundaries in such a way as to make its Senate majority almost unassailable; for example, a Democratic majority might divide Democratic Texas into five States while consolidating several normally Republican midwestern States into one State.

One of the chief consequences of this provision today is that there is no easy way of making more equal the representation of such population giants as California and such population midgets as Nevada. Moreover, it thwarts the proposals of some planners who argue that such interstate metropolitan areas as New York City, Chicago, Philadelphia, St. Louis, Kansas City, and Cincinnati should be established as separate States. The State legislatures would almost certainly oppose these projects, if only because of the tax receipts and power the State governments would lose.

Protection from Foreign Invasion and Domestic Violence: The Constitution provides that the national government ". . . shall protect each [State] . . . against invasion, and on application of the legislature, or of the executive (when the legislature cannot be convened) against domestic violence" (Art. VI, sec. 4). Of course, invasion of a State would be an invasion of the United States, so that a guarantee of this sort is rather needless. Ordinarily a State is expected to cope with local disorders by means of its own police forces and its militia. If a State cannot do so, however, and if either the governor or the State assembly applies for federal assistance, the national government will probably intervene. If the disorders destroy property of the federal government or interfere with some federal function, the national government may intercede without any request for aid from the State government (see, for example, the lead illustration to Chapter 21).

Prohibitions on the States

The Constitution imposes a number of prohibitions on the States, in that it forbids them to carry on any of a number of types of actions. Several of these prohibitions cover fields in which the federal government is presumed to have exclusive powers; they are fields in which State activity would severely contract the power of the national government to enact and execute laws dealing with all the American people. Other prohibitions are designed to secure the people in their persons and their property; they are similar to limitations which the Constitution sets for the national government as well. These prohibitions on State activity are discussed at length in the various chapters dealing with the functioning of the national government; but it would be well to enumerate the principal prohibitions on the States at this point. These prohibitions forbid the States to negotiate treaties or alliances with foreign powers; maintain armed forces; tax federal property; levy import or export duties; regulate interstate commerce; coin money; make anything but gold or silver legal tender; impair contracts; deny a citizen of another State the privileges and immunities of American citizenship; deny any person the equal protection of the laws; or deny any person due process of law.

INTERSTATE RELATIONS

Interstate obligations

The federal Constitution sets certain obligations that the States must respect in their relations with one another. These obligations will be discussed more fully in the chapters dealing with governmental functioning. Briefly, States must give "full faith and credit" to the public acts and records of all other States; and they must guarantee citizens of other States all the "privileges and immunities" of an American citizen.

"Full Faith and Credit": If the States were independent powers, as foreign states are to one another, any person might escape the laws and court judgments of his home State by moving to another State (unless the two States had a treaty governing such cases). For example, if he owed money in Alabama, he might not be held liable for the debt if he went to Arkansas. However, the "full faith and credit" clause of the Constitution resembles a universal treaty binding all the States to regard each other's laws as their own laws. A business that secures a charter of incorporation (a legal document) from one State may operate in another State so long as it obeys the laws that most States have enacted to regulate "foreign" corporations. If a court in New York decides that a man must pay a debt, and the man flees to California, his creditor can, without having to try the case over again, get the California courts to enforce the decree of the New York court. There is one area in which recently the "full faith and credit" clause has faltered: divorces. Some court decisions in the past few years have cast doubts on the validity of Nevada divorces in other States. Despite the tendency of the States to have many different laws, this clause binds them together and makes business and personal affairs much more stable than they would otherwise be.

"Privileges and Immunities": In another important way, the Constitution acts as a super-treaty among the States. It prevents any State from discriminating against a citizen of any other State. For instance, a State cannot block a resident of another State from using its courts and police on equal terms with its own citizens. It cannot keep other Americans from freely entering its territory. Its recreational parks, its roads, its harbors, and its other public facilities are open to all Americans without distinction. If someone from another State wishes to sell products or perform work in the

State, he is entitled to do so with only such restrictions as are imposed upon citizens resident in the State.

However, some limits to the grant of all privileges and immunities exist. Minor burdens can be placed upon non-residents to compensate the State for the difficulty of administering to non-residents. For example, an extra fee may be charged a non-resident applicant for a license to do business, on the ground that it costs more to investigate his application. Of greater importance are limitations upon non-residents that are justified on the ground that experience in the State is essential to the activity the non-resident wishes to engage in. For instance, the States require a term of residence as a condition to granting a newcomer the right to vote. Also, doctors, lawyers, and other professional people moving into a State may find it unusually difficult to practice their callings; they may feel that their qualifications are superior to those demanded of local residents. However, the federal courts have agreed with the States that special local conditions in these occupations permit unusual burdens to be placed upon non-residents or new residents. Naturally, the State organizations of the members of these professions encourage the imposition of such burdens so as to reduce the likelihood of competition from members of these professions immigrating from other States, and bring pressure upon their State government to enact appropriate laws.

Interstate agreements

One means whereby the States have attempted to solve problems related to more than one State without the intercession of the national government has been the interstate agreement or compact. The Constitution provides that a State may enter such a compact only with the consent of Congress (Art. I, sec. 10, cl. 3). However, the federal courts have consistently ruled that such a compact is permissible even without federal consent provided that it does not conflict with the political power of the national government, nor infringe upon its supremacy. For instance, an interstate agreement determining the allocation of water in an area in which the national government has its own irrigation project would be overthrown by the federal courts.

The States have negotiated over one hundred of such compacts, most of them in the twentieth century. A large number of the recent compacts deal with the allocation and conservation of natural resources; for example, seven western States in 1922 agreed to the Colorado River Compact distributing rights to the waters of that river among the States concerned. One of the most important compacts was that between New York State and New Jersey establishing the Port of New York Authority, which administers the harbor facilities in the two States that comprise the Port of New York— New York and New Jersey. The type of enforcement agency for administering the compact varies greatly. Often the States erect a commission for administrative purposes; but in the long run there is no superior authority to compel the States to abide by these compacts.

QUESTIONS AND PROBLEMS

1. The "supremacy clause" (Art. VI, cl. 2) is of great importance to the federal structure of the United States. What function did it serve and what forces operated afterward to make these few words more than a mere gesture of intent to create federal supremacy?

2. Define and contrast briefly the following doctrines: delegated and inherent powers; expressed and implied powers; exclusive and concurrent powers; strict and broad constructionism.

3. What are the possibilities, in your opinion, that the *inherent powers* doctrine might subvert the Constitution?

4. Opponents of the grants-in-aid programs have alleged that the States are selling their birthrights for a mess of pottage. Criticize this assertion in its three phases: *selling; birthrights;* and *mess of pottage.*

5. Suppose that Congress wished to admit the constitutional and democratic kingdom of Belgium to the Union as a State. The allegation is made that the action is unconstitutional. Compose a legal argument favoring the action of Congress.

6. Compare the form of the interstate compact with that of confederational government. Are they similar? How?

PART III

The Public

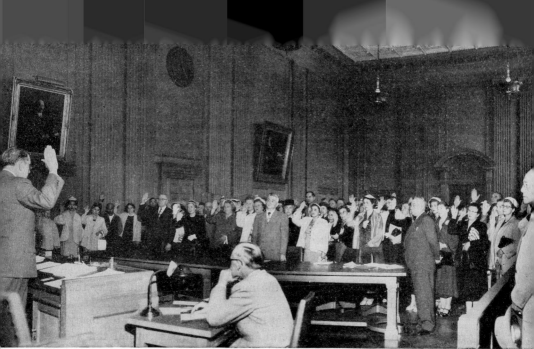

THE CITIZEN

A CITIZEN is a member of a political community who has some voice in the government of that community. He is not a subject, a national, a slave, or an alien. These terms vary in meaning from time to time and country to country. Like the word "republic," the word "citizen" has been fouled in the nets of political propaganda. Where the word has a favorable sense, people call themselves by it, even though they may in fact be slaves. Throughout world history most people have been subjects, not citizens. Since the American and French Revolutions, however, there have come to be only a few countries whose inhabitants do not view themselves as citizens.

A subject is a member of a political community who owes allegiance not so much to the community as to the ruler or the ruling group of the community, and who is authorized to take little if any part in the governing of the community. Yet at ceremonial functions Queen Elizabeth II of Great Britain may be addressed by her "loyal subjects." Moreover, although the inhabitants of the Soviet Union and of other totalitarian powers are called "citizens," they cannot take part in the governing process of their countries to the degree that American citizens can in the United States. In terms of political participation, the citizen is also to be distinguished from the *national*. A national occupies a status much like that of a subject save that the term usually connotes a republican form of government whereas the term "subject" connotes a monarchy. An inhabitant of Samoa today

125

is a national of the United States; an inhabitant of France in 1700 was a subject of King Louis XIV.

In terms of his allegiance to the political community in which he resides, a citizen is to be differentiated from an *alien*. An alien is a citizen or subject of one country who is residing in another country. Usually the alien may take no part whatsoever in the ruling process of the country in which he resides; however, there have been occasional exceptions to this principle. On the other hand, the alien enjoys to a large extent the protection of the laws regarding his person and his property.

Citizenship in the United States

Today most of the people in the United States are citizens. At one time a large percentage of the population consisted of aliens. However, the barriers against immigration, and the public pressure to become citizens brought on those aliens who had taken up permanent residence in the United States, have so reduced the number of aliens that today there are only about three million.

The actual nature of citizenship in the United States was for many years rather vague. Although the term "citizen" appears several times in the Constitution, it is nowhere defined in that document. Indeed, prior to the War between the States many Americans tended to think of themselves first as citizens of a specific State, and only second as citizens of the United States; they had not yet adapted themselves to the concept of a powerful central government. At length, after the War between the States, chiefly in order to protect the southern Negroes, Congress proposed and the States ratified the Fourteenth Amendment to the Constitution, which asserts that "All persons born or naturalized in the United States, and subject to the jurisdiction thereof, are citizens of the United States and of the State wherein they reside." Hence all American citizens in the United States save those residing in the District of Columbia or other federal territory possess dual citizenship: of the United States, and of the State in which they live.

Acquisition of Citizenship: Citizenship *by birth* in the United States has been extended to mean birth in an American territory, such as Alaska or Puerto Rico. It has been limited so as to exclude infants of foreign diplomatic personnel in the United States. There are other minor conditions that need not be delved into here, although they sometimes bring about interesting and complicated cases in court. Similarly, under certain circumstances, the children of Americans abroad are citizens by birth.

Citizenship *by naturalization* has been of great concern in American history because the nation was formed almost entirely of immigrants. The problem of naturalization of whole groups of people arose early in the history of the republic. The Louisiana Territory (1803), Florida (1819), Texas (1845), the lands taken from Mexico (1848), Alaska (1867), Hawaii (1898), Puerto Rico and Guam (1898), and the Virgin Islands (1917)

New Citizens Taking the Oath of Allegiance. Federal Court House, Portland, Oregon, U. S. District Court.

brought new groups into the nation. Sometimes immediately and some-times with a brief delay, their residents were granted citizenship. The Fourteenth Amendment affirmed that Negroes are American citizens by birth, along with all other native-born residents. All native-born Indians were declared citizens in 1924.

Naturalization of individuals is a power of Congress under the Con-stitution (Art. I, sec. 8, cl. 4). Many laws have been passed under this clause, beginning in 1790 and ending for the present with the Immigration and Nationality Act of 1952, which supersedes all previous legislation. An alien can become a citizen by satisfying a number of conditions and passing successfully a court examination in any one of about 2,000 different courts at the federal or State level. The courts in turn rely heavily upon the advice of the Immigration and Naturalization Service of the Department of Justice. The conditions to be satisfied are in general the following: the alien must be eighteen years of age or more; he must have entered the United States legally; he must have resided in the United States continuously for five years and in his State for six months; he must speak, read, and write the English language; he must know the essential principles and facts of the American government; he must be of "good moral character" and must be attached to the principles of the Con-stitution; he must renounce his foreign allegiances and swear to defend the United States against all enemies.

The alien asserts that all these conditions are satisfied when he petitions the court for naturalization. The Immigration and Naturalization Service investigates the assertion. Some of the conditions can be readily confirmed. Difficulty is often caused by questions of moral character and of loyalty to the United States. Since the government and the public recently have been more agitated by these questions than in times past, an alien is scrutinized far more closely in these regards than he would have been ten, twenty, or one hundred years ago, or, in fact, ever before.

Loss of Citizenship: Recent attitudes and laws have made retaining citi-zenship more difficult. A naturalized citizen is almost certain to lose his citi-zenship if, within ten years of his being naturalized, he refuses to testify concerning alleged subversive activities on his part before a congressional investigating committee, and is subsequently convicted of contempt of Con-gress; if, within five years of his being naturalized, he joins any subversive organization, membership in which would have barred him from citizen-ship at the time he took the oath of allegiance; if, within five years of being naturalized, he establishes a permanent residence in any foreign country; if he resides for three years in the country of which he was once a national, or for five years in any foreign country; or if it is discovered, at any time after he is naturalized, that he has falsified any material fact in his application for naturalization.

Any American citizen, natural-born or naturalized, may be threatened by loss of citizenship if he obtains naturalization in another country; swears allegiance to another country; serves in the armed forces of another country without written permission from the United States government;

secures employment with the government of another country which provides that he must declare allegiance to that country to obtain the employment, or acquires citizenship in that country by accepting the employment; is convicted of committing treason against the United States; votes in a political election in another country, or in a plebiscite to fix geographic boundaries; deserts the United States armed forces in time of war, is convicted thereof by court martial, and receives a dishonorable discharge; or leaves or stays out of the United States in time of national emergency so as to avoid military service.

Problems of Dual Citizenship: Conceivably a person may be claimed as a citizen by more than one country. Many countries have not permitted expatriation—the act of voluntarily surrendering one's citizenship—until the recent past. Hence a person might or even may still possess dual citizenship if he was or is a naturalized American citizen. This situation may prove embarrassing; for, should such an American visit his native country he might be convicted of evading military conscription, since in the eyes of that government he is still a citizen. Under such circumstances there is little that the government of the United States can do.

THE VOTER

In recent years, the title of citizen has come to imply the title of voter as well. The very idea that a citizen is an active, responsible member of the community demands a channel for expressing that role. The basic channel is the vote for the selection of public officials, a channel that is also termed the suffrage. In the national, State, and local governments the voter chooses the legislative branch, which, although it may have yielded some of its initiative to the executive, still formally establishes the policy of the government; moreover, the legislature appropriates the money which finances the operations of the government. In the national and State governments, and in many local governments, the voter also names the chief of the executive branch; and in most States he elects the judiciary. Also, thanks to the practice of periodic elections, the voter exercises a constant check upon elected officials; should their behavior displease him, he may vote to replace them at some future election. Furthermore, in many localities the voter takes a direct part in the enactment of laws and the ratification of constitutional amendments through the initiative and the referendum. Finally, during political campaigns the voter becomes the most ardently courted man in America; virtually all the activity of the party leaders is aimed at winning his sometimes reluctantly given favors. Hence American politics revolve about the voter.

Emergence of the suffrage

The suffrage, or franchise, has existed in many societies since ancient times. In numerous primitive communities the chief of the tribe was elected by the heads of the principal families, usually out of their own number. Indeed, there is evidence to show that hereditary succession to the throne—that is, succession by the nearest blood relative or descend-ant—was sometimes a later principle that was adoped partly in an effort to avoid the disorders often incident to the election of a king.   Practically every culture that man has developed in historic times has on occasion showed signs of the doctrine that the people must consent to the choice of their rulers by some open manifestation of approval.   But it is a far cry from most of these practices to the elaborate apparatus of modern voting systems.

The beginnings of the modern theory of the suffrage are to be found in medieval legislatures such as the British Parliament, the French Estates-Gen-eral, the Sicilian *Parlamento,* and the Spanish *Cortes.*   Although many members of these assemblies held their seats through personal rights, many others obtained them through election by groups of qualified voters. These bodies came to represent the distinctive interests of the Church, the landed nobility, and the townspeople.   Moreover, for a time they afforded a strong check upon the actions of the hereditary king.   The constitutional history of these countries is the account of the struggle between the king and the legislature for preeminence.   By the time of the American Revolution, the king had been victorious on the European continent, so that the suffrage had all but disappeared.   In Great Britain, on the con-trary, the legislature was paramount; and the elected colonial legislatures had come to control strictly the prerogatives of the colonial governors. Hence early American leaders, nearly all of whom were of British descent, viewed a legislature named by the voters as the surest rein upon arbitrary government and the best guarantee of a regime founded upon the rule of law.   Thus from the beginning the voter has had a major role in the American government.

Evolution of the suffrage in the United States

However, few early American leaders believed that all adults should have the vote.   Therefore the present suffrage in the United States ends a process whereby the power of voting, which was extended to only a small percentage of the population when the Constitution was adopted, has been granted to almost all the adults in the country.   This change, occupying 150 years, has had three phases: extension of the suffrage (1) to all white men, (2) to all white women, and (3) to all Negroes.   Figure 19 shows how the huge potential vote of 102,743,000 persons in 1956 was distributed among the forty-eight States, and also what proportion of such persons actually voted in each State in the November presidential election.

State Control of the Suffrage: The evolution of the suffrage in the United States has been strongly conditioned by one important factor: the States, not the national government, determine the composition of the electorate, or the persons qualified to vote.   Hence every extension of the suffrage has had to cope with the social, economic, and political structures of the separate States.   Although the suffrage is a function of national citizenship, the national government cannot extend the suffrage to anyone.   This fact is visible in the qualifications that the federal Constitution sets for the electors of the House of Representatives, who "shall have the qualifications requisite for electors of the most numerous branch of the State legislature" (Art. I, sec. 2, cl. 1). The Seventeenth Amendment provides that the electors of members of the United States Senate shall have the same qualifications. These qualifications, of course, are established by the individual States. The only power of the national government with respect to the requirements for the suffrage is to forbid the States to fix certain qualifications, as it did in the Fifteenth and Nineteenth Amendments.

Extension of the Suffrage to Adult White Men: When George Washington was elected to his first term as President, fewer than ten per cent of the population may have possessed the suffrage. In no State were women authorized to vote; and in every State many if not most men were denied the suffrage by taxpaying or property-owning requirements. This sort of limitation on voting had been common during colonial times; but even during the period of the Confederation, a movement to broaden the suffrage was becoming evident. For example, in New York all adult males were empowered to vote for the members of the convention which was to ratify the Constitution.

Then, in 1791, the State of Vermont was admitted to the Union with a constitution that enfranchised all adult males. Vermont, which was then

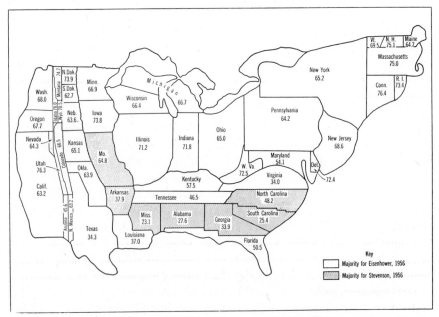

Based on unofficial and incomplete returns by the Associated Press, Nov. 9, 1956. In every case where returns were incomplete, an unweighted projection was made from the votes counted to the votes remaining unreported. Potential vote by States was taken from the Bureau of Census Series P-25, No. 143, Oct. 5, 1956.

Figure 19. The Potential and Actual Vote in 1956. The States are shown on a scale nearly proportionate to their potential vote (and, incidentally, this scale is fairly close to their proportionate electoral vote and population, too). The figure within each State is the per cent of the potential vote that actually voted for President in November, 1956. The potential vote is the number of civilians over twenty-one years of age in every State except Georgia and Kentucky, where the voting age is eighteen.

a western frontier State, set a pattern for other new States, which were successively admitted to the Union with universal, or almost universal, adult white male suffrage. In these western States land was so plentiful that its ownership did not set one man off from his fellows. Moreover, there was a rough equality among the western population that discouraged economic requirements for the suffrage. Too, western States felt that widening the franchise would tend to attract immigrants from the older coastal States, where restrictions on voting barred many of the less prosperous people from the polls. Eventually, especially after the election of Andrew Jackson as President in 1828, one eastern State after another also discarded its qualifications for voting, partly in an effort to avoid losing more of their already scanty labor force to the western States. In fact, this movement was simply the American contribution to a trend throughout the western world that was reflected in the European revolutions of 1830 and the English Reform Bill of 1832. The American movement was the most successful. By about 1850 universal adult white male suffrage prevailed in nearly every State, and America had the largest electorate in the world.

Extension of the Suffrage to Adult White Women: The nineteenth-century movement toward extending the franchise to women was one aspect of a process in western Europe and America wherein women were accorded general legal equality with men. Also it was but one of the many campaigns for reform, such as those to abolish slavery and to prohibit the manufacture and sale of alcoholic beverages, which agitated the United States during this era. The first State to grant women any power at the polls was Kentucky, which in 1838 authorized them to take part in school elections. Other States began to enfranchise women, especially after 1900, so that by 1918 more than half, particularly in the North Central and Far Western regions, had awarded women either partial or full voting authority.

Shortly after World War I, in 1919, Congress proposed a women's suffrage amendment and submitted it to the States. Within little more than a year the necessary three-fourths of the State legislatures had ratified this, the Nineteenth Amendment, so that women in every State could take part in the presidential election of 1920. The Amendment provides merely that "The right of citizens of the United States to vote shall not be denied or abridged by the United States or any State on account of sex." The Nineteenth Amendment, then, does not empower women to vote. It only forbids the States to bar a woman from voting because she is a woman.

Development of the Suffrage in the South: The development of the suffrage in the South, and the general conditions underlying voting there, are different from those in any other section of the country. The most obvious singularity of the South is the concerted effort to bar Negroes from the polls. However, the matter of Negro voting in the South is not only a racial issue; it also was part of a doctrine of "rule by the few" that goes back to colonial days in that region. The South was slowest to remove property qualifications and slowest to give the vote to women. After the Civil War the emancipated Negroes, for reasons of class as well as race, fell

TABLE 3. KEY DATES IN THE LEGAL HISTORY OF
NEGRO RIGHTS[1]

JAN. 1, 1863—President Lincoln puts into effect his Proclamation, declaring all persons held as slaves in rebel states to be free.

DEC. 18, 1865—Thirteenth Amendment ratified, abolishing slavery in the United States and its territories.

JULY 28, 1868—Guarantee of "equal protection of the laws" for all citizens is written into the Constitution as the Fourteenth Amendment.

MARCH 30, 1870—Fifteenth Amendment ratified, declaring that the right to vote should not be denied to anyone on grounds of "race, color or previous condition of servitude."

MAY 31, 1870—Enforcement Act, designed to bring Federal Government pressure to bear against any effort to circumvent the Fourteenth and Fifteenth Amendments, passed by Congress. (Six years later the act was nullified by the Supreme Court as exceeding the Federal Government's proper role.)

MARCH 1, 1875—Congress, in an act subsequently nullified by the courts, passes Civil Rights Law guaranteeing all persons, regardless of race, the use of "inns, public conveyances on land or water, theatres, and other places of amusement."

MAY 18, 1896—Supreme Court, in Plessy v. Ferguson, establishes principle of "separate but equal" facilities for Negroes, in a decision upholding a Louisiana railway segregation law as not violating "equal protection" clause of Fourteenth Amendment.

JUNE 21, 1915—Supreme Court declares unconstitutional the so-called "grandfather clause," a voting-qualification device employed by Southern states to restrict Negro suffrage. The clause exempted persons who had voted or whose progenitors had voted prior to 1867 from the fulfillment of educational tests and property qualifications required of other voters.

MARCH 7, 1927—Texas law barring Negroes from voting in Democratic primary elections is unanimously overruled by Supreme Court. (Five years later, Texas Democrats' attempt to bar Negroes from primaries by party resolution is declared illegal by the Supreme Court.)

DEC. 12, 1938—Supreme Court rules a state must admit a Negro to its law school or establish comparable separate facilities.

NOV. 25, 1940—Conviction of a Southern Negro is overturned by Supreme Court on grounds that Negroes had been barred from jury service at his trial.

JUNE 25, 1941—President Roosevelt establishes Federal Fair Employment Practices Commission, with instructions to seek the elimination of discriminatory practices in industry.

DEC. 18, 1944—Supreme Court rules that Railway Brotherhoods cannot act as bargaining agents under Railway Act of 1934 unless they grant equality of membership rights to Negroes.

MARCH 12, 1945—New York passes first state Fair Employment Practices law forbidding "discrimination because of race, creed, color or national origin" in employment, and sets up a State Commission against discrimination.

JUNE 3, 1946—Jim Crow practices on interstate buses barred by the Supreme Court.

OCT. 29, 1947—President Truman's Committee on Civil Rights calls for an end to all forms of segregation.

MAY 3, 1948—Supreme Court rules that "racial covenants," private real estate agreements involving residential race restrictions, cannot be enforced by the courts.

JULY 26, 1948—President Truman issues executive order establishing as a policy for the armed forces "equality of treatment and opportunity for all persons . . . without regard to race, color or national origin."

---

[1] From *N. Y. Times,* May 23, 1955, p. E5.

Table 3 (*Continued*)

JAN. 7, 1949—Alabama constitutional provision giving local registrars wide powers to deny franchise nullified by a Federal court.

JUNE 5, 1950—Segregation in railroad dining cars is banned by the Supreme Court.

JUNE 5, 1950—Supreme Court, in a decision acknowledging that inequality is inherent in segregation, directs University of Oklahoma to stop segregating a Negro student in classrooms, library and other facilities.

MAY 17, 1954—Supreme Court, in a ruling based on the principle that separate facilities are inherently unequal, outlaws segregation in public schools as "a denial of the equal protection of the laws" guaranteed by the Fourteenth Amendment.

into the category of the impoverished groups that the southern ruling group was wont to disfranchise, or at least to discourage from political activity. In those States in which payment of a poll tax (a small sum, such as a dollar or two, levied per person yearly) is a qualification for voting, the tax probably disfranchises many whites as well as Negroes. Furthermore, many southern whites, as well as Negroes, seem to have been convinced, or to have convinced themselves, that they need not or should not take part in elections. The proportion of the potential electorate that votes regularly in the southern States is smaller than that in any other part of the country.

The situation is changing. The economy of the South grows daily more complex and productive. Durable factions are springing up. Lumber, cattle, citrus fruits, chemicals, oil, and other industries are introducing a new way of life to many Southerners. More Northerners have migrated to the South. More Southerners, both white and Negro, have fanned out to the North and West. A new middle class of business and commerce is growing up in the cities, both large and small. The old South, as pictured by Northerners, is vanishing; the magnolia trees, sleepy hamlets, and slow-moving country folk belong to the historical motion pictures rather than to the modern South. Southern universities have greatly expanded and improved.

Reflecting these cultural changes, both white and Negro electoral participation has risen. The number of registered Negro voters in the southern States increased from 650,000 in 1947 to 1,100,000 in 1952. All competent observers agree that this figure will steadily grow. Despite frequent evidence of hostility from the "white supremacy" groups, leaders and agents of Negro civic organizations continually penetrate new areas of the South, ingeniously probing for opportunities to extend the privilege of voting to local Negroes. The watchful eye of the federal government under both Democrats and Republicans guards against many of the worst incidents that might occur; too, there is a growing willingness among Southerners to allow the extension of the suffrage, which makes the position of the white supremacists not at all so comfortable as it is portrayed by many Northerners. Table 3 gives some of the most important dates in the recovery of rights that the Negroes possessed in the Reconstruction Era and lost shortly thereafter.

The major restrictions that remain on Negro voting are the following:

(1) The anti-Negro sentiment that intimidates Negroes from time to time and place to place, especially in the rural, predominantly Negro sectors where the sentiment is strongest. This restriction is supported by those less hostile but tradition-minded county registrars and election officials who make it as difficult as possible for a Negro to vote.

(2) The apathy and fear of many Negroes that deter them from "taking chances" for an "unimportant" benefit.

(3) The absence of an opposition party that can seek votes from among the non-voters.

(4) The payment of a poll tax, disfranchising poor whites as well as poor Negroes, that is used in five States of the South as a requirement for voting. The Alabama and Virginia laws are most difficult to comply with and therefore are most effective in excluding voters.

(5) The literacy requirements, ranging from a demand that voters know their ABC's to a stipulation that they be able to "interpret" the federal and State constitutions. This kind of requirement is often administered loosely for whites and rigidly for Negroes.

It should be realized that all of this struggle was conducted within a framework of legal statement in the Constitution that specifically demands the equal treatment of Negroes. As such, it is an object lesson of what can cause a law, even a constitutional clause, to be null. The Fifteenth Amendment states that "The right of citizens of the United States to vote shall not be denied or abridged by the United States or any State on account of race, color, or previous condition of servitude." Furthermore, Section Two of the Fourteenth Amendment penalizes any State for establishing restrictions on the suffrage of twenty-one-year-old male citizens (with some minor exceptions) by reducing their representation in the House of Representatives proportionately. Thus, if a State, half of whose population is Negro, were to prevent Negroes from voting, the delegation of the State in Congress would be halved. (Of course, the exclusion of Negroes would have been unconstitutional in the first place under the later —1870—Fifteenth Amendment.) Needless to say, Congress and the President found it convenient over many years to ignore this clause, and even the Fifteenth Amendment itself, so disciplined was the southern public, so inarticulate the Negroes, both North and South, and so preoccupied the northern and western people and their leaders with other issues.

General qualifications for voting in the United States

Aside from the diminishing fact of Negro exclusion in the South, there exist few significant restrictions on a universal adult suffrage in the United States. There are only three general qualifications for voting: citizenship, age, and residence. Beyond these, there are two special qualifications which have been set in some of the States: taxpaying or property-owning, and literacy. Insanity and conviction of a felony usually bar an individual from the polls. Finally, there is a qualification that is at the same time an assertion that other qualifications have been satisfied: registration.

Citizenship: Voting actually follows citizenship; but in certain periods of history, citizenship was not in fact required of voters. Aliens who had declared their intention of becoming citizens were enfranchised in some of the early western States; this authorization was probably made chiefly in order to attract population. (Argentina had a similar law.) Since Arkansas did away with this practice in 1926, every State has extended the vote only to citizens of the United States.

Age: It is traditional that the vote is granted only to those who are twenty-one years of age or older; in fact, that age is specifically named in the Section of the Fourteenth Amendment cited above. However, in 1943 the government of Georgia lowered the required age to eighteen years, partly in the belief that "those who are old enough to bear arms are also old enough to vote"; in 1955 the government of Kentucky did likewise. It has been urged (by President Eisenhower, for instance) that the federal Constitution be amended so as to lower the voting age to eighteen for all federal elections. Moreover, a number of States have received like proposals in their legislatures. Actually, the effect of lowering the voting age in Georgia seems to have been rather slight. It may generally produce an accenting of "liberalism" in the electorate, that is, of the feeling that the government should take a more vigorous role in managing the national economy for the direct benefit of the lower-income groups. At present, younger people are more negligent in exercising the suffrage than older people are—at least up to the age of sixty. It is possible that a lowering of the voting age throughout the country, although it is not apt to work any major change in the composition of the electorate or in the machinery of government, would start the voting habit early in life, before the problems of jobholding, marriage, and homebuilding sap people's interest in casting ballots.

Residence: Every State demands that the citizen have a certain period of residence in the State; and most States demand residence also for shorter periods in the county and the voting district. This qualification has been established largely to prevent party agents from bringing added voters into a district in which a close contest is foreseen. Some southern States demand unusually long residence periods mainly in order to disfranchise migrant farm workers and other relatively unsettled persons who might vote against the *status quo.* By contrast, some central and western States have rather short requirements: Nevada, for example, asks six months in the State, thirty days in the county, and ten days in the district—probably in order to attract settlement. Over the whole country, the residence qualifications average about one year in the State, three months in the county, and one month in the district.

Taxpaying and Property-owning: Although a taxpaying requirement for the suffrage was fairly common at one time, today it has almost everywhere disappeared save under exceptional circumstances. As noted above, five southern States make payment of a poll tax obligatory for voters, in order to disfranchise Negroes and also the less prosperous whites. The once widespread property-owning qualification has virtually everywhere been abandoned. However, in Michigan, Montana, Nevada, New Mexico, Texas, and Utah, only property-owners are permitted to vote on bond issues, probably from the fear that those who do not own property might combine to pass a bond issue that would fall directly on property-owners alone. Finally, in South Carolina property-owning is an alternative qualification to the literacy test.

Literacy Tests: Seventeen States now require evidence of the ability to read or write English, or both, to qualify an individual for the suffrage. Seven of these States are in the South (in South Carolina the test is an alternative to property-owning); five are in the Far West; four are in New England; and the last is New York. The ability that is demanded, and the way in which the test is administered, vary widely from State to State. In the South the principal function of the test is to disqualify Negroes. Generally these tests are supervised by election officials; hence passage or failure depends upon the discretion and will of the officials. In New York, however, the test is administered by the State department of education, and is required only of those persons who cannot prove that they have completed the fifth grade in public school, or secured equivalent instruction elsewhere.

Registration: Every State save Arkansas and Texas requires all voters to register in one way or another, so that at election time officials may quickly establish who shall be permitted to vote. In the two exceptional States, the Texas constitution empowers cities of more than 10,000 population to institute registration, but the power has never been used; the Arkansas constitution forbids personal registration. In these States poll tax receipts serve to register voters.

Registration may be either permanent or periodic. That is, a voter may be required to register only once for any given address, so that his name will remain on the list until he moves away or dies. On the other hand, he may have to register periodically, since all names are cleared from the list after a certain lapse of time. At one time periodic registration was the more common. However, it has in late years been generally supplanted by the permanent registration system; for although periodic registration is apt to be more nearly accurate, it is expensive and imposes on the voter the need for keeping his registration current. Today thirty-three States have permanent statewide registration, and eleven others have it in some areas. Periodic registration is used in all areas in only two States: South Carolina and Wyoming.

Conclusion: Existing citizenship, tax, property, residential, literacy, and registration requirements bar about 22 million American adults from the polls. That is, although there were about 102 million potential voters in 1956, there were only about 80 million legally qualified electors entitled to vote for President. Nevertheless, America, which started out far ahead of the rest of the world in the extension of the suffrage to adult males, and which was bogged down in bitter quarrels over racialism for seventy-five years, is assuming presently the condition of universal suffrage with none save truly administrative restrictions. This condition is normal in the contemporary world, where every large nation possesses universal suffrage.

QUESTIONS AND PROBLEMS

1. Distinguish among a citizen, a subject, a national, and an alien.

2. Interview one foreign-born person whom you know regarding the procedures he followed in getting to America; describe his or her present status. (Note: The foreign-born person may be a foreign student, a naturalized citizen, a visitor, or a resident alien.)

3. List the conditions that may cause a loss of citizenship and in each case give a doctrine or reason that to your mind can be used to justify the action.

4. Using the index to this book and going back to previous chapters, write an essay of 400 words on the changing attitude toward universal suffrage from 1620 to the Civil War.

5. Repeat problem (4) above for the period from 1865 to the present.

6. Using *The World Almanac*, compute the average proportion of the qualified electorate in 1952 voting in the South, West, Midwest, and Northeast regions. Which region showed the heaviest and which the lightest, turnout?

7. Using figures obtained from *The Book of the States* or elsewhere, determine what region of the country has the shortest, and which the longest, residence requirements for voting. Can you give any reasons for these requirements?

10. Political Rights and Guarantees

Bettman Archive

$\mathbf{A}$ RIGHT is an act that an individual is in every sense capable of performing and for the performance of which he has the protection of the government. A right is to be distinguished from a liberty, which may be defined simply as an act that an individual is able to carry out. A right, then, is a liberty that is protected by the government.

There are several ways of classifying the rights that are enjoyed in the

United States.   One widely accepted way, which will be used for the purposes of this text, terms rights either political, judicial, or property. Political rights, which are to be the topic of this chapter, refer to the relationships between the individual and the state in the governing process. These rights include (1) a guarantee against involuntary servitude; (2) an assurance of the equal protection of the laws; (3) freedom of speech and the press; (4) freedom of assembly; (5) freedom of religion; (6) the right to bear arms; (7) a clear definition of treason; and (8) protection against being deprived of life or liberty without due process of law.

Judicial and property rights are to be discussed in later chapters which deal with issues regarding which these rights become vital. Judicial rights comprise the numerous guarantees against unfair treatment in conjunction with a case at law. They include (1) a prohibition against bills of attainder; (2) a prohibition against *ex post facto* laws; (3) assurance against unreasonable search and seizure; (4) a prohibition against excessive bail; (5) indictment by a grand jury; (6) the writ of *habeas corpus;* (7) a speedy, public trial by jury; (8) a defense attorney and witnesses for the defense; (9) protection against self-incrimination; (10) a prohibition against double jeopardy; (11) a ban on cruel and unusual punishments; and (12) a guarantee of due process of law throughout the trial proceedings. Property rights concern guarantees given to property-owners against actions of the government. Property rights include (1) a guarantee of the inviolability of contracts; (2) limitations on the power of eminent domain; and (3) the requirement that the seizure of private property by the state be done only according to the due process of the law.

One of the most important aspects of all rights, whether political, judicial, or property, is that none of them is absolute. That is to say, there is no right that has no limitations upon it. These limitations may be imposed for many different reasons, such as the fact of a state of war between the United States and a foreign power, or for the protection of the public. Indeed, it is this latter reason which probably occasions the greatest contests over rights. It is in general the function of the States, through their police power, to enact laws for the protection of the public; and it is this State legislation that most frequently clashes with the essence of rights.

SOURCES AND GUARANTEES OF RIGHTS

Documentary sources

The principal sources of rights are the Constitution, its Amendments, federal laws, and court decisions. Many of these are derived from the principles of Christianity and Roman Stoicism; such British documents as

---

The Trial of Aaron Burr, 1807. William Wirt is delivering a famous speech in prosecution of the former Vice President (1801–1805). In the background sits Chief Justice Marshall. Burr was acquitted for lack of two witnesses to the overt act of treason in levying war against the United States. The trial gave early proof of the difficulty of convicting anyone of treason under the Constitution.

the Magna Carta, the Petition of Right, and the Bill of Rights; and colonial practices. The federal Constitution itself contains few explicit statements of rights; but for many people it is an implicit assertion of rights in that it confers only delegated powers upon the national government. The Amendments, especially the first ten, the Thirteenth, and the Fourteenth, are major sources of rights; in fact, the first ten Amendments, the Bill of Rights, were adopted in 1791 to provide guarantees of rights that many Americans had expected in the Constitution proper. The Thirteenth and Fourteenth Amendments, which were originally designed to apply chiefly to the newly emancipated Negroes, have since been applied to all persons regardless of race, and even to business corporations, which are "legal persons." On the basis of the authorizations in the Constitution and its Amendments, Congress has from time to time passed laws providing for further rights. Finally, through judicial decisions the federal courts, notably the Supreme Court, have interpreted and defined many of these rights in cases in which one of these rights, or a limitation on a right, has been challenged.

The federal Supreme Court as guarantor of rights

In practice the federal Supreme Court has been the ultimate guarantor and defender of rights. A question involving a right originates in some federal or State law. An executive, either federal, State, or local, complies with the terms of this law in enforcing it. An individual, or group of individuals, may charge that the law violates a right based on the Constitution or some other foundation. A case arises from this charge which, if it concerns some federal right, will eventually come into a federal court and perhaps finally into the Supreme Court. It is then the task of the Supreme Court to determine if a right exists under the circumstances of the case and if it has been violated.

Presumably there is no appeal from the decision of the Supreme Court. However, cases containing similar issues have come before the Court separated by a period of years during which the personnel of the Court may have changed, or during which some members of the Court may have adopted other ideas, so that their decisions in the two cases may differ. Hence a right may be affirmed where it was once denied, or denied where it was once affirmed. Rights, then, are not necessarily permanent. Partly for this reason many persons have disputed the power of the Supreme Court in deciding cases involving rights, and have argued that the legislatures which have enacted the laws should be allowed greater discretion. Yet as matters stand today, short of constitutional amendment the Supreme Court is the final arbiter of rights.

The function of public opinion

It is sometimes maintained that the final judge in the case of political rights is public opinion. Indeed, in the early debates over the desirability of incorporating a bill of rights into the Constitution, Alexander Hamilton wrote in *The Federalist*, No. 84: ". . . [a political right] whatever fine declarations may be inserted in any constitution respecting it must altogether depend upon public opinion, and on the general spirit of the people and of the government. And here, after all . . . must we seek for the only solid basis of our rights."

Perhaps it is true that many rights draw their principal strength from public opinion. It might be more nearly accurate, however, to assert that the public, or at least any given interest group within the public, supports rights usually only for those who agree with them; but the same group would forbid rights to those who disagree with them. For example, in recent years in various American communities members of the sect of Jehovah's Witnesses have been physically assaulted and have seen their property destroyed by mobs. Yet the Supreme Court has upheld the right of their children not to salute the American flag in schools. Here is only one of the many instances in which the Supreme Court has upheld a right in defiance of public opinion.

Perhaps the most important role played by public opinion in the matter of rights is that of supporting Supreme Court decisions as final. Again, it is only those groups that want the decision which will accept it without complaint; after the Supreme Court, in 1954, overthrew many State laws providing that the white and Negro races must be segregated in the public schools, certain groups in the southern States inaugurated immediate campaigns to keep segregated education. Yet a Supreme Court decision affirming a right will greatly add to its acceptability in many circles of society.

THE CHIEF THREATS TO RIGHTS

Government

The chief threats to rights in the United States come from the various units of government and from the public. Judging from numerous decisions of the Supreme Court respecting rights, the federal government only rarely has denied a citizen his rights. However, the laws and ordinances of State and local governments have frequently been overturned as destructive of a right guaranteed by the federal courts. As indicated above, the background of such a ruling has usually been that the State or local government has exercised its police power to regulate people's activities in such a way that an individual or group has felt his or its rights infringed.

One of the most important legal developments over the years has been the expansion of certain parts of the federal Bill of Rights so that it restrains State governments. Originally it was denied that the Bill of Rights limited State behavior, if only because the State constitutions normally had their own bill of rights. However, parts of the Fourteenth Amendment were deliberately phrased so as to apply specifically to State governments; the dominant northern Republicans at the time feared lest some of the southern States restrict the political life of the former slaves. With the passage of time, successive court rulings have gradually extended a large part of the Bill of Rights to State governments. A crucial turn came when the Supreme Court ceased to interpret the word "liberty" in the Fourteenth Amendment as meaning simply "freedom from arrest," and expanded its interpretation to include such matters as "freedom of speech" and "freedom of the press." It must be emphasized that the Supreme Court has held most *political* rights to be protected from State interference by the Fourteenth Amendment, especially by its due process clause; many *judicial* rights, on the other hand, are not within the scope of the Amendment.

The public

It is sometimes forgotten that the public, in one form or another, may be a menace to rights. This forgetfulness stems in part from one interpretation of the concept of popular sovereignty, an interpretation which holds that the public not only is the source of all the powers that it confers upon governments but also that it cannot be restrained in the exercise of those powers that it withholds from governments. At the same time, save in cases concerning infractions of the Thirteenth Amendment, it is usually quite difficult to secure favorable court judgments for those who charge that an individual or group, by contrast to a government, has violated one of their rights.

The federal Constitution is almost entirely concerned with protecting individual rights from violation by the federal and State governments. What, then, would be needed to protect individuals' liberties from interference by other people and private groups? The answer is that the federal government must pass legislation to protect any liberty from private interference; this legislation would convert the liberty into a right. In connection with some liberties, the federal government has acted against private obstacles; for example, federal law prohibits conspiracies by groups, such as the Ku Klux Klan, to prevent Negroes (or, in some cases, whites) from enjoying the freedom of speech, the freedom of assembly, and other liberties, as well as the power to exercise the suffrage.

In other cases, however, there are no federal laws to protect liberties that many people possess or desire to possess. Sometimes actual crimes are perpetrated against liberty; then the only recourse of the injured, or of those affected by the crime, is a government prosecution on some ground other than that of the denial of the liberty. This would have been the only way to deal with the mob that denied freedom of the press to Elijah Lovejoy (an abolitionist newspaper editor of Alton, Illinois) and lynched him, in 1837; they might have been tried for murder. Likewise, this sort of prosecution would have been the only defense against the mob in Carthage, Illinois, that in 1844 denied freedom of religion to the Mormons and shot their leader, Joseph Smith.

In yet other cases, however, no crime is committed; hence no recourse at all is available to those deprived of liberties save to agitate for the passage of favorable laws. For example, an organization, such as a business corporation that founds so-called "company towns" in which the corporation owns virtually all the property and in which only corporation employees live, may forbid practically all political liberties to the inhabitants of the town. An organization of workers may in the same fashion refuse individuals a political liberty. For instance, in 1951 the Brotherhood of Locomotive Firemen and Enginemen negotiated a union shop agreement with the New York Central Railroad, providing characteristically that all employees of the railroad performing types of work under the jurisdiction of the Brotherhood must become members. Subsequently the railroad was compelled by the Brotherhood to discharge two employees whose religious convictions prohibited their joining a labor union.

Another commonly resented private practice is racial discrimination in the hiring of workers. People who are as poor as most Negroes find it a great disadvantage to be barred from many kinds of work because of their color. Consequently, many persons and groups have besought Congress to enact a fair employment practices law designed to prevent employers from discriminating against any person on the ground of his or her race, creed, or national origins, when selecting workers. To this date, Congress has not enacted such a law; however, several States and cities have. In this case, as in the two others noted immediately above, the nation-wide protection of the desired liberty requires a federal statute.

THE PROHIBITION ON INVOLUNTARY SERVITUDE

Involuntary servitude is prohibited by the Thirteenth Amendment, which forbids "slavery or involuntary servitude, except as a punishment for crime whereof the party shall have been duly convicted. . . ." Freedom from involuntary servitude is one right that is guaranteed against both governments and private parties. Although intended principally to abolish slavery, the guarantee protects individuals from other forms of compulsion. Its real force rests in the interpretation made by the courts of the term "involuntary servitude." For instance, conscript military service is not involuntary servitude; it is held to be a duty to the country. On the other hand, because of their obligations to the passengers, sailors and railroad employees may be compelled to complete a voyage or a trip. By contrast, a State may not enact legislation making it a criminal offense for an individual to fail to do work for which he has received payment in advance. An individual cannot be held to work by threat of criminal prosecution; if he refuses to do the work for which he has been paid, he may only be sued for obtaining money under false pretenses.

THE RIGHT TO EQUALITY UNDER THE LAW

The right to equality under the law is stated in the Fourteenth Amendment, which forbids any State to "deny to any person within its jurisdiction the equal protection of the laws." This Amendment was at first designed to prevent the southern States from discriminating against Negroes; in practice, however, it has come to be applied in litigation having no bearing upon race, and even to corporations. This Amendment does *not* prohibit the classifying of persons or things into different categories, and then the application of different treatments to the various categories. For example, a State may impose one tax rate upon locally-owned stores and another upon chain stores. The whole working of the progressive income tax demands first a classification of the population according to income. Indeed, one of the most important aspects of law is the fact that it classifies. What the courts resist, when a law is questioned, is impropriety in classification; in other words, the courts examine the intent of the classification and its consequences. For instance, should a State attempt to pass laws or otherwise to prevent people from other States moving into it to live and to work, the courts would find the State action to be an unconstitutional act in violation of the "equal protection" guarantee.

Education

The most notable cases arising under the "equal protection" clause have been those concerning race relations, especially with respect to education, transportation, and housing. All the southern States have insisted since the Civil War that whites and Negroes must not attend the same schools; and these States have enacted and strictly enforced laws providing for racial segregation in the public schools. In 1896 the Supreme Court, although not by a unanimous decision, held that segregation was permissible so long as the facilities for the Negroes were equal in quality to those for the whites. However, the "separate but equal" principle has been slowly undermined. For example, in 1938 the Supreme Court ordered the State of Missouri either to establish a separate law school for Negroes or else to admit Negroes to the law school at the white University of Missouri. In subsequent years the Court directed other State universities in the South to admit Negroes to their graduate and professional schools. Finally, in 1954 the Supreme Court rejected the entire system of segregated education and instructed the southern States to admit both Negroes and whites to the same schools (*Brown* versus *Board of Education*).

Transportation

With respect to transportation, cases involving equality before the law again have usually been concerned with the segregation of Negroes from whites in the southern States. Actually, where the Supreme Court has been able to overthrow State and local ordinances it has done so not on the ground that segregation has violated the right of equality before the law but that it has comprised an interference with interstate commerce. Using this as a basis, the Court in 1946 ruled that segregation on interstate transportation amounts to a violation of the federal Interstate Commerce Act (*Morgan* versus *Virginia*).

Housing

Segregation in housing has been much more widespread than that in education or in transportation; for it has concerned most of the States, not merely those in the South, and it has involved not only Negroes but also such other non-white nationalities as the Chinese and the Japanese. The means used to exclude members of the unwanted race or nationality has been the so-called "restrictive covenant," a document which amounted to a contract signed by all the property-owners of a given district agreeing that they would not sell their property to a member of an unwanted group. Courts from time to time have held that any person who violated such a covenant might be sued for breach of contract. In 1948, however, in the case of Shelly *versus* Kraemer, the Supreme Court ruled that whereas property-owners might negotiate such agreements among themselves, the agreements are unenforceable in court. The Court declared that "the Constitution confers upon no individual the right to demand action by the State which results in the denial of equal protection of the laws."

FREEDOM OF SPEECH AND THE PRESS

Freedom of speech and the press is declared in the First Amendment: "Congress shall make no law . . . abridging the freedom of speech or of the press. . . ." According to this section of the First Amendment, Congress may enact no restriction upon the freedom of speech or the freedom of the press. Moreover, through decisions of the Supreme Court this Amendment functions by the agency of the Fourteenth Amendment as a restraint upon State and local authorities as well. Yet the very way in which these freedoms may be used and abused has made them the object of frequent limitations at all levels of government, limitations which for various reasons have been sustained by the courts.

Prohibition on censorship

One principle to which the courts have adhered under almost all circumstances is that speech and the press may not be subjected to censorship, or, in legal terminology, "previous restraint." That is to say, under almost all conditions, no laws may be enacted that will inflict a penalty upon any utterance or publication before evidence is given that some damage has been incurred. In other words, a person is to be free to say or print what he pleases, with the understanding that he may have to suffer the consequences; but he is not to be prohibited beforehand from saying or printing what he chooses.

Limitations on seditious utterances

Wartime Restraints: Under conditions of warfare even the ban on censorship may be lifted, so as to forbid seditious utterances, or utterances that will tend to promote uprisings against the government. The first of such limitations was the Sedition Act of 1798, ostensibly to prevent hindrance with the undeclared American war against France being waged at the time, but actually to curtail Republican criticism of the Federalist administration and Congress. During the Civil War and the two world wars Congress passed sedition acts, on these occasions with the clear intent of protecting the government from its enemies rather than the party in power from its political rivals. The legislation in World War II was indeed less severe than that in World War I, certainly because the newspapers censored themselves from 1941 on and also perhaps because the second war was more generally, if less enthusiastically, supported.

Peacetime Restraints: During the past four decades, almost entirely because of the world revolutionary aims of the Soviet Union, various governing agencies have imposed certain peacetime restraints on the freedom of expression. States and localities, especially after the Russian Revolution of 1917, have passed laws designed to curtail utterances that might tend toward domestic upheavals. These laws often have been called "criminal syndicalism" acts, probably because the chief group of political radicals in the United States before 1918, the Industrial Workers of the World (I.W.W.), was syndicalist rather than communist. The revolutionary syndicalists urged the violent overthrow of government by labor unions. Under the provisions of these acts, State and local officials have attempted to silence not only those groups that were indisputably subversive but also certain organizations whose beliefs, although comparatively harmless, clashed with those of most people.

Beginning in 1940, the federal government likewise has enacted peacetime restraints on seditious activities. Congress in that year passed the Alien Registration (Smith) Act, the first of a series of laws designed to limit freedom of speech and of the press on the part of those who would seek to overthrow or disrupt the federal government not only in time of war but also in peacetime. The Smith Act makes it a federal offense to persuade members of the armed forces to mutiny, to conspire to teach the violent overthrow of the American government, to advocate the overthrow of the government, or to publish material designed toward that end. In the following year, eighteen members of the Socialist Workers (Trotskyite) Party were convicted of violating the Smith Act and were sent to prison. In 1949 eleven leaders of the Communist Party were convicted of violating the Smith Act; and on hearing their appeal, the Supreme Court upheld both the decision of the lower court and the constitutionality of the Act. Later numerous other important communists were arrested and jailed under the terms of this Act. In these decisions the Court seems to be holding to the precedent set by Associate Justice Oliver Wendell Holmes in 1919 that the accused had used words in a fashion which would "create a clear and present danger that they [the words] will bring about the substantial evils that Congress has a right to prevent." However important the Smith Act has been, it probably will be superseded as a weapon against communists by the Communist Control Act of 1954 (see below, under "Freedom of Assembly").

Other restraints on speech and the press

Libel and Slander: Freedom of speech and the press is also limited by the penalties that the speaker or publisher may have to suffer after the act is committed. For instance, one may not state openly or publish materials that are intended to damage the character or the social or professional standing of another individual. Such an act, if spoken, constitutes *slander* and, if written, *libel*. However, most cases of libel and slander reach court as civil trials, that is, as trials in which one person sues another for damages, with the government as referee; and in such cases, if the truth of the statement can be shown, no damages can be allowed. The more severe instances of libel may be tried as criminal cases, in which the offense is deemed to be against the State, and in which the punishment is fine or imprisonment; under such circumstances, the proof that the statement is true may not be a defense, since certain truths may be regarded as indecent or injurious to public morals.

Blasphemy and Obscenity: Freedom of speech and of the press may also be limited by laws against blasphemy and obscenity. This sort of law is almost invariably an enactment of a State or local government, as a function of its police power; however, the federal government forbids the sending of obscene matter through the mails. In ruling on cases in which blasphemy or obscenity has been charged the courts have usually been rather lenient. For example, if a city directs its police commissioner to remove obscene publications from public magazine stands, the courts may hold that a police commissioner is not a qualified judge of literature. Actually there are on the statute books of many States laws regarding obscenity in literature which are completely inapplicable to modern tastes; these the courts simply do not enforce. However, courts rarely rule such a law unconstitutional.

Limitations on mechanical devices

In the wake of modern technology have come several new means of mass communication whose regulation the Constitution makes no provision for; principal among these new means are motion pictures, radio, television, and electronic sound-amplifying devices. In some respects, their regulation differs from that imposed upon speech and the press.

Motion Pictures: Local and State governments have established boards of censorship for motion pictures, to purge them of matter that may be obscene, sacrilegious, overly suggestive, or, in the opinion of the censors, contrary to the public welfare. In 1915 the Supreme Court upheld such boards by ruling that motion pictures are purely a form of business and therefore not entitled to the protection of the First Amendment. The motion picture industry, however, never ceased demanding this protection. Ulti- mately its efforts were in part rewarded; for, in 1952, the Supreme Court ruled not only that the State of New York had acted improperly in banning the film "The Miracle" on the ground that it was sacrilegious, but also that motion pictures in a sense are sheltered by the protection of the First Amendment. However, the Supreme Court admitted that because of its peculiar nature the motion picture industry might be subjected to restraints different from those imposed upon any other medium of mass communi- cation. Hence in 1956 certain State and local boards of motion picture censorship were still functioning. The Supreme Court was probably directed to its recent decision partly because of the change in public tastes and also partly because the industry has organized its own board of censorship and production code to regulate itself.

Radio and Television: The very nature of radio and television lays certain restrictions upon their freedom. There are only a limited number of wave lengths available for transmitting purposes; and the unrestricted use of these wave lengths would produce such chaos that broadcasting would be impossible. Consequently the privilege of using these wave lengths is distributed and administered by the Federal Communications Commission (FCC), a bipartisan board created by Congress in 1934, whose seven members are appointed by the President and confirmed by the Senate. The control of broadcasting is exercised chiefly through the license that every commercial broadcasting station must have and that must be renewed every three years. Since the FCC is directed to consider the "public interest, convenience, or necessity" in granting these licenses, it can to some extent censor radio and television programs; a few licenses have been withheld on the ground of objectionable practices. In fact, the FCC has not greatly interfered with these media; and federal law does prohibit overt censorship by the FCC. The federal government has tried to prevent any station from being monopolized by any one political party; for it requires that if any station give program time to a candidate of one party, it must make an equal amount of time available to candidates of other parties for the same office.

Electronic Sound Amplifiers: Electronic devices for the amplification of sound have become important parts of political campaigning. Frequently such devices are mounted on trucks to broadcast a candidate's message through the streets of a city. Some local authorities have passed ordinances restricting the use of such mobile devices on the ground that they are public nuisances. In 1948, however, the Supreme Court struck down such an ordinance in Lockport, New York, which had authorized the city chief of police to grant or deny permits for the use of sound trucks; the Court held that the ordinance amounted to a violation of the freedom of speech. In 1949, on the other hand, the Court upheld an ordinance of Trenton, New Jersey, which banned the projection of "loud and raucous" sound from a moving vehicle on the city streets. The Court probably found a distinction between the two cases in that the Trenton ordinance was specific whereas the Lockport ordinance was so loosely phrased that it might have been invoked only against the political foes of the municipal government.

Picketing

Another form of expression unknown to the Founding Fathers is picketing. Its protection has been a matter of litigation in recent years. Picketing is any stationing of people, by workers, before a place of employment. Picketing may be designed to urge workers not to enter a factory whose labor force is on strike; or it may be aimed at persuading the public not to patronize an establishment which presumably engages in unfair labor practices or refuses to recognize a union. In the past, municipal governments dominated by employers' interests have enacted restraints against picketing, even though it was peaceful. However, in 1940 the Supreme Court ruled that picketing for the purpose of informing the public about labor disputes enjoyed federal protection against prohibition by the State or the local governments.

THE FREEDOM OF ASSEMBLY

The freedom of assembly is protected by the First Amendment, which declares that "Congress shall make no law . . . abridging . . . the right of the people peaceably to assemble. . . ." This provision assures the American people the right to meet for the purpose of discussing political matters, and the right to organize political associations to influence the government. It should be apparent that this right has a close functional relationship with the freedom of speech, since the freedom to assemble for political ends presumes the right to speak in the assembly. Like other rights, the freedom of assembly may be restricted for the sake of the public welfare or the safety of the government. However, basing its action on the due process clause of the Fourteenth Amendment, the Supreme Court has overturned many State and local prohibitions on the freedom of assembly, owing to the fact that these prohibitions were not intended for the benefit of the public but were designed to limit lawful political activity which might threaten to oust the group in power without subverting the government itself.

For some time the most sensitive issue connected with the freedom of assembly has been the Communist Party. In the past decade there has been wide public demand that the Communist Party be made illegal. States have attempted to use their criminal syndicalism acts noted above not only to stifle disloyal utterances but also to disperse subversive organizations; usually, however, the Supreme Court refuses to uphold such legislation unless the "clear and present danger" formula is satisfied. At length, in 1954 Congress passed the Communist Control Act, which at least on paper outlawed the Party.

The Communist Control Act specifically terms the Communist Party an "instrumentality of a conspiracy to overthrow the United States government" and includes a long description of the Party and its purposes. By this definition Congress has greatly simplified reaching convictions under the Smith Act, since it no longer will be necessary to prove that the Party is a conspiracy aiming to subvert the American government. Then the Act in effect outlaws the Party, for it declares that the Party is "not entitled to any of the rights, privileges, and immunities" of lawful bodies organized in the United States. The Act provides for the possibility that the Party may change its name. It further states that any person knowingly joining the Party in full awareness of its nature (something that may be very difficult to prove in court) shall be denied the rights of citizenship, including the right to hold a federal civil service post or to work in a defense plant. Members of the Party must register with the Department of Justice (a requirement similar to one in the Internal Security Act of 1950, which had not been enforced six years later). Communist-infiltrated unions may not represent workers in industry for collective bargaining purposes under the National Labor Relations Act; and the Act fixes a number of standards whereby communist infiltration may be detected. If a small percentage of the workers in a factory wish, an election shall be held to determine what union shall be their bargaining agent; and no communist-infiltrated union may appear on the ballot.

Another freedom, one related to that of assembly, is the right to petition Congress. One of the earliest functions of the British Parliament was the drafting of a "petition of grievances" for the king, enumerating wrongs that the members of Parliament wished to see righted. Whereas this practice formerly was of great importance in the legislative process, today it occupies a primarily ceremonial status. There are so many pressure groups that draw up and submit petitions to Congress today that these documents usually receive only cursory note. In short, the freedom of petition does not include a guarantee that the grievances will be attended to, or even that the petition will be read.

THE FREEDOM OF RELIGION

Prohibition against an established church

The freedom of religion is guaranteed by the First Amendment, in the statement that "Congress shall make no law respecting an establishment of religion, or prohibiting the free exercise thereof . . . ." An established religion is one in which the church in one way or another is supported by the state. The established church in any country has an obvious advantage over any other faith, in that it can rely upon the support of the government in any doctrinal or jurisdictional questions. At the time of the American Revolution, as it is today, the Anglican Church was the established church in England; and members of many of the dissident faiths, such as the Puritans, came to the American colonies rather than suffer the harsh treatment meted out by the English government and the Anglican clergy. The First Amendment was designed to prevent this situation in the United States by separating the churches from the federal government.

There has never been a determined effort to found an established church under the national government of the United States. However, for some years after the Revolution, certain New England States retained the system of established churches that they had inherited from the colonial era; the last of the State-established churches, the Congregational in Massachusetts, was not separated from the government until 1833. Today, since the limitations of the First Amendment are now held to apply to State governments as well as to the federal regime, it is difficult to see how a State might organize an established church even in the improbable case that the people would want one.

However, it is sometimes alleged that the principle of the separation of church and State is being violated with respect to government services that are extended to students of parochial schools. For example, when the

State of New Jersey in 1941 began to pay for school-bus transportation to students in church-operated schools, some observers declared that the State was thereby contributing, through public taxes, to the churches. However, in a suit at law which arose over this dispute, the Court in 1947 ruled by a five-to-four margin that religion was only incidental to the issue and that by providing this service the State was avoiding discrimination against some children. The opinion of the majority of the Court, then, was that this service was primarily educational, not religious (*Everson* versus *Board of Education*). By contrast, in the following year there came before the Court a case testing the practice of "released time," in which school authorities excused students from their regular classes at a certain time during school hours to receive religious instruction from a teacher of the sect of their, or their parents', choice, employed by church authorities (*McCollum* versus *Board of Education*). In this instance the Court ruled that the school administrators were collaborating with the religious bodies so as to disseminate religious beliefs with public money. This issue has also been raised in debates over federal aid to education.

The free exercise of religion

The letter from George Washington to the Jewish congregation of Newport, Rhode Island, reproduced in Figure 20, is an excellent example of the attitude fostered by the constitutional guarantee of the right to the free exercise of religious belief. But the members of the various faiths may be subject to local or federal police restrictions. For example, the Mormons in Utah taught and practiced the belief in polygamy, the family structure in which one man has more than one wife. Yet, acting under its authorization to legislate for the territories, Congress while Utah was a territory forbade the institution of polygamy; and the Supreme Court upheld the legislation. In late years the religious group most commonly at odds with the governing power has been the Jehovah's Witnesses. This sect has aroused public wrath in many communities by its refusal to abide by some of the customs of the community and by its contention that civil government is evil. Members of this faith teach their children not to salute the flag during patriotic observances at school. Local authorities have enacted a host of ordinances aimed at curbing the Witnesses, notably requirements that any person soliciting funds from the public be licensed. The Witnesses have brought many cases involving violations of these ordinances into the federal Supreme Court on the ground that the ordinances comprised denials of the freedom of religion; and the Court has tended to uphold the sect. In recent cases the Witnesses have been guaranteed their right not to salute the flag, and the freedom to sell their literature without a license provided that they create no public disturbance. The Constitution provides further assurance of the separation of the government from all religious faiths in its guarantee that ". . . no religious test shall ever be required as a qualification to any office or public trust under the United States" (Art. VI, cl. 3).

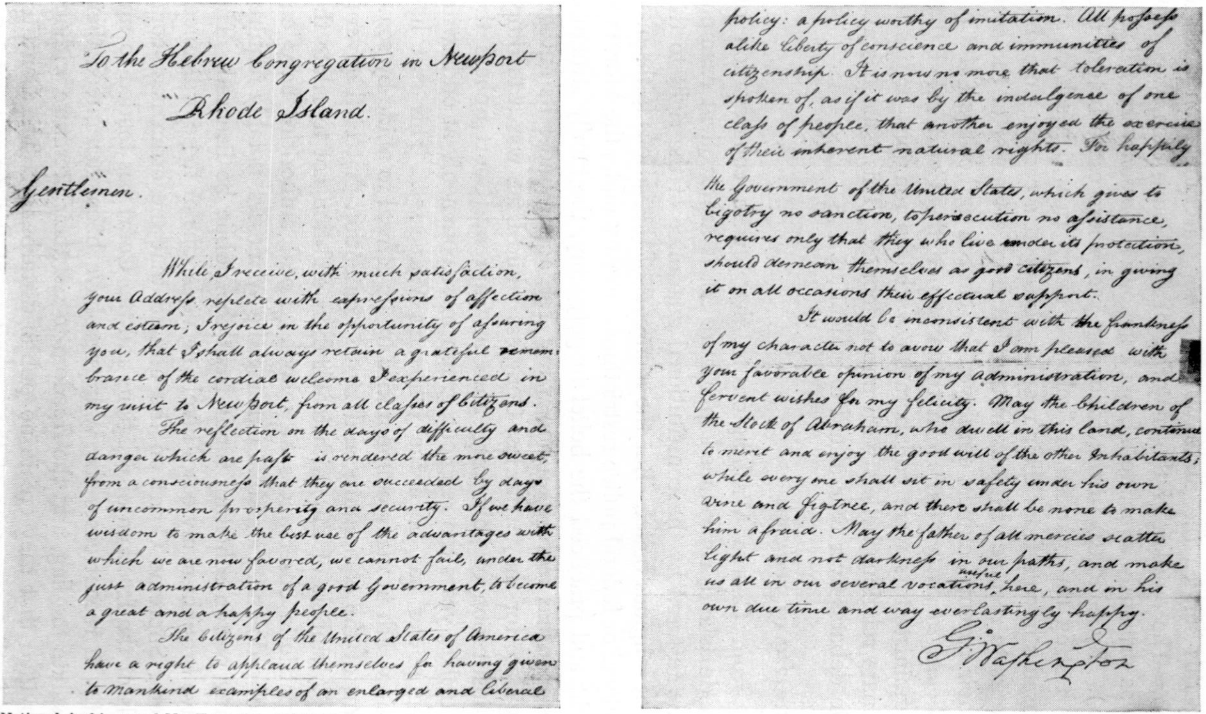

To the Hebrew Congregation in Newport
Rhode Island.

Gentlemen.

While I receive, with much satisfaction, your Address replete with expressions of affection and esteem; I rejoice in the opportunity of assuring you, that I shall always retain a grateful remembrance of the cordial welcome I experienced in my visit to Newport, from all classes of Citizens.

The reflection on the days of difficulty and danger which are past is rendered the more sweet, from a consciousness that they are succeeded by days of uncommon prosperity and security. If we have wisdom to make the best use of the advantages with which we are now favored, we cannot fail, under the just administration of a good Government, to become a great and a happy people.

The Citizens of the United States of America have a right to applaud themselves for having given to mankind examples of an enlarged and liberal policy: a policy worthy of imitation. All possess alike liberty of conscience and immunities of citizenship. It is now no more that toleration is spoken of, as if it was by the indulgence of one class of people, that another enjoyed the exercise of their inherent natural rights. For happily the Government of the United States, which gives to bigotry no sanction, to persecution no assistance, requires only that they who live under its protection, should demean themselves as good citizens, in giving it on all occasions their effectual support.

It would be inconsistent with the frankness of my character not to avow that I am pleased with your favorable opinion of my administration, and fervent wishes for my felicity. May the Children of the Stock of Abraham, who dwell in this land, continue to merit and enjoy the good will of the other Inhabitants; while every one shall sit in safety under his own vine and figtree, and there shall be none to make him afraid. May the father of all mercies scatter light and not darkness in our paths, and make us all in our several vocations useful here, and in his own due time and way everlastingly happy.

G. Washington

National Archives and Mr. Howard L. Milkman

Figure 20. Washington's Letter on Freedom to the Newport Synagogue. In response to a letter of welcome from the Sexton of the Hebrew synagogue, on the occasion of his visit to Newport, R. I., in 1790, President Washington penned this reply. It is an elegant and clear interpretation of several key doctrines of the Constitution and Bill of Rights.

THE RIGHT TO BEAR ARMS

The right of every citizen to possess firearms is protected by the Second Amendment, which declares that "A well-regulated militia being necessary to the security of a free state, the right of the people to keep and bear arms shall not be infringed." This guarantee was far more important at the time it was adopted than it is today; for it was assumed that the armed forces of the United States would consist primarily of the State militias. One of the chief aims of this Amendment, then, was to discourage the development of a professional, mercenary army such as the British had used in their efforts to quell the American Revolution. For many years, however, the United States has supported professional military forces; and in any event, the average citizen today could not afford to furnish himself with modern weapons. Moreover, at the time the Amendment was ratified, many people fed themselves and their families by hunting; today, by contrast, there are few areas in which many people provision themselves in this manner.

The right to bear arms may be, and has been, restricted on behalf of the public welfare. Local authorities demand that weapons be registered, and enact ordinances prohibiting the carrying of concealed weapons. The federal government, too, through both its taxing powers and its control over interstate commerce, has enacted laws against the sale, use, or possession of certain types of arms such as sawed-off shotguns.

LIMITATIONS ON TREASON TRIALS

No person in the United States may be lightly convicted of treason against the federal government, for the Constitution states that treason ". . . shall consist only in levying war against [the United States], or in adhering to their enemies, giving to them aid and comfort" (Art. III, sec. 3, cl. 1). The same Article fixes definite procedural requirements in treason trials, for it provides that "No person shall be convicted of treason unless on the testimony of two witnesses to the same overt act, or on confession in open court." In many countries rulers have been able to dispose of their enemies by charging them with treason on quite indefinite grounds and having them convicted, perhaps with no more evidence than a confession exacted under torture. However, in the United States the Constitution defines the crime narrowly and fixes the trial procedure; moreover these can be changed only by constitutional amendment.

On the other hand, the federal government is free to legislate with regard to the act of sedition, which consists in urging others to commit treason, or in committing acts that approach treason but do not include an overt act. It may also create laws to deal with subversion and espionage. No person was executed in peacetime for an act of espionage until 1953, when Julius and Ethel Rosenberg were executed after being convicted of having given secret information regarding the atomic bomb to the Soviet Union during World War II. In 1954, Congress passed a law providing for capital punishment in cases of peacetime espionage. Actually, with the changed concepts of warfare, it is very difficult to tell precisely when peacetime shades into wartime; hence this action by Congress may not mean a great deal.

ASSURANCES OF DUE PROCESS OF LAW

Life, liberty, and property cannot be taken without due process of law, say the Fifth Amendment (regarding the federal government) and the Fourteenth Amendment (regarding State and local governments). This protection gives, at one and the same time, a political, a judicial, and a property right. Commonly, it is asserted as a judicial right, and it will be discussed as such in a later chapter. Sometimes it is also used in a substantive sense to create or assert rights that are not otherwise mentioned in the Constitution: rights of an economic or political type. The economic rights of this character will be treated in yet another chapter, but the political rights must be mentioned here.

With regard to the Fourteenth Amendment, the Supreme Court has come to the view that words in it mean that a number of the political rights protected by the Bill of Rights with reference to the federal government are also protected with reference to the States and localities. Hence, when a State violates the rights of free speech, of free assembly, of petition, or of other political rights, it may be restrained by the Supreme Court in the language of the Fourteenth Amendment.

The Fifth Amendment refers to the federal government. An example of how it adds to the substantive rights of Americans is afforded by a recent case concerning a passport to travel abroad. The United States Court of Appeals held that the Department of State could not treat the desire to travel abroad as a mere privilege that could be granted or withheld at will. Rather, to "go from place to place" is a "natural right subject to the rights of others and to reasonable regulation under law." The Fifth Amendment was thus given new meaning; the substance of political rights was increased by prescribing due process of law for what could previously be denied without due process of law.

QUESTIONS AND PROBLEMS

1. From a merely preliminary reading of the three lists of political, judicial, and property rights, which group of rights, if any, would you guess to be most necessary to the survival of constitutionalism (see Chapter 6)? Explain your answer.

2. Suppose a would-be Hitler wishes to deliver a speech in Washington Square, New York City, and on arriving at the Square reads a sign saying, "No speeches permitted, by order of the Department of Police." What might he do from that point on and how might the authorities react?

3. In your opinion, are threats to political rights today more likely to come from government or from the public or from other sources? Explain your answer.

4. Although the Fourteenth Amendment specifically guarantees "equal protection of the laws," is the equivalent right of equal protection of the laws

implied and provided by other parts of the Constitution? Explain your answer.

5. As a "friend of the Court," write a 300-word argument justifying a village ordinance banning loudspeaker trucks of all kinds.

6. What limitations, penalties, harassments, and embarrassments can be expected by a person who is a member of the American Communist Party today?

7. When Congress refused to admit Utah to the Union until the Mormons abolished polygamy, was its action not a violation of the First Amendment? Explain your answer.

11. Public Opinion and Activity

Courtesy of Northwestern University Publicity Office

Pᴜʙʟɪᴄ opinion is the attitudes or beliefs of people about a political issue. The people concerned need have no organization, need not inhabit the same geographic area, and may have no personal acquaintanceship. The attitudes or beliefs must revolve about an issue; that is, a controversy must exist. For the purposes of this chapter and text, public opinion will be viewed as concerning only those matters that are related to government. Whether an eight-cylinder automobile is superior to a six-cylinder model, or whether Beethoven is preferable to Brahms, are matters of private judgment or of taste, at least until such time as some people appeal to the government to prefer one to the other. Thus, if a public statue of a great

156

composer is to be erected, preference for Beethoven or for Brahms enters the area of public opinion. A discussion of public opinion demands a treatment of (1) the origins of opinions, (2) the characteristics of opinion in action, and (3) the role of public opinion leaders.

THE ORIGINS OF PUBLIC OPINION

Cultural limits on opinion

Public opinion is founded upon needs that people feel as a result of their background and training. Opinions are only made possible, and are thereafter limited, by the culture in which the individual lives. Men do not have in all places and at all times the same wants or beliefs; rather, the wants and beliefs have stemmed from the culture—the totality of social relationships—in which they have lived. Thus what may be an opinion in one culture may not even exist in another. In the United States, for example, under present social security legislation a widow over sixty-two years of age receives monthly checks from the government provided that her husband was employed in a vocational field covered by this legislative system. Here opinion may differ as to whether or not such a system should exist, and as to how much the widow should receive. Assume that a comparable system of government annuities for widows was organized in a Moslem country, where a man may have more than one wife. Now public opinion could develop over the issue of how the money should be divided among the widows: for example, should each receive an equal portion, or should a kind of seniority principle determine the size of the portions? In the Moslem country, then, heated public debate could arise over an issue that could not even exist in the United States, whose culture forbids the institution of polygamy.

Social forces and opinion formation

Moreover, within the culturally determined limits of opinion, other special forces prescribe the opinions of individuals. Some of these forces are: the family, the neighborhood, the rural or urban nature of the community, the section of the country, vocation, income level, race and ethnic grouping, and religion. Each individual is prepared by most of these forces to look for certain kinds of issues, and to take only certain sides on those kinds of issues when they appear. All persons, consequently, do not have the same interests, nor do they take up the same sides on issues.

As an illustration, one may take the field of the family and opinions related to higher salaries for public school teachers. An individual who has

Top. **Great wheels bear petitions presented to Congress in 1893 for the establishment of a national department of roads.** The right to petition the government is guaranteed by the First Amendment (National Archives).

Bottom. **Northwestern University Students conduct a model United Nations meeting to develop interest in foreign affairs, discuss outstanding international issues, acquire skill in parliamentary procedure, and understand the viewpoints of the many UN nations.** Here Mrs. Edith Sampson is delivering the keynote address to the model General Assembly, January 26, 1955.

no children, who is perhaps himself uneducated, or who has had little education, is likely to pay little attention to the matter of public schools; he may have no opinion about teachers' salaries. A man who has children of school age, who is not sufficiently wealthy to send his children to a private school, whose family owns little if any taxable property, who believes that children should have a good education, and who feels that higher salaries for teachers will assure a good education for his children, will probably adopt the opinion that teachers' salaries should be increased. As a third case, a man whose children are beyond school age, or who has been financially able to send his children to a private school, whose family owns property that would bear the burden of increased school costs, and who feels that there is no need for trying to improve public school education by raising teachers' salaries, will probably be of the opinion that teachers' salaries are high enough.

The Family and Opinion: The family is probably the most important source of opinion for most people. It furnishes most individuals with their first experience in a sort of government, including such principles as authority and obedience, leadership and followership, and the like. Utterances by the parents often make lasting impressions and convictions. Relationships between the individual and his parents, and the individual and his brothers and sisters, may be the chief determinants of his political ideas; a hated and domineering father, for instance, may conduct an individual toward a hatred of all authority, reflected in the political field by a distrust or dislike of political leaders and the government in all its manifestations. Such was the background and resulting behavior, for example, of Giuseppe Zangara, who tried to assassinate President-elect F. D. Roosevelt in 1933.

The family, too, is likely to condition an individual's attitudes toward many other fields. It may relatively or even absolutely determine his choice of an occupation. It is important in establishing his income level. Its environment, the neighborhood in which the home is situated, its location in an urban or rural setting and in a particular region of the country, influence the individual in his opinion regarding these matters. The family establishes the racial and national grouping of the individual, and, especially in the cases of minorities, fixes his attitudes toward his own and other groups. For instance, in her novel *Strange Fruit,* a comparatively objective tale involving interracial conflict in Georgia, Lillian Smith portrays a Negro mother beating her son for having jeered at a white girl, to teach him submission to white people. It can be seen from the scope of its molding effects that the family is the actual origin of a vast body of specific opinion.

The School and Opinion: It is difficult to assess the importance of the school as a source of opinion. Of course, a parochial school will plant in the child the opinions that the parent church itself propagates; and it is likely to urge greater use of public funds for the support of the school. A private, non-sectarian school, since it is designed for children of upper-income groups, is apt to instill the opinions, attitudes, and values of those groups. Public schools, however, are presumably unbiased. Certainly the schools mirror the culture of their environment, and probably teach few if any opinions that clash violently with the culture.

Exactly what opinions the schools may and do teach are matters of considerable dispute. On the one hand are those holding the traditional view that teachers with rare exceptions are very "conservative" and timid in their political and economic beliefs; these observers insist that any teacher deviating even a trifle from the beliefs of the community is apt to be dismissed on the spot. By contrast, there are those who argue that public school teachers are excessively "liberal" in their opinions, and that they are endeavoring to plant in their students a belief in the need for a state-planned economy. As with many disputes, the truth lies somewhere between these two extremes. Probably many teachers seek little if any change in American society; teachers are recruited primarily from families of the lower-middle income level, a group that tends to adhere to conventional values. By contrast, one faction among the educators, whose influence over the whole public school system is difficult to weigh but which is not preponderating, sees the schools as implements whereby to refashion society.

The Church and Opinion: The degree to which the church or religious body contributes to the formation of public opinion varies greatly from one church to another. Perhaps the greatest religious influence upon modern American public opinion stems from no church body today but from the seventeenth-century Puritans who colonized New England, bringing with them their powerful credo of thrift and profit. It should be remembered that the northern and western regions of the United States were civilized by one of the most benevolent manifestations of cultural imperialism in history, that of Massachusetts and Connecticut. The broadcasting of these Puritan doctrines gave the stimulus for much of the economic expansion of the United States, and furnishes it with a substantial portion of its justification today.

So far as churches of this century are concerned, studies have shown in the case of many large congregations that people tend to join churches containing other people with similar political, economic, and social backgrounds. Hence these churches follow, rather than lead, the opinions of their members. Of course, there are exceptions to this general principle; John D. Rockefeller all his life was associated with the Baptist Church, a body that attracts most of its membership from the lower income groups. Jewish congregations, although made up of individuals as prosperous as the average of well-to-do Protestant groups such as the Presbyterian, also number a greater proportion of people supporting the enactment of laws favoring working people. Certain church bodies lead their members' opinions more than other churches do. The Catholic Church, for example, with its stress on the family, emphasizes the desirability of certain kinds of social legislation.

Media of mass communications

The Press: 1. NEWSPAPERS.   Among the various mass communications media associated with the press, that is, newspapers, magazines, and books, newspapers have the widest and most persistent influence upon public opinion.   However, it is easy to overestimate the importance of newspapers in the formulation of public opinion; and almost certainly they are not, for a number of reasons, as influential as they were during much of the nineteenth century.

Newspapers reach a vast number of people.   In 1956 there were 1,841 daily papers, with a total circulation of 55,837,834.   The first figure, however, represents a net decline of nineteen papers by comparison with 1955, and continues a trend of decline that set in about 1910.   Many newspapers under the pressure of economic want have merged, to yield such names as *The New York World-Telegram and the New York Sun,* obviously a compound of three once independently-owned papers.   There have developed such newspaper chains as the Hearst, Scripps-Howard, Gannett, and Knight groups.   However, the largest chain, the Hearst group, in late years has considerably retrenched: for example, in 1956 the last of three Hearst newspapers once published in Chicago was sold; and no American chain approaches the dominance over the American press that the Beaverbrook papers have in England.

Yet there is a trend that is constantly increasing the number of cities in which only one paper is published, so that today there are only about one hundred cities that have more than one paper owned by different interests.   Consequently, where a city has but one paper the readers may be given only one side of political events.   However, the dangers in the situation have been rather overdrawn; for in many of the smaller, "one-paper" cities it is possible to secure home delivery of a paper from a neighboring metropolis which may maintain a local correspondent who is not affiliated with the local ruling group.   Besides, the radio stations, news magazines, and other media bring in comment on the outside world.

Newspaper owners and publishers move in the same circles as the captains of industry, commerce, and finance.   Consequently most newspapers tend to reflect the outlook of these circles.   It is often charged that newspaper policy is controlled by advertisers, since newspapers obtain 70% of their income from publishing advertisements.   However, metropolitan newspapers are larger than most of their advertisers, so that a single advertiser is not likely to have the power to sway the policies expressed by the paper.   Even when the papers are not larger, their ready access to public opinion fortifies their position.   For example, the withdrawal of advertising from the *Wall Street Journal* by the General Motors Corporation in 1954, for an alleged violation of confidence in publishing information about 1955 models before the information was to be released, stiffened the backs of the publishers.   Although it was far more wealthy than the newspaper, the Corporation found it best to resume advertising relations.

In general American newspapers are probably more nearly balanced and complete than those of any other large country in the world. Newspapers want to carry enough news to please their current readers and to attract new readers; for it is chiefly by amount of circulation that newspapers win advertising. European papers, especially in France, are in the majority owned and operated by political parties or factions. They probably do more to divide the public into separate worlds of discourse than the American press does.

2. MAGAZINES AND BOOKS. Magazines and books, the two chief products of the press apart from newspapers, also play an important role in the formation of public opinion; this role, especially in the case of books, may be indirect. In 1956 there were 7,907 periodicals of all sorts, an increase of 259 over 1955. Only a few of these publications have a large circulation. Traditionally magazines are devoted primarily to literature. However, one significant development in recent years has been the tendency of mass-circulation periodicals such as the *Saturday Evening Post* and *Collier's* to publish in each issue one article or more recounting political, economic, or social matters. There are also at least three large and influential "news magazines": *Time, Newsweek,* and *U.S. News and World Report.* The magazine with the largest circulation in the United States, and perhaps in the world, *Reader's Digest,* includes many articles of political import.

However, periodicals do not directly reach a majority of the population; only one-third of the people, mainly from the upper educational levels, read any magazines. Yet many of these persons, such as newspaper editors and columnists, themselves contribute directly to opinion formation; and others of them are politically active and influential. Furthermore, numerous small periodicals have considerable weight, though their scope is usually narrow, particularly the professional journals such as that of the American Medical Association. Magazines in general are much more forthright about their prejudices than newspapers are; hence a prospective reader, especially one with strong political sensitivities, is apt to be careful in choosing only those publications that coincide editorially with his beliefs.

More than 10,000 different book titles are published annually in the United States; in 1955 the total was 12,589, of which 10,226 were new books and 2,363 new editions. The vast majority of these have little if anything to do with opinion formation, since they are light escapist reading. Moreover, books treating political matters rarely have a large sale. On the surface, then, books would seem to take a small role in fashioning public opinion. However, among those few who do read books may be the most influential persons in the community: as opinion leaders (see the following section) they can give the book an importance completely out of proportion to its sale. Moreover, some magazines, notably the *Reader's Digest* and the *U.S. News and World Report,* publish condensations of books the editors consider important. Such condensations may give the books unexpected and tremendous weight.

Radio and Television: In the past three decades radio and television have assumed an important role in the shaping of public opinion, radio after World War I and television after World War II. The structure of the radio broadcasting industry is quite different from that of newspaper publishing. In 1956, there were 2,896 AM and 530 FM radio broadcasting stations in the United States, reaching into an estimated forty-seven million homes by means of 125 million receiving sets. A considerable fraction of stations, including almost all of the powerful transmitters, are associated with one of the four great networks: National Broadcasting Company (NBC); Columbia Broadcasting System (CBS); American Broadcasting Company (ABC); and Mutual Broadcasting System (MBS). Station revenues come from the sale of advertising and talent, and amounted to $700 millions in 1955; about 100 educational and other stations are subsidized.

Only a minute portion of radio programs aim deliberately at swaying or even arousing public opinion; this portion includes discussion forums, news announcements and commentaries, and speeches by public officials and other opinion leaders. Speeches, of course, can hardly escape the prejudices of the orator and the group behind him. Simple news announcements are apt to be rather free of bias, for often the announcer does little more than read press service releases. With radio, because of the time factor, the possibility of omitting significant events is even greater than it is in the case of newspapers. News commentators are expected to reveal their slant in their commentaries. Discussion forums frequently present spokesmen for more than one side of the issue under debate, so that public opinion may be stimulated rather than attracted.

Radio in the main is directed at those on the lower educational levels. College-educated people tend to get their daily news from the papers. These differences persist among both men and women, but more women than men get their daily news from the radio. In explanation of these facts, several points require note. Most radio programs are pitched at a "low-level" audience; the news cannot be fully analyzed; radio gives a sense of personal contact; and it continues to play while women are busy around the home.

Television may have ultimately more effect upon public opinion than radio and perhaps more even than newspapers. By 1956 there were 36 million television receivers in the United States. There were 516 television broadcasting stations, with a revenue of $1.2 billions for the preceding year. The financial organization and the programming methods of television are very similar to those of radio, largely, of course, because television comprises an expansion of radio techniques to the visual field. In the past few years it has been shown that television has had a great effect upon public opinion. It has the unique capacity of creating the illusion that the viewer is at the scene of action. Among the most widely seen of all television broadcasts were those of the national party conventions in 1952 and 1956, and of the ensuing presidential campaigns. A sample of the United States population was asked what medium of communication had been the most important in informing them about the 1952 campaign; television took first place in its impact. Not surprisingly, a large part of all campaign funds goes to pay for television programs.

DIMENSIONS OF PUBLIC OPINION

Public opinion, like a geometric figure, has dimensions. These dimensions are not susceptible to such precise measurements as those in geometry, and as a result do not provide absolute numerical data as to the "size" of opinion. Yet, the dimensions suggest what may be the relative influence of various opinions. These dimensions include (1) the intensity with which opinions are held, (2) the number of persons or groups holding the opinions, (3) the political power wielded by those holding the opinions, and (4) the shifts that may occur among those holding the opinions.

Intensity

The intensity of a public opinion is based upon how much that opinion matters to the persons holding it. In any controversy, although an equal number of persons may have taken opposite stands on the issue, the persons on one side may be far more concerned than those on the other in having their opinion prevail. Often a large number of persons only moderately concerned with an issue may be counterbalanced by a very small group deeply attached to its opinion. Just how intensely these individuals hold their opinion can be sometimes seen from the precision, clarity, and detail of the arguments with which they endeavor to convince others of their rightness. At other times, intensity of conviction is reflected in sheer vehemence, and a liberal use of crude slogans.

Number of persons or groups

On any given issue there are almost always different numbers of people or groups holding distinct opinions. Number in itself is not decisive in fixing the weight of an opinion; intensity, for example, as noted above can conquer number. At the same time, if a very large number of people become attached to an opinion, that opinion has a better chance of prevailing in a contest with an opinion held by a few people, even if they are closely organized.

One important consequence of an intensely-held conviction may be that those sharing the opinion will create an organization to further their ends, making the opinion the property of a group. Now those holding the opinion have a tremendous advantage since, in politics as in war, a group tightly organized about a conviction can easily dispose of a much larger number of comparatively disinterested and isolated individuals. This is one of the reasons for the frequent success of the Communist Party in dealing with apparently overwhelming majority opposition.

Political power

However intensely people may hold an opinion, and however many persons or groups may hold it, the opinion may come to naught because those behind it have little political power. Political controls in this context include the means that those holding an opinion have for influencing the government, such as political office, wealth, prestige, or management of mass communications media. One of the prime differences between a representative government and a totalitarian regime is that in the representative government almost any opinion has the possibility of winning some audience. An apt illustration of the effect of political control upon the force of opinion lies in federal legislation benefitting industrial workers. For many decades there has been a widely shared opinion that Congress should enact statutes for the welfare of laborers. However, this opinion was generally unheard at the level of the federal government (with important exceptions in Wilson's first term) until 1933. Beginning in that year, however, this opinion carried far greater weight because for the first time it was shared by many politically influential persons in Washington. To take another illustration, one of the reasons why Indian welfare was commonly neglected in American politics was that Indians had no vote, no power, and no organization to present their needs to officials in Washington.

Shifts in public opinion

Whatever may be the strength of an opinion, as measured by its dimensions of intensity, number, and political controls, it is never constant, but always varying. An opinion is continually losing and winning adherents. In the case of the minimum wage law cited above, if the managers of a factory should raise all wages so that none would be below the minimum sought by law, the number of persons behind that opinion would probably be diminished by the withdrawal of some workers at that factory; probably not all the workers would desert the opinion, since opinions are not held solely on the basis of immediate self-interest. Opinions also may be discarded, or at least their intensity may be lessened, in order to advance other causes. For instance, after American involvement in World War II, President Roosevelt urged that "Doctor New Deal" be superseded by "Doctor Win-the-War." Thus the outbreak of the war paved the way for a reconciliation between capital and labor, which had been divided over Roosevelt's domestic undertakings, so that they could unite in the effort to defeat Germany, Italy, and Japan. This sort of procedure is more possible in the case of organized interest groups, in which the leaders may have substantial control over the opinions and actions of the followers.

OPINION LEADERS AND PUBLIC ACTIVITY

Opinion leaders are those individuals who, for any one of many reasons, have over the opinions of others an influence that is above average. Opinion leaders are a minority in the population. One study made in 1946 disclosed how unaware most people are of major political events. A sample of the American people, consisting of 1,292 persons, was interrogated about their awareness regarding five important issues of the time: the Report of the Anglo-American Committee on Palestine; the Acheson-

Lilienthal report on atomic energy; the Paris meeting of the Big Four Ministers; the proposed loan to England being debated in Congress; and the fact that Palestine was then ruled by England. Twelve per cent of the sample had heard of all five issues. Nineteen per cent had heard of four of the issues; seventeen per cent, of three; twenty per cent, of two; eighteen per cent, of one; and fourteen per cent of the sample had heard of none of the issues.[1]

Probably less than half the adult population is aware of half or more of the concrete issues that agitate the nation at a given moment. An even smaller fraction of the population contributes to the public debate on any single issue or group of issues. A demonstration of this came from the 1952 presidential campaign, which evoked more public interest than most, and which, since it was a campaign, probably found more persons using their powers of persuasion than in ordinary months. When a sample of 1,614 American adults were asked by the Survey Research Center, "Did you talk to any people to try to show them why they should vote for one of the parties or candidates?" only twenty-seven per cent answered "Yes."[2] Probably many of these people who answered "Yes" were not even aware that they were engaging in an uncommon activity.

Other studies, aiming at a clearer proof of opinion leadership (as opposed to simple knowledge about issues, or an occasional urging of people to take a certain viewpoint), have revealed an even smaller minority of opinion leaders. For instance, R. K. Merton reported interviews with eighty-five persons in a small Atlantic seaboard city in which respondents were asked to name persons whose opinions influenced them and who were generally sought out for advice regarding personal decisions. Respondents mentioned 1,043 names; but owing to duplications there were but 379 different persons. Of this total, fifty-seven were mentioned four or more times, and a few were mentioned thirty or more times.

In another study of farm operators in four townships in Iowa, Bryce Ryan asked a large sample to name persons to whom they would go for advice on local problems of schools, farm taxes, scarcity of farms, land use, and local roads. Again, many people were named once, and a very few men were named several times. The conclusion is that opinion leaders may influence from a very few to very many other people, and that the highly influential opinion leaders are very few in number. Of course, when opinion leaders "get into the business" of influencing others—as public relations counsels, professors, newspaper publishers, or politicians—they greatly increase their range of influence.

An opinion leader may or may not be an officer in a pressure group. In the case of a pressure group, there is some sort of definite organization or structure within which the leader functions. The opinion leader can, and often tries to, operate within the framework of an organization; but so far

---

[1] Hyman, H. H., and P. B. Sheatsley, "Some Reasons Why Information Campaigns Fail," *Public Opinion Quarterly*, 11 (1947), pp. 412–423.

[2] Campbell *et al.*, *The Voter Decides*, p. 30.

as his role of opinion leader is concerned, he can also address persons to whom he has no formal attachment. If he is an official of a public or private group, some are likely to hearken more closely to him than other people do.

Opinion leaders appear at many levels in society, and in many different vocations. They include, among others: the policy-making officials of the government; party bosses; pressure group chiefs; officers of political research bodies and of reform groups; captains of industry and labor union presidents; directors of mass communications media; members of certain professions, especially those who, like lawyers and teachers, deal closely with the public; and certain types of businessmen, such as building contractors and real estate brokers, who are apt to have economic ties with the government. On the neighborhood level the opinion leader may be an individual on a far more modest plane, such as a perceptive, vocal, and aggressive barber or bartender. Whatever their political, economic, or social standing, opinion leaders are men and women whom other people listen to and from whom they get ideas and convictions. Their activity constitutes an important type of political participation.

However, the influencing of opinion by members of the public is only one kind of activity. Ordinary people cannot only convince others of their point of view, but also can vote, give money to political movements, take part in rallies, ring doorbells for their candidates, be active in associations of many kinds, and do other things. Just as one can conceive of the completely inert citizen who is politically a blank page, so also can one conceive of the highly active citizen who does all of these things and more, without necessarily holding public office.

Voting

Voting is perhaps the most obvious and common kind of political activity. However, in the United States at a presidential election, fewer than seventy per cent of the potential voters go to the polls. Indeed, at elections other than those for the presidency, the rate of voting participation may fall far below fifty per cent; sometimes only one voter in three casts a ballot. Americans do not vote in such proportions as the people of western European nations, regardless of the type of election. Figure 21 shows the voting rate in recent years, and Figure 19 pictures the situation in the general elections of 1956.

The Americans who fail to vote fall into certain distinguishable categories. Voting in the southern States, whether or not there is a poll tax, lags far behind voting elsewhere in the country; in fact, when the proportion of American voters outside the southern States is computed, it does not fall far behind the percentages of western Europe. More men than women vote; the sharp rise in the curve of potential voters about the year 1920 shown in Figure 21, which was occasioned by the Nineteenth (Women's Suffrage) Amendment, was not paralleled by a comparable rise in actual voting. Persons with a college education vote more frequently than those without. Managerial employees and office workers vote more often than farmers and unskilled laborers. A higher proportion of union members than of non-union workers go to the polls, a situation that testifies to the success of unions in getting out the vote. City dwellers vote in greater proportion than country dwellers. More Republicans than Democrats vote, save where the latter are highly organized.

Proposals are sometimes made that steps be taken to increase the proportion of those voting. It is occasionally suggested that States enact compulsory voting laws, imposing a fine upon, or removing a tax exemption from, those who fail to vote. Certain foreign countries, such as Belgium, and even some American States, such as Georgia, have enforced compulsory voting. Neglect, not ignorance, is said to cause non-voting; also, the duty to vote, it is felt, will impel people to study the candidates and issues,

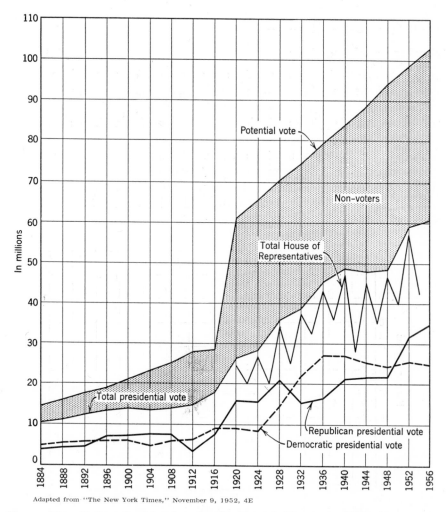

Adapted from "The New York Times," November 9, 1952, 4E

Figure 21. Voting Participation in Presidential Elections (1884–1956) and Midterm Elections (1920–1954). Note the sharp decline in participation in midterm elections of the House of Representatives.

and create a more intelligent public. However, this sort of voting raises some questions. Those who go to the polls today are better-informed about current events than those who do not. Would compelling present-day non-voters to cast ballots add to the "intelligence" of the vote? Furthermore, would compulsory voting be an imposition upon those persons who have scanned the lists of candidates and have concluded that they positively reject all aspirants for office? Also, following the principle that one may attract more flies with sugar than with vinegar, might it not be possible to draw more persons to the polls by reducing the number of elections during the year, shortening the list of offices for which people must vote, and simplifying the election procedure? Finally, the most obvious effect of compulsory voting would be to reward the political party that gets the largest proportion among those who previously have been non-voters; in America, the Democrats would benefit. Is compulsory voting then still desirable, on general principles?

Scoring people's activity

Voting, like urging one's opinions upon others, is again only a simple activity. Some part of the people do much more than talk and vote. They work in different ways in politics. What do they do, and how many do so? The chart in Figure 22 plots the number of American adults who were found during the 1952 presidential campaign at each level of activity, from complete inactivity to high activity. On the next page is the scoring system that was used to give each respondent his or her score. Perhaps the most remarkable feature of the chart is the sudden, sharp decline in political activity upon moving from the modest scores of 5–8 to the higher scores of 9–14. Also, the large number of inactive citizens in the scoring

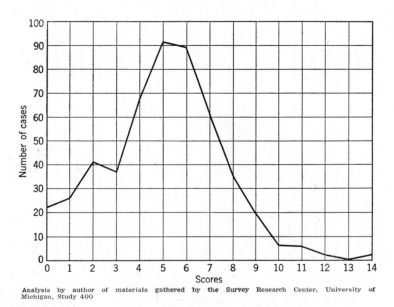

Analysis by author of materials gathered by the Survey Research Center, University of Michigan, Study 400

Figure 22.   Political Activity Scores of Americans, 1952.

HOW AMERICANS WERE SCORED ON POLITICAL ACTIVITY

Possible Points	Area of Activity	Description of Scoring Method
3	Voting	A person scores 1 point if he voted in 1952. He scores 2 additional points if he says he has always or almost always voted. A person scores 1 point if he states that he has sometimes voted in the past. Persons who were under 21 in 1948 were given 1 additional point if they voted in 1952, thus scoring 2 points.
2	Media use	A person scores 1 point if he said he read a lot about the campaign in newspapers or magazines or both. He is given ½ point for reading both not very much. Another point is given for radio or television listening or viewing under the same rules.
1	Persuading others	A person scores 1 point if he answered "yes" to the question: Did you talk to any people and try to show them why they should vote for one of the parties or candidates?
1	Financial contributions	Same for question: Did you give any money or buy tickets or anything to help the campaign for one of the parties or candidates?
1	Attending meetings	Same for question: Did you go to any political gatherings, meetings, dinners, or affairs of that nature?
1	Party work	Same for question: Did you do any other work for one of the parties or candidates?
1	Political club member	Same for question: Do you belong to any political club or organization?
2	Member of formal organization	Four or more memberships score 2 points, one to three score 1 point.
1	Member of informal club or group	Four or more memberships score 1 point, one to three score ½ point.
2	Active in formal organization	Being active in three or more scores 2 points, active in one or two scores 1 point.
1	Active in informal organization or group	Being active in four or more scores 1 point, active in one to three scores ½ point.
16	Total possible score	(In totalling individual scores, wherever a person scored a fractional sum, the half-points were rounded off alternately whenever they occurred to the next higher and next lower number.)

range below 5 is worthy of note. The picture of American public life suggested by the chart shows the "average man" to be far from a "model citizen" as painted by a Fourth of July orator. The "examination" was not meant to be difficult to pass, but only a small minority of citizens made high grades. About 14% of the 505 respondents scored eight points or more. The "active" score of 10 or more was achieved by only three per cent of the number.

Referring back to Figure 5, in Chapter 2, the American public appears to fit diagram (C) better than it does any other of the diagrams. The *active* public is small, numbering about one out of every thirty-five adult Americans. They have been called sometimes the *politists*, that is, people who are especially occupied with politics. Many of the contacts of the government with the whole public are filtered through the politists. Much of the control and influence exerted upon the most active and powerful sector of the public—the political leaders of the government—emanate from the politists. All the one hundred million adults of the United States might conceivably be active in politics; but the fact is that the active public is made up of no more than three million Americans.

Chapter 18 will describe the top leaders of the nation in some detail. As might perhaps be expected, the whole body of politists, or active citizens, has traits that place it midway between the inactive citizens and the highly influential citizens. The politists, in comparison with the inactive citizens, contain a greater proportion of well-educated, upper-income, white persons of skilled and professional occupations living in urban centers. A study, by Professors Ralph H. Smuckler and George M. Belknap, of a Michigan city indicates also that the politists are more aware of technical and administrative problems of government than are the inactive citizens, even when both groups are interested in the same type of problem; a psychologist would say they have a greater "reality orientation" in that they see the way the governmental machinery actually meshes. The active citizens also are concerned more with local community problems as well as national problems, whereas the inactive citizens tend to be interested solely in national affairs.

QUESTIONS AND PROBLEMS

1. Can you think of one debatable question of any kind that has never, to your knowledge, been the subject of public opinion? If so, can you also state that the class or type of problem it represents has never found itself a subject of public opinion?

2. Give one example, not used in the text, of each force working to create opinion: culture, family, neighborhood, school, and church.

3. Using one issue of any daily newspaper, list all the expressions of opinion to be found outside of the sports section, and give the source of each. What part of the total is supplied by the editors, would you estimate?

4. Select what appear to you to be the five most prominent national issues of the week. Interview five friends or other people to determine whether they have heard of the issues, and, if so, how much they know about them. Report your study in 400 words.

5. Can you think of any kinds of political activity that were left out of the test reported in the text? If so, do you believe that including it or them would change the total pattern of activity? Explain your answer.

6. What differences of trait and behavior distinguish the active from the inactive citizens, as groupings?

A POLITICAL interest is a desire to obtain some satisfaction from the government. Most interest groups are private organizations of people aimed at winning satisfaction for some collective desire. However, government agencies may also function as interest groups, in their efforts to persuade another organ of the government to perform some action advantageous to them. The effort to get the government to do what one wants can be

172

called "pressure." Consequently, interest groups are also termed pressure groups.

Pressure, despite its bad connotation, means only the attempts to convince government officials that an interest exists that they "should" satisfy. An interest is not necessarily evil or good as such. Everybody has interests, although not the same ones. If people want their property protected, and do not wish to pay for privately-employed custodians, they go to the government and ask for police protection to be paid for out of tax moneys.

Whether particular interests and their accompanying pressures are good or bad, therefore, depends on one's viewpoint. A *general* interest, or an interest that everyone has, is almost exclusively found among broad background issues such as "law and order," "honesty," or "humanitarianism in government." Such interests have their principal spokesmen in the general representative qualities that human beings of the same culture possess and carry with them when they enter public office. Conceivably one might say that national defense is a general interest; however, it is related to foreign affairs, and even in foreign relations the general interest is often only apparent. For instance, although it is true that most people's attachments with other people stop at the water's edge, a fair number consider the general interest to be an interest in the well-being of mankind. Again, some people believe that the use of force in world affairs is always a bad policy, whereas others consider it necessary from time to time. The fact is that many groups of opposing viewpoints are interested in foreign affairs, each one claiming that it represents the "general interest." Whatever the nature of an interest, its fulfillment is apt to be harmful or displeasing to some persons. Thus interests clash; and the efforts to realize these interests bring their advocates into unending struggle.

CHARACTER AND DEVELOPMENT OF PRESSURES

Individuals and interest

Individuals and small unorganized groups who seek fulfillment of their interest do so generally through means of direct personal contact with the governing official concerned. As weapons, these persons tend to rely upon their influential status in the community or their relationships with particular officials. Examples are legion. One consisted of the notorious so-called "five-percenters" of recent years, who were individuals who supposedly had access to national agency chiefs from whom they could obtain profitable business contracts with the government, and who charged five per cent of the total business they secured as their fee. The attempts of General Billy Mitchell in the 1920's to persuade other Army generals via public discussion that air power would be decisive in any future war also typified this sort of pressure. A wealthy roadhouse owner may telephone

National American Legion Office Building in Washington. Center of capital operations of one of the most influential of American civic associations, it houses the legislative, economic, and veterans rehabilitation staffs.

a sheriff, whom he has helped elect, to have a deputy give closer protection to the premises on Saturday night, when the "take" is large. A group of store proprietors all doing business near one unguarded street intersection may agree among themselves that the traffic congestion is bad for business; each may then write the chief of police urging installation of traffic signals at the intersection. Another campaign contributor may suggest to the district attorney's office that his son, who has just graduated from college, needs a job. A mother may telephone the school superintendent to complain about a teacher's methods of instruction. This sort of interest, and the unorganized means by which the individuals seek to have it satisfied, are the most common of all.

Pressures as a universal trait

Every day many thousands of instances of individual, unorganized pressures bombard the government throughout the land. Hence every form of government must have a way for coping with them. In an absolute monarchy, the king and his ministers receive countless petitions. (It should be recalled how the American colonists felt that they had poor access to the faraway royal court, and how the Constitution assures the right to petition for a redress of grievances.) In the Soviet Union, which strives to be a totally planned society, there are many planned (and controlled) ways of putting pressure upon the government. In addition to an elaborate apparatus of *soviets* (councils or assemblies), Soviet Russia has thousands of grievance committees; moreover, a giant government newspaper such as *Trud* (*Labor*), published for the workers, carries many selected "letters to the editor" making suggestions and complaining about difficulties and shortcomings in the national economy. In small and in great societies, in unorganized and in tightly organized societies, and in free and in despotic societies, there will always be pressure and some means for channeling the pressure into the government.

Role of interests in representative government

One outstanding function of representative government is to give a means for the channeling of pressure. The very origins of representative government reveal this fact. In the thirteenth century, various European kings were beset by difficult problems of finance and of administration; they needed the cooperation of the people, and sought some orderly way of obtaining it. The most imporant new elements of political and economic power of the day were the knights of the country areas and the merchants and artisans of the cities; they controlled much of the wealth and energies of the nation. Consequently, assemblies were formed to which they were invited, there to seek satisfaction of their interests and to be asked to aid the crown.

Practically every country in the world today has such an assembly, legislature, or parliament. Also, through elected or appointed delegates, the various interests of the nation are channeled to the government. Even today the American Congress gives vent to a great many interests. California, Alabamans, Iowans, and New Yorkers, like the congressmen from all the other States, speak up for local needs. Representatives of working-class districts defend the position of labor; representatives from rural areas present the interests of farmers. Furthermore, the age-old function of kings and appointed officials in dealing with grievances, complaints, and demands continues. In America the President and the many Departments of the government are still the targets of numerous pressures.

However, modern society is especially busy and complicated. Pressures have mounted in number and intensity beyond the capacity of the legislative and executive branches to cope with them. One response of the political system was to develop political parties as subsidiary or auxiliary channels. If the banks of a river cannot contain its flood, the water will wash over the banks or create new channels in its inevitable course downstream. As will be described in a later chapter, the political party functions so as to gather in, arrange, and direct a portion of the pressure of interests.

But not even the parties could manage the flood of interests after the Industrial Revolution; new rains fell continuously over the period beginning about 1750 and extending up to the present day. Those rains are still falling. Thousands of new occupations, enterprises, and activities have developed; even more important, the vote was given to virtually all adults, and, with the vote, an invitation to bring one's problems to the government. The response of the political system to the fresh rains—and especially the response of the American system—was the creation of innumerable rivulets, called associations or pressure groups, that wind about seeking access to the main channel of law-making, or to the party channels, or that tumble down toward the direct determination of policies themselves.

Further distinctions of interest groups

The weight of interest groups can be felt at almost every stage in the making and enforcing of laws. Yet, like political parties, they have grown up outside the structure of the government; with few exceptions, they have no legal connection with the legislative, executive, or judicial organs. In the eyes of the law they are chiefly private agencies. They conduct various types of political activities, some groups more or less restricting themselves to one type of activity and others carrying on two or more types. Some attempt to promote the nomination of some candidates and to block that of others. Some campaign vigorously for the election of candidates they favor and against the election of the ones they oppose. Some seek to obtain the enactment of bills they think would be advantageous and prevent that of bills they believe would be disadvantageous. Some urge strict enforcement of laws they find helpful and lax enforcement of the ones they feel burdensome. Some constantly aim at swaying public opinion toward adopting their attitudes. Interest groups appear to have goals similar to those of political parties; however, to the extent that they do, the emphases are different. For parties, candidates take first rank; for interest groups, principles. Parties seek to win elections; interest groups strive to win adoption of their policies.

NUMBER AND TYPES OF INTEREST GROUPS

Extent

Interest groups in the United States are extremely numerous. According to one estimate, there are upwards of 100,000 interest groups of an organized formal kind. They show great variations in size, wealth, and the influence they wield. They exist at the national, the State, and the local level of government. They seek to achieve their ends in many different ways. The great number of interest groups makes an exact and detailed system of classification quite difficult. Certain major functional tyes stand out: economic associations, comprising those in the three great fields of business, labor, and agriculture; organizations of professions; comparatively non-economic bodies such as the groupings of veterans and of national and racial minorities; and the adherents of plans for reforms. Finally, many agencies of government are themselves interest groups.

Types

Business: Two great organizations attempt to state the attitudes of all American business: the United States Chamber of Commerce and the National Association of Manufacturers (NAM). Each has a heterogeneous membership, that of the Chamber of Commerce being even more diversified than that of the NAM; in fact, the Chamber is more nearly a federation of numerous local business interest groups across the country. Too, many large business interests have erected their own national bodies, such as the Independent Petroleum Association, the National Association of Real Estate Boards (see Figure 24), and the American Bankers' Association. There are many comparable groups at the State level, such as the Pennsylvania Manufacturers' Association. These organizations have a relatively small membership; they cannot, like certain other groupings, deliver large blocs of votes from their own numbers. In proportion to membership, however, they are the wealthiest type of grouping. They tend to promote those policies which appear most favorable to the business community; on many issues, however, they may be silent. This is especially true of the U.S. Chamber of Commerce, whose members, owing to their diversity, may not agree on some public questions.

Labor: Until 1955 there were two great labor organizations: the American Federation of Labor (AFL), which then claimed over 10,000,000 members; and the Congress of Industrial Organizations (CIO), claiming over 5,000,000. Besides the AFL and the CIO there were many unions, such as the railroad brotherhoods, that were not affiliated with either major body. These so-called "unaffiliated" groups had a combined asserted membership of 2,500,000. In 1955, however, the officials of the AFL and the CIO agreed to merge the two bodies into a single giant group, the AFL-CIO.

The new union did not immediately embrace the unaffiliated unions, but additional mergers are still possible.

This new combination, like the AFL and CIO before it, has a federal structure. Its chief governing agency is the Convention, which meets every two years. There the delegates from all member unions have a number of votes in proportion to the size of their membership. Between meetings of the Convention, the Federation is managed by an Executive Council composed of twenty-nine members, ten from former CIO bodies and nineteen from former AFL organizations. In turn the Council delegates most of its work to an Executive Committee, made up of the President and the Secretary-Treasurer of the Federation, three Vice Presidents from unions formerly in the AFL, and three Vice Presidents from unions formerly in the CIO. Figure 23 gives the estimated membership of the new union and the proportions that come from the AFL and the CIO.

Labor groups follow tactics sometimes similar to, and sometimes con-

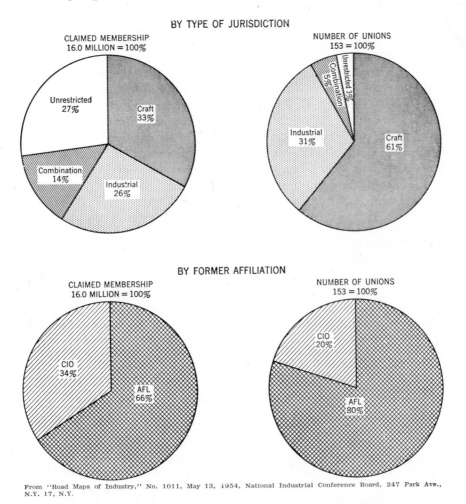

From "Road Maps of Industry," No. 1011, May 13, 1954, National Industrial Conference Board, 247 Park Ave., N.Y. 17, N.Y.

Figure 23. The AFL-CIO: Composition of the New Labor Federation.

siderably different from, those of business groups; and labor tactics have altered greatly since the founding of the AFL. Like business groups, labor unions maintain lobbies in Washington in profusion. Yet because labor groups unlike business groups count far more upon numbers than upon wealth, they are very active in election campaigns. Originally the AFL refused to become associated with any political party, and clung to the practice of rewarding its friends and punishing its enemies regardless of party. In fact, the AFL at first planned to rely almost entirely on traditional economic weapons such as the strike, the boosting of the union label, and the boycott of non-cooperating businesses. The CIO, by contrast, was rather steadfast to the Democratic Party, largely because it was indebted to that party for its very origins and also because since 1933 the party in the northern States has been quite favorable to labor unions. Too, the unskilled laborers who were the backbone of the CIO were more likely than the skilled artisans of the AFL to vote Democratic in any case. In 1952 for the first time the national leaders of both the CIO and the AFL supported a major party presidential candidate when they campaigned for Adlai Stevenson, the Democratic Party nominee.

In recent years, as unions have gained power, wealth, prestige, and dignity, labor leaders have extended their activities to the promotion of legislation and have emulated business groups in their efforts to "educate" the public. The AFL-CIO carries on this work chiefly through its Committee on Political Education (COPE). The new Federation, speaking through the two leaders most responsible for its creation, George Meany of the AFL and Walter Reuther of the CIO, disavowed any plan to convert the new group into a third party. Pressure and election activity for favored candidates were to remain the tactics of labor. Said Meany, when the new combination was announced:

> As long as I have anything to say about it, the AFL will not tie itself to any political party. I don't believe in a labor class or a labor party along class lines such as the British Labor Party. I don't believe in it just as I don't think there should be a political party in this country along denominational lines.
> There will be increased political action by labor in 1956. But political action by organized labor doesn't mean we will tie ourselves to any party. There is talk that labor is going to join forces with the Democratic party. Well, I'm not going to tie the AFL to any party, any time, anywhere.
> That doesn't mean, of course, that we won't support more Democrats than Republicans because that probably will be just the way it works out. The facts are that more Democrats have favorable records from our point of view than Republicans.

Reuther spoke in agreement:

> Building third parties will get no one anywhere. Every try has failed miserably, not because the motives or the reasons or the morality behind it was wrong, but because we are dealing with a structure in America that does not lend itself to the creation of third party movements. . . .
> Basically what we are trying to do is work within the two-party system of America and bring about within that two-party system a fundamental

realignment of basic political forces so that political parties can become responsible. . . .

Agriculture: There are three national agricultural groups: the Patrons of Husbandry, or the Grange, with nearly 1,000,000 members; the American Farm Bureau Federation, with about 1,600,000 member families; and the Farmers' Union, with about 260,000 members. The greatest strength of the Grange is in the northeastern States; of the Farm Bureau Federation, in the midwestern and southern States; and of the Farmers' Union, in the Great Plains States.

These groups represent considerably different economic levels and different ideas of government. The programs of the Farm Bureau Federation sometimes resemble those of the NAM. For instance, on August 31, 1955, the AFBF filed testimony with the Senate Antitrust and Monopoly Subcommittee, asking that labor unions be made subject to the same antimonopoly laws as business concerns. On the other hand, the aims of the Farmers' Union occasionally are similar to the aims of the CIO. For example, it cooperated with the CIO in drafting and urging passing of full employment laws at the end of World War II.

There are many lesser groupings for the particular types of farming, such as the American Sugar Cane League. Occasionally this type of organization on a local scale may be extremely powerful, especially if it covers the leading pursuit of the region; for instance, during the 1870's and the 1880's the Wyoming Stock Growers' Association was the virtual government of Wyoming Territory.

Like labor unions, agricultural groups can rely upon number as a means of exerting pressure. It has already been noted that the farming areas are overrepresented with respect to their populations in both Congress and the State legislatures; therefore the work of farmers' organizations is more openly conducted than that of either business or labor groups. The agricultural groups have had so much influence in Congress that since the 1920's their interests have been upheld in each chamber by a bipartisan union of congressmen termed the Farm Bloc.

The Professions: Each major profession is represented by one or more national organizations, such as the American Bar Association, the American Medical Association, and the National Education Association. Similar bodies exist on the State level. The power of these groups is derived largely from their wealth and the social standing of the profession itself. Professional groups confine their activity almost entirely to the enactment and execution of laws regulating their particular interests. They are especially concerned with statutes fixing qualifications for admittance to the profession. Since the members of most professions are privately employed and are paid on a fee basis, their interest group can do little respecting their income. Public school teachers, by contrast, are employed by the public and receive salaries; hence the National Education Association emits a great deal of publicity favoring an increase in teachers' salaries. Sometimes the professional interest groups, or at least their leaders, will take a stand on issues not directly connected with the group itself.

Veterans: Beginning with the American Revolution, every major war in which the United States has fought has spawned one or more associations of veterans. The most important of these associations are the American Legion, largest of all; the Veterans of Foreign Wars (VFW), next largest; the American Veterans Association (Amvets); and the American Veterans Committee (AVC). Presumably the chief goal of these organizations has been to preserve the sense of cameraderie attained on the battlefield. They have also been very much concerned with government treatment of the veteran. The defeat of President Grover Cleveland in 1888, after he had established a reputation for vetoing private military pension bills, was achieved largely by the Grand Army of the Republic (GAR), a group composed of Union veterans of the Civil War. The numerous benefits enacted by Congress after each of the two world wars were promoted by veterans' associations.

Veterans' organizations have been sponsors of other types of legislation. Understandably, they have urged a strong national defense system. In common with veterans' groups across the globe, they have been very nationalistic, and have been among the strongest supporters of internal security laws. Often these groups take a stand on broad economic issues. There is good evidence to show that the Order of the Cincinnati, composed of former officers in the American Revolution, was influential in securing ratification of the Constitution, since prosperous members of the Order expected to flourish under the proposed government and others were quite nationalistic. Most present-day veterans' organizations have tended to uphold economic policies similar to those of the NAM. The outstanding exception is the AVC, which frankly aligned itself with President Truman's Fair Deal program; in fact, the Communist Party made a determined but unsuccessful effort to capture the AVC, evoking a contest that almost destroyed the organization.

In seeking to bring pressure upon the government, the large veterans' groups have both numbers and wealth at their call. Supposedly these bodies do not affiliate with any one party, nor do they promote the election of particular candidates, but they do support candidates and bills that will aid veterans. The great exception to this rule was the GAR, which for many years was the cornerstone of the Republican Party. Veterans' organizations have direct ownership and control of two large periodicals: the *American Legion Magazine,* with a circulation of 2,750,000, fourteenth largest in the nation; and the *VFW Magazine,* with a circulation of more than 1,000,000.

National and Racial Minorities: Most American interest groups are paralleled to some extent in the industrialized countries of western Europe; but the organizations of national and racial minorities are more prominent in the United States than in any other country in the world. Their existence and importance in the United States are due to the fact that the New World was colonized by successive waves of immigrants from many nations, and that a large racial minority consists primarily of descendants of chattel slaves. Hence there are a vast number of associations for members of virtually every nationality and racial group that has emigrated to the United States. Many of these associations seem to be confined to small areas; however, there is a major country-wide organization of Negroes, the National Association for the Advancement of Colored People (NAACP).

Only a small proportion of any national or racial grouping in America is organized into a formal interest body. The appeal of national clubs is principally for the first generation, who are most uncertain of the new life and most attached to the old. In the second generation and thereafter the cohesion of the national group disintegrates until one finds few enthusiasts left to organize around "old country" sentiments. The only kind of political event that henceforth excites them to antagonism is some "slur" or "injustice" aimed at their origins or onetime homeland.

In their tactics these organizations, like other interest groups, try to appear as representative of all people in whose name they operate. Only in a few legislative districts do the people they claim to speak for constitute a sizable fraction of the population. Hence national and racial organizations may be effective in some campaigns for nominations and elections to State legislatures and to the national House of Representatives. Yet in these very constituencies they are most likely to be split into opposing factions, one Republican and the other Democratic.

The influx of immigrants has also led to the rise of many "nativist" groups, or groups opposed to national and racial minorities. Considered by many to be a sort of "lunatic fringe" of American politics, these groups include such bodies as the Ku Klux Klan, the Knights of the White Camelia, and the Know-Nothing Party. Their principal aims have been to limit the political and economic lives of the national and racial minorities already in the country and to prevent further immigration by these peoples. Whereas these groups may speak at length of such goals as "national homogeneity" and "racial purity," actually they have often had the powerful economic motive of wanting to exclude laborers from Europe, Asia, or even the southern States, who would work for lower wages and thus "deprive" Americans or merely northerners of jobs. In 1954, to protest against the Supreme Court decision regarding racial segregation in southern schools, there emerged in the South an organization calling itself the National Association for the Advancement of White People.

Most of these groups operate at the local rather than at the national level, since feeling against minority groups can be more readily aroused at the community level. Even a supposedly national body such as the Know-Nothing Party was most successful in elections for local candidates. The Ku Klux Klan during the 1920's succeeded in dominating the government of at least one northern State, Indiana. This same group, which was hostile to Catholics as well as foreigners and Negroes, did have an important effect upon national politics, for it helped to block the nomination of Alfred E. Smith as Democratic candidate for the presidency in 1924, and was one of the elements contributing to his defeat in the election of 1928.

Reform Adherents: The groupings of reform adherents include the advocates of many types of policies and candidates. In a sense, all interest groups might be concerned with "reform." But custom has reserved the use of the "reform group" label for the miscellaneous associations that have been organized for "non-selfish" purposes. These groups include such bodies as "good government" leagues, voters' societies, and taxpayers' associations; religious agencies such as the National Council of Churches of Christ in the U.S.A.; prohibition groups such as the Women's Christian Temperance Union; and a host of others.

Ostensibly these groups, more than any other sort, are aiming at a certain intangible goal called "the general welfare." However, many have rather clearly discernible ulterior motives. For example, a taxpayers' association may have as its overt goal the reduction of taxes; but to achieve this goal the group may demand large reductions in important governmental services such as the public school. It may then appear that the group actually consists not of persons chiefly concerned with reducing taxes but of individuals opposed to the public school administration who are using the argument of high taxes to camouflage their real intentions. Reform groups operate at all governmental levels; usually they are small bodies concerned with local issues. They support candidates for office and seek to win public confidence in their aims. Probably the most effective reform group in American history was the Anti-Saloon League, which showed tremendous power over both voters and officeholders, and which helped greatly in the enactment of the Eighteenth Amendment.

Government Agencies and Interests: Another type of interest group is to be found in the organs of government itself. Because of the vast expansion of its machinery, government contains a huge number of agencies each of which has many interests; and government officials attached to these agencies seek by a variety of means to have these interests satisfied. Today all the larger agencies have established offices and employed representatives for stating their cases before Congress, the President, and the public. Agencies vie with one another for the support of Congress. One outstanding instance of this sort of competition in the past decade has been that among the Army, the Navy, and the Air Force, for larger shares of the total defense appropriations. Another is the struggle between the Reclamation Service of the Interior Department and the Army Engineers Corps in the field of conservation and public power development.

Agencies must take care, of course, in attempting to influence legislation. They are targets for hostile criticism as much as private lobbies are. For example, in June, 1950, a *Washington Times-Herald* article declared: "For many weeks, it was learned, Secretary Acheson and a corps of assistant secretaries have been endeavoring to soften up Congress by inviting groups of Senators and Representatives to drink and make merry in one of the capital's show places." In August, 1950, Jack K. McFall, Assistant Secretary for Congressional Relations of the State Department, had to write a lengthy explanation of the proceedings for a congressional committee on lobbying, showing that the expenses of the gatherings had been privately contributed by State Department officials and stating that the object was to exchange views and foster better working relations.

Catching the ear of the President and his closest advisers is not easy, considering the many demands bombarding them. Hence an agency that has officials who are intimates of the men about the President can regard itself as fortunate. One of the reasons for expanding the powers and personnel of the Bureau of the Budget in recent years was to fend off agency interests that had been coming directly to the President with various proposals and plans. (Another reason, even more important, was to prevent agencies from going directly to congressmen without receiving presidential approval of their proposals. In short, the President and his advisers wanted agency "lobbying" to change its direction and then wanted it taken care of before it reached the President's desk.)

Nor do the agencies neglect the public. Despite laws prohibiting spending public money for influencing legislation, they find means for communicating their wants to the public and to private interest groups which then bring pressure upon the organs of government. Two examples will suffice here. The first comes from the indignant lips of Congressman Clarence J. Brown at a hearing on lobbying:

> The Customs Service had asked for an increase in their appropriations and the House Appropriations Committee, upon investigation, found that they had given Customs an increase, I think, of 25 per cent the year before. The Committee refused to give a further appropriation increase because of evidence of waste and extravagance, but within 24 hours after the Congress, or the House, refused to grant any further money to the Customs Service, a great propaganda campaign was put on throughout this country and it was traced directly to the head of the Customs Service, to force Congress to give the Service the appropriation requested. The whole nefarious scheme was exposed, and upon protest by Congress the Secretary of the Treasury finally relieved from duty the head of that agency. . . .

Another example of agency relations with the public aimed at promoting the program of the agency is partially described in the following newspaper article (excerpted):

(From the *Washington Post*, Washington, Wednesday, May 5, 1948)

HEALTH ASSEMBLY IS ACCLAIMED AS TOP SUCCESS AT ITS CLOSING

(By Mary Spargo, *Post* reporter)

The National Health Assembly ended 4 days of intensive sessions here yesterday with the acclaim of both medical and public delegates as the most successful event of its kind in the history of the United States.

The assembly was called by Federal Security Administrator Oscar Ewing in response to President Truman's request to outline a 10-year program for the health and welfare of this country.

It was financed, Ewing told a press conference yesterday, through $45,000 in contributions from private medical and charitable foundations.

The 800 delegates comprised a cross section of American life and interests. Attending were leading authorities in all fields of health and representatives of a vast number of labor, farm, consumer, cooperative, parent-teacher, and other organizations.

Representatives of the public and medical authorities evidenced complete unanimity in favoring United States participation in the World Health Organization. Although the conference could not pass resolutions on pend-

ing legislation because some Government funds were involved in its operation, delegates left no doubt of their sentiments.

The unanimous report of WHO, it is believed, has helped to bring about
the recent decision to get the blocked measure to the House floor.

The National Health Assembly failed to find any agreement on national
compulsory health insurance, for which President Truman reiterated his
support in an address to the delegates.

Labor and some farm groups favored such a step, but the American
Medical Association maintained its determined opposition.

Nevertheless, even in this field, the most controversial before the delegates,
there was substantial progress made that pleased both sides.

State and Local Government Interests: A final type of interest may be
mentioned. The State and local governments have a large interest in
national legislation. National grants-in-aid concern both States and cities.
National taxes affect both State and local tax policy. Many other happenings on Capitol Hill and in the White House influence States and
localities. Therefore governors, mayors, and other local officials are frequently in touch with Washington. In addition there are special groups,
the most notable of which are the Council of State Governments and the
Conference of Mayors, that steadily observe and gather information on
pertinent national affairs, and from time to time advise national officeholders about subjects upon which the States or cities have already made
their policy decisions. Members of Congress themselves, being elected
from specific localities, have an important part in the satisfaction of local
interests. Indeed, their continuance in office ordinarily depends upon this
satisfaction, since the local interests have aided their election largely in
order to have their wants fulfilled.

THE STRUCTURE OF PRIVATE INTEREST GROUPS

The organization of private interest groups shows wide variations from
one group to another. Some groups have a highly centralized structure;
others may be quite decentralized. For example, as drawn in Figure 24,
the National Association of Real Estate Boards is a federated group of
1100 member boards; it also organizes Institutes and Councils to which
individual members may belong. It is a most complicated structure. In
each State there is also a central council. This type of structure was
adopted not merely to imitate the government of the United States, but
also to facilitate dealing with the two major levels of the American government, the national and the State authorities. Some interest groups are
akin to holding companies, in that they are the parent bodies for numerous
subsidiaries whose goal may be even more precise than that of the parent
organization; too, by this means an organization may hope to conceal the
actual inspiration for a particular campaign. The Communist Party (which
is not nearly so much a "party" in the American sense as it is an interest
group, since it aims not at winning elections but at spreading propaganda
and policies) is the arch-practitioner of the holding-company device. It
has put forth shoots with a variety of sheltering foliage, such as an organi-

zation to recruit youth, the now defunct American Youth for Democracy; protective bodies like the International Labor Defense; and many single-purpose associations like the Harry Bridges Defense Committee. Among holding-company groups there often appears another institution reminiscent of high finance and great industry, the interlocking directorate; for the same person may be a member of the board of directors of twenty or thirty organizations.

Whatever the peculiarities of its structure, an interest group furnishes a sort of "little government" for its members. They owe it an allegiance that presumably is secondary to their loyalty to the United States, although on occasion, and for some persons, the interest group has seemed prior to the national government. In most cases, the group does have a set of rules or laws, with a disciplinary agency to punish violators. This agency is usually not very strong. However, in the case of certain economically

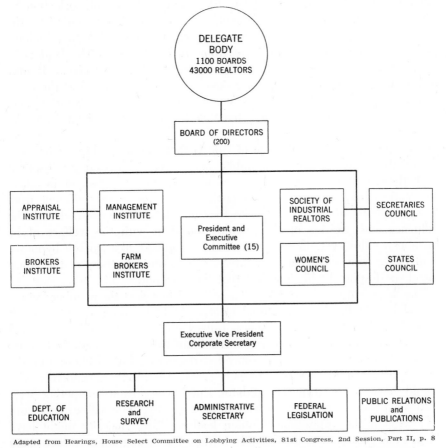

Adapted from Hearings, House Select Committee on Lobbying Activities, 81st Congress, 2nd Session, Part II, p. 8

Figure 24. Organization of a Large National Interest Group. The structure of the National Association of Real Estate Boards, an important interest and pressure group. Note three different kinds of structure are involved: popular representation through the Delegate Body and (though not pictured) within the separate institutes and councils; functional representation of different kinds of realtors; and federal representation in the State councils. On the bottom level, one sees the executive branch of the NAREB.

oriented groups, such as labor unions and retailers' associations, the agency may be quite ruthless in employing its power of expulsion, which, in the instance of the closed shop, can be a sentence to the loss of a lifetime skill and career. The group also has conventions, or conferences, which ideally are policy-framing bodies where the rules are adopted; and it has a board of directors, or a comparable agency, to execute the rules.

The most noteworthy fact about interest groups, and the trait that almost all hold in common, is the great power of the executive or administrative branch of this "little government." In interest groups there is almost invariably a ruling clique or elite which dominates the conventions and which usually serves officially as the administrative branch. Frequently, unless the rules of the organization prohibit it, the same officers are elected year after year with little opposition; when they decide to step down they often in effect name their successors, as Dan Tobin, retiring President of the AFL Teamsters' Union, chose Dave Beck as new President. Election by the convention is ordinarily a formality. Likewise, policy-framing by the convention may also be a formality, since it may do no more than endorse policy recommendations that issue from the leadership. The leadership has several means for throttling any opposition that does arise. It may resort only to simple parliamentary devices at the convention; at the other extreme, where controls over employment exist, the administration may deprive its antagonists of their livelihood by expelling them from the group.

The consequence of this type of rule is that the leadership, which represents the interest group to the public, may express policies quite dissonant with those of the majority of the members. Once entrenched in office, the leaders may acquire a set of goals and values totally different from those of the members out of power; they may be more concerned with the influence and prestige of the organization than with the welfare of its members. However, in many cases, by a process akin to self-hypnosis, leaders are convinced that their interests are genuinely those of the group members despite the obvious fact that they are not.

The degree to which group leaders may fail to reflect the members' views was shown in the 1950 senatorial election in Ohio when, despite violent opposition by labor leaders, Senator Robert A. Taft, a Republican, carried this highly industrialized and unionized State by an unexampled majority. Two points should at once be conceded respecting this election: (1) the Democratic candidate was extremely weak, for all the Democrats who would have made strong candidates shied away from competing with Taft since defeat might have ended their elective political careers; and (2) without the opposition of union leaders, Taft's majority might have been even greater. As another illustration, the strong support that many midwestern farmers gave to Harry Truman in 1948 was also in contrast to the coldness or antagonism to him found among most prominent leaders of farm organizations. In the long run, group leaders are actually trying to form the opinions of their members, and they become significant agents in the framing of public opinion.

THE ARENAS OF INTEREST GROUP STRUGGLE

Where do interest groups clash? Every contest must have an arena; the contests among interests occur in several parts of the political process: in (1) elections; (2) legislation; (3) administration; and (4) public debate.

Elections

Interest groups find it important to have sympathetic public officials; hence some of them strive to influence elections in their favor. It is at this juncture that these groups attempt to secure adoption of their beliefs by one or both major parties. They press party leaders to incorporate the policies of the group into the party platform. Of course, there are many competing groups with contradictory policies; since on the national level no party leader wishes to alienate any important group, the party platform is likely to contain a diluted version of the policies of several powerful groups. By contrast, in a smaller area, such as a constituency for the House of Representatives, where one interest may predominate over all others, each party may submit a platform especially sensitive to that interest. In the election process itself, groups active at this stage in the political process may try to obtain first the nomination, then the election, of desirable candidates. In these endeavors, depending upon their nature the groups may resort to numbers, wealth (within the limits of the law), or both.

Legislation

Perhaps the most notable work of interest groups takes place in the legislative arena; it is here that they carry on their lobbying activities. By lobbying is meant simply the attempt to influence officials by personal relationships. The success or failure of a lobbying campaign depends at first perhaps most heavily upon the access that a group has to the legislative official whose favor is most essential for the realization of group aims. Access is easier after a group has aided the election of a legislator. Access also depends upon the personality and skill of the lobbyist himself. Lobbyists are usually drawn from the ranks of lawyers, journalists, and former legislators; indeed, the roster of group representatives to Congress normally includes the names of several former Senators and Representatives. In 1956, according to the *Congressional Quarterly Weekly Report* (p. 326), thirteen former Senators and eighty-three former Representatives had registered as lobbyists.

It is at the standing committee stage in the legislative process, that is, the stage at which one of the standing or permanent committees (into which a legislature divides itself to conduct its business) examines a proposed law, that the lobbyist is apt to be most conspicuous. The importance of the standing committee stage for lobbying may perhaps be attributed to the fact that this is the most critical stage in congressional handling of a bill; as will be seen in a later chapter. standing committees of Congress are the actual policy-framing bodies of the United States government. Furthermore, it is at this stage that the most coherent and pertinent discussion respecting a bill occurs. There are also other stages that lend themselves to his needs. For example, he may even take a hand in drafting a piece of legislation for friendly congressmen. Also when a bill is being debated in either house, it may be the subject of some influence for or against its passage. Presumably all private citizens are barred from the floor of both chambers; however, any former congressman is authorized to go on the floor, a privilege that helps to explain the desirability of ex-congressmen as legislative representatives. (It would be instructive to know what proportion of such privileged visits come from interested parties.)

The very number of stages in the American legislative process is a great advantage to many lobbyists, especially those representing business groups. As will be shown in a later chapter, the principal goal of the lobbyist may be not promotion but interception of legislation; each stage for this reason lends itself to the blocking of proposed laws since all the lobbyist need do is assure inaction. Today forthright bribery seems to be quite rare, for legislators at least on the national level tend to be comparatively honest men and also because there are many means for subduing legislators' objections without violating laws. A legislator who is a lawyer can be promised, and actually be given, company business; since income tax returns are confidential, there is no way of stating whether many congressmen today are counsellors for business organizations. Sometimes legislators are given the opportunity to purchase shares of corporation stock at prices far below market quotations; other legislators may be assured lucrative jobs when they leave office. Lobbyists may inspire a torrent of letters from constituents to their Senators and Representatives. Sheerly coincidental agreement may bring the lobbyist his triumph: the lobbyist may represent an interest with which the legislator has identified himself. The multiplicity of tasks engaging the lobbyist may be seen from the following letter:

> American Enterprise Association [AEA]
> 4 East Forty-First Street
> New York,
> January 26, 1949

Mr. Sinclair Weeks
1014 Statler Building, Boston, Mass.

Dear Senator: To inform you of happenings and opinions on certain matters occurring since Monday, 17th of January, I am setting down those things in which you may be interested, in chronological order.

Monday. Lunched with Clarence Brown on the Hill. He is much interested in proposed unofficial advisory group from Congress for activities of AEA in Washington. Mutually decided to go slow and pick most congenial, helpful, and potential leaders of various groups in both parties. Will help in selection and formation from both parties. Discussed federal aid to medical care. Interested in getting AEA Reporter as soon as possible. Thinks new bill analysis good improvement.

Office appointment with Gene Cox. Told me to disregard letter re McCarthy recommendation, which I showed you, for reasons which I suspected and explained to you. Offered strong help for AEA operations in his group; stated our Washington activities, as now set up and proposed, can be very important. Much pleased with new bill analysis and feel AEA Reporter will be most valuable. Volunteered assistance is [sic] obtaining new finances; will take immediate steps with Guaranty Trust, New York group, who have asked how and where they can help.

Office appointment with Dan Reed. Very pleased with new bill analysis. Called Gordon Grand, minority clerk, Ways and Means Committee, into conference and told him of valuable AEA assistance, including proposed AEA Reporter. Grand offered help in getting new bills quickly to AEA for timely analysis. Got copy of foreign trade bill 1 hour off the press, which was sent at once to our lawyers—analysis ready Monday or Tuesday this week. Reed for advisory group idea with good suggestion that groups be called in separate party groups; first, starting with majority party, then brought together when deemed necessary by recommendation of members —rather than AEA. Reed disturbed by let-down attitude of some Republican Members and feels need for strong leadership to inspire and guide minority.

Reed commented on futility of some operations in which industry is active, so far as aid to Congress is concerned. Particularly mentioned NAM literature, which he stated, for the most part, went into the waste basket.

Office appointment with Roy Woodruff. Most appreciative of new AEA bill analysis and Reporter, strongly in favor of unofficial advisory group; feels as does Reed, that minority Members are low in spirit and need vigorous leadership.

Call from AEA office reporting request from Donald Jackson of California for 25 extra copies bill analysis of S. 246, aid to education; is personally mimeographing 350 extra copies to go to constituents. Highly complimentary re analysis and new form. (This 2 hours after first delivery of bill.)

Called on Joe Martin and in his absence talked with Jim Milne. Particularly dejected atmosphere as to future. Impressed with new set-up of bill analysis and potentialities of AEA Reporter, offered all help possible.

Tuesday. Attended Truman-Barkley Club dinner, at table with Mr. and Mrs. Elias, editor Winston-Salem newspaper, Secretary of the Army and Mrs. Royall, and Mr. and Mrs. Joe Blythe, treasurer of the National Democratic Committee. Met many Democratic committee and congressional members through Judge Alan T. Goldsborough's daughter-in-law, who is secretary to treasurer of National Democratic Committee.

Met with lawyers to discuss slight changes in bill analysis, also general program aiming to cover all important legislation but not pad with unimportant bills just to make a showing of volume.

Lunch and extended meeting with Les Arends at his request. Very pleased with new bill analysis and heartily agreeable to signing letter which he asked us to draft, to accompany bill analysis to new members and nonusers, explaining use and value of AEA assistance. Considerable favorable discussion of suggested AEA unofficial advisory committee of Members of Congress. Offered assistance with both Republicans and certain Democrats. Arends also perturbed by discouraging attitude of some Members. Expressed feeling that AEA has opportunity to do a big job in field of coalition on objective source material. Much interested in possibilities of AEA Reporter.

Appointment with Coordinator of Information Cecil Dixon and Assistant Felix Sklagen. Offered our continuing assistance, which was gratefully received. New bill analyses favorably commented upon as was China section of AEA Reporter, other sections looked forward to with interest.

Long telephone conversations with Charlie Abbott and later with Dwight

Eckerman (editing AEA Reporter). Abbott's requirements that writers sign articles and that Eckerman be listed as executive editor were readily agreed to, were in fact under serious consideration. Suggested changes in tax section to be further considered. Suggested amplifications to medical-care article not wholly concurred in by Eckerman and myself because of fear it would extend subject into realm of our economic study. Believe changes made will satisfy Abbott. Publication has been delayed a week; is going to printers Wednesday, January 26. Wrote letter to accompany first issue, stating care being taken to make this publication as objective, nonpartisan, and constructive help, as are other AEA materials.

Wednesday. Return appointment with Les Arends. Letter to all House Republicans approved and AEA office notified to proceed with typing. Arends will talk with Percy Priest, Tennessee, to request his similar action with House Democrats.

Luncheon with Jim Reinhold, assistant to president of Santa Fe Railroad, and Ed Carr, president, National Homebuilders Association; both interested in AEA and expected contribution. Santa Fe we hope for $2,000. Carr trying to get group of large builders at $500 apiece.

Further edited material for Reporter.

Thursday. Filled with inauguration activities and meeting with number of prominent Democrats. Finished off at inaugural ball with a 2 a.m. talk with Senator Brewster of Maine. He asked if you still went along with Dewey. Replied that I couldn't answer as to whether you ever had or not. Also asked if you intended to back up Taft. Again stated that I would not answer for you. Brewster expressed himself as believing that industry was going to get just what is deserved for not backing Taft and Taft-Hartley bill before elections.

Friday. Long session with Gwinn, New York, who is crusading against Federal housing. Had asked AEA last year for assistance but wanted strictly slanted material which we could not afford to publish. Has started personal drive for funds to set up research organization and to supply material he wants. Nicholas Noyes received an appeal and wrote me asking if duplication of activities was involved. Gwinn disturbed that his letter for funds has been so misinterpreted and is writing me a letter, with permission to use, explaining need for AEA continuance and different purpose of his efforts.

So ended an arduous week.

Sincerely,

Guy E. Wyatt[1]

Administration

Administration has provided an arena for lobbying whose importance has risen in recent years. At one time it was believed that if the group was successful in dealing with the legislature it had won its battle. Today, however, groups assume that they must pay attention to the administration of laws as well as to their enactment. The present conviction is the result principally of the fact that administrative agencies today far more than in the past have policy-making functions.

One important phase of lobbying in the administration concerns influence over executive appointments. It may be noted at this point that here is

---

[1] 81st Congress, 2d Session. House Report No. 3233. American Enterprise Association. *Report* of the House Select Committee on Lobbying Activities. House of Representatives. Eighty-First Congress, Second Session. Created Pursuant to H. Res. 298. United States Government Printing Office, Washington: 1950. Pp. 39–41.

virtually the only place at which interest groups attempt to sway the judicial branch of the government. Any other action to deal with the judiciary (save, naturally, in the legitimate role of an attorney pleading his case before the bar) would probably fall into the category of a serious felony known as tampering with justice. Groups do try to prevent the naming to the bench of persons known to them as foes of their interests. Also, lobbyists try to persuade the President or other appointing officials to name Cabinet members and other administrators favorable to their groups. Lobbyists also seek to obtain principles of law enforcement that will redound to their advantage. Again, in the case of business interests, it sometimes suffices to procure non-observance or non-enforcement of certain undesirable statutes. Finally, just as they are for legislators, lobbyists may be important sources of information for administrators.

Public opinion

Most interest groups take great pains to cultivate public opinion. In doing so, they disseminate what they term "facts" and what their opponents denounce as "propaganda." The arguments of interest groups are seldom deliberately false; those who utter false statements on behalf of interest groups are often fully convinced that the statements are true. In fact, not many interest group assertions are false; the spokesmen for these groups do not wish to discredit themselves before the public. Interest group utterances, then, usually comprise carefully chosen facts to buttress their own position. Hence groups may be said to rely upon indoctrination, a practice that has been defined as the presentation of the facts of only one side in a dispute under the pretext of recounting both sides. Groups may be clear of malice even regarding indoctrination, since they may believe that they are submitting an impartial recital.

Efforts to influence public opinion may be either short- or long-range. The short-range undertaking is much less costly but of course is related to only one issue or body of issues. A paid advertisement entered into a newspaper by a local teachers' association pleading for enactment of a bond issue to erect new schools represents one type of short-range project. Long-range projects demand far greater funds and are devoted not so much to specific issues as to extended political, economic, and social questions. As an illustration, the Association of American Railroads has sponsored a lengthy series of institutional advertisements extolling the American economic system in general and depicting the advantages of railroads over other modes of transportation in particular.

REGULATION OF INTEREST GROUPS

Today the federal government, and about three-fourths of the State governments, have enacted laws to regulate interest groups. The principal aim of these regulatory statutes is not to bar the operations of interest groups but to publicize their attempts to influence legislation and legislators. The federal Regulation of Lobbying Act was passed as one section of the

Legislative Reorganization Act of 1946. It provides two chief requirements: (1) lobbyists must register with Congress; and (2) lobbyists must report all contributions over $500 and all expenditures over $10. These data are a matter of public record. Table 4 indicates what groups made the largest expenditures during 1955.

TABLE 4. THE TWELVE LOBBIES REPORTING THE LARGEST EXPENDITURES IN 1955[1]

National Association of Electric Companies	$114,836
American Federation of Labor	114,090
American Farm Bureau Federation	113,610
Congress of Industrial Organizations	111,788
Association of American Railroads	104,806
Southern States Industrial Council	100,245
United States Cuban Sugar Council	99,275
National Association of Real Estate Boards	93,802[2]
American Legion	91,794
National Federation of Post Office Clerks	90,552
General Gas Committee	87,710
Friends Committee on National Legislation	86,221

[1] CQ Weekly Report 1956, p. 137.
[2] Nine months' expenditures.

One other type of control over interest groups is the requirement that administrative officials, before they enter office, divest themselves of financial ties with organizations that might receive government contracts. During the first month of President Eisenhower's administration, the Secretary of Defense-designate, C. E. Wilson, President of the General Motors Corporation, was faced with the difficult choice of either selling his enormous holdings of General Motors stock, or else withdrawing from candidacy. He chose to sell the securities.

Another example of the efforts made to restrict the pressure of interest groups upon administrative officers is the law that forbids any person who has been employed by any government agency to act as "counsel, attorney, or agent for prosecuting any claims against the United States," for any firm with which he had dealings while employed by the government, within two years of his leaving government service. The intention here is to block attempts of private corporations to secure favorable treatment by offers of remunerative employment.

THE EFFECTS OF PRESSURE GROUPS

It is difficult to make an accurate computation of the effect of interest groups. Comparable problems arise when one tries to calculate whether the Soviet army could have expelled the German army without American Lend-Lease materiel, or whether the American colonists could have won the Revolution without the aid of France. Similarly, it is difficult to assert when the fate of legislation or administration, or the formulation of public opinion, has unquestionably been the consequence of interest group activity. One study of ninety laws enacted between the Civil War and World War II concludes that only a handful might be attributed to interest groups. From these findings one might decide that interest groups and their lobbyists have little effect upon Congress. However, such a conclusion would neglect one of the most important functions of lobbyists—the prevention of legislation. Analysis of bills that have failed of enactment might reveal a far greater role for interest groups in this regard, since many of the best-financed lobbies are much more concerned with blocking laws than with promoting them.

Both legislators and administrators are prone to be cautious in dealing with interest groups. They are loath to give much credit to obviously inspired letter-writing campaigns, especially when the letters may be mimeographed, requiring no more than the sender's signature. Congressmen appear far more likely to heed a single letter or telephone call, particularly one from a person or group that assisted in the congressman's election. Congressmen are also wary of the claims that interest group spokesmen may make for the power of the organization behind them; any individual can obtain an impressive letterhead. Legislators also bear in mind that not all persons sharing a given interest will be members of an organized group; only a minority of industrialists belong to the NAM, and only one quarter of all American workers are affiliated with a labor union.

It is also noteworthy that lobbyists do not devote much time or money to attempts to convert unquestioned opponents. They give most of their attention to their adherents, or to any waverers whom they might win to their side. When the lobbyists turn to influencing public opinion, they direct their institutional advertisements again to those who are already susceptible to their message. Hence in the large—and many instances of corruption or near-corruption aside—interest groups and lobbyists have two significant effects upon the governing process: (1) They make many legislators, many administrators, and part of the public aware of a set of facts or attitudes that might otherwise not be forcefully revealed; they furnish the United States with a sort of functional representation. (2) They strengthen the morale of their public and private supporters to continue steadfastly the fight for their point of view.

QUESTIONS AND PROBLEMS

1. Give two examples of individual pressures that you would consider "good" and two that you regard as "bad." Explain how you distinguish between the two types of pressure.

2. Name and identify in two sentences a prominent interest group that represents some part of: (a) labor; (b) business; (c) farmers; (d) a profession; (e) veterans; and (f) Negroes.

3. Describe how a government agency often functions as a pressure group.

4. State one method by which interest organizations operate in the area of: (a) elections; (b) legislative proceedings; (c) administration; and (d) public debate.

5. Summarize the functions of interest groups in American government today.

PART IV

The Party Process

13. Composition and Structure of Parties

First Republican Convention Held at Lafayette Hall, Pittsburg, Pa. Feb. 22ᴰ 1856.

Parties, as they shall be discussed here, are groups publicly organized to capture, through elections, the control of the government. Parties are the principal forms through which interest groups and factions wage political combat. Interest groups aim at acquiring special benefits from the government; factions are groups, not officially recognized, seeking to win political power. Government without parties is possible; but government without interest groups and factions is not. Many governments have prohibited people from organizing parties in opposition to them. The leaders of Fascist Italy and Nazi Germany tolerated no party save the Fascist or Nazi Party. The Soviet Union permits only the Communist Party. In such countries, the single party dominates the government, or, in a sense, actually *is* the government, and sees to it that no other group is allowed to seek power.

195

Weakness of American minor parties

In the United States only two great parties—the Democratic and the Republican Parties—have followings, resources, and influence. England for a time supported three great parties—the Liberal, Labour, and Conservative Parties—until the Liberal Party lost its major role in the years after 1920. On the European continent and elsewhere in the world of democracy, several major parties and some minor parties typify the political systems. The minor parties of the United States only rarely threaten to develop large proportions. The Socialist Party, the Prohibition Party, the American Party, the Independent Progressive Party—and in the past such parties as the Free Soilers, the Know-Nothings, the Populists, and the Progressives— engage merely in marginal skirmishes with the two great parties except upon occasion. The Republican Party is the only minor party in the United States that has ever succeeded in transforming itself into a major party. In 1948 all minor parties together achieved only 5.4 per cent of the ballots cast for President; in 1952 the figure was about 0.5 per cent, and in 1956 it was even less. The minor parties do not always run candidates; they do not run candidates for all offices; they do not get on the ballot in all States. Most of the time their influence is negligible.

Perhaps their major impact on politics is that they publicize certain issues such as alcoholism, government ownership of railroads and industry, race conflict, or a communist threat. They force these issues upon public attention, with the result that action upon some of them by the major parties is hastened. The issue sometimes finds its way in more or less reworked form into the disputes of the major parties. For example, a personal income tax to be levied by the federal government was advocated by several small American parties before the major parties incorporated such a demand in their platforms. A minor party also may convert itself into a faction of a major party, and then strive to capture that party from its dominant faction. For instance, supporters of the People's Party, which ran its own presidential candidate in 1892, in 1896 became the leading group in the Democratic Party and named their candidate for President, William Jennings Bryan, on the Democratic ticket. The remnants of the People's Party, whose convention in 1896 met after the Democratic convention, also nominated Bryan.

THE INTERNAL ORGANIZATION OF PARTIES

The two great American parties are organized in a very complicated manner. About the year 1800 neither the laws of the federal government nor those of the States said anything about parties. Each party developed its own organization; and since the States were and are important units of government, each party was organized a little differently in each State. Later on, every State enacted its own laws, partly legalizing the existing party organization and partly changing it to conform to the then current beliefs about better forms of organization. Afterward came new changes in practice, then changes in laws, and still later more changes in both fields so that today each State has an elaborate and complex code of rules governing the way parties shall be organized. The national government has left practically all such legislation to the States, including the conduct of parties in the election of national officers. In this latter context, however, the national government has been concerned with the protection of the right of citizens to vote and in the honesty with which national elections are managed.

Legal regulation of American parties has occurred in three principal areas that can be treated separately below: (1) parties have been given a status as collective or corporate bodies or associations, and their membership rules have been controlled; (2) party organization has been prescribed in detail by the laws; and (3) party activities, especially electioneering, have been regulated.

Legal status of parties

Uncertain Legal Definitions of Party: In the first place, the very legal status of the political party is uncertain. At an early date, the party was considered a completely voluntary association of people who wished to pool their forces in political campaigns. As such, it was thought to be not subject to law. But at the present time the American parties labor under more detailed legal control than the parties of France or England, although not so much as the Communist Party in Soviet Russia. Unlike certain "inherent" or guaranteed rights that Americans are given by their federal and State constitutions, the right to form political parties is not protected explicitly by fundamental constitutional documents. The freedom of assembly guaranteed by the federal Constitution might very well guard the liberty of a party, however, should it ever need to defend its existence. Though practically all State constitutions mention political parties, and presumably thus encourage their existence, they do not assure them the right to exist. The federal Constitution does not even mention political parties. Some States have "abolished" the political party in certain local, "non-partisan" elections. Some States too have outlawed "subversive," "revolutionary," or "treasonable" parties, and the national government has outlawed the Communist Party. However, it would have to be an extreme emergency indeed that might bring the outlawing of the major political parties, for they are firmly embedded in tradition, practice, and belief. It is difficult to imagine American government without them. Certainly factionalism would not be stilled; and factionalism itself is even protected by the First Amendment to the Constitution, in its guarantee of the right of peaceful assembly.

Control of Party Membership: A party has two sometimes conflicting aims. First, it has reasons for enrolling every possible person in order to win elections; and in this drive it asks nothing but a vote from its "members." Second, and contrariwise, it has reasons for being exclusive, in order that its leaders can work their wills upon its activity and in order to keep the rather weak unity of belief found among its members from being more diluted by non-believers. The States have cooperated with the parties respecting these aims, but also have controlled the aims. Party membership is defined by law: almost always a test is set up to determine who is a party member eligible to share in party proceedings, especially the party primary elections. The test is aimed at permitting only Republicans to take part in Republican proceedings and only Democrats in Democratic proceedings. The reason for the test is to help the party to stand for its principles by excluding people who do not share them. But the test is never strict and is often loose. Unlike many parties abroad and most minor parties at home, the major parties do not require payments of dues or any other strong test of party adherence. In some States, the party itself administers such tests; in others the government does. The party is never entirely free to limit its membership, and the amount of federal and State control of this freedom is increasing. At most, a person must prove that he has been of the party persuasion at some time in the past in order to have his claim of membership accepted at the time he is examined. At the least, in Washington State, any person may join in either party's proceedings at will, a situation in which of course there is no test at all. It is noteworthy, too, that a party cannot legally bar individuals from its proceedings on the ground of race; that is, it cannot make racial origins a test of membership. This right to participate in party nominations as well as in general elections is guaranteed persons of all races by the fact that all stages in the election of federal officers are governed by Congress (see Art. I, sec. 2 of the Constitution) and also by the Fifteenth Amendment, that forbids anyone from barring Negroes from the suffrage.

The party machinery

The party machinery must conform with State laws, whose requirements sometimes detract from the effectiveness of the organization. For example, the law in most States declares what kinds of party committees should be formed, how many of them there should be, and what their functions should be. Laws also define the ways in which parties should organize conventions and should elect delegates to the national presidential nominating conventions

The net result of the great body of laws governing parties is a loosely-knit national organization of forty-eight generally similar sections, but with the details from one section to another so varied as to encourage strong parties in some States and weak parties in others. For example, although in their main outlines the parties of California resemble those of New York and Michigan, the details of the laws—the small print, so to speak—weaken party organization in California and strengthen it in New York and Michigan. In general, the party organizations of the western States are thus rendered weaker than those of the East, despite certain overall similarities that can now be described.

The typical blueprint of party structure and organization in the American States shows a formidable array of committees at all levels. From the level of the nation down to that of the voting precinct, the picture seems to represent an army; but only an insider will know that the lines of command do not go from top to bottom, nor from bottom to top, nor certainly sideways, but that they move in all directions. Yet the formal structure is well worth knowing, as it is presented in Figure 25.

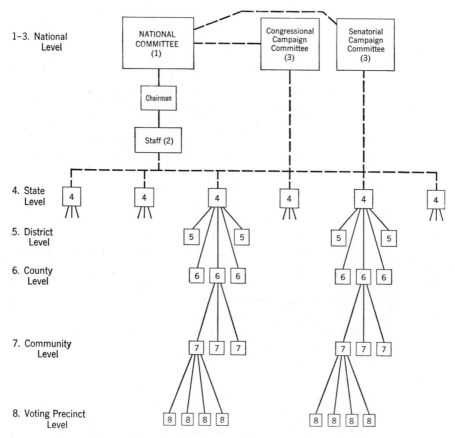

Figure 25. Structure of an American Major Party.

1. At the top of each party there is a National Committee composed of one man and one woman from each State, with a few additional members.

2. Working under its chairman is a headquarters staff.

3. Independent of both are found a committee to manage Senatorial elections and another to manage House elections. These are most active during midterm congressional elections.

4. Below these are forty-eight State Central or State Executive Committees that are created by State law and owe only voluntary allegiance to the national groups.

5. From each of these stem various district committees for congressional, judicial, and other elections.

6. Below these are the 3,049 county central committees, one for each county.

7. Below these are the ward, township, town, and city committees.

8. This whole tower reposes upon precinct committees or precinct captains, one in each of the approximately 154,000 precincts in the United States.

Beginning at the State level and moving down the diagram, one would have a different drawing for each State. Large cities have their own peculiar organizations very often, such as the famous Tammany Hall Democratic organization of New York City.

Special Machinery: Conventions: Even this complicated apparatus does not comprise all party machinery. Some States require the parties to summon nominating conventions for the election of certain party officials and the choice of candidates for certain public offices. The rules for these conventions are lengthy and detailed. Many additional offices are created if only for the special occasion. The presidential nominating convention itself is an exceedingly complex mechanism that reflects and takes into account the laws of the forty-eight States and the traditions and rules of the preceding conventions.

Informal and Associated Machinery: Furthermore, there are innumerable caucuses and shadow committees of an informal nature that cannot be ignored; they develop to avert the natural effects of the legally prescribed organization or to coordinate the many relations a party has with the interest groups, candidates' campaign committees, governmental agencies, personal cliques, and neighboring bodies. There are many examples of men who hold several offices. It would not be unusual, for instance, for an active party official to find himself a ward leader or committeeman, an alderman, the campaign manager of a State-wide campaign, a member of the county central committee, a member of the State central committee, a delegate to a national nominating convention, the chairman of the platform committee of the State party convention, and a member of the platform committee for the national presidential nominating convention. At the same time, he might be a member of the elections committee and of other committees of the city council, the attorney for several interest groups, a member of several informal cliques such as a "kitchen cabinet" and a "city hall gang"; and he may belong also to the American Legion, civic and business organizations, and a church.

He probably realizes full well his burdens and regrets his numerous and far-flung memberships, but there is little he can do about it; if he does not remain in all his posts, someone else will be able to take them over and obstruct his efforts. Any single post will give him only a small part of the power he needs to make his will felt beyond a very small area. In fact, for the party to be anything but a completely helpless mass of petty officers stumbling over one another, and for it to make and keep any large or useful promises to any or all interests in the locality or nation, it must have such active and office-ridden individuals. Some persons must reach out in all directions to give the mere elements of coordination, consistency, and movement to the political party. Far from being a concerted, driving machine aimed at the supreme goal of capturing the offices of the government—as a party often is in such centralized countries as Japan, France, England, Germany, Italy, and Turkey—the party in America is a floundering, awkward, pieced-together device with only the amount of unity that a few dedicated men and women working informally and partly in the background can give it.

Location of Power in the Structure: Where the "real power" lies in this enormous structure is practically impossible to determine. The answer may well be "nowhere." Power is strewn throughout the structure; moreover, shifts of power occur constantly. Conditions vary from State to State, county to county, district to district, and even from precinct to precinct. In the same unit of the structure they vary from time to time. In Illinois the most powerful person in one county may be the chairman of the county central committee; in another the most powerful may be an elected State senator. In California, a large contributor to the party coffers may have the principal influence in one county, a newspaper editor in another, a county central committee chairman in yet another. Great sections of the country have no effective party organization, to the point where no precinct committeemen or captains exist and where no candidates appear to seek posts on the county central committees. Men will fight desperately to achieve ward leadership in Chicago; even murder has been used as a means toward this end; but in Oregon a similar post will go begging for candidates.

A sheriff may be the party power in an Indiana county; a probate court judge in a South Carolina county; a group of ranchers in a Colorado county; an oilman in a Texas county; a machine boss in a Tennessee county; a mining company manager in a Montana county. In one place or time, a single individual will draw power into his hands; in or at another, a close-knit group may share it; more commonly, a scattered and not very cohesive group of people will hold power to decide some, but not all, questions. A State boss is not unknown; city and county bosses are more common. Or, despite a voluminous set of laws and regulations, a State may be bereft of any effective formal party organization, and the fate of a party may be in the hands of a few businessmen.

The strength of the national party organization also varies fom time to time, but it is never very great. In the McKinley era, Marcus Alonzo Hanna of Cleveland had the reputation and some of the power of a national, Republican boss. Perhaps the early years of the New Deal of Franklin D. Roosevelt represented the period when national party leadership achieved its greatest dominance in this century. A vast number of jobs were available for distribution among the disciplined following of the Democratic Party; millions focused their beliefs in a new type of society and economy upon the White House, and lent their support to the national leadership. For a few years it appeared that the American party system might become truly national and centralized. Moreover, World War II fostered additional centralization of men, money, decisions, and attention at Washington. But the extraordinary structure and tradition of American politics finally halted the development. When Eisenhower was elected President in 1952, he was most reluctant to don the mantle of party leadership and to aggressively control the party and the government. Today

the party system in the United States is about as decentralized, uncoordinated, and variegated internally as it has been at any time during
the century.

Regulation of party elections and campaigning

The role that parties play in elections is defined in both federal and
State law. In most States the laws declare whether nominating conventions
or direct primaries shall be used to select party candidates to run against
the candidates of the opposing party; in some few States the issue is left
to the discretion of party leaders.   The form of the party ballot is
regulated for party elections, and the ballots are printed at public expense.   The administration and costs of elections of party officials, as
well as of candidates for government office, are assumed by the State
governments.

An important body of federal and State law controls and polices the
conduct of campaigns.   Bribery, tampering with the ballot-boxes, and
many other practices, are forbidden in both party and general elections.
Legislation also governs campaign expenditures.   In September, 1956, Professor Alexander Heard estimated that campaign expenditures on all levels
of politics amounted to $140 millions in 1952 and would amount to about
$175 millions in 1956.   Such heavy spending invites controls.

Hence, election campaign expenditures have been limited and regulated
with respect to both primary and general elections.   The laws of most
governments must take for granted, however, that the party is not accountable for funds spent in behalf of candidates of that same party who are
in a contest for the party's nomination.   Hence the individual candidate
is the chief target of regulation in primary elections, whereas both candidates and parties come under the rules governing general elections.

Most States require a reporting of campaign expenditures by the candidates in both primary and general elections.   Most also prohibit expenditures for certain purposes, such as employing excessive numbers of
workers on election day.   Most limit the expenditures of a candidate for
office.   Finally, most States ban financial contributions by corporations,
and a few restrict those of labor unions as well.

Through several important laws, notably the Corrupt Practices Act of
1925 and the Hatch Acts of 1939 and 1940, the federal government has
entered the field of campaign regulation.   It requires reports of money
spent by the candidates. It limits expenditures by candidates and parties in
national elections.   It forbids contributions by corporations and by labor
unions to a campaign, and holds individual contributions to a maximum
of $5,000 to any one candidate or political committee.   Finally, it bars
the solicitation of contributions from federal employees by other federal
employees or by anyone on federal premises.   Only the last of these types
of control extends to primary elections, although there is little doubt now
that the federal government could, if it wished, regulate expenditures in
primary elections.   A bill is presently before the Senate, with this aim
in mind; the same bill would require a more nearly complete reporting

of funds, and also would increase the amount that a candidate is allowed to spend in his campaign.

Some experts believe that the federal government might as well have no laws at all; for the laws generally have proved only modestly effective. There are many ways of supporting a candidate for which the laws prescribe no reporting or accounting. Moreover, parties and candidates often are in such dire need that they are not above trickery. Hence laws can only partly stem the flow of money into elections. For example, although the limit set for expenditures by the National Committee of each party is $3 millions, it is estimated that the parties each spent from $30 to $60 millions in the 1952 presidential elections. The difference between the legal and the estimated actual figures was spent by dozens of special committees, State central committees, interest groups, and individuals. Too, the limitation on individual contributions is not very effectual. One person may contribute any amount not exceeding $5,000 to several committees; also, one person may contribute sums in the names of family members. After the elections of 1954, twelve persons, each from Delaware and each bearing the last name "du Pont," reported altogether twenty-one contributions to various political committees, each contribution amounting to $1,000 or more. Perhaps the only way to control both the total amount spent and the reporting of the total is to raise the allowable maximum greatly and to oblige all committees to report, under pain of fine and imprisonment. The above-mentioned bill contains such provisions.

In conclusion, it may be remarked that the difficulties of regulating party finances issue in part from the complexities of party organization. A great number of the problems confronting the American party system result from the baffling legal differences among the States. When one turns to the subject of the beliefs that the party leaders and party followers hold, he can see the same clutter and profusion of ideas. Hence one finds not only that party organization varies from State to State, but also that party beliefs are distinctive among the several States.

These varieties of beliefs are to be the next topic for discussion. However, before entering this discussion, it is well to consider the old riddle: Which came first, the chicken or the egg? It happens that the party system is afflicted by the same riddle. Although it is true that local complications of organization produce national parties composed of people of different ideas, is it not also true that people of different ideas prefer local organizations that are independent? The answer cannot be simple. Just as the hen lays the egg, but the egg yields the hen, so a host of different semi-independent organizations produce different beliefs, but different beliefs also yield semi-independent organizations and encourage differing laws everywhere.

THE PARTY FOLLOWING

Whereas the preceding section described the structure of the American major parties, it did not detail how many people belong to each party, or what they believe in. It is the task of this section to respond to those questions.

The two-party shift over time

Whatever may be the theoretical merits of third or minor parties, the overwhelming majority of Americans affiliate with either the Republican or the Democratic Party. A two-party condition has persisted from the beginning of the republic and has produced, on the national level, a rather simple cycle of in-again, out-again party politics, especially since 1864. Figure 26 shows this pattern of shifting power. One party stays in control until it wins a certain amount of disfavor throughout the country; then the other party, acting as the champion of the discontented, takes office. However, owing to the separate elections of the President, the House, and the Senate, a given party sometimes controls one or two of these agencies but not all three. As Figure 26 reveals, the longest period of presidential control by a single party from 1856 on (that date being chosen because the 1856 presidential election was the first in which the present Republican and Democratic Parties confronted each other as the two major parties of the country) occurred between 1860 and 1884, with the Republicans in power. On the other hand, the longest period of supremacy of a party

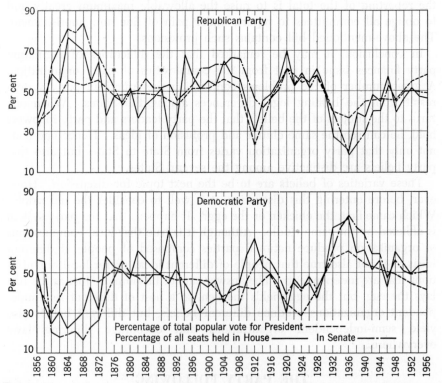

Figure 26. A Century of Two-Party Government. In 1876 and 1888, Republican candidates Hayes and Harrison were elected President by a majority in the Electoral College but received less popular votes than their Democratic opponents. Otherwise, throughout the century, the major party candidate with the greater number of votes was elected President.

in both the presidency and Congress occurred between 1896 and 1910, with the Republicans in power, and in the equally long period from 1932 until 1946, with the Democrats in power.

The margins between victory and defeat are often close, but the accepted majority principle takes no cognizance of that: "a miss is as good as a mile." In the 1954 congressional elections, for example, out of 435 House contests, ninety-four were won by less than five per cent, and eighty-eight more by from five to ten per cent. Of the remainder that were won by more than ten per cent, a large number of them were taken by southern Democrats in districts where Republican opposition is non-existent or at most token.

Pattern of party affiliations in the United States

The party affiliations of Americans help to explain why a large number of elections are close. Some Americans are very loyal to the party of their choice; others are not so faithful. Few are completely independent of party ties. During the presidential campaign of 1952, the Survey Research Center asked a representative sample of American adults about the strength of their party loyalty or the strength of their feelings of independence. People were then sorted according to their replies into seven grades of partisanship, ranging from Strong Democrats to Strong Republicans. Table 5

TABLE 5. PARTY AFFILIATIONS OF AMERICANS, BY REGION, 1952[1]

		REGION			
Party Identification	Total Sample	Northeast	Midwest	South	Far West
Strong Democrat (SD)	22%	18%	17%	31%	22%
Weak Democrat (WD)	25	18	25	32	24
Independent Democrat (ID)	10	13	9	8	10
Independent (Ind)	5	8	7	2	7
Independent Republican (IR)	7	9	8	5	6
Weak Republican (WR)	14	18	15	8	13
Strong Republican (SR)	13	14	18	6	16
None, minor party, or not ascertained	4	2	1	8	2
Total	100%	100%	100%	100%	100%
Number of cases	1,614	390	580	440	446

[1] Campbell et al., The Voter Decides, p. 93.

shows what party Americans say they belong to, if any, and how strongly they feel about their attachment. The percentages given for the whole nation are followed by separate percentages for the four major regions of the country.

A number of facts visible from the table bear emphasis:

1. The proportion of true independents is quite small (5%) by comparison with what is generally believed.

2. Only an insignificant number of people belong to third or minor parties.

TABLE 6. PARTY PREFERENCES VERSUS PRESIDENTIAL
PREFERENCES OF VOTERS[1]

Party Affiliation

Presidential Preference of Voters	Strong Democrat	Weak Democrat	Independent Democrat	Independent	Independent Republican	Weak Republican	Strong Republican
Voted for:							
Eisenhower	12%	26%	28%	57%	73%	73%	91%
Stevenson	63	42	44	14	5	5	1
Did not vote	24	31	26	26	22	22	8
Other, or not ascertained	1	1	2	3	0	[2]	[2]
Total	100%	100%	100%	100%	100%	100%	100%

[1] Adapted from Campbell and others, *op. cit.*
[2] Less than one-half of one per cent.

3. Only about one out of three Americans is a staunch supporter of a political party.

4. Almost six out of ten Americans have some party tie, but will break it under what they regard as unusual circumstances.

5. Democrats outnumber the Republicans in the country as a whole (57%–34%) and in every region in the country too.

6. Outside the South, the West is the most Democratic region (it includes the eleven western States).

7. About one out of every five southerners is a Republican of some kind.

Changing party affiliations

These proportions can change. The historical record shows that the Democratic Party received a considerable number of its present adherents in the North during the 1930's and 1940's. Where registration figures are kept that indicate the party affiliation of the registrants, as in Pennsylvania and California, a steadily mounting Democratic registration can be noted. Under changed conditions a reverse trend might set in. Furthermore, an unusual occasion may send throngs of voters into the opposing camp, at least temporarily, and in some part to stay. This is what happened in 1952, as Table 6 shows. Dwight Eisenhower obtained the solid support of all kinds of Republicans and also deeply invaded the Democratic lists. As could be expected, his support among Strong Democrats was the least of all.

A substantial number of people split their tickets, too, even when they vote chiefly for one party. For instance, in 1952 and 1956 many who were Democratic and voted for the Republican candidate, Eisenhower, voted for Democrats in the contests for United States Senator, State Governor, and other offices. The extent of such split-ticket voting changes from one region of the country to another. The local tradition, the strength of party organization, and the order in which the names appear on the ballot, are three of the factors that make split-ticket voting more common in some places than in others. Thus, in 1952, according to a Survey Research

Center poll, 83% of the voters of the Northeast cast straight tickets, that is, voted for members of only one party. The corresponding figure in the Midwest was 66%, in the South, 79%, and in the Far West, 57%. The remainder split their votes among the candidates of both parties. Thus, along with a long-range shift in party affiliation and along with a temporary switch to the opposing party, there is to be found a considerable amount of split-ticket voting that breaks up the tendency to prefer the whole slate of one's party.

Extent of party tradition in individuals

The stronger the attachment to a party, of course, the less likely a complete change and the longer that change takes. A considerable part of the American public belongs to the party of its parents. Many vote as their fathers and grandfathers did. Long-standing habit blocks a switch of voting, even when a person's new ideas and preferences for a candidate may urge him to change.

It is a well-known fact that the southern States ordinarily have larger Democratic votes than the northern or western States. Indeed, over much of the South, the Republican Party scarcely exists as an organized force. However, many people do not know that, as individuals, southerners are almost as changeable as northerners in their voting. That is, the chances that in a presidential election a southerner will cast a vote different from his parents' votes are almost as great as the chances that a northerner will vote differently than his parents did. Table 7 shows this to have been true in 1952. Hence one should not assume that southerners as individuals are bound by tradition, nor that northerners vote freely without reference to the past.

Thus tradition is often misunderstood. In its pure sense, it is a habit and a nostalgia that works on a person to vote as his family has always voted. Sometimes a tradition-motivated person will explain his vote in

TABLE 7.   TRADITIONAL VOTING: PARENTS AND THEIR CHILDREN'S VOTE IN 1952[1]

Per Cent of the Children of Two Democratic Parents Who in 1952 Voted:	South		North	
(a) Democratic	59%	(82)	55%	(183)
(b) Republican	41%	(57)	45%	(149)
Total	100%	(139)	100%	(332)
Per Cent of the Children of Two Republican Parents Who in 1952 Voted:				
(a) Democratic	33%	(13)	20%	(56)
(b) Republican	67%	(27)	80%	(226)
Total	100%	(40)	100%	(282)

[1] From author's analysis of Survey Research Center materials.

TABLE 8.　SOCIAL CONDITIONS RELATED TO
PARTY AFFILIATION, 1952

Party Affiliation (Per Cent)[1]

CONDITIONS	SD	WD	ID	Ind	IR	WR	SR	Apoly	No. Cases
SEX:									
Men	24	23	11	7	7	13	13	1	814
Women	21	27	8	5	7	15	14	4	970
AGE:									
21–34	21	29	10	6	11	13	7	4	543
35–44	21	31	11	6	6	14	10	2	427
45–54	23	21	13	6	6	14	15	2	308
55 and over	24	18	7	6	5	14	22	3	481
RELIGION:									
Protestant	20	24	8	5	7	16	16	4	1,272
Catholic	29	27	12	7	7	10	8	2	386
RACE:									
White	21	25	10	6	10	12	14	2	1,607
Negro	31	22	10	4	5	7	5	17	169
AREA TYPE:									
Urban Metropolitan	25	24	11	7	5	15	12	1	295
Suburban Metropolitan	16	19	10	8	10	14	21	2	142
Cities over 50,000	25	22	14	6	8	9	12	4	297
Cities 2,500 to 50,000 (South)	31	37	4	1	3	8	6	10	142
Cities 2,500 to 50,000 (North)	15	21	9	7	9	19	19	1	244
Cities under 2,500 (South)	38	31	8	2	2	6	7	5	143
Cities under 2,500 (North)	15	21	9	7	8	18	18	3	211
Open Country (South)	30	32	2	2	4	11	8	11	122
Open Country (North)	8	28	12	7	10	20	14	1	154
EDUCATION:									
Grade School[3]	25	26	8	7	5	12	11	5	706
High School[4]	21	27	11	5	7	14	13	1	784
College[5]	16	18	13	3	12	17	21	—	261
OCCUPATION OF HEAD OF HOUSEHOLD:									
Professional and Managerial	17	24	11	7	8	14	18	1	381
Other White Collar	20	22	9	7	6	20	16	1	176
Skilled and Semiskilled	23	28	12	6	6	13	10	1	527
Unskilled	30	23	7	4	5	10	7	14	207
Farm Operators	19	29	7	4	8	15	14	3	209

TABLE 8. SOCIAL CONDITIONS RELATED TO PARTY AFFILIATION, 1952 (*Continued*)

Party Affiliation (Per Cent)[1]

CONDITIONS	SD	WD	ID	Ind	IR	WR	SR	Apoly	No. Cases
UNION MEMBER IN HOUSEHOLD:									
Yes	25	28	11	5	6	13	11	1	419
No	21	24	9	6	7	14	15	4	1,287
FAMILY INCOME:									
Under $2,000	27	23	7	4	5	10	14	10	350
$2,000–2,999	25	24	9	8	6	14	11	3	274
$3,000–3,999	22	29	9	5	8	14	12	2	397
$4,000–4,999	21	27	14	5	8	13	12	—	259
$5,000 or more	16	24	11	6	8	17	18	—	457
GENERATIONS IN AMERICA:[6]									
First	29	23	11	8	6	13	9	2	132
Second	19	26	10	8	6	14	15	1	408
Third	17	20	13	7	11	15	16	1	388
Fourth	25	28	7	4	5	14	13	4	726

[1] From author's analysis of Survey Research Center materials, with the assistance of Mr. Glenn West. Percentages have not been rounded out to total 100 per cent and hence in some cases equal 99 or 101.

[2] Less than one-half of one per cent.

[3] Those completing grade school, and those with some grade school.

[4] Those completing high school, those with some high school, those with some high school and some non-college special training, and those completing high school and some non-college studies.

[5] Those completing college, and those with some college.

[6] First generation includes persons born abroad; the second, persons one or both of whose parents were born abroad; the third, persons one or more of whose grandparents were born abroad; and the fourth, persons all of whose grandparents were born in the United States.

this manner: "All my ancestors all the way back have always voted Democratic and I felt like it would have made my poor daddy turn over in his grave if I voted any other way." Much of the traditional voting as shown by the chart may be quite different. If a son of a well-to-do family is himself well educated, well-to-do, of the same religion, and of the same social class as his parents, he may very well vote the same way as his parents without any feeling of habit or tradition; he simply has the same reasons as they for voting the way he does.

Forces determining the vote

Pure tradition is only one of a number of forces that may be working on a person to make him vote regularly for a certain party. There is no exact computation of the strength of these numerous forces impinging on the person to fix his party affiliation; however, political science has advanced enough to discover what these social forces are and how they influence people to have specific political opinions. Table 8 lists the major conditions in which are found these forces that act upon a person's party attachment. It shows in detail in what segments of the population Republicans or Democrats are more likely to be found. For example, the table shows that younger people tend to include more Democrats than older people, as do people of grade-school education, by contrast with people of college education. The 1956 elections somewhat altered alignments, as each election does. Some Negroes, for example, changed to the Republicans.

THE PARTIES AS SEEN BY VOTERS AND LEADERS

How voters view the parties

From knowing the tendency of various groups to favor one party or the other, one might estimate the character of each of the two parties. The task would be made difficult, of course, by the obvious fact that none of the groups supports overwhelmingly either one or the other party. In some cases, barely over half a group prefers one party to the other. Evidently the people holding those traits are not unanimously convinced that one party alone stands for their specific interests. However, one might predict that since lower-income groups, for example, favor the Democrats more than upper-income groups do, for that reason the Democratic Party would have the reputation of being friendly to the "common man."

That, it so happens, is the case. The Democratic Party, which is liked and is disliked for many reasons, is credited by quite a few with being well-disposed to the "little fellow". In 1955, a Gallup poll of a sample of adult Americans asked the following question: "Suppose a young person, just turned twenty-one, asked you what the Republican party stands for today—what would you tell him?" (The same question was asked regarding the Democratic Party.) Table 9 shows what people said the two parties stand for.

From the table, one notes that many Americans view the Republican Party as the party of big business and the Democratic Party as the party of the lower income groups. Some say that the Republican Party is more concerned with peace, free enterprise, economy in government, and conservatism generally. Some say that the Democratic Party is more devoted to bringing prosperity and jobs to all. A very high proportion of the public confess that they cannot say what the parties stand for. A large yet minor fraction assert that the two parties stand for the same things.

The results of this poll are crude, of course. Actually it has been shown in other studies that almost everyone can give a more detailed description of the parties if pressed to do so. However, whether there are few or many details in the description, two elemental facts emerge: (1) people of one party disagree about what the people of the other party are like; and (2) people of one party disagree about what their own party is like.

Many people have strong notions about the nature of the other party. Staunch labor-union people on the Democratic side find it difficult to believe that many workers favor the Republicans. Some confirmed Republicans who are well-to-do are convinced that all Democrats come from "the

TABLE 9. THE PARTIES AS THE PUBLIC SEES THEM[1]

What Republicans Stand For[2]

Big business, privileged few	19%
Avoid war	5
Conservative, more to right	5
Economy, pay-as-you-go	4
Higher standard of living	3
Honesty in government	2
Average man, common people	2
Higher tariffs	2
Free enterprise, capitalism	2
All others	12
Same as Democrats	9
Don't know	43

What Democrats Stand for

Common man, labor, all the people	27%
Socialism, liberal, more to left	6
Better living conditions	4
Big spending	4
High farm prices; farm program	2
War	2
All others	13
Same as Republicans	9
Don't know	39

[1] From the American Institute of Public Opinion.

[2] Each table adds to more than 100% because some people named more than one trait. (Release of February 23, 1955.)

other side of the tracks," and are a trifle shocked when people of their own standing vote Democratic. In actuality, there are few great differences between the followers of the two parties (as one will recall from his reading of Table 8). The one-party South is an exception, in that it can be said that four out of five southerners are Democrats, but that only about half the northerners are.

What is just as striking is that people of the same party will see their own party in many different ways. Most people live in their own worlds and readily distort the worlds that others inhabit. A Chicago professional Democrat, a California liberal Democrat, and a southern conservative Democrat often think and behave as if the Democratic Party were composed entirely of people of their ilk.

One result of the belief of members of each party that people like themselves belong to it is that they will follow the party even when most other members of the party lead it along a disagreeable route. Thus it comes about that the American parties are quite varied internally, and yet can arouse a sense of unity among a great many people.

Agreement on issues among party followers

Up to this point it has been shown that the parties are composed of differing numbers of the various kinds of people. It has been disclosed that voters have different notions of what the parties mean and of who belongs to each party. Now some evidence can be brought forward to show how members of both parties stand on some major issues of the day.

Differences of viewpoint are almost as common among members of the same party as between members of the two parties. To show this feature of the party system, Table 10 is introduced. Seven major issues of public policy in 1952 were selected. On each one, the Democratic Truman administration took a fairly clear position. Then, a sample of the American public was asked their opinion on these issues. Only those who said they had voted were included in making up the table. A person was scored as holding a Democratic, a Republican, or a neutral or uncertain position, as follows:

| | Answer | | |
Question	Democratic	Republican	Neutral or Uncertain
1. Whether the attention of the government to social welfare activities was adequate	More legislation needed	Less activity desirable	Present Situation adequate, or other replies
2. Whether the Taft-Hartley Act should be repealed or revised	Yes, pro-labor	No, or yes, pro-management	Other replies
·3. Whether the national government should take action against racial discrimination in employment	Yes	No	Other replies
4. Whether the U.S.A. has become too involved in foreign affairs	No	Yes	Other replies
5. Whether the American government is to blame for China's going communist	No	Yes	Other replies
6. Whether the American government was right to send troops to Korea	Yes	No	Other replies
7. What should be the American policy in Korea (October, 1952)	Keep trying for a peaceful settlement	Bomb Manchuria and other stronger steps or pull out of Korea	Other replies

As a whole, Table 10 shows that the Democratic voter was more likely than the Republican voter to cling to Truman's position. On the first two questions, over half the people of both parties had no clearly defined stand; and on two others (nos. 5 and 6) the neutrality amounted to a quarter or fifth of the total. On action against racial discrimination, Democratic voters held the "Democratic" position only slightly more often than Republican voters held it. Half the Republican voters agreed with the

TABLE 10. CONSISTENCY OF VOTERS ON
PARTY AND ISSUES, 1952[1]
(in percentages)

Question Number	Vote in 1952	Support Democrat Position	Neutral, Uncertain	Oppose Democrat Position	Total
1. Government Activity	D	33	62	5	100
	R	19	50	31	100
2. Taft-Hartley	D	32	56	12	100
	R	9	55	36	100
3. FEPC	D	51	4	45	100
	R	40	6	54	100
4. Foreign Involvements	D	43	13	44	100
	R	28	7	65	100
5. China Policy	D	60	23	17	100
	R	38	24	38	100
6. Entry in Korean War	D	52	16	32	100
	R	34	20	46	100
7. Korean Policy	D	52	7	41	100
	R	36	8	56	100

Note: Number of cases in the sample: Democratic voters, 494; Republican voters, 687.

[1] Campbell, Angus, Gerald Gurin, and W. E. Miller, "Political Issues and the Vote: November, 1952," *American Political Science Review*, 46 (1953), 359–385. Also author's analysis of Survey Research Center materials.

majority of Democrats on China policy. Half the Democrats agreed with the majority of Republicans on foreign involvement.

Such qualifications to party agreement are easy to make from this table. A further qualification can be added: only the voters were considered (74% of the total sample); hence, since non-voters are generally less informed than voters, the extent of agreement in the whole population is less than shown here. A more striking fact can be learned from a few simple calculations. Issue no. 7, on what to do in Korea, may be used for illustration. The issue divides the followers, but not in an extreme manner. Yet only about 54% of the whole population took up positions on the issue that coincided with that attributed to their party.[1] (If any other position were attributed to their party, the proportion would be less.) The case with some of the other issues shows that individual deviation from party policy is even more common. For example, the governmental activity issue shows only a rough third of the population holding a position consistent with their "presumed" party position.

The extent to which party members differ from one another in their beliefs can be shown in one other manner. A more severe critic may say:

---

[1] The reader can make the calculations himself by determining the numbers contained in the 52% and 56% figures, and then, after adding them, computing what percentage the total (642) is of the total population sample (1181).

"One swallow doesn't make a summer, nor one issue a party ideology. How many people hold to one, two, or more of the seven 'Democratic' positions, and how many hold to one or more of the 'Republican' positions?" To answer his question is not impossible. Table 11 has been developed for the purpose. Four of the previous questions can be used: nos. 1, 2, 4, and 5. Depending upon how he answered these questions, a person might score in any one of five different ways. In Table 11, each letter indicates an answer to one of the questions, "D" representing a Democratic answer; "R" a Republican answer; and "?" a neutral stand. Each set of four symbols illustrates a combination of responses that would place a person in a specific category (A to E). The arrangement of the letters is not related to the order of the four questions.

TABLE 11. EXTENT OF A DEMOCRATIC OR REPUBLICAN IDEOLOGY, 1952[1]

A	B	C	D	E
	Democratic		Republican	
Democratic,	with	No Party	with	Republican,
no Conflict	Conflict	Dominating	Conflict	no Conflict
DDDD	DDDR	DDRR	RRRD	RRRR
DDD?	DDR?	DR??	RRD?	RRR?
DD??		????		RR??
D???				R???

Number of Cases in Each Category

A	B	C	D	E
357	252	391	268	346

Percentage of Total Population in Each Category

A	B	C	D	E
22%	16%	24%	17%	21%

[1] Campbell *et al.*, *The Voter Decides*, p. 123.

These figures show that over half the American people probably do not hold to a party line, or hold to it only in part. They disagree either wholly or in part with one party's position. (It should be noted, too, that even some part of the consistent Democratic or Republican issue-supporters in the categories A and E did not "know" whether their position *was* a party position; and some were, in fact, voting for a candidate of the party opposing their issue stand.) A portion of the remaining half who were "consistent" took neutral or uncertain positions on some issues. The two major American parties certainly have not succeeded in aligning people into two antagonistic ideological camps. Perhaps one should presume that no issue is a party issue so far as the whole public is concerned.

Lack of unified belief among leaders

Just as the party rank and file do not have firm and homogeneous political convictions, so too the leaders lack unity of belief. The leaders, however, are more aware than the rank and file that they are split within the same party. Deep chasms of attitude differences separate leaders of the same party. The left wing of the Republican Party is as far left as the left wing of the Democratic Party, and the right wing of the Republican

Party is no farther right than the right wing of the Democratic Party. There is again, as with the party followings, some difference of degree, giving an aura of "liberalism" to the Democratic Party leadership and one of "conservatism" to the Republican leadership. In addition, when the leaders of a given party have to campaign together or work in a legislature together, they subdue some of their differences; under those circumstances it often appears that the leaders of the party have more in common than they actually do have.

A glance at the record of the Eighty-third Congress will illustrate some of these points. There were 407 roll-call votes in all during that Congress, which met in 1953 and 1954. By the calculations of the *Congressional Quarterly*, President Eisenhower had taken a clear position on 198 of them. Each congressman's votes were compared with the President's stand on the issue and the total percentage of his agreement with the President on all issues was computed. Then the average of the percentages for all Democratic congressmen was calculated, as well as that for the Republicans. It was discovered that in the Senate the Republican score for cooperating with Eisenhower was 73%; in the House, 71%; and in both chambers together, 72%. By contrast, the Democratic composite cooperation-with-Eisenhower score on the 198 issues was 38% in the Senate, 44% in the House, and 43% in both houses together. The Republicans thus voted with the President in seven out of every ten cases, the Democrats in four out of every ten. Obviously the Republicans in Congress supported Eisenhower more than the Democrats did.

Yet the Democratic support was by no means negligible. Neither party could make a blanket statement of full support or full opposition to the President. Moreover, it would be politically risky to accuse the opposition party of stiff-necked obstructionism, as several new figures can show. In 164 of the 198 cases, the vote was concurrent with Eisenhower's wishes. However, eighty-seven times in the Senate and thirty-four times in the House, the measures would have failed without some Democratic assistance because, although the Republican Party possessed slender majorities in both houses, some Republicans were absent or antagonistic on the roll-calls. Only in sixteen cases in the Senate and twenty-seven in the House was Democratic support not needed for carrying the measure. In some areas of public policy, the amount of overlapping between the parties was even greater. For example, in all, fifty-four votes were cast in the Senate of the Eighty-third Congress on questions of foreign policy. In 72% of these cases (thirty-nine out of fifty-four), a majority of Republicans voting agreed with a majority of Democrats voting. Foreign policy voting could therefore be termed bipartisan.

Confronted by the myriad differences and complexities of the American party system, the bemused citizen may feel that no statement about it can be true. This is not the case. One must only bear in mind: (1) that only vague general statements can be used to describe its vast, rambling organization; and (2) that only statements of degree can be made with respect to the people who compose each party and to the issues they stand for. Although the whole of the next chapter is devoted to a description of the functions performed by these organizations and people, it may be well to say in advance that the same kind of situation prevails with respect to party functions: parties perform a number of tasks, but do so in an erratic fashion.

QUESTIONS AND PROBLEMS

1. Summarize the victories and the failures of the major parties since the Civil War; do likewise with the minor parties.

2. Explain what is meant by this statement: "The American political party has on paper the structure and rules of a disciplined army; but it behaves like a rabble."

3. In what major respects are the American political parties regulated by law?

4. Describe the pattern of party affiliations among Americans.

5. List the major forces working to determine the way Americans vote. Give an example of how each worked in 1952.

6. What are the major reasons for which people like and dislike the two major parties?

7. Show both how Democratic voters stand together on some issues and how they overlap with Republicans or disagree sharply among themselves on other issues.

8. Do you think that the party leaders agree among themselves *more* or *less* than the party's rank and file? Explain your answer.

14. Party Functions

Photograph by Sam Falk. Reproduced by courtesy of The New York Times

THE purpose of this chapter is to describe what the political party does. The student must keep in mind at all times the vast physical spread of the party over the country, its huge membership of people from all walks and stations of life, and its elaborate formal and informal organization. These important facts, depicted in the preceding chapter, underlie the party at work. They indicate the variety of functions that must be occurring and also set the rules and limits on what functions can actually be fulfilled.

Two types of functions

A necessary first step is to distinguish two general types of functions a party performs. Some functions are acknowledged openly to be the party goals, such as winning elections. Other functions occur without fore-thought or plan, and may even be disliked by many people. The former are termed *professed* functions; the latter are called *latent* functions. They can be compared to the functions of a fishing trip that a man may under-take. Catching fish is the professed function of his actions. Yet other functions of the trip may be to relax his nerves, to think over some per-sonal or business problems, to get away from his family, and so on. These are the latent functions of the fishing trip.

Just as fishing trips have professed functions, so has the political party. They are (1) proposing goals for society to follow; (2) putting forward candidates for office; (3) waging political campaigns; and (4) operating or criticizing the government. The latent functions of the political party include (1) the fulfillment of personal ambitions; (2) the obtaining of profitable group concessions; (3) the expression of social sentiments; and (4) the provision of means for social mobility. The two groups of functions may be taken up in order.

THE PROFESSED FUNCTIONS

Proposing goals for society

The American parties are the objects of much scorn for not fulfilling what is regarded as an essential function of a political party: the declaration of noble human goals toward which the party can lead the nation. The chief reason for wanting parties, many say, is to give society some sense of direction, some possible plan for achieving social happiness. In truth, back of most political parties there does lie an evangelistic origin: they were born "to save the community from a horrible fate." But few parties have ever struggled into adulthood and power without shedding most of their evangelism. Their creed and gospel are transformed by the toil of campaigning and by the compromises needed to secure power; indeed, parties are often converted to a new gospel before they have had time to succeed with the old. The Democratic Party has stood for many things at different times and even at the same time: it has been the party of pure democracy, the party of States' rights, the party of slavery, the party of immigrants, the party of great liberal reform, and the party for liberat-ing the world from tyranny. The Republican Party, in its briefer life-span, has been the party of homesteading farmers, of anti-slavery, of saving the federal union, of the monopolies, of free enterprise, and of peace and nationalism. *& of racism*

Such great issues exist in the history of the parties, and echoes of them resound even in contemporary political campaigns. But the problem of the party leaders at any moment is more short-term and humble. It is that of winning the next election. And great issues do not run off ticker tape into their campaign headquarters. To be fair to many politicians, it must

Public Opinion Generates Often in Small Groups Gathered at Stores, Barber Shops, Clubs, Taverns, and Hotels. Here is a prize-winning picture of the traditional general store, pot-bellied stove, and informal group of citizens.

be said that they are pathetically eager to find a campaign issue—always with the proviso, however, that they can take a stand on it without losing an election. There is a statement in training troops for war that "a dead soldier is not a good soldier"; in politics, a losing politician is not a "good" one. Hence a "good" politician strains for the issue (1) that wins more votes than it loses and (2) that he believes is good for the country, or for whomever he wants to do good.

Difficulty of Creating Issues: On the whole, "natural" issues are more effective than "created" issues. Many politicians—and a large fraction of the public and the press agree with the belief—think that they can create issues. But they can do so only in a limited sense; for issues are very difficult to create. The public, or a large part of it, is generally paying some attention to the political process; but the attention is at a low level and is difficult to manipulate because of its ponderous and vague character. "War or peace," "jobs or unemployment," "honesty or corruption," and "Communism or Americanism" are some of the large issues that have found their way into recent campaigns. These issues cannot be raised from the dead; they can be played upon only for what they are worth, and events that are far beyond the ability of politicians or parties to affect give rise to them and give them most of their force.

Other issues of a more specific character, such as the repeal of the Taft-Hartley Act, the creation of a national Fair Employment Practices Commission to prevent discrimination against Negroes in employment, or a withdrawal of diplomatic recognition from the Soviet Union, are in the air, certainly. However, they reach only limited segments of the public, and, when they lack exciting possibilities, can be acclaimed vociferously to little avail. Both with the very general issues and with such specific issues, the political party can have only a most limited freedom; the political party or some section of it cannot make an issue effective when the public, and perhaps also the press, are bored with the subject or little interested in it.

Modest Role in Setting Goals: Is then this function of proposing goals for a society one for which the parties must be ill-equipped and inadequate? In the absolute sense, yes; in a relative sense, however, there can be little doubt of the educative effect of parties. The level of public discourse may be generally not high; yet even the attainment of that level is due, in part, to the efforts of politicians and the rank and file of the party. The fact is, and several recent studies reveal it clearly, that the most vocal, active, informed Americans on the issues that are before the country in a practical form for action are the strong supporters of one party or the other. Those who know the issues, who are aware of what is happening locally, regionally, and nationally, who stir up argumentation, are the stauncher Republicans and Democrats. Hence party activity has some educative effect upon party members and the public in general.

Furthermore, in a number of localities, particularly in urban areas, campaigns are often waged over heated issues that are of vital concern to the voters. A real choice between pro-union and pro-business policies, or between other important alternatives, is offered in the character of the candidates. For example, a working-class area in Detroit may send a spokesman to Congress to strive for the repeal of the Taft-Hartley Act. Or the Harlem district in New York may elect a representative to Congress to fight for the equal rights of Negroes. Or Arizona may expect its congressmen to argue for water rights in the Colorado River basin. In such cases, parties (or portions thereof) do set up goals for society.

However, these local calls to arms do not summon a disciplined response from the two parties in Congress. The candidates can truly promise no more than to fight for their goals if elected; they cannot guarantee the achievement of the goals. When elected, they must content themselves with marking time, with delivering pleas on behalf of their cause, and with watching for those fleeting opportunities when they can work their ideas into legislation.

Putting forward candidates

Beside fulfilling an expressed function of proposing various goals for the community, a party has the task of putting forward candidates who are to occupy the many thousands of elective offices throughout the nation. Candidacy is no simple matter akin to stepping forward to give blood for a Red Cross blood bank. To be a candidate for public office one must satisfy certain eligibility rules that the laws lay down: residence, citizenship, age, and a few other minor requirements. There also are social eligibility rules that are outside the law but important, nevertheless: length of residence in the community, marital status, and veteran's status. Additional social considerations include some that are general, such as pleasing manners and appearance, and the lack of a penal record; and some that are peculiar to the constituency, such as religion and national origins. There are qualifications of skill and experience—what would make people believe that the candidate is able to do a good job? Can he deliver a speech well? Does he have some acquaintance, no matter how tenuous, with the post he hopes to occupy? There are also a number of routine (and sometimes technically involved) requirements for proposing candidacy: what does one do to file; how many people must support one's candidacy; what are the dates of filing; how closely are the applications scrutinized; how much money is needed; and more questions of the same type.

Many people are eliminated as candidates by their inability or incapacity to run the gantlet described. But more serious considerations then arise: How does one find a man with the stated qualities? Having found him, how does one persuade him to run for office? Probably most men and women are unable to contemplate themselves as candidates for public office. Some are physically incapable of the strain of running. Others are psychologically quite unsuited to subjecting themselves to the sardonic or even sympathetic scrutiny of thousands of eyes. A great many never regard the matter seriously, and no one suggests that they do. The possible candidates must be chosen from the very few people who can stand the gaff.

Still, however, these few must have jobs that will permit them leave or time to campaign. The nature of their work must not preclude politicking either because they would lose customers or earnings, or because they derive their salary from a government agency so that they are prevented by law from politicking. Personal considerations enter again, in that often incompatible plans have been laid that would be upset by campaigning— perhaps a vacation or a temporary residence in another place.

Then enter all the partisan considerations: Is the person a loyal party man, or at least has he or she been silent about his or her politics? What enemies has the potential candidate made among the party regulars, among those who must be counted on to do the work of advocating his candidacy? Furthermore, does the potential candidate hold the "right" views on the issues, such as they may be? Does he share more or less the morality of the party workers? Does he have money to support his campaign and that of others, or does he have friends or acquaintances who would put up money to see him run?

By the time that all of these considerations, or even a part of them, are satisfied, very few candidates are left for the 800,000 elective offices that the State constitutions and legislatures have created. It is little wonder that the voter is often confronted on his ballot with the same scarred and spavined old war horses with whom he has become familiar through many an electoral campaign. At least, to the eternally timid leaders, catastrophe is unlikely with such reliable and tested candidates. Furthermore, having campaigned before, the candidates of yesteryear have names and faces that are known by many of the voters. And, of course, although the federal elective offices are few, it is asking a great deal of the party or its candidates to entrust those candidacies to untried persons who have served the party little or not at all in times gone by. Therefore, it is largely true that in a democracy, whereas many common citizens feel that they are potentially ideal candidates for public office, the political party finds all too few candidates, even among those who are not illustrious.

Waging political campaigns

The parties conduct campaigns, but candidates do likewise. Sometimes the one overshadows the other. The party is often well organized, with a machine that carries the candidate along with it, leaving only certain specialized functions to him. At other times, the party is almost non-existent, so that the candidate must found his own organization, such as it is, as he goes along. There is, in other words, a maximum and a minimum party role in campaigns. Since great differences in campaigning come about because of party strength and weakness, it is perhaps most useful to depict two types of campaign, one in an area of well-organized parties and the other in an area where the party mechanism is extremely feeble. A great many jurisdictions, of course, fall between these two poles, and share the characteristics of each.

Campaigns by Strong Organizations: At its peak of efficiency, a party closely resembles a disciplined army. It is professional; its rank and file as well as its leaders derive much or all of their income from party work and its legal and illegal sources of revenue. It is fully manned; all posts are filled down to those of precinct captain and assistant precinct captain in each voting district of the area. It is cohesive; loyalty is strong among leaders and followers. It has a single leadership, and the leaders have distinct lines of command down to the precinct workers. It has a specialized staff for public speaking, propaganda, treating with friendly interests, collecting money, purchasing supplies, and making arrangements for meetings; it has espionage and counter-espionage agents, and a central secretarial and clerical staff.

It is not very concerned with issues and the flights of fancy that sometimes overtake amateurs, whether in war or politics; its operations are humdrum and detailed, conducted soberly, with planning and forethought; they are somewhat cautious, and without illusions. It tends to favor slow change in most political, economic, and social matters; no political machine in the United States that strove to accelerate the pace of change has lasted for more than a few years. The party sometimes has "liberal" candidates on its ticket, often to counteract the presence of candidates temporarily in bad odor. It reaches out in all directions for sources of support and revenue, asking little of the ideology of the sources but as much as it can of their favors and money.

In its strongest form, the party usually maintains a number of corrupt connections, even when it has rich financial support from entertainment businesses, public utilities, and all sorts of private enterprise. One reason for the underworld character of some of its operations lies undoubtedly in the unfortunate circumstances from which most of the rank and file, and even the top managers, have risen. Another is the greater reliability of supporters who are dependent upon police protection, which is controlled by the organization.

The candidates are picked as a team and run as one. Most have long periods of service to the party, justifying their public promotion, even though their merits be inconsiderable in the eyes of the population as a whole. A measurement of merit becomes difficult for the public to make, except upon some absolute scale, since candidates that correspond to the specifications of a reform group or a professor of philosophy infrequently present themselves for comparison. Where the machine is not menaced by the other major party, it fills its slate of candidates by internal priorities; the men who are the most deserving by the criteria of the machine achieve the most desirable places. Where defeat is possible, a balanced ticket is made up that is calculated to appeal to the outside world.

Long practice has made the organization expert in coping with the great volume of legal detail surrounding the operations of the party system. Its files, traditions, experienced personnel, and habits give it a group memory. Amateurs, reformers, "johnnies-come-lately," and unorganized opponents lack such advantages. The party knows when to begin preparations for conventions or primary elections, when to file for candidates, and how to circulate nominating petitions quickly in legal fashion. It knows all about the convention—where it is to be held, who will be there, how it will work, and how it will be controlled—because it has had a hand in deciding all these matters. It knows what can be spent on a campaign, how much it can collect, and where the money can be obtained. It remembers to get its supporters on the election boards in the precincts. Its precinct captains make personal calls on all the voters, urging their support of the slate with arguments suited to the individual rather than to the predispositions of the captain (he is helped in this by the group memory again, because the voter's ideas and past behavior are known and often recorded).

On election day, the machine is busy before dawn, making sure that all the polls are staffed and that the machine is represented when the new ballots come into the polling places. Approaches to the polls are placarded so far as is legally permitted. All friendly voters are urged to vote, for a great many elections are decided not by the *general* public's opinion but by the *voting* public's opinion, a difference in some cases of 60%. Under such circumstances the party that can get out the favorable vote has a great advantage, regardless of everything that has been said and done throughout the campaign.

How Machines Are Broken Up: How does change come to such an area? The greatest chance of change in the short run comes from deserters or factions. Occasionally a subordinate or a clique of subleaders becomes alienated by the leaders' practices and moves to evict them either by maneuvers within the organization, or by opposing them in a primary election, or by joining the opposition in a general election. Sometimes one of the higher committees, such as the county or State central committee, splits into factions; the contestants then seek support down the line, thus splitting also a large number of local organizations. Other more long-range causes of the overthrow of machines are a severe economic crisis that alienates even the voters traditionally friendly to them, or a program of social security measures and full employment that causes people to be less dependent on the charitable aspects of the organization's function.

Campaigning in Weak Party Areas: Very few parts of the United States today have strong party organizations; the remaining cases are found in some sections of a number of the older eastern and midwestern cities. A somewhat larger number of areas have party organizations that try to model themselves on the type. The vast majority of American localities are organized politically by networks of men in shifting alliances, which ordinarily stop short of crossing party lines. The campaign functions of the political parties under these circumstances are not nearly so numerous or important. The party, instead of acquiring what seems like an existence or character of its own, is quite simply represented in the characters of a few individuals and in the laws governing parties, which the courts compel these men to follow.

In an area of extreme party disintegration, the elaborate set of committees still exists, for the laws are fairly uniform throughout the United States; however, vacancies often occur on the committees, for the men and women who hold posts on them are not professional politicians or necessarily influential citizens. There are usually a few old hands in the area to whom one goes for information and aid on party matters. They have served on such committees, or have run for office in the past. They may be officials of the government administering the law of parties. They may have connections with the national and State party leaders, or may have held patronage appointments under previous administrations of their party. Sometimes they have given money and time to political work before. There may be no more than two or three dozen such men in a party in a county with 100,000 people; the number rarely exceeds 150.

There are no precinct captains in an area of extreme party disintegration. In their place are a number of persons who in the past have helped a candidate of the party, and who are known to the first group of "old-hand" leaders; in addition, each candidate brings with him a certain number of friends, relatives, and new acquaintances who are attracted by some belief or trait he possesses. Some of them will not be of the same party.

The potential candidate need have served the party little in the past, and there is little the party can do for him in the present. He obtains a certain amount of good will from the old hands and their networks of acquaintances, some good advice, and much of the money he is apt to obtain. Also, he gets the benefit or harm of the party label beside his name on the ballot. In middle-sized communities and in most constituencies of more than a few thousand voters, fewer than half the voters will know one name from another on election day; a candidate will be carried along or cast ashore by general tides over which he has little control. Of the small proportion of voters who stoutly refuse to accept a party label as meaningful, the largest part will not know the candidates either. They will vote for an incumbent, or the man whose name appears first on the ballot, or toward whose name they are drawn. They may select one whose occupation or address pleases them, or for whom they have some affinity owing to some snatch of news about him that has come to their attention in the campaign. It is the task of the candidate and a half-dozen friends to set up his campaign committee, circulate petitions for nomination, distribute campaign materials, and otherwise conduct the campaign.

The candidate who is an incumbent has a good chance of election under the conditions of an unintegrated party system. Holding office gives him the advantage of access to all those people in the area who are normally concerned with the operations of the office. He has therefore a network of influence that is already activated and that substitutes for the kind provided by the party in a well-organized area.

Also, an unintegrated party system favors the party whose candidates have money, or who come from or represent the professional, managerial, and brokerage occupations. The former is true because money can, up to a point, buy the special services needed; indeed, in areas such as the one being described, the rise of professional campaign managers, usually going under the title of public relations consultants, is marked in recent years. The latter is true because candidates who come from such social circles know more people who are engaged in work necessitating human contacts.

especially with the more affluent and important members of society. On the whole, in consequence of these greater uses of money and contacts, Republicans hold an edge over Democrats, who generally come from, or depend upon, less tightly-knit groups of people and the support of individuals who work with things rather than with other human beings, such as clerks, semi-skilled and unskilled workers, and owners of small farms.

In an unorganized party area, the amount of "independent" voting is considerable. Candidates of the one party make frequent, successful raids on the membership of the other party. Only in a narrow sense can the voters of the area be called non-partisan. Their liking for one or the other party remains; however, being under little party pressure to vote the straight ticket, they naturally do not carry out their party's wishes seriously. When party disorganization is further supplemented and assisted by open primaries and other election laws that encourage split-ticket voting, many people will vote split tickets so that an independent candidacy is stimulated further, to the point often of the candidate's refusing to identify himself with the views of either party—although he still shuns identifying himself with a third or minor party.

The party system in much of the South is a one-party replica of both extremes of party organization described here. In a few places, factions of the Democratic Party are well organized and fight one another as machines, in, for example, New Orleans. By contrast, in most southern districts party organization may be almost absent, and the situation will strongly resemble that of similar areas in the North and the West.

Operating the government

In victory or defeat, the American major party plays a role in the operation of government. If triumphant at the polls, the party's candidates become President and congressmen. The details of how the President and congressmen behave as party leaders are presented in a series of chapters to come. Here only a few general remarks about party government need expression.

Both the majority party and the minority party organize themselves in Congress. Members of the majority party in either chamber of Congress enjoy certain powers and offices that are denied to the minority party members. At the same time, the defeated party is not plunged into oblivion. It has the critic's functions. It has no representation, it is true, in the executive establishment, although from time to time, especially in foreign affairs, appointments of men from the minority party are made. But in Congress, the minority party members have the rights of representation upon all standing committees, of debate, and of introducing bills no matter what may be the likelihood of their passage. From their position in Congress they may denounce the majority and the President almost at will. They have their own group of congressional leaders who are ready to assume the direction of Congress should another election restore their majority status.

Furthermore, one faction of the minority party may find itself more at home with the majority leadership than with its own majority faction, not only on one issue but on a series of issues. Hence the defeat of the party in general does not mean necessarily a defeat for certain segments of the party. A number of "conservative" Democrats do not fear greatly an upset of "liberal" congressmen of their own party, even if it means a loss of their own committee chairmanships and of other perquisites of majority party members. The same is true of some "liberal" Republicans when their party loses control of their branch of Congress. Practically every member, however, regrets his party's loss of the presidency, because possession of that office is gratifying in so many ways that it tends to nullify any antagonism he may feel toward the ideas of the President himself.

LATENT FUNCTIONS

A second group of functions of the American political party may be called latent functions. These consist of those several party goals and activities that are not proclaimed openly as the goals of the party but are either given quiet recognition or are even condemned as unfortunate or harmful consequences of party activities.

Fulfillment of personal ambitions

The first of the latent functions of the party is to provide ambitious people with an avenue and a means to success. Over a hundred years ago Alexis de Tocqueville penned words that are as true now as they were then:

> The pains which are taken to create parties are inconceivable, and at the present day it is no easy task. In the United States there is no religious animosity, because all religion is respected and no sect is predominant; there is no jealousy of rank, because the people are everything and none can contest their authority; lastly, there is no public misery to serve as a means of agitation, because the physical condition of the country opens so wide a field to industry that man only needs to be let alone to be able to accomplish prodigies. Nevertheless, ambitious men will succeed in creating parties, since it is difficult to eject a person from authority on the mere ground that his place is coveted by others. All of the skill of the actors in the political world lies in the art of creating parties. A political aspirant in the United States begins by discerning his own interest, and discovering those other interests which may be collected around and amalgamated with it. He then contrives to find out some doctrine or principle which may suit the purpose of this new association, and which he adopts in order to bring forward his party and secure its popularity.

Practically every desire can find a congenial environment in political activity. Men enter party work to increase their incomes, to acquire prestige, to enjoy human companionship, to seek enlightenment about world events, to gain power, to vent their inner rages upon a legitimate object— the opposing party—and to practice a skill that they enjoy. They may not only wish one or more of these values for themselves, but may also wish them for others—in which event they can be called altruistic. And, of course, if this altruistic idea seems full and complete, they can then function in psychological accord with the professed aim of the party to set goals for the society and to achieve those goals. Rarely does a person have such a well-integrated character, or do people agree that he has; consequently there almost always is not only a question of individual ambition in any political action, but also a considerable amount of evidence to that end.

Obtaining profitable group concessions

Not only individuals but also organized groups find fulfillment of needs in the party process. The hundreds of functions of government impinge upon thousands of groups. Consequently, groups engage in politics, for politics in some measure directs their lives. Of course, as the chapter on interest groups showed, many relations between groups and government consist of external negotiations between representatives of the parties and of the groups, or between permanent non-partisan officials and group representatives.

However, there remains an important fraction of the parties themselves that is composed of the groups or their representatives. It is well, for instance, that the Brewers' Association gives advice and applies pressure to party candidates; yet it is also effective to have agents or retainers as party officials or public officials. It is excellent for delegates from cities to express urban needs at a hearing before Congress; it is also useful to have mayors in prominent party posts. Greek maritime shippers may make effective representations to congressmen and to public opinion; they also do well if some of their important stockholders are also politicians. The National Association for the Advancement of the Colored People and other organizations work hard and successfully to promote the rights of Negroes, but they are pleased when Negro members of legislatures and Negro party leaders are also in a position to help. The list of cases could be extended indefinitely. It proves that the argument that pressure groups arise because the parties are too large to represent them, is not the whole truth; the parties themselves are to a degree interest group representatives.

Expression of social sentiments

The party is also an association of like-minded persons for the expression of social sentiments. A coldly objective analysis of all aspects of party activity will reveal that a "disproportionate" quantity of energy goes into this latent function to the "detriment" of the function of winning votes and capturing office. For every tea or picnic that is given to impress potential recruits and undecided voters, at least another is given for purely social intercourse among those already converted. It is often impossible to direct political clubs and cliques of party workers at their professed aim of winning elections, so enthralled are they by the cameraderie of fellow-believers.

Nor does it commonly occur to party workers to engage the opposition except formally and in a few picturesque encounters such as on a radio program or in a pamphlet. At some times the parties behave like the famous medieval Chinese mercenary armies that disturbed their pleasant existences only to execute ritualistic maneuvers, replete with bugles, fire-crackers, and gaudy uniforms, that were the prelude to a brief clash of arms followed by a prearranged armistice and a negotiated peace. Even in destructive modern times armies are plagued by the vast number of service troops and the small number of men on the firing line, many of the latter being found by intensive research to be loath to discharge their weapons.

Similar surveys of party workers disclose a comparable situation, with a great proportion of party workers supplying each other with information, ideas, plans, bulletins, slogans, transportation, and sympathetic audiences. Discussing at length what they should do and how they feel, they occasionally even speak disapprovingly of the few workers who labor among the undecided and the opposition, for, among those engaged in actual political struggle, embarrassing incidents, defeats, unseemly noises, recriminations, and other unpleasant encounters inevitably occur. True campaigning, in which energy is directed at the most vulnerable points of the opposition, is often arduous, routine, laborious, apt to incite counter-attacks, undignified, and misunderstood. Many times it leaves scars. It is out of tune with the expression of congenial social sentiments.

A means of group mobility

In an early textbook on political parties Professors C. E. Merriam and H. F. Gosnell, of the University of Chicago, wrote that parties speeded up the process of Americanization. Over several generations the party helped millions of newcomers to obtain citizenship, to get jobs, to understand some of their constitutional rights, to see how other Americans lived, and otherwise to fit into American society. Large-scale immigration to the United States is ended, but the same general function remains. Although parties have not developed consciously for the purpose, they have constantly contributed aid to "under-privileged" groups of Americans.

The story of this function, even apart from its Americanization side, goes back to earliest America. Then the formation of parties was contemporary with such events as the birth of a free educational system and the distribution of free land, and operated with them as means by which the socially downtrodden groups of the backwoods, the hills, or the cities could climb upward economically and socially. Entrance to the upper levels of business and social leadership has never been so free as entrance to the upper levels of politics; furthermore the greater freedom of opportunity in politics has made the other areas more free than they would otherwise have been.

Today politics is still one of the most unguarded ladders of opportunity in America for individuals, and, by the same token, for numbers of individuals from the less privileged sections of society. Many American politicians have come from the poorer parts of the South, the melting-pot areas of the cities and country, and from that group of persons who are frustrated by purely personal circumstances from getting ahead.

Examples abound, although they are not often thought of in this light. A survey of Norwegian-Americans in Wisconsin politics, for instance, shows that the first two Norwegians to be elected to public office were intellectuals who were chosen in 1847 and 1859. In 1850, Norwegians comprised about three per cent of the State's population. From 1861 to 1868 the payroll of the State legislature carried only a doorkeeper and a fireman who were Norwegian. Yet by 1870 four counties were from twenty to forty per cent Norwegian. During the decade after 1868, several Norwegians were elected to State office. One, Knute Nelson, later became a United States Senator from Minnesota.

The first generation is usually poorly represented in political leadership; the second generation is much better represented. In another instance, the Irish immigrants to New York City in the 1800's were given aid and comfort by Tammany Hall; their descendants inherited the organization

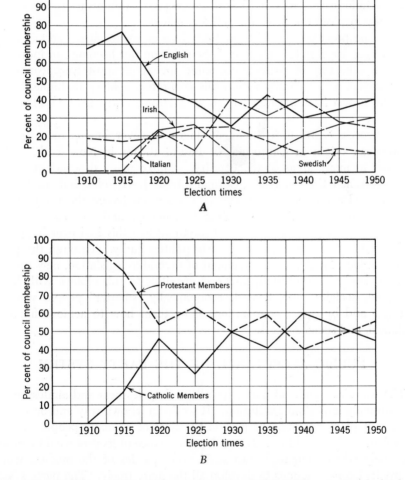

Figure 27. **Politics and Social Change in a City, 1910–1950.** A. Trend of Ethnic Names in the City Council; B. Changing Religious Affiliations of City Councilmen. (The city in question is under 50,000 population and located south of Providence, R. I. The Council held 16 members until 1930 and thereafter 20 members.)

itself. By the time of the Civil War, most New York police were Irish, and the Irish were moving from politics into all kinds of businesses that had to do with politics—moving in sidewise, often, as partners, instead of from the bottom. A survey of appointed judgeships in New York City over the last two generations reveals an increase first of Irish, then of Jewish, and finally of Italian, names.

The two graphs in Figure 27 show how members of several principal ethnic strains in a New England town developed political prominence. An equilibrium seems to have recently been established among the national origins of council members. The achievement of such "proportional" representation generally signifies the decline of true ethnic representation in American politics, contrary as it may seem. That is, the index used—the nationality of people's names—comes to lack any real ethnic meaning. Once the point of equilibrium has been reached there is no longer a strong, conscious ethnic drive. As time passes, success itself diminishes the force that originally inspired the drive for political office.

Once the process of political mobility in a group reaches a certain speed it no longer appears to be a group phenomenon but becomes an individual process. The rate of political-economic success of most European immigrant groups will probably within this generation achieve its highest speed and the group itself rapidly vanish as a strong component in individual behavior.

The process is still in its incipient stages, however, among recent groups of Mexican origin in California, of Puerto Ricans in New York, and of Negroes in many areas of the country. Unlike many descendants of the backwoodsmen, Scandinavians, Germans, Irish, Jews, Poles, Italians, Czechs, French, and southerners, who can now afford to ignore the usefulness of party as a means of achieving political, economic, and social security, and who are indeed quite unaware that anything like this had ever happened, these contemporary groups need party politics badly. Through the party, they find jobs, legal aid, advancement of favorable legislation, new prestige as their leaders are elected, and opportunities to rub elbows with better educated, socially sophisticated, economically "smarter" people who, by example and by direct cooperation, show them how to achieve financial, technical, and social success.

PUBLIC ACCEPTANCE OF THE PARTY SYSTEM

The American political party, for all its shapelessness and aimlessness, is an extremely important institution. It works in its own way and on its own terms. It plays a significant part in the lives of as many people as go to church or are baseball fans. Its weak performance of its professed functions, especially when compared with some other parties of the modern world, allows its latent functions to develop all the more freely. The party system can be taken to task for not being something other than it is. But what it is can be clearly comprehended, if one seeks seriously to understand it, and can be stoutly defended on a respectable basis.

Public attitudes toward party differences

What does the American public think of this kind of party system? Do they know that it exists? Are people bitter about it? Would they welcome some alternative party system? Apparently a large part of the public is aware of the nature of the party system. They know what is occurring therein. In a survey in 1952 of a national cross-section of Americans, about half the population saw only minor differences or no differences at all between the parties. They made this judgment, too, in the middle of an exciting presidential election campaign. Less than fifteen per cent of the public believed that many important differences existed between the two major parties.[1] Furthermore, when asked whether they thought it would make a great deal of difference to the country whether the Democrats or the Republicans won the elections, or whether it would not make much difference which side won, one-third of the sample said that it would make no difference. About forty per cent declared that it would make some difference or minor differences. Only twenty-one per cent felt that it would make a great deal of difference who won. A large majority of the American people believe that the parties do not represent sharp alternatives.

Apathy toward "liberal" or labor parties

There is little to suggest that people are bitter about the lack of burning issues or that they would like to demand such issues. Perhaps the best evidence of this comes from asking people whether they would prefer a different kind of party system, one which gave them more to choose from. In five polls of a sample of the American public by the American Institute of Public Opinion, conducted in the years from 1937 to 1947, people were asked whether they would favor giving up the two present major parties for a system with a "liberal" and a "conservative" party. The percentages favoring such a change ranged from twelve per cent to twenty-four per cent. The percentages opposing any such change ranged from fifty-two per cent to seventy-two per cent (the balance had no opinion on the subject and could hardly be considered therefore as favoring such a change). In May, 1946, only ten per cent said that they would join a third, labor party should one be organized. Many people are unclear about what their party stands for (and the fact is that they have good reason for being unclear); few people —perhaps one out of fifty—are interested enough in their party to work a little for it; yet a large majority of present-day Americans are still hesitant to regard any other system as better.

QUESTIONS AND PROBLEMS

1. Name and describe briefly the professed functions of an American political party.
2. Name and describe briefly the latent functions of an American political party.

---

[1] Analysis by the author of Survey Research Center materials.

3. Which professed function of the party do you think is most thoroughly performed? Explain your answer.

4. Which latent function of the party do you regard as most important? Explain your answer.

5. Contrast the conduct of a political campaign in an area where a party is highly organized with its conduct in an area where a party is loosely organized.

6. What are the legal and other institutions that limit the number of candidates for office?

7. Give an example of each professed party function as it is carried out in some part of America (but do not use the example given in the text). Use the *New York Times, Time* magazine, or your local newspaper files to discover examples if you cannot readily think of them.

8. Repeat the problem in question (7) for each latent party function.

Courtesy of the City Art Museum, St. Louis

Nomination and election are the two formal stages in the process whereby the voters choose certain officials of the government. Essentially, the nomination determines what person each political party will support as its candidate for a given office; and the election decides which of the two or more candidates shall hold that office. Nominations and elections, then, each end one stage of party struggle. A nomination is the outcome of an *intra*party contest; in other words, it constitutes a victory of one party faction over the other faction or factions, all of which may have been supporting separate aspirants for the candidacy. An election is the result of *inter*-party conflict; it comprises a triumph for the party whose candidate is elected to office, or at least the faction of the party that first promoted the candidate. (One should remember, of course, that candidates often may win nomination or election without intraparty or interparty opposition: no one runs against them.)

Today most nominations and all elections are functions of the government. Elections, of course, were governmental functions from the outset; they existed before parties did. By contrast, for a long time nominations, whether by primary election or in caucus or convention, were viewed as party affairs, or as the concerns of private organizations. Then, over the past century, States have enacted many laws controlling party affairs and nominations. Also, in the past two decades, partly because of certain federal Supreme Court decisions, most primary elections have come under the jurisdiction of Congress and of the State legislatures. Hence today in many States the primary elections and the general elections are governed by a code of State laws. In addition, some federal laws regulate both primary and general elections in which candidates are running for federal office; the future will probably see more of such federal laws. Since parties themselves are the objects of much legal regulation, other means for nominating candidates are also public rather than private matters. Thus nominations are linked with elections as stages in the choosing of public officials, and both are equally viewed today as governmental functions.

NOMINATIONS

The commonest means for nominating candidates for federal offices today is the primary election. Candidates for many State elective posts are chosen by the same method. However, there are other means for selecting candidates which are entitled to a brief note.

Nominating methods other than the direct primary

Write-in: The easiest, least expensive, and least effective means for nominating a candidate is by writing in his name on the general election ballot. Ballots in general provide blank spaces where the voter may insert the name of an individual for whom he wishes to vote in the event he does not choose to vote for any person whose name is printed on the official ballot. Usually the write-in procedure has little if any organization backing it; consequently it is almost certain to fail.

Petition: The petition is another means for nomination which may or may not have the support of an organization. In most States the election laws provide that an independent nomination may be procured for an individual who can submit petitions seeking to admit him to the ballot. These petitions must bear enough names of registered voters to equal either a certain percentage of the vote in a preceding election or a stipulated number. Sometimes a prospective candidate must deposit a specified sum of money which he will forfeit if he does not secure a required proportion of the total vote cast; the purpose of this rule is to block the names of publicity seekers from cluttering the ballot. One difficulty with this sort of nomination, especially when a large number of signatures must be obtained, is that many signatures may be erroneously written or even fraudulent. Sometimes eager citizens gather in the signatures. At other times, those circulating the petitions are paid a flat rate per signature. Not rarely, handwriting

"The County Election" by George Caleb Bingham.

experts have found, in the case of challenged petitions, that hundreds of names have been contributed by the same hand. The most common source of nomination by petition in federal elections is the minor parties, for whom primary elections may not be possible.

Caucus: The caucus comprises simply a gathering of party members or of a clique within a party. Today the caucus as a formal nominating device is relatively unimportant save for local offices. It does play one important nominating role at the national level: the party caucuses in Congress nominate the party candidates for the various congressional offices, including such posts as the House speakership and the standing committee chairmanships. *Informal* caucuses, however, are as abundant as ever. Behind practically all nominating conventions or elections stands a small group of leaders who put forward the candidates most likely to succeed.

Convention: The convention, which was also noted in the previous chapter, has to a great degree been displaced in the nominating process; however, it is still employed to choose many candidates. A national convention of each party chooses presidential candidates; in some southern States, the Republican Party makes wide use of conventions; and in many States, conventions select candidates for local offices.

In short, the convention has not surrendered all of its nominating functions to the primary, as many reformers half a century ago expected. These reformers denounced conventions as tools of the party bosses and of "special interests." In a sense, perhaps, conventions were the tools of the bosses; however, party leaders have since learned ways by which they can manipulate primary elections, which were depicted by their promoters as immune to party chicanery. It might also be said that conventions were the devices of special interests; yet the reformers themselves were no less a special interest or group of such interests. In other words, the "Old Guard" party factions controlled the conventions; the "reform" or "progressive" faction relied upon the primary to unseat them.

Moreover, the convention has at least two asserted advantages over the primary election. In the first place, a convention is able both to nominate candidates and to draft a platform; then it may reconcile, or at least attempt to reconcile, the details of the platform with the professed aims of the candidates. A primary election cannot produce a lengthy platform. In an effort to cope with this shortcoming, South Dakota once required that each party hold a convention before the primary, draft a platform, then condense it to eight words which were to appear on the ballot. The result was such programs as that of Major General Leonard Wood in 1920: "Patriotism, Prosperity, Peace, Agriculture Promoted, One Flag."[1] Why the General did not avail himself of his full quota of eight words is unknown. In any event, the law was repealed. Other States have tried to overcome this difficulty of the primary and have been equally unsuccessful.

The other asserted advantage of the convention is that it can assume a greater responsibility for candidates. It is true that a convention assembles

---

[1] Penniman, H. R., *Sait's American Parties and Elections* (New York: Appleton-Century-Crofts, 1952, 5th ed.), p. 383.

for no more than a few days to do its tasks; to assign collective responsibility in its case is very ticklish. Yet the convention usually follows its leaders; the leaders have party stature apart from their convention office, often occupying high elective posts in the government. By its direct power to hold convention leaders responsible, the public can indirectly hold the entire convention responsible. There is no comparable means for assigning responsibility in a primary election.

The direct primary

The direct primary today is used in every State to choose candidates for Congress and for a host of State and local offices. The primary developed, as indicated above, in opposition to the party factions that had become entrenched through the convention system. The primary was first instituted in 1868 in Pennsylvania, on a local scale. It was adopted in South Carolina in the 1890's for elections to many offices. By about the year 1900 strong pressure had built up to install it on a State-wide basis. Wisconsin and Oregon both adopted the State-wide primary in 1904; after that date it expanded quickly, first in the West and South, and finally in the East. However, as noted above, for certain offices other means of nomination are still used in some States. Furthermore, in a few States the parties hold preprimary conventions to give official endorsement to aspirants for the nomination.

Types of Primaries: There are two main types of primary elections for federal office: closed and open. The principal distinction between these types is in the strictness with which party lines are enforced. Figure 28 contains a facsimile of a ballot for each type of primary.

1. THE CLOSED PRIMARY. A closed primary is a primary election in which an individual may vote only for candidates from that party in which he can prove membership. In other words, the primary is "closed" to non-party members. The closed primary today is used in thirty-five States. There are various methods for proving party membership. According to one method, known as *enrolment,* when the voter registers he must state his party membership in order to vote in party primaries. If, as in California, he declines to state a party affiliation, he can vote only in non-partisan primaries such as for sheriff and county supervisors. If, on the other hand, he has declared a party affiliation, he is given a ballot for the party of which he has said he is a member. In some other States, enrolment occurs not at registration but at the primary.

Another means for enforcing the closed primary is termed the *challenge* system. In the States using this means, the voter must publicly ask at the polls for the ballot of one of the parties; then his right to vote for that party may be challenged by any party member present. He may be compelled to swear that he supported that party in the past, or that he will support it in the future. Of course, since voting is secret, it would be very difficult to sue any person for violating his oath.

The ballot for the closed primary, as shown in Figure 28, bears the names of all the aspirants in the party, grouped according to the offices

OFFICIAL REPUBLICAN PRIMARY BALLOT

6th Senatorial District   13th Congressional District

FOR PRESIDENT OF THE UNITED STATES
(Vote for One)
- [ ] RILEY ALVIN BENDER
- [ ] ROBERT A. TAFT
- [ ] HAROLD E. STASSEN

FOR GOVERNOR
(Vote for One)
- [ ] WILLIAM N. ERICKSON
- [ ] PARK LIVINGSTON
- [ ] ANTHONY A. POLLEY
- [ ] RICHARD YATES ROWE
- [ ] WILLIAM G. STRATTON

FOR LIEUTENANT GOVERNOR
(Vote for One)
- [ ] PATRICK S. CLARY
- [ ] JOHN D. BIGGS
- [ ] JOHN WILLIAM CHAPMAN

FOR SECRETARY OF STATE
(Vote for One)
- [ ] HAROLD R. COLLIER
- [ ] GEORGE R. HEDGES
- [ ] WARREN E. WRIGHT
- [ ] CHAS. F. CARPENTIER

FOR AUDITOR OF PUBLIC ACCOUNTS
(Vote for One)
- [ ] LOUIS E. NELSON
- [ ] RICHARD J. OGLESBY
- [ ] WILLIAM H. BROWN
- [ ] RALPH WALDO EMERSON
- [ ] JAMES E. HILL

OFFICIAL DEMOCRATIC PRIMARY BALLOT

7th Senatorial District   4th Congressional District

FOR PRESIDENT OF THE UNITED STATES
(Vote for One)
- [ ] ESTES KEFAUVER

FOR GOVERNOR
(Vote for One)
- [ ] ADLAI E. STEVENSON

FOR LIEUTENANT GOVERNOR
(Vote for One)
- [ ] SHERWOOD DIXON

FOR SECRETARY OF STATE
(Vote for One)
- [ ] EDWARD J. BARRETT

FOR AUDITOR OF PUBLIC ACCOUNTS
(Vote for One)
- [ ] BENJAMIN O. COOPER

FOR STATE TREASURER
(Vote for One)
- [ ] FRED A. CAIN

FOR ATTORNEY GENERAL
(Vote for One)
- [ ] JOSEPH P. BURKE
- [ ] IVAN A. ELLIOTT
- [ ] JAMES L. ...

FOR DELEGATES TO NATIONAL NOMINATING CONVENTION
4th Congressional District
(Vote for Two)
- [ ] LESLIE V. BECK
- [ ] PAULINE VYZRAL

FOR ALTERNATE DELEGATES TO NATIONAL NOMINATING CONVENTION
4th Congressional District
(Vote for Two)
- [ ] JOHN A. JOHNSON
- [ ] LEO F. KENNEDY

FOR STATE CENTRAL COMMITTEEMAN
(Vote for One)
- [ ] JOHN M. SZYMANSKI

FOR REPRESENTATIVE IN GENERAL ASSEMBLY
7th Senatorial District
(Vote for One)
- [ ] JOSEPH J. LELIVELT
- [ ] LeROY E. STEVENS
- [ ] WILLIAM E. MUSIL
- [ ] MICHAEL HUNT

FOR MEMBERS SENATORIAL COMMITTEE
7th Senatorial District
(Vote for Three)
- [ ] HARRY A. SULLIVAN

FOR STATE'S ATTORNEY OF THE COUNTY OF COOK, ILLINOIS
(Vote for One)
- [ ] JOHN GUTKNECHT
- [ ] JOHN S. BOYLE

FOR RECORDER OF DEEDS OF THE COUNTY OF COOK, ILLINOIS
(Vote for One)
- [ ] JOSEPH T. BARAN

FOR CLERK OF THE SUPERIOR COURT OF THE COUNTY OF COOK, ILLINOIS
(Vote for One)
- [ ] HENRY SONNENSCHEIN

FOR CLERK OF THE CIRCUIT COURT OF THE COUNTY OF COOK, ILLINOIS
(Vote for One)
- [ ] JOHN E. CONROY

FOR CORONER OF THE COUNTY OF COOK, ILLINOIS
(Vote for One)
- [ ] A. L. BRODIE

A. Portions of the Illinois "closed-primary" ballots.

SAMPLE PRIMARY ELECTION BALLOT
CLARK COUNTY
TUESDAY, SEPTEMBER 9, 1952

To Vote for a Person Mark a CROSS (X) in the Square at the right of the Name of the Person for Whom You Desire to vote

UNITED STATES SENATOR	Vote for One	STATE TREASURER	Vote for One	JUDGES OF THE SUPERIOR COURT Position No. 1—Non-Partisan	Vote for One
HENRY M. JACKSON	Democrat [ ]	EDWIN S. KIEHL	Democrat [ ]	CHARLES W. HALL	[ ]
CARL VIKING HOLMAN	Republican [ ]	CHARLES R. MAYBURY	Republican [ ]		[ ]
HARRY P. CAIN	Republican [ ]	WILLARD F. ROUSE	Republican [ ]		
ED F. OLDFIELD	Republican [ ]	PHIL H. GALLAGHER	Democrat [ ]	Position No. 2—Non-Partisan	Vote for One
	[ ]		[ ]	EUGENE G. CUSHING	[ ]
CONGRESSMAN-AT-LARGE	Vote for One	STATE AUDITOR	Vote for One		[ ]
FRANK T. BELL	Democrat [ ]	FLOYD OLES	Republican [ ]	STATE SENATOR—(17th District)	Vote for One
ALICE FRANKLIN BRYANT	Democrat [ ]	THOR A. ROMSTAD	Republican [ ]	DALE McMULLEN	Republican [ ]
NAT WASHINGTON	Democrat [ ]	CLIFF YELLE	Democrat [ ]	W. E. CARTY	Democrat [ ]
REUBEN T. SMILEY	Democrat [ ]		[ ]	HERBERT D. GREEN	Republican [ ]
DON MAGNUSON	Democrat [ ]	ATTORNEY GENERAL	Vote for One		[ ]
EPHRAIM D. MILLS	Republican [ ]	SMITH TROY	Democrat [ ]	STATE REPRESENTATIVE—(17th District)	
JANET TOURTELOTTE	Republican [ ]	DON EASTVOLD	Republican [ ]		Vote for Three
JOHN T. McCUTCHEON	Democrat [ ]		[ ]	MISS ELLA WINTLER	Republican [ ]
DAVID J. WILLIAMS	Republican [ ]	SUPERINTENDENT OF PUBLIC INSTRUCTION Non-Partisan	Vote for One	MARK V. HOLLIDAY	Democrat [ ]
AL CANWELL	Republican [ ]	PEARL A. WANAMAKER	Non-Partisan [ ]	MORRIS S. SWAN	Republican [ ]
TOM SMITH	Democrat [ ]	HENRY W. TURNER	Non-Partisan [ ]	C. A. ANDERSON	Republican [ ]
GLEN S. CORKERY	Republican [ ]	AGNES M. GEHRMAN	Non-Partisan [ ]	P. L. "Louie" RASMUSSEN	Republican [ ]
LINUS PEARSON	Republican [ ]			VERN TUCKER	Democrat [ ]
WILBUR R. P...	Republican [ ]			JOHN E. MORSE	Republican [ ]

B. A portion of the Washington "open-primary" ballot.

Figure 28. Primary Election Ballots.

sought. The voter marks an "X" in the space beside the names of the persons for whom he wishes to vote; but he votes for no more aspirants than there are offices to be filled. In California there is a unique variation in the closed primary ballot. There, by the practice known as *cross-filing*, an aspirant from one party may run, or file, in the primary of as many parties as he wishes; if he wins his own party's primary race, then he becomes the candidate for any other party whose primary he wins. Hence if an aspirant should become the candidate of both the Republican and the Democratic parties, he would be certain of election since he would have to compete with only the minor party candidates in the general elections. In the past, many individuals have succeeded in becoming the candidate of both major parties.

Before 1954, the ballots did not even carry the party affiliation of the candidate; then, in the 1954 primary, for the first time the California ballots carried the party affiliation of the candidate after his name. The results were striking: very few aspirants won candidacy in both major parties; moreover, the Democratic Party achieved a complete slate of candidates for State offices, a goal they had never before accomplished under the direct primary. This was impressive evidence that the former type of ballot favored the Republicans because of their "natural" party organization, that is, the informal support they enjoy from such business groups as chambers of commerce and local real estate boards.

2. THE OPEN PRIMARY. The open primary is a primary in which a voter may participate in choosing the candidates of any party regardless of his attachments. It prevails in thirteen States, all of them in the West. It is very instructive that this sort of primary, which tends to weaken party organization, like the non-partisan primary should have emerged in the section of the country that is typified by a fluid population and rapidly shifting party allegiances. The open primary is administered in several different ways. In some States the voter is given a ballot for each party, all ballots being identical in size and color. He marks one and, after folding it so that the party label cannot be seen, places it in a box for marked ballots; he folds the other ballots similarly and places them in a box for unmarked ballots. The contents of the second box are destroyed without being examined. In other States all parties appear on a single ballot in separate columns; the voter chooses candidates only in one party.

The State of Washington has a unique ballot, on which aspirants of all parties for a single office are grouped together; the voter may choose a candidate from one party for one office, and a candidate from a second party for another office. This is called the "blanket" primary.

The open primary has been criticized on two important grounds. In the first place, it is held to be destructive of party responsibility. That is, the candidate who finally is elected to office may owe his nomination to a large number of members of both parties. Since he is not absolutely indebted for his nomination to the party in whose name he ran for office, that party cannot be so responsible for his actions as it could be if it alone had placed him in nomination. In the second place, the open primary in fact makes it possible for voters of one party to invade the primary of another party, with the aim of choosing weak candidates. For example, if the Democrats were presenting only one aspirant for the office of State Governor and the Republicans were offering two, and if one of the Republicans was so weak that the Democrats would be certain to win the election against him, Democrats might vote in the Republican primary so as to make the weak Republican the candidate of his party for the office. In so doing, of course, the Democrats in any State except Washington would be sacrificing their right to vote for Democrats seeking all other offices, but they might willingly make this sacrifice in order to assure winning the one important office through the primary. Actually this is an imaginary situation that would require an exceptionally efficient Democratic Party organization to so educate its voters; yet it is a specter that has been evoked by party leaders hostile to the open primary. Perhaps the most important virtue of the open primary is that it gives added safeguards for the secrecy of voting, in that a person's party affiliation need not be disclosed at the polls or on the registration lists.

Procuring a Majority Vote in the Primary: In most States, the nominee securing the largest number of votes in the primary, whether or not it is a majority of the total cast, becomes the candidate of his party for the office. However, in some States it has appeared desirable to require further indication of party support if no nominee has won an absolute majority. Two different means are employed in the United States for establishing the existence of this support:

1. THE POST-PRIMARY CONVENTION. In Iowa and South Dakota, a post-primary convention is summoned when no aspirant for certain offices receives as much as thirty-five per cent of the vote. In Iowa the rule is used in the case of all State and local offices; in South Dakota it applies to the nominations for the offices of Governor, United States Senator, and United States Representative. This sort of convention has been called with great rarity, since almost invariably one aspirant wins at least the minimum percentage, if not a clear majority, in these States.

2. THE RUN-OFF PRIMARY. In eleven southern States, in the event no aspirant wins a clear majority, the two individuals at the top of the list must run in a second primary. Most people find this procedure desirable there since victory in the Democratic primary is tantamount to election. On the surface it might appear that the aspirant who won the largest number of votes in the first election would be certain of triumph in the run-off; however, this is not necessarily the case. It can happen, and has happened, that the leading aspirant in the first election is an adherent of some type of legislation that many powerful southern interests oppose, such as the establishment of a federal Fair Employment Practices Commission. Under these circumstances the opponents of this sort of measure, who perhaps have divided their votes among several nominees in the first primary, will so concentrate their efforts in the run-off that they can give their candidate a majority even though he lagged considerably in the first trial. For example, in North Carolina in 1950, incumbent Senator Frank P. Graham

secured the largest number of votes, although not a majority, in the primary; but in the run-off he was defeated by Willis Smith. The positions of Graham and Smith were precisely as indicated above.

Criticisms of the Direct Primary: Many people, including both disgruntled machine politicians and other observers who have a less direct personal stake in the matter, have leveled severe criticisms at the direct primary as a nominating procedure. Two of these criticisms have already been noted: that the primary tends to dissolve party bonds and party responsibility; and that the primary cannot yield a platform with the candidates. Other important criticisms are:

1. The primary imposes another duty upon the already overburdened voter. In some areas voters troop to the polls at least once a year for general elections to fill political offices; obliging them to name the candidates in the primaries is demanding more than they can reasonably and intelligently perform. Certain election laws tacitly acknowledge the fact that voters cannot know the qualifications of all aspirants by requiring that names be rotated on the ballots, lest one person whose name might appear always at the first of the list should profit from this accident.

2. The primary adds to the public cost of electing officials. Since primaries generally fall under the supervision of the government, they add to the tax load. They also require further expenditures on the part of office-seekers; for instance, a nine-month leave, as against a three-month leave from work, is often necessary.

3. Where there is no post-primary convention or run-off election, the primary may yield minority candidates. This shortcoming is exaggerated by the fact that only a small proportion of registered voters take part in primary elections; hence an individual supported by a small but energetic and well-organized faction of the party may win the nomination. It is significant that in the South, where the Democratic primary is often more important than the general election, three or four times as many voters may participate in the primary as in the general election. This situation probably derives from the fact that the party segments that are contesting the nomination are more active in getting out the vote for the primary than the whole party is for the general election.

GENERAL ELECTIONS

General elections are the elections at which the voters choose their officeholders. Such elections have a discontinuous history reaching back to prehistoric times. Today they have become so highly organized that for most people they require nothing more complicated than marking a ballot containing the names of the candidates; yet they are for the people certainly the most exciting aspect of the governmental process.

The Australian ballot

The Australian ballot, which gets its name from the country in which it originated, is prepared and distributed by the government. In the United

States every State save South Carolina employs it. Voters in the past have had many ways for expressing their will. The commonest means of all—one still used in legislatures and conventions—is by voice vote, or *viva voce*. Sometimes, on matters requiring only a simple "yes" or "no" response, voters have used colored beans, balls, or other objects. During the nineteenth century in the United States, when it became possible to assume that most voters could read, political parties began to print ballots and issue them to voters as they entered the polls. Since the ballots contained, of course, only the candidates of the party concerned, and since they were usually on paper of distinguishing color, they made it easy for party officials to determine how people were voting and whether or not those persons whom they had influenced or bribed to vote for their candidates had carried out their part of the bargain. Beginning with Kentucky in 1880, one American State after another instituted the ballot that had been developed in Australia in the 1850's, until all but South Carolina required it by law. Not only is the Australian ballot produced by the State; it also contains the names of candidates of all parties that have a right to appear on the ballot, and it is marked secretly in a voting booth. There are two major forms of the Australian ballot, and each form has an important variant. Figure 29 gives examples of these forms.

The Office-Group Ballot: The office-group ballot, which is used in eighteen States, and is sometimes called the Massachusetts ballot since it was first

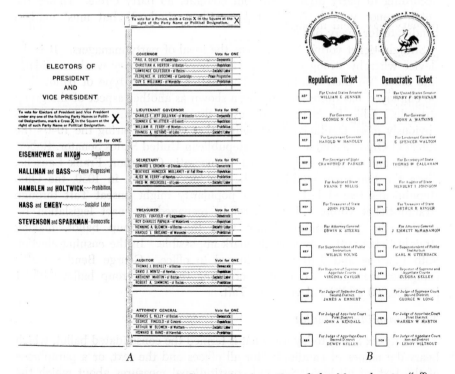

Figure 29. General Election Ballots. *A.* A portion of the Massachusetts "office-group" type of ballot. *B.* A portion of the Indiana "party-column" type of ballot.

employed there, lists the candidates according to the office they seek. That is, candidates for the presidency are in one block, each name followed by the party affiliation; candidates for the Senate and House may follow; next may be those for State and local positions. The voter indicates his choice by placing a mark, usually an X, in the blank spaces before the candidates' names.

The chief variant of the office-group ballot is found only in Pennsylvania. There the ballot is identical to that used in Massachusetts, save that at one side the name of each party is listed alone, accompanied by a large space, known as the "party circle," to be marked. If the voter places an X before the name of one of the parties, he indicates that he wishes to vote for all candidates of the party; in other words, he votes a "straight ticket." He then has no need to mark the names of individual candidates.

The Party-Column Ballot: The party-column ballot, which is used in twenty-nine States, and which is also called the Indiana ballot from its place of birth, lists the candidates in separate columns according to their parties. As on the Massachusetts ballot, there is a space beside the name of each candidate to be marked by the voter. At the top of each column is the name of the party, and sometimes a party emblem, together with a party circle for straight-ticket voting.

The variant of the Indiana ballot, which is employed in New Jersey, North Dakota, Washington, and Wyoming, similarly lists the candidates according to party attachments but contains no party circle. Hence the voter cannot vote a straight ticket with a single X, but must mark a candidate for every office.

Straight-ticket voting is, of course, the ideal of party managers. It is the device whereby strong candidates, it is hoped, will carry weak candidates into office "on their coattails." The matter of which type of ballot shall be employed has quite recently been shown as another aspect of the group struggle. Ohio for many years used the party-column ballot, which is obviously more conducive to straight-ticket voting. During the 1940's the voters of Ohio elected a powerful Republican United States Senator, Robert A. Taft, and an extremely popular Democratic Governor, Frank Lausche. Since the two men would both be seeking reelection in 1950, the Ohio Republicans feared lest Lausche's popularity might unseat Taft through straight-ticket voting. They therefore managed to enact legislation replacing the party-column ballot with the office-group ballot, making straight-ticket voting by a single mark impossible. In the ensuing election both Lausche and Taft were returned to office. George Bender, Taft's campaign manager, is quoted as crediting the office-group ballot with at least 150,000 additional votes for Taft.

The consolidated ballot

Twenty-six States today use what is termed the consolidated ballot, which bears the names of candidates for all offices and the text, or a paraphrase of the text, of all legislative and constitutional measures about which the voters have a choice. This may produce an enormous sheet of paper; Indiana voters once were faced with a ballot covering fourteen square feet. Other States may use two or more ballots at the same election, including perhaps one for national and State offices, a second for local offices, and a third for legislative and constitutional matters.

Voting machines

Voting machines (see Figure 30) today are authorized by law in forty-three States, and the law has been applied in thirty-eight. Use of the machines is compulsory in every precinct in the States of Connecticut, Delaware, Louisiana, Maryland, New York, and Rhode Island. They are employed widely in Florida, Illinois, Indiana, Iowa, New Jersey, Pennsylvania, and Washington; elsewhere they appear only in scattered urban precincts. On June 1, 1956, over 80,000 voting machines were in use in the nation.

The machines have several important advantages, some of which collide with the wishes of venal politicians. First, they make it impossible to manipulate the ballots or to stuff the ballot box, because there are neither ballots nor ballot boxes. Secrecy is provided in that the machine does not begin to function until a curtain has been pulled behind the voter; withdrawing the curtain to provide an exit registers the vote and clears the machine for the next voter. Too, the machines are constructed so as to remove almost all possibility of casting a defective ballot. For instance, if a voter using a paper ballot should inadvertently mark both the Democratic and Republican candidates for Governor, he would lose his vote for that office and in some States invalidate the entire ballot. With a voting machine, however, he could not move the lever to vote for any other candidate for an office once he had voted for one candidate.

Although voting machines cost more than $1,000 apiece, and impose hauling and storage costs, they still materially reduce election costs. They obviate the expense of printing ballots. Because the total vote at the end of the day need only be read from the machine, they further reduce the number of polling officials needed, and the time the officials work. Since they make counting faster, they offer the possibility of lessening the number of voting places. The principal shortcoming of voting machines appears to be that they confuse the voter; one study indicates that more straight tickets are cast on machines than have been cast on paper ballots during previous elections in the same locality. Also the machines are not an answer to most forms of vote corruption, and even lend themselves to new forms. Voters may still be bribed. The machine counter may be tampered with before the polls open. Unscrupulous officials may enter and remain behind the curtain with the voter as he moves the levers in order to control the vote. Finally, the recording of the count may still be distorted. Early machines had a tendency to break down fairly often; modern machines, however, are mechanically excellent, with almost negligible maintenance costs. The chief barriers to their use seem to be their apparently high initial cost and the opposition of those who have a vested interest in paper ballots.

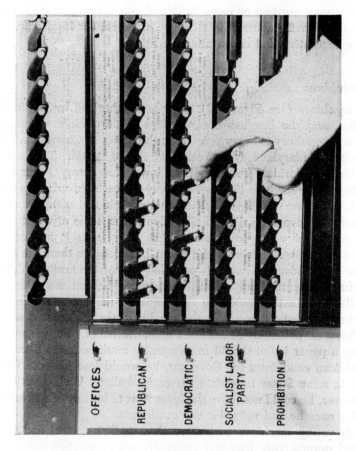

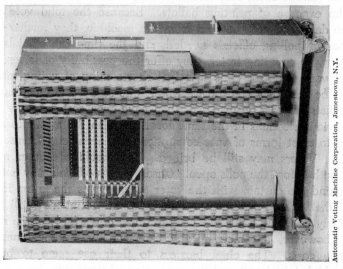

Figure 30.   A Voting Machine.

ELECTION ADMINISTRATION

Polling places

The geographic unit for voting purposes is the precinct or election district. There are about 154,000 precincts and districts in the United States. Consequently, with a total population in the United States of more than 168,000,000 in 1956, the average precinct has about 1,100 people and about 700 potential voters; actually fewer than 300 votes were cast in the average precinct during the 1956 presidential election, and fewer than 300 in the 1954 congressional elections. Therefore most voters live close to the polling place in their precinct or election district. The place is apt to be crowded with voters only just after it opens and just before it closes (although party watchers or hangers-on may abound at all times). The polls are usually open about twelve hours on election day.

The polling place itself may be situated in either a public or a private building. Until the beginning of the twentieth century, almost all voting was conducted in private buildings, such as shops and homes. However, this sort of locale is expensive for the government, which has to pay rent; it sometimes may be a lucrative source of graft for machine politicians, who can collect a portion of the rent in exchange for having negotiated the rental agreement; and the surroundings may degrade the election process. Today, by contrast, some States authorize the use of public buildings, such as schools and firehouses; and others, such as Michigan, require their use. In this respect the United States differs from most other major countries, where the employment of public buildings is mandatory.

Precinct voting officials

Although conditions may vary somewhat from one precinct to another, in general there are three chief officials at each polling place, termed judges or inspectors. Usually they have the assistance of two clerks. In most places these boards are bipartisan; no more than two of the three judges or inspectors may belong to the same party. The principle appears to be that Democrats will check Republicans, and vice versa. In fact, collusion is quite possible; judges of the two major parties may agree to withhold votes from a third or minor party, which is not represented on the precinct board, or they may exchange presidential ballots for congressional ballots. Precinct officials usually are chosen by a local governing body such as a town council, or by a county election board. These appointments are sponsored by the precinct committeeman where the party organization is strong; in other areas, applications are sought from the general population. Only in a few cases is any knowledge of election laws demanded, tested, and proved. Precinct boards in most places administer registration, primary elections, and general elections.

Election procedure

Election procedure includes the opening of the polls, the voting itself, and the counting of the ballots. An hour or less before the polls open the judges or inspectors arrive and examine either the ballot boxes, to see that they are empty, or the voting machines, to see that no votes have been tallied on the counters. The boxes or machines are then locked. As the voters appear they must identify themselves and sometimes sign their names for comparison with the register. One judge hands each voter a ballot; in some States the ballot carries a detachable stub with a number that is placed after the voter's name. The voter then retires to a booth to vote. When he finishes, if paper ballots are used, he gives the ballot to another judge, who puts it in the box. Where the ballots have numbered stubs, the number is compared with that listed after the voter's name; the stub is then removed so that the ballot cannot later be identified. The stub is designed to prevent a voter from bringing a previously marked ballot into the polling place and leaving with a clean ballot which likewise can be marked outside, resulting in an endless chain process called the "Tasmanian Dodge."

Ballot counting generally does not begin until after the polls have closed, which usually takes place about twelve hours after they open except, as sometimes happens, when all the registered voters in the precinct have cast their ballots. In precincts using machines, all that is needed is to unlock the machines and read the counters. Elsewhere the tallying may take many hours. Often disputes will arise and errors occur, adding to the time consumed. Since the board may have been in attendance for twelve hours or more prior to the counting, its members are neither alert nor calm; hence to shorten their work they may arrive at peculiar compromises over counting disputes. To remove this difficulty, some States have installed double election boards, one to supervise the voting and the other to count the ballots.

When the results are finally known, the precinct totals are sent to a central board. Unofficial results, which are rarely much different from the final count, are available early in the morning after an election. The official tally is not known until after the county and State canvasses, which take place some days or weeks after election day. The ballots are preserved for a considerable period after the official canvass, in case a recount is demanded. Long before this time, however, the people normally have accepted the verdict of the polls and the newly elected officials have prepared to enter their governmental posts.

QUESTIONS AND PROBLEMS

1. Name and describe briefly the various methods for nominating candidates for office.

2. Compare the costs and results of the convention and the direct primary systems of nominating candidates.

3. Contrast the workings of the closed and the open primaries. Which is more common? Are there degrees of "openness"?

4. Does the primary election insure that a candidate will represent a majority of the voters of his party? Explain your answer.

5. Identify briefly the following terms: *viva voce;* Australian ballot; office-group ballot; party-column ballot; straight-ticket voting; voting precinct.

6 Describe the process of election administration.

16. Electing Congress

Remington Rand

I<small>N EVERY</small> even-numbered year the voters of the United States elect a new Congress, their national legislature. That is to say, in those years they name all the 435 members of the House of Representatives. At the same time, they choose one-third, or a few more than one-third, of the 96 members of the Senate; although thanks to the overlapping six-year terms of Senators the voters may change only a minority of its membership at any given election, yet in three successive elections the people may elect an entirely new Senate. Thus the people determine who shall be their national legislators.

ELECTORAL AREAS

Every congressman is elected from a specific geographic area by some of the people residing in that area. These people, whether or not they voted or could vote for the congressman, individually are termed "constituents" and all together a "constituency" (a term sometimes loosely applied to the district rather than to its residents). The constituents or constituency is what the congressman represents in Washington.

There is a great difference between the electoral area of a Senator and that of a Representative. Every Senator represents a State; the citizens of the entire State are his constituency. By contrast, a Representative, with few exceptions, represents a congressional district that is smaller than a State. In the Eighty-fifth Congress the exceptions are the single congressmen from Delaware, Nevada, Vermont, and Wyoming—four States whose population is so small that each is assigned only one Representative—so that the single electoral area is coterminous with the State; and the congressmen-at-large from Connecticut, New Mexico, North Dakota, Texas, and Washington, five States which all have more than one Representative but which, for reasons to be discussed later in this chapter, have been unable to fix electoral areas for every Representative.

Apportionment of Representatives

Members of the House of Representatives are apportioned among the States according to their respective populations. Foreseeing that the population in some sections of the country might increase more rapidly than that in others, the Founding Fathers provided that Congress should calculate the apportionment on the basis of a national census, which was to be taken every ten years (Art. I, sec. 1, cl. 3). Thus the census, which now occupies a major rank in the Department of Commerce, was originated partly for the purpose of distributing the seats in the House.

Today the apportionment is computed not by Congress but in the office of the President. Congress has by law provided that after each census the President shall notify the House of the population of each State and the number of members assigned to each State. Congress has ceded the initiation of apportionment to the executive branch because the apportionment evoked so much partisan sentiment and loyalty to State interests that the House was unable to implement its power. Beginning with the first census in 1790, Congress drafted a reapportionment in keeping with every census through that of 1910. After the 1920 census so many States would have lost members (unless the seats were so increased in number as to make the House unmanageable) that their delegations were able to block all action. Although the Constitution plainly directs that seats in the House shall be redistributed after each census, there is no means for compelling Congress to act. Finally, in 1929 Congress enacted the present rule.

Henceforth the total membership is to be fixed at 435; actually, since no Congress may bind the action of its successors, the failure of Congress

---

Univac: An automatic calculating machine that was used by the Columbia Broadcasting System on election night to store information about the past voting patterns of the nation and the early voting results in order to forecast the trend of the presidential elections. The Central Computer is in the background and the Supervisory Control panel is in the foreground. Information is stored inside the Central Computer cabinet. The tape-handling machines at the right feed facts into the computer and take off the results of computations. Experience in 1954 showed that not enough was known about patterns of change in voting to set the machine accurately at early stages of the election.

to change the total since immediately after the census of 1910 may best be attributed to the inability of the members to agree on any other number. After the decennial census has been completed, mathematicians in the White House Office divide the total population of the United States by 435 to obtain the ratio of representation. Then, using one of the several complex possible methods, the mathematicians calculate the number of seats to which each State is entitled. These data, after being sent to Congress, are transmitted by the Clerk of the House to every State Governor.

After each census it may be expected that some States will lose, and others gain, seats, reflecting the population changes of the preceding ten years. In 1950, Caalifornia gained seven seats; Florida, two; and Maryland, Michigan, Texas, Virginia, and Washington, one each. Meantime Pennsylvania lost three; Missouri, New York, and Oklahoma, two apiece; and Arkansas, Illinois, Kentucky, Mississippi, and Tennessee, one each. These changes only mirror the greatly increased population of the West Coast, Miami, Houston, Dallas, Detroit, and Washington, D.C., along with the rather slowly rising or actually declining population of the industrial Middle Atlantic region and of the agrarian parts of the South and Midwest. The map in Figure 31 shows how the 1952 reapportionment only continued a trend that has been going on since 1912.

Establishing congressional districts

After the seats have been apportioned among the States following a census, and the State Governors have been duly notified of the size of their congressional delegations, each State with more than one Representative

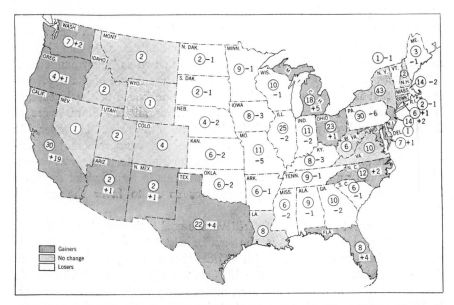

Figure 31. Changes in State Representation in the House Since 1912. Figures in circles stand for the total number of Representatives per State. Gains and losses are shown by plus and minus signs outside the circled figure in each State.

is to be divided by its legislature into as many congressional districts as there are Representatives from the State. Congress has in the past enacted several laws to regulate the districting within States, providing among other things that the districts must be compact, contiguous, and as nearly as possible equal in population. However, in the face of these congressional enactments the State assemblies continue to draw many district lines according to the relative power of the several factions in the respective assemblies; for there is no means for compelling State assemblies to heed congressional directions.

The districting process, then, affords another battleground for the struggle among political groups. Sometimes the opposing forces in an assembly are so nearly equal that after an apportionment giving a State changed representation it may be impossible for the assemblymen to agree upon new district lines. Under these circumstances one, or even two, of the members of the House will be elected "at-large," or with the whole State as a congressional district, a situation which in 1956 prevailed in Connecticut, New Mexico, North Dakota, Texas, and Washington.

Usually, however, there is not so close a balance of forces in the State assembly. Under conditions of markedly unequal forces, the groups that are superior tend to set the district lines in a manner that will be most advantageous to themselves without so enraging the minority that it will not collaborate in legislation. There are two principal types of contest that arise over the districting process: (1) a regional group clash, especially between rural interests and urban interests; and (2) a partisan dispute, between Democrats and Republicans. To satisfy their ends, the stronger forces may manipulate district boundaries in either one of two ways: (1) they may establish a pattern of districts in which one district has two or three times as great a population as certain others; and (2) they may draw districts with very irregular limits so as to include only selected groups within the districts, a practice known as "gerrymandering."

The Rural-Urban Clash: One outstanding characteristic of State governments is that in virtually every State at least one house of the legislature is dominated by rural, agrarian interests. After all, the States were at first chiefly rural; only later in their history did cities arise. However, the rural groups that had secured control at the first were reluctant to surrender their power. The districting within the States for their own assemblies favors the rural interests; and these interests in turn district the State for the national House of Representatives so as to favor the agrarian groups.

The commonest means used to achieve this goal is the creation of districts greatly unequal in population, the smaller districts being predominantly rural and the larger, urban. With 435 districts and 150,000,000 people in the United States according to the 1950 census, the average district should have about 345,000 people; however, States rarely settle upon the average. In 1954 the State showing the greatest disparity in the population of congressional districts was Texas; there the Eighth District (metropolitan Houston) contained 806,701 people according to the 1950 census, whereas

the Fourth contained 227,735 and the Seventeenth, 226,739. The Houston
district was the most populous in the country; the least was the South
Dakota Second, with 159,099. Other metropolitan districts were and usually
are similarly oversized. The Georgia district that includes Atlanta has a
population of 618,431; the Alabama district containing Birmingham, 558,-
928; Cook County, Illinois (Chicago), districts have more residents than
those of downstate Illinois.

The main consequence of this districting technique is that the agricultural
interests of the nation have a disproportionately large representation in the
House. Figure 32 shows the percentage
by which the average population of each
of four types of congressional districts—
rural Democratic, rural Republican, urban
Republican, and urban Democratic—either
exceeds or falls short of the average population of all congressional districts in each
State in which these districts are located.
An urban district is one containing one city
of 100,000 or more people according to the
1950 census; all other districts are rural.
A district is identified with one party or the
other if it elected a Representative from
that party in both the 1952 and the 1954
elections; twenty-eight other districts are
omitted. (Eleven seats elected from a
State at large are also omitted.) There
are 111 rural Democratic districts (74 in
the eleven southern States); 122 rural
Republican (3 in the South); 70 urban
Republican (2 in the South); and 93 urban
Democratic (23 in the South).

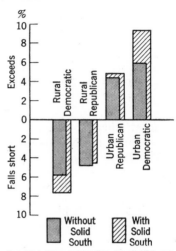

Computed from information by district contained in a speech by Senator Paul H.
Douglas before the Senate, mimeographed
release of March 26, 1956, citing in turn an
unpublished manuscript of Mr. Gus Tyler

**Figure 32. The Rural Advan-
tage in House Apportionment,
Regardless of Party.** Percentage
by which the average populations
of four different types of congressional districts either exceed or fall
short of the average population of
all congressional districts in their
State.

The significant point to observe in this
figure is that so far as the drawing of congressional district lines is concerned the
rural areas, regardless of which major party
predominates, have the advantage over the
urban areas. That is, both Democratic and Republican *rural* districts tend
to have smaller populations than the average district, and both Democratic and Republican *urban* districts tend to have larger populations than
the average district. In other words, rural areas across the country tend
to be overrepresented in Congress, and urban areas tend to be underrepresented. This advantage for the rural areas stems from the fact that
State legislatures, which lay out congressional districts, are dominated by
rural areas themselves. It is noteworthy that the disproportion is greater
in the South than in the remainder of the country, partly because it is more
rural than the rest of the country; also, because it is dominated by one
party, there is little if any possibility of gerrymandering according to party

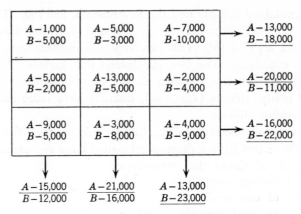

Figure 33. The Mechanics of Gerrymandering. Note that if the State (or other governmental unit) were cut into three districts horizontally, Party B would thereafter win two out of three districts whereas if it were cut vertically, Party A would win two of the three districts.

concentrations, a practice which further aggravates inequalities of apportionment in the North and West.

The Party Dispute: Although, as Figure 32 reveals, there is some connection between political party membership and a disproportion in the population of congressional districts, the chief impact of party membership upon legislative districting has to do with the actual contours of the districts, that is, the areas they include. Each of the two major parties in a State legislature normally aims to have the State districted according to its wishes; for the boundaries of the congressional districts play a large role in determining the percentage of seats that each party will hold in the State's entire delegation to Congress. One outstanding trait of politics is that there are many "blocs" of voters distributed according to geographic areas; that is to say, there are a great number of small land units—precincts, wards, townships, and even counties—in which one party is preponderant. Furthermore, barring an extraordinary change in the economic, social, or demographic complexion of a given unit, the dominance enjoyed by the party is sufficiently permanent that it may be assumed in any given election. This concentration results not from the fact that Democrats or Republicans tend to flock together but from the fact that a common background of social, economic, and regional interests is apt to induce most people of a specific locality to attach themselves to the same party. For example, northern suburban areas are usually Republican; southern rural districts are generally Democratic.

Because American voters are often formed in blocs, the majority party in the State legislature can draw the lines of congressional districts in such a way that although the districts may have relatively equal populations they will include utterly different patterns of party affiliation and concentration. As an illustration, let us assume a State to which three Representatives have been assigned; the State has nine counties; each congressional district shall include three counties. The approximate vote of each county is known in advance. If party *A* controls the assembly, it will draw the districts vertically, or from north to south, so as to carry two of the three. If party *B* controls the assembly, it will draw the districts horizontally, or from west to east, so that it can carry two (see Figure 33). Notice that when the districts are drawn vertically, *A*'s margin of victory in either of the two districts it carries is smaller than its margin of defeat in the district it loses; the

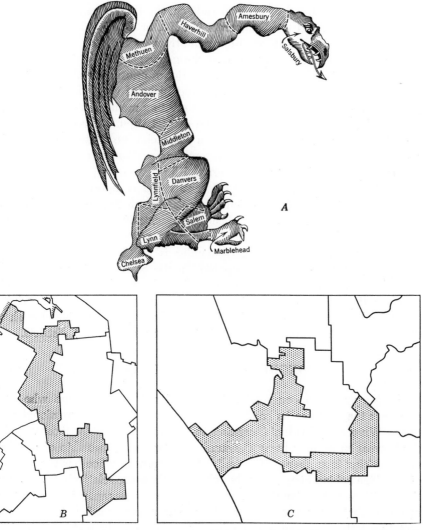

Figure 34. The Original Gerrymander and the Gerrymanders of the New York Twelfth and California Twenty-sixth Districts Today. *A*. The original "Gerrymander," so named because of the distorted district's resemblance to a salamander; Governor Gerry was the power behind the peculiar districting. *B*. The "Brooklyn baseball rooter," the New York Twelfth District, was carved out of strong Democratic areas to assure a Republican district where none had existed before. *C*. The "tin lizzie," California's Twenty-sixth District, was designed to collect various Democratic strongholds into a single district so as to allow the surrounding districts a greater chance of electing Republican congressmen.

same holds true for *B* when the districts are laid out horizontally. Indeed, *A* actually has fewer votes than *B* in the entire State, 49,000 to 51,000; yet by careful planning of the district limits *A* can elect two congressmen to *B*'s one. This illustration, it must be admitted, portrays an imaginary situation. However, in many of the States that send large delegations to the House, the lines are drawn so that a small popular majority may be translated into a great edge in the delegation itself. For example, in 1952, in the total congressional vote in all districts in Indiana, the Republicans had 1,094,000 ballots, or 56.5%, and the Democrats 831,000, or 42.9%. Yet the Republicans elected ten of the eleven Representatives, or 90.9%.

This type of districting is known as the *gerrymander.* In its exact sense, a gerrymander is an act of creating a district of unusual or absurd shape or size so as to comprehend several scattered blocs of voters attached to one party, thus increasing the possibilities of electing members of the dominant party. The term may also connote the district itself. The expression was coined in the early 1800's to describe a Massachusetts State legislative district—not a congressional district—resembling a *salamander,* that would be advantageous to the party of Governor Elbridge *Gerry.* The best-known gerrymander devised after the 1950 census and reapportionment was the New York Twelfth District, which connects enough Republican enclaves in Brooklyn to elect the only Republican Representative from that borough in Congress; it has the appearance of an enraged Brooklyn baseball fan. Another famous present-day gerrymander is the Twenty-sixth California "tin lizzie" District, the most populous in the State, which was drawn to include as many Democrats as possible in order to insure Republican victories in the adjacent districts. Figure 34 shows a copy of the original gerrymander cartoon of the artist Gilbert Stuart, and also gives the shape of the present-day Brooklyn (12th) and Los Angeles (26th) districts.

CONGRESSIONAL NOMINATIONS

The purpose of a congressional nomination is to determine who shall represent the party as its candidate in the forthcoming congressional elections. When an individual is seeking nomination, perhaps the most valuable single weapon he may have is incumbency, or the sponsorship of a voluntarily retiring incumbent. The individual already in office has the prestige of the office behind him; and, although today there are relatively few appointive positions not under the merit system, the congressman is in charge of much of what patronage remains. It is quite rare that a Senator or Representative fails to secure a renomination he is actively seeking. In 1938 President Roosevelt campaigned in several southern States at the time of their Democratic primary elections, seeking to block the candidacy of those individuals who opposed the New Deal. Roosevelt was not very successful in his efforts to influence these nominations. This episode is often cited as an illustration of the impotence of the chief executive when he tries to oust members of Congress. Since all the incumbent Senators were nominated regardless of Roosevelt's position on his candidacy, the episode also demonstrates the fact that it is extremely difficult to deny an incumbent Senator—or Representative, for that matter—the nomination of his party.

Concerning the choice of a candidate by the party out of power, it appears that more often than not the aspirant commanding the largest sum of money is apt to win the prize. Of course, there have been many instances in which an individual of exceptional prestige or organizational ability has succeeded in winning the nomination. The crucial point is whether the aspirant can either capture the support of the dominant faction in the party organization, or transform into the dominant faction a lesser faction that is backing him. If he can perform either of these alternatives he will secure the candidacy; if he cannot perform either, he will not be nominated.

The actual mechanics of the nominating process have been analyzed at length in the preceding chapter. It suffices to say that in most States today congressional candidates are nominated in direct primary elections; that a simple plurality in the bulk of these States wins the nomination; and that in a few States, when no person receives a majority in the primary, the candidate is finally chosen in a second, "run-off" primary, or in a convention.

CONGRESSIONAL CAMPAIGNS

The local aspect

Congressional campaigns are waged to a large extent on local issues; and the brunt of the campaign is shouldered by the organization of the electoral area concerned—the State or the district group, depending upon whether the election is for the Senate or the House. The campaign, then, to a great degree embraces discussions of what the national government has done or is going to do with respect to local problems; in his campaign the incumbent himself stresses what he, rather than the national government, has done or plans to do. In 1954 a typical congressional campaign was that of Republican Representative Charles S. Gubser, candidate for reelection from the California Tenth District (San Benito, Santa Clara, and Santa Cruz counties). Gubser's campaign literature claimed twenty-six accomplishments for his current term. Of these accomplishments, twenty-two are directly related to the concerns of his district (marked with asterisk):

* Brought $21,000,000 V.A. Hospital to Palo Alto
* Won Reber Plan Survey Funds
* Fought for More Hospital Funds for California
* Met Humanitarian Needs Here
* Active in Narcotic Education Legislation
* Led Fight to Restore Local Airport Funds
* Prevented Removal of Navigation Aids from San Jose Airport
* Worked for Prune Price Support and Export Program
* Helped Move $5 Million Worth of Santa Clara County Prunes
* Helped Move Multi-Millions in Canned Peaches-Apricots
* Helped Get Funds for Mexican Fruit Fly Fight
* Worked for Better Domestic Quicksilver Production and Prices
  Gained Approval for American Business Census
* Supported Bill for $1.3 Million Moffett Field Program
* Worked for Port of Redwood City Facilities

     * Corrected Injustices against Local Foreign Born
     * Presented Gubser Plan to Alleviate 20% of Our Water Shortage
      Supported the Eisenhower Legislative Program
      Fought Waste on the National Level
      Helped Reduce Excise Taxes
     * Made Possible Additional TB Beds for Santa Clara County
     * Appointments Made on Merit, not Politics
     * Fought for Postoffice and Civil Service Employe Pay Raises
     * Active Supporter of Postoffice and Civil Service Programs
     * Supported Realistic Programs of Old Age Security
     * Supported First Constructive Step for Solution of Health Insurance Problems

Congressional campaign committees

Congressional candidates may also look for support to the congressional campaign committees. Each major party has such a committee in each chamber of Congress. In the House the committee of each party is made up of one member from each State which has at least one Representative from the party. The State delegations decide which of their members shall be on the campaign committee. In the Senate the committee members are named by the chairman of their respective Senate party conferences or caucuses. These committees are not subordinate to, but are coordinate with, the national party organizations; in other words, they do not receive instructions from the national committee. The principal campaign activities of the committees include soliciting funds, providing speakers, and working to unify party support for the candidates. They concentrate their efforts upon closely contested districts, since the loss of only a few districts may entail the loss of the majority in either house to the opposing party.

THE ELECTION PROPER

The election proper occurs, in every State save Maine, on the first Tuesday after the first Monday of November in every even-numbered year. The earlier election in Maine is based on an escape clause in the federal statute fixing the time of elections, which exempts from the requirements of the statute any State that would have to amend its constitution in order to comply; the election date in Maine is established by a provision in the Maine constitution. Over a century ago there arose a notion that Maine afforded a barometer for election trends throughout the country: "As Maine goes, so goes the nation." After the 1936 Republican disaster, James Farley amended the axiom to read: "As Maine goes, so goes Vermont." Actually, Dr. J. Gordon Hall has shown that, in six of the seven elections between 1944 and 1956, the vote for congressional candidates of the Republican Party in Maine has generally moved in the opposite direction from the vote for Republican candidates in the nation as a whole.

There appear to be two major differences between presidential-year elections and midterm elections. The first difference is sheerly quantitative; as shown in Figure 21, far more votes are cast in the years of presidential elections than in those of midterm elections. The explanation is simple: as public opinion polls unanimously show, fewer voters know the names of congressional candidates than know the names of presidential candidates. The election of congressmen simply does not evoke the interest that the election of a President does. Hence less than half the adults of voting age go to the polls in a midterm election.

The other great difference between midterm and presidential year elections is that in the presidential year the same party almost always carries both the executive and the legislative branch; but in the midterm elections, the presidential party almost always loses representation in Congress, and sometimes loses its majority.

There are exceptions to both rules. In 1956, for the first time since 1848, the President and the congressional majorities were of different parties. The voters re-elected President Eisenhower by a great majority, but chose at the same time a majority of Democrats in the House and Senate; on several other occasions, either the House or the Senate alone was of different political persuasion from that of the President. The second rule is pictured for the House in Figure 35, where each line connects a presidential year House election with the first succeeding midterm House election. The graph shows that in every midterm election beginning with that of 1882, save only that of 1934, the presidential party has lost seats in the House. Indeed, the Republican loss of five per cent in 1954 was trifling by comparison with the Democratic loss of thirty-two per cent in 1894; and out of these nineteen midterm elections, in eight the administration party has become the minority group in the House. Apparently the midterm

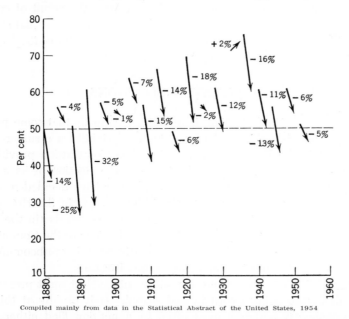

Compiled mainly from data in the Statistical Abstract of the United States, 1954

Figure 35. Administration Party Losses (or Gains) in House Membership at Midterm Elections, 1880–1954. Note that the only gain ever registered by the party in power was in 1934, in the middle of Franklin Roosevelt's first term.

elections give the voters the opportunity to express their distaste for national policies, as they conflict with local interests.

The relationship between presidential and congressional elections offers a problem: does the presidential candidate bring about the election of congressmen; or do the congressional candidates effect the election of a President? Who, so to speak, rides into office on whose coattails? The solution of this problem is extremely difficult; as of today, it appears to depend upon certain facts about elections that cannot be extracted from the voting figures alone.

One new method for solving this problem that gives promise of success is based upon public opinion surveying. It was first determined what proportion of a sample of the population had in 1952 voted for Eisenhower or Stevenson on the ground of personalities, rather than on that of issues or party loyalty; this group would be the one to manifest a "coattail effect." This group was then further broken down in terms of how many had voted a straight ticket, since straight-ticket voting would specifically indicate this effect. It appeared that a far greater number of Democrats and independents had been induced by Eisenhower's personality to vote a straight Republican ticket than the number of Republicans and independents who were led by Stevenson's personality to vote a straight Democratic ticket. The conclusion was that if the average coattail effect of Eisenhower were spread evenly across the country it would account for the Republican victories in thirty-nine House elections and thirteen Senate elections. Hence the Republican majorities in both House and Senate of the Eighty-third Congress might well have been the result of congressmen who rode to office on Eisenhower's coattails. These data are not available for the study of previous elections, so that the coattail effect in the past cannot be computed by this method.

CONTESTED ELECTIONS

After a congressional election, it sometimes happens that some person— occasionally a defeated candidate—contests the right of a member-elect to take his seat in the House or the Senate. The Constitution provides that each house of Congress shall be the judge of the election of its members (Art. I, sec. 5, cl. 1). Since 1789 the two houses have decided nearly 700 cases involving challenged seats, the majority of them in the House. The two chambers employ similar bodies to hear these contests: in the Senate, the Standing Subcommittee on Privileges and Elections of the Committee on Rules and Administration; and in the House, the Standing Subcommittee on Elections of the Committee on House Administration.

At the opening of a new Congress, all members-elect must present their credentials before being sworn in and seated. It is usually at this point that the contest is initiated, most often by a petition filed either by the defeated candidate or by one or more private individuals, arguing that a specific member-elect is not entitled to his credentials and seat. Sometimes the chamber will then vote to deny the individual his seat until the appropriate committee has investigated the charges; at other times the member will be seated pending the investigation. Grounds for such contests may be that too much money was spent in the campaign, or that the candidate resorted to improper campaign practices, or simply that the election was fraudulent. In 1950, for example, the election of Senator John Butler of Maryland was bitterly contested, chiefly on the ground that outsiders, notably Senator Joseph McCarthy of Wisconsin, had intruded upon the Maryland election and had spread defamatory literature concerning Butler's opponent, incumbent Senator Millard Tydings. Butler was nevertheless seated, but not without strong criticism of the campaign methods utilized.

In 1952 the election of Senator Dennis Chavez of New Mexico was challenged on behalf of his opponent, Patrick Hurley, on the basis of election fraud. The election committee reported that it had unearthed evidence of fraud on both sides, and recommended that Chavez be unseated. In spite of this recommendation, and although Chavez as a Democrat belonged to the minority party, the Senate voted to seat him. In the past those who have contested an election have usually lost their cases; apart from this fact, the decisions have tended to favor the majority party. Today Congress inclines toward the belief that unless one-sided election fraud can be proved, the people of the State or district have in fact elected the challenged congressman, and they are entitled to the representative they have chosen.

Congress on occasion has been as bold to reject new members on moral and political grounds as it has been reluctant to refuse admission on charges of fraud at the polls. In 1900, for example, the House denied a seat to Brigham H. Roberts of Utah, on the ground that he was a polygamist; also, in 1918, it rejected Victor L. Berger, a Wisconsin Socialist who had been accused of sedition and un-American behavior in World War I. In these cases and in others, the House showed an inclination to establish qualifications for membership other than those specifically mentioned in the Constitution. There remains today some question whether such "additional" qualifications, if they may be so termed, would pass muster before the Supreme Court.

FILLING CONGRESSIONAL VACANCIES

Occasionally, because of the death, resignation, or expulsion of a congressman, a seat in the House or the Senate may become vacant. The means for filling a Senate vacancy are quite different from those in the House; for, as will be shown, a Senate vacancy may be filled almost immediately, whereas a vacant seat in the House may not be filled for several months. The reason for this probably lies in the fact that each State has only two Senators, and that a Senate vacancy means that the State is deprived of one-half of its representation in that chamber. This consideration is reinforced by the constitutional provision that no State without its permission may be denied an equal voice in the Senate (Art. V); the institution of two

Senators is a zealously guarded symbol of the equality of the States. By contrast, in 1956 only thirteen States had as few as two Representatives; therefore a House vacancy for the majority of States would not mean the loss of half their delegation. Moreover, there is no concern with State equality in the House.

House vacancies

With regard to the House, the Constitution provides that when there are vacancies in the delegation of any State, "the executive authority thereof shall issue writs of election to fill such vacancies" (Art. I, sec. 2, cl. 4). In other terms, the Governor of the State authorizes the voters to choose a new Representative. Sometimes the election is set at a date shortly after the vacancy occurs; at other times it may be postponed until the next general election to be held in the State, which perhaps does not occur until November. As a result, the House often does not have its full complement of 435 members. Recently there have been suggestions that since an atomic or hydrogen bomb explosion could wipe out the entire House, the Constitution should be amended so as to empower the governor to appoint a new delegation, in order that the national government would not cease to function.

Senate vacancies

So far as the Senate is concerned, the Constitution states that in the event of vacancies, "the executive authority of such State shall issue writs of election to fill such vacancies; provided, that the legislature of any State may empower the executive thereof to make temporary appointment until the people fill the vacancies by election as the legislature may direct." Thus, as in the case of the House, the Governor authorizes the voters to choose a new Senator; but, as distinct from the House, the legislature of the State may empower the Governor to appoint a new Senator who will serve until the election. The legislature always grants this power simply in response to the will of State political leaders that they should not lose their voice and equal vote in the Senate; hence no Senate seat is long vacant. As matters now stand, the Governor's appointee serves until the next election, which must occur no later than the regular senatorial election that falls in November of the next even-numbered year.

A Senator elected to fill a vacancy does not serve for six years; he serves only to the end of the unexpired term. However, his term commences with the election, not in the following January, so that the vacancy will be filled at once. Therefore such a Senator might serve only two months, if the term were scheduled to end in the following January.

FREQUENCY OF REELECTION TO CONGRESS

One of the most important characteristics of Congress is that in each house a large majority of the members have served more than one consecutive term. Figure 36 contains two graphs, one for the Senate and one

for the House. Each graph depicts the membership of the Eighty-second
Congress (1951–1953) at the end of 1951, and the Eighty-third Congress
(1953–1955), at the end of 1953. In the drawing of these graphs, fractional
terms were computed as whole terms. For example, any member of the
Eighty-second Congress who took office between January 3, 1949, and
January 2, 1951, was included in the hatched bar over "1." Thus these graphs
show how many consecutive times a congressman has been reelected. The
graphs show, as might be expected, that the curve of the number of members falls as the number of consecutive terms, or reelections, rises. In the
case of the House, at least, the average experience of members in the
Twentieth Century is about double what it was in the Nineteenth Century.
Another significant trait of Congress shown by these graphs is that whether
a given election keeps the majority party in power or whether it converts
the previously minority party into the majority party, the total change in
the personnel of Congress is relatively small. The Eighty-first and Eighty-
second Congresses each had a Democratic majority; the Eighty-third Con-

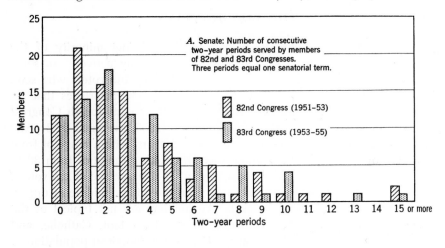

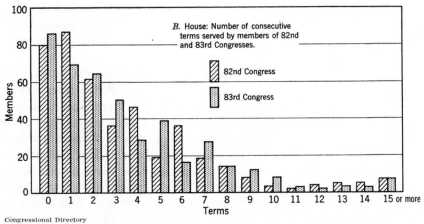

Congressional Directory

**Figure 36.   Number of Consecutive Two-year Periods Served by Members of the
House and Senate of the 82nd and 83rd Congresses.**

gress had a Republican majority. Therefore the Eighty-second Congress represented a maintenance of party control; the Eighty-third Congress represented a shift in party control. Note, then, how in the Senate of each Congress there were the same number of Senators—twelve—who had not held seats in the preceding two-year period. Note also how in the House there were eighty members of the Eighty-second Congress who had not served in the Eighty-first, and only eighty-six members of the Eighty-third who had not served in the Eighty-second. Moreover, a substantial proportion of these new members belonged to the same party as the previous Senator from the State or Representative from the district. The point to be made is that the most congressional electoral areas are more or less "safe"; they may be expected to elect the same member—or a member from the same party—term after term. Only a minority of States or districts waver in their party attachments. When a shift in party control occurs, then, it does not mean a great change in congressional personnel.

THE CONGRESSMAN

Congressmen, as individuals, belong to that distinct minority of the American population that is known as the "politically active." In some respects Senators and Representatives are not unlike the voters who send them to Congress; however, they do have certain characteristics that set them off from their constituents. Members of the Eighty-fourth Congress (1955–1957) at its first meeting, on January 5, 1955, averaged 52.2 years of age. In the Senate the average age was 57.2 years, with a range of from 36 to 87. In the House the average was 51.3, with a range of from 30 to 79. Thus both houses exceeded considerably the average age of the voters. Members of both houses tended to come from the middle-middle or upper-middle economic and social brackets. Again, they are not typical of the American population. They belonged to the Protestant, Catholic, and Hebrew faiths in about the same proportion as the American population at large. Somewhat more than half the members of each house had served in the American armed forces during either the First or the Second World War; this proportion is about twenty per cent higher than the proportion of veterans in the total adult male population.

In other and more specific ways congressmen differ from the voters. The majority of Senators and of Representatives have graduated from college. More than a majority in each chamber in 1955 listed themselves as lawyers by profession. It is a fact that a good number of these lawyers had never tried a case before the bar; but graduation from law school appears to be a stepping-stone for a career in politics, perhaps because law, like politics, is a "talking art." Other congressmen reported themselves as teachers— another group of "talking artists"; however, it appears that few who so described themselves had been teachers long or seriously. Still others indicated business or industrial activity. A handful termed themselves engineers or doctors. Congressmen, it is evident, have considerably more formal education than the average American.

Also, congressmen have had a great deal of political experience. In the last section it was noted that a large majority of congressmen have been reelected consecutively. Still others—whose inclusion in the graph would not greatly change the contours of the graph—have been reelected to nonconsecutive terms. Most congressmen, whether they are serving their first term or their tenth, have held some other elective office. A large number of Senators have been Representatives, and about an equal number have been State Governors. Both Senators and Representatives have previously been elected State legislators, city councilmen, or district attorneys. Even when congressmen have held no other political office, they frequently have occupied elective positions in private organizations such as the Junior Chamber of Commerce or the American Legion.

Congressmen therefore may be described as persons absorbed in the manipulation of interests, in dealing with people. They either share, or can persuade their listeners that they share, the concerns of a large number of individuals; although somewhat different from their constituents they have not been regarded as apart from the mainstream of American life and habits. Moreover, they have swayed their audiences to the belief that they can represent and symbolize the common concerns. In short, one can describe the congressman as Harold Laski once defined the President: "an uncommon man of common ideas."

QUESTIONS AND PROBLEMS

1. Summarize in 350 words how apportionment is carried out in the federal government, explaining particularly the part of the State legislatures in establishing districts for the House of Representatives.

2. Explain the various forces that cause emphasis on local needs among Representatives.

3. If you were a member of the Senate, and wished to contest the election of another member, how would you go about the task?

4. Contrast the means for filling vacancies in the House with those for filling vacancies in the Senate.

5. Describe the situation that exists regarding the length of service of the average congressman. How, if at all, do you think this situation influences legislation?

6. What are some of the social characteristics of congressmen? How do you suspect that they affect the quality of the laws produced?

17. Electing the President

Photograph by The New York Times

THE election of the President is probably the most important event, and certainly the most spectacular, in American domestic politics. A quadrennial occurrence, the presidential election appropriately falls in Leap Year (and century years as well, such as 1800 and 1900, which were not Leap Years), a period that legend has already dedicated to a singular type of courtship. As the maiden turns about to court the reluctant lad, so the presidential aspirants and their supporters court the people: "choosing the President" is perhaps more truly said as "the candidate causing himself to be chosen." Formally, the choice of a President requires two stages: nomination and election. In fact, the process is virtually continuous. Parties and potential candidates are unfaltering suitors of the electorate, only awaiting election year to announce their quest.

THE NOMINATING CONVENTION

For more than a century, candidates for the presidency have been nominated by a convention of party members. In appearance the convention is the legislature of the party. Actually the convention is so large, and most of its members so untutored politically, that it is in fact guided by the party executive—the national committee—and the few outstanding politicians among its members. A convention rarely is a unified organization. Rather, it is an aggregation of party factions, each seeking to dominate the whole. At convention time these factions center upon both a geographic region and a governmental policy, but, more than either, upon a potential candidate. The principal aim of the convention is, of course, to name the party presidential candidate; it also has the comparatively secondary aim of drafting a party platform. The choice of the candidate and the contents of the platform depend upon what faction secures control over the convention. Yet the candidate and the platform must be such that the defeated factions can accept them; otherwise these factions may secede to form new parties, such as the Progressive in 1912 and the States' Rights in 1948.

Summoning the convention

A convention is officially summoned by the national committee of the party. About half of the conventions of each major party have met in Chicago; but conventions have been held as far east as New York, as far south as Houston, and as far west as San Francisco. The Democrats have shown a greater willingness than the Republicans to choose different sites for their gatherings, a fact suggesting that Democrats are more evenly distributed about the country than Republicans are. Ordinarily the conventions have assembled in late June or early July, the Democrats traditionally about two weeks after the Republicans. However, the conventions of 1956 were held in August, in order to avoid the heavy costs of a long campaign, which modern methods of communication may have made needless since a candidiate may now address the entire nation with a single speech. Usually, in January of each election year, the national committee nominates candidates for the temporary official positions at the convention. The choices made tend to show which potential candidate has the greatest support among the members of the national committee.

The delegates

Apportionment of Delegates: Today the convention of each major party contains more than 1,000 delegates; in 1956 the Republican convention numbered 1323, and the Democratic, 1372.[1] These delegates are apportioned

---

[1] Throughout this chapter the term "delegate" is used as a synonym for "vote." It occurs rather often, especially at a Democratic convention, that a State will send more delegates than it has votes, so that each delegate has only a fraction of a vote. Sometimes, for instance, two factions of a party in a given State will each send as many delegates as the State has votes; a compromise may be reached whereby both delegations will be seated, each delegate having one-half vote.

Chief Justice Fred M. Vinson Administering the Oath of Office to President Harry S. Truman. Just to right of Truman stands Vice-President Barkley and Associate Justice of the Supreme Court Stanley Reed.

among the States in relation to two factors: (1) the representation of a given State in Congress; and (2) the number of voters that the party may claim in the State. The latter factor today is of great significance, particularly with respect to the Republican party.

It is difficult to decide which party uses the more complicated apportionment system. In the Republican convention of 1956, every State had two delegates-at-large for each Senator and congressman-at-large, and one delegate for each of its congressional districts casting 2,000 or more Republican votes for the presidential candidate in the last election. Furthermore, every State was granted one additional delegate for every congressional district in which 10,000 or more Republican votes were cast. Finally, each State that had cast its electoral votes for the Republican candidate for President in the last presidential election, or that had since elected a Republican Governor, was awarded six additional delegates. Among the territories, Alaska was given four, and Hawaii six; each was granted four more if it had chosen a Republican delegate to Congress at the last election. The District of Columbia was allotted six delegates; Puerto Rico, three; and the Virgin Islands, one.

Delegates to the Democratic convention were assigned principally on the basis of two for each Senator, Representative-at-large, and Representative; fundamentally, then, each State had twice as many delegates as it had electoral votes. As a bonus for concentration of Democratic voters, each State that had voted Democratic in the 1948 presidential election was given four additional delegates. Also, each State voting Democratic in the 1952 presidential election, or electing a Democratic Governor then or later, received four more delegates. Finally, every State was awarded two delegates for each congressional district it had lost as a result of the reapportionment following the 1950 census. The District of Columbia, Alaska, Puerto Rico, and Hawaii were given six delegates each; and the Virgin Islands and the Canal Zone, three apiece.

Selection of the Delegates: At some time between the January meeting of the national committee and the gathering of the convention, the party organization in each State must choose the delegates for the State to the convention. The means of choosing these delegates is in the main at the discretion of each State central committee. In most States, the delegates are chosen by party conventions. In some States, all the delegates are named by the State convention; in others, the delegates-at-large are selected by the State convention, and the district delegates by district conventions. In a few States, the party central committee names the delegates.

In a minority of the States the delegates are chosen in direct primary elections. In 1956, some or all Democratic delegates were named by primaries in sixteen States, and some or all Republican delegates in fifteen. In some States the delegates are pledged to cast their votes at the convention for a specific potential candidate; in other States the delegates are unpledged. In a handful of States the voters at the primary merely indicate their preference for a presidential candidate; the delegates themselves are named by the State convention.

The so-called "presidential primary" emerged about fifty years ago as one phase of the Progressive movement to bring the government closer to the people. Agitation for this sort of primary was so widespread that many observers predicted a quick end for convention nominations; President Wilson in 1913 called for a constitutional amendment requiring nomination by this means. However, even before 1920 the enthusiasm it had kindled was beginning to wane, and several of the States that had adopted the primary later discarded it. On the other hand, between 1952 and 1956 two more States, Indiana and Montana, adopted it.

These primaries have had a considerable effect upon the national conventions. Surely the choice of many Eisenhower backers in the 1952 primaries aided in Eisenhower's ultimate nomination at Chicago. When Wendell Willkie lost the Wisconsin primary of 1944, he accepted the loss as conclusive proof that he could not win the Republican nomination that year, and withdrew from contention. Yet certain facts about the primaries as they exist today greatly reduce their effectiveness. In the first place, they are not held at the same time; hence one primary almost certainly will affect all those following it. In the second place, any person seeking the presidency may or may not enter a primary, just as he chooses. A potential candidate is apt to avoid States in which a native politician, or "favorite son," is campaigning; also, in States where delegates are elected by districts, an aspirant may avoid unfortunate collisions by remaining out of contests in districts where the favorite son is strong. When Harold Stassen competed in the Ohio primary of 1944 against Senator Robert A. Taft, he was careful to enter only in those districts where his managers had assured him that Taft was weak. Another shortcoming of the primaries is that they are not identical; each of the different types measures a different kind of public sentiment.

In 1956 most of the presidential primaries fell into three broad classes. One class, such as the primary in New York, provided for the direct election of convention delegates whose votes were not pledged to any candidate for the presidency. The second class, typified by the California primary, combined a vote for a presidential candidate with a slate of delegates pledged to that candidate for at least the first roll-call vote at the convention. The third class, exemplified by the Massachusetts primary, contained the direct election of convention delegates who could by one means or another show on the ballot which presidential candidate they intended to support. Finally, the primaries in a few States did not fall into any of these categories.

General Background of the Delegates: The delegates to the national convention are, of course, all persons for whom politics is either a vocation or an avocation. The leading figures at a convention are almost always Governors, State party chairmen, Senators, and Representatives. In 1956, the California delegation to the Republican convention included the Vice President of the United States, the State Governor, and two United States Senators. Many other delegates are former officeholders or important party figures in State politics. Private citizens who are delegates frequently are lawyers, journalists, and real estate brokers. The 1956 Democratic convention had many delegates from the AFL–CIO.

Organization of the convention

At its outset the convention, like a full-fledged legislative body, must adopt an organization; it must have officers, rules, and committees. However, a national convention meets for only a short period. Ideally it will last no more than four days; some conventions have extended considerably beyond this period, that of the Democrats in 1924 going on for almost two weeks. However, delegates rarely are prepared to finance so long a stay; hence convention leaders are under pressure to terminate business as quickly as possible lest delegates leave, taking with them, of course, their votes. Owing to the short duration of the convention, therefore, the process of organizing the convention and the other activities of the convention occur simultaneously during the first two or three days of the meeting.

The first important event at the convention is the keynote speech, which is delivered by the temporary chairman or another dignitary. In 1952 at the Republican convention the keynote address was delivered by General Douglas MacArthur, who since he had announced his opposition to a military leader as candidate was assumed to be more favorable to Taft than to Eisenhower. The keynote speech is the first of the many devices at the convention to exalt party morale and seek to consolidate the party at the time when factional divisions are certain to be widest. The speech extols the achievements of the party and denounces the work of the opposition.

Early in the convention, four committees are appointed: credentials, permanent organization, rules, and resolutions and platform. After the keynote speech has been delivered, their members are officially elected by the convention. Each State sends one delegate to each of the first three committees, and two delegates, one man and one woman, to that on resolutions and platform. The committee members actually are nominated by the chairmen of the State delegations. The work of these committees is to a large extent directed by the predominant faction of the national committee. Ordinarily these committees report to the convention in the above order.

The function of the committee on credentials is to determine the right of each delegate present to have his seat. Usually there is little question of this right. The chief task of the committee on permanent organization is to name the candidate for the post of permanent chairman of the convention. Each faction of the party strives to name one of its adherents to this post because of the power it may win for the faction. The purpose of the committee on rules is simply to prepare those rules under which the convention will operate. These rules are very similar to those of Congress. Customarily this committee does little other than recommend that the convention adopt the rules used four years before by its predecessor.

The work of the committee on resolutions and platform is in a sense more important than that of any other of the committees; it is the only work that is submitted not merely to the convention but also to the whole public, and that has a direct influence upon the voter. Members of this committee—or at least the principal members—are unofficially selected by the national party committee long before the convention gathers, and these individuals have already begun drafting the platform when the convention meets. This committee always includes some outstanding party figures; chairman of the Republican resolutions and platform committee in 1952 was Senator Eugene Millikin of Colorado, who in the Eighty-third Congress became chairman of the Senate Finance Committee. Prior to completing its work the committee hears representatives for a multitude of interest groups of all sorts. After hearing petitions for support from varied and conflicting interests, the committee writes the party platform. The platform tends to be specific only on matters that are already settled; on controversial issues it is intentionally vague, so as to avoid offending any major faction. Those who criticize platforms for their lack of a definite stand on disputed matters forget that each major party contains factions that directly oppose one another on certain questions, and that alienation of any large faction may mean loss of the election. Only a small group such as the Socialist or Prohibition Party that has no hope of winning an election can ordinarily afford the luxury of an unequivocal platform.

Nominations

The nominations for the presidency and the vice-presidency are the culmination of the convention. The first two or three days are occupied with the organizational work detailed above. This work actually is carried out by approximately one hundred leading personages at the gathering; the bulk of the delegates, who are consequential for little more than their votes, are kept entertained by a large number of speeches from other party leaders. Finally, after all the committees have reported and the convention has voted on their decisions, the delegates turn to the nominations.

To secure nominations for the presidency, the chairman calls the roll of the States in alphabetical order. Presumably any delegate from any of the States, beginning with Alabama, may propose a candidate. However, the floor managers for each of the strong contenders invariably have arranged with the chairman of the delegation from one of the first States to be called that he should yield to another State, where one of the managers may submit a nomination. Nominating speeches have a unique quality; they consist of a long and flowery oration which is terminated and climaxed by what virtually everyone present knew long before—the name of the proposed candidate. At the end of the speech there breaks out a demonstration punctuated by snake-dances, war whoops, and the popping of noisemakers, an almost totally artificial outbreak that has been carefully staged by the nominee's managers. Following the nominating speech come seconding speeches which were numerous in the past but are now limited to a maximum of four. The seconding speeches do have the important function of indicating some of the States that will support the nominee during at least the first ballot. This same procedure is followed for every name proposed, until there remain no more candidacies to offer.

The balloting follows the nominating speeches, each State again being called upon in alphabetical order. Winning the nomination of either party today demands a simple majority vote at the convention. Precisely how many ballots will be cast by the convention before such a majority is obtained depends largely upon who are the potential candidates and what is the skill of their floor managers. Should no candidate secure a majority on the first ballot, managers will dash about in quest of further votes, negotiating agreements and concessions in return for greater support. One ballot may follow another until finally, when it appears that one person is on the verge of nomination, several States will vie for the honor of giving the margin essential for triumph, as California and Texas did on the fourth ballot at the 1932 Democratic convention. Once an individual has a clear majority, the supporters of the other aspirants may flock to his side, resulting in a huge margin of victory. For example, at the 1952 Republican convention, before Minnesota shifted from Stassen to Eisenhower, the count stood at 595 for Eisenhower, 500 for Taft, and 111 scattered votes; yet the final tally on the same ballot, owing to rapid reversals, was 845 for Eisenhower, 280 for Taft, and 81 scattered.

Types of Support Behind Successful Nominees: Recent studies by Drs. Paul David and Ralph Goldman have classified the kinds of men who win nomination according to the type of support they receive before and during the conventions. Since the first presidential nominating convention of a major party in 1831, there have been 63 major party nominations in convention. Table 12 reveals the source of the push that carried all of these men successfully through the convention of their party. There it will be noted that Presidents are almost always nominated when they want to run for a second term; even slightly more numerous as candidates are the nominees of factions of the party (18) who may be either in revolt against the party leadership or representatives of special interests not uniform in the party. Former nominees, or titular leaders, are few; so are protégés of incumbent Presidents, and surprisingly, the "dark horse" or compromise candidates. In ten cases the inner leadership, or ruling clique, picked the nominee. Thus six different modes of achieving the nomination emerge from the history of the 63 successful convention nominees.

Nominating the Vice President: Having chosen its presidential candidate, the convention turns to the vice presidency. Several considerations influence the choice of the vice presidential candidate. Today perhaps the most important is the will of the presidential candidate. He may virtually dictate the choice, as Roosevelt did in 1940 in the case of Wallace; or he may let several names be contested, as Roosevelt did in 1944; or he may let the convention freely decide, as did Stevenson in 1956.

The presidential candidate, his managers, and the other party leaders mull over various points. Sometimes it may be well to select one of the strong contenders so as to form an alliance with his backers during the campaign; this was certainly the case with Garner, and probably told in the choice of John Bricker in 1944. Too, it may be well to name a candidate from a party faction distinctly opposed to that of the presidential candidate, as Senator John Sparkman in 1952. Moreover, the vice presidential can-

TABLE 12. TYPES OF LEADERS NOMINATED AS PRESIDENT BY THE TWO MAJOR PARTY CONVENTIONS, 1831–1956[1]

	Leadership Confirmation			Leadership Succession		
	President Renominated (Including former Vice President who has succeeded to Presidency)	Titular Leader (Former Nominee Renominated)	Inheritance by Understudy or Previously Outstanding Leader	Inner Group Selection	Factional Leader	
					Successful Factional Candidate	Compromise Candidate
DEMOCRATIC PARTY	Jackson, 1832; Van Buren, 1840; Cleveland, 1888; Wilson, 1916; F. D. Roosevelt, 1936, 1940, 1944; Truman, 1948	Cleveland, 1892; Bryan, 1900, 1908; Stevenson, 1956	Van Buren, 1836; Smith, 1928	Cass, 1848; McClellan, 1864; Greeley, 1872; Hancock, 1880; Cleveland, 1884; Parker, 1904	Buchanan, 1856; Douglas, 1860; Tilden, 1876; Bryan, 1896; Wilson, 1912; Cox, 1920; F. D. Roosevelt, 1932; Stevenson, 1952	Polk, 1844; Pierce, 1852; Seymour, 1868; Davis, 1924
NATIONAL REPUBLICAN, WHIG, AND REPUBLICAN PARTIES	Lincoln, 1864; Grant, 1872; B. Harrison, 1892; McKinley, 1900; T. Roosevelt, 1904; Taft, 1912; Coolidge, 1924; Hoover, 1928; Eisenhower, 1956	Dewey, 1948	Clay, 1831, 1844; Taft, 1908; Hoover, 1928	Fremont, 1856; Grant, 1868; Hughes, 1916; Landon, 1936	W. H. Harrison, 1840; Taylor, 1848; Scott, 1852; Lincoln, 1860; Blaine, 1884; B. Harrison, 1888; McKinley, 1896; Willkie, 1940; Dewey, 1944; Eisenhower, 1952	Hayes, 1876; Garfield, 1880; Harding, 1920
Totals: 61	17	5	6	10	18	7

[1] Adapted from Paul T. David and Ralph M. Goldman, *The Politics of National Party Conventions* (Brookings Institution, 1956, publication pending). Items concerning the 1956 nominations have been added by the author.

didate is usually chosen from a different sector of the country; the Truman-Barkley ticket in 1948 was the only one in recent years in which the two candidates were from adjacent States (Missouri and Kentucky), and the Eisenhower-Nixon combination was unusual in that both candidates were born west of the Mississippi (Texas and California).

Concluding Work of the Convention: Once the convention has named the presidential and vice presidential candidates, it has little to do other than to elect the national party committee that will serve until the next national convention. (In more general terms, the legislature chooses its executive and gives it legislative powers.) The election of the national committee is little more than a formality; the convention merely accepts the man and the woman from each State that the State party organization has presented as candidates.

In 1952 the Republican convention made a significant change in the composition of the national committee: it added to the man and woman from each State the chairman of the party organization of every State that cast a Republican majority in the election for the President, the Governor, or Congress. The principal opposition to this move came from the women of the party, who declared that since the State chairmen were all men, the undertaking would deprive women of their equal status on the national committee. In fact, a much graver consequence appears to be that it will lessen the proportionate representation of the South, with its small Republican vote, on the committee. Having completed its work, the convention now disbands.

THE DESIRABLE CANDIDATE: "AVAILABILITY"

The desirability of any individual as a presidential candidate is measured by an intangible quality termed "availability," a compound of several personal and political traits. The task of computing availability is greatly simplified for the party in control of the White House. As noted above, a President who has served only one term is the most "available" candidate. When the President is about to retire, the nominee with his support usually is the most available. For instance, Theodore Roosevelt in 1908 almost forced the choice of William Howard Taft upon the convention.

Certain other factors may be very influential; however, their effectiveness in at least some cases is questionable. It is generally believed that a candidate should come from a so-called "pivotal" State, that is, one that does not almost invariably cast its vote for one major party. It is also felt desirable that the candidate come from a populous State, with a large electoral vote. Two States that fit both these criteria are New York and Ohio; of the forty-four major party candidates since the end of the Civil War, counting all the candidacies of each person, New York has provided seventeen candidates and Ohio, eight. Yet many a presidential candidate has not carried his own State (even excluding those elections such as 1904 and 1920 in which both candidates came from the same State); moreover, a shift in the electoral vote of New York from one side to the other would have changed the outcome of no election since that of 1884.

It is also important that the candidate has had some political experience, preferably in an elective office. At one time many candidates were selected from Congress; today, however, the tendency is to choose a State Governor, for he has not had to take a position on national issues, and is acquainted with administrative procedure. Since 1900 both Roosevelts, Woodrow Wilson, Charles Evans Hughes, James M. Cox, Calvin Coolidge, Alfred E. Smith, Alfred M. Landon, Dewey, and Stevenson all had been Governors. Over the same period, Eisenhower and Wendell Willkie were the only candidates who had never held a political office; yet each, and especially Eisenhower, had been in a position in which he had had to deal with men. Particularly after the Civil War, military experience was an advantage; every Republican President from Grant through McKinley had been a Union officer. It is thought well for a candidate not to be a businessman—Willkie is again the exception. Finally, a candidate will fare better if he has an unsmirched personal background. James Blaine's financial dealings blocked him from the nomination in 1876, and they caused many Republicans to default to the Democrats in 1884 after he was nominated; yet when it was discovered, after Cleveland was nominated in 1884, that he had fathered an illegitimate child, he admitted it publicly. It would be well to add to this list that great catalyst of eminence: luck, or the good fortune to be standing where one is when the lightning strikes.

THE CAMPAIGN

The presidential campaign in most qualitative respects is similar to other political campaigns. It is bigger and louder; and it is probably longer, for although it does not officially start until September it is in fact a struggle that may have been going on since the last presidential election.

The campaign forces

The commander-in-chief of the campaign forces is the national chairman of the party, who is chosen by the presidential candidate. Certain campaign managers, notably James A. Farley, have become important political figures in their own right. In late years, however, especially in the case of F. D. Roosevelt and Truman, the candidate himself has been the highest officer in the campaign. It is difficult to say whether this represents a trend associated with the emergence of the President as the chief of his party, or whether it is to be associated with the unusual fondness each of these two men had for political combat.

Below the candidate and the campaign manager are the rather disorganized echelons of supporters, both in and out of the formal party structure. It would be inaccurate to say that there is a large national organization behind the candidate since even at election time a strong national party organization scarcely exists in the United States. However, each State party organization—a body that may have great coherence and direction— is ordinarily at the service of the candidate. Beneath, and supposedly obedient to, this State organization is a hierarchy of local political bodies at the district, county, city, ward, and precinct levels. However, there may be all varieties of disputes among party units, for reasons both of personalities and of policies. It is the task of the campaign manager to compromise differences and to bridge lines of separation so that the party will be unified at least during its greatest effort—the drive toward conquest of the White House.

Aside from the party there may be many other groups working for the candidate. One of the most active in recent years has been the Political Action Committee of the CIO (CIO-PAC), a group that in some areas has been more effective than the party organizations themselves in getting out the vote. A parallel subsidiary of the AFL, Labor's League for Political Education (LLPE), although perhaps not so effective as the CIO-PAC, has nevertheless seemed to have considerable influence in some localities. Both organizations were joined into a single political action group, the Committee on Political Education (COPE), in 1955. Another nation-wide group is the Americans for Democratic Action (ADA), which, although structurally not affiliated with any labor organization, seeks the election of candidates and the adoption of policies favorable to labor unions as well as the general policies of the New Deal and the Fair Deal. Leading figures in the ADA have included Walter Reuther, President of the CIO, and Senator Hubert Humphrey of Minnesota.

Probably the nearest approach to such organizations on the Republican side was the ill-starred Liberty League that backed Landon in 1936. In 1952 there did appear one group which, although it did not work for the election of the entire Republican ticket, did seek the election of the Republican presidential candidate: the National Citizen's Committee for Eisenhower. Yet a third Republican group is For America, which usually has supported candidates who have pursued the policies of the late Senator Taft of Ohio and General Douglas MacArthur.

Speeches: Since time immemorial, speeches have been the principal means for communication during a political campaign. Candidates make widely differing uses of speeches. For example, a candidate who is already President may during the campaign speak only a few times, remaining in Washington so as to give the impression of being preoccupied by the cares of office. This definitely was the program of Roosevelt in 1940, when he made only one brief tour shortly before election day. His opponent, Willkie, meantime was following the reverse policy, that of speaking as often and at as many places as possible. The achievement of William Jennings Bryan of speaking sixteen times in one day led one Republican politician to ask, "When does he think?"

The candidate may devote his speeches to particular issues, as Truman did in 1948; or he may confine himself to generalities, as Dewey did in the same campaign. Every candidate prior to his campaign vows to forego injurious personal remarks; yet abuse and misinformation are still rife today.

Supposedly the low in campaign vilification occurred during the 1884 campaign when the Republicans, after discovering that Cleveland although a bachelor was a father, chanted in their parades:

"Ma! Ma! Where's my pa?"
"Gone to the White House!"
"Ha! Ha! Ha!"

One frequent consideration is the amount of attention that should be given to the other candidates. Many experienced politicians argue that the less notice paid to the adversary, the better. During the 1940 campaign, for example, Roosevelt scrupulously avoided naming Willkie. One observer of the 1916 campaign noted that the real failure of the Republicans lay in the fact that in their speeches "Hughes talked about Wilson. Taft came out and talked about Wilson. Roosevelt came forth and talked about Wilson and Wilsonism. And now and then in calm pauses Wilson would come out onto the porch of Shadow Lawn and talk about Taft and Roosevelt—and Wilson. Nobody talked about Hughes."

Today the delivery and effectiveness of speech are closely related to three mass media: the press, radio, and television. Of the three, newspapers by their very nature must be the most carefully cultivated by the campaign manager; for newspaper reporting of a speech is in a sense "free" whereas radio and television time must be paid for. Radio and television have emphasized one element that is absent from the press, and appears only to the actual audience—the speaking ability and mannerisms of the candidate. One of Al Smith's greatest handicaps in 1928 was the fact that he was obviously a born and bred New Yorker. On the other hand, F. D. Roosevelt's already great speaking talent was enhanced by the nation-wide transmission of his speeches over radio. Network radio and television broadcasting also influences campaigning by making it more hazardous for a candidate to express contradictory remarks in different parts of the country. Television, although a new medium, has become extremely important. During the campaign, too, all candidates devote vast sums to the dissemination of literature and other forms of publicity, such as brief radio announcements and billboards. Literally millions of pieces of literature are produced for distribution among the electorate.

The effects of campaigns

The effects of presidential campaigns when viewed in one way seem rather inconsequential, and when viewed in another appear of the greatest moment. In *The Western Public*, this author said of the 1952 election:

> The big lesson of political tactics, one which can never be well enough explained to political amateurs, and, indeed, to a great many professionals, is that the contest for power is perhaps three-quarters settled before the encounter of an election comes about. The traditional affiliations, economic conditions, general issues, the average of personalities on both sides—such assured general features account for most of the strength of both sides. Sometimes these basic conditions may differ from one election to another, but they tend toward constancy.
> But beyond the durable resources of the parties and the short term condi-

tions of economic life and ponderous international events comes the multitude of minor, often trivial, events that create the margin of victory. . . . If it is discovered in a poll, as it was discovered in 1952, that the issue of Nixon's sources of financial support caused a bare flicker of the needle of public emotion, then this was a big issue of the campaign. So weighty and immobile are the general conditions under which the campaign is fought that a few hundred changed votes constitute a major change in the determination of the campaign's results.

American presidential elections are close contests; the great margins that appear in the Electoral College are huge exaggerations of the popular vote. The highest percentage of the popular vote taken by any candidate since 1820 was that of Harding: 61%. In the Democratic landslide of 1936, Roosevelt won only 60.7%. In 1956, Eisenhower won 57.8%. If it be assumed that three-quarters of the vote is settled before the campaign, and that the three-quarters were equally divided, the remaining quarter still allows a swing of from 37.5% to 62.5%, the latter figure being larger than Harding's winning percentage. Table 13, which is based on two national sample surveys of the Survey Research Center, by showing when people made up their minds about how they would vote, is helpful in deciding what is the effect of a campaign:

TABLE 13.   WHEN THE VOTERS MADE UP THEIR MINDS, 1948 AND 1952

	1948			1952		
Time of Decision	Dewey	Truman	All	Eisen-hower	Steven-son	All
Before conventions	42%	36%	37%	27%	35%	31%
At time of conventions	34	22	28	40	27	34
During campaign	13	14	14	18	24	20
Within two weeks of election	3	14	9	10	7	9
Election Day	2	3	3	1	4	2
Other	6	11	9	4	3	4
Number of cases	178	212	421	687	494	1195

It may be concluded, then, that campaigns have two major effects. In the first place, they help to consolidate the party organizations and to elevate the morale of the consistent party followers, so that a large proportion of those certain to vote for a specific party will come to the polls. In the second place, campaigns serve to convince the so-called "independents"— that is, persons without strong party attachments—that they should vote for a specific candidate or party. It is in either or both of these two effects that a campaign may give birth to the narrow margin that will yield victory.

THE ELECTION PROCESS

The President of the United States is not elected directly by the people; rather, he is elected by a group of persons from each State known individually as Electors and collectively as the Electoral College, who today are chosen by the people. Yet in certain respects the election of the President in its current form differs widely from popular election, for it is the Electoral College that in fact names the President.

Procedure of the election

Apportionment of Electors: Electors are apportioned among the States according to their respective representation in the two houses of Congress. Each State has one Elector for each Senator and each Representative. Thus Delaware, with one Representative, has three Electors or electoral votes; and California, with thirty Representatives, has thirty-two Electors or electoral votes. Hence each State gains or loses electoral votes every time it gains or loses Representatives in the reapportionment following the decennial census. Today there are 531 members in the Electoral College. The map in Figure 31 in the preceding chapter shows how the electoral vote has changed along with seats in the House.

Choosing the Electors: The Constitution provides that "Each State shall appoint, in such manner as the legislature thereof may direct, a number of Electors. . . ." (Art. II, sec. 1, cl. 2.) At first in most States the Electors were named by the State legislatures; it is for this reason that there are no reliable figures for the popular vote in any presidential election before that of 1824. However, since the end of the Civil War all Electors have been chosen at large on a general ticket. Each State party organization today names as many candidates for the Electoral College as there shall be Electors from the State concerned. In a minority of States the name of each candidate for the Electoral College appears on the presidential ballot under the names of the candidates for the presidency and the vice presidency. By 1956 thirty States had adopted the so-called "short presidential ballot" on which only the candidates for the presidency and the vice presidency are printed. However, in casting these ballots the voters actually are choosing Electors.

Functioning of the Electoral College: On the second Wednesday of December following a presidential election the Electors of the party that received the largest number of votes in the election in their State gather at the State capital and cast all their votes for the candidate of their party. In other words, the presidential candidate who wins a plurality of the State popular vote secures all the electoral votes of the State. Today it rarely occurs that an Elector does not vote according to the directions of his electorate; the Tennessee Elector who in 1948 cast his vote for Strom Thurmond, States' Rights candidate, instead of for President Truman, who had carried the State, was committing a very unusual action. There is nothing in the Constitution nor in federal law to prevent the Electors from disregarding completely the instructions of the voters and making whomever they please President. However, an Elector is an officer of his State government; hence California and Oregon have acted within their authority in passing laws that require the Electors to heed the decision of the voters. More important, a turncoat Elector would invite great social disapproval.

The Official Count: The ballots of the Electoral College are officially counted, and the victorious candidate proclaimed, at a joint session of Congress that meets on January 6, after the election. When the Electors in the several States have cast their votes, they transmit the results to the General Services Administration in Washington. This office then sends the results to the presiding officer of the Senate—the Vice President of the United States or the President pro tem of the Senate, whichever the case may be. The House and the Senate convene in the House chamber on January 6. Each house appoints two tellers, one from either major party. The result of the electoral vote from each State is now tabulated by the four tellers. The totals yield the official outcome of the election, an outcome that has in fact been known to the public for two months: the candidate receiving a majority of the electoral vote—266, today—is declared to be President.

Procedure in the Event of Dispute: In the case of a very close election, the circumstances under which the electoral vote is counted make it possible, although not probable, that a dispute may arise. It should be noted that on January 6, the Congress that has been elected in November is now in session; however, the presiding officer, if the Vice President, was elected four years ago and in the immediately preceding November election may have been defeated. The Constitution does not make it clear precisely *who* is to "count" the vote: does the presiding officer, do the tellers, or do the congressmen "count" the vote? Since the presiding officer may be of one party and the congressional majority of another, in the event that a State sent two sets of electoral votes to the General Services Administration it would be difficult to reach a decision as to which set would be honored.

Once in American history, after the election of 1876, such a dispute did arise. On that occasion a commission of five Senators, five Representatives, and five Supreme Court justices was appointed to settle the conflict. The commission, which included eight Republicans and seven Democrats, achieved a decision on a purely partisan basis, awarding all the contested votes to the Republican candidate, Rutherford B. Hayes. Since that time there has been no other disputed electoral vote.

In 1887 Congress enacted legislation providing for a method of resolving any future disputes of this type. The law operates on the generally accepted theory that Electors are State, not national, officers; hence the burden of ultimate decision lies upon the State. When the electoral vote of a State is disputed, the question is first turned over to any authority that the State may have established by law or constitutional provision, for resolving such an issue. If the State agency cannot reach a decision, the matter is then submitted to Congress, where each house deliberates it separately. In the event the two houses of Congress cannot agree—a likely outcome if they are dominated by different parties—the contest reverts to the State: any set of returns certified by the Governor will be accepted as official. If the Governor cannot or will not act, the State loses its electoral vote. Such a conclusion is, of course, very improbable; for, confronted by the possibility that their State might lose its voice in naming the President, the leaders of the two parties in the State almost certainly would compromise their differences.

Procedure in the Absence of an Electoral College Majority: In case no candidate receives a majority of the votes in the Electoral College—an event that has not occurred since 1824—the election of the President falls to the House of Representatives, which chooses the President from among the three candidates receiving the largest number of electoral votes. Each State delegation has one vote; the majority of the delegation determines the vote of the State. Should the delegation be unable to reach a decision, the State loses its vote. A majority of the votes elects the President. In the event no candidate receives a majority of the votes in the House, the Vice President-elect acts as President until a President has been named. If the Electoral College does not cast a majority of its votes for any vice presidential candidate, the Senate, with each Senator voting individually, by a majority vote chooses the Vice President from between the two candidates receiving the largest number of electoral votes.

Proposed reforms of electoral procedure

Criticisms of the Electoral College: The Electoral College has been criticized on a number of grounds: (1) It long ago ceased to operate as its designers intended; and it clashes with the spirit of American government today. (2) It gives undue weight to the smaller States. If the votes in the Electoral College were distributed according to the delegations of the States in the House of Representatives alone, the apportionment of electoral votes would be fairly consistent with the populations of the States. However, since Senators are also computed in the distribution, and since every State has two Senators, the apportionment in the Electoral College is distorted in favor of the smaller States. In the 1956 election, each Elector from Nevada represented only about 55,000 people; each Elector from New York, nearly 350,000. (3) The system whereby the candidate winning the largest number of votes in the State secures all the electoral votes of the State denies their vote to all who voted for the other candidates. In the event candidate A received 300,000 popular votes, candidate B 250,000, and candidate C 200,000, candidate A even though he had received only forty per cent, or a minority, of the total popular vote would be given all the electoral votes of the State. (4) The Electoral College may send to the White House a candidate who has not even received a plurality of the popular vote. There have been several cases in which the victorious candidate has received the largest popular vote, although it has been a minority of the total: Polk in 1844; Taylor in 1848; Buchanan in 1856; Lincoln in 1860; Garfield in 1880; Cleveland in 1884 and 1892; Wilson in 1912 and 1916; and Truman in 1948. However, twice the President has received fewer votes than his opponent: Hayes in 1876, and Harrison in 1888. It is noteworthy that in each case the loser was a Democrat. Because a candidate receives all of the electoral votes from a State in which he has a bare plurality, and because the proportion of Democrats is very high in the southern States, the Democratic vote from that section is in a sense "wasted." One might say that through "natural" processes the United States is slightly "gerrymandered" in favor of the Republicans.

Suggested Changes: Many types of changes have been suggested to alleviate these shortcomings in the Electoral College. Any of them would require a constitutional amendment. Of these suggestions, three have won serious consideration:

1. The suggestion that would create perhaps the slightest change has been that the Electoral College as a group of persons be eliminated. Following this suggestion, each State would retain its electoral vote, and the votes would be awarded as at present. This proposition does little more than assure that no Elector could override the will of his constituents; for this reason it might be opposed by those southern States that may be attached to the Democratic Party but not to its candidates.

2. One of the most extreme recommendations has been that the Electoral College be abolished entirely, and that the President be chosen by a simple majority of a nation-wide popular vote. This suggestion would encounter several barriers. First, it would be opposed by the small States since, as noted above, they have a disproportionately large representation in the Electoral College. Second, it would be opposed by many States regardless of size, because it would expunge a number of powers, especially that of fixing the means for choosing Electors, which the States would not readily surrender. Finally, it would be opposed by southern Democrats, since it would make the Republican vote in the South effective in the national totals, and thereupon encourage greater Republican organization and turnout of voters.

3. Standing between these two suggestions are various plans for distributing the electoral vote of each State among the candidates according to their popular vote. The most recent of these proposals, called after those who introduced it to Congress the Lodge-Gossett Plan, would make the proportion of the electoral vote of a State that a candidate receives equal to the percentage of the popular vote that he receives in that State. It further would provide that a candidate who receives the largest number of electoral votes, whenever that number amounts to forty per cent or more of the total electoral votes, will be President. The Lodge-Gossett Plan does not deprive the smaller States of their exceptional weight in presidential elections, and it furnishes a method for respecting the minority popular vote.

When first offered to Congress as a joint resolution for amending the Constitution, the Plan was warmly greeted and was adopted by the Senate. Later, however, sufficient opposition arose to effect its rejection by the House. The opposition was based on the fact, as shown in a group of calculations, that the Plan would take away from the Republican Party the advantage it has (noted above) in the Electoral College; that is, it would impose, because of the distribution of Republican voters, such a severe handicap on the Republican Party that it might never elect a President. Another group charged that the Plan would encourage the rise of splinter parties, inasmuch as a small party, with only a small fraction of the total vote in a State, would still receive some electoral votes. Still others asserted that it would weaken the Democratic Party in the North and turn control of the Party over to its southern elements, because a medium-sized State in the Solid South might cast as many

Democratic electoral votes as a pivotal State in the North; thus, a southern presidential candidate might be more eligible than one from a great industrial State. Hence no change in the method for electing the President is likely in the near future.

QUESTIONS AND PROBLEMS

1. Contrast the methods of apportioning seats in the Republican and the Democratic Party presidential nominating conventions.

2. What are the various means during the nominating process by which one candidate can receive preference over another, and thus increase the chances of his being nominated?

3. Describe one major proposal that would alter the presidential nominating system and another that would alter the election system. Why have these proposals not been adopted?

4. Describe the internal organization of the nominating convention.

5. Suppose your three closest friends were an impressive orator, a skilled organizer, and a financial wizard, and that you were an aspirant for the presidential nomination and election. Where would you place your friends from the very beginning of the campaign through the various stages of the process, so as to help your cause the most?

6. List three Republicans and three Democrats who are potential presidential candidates at the next election. Discuss the "availability" of each.

7. According to Table 13 on page 276, would you have preferred to be Truman or Stevenson two weeks before the election? Why?

18. Leadership in the Federal Government

A LEADER is a person who has extraordinary influence on decisions that are made in a given situation. He may exert his influence either by means of his personal qualities or because of the position he holds, or by some combination of the two factors. Bernard Baruch, whose advice was heard and followed by several Presidents even when he held no political office, is an example of personal leadership. The newspaper photographs showing him at his favorite park bench symbolize the fact that his role contained no official character. In contrast stood Calvin Coolidge, whose authority and power as President came almost exclusively from his government office rather than from the unassuming personality that earned him the nickname "Silent Cal." The influence of most political leaders is a sum of both personal and official qualities.

The political leaders who have been encountered thus far in the text have been using both their personal and their official qualities to influence public policy or achieve public office. In the search for political influence, men typically use their personal qualities to gain some office, and then combine both the personal and the official qualities to reach out for more influence. When, blessed by fortune and the appropriate combination of personal and official qualities, a man acquires great power, he moves into the select company of those who govern America. Whether his power stems from unofficial influence does not matter much in his being counted in that company. The primary fact is that he has arrived, that he has made a place for himself and must be taken into consideration when some important decisions are made.

It has long been a question whether any particular number of men can be said to rule America, whether one group or another does so, and how many people can be said to make decisions for the whole population. Some answers may be given to each of these questions here.

THE RULE OF LAW

A strong argument can be made to deny that America has any set of rulers. One can say: no one rules America; it is ruled by laws, not by men. The laws tell leaders what they must and what they must not do, what they may and what they may not do. The Constitution, the court decisions, and all of the laws governing rights, interest groups, political parties, and government officials, are in effect *impersonal* leaders.

That is so. People not living under constitutionalism, and people who are living under it but do not realize it, fall very easily into the false position that men are without limits, save as the "law" of the political jungle sets such bounds. In fact, the laws "lead the leaders" in two general ways:

1. They stand as constant reminders to the leaders regarding how they should behave. For instance, the statement in the Constitution that no man shall be convicted of a crime without due process of law is not only an instruction to the courts; it is an ethical principle that guides a great many men and their leaders to respect the rights of others, even in the hurly-burly of politics.

2. The laws also limit the behavior of leaders in specific senses. For instance, the Attorney General, who is chief of the Department of Justice and who therefore is the overall head of the Federal Bureau of Investigation, cannot use these federal police to suppress free speech nor to censor the press of his opponents without risking impeachment or indictment, trial, and conviction on several counts. To take another example, men who wish

Bernard Baruch, Seated at a Bench in New York's Central Park, Where He Often Has Chatted Informally with Political Leaders.

to achieve certain kinds of power over their fellow citizens must go through the process of being nominated, elected, and sworn into public office; the laws of the land are aimed at giving the most important political powers only to men who have thus qualified themselves.

The body of laws is the work of many generations of leaders. The Constitution, for instance, owes much to the seven thousand years of western civilization that preceded it, to the leaders who drafted it, and to the generations of leaders who have carried it forward. Today it is part of the mental and moral heritage of American political leaders; and, through the institutions that it sets up, it limits the ability of one leader or a set of leaders to avoid its injunctions and intent. Therefore the leaders of today rule America only to the extent allowed by the laws and by their training in obeying the laws.

THE NUMBER OF LEADERS TODAY

The laws govern leaders; but they also have an especial effect upon the number of leaders. They permit every person to become politically active to the full measure of his desires and ability. Under American law, practically every adult could be active in politics twenty-four hours of the day. Furthermore, the laws of the United States are hostile to the concentration of power in a very few hands. The details of this division of powers have been treated in earlier pages. The federal system of government, which divides power between State and nation; the decentralized and chaotic party structure that makes personal power hard to acquire and to retain in large amounts; and the division of the federal government (and the States too) into legislative, executive, and judicial branches with strong legal defenses against invasions from one another—all these laws guarantee that the number of men of great importance in government will exceed the tens, dozens, or few hundreds that have ruled many other governments, past and present.

Before settling more closely, however, upon the estimated number of determining voices in national affairs, it is well to remember how few Americans have demonstrated some amount of political activity. It will be recalled from the chapter on public opinion that only a small fraction of the population engages in a modest degree of political activity in the midst of a political campaign. Figure 22 showed precisely the results of the latest of several studies of the political activity of Americans. Its central point was clear: although the laws may permit and foster universal political activity, only about one out of every thirty-five American adults engages in even that minimum of political activity from which leadership must spring. Whatever kind of leadership one is talking about will have to come from a group of Americans numbering fewer than three millions, for a completely inactive and non-participating leader is an impossibility akin to an "illiterate reader."

Some people may be shocked, and others consoled, by these figures; in either event, politics can be understood only in their terms. Whether other lands have experienced a condition of greater activity can only be a matter for speculation. However, it is doubtful that other peoples have been much more active than the Americans of today. The short-lived Athenian democracy had its multitude of slaves, aliens, and inactive citizens. The laws of the Roman Republic permitted a very small ruling group during most of its history. No information is available on the great modern democracies, save that until a generation ago they could not have supported even under the law as large a proportion of active citizens as is found in the United States. James Bryce once declared that the politically active Englishmen of the late nineteenth century numbered no more than 3,500. Indeed, it is probably fair to say, disconcerting as the situation may appear to some, that America has one of the most active citizen bodies in history. If the proportion of Soviet citizens exceeds it, and such is probably the case, the reason lies in the intense agitation within the Soviet Union to make people active in civic affairs, always provided that the activity is controlled rigidly in the interests of the Communist Party. Obviously, in the Soviet case, one is then talking about an administrative machine, not the free and general political activity that is in question here.

Size of the national leadership

The still considerable number of citizens who may be termed "active" is, however, reduced considerably by the demand that they exhibit some real influence before they may be admitted into the ranks of those leaders who make the vast majority of top decisions of the federal government. Previous chapters have given leads to how many of these three millions are leaders of consequence.

1. A few of them are elected federal officials and judges, about 900 in all.

2. Some are appointed federal officials of high authority and responsibility, such as Cabinet members and their principal aides, numbering about 800.

3. Some are leaders of opinion, including publishers, editors, writers, professors, actors, and the like, totalling perhaps 800.

4. Many are leaders of national interest groups such as the National Association of Manufacturers, the American Federation of Labor, the American Legion, and the Farm Bureau Federation, numbering perhaps 400.

5. Many, about 800, are party leaders and defeated or aspiring candidates for office.

6. Some are drawn from particularly interested State and local officials, both elective and appointive; others are the counterparts of categories (3), (4), and (5) above, on the State and local level, making perhaps 1,500 in all. In connection with this category, it is well to remark again on the effect that the laws and character of the country have upon federal leadership. State Governors and mayors often have a good deal to say about national questions. A county political leader, for example, although he may have little interest in or knowledge of national affairs, may hand-pick a congressman or control a high federal appointive officer. The many thousands of people in this category are for the most part unconcerned with national affairs. However, they are potentially powerful; on occasions and in matters

that involve their immediate interests (as in a party struggle, an election campaign, or a legislative debate), they will rise to the defense of their views. As officeholders or party workers of considerable skill, they can command attention and respect. They are not to be relegated to the ranks of unconnected, uninformed outsiders, or uninformed and powerless people at large.

7. Others, perhaps 500 in all, are private individuals of important financial and industrial connections.

8. A number are "political personalities without portfolio." These are the trusted advisers, assistants, and confidantes of congressmen and other leaders, Washington hosts and hostesses, and even a handful of foreign diplomats, totalling altogether approximately 1,000.

Summing up, the number of highly placed and influential leaders in national affairs does not appear to be large. The rough calculations above yield about 7,000 persons. It is unlikely that the whole range of federal government occupies the direct initiative, ideas, interests, and actions of more than 10,000 persons of first-ranking importance. To be on the safe side, one may keep in mind the figure 10,000. Beyond them stand perhaps ten or twenty times as many persons who are quite active but who have a hand in making important policies only occasionally. Behind these, in turn, come probably another million or thereabouts who contribute modest leadership in building up pressures, carrying out decisions, modifying details, and operating the vast machinery of the governmental process. The remainder of the three millions of at least minimum activity accomplish that minimum and little more; yet in view of their small number in comparison with the total population, their contribution to the political process cannot be viewed as negligible. One might add, too, that about another six million people work for the government or in relation to the government, but in non-political jobs.

Relations among the top leaders

The 10,000 that constitute the national top leadership are not organized. They form no clique. The American government is not run by "Wall Street," as communists invariably argue. It is not ruled by "labor," by "Jews," by the "city machines," by the "farmers," by a "brain trust," by "business interests," or by "communists," for that matter. Such simple assertions contain at best the grain of truth that a hundred similar assertions would have when made about a hundred different groups; "even a stopped clock is right twice a day." They arise, of course, out of a profound ignorance of how the government functions and out of a hostility to some one element of the population. It would be more nearly correct, although still scarcely worthy of consideration, and probably a good deal healthier for national unity, if one accepted as fact that 100 million American adults have equal voices in the making of public policy.

More nearly true is the assertion that the top leaders of the nation, like the politically active citizens who were described earlier, are drawn in the majority from the better-educated, more skilled occupational groups. Furthermore, their parents, on the whole, are more prosperous and give them more opportunities than are afforded the average American. Probably the most conclusive proof for this statement is to be found in an examination of the occupations of the parents of the top 10,000. Regrettably, complete information on this subject is not available; but Table 14 shows the situation found among large parts of the top leadership. Note the special representation of segments of the population by labor and business leaders.

TABLE 14.   OCCUPATION OF FATHERS OF AMERICAN TOP LEADERS[1]
(in percentages)

Occupation of Father	Pres., V. Pres., Cab. Memb., 1789– 1934	High Civil Serv., 1940	U.S. Sen., 1949– 1951	U.S. Hse. Rep., 1941– 1943	CIO, AFL Ldrs., 1940's	Bus. Ldrs., 1930's	Occupations of Labor Force, 1890
Professional	38	28	22	31	1	14	5
Proprietors & officials	20	30	33	31	16	58	6
Farmers	38	29	40	29	15	12	26
Low-salaried workers	0	3	1	0	8	5	5
Wage earners	4	10	3	9	60	11	36
Servants	0	0	0	0	0	0	7
Farm laborers	0	0	0	0	0	0	15
Unknown, unclassified	0	0	1	0	0	0	0
Total	100	100	100	100	100	100	100
Number	311	180	109	186	356	8,396	

[1] Data of first four and last columns from Matthews, D. R., *The Social Background of Political Decision-Makers* (New York: Doubleday and Company, 1954), p. 23. Data on labor leaders derived from Mills, C. Wright, *The New Men of Power* (New York: Harcourt, Brace, 1948), pp. 88–90, and on business leaders from Taussig, F. W., and C. S. Joslyn, *American Business Leaders* (New York: The Macmillan Company, 1932), p. 78.

Figures on education support the conclusion: for example, 88% of the House of Representatives during 1941–1943 had college educations; 87% of the Senate of 1949–1951; 77% of the State Governors during 1930–1940; and 79% of all Presidents, Vice Presidents, and Cabinet members during 1877–1934. But only about 10% of the entire population more than twenty-five years of age has received a college education. Today more than ever, the chances that a boy or girl may achieve great political success are bettered if he or she comes from a family that is well-to-do and if he or she receives a college education.

Certain among the States, too, seem favored so far as producing leaders is concerned. Between the year 1900 and the middle of 1955, thirty-two different men were named to the federal Supreme Court and 152 different persons to Cabinet posts. Four States—New York, Massachusetts, Ohio, and Tennessee—supplied sixteen, or half, of the new justices; yet the combined population of these States according to the 1950 census was only about 30 millions, or 20% of the national total. The twenty-nine States that have furnished no justices during this period have a total population of 60 millions, or twice as great as these four States. Seven States—New York, Pennsylvania, Massachusetts, Missouri, Illinois, Iowa, and Ohio—have provided eighty-nine, or 59%, of the Cabinet members chosen since 1900. Yet these States together have only 35% of the entire population of the country. The reasons for this concentration are numerous; perhaps most important are the facts that at least some of these States are pivotal in national elections, and also that Presidents have been indebted to the ruling circles of these States.

Considering the vast size of the nation, its heterogeneity, the manner in which the 10,000 are chosen, and the utterly divergent and multitudinous people to whom they owe their positions, it must be concluded that they are a very mixed group. Indeed, many of them are bitter political opponents. The 10,000, however, do have an important trait that merits comment: it is probable that any one of them will know scores or hundreds of the others. It is likely that any one of them could come to know any other member of the 10,000 by asking for an introduction through a mutual friend in the group. Very few people among the remaining 100,000,000 American adults could do the same. Hence it would be permissible to view the national leadership as a very loose network of people who are informed about many of the same things, who tend to know people of the same type, who perhaps share some attitudes and habits in greater numbers than do the rest of the population. However, they cannot be regarded as a clique, a social class, or an organized group.

Divisions of the influentials by scope

One can decide that, although the 10,000 may be lumped together from the fact that they all have considerably more power in national affairs than the rest of the people, their influence is in almost all cases restricted in scope. One restriction of scope is *functional*. For example, a congressman cannot judge a court case, even if he should care to do so. No doubt many times, as when the Supreme Court struck down New Deal measures of the 1930's or when the Court in 1954 ruled that segregation by race in public schools is unconstitutional, a President or some congressmen would have liked to reverse the Court; however, no President or congressman has ever attained such power, although Presidents Jackson, Lincoln, and F. D. Roosevelt nearly performed the feat.

The President and Congress are allowed more leeway in invading each other's powers; still, the record, as a subsequent chapter will show, contains more drawn decisions than victories for one or the other. These are but two examples of the way in which the 10,000 are split up into groups that are charged with proposing policies, urging their adoption, propagandizing about them, legislating, administering the laws, judging them, and policing the judgments. Each of the clusters of leaders in these functional categories meets severe restrictions both from the law and from the other leadership clusters when it moves out of its customary range of power.

Overlapping these functional clusters and running parallel to them are geographic clusters of leaders. For instance, a Virginia party leader has little influence in North Carolina and less in New York; the head of the California Federation of Labor has little to do with the legislative policies of the Illinois Federation of Labor; and the Senate as a whole can do little about the party machinery in a State that sends an unpopular colleague into their midst. Other clusters of leaders are divided according to the *topical* subjects their chiefs are entitled to, or directed to, treat with. The Court of Customs and Patent Appeals has no purview over a violation of the federal law against kidnapping, which falls in the jurisdiction of the Department of Justice for prosecution and the regular federal district court for trial. The Secretary of Commerce has little influence over the Federal Reserve Board. The President cannot, even after several years of power, influence strongly the policies of the Interstate Commerce Commisssion. Most defense policies are made without the consent of the Secretary of Labor. The National Association of Manufacturers reaches its policies on international trade without consulting the Department of State.

The hierarchy within the clusters

Besides being divided up according to the scope of their powers, the 10,000 are arranged differently within their clusters. For example, the cluster of the executive branch is arranged internally so that the President has potentially at least the power of making personally most important decisions that the Department heads or the White House staff can make. On the other hand, the power cluster of the Senate comprises ninety-six men of relatively equal power, at least by contrast with the presidency; its collective decision, represented by the majority vote on an issue before it, of course has great weight in telling the executive branch what to do. It has such great weight, in fact, that the individual Senators derive much personal power in and out of Washington from the part they take in that collective decision.

A wealthy, active interest group of many members may resemble either the presidency in the way its influence is focused in one man (e.g., John L. Lewis of the United Miners Union), or the Senate in the way its influence is divided among several men (e.g., the National Association of Manufacturers). The most important newspaper publishers of the country ordinarily act without consultation and apply their strong individual pressures without the collective force of a senatorial vote. Such a cluster is, within its own scope, an anarchy, a condition without any central authority.

Interlocking clusters

Some of the clusters are so closely related to one another that they contribute to the making of the same decisions and policies. Others are isolated. There is, however, no master network that has scope over everything and in which power is concentrated in a few hands. Perhaps the closest approach to such a master network is the presidency. The President and his subordinates can sometimes effectively dominate the executive branch of the government. They can sometimes rule a majority of both houses of Congress on a sizable proportion of all matters coming before Congress. They can sometimes influence strongly a part of the press, a number of key interest groups, and several of the independent administrative agencies of the government such as the Interstate Commerce Commission.

Yet this uncommon and vast network of control is the closest the United States has ever come to an oligarchy or a totalitarian government, and it is too far from these conditions to be called by either of those names. One notes, moreover, that, in such a rare event, strong and hostile minorities are still to be found everywhere save in the executive branch. Nor does the unusual condition embrace the courts, the many State and local party organizations and governments, or the numerous autonomous facets of society— churches, schools, and the like—that escape the network's influence entirely.

Comparison with foreign networks

Compared with the top leadership of other large countries the American structure is very large, loose-knit, and lightly powered. The Soviet government, for example, concentrates most of its vast authority in the hands of a very few men of the Presidium (or Executive Board) of the Central Committee of the Communist Party, the Presidium of the Supreme Soviet (a cabinet of the parliament), and the Presidium of the Council of Ministers (a cabinet of the chiefs of administrative departments). The very highest leaders occupy posts in more than one of these three groups. Probably a hundred men, or even fewer, make the vast majority of decisions in all spheres of social and political life. No independent leadership cluster exists outside this group. All opposition to the leadership, save where directly solicited by it and permitted by it, is extremely hazardous. Members of the innermost circles strike up independent tones at their peril. Vast numbers of Soviet citizens are politically active, but they are bridled, saddled, and ridden, by the top leadership.

The English leadership is also a much smaller group than the American, even in relation to the smaller population of the country. Probably no more than one thousand Englishmen can be said to possess significant ability to influence their government's policies in the regular course of governing. Unlike American congressmen, a sizable proportion of members of the House of Commons would not qualify as members of the top leadership. They are so tightly controlled by their party chiefs that they cannot contribute independently to public policy. The contrast of the English situation with the Russian is nonetheless striking, for two reasons: English constitutionalism severely restricts the behavior of English top leadership; and, as a salient facet of such constitutionalism, a potential elite in the form of the opposition political party is always ready to take over the government. Even when out of power, the party's leadership must be counted as directly influential upon the government's decisions. Perhaps nowhere in the world is an opposition as carefully organized, given such license to criticize, and as accurately focused, as in England.

The French, German, and Italian republics possess a more diffuse top leadership structure than the English. In each of them there is a type of localism—provincialism in France and in Italy, provincialism and federalism in West Germany—that decreases the freedom of action of the group that controls the central government. Also, each country has a multi-party system whose leaders must be counted among the persons with strong influence upon public policy. Probably for both reasons, the number of individuals involved in the top leadership goes well beyond the number in England without, however, approaching the total number of American national leaders of first rank.

A survey of American national leadership and a comparison of it with foreign examples indicates that the American government is conducted in an immediate and direct sense by a few thousands of individuals who combine official and unofficial roles in varying degrees. They are limited by the laws; their scope of action is restricted; they are not well coordinated; they do not share uniform views; most owe their power to different sources of public esteem in the various sections of the country, in private enterprises, in appointments by public or private bodies, in long party service, or in intellectual and scientific skills. The forces blocking a unification of these separate clusters are very strong. When, as will be seen in the next chapters, an institution such as the presidency has expanded its leadership function relative to the rest of the 10,000, it has been not so much at the expense of the other leadership clusters as it has been the outgrowth of performing new or augmented functions.

QUESTIONS AND PROBLEMS

1. Distinguish between official and personal leaders. Give an example of each from your student community.

2. What are some educational and other traits found among the top leadership in different proportions than in the national population as a whole?

3. What are the institutional limits to the full power of the top leadership of the nation?

4. To what extent are the national leaders independent of one another, rather than being a single clique?

5. Is the American national leadership a tighter network than the leadership of England or of the Soviet Union? Explain your answer.

PART V

The Presidency

19. Office of the President

Photo by Abbie Rowe. Courtesy National Park Service

CONSTITUTIONAL POSITION OF THE PRESIDENT

THE executive power shall be vested in a President. . . ." So reads the Constitution. This bare, curt statement defines what is now the most powerful office in the world outside the dictatorships. As chief executive the President possesses broad functions—broader, in fact, than those of any other single executive in any other representative government. In addition, like the British monarch and the French President, he must represent the nation in numerous ceremonial roles.

The ceremonial or expressive role takes much of his time. Some of it, such as the entertaining of foreign dignitaries, finds counterparts throughout the world. Other parts of it, such as throwing out the first ball to open the major league baseball season, are peculiar to the United States. Hardly a day goes by without some example of such symbolic functions, in which the President typifies the nation.

293

Along with these decorative and expressive functions the President must move men and things. That is, he must perform tasks which in Great Britain, France, and other nations with kindred governments are the obligation of the Prime Minister or some other executive official. For example, the President must see to the execution of federal laws. In so doing, he supervises directly or indirectly the work of more than two million administrative employees. The President is also Commander in Chief of the armed forces of the United States. Finally, he represents the United States, in an active as well as in a symbolic sense, in relations with the nations of the world.

Moreover, in keeping with the principle of checks and balances, the President has considerable power outside his executive functions. He possesses considerable judicial authority. He has extensive legislative powers, through his authority to approve or to veto laws, to send messages to Congress, and the like. Hence the President not only is head of the executive branch but also plays an important part in each of the other two branches of the government as well.

DEVELOPMENT OF PRESIDENTIAL LEADERSHIP

Today the President occupies a position superior to that originally intended by most supporters and opponents of the Constitution. He is now the political leader of the American people. Almost certainly the authors of the Constitution did not intend that the President should achieve this stature. Rather, they aimed at creating a government whose three branches should be approximately equal in power. However, their philosophy did not comprehend the changes that might stimulate growth in the executive branch; nor could they predict the vigorous competition that has occurred among the three branches of government for power and prestige. Hence despite their efforts to perpetuate equality among these branches, Congress has lagged relatively; the judiciary long ago enjoyed its one great gain, the power of judicial review; but the President has vaulted far ahead of both.

Executive preeminence can be illustrated from the transformation of the legislative process. The authors of the Constitution expected that Congress would take the initiative in legislating; they felt that the representative body should assume the burden of steering government policy. It was anticipated that from time to time the President would have certain recommendations to make about legislation he desired; yet the legislative role of the President was supposed to lie chiefly in the field of approving or vetoing bills that had been originated in Congress. Today the bulk of legislation is proposed by the White House; it can be maintained that Congress does not so much initiate legislation as it approves, amends, or rejects the President's legislative program.

The President has secured this predominance in the government through a number of means, both constitutional and extraconstitutional. Of the two categories the constitutional has been the less important; the emergence of

The White House.

presidential leadership can be ascribed largely to means outside the letter of the Constitution—although, of course, quite legal. For example, the President has been able to exploit the unity of his office—by comparison with the plurality of Congress—to show the public greater determination and singlemindedness in time of need. Undoubtedly the public reciprocates by looking toward the President as the one man who can provide the leadership it seeks; the public sees a symbol in the President. This situation was dramatized in the depression of 1929, when a part of the people sought leadership from President Hoover toward recovery, was disappointed in "seeing" none, turned to Franklin D. Roosevelt in 1932, and at once followed the leadership he offered.

Congress has sometimes accelerated this process by turning its leadership on some matters over to the President. For instance, by creating the Bureau of the Budget and establishing it in the Executive Office of the President, Congress lost some of its financial initiative. Moreover, Presidents Theodore Roosevelt, Wilson, F. D. Roosevelt, and Truman, while in office, frequently asserted their belief that they must lead the country. Wilson wrote and spoke eloquently in defense of the belief; he admired the chance for decisive leadership that the Prime Minister of Great Britain had. Finally, various Presidents have used their executive powers to take the leadership of their political party, and then, completing the circle, have used their party leadership to increase their control of Congress and of party policy. Many more details of the development of the powers of the chief executive are contained in the subsequent description of the presidency and Congress.

QUALIFICATIONS FOR THE PRESIDENCY

Constitutional qualifications

The Constitution briefly establishes three qualifications for the President that are effective today (Art. II, sec. 1, cl. 5). He must be "a natural-born citizen"; he shall "have attained to the age of thirty-five years"; and he must "have been fourteen years a resident within the United States." The requirement of natural-born citizenship excludes anyone born a foreign subject or national. The age limit has probably never interfered with any serious candidacy, and almost certainly never will. The residence requirement has not been thought to mean the fourteen years immediately prior to the election or inauguration, for Herbert Hoover was out of the United States for lengthy periods during the era from 1914 to 1928.

Term of office

It has already been noted that the question of the President's term excited long discussions at the Philadelphia Convention. A four-year term was ultimately selected, with no bar to reelection. Probably the Founding Fathers agreed that a President might be reelected an indefinite number of times. President Washington retired after two terms, doubtless in part from age, fatigue, and resentment at the attacks directed at him by his opponents. Also, he probably felt that after eight years of successful functioning the government was well enough launched on its course to have no further need of him.

The third President, Thomas Jefferson, who retired at the end of his second term, stated his belief as a general principle that no President should serve for more than two terms. This assertion should not be interpreted as a justification for any belief on Jefferson's part that he was faced by defeat in 1808; for it is widely acknowledged that he chose both of his successors, James Madison and James Monroe, each of whom served two terms. This display of Jefferson's influence suggests that he might have been reelected as many times as he sought office. Hence his statement that no President should serve more than two terms can be accepted as a principle rather than an expedient.

The two-term tradition established by Jefferson lasted more than a century, until 1940, when it was smashed by President Franklin D. Roosevelt. It can never be known definitely what the President might have done had World War II not begun in 1939; but there are grounds for surmising that he might have offered himself as a candidate in any case. Roosevelt enjoyed the exercise of power; he had suffered a defeat in the midterm elections of 1938, partly at the hands of his own party, which he probably wanted to recoup; and as a good politician Roosevelt knew that there were few if any prominent Democrats to succeed him (some say that he saw to it that no eligible politicians became prominent).

However, the advent of the war offered Roosevelt and the American people a strong justification for a third term: the argument that he was the only American who was well enough acquainted with the diplomatic situation to pilot the American government in the crisis. Prior to the Democratic convention of 1940, Roosevelt refused to commit himself when asked his intentions about reelection. There was some pre-convention discussion about other candidates, such as James Farley and John Nance Garner; nevertheless, at the convention Roosevelt was nominated on the first ballot. Four years later, before any "three-term tradition" had had an opportunity to crystallize, Roosevelt was nominated for, and elected to, a fourth term.

Today a barrier has been erected against unlimited presidential reelection, so that no future President may hope to emulate Roosevelt's achievement. The Twenty-second Amendment, which completed the ratification process in 1951, provides that no person shall be elected to the presidency more than twice, and that no person who has served more than two years of a term for which some other person was elected may be chosen more than once. Thus no person may possibly be President for more than ten years. Springing in part from Roosevelt's achievement, this Amendment was proposed in 1947 by the Eightieth Congress, the first to be dominated by the Republican Party after Roosevelt's death.

Salary

Although some leaders at the Philadelphia Convention, particularly Benjamin Franklin, expressed the wish that the President would serve without salary, the Constitution provides that the President shall receive a salary. It is further provided that this salary may not be increased or diminished during the President's term (Art. II, sec. 1, cl. 6); thus Congress can neither reward nor punish a President for his official actions by raising or lowering his pay. Originally Congress set this salary at $25,000 per annum. It was increased by steps over the years until, in 1949, Congress fixed it at $100,000 plus a $50,000 expense account that was tax-exempt and up to $40,000 additional for entertainment and traveling. At the request of President

TABLE 15. A PRESIDENT'S PAY AND ALLOWANCES[1]

Salary, expense allowance	$150,000
Travel allowance	40,000
Servants' pay, upkeep of White House	443,000
Upkeep of airplanes, pay of crew	310,000
Protection by Secret Service and White House police	945,000
Upkeep of cabin cruisers, pay of crew	50,000
White House chauffeurs	50,000
Other (including upkeep of Camp David and cost of White House military detachment)	150,000
Total	$2,138,000 per year

These Things Are Furnished to the President:

A mansion and grounds worth	$25,000,000
Two airplanes worth	3,075,000
Cabin cruisers worth	500,000
A retreat (Camp David) worth	100,000
An automobile worth	30,000
Total	$28,705,000

These People Work Directly for the President:

White House office workers and aides	289
Servants at the White House	72
White House police	151
Airplane crewmen	10
Cabin-cruiser crewmen	23
Total	545

[1] From *U.S. News & World Report*, an independent weekly news magazine published in Washington. Copyright 1953, United States News Publishing Corporation, July 22, 1955, pp. 31–32.

Eisenhower, Congress in 1953 removed the tax exemption from the expense account. Beyond this, numerous other goods and services are attached to the presidency, such as the White House, the presidential yacht, and a large secretarial staff. Altogether the President receives the equivalent of over two million dollars annually (see Table 15).

Privileges and immunities

Before George Washington was inaugurated as the first President, there were long debates as to what privileges the President should enjoy, by what title he should be addressed, and whether he should wear some sort of distinguishing attire. Washington felt some affection for kingly protocol, and

Vice President John Adams was at first quite insistent upon special recognition for his office. However, the steady infusion of the American government with the special notions of what is correct for a democratic representative regime ended many of these claims and practices.

The President does retain one major immunity: he cannot be sued or prosecuted in court, unless he waives his immunity. This privilege is not stated in the Constitution. It is a custom based on the principle of the separation of powers; if the President were subject to court action, it would mean that the executive branch of the government was subordinate to the judicial branch. Therefore the only judicial action to which the President is liable is impeachment; moreover, a conviction following impeachment may result in no more severe penalty than removal from office and disqualification for further officeholding. However, this immunity extends to the office, not to the person; hence once a President is removed by impeachment, he may be tried in court in the same fashion as any private citizen. Finally, the President is immune from interrogation by Congress, or any congressional committee, just as he is immune from court trial. He does not have to respond to a subpena, which is an order by a committee or court to appear as a witness.

In 1953 the question arose whether this immunity extended to a former President with respect to events occurring while he was President. Chairman Harold Velde of the House Un-American Activities Committee subpenaed former President Truman to testify concerning events that had occurred during Truman's term of office. Truman rejected the subpena, claiming immunity; before his claim had an opportunity to be tested, however, Velde withdrew the subpena.

THE VICE PRESIDENT

Until recent years the office of the Vice President has appeared to be one of the least significant executive positions in the American government. John Calhoun resigned from the vice presidency in order to enter the Senate. Theodore Roosevelt when President is said to have ordered that the large glass chandelier over his desk be transferred from his office to that of the Vice President, where the tinkling of the glass in the wind might keep its occupant awake. The Democratic Party candidate for the vice presidency in 1904 was more than eighty years old.

Succession to the presidency

Constitutionally the principal function of the Vice President is to assume the office of President should the incumbent die, resign, become incapacitated, or be removed through impeachment proceedings. Thus the Vice President provides the citizenry with reassurance that national leadership will continue in a crisis and that no free-for-all political struggle will ensue. The question has arisen as to whether the Vice President *becomes* President, or merely *occupies the office* of President. The problem was resolved largely by the determined personality of John Tyler, who in 1841 became the first Vice President to succeed a deceased President. Congress, then relatively stronger than it is today, and containing such powerful members as John Calhoun, prepared to assume leadership of the country. However, Tyler refused to bow to Congress and insisted on being dealt with as President in fact. Tyler's success in his endeavors founded the principle that the Vice President upon succeeding becomes as surely President as if he had been elected to that office. Section Three of the Twentieth Amendment formally clarifies the situation to some extent in providing that if the President-elect should die before his inauguration, the Vice President-elect "shall become President."

Presiding officer of the Senate

While the Vice President is marking time, so to speak, he serves as the presiding officer of the Senate. However, he has only a casting vote; that is, he may vote only to break a tie. The Senate does not often regard the Vice President very highly, especially since he may be a comparative newcomer in politics; and it will countenance little if any criticism of its procedure by an impatient Vice President, if only because such action constitutes executive interference with the legislative branch, and because of the Senate's jealousy of its privileges. In any case the chair in the Senate frequently is occupied not by the Vice President, who may be absent on other business, but by the President *pro tem.*

Evolution of the vice presidency

The potentialities of the vice presidency have fluctuated considerably since 1788. The pressure of recent events has compelled the Vice President to assume a more weighty role in American politics than he did in the past. The President has become so burdened with duties that the Vice President has had to accept some of them, especially those dealing with ceremony—the entertainment of foreign potentates, visiting other countries, even substituting for the President in certain American political rituals. For example, in 1953 Vice President Richard M. Nixon made a trip around the world, visiting chiefly the nations of Asia, as the personal representative of President Eisenhower, to assure their governments of the good intentions of the United States.

Too, Vice Presidents have begun to take more seriously the possibility that the President may die in office; most Vice Presidents since Coolidge have attended cabinet meetings if only to grasp the general policy of the administration. Moreover, as presiding officer of the Senate, the Vice President can furnish liaison between the White House and Capitol Hill; this function can be very well implemented by a Vice President such as Alben Barkley, who had long been an influential and respected member of the Senate. Finally, Congress has added to the strength of the Vice President by making him a member of the National Security Council. Congress, however, probably cannot go very far in giving power to the Vice President without encountering vigorous opposition from the President, who can cite the Constitution as making the presidency the paramount executive.

Careers of some Vice Presidents

Seven Vice Presidents have succeeded to the presidency upon the death of the President. (Three more—John Adams, Thomas Jefferson, and Martin Van Buren—were elected to the presidency after completing their vice presidential terms.) Thus, about one out of five Vice Presidents has been summoned by fate to the highest office. Of these, only the last three—Theodore Roosevelt, Coolidge, and Truman—were afterward nominated for, and elected to, the presidency. All of the first four experienced difficulties with their party; and two, Tyler and Johnson, collided head-on with Congress. Of course, Johnson's case was unique; he was a Democrat who owed his nomination to the fact that he had been the only Senator from a seceded State who had not abdicated his seat in Congress prior to the Civil War. Sudden accession to the presidency has evoked different types of reactions from these men. In the case of Chester A. Arthur it called forth a sense of responsibility that amazed the nation and staggered his faction of the Republican Party. In 1878 he had been removed by President Hayes from his office as collector of the port of New York, for practicing too assiduously the spoils system; but as President (1881–1885) he urged adoption of the Pendleton Act, which set up a merit system in the Civil Service.

Qualifications and salary

For some reason the Constitution is mute as to the qualifications of the Vice President; probably the omission was due to the original mode of filling this office, whereby it was a sort of consolation prize for a man who had tried to win the presidency but had failed. In any event, the Twelfth Amendment, which establishes the present means for filling the office, also established the same qualifications for the Vice President that the Constitution demands of the President. As in the case of the President, there are numerous types of "eligibility" demands that change with the circumstances. The Vice President receives an annual salary of $45,000. Not only is his salary considerably less than that of the President; so likewise are the perquisites of his office. Since the Vice President today must assume heavy and expensive social tasks, it is widely argued that the government should at least provide him with a suitable house.

SUCCESSION TO THE PRESIDENCY

The Constitution furnishes the Vice President as the immediate successor to the President; however, it leaves to Congress the fixing of a further line of succession (Art. II, sec. 1, cl. 6). Up to the present there has always been a Vice President to succeed when a President has died in office. However, seven Vice Presidents have died in office, and another has resigned. Hence arrangements for an extended line of succession to the presidency have been thought essential.

Congress twice, in 1792 and in 1886, provided for succession in the absence of both the President and the Vice President; each method was later found unsatisfactory. The present arrangement, established by Congress in 1947, confers the presidency first upon the Speaker, then the President *pro tem,* and finally upon the Cabinet members in the order in which the cabinet posts were created.

A poet, impressed with the problem of succession in a republic, penned the following doggerel to celebrate the latest law:

> *American law leaves nothing to chance*
> *and makes its choice before death's dance.*

> *Should the President unfortunately die*
> *it's the Vice Presidential turn to try.*

> *If the V.P. falters*
> *and his grip gets weaker*
> *the scepter is placed*
> *in the hands of the Speaker.*

> *The Senatorial President pro tem*
> *comes next in line after them;*

> *and should the latter pass away*
> *the Secretary of State comes into play.*

> *State's demise gives Treasury the prize.*

> *To take it with him would create offense*
> *were the financier to mount his bier,*
> *so he must pass it to Defense;*

> *and should the Bomb shake his aplomb,*
> *shunning unpatriotic fright*
> *the Attorney-General must plight.*

> *Then Post, Interior, and Agriculture rate*
> *while Commerce and Labor await a fate*

> *whose chances to befall*
> *are not very good at all.*

QUESTIONS AND PROBLEMS

1. The structure of the presidential office has been changed under the pressure of numerous demands upon it. What are some of these demands?

2. What have been some of the legal and extralegal means whereby the office of the President has expanded its powers?

3. Is it likely that the Twenty-second Amendment is as durable as the average provision of the Constitution, or is it likely to be changed whenever a President who is popular wishes a third term?

4. Consulting a good encyclopedia on the subject of monarchy or kingship, compare the American presidency with the traits and powers commonly found among kings. What are the important similarities and differences of training, selection, powers, functions, respect, and political difficulties?

5. What are the vice presidential duties that have evolved beyond those stated in the Constitution? Would you suggest others that might be undertaken? Explain your answer.

6. Suppose a Vice President who has become President on April 2, 1958, runs again for the presidency in 1960 and is elected. Could he run again in 1964?

THE Cabinet and the presidential staff, along with a varying number of other individuals and small groups, make up the President's family of direct advisers. They are pictured in Figure 37 as they will be discussed in this chapter. Since time immemorial, the executive chief has possessed a body of advisers or counsellors. Where government is primitive and the state small, the counsellors group around the ruler as relatives, co-warriors, or as a council of elders. Where government is complex and the state large, the same small groups persist but a large body of officials also develops. American government, of course, was never, save among the Indians, of the first type. Rather, it began as a somewhat complex organism and has become increasingly complicated. To carry out the various governmental operations the executive has needed expert advice from people trained in these operations. Examples here include those men in the Bureau of the Budget who are specialists in the financial affairs of the different agencies of the government. The executive also requires the advice as well as the obedient services of the men who directly manage the numerous operations. The heads of the Departments illustrate this type of adviser.

Furthermore, the various agencies of the government become themselves representatives of newly arisen economic and social interests, such as farmers, businessmen, and industrial workers; and the President keeps informed of group needs through his agency chiefs. The Secretary of Health, Education, and Welfare is the national spokesman for, among others, some of the most vocal and potent lobbies at many State capitals—the vari-

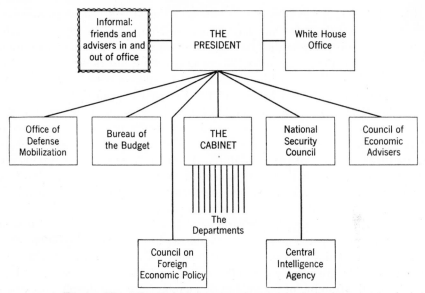

Figure 37.   The President's Family of Direct Advisers.

ous organizations of public elementary and secondary school teachers.   On the other hand, giving an economic or social grouping access to the executive commonly entails, in the near future, new government functions in behalf of that grouping.   The creation of the Department of Commerce, with its chief in the Cabinet, soon brought the vast information resources of the executive branch to the assistance of the business community, as a stimulus to domestic and international trade.

TWO GREAT EXECUTIVE REVOLUTIONS

The history of counsellors to the executive over the last 800 years throws into sharp light an important problem of politics in America and the world today.   Congress itself is the living descendant of a group of executive counsellors that goes back to the late Middle Ages.   Although it bears as remote a resemblance to its ancestors as modern man does to the first recognizable human beings, it has sprung from the ancient practice of the king to summon to his court the nobles and high clergy (as in the ancient House of Lords) and the commoners (as in the first House of Commons) to lend aid and advice.   Gradually these advisory bodies came to give mandatory "advice."   Finally, in a series of revolutions beginning in England in 1640 and continuing there, in America, in France, and elsewhere, the legislatures came to be the primary law-making bodies.   Through this evolution the king became a subject.   The nineteenth and early twentieth centuries, in fact, may well be called the Age of Legislatures.

Amidst the first series of revolutions grew the second series, quietly, persistently, and after 1914, strongly.   The second series threatened the first,

A Meeting of the Cabinet, October 25, 1954, the First to be Viewed by a Television Audience.

although in fact it was of the same type save that it was 800 years younger. This comprised the development of executive counsellors in the new executive that had grown from the new, supreme legislatures. The new institution in America was the President and his executive staff; in France and England it was the Prime Minister, the cabinet, and the department heads; in Italy, Mussolini and the Grand Council of the Fascist Party; in Germany, Hitler and the Nazi chieftains; and in the Soviet Union and other communist states, the Central Committee of the Communist Party. These new executive leaders, even in their weakest form, now share, and threaten to embrace more of, the powers of the legislature. The fact that these new groups are not called legislatures does not prevent them from making laws. The fact that sometimes they are called "non-partisan" does not deter their members from acting in all other respects like politicians.

It would be tempting but hazardous at this juncture to distinguish who among the presidential counsellors are devoted to policy, and who are concerned with administration. No such categorical distinction is possible, for the two fields are closely intermingled. For instance, the cabinet gives advice on the framing of policy, but its members are also deeply concerned with administrative problems. Moreover, the Executive Office of the President was designed with an eye to easing his administrative chores; yet it makes outstanding contributions to the framing of policy.

THE CABINET

Origins

The Cabinet had its origins during President Washington's first term. The Constitution makes no provision for a Cabinet; however, its authors surely were aware that the President would want to surround himself with a body of competent advisers. Perhaps they expected that he might ask counsel of the Senate. At that time a small (twenty-six members in 1789) deliberative body, the Senate was somewhat analogous to the upper houses of the colonial legislatures, which had on occasion provided counsel to colonial governors. Finally, it possessed executive powers, in that it could accept or reject both presidential appointments and treaties with foreign nations. However, the Senate displayed resentment at Washington's efforts to consult with it in the senatorial chamber. The Supreme Court, too, might have been expected to yield counsel; however, whereas certain colonial courts had rendered advisory decisions, the Supreme Court refused to do so, and restricted its decisions to actual cases at law.

Thus rebuffed, Washington turned to the heads of the executive Departments for a consultative body. The President was already constitutionally empowered to seek their opinion, in writing, concerning the affairs of their respective Departments (Art. II, sec. 2, cl. 1). Calling upon these departmental chiefs in a body for their advice required at most only a slight expansion of this constitutional grant. The practice of terming the body a "Cabinet" seems to have developed about the year 1793, and to have continued from that date to the present. However, the Cabinet was not mentioned by name in a statute until the twentieth century. Even the Reorganization Plan No. 1 of 1953, which laid the foundation for the Department of Health, Education, and Welfare, did not use the word; it provided simply for the establishment of an "executive Department" under a "Secretary." Thus the Cabinet is an important part of the American government that is not founded specifically by the Constitution.

Choice of Cabinet members

The choice of Cabinet members is almost entirely at the ultimate discretion of the President. The Senate seldom questions the President's nominations; and it has no control over his dismissals. It might almost be said that the chief prerequisite for Cabinet members is that they be satisfactory to the President. However, there are certain broad considerations which modify his selections.

Party Attachment: In the first place, the Cabinet nearly always consists entirely of members of the President's party. In the very first Cabinet, President Washington underwent difficulties from the clashes between his Antifederalist Secretary of State, Jefferson, and his Federalist Secretary of the Treasury, Hamilton. Washington's experience, and the demands of the party system, laid down the general principle that Cabinet members should be solely of the President's party. However, there have been exceptions to this principle. Shortly before the election of 1940 President Roosevelt enlisted two Republicans, Henry Stimson and Frank Knox, in his Cabinet as, respectively, Secretary of War and Secretary of the Navy. Roosevelt's intention in this case seems to have been to make bipartisan the formulation of American policy toward the war in Europe, and at the same time to cut the ground from beneath Republican opponents of the presidential foreign policy. Then, in 1953, President Eisenhower named a southern Democrat, Mrs. Oveta Culp Hobby, as the first Secretary of Health, Education, and Welfare. Her appointment was probably aimed at rewarding the many southern Democrats who had voted for Eisenhower, enabling him to capture the electoral vote of several southern States, among them Texas.

Other Considerations: In the second place, Cabinet members are commonly selected so as to represent the different factions of the party. President Wilson named as his Secretary of State William Jennings Bryan, who led the Populist, free-silver wing of the Democratic Party. Third, Cabinet members are usually chosen in such a way as to represent the various regions of the country. President Eisenhower's original Cabinet included two men each from New York and Michigan; one each from Ohio, Oregon, Utah, Illinois, and Massachusetts; and Mrs. Hobby, from Texas. By contrast, on January 1, 1941, four of the ten members of the Cabinet hailed from New York State; indeed, Franklin Roosevelt was often accused of naming too many Easterners to his Cabinet. Probably the extent to which each of the above two considerations will prevail depends somewhat upon how much control the President exercises over his own party and how large his popular and electoral majorities were; a President who is politically powerful dares be rather insensitive about the demands of factions and regions.

In the fourth place, Cabinet appointments may be rewards for faithful party service or for major contributions toward campaign expenditures. The multimillionaire W. Averell Harriman could probably thank his gifts to the party coffers for his post as Secretary of Commerce under President Truman. It must be borne in mind that Cabinet members receive no salary as such; they must seek compensation in intangibles such as prestige and influence, which can be great. However, as Department heads they each receive an annual stipend of $25,000. Frequently the Postmaster Generalship is awarded to the national party chairman, as in the cases of James Farley, Robert Hannegan, and Arthur Summerfield. Too, the President may choose for a Cabinet position an individual notable principally for being a close friend of the President, as F. D. Roosevelt apparently did in naming William Woodin Secretary of the Treasury. Moreover, certain special qualifications are attached to some of the Cabinet posts. For instance, the Attorney General must be a lawyer; the Secretaries of Commerce and of Labor must not be disagreeable, respectively, to the major business interests and to the major labor organizations.

Experts: Finally, Cabinet positions are offered with growing frequency to experts in the work of the Departments. Secretaries of Agriculture Henry Wallace and Ezra Taft Benson each were closely affiliated with farming. President Eisenhower's first Secretary of Labor, Martin Durkin, was President of the AFL Plumbers' Union. Secretary of State John Foster Dulles had had more than three decades of experience in diplomacy prior to his appointment to the Cabinet. Even the tradition of Postmasters General was broken in 1947 by the nomination of Jesse Donaldson, who had been in the career postal service for many years.

The evidence of a changing composition of the Cabinet can be read in a few statistics prepared by Mr. Richard Fisher at the Hoover Institute and Library of Stanford University. Between 1889 and 1921, 27% of the Cabinet members belonged to professional organizations such as the American Bar Association. In contrast, about 45% of the Cabinet members since 1921 belonged to such organizations. A similar rise has been recorded in their membership in community service and fraternal organizations. The proportion of Cabinet officials who had held lower federal appointive positions was 18% for the period from 1889 to 1921, but about one-third since that time. However, the percentage who had once been congressmen declined from 35% to 18% in the two periods. Moreover, the number of Cabinet members who had once held State and local office also declined after 1921.

The trend toward choosing experts rather than politicians as Cabinet members illustrates the acceptance of the notion that the government is to play an affirmative role with respect to American life. At the same time, the choice of experts tends to diminish the ability of the Cabinet to provide counsel on broad policy questions; for by their very training experts are apt to have political views limited to the area of their especial competence. Moreover, Cabinet members rarely continue in office under a succeeding President, even of the same party. In fact, a Vice President rising to the presidency usually disposes fairly quickly of the Cabinet that he has inherited; for example, before the end of 1946 Truman had replaced all of Roosevelt's appointees except Secretary of the Navy James Forrestal. Finally, Cabinet office carries with it pressures, conflicts, and personal inconvenience to the extent that the average term in office of Secretaries between 1933 and 1948 was forty-nine months. Between 1948 and 1952, it was 42.5 months. Hence the Secretaries' expertness hardly has time to take effect; the Departments therefore must look instead to the permanent subordinates who can carry on despite changes in regime.

Functioning of the Cabinet

Precisely how the Cabinet functions, and exactly how much it can accomplish, are matters at the will of the President. From Washington to John Quincy Adams, Presidents tended to give considerable respect to Cabinet opinions. Andrew Jackson, however, found the principal source of his advice elsewhere, in his "Kitchen Cabinet." Jackson's immediate successors placed varying reliance upon their Cabinets. Franklin Pierce seems to have had great dependence upon his, for it was the only Cabinet that survived a presidential term intact. But Lincoln, Johnson, and Grant had major disputes with members of their Cabinets. Wilson, who held the British cabinet system in high honor, attempted to manage his Cabinet in that pattern. Harding was the last President who depended a great deal on his Cabinet. Presidents since Harding have relied mainly upon other sources for counsel regarding general policy. However, President Eisenhower has shown considerably more deference to Cabinet opinions than did his two predecessors.

The American Cabinet must be carefully distinguished from European Cabinets. In Europe the Cabinets are accountable more or less as a unit to their legislatures; on the continent, they usually can be unseated by an adverse parliamentary vote. Prime ministers are little more than the equals of other Cabinet members; in France the overthrow of the Cabinet by the parliament may produce a new Cabinet in which the new Prime Minister was previously a Cabinet member, whereas the past Prime Minister still holds a powerful ministerial portfolio. By contrast, American cabinets are totally the creatures of the President; he may dismiss individual members as he chooses. At the same time, American Cabinet members are not responsible to anyone but the President. Congress can discharge a Cabinet member only through conviction following impeachment.

At its meetings the Cabinet deals with two different levels of business; and the nature and role of any given Cabinet depends upon which of these levels tends to be emphasized. Cabinet members, after all, perform two roles. First, they are part of an advisory body to the President; and second, they are chiefs of the executive Departments. In its functioning, then, the Cabinet may present advice respecting the general policy of the administration; or it may discuss the operation of individual executive Departments. In their first role, Cabinet members operate more or less collectively; in their second, they operate as individuals. In general, the trend has been toward a greater stress of the second type of function; for little by little the Cabinet has been losing significance as a unit for providing advice on questions of broad policy.

This condition has arisen to a considerable extent from the fact that the Cabinet has become in late years more a body of specialists than a group of seasoned politicians used to dealing with all kinds of political and social questions. This change has already been noted above in the figures on the backgrounds of secretaries.

Secondly, the Cabinet has become decreasingly representative of the whole executive branch of the government. Under President Eisenhower, Cabinet meetings are attended not only by the traditional Department heads but also, occasionally and on invitation of the President, by the Chairman of the Civil Service Commission, the Director of the Council on Foreign Economic Policy, the American Ambassador to the United Nations, the Assistant to the President, and the Director of the Budget. The Vice-President, too, frequently attends Cabinet meetings. Yet there is no spokesman for the great quasi-judicial bodies such as the Interstate Commerce Commission, nor for government corporations such as the Tennessee Valley Authority. Furthermore, it is precisely those bodies and their chief personnel which in late years have often been productive of important plans and policies. These proposals must be delivered to the President and the public through channels other than Cabinet meetings. Hence the President must rely for policy counsel upon numerous individuals and groups outside his Cabinet.

Moreover, the Cabinet has become too large for intimate give-and-take discussions. Cabinet meetings, therefore, do not often generate the fundamental ideas under which the government operates today. At one of these meetings, which take place at the White House every Friday morning, there may be a rather perfunctory discussion of broad policy issues. Too, an individual member may submit for debate a departmental project, so that the Cabinet may collectively examine its possible effect upon the whole administration, and on the administrative program as well. But in the recent past it has been much commoner for members to seize the opportunity to have a private conversation with the President regarding administrative problems, while other members have chatted among themselves or dealt with other concerns.

Whatever new policy departure the President may sketch, the Cabinet has no control over presidential plans; the President may carry on his projects in the face of unanimous Cabinet disapproval. Cabinet votes are not officially recorded, and in the past no minutes have been kept of Cabinet meetings. The President is at liberty to deal with the Cabinet as he chooses. Some Presidents, notably Lincoln and F. D. Roosevelt, have found it desirable to enliven Cabinet meetings by telling funny stories. It is reported, however, that Eisenhower's Cabinet meetings show considerably greater decorum. But it is probably safe to predict that, barring a continued drive by the President to strengthen the Cabinet, it will decline as a policy-framing organ.

President Eisenhower has endeavored somewhat to reinvigorate the Cabinet by having major policy statements issue from Cabinet meetings rather than from the White House Office. Furthermore, he created a new post, Secretary to the Cabinet, in 1954. The Cabinet Secretary now keeps a central record of proceedings, and follows through afterward to see that Cabinet decisions are made known and their effects reported upon in subsequent meetings. He also prepares an agenda for each Cabinet meeting and distributes copies among the Cabinet members.

A few words may be inserted here, however, about the Bureau of the Budget, apart from its later treatment, for it is quite close to the President. Besides its great and detailed financial tasks, its Director and his associates are constantly consulted by the President and other leaders of the executive branch regarding the need for changes in the organization of the government and the desirability of increasing or decreasing emphasis upon certain operations of the government. These features of the work of the Bureau need surprise no one, for its vast knowledge of the innumerable financial details of the state puts it in an unmatched position for giving advice to the President on what he can and cannot do regarding many areas of policy.

THE PRESIDENTIAL STAFF

General structure

The formal presidential staff consists of a group of agencies loosely associated under the direct supervision of the President and known as the Executive Office of the President. It was created by Congress in 1939 primarily to lessen the enormous administrative burdens of the chief executive, to provide new bodies to assist the President in the formulation of policy, and to improve the means for executing and administering the presidential programs. The organizations making up the Executive Office have been subject to frequent experimentation and change; they include (1) the White House Office; (2) the Bureau of the Budget, which controls the fiscal planning of the government; (3) the Council of Economic Advisers, which supplies the President with information on economic affairs; (4) the National Security Council, which plans foreign policy and which has an important subordinate office, the Central Intelligence Agency; (5) the Office for Emergency Management, which is a mere shell of an organization for wartime preparedness; and (6) the Office of Defense Mobilization, which continuously organizes and plans economic resources for war. Of these six bodies, all but the first have distinct relationships with specific functions of the government, and are consequently discussed elsewhere in the book, in the context of those functions.

The White House Office

The White House Office is designed to carry out many administrative functions directly attached to the Office of the President. Authority for the formal creation of the Office was granted by Congress in 1939 pursuant to recommendations of the President's Committee on Administrative Management in the Government of the United States.

However, Congress at that time empowered the President to make any or all of numerous modifications in the Office; it has in fact seen many changes since 1939. The nucleus of the White House Office comprises six presidential assistants, three of them "special" and three "administrative." These assistants provide liaison between the President and the various agencies of the executive branch. They relieve the President of seeing many people whose problems are not so important as to merit his direct attention. The White House Office also contains a Press Secretary to deal with the media of publicity; military, naval, and Air Force aides, to advise the President with respect to the armed forces; the Economic Adviser to the President; the Physician to the President; the Special Counsel to the President; and a large secretarial staff to handle relationships with Congress and the public.

Under President Eisenhower the leading personage in the White House Office is the Assistant to the President, an office established by the President. The powers of the Assistant actually are as great or as small as the President may decide. Under a weak President—should he see fit to continue the office—the Assistant conceivably might gain a position roughly analogous to that of the Carolingian *major domo* under the last Merovingian rulers of the Frankish Empire in the eighth century; in other terms, he might become the real power behind the throne. In any case, he holds an office in which he can bring great influence upon the presidential policy; hence his appointment may be a matter of considerable intraparty maneuvering about the President. However, he is subordinate to the President, and may be dismissed at the latter's discretion.

The relationship between President Eisenhower and his Assistant, Sherman Adams, former governor of New Hampshire, may also be compared with that of an infantry lieutenant to his platoon sergeant, in which the latter assumes the more distasteful obligations, especially those of partisan political significance. For example, it was Assistant Adams rather than President Eisenhower who in 1954 asked the resignation of the controversial Dean Clarence Manion, Chairman of the Commission on Intergovernmental Relations, who had publicly supported issues that Eisenhower had opposed, and who was associated with a faction of the Republican Party that had opposed the nomination of Eisenhower. Had Eisenhower, not Adams, asked Dean Manion's resignation, the action might have led to more disturbance within the Republican Party than it did.

OTHER PRESIDENTIAL ADVISERS

The freedom of presidential choice

The President has almost complete freedom to select whatever advisers he may wish apart from the Cabinet and his Executive Office. Many chief executives throughout the world have been, and may still be, isolated from affairs by a clique that rules in the executive's name; one outstanding example of such a regime in modern times was that of the aged President Hindenburg in pre-Hitlerite Germany, in which the governing policy appears to have been almost completely dictated by a cabal surrounding the senile Field Marshal. Even the American President is to some degree the captive of his office and his party.

However, it would be idle to attempt to insulate the President wholly from the political world about him, since it would be almost impossible to sever all his channels to the outside. Few Presidents, if any, would allow themselves to be denied the morning newspaper. Consequently many Presidents, sensing that the counsel furnished by their traditional and formal advisers was inadequate or unsatisfactory, have utilized this freedom to go outside their official families to seek counsel. The nature of the source to which the President may turn will depend largely upon circumstances and to a great extent upon the very personality of the President himself. President Eisenhower appears to have employed so-called "stag dinners" at the White House to obtain counsel from private individuals. The *U.S. News and World Report* in its issue of February 4, 1955, stated that altogether 555 persons had attended thirty-eight of these gatherings. Among the 555, 294 were businessmen; eighty-one, administration officials; fifty-one, editors, publishers, and writers; thirty, educators; twenty-three, Republican Party leaders, and smaller numbers of scientists, artists, sportsmen, old friends from military days, heads of foundations or charities, farmers and farm leaders, union officials, church leaders, Eisen-

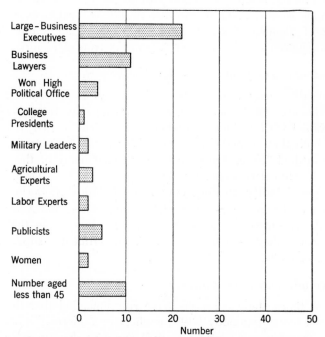

Adapted from "U.S. News and World Report," an independent weekly news magazine published at Washington. Copyright 1953, United States News Publishing Corporation, January 30, 1953, pp. 21—23

Figure 38. Eisenhower's Fifty Chief Assistants.

hower relatives, and State and local officials. It is instructive that following publication of this article the identity of the White Houses guests was
ordered henceforth withheld. In general, as Figure 38 shows, President
Eisenhower has favored leading businessmen for official appointment as
well.

Individual friends

Some Presidents have resorted to individuals and confidential advisers;
two noteworthy cases of this practice were Colonel E. M. House under
President Wilson and Harry Hopkins under F. D. Roosevelt. Whereas
Colonel House occupied no significant post in the executive branch, he was
a constant spring of advice, especially regarding foreign policy. Harry
Hopkins did hold important offices, such as administrator of the Works
Progress Administration and Secretary of Commerce; however, for some
years his influence pervaded so many aspects of the government that it
will probably never be established to what degree the elusive—and to
some people sinister—personality of Hopkins directed American foreign
and domestic policy.

"Kitchen Cabinets"

Other Presidents have had recourse not to one but to several friends
outside the government. This sort of presidential council was first publicized under President Jackson, whose group of behind-the-scenes councillors
won the name of "Kitchen Cabinet." In recent times, Presidents Harding
and Truman have availed themselves of kitchen cabinets, the former's
consisting of elements from the so-called "Ohio Gang" and the latter's
of friends (journalistically termed "cronies") from Missouri.

Additional advisers from the executive branch

The President may also create an advisory group from government
officials who are not Department heads; or he may bring such officials
to collaborate with Cabinet members. President F. D. Roosevelt resorted to both these expedients. One of his better-publicized innovations
was the so-called "Brain Trust," which provided many of the social, economic, and political concepts fashioning the early New Deal. Its members—Raymond Moley, Rexford Guy Tugwell, Adolf A. Berle, and others
—were generally imaginative young Under Secretaries and Assistant Secretaries in the executive Departments; but for a time, from their positions
as "idea men," they overshadowed their departmental superiors in the
President's councils.

Legislative advisers from Congress

In recent times many observers have recommended that the President
take counsel more frequently with members of Congress. President Truman, who as a former Senator was well acquainted with many congressmen, often entertained leaders of Congress at the White House. Under
various recent Presidents, but especially under President Eisenhower, whose

relationships with Congress are considerably less personal than Truman's, there has developed a form of legislative-executive cooperation that bids fair to become a permanent institution. For instance, the practice under President Eisenhower has been that every Monday morning the Republican leaders of each house convene with the President to discuss new legislative proposals. For specific matters the committee chairmen and Cabinet members involved may also be invited. Democratic Party chieftains may also come, to give their reactions. Continuation of this practice may bring the executive and legislative branches much closer together than ever before. At the same time, this agency may enable the President to place even greater pressure upon Congress to enact his program.

QUESTIONS AND PROBLEMS

1. Why does a counselling group grow up around an executive?

2. Does the history of executive power help explain the theory that leadership of a revolution always springs from the bosom of the old leadership?

3. Why do you think the Constitution did not provide specific presidential advisers or staff (even the vice presidency being considered a quite separate office)?

4. From the *United States Government Organization Manual* (current issue), the *Encyclopedia Britannica Yearbook*, or some other source, find who compose the present United States Cabinet. Read their brief biographies in *Who's Who* or in an article (consult the *Reader's Guide to Periodical Literature*) published when they were appointed. Suggest, in each case, the major reason why each may have been appointed to the Cabinet.

5. What are some of the different modes in which various Presidents sought counsel?

Bettman Archive

THE executive powers of the President may be defined as the powers that enable the President to carry out the policies—as stated in laws —that have been framed by Congress. Presumably, then, in using his executive powers the President is adhering to policies established not by himself but by an outside force, Congress. Actually in exercising these powers the President frequently reveals and even emphasizes his own policies, particularly in the case of laws that oppose his ideas.

The executive powers of the President are many and varied. The President is charged by the Constitution with supervising the execution of the laws. He appoints thousands of administrative leaders. He can remove many administrative leaders from their posts. He is the managing director of the vast administrative machinery of the United States, to which he gives

314

direction by executive orders and other types of oral and written commands. He is in a sense also the business manager of the national government; the national budget is prepared in the Bureau of the Budget, which is in the Executive Office of the President. He is the Commander in Chief of the armed forces of the United States. He is the principal representative of the United States to the other nations of the world. Indeed, in his executive functions alone the President may be regarded as filling many political roles. For making bare, initial comparisons, the clauses treating of the executive power from several constitutions of the modern world are presented on page 316.

The subject matter of this chapter includes only four of the presidential executive powers listed above: the execution of the laws, the appointment of administrative chiefs and of judges, the removal of administrative chiefs, and the supervision of the national administration. The other executive powers of the President will be dealt with in subsequent chapters where they may be more appropriately treated as phases of the functioning of the government.

THE EXECUTION OF THE LAWS

The Constitution provides that the President ". . . shall take care that the laws be faithfully executed. . . ." (Art. II, sec. 3.) This clause establishes the President as the chief executive officer of the United States. It contains the assumption that the President himself is not to execute the laws but to supervise those who do. It is sometimes overlooked that laws are not self-executing; legislation by Congress is meaningless until executed, or carried out, by the President's subordinates. Hence, the execution of federal law involves in one way or another all of the more than two million civil service employees, and, in time of need, the armed forces of the United States. Only a small part of the executing of the laws is composed of police work by such agencies as the Federal Bureau of Investigation; indeed, most police work falls in the province of the State and local governments. The federal executive branch is composed of people who carry out laws of many kinds, from collecting taxes to building electric power stations.

There is no formal means for compelling the President to execute the laws. Owing to the principle of the separation of powers, Congress can only legislate. Hence in the execution of the laws a President may often display policies that differ widely from those of Congress. For example, President Truman frequently refused to invoke certain clauses of the Labor-Management Relations (Taft-Hartley) Act of 1947 even though the Act had been passed by an extraordinary majority over his veto, showing great

Troops Escorting a Train Past Railroad Strikers, Chicago, July 10, 1894. President Cleveland, over the protests of Governor Altgeld and Mayor Hopkins of Chicago, ordered a regiment of federal troops to enforce a federal court injunction against the Pullman Company workers and the American Railway Union. The strike was broken after bloody rioting.

LOCATION OF THE SEAT OF EXECUTIVE POWER ACCORDING TO VARIOUS CONSTITUTIONS AND ORGANIC LAWS

Argentina: "The executive power of the Nation shall be vested in a citizen with the title of 'President of the Argentine Nation'." (art. 75)

Brazil: "The executive power is exercised by the President of the Republic." (art. 78)

Ceylon: "The executive power of the island shall continue vested in His Majesty [the British monarch] and may be exercised, on behalf of His Majesty, by the Governor-General in accordance with the provisions of this Order and of any other law for the time being in force." (art. 45)

Communist China: "The State Council of the People's Republic of China, that is, the Central People's Government, is the executive of the highest organ of state power; it is the highest administrative organ of state." (art. 47)

Greece: "The executive power belongs to the King, and is exercised by the responsible ministers appointed by him." (art. 27)

Japan: "Executive power shall be vested in the Cabinet." (art. 89)

Luxembourg: "The Grand Duke alone exercises the executive power." (art. 33)

The Netherlands: "The executive power shall be vested in the King." (art. 56)

The State of New York: "The executive power shall be vested in the governor. . . ." (Art. IV, sec. 1)

Saudi Arabia (The Hejaz): "The entire administration of the Kingdom of the Hejaz is in the hands of His Majesty Abdel Aziz I ibn Abdel Rahman Al Faisal Al Séoud." (art. 1)

Switzerland: "The supreme directing and executive authority of the Confederation is exercised by a federal council composed of seven members." (art. 95)

Syria: "The executive power shall be entrusted to the President of the Republic, by whom it shall be exercised, with the assistance of the ministers, under the conditions laid down in the present Constitution." (art. 31)

Thailand: "The King exercises the executive power through the Council of Ministers." (art. 9)

Turkey: "The Grand National Assembly exercises its executive authority through the person of the President of the Republic elected by it, and a council of ministers chosen by the President." (art. 7)

The Union of Soviet Socialist Republics: "The highest executive and administrative organ of the state power of the Union of Soviet Socialist Republics is the Council of Ministers of the U.S.S.R." (art. 64)

The United States of America: "The executive power shall be vested in a President of the United States of America." (Art. II, sec. 1, cl. 1)

Vatican City: "The Sovereign Pontiff, sovereign of the City of the Vatican, has full legislative, executive, and judicial powers.
"During a vacancy in the pontifical see, these same powers belong to the Holy College [the College of Cardinals]. . . ." (art. 1)

The Commonwealth of Virginia: "The chief executive power of the State shall be vested in a Governor." (sec. 69) congressional enthusiasm for the law; for President Truman was deeply in-debted politically to those labor union leaders against whom he would be using the Act. The Sherman Antitrust Act was passed in 1890; however, during its first decade it was rarely invoked, since Presidents Benjamin Harrison, Grover Cleveland, and William McKinley felt scant desire to regulate corporations and were in fact assisted by certain large corpora-tions in their campaigns for office. However, after 1901 Presidents Theo-dore Roosevelt and William H. Taft enforced the Sherman Act vigorously since certain other interests had brought strong pressure on them to do so.

Whereas there may be no formal means for compelling the President to execute the law, there quite decidedly are informal, political compulsions. One of the President's greatest duties is to uphold his party; even though he may be in his second term and is consequently ineligible for another term, he must so conduct himself as not to weaken his party for the coming elections. In the same way the President is obligated to those who sup-ported him for office, and who expect some sort of compensation for their support. An obstinate refusal to execute the laws may cost him and his party the following of some of the public, and will perhaps be unrewarding for those who aided his campaign. Indeed, the majority of the twentieth-century American public would not long tolerate a President who did not act. In the long run, then, the President's decision to execute or not to execute a given law must be modified by political as well as by con-scientious considerations.

THE APPOINTMENT OF EXECUTIVE OFFICERS AND OF JUDGES

One of the weightiest presidential powers is that of appointing executive officers and judges. The Constitution states that the President "shall nom-inate, and, by and with the advice and consent of the Senate, shall appoint ambassadors, other public ministers and consuls, judges of the Supreme Court, and all other officers of the United States, whose appointments are not herein otherwise provided for, and which shall be established by law; but the Congress may by law vest the appointment of such inferior officers, as they think proper, in the President alone, in the courts of law, or in the heads of departments" (Art. II, sec. 2, cl. 2). Thus every member of the executive branch of the national government except the President and the Vice President—more than two million people—is either directly or indirectly appointed by the President. In keeping with this constitutional authorization, the appointment of most of these persons, including all those under the merit system in the Civil Service save postmasters, has been vested in the heads of Departments. The direct presidential appointees number about 20,000, approximately one per cent of the total.

Following the Constitution, the process of appointment would appear to take a path wherein the President nominates, the Senate consents, and the President then officially appoints. In the case of Cabinet members, federal judges, diplomatic officials, and military commissions, this is roughly the path to appointment. The Senate rarely fails to confirm a Cabinet nomination since it regards these officers as belonging to the presidential family and such close advisers of the President that he should have virtually unlimited discretion in his choice. The Senate is less ready to accept the presidential choices for judges and diplomatic officers. For example, there were major disputes over the confirmation of Associate Justice Hugo Black and of Charles Bohlen as Ambassador to the Soviet Union.

In the case of some thousands of other appointive offices, however, although the process formally adheres to the text of the Constitution, in practice it might almost be said to reverse the Constitution, so that the Senate actually nominates and the President confirms. In the case of a federal appointive officer such as a United States marshal, the President consults with the senior Senator of his party from the State in which the office is located. Should there be no senior Senator of his party from the State, the President may confer with a Representative or even with State party leaders. From these advisers he can receive the name of a competent person for the post whom the adviser may well wish to reward for some past political favor. The President may then proceed to nominate the individual suggested; presumably the Senate will consent to the nomination, and the President can then make the appointment official.

With the bulk of presidential appointments being effected through recommendations from the Senate, there has developed a practice termed "senatorial courtesy." This practice is aimed at curbing the independence of the President when making appointments. If the President should make an appointment without consulting his party's Senator or Senators from the State concerned to a post whose incumbent is normally recommended by the Senators from the State, and if the individual whom the President has nominated is in some way undesirable to one or both of those Senators, they may state on the floor of the Senate that the presidential nominee is "personally obnoxious" to them. Indeed, since most appointments are first referred to the relevant Senate standing committee, the Senators may make the declaration of opposition at a committee hearing. Under the operation of senatorial courtesy, the Senate will refuse to consent to the appointment of the presidential nominee. The working of senatorial courtesy is not inevitable; but it is so nearly so that a President will not often attempt an appointment without prior assurance from the Senate that his nomination will be confirmed. Senatorial courtesy is, of course, a device whereby the Senators strengthen their influence on the party organizations in their own States and prevent the national party organization, which may be hostile to the local group although of the same party, from invading the Senators' realm.

Through his power to appoint the chief administrative officers of the federal government, the President may go far in the execution of his own policies. For example, with the election of a Republican President and Congress in 1952, it was expected in some circles that certain federal regulatory bodies, such as the Federal Trade Commission, might have their powers shorn in behalf of the interests that opposed federal controls over business and industry. Actually, little if any legislative change was made in the structure or functioning of these regulatory bodies. However, whenever a vacancy appeared on one of these groups, President Eisenhower tended to name to the post an individual known to dislike strong federal restraints on the national economy. By these appointments President Eisenhower accomplished about the same results that would have been attained by legislative change; his appointees in general exercised only a fraction of the regulatory powers with which they were endowed.

Likewise, in his function of selecting federal judges, the President may have great influence over policy. This principle has been recognized in the federal government for many years; the first real "court-packing plan" was that of the Federalists in 1800 and 1801. After they had lost the election of 1800 to the Republicans, but before they had left office, the Federalists in Congress passed the Judiciary Act of 1801, which created a number of new federal judgeships; retiring President John Adams quickly filled them with Federalists. This project met an early defeat, for one of the first acts of the Republicans was to repeal the law, thus doing away with the new judicial posts. However, the Republicans could not unseat John Marshall, whom Adams had lately chosen as Chief Justice. For three decades afterward, the decisions of the Supreme Court bore the imprint of the Federalist point of view although the Federalist Party never won another national election.

THE REMOVAL OF EXECUTIVE OFFICERS

Another major presidential executive power, closely associated with the appointive function, is that of removing executive officers. The Constitution provides means whereby executive officers may be removed by Congress through impeachment; however, this is a long process, and can be used only in the case of "treason, bribery, and other high crimes and misdemeanors." Congress has been unable to expand this process so as, for partisan reasons, to be able to remove presidential appointees. In 1805 the Republican Congress impeached an associate justice of the Supreme Court, Samuel Chase, who had made himself notorious for his unbridled public utterances of Federalist principles. However, the Senate refused to vote for conviction, thereby establishing the precedent that the impeachment process cannot be used for partisan causes. Success in this impeachment effort would probably have brought prompt impeachment and conviction of all other Federalist justices, and ultimately the subordination of all presidential appointees to the majority party in Congress.

It was evident at the outset, however, that the President must have means available for removing those officers who do not share his policies. This, of course, refers strictly to events that may occur during the President's term of office. Normally cabinet members and other high executive officers will tender their resignations whenever a new President is elected, even though the same party is in power; they are apt to do so when a Vice President succeeds to the presidency. Hence the problem of removal almost invariably concerns some officer whom the President himself has named. The chief dispute over the means of removal came to revolve about the question of whether the President alone might dismiss an officer who had received his post through presidential nomination and senatorial confirmation, or whether the Senate must confirm the removal. Until the Reconstruction Era (1865–1877) it was generally admitted that the Senate should take no part in removals, and that the President should have a free hand.

However, during the contest between the Radical Republicans in Congress and President Andrew Johnson, Congress in 1867 enacted the Tenure of Office Act, requiring the consent of the Senate for the removal of any officer whose appointment had been confirmed by that body. The purpose of Congress at this time was to ensure that the President would remove no officer who appeared to obey congressional rather than presidential guidance. Johnson and his supporters argued that the Act was unconstitutional, in that it denied the President the right to surround himself with aides who would follow his directives; hence in 1868 the President removed Secretary of War Edward M. Stanton without consulting the Senate. Shortly thereafter Congress impeached the President, in part for the alleged violation of the Tenure of Office Act; however, the Senate failed by one vote to convict Johnson. Eventually the Act was repealed.

However, there can be and are limitations imposed upon the presidential power of removal. The President has no power to remove federal judges; for the Constitution declares that they shall hold office "during good behavior" (Art. III, sec. 1). The aim of this provision is clearly that of assuring the independence of the federal judiciary. Moreover, the President may not remove the members of federal bodies that are partly administrative, partly legislative, and partly judicial, such as the Interstate Commerce Commission, whose terms of office have been fixed by the congressional act establishing the body.

This point was settled by a case in the 1930's. In 1933 President F. D. Roosevelt removed William E. Humphrey from his post on the Federal Trade Commission. Humphrey, a Republican who had been appointed by President Coolidge, evidently committed no offense other than that of opposing Roosevelt's policies. Humphrey shortly afterward died, but the executor of his estate brought suit in federal court for Humphrey's salary from the time of his dismissal until his death. It was pointed out that the law creating the Federal Trade Commission had set its members' terms at seven years, and that it had permitted their removal only for reasons of "inefficiency, neglect of duty, or malfeasance in office," all of which were non-partisan. Finally, in 1935, in the case of Rathbun [Humphrey's executor] *versus* United States, the Supreme Court ruled that Humphrey's dismissal had been wrongful. Evidently such bodies as the Federal Trade Commission are to be regarded as nonpartisan—it is true that Congress generally requires that their members be almost equally divided between the two major parties—and that they are not responsible to the President alone, but to Congress as well.

However, in the case of executive officers responsible only to the President, such as the heads of the executive Departments, the presidential power of removal is not subject to limitations. Such was the ruling of the Supreme Court in the case of Myers *versus* United States (1926). Myers, a postmaster, had been dismissed by Wilson and could not regain his job by citing a congressional act giving him a longer term of office.

The power of the President to remove executive officers is always conditioned by political needs. It has been pointed out in the previous chapter that the President may make appointments in order to conciliate the different factions of his party, even though he may be at odds with them. Often the President and some other members of his party may have to tolerate a good deal of undesirable behavior from such officers for the sake of party unity.

SUPERVISION OF THE NATIONAL ADMINISTRATION

Another important executive power of the President is the supervision of the national administration, a function that makes the President in effect the managing director of the United States government. It must be remembered that Congress creates all parts of the national administration, gives a general description of their purposes, and endows them with the funds for their operation. However, Congress leaves to the President the task of determining the day-to-day obligations of the administration. First the President must decide what these obligations are to be; then he issues instructions to the relevant agency in any one of several forms. Very commonly these instructions are delivered orally, in person or over the telephone. They may be written, as memoranda or letters of command. The most formal type of instruction is the executive order; Congress usually establishes by law the conditions under which an executive order may be issued. Whatever their form, these instructions reach the Department heads, who transmit them to their assistants, and so on down the line to the individuals who actually perform the prescribed duties. Figure 39 contains facsimiles of different types of presidential papers.

Many of the executive orders have the force of law. Congress in creating an administrative office or function may declare only in the broadest terms the general aims of the office or function; the essential details must be stated in one or more executive orders. For example, under the Reciprocal Trade Agreement Act of 1934 Congress fixed the principle of lowering tariff duties in order to encourage a revival of international trade. However, the decisions concerning which duties were to be lowered, and by how much, were left almost entirely to the President, to be based on the success he and his aides achieved in bargaining with foreign powers. In this way Congress may almost seem to delegate lawmaking powers to the President. Yet Congress must not surrender its legislative initiative to the President. One of the reasons for which the National Industrial Recovery Act was declared unconstitutional in 1935 was that through this Act, which was intended to assist industry to regain its normal levels of production, Congress was conferring legislative functions upon the Presi-

A. "State of the Union" Message to Congress. First page of President Wilson's text for his annual message to Congress, December 2, 1913. Written on the President's own typewriter, with corrections in his handwriting.

B. Memo to an Agency Chief. Original letter by President Wilson to Herbert Hoover, the Food Administrator, Feb. 19, 1918, directing Hoover to apply pressure to the packing trade.

Figure 39. Types of Presidential Papers.

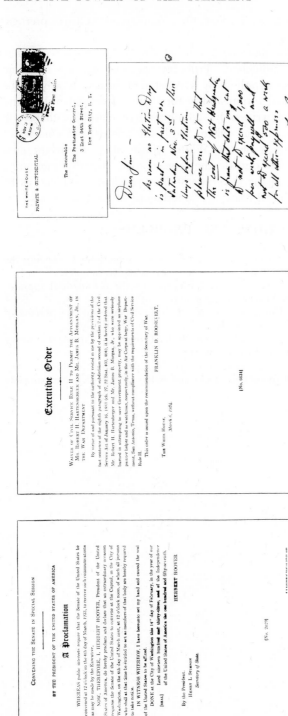

C. A Presidential Proclamation.

D. An Executive Order.

E. The President as Party Chief. A memo to James Farley sharply curtailing Democratic overhead facilities, Nov. 3, 1934.

Figure 39. *(continued)*

A, B. From: "Woodrow Wilson; Life and Letters," by Ray Stannard Baker. Copyright 1927, 1939 by Doubleday & Company, Inc., reprinted by permission of Mrs. Rachel Baker Napier and Doubleday & Company, Inc.; E, Reprinted by permission from "Jim Farley's Story," published by McGraw-Hill Book Co., Inc., copyright 1948, James A. Farley.

dent. The formulation of general policy, then, remains an exclusive prerogative of Congress.

It must not be thought that the President drafts his executive orders independently of outside influence. Probably the vast majority of them are based on information supplied by Department heads; however, the President must assume final responsibility for them. Informal orders and memoranda may even be written by administrative chiefs. Others will be drawn up in the presidential offices, with the advice and counsel of Department heads, members of the White House Staff, important congressmen, and party leaders outside the government. In his functioning as the managing director of the government the President is subject, as he is in each of his other political roles, to the influence of political needs.

QUESTIONS AND PROBLEMS

1. What are the reasons that may impel the President sometimes to execute the laws meticulously and at other times loosely or in an extended manner?

2. What are the formal and the informal limitations on the presidential appointing power over the executive branch of the government?

3. Compare the roles of Congress and of the federal courts in the process of presidential appointments and removals.

4. What controls do Congress and the courts have over the President's power to supervise the administration of government?

5. Of the four major types of presidential powers described in this chapter, which do you believe is most subject to checks and balances? Which least subject?

22. Legislative Powers of the President

Photograph by New York Times

$\mathbf{T}$HE legislative powers of the President comprise all the legal and political influence that the President is able to impose for or against the initiation or enactment of a law by Congress. These legislative powers include the various means whereby the President may cause a bill to be introduced, promote the passage of a bill, and block the passage of a bill. (Furthermore, he may use the same means to advance or block some special provisions of a bill.) Originally the office of President was intended chiefly for executive purposes; it was supposed to administer the laws that Congress had framed. For a number of reasons the legislative powers of the President have expanded far beyond the intentions of the Founding Fathers, so that today the President has a major positive role in framing as well as in executing the policy of the government. The public expects him to propose and work for a legislative program.

SOURCES OF THE LEGISLATIVE POWERS
OF THE PRESIDENT

Constitutional legislative powers

The sources of the legislative powers of the President are both constitutional and extraconstitutional. By the term "constitutional legislative
powers" is meant here those powers given the President specifically for legislative purposes. The President is directed (Art. II, sec. 3) to "from time
to time give to the Congress information of the state of the Union, and
recommend to their consideration such measures as he shall judge necessary and expedient"; here the President also is authorized "on extraordinary
occasions, [to] convene both houses, or either of them, and in case of disagreement between them, with respect to the time of adjournment, he may
adjourn them to such time as he shall think proper." In a different
passage (Art. I, sec. 7, cl. 2), in describing the mechanics of enacting a
bill, the Constitution sets forth the role of the President in signing or
vetoing a bill.

An important legislative power is specifically assigned the President in
connection with making treaties with foreign powers. "He shall have
power, by and with the advice and consent of the Senate, to make treaties,
provided two thirds of the Senators present concur; . . ." (Art. II, sec. 2).
This clause could be interpreted to mean that the President and the Senate
should *together* draft treaties with other nations, but in fact treaty-making
has been monopolized by the presidency; on many occasions, leading
Senators have been consulted by the President in early stages of the negotiation and drafting of a treaty, but in general the Senate can expect to
have a hand in the proceedings only at the point of debate and voting on
its approval.

A treaty, once approved by the Senate and ratified by the President,
becomes part of the law of the land, like domestic laws. Two other forms
of international action express additional legislative powers of the President. One is a statute passed by both houses of Congress and signed by
the President, which delegates to the President the authority to engage
in agreements with foreign powers in certain areas and under certain
restrictions. For instance, under the Trade Agreements Act of 1955 the
President is authorized to negotiate rules for the regulation of trade,
including exports and imports, with other nations.

Another kind of legislative power of the President in foreign affairs is
the power to make executive agreements with other countries concerning
matters within the scope of the executive authority. For example, without an act of Congress, the President authorized the Rush-Bagot agreement of 1817 with Great Britain that restricted naval forces on the Great

Presidential Press Conference. Close-up of a forty-four-year-old American institution, developed to provide a regular channel of communication between the President
and the nation's press. Here President Eisenhower listens to a question being posed
by a correspondent.

Lakes. Later, the agreement was transformed into a treaty because the British feared that executive agreements were too dependent upon the goodwill of the incumbent President. A more detailed discussion of this and the other international activities of the President is contained in Chapter 48 of this book.

Extraconstitutional legislative powers

The term "extraconstitutional legislative powers" denotes all the legislative powers that are not directly authorized by the Constitution as parts of the legislative process. Some of these powers are explicitly awarded by the Constitution, but not for legislative ends. For example, the President is empowered (Art. II, sec. 2, cl. 2) to "appoint ambassadors, other public ministers and consuls, and all other officers of the United States. . . ." Although the presidential appointing function is not intrinsically a legislative power, it has been transformed into one under certain circumstances by different Presidents, as shall be shown below.

Other extraconstitutional legislative powers are derived not from constitutional grants but from some political development not formulated in the Constitution but not contradictory to it. One of the most important of these sources is the President's position as party leader. Of course, if the majority in one house or both houses of Congress is of an opposing party, the President cannot exercise his leadership to a very great extent. However, when the President and the majority in both houses are of the same party, the President as leader of this party can wield broad influence over lawmaking. It has been shown previously that the major political parties are not united in their beliefs, and that their members cannot in every case be obliged to vote according to the dictates of party chiefs. However, congressmen and the President have a common aim, that of winning re-election. When the President introduces a widely accepted legislative program, and Congress enacts it, a public atmosphere favorable to both is likely to result.

Another important source of presidential legislative powers resides in the unity of the presidential office. This condition is often cited in justification of the near-monopoly that the President enjoys in the conduct of foreign relations. The unity of direction there is supposed to be beneficial to the delicate problems of treating with foreign powers. At the same time it affords a major advantage in the direction of internal policy. The nature of the presidential office is such that the President cannot be blocked by an adverse vote in the executive branch. In other words, the President is supreme in his own office; every other official in the executive branch is his subordinate. He may be influenced more by some officials than by others, and may at any time be deflected from his course for reasons of political expediency. Yet ultimately every decision is his responsibility. The President, then, is capable of a singleness of aim that Congress cannot rival. The President may appeal to some congressmen for the purpose of influencing some other congressmen, who are their equals. Congressmen may appeal to members of the presidential staff or the cabinet to sway the President; however, these men are always the subordinates, never the equals, of the President.

Limitations on the legislative powers of the President

The principal limitation on the legislative powers of the President is the profound congressional separatism that is built into the American system of government. Naturally, when a majority of either house of Congress is not of the President's party, the President is likely to meet great opposition to his legislative projects. However, this circumstance is the exception rather than the rule; for of the forty-five Congresses elected since the end of the Civil War, in thirty, or two-thirds, the presidential party had a clear majority in each house.

Another less apparent, but perhaps more significant, barrier lies in the existence of conflicting groups within the party that may represent sectional, economic, or political interests different from those supporting the President. Such groups may combine with the minority party to make a congressional bloc that is a majority sufficient to defeat the President. Franklin D. Roosevelt from 1938 on was opposed by this sort of coalition, made up principally of midwestern Republicans and southern Democrats; Harry Truman inherited the coalition and never broke it. Dwight Eisenhower, the candidate primarily of eastern Republican leaders, has frequently met resistance from the midwestern members of his party.

The ultimate source of such conflicts, however, lies in the nature of the American government. It is a part of the unending struggle between two groups of American political rulers—the executive and legislative branches of the government—for supremacy, a struggle that may be interrupted only in the event of war or economic catastrophe. The Congress has its own ego, its own sense of autonomy and mission. It tends to resent efforts by the President to introduce a program or to take steps to ensure its passage; Congress interprets such actions as improper encroachments upon what it deems its exclusive area of action. The center of this resistance consists, not surprisingly, of the chairmen of the congressional committees. Most of these chairmen have served in Congress for more than two presidential terms; and many of them have, or at least feel they have, knowledge in the field of their committees equal to or superior to that of the President.

THE EXERCISE OF THE PRESIDENTIAL LEGISLATIVE POWERS

Presidential legislative powers may be divided into the three processes of introducing legislation, promoting legislation, and blocking legislation; they will be analyzed under these three headings. It is important to bear in mind, however, that this division is somewhat arbitrary, since some of the instruments described below may be employed in more than one of the three processes. Figure 40 diagrams what might be called the presidential legislative process; that is, it pictures the legislative process as it operates when the President takes the initiative in it.

Introducing legislation

Neither the President nor any other member of the executive branch may formally introduce a bill into Congress. Legislation can be initiated only by a member of one or the other house of Congress. However, the President has certain means for procuring, or at least stimulating, such initiation.

Drafting Bills: Though Congress at one time was responsible for drafting most bills, today more and more bills are drafted in the executive branch of the government and are subjected to presidential review. In drafting legislation the President can exploit the distinctive nature of his office: its unity; its access to almost unlimited sources of information; the fact that, as one author puts it, the President is "always in session"; and his eminence in the eyes of the electorate.

Although individual bills may be drafted at almost any time, the usual period for drawing up a comprehensive legislative program falls between the sessions of Congress; that allows the President to be ready for the early January meetings in which he delivers his three great messages (see below). In the drafting of bills the President relies upon his many advisers and subordinates in the Bureau of the Budget and the executive branch, especially Department heads and commission chiefs. He also tends to seek counsel from the chairmen of congressional committees, not only because they may have great experience in a particular field but also because by deferring to them the President may win their support in the Senate and House. Furthermore, he consults with party leaders to determine just what sort of program the people want.

Eventually the President and his aides draft a comprehensive group of bills incorporating the whole presidential program. Then they persuade

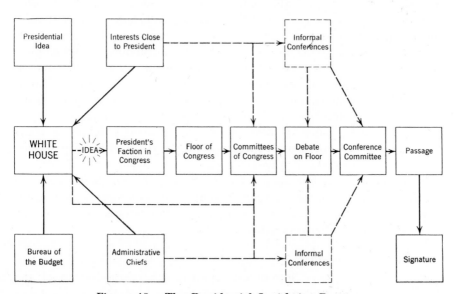

Figure 40.   The Presidential Legislative Process.

or permit one congressman or more to introduce this project to Congress, either as a unit or piecemeal, whichever may seem the more expedient. Since the President—apart from the Vice President—is the only official who is elected by the people of every State, he may claim to be in a better position to draft such a group of proposals on the ground that he is the only representative of all the people. He is also in a better position than Congress to frame legislation that will assist in his reelection and in the maintenance of a congressional majority. Indeed, the presidential drafting of legislation provides a mighty instrument for the strengthening of the President's party.

Presidential Messages: Presidential messages today exert great influence upon the initiation, and the enactment as well, of significant legislation. The President may deliver these messages in either oral or written form, and as frequently as he thinks necessary and proper. Washington and John Adams presented their messages orally; thereafter, until Wilson, Presidents did not appear before Congress but sent their messages in writing. President Wilson revived the oral message, as another phase of his theory of presidential leadership. However, Wilson's three immediate successors—Harding, Coolidge, and Hoover—relied mainly upon written messages. F. D. Roosevelt, Truman, and Eisenhower appeared considerably more often before Congress to state their aims.

Normally during the first few days of every regular session of Congress the President delivers three cardinal messages. In the first of these, the State of the Union message, the President usually does no more than indicate general conditions across the country, roughly outline the policy he intends to follow in the coming year, and exhort Congress to unified action. Another message deals with the budget; though it can hardly explain all the items in the budget, it does contain a justification of the fiscal policies that the budget reveals. The chief purposes of this message, which is drafted with the advice of the Bureau of the Budget, are to introduce the budget and to urge congressional acceptance, at least in its broad outlines. The third message is an economic report, or "national production and employment budget," as it is termed by the Employment Act of 1946. In this message, written with the assistance of his economic advisers, the President submits the legislation that he believes essential to stimulate the national economy, with especial regard for a high level of employment. Apart from these three customary messages the President may deliver as many as a dozen or more messages related to particular issues of the day. These comparatively irregular messages, however, often are directed at bringing about the passage of bills rather than their introduction. Some messages of the past have presented highly important declarations of policy; for example, President James Monroe in his annual message in December, 1823, set forth the Monroe Doctrine.

Promoting legislation

That a bill has been introduced into Congress with the aid of the President is no guarantee of its passage, especially if the President has only a small majority in each house. Hence the President may intervene in any one of several ways to win votes for measures he favors and to procure their enactment.

Presidential Control over Sessions of Congress: According to the Constitution (Art. I, sec. 4), and the Twentieth Amendment, Congress has regular annual sessions. The President has no control over the meeting of the regular sessions. He is authorized (Art. II, sec. 3) to adjourn Congress in the event that the two houses cannot agree on a date for adjournment. This is a power that Congress has never allowed the President to exercise, since the houses have always agreed on the day of adjournment; for if the precedent were once established, the President might eventually secure the power to dismiss Congress almost at will. Then the American condition would be like the English: one of the most important legislative powers of the British cabinet is that of dismissing Parliament, in case of an adverse vote, and calling for elections for a new Parliament.

However, the President has often used the power, conferred by the same section of the Constitution, to summon Congress for extraordinary or special sessions. Presidents have convened special sessions before a regular session was scheduled to meet, so as to have a body of proposed legislation enacted as quickly as possible. On other occasions, as in 1939, the extraordinary session was called after the regular session because, with the outbreak of war in September, President Roosevelt wanted neutrality laws altered so that war materiel could be sent to Great Britain and France. Today only the latter type of extraordinary session, meeting after the regular session, may be summoned. Prior to the adoption of the Twentieth Amendment, a Congress did not meet in regular session until the December thirteen months after the November in which it had been elected. Hence a President inaugurated in March would summon Congress in extraordinary session if he had an urgent legislative program. The Twentieth Amendment rearranged the schedule of the national government so that Congress now meets in January, two months after the elections; as a result it is already in session when the President is inaugurated. Consequently the need for a special session at this time no longer exists.

It must be remembered that the President cannot force a special session of Congress to deal with his requests. The members may gather after being called but do nothing that the President has asked. To secure what he wishes from an extraordinary session the President must rely upon his own prestige, his leaders in Congress, and the demands of the people. Normally the President would not call such a session unless he had been assured by congressional leaders that a majority of the members would follow his lead. It is perhaps for this reason that no special session of Congress has been called since the one in 1939.

Patronage: Patronage, or the executive appointing power, has become a weighty instrument for promoting the presidential legislative program. The President is in a position to influence congressmen by his willingness or unwillingness to appoint those persons whom the congressmen may suggest for appointments. It should not be thought that these appointments become actual objects of a bartering process; however, the congressman may be given to understand that his requests for appointments will be honored much more rapidly if he supports the presidential program.

In the future, patronage is apt to be less and less important to the President as a means for promoting his legislative program. This is true largely because a growing percentage of federal appointive positions are being placed under the classified civil service, in which case the incumbents may be dismissed only for such causes as improving the efficiency of the service. It must be remembered that it is the function of the President to classify these appointive positions; by classifying these positions a President just before leaving office may freeze thousands of administrative employees in their offices regardless of party connections.

Interference in Congressional Elections: The President may also try to promote enactment of his legislative proposals by interfering directly in congressional elections, in order to remove opponents from office and also to secure the election or reelection of congressional supporters. This kind of activity usually occurs in the midterm elections, since at the time of a presidential election the President is too concerned with his own office to be able to bring much pressure upon congressional contests. The President may direct his attention to either a primary or a general election. He may publicly endorse a candidate, and go so far as to speak in the candidate's district on his behalf. On the other hand, he may as party leader withhold party support from the campaign of an incumbent who has voted against the presidential program. The President's control here is not absolute; the candidate may be supported by the State party leaders and funds in spite of the President.

Conferences with Congressmen: In late years the President and his aides have relied more and more upon conferences with congressmen to promote the presidential program. The extent to which a President may employ this instrument, and the degree of success he may expect, depend upon many factors. A President such as Herbert Hoover, who was not a master of the political art, may confer seldom with congressional leaders and may have little success when he does. On the other hand, a President such as Harry Truman, who is a talented politician and who prior to his accession to the presidency was a well-liked member of Congress, may frequently confer with congressmen, sometimes merely because they are personal friends, and may win considerable support through these conferences. Under conditions of emergency, such as war or depression, the President and congressional leaders may confer more often than in more nearly normal times.

Another important group of informal conferences among members of the executive and legislative branches takes place in the Capitol itself. Here the President is absent; he is represented by any one of the leading administrative chiefs, such as a Department head or a commission member, along with White House assistants for congressional relations and others from the White House staff. The administrator is usually requesting action on some bill relative to his Department or commission, or may simply be trying to secure a larger appropriation after Congress has threatened to pare the President's original figure in his proposed budget. Fundamentally, this type of conference is equivalent to lobbying by the executive branch; in this activity the so-called "presidential lobby" is one of the most potent on Capitol Hill.

Appeals to the People: The President has almost countless avenues for appealing to the people. Messages to Congress, for example, through being published may be more effective with the people than with Congress, and may be actually designed chiefly for popular consumption. Too, the President addresses meetings of many organizations, where he can aim his words at a national audience. Today thanks to radio the President can speak to virtually the whole population of the country. F. D. Roosevelt in his first months as President used the radio to inform the people of his plans for dealing with the economic situation; through his so-called "fireside chats" he doubtless won great support, if only by creating the illusion that he was taking the people into his confidence. This means for diffusing the President's words has furthered the rise of a new profession, that of presidential speech-writer; notable members of this profession include Robert Sherwood under Roosevelt, Clark Clifford under Truman, and Kevin McCann under Eisenhower.

The press is another important means through which the President may appeal to the people. The presidential press conferences (see the lead illustration to this chapter), at which representatives of American and foreign newspapers and press associations interview the President, were originated during Wilson's time, and afford another illustration of his concept of presidential leadership. Harding, Coolidge, and Hoover banned spontaneous oral questioning and required that questions be submitted in advance in writing. F. D. Roosevelt reverted to the oral form of interview, a sort of procedure that he obviously enjoyed and that cultivated excellent relations with the press. Truman continued these conferences in the same manner, but, after several unfortunate errors and displays of temper, Truman was persuaded to adopt a more restrained manner than Rooseevelt had shown.

President Eisenhower likewise holds regular press conferences at weekly intervals; but perhaps because of his comparative lack of political experience he has conducted these conferences in a quite formal manner. Yet Eisenhower has permitted a significant innovation: his conferences are broadcast over television, and recorded for later radio transmission. These conferences are not so spontaneous as they may seem; the President or one of his aides may have a reporter friendly to the administration ask a question designed to light up some important aspect of the presidential program. However, these press conferences are among the most important means whereby the President acquaints the public with his intentions and seeks to win public backing.

Blocking legislation: the veto

In order to block legislation the President may impose his veto upon bills, as authorized by the Constitution (Art. I, sec. 7, cls. 2–3). In the veto the President has a legislative weapon enjoyed by almost every executive chief in a representative government. Depending upon the type of veto used, this presidential action may be either suspensive or final for any given session of Congress.

Nature of the Veto: The Constitution requires that every bill, order, resolution, or vote needing the concurrence of both houses of Congress must be submitted to the President for his approval or rejection. Once the measure is in the hands of the President, any one of four sequences of events may follow:

1. The President may register his approval by signing the bill, making it law. On some occasions, he will deem it necessary to sign a bill, thus expressing formal approval, but will accompany his action with a message to Congress stating that he objects to parts of the bill and requests Congress to remedy the alleged defects.

2. He may show disapproval by vetoing it and returning it to the house in which it originated, together with a message stating the reasons behind his disapproval. The message may be phrased simply as an explanation to Congress, sometimes including suggestions for changes that will make the bill acceptable; then again, it may be directed over the head of Congress to the people, appealing for support against the bill. Congress may take no action, in which case the veto stands. On the other hand, Congress may vote in an effort to override the veto, an action that requires a two-thirds majority vote of those present and voting in each house. Failure to muster this majority sustains the veto. Since this type of veto can be overridden, it is suspensive only.

3. The President may do nothing concerning the bill; if Congress is still in session ten days later, the bill becomes law without the President's signature. In this way the President may avoid going on record for having signed legislation of which he disapproves, yet which he fears to veto because of the possibility that the veto may be overridden so as to cause him to lose prestige.

4. The President, as in the above instance, may do nothing with respect to the bill; if Congress adjourns within ten days of his receiving the bill, it is vetoed. This step, which is known as a pocket veto, differs from the regular or messaged veto in that it is final; for since Congress has adjourned, it can do nothing about the bill. It can revive the bill in the next session only by reintroducing it as a new measure. The pocket veto is of course possible only with measures that are sent to the President just before Congress adjourns. However, so many bills are passed by Congress in the last few days of a session that the President has considerable opportunity to impose a pocket veto.

Naturally the President rarely decides in solitude upon a veto or upon the type of veto to exercise. A decision of this kind is usually far too complicated for such easy determination, especially since, at the end of a session of Congress, he is deluged by up to several hundred bills that have passed Congress and require attention within, at the most, ten days. Consequently, he relies greatly upon the Bureau of the Budget to review and express a considered opinion regarding the legislation he must act upon.

Use of the Veto: The authors of the Constitution, according to one of *The Federalist* papers, intended that the President use the veto to defend himself from congressional invasion of his authority, and to prevent undesirable bills from becoming law. Early Presidents appear to have used the veto almost exclusively to block legislation that they thought unconstitutional. Hence the Presidents from Washington to John Quincy Adams imposed the veto only ten times altogether; neither of the Adamses, nor Thomas Jefferson, used the veto at all.

Andrew Jackson introduced a new concept of the use of the veto, that of blocking legislation he opposed for partisan reasons. His twelve vetoes, five regular and seven pocket, displayed his belief that the President was empowered to bar legislation he felt contrary to his principles of government. These vetoes illustrate also Jackson's notion that one function of the presidency is to defend the people against improper legislation by Congress, a function much like that of the tribune in republican Rome. Finally, Jackson more than once employed the veto in a manner calculated chiefly to win public favor for himself, his party, and his ideas. But in spite of the precedent set by Jackson, succeeding Presidents did not often avail themselves of this power.

Since the Civil War the use of the veto has been much more common. The greater use of the veto in recent years shows that the President is taking an increased role in the legislative process, and that the President may sometimes feel that his judgment is superior to that of Congress. The actual proportion of bills vetoed is not large. Even Franklin Roosevelt averaged only slightly more than fifty vetoes per year, at a time when Congress was passing several hundred bills each session.

The overriding of a veto is a rare occurrence; of the 1,190 regular vetoes up to the end of 1952, only seventy-one, or about six per cent, had been overridden. When Congress overrides a veto, the action often reveals that the executive and legislative branches are in the midst of a serious dispute. Probably at no time were relations between the President and Congress more envenomed than in the era of Andrew Johnson; Johnson saw fifteen vetoes overridden, more than any other President. Harry Truman, who had twelve vetoes overturned—three in four days—was also frequently on bad terms with Congress. On the other hand, the fact that five of Franklin Pierce's nine vetoes were overridden intimates, as do many other happenings of his presidency, that he had little effective control over Congress. The number of vetoes that have been overridden may also have been reduced by the fact that the President has refused to veto a bill when he knew his veto would be overridden, but instead permitted it to become law without his signature.

Among the important bills passed over a presidential veto in recent years

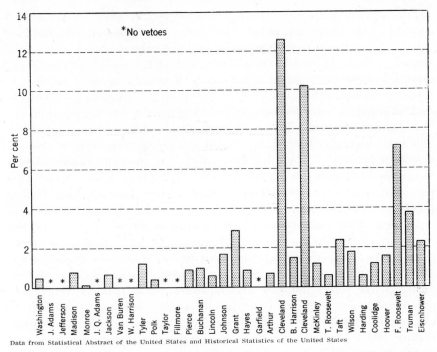

Figure 41. **Percentage of All Bills and Resolutions Vetoed by Each President.**

were the War Disputes (Smith-Connally) Act of 1943, the Labor-Management Relations (Taft-Hartley) Act of 1947, the Internal Security (McCarran) Act of 1950, and the Immigration and Nationality (McCarran-Walter) Act of 1952. Significantly, each of these acts was opposed by labor union leaders, and each was sponsored by a congressman or congressmen hostile to the administration; only one—the Taft-Hartley Act—was passed by a Congress in which the President's party was in the minority. The graph in Figure 41 shows what percentage of the bills presented to him for his signature each President has vetoed.

Suggested Changes in the Veto Procedure: A number of changes have been suggested for the veto procedure. One common suggestion is that the President be empowered to veto single items, or clauses, in bills, especially those appropriating funds, as the Governors of thirty-eight States may now do. As matters stand, the President must accept or reject a whole bill. This situation has given birth to the practice of attaching so-called "riders" at the end of appropriation bills. A rider is a legislative proposal which, if introduced and passed as an independent bill, would probably be vetoed by the President; when attached to another bill favored by the President, it has a better chance of escaping the veto; when attached to an appropriation bill, it is almost certain of receiving the presidential signature, since the President will not often veto a measure providing funds for the operation of the government.

Sometimes the rider constitutes an appropriation for purposes that the President considers unjustifiable. On other occasions the rider may not appropriate money at all, but have an entirely different function. For example, "fair trade" agreements, whereby manufacturers fix prices on branded goods in interstate commerce in apparent violation of antitrust legislation, were authorized by a rider on the District of Columbia Appropriation Act of 1937. A rider on a general appropriation bill in 1950 that opened the way for an American loan to Spain was vigorously criticized by President Truman, who opposed the Franco regime.

However, giving the President the power to veto items in an appropriation bill would increase his power over the budget and thence over the government's policy as a whole. Whereas those who support the item veto say that the President might then strike down many "undesirable" actions, their opponents can equally well declare that the item veto would empower the President to remove those items he was hostile toward, or his enemies had supported, regardless of the virtue of the items. Up to the present, the efforts of several Presidents to secure the authority to veto items have been unsuccessful.

QUESTIONS AND PROBLEMS

1. List and describe all presidential legislative powers that come originally from the *executive* powers granted by the Constitution.

2. What legislative powers emanate from the status of the presidency in itself (that is, regardless of its allocated or derived powers)? Use materials from preceding chapters also in answering this question.

3. How might you go about better ascertaining the results of presidential messages, which the text terms "incapable of accurate measurement"?

4. Name one or more of the limitations on each of the President's legislative powers described in the text.

5. The vetoes resemble rifles; the messages and conferences time bombs. In the long run, which do you think make the more important contribution to the powers of the President?

6. Is there any part or action of the American government, according to your knowledge at this point, in which the President cannot conceivably interfere with considerable force? If so, describe it or them. If not, describe the parts or actions most nearly immune to presidential activity.

PART VI

Congress

Photograph by The New York Times

Congress performs several broad functions. Presumably the legislative, or law-making, is the most important. However, partly because of the principle of checks and balances, and partly because it requires aid in performing its legislative powers, Congress possesses other types of functions. It enjoys wide powers of investigation. It has certain executive and judicial powers. It possesses duties in conjunction with national elections. It has administrative functions, in that it creates and supervises all administrative agencies of the federal government. It plays a significant role in the formal and the informal amending of the Constitution. Finally, it has a major representative function; as much as, or more than, any other organ of the government, it may be said to speak and act for all the people.

THE REPRESENTATIVE FUNCTION

The representative function of Congress in a sense underlies all its other functions. The government of the United States is often termed a "representative government"; it was Congress more than any other branch of the government that was originally designed to fulfill this representative function. Of course, the President too may be said to represent the people; so, likewise, may the officials of the executive branch and the justices of the federal courts. A working man, for example, might claim to be represented by the Secretary of Labor; however, he is also represented by the Secretary of Health, Education, and Welfare to an almost equal degree, by every other member of the Cabinet, and by the chiefs of the independent agencies, only to a lesser degree. Many of the agencies of government have so sprawled out that citizens sometimes are in closer contact with their officials than with their congressmen. In addition, millions of people have come to see their pressure groups as their genuine, direct contact; and they leave it to their pressure group leaders to deal with congressmen and officials alike. Yet each individual living at a definite address in any one of the forty-eight States may claim to be represented by two Senators and one Representative. And these representatives have a unique power over, and relationship to, their constituents.

Congress, then, represents the people of the United States in and to the national government. Presumably in carrying out any of its other functions it operates at the behest of those it represents. It expresses public opinion; in return, through its words and acts Congress contributes to the formation of public opinion. Although the Founding Fathers probably intended that Congress be the chief organ of the national government, today Congress certainly does not govern the country; the administration, under the President, does the actual governing. Congress, however, stands between the people and the administration, often acting as a buffer to lessen or prevent the shock of collisions.

THE CONSTITUENT FUNCTION

The constituent function is that which is associated with amending the supreme law, or the Constitution. "Constituent" in this sense has a different meaning from that of a "constituent" of a congressman. Congress has a hand in each of the formal means for amending the Constitution: it proposes amendments by joint resolutions adopted by a two-thirds majority in each house; and it summons a constituent convention on petition of the legislatures of two-thirds of the States (Art. V). Also, by enacting laws to fill out the framework of government and to execute the general principles of the Constitution, Congress has an important part in the informal amendment of the supreme law.

THE ELECTORAL FUNCTION

Congress has several duties connected with the election of federal officials. It may make regulations concerning the ". . . times, places, and manner of holding elections for Senators and Representatives . . . except

Joint Session of Congress to Hear a State of the Union Message. The President of the Senate and Speaker of the House sit directly behind President Eisenhower.

as to the places of choosing Senators" (Art. I, sec. 4, cl. 1). Moreover, "Each house shall be the judge of the elections, returns and qualifications of its own members, . . ." (Art. I, sec. 5, cl. 1). With respect to presidential elections, "The Congress may determine the time of choosing the Electors, and the day on which they shall give their votes; which day shall be the same throughout the United States" (Art. II, sec. 1, cl. 4). The Electors cast their votes, then send them "sealed to the seat of the government of the United States, directed to the President of the Senate. The President of the Senate shall, in the presence of the Senate and House of Representatives, open all the certificates, and the votes shall then be counted" (Art. II, sec. 1, cl. 3).

In the event some electoral votes are contested, as in the Hayes-Tilden race in 1876, Congress arranges for a commission to settle the dispute, or enacts legislation providing for another mode of settlement. In the event no candidate for the presidency receives a majority of the electoral vote, the House of Representatives shall choose the President from among the candidates receiving the three largest numbers of votes. If no candidate for the vice presidency secures a majority of the electoral vote, the Senate shall choose as Vice President one of the two candidates receiving the largest numbers of votes (Twelfth Amendment). Congress also determines by law who shall succeed to the presidency in the event there is neither a President nor a Vice President (Art. II, sec. 1, cl. 6).

THE LEGISLATIVE FUNCTION

The legislative function of Congress includes chiefly the powers associated with framing and declaring the policy of the national government. The legislative powers of Congress, at least with respect to internal affairs, comprise almost all the stated powers of the national government. It is apparent from the structure of the Constitution that its authors intended that any undertaking of the government in domestic matters should be initiated by Congress. Article I, section 8 of the Constitution lists the bulk of these powers, such as levying taxes, borrowing money, regulating commerce, coining money, establishing a postal system, and the like.

Today, whereas the proposals for legislation may not originate from Congress, the formal enactment of laws still must take place there. Congress may not delegate legislative power to any other agency of the government. One of the reasons for which the federal Supreme Court ruled that the National Industrial Recovery Act of 1933 was unconstitutional was that through it Congress had provided for the delegation of legislative functions to the President in the matter of drafting codes for manufacturers. Congress may empower agencies to lay down the details of their procedure; for instance, it has authorized the Interstate Commerce Commission to fix railroad rates. But Congress must always set forth the general rules under which the agencies are to function; it cannot abandon its policy-making role to an adminstrative office.

THE INVESTIGATIVE FUNCTION

The investigative function embraces the authority of Congress to examine the behavior and value of any agency in the federal government, and any activity in which the federal government is engaged or which it proposes to undertake. For instance, if Congress must legislate on interstate commerce, it, or one of its committees, must learn all it can about the problems of interstate commerce. Often, when Congress has not passed laws on a certain subject at all, as, for example, on the question of connections between gamblers in Nevada and Louisiana, it must and can, through one of its committees, look into the subject and perhaps develop laws governing interstate gambling rings. Thus the range of congressional inquiry can be very wide; it can gather written materials, seize records, and question witnesses under oath, to collect information that may be useful for amending or evaluating present laws and for proposing new ones. In addition to these overt functions of the investigation of social questions, congressmen can, in the course of their investigations of controversial issues, stir up public attention and indignation that may be helpful to their reelection.

THE EXECUTIVE FUNCTION

The executive function of Congress comprises its activities with relation to two particular fields: presidential appointments, and treaties with foreign powers. The executive function, in name at least, is limited to the Senate, which in that respect was modeled after the upper house, or governor's council, in many of the colonial assemblies. Actually the House often enters into this function. In the case of appointments, when there is no Senator from a given State who belongs to the President's party, the President may consult with a Representative from his party concerning an appointment. Moreover, in the negotiation and ratification of treaties, the President must consider the willingness of the House to appropriate money for the execution of the treaty. With respect to presidential appointments, there are more than twenty thousand positions whose appointees must be confirmed by a simple majority vote of the Senate. In regard to treaties, all treaties must be approved by a two-thirds majority vote of the Senate. In the area of international affairs the competence of Congress reaches beyond the approving of treaties; only Congress may declare war, provide funds for the armed forces, and establish rules for the government of the armed forces (Art. I, sec. 7, cls. 11–14).

THE ADMINISTRATIVE FUNCTION

The administrative function of Congress includes congressional creation of all administrative agencies, its statement of their purposes, and its supervision of their operations. It bears repeating that a law is not self-executing; an agency must be established to enforce the law. For example, the passage of the Clayton Antitrust Law in 1913 necessitated the erection of the Federal Trade Commission to implement the provisions of the Law. Only Congress can appropriate the money for the operations of these agencies; furthermore, Congress can, as it did in the case of the National Youth Administration, terminate the existence of such an agency by refusing to vote funds for its continuance.

Congress also sets the rules which the agencies shall observe in their operations, and in one or another fashion Congress oversees these operations. The House Committee on Appropriations is especially equipped, by virtue of an unusually large staff, to function as an overseer. Too, Congress may create a standing, so-called "watchdog," committee to supervise the administration; for example, the Joint Committee on Atomic Energy supervises the Atomic Energy Commission. Individual congressmen frequently engage directly in relations with officials of the executive branch. Such contacts are for many purposes. Often congressmen call to point out specific "abuses" of administration, or to draw attention to needs of their constituents, or to introduce friends and constituents to officials, or to ask advice on pending legislation. Finally, Congress exercises some control over administration by confirming, or refusing to confirm, presidential appointments to administrative agencies.

THE JUDICIAL FUNCTION

The judicial function of Congress has two important aspects. First, Congress, as authorized by the Constitution (Art. I, sec. 8, cl. 9), establishes all federal courts below the Supreme Court, and defines the geographic areas of their jurisdictions. Furthermore, Congress fixes the number of judges in all federal courts, determines the justices' salaries, and appropriates funds for the operation of the judicial branch of the government. However, this aspect of the judicial function of Congress in fact is but another phase of the congressional power to work out structural details of the government that were only roughly sketched by the Constitution. Congress has another judicial function that contributes to the system of checks and balances that is fundamental to the American way of government: impeachment, or the legislative method of removing corrupt or incapable executive and judicial officers.

The grounds for impeachment

The Constitution provides (Art. II, sec. 4) that "The President, Vice President and all civil officers of the United States, shall be removed from office on impeachment for, and conviction of, treason, bribery, or other high crimes and misdemeanors." The nature of treason and bribery are clear enough. Whereas "high crimes and misdemeanors" may be variously defined, they have been usually held to denote acts involving moral turpitude. Owing to this constitutional definition, impeachment proceedings may not be instituted for solely partisan causes; if they could, executive and judicial officers would be subordinate to Congress.

Persons who may be impeached

The term "civil officers" in practice has come to include only the civilian officials of the executive and judicial branches of the government. Military officers are subject, not to Congress, but to courts-martial; when President Truman dismissed General Douglas MacArthur in 1951, he did so not in a civilian role but as Commander in Chief of the United States Army. Members of Congress are not "civil officers." The first impeachment case in the United States was brought against Senator William Blount of Tennessee in 1797. After being charged with treason, he was expelled from the Senate. Subsequently the House voted to impeach Blount, but the Supreme Court ruled that since Blount had been expelled from the Senate he was out of the jurisdiction of the House. Actually the tedious procedure of impeachment is quite needless in Congress, for either house may far more easily expel a member by a two-thirds majority vote, without recourse to the other house. Since Blount's case there has never again been an attempt to impeach a congressman.

The impeachment procedure

The impeachment procedure must be initiated by the House, which shall by a majority vote adopt specific articles of impeachment. Having declared its intention to impeach an official, the House now appoints certain of its members to serve as "managers" to present the case. In a sense the whole House functions as a prosecuting attorney, but the managers do the actual legal work. Once the House has prepared its case, it brings it before the Senate, which must hear the case. In the proceedings, then, the Senate functions as judge and jury. The Vice President holds the chair during impeachment trials save when the President is being impeached; then the Chief Justice of the United States holds the chair, since the Vice President might be prejudiced. At the trial the House first seeks to show cause why the accused should be convicted. The accused, who at all times is entitled to legal counsel, may then present evidence in an effort to prove his innocence. After all the evidence has been offered, the Senators vote for or against conviction. A two-thirds majority is necessary to convict.

Penalties upon conviction

Since an impeachment trial is essentially a political affair, the penalties that may be imposed also are political. An official convicted by impeachment may only be removed from office, and disqualified from holding any other "office of honor, trust or profit under the United States" (Art. I, sec. 3, cl. 7). Conviction in impeachment cases, then, cannot result in fine or imprisonment. However, after removal from office the individual loses any legal immunities that he may have previously enjoyed, and he may thereupon be tried and sentenced as any other private citizen. In fact, the articles of impeachment may be brought as the ground for legal action, without exposing the individual to double jeopardy.

Impeachment trials in American history

Only twelve persons have been impeached in the United States. Of these, four, all members of the judiciary, were convicted. In each of five remaining cases, the defendant was a federal judge; in the sixth, Senator Blount; the seventh, a Cabinet member; and the eighth, President Andrew Johnson. Johnson escaped conviction by only one vote; his acquittal can be attributed to the votes of seven Republican Senators, who by supporting Johnson effectively terminated their political careers. The impeachment of Johnson was inspired solely by partisan motives; consequently it is not difficult to imagine that, had the Senate voted to convict, the presidential system would have been replaced by a parliamentary sytem in which a President who clashed with Congress would be removed by impeachment. The threat of impeachment has persuaded certain other officers to resign. However, impeachment is a lengthy and expensive proceeding, taking time that the Senate today can ill afford to withdraw from its other concerns. Only grave offenses or a great partisan crisis can excite the cumbersome machinery into motion.

QUESTIONS AND PROBLEMS

1. If a congressman is elected by a plurality of votes in his district, what forces can operate upon him to make him concerned with the fate of other parts of the nation?

2. Could Congress set up a bureau to administer all federal elections? Explain your answer.

3. List the functions of Congress and describe each in one sentence.

4. What are the reasons why only twelve persons have been impeached in the history of the United States?

24. Structure of Congress

Photo by Abbie Rowe.   Courtesy National Park Service

THE functions of Congress are carried out by a corps of men and women operating within a structure and according to established procedures.   This chapter is concerned with the structure of Congress, which may be viewed as the bare framework of the body.   It is followed by a chapter discussing the organization of Congress, which may be regarded as an analysis of the organs of Congress that give it motive power. The distinction between *structure* and *organization,* then, is roughly similar to that between skeleton on the one hand and musculature combined with nervous system on the other.   These two chapters on structure and organization, which in a sense treat of anatomy, are followed by a description of the procedure of Congress, which is akin to its physiology.   In all, the reader may obtain a description of what is probably one of man's most complex creations which, like other ingenious institutions, is not fully responsive either to its own will or that of its creators.

BICAMERALISM

The nature of bicameralism

Congress is a bicameral, or two-chambered, legislature, consisting of the House of Representatives and the Senate. At the time that the Constitution was drafted, most of the States had comparable bicameral assemblies; the majority of the colonial assemblies before the Revolution had also been bicameral. The authors of the Constitution, then, were probably doing little more than imitating that legislative form which was most familiar to them. At the same time they may have been reacting against the unicameral, or single-chambered, national Congress under the Articles. It seems also probable that by providing different constituencies, methods of election, lengths of term, and qualifications for members in the two houses, the Founding Fathers planned that the Senate and the House should represent distinct interest groups, just as the contemporary House of Lords and House of Commons did in England. Indeed, these distinguishing traits were so assigned that the Senate was to be unmistakably an "upper house," and the House of Representatives a "lower house," in terms of membership, groups represented, and prestige.

Also, the coexistence of two legislative chambers, especially since they would represent differing interest groups, was designed to contribute one more barrier against despotic government, for the two houses would check and balance one another. Finally, the bicameral Congress afforded a means whereby the conflicting demands of the large and the small States might be reconciled, in that one chamber could represent population and the other, the States. However, it is important to remember that the Virginia Plan, which proposed a bicameral legislature, was approved by the majority at the Philadelphia Convention during its first few days; the Connecticut Compromise was simply adapted to a legislative structure that had already been accepted.

The results of bicameralism

The results of bicameralism have been significant, although perhaps not so much so as either the Founding Fathers planned or the modern critics of Congress declare. It is true that some bills have passed in one house but failed in the other, and that some constitutional amendments have been proposed by one house but rejected by the other. It would be somewhat presumptuous to attempt an estimate of what good or harm this apparent blocking of legislation may have done the country; most of these bills probably would have served some interests well and others ill. However, the very fact that they failed of enactment suggests that there was not an outstanding majority of the national electorate that positively wanted them enacted; most congressmen are too interested in reelection to be deaf to a loud call from the voters. It has also been charged that in the event of an emergency the existence of two houses might delay needed

The United States Capitol.

legislation. This complaint is somewhat academic; an emergency almost always demands action from the executive, not from the legislature. Too, when emergency legislative action has been required, as a declaration of war against Japan after the attack on Pearl Harbor, it has been produced in a single meeting of Congress.

It is occasionally urged that Congress be transformed into a unicameral body; most cities now have unicameral councils and the State of Nebraska has a single-chambered assembly. However, tradition and the many vested interests in the bicameral system—notably, the committee chairmanships in each house—militate against any such change in the near future. It should, finally, be observed that the Senate was designed to serve as a check upon impulsive action by the House. Through American history, however, the House has often reined in what it deemed radical proposals on the part of the Senate.

DISTINGUISHING TRAITS OF THE TWO HOUSES

In most details of their respective structures the two houses of Congress are similar or even identical. However, in certain matters they are different from one another. The principal distinguishing traits are the constitutional qualifications for the members; the terms of the members; and the geographic areas which the members represent. Furthermore, owing to the difference in the size of the two houses, the chambers in which they meet are somewhat dissimilar. This section describes the two branches of Congress with regard to these distinctions.

The Senate

The Senate Chamber: The Senate chamber is located in the north wing of the Capitol. On the floor of the chamber are ninety-six seats and desks arranged in four rows about a semi-circle, with a center aisle. At the beginning of a session each Senator is assigned to one of the desks. Facing the Senators is a dais supporting the chair of the presiding officer—the Vice President or the President *pro tem*—and desks for the Sergeant at Arms, the Parliamentarian, and the various secretaries and clerks. The Senators are seated so that the Republicans are at the left hand of the presiding officer and the Democrats at the right; the seats can be moved from one side of the aisle to the other for a changed party distribution after an election. For the many who regard the Democrats as "liberals" and the Republicans as "conservatives" the congressional seating arrangement is the reverse of that which arose during the French Revolution and is currently employed in continental European legislatures, in which "liberals," or the Left, sit on the presiding officer's left, whereas "conservatives," or the Right, sit on his right. In the typical multiparty continental parliament the numerous factions make up a rainbow of doctrines shading from Right to Center to Left.

The American system also differs from that of Great Britain; for seats in Parliament are ranged along two opposite walls in the chamber so that the majority and the minority parties face each other. Arguing fervently in behalf of this system before Commons underwent the rebuilding necessitated by bombings during World War II, Prime Minister Winston Churchill contended that since the members face one another they are more likely to discuss than to orate; he also argued that the clear separation between the two parties discourages ready shifting from one side to the other and the rise of a multiparty system. One other remarkable trait of the House of Commons is that there are insufficient seats for all the members; hence deliberation does not take place in the air of vacancy that sometimes characterizes both houses in the American Congress.

Outside the chamber proper are the coatrooms, lobbies, and other areas to which members may retire to discuss issues among themselves and with interested private citizens. Elevated above the floor about fifteen feet are balconies on all four sides of the chamber, known as galleries; these hold several hundred persons. Admittance to the galleries has been strictly regulated since a handful of Puerto Rican fanatics sprayed the House of Representatives with gunfire in 1953.

Constitutional Qualifications: The Constitution provides that a Senator must be at least thirty years of age, have been a citizen of the United States for at least nine years, and be an inhabitant of the State from which he is elected (Art. I, sec. 3, cl. 3). There have been instances in which persons under thirty years of age have been appointed or elected to the Senate, for instance, Henry Clay in 1806 and Rush D. Holt in 1934. However, such instances are rare; the odds are great that an individual must be considerably more than thirty years old before he is politically "available" for the Senate. Likewise, the qualifications of citizenship and residence, because of political considerations, seldom operate so as to block a candidacy.

One other constitutional requirement is that no Senator may hold "any office under the United States" (Art. I, sec. 6, cl. 2). This provision, which is designed to ensure the separation of powers, forbids a Senator to hold any permanent position in the executive or judicial branch of the federal government. He may, for example, like Senators Arthur Vandenburg and Tom Connally—each of whom was at one time chairman of the Senate Foreign Relations Committee—serve as a presidential appointee to an international conference. However, he may not be a member of the Cabinet or a military officer. This requirement helps to bar the introduction of the parliamentary cabinet system into the United States.

Term: The term of office for Senators is six years. This term, the longest for any federal elective official, was doubtless instituted to guarantee that the Senate would be an essentially conservative body, again like an upper house. Furthermore, because the authors of the Constitution wanted to block any sudden change in Senate membership, they made the terms of Senators overlap one another. Hence there are elections for the Senate every two years; but, excluding deaths, resignations, or removals, only one-third of the seats will be at stake. Thus the entire membership of the Senate can be replaced only after three elections, or a lapse of four years.

The Constitution provided that the first Senate elected should at once divide itself into three classes of equal size, made up respectively of those who would serve two, four, and six years (Art. I, sec. 3, cl. 2). At this time the Senate arranged that the Senators from the same State would not fall into the same class; and Senators from the States thereafter admitted to the Union were similarly classified. Hence normally a State does not choose more than one Senator at a given election.

Geographic Area Represented: The Senate was designed to represent the States; hence each State has two Senators. Indeed, the Senate was intended to be in limited respects an assembly of ambassadors from the States, somewhat akin to the Congress under the Articles. Actually, popular election of Senators has placed them on virtually the same plane as that of Representatives so far as their relationship to the voters is concerned; yet it is noteworthy that members of the Senate are still referred to as "the Senator from Ohio" or "the Senator from Colorado."

Whereas the Senators from any given State in a legal and a constitutional sense equally represent the people of that State, by no means do they necessarily represent the same interests in the State. It is true that in some States, particularly in the South and the Midwest, a single interest or coalition of interests may so dominate State politics that it can succeed in electing both Senators. In the Eighty-fourth Congress, for instance, Senators Homer Capehart and William Jenner of Indiana could be said to represent the same groupings; the same also was true of Senators Walter George and Richard Russell of Georgia.

By contrast, Senators Joseph McCarthy and Alexander Wiley of Wisconsin, although of the same party, stood for policies that sometimes clashed. Where the two members came from opposing parties, as in the case of Paul H. Douglas and Everett M. Dirksen of Illinois, they quite commonly represented antagonistic groups. Where a State is divided into two geographic sections each party may try to elect one Senator from each section. This practice is normal where a State contains one vast metropolitan district and an agricultural hinterland; in Michigan, for example, Democratic Senator Patrick V. McNamara was from Detroit, and Republican Senator Charles Potter came from Cheboygan. Northern and southern California have such diverse interests that almost invariably one Senator is named from metropolitan Los Angeles and the second from in or near San Francisco. It should be quite apparent from these examples that although Senators may be elected by the voters of the whole State they cannot be said to represent all the voters of the State, or even all those of their party.

The House of Representatives

The House Chamber: The House chamber is located in the southern wing of the Capitol. On the floor of the chamber are 444 seats, with no desks, arranged in eight semi-circular rows, with parts of a ninth row in each of the two far corners. These seats are divided into eight more or less equal wedgelike sections by the center aisle and the three lesser aisles at like intervals on either side. Representatives are not assigned to seats, but merely take a seat to their liking upon entering the chamber. As in the Senate, Democrats sit at the Speaker's right, Republicans at his left. However, members of the majority party may sit on either side if they wish; it is rare that there are enough members of the majority party present to overflow their own side. Whereas the members do not have individual desks, there are two large desks on each side of the center aisle in the third row of seats, to accommodate the floor leaders and the members of a standing committee charged with a bill that is being considered. As in the Senate, there is a large dais containing the House officers and the clerks. The House, too, has its coatrooms, lobbies, and galleries.

Constitutional Qualifications: The Constitution provides that a Representative must be at least twenty-five years of age, have been a citizen of the United States for at least seven years, and be an inhabitant of the State from which he is elected (Art. I, sec. 2, cl. 2). The lesser age and shorter citizenship requirements for the House show the intention of the Founding Fathers that this be the lower house, reflecting the interests of the less powerful and wealthy groups. As in the Senate, these minimal requirements can be said to have seldom barred entry to House membership; most Representatives are native-born citizens of the United States and of the State from which they are elected, and their average age is more than twice twenty-five. Interestingly enough, the average age of Senators is about five years greater than that of Representatives, just as there is a five-year difference in the constitutional requirement. Representatives like Senators may not hold any office in the executive or judicial branch of the government.

Term: The term for Representatives is two years. It was set at this length in keeping with the doctrine that members of the lower house, or popular assembly, should be subject to frequent checking by the electorate. However, this short term has greatly contributed to the fact that many Representatives, especially those from areas in which both major parties are strong, tend to mirror local rather than national interests; only by bringing about legislation favorable to their own constituencies may they hope for consistent reelection. Not only do Representatives seek to limit the duration of congressional sessions in order to devote their time to campaigning; they also are apt to modify their congressional decisions according to the wants of their constituents, and thus in a sense campaign from Capitol Hill.

Geographic Area Represented: Properly speaking, Representatives do not speak for a geographic area but for the people in general; they differ from Senators, who are chosen to represent specific areas—that is, the States— and who were once named by the elected assemblies of the States. Representatives are assigned to the States in proportion to the population of the States; then, because most of them have more than one Representative, the States in turn usually are divided into districts, from which the Representatives are named. However, these districts do not have distinct governments of their own unless, as rather infrequently occurs, their boundaries happen to coincide with those of a county or a State. Moreover, the State legislature may change the boundaries of the districts at any time. Hence the

Representative has never been viewed as the delegate of a government, in the way Senators were, and sometimes are, even today.

RELATIVE STATURE OF THE TWO HOUSES

Today there does not appear to be much difference in the stature of the two houses of Congress. It has already been shown how the electorate and the qualifications for membership in the two houses are either very similar or identical to one another. Also, there are only a few noteworthy distinctions in the functions of the two houses. The Senate does have major executive powers, such as consenting to treaties and confirming presidential appointments—powers reminiscent of the exceptional position of the upper houses of colonial and early State governments. On the other hand, the House alone may initiate bills for the levying of taxes, in keeping with the pattern set by the English House of Commons. In practice, however, the leaders of each house sometimes consult informally with leaders of the other before exercising what are only theoretically its exclusive powers.

The statement that the two houses are approximately equal in stature sets the American Congress off from almost all other national legislatures, for during the past century most upper houses have become virtually impotent by contrast with lower houses. In Great Britain, for instance, the House of Lords has practically no legislative power. The Council of the Republic in the French Fourth Republic (analogous to the Senate in the Third Republic) may initiate bills only under special conditions, and also has only a suspensive veto. It is true that constitutionally the two houses of the Soviet national legislature, the Supreme Soviet of the USSR, have equal powers; however, most observers agree that these powers are small. Hence the American Senate is without question the most powerful upper house in the world.

So far as congressmen themselves are concerned, the Senate appears to be by far the more attractive body. As an illustration, in the Eighty-fourth Congress more than one-fourth of the Senators had been members of the House; a smaller fraction had been State Governors. A handful had been both Representatives and Senators. By comparison, the House included neither a former Governor nor a former Senator. This obvious preference probably arises from the greater public respect accorded Senators, the more leisurely pace of the Senate, the smaller degree of party dictation and management in the Senate, and the security of the six-year term.

COMPENSATION, PERQUISITES, STAFF

Compensation

Congressmen receive an annual salary for their services. Beginning with March 1, 1955 members of both the House and the Senate have been paid $22,500 per year; they are also allowed, for tax purposes, to list up to $3,000 of this sum as a business expense incurred through maintaining a second residence in Washington. The presiding officers—the Speaker of the House and the Vice President or the President *pro tem* of the Senate —each receive $45,000 annually.

The Constitution provides that Senators and Representatives shall be paid for their services (Art. I, sec. 6, cl. 1); Congress itself by law fixes the amount of its members' compensation. Whereas a regular stipend for legislators today is more or less taken for granted, it should be borne in mind that at the time the Constitution was adopted this was a revolutionary provision. It made holding a seat in Congress neither a privilege nor an obligation, but a salaried vocation. What was revolutionary was the fact that it made it at least in theory possible for a man with no other means of support to become a national lawmaker; in practice today a congressman has such large expenses that he is almost compelled to have an outside income. By contrast, members of the British House of Commons received no stipend until 1911; before that time they had to live entirely on their own resources, so that only the wealthy could afford a seat in Parliament. Moreover, even as late as 1955 their salary was only about $4,200 per annum, with few of the perquisites attached to a seat in Congress.

It is often urged that congressional salaries be raised much higher, so that the country might have "better" Senators and Representatives. Aside from the fact that this suggestion is a gratuitous insult to the present members of Congress, there is no concrete evidence that a higher salary would necessarily induce a "better type" of person to campaign for office. There are many persons who might make desirable legislators who would not seek office regardless of its financial attractiveness. On the other hand there are occasional mediocrities in Congress today who would be even more firmly attached by a higher income. Certainly the cost of living for a congressman in Washington is so high that no Senator or Representative grows rich on his salary alone; many, in fact, go into debt. Yet congressmen, particularly lawyers, make associations that can be extremely profitable once they leave Capitol Hill. Finally, the rewards in the form of such intangibles as influence and prestige can be very important.

Perquisites

Congressmen enjoy many perquisites of office apart from their salary. One of the most significant, and one that has only recently been devised, is a retirement system. Under this system, established by the Legislative Reorganization Act of 1946, Senators and Representatives each contribute six per cent of their annual salaries to a retirement fund. Those who hold office for six years or more, and who at some time after reaching the age of sixty-two no longer hold a seat in Congress or any other position under the federal government, may then draw a pension based upon the length of their tenure.

Members of Congress are also granted an allowance of twenty cents per mile for one round trip annually from their homes to Washington. They are given a certain amount of stationery and of air mail stamps; they also receive up to a specified maximum of free telephone and telegraph service —a limit, it might be said, that is usually exceeded. One of the more noteworthy perquisites is the postal frank, enabling them to send an unlimited amount of railroad mail free. Congressmen from time to time utilize the frank quite openly to assist themselves in campaigns; for example, in 1954 Congressman Sam Yorty of California, seeking the Democratic nomination in the primary as a candidate for the Senate, mailed under his frank four million copies of one of his speeches to the voters of California. Another important perquisite is the office space furnished to congressmen in the House and Senate Office Buildings. (Incidentally, members of the British House of Commons do not have free office space.) A congressman desires this privacy where he may be closeted with a constituent to discuss matters of only State or district importance.

Staff assistance

One of the outstanding developments in Congress over the past half-century has been the emergence of a professional staff system. This "legislative bureaucracy," as it might be termed, includes clerks, secretaries, and experts in a host of fields related to different types of legislative activity. A prime function of this personnel, especially the experts, has been to give Congress and its members sources of information that are at least formally independent of other branches of the government and of outside interests. Previously, when congressmen sought the facts regarding an issue destined for legislation, they were compelled to resort either to experts in the executive branch or to lobbyists, or to both. Under such circumstances the data provided would often carry the impress of forces external to Congress and perhaps even hostile to its purposes.

Starting in the twentieth century, however, Congress has instituted several organizations of its own to furnish data to its members. These organizations may be said to exist on three levels. First are those for Congress as a whole: the Legislative Reference Service and the Office of Legislative Counsel. Second are the staffs of the standing and special committees. Third are the staffs of the individual congressmen. This section will treat of the first and the third categories, for a discussion of committee staffs can be better understood in conjunction with the later discussion of committees themselves.

Staff Assistance for Congress as a Whole: What may be called staff assistance for Congress as a whole is so termed chiefly because these staffs are employed by the entire Congress, and are responsible to the whole body. They do not advise Congress as a unit, but their services are available to all members of Congress and to every legislative committee. One of these staff bodies is the Legislative Reference Service. Now a department of the Library of Congress, the Service was created in 1914. It comprises seven groups: history and general research, foreign affairs, economics, government, American law, senior specialists, and library services; the staff numbers over 150 persons. Its purposes are to gather and analyze materials bearing upon proposed legislation, to aid members and committees of Congress in such undertakings, and to publish summaries of committee hearings and digests of bills. Specialists from the Service may be retained as advisers to congressional committees. Another staff body is the Office of Legislative Counsel, established in 1918. The Office is divided into two branches, one for each house of Congress. Its staff includes about thirty lawyers, their assistants, and clerks; the two chief counsels, one for each house, are named by the presiding officers of the houses. The function of this Office is to assist members in the drafting of bills, so that they may reach the floor in appropriate legal terminology.

Staffs of Individual Congressmen: Each member of Congress receives an allowance for clerical help. Every Representative is granted a basic sum of $12,500, which is sufficient to hire one secretary and two clerks. Senators receive considerably more; those from the more populous States receive larger allowances than those from the less populous. Since a Senator from California normally is sent more correspondence than one from Idaho, he is presumably entitled to a larger staff for answering this correspondence. Furthermore, this arrangement in a very rough way tends to equalize the allowance given to Senators and to Representatives from any given State. Beyond their clerical help, Senators may each employ one administrative assistant, at a base annual salary of $10,000. Bills authorizing Representatives to hire similar assistants have been several times proposed but never enacted.

The degree to which a congressman's staff provides him with expert advice depends largely upon the individual congressman; it is he, after all, who chooses his staff members. Very commonly these staffs are named on a patronage basis; also, many members name wives and relatives to their staffs. The assistants to the Senators in a few cases have afforded outstanding research and counselling advice; yet it appears that many if not most Senators simply promoted their secretaries to the new and higher status when it was created by the Legislative Reorganization Act of 1946. Even without professional experts, these staffs can relieve and have relieved congressmen of many trivial duties in connection with meeting the public.

IMMUNITIES

A seat in Congress grants to a Senator or a Representative, at least in theory, immunity from certain types of judicial action. These immunities may be ascribed to the somewhat higher rank in society occupied by congressmen than that held by private citizens. However, it would perhaps be more nearly accurate to attribute them to the fear that was present in the eighteenth century that legislators must be protected from arbitrary acts of the executive. It is probably because this fear has vanished that some of these immunities are virtually inoperative today.

Immunity from arrest

The Constitution provides that congressmen "shall in all cases, except treason, felony, and breach of the peace, be privileged from arrest during their attendance at the session of their respective houses, and in going to and returning from the same. . . ." (Art. I, sec. 6, cl. 1.) This immunity today is practically meaningless, for "breach of the peace" has been interpreted to cover almost any violation of the law. A congressman today may be held to trial for a traffic offense, regardless of this immunity.

Immunity from suits for libel or slander

The Constitution states that ". . . for any speech or debate in either house [congressmen] shall not be questioned in any other place." (Art. I, sec. 6, cl. 1.) A Representative or Senator, then, may make any sort of statement he wishes about any person from the floor of Congress, without fear of being sued for libel or slander. This immunity extends to committee hearings and to materials published in the Congressional Record. Indeed, newspapers, periodicals, books, and any other type of publication may freely quote the Record, with complete immunity from prosecution. This protection, which is as valid today as it was in 1789, was designed to assure congressmen freedom of debate respecting legislative matters. However, certain members of Congress—the most notable case in recent days being Senator McCarthy of Wisconsin—have been accused of exploiting this immunity so as to utter statements from the floor that they would not express without the immunity.

There are limits on this protection. One limit is that a congressman may be brought to court for statements made off the floor, just as any private citizen. Another limit is that congressmen may not criticize each other in the same terms as those used against persons outside Congress; as will be seen below, each house has extraordinary, if rarely used, means for punishing its own members. Finally, a congressman must be wary of arousing public opinion against himself through his utterances, for what he says may cost him his seat. Of course, after he has been voted out of office, he may not be held for what he said as a congressman.

DISCIPLINING OF CONGRESSMEN

The Constitution empowers each house of Congress to ". . . punish its members for disorderly behavior, and, with the concurrence of two-thirds, expel a member" (Art. I, sec. 5, cl. 2). The canons of behavior that the houses of Congress enforce upon their members may often appear strange to the onlooker. It has already been noted that congressmen are permitted unusual liberties in what they may say about persons who are not members of Congress. In a sense they are permitted almost equally great liberties in speaking of other members of Congress and of the executive and judicial branches, provided that certain restraints are carefully observed. The principal restraint is that on the language used; that is, insults must be phrased in courtly terms.

Also, it is considered extremely reprehensible to insinuate that a fellow member had improper motives for a given act. When Senator McCarthy was condemned by the Senators in November, 1954, it was in part for calling the Senate session that had gathered to consider disciplining him a "lynch party" and a "lynch bee," and for having termed the special committee that investigated his behavior the "unwitting handmaiden," "involuntary agent," and "attorney-in-fact" of the Communist Party. So far as actions are concerned, congressmen are perhaps most alert to detect and punish any that might cast discredit upon their house. However, as Professor H. H. Wilson has pointed out in *Congress: Corruption and Compromise*, strict disciplining of members is a very rare occurrence.

There are three forms that discipline may take, which, in an ascending scale of severity, are: calling a member to order; censure; and expulsion. A member can be called to order simply by the presiding officer, for an utterance that the Speaker or Vice President may feel crosses the bounds of propriety. A censure is considerably more formal; it customarily includes the filing of specific charges by one or more members, a committee investigation of the charges, a report to the whole house, and finally a majority vote of those present. The Senate followed this pattern in disciplining Senator McCarthy in 1954, save that at the last the verb "condemn" was substituted for "censure." The vote was sixty-seven to twenty-two, with all forty-four Democrats voting for condemnation. A censure is the customary punishment for an act that congressmen feel may reflect upon the honor of their house. Expulsion, the extreme penalty, requires formal charges, a committee investigation and report, and a two-thirds vote in the house concerned. It is resorted to only in exceptional cases such as disloyalty to the country; some congressmen were expelled at the outbreak of the Civil War.

QUESTIONS AND PROBLEMS

1. What are the origins and effects of the bicameralism of Congress?
2. Compare the qualifications for membership in the House and in the Senate.
3. What can you suggest as the possible effects of the equal apportionment of States in the Senate? How can the present arrangement be changed?
4. Does membership in the Senate or in the House carry more prestige among most people? How do you explain your answer?
5. Compare the congressional retirement system with that in use among the faculty of your college. Which is more generous to its beneficiaries?
6. Compare the staff assistance given the individual congressman with that provided the President.
7. Compare the immunities of congressmen with those of the President.

$\mathbf{T}$HE organization of Congress is designed fundamentally to enable Congress to perform its work. Without certain major elements of organization, Congress would be little more than an unwieldy crowd. Yet, since the very soul of Congress is disagreement over ideas, Congress does not nearly approach the neat and simple organization of an army unit or a typical government agency. Rather, the organization of Congress is a compromise between order and chaos. Its form is that produced by an intimate union of party politics and the need to get business done. Hence, in order to understand the organization of Congress, the student must pick his way carefully through a series of interlocking offices and groups—some of them established by a law or a rule of the chamber and others created by the individual parties for their own guidance.

Six principal features of the organization of Congress merit distinct

358

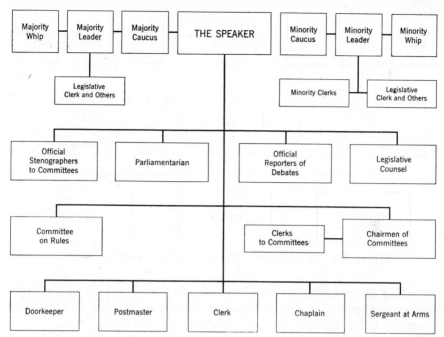

Figure 42. Legislative and Party Organization of the House of Representatives.

treatment. These are: (1) the constitutional basis of congressional organization; (2) the caucus of the majority party, which introduces party politics into the two chambers; (3) the congressional officers, who merge their party functions into the overall operation of Congress; (4) the several party devices for assuring control of lawmaking by the majority party; (5) the rules for conducting work and those who manage the rules; and (6) the committee system that screens and guides proposed laws. Figures 42 and 43 summarize the details of both the political and legislative organization of the House and the Senate as they are discussed in the text that follows.

SOURCES OF CONGRESSIONAL ORGANIZATION

The constitutional basis

One outstanding fact about congressional organization is that it has been created largely by Congress itself, as needs have arisen. The Constitution makes little provision for organizing Congress. It authorizes the House of Representatives to choose "their Speaker and other officers" (Art. I, sec. 2, cl. 5); declares that "The Vice President of the United States shall be President of the Senate, but shall have no vote, unless they be equally divided" (Art. I, sec. 3, cl. 4); empowers the Senate to choose a President *pro tem,* and other officers (Art. I, sec. 3, cl. 5); and permits each house to "determine the rules of its proceedings" (Art. I, sec. 5, cl. 2). Apart from these few general provisions, however, the Constitution is mute

The House of Representatives on the Opening Day of Congress.

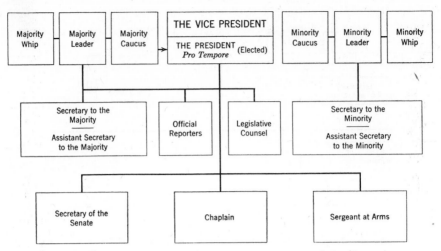

Figure 43. Legislative and Party Organization of the Senate.

respecting the organization of Congress. Hence almost all of the complex apparatus under which Congress functions has been devised by Congress; it has developed piecemeal, with no underlying plan.

The organization of the House and of the Senate is similar but different features receive emphasis in each. The same organizational elements appear in each house in about the same form. However, the organization of the House is much stronger and far more important in the legislative process than it is in the Senate. This condition prevails for several reasons. First, the House has nearly five times as many members as the Senate; it is axiomatic that the need for leadership in a legislative body increases as the size of the body increases. Second, members of the House tend to be younger and less experienced than those of the Senate, so that they need and even demand more leadership. Senators, by comparison, are apt to be more individualistic and to resist efforts to compel their obedience. Also, because members of the House serve for only two years whereas Senators serve for six, Representatives must devote a considerably higher proportion of their time and attention to the problem of reelection; therefore the organization of the House must be capable of marshaling their votes on significant issues.

Important results flow from the fact that the House must organize itself anew every two years, after each congressional election, whereas the Senate is permanently organized. Members of the Senate have overlapping terms, so that only one-third of the seats—perhaps slightly more than one-third, in the event of deaths, resignations, or removals from office—are voted on in any one election. Hence after an election only a minority of the Senate will consist of new members, so that senatorial organization continues from one session to the next. At the beginning of a session it is necessary merely to execute certain organizational details, such as the assignment of new members to committee vacancies.

At the beginning of a session of the House, however, since each member has just been elected or reelected, the whole body must organize itself anew. At the outset of the first meeting there are neither officers, nor rules, nor committees. The clerk of the preceding House calls the members to order and reads the roll according to the alphabetical order of the States. Now the House proceeds to elect a Speaker, from two candidates each of whom has been nominated by one of the major parties. The candidate of the majority party is of course elected; he is brought to the chair by the other candidate, and is there sworn in usually by the Representative with the longest term of service in the House. The Speaker now swears in all the other Representatives. Other House officers have been elected with the Speaker. The House then adopts its standing rules for procedure, ordinarily those of the preceding House, and it chooses the members of its committees. This last act completes the formal organization of the House.

THE CAUCUS OF THE MAJORITY PARTY

The majority caucus, or caucus of the majority party, apart from the few constitutional provisions is the starting point of all congressional organization. A congressional caucus—or, as members of both parties in the Senate and the Republicans in the House prefer to call it, a conference—is an assembly of all Senators or Representatives who belong to one or the other of the two major parties. In this respect the caucuses today have lost importance. The Republican caucuses in both houses have relatively little control over their members' actions. The Democratic caucus of the House can bind its members by a two-thirds vote, provided it is a majority of all Democratic Representatives, but not if the caucus decision violates a commitment that the congressman may have made to his constituents, or if it comprises, in the judgment of the congressman, a threat to his reelection. Caucus meetings from time to time do consider legislative programs; they also may punish party irregulars by limiting their patronage or by refusing party funds to aid them in campaigns for reelection. However, this in general is now only a minor function of a caucus; inasmuch as each major party is composed of distinctive and sometimes clashing blocs, neither can have a comprehensive program to which all its members will subscribe.

The major role of the caucus lies in the organizing of Congress. At some time between a congressional election and the first meeting of a new Congress, the members of each major party from each house assemble in caucus. First they choose one of their members as chairman of the caucus, and another as secretary. The caucus then prepares a slate of candidates for the congressional offices, such as the speakership. Also, in each caucus a committee on committees is named, to select the party candidates for committee posts and committee chairmanships. Moreover, the caucus names members for important congressional party instruments, such as the floor leaders and the whips. The caucus nominations and elections sometimes evoke important contests between the two or more chief blocs making up the party, and the outcome of these choices often indicates which bloc or coalition of blocs is to predominate. The reason for designating the *majority* caucus as the starting point of congressional organization is that in partisan contests for congressional offices—for example, the speakership—its candidates are invariably elected.

CONGRESSIONAL OFFICERS

Congressional officers may be defined as those officers whose posts are created by the Constitution or by statute and who officially represent the whole membership of either house, not simply one party in a house. The congressional officers include the Speaker of the House of Representatives, the Vice President of the United States, the President *pro tem* of the Senate, and the incumbents of several minor posts.

The Speaker of the House of Representatives

Nature and Origin of the Speakership: The Speaker of the House of Representatives is the presiding officer of that house. He is the most powerful member of Congress and is perhaps next to the President the most powerful elected official in the entire federal government. He draws strength not only from his constitutional position as the chief officer of the House, but also from his high rank in his political party. Therefore his performance of his congressional functions is always modified by partisan requirements.

The office of the Speaker of the House is derived from that of the presiding officer in the British House of Commons, who is also called the Speaker. The name originated from the fact that this officer alone was privileged to speak with the king and to communicate to him the grants and petitions of Commons. In this way he came to be the spokesman for all the interests represented in Commons. However, the British Speaker long ago yielded his preeminence in Commons to the Prime Minister. Today the British Speaker is absolutely distinct from his American counterpart in one major respect: he is chosen on non-partisan grounds, and is expected to conduct himself in a non-partisan fashion.

Selection of the Speaker: Officially the Speaker is elected by the House of Representatives at its first meeting after a congressional election. Actually the caucus of each major party offers its candidate at this meeting; the House chooses between the two candidates, voting almost invariably along party lines. Consequently it is more nearly accurate to say that the Speaker is chosen by the caucus of the majority party; it might be even closer to the truth to say that he is named by the dominant faction at the party caucus. Contests for this office rarely occur on the floor at the time of the election, and are little more common at the caucus nomination.

Today the Speaker is without exception a member of the House of many years' standing who has never failed of reelection and who has climbed a ladder of offices in Congress. He has been able to achieve this continuous service because he represents a virtually one-party district; hence Republican Speakers are usually from the Northeastern or North-

Central region, whereas Democratic Speakers almost always are from the South.

Functions of the Speaker: One significant function of the Speaker is to recognize and give the floor to those members who wish to speak. On the surface it might seem that through this power the Speaker could prevent the voicing of all dissenting opinions, for the Speaker may ask any member for what purpose he rises before extending recognition to him. However, the members of the minority group are actually granted considerable time in which to present their case. Indeed, it would be erroneous to imagine that there are frequent contests among members to secure recognition. Usually, prior to the introduction of a bill, the leaders of each party meet to arrange a distribution of time among those Representatives who wish to speak on the matter; then, when the bill is introduced onto the floor, the speaking time has been allocated in advance, chiefly to the leading members of the standing committee that has been handling the bill. However, the Speaker does use his power of recognition at his own discretion in order to block so-called "dilatory motions," motions, that is, whose sole aim is to delay business. In this way the Speaker can expedite House business. Furthermore, if such a motion should succeed in reaching the floor, the Speaker in accordance with his own judgment may refuse to put it to a vote. However, such a refusal, like any other ruling by the Speaker, may be appealed and overturned by the House.

The Speaker has many other important functions. With the assistance of the Sergeant at Arms, he keeps the House in order. He interprets and applies the complex rules governing House procedure; should the situation become too knotty for him to unravel he may resort to the aid of the House Parliamentarian, an expert on parliamentary law. In controversial cases he decides to which standing committee a bill shall be referred; through this power he may decree the fate of a bill by sending it to a committee known either to favor or oppose the bill, as the Speaker's own will may dictate. He appoints all members of special House committees, and House members of joint conference committees. There has emerged a formula for the choice of conference committee members, so that the Speaker cannot have much influence over a bill through this function; however, since he is virtually unrestrained in his power to select members for special committees, he can bring considerable force to bear in confining or expanding their potential achievement. He puts all questions and motions to a vote. Like any other member of the House, he may speak and vote on issues; the fact is, however, that he rarely does speak or vote. Since the Speaker always yields the chair when the House is organized as a committee of the whole he is frequently in a position to participate in discussion.

The Vice President as presiding officer of the Senate

The Vice President of the United States is the presiding officer of the Senate. In this post he holds no such commanding role as the Speaker of the House. He is a member of the executive branch of the government and is not a Senator. He is elected by the people of the United States, not by the Senate. Since the Civil War, four Vice Presidents were members of the minority party in the Senate for two years. One of them, Thomas R. Marshall (1913–1921), made the remark, "What this country needs is a good five-cent cigar," in a moment of tedium during a Senate meeting. Hence the Vice President does not manage the Senate in the manner in which the Speaker dominates the House.

He does have the power of recognizing those Senators who wish the floor; however, he may not question the reasons for which the Senators wish to speak, nor does he exercise this power with much consideration for party needs. Vice-presidential decisions with respect to the Senate rules may always be appealed to the Senate itself, and sometimes the Senate may be consulted before the Vice President makes his ruling. The Vice President does choose the members of Senate special committees and the senatorial delegates on joint conference committees. He has no voice in Senate debates; his only vote is a casting vote, that is, a vote in the event of a tie vote by the Senators themselves.

The President pro tem

The President *pro tem* is the presiding officer of the Senate whenever the Vice President is absent. After a President of the United States dies, a President *pro tem* takes over the chair of the Senate until the next presidential election, when a new Vice President will be chosen. Otherwise the President *pro tem* holds the chair only at intervals. The choice of the President *pro tem* is much like that of the Speaker; that is, the Senate chooses between two candidates, each of whom has been nominated by the caucus of one of the major parties, with the candidate of the majority party always victorious. He has, however, only a tiny fraction of the Speaker's powers.

Indeed, his office is the same as that of the Vice President; however, he is in a slightly different position inasmuch as he is always a member of the majority party of the Senate and is a member of the legislative rather than the executive branch. It is noteworthy, however, that this election does not necessarily take place at the first meeting of a new Congress. Since the President *pro tem* is a Senator, he may take part in debates and vote on questions. Hence his personal influence over the Senate is apt to be greater than that of the Vice President. Finally, he follows the Speaker in the line of succession to the presidency.

Other congressional officers and employees

Apart from the Speaker, the Vice President, and the President *pro tem*, there are several other congressional officers whose posts are not established by the Constitution and who are elected by their respective houses. They are to be distinguished from congressional employees, whose positions are usually established by law and who are appointed not by the whole membership of either the House or the Senate but by one or more members of either body. None of these officers or employees are congressmen. Officers almost always are connected with the majority party; when one party loses control over Congress, the officers lose their posts. Employees, on the other hand, may hold their posts through a number of party changes.

Officers: One important post is that held by the officer known in the House as the Clerk and in the Senate as the Secretary. The incumbents of these posts have quite similar duties, chief among which are keeping a record of the proceedings of his chamber of Congress, which becomes the Journal, and making copies of this record available to every member of his house. The Clerk or Secretary also issues the subpenas directed by his house; he arranges for all labor and supplies required by his chamber; and he is the paymaster of the many employees and officers of his branch of Congress. The Clerk of the House has one additional function, which is based upon the difference between the two houses. Since the organization of the House lapses after a congressional election, it is provided that the Clerk shall retain his post in the newly elected House until his successor is chosen. Hence the Clerk drafts a list of Representatives-elect and presides over the first meeting until the Speaker has been named. Since the organization of the Senate is continuous, the Secretary of the Senate does not have this function.

The Clerk and the Secretary are more than administrators of detail. Their positions make them political figures of some prominence, somewhat as the trainers of baseball teams have some effect upon the players' games. As masters of many small affairs, they are often called upon by the members for help on weightier legislative subjects. Naturally, since the majority party chooses them, their sympathies incline them toward the problems of the members of the majority party; thus they contribute somewhat to the general leadership of Congress.

Among the other officers, the Sergeant at Arms in each house is probably the most important. His most obvious function is that of preserving order during congressional meetings. He is also authorized to summon absent members in order to make a quorum for a vote. He serves congressional subpoenas. He pays the members of his house their salaries and mileage allowances. A third officer is the Doorkeeper of the House (the Sergeant at Arms of the Senate is also its Doorkeeper), who is entrusted with supervising the admission of the public audience to his house and is also held to account for the books, furniture, and other items belonging to his chamber. Two other officers are the Postmaster and the Chaplain in each house; their functions are evident from their titles.

Employees: Probably the most significant employees are the Parliamentarians of each house. The Parliamentarians are chosen by their respective presiding officers. Their principal function is to serve as authorities on questions of parliamentary law, the law that governs congressional procedure. Another important task of the Parliamentarians is to refer all bills to standing committees; in this task he is subject to the will of the presiding officer. Also, the Parliamentarians frequently give advice to the rules committees, particularly in the House. Other employees include the journal clerks, enrolling clerks, reading clerks, bill clerks, and house tally clerks.

There are numerous minor posts filled by congressional employees whose appointment is almost entirely a matter of patronage, such as the elevator operators in the Capitol.

PARTY DEVICES FOR ASSURING CONTROL

The party devices for assuring control of Congress consist of arrangements whereby congressmen can occupy posts that are significant in the guidance of congressional action. Such arrangements draw their authority not from the Constitution but from the political parties. The principal sheerly party implements are the caucus, which has already been discussed; the steering and policy committees; the floor leaders; and the whips.

The steering and policy committees

Each major party has either a policy or a steering committee in each house of Congress. In the House of Representatives, the Democratic Steering Committee includes the floor leader; the whips; the caucus chairman; the Speaker—if the Democrats are the majority party; the principal Democratic members of the Appropriations, Ways and Means, and Rules Committees; and fifteen other members, each from one of the regions into which the country is divided for this purpose, and each chosen by the Democratic Representatives from the region. The Republican Policy Committee in the House comprises the five chief Republican congressional leaders plus seventeen other members selected like their Democratic counterparts on a regional basis.

In the Senate, the Democrats have both a Steering and a Policy Committee. The former apparently does little more than serve as a committee on committees (see below). The latter includes nine Democratic Senators, among them the whip and the conference secretary; its chairman is the Democratic floor leader, who also names its members, as he names the members of the Democratic Steering Committee. The Senate Republican Policy Committee at the beginning of the Eighty-fourth Congress in 1955 was enlarged from twelve to twenty-three members. Under this new arrangement, ten of its members were former chairmen of standing committees (the Democrats being the majority party in this Congress, there were no Republican standing committee chairmen). Furthermore, all seventeen Republican Senators whose seats faced contests in the 1956 elections belonged to the Policy Committee. One important aim of this change was to give a voice to every faction in the party. The Senate Republican Policy Committee is elected by the Republican conference, on nomination by the conference chairman; it includes a chairman, the conference chairman, the conference secretary, the whip, and the Republican floor leader.

The function of the policy or steering committee, as the name implies, is to formulate party policy and to steer legislation. The Senate policy committees have been far more effective than those of the House in the consideration of party programs. This fact may in part be ascribed to the great role played by the House Rules Committee in drafting party programs; it may to a lesser degree be attributed to the fact that the Senate committees have employed considerable advisory staffs, whereas the House committees have not. Consequently the principal function of the policy and steering committees, aside from the Senate Democratic Steering Committee, has been the planning of a legislative schedule, in cooperation—in the case of the House—with the Rules Committees.

The floor leaders

Each major party in each house possesses a floor leader, whose task is the direction of his party from the floor of Congress. The floor leaders are chosen in their party caucuses. So far as the House is concerned, floor leaders always are among the chief figures in their parties, and have been consistently reelected to their seats, so that, like the Speaker, they usually come from States or districts controlled by one party. The majority floor leader of the House holds the unofficial rank of assistant Speaker; he may expect to become Speaker if the incumbent Speaker dies, retires, or fails of reelection while his party remains in the majority. The minority floor leader in the House is the leading Representative of his party, and is almost certain to become Speaker should his party achieve a majority in the House. In the Republican-controlled Eightieth Congress (1947–1949) Republican Joseph Martin of Massachusetts was Speaker, and Democrat Sam Rayburn of Texas was minority floor leader. In the Democratic-controlled Eighty-first and Eighty-second Congresses, Rayburn was Speaker and Martin minority floor leader. Since the Republicans won control of the Eighty-third Congress, the two men again exchanged positions; then they exchanged once more in 1955 after the Democrats became the majority party in the Eighty-fourth Congress. In the Senate the floor leaders of course do not aspire to hold the chair, because it is conferred by the Constitution upon the Vice President; in fact, the Senate floor leaders may be, as in the cases of William Knowland and Lyndon Johnson in 1955, comparatively young men and relatively secondary party figures in their chamber at the time they are chosen.

The functions of the floor leaders are to guide the work of their parties in their respective houses. In this regard the House majority leader is by far the most active, for he has the direct support of the Speaker. He helps determine what member or members shall speak on a given question, and what phases of the question shall be emphasized; in cooperation with the minority leader he allocates speaking time to members of each party for and against a measure. He shares with other majority party leaders the task of deciding in what order proposals shall reach the floor. In case of intraparty disputes, he may summon a party caucus, where he can urge party unity. He directs the work of the majority whip and his assistants, and bases his plans to a considerable degree upon the information they give him. Usually the majority leader's stand on any issue is the official stand of his party; a recent exception to this condition was Senator William Knowland's opposition to several foreign policies of the Republican administration.

The functions of the minority leader in many respects are similar; they are of course different inasmuch as his party does not control the House. It may perhaps be said that the principal aim of the minority leader is to create party unison so as to oppose the majority party and to win support for the next election. Floor leaders in the Senate, although important figures, cannot so readily direct the course of debate if only because the rules of the Senate allow great personal independence.

The whips

Each party in each house has a whip, or assistant floor leader. The Democratic whips are named by the floor leaders; the Republican whips are named by the party committees on committees, whose chairmen, incidentally, are the Republican floor leaders. Each whip in turn names about a dozen assistants, chosen with an eye to representing all regions of the country. The whips canvass their party members as to their stand upon issues, so as to be able to inform the floor leaders of the probable outcome of future congressional voting. They also notify party members when important issues are to be put to a vote; finally, they insure that the party members are present for the voting.

Congressional Rules Committees

Function: Each house of Congress has a standing committee to supervise its rules, known as the Committee on Rules in the House and the Committee on Rules and Administration in the Senate. The Senate committee is not particularly important. It is normally composed of a few of the more elderly members of the Senate (the chairman at the beginning of the Eighty-fourth Congress was eighty-seven years old); its prime goal is to block any proposals for a radical change in the Senate rules. The House Committee on Rules, by contrast, is an extremely powerful body. In recent years it has contained twelve members, eight from the majority party and four from the minority regardless of the party proportion in the House itself. It is composed principally of conservatives from both parties; Democratic members tend to come from the South, and Republicans from New England and the North Central States.

Thanks to its powers and to the extraordinary proportion of its majority party members, the House Rules Committee is an important cog of the majority party machinery that governs the House. It is one more device for getting favored bills quickly to the floor, and for preventing bills opposed by the majority party leaders or by its conservative members from securing House deliberation. In working toward these ends the committee must frequently coordinate its work with the operations of other party instruments such as the Speaker, the majority floor leader, the whips, and the steering committee. Yet, this coordination sometimes does not spring from fundamental agreement of policies, for the Committee may be at odds with the other leaders in such respects; nor does the Rules Committee have to bow to the other leaders unless they appear to have a solid majority of the House behind them.

The House Rules Committee has unique authority. Supposedly its principal function is the consideration of proposals for amending the standing rules of the House; usually its action is to smother these proposals. Through the years, however, it has won for itself many other powers. Apart from the Committee on Government Operations and the Committee on Un-American Activities, the House Rules Committee is the only standing committee that may meet while the whole House is in session without special permission. No bill may reach the House floor unless escorted by special rules; it is the Rules Committee that drafts all special rules. Its proposals have the right-of-way over those of all other standing committees. Hence at any sign of rebellion in the House, the Rules Committee may meet hurriedly, draft special rules to control the uprising, and present them on the floor in the midst of whatever other discussion may be occurring except that of a conference committee report. It may present amendments to any bill, and it may draft a rule that any given bill may not be amended. It fixes the time allowed any member for the debate of a bill, and it can propose a rule barring all debate on a bill. In fact, it can on its own initiative draft a bill and rush it to the floor with privileges over almost any other business.

STANDING COMMITTEES

The standing committees of Congress are the bodies in which the bulk of proposed federal legislation in the United States is sifted, judged as to its desirability, and readied for formal enactment by Congress. Congress has subdivided itself into these committees to do the work that it, as a unit, would be incapable of completing. Most parliamentary bodies across the world possess a system of standing committees, although probably none is so elaborate as that of the United States. One reason for this is the fact that most other large countries with elective, representative governments have a parliamentary system, in which administrative agencies supervised by the cabinet members do most of the preparatory work on the legislation. Because of the presidential system in the United States, Congress may often refer for advice to administrative agencies but does most of the preparatory tasks itself.

Number: In 1946 Congress enacted the Legislative Reorganization Act, which set the number of committees at nineteen in the House and fifteen in the Senate, making more or less parallel committee structures in each house, and which established distinct regions of legislation that each committee was to supervise. The act further provided that a Representative might serve on no more than one committee, save for certain committees that had relatively little work to do, and that a Senator might serve on no more than two committees, with similar exceptions. As will be noted below, circumstances have compelled the acceptance of some changes in this last provision. The present standing committees, together with their membership in the Eighty-fourth Congress excluding the territorial delegates' seats, are as follows:

House	Senate
Agriculture (36)	Agriculture and Forestry (15)
Appropriations (50)	Appropriations (23)
Armed Services (37)	Armed Services (15)
Banking and Currency (30)	Banking and Currency (15)
District of Columbia (25)	District of Columbia (9)
Education and Labor (30)	Labor and Public Welfare (13)
Foreign Affairs (32)	Foreign Relations (15)
Government Operations (30)	Government Operations (13)
House Administration (25)	
Internal and Insular Affairs (29)	Internal and Insular Affairs (15)
Interstate and Foreign Commerce (31)	Interstate and Foreign Commerce (15)
Judiciary (32)	Judiciary (15)
Merchant Marine and Fisheries (29)	
Post Office and Civil Service (24)	Post Office and Civil Service (13)
Public Works (34)	Public Works (13)
Rules (12)	Rules and Administration (9)
Un-American Activities (9)	
Veterans' Affairs (24)	
Ways and Means (25)	Finance (15)

Figure 44 is a diagram of the organization of one of the standing committees. Despite the reduction in the number of standing committees, there is still considerable fragmentation in legislative work because of the many subcommittees. Any committee chairman may appoint some members of his committee to form a subcommittee in order to deal with one particular bill or phase of a bill. Subcommittees have great power, especially in the case of those of the two Appropriations Committees, so that their reports may be the final judgment of the committee itself. It has been charged that since the enactment of the Legislative Reorganization Act of 1946 the number of subcommittees has greatly increased; however, this is not the case, for the number is approximately the same as it was before the Act was passed. In the Eighty-fourth Congress, First Session (1955), there were 156 standing subcommittees, seventy-five in the Senate and eighty-one in the House.

Selection of committee members

The selection of standing committee members is purely a party affair, although the selections receive a formal endorsement by the houses. After an election, but before the first meeting of a new Congress, each party caucus names a committee on committees to choose party candidates for the various standing committees. In the House, the Democratic caucus first selects its members for the Ways and Means Committee; this delegation then names the Democratic candidates for the other committees. The House Republican committee on committees consists of one Republican from each State having at least one Republican Representative; each member has as many votes as there are Republican Representatives from his State. In the Senate, the Democratic Steering Committee functions also as a committee on committees; the Republican committee on committees is chosen by the Republican conference chairman. It is noteworthy that in the House the Republican floor leader is ex officio chairman of the committee on committees, but that in the Senate the Republican floor leader is not even a member of this committee.

At the very outset the committee on committees of the majority party in each house has a great advantage, for it determines how the committee positions shall be apportioned between the two major parties. Usually it sets a ratio that is similar to the party division in its house. However, when the majority party has only a small numerical superiority over the minority party, the majority committee on committees may set no fixed ratio; instead it will provide safe majorities, despite the ratio of the parties in the Congress, on the most significant committees and give itself only a bare majority in the comparatively unimportant committees. It is forced to this resort because congressmen may normally sit on only one House committee or two Senate committees.

The standing committee assignments made at the beginning of any Congress are decided almost entirely on the basis of seniority, that is, upon the number of consecutive terms the members have been elected to their house, and the number of consecutive terms they have served on a given committee. Since the majority of congressmen are reelected at any election (in the House of the Eighty-fourth Congress, 379 of the 435 Representatives, or 87%, had been members of the Eighty-third Congress) the committees on committees have only to assign them to their previous posts. They must also entertain requests that members be assigned to other, and presumably more important, committees. New members must then accept the remaining committee posts; hence they generally commence in one of the less significant committees. If a congressman fails of reelection for one term, he reverts to the bottom of the seniority list when he again appears in Congress, ranking above only those newly elected members who have never before served. For instance, Representative B. Carroll Reece despite fourteen terms in the House was at the end of the seniority list in the Rules Committee in the Eighty-third Congress because his terms were not consecutive.

A Senator or Representative is not apt to suffer with respect to his committee assignments because of his congressional voting record. However, he may be punished if he has not supported his party in an election. In the Eighty-third Congress, for example, Senate Wayne Morse was taken off the Armed Services and the Labor and Public Welfare Committees—both significant bodies—and installed on the District of Columbia and the Public Works Committees—two relatively minor bodies; this was done because he had refused to support the Republican presidential candidate, Dwight Eisenhower, in 1952, and had proclaimed himself an independent. His demand that he be given his old assignments as a member of the Independent Party was voted down. In 1955, in organizing the Eighty-fourth Congress, the Democrats awarded him a coveted seat on the Foreign Relations Committee. In 1949, by contrast with Morse's experience, the southern Democrats who had supported the States' Rights Party candidate in 1948, because they formed part of the core of the Democratic Party

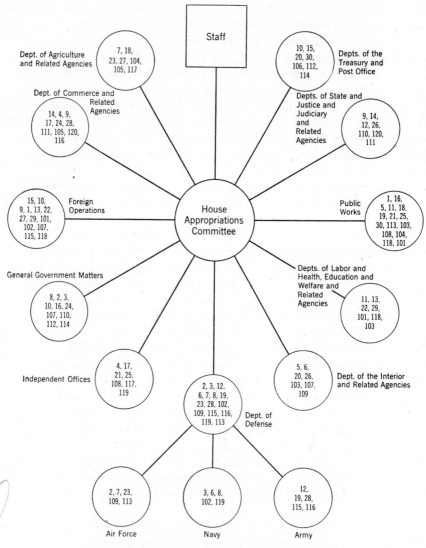

Figure 44.   Organization of a Standing Committee.

The House Committee on Appropriations
Eighty-fourth Congress, First Session (1955)

Membership

Democrats

1. Cannon, Mo. (chairman)
2. Mahon, Tex.
3. Sheppard, Calif.
4. Thomas, Tex.
5. Kirwan, Ohio
6. Norrell, Ark.
7. Whitten, Miss.
8. Andrews, Ala.
9. Rooney, N. Y.
10. Gary, Va.
11. Fogarty, R. I.
12. Sikes, Fla.
13. Fernandez, N. Mex.
14. Preston, Ga.
15. Passman, La.
16. Rabaut, Mich.
17. Yates, Ill.
18. Marshall, Minn.

and because their votes and influence were needed by the Party, were not penalized in their committee assignments.

Committee Chairmen: Committee chairmen are the presiding officers of their respective committees. They achieve their posts through consistent reelection; in short, they rise to leadership of their committee by virtue of the seniority system—provided, of course, that their party is in power. Hence committee chairmen, like Speakers of the House, tend to come from States or districts controlled by one party; they usually are concentrated in the region where their party is strongest.

In a Democratic Congress, most committee chairmen will come from the South, with a few from northern large cities; in a Republican Congress, most will come from New England and midwestern small towns. In the House of the Republican Eighty-third Congress, fourteen of the nineteen chairmen came from the area west of Pennsylvania, east of Utah, and north of the Ohio River and the Missouri Compromise line; five were from Illinois alone. In the House of the Democratic Eighty-fourth Congress, eleven of the nineteen chairmen were from east of the Mississippi and south of the Ohio River and the Mason-Dixon Line; two more were from Texas; two, from New York City; and one, from Chicago.

It is noteworthy that in recent decades the presidential candidates of both parties have usually come from regions other than those in which the party's committee chairmen are concentrated, or at least the candidates have been supported by a faction of their party hostile to that providing their chairmen. Such presidential nominations have been made, of course, because the party leaders can be rather certain of winning the area that supplies the chairmen, and desire to appeal to other areas by means of

---

19. Riley, So. Car.	25. Boland, Mass.
20. Sieminski, N. J.	26. Magnuson, Wash.
21. Evins, Tenn.	27. Natcher, Ky.
22. Lanham, Ga.	28. Flood, Pa.
23. Deane, No. Car.	29. Denton, Ind.
24. Shelley, Calif.	30. Murray, Ill.

Republicans

101. Taber, N. Y.	111. Clevenger, Ohio
102. Wigglesworth, Mass.	112. Wilson, Ind.
103. Jensen, Iowa	113. Davis, Wis.
104. Andersen, Minn.	114. James, Pa.
105. Horan, Wash.	115. Ford, Mich.
106. Canfield, N. J.	116. Miller, Md.
107. Fenton, Pa.	117. Vursell, Ill.
108. Phillips, Calif.	118. Hand, N. J.
109. Scrivner, Kans.	119. Ostertag, N. Y.
110. Coudert, N. Y.	120. Bow, Ohio

The members of the committee are listed here in the order of their committee seniority. In the figure they are listed in the subcommittees in order of their subcommittee seniority; the first subcommittee member listed is the chairman of the subcommittee. Note that half the Democratic members of this unusually important committee come from southern States, and that almost half the Republican members come from midwestern States.

the presidential candidate. However, as a result of this practice, the struggle between the legislative and the executive branches of the government is apt to be intensified in the years after the election.

Generally speaking, the chairmen have great power in their committees. They summon committee meetings, determine the subjects for discussion, control the discussions, and report their results to their respective houses. In the main they operate the committees under the rules of their houses whenever the rules apply. Hence they can be voted down by a committee majority. Furthermore, if they refuse to call a committee hearing, they may be compelled to by a specified number of committee members. It can be said, however, that they stand in about the same relation to their committees as the Speaker to the House.

Committee staffs

The staffs of congressional committees perform the administrative, research, and investigative tasks of the committee. Under the Legislative Reorganization Act of 1946, each standing committee may appoint a professional staff of up to four members. Whereas the staff members are assigned to the committee chairman and to the ranking minority member, they usually work for the committee as a whole. Committee staffs have an important function beyond their evident task of keeping Congress informed; as experts, they can serve as a counterbalance to the analogous counsellors of the executive branch. Hence at hearings the committees do not have to rely solely upon representatives of the administration for information respecting proposed legislation; they may turn to their own staff experts for corroborative or contradictory testimony. Thus the staffs may enable Congress to protect its legislative initiative. However, the committee staffs so far have not carried out this function so successfully as was hoped; committee members still rely to a large degree upon special staff personnel who are provided them temporarily by the executive branch, and also upon experts from various pressure groups, for their information.

Joint standing committees

A joint standing committee is a committee created by law, which contains members from both houses of Congress, usually in equal numbers; it may sometimes include members of the executive branch as well. The establishing law normally fixes the means whereby the members are chosen; sometimes the selections are made in the same fashion as those for ordinary standing committees, and at other times they are made by the presiding officers of the two houses, after consultation with congressional and party leaders. Generally representation is accorded to the two parties in rough proportion to their seats in Congress. Customarily the first-named Senator becomes chairman of the joint standing committee; but in the Eighty-third Congress, Representative W. Sterling Cole of New York was named chairman of the Joint Committee on Atomic Energy; in the Eighty-fourth Congress, however, Senator Clinton P. Anderson of New Mexico became chairman.

Joint standing committees have almost always had only supervisory and investigative functions. The Joint Committee on Atomic Energy is unique in having legislative power as well; that is to say, it may not only conduct studies of a particular activity of the government but may also draft and introduce bills to regulate that activity. The refusal to extend legislative power to these committees probably arises chiefly from the unwillingness of the two chambers to surrender their legislative initiative, which they might lose if joint committees had the power to review, recommend, or shelve proposed bills. Typical of the supervisory joint committees are those on printing and on the Library of Congress. The Atomic Energy Committee is the outstanding instance of a joint committee organized for not only supervisory but also investigative and research functions. This committee maintains a large staff of experts that has produced some scholarly reports. Another joint committee of comparable efficiency is that on the Economic Report, which was created in 1946 to deal with the presidential economic message.

Select or special committees

A select or special committee is a committee made up of members of either house of Congress, or of both houses, that has been named to deal with one specific piece of legislation or one field of legislation. The members of all select committees are named by the presiding officer of the house concerned. At one time, as was indicated earlier in this chapter, select committees played an important part in American legislation. In recent years, however, they have appeared less and less frequently. Since 1946, however, there have been a few select committees, created chiefly for investigative functions.

THE INVESTIGATIVE FUNCTION OF COMMITTEES

In a general sense, every hearing with respect to a bill before a standing committee is an investigation, in that the committee is seeking information that will either justify the enactment of the bill into law or demonstrate that the bill should die in committee. In a more specialized sense, however, the investigative function refers to hearings that are particularly designated as investigations.

Congressional investigations are almost always conducted by one form or another of bipartisan committee. Some investigations are carried on by standing committees, such as the House Un-American Activities Committee. In fact, it was believed that after the passage of the Legislative Reorganization Act of 1946 all investigations would be entrusted to standing committees. Although this has not been the case, a larger proportion of investigations than before are now handled by standing committees. Some investigations are executed by subcommittees of congressional standing committees, such as the Subcommittee on Permanent Investigations of the Committee on Government Operations, whose controversial head during the Eighty-third Congress was Senator McCarthy. Other investigations

are assigned to select committees, such as the Special Committee to Investigate Tax-Exempt Foundations in the Eighty-third Congress; it is
noteworthy that whereas such special committees were once numerous, in
the first session of this Congress there were only two. Matters of greater
complexity may be turned over to a joint special committee, such as that
which investigated the Japanese attack upon Pearl Harbor. Finally, some
investigations are made by groups containing members from each house
of Congress and from outside Congress as well, such as the Commission
on Intergovernmental Relations, which included Senators, Representatives, deputies from the executive branch, State governors, and interested
private citizens.

Committee powers to secure facts

Since the broad purpose of investigating committees is to gather facts
related to present or possible laws, it is of considerable significance whether
they have the power to force the yielding of the facts. Today most investigating committees receive from Congress the power to subpoena witnesses and relevant documents or other objects. Normally a witness who
refuses to testify after being subpoenaed may be held in contempt of
Congress and sentenced to jail. Such a refusal may emanate from the
witness' belief that he is being denied his judicial rights and privileges,
especially that of cross-examination. But a congressional investigation is
not a court trial, and need not be conducted according to the principles
of court procedure; if a witness is authorized to cross-examine others, he is
given the authority as a privilege by the committee.

Use of Fifth Amendment: A more reliable protection that some witnesses
invoke is the clause in the Fifth Amendment that guarantees all persons
the right to withhold answers to any questions when the answers might
tend to incriminate them. For example, should a person be asked by a
committee to state his income in a certain year, and should the answer
to this question lay him open to prosecution by the Department of Justice
for failure to pay his income tax, he may decline to answer the question.
To take a second instance, should a committee inquire whether the witness was a member of the Communist Party, and should the witness feel
that an answer to the question might possibly subject him to prosecution
for criminal conspiracy or for asserting a criminal falsehood on a previous
occasion, the witness might again refuse to answer, citing his right under
the Fifth Amendment.

Obstacles by the Executive Branch: Owing to the doctrine of the separation of powers, Congress has striven in vain to compel officers of the executive and judicial branches of the government to testify, or to surrender
documents that chiefs of those branches may refuse to yield. The precedent
for these refusals was set by George Washington, who, after being asked
for certain papers, declared "that the executive ought to communicate
such papers as the public good would permit and ought to refuse those
the disclosure of which would injure the public."

The Truman administration refused to produce documents for Congress on at least nine important occasions. On March 4, 1948, the Secretary of Commerce refused to give over an FBI letter-report on Dr. Edward U. Condon, Director of the National Bureau of Standards. On March 15, 1948, President Truman issued a directive forbidding the departments and agencies to furnish information pertaining to the loyalty of their employees to any court or committee of Congress, unless with presidential authorization. The same month, Dr. John R. Steelman, Confidential Adviser to the President, was directed by the President to refuse to appear before the House Committee on Education and Labor, despite two subpenas that the Committee served upon Steelman. On August 5, 1948, the Department of Justice refused to provide the chairman of the Senate Investigations Subcommittee with material on the case of W. W. Remington. On February 22, 1950, the President denied access to State Department loyalty files after the Senate had passed a resolution demanding them; the Attorney General and FBI Director, J. Edgar Hoover, supported his position during the following month of argument. On May 16, 1951, General Bradley declined before the Senate Foreign Relations and Armed Services Committees to discuss the deliberations of the executive branch that led to the dismissal of General MacArthur. On January 31, 1952, the President ordered the Secretary of State to refuse to give the Senate Internal Security Subcommittee the reports and views of Foreign Service officers. On April 22, 1952, the Attorney General declared that the files on "open cases" would not be shown to the Committee on the Judiciary. On April 3, 1952, the President ordered all security and loyalty files on employees to be withheld from the Senate Appropriations Subcommittee.

These and other precedents were cited by President Eisenhower when he too directed the Secretary of Defense to withhold from Congress information concerning internal agency conversations and communications. The letter containing the instructions is reprinted below as it was issued in the prolonged hearings on the controversy between Senator McCarthy and Army Department officials. It should be especially noted that two separate doctrines are used in cases like this one: the national security and the principle of the separation of powers.

THE WHITE HOUSE,
May 17, 1954

The honorable the SECRETARY OF DEFENSE
Washington, D. C.

DEAR MR. SECRETARY: It has long been recognized that to assist the Congress in achieving its legislative purposes every Executive Department or Agency must, upon the request of a Congressional Committee, expeditiously furnish information relating to any matter within the jurisdiction of the Committee, with certain historical exceptions—some of which are pointed out in the attached memorandum from the Attorney General. This Administration has been and will continue to be diligent in following this principle. However, it is essential to the successful working of our system that the persons entrusted with power in any one of the three great branches of Government shall not encroach upon the authority confided to the others.

The ultimate responsibility for the conduct of the Executive branch rests with the President.

Within this Constitutional framework each branch should cooperate fully with each other for the common good. However, throughout our history the President has withheld information whenever he found that what was sought was confidential or its disclosure would be incompatible with the public interest or jeopardize the safety of the Nation.

Because it is essential to efficient and effective administration that employees of the Executive Branch be in a position to be completely candid in advising with each other on official matters, and because it is not in the public interest that any of their conversations or communications, or any documents or reproductions, concerning such advice be disclosed, you will instruct employees of your Department that in all of their appearances before the Subcommittee of the Senate Committee on Government Operations regarding the inquiry now before it they are not to testify to any such conversations or communications or to produce any such documents or reproductions. This principle must be maintained regardless of who would be benefited by such disclosures.

I direct this action so as to maintain the proper separation of powers between the Executive and Legislative Branches of the Government in accordance with my responsibilities and duties under the Constitution. This separation is vital to preclude the exercise of arbitrary power by any branch of the Government.

By this action I am not in any way restricting the testimony of such witnesses as to what occurred regarding any matters where the communication was directly between any of the principals in the controversy within the Executive Branch on the one hand and a member of the Subcommittee or its staff on the other.

Sincerely,

DWIGHT D. EISENHOWER

Of course, a President, in refusing to cooperate with congressional committees, may have in mind no such high purpose as Washington and others have specified; he may only resent congressional efforts to investigate the functioning of the executive branch, or more simply may not wish to reveal documents that might embarrass his administration. By the same token, a President may gladly surrender documents when the publicity secured by revealing their contents may serve him, his administration, or his party. For this reason it can be expected that any change in party control of the White House may be followed by the publication of certain documents heretofore withheld from Congress.

Criticism of investigating committees

Investigating committees have been the objects of persistent criticism down through the years. One of the chief criticisms has been that the committees have disregarded the principles of constitutional legal procedure. However, as pointed out above, an investigating committee is not a court of law, but an arm of Congress; therefore it is not obliged to follow those principles. From time to time, committee chairmen and members have abused witnesses, made reckless charges against persons or groups, and sometimes damaged the reputations of innocent persons. The committee hearings provide an easy way to get publicity, and the temptation to make

A SELECT COMMITTEE OF ENQUIRY HARD AT WORK.

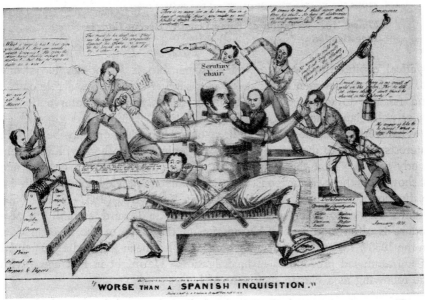

"WORSE THAN A SPANISH INQUISITION."

Figure 45. Conflicting Views of a Congressional Investigation in the Administration of Van Buren (1839). In the top cartoon, the contention is that the President is being "whitewashed" by the Committee. In the bottom cartoon, the complaint is that he is being tortured. Note his weak appearance in the upper cartoon and his Herculean physique in the lower.

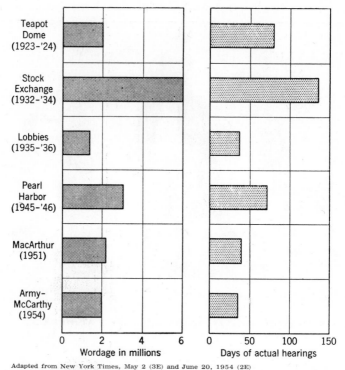

Adapted from New York Times, May 2 (3E) and June 20, 1954 (2E)

Figure 46. Duration of Some Lengthy Recent Congressional Investigations.

political capital from exaggerated showmanship is sometimes too strong for certain congressmen to resist. Under such circumstances, a rule of law and fairness to witnesses can be preserved only by the intervention of other politicians, the press, and representatives of interested groups.

Whatever the methods and findings of an investigation may be, certain interests are apt to denounce them as too lenient and others will find them overly severe. That these two positions existed more than a century ago is shown by the two cartoons illustrating divergent viewpoints on an investigation during the presidency of Martin Van Buren (1837–1841). (See Figure 45.) Moreover, the observer's attitude toward committtee procedure is often modified by his opinion of the value of the investigation. In the 1950's, for example, Senator McCarthy has been the leading exponent of untrammeled procedures in investigation. He might in fact agree with the following as a classic statement of his position:

> The question is not whether people's feelings, here and there may be hurt, or names "dragged through the mud," as it is called. The real issue is whether the danger of abuses and the actual harm done are so clear and substantial that the grave risks of fettering free congressional inquiry are to be incurred by artificial and technical limitations upon inquiry.
> The procedure of congressional investigation should remain as it is. The power of investigation should be left untrammelled, and the methods and forms of each investigation should be left for determination by Congress and

its committees, as each situation arises. The safeguards against abuse and folly are to be looked for in the forces of responsibility which are operating within Congress, and are generated from without.

Thus wrote a staunch liberal in the May 21, 1924, issue of the *New Republic* magazine; he was Professor Felix Frankfurter of Harvard Law School, later Associate Justice of the federal Supreme Court. Obviously some measure of tolerance depends upon whose ox is being gored.

Regardless of the criticism that investigations provoke in some quarters, Congress will vote investigations whenever they serve the interests of the majority. For example, for the period 1953–1954 the Eighty-third Congress carried out 228 investigations, and appropriated over eight million dollars to conduct them. As Figure 46 shows, certain investigations in late years have consumed much time of the members of Congress.

QUESTIONS AND PROBLEMS

1. Contrast the *legislative* organization of the House with that of the Senate. How do you explain the major differences?

2. Contrast the *party* organization of the House with that of the Senate. How do you explain any differences?

3. Sometimes during the nineteenth century the Speaker of the House was regarded as being more powerful than the President. Considering the respective (but changing) powers of the two offices and of the personalities that might occupy them, how do you think that this could have happened?

4. What are the functions and powers of the Committee on Rules of the House?

5. Define the following terms in one sentence: standing committee; joint standing committee; special or select committee; committee on committees of the Democratic Party of the House; steering committee; policy committee; subcommittee.

6. How is seniority in the Congress determined for the purpose of assigning committee memberships?

7. What are the powers of the chairman of a congressional standing committee?

8. Do you think a line should be drawn between ordinary legislative committees and investigating committees? Explain your answer.

9. What are the major criticisms that have been voiced against congressional investigating committees?

THE legislative procedure comprises the most important activity of Congress—the making of laws. This procedure involves essentially the introduction, study, possible amendment, and passage of a bill in one house; the same steps in the other house; the reconciliation of any differences in the two versions; final passage in identical form; and submission to the President for his signature, whereupon the bill becomes law. Figure 47 pictures these essential parts of the legislative procedure.

THE RULES

This procedure is ostensibly hedged about by two sets of detailed, standing rules, one for each chamber, those for the House being even more

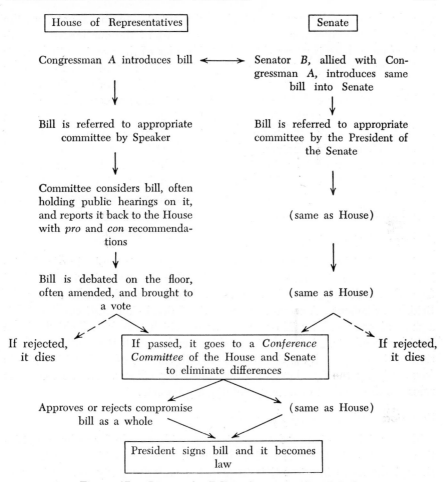

Figure 47.   Career of a Bill in Congress (Simplified).

complex than those for the Senate.   Actually, these rules may be amplified, superseded, or even contradicted at any time by special rules, which are devices that crop up far more frequently in the House than in the Senate.

The status of the rules in the House is somewhat different from that in the Senate.   House rules are viewed as ending with every Congress.   One of the first acts of a new House, therefore, is to acquire a body of rules. Usually one of the senior Representatives, often the chairman of the Rules Committee, moves that the rules of the previous House be adopted; and it is at this time that any insurgents have the best opportunity for procuring a change in the rules.   However, since the bulk of the Representatives normally have a vested interest in the perpetuation of the old rules, any change even at this time is extremely difficult to accomplish.   Conse-

Public Hearings of a Senate Investigating Committee.   Under the chairmanship of Senator Estes Kefauver (Tenn.), the Senate Committee to Investigate Organized Crime in Interstate Commerce sits at the Federal Court Building in New York City, March 13, 1951.   Television cameras brought tremendous publicity to bear upon the proceedings.

quently the old rules are almost always adopted. In the Senate, on the other hand, the rules are considered to be part of the continuous organization; hence there is no need to adopt the rules of the previous Senate.

Occasionally an uprising may break out at the first meeting of a new Senate, in which a Senator or group of Senators desirous of enacting certain legislation will argue that the rules of the Senate are not continuous, so that they can secure new rules that will assist their legislative project. Such an uprising took place at the beginning of the Eighty-third Congress, when a group of Democratic Senators, including Herbert Lehman of New York and Clinton Anderson of New Mexico, sought to bring about the adoption of new rules that would enable them to push a body of civil rights laws through the Senate. The attempt was voted down when Robert A. Taft, Republican floor leader, rallied the opposition to the proposals.

Sources of the rules

Congressional rules have numerous sources. One is the body of rules inherited from the Congress of the Confederation, a set of rules itself derived from those of early State legislatures, colonial assemblies, and finally the British Parliament. A second source is the federal Constitution. A third is a manual compiled by Thomas Jefferson, which was based chiefly upon British precedents. A fourth lies in the amendments that are adopted from time to time, especially in the House. A fifth consists of the decisions made frequently by the Speaker and other presiding officers. In the main the rules are the product of a long evolutionary process.

Function and nature of the rules

The official function of the rules is to provide a code for orderly legislative procedure in Congress. The unofficial function, which may be considered the more important, is to give the majority party, particularly in the House, a group of regulations that will furnish that party an additional means for enacting its program while fending off opposition from the minority party. The rules have a dual nature, formal and informal. The formal rules are extremely complex, so that even so skilled and experienced a congressman as the Speaker must occasionally refer to the Parliamentarian for clarification of points of order. Actually Congress does a large part of its work under a second set of rules, which may be termed informal. Under the practice known as "suspension of the rules," the formal rules of the House may be made temporarily inapplicable, in order to expedite business. This suspension is possible, however, only if no member present offers an objection. The procedure for expediting business in the Senate is termed "unanimous consent"; under this procedure, all members agree to limit the length of debate on a measure.

TYPES OF LEGISLATIVE MEASURES BEFORE CONGRESS

A legislative measure is one that has to do with the process of law-making, or of framing policy. It is to be distinguished from an executive measure, which is related to a congressional action such as the confirmation of a presidential appointment; or a judicial measure, which is related to a congressional action such as an impeachment. There are four principal types of legislative measures that come before Congress: a bill, a joint resolution, a concurrent resolution, and a simple resolution. Two of these, it will be seen, are concerned with the actual substance of the laws; the other two are more closely associated with the procedure of enacting laws. Figure 48 provides facsimiles of the first pages of all four types, and of a public law as well.

Bill (See Figure 48A)

A bill is the customary form taken by a legislative proposal, or a proposed law. The bill has a maximum life of two years—that of the Congress to which it is submitted. Bills submitted after the opening of a Congress are alive only during that Congress. There are two general types of bills: *public* and *private.* A public bill is one that is of general application, such as an income tax proposal. A private bill applies to one person or a few persons, or perhaps an institution; under President Cleveland, for example, there was a torrent of private bills to grant pensions for Union veterans of the Civil War who did not qualify under the general pension law. Today there are not so many private bills as there were in Cleveland's day, because of legal restrictions.

Normally a bill has eight parts: a title; a table of contents; an enacting clause; a definition of terms; the body of the proposed law; exceptions to the general principles of the proposed law; a so-called *separability clause*, providing that the invalidation of one part of the law will not affect the other parts; and a clause giving the date or dates at which the act would become effective.[1]

Joint resolution (See Figure 48B)

A joint resolution is almost identical to a bill. Like a bill, it must win a majority vote from each house; however, a bill is thereby *passed*, whereas a resolution is *adopted*. Like a bill, a joint resolution must be signed by the President to become effective. Matters proposed in joint resolutions usually are planned to be of shorter duration than those encompassed in bills; for example, an emergency appropriation to carry on the activities of an agency when Congress has been unable to agree on a general appropriation bill is usually made by a joint resolution. One of the most important joint resolutions was that making peace with Germany after World War I, when the Senate refused to approve the Versailles Treaty. When the two houses of Congress propose an amendment to the Constitution, they do so in the form of a joint resolution. On this occasion the resolution does not require the President's signature, for an amendment is not a legislative measure.

---

[1] Cf. Galloway, George, *The Legislative Process in Congress* (New York: Thomas Y. Crowell Company, 1953), p. 51.

C. A Public Law (First page).

[PUBLIC LAW 101—80TH CONGRESS]

[CHAPTER 120—1ST SESSION]

[H. R. 3020]

AN ACT

To amend the National Labor Relations Act, to provide additional facilities for the mediation of labor disputes affecting commerce, to equalize legal responsibilities of labor organizations and employers, and for other purposes.

Be it enacted by the Senate and House of Representatives of the United States of America in Congress assembled,

SHORT TITLE AND DECLARATION OF POLICY

SECTION 1. (a) This Act may be cited as the "Labor Management Relations Act, 1947".

(b) Industrial strife which interferes with the normal flow of commerce and with the full production of articles and commodities for commerce, can be avoided or substantially minimized if employers, employees, and labor organizations each recognize under law one another's legitimate rights in their relations with each other, and above all recognize under law that neither party has any right in its relations with any other to engage in acts or practices which jeopardize the public health, safety, or interest.

It is the purpose and policy of this Act, in order to promote the full flow of commerce, to prescribe the legitimate rights of both employees and employers in their relations affecting commerce, to provide orderly and peaceful procedures for preventing the interference by either with the legitimate rights of the other, to protect the rights of individual employees in their relations with labor organizations whose activities affect commerce, to define and proscribe practices on the part of labor and management which affect commerce and are inimical to the general welfare, and to protect the rights of the public in connection with labor disputes affecting commerce.

TITLE I—AMENDMENT OF NATIONAL LABOR RELATIONS ACT

SEC. 101. The National Labor Relations Act is hereby amended to read as follows:

"FINDINGS AND POLICIES

"SECTION 1. The denial by some employers of the right of employees to organize and the refusal by some employers to accept the procedure of collective bargaining lead to strikes and other forms of industrial strife or unrest, which have the intent or the necessary effect of burdening or obstructing commerce by (a) impairing the efficiency, safety, or operation of the instrumentalities of commerce; (b) occurring in the current of commerce; (c) materially affecting, restraining, or controlling the flow of raw materials or manufactured or processed goods from or into the channels of commerce, or the prices of such materials or

---

B. A Joint Resolution (First page).

80th CONGRESS
1st Session

H. J. RES. 99

IN THE HOUSE OF REPRESENTATIVES

JANUARY 7, 1953

Mr. MACHROWICZ introduced the following joint resolution; which was referred to the Committee on the Judiciary

JOINT RESOLUTION

Proposing an amendment to the Constitution of the United States to abolish the electoral college system and to provide for the election of the President and Vice President.

1   *Resolved by the Senate and House of Representatives*

2   *of the United States of America in Congress assembled*

3   *(two-thirds of each House concurring therein),* That the

4   following article is hereby proposed as part of the Constitu-

5   tion of the United States, which shall be valid to all intents

6   and purposes as part of the Constitution when ratified by the

7   legislatures of three-fourths of the several States:

8   "ARTICLE —

9   "SECTION 1. The executive power shall be vested in a

10   President of the United States of America. He shall hold

11   his office during the term of four years, and together with

I

A. A Bill introduced in the Senate (First page).

80th CONGRESS
1st Session

S. 2585

IN THE SENATE OF THE UNITED STATES

AUGUST 3, 1953

Mr. LEHMAN (for himself, Mr. GREEN, Mr. HUMPHREY, Mr. KEFAUVER, Mr. MOSES, Mr. MURRAY, Mr. PASTORE, and Mr. MAGNUSON) introduced the following bill; which was read twice and referred to the Committee on the Judiciary

A BILL

To amend and revise the laws relating to immigration, naturalization, nationality, and citizenship, and for other purposes.

1   *Be it enacted by the Senate and House of Representa-*

2   *tives of the United States of America in Congress assembled,*

3   That this Act, divided into titles, chapters, and sections

4   according to the following table of contents, may be cited

5   as the "Immigration and Citizenship Act of 1953".

TABLE OF CONTENTS

TITLE I—General

J. 26001—1

Figure 48.   A Congressional Bill and Resolutions, and a Public Law.

84TH CONGRESS
1ST SESSION
H. RES. 5

IN THE HOUSE OF REPRESENTATIVES

JANUARY 5, 1955

Mr. SMITH of Virginia submitted the following resolution; which was considered and agreed to

RESOLUTION

1 *Resolved*, That the rules of the House of Representatives
2 of the Eighty-third Congress, together with all applicable
3 provisions of the Legislative Reorganization Act of 1946,
4 as amended, be, and they are hereby, adopted as the rules
5 of the House of Representatives of the Eighty-fourth
6 Congress.

v

E.   A Resolution of the House.

85th CONGRESS
1ST SESSION
S. CON. RES. 1

IN THE SENATE OF THE UNITED STATES

JANUARY 3, 1953

Mr. JENNER submitted the following concurrent resolution; which was considered and agreed to

CONCURRENT RESOLUTION

1 *Resolved by the Senate (the House of Representatives*
2 *concurring)*, That the two Houses of Congress shall meet
3 in the Hall of the House of Representatives on Tuesday, the
4 6th day of January 1953, at 1 o'clock postmeridian, pur-
5 suant to the requirements of the Constitution and laws re-
6 lating to the election of President and Vice President of the
7 United States, and the President of the Senate shall be their
8 presiding officer; that two tellers shall be previously appointed
9 by the President of the Senate on the part of the Senate
10 and two by the Speaker on the part of the House of
11 Representatives, to whom shall be handed, as they are
12 opened by the President of the Senate, all the certificates

v

D.   A Concurrent Resolution (First page).

Figure 48. (*continued*)

Concurrent resolution (See Figure 48D)

A concurrent resolution is a measure adopted by both houses that is usually designed either to express the feelings of each house or to establish some rule fixing the behavior of the two houses. For example, Congress may by concurrent resolution tender its congratulations to a foreign monarch for achieving twenty-five years of rule. The House and Senate generally set the date for their adjournment by this means. This sort of resolution does not require the signature of the President; hence it can be used on occasion to bypass the will of the chief executive.

The Reorganization Act of 1945 (which, of course, was a regular bill, signed by the President) provided that certain plans might be drafted by the President concerning the reorganization of administrative offices and that these plans were to take effect unless Congress by concurrent resolution should disapprove of them. Congress had thus inserted a method for preventing the President from vetoing congressional rejection of his reorganization plans; on the other hand, the method described transferred great powers of legislative initiative to the President in the area of administrative reorganization. Indeed, it is this latter fact that may have the greater importance for the future. It is possible that the President might be delegated wide discretion to make law on many subjects, limited only by what would turn out to be in fact a "congressional veto."

Resolution (See Figure 48E)

A resolution is similar to a concurrent resolution in aim, but is adopted by only one house. For example, a special rule proposed to the House by the House Committee on Rules is submitted in the form of a resolution. As in the case of the concurrent resolution, Congress has used the simple resolution to block a presidential veto of a congressional act; thus the Reorganization Act of 1949 stated that either house could reject an executive project by a simple resolution to that effect adopted by a majority vote of the entire membership of the house concerned.

PROCEDURE IN THE HOUSE

The continuous restraints imposed by the rules accompany a bill throughout its career. This can be seen in tracing the passage through Congress of a bill that has been introduced in the House. (The House example, rather than a Senate one, is chosen solely for convenience.) Every recent session has seen hundreds of bills that have successfully passed both houses of Congress. Some even refer to Congress as a legislative mill, grinding out bill after bill. As Figure 49 shows, the mill has been increasingly busy as time has gone by; its passage of bills has grown tenfold since the first decade of the Republic.

Introduction and referral of a bill

The introduction of a bill to the floor of either chamber begins the process of enacting a law. Any type of bill may be introduced into either house, save for bills levying taxes, which the Constitution states must originate in the House (Art. I, sec. 7, cl. 1), and bills providing for expenditures, which custom dictates shall start in the House. Generally, when a bill is so important that it has sponsors in both houses, its introduction into one or the other house is often the consequence of long reflection and debate over legislative tactics and strategy, since the position assumed by one house may have considerable influence over that assumed by the other. For example, when a bill is very controversial, its sponsors may feel that it should be introduced into the house with the larger proportion of supporters on the theory that passage in one house may convert enemies in the other house into friends.

Every bill, whatever its source, must be introduced by a congressman. A bill drafted by a single congressman will be introduced by him. A bill prepared by a congressional committeee (and many important ones are) is usually introduced by the chairman of the committee. Bills written in the executive branch are turned over to a friendly congressman for introduction. Bills drafted by people outside the government will be introduced on occasion by the congressman from the district of the person or persons affected, by the chairman of the committee handling bills in this legislative area, or perhaps by one of the several members of both chambers who are known to introduce privately drafted bills readily. The mechanics of introduction in the House are simple: the member merely places the bill in a box, or "hopper," at the Speaker's desk.

The bill is then referred to a standing committee by the House Parliamentarian, under the supervision and ultimate authority of the Speaker. Since the Legislative Reorganization Act of 1946 describes in detail the types of

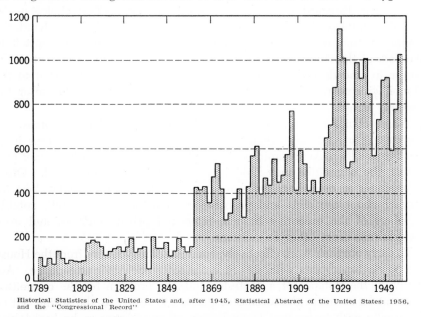

Historical Statistics of the United States and, after 1945, Statistical Abstract of the United States: 1956, and the "Congressional Record"

Figure 49. The Number of Public Bills and Resolutions Passed by Congress, 1789–1956, First Through Eighty-Fourth Congress.

legislation that the committees are to handle, the referring is usually quickly determined by the contents of the bill. On occasion, however, a bill may deal with matters that fall within the province of more than one committee; hence a contest may arise between supporters and antagonists of the proposed measure as to which committee shall deal with it, the supporters hoping for a sympathetic committee and the antagonists seeking a hostile one. Meanwhile the chairmen of the committees involved themselves may struggle over the bill, since having it referred to their committee may add to their prestige. The House can, by a majority vote, override the Speaker's decision and refer a bill to a committee of its own choice; however it does so rarely.

At the time that the bill is referred, it receives the first of its three readings, generally by title only. It gets a designation—"H.R." for a bill, and "H.J.Res.," "H.Con.Res.," or "H.Res.," if a joint, concurrent, or simple resolution; it also acquires a number. It is then printed, with copies made available to all members of Congress, and turned over to the committee.

Committee treatment

The action of the committee almost always determines the fate of the bill. Inasmuch as members of the House cannot expect to know more than a few bills very well, and inasmuch as they tend to regard committee members as comparative experts in their especial field, Representatives customarily accept the decisions of the standing committees. Hence it is in and during committee functioning that one finds perhaps the most intense form of the legislative struggle. In dealing with a bill a committee has a number of choices. It may give it only a cursory examination, then "pigeon-hole" it, or even disregard it completely; this is the commonest choice made, and almost always is a death sentence for the bill. On the other hand, the committee may devote more attention to the bill, and finally report it to the floor of the House with a recommendation for passage; report it to the House in amended form, with a similar recommendation; report it to the House with no recommendation; or report it entirely rewritten after the enacting clause.

Which choice the committee makes is the product of many forces. In the case of a relatively insignificant bill, if the committee concerns itself at all it usually makes a rapid decision. In the case of more important proposals, the committee may hold hearings, either open or closed. Often it summons to open hearings those persons who are presumably best informed about the aims and probable consequences of the bill, notably members of the executive branch, interested private citizens, and even congressmen from other committees.

To carry out their work effectively, committees may secure from the House the power to subpena witnesses in order to compel their attendance. Actually, in the instance of a contested bill, the problem for the committee may not be so much the forcing of persons to testify as the sifting out of those who wish to speak. The selection of the persons to be heard, and the manner in which their testimony is received, is ordinarily settled by the party attachments and the economic and sectional interests of the committee members. Indeed, the very time at which the hearings are held—the lapse of time between the introduction of a bill and its consideration—is often a matter of political tactics.

At the conclusion of the open hearings the committee may hold closed, or executive, sessions, to decide its action on the bill. It is now that the bill may be amended or rewritten. Eventually, the committee reaches its decision by a majority vote of its members. Usually, whether or not the decision is to bring the bill to the floor, the details of the open hearings are ordered to be printed and made available to members of Congress. If the committee decision is favorable, the bill is reported to the floor. Only a small minority of all bills introduced survive committee treatment. In the first session of the Eighty-fourth Congress, 5,361 public bills were introduced into the House, and 1,758 into the Senate. Yet Congress in this session enacted only 390 public laws. Of course, bills introduced in one session are "active" during the whole of a Congress; if not reported out in the first session, they may be in the second. Hence some of these bills did become laws during the second session. The vast majority of them, however, were buried in committee.

Action on the floor

The House Calendars: When a bill is reported out of committee, it is placed on one of the calendars that the House maintains for pending business. Public bills and resolutions that provide for the levying of taxes or the expenditure of money are placed on the Union Calendar. Other public bills are listed on the House Calendar. Private bills are put on the Private Calendar. When a bill is not controversial—that is, when passage by unanimous vote appears a certainty—it may be removed from any of these calendars and placed on the Consent Calendar.

A fifth calendar, the Discharge Calendar, is related to the process of dislodging a bill from a committee whose majority does not want to report it to the floor. The discharge process, which was inaugurated in 1910 and has since been amended several times, is effected in two stages. First, a congressman files with the Clerk of the House a petition signifying his wish to have a committee discharged of further consideration of a bill that has been in the custody of the committee for at least thirty days. Then, when and if 218 Representatives—a quorum, or one-half of the membership of the House—sign the petition, the bill is taken from the committee and placed on the Discharge Calendar. This proceeding is usually initiated several times during each session, but is rarely completed. Only one bill that has been discharged from a committee has ever been enacted into law: the Fair Labor Standards Act of 1938.

Bringing a Bill to the Floor: Although the calendars appear to be devices for arranging the order in which business comes to the floor, actually public bills are withdrawn from them with little regard for numerical sequence; private bills, it is true, are normally taken from their calendar in sequence. Certain types of bills enjoy precedence, or privilege, under the standing rules of the House. Resolutions of the Rules Committee, which lead to the adoption of special rules for legislating, take precedence over almost all other business. Bills from certain committees, such as that on Ways and Means and that on Appropriations, are privileged business.

Moreover, certain days are set aside for dealing with classes of bills not otherwise privileged. On the first and third Monday of every month, bills may be called from the Consent Calendar and passed by the House so long as no Representative objects. On the same days, after the Consent Calendar business has been completed, any Representative may move that the standing rules be suspended and that a certain bill be passed; if the members concur by a two-thirds majority vote, the rules are suspended and the bill passed at the same time. Special days are similarly reserved for matters on the Private and Discharge Calendars. On the second and fourth Mondays, Congress may function almost as a city council, in that it deals with District of Columbia affairs. On Calendar Wednesday, each standing committee is called upon in alphabetical order, at which time a committee may bring from the calendars any bill not otherwise privileged.

Actually, most bills, apart from those on the privileged days, come to the floor on the basis of a legislative schedule drafted by the leaders of the majority party. Even reports from such privileged committees as that on Ways and Means are brought forward only when the leaders deem the moment propitious. Legislative timing is the product, then, of frequent conferences among the Speaker, floor leader, whip, committee chairmen, policy and steering committees, and, if the administration is of the same party as the majority in Congress, deputies from the executive branch or even the President himself. It is the special rules drawn up by the Rules Committee and adopted by a majority vote that pave the way for bills coming to the floor.

Treatment on the Floor: The prospect of the House floor is usually rather disappointing, if not actually depressing, to the spectator. Often many seats are empty; those Representatives who are present may appear to be paying little if any attention to the speaker. The contents of the debates may sound absurd. It should be apparent by now, however, that the real work of Congress takes place in committee meetings. The purpose of floor treatment has come to be little more than formal endorsement of committee work, the strengthening of partisan bonds, or the justification of a congressman's stand to his supporters.

To expedite its work, Congress uses an efficient legislative device, originally English, known as the Committee of the Whole. This Committee, which today is used almost solely by the House, is fundamentally an implement of the House. It consists of the total membership of the House operating under different rules from those of the House. All bills on the Union Calendar must be discussed in the Committee of the Whole; in practice, most bills are so treated.

The House is converted into the Committee of the Whole when a single member moves that the House shall resolve itself into this Committee, and the motion is carried by a majority vote. The Speaker now appoints another

Representative to serve as chairman, then steps down. In the Committee a quorum consists of only 100 members; the time for speaking is limited, and no roll-call votes are taken. First the bill concerned is debated; time for the debate is divided equally between supporters and opponents of the bill, whose forces usually are captained, respectively, by the chairman and ranking minority member of the standing committee in charge of the bill. After debate has been concluded, the bill is read, section by section or article by article, by the Clerk—the second reading of the bill. At this time amendments may be proposed for any of the sections, with those for and those against the amendment each being allotted five minutes for speaking. After the bill has been debated and amended, some member moves that the Committee of the Whole rise and report to the House. The Speaker then resumes the chair, and the House is again in session.

The House must now pass upon the bill as debated, amended, and reported by the Committee of the Whole. Thereupon, the question is put as to whether the bill shall be read a third time and "engrossed," or reprinted as amended. Whatever debate occurs in the House sessions proper almost invariably takes place at this point. Debate, which is often designed solely to slow proceedings, and other delaying maneuvers, are rather strictly limited in the House; for example, a Representative must speak to the point, and is, in fact, duly recognized by the chair only after having stated his purpose for wishing to speak. It is now that one Representative—generally the standing committee chairman—addresses the whole House in behalf of the bill; and the leading opponent likewise presents his cause. However, no member may speak for more than an hour. Normally delegates from the two major parties have agreed about the apportionment of discussion time.

However, those who wish to delay have several instruments at their disposal. One of the commonest delaying tactics is to demand a quorum call, to determine the presence of the necessary 218 members for the conduct of business. Should a call of the roll show that there is not a quorum in the chamber, the Speaker may order the doors locked and the Sergeant at Arms with his aides to arrest all absent members; meantime all business is suspended. Those who seek to delay the proceedings do so under the assumption that in the additional time they may convince some waverers to adopt their side. Yet, it is possible for a member of the House to halt all debate, by "moving the previous question." If the motion is adopted by a majority of those present, the House must proceed without further debate to vote on the measure before it.

Methods of Voting: There are four methods of voting in the House. The first is a simple voice, or *viva voce*, vote, wherein the Speaker calls first for the "Ayes," then the "Noes," and declares which have a majority. Should any single member dissent, the Speaker may order a standing vote, or "division," again announcing his conclusion, by rough estimate of the numbers standing, as to which side carried the vote. At this point, if one-fifth of a quorum (forty-four in the House, twenty in the Committee of the Whole) require, he may call a "teller" vote. The members leave their

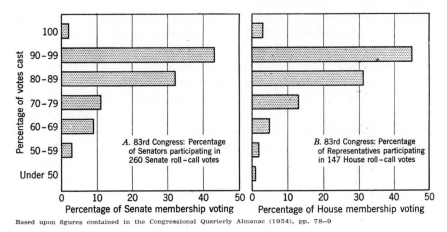

Based upon figures contained in the Congressional Quarterly Almanac (1954), pp. 78–9

Figure 50.   Participation in Roll-Calls by Members of the 83rd Congress.

seats and gather in the "well" of the chamber before the Speaker's desk. Two tellers are appointed, one for each side.   First the members favoring the measure pass between the tellers to be counted; those opposed follow. Finally, in the House but not in the Committee of the Whole, if one-fifth of those present ask it, the Speaker may order a roll-call vote, in which each member is to state his position.   According to the rules, every member present must vote "Aye" or "No."   However, no means has ever been discovered to force a member unwilling to commit himself to declare himself.   Actually it is not necessary to run through the entire gamut of voting methods; if one-fifth of those present demand it immediately after a *viva voce* vote, the Speaker must at once order a roll-call vote.

The roll-call vote can be of great importance.   It is the only one of the four types of voting in which each member's position on a specific bill may be determined (except, of course, in the case of non-controversial bills passed under unanimous consent agreements).   One group in the House may demand a roll-call vote in the belief that certain members will change their votes in order to placate their constituents, or to prove that they are keeping faith with their party leaders.

The proportion of Representatives declaring themselves on roll-call votes is quite high; the average Representative responded to about 90% of the approximately 150 such votes.   Figure 50 shows that only a small percentage averaged below 70%.   It is somewhat dangerous to criticize Representatives very harshly for being absent from a number of roll-call votes.   Indeed, some of those who are most punctual are viewed by their colleagues as relatively unimportant members of the House.   Absences may be occasioned by exceptional attention to committee tasks, which may keep the Representative out of Washington.   It should be noted that a House roll takes about three-quarters of an hour to call; the Clerk calls each name in alphabetical order once, then calls again the names of all those absent.   Hence, on being notified of the imminence of a vote, a member may make his way across the whole District of Columbia to the Capitol in time to state his position.

Some observers have deplored the fact that this method of voting uses a great deal of time that might be employed more profitably, and have urged that Congress install electrical voting devices like those now employed in numerous State assemblies. However, the roll-call vote as it now stands is adaptable to delicate political stratagems that would be obliterated by mechanical appliances; hence congressmen are apt to continue the present voting system.

Once a bill has been passed by the House, it is certified by the Clerk of the House, renamed an "act," and sent to the Senate.

PROCEDURE IN THE SENATE

The legislative procedure in the Senate is very similar to that in the House. There are, however, a few notable differences, which are based largely upon the smaller number of members in the Senate and the lesser degree of party management and dictation there; the latter fact is quite evident from the comparative impotence of the Senate Committee on Rules and Administration.

Introduction and committee handling of an act

A bill passed by the House and thereby converted into an "act" is transmitted to the desk of the presiding officer of the Senate. It is then, as in the House, referred to a standing committee. Committee hearings in the Senate have the same purpose as those in the House, that of ascertaining the desirability of the proposed law. When the Senate is the second chamber to deal with projected legislation, however, its committee hearings may be somewhat different. On occasion a bill originating outside of Congress, especially one drafted in the executive branch, is introduced simultaneously into each house of Congress. The two houses, then, may have held their committee hearings at about the same time. If this be the case, a House-passed bill that has been delivered to the Senate may be stricken out after the enacting clause, and the bill that has emerged from the Senate hearing inserted in its stead. Sometimes, with a bill introduced into each house at the same time, the two chambers may hold joint committee hearings. When the House has held lengthy hearings on a bill, the Senate hearings may be abbreviated inasmuch as the Senators can rely upon the printed accounts of the House hearings for their information.

Senate committee hearings otherwise resemble those in the House, with the testimony of witnesses for and against the proposed legislation. Ralph K. Huitt, analyzing Senate committee operations in "The Congressional Committee; a Case Study," an investigation of hearings before the Senate Committee on Banking and Currency in 1946 respecting price control legislation, concluded that members of a committee in these proceedings tend to adopt specific roles for themselves, such as defenders of sectional interests, protectors of their own economic fields, and the like. Professor Huitt also noted how committee members tend to shift roles according to the subject matter being dealt with, and the position of the person being interrogated. As a fact-finding agency, "quantitatively" the committee did "an impressive job." However, two sets of "facts" emerged: one set for the advocates of price control, and one for its enemies, each based upon the frame of reference of the individual committee members.

When the committee has finished debating, amending, and rewriting the act, it may report it to the floor. In the event a committee will not return an act to the floor, a Senator may move that the committee be discharged; if the motion is adopted by a majority vote, the act is brought to the floor. However, the Senate more often takes the bill from one committee and refers it to another that will treat it more favorably. The act can now be placed on a Senate calendar: for ordinary legislative matters there is but one, the Calendar of General Business. Once on this calendar, the act becomes part of the pending business of the Senate.

Floor maneuvers

Maneuvers on the Senate floor are in general much less restrained than those on the House floor. The Senate does not have an elaborate schedule of days for privileged business like that in the House. Furthermore, for legislative business the Senate does not resolve itself into a Committee of the Whole, which, because of its peculiar rules, imposes considerable limitations upon House debate. Members of the Senate do not have the power to "move the previous question." In fact, save for the temporary rule of unanimous consent, adopted for handling single, particular bills, resolutions, or acts within a specified time, the Senate permits virtually no limits on debate. Since World War II an average year has seen the rule of unanimous consent used a score of times. The usual absence of restrictions on speaking has led to the institution of filibustering.

Filibustering: Filibustering is simply the effort made by one man or several, through protracted speaking, so to delay business in the Senate that his or their opponents, who may be in the vast majority, will yield on a given point or group of points in order to be able to undertake other business. It can flourish in the Senate because the rules do not compel Senators to speak to the point on a measure unless the rule of unanimous consent has been adopted. Filibustering is a very old practice. Plutarch, the biographer of Greeks and Romans who lived more than two thousand years ago, recounts how Julius Caesar sought to campaign for the consulship, the highest executive office in the Roman Republic, without appearing in person in Rome as the law required him to do. Plutarch says that Marcus Porcius Cato, one of Caesar's foes, seeing that Caesar's supporters numbered a majority in the Senate and would be able to exempt him from the law, "wasted the whole day of the Senate in talking." This filibuster succeeded, for ultimately Caesar yielded and came to Rome.

Filibustering in the American Senate has been especially common during the twentieth century. The longest individual filibustering speech in American history was twenty-two hours, twenty-six minutes long; it was delivered April 25, 1953, by Wayne Morse of Oregon, who sought to block enactment of a law giving oil-bearing lands off the coasts to the States. Fittingly,

Morse had been one of the severest critics of filibustering. A small faction, by carefully maintaining unity, can delay business for days or even weeks, with one speaker following another to the floor. Custom forbids the presiding officer to a call a Senator to order for discussing irrelevant matters. Hence the contents of a filibustering speech may be almost anything; one Senator once read the telephone directory of Washington, D.C.

Through the years a number of measures have been the targets of filibusters. In recent times the commonest object has been proposed federal legislation aimed at curtailing racial discrimination in the South. One of the most celebrated filibusters was that delivered in 1917 against the proposed arming of merchant ships. The outcome of a filibuster appears to depend to a considerable degree upon the actual forces against the debated measure. At one time, Senator George Malone of Nevada filibustered for more than eleven hours against a bill aimed at limiting the interstate shipment of gambling devices; Malone's effort failed for lack of concurring sentiment among the other Senators, and lack of support from private interests. On the other hand, when a number of durable Senators attempted to filibuster in behalf of a veto by President Truman against an internal security act, the pressure from certain groups such as veterans' organizations in favor of the act drove the majority to wear down the filibusters and override the veto.[1]

Closure: After the success of the 1917 filibuster over the arming of merchant ships, and President Wilson's denunciation of those concerned, the majority in the Senate introduced a means for shutting off Senate debate, known as *closure.* As amended in 1949, the adoption of closure requires two distinct steps. First, a petition for closure, to end debate on a certain matter, signed by one-sixth of the Senate membership— now sixteen Senators—must be submitted to the chair. Then, two calendar days after the petition is filed, the Senate must indicate by a roll-call vote whether debate shall be closed. Adoption of closure needs a two-thirds majority vote of the entire Senate membership—now sixty-four Senators. Closure is effective not only with regard to legislative measures but also with motions or other matters before the chamber; however, motions to change the Senate rules are exempted, so that any move to make closure more easy could itself be filibustered to death. Between 1917 and 1953, twenty-three closure petitions were filed, but in only four instances was the required majority attained. Furthermore, each of these instances occurred prior to 1949, at a time when the vote needed to be only two-thirds of those present.

The probability of instituting an effective curb on Senate debate is very slender. Many Senators regard unlimited debate as the principal bulwark for a minority against a potentially despotic majority, and they know that a turn of fate may bring them into the ranks of the minority. Senator Morse is not the only member of the upper house to have once denounced unlimited debate, then exploited it himself when the occasion demanded. Supporters of the filibuster contend that it may serve to introduce delay where

[1] Cf. Gross, Bertram, *The Legislative Struggle* (New York: The McGraw-Hill Book Company, 1953), pp. 376–377.

haste might be fatal. Opponents reply that much desirable legislation has been blocked; supporters contend that the only bills that have been permanently blocked have been those designed to curtail racial discrimination, a field of law which, they argue, falls in the province of the State and local governments. Since any plan to alter the closure proceeding itself could be filibustered, it seems that only an extraordinary parliamentary coup at the beginning of a Senate session, when the issue of the continuity of Senate organization may arise, could ease the adoption of closure. So long as a majority of Senators, for various reasons, wish to preserve the institution of filibustering, no such coup could be carried out.

Voting

The Senate has three means of voting: *viva voce*, division, and roll-call. There is no teller vote in the Senate as in the House. Like Representatives, Senators average nearly ninety per cent on roll-call votes. Although their percentage is slightly below that of Representatives, it should be remembered that Senators are members of two or more standing committees, but most Representatives are members of only one. As with members of the House, some Senators show comparatively low percentages probably because of their devotion to committee work. Figure 50 shows that senatorial attendance at roll-call votes is quite high.

Disposition of an act after passage in the Senate

What happens to an act after it has been passed by the Senate depends largely upon whether that body has passed the measure in the same form as the House. If it is in the same form as that passed by the House, the bill is returned to the House, enrolled on parchment, signed first by the Speaker and then by the presiding officer of the Senate (even if the bill originated in the Senate it is signed first by the Speaker), and finally transferred to the President for his signature. If, however, the Senate passes the bill in an amended form, it may at once ask for a conference committee to remove the differences between its version and that of the House. On the other hand, it may return the amended bill to the Speaker's desk to await House action. In the latter case, when the amendments are minor, the House may accept them. Certainly there is enough intercommunication between the two houses for the Senate to be fairly well advised as to the probable reaction in the House. If the House does accept the amendments, the bill is enrolled and signed by the presiding officers. If, on the contrary, the House rejects the Senate amendments, or if the Senate at the outset has requested a conference, the bill must go to a conference committee.

THE CONFERENCE COMMITTEE

The function of conference committees is apparently no more than that of removing differences from the House and Senate versions of a bill. However, because of their membership and their proceedings, and because most important bills must be dealt with in conference, these committees occupy a singularly important place in the legislative process.

Membership

Each major party in each house is represented on a conference committee. Officially the presiding officer in each chamber appoints the members of these committees; actually, custom has almost entirely relieved the Speaker and the Vice President of this function. Congressional practice dictates that each house shall have at least three deputies to a conference committee: the chairman, ranking majority member, and ranking minority member, from the standing committee that has handled the bill in each house. These members are chosen habitually to serve as managers for the position assumed by the majority in their house. Actually it often happens that the personal views of these managers do not coincide with the will of the majority; in such cases they do not truly represent that will. Yet efforts to select more representative managers usually surrender to custom. At his discretion the presiding officer may send more than three deputies, or he may be directed to do so by a majority vote of his house. It is not necessary that the two houses be equally represented, for the delegates from each house vote separately from those of the other house. The decision of a conference committee, then, is carried by a majority vote of the deputies from each chamber.

Proceedings

Perhaps the most striking aspect of the proceedings of a conference committee is that they are conducted in executive session, or behind closed doors. Behind this wall of secrecy a conference committee can, and often does, act as a third legislative chamber. Presumably a conference committee is empowered only to adjust differences between the two houses; in practice, however, it sometimes writes what amounts to a new bill. The House, at least, may give instructions to its appointees; however, these instructions must be adopted by the House before the managers are named. In the committee sessions, if the managers for the two houses cannot reach a compromise on the differences, the bill is dead. If, on the other hand, the differences are reconciled, the committee drafts a report of its proceedings and submits it along with the amended bill to each house.

It is an interesting problem to determine which of the two houses yields more to the other in a conference committee. It is generally assumed that the House is apt to yield more than the Senate, because Senators on the average admittedly have more experience than Representatives, and because the ranking Senator becomes chairman of a conference committee. Yet Gilbert Y. Steiner, after examining conferences dealing with fifty-six major bills between 1927 and 1949, concluded that the House carried substantially more weight than the Senate in determining the final version of these bills; he credited the House with nearly sixty per cent of the victories and the Senate with less than thirty per cent; he found in roughly fifteen per cent a drawn contest.[1] Yet the House is still very sensitive about its al-

---

[1] Cf. Steiner, Gilbert Y., *The Congressional Conference Committee: Seventieth to Eightieth Congresses* (Champaign: University of Illinois Press, 1951).

leged inferiority; Representative Fred Hartley has been quoted as saying that the House deliberately made its version of the Labor-Management Relations (Taft-Hartley) Act of 1947 as severe as possible, so that after the Senate had finished cutting it down in conference there would still remain an effective law.

Conference committee reports on the floor

In each house a conference committee report, including the bill, is highly privileged business. Once on the floor, the report may be debated; the chairman of the standing committee that dealt with the bill manages the debate. However, the bill cannot be amended save by concurrent resolution, for amendment by one house would produce again two versions of the bill. It is partly for this reason that a conference committee may function as a lawmaking agency; the Senate and the House may accept a bill, no matter how repugnant they may find the conference committee report, rather than reject the report, which would kill the measure. At the conclusion of debate, the members of each house vote on the report. If each house adopts it by a majority, the act then goes through the stages prescribed for a bill initially passed in the same form by each house, terminating with the President's signature.

PROCEDURE WITH REGARD TO PRESIDENTIAL VETOES

Any bill vetoed by the President, unless by pocket veto, is returned to the house in which it originated, with a message stating the President's reasons for his disapproval. The vetoed bill and the message take precedence over almost any other legislative matter in the house. Perhaps the most important considerations for supporters of the bill are that a two-thirds majority vote is needed to override the veto and that the vote of each member present must be recorded. Hence, if it appears that such a majority will not be forthcoming, the supporters may move to "table" the bill, or, in other words, to postpone indefinitely its consideration, in which case the veto actually is sustained. Proponents of the measure can tacitly admit defeat by this maneuver without the embarrassment of failing to secure the needed majority. If, on the other hand, an overriding majority appears certain, congressional leaders will call for a vote at once. If the veto is overridden in one house, the bill is transmitted to the other house to be voted on similarly. If the veto is overridden likewise in the second house, the bill becomes law without the President's signature.

PUBLICATION OF CONGRESSIONAL PROCEEDINGS

The proceedings of Congress appear in several different publications. The Constitution states that "Each house shall keep a Journal of its proceedings, and from time to time publish the same, excepting such parts as may in their judgment require secrecy; . . ." (Art. I, sec. 5, cl. 3). This Journal, however, is a bare record of official acts such as the introduction of bills and the taking of votes. Since 1873 what purports to be a detailed account of all debates has been published daily in the *Congressional Record.*. Actually the *Record* does not recount precisely what occurred on the floor. Members of both houses can and do edit their speeches, and introduce material never heard on the floor, such as newspaper editorials, magazine articles, and correspondence. Representatives, but not Senators, may even procure the insertion of speeches that they did not deliver. Laws after their passage are sent to the General Services Administration to be placed in the national archives. At the end of each year the government publishes a two-volume text, the *Statutes at Large of the United States*, containing all laws enacted during the year, with the public acts and joint resolutions in one volume and the private acts, concurrent resolutions, resolutions, treaties, and presidential proclamations in the other.

QUESTIONS AND PROBLEMS

1. Name and describe briefly the elements of a congressional bill.
2. What do you think accounts for the great increase in the number of bills passed over the history of Congress (as shown in Figure 48)?
3. What are the several forms of legislation that can be passed by one or both houses of Congress?
4. To what extent do outside groups contribute to the legislation passed by Congress?
5. Describe the procedure for passing a bill through the House.
6. Describe the procedure for passing a bill through the Senate.
7. What are the functions of legislative debate? What might happen if all debate were simply cut out of the legislative process?
8. Describe the various forms of voting on questions before the House.
9. What reasons do some people have for retaining the filibuster, and others for abolishing it? How steadfast are these reasons? Are they matters of principle or of expediency?
10. What is the importance of the work of the conference committee?

PART VII

The Judicial Branch

27. Structure of
the Federal Judiciary

Photo by Abbie Rowe.   Courtesy National Park Service

A court is a governmental institution for the peaceful solution of disputes over matters of law.   Laws, as has been seen in previous chapters, either are enactments of a legislature (statutory law), or stem from a vast body of tradition and custom belonging to the people (common law).   When these laws are being executed, certain disputes may arise that must be resolved in, if possible, a peaceful manner.   Legal disputes fall in the main into any one of three great classes, depending chiefly upon who or what are the parties to the dispute: (1) two or more private individuals or groups; (2) one or more private individuals on the one side and the government, functioning as the embodiment of society, on the other; and (3)

403

one or more individuals on the one side, and one or more government officials or agencies on the other. These three classes involve, respectively, civil law, criminal law, and administrative law. In the American national government, cases pertaining to civil law and to criminal law, and some cases pertaining to administrative law, fall into the sphere of the main American judicial system, the *constitutional* courts. Certain types of cases related to administrative law are dealt with by one or another of the special judicial bodies called *legislative* or *administrative* courts.

THE PLACE OF THE COURTS IN
THE AMERICAN GOVERNMENT

With regard to the place that they occupy in the government, American courts have two important traits that make the American judicial system unique by comparison with the systems of other great powers. In the first place, the American court system is dual: there is a system of national courts under the authority of the national government, and there is a parallel and independent system of State courts for every State government. In the second place, at both levels the courts are independent of, and constitutionally equal to, both the executive and the legislative branches of the government.

A dual court system

In the United States there is a dual court system composed of a national judiciary and forty-eight State judiciaries. This dual court system is but another reflection of the American federal form of government. Under the Articles of Confederation there were only State courts. Conceivably under a federal system there might be only State courts or only national courts. Canada and Australia, both of which have federal governments, have single court systems. However, the authors of the Constitution had to respect State fears of annihilation by a powerful central authority. Therefore they made no effort to prevent the States from continuing their own judicial organizations. On the hand, the Constitution requires only a Supreme Court at the national level, leaving the establishment of inferior courts to the discretion of Congress. However, the early federal leaders feared to rely solely upon the State courts for interpretations of federal law, short of cases that came before the Supreme Court; the State courts might have blocked the growing nationalism to the utmost of their ability. Hence a complete set of federal courts was established.

The national and State systems of courts are independent and co-equal, each in its own sphere. Federal courts do not possess powers superior to those of the State courts. Cases that originate in a State court and that conclude with decisions intolerable to one of the parties to the dispute may not simply for that reason be transferred to a federal court. A case may come into a federal court only when it clearly falls within the jurisdiction of the federal court system. The broadest limits of this jurisdiction

The Supreme Court Building.

are set forth in Article III, section 2 of the Constitution (see below). Congress may by statute clarify these limits and may further constrict them; however, it cannot expand them since, as the Court itself once ruled, such a law would consist of an amendment to the Constitution by unauthorized means. The jurisdiction of State courts occupies the vast unconfined region outside federal court jurisdiction. For this reason, the great majority of cases arising in an American court never leave the State courts; a case enters a federal court only when it can be shown that the case concerns a national issue of the sort described by the Constitution or by an act of Congress. The apparently superior powers of the federal court system repose in the supreme law—the Constitution, federal laws, and treaties—that the federal courts judge.

Equality of the judicial branch

The judicial branch of the national government (and of each State government as well) is constitutionally equal to the executive and the legislative branches. Ideally, under the principles of either Roman or Anglo-American law, a court must reach its decision independently of the status of the litigants, or parties to the dispute; thus the goddess of justice is portrayed as being blindfolded, so that she cannot see who are the litigants. But the ideal of an independent judiciary is difficult to achieve within a practical framework of government. A comparison of two other great and widely imitated juridical systems, the French and the British, with that of the United States will show how the American courts, both national and State, come closer to independence than those of European countries do.

It is important to stress that in each of these countries the judges are presumed to be unprejudiced, as contrasted with the Soviet courts, which must adapt their rulings to the needs of the state as set forth by the Soviet leaders. The real distinctions among the French, British, and American court systems lie in their relationships with the other branches of the government. In France the courts are in fact a part of the executive branch of the government. The court system is under the Ministry of Justice, whose administrative chief is a member of the cabinet. The process of recruiting French judges illustrates the position of the courts in the French government. Judges in France are chosen in a manner similar to that for naming any highly skilled civil servants. A person seeking to become a judge in France follows a special law school curriculum to prepare himself for the bench; he must then pass a typical civil service examination; and, if successful, he is assigned to a minor judicial post, whence he rises in the court system through promotions.

In Great Britain the courts are subordinate to Parliament. Indeed, the supreme tribunal in the British court system is the House of Lords, or more properly those members called the "Law Lords"; historically, the judicial functions of Parliament antedate the legislative. Judges in England are recruited much as they are in the United States, with one outstanding exception: the Lord Chancellor, who is the judicial and administrative head of the British court system, occupying a position roughly analogous to that of the American Chief Justice, is replaced every time the party control of Parliament changes hands; he is a cabinet member and normally is chosen because he is a trained lawyer who supports the policies of the majority party in the Commons.

American courts at both the national and the State levels enjoy an independence surpassing that of either French or British courts. All American court systems (aside from certain administrative courts, which are a comparatively minor fraction of the whole) are established by the supreme laws, or constitutions, of their respective governments, as organizations independent of and equal to either the executive or legislative branch. The Department of Justice, supervised by the Attoney General, who is a member of the cabinet, is in charge only of prosecutions; hence in the American national government a case is preferred by one branch of the government—the executive—and decided by another—the judicial. In France, by contrast, the prosecuting and the judging of a case are both handled by the Ministry of Justice.

JURISDICTION OF THE AMERICAN FEDERAL COURTS

The jurisdiction of the federal courts of the United States, which comprises the cases that these courts will decide, is succinctly outlined in Article III, section 2, of the Constitution. It was the intention of the Founding Fathers to assign to the federal courts only those types of cases which the State courts would be incompetent to handle; the Tenth Amendment, assuring the States their reserved powers, clearly turns over to the State courts all other types of cases. The Constitution empowered the federal courts to deal with cases on the grounds of two criteria: (1) the nature of the dispute; and (2) the parties to the dispute. Congress may at any time enact legislation to define the constitutional grant of jurisdiction, and has on occasion limited it; nevertheless, the federal courts may deal with no other classes of disputes than those named in the Constitution.

The nature of the dispute

The federal courts have jurisdiction over all cases arising under the "Constitution, the laws of the United States, and treaties made, or which shall be made, under their authority." They also hear "all cases of admiralty and maritime jurisdiction." All such cases plainly are matters of national concern. Indeed, cases revolving about treaties or admiralty law would seem to fall within the province of the national courts even without a constitutional grant, since the national government has admittedly inherent powers to administer relations with other countries; however, that these powers are inherent had not been stated at the time the Constitution was adopted.

The parties to the dispute

The federal courts have jurisdiction over "all cases affecting ambassadors, other public ministers and consuls"; cases in which the United States is a party; and the so-called "diversity of citizenship" cases, that is, cases between two or more States, between one State and a citizen of another State, between citizens of different States, between a State and a foreign country, and between an American citizen and a foreign country. These constitutional grants have subsequently been diminished by constitutional amendment and by legislation. For example, owing to the Eleventh Amendment, federal courts no longer hear cases in which a citizen of one State sues the government of another State; to the adherents of States' rights in the eighteenth century this power seemed an invasion of State sovereignty. Also, it is provided by congressional statute that unless a controversy between citizens of different States involves a sum greater than $3,000, the case cannot come into a federal court; the federal courts are overwhelmed with business as it is. Congress may in the future delegate more of these judicial areas to the State courts.

THE HIERARCHY OF COURTS

The federal courts of the United States are ranged in a hierarchy from the district courts at the base to the Supreme Court at the apex. With respect to the authority underlying their establishment, and with respect also to their function, these courts may also be divided into two classes, *constitutional* and *legislative;* it is in terms of this classification that the courts will be discussed.

Constitutional courts

The constitutional courts of the United States are those that have been created by the constitutional warrant expressed in Article III, section 1: "The judicial power of the United States, shall be vested in one Supreme Court, and in such inferior courts as the Congress may from time to time ordain and establish."

District Courts: The district courts stand at the base of the constitutional court system. The United States is divided into eighty-five districts, each with one court. In a legal sense, Hawaii and Puerto Rico each comprise districts also, although the courts on those islands have been created by legislative rather than by constitutional warrant; yet their jurisdiction is the same as that of district courts on the mainland. Each State contains at least one district; that is, no district crosses a State line. However, some States have two or three districts; New York and Texas each have four. Presumably States are divided into more than one district to cope with a large volume of litigation. However, it is noteworthy that Oklahoma, with 2,233,351 people according to 1956 estimates, has three districts; but Ohio, with 7,946,627, or more than three times as many people as Oklahoma, includes only two districts. Indeed, the southern States have proportionately far more districts than the northern and western States, as can be seen from the map in Figure 51. A reasonable explanation may be that judicial districting, which is executed by Congress, may be a source of patronage; for every district has appointive officers such as district attorneys.

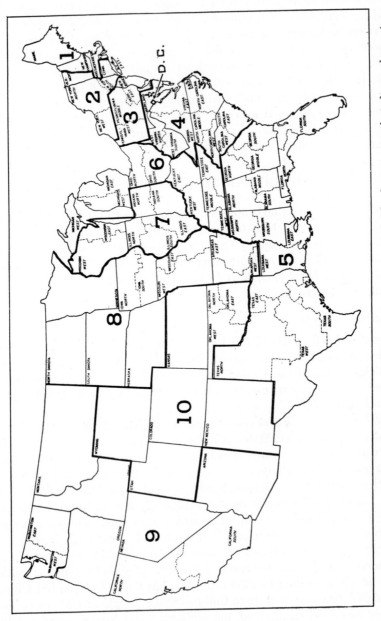

Figure 51. United States Federal Court Districts and Circuits. (1) The large numerals indicate the various Courts of Appeals and the heavy lines represent the jurisdictional boundaries of each circuit; (2) The broken lines represent jurisdictional boundaries of District Courts in States having more than one District.

The amount of business determines not so much the number of districts as it does the number of justices in a district, which may range from one, as in Maine, to sixteen, in the New York Southern District, which includes Manhattan Island. There are about two hundred federal district judges. Congress determines how many judges shall be permanently installed in a district, but judges may be temporarily assigned out of their districts when they are needed elsewhere. A case is heard by only one judge.

District courts handle most of the business that comes before the federal judiciary. A district court is a so-called *court of first instance,* or of *original jurisdiction;* as a trial court, it is the location for the first hearing of almost all federal cases, and also for the last hearing of a large majority of these cases. Its function is to determine the facts in a controversy, to decide what law shall be applied, and to render a judgment.

In the year ending on June 30, 1955, 59,375 civil cases were commenced before all district courts (see Figure 52); in thirty-four per cent of the cases, the United States was a party. Of the balance that were private cases, thirty-two per cent involved diversity of citizenship; only twelve per cent concerned a federal question, that is, some dispute revolving about a federal law, the federal Constitution, or a treaty. In the same year, 41,149 persons were accused of crimes in cases commenced before the district courts (see Figure 53). Of these cases, twenty-four per cent were charged with violating immigration laws; thirty-five per cent were accused of larceny, fraud, or other theft; and fourteen per cent of liquor and internal revenue law violations. During the year before, 1954, the federal district courts disposed of 42,989 adult criminal defendants, finding only 1,277 not guilty and dismissing 3,571 for various reasons. Of the balance, nearly half were given suspended sentences and put on probation, or fined; the average sentence of imprisonment for the other half was 18.3 months.

Courts of Appeals: The courts of appeals rank second in the federal court hierarchy, being intermediate to the district courts and the Supreme Court. The United States is divided into ten circuits, each of which has a court of appeals; the District of Columbia constitutes an eleventh circuit. The practice of terming these judicial areas "circuits" descends in a direct line from the medieval English institution whereby royal justices were sent out "on eyre" (derived from the Latin verb *ire,* "to go"), "riding a circuit," to hear cases in different parts of the realm under the principles of royal law. Courts of appeals today may or may not move about their circuits, depending upon circumstances. The composition and procedure of circuit courts differ from those of district courts; each circuit has at least three, and possibly as many as nine, justices. There are sixty-five federal appellate judges. Furthermore, at least two judges must hear a case in a court of appeals; three is the usual number. Each Supreme Court justice is assigned to one or two circuits, but he no longer "rides the circuit."

Courts of appeals have solely appellate jurisdiction; that is, they hear only the cases that have already been tried in a lower court, and that the losing party has appealed. It was stated above that district courts determine facts and apply law. Conceivably an appeal might be raised on the basis of either facts or law. However, the presumption is that the trial court has discovered the pertinent facts; hence appeals are brought almost entirely on the ground of improper law. Thus a court of appeals does not need to retry the case; it needs only to review the court records to decide whether or not the judge in the lower court has applied the relevant law. If the court of appeals rules that the lower court has applied the proper law, the lower court decision stands unless the aggrieved

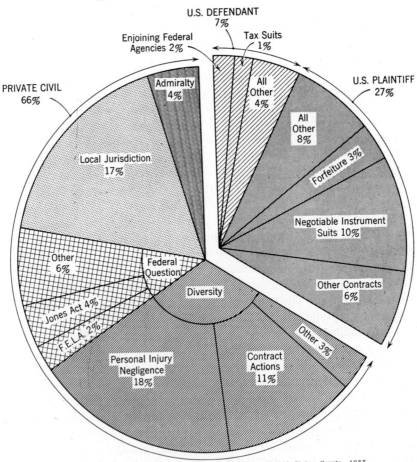

Total Number = 59,375

Annual Report of the Director of the Administrative Office of the United States Courts, 1955

Figure 52. District Courts. Civil Cases Commenced during Fiscal Year 1955.
Several terms used in the chart require brief explanation: Negotiable instruments are promises to pay things or money which are not legal tender (money) themselves; they are contracts. By "diversity" is meant cases mainly where citizens of two states are involved. A federal question concerns an act of Congress; the Jones Act concerns injuries to seamen; the F.E.L.A. is the Federal Employers' Liability Act. Cases of local jurisdiction are ones that arise directly in places under the jurisdiction of the Federal government, such as reservations, the high seas, or the District of Columbia.

party manages to bring the case to the Supreme Court—a rare achievement. On the other hand, if the court of appeals rules against the lower court, the case must be retried in the lower court; the lower court judge will thereupon bring his interpretation of the law into conformity with the decision of the appellate court.

Courts of appeals were first established in 1891 to relieve the Supreme Court of some of its burdens; and from time to time Congress has expanded the work of these appellate courts, so that they are the last courts for most cases that are appealed. Their principal function is to review cases appealed from the federal district courts in their circuits and rulings of administra-

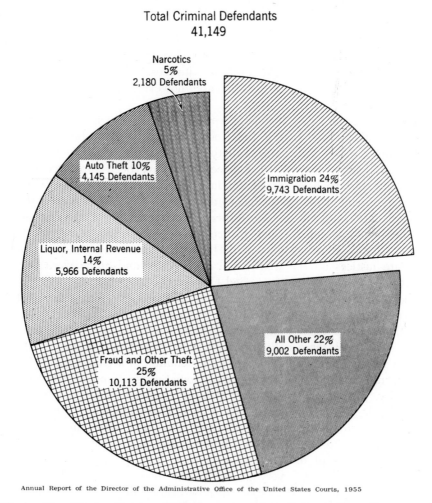

Total Criminal Defendants
41,149

Narcotics
5%
2,180 Defendants

Auto Theft 10%
4,145 Defendants

Immigration 24%
9,743 Defendants

Liquor, Internal Revenue
14%
5,966 Defendants

All Other 22%
9,002 Defendants

Fraud and Other Theft
25%
10,113 Defendants

Annual Report of the Director of the Administrative Office of the United States Courts, 1955

Figure 53. District Courts. Defendants in Criminal Proceedings Commenced during Fiscal Year 1955. "All other" includes anti-trust law violations (190), food and drug act violations (589), impersonation of federal officer (180), juvenile delinquency (1235), migratory bird act (839), selective service acts (477), illegal use of uniform (109), offenses on high seas or U.S. reservations (2080), and others. "Fraud and theft" includes 529 income tax defendants.

tive courts and agencies (see below). For example, in the year ending on June 30, 1955, 3,695 cases were filed in all the courts of appeals; of these, 3,004 or eighty-one per cent came from the various district courts and 691 from administrative agencies and courts, chiefly the United States Tax Court and the National Labor Relations Board. Federal courts of appeals hear no cases brought up from State courts. However, in cases such as those involving diversity of citizenship where there is no federal question, and in criminal cases where less than $1,000 is at stake, the court of appeals is the last resort unless the federal Supreme Court deliberately brings the case within its purview.

The Supreme Court: The Supreme Court is the pinnacle of the federal court system. It is the only federal court that is specifically named in the Constitution and that it was mandatory for Congress to establish. However, Congress has numerous controls over the Supreme Court that will be subsequently indicated. Congress, for instance, fixes the number of justices on the Court. Today there are nine justices. Supposedly the entire membership of the Court hears a case; however, six members make a quorum.

The role of the Chief Justice is worthy of note. He is not necessarily the predominant member of the Court; rather, he is simply its presiding member. Today he is as well the administrative head of the whole federal judiciary. Since 1789, fourteen men have been appointed to this post; only thirteen have served, for in 1795 the Senate refused to confirm the appointment of John Rutledge, evidently because the Federalist majority in the Senate could not tolerate Rutledge's extremely anti-Federalist views. Of the men appointed Chief Justice, only four—Rutledge, Edward D. White, Charles Evans Hughes, and Harlan F. Stone—had previously been associate justices on the Court; and only White and Stone were on the Court at the time they were named Chief Justice.

The Supreme Court has both original and appellate jurisdiction. It is the court of first instance in all cases concerning the diplomatic representatives of foreign powers, and all controversies in which a State is a party. However, there is little possibility that the Court will ever hear a case in which a representative of another country is a party, since ambassadors, ministers, consuls, and other diplomatic agents possess diplomatic immunity, guaranteeing that they will be tried only in courts of their native land. On occasion States do bring suit, as in the case of the perennial litigation over the diversion of water from Lake Michigan by the city of Chicago, where the State of Illinois is the party since Chicago is a legal dependency of the State government. But the original jurisdiction of the Supreme Court is very small. In the three sessions of 1952, 1953, and 1954, none of the 3,950 cases disposed of by the Court was an original case. Only 11 of the 4,466 cases on the Court's docket were original cases.

Cases brought up on appeal, therefore, make up the bulk of the controversies before the Supreme Court. Whereas at one time a large number of types of cases could be brought before the Court on appeal, today there are only two classes that the Court will deal with: (1) those in which it is held that a right or privilege guaranteed by the federal Constitution or by a federal law has been violated; and (2) those in which it is held that a State law or a clause in a State constitution violates some federal law or a clause in the federal Constitution. Cases, then, come to the Supreme Court from any one of three main sources: (1) a federal district court; (2) a federal court of appeals; or (3) a State supreme court. Hence the real function of the Court today, apart from the few cases it handles in original jurisdiction, is to hear cases that involve an interpretation and application of some part of the federal Constitution. It is important to bear in mind also that the Constitution determines the original jurisdiction of the Court, but that Congress fixes the appellate jurisdiction of the Court.

A further limitation on the amount of business that the Supreme Court will handle arises from the means by which a case may be brought before the Court, that is, by the so-called writ of *certiorari* (from the Latin, "to be certified"). Many disputants seek to plead their cause before the Supreme Court; however, the Court itself chooses most of the litigation that is to come before it by issuing a writ of *certiorari*, which is an order to a lower court to send up the certified record of a case so that a superior court—in this instance, the Supreme Court—may deal with it. Those who wish to obtain a Supreme Court hearing, then, must normally submit a petition for a writ of *certiorari;* and the crucial point is the decision of the Court as to whether or not it will honor this petition by issuing the writ. Most such petitions are rejected; in the session ending in June 1955, the Court dismissed or denied 494 and granted only twelve of them.

These petitions make up the largest proportion of the work of the Court. In a normal year the Court hands down no more than 200 decisions apart from acting on petitions for writs of *certiorari;* fewer than 100 written opinions are handed down. Yet it is still somewhat behind its docket, or schedule of cases, although not so much as in the past when more cases could be brought before it. The subject of judicial review, a prime function of the Court that involves the probing of State and federal laws to see if they conflict with the Constitution, will be discussed in a later chapter.

Legislative courts

A legislative court is a court that has been created by Congress for the purpose of carrying out any one of the powers of Congress authorized by the Constitution; the warrant for the creation of most of these courts lies in Article I, section 8, which enumerates the various congressional powers. A number of these courts may be called *administrative* courts, since they deal with administrative law. However, as will be shown, not all legislative courts are administrative courts; nor are all federal administrative courts included under the heading of legislative courts. Some of the most important administrative judicial bodies in the national government are known as *administrative agencies,* such as the Interstate Commerce Commission and the Federal Trade Commission, which have executive and quasi-legislative powers as well as judicial functions; these will be described in the chapter entitled "The Departments and Independent Agencies."

The group of administrative courts in the United States is markedly different from the administrative court structure in France. In the United States these courts are all inferior courts that have been established in quite haphazard fashion. In France, by contrast, the administrative courts make up a judicial hierarchy both equal and parallel to the French civil and criminal courts. The implication seems to be that the power of the French executive branch demands this sort of juridical edifice to protect French citizens from governmental excesses.

Territorial Courts: Territorial courts are the courts that Congress has established in Alaska, Guam, the Virgin Islands, and the Canal Zone, under its constitutional power to govern the territories (Art. IV, sec. 3, cl. 2) and in the District of Columbia, under its authority to rule the seat of the national power in the United States (Art. I, sec. 8, cl. 17). In most respects these courts are similar to those of Hawaii and of Puerto Rico. However, by law the courts of Hawaii and of Puerto Rico are classed as federal district courts; furthermore, the courts of Alaska, Guam, the Virgin Islands, the Canal Zone, and the District of Columbia hear many cases that are normally in the province of the State courts, such as suits for divorce. There are four judges of the territorial court of Alaska, one in each of the other outlying territories, and fifteen in the court of the District of Columbia. It has already been noted that the District of Columbia also has a court of appeals, similar in every respect to other federal courts of appeals.

Court of Claims: The Court of Claims hears suits for damages filed against the government of the United States. These suits are typical of those found in civil law; they involve chiefly breaches of contract and torts, the latter being such civil wrongs as trespassing. A building contractor who holds that the federal government has damaged him by breaking a contract providing for some construction work, or a person who has felt that government employees while at work have been improperly entering his land, brings his case to the Court of Claims. The establishment of this court has largely abolished the former procedure whereby a citizen might sue the federal government only when authorized to do so by a special act of Congress. The findings of this Court are transmitted for enforcement either to Congress or to the appropriate agency. The Court contains a chief justice and four associate justices, who hear cases as a unit. Authority to create this court lies in the congressional power to pay the debts of the United States.

Customs Court: The Customs Court hears complaints from importers of goods from foreign countries who maintain that they have been obliged to pay an unduly high tariff on some commodity. For example, a merchant may import a beverage which he contends is for medicinal purposes and on which the tariff rate should be low; the customs inspectors, however, may declare that the beverage is nothing more than an exotic intoxicating liquor on which a high tariff rate should be imposed. This sort of controversy is brought to the Customs Court. This Court includes a chief justice and eight associates, who hear cases in teams of three judges each. No more than five of these judges may be of the same political party. The power to establish this Court lies in the warrant of Congress to regulate foreign trade.

Court of Customs and Patent Appeals: The Court of Customs and Patent Appeals hears two types of cases: (1) disputes that are appealed from the Customs Court described above; and (2) controversies arising with respect to decisions of the Patent Office in the Department of Commerce over new mechanical devices and trade marks. The Court is made up of a chief justice and four associates, who hear cases as a unit. Authority to create this Court is derived from the congressional powers to regulate foreign trade and to grant patents.

Court of Military Appeals: The Court of Military Appeals reviews all cases of courts-martial in which a general or admiral has been found guilty, or in which any member of the armed forces has been sentenced to death. It also reviews cases that have been turned over to it by the Judge Advocate General—the highest judicial officer—of the Army, the Navy, or the Air Force. This Court is located in the Department of Defense. It contains three judges, all civilian lawyers, no more than two of whom may belong to the same political party. Congress is empowered to erect this Court through its authority to regulate the armed forces.

Tax Court of the United States: The Tax Court of the United States handles disputes arising over the excessive payment, or deficient payment, of federal income, excess profits, estate, and gift taxes. Decisions of this Court in some types of controversy are final; in others, they may be appealed to a federal court of appeals and even to the Supreme Court on a writ of *certiorari.* It also hears cases concerning the refund of certain federal taxes. The Court includes sixteen divisions, each headed by one justice; one of these justices is biennially chosen to be Chief Judge for a two-year term. The Court has been established on the congressional warrant to levy taxes.

FEDERAL JUDGES

Appointment, tenure, salary, and retirement

Appointment: All of the approximately three hundred federal judges, regardless of the court in which they serve, are similar or even identical with respect to appointment, tenure, salary, and retirement. All federal judges are appointed by the President with the advice and consent of the Senate. Appointments to the inferior courts are usually made upon the recommendation of a Senator, Representative, or party chief, from the area concerned; however, the President normally names appointees who will be satisfactory to the Attorney General. Appointments to the federal Supreme Court usually reflect among other influences the wishes, or at least suggestions, of the Department of Justice. These appointments are also modified by the practice of having most if not all of the sections of the country represented on the Court, and the custom of choosing experts in different fields of law. Other considerations in the appointment of Supreme Court justices can be seen from the analysis of their backgrounds given below. The Senate rarely rejects a judicial appointment; the unusual case of John Rutledge has already received comment in this text.

Tenure: Judges in all the constitutional federal courts and most of the legislative courts are appointed for life, or for "good behavior." Judges in the territorial courts, by contrast (save those in the District of Columbia) have specified terms; for instance, those in Alaska and the Virgin Islands serve for four years. The aim of life tenure was undoubtedly to raise judges above partisan activities, since it protects them from removal for partisan causes. Justices hold their seats for long terms; the seventy-nine Supreme Court judges who between 1789 and 1954 were appointed to, and subsequently departed from, the bench averaged almost sixteen years in office. This average far exceeds the average tenure of any federal elective post. However, the longest period served by any Supreme Court justice, the thirty-four year terms of John Marshall, Stephen J. Field, and John Harlan, does not equal the forty-four consecutive years that Adolph J. Sabath represented the Illinois Seventh District in the House.

Federal judges may be removed only by impeachment. Nine judges have been impeached; one was an associate justice of the Supreme Court, seven were district judges, and one was a member of the now-defunct Commerce Court. Four, including the Supreme Court justice, were acquitted; four were convicted and removed from office; and the ninth resigned after the House had voted his impeachment. The articles of impeachment for these justices included such counts as misconduct in office, drunkenness, improper financial transactions of various types, and tyrannous treatment of counsel (meaning abuse of an attorney in court). The specified terms for territorial justices were probably designed to make these benches subjects of patronage. Actually, since most American territories are administered by the Interior Department, it is certainly a contradiction of the principle of an independent judiciary to have their justices of the same party as that of the Secretary of the Interior.

Salary and Retirement: All federal judges receive an annual salary that may not be reduced during their tenure of office; in this way a hostile Congress may not threaten to diminish their income for an unfavorable ruling. Judges in the district courts, the Customs Court, the Tax Court, and the territorial courts, are paid $22,500 yearly; those in the courts of appeals, the Court of Customs and Patent Appeals, and the Court of Claims, $25,500; and the justices of the Supreme Court, $35,000. These salaries hardly match what many justices can earn, and what some have earned prior to their appointment, in private law practice. However, especially in recent years, public respect for the courts has conferred exceptional prestige upon a federal judgeship; and life tenure gives the position great security. Because in the past some judges have abused this security so as to remain on the bench after they had become senile and mentally incompetent, Congress has provided that any federal judge who has served at least ten years and who had reached the age of seventy years may retire on full salary.

The backgrounds of federal judges

Federal judges, especially those on the Supreme Court, from 1789 to the present show considerable similarity in their backgrounds; however, in recent years a growing number of justices have possessed types of experience and training seldom encountered in earlier days. This evolution reflects the changed attitude toward the Supreme Court assumed both by the public at large and by the officers in the other two branches of the federal government. This attitude can be summed up as a greater respect for the Court united with the belief that the justices should be legal technicians who have a broad education in the social studies, rather than politicians who have studied law. The following data refer to all Supreme Court members from 1789 through the appointment of John Marshall Harlan as associate justice in 1955, eighty-nine men in all.

All Supreme Court justices have been lawyers. Those in the first half of the Court's history had prepared for the bar by independent study in an older lawyer's office, for there were no law schools at that time. However, all justices have been admitted to the bar. Some have had little legal practice; they were occupied with other concerns, such as political office. Others prior to their appointment have held no governmental posts; men such as George Shiras, who sat on the Court from 1892 until 1903, have been known exclusively as wealthy and influential lawyers.

Most Supreme Court justices have been deeply immersed in politics; however, this trait was more nearly universal among early justices than of those today. Thirty-nine justices have been members of State legislatures; however, only Wiley Rutledge among jurists of the past three decades was once a State legislator. Thirty-two justices have been members of Congress, more often the Senate than the House; Justices Harold Burton, Hugo Black, and Sherman Minton on the 1955 Court were all former Senators. Twelve justices have held some cabinet post apart from the attorney generalship, none of them on the 1955 Court. Chief Justice William H. Taft had been President of the United States; and Chief Justice Charles Evans Hughes had been almost victorious as Republican candidate in 1916. Eight justices, mainly in the nineteenth century but including Earl Warren, have been State governors.

Many justices have been very active in party affairs; Associate Justice David Davis took a leading role at the 1860 Republican national convention in procuring the nomination of Abraham Lincoln, and later worked for his election. It is probable that Lincoln appointed Davis to the Court as a reward for his actions, and that he named Salmon P. Chase as Chief Justice to thwart Chase's inordinate political ambitions. Almost without exception, justices have been of the President's party; during the twenty years from 1933 until 1953 when the Democrats held the White House, Roosevelt and Truman between them named thirteen Supreme Court justices but only one Republican, Burton, who had been a close friend of Truman in the Senate.

Supreme Court justices have had varying degrees of experience in the public practice of law before their elevation to the Supreme Court. Only nineteen, or about one-fifth, had held a position in the inferior courts, and all but three of these have been men appointed since 1880. However, more than forty justices, most of them in the nineteenth century, had occupied a State bench; about a dozen had been chief justice in their State, but only Associate Justice Benjamin Cardozo in recent years. By contrast, more than a dozen, chiefly since 1880, have been prosecuting attorneys at the State level. Nine justices, seven of them since 1890, have been Attorney General of the United States; three members of the Roosevelt-Truman Court, Associate Justices Frank Murphy, Robert Jackson, and Tom Clark, had previously been Attorney General, and Stanley Reed had been Solicitor General, a position equivalent to that of assistant to the Attorney General.

The desire to secure justices who have special competences can be seen in the appointment of men who have served as lawyers in important administrative agencies; for instance, Reed had been with the Reconstruction Finance Corporation, and Douglas and Jackson with the Securities and Exchange Commission. Perhaps the most significant index for the conviction that justices must be above partisan affiliation is in the growing number of professors of law who have been named to the Supreme Court. Many justices have occasionally taught a few courses in law schools to increase their incomes; however, only about a dozen justices could be described as career professors of law. Ten of these have been appointed since 1880; on the 1955 Court, Justice Felix Frankfurter had been a professor at the Harvard Law School, and Justice Douglas had long been a professor of law. One might be wise in suspecting, however, that this trend indicates an increasing participation by professors of law in political affairs; Justice Frankfurter never held any other public office before entering the Court, but he was a powerful factor in Massachusetts, and then in national, politics while he was a notable professor at Harvard Law School.

Supreme Court justices are men of mature years. As can be seen from Figure 54, which gives the average age of the justices at the inauguration of each regularly-elected President, only twice has the average been as low as fifty years. Since about 1840, or for more than a century, it has almost always exceeded sixty years; meanwhile, the age of Presidents has dropped greatly, with Eisenhower being the oldest President inaugurated for his first term since James Buchanan. President F. D. Roosevelt, exasperated by several contrary rulings of the Court, gave great publicity to the age of the justices in 1937. True, at that time the average was seventy-two years, higher than at any other time in American history. However, the age of the justices at this time gave Roosevelt a convenient talking-point for his aim of selecting justices who would not rule against laws he had sponsored; actually, one of the oldest justices in 1937, Louis Brandeis, was a staunch supporter of New Deal legislation.

Doubtless another significant point was that during his first term Roosevelt had not had the opportunity to name a single justice, so that he may have felt cheated. The fact is that in the 144 years from 1789 until 1933, when Roosevelt was first inaugurated, there had been seventy-eight appointments to the Court, an average of one every twenty-two months; hence in a four-year term a President might expect to appoint two or three members of the Court. As matters worked out, Roosevelt was able to make five appointments in his second term, double the average rate; at the end of this time, the average age of the justices had dropped to sixty years. After a further decline in 1945, the average once more began to rise. The youngest man ever named to the Court was Joseph Story, who was appointed in 1811 at the age of thirty-two; the youngest member in recent years was William O. Douglas, named in 1939 at the age of forty-one.

Although some appointments have been made with an eye to representing different sections of the country, a few States have contributed a large proportion of the Supreme Court justices. Eleven justices have come from New York, eight from Massachusetts, and eight from Ohio. Only eleven justices—fewer than fifteen per cent of the total—have come from States west of the Mississippi. In proportion to population the South has been very heavily represented, with Virginia, Maryland, Kentucky, and Tennessee all sending five justices apiece. One explanation may be that lawyers from these States, particularly from New York, are in a position to make themselves better known in Washington than lawyers from States far from the District of Columbia. Unquestionably the need for paying political debts has played a role also. Of course, too, these are among the oldest States in the country, and New York is the most populous.

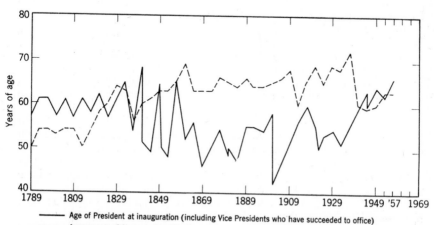

Age of President at inauguration (including Vice Presidents who have succeeded to office)
- - - - Average age of Supreme Court justices at each regular quadrennial presidential inauguration

Analysis of data in World Almanac (1955), adapted

Figure 54. Comparative Age of Presidents at Inauguration and Average Age of Supreme Court Justices at Each Regular Presidential Inauguration, 1789–1957.

This summary of Supreme Court justices' backgrounds shows, then, that justices are not, and never have been, persons isolated from the main stream of public concerns. Rather, they have been, in one fashion or another, political leaders; in fact it has been only in recent years that influential circles of opinion have expected and demanded that the justices have achieved a high level of scholarship and civic reputation. Supreme Court justices have not had feet of clay; on the other hand, their backgrounds have not been such as to cushion them from partisan considerations. It seems very improbable that a politically neutral individual, regardless of the excellence of his training, could secure an appointment to the Supreme Court, or, for that matter, to any federal court. On the other hand, appointment to the Supreme Court or inferior courts brings a great change to the lives of the judges and to the rules of conduct which they observe. The following interview of Chief Justice Warren by a newspaper reporter brings out these changes clearly:

Excerpt from the San Francisco Chronicle, Sunday, July 11, 1954, pages 1, 10.

Earl Warren was back in San Francisco last week. He was working at his new job as Chief Justice of the United States and Chairman of the Judicial Conference of the United States by attending the annual meeting of Federal Judges of the Ninth Circuit. Between sessions, he talked to a Chronicle reporter about how things were going with him in Washington.

By Kevin Wallace

After 31 years in the hurly burly of ever-temporary (that is, elective) employment, as deputy and district attorney and Governor, Earl Warren has wound up his first season in a new job that is seasonal but serene and, in the long range, steady.

"It was a great change and, initially, something of a shock," he told friends who reunioned with him here this week.

Being fourteenth Chief Justice of the United States and head of the Nation's judicial system, keeps him away from home—which, in point of legal residence, is and always will be Oakland—during the long October-to-June Supreme Court season.

And all of Mrs. Warren's house-hunting hasn't pried anything more than a rented apartment out of Washington's tight real estate situation, to make a home-away-from-home.

And the peculiarly discreet nature of the new job forbids Earl Warren from so much as hinting as to which California gubernatorial candidate he'll check on the absentee ballot he mails in next November.

But just the same:

"While I enjoyed my experience in public service very greatly, I have no longing to be back in it—I'm happy in this new work," he said.

"As you can imagine, it's been a big change—initially, something of a shock—and I've spent this year becoming oriented to new conditions.

"A Justice who joined the Supreme Court when Chief Justice Hughes was there told me Hughes warned him it would take three years to learn the limitations of the job, and it did. That's always encouraging—to know it's not unique with you, when you take time getting used to a complete change in your way of living.

"There were a number of things I'd wondered about.

Special help

"For ten years before in an executive position (as California's first three-term governor), I had a very large and highly specialized and organized administrative organization, supplying basic material essential to make my decisions.

"When I went to Washington, I found that my total entourage consisted of two secretaries and three law clerks and a messenger. My decisions—not just formal opinions, but my own decisions—were, from that day on, largely the result of my own personal research.

"But I've found the quiet of my chambers and of the (Supreme Court Building's) library a very soothing thing, after the hectic years I put in as an executive.

Speech-making

"Then there's the matter of making speeches. A governor has to make speeches, day and night, all kinds, all over the State—it's part of his job to let people know his views. I did a lot of it.

"But now it's just the opposite. A Justice who started expounding informal opinions would never know when their subject matter might come before him in court.

"Any other judge who disqualified himself that way could simply step aside for another judge to sit in his place. But there aren't any substitutes available to replace a Supreme Court Justice on a case."

And is this limitation frustrating?

"No—I never made a speech I really wanted to. I don't mind telling my views, but making speeches was never an experience I really enjoyed."

Aloof nature

The somewhat aloof nature of the new job also provides the Warrens with a perfect out from the deluge of invitations to political luncheons and receptions that naturally descend on the top man in one of the government's three branches.

"When I was governor, I'd finish my day's work and then fly down from Sacramento to Los Angeles for a meeting and then back again that night, perhaps 60 times a year—or, just as often, I'd drive down here to San Francisco and back.

"And the luncheons.

"But now I have a few ground rules I can go by. Since I've been in the new work, I've left the office at noon only three times—and only to go to the White House.

"I pass up almost all the receptions except the formal ones that require the attendance of the Chief Justice.

"And I get to go home nights. . . . ."

Other court personnel

Attached to each federal court are certain non-judicial employees who are appointed by, and responsible to, the justice or justices of the court. Each district court has a commissioner, who occupies a position somewhat akin to that of a justice of the peace in State courts; he conducts preliminary hearings and binds over criminal suspects for trials. Each federal court has a clerk, who must keep the records of court proceedings. The Supreme Court has a marshal to make arrests, a librarian, a reporter, and three deputy clerks.

THE ADMINISTRATIVE ORGANIZATION OF THE COURTS

The administrative organization of the federal court system coordinates the work of the individual courts, strives to establish uniform standards of justice throughout the system, and manages most of the non-judicial business of the courts. It performs tasks that in France or some other country with a judicial structure analogous to the French would be carried out by the Ministry of Justice. In the United States, however, this administrative organization is part of the judicial branch rather than of the executive.

Federal Judicial Conference

The Federal Judicial Conference includes the Chief Justice, who is its presiding officer; the senior judge from each of the eleven federal courts of appeals; and representatives from the judiciary committees of both houses of Congress and from the Department of Justice. Through the Conference the Chief Justice functions as the administrative chief of all federal courts. It meets annually to report on the amount of judicial business in the various circuits and districts; to recommend the transfer of a judge from one district to another, or even from one circuit to another, to equalize the burden of cases; to urge Congress to create new judicial positions; and to seek the uniform interpretation of federal laws throughout the federal court system.

In each circuit there is a judicial council similar to the Federal Judicial Conference, made up of all the federal judges in the circuit. The presiding officer of each circuit council is the senior judge from the court of appeals in the circuit. Often the leading members of the bar in the circuit are invited to attend. At the annual gathering of these circuit councils the senior judge transmits the recommendations of the Federal Conference and in turn receives suggestions for the Conference to examine.

Administrative Office of the United States Courts

The Administrative Office of the United States Courts manages the routine housekeeping details of the federal court system. It handles clerical and accounting matters; disburses the moneys provided for the maintenance of the courts; purchases the supplies needed by the courts; and furnishes janitorial services for federal court buildings. The Office also prepares statistics on the weight of court business for the Federal Judicial Conference. The principal officers of the Office are the Director and the Assistant Director, who are appointed by the Supreme Court and supervised by the Federal Judicial Conference.

THE DEPARTMENT OF JUSTICE

The Department of Justice is entrusted with the general enforcement of federal laws, detecting and prosecuting crimes against the federal government, representing the government in civil cases, and advising all other agencies of the government regarding legal questions. Whereas the Department of Justice is functionally related to the federal judiciary, it is structurally and administratively distinct; it is a part of the executive branch of the government and is responsible to the President. Hence it has no formal power over any of the federal courts.

The administrative head of the Department is the United States Attorney General, who is a member of the Cabinet. He is the chief legal officer of the federal government; he represents the government before the Supreme Court in extremely important cases. Yet most of his work revolves about managing the affairs of the Department and giving legal counsel to the President. His principal aide, the Deputy Attorney General, maintains relations with Congress and supervises the employees of the Department. The Solicitor General actually pleads most Supreme Court cases for the government, under the guidance of the Attorney General.

The Department of Justice has a number of important offices and divisions. Several of them may be briefly described. The Office of Alien Property administers assets in the United States that were owned by enemy aliens and confiscated by the government. The Antitrust Division enforces laws prohibiting the formation of trusts and monopolies. The Tax Division handles cases involving federal taxes. A Civil Division deals with civil suits against the government, and a Criminal Division prosecutes individuals charged with violating federal criminal laws. Undoubtedly the best-known office of the Department is the Federal Bureau of Investigation (FBI), whose function is to investigate, but not to prosecute, alleged infractions of all federal laws except those that have been assigned by Congress to some other agency. The FBI also collaborates with State and local police agencies in matters such as providing information about suspected persons and distributing educational materials on innovations in police methods. Another major section of the Justice Department is the Immigration and Naturalization Service, which administers all aspects of the immigration and naturalization laws. Finally, the Department contains a Bureau of Prisons to manage the various penitentiaries, such as that at Atlanta, reformatories (Chillicothe, Ohio), correctional institutions (Milan, Michigan), and camps (McNeil Island, Washington), where the federal government detains its prisoners.

The Department also maintains a considerable personnel in each of the court districts and territories. In each there is a district attorney who, with his several assistants, files suits on behalf of the government and prosecutes those charged with breaking federal laws. The other chief agent of the Department in each court district is the United States Marshal, whose chief functions are the arresting of suspected persons and the serving of federal warrants; the marshal, then, fills about the role that the sheriff has in the county. These officers, like federal judges, are appointed by the President; unlike federal judges, they do not hold office for life, so that their positions are an important source of federal patronage.

QUESTIONS AND PROBLEMS

1. What are the sources in law of constitutional courts and of legislative courts?

2. Define briefly the following terms: a dual court system; jurisdiction; a case on appeal; writ of *certiorari;* administrative courts.

3. List the classes of cases over which the Supreme Court has original jurisdiction.

4. Which of the legislative courts would you regard as being closest to the constitutional court system? Explain your reasons.

5. Describe some of the social characteristics of justices of the Supreme Court. What changes have occurred since the inception of the Court?

6. What are the duties of the Chief Justice of the Supreme Court as administrative chief of the federal judicial system?

7. What are the various ways in which the Department of Justice performs services necessary to the federal court system?

28. The Judicial Process

United Press Photo

THE judicial process consists of the practices that are followed by a given court system in hearing and judging the cases before it. Details of the judicial process vary widely from one country to another. The countries of Western legal type fall into three main classes with regard to the judicial process they maintain: (1) the United States, Great Britain, and other nations such as Canada and Australia that adhere to Anglo-American legal procedures and ideas; (2) France, the Lowlands, Italy, Germany under the Bonn government, Latin-American states such as Uruguay that are not dictatorial, and Japan—all governments that have adopted some form of the Napoleonic Code; and (3) the Soviet Union and the countries in its orbit. Within each class of countries there are important differences; and between any two classes there are numerous similarities. For instance, the French trial process contains features that are familiar to an American attorney. Also, for example, the Soviet Union has a federal court structure comprising

425

supreme courts of the republics, that resembles the American dual court system more than it does the French or English.

It is probably true, however, that the *theory* of Anglo-American justice is extremely generous to the defendant and to private property, that the Franco-Roman theory is less so, and that the Soviet theory is least so. To put it in other terms, from the first to the third class one finds diminishing amounts of sensitivity, especially in criminal trials, to the protection of the defendant from the caprice of the state. Often the difference is purely philosophical, for in the states depending on the Napoleonic Code (itself derived largely from Roman Law principles) more orderly court processes exist than are to be found in America; these may in the end give greater protection in law both to the defendant and to those whom he has been alleged to harm. On the other hand, it cannot be denied that orderly and fair judicial procedures are not available in many political cases in the Soviet Union. Perhaps not even the Nazi ruling group has surpassed that of Soviet Russia in utilizing the judicial process to dispose of leaders, such as Minister of the Interior Lavrenty Beria, who have fallen from grace.

A rule of thumb is that the judicial process mirrors the extent to which a government permits general freedom to individuals. A despotic government usually has a prejudiced court system. A government that upholds the freedom of speech is apt to provide numerous assurances against judicial whim in the courtroom. In turn, the protection of a person inside the courtroom assists him in exercising freedom outside the courtroom. For example, the institution of *habeas corpus* makes it difficult for the police to hold an individual without a specific charge, and thus is one more defense for freedom of speech.

The judicial process includes three principal steps. (1) A case must be brought to court. Courts do not seek business; they must be persuaded that there is a legal dispute that merits a court hearing. (2) The case must be heard in court; facts must be presented, law applied, and a decision reached. (3) The losing side must be permitted to appeal the decision to a higher court. American courts deal with three types of law: criminal, civil, and equity. Each type of law possesses its own judicial process; yet the process for each type includes the above three steps.

The processes for civil and for equity law are relatively simple. Since cases under each of these types of law usually involve private disputants who are theoretically equal before the law, the judicial process is chiefly concerned with guaranteeing that equality. The process for criminal law has far more ramifications, for in a criminal case one party is the government, and the court in which the accused is being tried is a gear in the machinery of that government. Many phases of the criminal judicial process were devised as protections in an era in which governments used courts to dispose of political opponents, as English kings of the sixteenth and seven-

---

The Supreme Court, 1955. Left to right, seated: Associate Justices Felix Frankfurter, Hugo L. Black; Chief Justice Earl Warren, Stanley F. Reed, and William O. Douglas. Back row: Tom C. Clark, Sherman Minton, Harold H. Burton, and John Marshall Harlan.

teenth century were wont to do, a fact well known to the authors of the Constitution. Even today, when the number of crimes against the state is very small by comparison with the number of those against the person and against property, these safeguards remain in the criminal judicial process.

CRIMINAL PROCEDURE

Criminal procedure is hedged about with many barriers for the protection of the accused. In practice these barriers have been much more difficult to surmount in the federal than in the State courts, for, acting under their reserved police power, the States enact most laws regarding crimes such as murder and robbery. However, Congress has found authority to enact statutes defining federal crimes and establishing penalties in two fields: (1) offenses against federal property and services, as counterfeiting the money of the United States or failing to pay income taxes; and (2) offenses that are interstate in nature, as the transportation of stolen property across State lines. Federal criminal procedure, then, applies to trials of persons accused of federal offenses.

Preliminary guarantees

Ban on Ex Post Facto *Legislation:* Any person accused of a crime is assured that the act with which he is charged constituted a crime when he committed it, and that no law has been passed after he committed the act making it easier to convict him or increasing the penalties that he might suffer. Legislation that transforms a previously innocent act into a crime to the disadvantage of the accused, which is termed *ex post facto* (Latin, "from what is done afterward"), is prohibited by the Constitution (Art. I, sec. 9, cl. 3). The ban on *ex post facto* legislation applies only to criminal law, and only to laws that would work to the disadvantage of the accused. Civil law, and laws working to the advantage of the accused, do not fall under this ban. An example of an *ex post facto* law that the Supreme Court held to be unconstitutional was a Missouri statute of the 1860's. This law required public officials, clergymen, teachers, and others to swear an oath, in order to practice their calling. The oath stated that they had *not* committed in times past a large number of acts, some of which were not previously crimes and others of which had been. The Court, in striking down the law and oath, declared that many people might now be penalized (through losing their profession) for acts that were legal at the time they were performed. The Court added that even when certain of the acts had been *illegal* before, the individuals concerned were now being given further penalties that applied to their past actions.

Guarantee of a Court Trial: Any person charged with a crime is guaranteed a court trial for his offense. This provision was not written idly; history is full of trials by torture, duels, mobs, tyrants, and police. The Fifth Amendment, however, plainly demands a court trial in declaring that no person may be deprived of life, liberty, or property, without due process of law. Conceivably, without this Amendment, some agency apart from the judiciary might pass sentence on the accused man; he might, for example, be sent to prison for an indefinite term by the arresting officials, quite a common happening in Europe three centuries ago in the epoch of the absolute monarchies.

Ban on Bills of Attainder: Another once-common device for procuring convictions without court trials was the *bill of attainder,* which was simply an act by a legislature stating that an individual was guilty of a certain crime. The name of this action stems from the practice of extending guilt to the individual's descendants, so that their blood was "attainted." The Constitution (Art. I, sec. 9, cl. 3) prohibits Congress from enacting bills of attainder, thus guarding against one method for securing convictions that was peculiar to certain eras.

In 1943, in order to remove from office three government employees who had been accused of affiliation with the communist movement, Congress in a bill appropriating money for government employees' salaries provided that none of this money was to be used to pay the salaries of any of the three employees unless they were reappointed by the President and reconfirmed by the Senate. The assumption was that the Senate would not confirm their appointment in light of the charges brought against them. After working for a short period without receiving their salaries, the employees brought suit for the sums due them; and ultimately the Supreme Court upheld their plea, ruling that the congressional act was a bill of attainder.

Pre-trial guarantees

After it is known, or even suspected, that a federal law has been violated, two acts must be carried out before a trial may begin. One or more persons must be arrested, and he or they must be formally charged with the crime, or indicted by a grand jury. These steps are essential for demonstrating to a court of proper jurisdiction that it should hold a trial. The arrest may precede or follow the grand jury charge, depending strictly upon the circumstances of the crime; hence the order followed in the subsequent paragraphs is purely arbitrary.

Prohibition on Arbitrary Arrest: A police officer must have solid ground for arresting a suspect. Of course, an officer finding any person in the act of committing a crime may seize him forthwith. However, an officer may not take an individual from his home without first obtaining from a court a warrant for arrest that specifically names the suspect (Fourth Amendment). Yet the courts have ruled that a person in a public place such as a hotel or restaurant does not enjoy the protection he has under his own roof, since he may leave a public place never to return.

Prohibition on Arbitrary Search: Usually it is necessary to provide material evidence of guilt to secure court conviction of a suspect. According to the Fourth Amendment, a police officer may not search any place for such evidence without procuring a warrant describing the place to be searched and the object or objects being sought. This guarantee is designed to buttress the common-law principle that "a man's home is his castle." The fact is that in recent times and with the development of certain mechanical devices, court decisions have in some instances relaxed this prohibition. For example, an officer may search an automobile, or any other vehicle, without a warrant; otherwise, while the warrant was being procured the vehicle with its incriminating evidence might disappear. Courts are also tending to legalize searches resulting in the discovery of items illegally in the possession of an individual, such as forged stamps, even though the search has not been authorized by a warrant.

One modern technique for securing evidence is a tap on a suspect's telephone line, so that police officers may listen to and record private conversations. As matters stood in 1956, federal courts refused to admit evidence gained through wire-tapping; however, it was then notorious that officers commonly employed such evidence as a guide to further evidence that would be admissible in court. Considerable pressure has been exerted upon Congress to enact legislation authorizing the use of wire-taps for the detection of communist activities. It is obvious that the telephone, by supplanting letters as a means of correspondence, has imposed a considerable handicap upon police officials. A letter is tangible evidence, but a private telephone call, unless recorded, has disappeared forever.

Assurance of the Writ of Habeas Corpus: Police officers must be able to show reasonable cause for arresting and detaining any person; that is, they may not summarily arrest an individual and hold him indefinitely without being able to show grounds for suspicion. Now, in the case of any person who has been formally charged with a crime through a grand jury indictment, that indictment suffices as a basis for detention until trial. However, when a person who has not been so charged is arrested and, according to his own reasoning, is unjustly held, he may (with certain exceptions) procure from a court, through his attorney, a writ of *habeas corpus* (Latin, "that you have the body" in an imperative sense). This writ is an order from a court to the arresting officers that they bring the person arrested before the court to show that there are grounds for suspicion. If the police can show no such grounds, they must release the individual concerned.

The writ of *habeas corpus* is a traditional and jealously guarded part of the judicial process in criminal trials. Even in 1787 it had become customary procedure to such a degree that the Constitution, rather than authorizing its issuance, provides instead that the privilege "shall not be suspended, unless when in cases of rebellion or invasion the public safety may require it [suspension]" (Art. I, sec. 9, cl. 2). Admittedly, then, in time of war or revolution, when police officers have arrested persons who might overthrow the government, the privilege may be denied those persons. Presumably, too, any section of the United States that is menaced by war or revolution may be placed under martial law, and the ordinary judicial process does not prevail under military rule.

However, it is nowhere specified *who* shall be empowered to suspend this privilege. During the Civil War, President Lincoln on his own authority suspended the writ, but a federal circuit court ruled that this suspension was illegal. Subsequently Congress enacted legislation permitting Lincoln to suspend the writ; this legislation after the war was pronounced constitutional, with respect to actual theaters of military operations, or areas under martial law where the regular courts are not in session. Outside these theaters, however, the Court held that the writ may not be suspended. The writ was also temporarily suspended in the Hawaiian Islands during World War II, but following the war the Supreme Court ruled that the suspension had been illegal. Evidently, then, the writ may be suspended only in an area of warfare and only by act of Congress.

Guarantee of a Grand Jury Indictment: Every person, apart from members of the armed forces, who is charged with a federal crime that may result in a long prison term or a death sentence upon conviction, must be indicted by a grand jury before being brought to trial, as required by the Fifth Amendment. The grand jury, which is an old English institution, was first designed to prevent police officials or executives from bringing persons into court for purely arbitrary causes. A federal grand jury today consists of from sixteen to twenty-three persons selected from the tax rolls or registration lists of a federal court district. The grand jury is the instrument through which the federal district attorney notifies the court that a crime has been perpetrated and that some individual is suspected as the perpetrator. To achieve this end the attorney submits to the grand jury the evidence that has been gathered by the police and by whatever detective forces he may have attached to his own office. The accused himself rarely appears at the grand jury hearing; he may do so only with the permission of the district attorney. The grand jury examines the evidence; and if it then decides that there is such an aroma of suspicion about some individual or individuals that a trial should be held, and that justice would be served by a conviction, it votes a true bill or indictment, which is a formal charge. The indictment must state the exact nature of the crime, for an individual may not be tried for any offense not contained in the grand jury charge.

A grand jury has powers whose enormous force is often not appreciated by the jury members themselves. It need not limit itself to the crime presented by the prosecuting attorney, and can strike out independently to make broad investigations. The grand jury has the authority to issue subpenas to compel the attendance of witnesses and the producing of testimony. Because of this authority a grand jury may initiate a study of allegedly corrupt public officials and of law enforcement programs. Hence it may transform itself from the prosecuting attorney's handmaiden into his nemesis. The relationships between the district attorney and the grand jury are thus delicately balanced. Political considerations sometimes cause trouble too, for the office of district attorney at any level lends a politically ambitious lawyer a stage and a usually sympathetic audience among the public.

Guarantee of Reasonable Bail: After the accused has been indicted, he is normally brought before a court for "arraignment": that is, he is asked by the judge whether he will plead guilty or not guilty to the charge. If he pleads guilty, the case is usually concluded on the spot; the judge passes sentence and the individual is remanded to jail to await transportation to a more permanent prison. If, on the other hand, the accused pleads not guilty, the court is obliged in most cases to fix a reasonable bail, or bond, that shall not be "excessive" (Eighth Amendment). That is, the amount must not be beyond the ability of the person to supply it. Bail consists of a deposit of money or some other token of wealth as a guarantee that the accused will appear at court for his trial. If he fails to appear, his bail is forfeited; yet he may be rearrested and still tried for the offense charged. The probable aim of allowing release on bail is to grant the accused the opportunity to seek evidence and witnesses in his own defense, on the principle that he is innocent until proved guilty. However, when the crime is murder or an especially outrageous crime, or when the suspect has already forfeited bail, or if it appears for some reason that he may forfeit bail, the judge may order that he be held in jail until his trial. The amount of bail fixed usually depends upon the nature of the crime. The judge himself sets the amount, usually a compromise figure between those asked by the district attorney and by the lawyer for the accused.

Trial guarantees

Assurance of a Speedy and Public Trial: A person accused of a federal offense is guaranteed a "speedy and public trial" (Sixth Amendment). No person may be tried behind closed doors, save in the rare cases in which a judge may decide that the nature of the evidence is such that it may prove harmful to public morals. In fact, a judge is very hestitant to bar the public since by that act he will also bar the press, thereby possibly winning himself hostile newspaper treatment; however, this consideration is less important for appointed federal judges than it is for elected State judges. The guarantee of a public trial constitutes one more attempt to block partisan justice.

Despite the constitutional provision for a "speedy trial," American justice is probably the slowest in the world. In fact, it is almost always the accused, for whose protection this guarantee was designed, who slows proceedings. There are many apparent advantages that the accused may win through delay: for example, public pressure on a jury to return a guilty verdict will diminish in time; witnesses may die, move away, or forget evidence; superior evidence of innocence may be unearthed. By the same token, it is with the aim of counteracting these potential advantages that the prosecution, once it has its evidence and witnesses, may demand a speedy trial. A remarkable case evoking the Sixth Amendment recently was that of ex-Sergeant John D. Provoo who was indicted in 1949 for treason committed in World War II, and who was sentenced to life imprisonment in 1953. The Supreme Court in 1955 upheld a district court ruling that he had been denied a speedy trial and confirmed the dismissal of charges against him.

Assurance of a Trial by Jury: Every person accused of a federal crime is assured of a trial by jury (Sixth Amendment). The trial jury, which is also termed a petty jury (French *petit,* "small") to distinguish it from the grand jury, consists of twelve persons residing in the district in which the crime was committed. The jury must be impartial; when its members are being chosen, both the district attorney and the counsel for the accused may dismiss a specified number of individuals for no particular cause and an almost indefinite number for possible bias, such as exceptional knowledge of the crime or previous conviction on a charge similar to that faced by the accused. The average petty jury ranks considerably below the average grand jury with respect to economic, social, and educational status. (Some say this situation prevails because lawyers find college graduates difficult to treat with as jurors.)

The function of the jury is to hear the evidence submitted by the prosecution and the defense, and upon the basis of these arguments to decide whether the accused is guilty or innocent. The decision of the jury must be unanimous; if the jury cannot reach a decision, or is "hung," it is discharged, and a new trial must be held to obtain a conviction. (A famous instance of a hung jury in recent years in a federal case was that in the first trial of Alger Hiss for perjury. A subsequent jury unanimously agreed to his guilt.) The jury is supposed to deal only in matters of *fact;* the court is held responsible for all matters of *law*, and must instruct the jury concerning disputed questions of law that may be related to the process of arriving at a decision.

Right of the Accused to Defend Himself: Any court trial essentially is a contest between two opposing parties, each striving to show itself in the right. To vie in this contest, each party must have witnesses and material evidence as troops for the fray, and an attorney to marshal these troops. In a criminal proceeding the government is certain to have witnesses, evidence, and an attorney, for without these elements it could not have procured an indictment from the grand jury. So that the contest may be waged on equitable terms, the accused must be allowed to produce the same elements for his defense. Hence, in a criminal trial the defendant has the right to have a lawyer; if he cannot afford to pay a lawyer's fee, the court must provide counsel for him. The defendant also must know the nature of the charges against him, and hear the testimony of adverse witnesses, so that with his attorney he can prepare a rebuttal. He may compel witnesses to attend court through the writ of subpoena, for ignoring which an offender may receive a summary conviction on the ground of contempt of court. With these rights, which are guaranteed by the Sixth Amendment, the defendant may have his side presented after the prosecution has made its plea for a conviction.

Ban on Self-Incrimination: The burden of producing evidence that proves guilt is entirely the responsibility of the prosecution. Neither before nor during the trial may the state force a defendant to testify so as to incriminate himself (Fifth Amendment). The original purpose of this guarantee was to bar confessions that had been extorted from the accused before the trial. Today, whereas it must be admitted that torture is sometimes employed upon suspects by State authorities, federal officers can rarely be charged with attempting to obtain pretrial confessions by this means.

In federal courts, then, the bar on self-incrimination operates chiefly with respect to trial proceedings. In late years this right has been invoked more frequently not in federal courts, but in hearings before congressional committees investigating charges of communism. A defendant may waive this protection so as to testify in his own defense; however, he must expose himself to the rigors of cross-examination by the prosecuting attorney, an interrogation in which he may lose more than he gained by his defense testimony. By a 1954 law, the Attorney General may apply to a federal court for permission to grant immunity from prosecution to a witness in a case involving the national security. If permission is granted, the witness may not refuse to answer on the grounds of self-incrimination, and may be punished if he does refuse.

Ban on Cruel and Unusual Punishments: The essence of the trial procedure thus comprises a series of witnesses, first for the prosecution and then for the defense. Each side has the right to cross-examine the witnesses of the other side, in an effort to shake their certainty about the facts they have presented or to demonstrate their personal unreliability to the jury. After all the evidence has been submitted, each attorney summarizes his case. The judge then instructs the jury respecting points of law related to the facts of the case, and the jury retires to determine the question of guilt or innocence. When the jury has reached a decision, it returns to the courtroom where the foreman of the jury states the decision.

If the jury finds the defendant guilty as charged, the judge sentences him according to the penalty for the offense that is established by law. Although the law usually grants the judge some discretion in setting the penalty, the judge may not fix any "cruel or unusual punishment" (Eighth Amendment). This provision again is chiefly a relic of the eighteenth century, when in England there were many comparatively minor crimes for which a death sentence was mandatory. Today this prohibition is rarely invoked. In one recent case involving a death sentence the electric chair failed to operate; counsel for the condemned man argued that to subject him again to the electric chair would constitute a cruel and unusual punishment. However, the Supreme Court rejected this plea.

Prohibition on Double Jeopardy: If the jury decides that the accused is innocent, the case has been concluded. The government may not try a defendant twice on the same charge, or, in the words of the Constitution, put him "twice . . . in jeopardy of life or limb" (Fifth Amendment). This ban is designed to prevent the government from trying a defendant several times on the same charge until it finally convicts him. The ban operates regardless of what new evidence may appear, after the jury has arrived at a verdict of innocence. However, there are certain loopholes in this prohibition. One is that in the commission of a single crime an individual may perform several indictable acts. A man who illegally brings five immigrants into the United States has committed five federal crimes, for each of which he may be tried and sentenced.

Another loophole exists in the federal form of government, wherein there are two distinct legal and judicial systems. A man who robs a national bank has violated both a federal law and a State law; he has committed two crimes. Indeed, in this type of case, if he happens to be tried and sentenced first in a federal court, he is apt to find authorities of the State government waiting for him when he steps out of a federal prison after completing his sentence, to return him for trial by the State. Also, the ban on double jeopardy does not apply when there is a hung jury or when the judge proclaims a mistrial, as he might if he were to discover, for instance, that a member of the jury was a cousin of the defendant. Finally, the defendant waives this protection if, after being found guilty, he appeals his case to a higher court.

Guarantee of the Due Process of Law: The entire judicial procedure must adhere to a broad group of principles known as the "due process of law." Due process is nowhere defined; the federal Supreme Court once asserted of due process that "the full meaning of the term should be gradually ascertained by the process of inclusion and exclusion in the course of decisions as they arise." Hence, due process is what the Supreme Court has said and now says it is, based on rulings which state that some practices are due process and that others are not. Due process is commonly identified with the "law of the land" mentioned in the Magna Carta, and with the rule of law, or constitutionalism. It is enforced upon federal courts by the Fifth Amendment, which forbids that any person "be deprived of life, liberty or property, without due process of law;" it is enforced upon State courts by a similar phrase in the Fourteenth Amendment. It refers to both criminal and to civil cases, to the *procedure* in these cases and to the *substance* of the law itself. At this juncture we are concerned with due process only as it is related to federal criminal *procedure*.

In criminal proceedings, due process can be said in the main to reinforce the constitutional guarantees regarding judicial procedure by peering into the spirit in which those guarantees have been executed. There are, however, some constitutional guarantees that are not due process. For example, although the Constitution assures a grand jury indictment for all persons charged with federal crimes, the Supreme Court has ruled that a State does not deny due process by reaching an indictment through other means.

Due process does insist that certain among the constitutional guarantees be observed not merely in form but also in spirit. As an illustration, the Constitution provides that a defendant must be allowed counsel for his defense. However, even if the accused has been provided with a lawyer, he has been denied due process if the lawyer has not had the time to prepare himself adequately for the trial. The Constitution requires that a defendant have a speedy and public trial and that his guilt be pronounced by a jury of his peers. However, if his whole trial has been completed in a very short time, if the public is extremely hostile, if it is known that any member of the jury voting for acquittal will incur great public rancor, the defendant again has been denied due process. An important requirement of due process that extends beyond sheerly procedural matters in criminal cases is that the law which the defendant is accused of violating is specific and comprehensible; a law that does not make clear precisely what act is a crime is a denial of due process. It is in its demand that criminal laws and proceedings be fair and predictable that due process can be identified with the rule of law.

Appeal proceedings

An individual convicted of violating a federal statute may not appeal his conviction simply as a matter of right. However, a fairly small percentage of the decisions in the federal district courts are brought into the courts of appeal; and a few bearing upon constitutional issues reach the Supreme Court. Since apart from the President (see below) the Supreme Court is the last resort of those convicted of federal offenses, and since it stands at the apex of the federal court system, its proceedings as an appellate court merit description. However, it should be recognized that a federal court of appeals conducts its hearings in much the same fashion, with variations in detail.

Sessions of the Supreme Court: The Supreme Court meets in regular annual sessions that open about the first of October and close in June of the following year. During these sessions, the Court sits five days a week, from Monday through Friday. The Court convenes at noon on these days and recesses about 4:30 P.M., with the half hour from 2:00 until 2:30 taken for lunch. A part of each Monday on which the Court sits is devoted to reading the decisions that have been reached during the previous week. The members of the Court generally spend Saturday in conference. The Court also ordinarily recesses for approximately two weeks out of each month during the session for conferences and the writing of decisions.

Court Hearings: During each Court hearing all nine members of the Supreme Court sit on individual chairs behind a single long desk, or "bench." The Chief Justice sits in the center of the nine; the senior associate justice, or associate justice with the longest term of service, sits at his right hand; the second senior associate at his left hand; and so on, in such a manner that the associate justice with the least seniority sits at the extreme left end of the bench. By contrast even with trial proceedings in a federal district court, appellate procedure in the Supreme Court is decorous. There is no jury in appellate hearings; indeed, there is no record that any jury has ever heard a case before the federal Supreme Court. The purpose of an appellate hearing is to resolve disputes that have arisen over questions of law; consequently only lawyers and the justices participate, since the facts have already been disclosed at the original trial. Therefore, the aim of the lawyer for the appellant (the person who claims that the original decision should be overturned) is simply to present his argument respecting the alleged faults of the trial; and the aim of the lawyer for the appellee or respondent (who is more or less analogous to a defendant in a trial hearing) is to rebut this argument and to support the procedure and the decision in the trial court.

Because of the amount of business before the Supreme Court, lawyers are rarely allowed more than an hour to present their case; and frequently this hour is punctuated by numerous questions from the members of the

Court respecting the points at issue. Hence lawyers orally can do little more than summarize their argument. However, each lawyer must present a brief of his argument in print, citing in full his authorities. Moreover, the trial court is obliged to send up the entire record of the original hearing, so that the Supreme Court justices may have access to the facts of the case. The justices, then, reach their decisions on the basis of the lawyers' oral presentations, the briefs, and the records from the trial courts.

Precedents: A great part of the argument of the lawyers is concerned with precedents, for precedents are the supreme guides to the Court's thinking. A precedent is the decision of the Court in the last case that most closely resembles the case at issue. Since life has infinite variety, a former case that is exactly the same as the one in hand is almost unheard of. Hence the lawyers on both sides compete with each other to find in the history of this Court, or a related court, precedents that will so closely resemble this case as to "rule" it. The judges will hardly ever defy a close precedent. On rare occasions a court will reverse itself and reject its own precedent; such an occasion always excites widespread comment and is looked upon as most dangerous to the rule of law. In many another case, however, the Court, without confessing to previous error, will find some distinctions between a precedent case and the one at hand, if the justices are absolutely bent on altering the law.

Decisions of the Supreme Court: The formulation of decisions commences in the Saturday conferences. There the justices advance their opinions regarding the cases that have been heard during the past week, the Chief Justice speaking first and the associate justices following in the order of their seniority. After each justice has aired his position on a case, all vote in reverse order of seniority, the Chief Justice voting last. Six justices must be present to make a quorum. One might expect that since there is an odd number of justices, one should always find one side having a majority. However, one justice may be absent; there may be an unfilled vacancy; or one or more justices may have disqualified themselves for one reason or another, such as having been Attorney General when the case was first prosecuted, and therefore being liable to prejudice. If under these circumstances the justices divide evenly in their vote, the case must be reargued; otherwise the decision of the lower court will stand.

If, as is much more common, one side of the dispute has a clear majority, the Chief Justice, if he is of the majority, will assign the writing of the majority opinion to one of the justices. He normally chooses the justice who has shown the greatest skill in presenting his argument at the conference, and whose field of specialization most nearly approaches the subject of the particular case. If the Chief Justice is not in the majority, the senior associate justice among the majority assigns the writing of the opinion. The senior associate justice among the minority of the Court assigns the writing of a minority or dissenting opinion.

It must be remembered that in the field of law there may be various ways of reaching the same decision, differing perhaps in the choice of legal precedents used to support an argument. In these instances, additional opinions may be written, which will be known as either concurring majority or concurring minority opinions. It must not be thought that dissenting opinions are wrong, or that in some way they lack judicial merit. Nor must it be thought that they are voices lost in the wilderness; as will be shown in the next chapter, with the evolution of political, economic, and social ideas, the dissenting opinion of one era may become the majority opinion of a later day.

Judicial Role of the President: In cases involving federal crimes, the President of the United States is the court of last appeal. It must not be thought that the President can or does intervene only after all other judicial resources have been exhausted. Rather, the President may intercede at any point in the judicial process, before, during, or after a trial. However, like most chief executives through history, the President has judicial authority superior to that of any court. There are only two constitutional limitations upon the judicial functioning of the President: (1) he has power only with respect to violations of federal law; and (2) he has no control over convictions following impeachment. Of course, there are many cases in which he is constitutionally empowered to act but where he is restrained by political obligations.

The President has four judicial weapons at his command: pardon, commutation, reprieve, and amnesty (Art. II, sec. 2, cl. 1). The pardon is an absolute weapon that restores the individual to the status he previously occupied in society, as if the event had never occurred; the individual regains all civil rights and privileges such as those of voting and of holding public office. Commutation is a relative instrument, through which the President may reduce a sentence from, for example, capital punishment to life imprisonment. Reprieve is a delaying implement, whereby the President may postpone the execution of a sentence so that the counsel for the convicted man may have more time to secure evidence for an appeal. Amnesty is a form of collective pardon customarily used with regard to political crimes, whereby the President may order the release of a group of persons convicted of rebellion.

The President exercises his judicial role only after consultations with a considerable number of people, for he has too many other burdens to be able to familiarize himself with the details of a criminal trial. Petitions for presidential action go to the Office of the Pardon Attorney in the Department of Justice, who prepares and analyzes the relevant data. The President also confers with the district attorney who prosecuted the trial and the district judge who heard it, as well as with the Attorney General. Ultimately, the President almost always follows the recommendations he is given by these officials.

CIVIL PROCEDURE

A case at civil law bears a strong resemblance to one at criminal law, in that two parties are contending before a theoretically neutral arbiter, each seeking to depict itself as in the right. The great distinction between the two lies in the fact that in civil cases the defendant does not stand in peril of life or limb; since civil cases deal chiefly with money or property, one or the other, or both, might be the defendant's principal loss. Too, whereas one party to criminal cases is always the government, both parties to civil cases are usually private persons or organizations. However, the federal government may be the plaintiff in a civil case, as when it brings suit for recovery against a person charged with income tax evasion; yet the defendant still foresees only a monetary loss. As a result, the constitutional and legal controls over civil proceedings are much less numerous and complicated than those over criminal proceedings.

Pre-trial proceedings

A civil case opens when one individual, who is termed the plaintiff, believes that he has suffered damages from an unlawful action by a second individual, to be known as the defendant. Such damages generally result from a *tort*, such as slander, or a breach of contract. This type of civil case reaches a federal court because of the diversity of citizenship among the parties, who come from different States or countries, and the sum of money involved. The plaintiff initiates action by filing a complaint with a court, stating the grounds on which he seeks recovery or compensation for his damages. The court informs the defendant of the action that has been taken against him; the defendant may now file with the court an answer, in which he endeavors to show his side in the dispute. There may ensue a series of amendments to the complaint and to the answer, until the court at last assumes jurisdiction over the dispute and orders a trial.

Trial proceedings

Trial proceedings at civil law have many of the elements of criminal trial proceedings. However, only one of these elements is guaranteed by the Constitution: the defendant is assured of the right to a jury trial in any case in which the stake is larger than twenty dollars, as provided by the Seventh Amendment. Actually, this figure is rather meaningless today; for any case arising out of the diversity of citizenship cannot come into the federal courts unless the controversy involves a sum greater than three thousand dollars, and cases of diversity of citizenship make up about half the work of the federal courts. Indeed, the jury is being discarded in civil suits just as it is in many criminal cases.

In a case at civil law, the plaintiff first presents his side, through witnesses and evidence; then the defendant states his side. Attorneys for each side may cross-examine witnesses for the other side. After all the evidence has been submitted each attorney makes a final plea to the jury, or, when there is no jury, to the judge. In the first instance, the judge then informs the jury concerning the law in the dispute. The jury withdraws to reach judgment favoring either the plaintiff or the defendant. If it agrees that the plaintiff is entitled to receive damages, it sets the figure. Where there is no jury, the judge, after studying the case, returns the judgment and the amount of damages, if any. Once a judgment in favor of the plaintiff has been pronounced, it is now the task of the plaintiff to discover what assets the defendant has that can make up the sum awarded to him.

Appeal proceedings

Appeal proceedings in civil law are also like those in criminal cases. Supposedly the trial court has discovered all the facts, so that only legal questions may supply a basis for appeal. The federal courts of appeal are the last resort for most civil cases; however, those revolving about a constitutional issue may come to the Supreme Court. In any case, hearings in an appeal follow approximately the same procedure, whether at civil or at criminal law. One outstanding difference, however, is that the President has no part in civil suits analogous to his role in criminal cases.

EQUITY PROCEDURE

Equity procedure today is considerably different from civil procedure, although the difference is not so great as it was some centuries ago. The most notable distinction is that in equity there is no jury; the judge renders the decision, which in equity is termed a *decree*. This difference is largely the result of the aim of a case at equity, that is, the prevention of damages before they occur; hence equity procedure is a great deal more summary than civil procedure. A case at equity is initiated when an individual who, as plaintiff, seeks to avoid suffering damages files a *bill* with a court of proper jurisdiction petitioning for aid and stating the circumstances of the case. The defendant must now file an *answer* under oath. At an equity hearing, which is held before a judge, the disputants are interrogated concerning the case. However, the written statements form a major portion of the testimony. In an equity proceeding the defendant enjoys a considerable advantage, in that his statements are presumed to be true unless there is strong evidence to the contrary.

Having heard and considered the evidence, the judge, if he decides in favor of the plaintiff, hands down the decree, which is an order of the court. A typical decree is an *injunction*, which is a command to the defendant not to perform a certain act. For example, a court may issue an injunction to the owners of a railroad that is under construction, ordering them not to lay their right of way across a certain field because the owner of the field, appearing as plaintiff, has shown that he will suffer damages if the railroad should cross it. Judges have extraordinary power to force obedience to an injunction. If the defendant can be shown to have disobeyed this order, the judge may immediately find him guilty of contempt of court, and without a jury trial may impose a fine or jail sentence upon him.

QUESTIONS AND PROBLEMS

1. Define briefly the following terms: *ex post facto* legislation; bill of attainder; *habeas corpus;* injunction; grand jury; petty jury.

2. Define briefly the following terms: bail; appeal; double jeopardy; plaintiff; a bill in equity; warrant.

3. Distinguish a "question of fact" from a "question of law" in the federal judicial process. What is the importance of the distinction in appellate trials?

4. What protections are afforded a person against *arbitrary* arrest, search, and detention?

5. When and by whom may the writ of *habeas corpus* be suspended?

6. Distinguish between civil and criminal procedure in the federal court system.

7. Does the doctrine of "due process of law" permit the courts to look behind the correct surface of police practices into the actual conduct of the police? Can you cite examples?

8. What are some arguments that might be made for and against the practice of publicizing dissenting opinions in Supreme Court cases?

29. Judicial Review

United Press Photo

JUDICIAL review is a process whereby a court during a case at law examines an act of some other branch of the government—often a legislature—to determine whether the act conflicts with the supreme law, or constitution, under which that branch of the government functions. Judicial review is an extreme form of the same power that judges exercise every time they hear a case; that is, they interpret and apply the law. If the judges hold that the law does conflict with the constitution, they are saying that the legislature has enacted an unconstitutional, or unenforceable, law. In other words, the court rebukes the legislature.   A serious political dispute may thereupon develop. Judicial review may thus be regarded as a *political* action; when exercising the power of judicial review, a judge is functioning as a legislator, in that he invades the area of the framing of government policy. When the court reviews an important rule or other act of an executive agency or officer, it again perforce takes part in the political process of making a policy; it functions in fact, if not in doctrine, as an independent executive.

441

THE EMERGENCE OF JUDICIAL REVIEW

The concept of supreme law

The foundation of judicial review in the United States is the constitutional proviso that "This Constitution, and the laws of the United States which shall be made in pursuance thereof; and all treaties made, or which shall be made, under the authority of the United States, shall be the supreme law of the land; and the judges in every State shall be bound thereby, anything in the constitution or laws of any State to the contrary notwithstanding." (Art. VI, cl. 2.) Without such an identification of a supreme law judicial review could not exist, for there would be no standard whereby to judge the constitutionality of a law.

The constitutional clause cited above is the authority under which federal courts determine the constitutionality of both State and federal laws. Hence the Judiciary Act of 1789 could empower the Supreme Court to review and reverse all decisions of State courts conflicting with a right guaranteed by the Constitution. Figure 55 shows how many State laws, acts of State administrative agencies, and municipal ordinances have been found unconstitutional by the Supreme Court.

Establishment of judicial review on the federal level

The principle of the judicial review of federal legislation was finally established by the Supreme Court in 1803, in the process of hearing a case at law. This establishment was intimately connected with partisan politics and with the contest among the three branches of the government for supremacy over the whole. In the elections of November, 1800, the hitherto dominant Federalist Party lost both the presidency and Congress. In an effort to retain control over one branch of the government, the Federalists in the "lame-duck" Congress that met in December, 1800, hurriedly created a number of new federal judgeships, and the retiring Federalist President, John Adams, named trustworthy Federalists to these posts. Adams also named his Secretary of State, John Marshall, to be Chief Justice of the United States.

At this time, a federal judge was not formally installed in office until he had been appointed by the President, his appointment had been confirmed by the Senate, and he had been given a commission for the office by the Secretary of State. In the waning days of the Federalist administration, however, the pressure of business was so great that Secretary of State Marshall was unable to issue all the commissions. Hence when the triumphant Republicans entered office in March, 1801, there were still some of the new federal justices who had not been duly commissioned. The new Secretary of State, James Madison, refused to deliver the commissions; and Congress soon abolished the new judicial posts. However, one of the so-called "midnight" judges, William Marbury, who had been appointed a

A Crowd Lined up in the Supreme Court Building Hoping to Hear Arguments Challenging the Constitutionality of Segregation in Public Schools, Dec. 6, 1953.

justice of the peace for the District of Columbia, turned to the Judiciary
Act of 1789, which empowered the Supreme Court to issue a writ of
mandamus (Latin, "we order"); he asked the Court to issue such a writ to
Madison, requiring him to deliver the commission on Marbury's demand.
It was this case, *Marbury* versus *Madison,* which came before the Supreme
Court in original jurisdiction, that gave Chief Justice Marshall, now arrived
on the bench, the opportunity to enunciate and claim the power of judicial
review for the federal Supreme Court.

In his opinion in *Marbury* versus *Madison,* Marshall established the basis
for all future decisions by the Supreme Court that a federal law is unconstitutional. In this decision, Marshall rapidly concluded that there was
no constitutional warrant for the judicial act empowering the Supreme
Court to issue a writ of *mandamus.* Said he, whereas the Constitution states
that the Supreme Court shall have original jurisdiction over "all cases
affecting Ambassadors, other public ministers, and consuls, and those in
which a State shall be a party. . . ." (Art. III, sec. 2, cl. 2), the Constitution
gives the Court *original* jurisdiction over *no other* type of case.

Marshall then asked "whether an act repugnant to the Constitution can
become the law of the land. . . ." He noted that in the Constitution the
people had asserted the principles under which they would be governed, and
had set limits upon their government. Since the United States has a government of limited powers, and since the Constitution is the supreme law,
Marshall went on, Congress may not alter the Constitution by simple
legislative act; otherwise Congress would no longer be limited, nor, con-

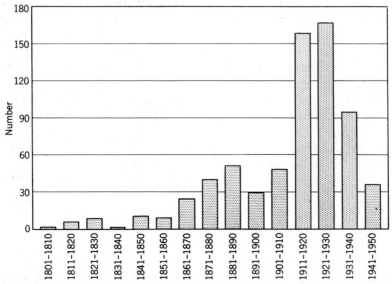

"The Supreme Court and Unconstitutional Legislation," Studies in History, Economics and Public Law, vol. LIV
(1913), no. 133, Columbia University, Faculty of Political Science: "U.S. Supreme Court Cases Declaring State Laws
Unconstitutional, 1912–1938," Library of Congress, State Law Index, Special Report no. 2, U.S. Government Printing
Office, Washington, 1938; Book of the States and correspondence with the Council of State Governments for the years
after 1938

**Figure 55. State Laws, Orders of State Administrative Bodies, and Municipal
Ordinances Ruled Unconstitutional by the Supreme Court, 1800–1950.**

sequently, would the government. Are the courts obliged to enforce a law that is patently repugnant to the Constitution? "It is emphatically the province and duty of the judicial department to say what the law is." Thus, when such a law appears, since the courts must obey the Constitution, they must disregard the law. If the courts do not disregard the law, Marshall declared, they would subvert the very principle of written constitutions. It was therefore the duty of the courts to hold as void any law repugnant to the Constitution.

The fact is that judicial review is an implied power of the Supreme Court. Indeed, there are those who are sufficiently hostile to term it a "usurped" power; they deny that it has any constitutional warrant. Certainly there were strong political motives behind Marshall's opinion in the Marbury case. Marshall's act was but one of the many that have taken place in the unending struggle among the three branches of the government for supremacy. Marshall himself was a vigorous politician. It should be noted that having been Secretary of State, he was himself implicated in the Marbury case; and he might have refused to take part in its adjudication on the ground of possible prejudice. Also it should be noted that he decided against Marbury, a fellow Federalist, sacrificing him for a greater Federalist principle. Marshall had espoused a body of principles, notably the strengthening of the central government and the defense of the propertied interests, that were identified with the Federalist Party. The Federalists now controlled only the judicial branch, but Marshall proposed through that branch to make the Federalist theory of government endure.

Marshall's reasoning in the Marbury case is open to question as to its logic. First it may be observed that the Constitution does not say or imply that the Supreme Court is a better judge of the meaning of the Constitution than is Congress or the President. Also, the clause in question does not say that the *original* jurisdiction of the Supreme Court is absolutely restricted to what is mentioned in the Constitution. In sum, the Marbury case will forever remain debatable. The decision could have been the opposite in law and logic, but the leadership of a powerful man, strategically situated at the proper moment, deflected the course of constitutional history.

Once this vast power of the judicial veto had been established, the Supreme Court was never to surrender it. One could not say that the Court has abused this power, for, as Figure 56 shows, since 1803 it has found only some eighty federal laws unconstitutional. Yet there was at least one occasion when the Court behaved almost as though it feared reconstruction by Congress and the President after having overthrown an unusually large number of laws. This behavior occurred in 1937, following a period of only four years in which the Court had voided eleven statutes, all of which were comprised in the New Deal program of Franklin D. Roosevelt.

After his tremendous victory in the 1936 elections, which he interpreted in part as a public mandate for his projects and a rebuke to the Court that had opposed them, Roosevelt began openly to ascribe the actions of the Court to the age of its members, which in 1937 averaged seventy-two years.

He urged that Congress empower him to appoint a new justice for each member over seventy years of age, an authorization that would have enabled him to name six new justices. (Incidentally, lest this plan be considered a diabolical invention of Roosevelt, it should be noted that its originator was James C. McReynolds, who proposed it in 1913 when he was Attorney General; the *same* Justice McReynolds was now a bitterly anti-New Deal member of the Supreme Court, threatened by the two-edged sword he had once forged and forgotten.) Since at this time there were three justices who usually upheld New Deal legislation, the appointment of six new members would have given the President a working margin of nine to six. However, this plan excited such opposition from some sectors of Congress and of the public that Roosevelt was unable to secure this authority. On the other hand, the Supreme Court beginning in 1937 suddenly curtailed the use of its judicial veto, as though fearful of being penalized by Congress or the administration. In fact, from 1937 until 1956 the Court declared only two minor laws unconstitutional, neither of them related to the fundamental policy of either of the branches of the government. Thus President Roosevelt lost his battle but won his war; the Supreme Court reacted as if it had accepted a new climate of opinion that fostered the New Deal. Today the Supreme Court is more restrained in holding acts of Congress unconstitutional.

THE PROCEDURE OF JUDICIAL REVIEW

The procedure of judicial review today illustrates the self-restraints that the Supreme Court has imposed upon itself. Among the various restraints, which were enumerated by Associate Justice Louis Brandeis in 1936, perhaps the most important is that the Court will make no ruling apart from an actual case at law. The supreme courts of some States render *advisory decisions* respecting the constitutionality of State legislation, but the Su-

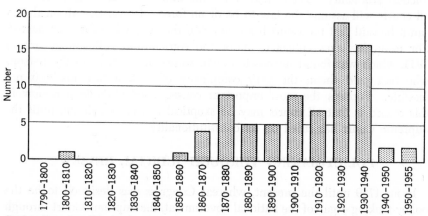

Based on figures from "The American Federal Government," by John H. Ferguson and Dean E. McHenry, copyright 1953, McGraw-Hill Book Co., Inc., pp. 72–3

Figure 56. Federal Laws Declared Unconstitutional by the Supreme Court, 1790–1950.

preme Court will not thus counsel Congress or the President. The Department of Justice is expected to render this service to the President. Should the Court do so, it is believed, the Court would become thoroughly involved in the policies of the executive and legislative branches; it might suffer a decline of its independence, and furthermore be plagued by numerous inquiries about imaginary issues. Also the case must involve a legal, not a political, question. It is difficult to fix an arbitrary line dividing the two categories; however, as an example, the Court has refused to state whether or not the Constitution has been properly amended, ruling that this is a matter for the political branches (Congress and the President).

Moreover, the question of constitutionality is not raised unless it is absolutely essential. If the Court may settle a case without raising the question, it does. Too, the Court always presumes the constitutionality of a law, as it does the innocence of a defendant. Also, the Court does not peer into the motives that prompted the legislature to enact the law. Finally, the Court declares unconstitutional only the part or parts of the law that is or are repugnant to the Constitution. The rest of the law remains effective, provided that it can be separated from the part that has been overthrown. Most laws today are drafted with a clause arranging for such a separation.

The net effect of a ruling of unconstitutionality is that the Court refuses to enforce or apply the law. The Court does not repeal a law; a law declared unconstitutional may stay forever on the statute books. What the Court does is simply to state that no person may be held guilty of violating this law, or that no person may be held liable in a civil suit under the terms of the law. Essentially, then, the Court has said that there is no law. Presumably, if a person were brought before a lower court after a ruling of unconstitutionality, the Supreme Court would bring the case within its own jurisdiction by a writ of *certiorari*, then repeat its original ruling. Actually, the Court numerous times has reversed past findings of unconstitutionality. Yet at least for some time after the original decision all courts will assume the law to be of no force. However, only in theory can it be said that the Court has acted as if the law had never been passed. For example, taxes collected under the Agricultural Adjustment Act of 1933, which was found unconstitutional, were not returned to the persons who had paid them; the very complexity of such a task made it not feasible. Perhaps the most important consequence of judicial review in this regard is that all courts may be skeptical of new legislation until the Supreme Court has ruled on its constitutionality.

POLICY-MAKING THROUGH JUDICIAL REVIEW

From 1789 until the present, whereas Congress was designed to be the policy-making organ of the national government, the Supreme Court through its power of judicial review has made great contributions to policy. Some of these policies have later been rejected; others remain to this day, although they too might be overthrown by adverse decisions. The following discussion is in no way exhaustive of the policy contributions of the Supreme Court; it is intended only to be illustrative.

Supremacy of the national government

The supremacy of the national government over the States was asserted by John Marshall in his opinion in the case of *McCulloch* versus *Maryland* (1819). This case revolved about the power of the State of Maryland to tax the Bank of the United States, a financial institution that had received its charter of incorporation from Congress. The litigation arose when the Bank refused to pay the tax. Marshall ruled first that the establishment of the bank was constitutional, his logic providing the classic statement of the theory of implied powers. He went on to assert that the government of the United States is a government of all the people and was created, not by the States, but by the people. This government, he argued, is supreme in its own sphere. However, "the power to tax involves the power to destroy." Maryland, or another State, could wipe out federal agencies and property by taxation. Since the constitution and laws of a State are controlled by those of the federal government, no State can have such power to destroy an agency of the federal government. Hence, Marshall declared, the Maryland tax is unconstitutional. This decision founded a principle that reigns today; practically all federal property is exempt from State taxation.

In later cases, Marshall dealt with particular governing spheres where the national authority is supreme. In *Cohens* versus *Virginia* (1821), Marshall formulated a powerful expression of national supremacy:

> That the United States form, for many, and for most important purposes, a single nation, has not yet been denied. In war, we are one people. In making peace, we are one people. In all commercial relations, we are one and the same people. In many other respects, the American people are one; and the government which is alone capable of controlling and managing their interests, in all these respects, is the government of the Union. It is their government, and in that character they have no other. America has chosen to be, and to many purposes, a nation; and for all these purposes her government is complete; to all these objects, it is competent. The people have declared, that in the exercise of all powers given for these objects, it is supreme. It can, then, in effecting these objects, legitimately control all individuals or governments within the American territory.

In *Gibbons* versus *Ogden* (1824), one of the most important of these cases, the Court ruled that a law of New York State giving one steamship company a monopoly of the traffic upon the Hudson River was unconstitutional, since it interfered with the power of Congress to regulate interstate commerce.

Defense of property rights

Almost from the very beginning, the Supreme Court functioned as a defender of property, a role that the Federalists had hoped it would adopt. One foundation for this role was the constitutional clause prohibiting a State from passing any "law impairing the obligation of contracts" (Art.

I, sec. 10, cl. 1). States were not, then, to enact legislation breaking a contract in any manner; the Court construed this ban so as to work in behalf of property owners. For example, in 1795 the State of Georgia for speculative purposes created a Yazoo Land Company to which the State sold lands that were disputed among Georgia, the United States, and Great Britain. It quickly transpired that the sale was fraudulent, since many of the stockholders in the company were members of the State legislature. The next legislature voided the contracts, but not before many private citizens had also invested in the stock. Later Georgia yielded these disputed lands to the United States. Meanwhile some of the private citizens who had purchased stock in the now defunct land company demanded reimbursement, on the ground that the State of Georgia had acted improperly in breaking the contract. Finally, in the case of *Fletcher* versus *Peck* (1810), the Supreme Court ruled that the Georgia legislature had acted in an unconstitutional manner in breaking the contract; and Congress appropriated eight million dollars to pay the claimants.

About a decade later, the Court reached a highly important decision involving breach of contract, in which it defined a corporation charter as a contract, with all its privileges. The State of New Hampshire sought, through legislative action, to transform Dartmouth College into a State institution. The College had received a charter as a private corporation from the New Hampshire colonial government; the State now proposed to alter the terms of the grant. In the case of *Dartmouth College* versus *Woodward* (1819), the Supreme Court held that a charter is a contract. Thanks to this broad interpretation of the term "contract," industrial and financial corporations (which, like Dartmouth College, receive their charters from the States) were able to obtain exceptional immunities for themselves which, because of the "full faith and credit" clause in the Constitution, they could enjoy in every State. States eventually found a sure means for protecting themselves by including in every charter a clause authorizing them to change the charter, or by fixing a constitutional limit on the duration of every corporate charter.

Limitations on social legislation

The Supreme Court during the years from the Civil War until about 1937 was a frequent barrier to the enactment and enforcement of social legislation by both the State and the national governments. This position, of course, in part complemented the role the Court had previously adopted as the defender of property interests. It must not be thought, however, that the Court invariably overthrew State and federal labor laws. For instance, in 1898 it upheld a Utah statute limiting the hours of work in mines. Then, in 1908, it favored an Oregon statute limiting the hours of work for women. Also, the Court accepted the constitutionality of federal laws regulating railroad workers, for these workers incontestably were engaged in interstate commerce and were thus within the province of congressional action. However, so long as the Court was capable of finding that manufacturing was only "incidental" to interstate commerce, it could overthrow any federal law regulating the conditions of labor in factories. In recent years the Court has enlarged greatly its definition of the scope of interstate commerce, thus allowing important new federal and State social legislation.

The defense of political rights

In late years, also, the Supreme Court has become a prime defender of political rights, not only against State legislatures but also against popular sentiment. It was once believed that the clauses of the Fourteenth Amendment forbidding any State to "make or enforce any law which shall abridge the privileges or immunities of citizens of the United States . . ." would serve to block State limitations on political rights. However, shortly after this Amendment was adopted, the Court ruled, in effect, that there are very few political rights that are attached to United States, or federal, citizenship; it said that most political rights are elements of State citizenship, and that it would not overrule State laws respecting the privileges and immunities of State citizenship. Only in recent times has the Court agreed to extend any of the first eight Amendments to the protection of individuals against *State* action. In the past two decades the Court has ruled against numerous State laws on the ground that they are repugnant to one or another of these Amendments.

Despite the obvious concern of the Supreme Court in recent years with personal civil and political liberties, many observers have felt that the Court is still too timid. In an article in *The Nation*, October 9, 1954, entitled "The Supreme Court and Our Civil Liberties," Professor Herman Pritchett wrote that the Supreme Court was no longer defending vigorously the rights of individuals and that it yielded too readily to Congress and the executive branch. He presented interesting data on fifty-one divided decisions of the Supreme Court between 1946 and 1953 involving government action against aliens (twenty-three cases) and general issues of civil

TABLE 16. SUPPORT OF PERSONS AGAINST GOVERNMENT
BY SUPREME COURT JUSTICES[1]

(percentage of cases in which individuals were upheld)

	Alien Cases	Civil Liberties Cases	Combined
Supreme Court (as a whole)	39%	21%	30%
Murphy (1947–1949)	100	100	100
Rutledge (1947–1949)	100	100	100
Black	100	96	98
Douglas	63	100	84
Frankfurter	82	44	61
Jackson	50	22	35
Burton	35	14	24
Vinson	30	11	20
Minton (1949–1953)	19	15	17
Reed	9	18	14
Clark (1949–1953)	14	10	12

[1] From Pritchett, Herman, "The Supreme Court and Our Civil Liberties," *The Nation,* October 9, 1954, p. 303.

liberties (twenty-eight cases). Table 16 gives the percentage of decisions in which each justice, as well as the Court as a whole, supported the individual's case against the government's.

The table shows that Murphy, Rutledge, and Black consistently leaned over backward to protect civil rights and liberties whereas, at the opposite extreme, Burton, Vinson, Minton, Reed, and Clark supported Congress and the Justice Department's view of individual liberties. It is well to note here, too, the strong evidence that the "law" can be read very differently by equally learned judges; the wide spread between the two groups of justices cannot be explained away as a coincidence.

CONSEQUENCES OF JUDICIAL REVIEW

It is impossible to make unequivocal, yet accurate, assertions regarding the consequences of judicial review, since almost everything that has happened in American history has been the product of more than one factor. However, it is possible to speculate about certain traits or tendencies that might have had a different emphasis, had judicial review never existed. For example, States might have shown a greater willingness to experiment in social legislation, and through this experimentation would have been less similar to one another in their governmental structures; the Supreme Court has overthrown a considerable number of early laws of this nature. The national government, too, would probably have a greater body of social legislation, and would be carrying out some services independently that it now administers cooperatively with the States through grants-in-aid. Indeed, without judicial review the federal government might own a great deal of industry that is "affected with a public interest," such as railroads. In the national government, Congress might have been emboldened to make the executive branch considerably stronger than it is now but for court restraints upon delegating legislative power to the President. Too, members of the legal profession might not have earned their current prestige and predominance in American politics. These differences, and many others, can be in part attributed both to actual decisions of unconstitutionality and the wish to avoid such decisions. The *potentiality* of judicial review has perhaps been as effective as the *actuality* of judicial review.

CRITICISMS OF JUDICIAL REVIEW

Judicial review has been the target of many criticisms from both inside and outside the government. Some persons have adopted a position already cited, that judicial reivew is a usurped power. Others maintain that it hampers legislators, and that it restrains their initiative. It is true that much of the time in the dispute over the propriety of judicial review, those who favor constant change in governmental machinery and functioning have supported legislatures against the Court; and those who have resisted change, or at least rapid change, have looked to the Court as an effective rein upon rash legislative action. (It is important to remember, in this connection, that much of the agitation depends upon whose ox is being gored. When a labor union is hurt by a court decision, it is likely to feel that judicial review is a usurped power; it is inclined to take the opposite view, however, when the Court knocks down a law restricting labor union membership.)

However, in any event it would not be correct to assert that the Court has always opposed change. For instance, Chief Justice John Marshall, in his insistence upon national supremacy, was a political radical in his own era. Associate Justice Oliver Wendell Holmes once made the following comment respecting judicial review: "I do not think the United States would come to an end if we [the Supreme Court] lost our power to declare an act of Congress void. I do think the Union would be imperilled if we could not make that declaration as to the laws of the several States." What Holmes meant was that on the federal level the Court in theory was no more than the equal of Congress or of the President, in interpreting the Constitution and that, if the Court lost its power of judicial review, the chief effect would be the substitution of one set of opinions regarding the meaning of the Constitution for another. On the other hand, he felt that the Supreme Court required the power of voiding State laws, lest the States encroach upon and restrict both the federal government and each other.

Opponents of judicial review have suggested various means for curtailing its use, or for enabling Congress to override a judicial veto. One common proposal has been to demand an extraordinary majority of the Court, such as six-to-three or even seven-to-two, for a declaration of unconstitutionality. Others have recommended that Congress be empowered to repass a law declared unconstitutional, perhaps by the same two-thirds majority necessary to override a presidential veto. Of course, Congress and the State legislatures together may collaborate against a judicial veto by amending the Constitution. This procedure has been followed twice: (1) the Fourteenth Amendment, with its definition of United States citizenship, reversed the Court's declaration that Dred Scott, as a Negro, could never be a citizen; and (2) the Sixteenth Amendment, authorizing Congress to levy an income tax without concerning itself about apportioning the tax according to population, reversed the earlier Court decision defining the income tax as a direct tax that must be apportioned among the States according to their population.

After the dramatic and important Supreme Court decision in 1954 that held racial segregation in public schools to be unconstitutional, the governments of some southern States held that they could overthrow this decision by a means known either as "nullification" or as "interposition." Nullification and interposition amount to approximately the same thing, although nullification is harsher. Each constitutes a protest against some action by the federal government which State leaders feel is an improper interference with State affairs; nullification is associated with the actions of the southern States just before the outbreak of the Civil War. As an example of nullification, the legislature of Alabama in 1955 declared that the Court decision outlawing segregation was "null, void, and of no effect." An instance of interposition came about through a resolution in Congress sponsored by seven Senators from the South; the resolution asserted that the Court had exceeded its authority in this decision and asked Congress to declare that the southern States are fulfilling their constitutional obligations so long as they maintain separate but equal schools. Inasmuch as the federal court system and machinery of law enforcement operate independently of State governments, these declarations had no formal effect upon the ruling of the Supreme Court. Actually, the Court itself has, under political pressure or because of changed personnel or philosophies, shown considerable flexibility through the years in rejecting or readjusting its own previous rulings. In any event, it appears that judicial review will remain a power of the Court so long as a great many politically influential Americans support it.

QUESTIONS AND PROBLEMS

1. Define judicial review. How does it contrast with other parts of the work of a court?

2. Compare the use and results of federal judicial review of State laws and of congressional enactments.

3. Supposing that you were the attorney for Marbury and knew that Chief Justice Marshall was considering the question of judicial review, how would you have argued against the principle of judicial review?

4. The periods when the greatest number of federal laws were declared unconstitutional coincided with periods when economic change and economic distress were most prominent. Offer some explanations for the existence of this relationship.

5. State briefly the principle of law involved in these cases: *McCulloch* versus *Maryland; Gibbons* versus *Ogden; Fletcher* versus *Peck.*

6. What do the data from Table 16 have to contribute to the theory that the Supreme Court is a political as well as a judicial body?

7. Write a 400-word report on the activities of the Supreme Court over the past two years, using as source material the *Encyclopedia Britannica Yearbook* or a comparable work.

PART VIII

Public Policy
and Its Administration

THUS far this book has carried its readers through an exploration of the roots of American government, the political process by which public policy is largely determined, and the most important organs that formulate and promulgate the law. From this point onward, its concern will be the tasks that the government performs, and the people who perform them. Specifically, the chapters that follow will examine the dozens of important functions of the agencies of the executive branch of government; describe how the agencies' workers are organized and controlled; and show how the public, interest groups, Congress, the President, and the courts enter again and again upon the decisions of those agencies.

To introduce such a large task demands an initial conception of the total problem of governmental activity. Else the grains of sand may blind one to the strand. Hundreds of different jobs are done by the federal government, and one might study each in turn without ever feeling that some overall question was involved—that question being: what does a whole society become as a result of its sum of governmental activities? Hence this chapter inquires in turn: How far does American government enter into the lives of the American people? Is this intervention little or great, in absolute terms? Is it modest or immense by comparison with other nations? Finally, what limits do law and opinion fix to the growth of governmental functions?

THE VARIETY OF TASKS OF THE FEDERAL GOVERNMENT

Foremost among the tasks of government, of course, are those that have already been dealt with at length. They include the passage of laws and rules, the administration of justice, and the control of parties and pressure groups. Each of these contains a host of detailed functions. Also, many tasks are involved in the selection and supervision of millions of federal employees. The federal government is by far the nation's largest employer of help. Controlling the money and banking system of the nation affords additional functions. Preparing the taxing, borrowing, and spending plans of the national government, and seeing that they are carried out, occupy many thousands of men and women throughout the year.

Dozens of programs in the fields of health, education, welfare, and working conditions, establish close relations between the government and the majority of Americans. Working conditions and wages are also a major concern of the government. Along with the attention that it gives to the human resources of the nation, the government makes efforts to conserve the natural resources of the land. It also has numerous agricultural activities. The intervention of the government in agriculture is paralleled by many activities in the field of commerce and industry.

Indeed, it is not an easy matter to name areas of human activity that are not in some way affected directly by the government. For instance, one might suggest newspapers, for it is true that newspapers are among the least affected of businesses. Yet censorship of various kinds is always a problem—as in cases of libel, obscenity, disclosure of government secrets or court records—and newspapers are also interested in postal rates, labor relations laws, the conservation of forests that supply newsprint, and many other concerns of government. Furthermore, nothing has been said of the hundreds of State and local government functions that often duplicate but more often complement federal functions.

Obviously, there is no question that the federal government is related directly to the everyday lives of the whole population. Just as obviously, one should have some method of judging the total meaning of this activity and its limits; an American farmer, for all the government attention he

"**Modern Justice**" **by Kindred McLeary.** This study for a mural in the Pittsburgh Post Office and Court House is a result of government sponsorship of the arts. It was produced in the period of the Great Depression under Federal Government sponsorship as part of a "New Deal" emergency program to provide work for the unemployed. Thousands of artists were employed and much of their work has found its way into public buildings throughout the land.

receives, may still not feel its weight as much as the Dutch farmer or the Russian farmer feels the weight of *his* government. Consequently, it is worthwhile to state carefully and systematically just what are the actual degrees of intervention found in American and foreign societies.

THE MEANING OF GOVERNMENTAL POWER OVER PERSONS

The word *power* has been used here and there so far to mean the ability to influence the behavior of people. Whatever their form, whatever the number of people who possess power, and whatever the ways in which they exercise power, all governments are alike in that they influence the behavior of the population. Furthermore, the more powerful members of the government influence the behavior of the less powerful members. When all is said and done, probably most people would say that to them the most important aspect of government is how much it absorbs of their lives, time, money, and energies. Therefore, one should have clearly in mind what is meant by the extent of power of any given government, whatever its form or typical means for executing its policies.

In order to perceive this aspect of government, one might chart the various interests of different individuals so as to show the proportionate role of the government with respect to each of these interests. Figure 57 illustrates the intervention of the state in the life of John Doe. Let us assume that John Doe has eight important interests in his life; one is his family role, another his occuption, a third his leisure, a fourth his participation in a larger public, a fifth his religion, and so on. Richard Roe, another citizen, may have only five such general areas of interest; a third, Jack Smith, might have a dozen or more such areas. In each case the interest would mean more or less to one man than to another.

Now, taking up the case of John Doe, let us suppose that a bar can be raised to the height on the chart corresponding to the proportion of his total interest that is occupied by each given interest. This is represented in Figure 57. Now let us block into each bar the proportion of that given interest that the government is concerned with, if at all. Then, let that portion of the interest bar showing the portion that the government is deeply concerned with be blacked over. That is, the government may be concerned with the family, but only to the extent of giving a small bonus for the children in order to increase the population. On the other hand, the government might be concerned with the family to the extent of making all sorts of rules about the parent-child relationship, about taking the child out of the family and putting him into public schools, teaching the child certain trades and political beliefs, placing the child in certain kinds of youth groups governed by officials of the state, and so on. Where the government exercises a complete, monopolistic, or *totalitarian* power with respect to a given interest, the whole bar would be blacked over.

Operating in the same manner with the other interests, one might build up a profile of any individual in the society showing the scope and in-

tensity with which the state intervenes in his interests. If this were done
for the whole of society and each individual were plotted similarly, one
would have a notion of the domain of the government. The *domain* of
the government differs from its *scope:* the former refers to the number
of people involved, whereas the latter is concerned with the number of
human functions the state is interested in. If, for example, a law were
enacted by Congress absolutely prohibiting llama-ranching in the United
States, the scope would amount to llama-ranching; the intensity of the state
interest would be one hundred per cent; but the domain of the interest
would be zero, since there are no llama-ranchers in the United States.

Thus power would have been broken down into the several elements
that measure its extent: the *scope* of the power, consisting of those things
or interests in which the government concerns itself; the *intensity* of the

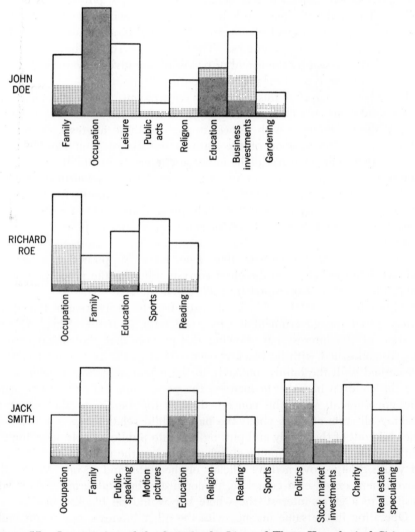

Figure 57.   Intervention of the State in the Lives of Three Hypothetical Citizens.

power, comprising the weight the government bears within the scope of its interests; and the *domain* of the power, embracing the number of people over whom the power is exercised. The perfect and complete totalitarian society would be one in which the whole society would have individual bar profiles that would be entirely blacked over in the technique shown here. Complete anarchy, or the absence of government, would see all humanity possessing white barred profiles, for there would be no government to exercise power.

The power of government, therefore, is measured as that part of all human activity in which the government to some extent intervenes, together with the actual degree of intervention and the number of people affected by it. The major areas of governmental intervention that are of past and present significance are the economic area, the religious area, and the cultural area. The problem of governmental power in these three areas will be introduced here, with especial reference to the United States.

THE EXTENT OF GOVERNMENTAL INTERVENTION

The economic power of government

The economic power of government may be measured by the extent, intensity, and domain of its interference with the economic life of the nation. No two governments exercise precisely the same degree of control over industry, commerce, finance, and agriculture. For the purposes of analyzing the economic role of the state, however, governments may be divided into socialist, regulatory or promotional, and laissez-faire regimes. In the order in which they stand, these categories represent a descending scale of governmental intercession, from well-nigh complete to almost non-existent.

The Socialist or Planned Economy: Under a planned economy, the government either owns, or more or less rigidly controls, all means of production and their output. A centralized or decentralized state planning commission fixes production quotas, allocates labor and raw materials, and sets prices. The extent to which the government actually owns the means of production may vary from one state to another. In the Soviet Union, for example, the government does own all the major facilities of agriculture, industry, transportation, and communication. In Nazi Germany, on the other hand, most of the facilities remained in the possession of their original owners; however, they were rather strictly regulated by the government. The relations of the individual owners to their property in Fascist Italy remained much the same as that in Nazi Germany; however, the industrial magnates in Italy, to an even greater degree than in Germany, were installed in government posts.

Under the regime of the Labour Party from 1945 until 1950, the British government came to own the railroads, the coal mines, and the steel industry, along with various other aspects of the British economy. This government also established crop quotas for farmers, and it threatened those farmers who disregarded these quotas with confiscation of their land. The Labour government also maintained a comprehensive system of rationing and price controls; probably these were more the consequences of World War II than they were of socialist inspiration. However, the Conservative Party was quick to abolish them.

It is quite evident that there are degrees to which an economy may be planned. One of the indexes to the degree of planning lies in the extent to which government ownership has superseded individual or private corporate ownership. On this basis Soviet Russia stands at the extreme of state planning; Nazi Germany, Fascist Italy, and England under the Labour Party are at a considerable remove from this extreme. There is a very rough pattern for the evolution of state ownership that governments progressing toward a planned economy may be said to follow. Such governments commonly own the so-called "natural monopolies"—the communication, transportation, and distributive industries, in which monopoly is an almost inevitable tendency because competition demands very expensive overlapping if the same customers are to be served. For example, it would appear somewhat ridiculous for two or more companies to try to pipe running water to a single community, since serving one customer on a block would require nearly as much pipe as serving twenty.

These governments likewise often own the munitions industries of the country. They may then, to a greater or lesser degree, expand their ownership to other heavy industries, frequently purchasing those segments that are losing money under private ownership; for instance, the British coal mines had been in an economic depression for many years. Then the socialist or communist government is in a position to enforce plans that it may draft for the whole national economy.

Planned economies have been numerous in both fact and theory down through the ages. Egypt under many of the Pharaohs might be termed a planned economy, as might also the later Roman Empire. One of the most attractive of such regimes was that proposed in a work entitled *Utopia* by Sir Thomas More (1478–1535), an English humanist who for a time held political office under King Henry VIII. Recent planned economies include not only those of Soviet Russia, Nazi Germany, Fascist Italy, and Great Britain under the Labour government, but also Falangist Spain, Titoist Yugoslavia, Communist China, and the Soviet satellites in Eastern Europe. It is important to bear in mind that in times of war all modern states adopt planned economies.

The motives beneath the foundation of a planned economy may be numerous. For those systems that exist only on paper, these motives often are quite humanitarian; for example, the system of More's *Utopia* was designed to permit each citizen to achieve moral and intellectual perfection. Upon close inspection, however, modern planned economies usually betray two cardinal motives whose proportion of the total vary according to circumstances; they are (1) to create domestic tranquillity, and (2) to prepare for foreign war. In Great Britain, however, preparation for war was certainly no more than a slight motivation; probably it played no role at all. Likewise, there was no question of maintaining or restoring domestic order. The principal goal of the Labour government appears to have been the reduction or removal of large differences in wealth among the British citizenry.

The Regulatory or Promotional Government: The regulatory or promotional government, as its name implies, tends to confine its interference in the national economy to regulating and promoting that economy. Under this sort of regime the various interest groups in the country compete vigorously for control of the government, so that they may employ its regulatory and promotional machinery to further their own interests. There may be some amount of deliberate governmental planning for the economy, but this planning almost always bears the stamp of one of the interest groups in the nation. Sometimes the government may own a small fraction of the national means of production, usually in the area of the "natural monopolies"; it may also exploit its ownership so as indirectly to regulate privately-owned facilities of the same type.

There have been many instances of regulatory and promotional governments. This sort of principle flourished, especially in England and France, during the seventeenth and eighteenth centuries, under the name *mercantilism.* This policy held that the wealth of a nation was to be measured by its stocks of gold and silver, and that the economic role of the government was to so stimulate the national economy that it would produce more than it consumed, so as to increase its supply of precious metals through selling its products abroad. Indeed, the founding of the British colonies in North America was partly motivated by mercantilism, for these colonies were expected to provide both raw materials and markets for British enterprise.

The early colonists themselves were often convinced of the necessity for strict regulation of industry, as illustrated in Figure 58. The United States throughout its history has never completely departed from such a regime. The Constitution provides such promotional devices as patents, to encourage inventors. Shortly after the adoption of the Constitution the government began to practice regulation through a tariff on imported goods, a tax aimed also at stimulating native industry. American legislation ever since has often sought to promote the interests of those in power and regulate the activities of those out of power, regardless of the nature of these groups. Since about 1900 the American government has engaged to a considerably greater degree than before in regulatory and promotional efforts; and much of this later activity has been at least presented in the form of assistance to very large parts of the population. At the same time it has constructed certain producing facilities, such as the Tennessee Valley Authority, one of whose functions is to regulate the cost of electric power in neighboring regions by threatening competition through tax-supported, low-cost electricity.

The Laissez-Faire Government: The laissez-faire government is one in which the government takes no part in the national economy beyond preserving the rudiments of law and order. Under a laissez-faire government the national economy regulates itself through the operation of various

Attachments. Bakers. Ballaſt. Barratrie.   **3**

produce, to which end any Court or Commiſſioners authorized by the General Court may adminiſter an oath to the partie or any others ſuſpected to be privie in concealing his eſtate, but ſhall ſatiſfie by ſervice if the Creditor require it but ſhall not be ſolde to any but of the Engliſh nation. [1641: 1647] *ſee ſect 1. page 1.*

Attachments.

It is ordered by this Court and Authoritie therof that no attachment ſhall be granted in any civil action to any Forreigner againſt a ſetled Inhabitant in this Juriſdiction before he hath given ſufficient ſecuritie or caution to proſecute his action and to anſwer the defendant ſuch coſts as the Court ſhall award him.   And further it is ordered that in all attachments of goods and chattels, or of lands, or hereditaments legall notice ſhall be given unto the partie or left in writing at his houſe, or place of uſuall aboad, otherwiſe the ſute ſhall not proceed ; notwithſtanding if he be out of this juriſdiction the cauſe ſhall then proceed to triall, but judgement ſhall not be entered before the next court.   And if the Defendant doe not then appear judgement ſhall be entered but execution ſhall not be granted before the Plantiſſe hath given ſecuritie to be reſponſall to the Defendant if he ſhall reverſe the judgement within one year or ſuch further time as the Court ſhall limit. [1644] *ſee actions. ſee El. writts. ſee Preſents. ſee Rates. ſee Accoſar.*

Forreigner ſhal not attach Inhabitats without cautiõ.

Reſpit of judgement
Of execution.

Bakers.

It is ordered by this Court and Authoritie therof, that henceforth every Baker ſhall have a diſtinct mark for his bread, & keep the true aſſizes as heerafter is expreſſed viz. When wheat is ordinarily ſold at theſe ſeverall rates heerafter mentioned the peñie white loaf by averdupois weight ſhall weigh when wheat is by the buſhell - - - - - - - at 3 ſs. 6 d. The white 11 ouces 1 qr. wheaten 17 ouc. 1 qr. houſhould 23 ouc. o.

at 3	6	10	1	15	1	20	2.
at 4	0	09	1	14	0	18	2.
at 4	6	08	1	11	3	16	2.
at 5	0	07	3	11	2	15	2.
at 5	6	07	0	10	2	14	0.
at 6	0	06	2	10	0	13	0.
at 6	6	06	0	09	2	12	2.

and ſo proportionably : under the penaltie of forfeiting all ſuch bread as ſhall not be of the ſeverall aſſizes as is aforementioned to the uſe of the poor of the towne where the offence is committed, and otherwiſe as is heerafter expreſſed: and for the better execution of this preſent Order ; there ſhall be in everie market towne, and all other townes needfull, one or two able perſons annually choſen by each towne, who ſhall be ſworn at the next county Court, or by the next Magiſtrate, unto the faithfull diſcharge of his or their office; who are heerby authorized to enter into all houſes, either with a Conſtable or without where they ſhall ſuſpect or be informed of any bread baked for ſale: & alſo to weigh the ſaid bread as oft as they ſee cauſe: and to ſeize all ſuch as they finde defective.   As alſo to weigh all butter made up for ſale; and bringing unto, or being in the towne or market to be ſolde by weight: which if found light after notice once given ſh ll be forfeited in like manner .   The like penaltie ſhall be for not marking all bread made for ſale.   and the ſayd officer ſhall have one third part of all forfeitures for his paines; the reſt to the poor as aforeſayd. [1646]

Penaltie.

Clerk of market.
Their power.

Butter.

bread not marked.
Clerks fee.

Ballaſt.

It is ordered by this Court and Authoritie therof; that no ballaſt ſhall be taken frõ any towne ſhore by any perſon whatſoever without allowance under the hands of the ſelect men upon the penalty of ſixpence for every ſhovel-full ſo taken; unles ſuch ſtones as they had layd there before.   2 It is alſo ordered by the Authoritie aforeſayd; that no ſhip nor other veſſell ſhall caſt out any ballaſt in the chanel, or other place inconvenient, in any Harbour within this Juriſdiction upon the penaltie of ten pound. [1646-1642]

Penalſie.

Penaltie.

Barratrie.

It is ordered, decreed and by this Court declared; that if any man be proved and

Reproduced by permission of The Huntington Library, San Marino, California

Figure 58.   Price Control in Puritan Massachusetts, 1646.   Facsimile of a page from an early code of laws, showing that thoroughgoing regulation of one sphere of life often accompanies the regulation of other spheres, such as the religious.

economic laws, primarily that of supply and demand. The concept of a
laissez-faire regime as it is expounded today stems largely from *The Wealth
of Nations*, a treatise on political economy directed chiefly against the
principles of mercantilism, by the Scottish moral philosopher Adam Smith
(1723–1790).

There probably has never been a purely laissez-faire government. It is
almost inconceivable that the political leading group—that is, the group that
held the reins of government—would not try to use the institutions of the
government to further its ideas of economic good. Certainly the United
States never had a truly laissez-faire regime, for under this system the
government does not even try to enact a tariff law, whereas the United
States has always had a tariff. Moreover, the American government has
consistently intervened into economic matters in ways other than by a tariff.
However, the importance of possessing a large, as against a small, sphere
of laissez-faire operations is great, for ensuring the flexibility of both the
economic and political systems.

The religious power of government

The religious power of a government may be computed by the scope,
intensity, and domain of its concern in the religious professions, attachments,
and behavior of its citizens. The power of governments with respect to
religion may end in a theocracy, a state religion, the separation of the
church and the state, or state repression of religion. The first three of these
categories comprise a declining scale of governmental interference with
religion; the last actually is a sort of theocracy in reverse.

Theocracy: A theocracy is a form of government in which the church
actually operates the state for the ends of religion, and in which the
principal officers of the church are also the leaders of the government.
There is today no important government that may be termed a theocracy.
Indeed, among all modern countries perhaps only Tibet might be classified
as a theocracy; since its absorption by the Communists it probably has
lost, or will soon lose, its theocratic nature, for it was reported in the
summer of 1954 that the lama, or ruler, had left Tibet for China to receive
his "brain-washing"—Chinese Communist jargon for "purging of all anti-
communist thoughts."

State Religion: A state religion is a religion that is closely associated with
and supported by the state; commonly the state exploits the teachings
of the religion to accomplish political ends. There are many varieties of
institutional arrangements among different state religions. Sometimes, as in
Spain during the sixteenth century, the whole population will be compelled
to hold the state religion, while all other faiths are persecuted. Elsewhere,
as in modern Spain, Sweden, and some Latin American countries, other
faiths will not be officially persecuted but will be discouraged. Governmental positions may be limited to members of the state religion, as in
the New England colonies. Sometimes the salaries of the clergy are paid
by the state, a system prevailing in France from the time of Napoleon
until the present century and in England from the Reformation to the

present day. Yet in England, although there is a state religion, all other faiths are tolerated.

Separation of the Church and the State: Under the system typified by the separation of the church and the state, the religious power of the government is confined to little more than preventing church members from violating commonly accepted principles of law and morality in their religious behavior. The United States is the outstanding example of a country in which church and state are separated. The First Amendment to the Constitution prohibits the American government from establishing a state religion. Although certain American States, notably Massachusetts, possessed state churches for a time after the Constitution was ratified, all have long since discarded these organizations. Furthermore, the American Constitution specifically bans the requirement of any religious oath for holding federal office.

Consequently all religions are officially tolerated. All that any American government, whether national, State, or local, may do with respect to religion is to forbid any person or group of persons to commit, in the name of religion, an act that would constitute a noxious crime under any other circumstances. For instance, there are laws and ordinances against disorderly meetings or assemblies; no church group may plead that the freedom of religion authorizes it to break such a law or ordinance because the meeting is for religious purposes. Under any conditions, however, the American national government has no institutional bond with any religious body.

State Repression of Religion: State repression of religion constitutes a political system in which the state represses, not one, but all religious faiths. It will be seen that such a system actually comprises a sort of theocracy in reverse, for the government that adopts this policy has done so chiefly because it believes that profession of any traditional faith amounts to disloyalty to the state.

The great exponent of this regime in recent times has been the Soviet Union. Under Soviet rule there emerged a government-sponsored organization called the Society of the Militant Godless whose function was to guide the Russian people away from Christianity. It must be remembered, however, that the fundamental doctrine for Soviet Russia, Marxism-Leninism, teaches that Christianity is but one of the many instruments used by the exploiting capitalist group to keep the toiling masses from claiming and enjoying their rights. It should also be borne in mind that the Russian Orthodox Church was a state church under the tsars which the government had employed as one means for controlling the population, and that this church was an immensely wealthy landholder.

Perhaps most important of all, an analysis of Marxism-Leninism as instituted in the USSR reveals that it in many ways partakes of the nature of a religion itself; it has its gods, its saints, its martyrs, its scriptures, and its Satan. Indeed, from one point of view the Communist Party of the Soviet Union is a religious body that has assumed political power. In fact, so far as morality is concerned—using the word in a neutral sense that means neither "good" nor "bad" but strict adherence to a system that teaches a special version of good and bad—the Russians under Communism are one of the most moral people on earth. Hence the Soviet repression of religion might be considered as only one phase in the evolution of a new theocracy, that of Marxism-Leninism governing the Soviet people.

The cultural power of government

The cultural power of government includes the scope, intensity, and domain of governmental intercession into such matters as the arts, sciences, education, ideas, and expression. The terms controlled culture, sponsored culture, and free culture may be used to indicate a decreasing power of the government in cultural activities.

Controlled Culture: Under a controlled culture, the state rigorously controls, or at least endeavors to control, all cultural matters as implements for achieving the ends of the government. The two outstanding instances of such a regime in recent times have been Nazi Germany and Soviet Russia. In Germany, for example, Adolf Hitler decreed that most forms of art were "decadent," and prescribed that only a few types—those that many foreign critics denounced as most banal—merited production in the Nazi Reich. German education likewise was bent to the needs of the regime. The only kind of philosophy permitted was that which exalted the Nazis and clung to the official Nazi philosophy as expounded in Hitler's *Mein Kampf* and by the leading Nazi theorist, Alfred Rosenberg, in his *Myth of the Twentieth Century.*

The Soviet government has paralleled the Nazi in regimenting culture. For example, the noted Russian composer Dmitri Shostakovitch was severely criticized by the government because certain of his musical works did not comply with the official notion of "proletarian music"; indeed, his Fourth Symphony has never been publicly performed, for this reason. The Soviets like the Nazis have converted their educational system into a means for recruiting and training leaders devoted to the Soviet state and its principles. "Soviet science" has even attacked the fundamental theory of biological heredity developed by the Austrian monk Gregory Mendel (1822–1884). Following a Marxist theory, the Soviet government has claimed that heredity may be influenced by environmental conditions.

Sponsored Culture: A government whose position with respect to culture may be viewed as that of a sponsor is one that tends to stimulate artistic production and to influence, but not absolutely command, it to the goals of the state. Many governments of Western Europe and the Americas today sponsor culture. Most, for example, maintain public school systems that teach pupils to pay due and patriotic homage to their governments; at the same time most of the countries permit the existence of private schools, either religious or not, whose teachings are seldom a concern of the government provided that they adhere to the academic standards required by the state of its own schools, and do not exhort disloyalty to the government.

In late years the national government of the United States has paid increasing attention to American public schools. American education was once thought to be the exclusive concern of State and local governments. However, the national government, which for many years did little more than grant the States a certain amount of land for the support of public schools, has begun to finance special educational programs, such as the teaching of agriculture and home economics at the high-school level. This new interest was signalized in 1953 by the creation of a new administrative Department and Cabinet post, the Department of Health, Education, and Welfare.

So far as the promotion of other facets of the national culture are concerned, the states of western Europe have probably been more active than the United States, where much of this promotion has been confided to private citizens and organizations. Even in this area the American government has shown some degree of interest; for it has exempted from federal income taxation the non-profit corporations or foundations, which have contributed vast sums to subsidize the arts and sciences, literature, and education. Finally, the Constitution itself contains one encouragement for culture, by empowering Congress to pass laws for the protection of copyrights.

Free Culture: A free culture would be one in which the state would show little or no interest and over which the state would exercise a minimum of power. Such a condition is inconceivable today, if only because no government can afford to relax its vigilance over its educational system. Moreover, national pride alone will demand that the government show some interest in, and promote to some degree, the artistic and literary creations of the population. Indeed, such has been and is the role of culture in society that a truly free culture would seem possible only in a state without recognizable culture.

Degrees of powers in different spheres

From the preceding discussion one may draw up a rough chart showing the various degrees of power that a government may employ in each of the three fields:

SPHERES OF POWER

Degree	Economic	Religion	Culture	All Spheres
Low	Laissez-faire	Church-state separation	Free culture	"Law and order"
Medium	Regulatory-promotional	State religion	Sponsored culture	Positive state
High	Planned economy	Theocracy	Controlled culture	Totalitarian

In this chart, the term "low" means some general agreement that in a given society the spheres in question are of little concern, involve few regulations, and affect few people. The term "medium" indicates a similar type of agreement that the government is moderately concerned with these matters, that it exercises considerable regimentation, and that roughly half the people in the country fall within the domain of any governmental activity. The term "high" embraces that sort of regime which practices almost total control over most of the activities of most people. Both the brief summary of the activities of American government and a comparison of its interests with those of other governments indicate its general placement. It is on the whole a positive government of the regulatory-promotional type, a somewhat reticent sponsor of culture and one that observes a separation of church and state.

THE LIMITS OF GOVERNMENT ACTIVITY

Although the technical capacity of governments to control thoroughly all spheres of life has greatly increased in the last hundred years, the development of such control is not inevitable, in the sense that human desires and ingenuity cannot restrict it. From its very beginnings the American way of government has experimented beyond all others in ways of limiting the rapid development of governmental activity. Most of these ways are incorporated into the Constitution and the interpretations placed upon it by political leaders in the courts. They are principally (1) the restriction of the powers of the national government to those delegated it by the Constitution, and (2) the rule that neither State nor nation should deprive persons of property without due process of law. Two related but narrower restrictions are the prohibition on State laws impairing the obligations of contracts and the requirement of payment of just compensation when any American government exercises its power of eminent domain —the taking of private property for public use. These are particularly the rights that will be discussed here; they are usually termed "property rights," and they are at issue in the many kinds of activity to be treated in the chapters to follow. However, it will be remembered that to these rights and limits must also be added those that guard against government interferences with freedom of religion and culture, which have been dealt with in earlier chapters. All three kinds of rights—property, political, and judicial—limit government activity or, at the very least, give it a special slant. Moreover, the barriers erected by the law are reinforced by public opinion. American opinion has numerous and strong resistances to government activity, as will be shown in conclusion.

Limits of delegated powers

The national government has powers of limited scope. Both the words of the Constitution and the prevailing opinion of judges and scholars attest to this fact. The Tenth Amendment declares that "The powers not delegated to the United States by the Constitution, nor prohibited by it to the States, are reserved to the States respectively, or to the people." The intent here was to avoid an expansion of federal powers and to permit an extension of State and individual activity. Yet this intent has not been fully borne out. The "reserved powers" Amendment has not proved to be a bulwark against increased federal action. In fact, like the French

Maginot Line its front was most formidable but its flanks were exposed to assault.

The fact is that federal activity has grown principally by way of victories in Congress and through new interpretations by the courts of other clauses of the Constitution—the interstate commerce clause, the taxation clauses, the "necessary and proper" powers clause, and the unmentioned "inherent powers" theory of federal authority. Plainly, when a broad construction was placed upon each of these clauses and theories of the Constitution, new activities might be undertaken by the federal government and justified as delegated powers.

"Substantive" due process

In earlier chapters, due process of law was mentioned in several connections. First it was pointed out that due process of law is a leading element in the principle of constitutionalism; that is, it is one of the cornerstones of the American system of preventing arbitrary, personal rule. Then later it was shown that due process of law is a principle under which the Supreme Court of the United States, in interpreting the Fourteenth Amendment, extended much of the Bill of Rights to the State governments; that is, free speech, free press, and the rights of a fair trial are implied in this phrase and hence must be observed by the State governments. Now, moreover, it should be understood that due process of law has been defined by the federal courts to limit the economic activity of State governments.

The federal courts have understood the proviso that no person shall be deprived of life, liberty, or property, without due process of law, to mean that burdensome State regulations on economic or other activities are unconstitutional. For example, the prohibition of private schools, or their severe restriction, in order to favor public schools, has been judged oppressive of liberty and a violation of due process of law. Until recent years, the Supreme Court was active in striking down attempts of State governments to regulate hours of work, wages, conditions of work, business practices, and prices charged by commercial and industrial enterprises. Many of such State laws fell victim to the due process clause of the Fourteenth Amendment. In a number of these cases, corporations were the beneficiaries of the Court's attitude; they were protected along with individual property-owners because the word "person" in the Amendment was held to include *artificial* persons, which is what legal theory views corporations to be.

In recent years, the federal courts have been more loath to strike down State regulation of business; many forms of regulation such as those limiting the hours of workers are regarded more tolerantly and considered "reasonable." Yet, if a State government should engage in some drastic interference with business, it is likely that the courts would again strike down the State law as a violation of the guarantee of due process of law. In general, the same reasoning can be applied to actions of the *federal* government; onerous and "unreasonable" regulations upon private business, even if they do not violate other constitutional rights, may be deemed unconstitutional for depriving persons of property without due process of law. In the cases of both the State and federal government, this kind of protection under the requirement of due process of law is called *substantive*, in contrast to the *procedural* protection given in court trials by the same requirement.

"Equal protection"

The Fourteenth Amendment also declares that no State shall deny to persons within its jurisdiction "the equal protection of the laws." This guarantee has come to be understood as demanding the same kind of "fairness" in controlling business as is granted by the due process guarantee. Generally speaking, any "shocking" discrimination against a particular business or class of business is likely to be considered a denial of the equal protection of the laws. However, any "reasonable" or administratively "necessary" distinctions among classes or types of business are regarded as constitutional. The quotation marks around the words "shocking," "reasonable," and "necessary" mean that these words are difficult to define and that the courts have the duty and power of defining them; nevertheless, it should be realized that their vagueness does not prevent them from warding off many potential and actual State laws and rules aimed at governing business and limiting property rights.

The obligation of contracts

Although Congress is not restricted in this manner, the State governments are denied the power to pass any law impairing the obligation of contracts. This constitutional provision has prevented State governments in a number of instances from taking the side of debtors against creditors. Today, it is true, the Supreme Court is more tolerant of State attempts to lessen the burdens of debtors during hard times; yet the degree of lessening is carefully watched, so that if it appears that a law will allow a substantial evasion of a private contract it will be declared unconstitutional. Furthermore, contracts that are against the public safety and morals are not granted protection against State prohibitions. Two men who have contracted to control the milk supply of a city cannot have their contract protected should the State forbid such agreements as being conspiracies.

Just compensation

The government has eminent domain; that is, it has the right to take private property for public use. This is a doctrine of law that is almost universally adhered to. In the United States, the doctrine has two narrowing limits: there must be reasonableness in the demand for the property; and the owner must receive "just compensation." For example, a vengeful Congress or legislature cannot simply decide that the government should own all mansions containing over fifteen rooms, even if it pays liberally for the transfer of rights. On the other hand, in the event that a road is being constructed on a line that traverses several such mansions, the properties may be "condemned" and, upon the payment of just compensation, be torn down to allow passage of the road. Moreover, should the government in time of war be pressed for hospital and rehabilitation buildings, it might perhaps take the entire famed collection of mansions at Newport, Rhode Island, upon payment of just compensation. The amount of compensation that is "just" is often not what the owners think is "just," but first what the government believes is "just"; then, should the owners launch a legal protest, the amount becomes what the courts say is "just."

Public opinion and government activity

Upon a review of the several kinds of restrictions that are placed upon the growth of government activities, several facts emerge. The most important legal limit to federal activity is the construction placed upon the powers delegated to the federal government by the Constitution. The most important limit upon the economic activities of the State governments comes from the due process clause of the Fourteenth Amendment (and of course the fact that the States are prevented from acting in areas over which the federal government has exclusive control, such as interstate commerce). Other constitutional protections of property, such as those provided under the rights of contract and just compensation, are directed principally at blocking arbitrary special actions.

The laws cited are sufficient neither in themselves nor all together to prevent a government of minimal activity from becoming very active. However, the laws do not stand alone. They do have considerable force in themselves, but they are also fortified by the many other ways in which both federal and State constitutions exhibit a profound respect for private property and free enterprise. In addition, the political leaders of the nation and State, on the whole, have from the very beginning of the nation been committed to free enterprise and opposed to socialism. Furthermore, at times when one segment of the leadership—a majority of Congress, or a President, or a political party, or a single State government—was most bent upon increasing the scope, weight, and domain of government intervention in the economy, that element met with resistance and hostility from one or more other powerful elements in the leadership. To take only the most recent and well-known example, President Truman's Fair Deal Program, which would have expanded the activities of the federal government, excited opposition in Congress and failed almost completely.

The principal increase in government activity has occurred since 1900. The machine age, wars, and depressions have caused most of the increase. The emergence of the factory system after the Civil War had by 1900 aroused a demand that persists today, calling for the national government to provide goods and services once supplied by private groups or local authorities. By 1900 the older "liberal" philosophy of the laissez-faire state had been elbowed aside by a political theory requiring a positive and active state. Each of the two world wars has introduced numerous functions associated with the waging of hostilities, and left behind it such concerns as the management of veterans' affairs that are the inescapable residue of military struggle. The great depression that began in 1929 evoked public insistence that the federal government bring relief to the suffering, recovery to business, and reform to the entire national economy.

Probably the beliefs of the many groups and people who make up the American public are not fixed on the question of "how much government." From decade to decade, year to year, and even from month to month, there are large changes in popular opinion regarding the virtues of a high level of government activity in general or of government intervention on a specific issue. Table 17 gives an example of change through time, showing that more Americans favored government ownership of the banks in the period before World War II than did so following the war.

TABLE 17.   AMERICAN OPINION ON WHETHER THE GOVERNMENT SHOULD OWN THE BANKS 1936–1946[1]

Date of Poll[2]	Yes	No, Leave Alone	Undecided, Don't Know	Total
(a) November, 1936	36%	56%	8%	100%
(a) December, 1936	37	49	14	100
(a) July, 1937	45	40	15	100
(b) August, 1937	40	42	18	100
(c) May, 1945	27	61	12	100
(d) September, 1945	25	64	11	100
(e) December, 1946	26	66	8	100

[1] From surveys of a national sample of Americans by the American Institute of Public Opinion, in Cantril, Hadley, and Strunk, Mildred (eds.), *Public Opinion, 1935–1946* (Princeton: Princeton University Press, 1951), p. 272.

[2] The precise wording of the question in each case was as follows:

(a) Do you favor government ownership of banks?

(b) Would you like to have the government own and control the banks?

(c) Do you believe the government should own the banks?

(d) Do you think the government should own the banks in this country?

(e) Do you think the United States government should own the banks in this country?

On the whole, over the past generation, large majorities of Americans have apparently favored social security measures, old-age pensions, job insurance, health insurance, aid for students, public works, relief in times of unemployment, and assistance to the sick and the young. A sizable proportion (depending on the issue) seems to favor government regulation of many businesses; and a minority is generally to be found supporting outright national ownership and operation of one or more businesses now in private hands.[1]

In 1952, a year in which power was transferred from a Democratic to a Republican administration in Washington, the public's appetite for more government activity exceeded its inclinations against greater activity; the two together did not quite equal the number of people who were satisfied with the present degree of government activity. A sample of Americans had this question put to them:

---

[1] Cf. the summaries presented in Cantril and Strunk, and also Bruner, Jerome S., *Mandate from the People* (New York: Duell, Sloane and Pearce, 1944), Part II.

Some people think the national government should do more in trying to deal with such problems as unemployment, education, housing, and so on. Others think that the government is already doing too much. On the whole, would you say that what the government has done has been about right, too much, or not enough?

The replies are presented in Table 18.

TABLE 18. BELIEFS ABOUT THE LEVEL OF GOVERNMENT ACTIVITY, 1952[1]

Extent of Government Activity	Number	Per Cent
Not enough	447	25
About right	878	49
Too much	322	18
Don't know	106	6
Not ascertained	46	2
Total	1,799	100

[1] From author's analysis of Survey Research Center Materials (Study 400).

The heavy weight of opinion, at that time at least, supported the existing level of national government functions. Under such circumstances, there is little incentive for any large number of political leaders to move vigorously to add to or cut government activities. Most changes are what might be called technical adjustments; for example, new groups of people are brought in under the Social Security Act, or various agencies receive budget cuts in the name of economy.

Yet, in conclusion, it should be repeated that this generally accepted level of government activity is by no means low. Though the level may be stable, and no longer controversial to most people, it is greatly above the level experienced by the fathers of modern college students when they themselves were of college age in the early 1930's. In turn, the level around 1930 was greatly higher than in 1900 or any previous time since 1789.

QUESTIONS AND PROBLEMS

1. Name ten specific functions of the national government in each of the following areas: law enforcement; health, education, and welfare; conservation of natural resources; business.

2. Following the method of Figure 57, as described in the text, prepare as best you can a series of bar charts that picture the degree of government intervention in *your* spheres of interest.

3. Describe briefly the characteristics of a laissez-faire government. How does it differ from a regulatory state and a planned economy?

4. Describe briefly the characteristics of a state religion. How does it differ from the condition in which state and church are separated and from a theocracy?

5. Describe briefly a culture controlled by the state. How does it differ from a sponsored culture and from a free culture?

6. What are the restrictions on the taking of private property for public use?

7. Assuming that the United States is at present a positive state, does the

country show any tendencies toward becoming a "law and order" state or a "totalitarian" state? Explain your answer.

8. What are the constitutional restrictions on the amount of economic activity in which the national government may engage?

9. What are the constitutional limits on the intervention of the American government into the sphere of religion and culture?

10. What are some of the limits, other than legal ones, to the intervention of the American government into the spheres of economics, religion, and culture?

11. Distinguish between the substantive and the procedural protections of the requirement of due process of law. Give an example of each.

12. Relating Table 17 back to what was learned of public opinion in Chapter 11, how would you explain the fluctuations in opinion as to whether the government should own the banks?

13. Under what circumstances could there occur a large rise in public demand for new or increased government activities?

DEPARTMENTS, non-departmental executive agencies, and commissions comprise the administrative branch of the federal government. That is to say, they administer the laws enacted by Congress; they do the actual work of governing. Moreover, they have large grants of authority from Congress and from the President; the powers they receive through these grants are so important as almost to make independent branches of government out of some large agencies. The vast array of these organizations testifies to the scope of the tasks carried out by the government (see Figure 59), and their extensive growth demonstrates how the people have come to expect a greater and greater number of services from the government. In 1789, the administrative organization was quite small, numbering only a few hundreds of employees; today it contains over two million persons in almost as many professions and trades as exist in private business.

SIZE OF THE ADMINISTRATIVE ESTABLISHMENT

The last chapter has revealed the sources and causes of many new government functions. Each new activity demands new personnel to administer it. Figure 65, on page 497, shows the number of civilian employees of the executive branch of government and the increase that was registered between 1884 and 1955, a period of seventy years. The number of *federal* government civilian and military employees has risen faster than the total number of workers in the nation; this fact is depicted in Figure 60. Finally, the relative size of the larger agencies of the government are pictured in Figure 61. One great agency, the Civil Service Commission, is created solely to manage part of the work of recruiting and controlling these employees; its work will be described in the next chapter.

There are many other evidences of the great volume of federal administrative work. The office space occupied by the many agencies takes up the equivalent of thirty-six Empire State Buildings. The records of the government alone consume twenty-four million cubic feet of space; if brought together they would fill an office building twenty stories high with a frontage and depth of about 280 feet. Aside from the tons of paper that go into pamphlets, manuals, bound volumes, packaging, and signs, twenty-five billion sheets of paper are used by the government each year. Government offices produce one billion letters annually. In 1912, fifty-five letters were mailed out for every federal employee; in 1953, 522 letters per employee were sent. For keeping each other informed, for overseeing their field work and subordinate offices, and for checking on the activities of business, federal agencies require 131,700 reports. The agencies demand about 100,000 reports annually in their internal work; they require 25,000 reports of field activities; they process 2,000 reports from one agency to another; and they demand 4,700 reports from commerce and industry. All these estimates were made by the Hoover Commission on Organization of the Executive Branch of Government from 1953 to 1955.

Comparisons with other great organizations

Probably the only administrative body in the world whose size exceeds that of the American federal government is that of the Soviet Union. In complexity, however, it is likely that any large nation of modern times has an equally staggering task of management. Moreover, so far as other types of institutions are concerned, the Roman Catholic Church has for centuries administered an enterprise just as challenging, conducting its operations in many different countries and often without the power to tax. Furthermore, a number of modern American business concerns are huge and complicated, with dozens of factories, offices throughout the world, and a large variety of products.

It is interesting to note the many parallels that exist among large concerns of all kinds, public and private. The problems of large-scale enterprise beset them both. For example, it is often believed that government management invariably is overwhelmed by paperwork, whereas private industry is unhampered by red tape. Yet recent studies cited by the Hoover Commission contrasting three private firms with the federal government

A New Department Chief Moves into the Open Air to Reach Personally His Hundreds of Employees. John Foster Dulles, shortly after he became Secretary of State in 1953, addressed a gathering of civil servants to introduce his new assistants and relate his administrative policies.

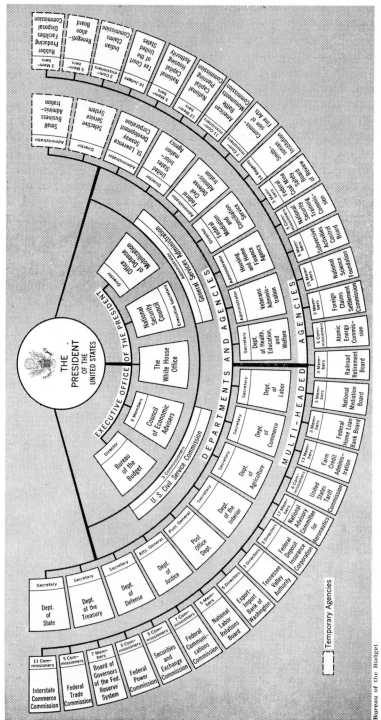

Figure 59. Executive Branch of the Government.

Bureau of the Budget

showed that government files were no more burdensome than private business files.

The General Services Administration

In the last few years, an agency has been created especially to provide over-all custody of, control of, and responsibility for problems of storage, paperwork, and purchasing. This is the General Services Administration (GSA), an organization that merits particular note at this point. The GSA, created in 1949, is one of the largest, most important, and least known of all federal administrative bodies. With more than 25,000 employees, the GSA has a payroll larger than that of any other independent agency except the Veterans' Administration. The Federal Supply Service in the GSA is the central purchasing agency for the whole national government; it also fixes standards and specifications for purchasing. The Emergency Procurement Service buys the goods that the government is stockpiling against the chance of war. The Public Buildings Service manages buildings owned by the federal government, and supervises the design and construction of new federal buildings. The National Archives and Records Service preserves the many documents of the federal government, and publishes constitutional Amendments, acts of Congress, executive orders, presidential proclamations, and administrative regulations. The chief executive of the GSA is the Administrator, who is appointed by the President and confirmed by the Senate.

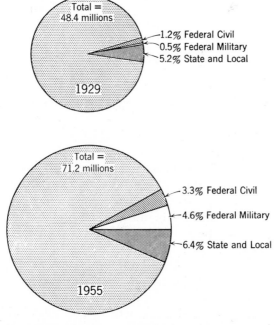

Figure 60. Percentage of Government Employees to Total National Employment, 1929 and 1955.

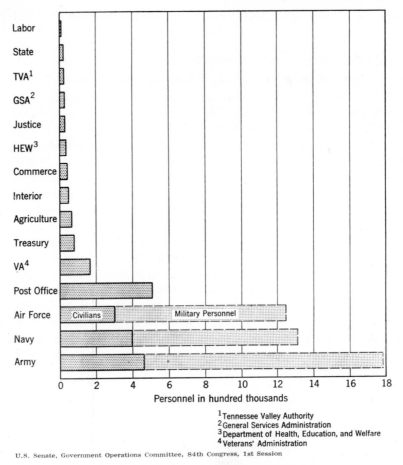

Figure 61. Number of Personnel in Selected Federal Agencies, January 1, 1955.

TYPES OF ADMINISTRATIVE BODIES

When an ordinary person thinks of the kind of organization that does large tasks in modern times, he is likely to think first of a corporation, so common is the corporation in business and economic life today. Yet the government does a host of things and usually does not accomplish them through corporations. In fact, there were only twenty-three agencies in 1955, among the several hundred in the government, that resembled strongly the well-known form of the private corporation. Of these, only seven were in fact leading separate and independent existences outside of any other government agency. The balance were inside a parent agency. The most famous government corporation is the Tennessee Valley Authority.

Government corporations are created by Congress and are given an initial sum of money to start their activities, together with a Board of Directors to guide them; they are free from direct control of the President, who merely appoints the Board members for fixed terms of office. Their financial affairs are watched by Congress. Also, like a private corporation, they issue stock, but all their stock is owned by the federal government. The reason why they are organized as corporations is that they are performing tasks, such as manufacturing electric power and operating the Panama Canal, that resemble the activities of private companies (although, for that matter, other government agencies, such as the Army Corps of Engineers, also perform tasks similar to those of private companies).

However, the corporate form is used to carry out only a few of the many activities of the federal government. The bulk of government functions is administered by three other types of major administrative bodies that lie outside of the Executive Office of the President.

There are sixty-six such separate administrative bodies in the federal government that are neither independent corporations nor part of the Executive Office of the President. (Some of the less important of these are omitted from Figure 59.) Of these, ten are Departments, nine are non-departmental executive agencies, and forty-seven are independent commissions (or boards). The fact that these three types are called by different terms conceals a great amount of similarity in their organization and operations. The simplest distinction among the three relates to the top figures of the agencies: the Departments have chiefs who are members of the Cabinet; the separate administrative bodies are organized like Departments save that their chiefs are not Cabinet members; and the independent commissions are headed by boards or commissions of several members, none of whom belong to the Cabinet. An example of the first type is the Department of Agriculture; of the second, the Veterans' Administration; and, of the third, the Interstate Commerce Commission.

A second distinction has to do with the relations of these leaders to the President. The Department chiefs and the non-departmental executive agency chiefs are appointed by the President, with the approval of the Senate, and may be removed by him whenever he pleases. The members of the independent commissions are appointed by the President, with the approval of the Senate, but serve for fixed terms of office and otherwise cannot be removed by the President, except for certain causes stated by Congress in statutes governing the agencies. These fixed terms are also overlapping, so that no board or commission may have its entire membership changed at the same time.

A third distinction among the three types of agencies is one that is not at all clear and is only partly true. That is, whereas the President, in the course of running the executive branch of the government, may direct the actions of the chiefs of Departments and non-departmental agencies at will, he has much control over the operations of some of the independent commissions but little control over the operations of others. An example of an independent commission over which the President exercises considerable control is the Civil Service Commission. An example of the contrary is the Federal Trade Commission.

However, regarding this third partial distinction, an additional fact must be remembered. At different periods of time, the personnel of the boards or commissions may come under different degrees of control by the President. Such variations may be due to laws of the Congress that change the relations between the agencies and the President; they may also be due to a coincidence of philosophy between a board and a President at a given moment. For instance, the Federal Trade Commission, when F. D. Roosevelt took office, was unfriendly to his policies, but, owing to his appointments over a period of time, became friendly to his ideas.

A fourth distinction among the three types of agencies concerns their function; this, especially, is a questionable distinction. Whereas the Departments and non-departmental executive agencies are supposedly engaged in operations of a hard-and-fast executive kind, those of the independent commissions are supposedly legislative, judicial, or advisory—as well as executive—in character.

It was, indeed, for this reason that Congress gave the form of boards and commissions to the top leadership of these latter agencies; Congress felt that a panel of "legislators" or "judges" or "experts" was called for to make "non-partisan" or "bipartisan" decisions on the matters entrusted to them by law. However, Departments and non-departmental executive agencies also exercise the same kinds of semi-legislative and semi-judicial powers, though perhaps not to so great an extent as the independent commissions. For example, in 1955, the Secretary of the Department of Health, Education, and Welfare, working through her subordinates, made rules regarding the standards of purity and excellence of the Salk anti-polio vaccine that had to be observed by all pharmaceutical firms. This ruling had no less force than a ruling by the Federal Communications Commission regarding the proportion of time that a television station must devote to public service programs.

Furthermore, the independent commissions frequently engage in the same kind of hard-and-fast executive work as do the other agencies. Much of the work of the Securities and Exchange Commission consists of registering stocks and bonds that are to be sold by stock and bond brokers, just as the Department of Agriculture carries on research in the improvement of livestock.

Also, within some Departments and non-departmental executive agencies, such as the Department of Commerce and the Veterans' Administration, are situated various boards to manage appeals and other types of judicial and legislative matters that the independent commissions also deal with. For example, one finds in the Department of Commerce the Board of Appeals in the Patent Office; this Board consists of the Commissioner of Patents, his assistants and nine Examiners-in-Chief. They hear and judge appeals from persons who have been denied patents. A similar board is the Board of Veterans' Appeals in the Veterans' Administration.

Hence, all three types of bodies, despite their different top structures, perform tasks of a similar nature—they execute programs of work, "legislate" or make rules, judge cases or "adjudicate," and give advice to Congress and the President. However, they do so in differing amounts and through different structures.

Beyond these distinctions (and similarities) thus far discussed, it is important to realize that there are additional fundamental resemblances in the work of all these bodies. Owing to these resemblances, the balance of this chapter can be concerned with some of the problems and features of administration in general. This can be done in the knowledge that what is said is true of all types of agencies.

THE CHAIN OF COMMAND

Supposedly public administrative organizations constitute a pyramidal body from the executive chief at the apex to the production workers at the base, with lines of control running down and lines of responsibility extending up. Figure 62 pictures a typical scheme for organizing a large-

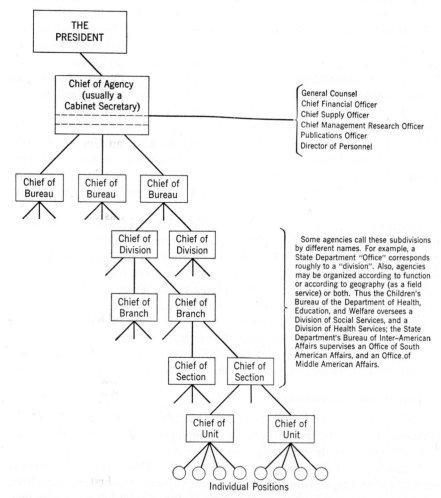

Figure 62. Typical Organization of a Federal Department. This same type of organization is found in a great many public and private enterprises throughout the world.

scale government agency. Public administration in the United States, however, betrays many deviations from this ideal. Theoretically the President is the executive head of the entire national government; yet, as has already been noted, the President does not directly control the independent agencies, nor are they absolutely responsible to him. Hence these agencies must at the outset be excluded from the pyramid. The Departments under the President do approximate more closely the theoretical structure; the Secretaries are generally under the control of the President. Within the agencies and Departments one encounters the chain of command again. In all Departments and in most agencies, authority moves from the top post down to the lower echelons.

Administrative chiefs

Each Department has a single chief, usually called the Secretary; the non-departmental executive agency chiefs are called usually a Director or Administrator; independent commissions are managed by several persons in a commission or board. Immediately below the chiefs of all types of agencies comes usually an assistant chief who may be an Under Secretary, an Assistant Administrator, or a General Manager or Director in the case of a commission. Also sometimes in commissions, the Chairman will become the chief executive of the will of the board or commission. In most of the Departments, immediately below the Secretary is an Under Secretary, who is the deputy of the Secretary; that is to say, he serves as Secretary in the absence of the latter. Under Secretaries sometimes become Secretary; Dean Acheson was Under Secretary of State before becoming Secretary. However, most Under Secretaries cannot safely anticipate this sort of promotion.

Beneath these two chiefs, and responsible to both of them, there normally are several Assistant Secretaries. Each Assistant Secretary customarily supervises one of the major branches or functions of the Department. For instance, in the Department of Agriculture there are four Assistant Secretaries: one each for Federal-States Relations, Marketing and Foreign Agriculture, Agricultural Stabilization, and Departmental Administration. The Under Secretary and the Assistant Secretaries, like the Secretary, are political appointees; in recent years, however, there has been an increasing tendency to name as Assistant Secretaries only persons who have some knowledge and training in the function they are to manage.

Administrative subdivisions

All Departments and most independent agencies contain a scale of subdivisions descending to the individual employee. The first level of subordinate grouping is generally called the *bureau*, although expressions such as *office* and *division* are sometimes used. The next inferior level is usually called the *division,* although again various other terms have been substituted. Depending upon the size of the establishment, there may be one or more subordinate ranks down to the unit worker. Agencies are also subdivided geographically, in that many of them operate offices

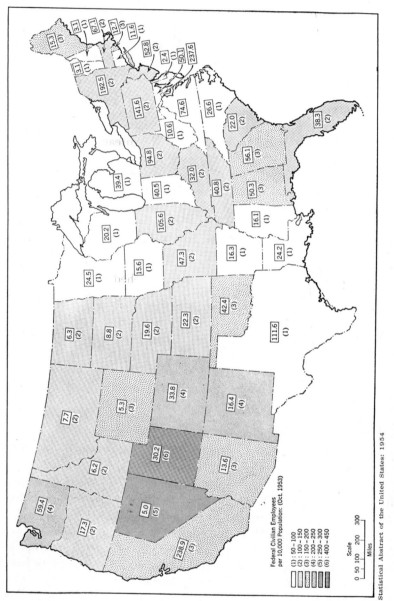

Statistical Abstract of the United States: 1954

Figure 63. Distribution of Federal Employees in the Several States: Total Number and Number per 10,-000 Population. Maryland and Virginia are unmarked because part of each is included in metropolitan Washington, D.C. Number in box is total of federal civilian employees (thousands omitted).

throughout the country; indeed, most federal employees work in the field, as Figure 63 discloses.

The chiefs at the bureau level customarily are the highest-ranking career officers; that is to say, neither their appointment nor their dismissal can arise from partisan political considerations. Theoretically, at this level there is an arbitrary line separating the policy-forming executives above from the non-policy-forming officers beneath; since bureau chiefs are presumed to be non-policy-forming, they hold their posts in spite of changes in the party control of Congress and of the presidency. The fact is that bureau chiefs are policy-forming only to a lesser degree than the executives superior to them. For example, a Secretary must rely upon his bureau chiefs for the information needed to make regulations; what information the bureau chiefs decide to submit, and the emphases they place upon it, play a great role in determining the contents of the regulations formulated by the Secretary. It is thus possible for an entrenched group of bureau chiefs to hamper the policy aims of the Secretary; this is especially true when, as sometimes happens, a bureau chief is a good friend of a congressman who is a member of the congressional committee that deals with the administrative organ concerned. Under such circumstances the ideal lines of control and responsibility are either very weak or even totally nonexistent.

THE POLITICAL AND LEGAL TOOLS OF ADMINISTRATIVE BODIES

Administrative bodies have certain political and legal means of carrying out their functions. These appear in such activities as influencing the President and Congress, informing people about the law, watching for violations of the law, prosecuting violations, and promulgating rules for individuals and groups.

The administrative legislative process

This text has already described two types of legislative process. One is the fundamental, congressional process dictated by the Constitution, whereby a bill is inspired, introduced, and enacted in the halls of the Senate and the House. (See Figure 47.) The second is the presidential legislative process, in which the initiation and the promotion of a bill emanated from the White House. (See Figure 40.) Besides these there is also the administrative legislative process, in which an administrative agency conceives a notion respecting legislation and works to have its notion enacted into law. (See Figure 64.) One of the clearest descriptions of this process appears in the *Foreign Service News Letter* of February 15, 1955, a publication of the Department of State:

> What does it take to get a bill through Congress and enacted into law? The answer to this question is not a simple one. The process is long and tedious, with the attrition rate on bills introduced in Congress extremely high.
> Actually, the [State] Department is in a better position than the average

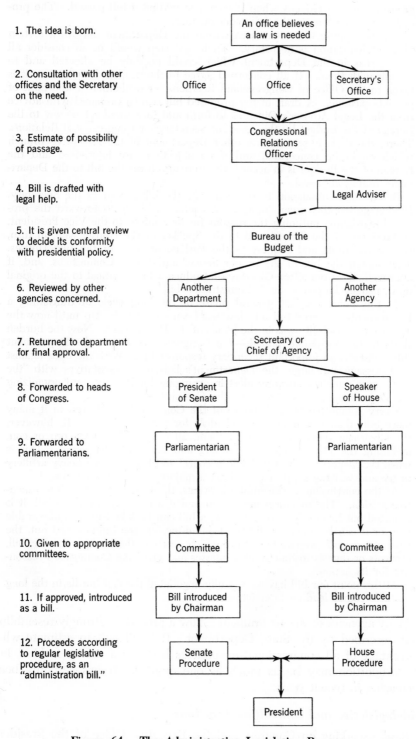

1. The idea is born.

2. Consultation with other offices and the Secretary on the need.

3. Estimate of possibility of passage.

4. Bill is drafted with legal help.

5. It is given central review to decide its conformity with presidential policy.

6. Reviewed by other agencies concerned.

7. Returned to department for final approval.

8. Forwarded to heads of Congress.

9. Forwarded to Parliamentarians.

10. Given to appropriate committees.

11. If approved, introduced as a bill.

12. Proceeds according to regular legislative procedure, as an "administration bill."

Figure 64.   The Administrative Legislative Process.

group of private citizens when it comes to getting a bill passed. The procedure might occur in the following manner:

Let us suppose that some area within the Department decides a certain piece of legislation is necessary. Their first step would be to consider all other areas in the Department which could possibly be affected and to consult with them. If all concerned agree to the proposed legislation, it is taken to the Office of Congressional Relations for evaluation in the light of possible passage. A draft of the proposed bill is then prepared with advice. from the Legal Adviser's Office as to form and forwarded for review to the Bureau of the Budget by the Assistant Secretary for Congressional Relations. There, the draft is sent to any other Department of the Executive Branch which might be concerned, and if no objections are interposed and the Bureau of the Budget is in accord, the Bureau returns the bill to the Department, noting approval.

Before final submission to the Congress the bill is sent to the Secretary. Having gotten this green light, the Secretary is ready to forward the proposed legislation, outlining the reasons for its request, to the Vice President, as President of the Senate, and to the Speaker of the House, who, in turn, submit the draft and request to the Parliamentarians of the two Houses. They assign the bill to the proper Senate and House Committees, and, if approved, the Committee Chairmen introduce a bill identical to the original draft, usually known as an "administration bill."

At this point the first general phase of the long cycle of translating a Department-sponsored bill into law has been completed. Up until now the primary responsibility was in the hands of the Department. Now the burden shifts to the legislative branch—the Congress. However, the Department still maintains an important secondary responsibility. With the odds against final passage still large, the Department's liaison representatives with "the Hill" must remain constantly alert in arranging for hearings and organizing the Department's presentation to the Committee.

Every committee of each house of the Congress has referred to it many more bills than it can possibly schedule for public hearings. If, however, the Chairman determines to hold them, all interested parties, pro or con, including the Department, are notified and invited to be heard. This is when the Department has its "day in court" and brings up its heavy artillery to try and win the support of at least a majority of the Committee.

At the conclusion of the public hearings, the Committee goes into executive session. The members are polled and if a majority favor the bill, it is reported out favorably. At this state, a bill can be killed by an unfavorable vote or it can be amended by the Committee. If the bill is voted out, the Committee staff prepares a report which sets out the reasons for the bill, excerpts or digests testimony of witnesses and gives the Committee's reasoning for its action.

At this point our bill has successfully negotiated the first hurdle in the long obstacle course leading to enactment.

Many agencies of the government follow a procedure strongly resembling that described by the State Department. It is difficult to estimate what percentage of all congressional enactments begin in a similar fashion, but the proportion may be as much as one quarter. It has certainly been increasing in recent years.

Sub-legislative and controlling functions

Beside working on Congress and the Executive Office of the President so as to alter the powers of their agencies, administrators must also carry out the decisions of their agencies, through the various means they have for influencing the American people. However, in any given circumstance, the administrator usually does not have a wide latitude in selecting the means for implementing his powers; rather, the means most often have already been fixed by Congress in establishing the administrative body. Where some range of choice is permitted, the administrator is apt to choose the means that will bring about his decision in the most efficient manner, yet will inflict the least possible discomfort on the people concerned.

Just what means are used also may depend upon what sort of relations the agency has with the people. For instance, the State Department has little direct impact upon American citizens; save with respect to those wishing to go overseas or already overseas, it needs to concern itself little with implementing its powers so far as Americans are involved. By comparison, there are agencies, such as the General Services Administration, that do not command the American people, but by buying huge quantities of materials have an impact on thousands of businessmen and workers. Finally, there are bodies, such as the Post Office Department, that carry out a direct service for the people. These distinctions in relations are tied in with the kind of means used.

Statement of Policy: The statement of policy is an effort to persuade the people to comply with a general line of behavior, without any punitive force against disobedience. Most high administrative officials upon assuming office issue statements of policy, such as the presidential State of the Union message. Another type of policy statement is illustrated by the declared embargo on trade with Japan before the Second World War, for which no penalties were established in the event of violations. The statement of policy tends to seek public cooperation, to appeal to a kind of "team spirit," without announcing any compulsion.

Education and Publicity: Education and publicity are somewhat more specific than a statement of policy, although they too contain no punitive machinery. They are likely to be more definite, to be concentrated upon single issues; and they are frequently delivered to only one section of the population. For example, the Department of Agriculture publishes a vast amount of literature about different farm procedures that the government would like to have adopted. The Department of Health, Education, and Welfare publicizes old age and survivors insurance, to convince people in the affected trades and professions that it is advantageous to them. Education and publicity may also strive for ends that are negative. The Federal Trade Commission, for instance, by noting so-called "unfair trade practices" may be recommending that people refuse to deal with certain business organizations.

Licensing: Licensing is a considerably stronger means for control than those described above. The government may require that any enterprise secure a license before it goes into business; and the government may establish the conditions that must be satisfied before the license will be granted. Licensing is a more important function for State and local authorities than it is for the national government; and for the lesser units, licensing, such as automobile registration, is a major source of revenue as well as a device for administrative control. However, on the national level, the Federal Communications Commission obliges every commercial radio broadcasting station first to secure a license; it may withdraw this license, or refuse to renew it, if the station can be shown guilty of certain practices; and the Commission may invoke the law in the event the station persists in operating without a license.

Rule-Making: Rule-making constitutes an administrative form of sub-legislation. Congress in creating the administrative body may authorize it to issue rules in the area of its competence. In recent decades Congress has relieved itself of a great amount of work by conferring this authority upon administrative agencies; it has neither the time nor the capability to make many of the rules essential for implementing policy. For example, Congress has empowered the ICC to fix the rates that railroads may charge for transporting freight, requiring only that the rates be "just and reasonable"; for Congress realizes that it alone could not find time to master the data on which the rates should be based. It is in the field of rule-making that a salient difference between Departments and independent agencies is revealed: rules made by the Departments are subject to reversal by the President, but rules made by independent agencies are not. It is for this reason that the interest groups associated with a phase of administration may urge that Congress create an independent agency, so as to avoid what amounts to a presidential veto on administrative rules. The intention to make a rule must be published in the *Federal Register,* and interested persons are allowed to testify in behalf of, or in opposition to, the proposed rule, much as in a hearing of a congressional committee.

Adjudication: Adjudication constitutes a subordinate form of judicial power enjoyed by many administrative bodies, especially certain of the independent agencies. The power of adjudication is employed in cases of disputes among private citizens, or between private citizens and the agency, arising over the rules issued by the administrative agency concerned. When the administrators discover that a rule has in fact been violated, they can impose specific penalties upon the violators.

It is particularly in the exercise of this power that the agencies betray the absence of the separation of powers in their functioning; for the same agency that has devised (legislative power) and enforced (executive power) these rules now undertakes to hear cases (judicial power) respecting violations of them. Moreover, officials of the same body both prosecute and render decisions in these cases; this proceeding should be contrasted with the typical federal court hearing, in which the prosecutor represents not the judicial, but the executive, branch of the government.

Partly in an effort to correct the results of this commingling of powers, Congress in 1946 passed the Administrative Procedure Act. This Act requires that the officials preparing cases involving infractions of the rules take no part in judging them; or, in other words, the Act separates prosecuting from judging. The Act also compels agencies to abide by certain concepts of normal juridical procedure; for instance, it states that every person testifying in a case shall be allowed counsel, and that all witnesses may be cross-examined. Doubtless the agencies hear many cases that the constitutional courts would refuse to take under their jurisdiction. At the same time, the courts have manifested great jealousy of administrative adjudication, and have often sought to remove cases from the authority of these agencies when the courts suspected that due process of law was being neglected.

CONTROLS OVER ADMINISTRATION

Administration has been frequently taxed with irresponsibility. It is true that some administrative bodies, especially the independent agencies, have from time to time won virtual immunity from control by other governmental units. Yet there are important means for the control of administration, which fall into four broad classes: administrative (or internal), legislative, judicial, and popular.

Administrative, or internal, controls

Controls within the Administrative Hierarchy: Administration is subject to a great number of controls from its own agents and officials. In a great number of cases, perhaps the most important control is the will of the individual employee that he perform his duties efficiently. Since administration is a hierarchical structure, higher officials may impose various instruments of discipline upon their subordinates, ranging from reprimand or censure to suspension or dismissal. It is true that on the lower levels the use of these instruments is restricted, since few employees at these levels may be disturbed in their employment for reasons of policy. However, on the higher levels administrators may be dismissed, or their resignations asked, for reasons of policy. Thus, for example, President Jackson needed to discharge two Secretaries of the Treasury before he could find one (Roger Taney) who would deal with the Bank of the United States as Jackson saw fit. In more recent times, President Truman secured the resignation of Secretary of Commerce Wallace for expressing views on foreign policy that conflicted with those of the White House.

Controls through Presidential Appointments: The appointive power is also a major implement of control. It is quite evident how the President can use this power with respect to the Departments. Congress, however, sought to protect the independent agencies from control by presidential appointment by fixing long and overlapping terms for commission members, and by requiring in the case of all important agencies that their membership be bipartisan. Yet, as has been seen, partisanship is not necessarily defined by party labels; some Republicans are closer philosophically to some Democrats than they are to some other Republicans. Hence a President through two or three appointments may, although adhering to the law, completely alter the principles dominating the work of the agency. On the lower levels, of course, the Civil Service Commission regulates almost all appointments.

Legislative controls

Congress has broad controls over administrative bodies. However, so far as policy-making is concerned, these controls have somewhat decreased in the past fifty years, as Congress has conceded to the President some of its initiative and renounced some of its detailed supervision of the agencies. For example, Congress has lately adopted the practice of granting funds for certain activities to the Defense Department for periods longer than one year. Furthermore, sometimes in response to the President's wishes and at other times in accordance with its own beliefs, an agency will work in such a way as to modify the general instructions of Congress. The manner of administration can make or break the aim of a statute. For instance, how meaningful are these first few words of a *New York Times* story on December 28, 1954: "The Eisenhower Administration has quietly dropped plans to ask Congress to modify the 'Buy American' Act which requires federal agencies to give preference to United States producers in placing orders. The official explanation is that the impact of the statute has been sufficiently eased by administrative action. . . ."

Yet Congress still creates agencies and endows them with funds for their operations; it wields its financial powers freely, even though committee hearings that concern these operations are certain to be well-populated with administrative officers anxious to testify respecting the needs of their organizations. Congress also may at any time alter the structure of administrative organs, as it did by creating the office of general counsel for the National Labor Relations Board (NLRB), to whom, under the pressure of anti-union interests, it gave sole power to initiate cases.

Congress, furthermore, sets the broad rules according to which administrative bodies shall function, and Congress may fix limits to the rule-making and adjudicating powers of these organizations. The Senate must confirm all appointments to high administrative posts. Congress may impeach the President and the other principal administrative officers; at the same time it can set, and has set, limits upon the removal power of the President with respect to the members of the independent agencies. Congress may also investigate the operations of administrative bodies; for example, a Senate investigation of the Reconstruction Finance Corporation in 1951 disclosed that some of President Truman's aides had brought pressure upon the Corporation to make loans to enterprises in which they were interested.

Judicial controls

The federal judiciary provides additional limits upon the federal administration. The prime concern of the courts with respect to administrative bodies is to insure that their actions are congruent with the rule of law. It should be remembered that Departments and independent agencies possess two types of powers: *ministerial* and *discretionary*. The ministerial powers are those that *must* be exercised; the discretionary powers are those that the administrators *may* exercise according to their own judgment. As an illustration, so far as the Post Office is concerned, the mail must be delivered, for that is a ministerial power; but how many daily deliveries shall be made is at the will of the Postmaster General, for that is a discretionary power. The courts are especially sensitive regarding abuse of discretionary powers.

Courts today cope with a great many cases emerging from a conflict of an individual or company with an administrative body, especially independent commissions. Courts enter a dispute when one party to an administrative controversy, feeling that the decision of an agency has been unjust, appeals his case to a higher tribunal. Courts have various methods for exercising their control. In some cases, the injured party may bring a civil suit; however, today most such cases come before the U.S. Court of Claims. In other cases that have been appealed, the court may issue an injunction forbidding the administrator to carry out an act. Then again, it may issue a writ of *mandamus,* ordering the administrator to exercise some ministerial power. Cases may be brought to the federal Court of Appeals, or even the Supreme Court, under the writ of *certiorari.* Sometimes the courts deal only with questions of law, holding that the administrative body alone is competent to determine the facts, and the court alone capable of establishing the law. Many observers demand that the courts use greater self-restraint to avoid transgressing beyond their competence into the region of fact, pointing out that the jurists may invite a hopeless volume of work if they insist upon retrying questions of fact.

Popular and pressure group controls

The people themselves have controls over administrative bodies. These controls may be either direct or indirect; that is, they can be brought to bear immediately upon the administrators, or they may come by means of public pressure upon Congress to alter some aspect of administrative structure or procedure. Public control may be exercised by one or more individuals who have no specific organization; or it may be implemented through a strong interest group. An interesting combination of pressures, public and otherwise, was imposed upon one administrative body, the Post Office Department, during the years 1953–1955. In 1953 the Post Office began to deliver circular mail (advertisements) bearing no other address than "householder" or "postal route patron" in all private mailboxes. This perhaps was a privilege extended businessmen as a form of subsidy that certain organized business interests had persuaded the Post Office to install. Soon, however, the general public—as an unorganized mass—began increasingly to express resentment at the delivery of this mail. At the same time the union of Post Office employees commenced uttering growing complaints about the added work connected with sorting and delivering this mail. One postman dramatized the situation by throwing away all the circulars he was to distribute on his route—a gesture that was, on a very small scale, an act of administrative policy-making; a judge contributed to the affair by doling out a very lenient punishment for what is ordinarily a serious crime. The Post Office reacted by abruptly terminating this service on April 1, 1955.

Certainly the current practice of admitting all interested persons to a hearing preliminary to the issuance of new administrative rules allows important groups to seek, and even to effect, controls over administrators. It is well to recall that such lobbying of administrators is not subject to as broad regulation as that imposed upon legislative lobbyists. The laws establishing some agencies—among them the Federal Maritime Board—require that lobbyists register with the agencies before attempting to deal with agency officers. However, there is no general law analogous to those provisions of the Legislative Reorganization Act that regulate lobbyists of Congress. The ultimate form of popular control, one that involves both individuals and pressure groups, is the ballot. The voters choose both the President, who is the chief administrator, and Congress, which creates, finances, and empowers all subordinate administrators.

QUESTIONS AND PROBLEMS

1. What are several distinctions commonly to be observed between federal Departments and independent agencies?

2. The independent commissions of government were called by one expert "the headless fourth branch of the government." What would you say in support of his term?

3. How is the General Services Administration organized and what are its functions?

4. Define the following forms of enforcement of the objectives of an agency: publicity; licensing; rule-making; adjudication.

5. How can the President control the operations of the Departments?

6. What controls does Congress exercise over the administrative agencies?

7. In what ways do the courts call administrative agencies to account for their actions?

8. What effects can public opinion have on administrative operations?

U.S.C.S. Commission

THE civil service consists of the men and women who work for the administrative branch of the government. That is to say, it includes the employees of the Departments, the non-departmental executive agencies, and the commissions, from the chiefs at the top to the individual clerks and mechanics at the bottom. All persons on the payroll of the federal government, except those in military uniform and the relatively few who are employed by Congress and the federal courts, regardless of the means by which they obtained their positions are considered members of the civil service.

It must be pointed out at the very first that the federal civil service can be divided into two main classes, and that one of these classes falls into two subclasses. The smaller of the two main classes comprises what might be called the "political" personnel of the government, or the personnel in charge of framing policy—the chiefs of the Departments, agencies, and commissions. The larger of the two main classes includes the "non-political," or "policy-obeying" personnel—the vast number of employees who follow orders and execute commands of the chiefs. The "policy-obeying" per-

493

sonnel may then be divided into those who (1) have been chosen for employment largely on the basis of their party attachments and who may expect to lose their positions should their party fall from power; and those who (2) have secured employment through competence demonstrated in tests, who usually plan to make government work their life career, and whose dismissal for partisan reasons is prohibited by law. The chapter is concerned with the problems facing federal authorities in the matters of procuring these persons who make up the civil service; of placing them in the appropriate offices; and of paying them, disciplining them, training them, promoting them, and determining what part they may play in the whole political process.

TABLE 19. POSTS RECOMMENDED FOR POLITICAL AND FOR NON-POLITICAL APPOINTMENTS

	Approx. No. in
Positions That Should Be in the Political Executive Group:	**All Agencies**
1. Heads of Departments and agencies and deputy heads	230
2. Assistant Secretaries and assistant heads of agencies	125
3. Department solicitors or general counsels	40
4. Heads of policy staff offices	50
5. Heads of departmental information offices	300
6. Political aides and assistants to political executives	10
Total	755
Positions That Should Be in Professional Administrator Groups:	
1. Administrative Assistant Secretaries and equivalent positions	60
2. Heads and members of departmental staff offices concerned with organic matters	250
3. Deputy heads and other members of departmental policy staff offices	40
4. Chiefs of line or operating bureaus	350
5. Assistant bureau chiefs, division chiefs, and others at lower levels	2,000
6. Heads of regional or district offices	1,000
7. Professional aides and assistants (in addition to political aides) at departmental level	300
Total	4,000

THE HIGH CIVIL SERVICE

In the administrative branch of government, political appointments are generally considered to be necessary only at high levels. There, the argument holds, the incoming President must be able to place men who share his confidence and his political principles. Without such personal aides

The United States Civil Service Commission Building.

for his program, he would be a figurehead; the permanent civil servants would have no fear of opposing him openly or secretly, because the President could not threaten to oust them.   Hence somewhat fewer than 800 persons should, according to this theory of the general management of the government, be appointed and hold office at the pleasure of the President.   How to determine what positions should be filled by "political" executives and which by permanent civil servants was one problem that the second Hoover Commission on Organization of the Executive Branch of Government (1953–1955) undertook to answer.   Table 19 tabulates the conclusions of the Commission.

The Hoover Commission, as the column of figures shows, also estimated the "proper" number of such political and career posts in the federal government.   Apparently ambassadors to foreign countries and special and permanent commission appointments were not included; nor were many thousands of presidential appointments to commissions in the armed forces and miscellaneous posts strewn through the executive branch of the government.   The White House staff was also omitted.   Of course, these recommendations for the top offices, and the distinction between political and professional, are the views of the Hoover Commission and not a matter of law.   Some such pattern, however, will work out in the future and is actually being roughly followed today.

Both now and in the future, however, one will find at the top levels of the executive establishment a combination of political and of non-political personnel.   The lower levels are, on the contrary, becoming exclusively the vocations of permanent, non-political, career civil servants; these levels and vocations are the chief subjects of this chapter.

EVOLUTION OF THE CIVIL SERVICE

The federal civil service has undergone a great process of evolution since 1789.   The permanent civil service of today is new.   One may discern three periods in all the time since 1789; in each a different method of choosing and maintaining civil servants has prevailed: (1) 1789–1829: competence for office, determined by the personal judgment (supposedly unbiased) of the appointing officer; (2) 1829–1883: the spoils system; and (3) 1883 to the present: the classified and permanent civil service.

Competence determined by personal judgment

The first six Presidents, Washington, John Adams, Jefferson, Madison, Monroe, and John Quincy Adams, in the main appointed officers who they thought were particularly competent to hold civil service positions.   It must be conceded that the party organizations which later had almost exclusive control over such appointments were at this time hardly in existence.   Even partisan sentiments played a comparatively small role in deciding administrative selections during this era.   True, John Adams sought especially at the end of his term to place Federalists in appointive offices; and Thomas Jefferson expressed regret that he had few opportunities to place his followers in office. Yet George Washington named such antagonists as Alexander Hamilton and Thomas Jefferson to be departmental chiefs; and John Quincy Adams even chose political opponents for administrative posts. It is important to recall that as late as 1820 there were only about 8,200 members of the civil service, and that the President named only a small fraction of these persons, the remainder being chosen by presidential appointees.

The spoils system

The spoils system for choosing federal officeholders prevailed from the accession of President Jackson in 1829 until the passage of the Pendleton Act in 1883, under President Arthur. Thereafter it diminished. The principle of the spoils system is merely that appointive offices should be held by members of the chief executive's party. Following this principle, each time party control is shifted by an election, all administrative personnel belonging to the minority party should be dismissed and replaced by members of the majority party. Such a system would tend toward a rapid turnover in appointive governing officials. This turnover, or rotation in office, was one of the goals of Andrew Jackson; he contended that long tenure was dangerous to the public weal. Jackson did not need to go far in search of agreement, for it was the creed of this era that "when annual elections cease, tyranny begins." Jackson also argued that the bulk of political offices require so little training that any normally intelligent man can perform them efficiently. Finally, as a Westerner, Jackson was convinced that the civil service was top-heavy with New Englanders. Hence Jackson became the first of a long series of American Presidents to appoint and dismiss officeholders on the basis of political partisanship.

Beginning in the 1850's Congress began to enact laws restricting the operation of the spoils system, a process that culminated with the passage of the Pendleton Act in 1883. These early laws, however, were quite weak, and their enforcement depended largely upon the discretion of the President and of the departmental chiefs. But by the opening of the 1880's an influential body of public opinion was on the side of changing the means for appointing civil service personnel. Then, in 1881, a rejected office-seeker assassinated President Garfield. This action crystallized public demand for civil service reform. In response, Congress in 1883 passed the Pendleton Act, which is the foundation for the modern federal civil service system.

Nature and application of the Pendleton Act

The Pendleton Act achieved two major steps in the restraint of the spoils system: (1) it established an administrative agency to supervise the entire civil service system; and (2) it provided means for the political neutralization of certain civil service posts. The administrative agency is the three-member Civil Service Commission, designed to control the recruitment, examination, appointment, promotion, and discipline, of all civil service employees, and the rating or classification of all civil service positions.

The means for political neutralization of civil service posts is the so-called merit system or classified civil service, which includes those positions whose incumbents can be chosen only on the basis of proved competence and can be discharged only on the ground of demonstrated incapacity.

The history of the civil service since 1883 has been largely that of the expansion of the merit system, so that the classified positions have made up a greater and greater proportion of the total. The graph in Figure 65 shows the rise of this proportion since 1883. The Pendleton Act placed about 14,000 posts, or approximately ten per cent of the total in 1883, under the umbrella of the merit system; far more important, it authorized the President to increase this number by executive order. Although Congress has added some areas of government employment to the classified list, the Presidents since Arthur have been chiefly responsible for the fact that about ninety per cent of federal employment today is embraced in the classified civil service.

The ten executive Departments have differing proportions of employees in the classified civil service; some of their employees are included in special classification systems. In 1955 practically all of the civilian employees of the Department of Defense (85.9%), the Post Office (97.1%), the Treasury (96.7%), Labor (89.3%), and Health, Education, and Welfare (90.5%) belonged to a single system administered by the Civil Service Commission. Smaller proportions of the other Departments also belonged:

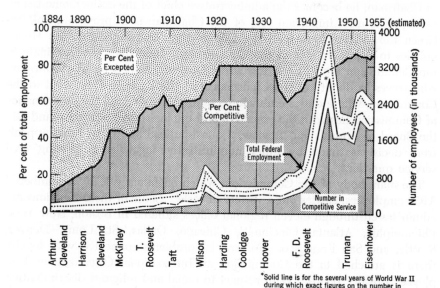

*Solid line is for the several years of World War II during which exact figures on the number in competitive service were not made available.

Commission on Organization of the Executive Branch of Government, "Personnel and Civil Service" (U.S. Government Printing Office, Feb., 1955), p. 6

Figure 65. Extension of the Competitive Civil Service, 1884–1955. The graph shows the growth of the competitive civil service positions in relation to the total number of positions in the national civil service (as shown by the rise in the heavy line along the left-hand scale of percentages). The graph also shows the rise in total numbers of civil servants (........) and total numbers placed in the competitive service (— · — ·), measured along the right-hand scale of numbers in thousands.

Agriculture (72.6%), Commerce (53.4%), Interior (72.6%), Justice (45.4%), and State (21.3%). But each of the last group has a special problem or system. For instance, the Census Bureau of the Commerce Department has a large number of temporary employees engaged in particular census work; there is a Forestry Service in Agriculture, a separate service for FBI agents in Justice, and the Foreign Service in State.

ADMINISTRATION OF THE CIVIL SERVICE

The administration of the civil service includes two factors: (1) a central agency, the Civil Service Commission, with subordinate bodies and associated groups, to supervise federal employees; and (2) a means for analyzing and sorting government positions, termed *classification*, to determine the duties of each position and the compensation to which the holder should be entitled.

Civil Service Commission

The Civil Service Commission, created in 1883, has as its executive head three commissioners chosen by the President with the confirmation of the Senate. No more than two commissioners may be of the same political party. The commissioners serve for indefinite terms and may be removed by the President at his discretion. The President names one commissioner as Chairman; he becomes the administrative chief of the entire Commission. Perhaps the most important role of the Chairman is to provide a link between the White House and the Commission, transmitting White House policies to the operations of the Commission. Immediately subordinate to the Commission are (1) the Executive Director, named by the Chairman, who serves as deputy of the Chairman; (2) the Executive Assistant to the Commission, whose duties embrace secretarial matters and the maintenance of Commission ties with the executive and the legislative branches; and (3) the Board of Appeals and Review, a quasi-judicial body that hears appeals from decisions made by other administrative agencies respecting civil service questions.

The main body of the Commission, which on January 1, 1956, numbered 3,950 employees, carries out a variety of tasks. Some of these functions are administered through eleven regional offices situated in Boston, New York, Philadelphia, Atlanta, Cincinnati, Chicago, Dallas, St. Louis, Denver, Seattle, and San Francisco. For special problems connected with loyalty there is attached to the Commission an International Organizations Employees Loyalty Board. With respect to racial and religious discrimination in government employment, the Commission depends upon the President's Committee on Government Employment Policy, an independent agency containing five members. The Commission has numerous branches, such as the Public Information Office, the Office of the General Counsel, and the Board of Appeals and Review. It is pertinent to note here that the Civil Service Commission does not actually *hire* any federal personnel, save for its own offices; rather, it sets the employment standards for the various personnel offices in the different administrative agencies, which do the actual employing for their organizations.

The classification process

The classification process is the technique whereby the Civil Service Commission evaluates each of the thousands of positions in the administrative branch, so as to determine what qualifications shall be required of the incumbent of the office, what tasks the incumbent shall perform, and what compensation the official should receive.

The classification process is administered by the Bureau of Inspection and Classification Audits of the Civil Service Commission; however, the classification itself is performed by administrative experts and analysts in the agencies themselves. Today the process is regulated by the Classification Act of 1949. This Act establishes two extensive categories of positions, into which each administrative post may be fitted; these categories are known as the General Schedule (GS) and the Crafts, Protective, and Custodial Schedule (CPC). In the General Schedule there are eighteen levels or classes; and in the Crafts, Protective, and Custodial Schedule, ten.

The level or class of each position is determined after an analysis of what the holder of the position does (not, it must be emphasized, by how well he performs his duties). The Act of 1949 supplies some general descriptions to aid the position analyst in making his decision as to which class the position belongs in; the analyst then designates the position by a number to indicate its class, as GS-9 or CPC-3. This conclusion determines what shall be the salary of the office; for the Act fixes the pay scale for each category, with the aim of assuring that persons doing similar or identical work shall receive the same stipend. For instance, the Act states that GS-1 positions include those whose duties are "to perform, under immediate supervision, with little or no latitude for the exercise of independent judgment, (1) the simplest routine work in office, business, or fiscal operations, or (2) elementary work of a subordinate technical character in a professional, scientific, or technical field."

APPOINTMENTS TO CIVIL SERVICE POSITIONS

Recruitment

Recruitment is specifically the process of getting persons to apply for civil service positions. In general the federal government takes a passive role in recruitment. In other words, the government expects the potential employee to take the initiative in seeking a federal post. Recruitment is chiefly a matter of publicizing the availability of offices. The usual procedure is that when the government seeks to fill certain positions, it issues circulars stating that vacancies exist and indicating where interested persons may secure information respecting the examinations. The commonest place to find such circulars is a post office; all post offices in major cities house representatives of the civil service.

The government often has been criticized for its failure to adopt a more aggressive policy regarding recruitment. It is held that many desirable persons are not now employed by the federal government because they do not linger about post office lobbies reading Civil Service Commission notices. In recent years the Commission has begun to communicate with colleges, universities, and professional societies, in recruiting candidates for posts demanding extensive preparation. Many agencies also actively seek candidates for the types of positions they offer.

Examinations

Before he can secure appointment to a post in the classified civil service, an individual must take an examination to prove his fitness for office. The nature of these examinations reveals several aspects of the federal civil service. In the first place, the government does not require an individual to pay a fee in order to take an examination; examinations, then, are open to all persons regardless of their economic status. Furthermore, a large number of the examinations are open to all adults irrespective of age and education. The absence of educational requirements is sometimes unfortunate, since certain people may undertake the time and expense of an examination which they cannot reasonably expect to pass because of their educational shortcomings. Civil service examinations are "practical"; they are designed to test the individual's capability of performing the duties imposed by the office.

Today the examination testing fitness for appointment is accompanied by an examination to determine the loyalty and security status of the candidate. "Loyalty" and "security" are not synonymous. Loyalty refers to the actual political allegiance of the candidate, to his formal associations and his predominant beliefs. Security is related to more general problems revolving about the personality of the individual. It might be said that loyalty is concerned with a *fact* and security with a *possibility*. The government for some time has had a loyalty program. For example, no person who is a member of an organization that the Attorney General's office has listed as subversive may be appointed to a federal post; moreover, the discovery that a functionary belongs to one of these groups is ground for prompt dismissal. The security program is most important with respect to the "sensitive" agencies such as the Department of State, that handle state secrets. In fact, in 1956, in a case involving a federal employee who had been discharged from his position on the ground that he was a security risk, the federal Supreme Court ordered him reinstated and ruled that a government employee in a "non-sensitive" post might not be discharged as a security risk under the fundamental security risk act of 1950. The program aims at detecting those traits in an individual that, although they do not constitute disloyalty, may yet unfit him for service. For example, a chronic alcoholic may be unquestionably loyal and yet have a propensity for telling government secrets when under the influence of intoxicants. An individual may have a character blemish making him a likely target for blackmail attempts, in which he is told that he can purchase silence only by turning over government information.

The loyalty and security programs are administered primarily by the agency chiefs; that is, the head of an office is responsible for the loyalty and security of his subordinates. The chiefs are authorized to dismiss any employee on the basis of derogatory information given to them about the employee. Such an employee may appeal his dismissal to the Security Review Board of the Civil Service Commission.

Presumably the administrative branch alone is to cope with situations involving loyalty and security. However, under its power to supervise the administrative agencies and to conduct investigations, Congress has probed the loyalty and security of officials in some parts of the administrative branch. These probes have been carried on chiefly by the House Committee on Un-American Activities, the Permanent Subcommittee on Internal Security of the Senate Judiciary Committee, and the Senate Government Operations Committee. Disputes have raged and are still raging over the effectiveness of this congressional activity. Supporters point to the fact that the House Un-American Activities Committee did unearth Alger Hiss and William Remington, two former government officers who were sent to a federal penitentiary for perjury committed by denying under oath that they were associated with the Communist Party. Certainly these committees have revealed cases of disloyalty to which administrative chiefs had paid little attention.

Opponents assert that the congressmen sometimes operate with so little factual justification that they threaten the morale of the personnel and dissuade competent men from seeking government office. For example, in 1950 Senator Joseph McCarthy accused the State Department of harboring eighty communists on its payroll. The Department denied the charge and was given a list containing the names of the supposed communists. Five years later Democrats in the Senate charged that not a single one of the eighty had been shown to be a communist. The State Department released a letter describing the history of the eighty before and during the intervening years. These persons fell into several classes, as follows: seven had never been employed by the Department; ten had moved to other government agencies; thirty-two had resigned, for reasons not given, before the date on which the list was given the Department; four had had limited appointments that had terminated; eight had been separated for reasons of economy; one had retired; one had died; one was discharged as unsuitable; three resigned during security proceedings; two were removed on security charges; and eleven presumably were still with the Department.

The picture presented is a puzzling one; no one, despite intensive investigation, had been shown to be a communist. Only two were removed as a result of security proceedings, and the rules of security were such as to exclude anyone regarding whose loyalty the government security officers might feel the slightest doubt. It is also possible that several of those who resigned were afraid of being discharged for security reasons. But the great turnover, with only eleven persons presumably in the Department, indicates very serious disturbances of an internal sort. One possibility is that the Department, frightened by the Senator's allegations, eased out a number of the accused by various means, including hints that promotion would be blocked. Another possibility is that a number of those who left did so because they were disgusted and dismayed by unfounded charges against their character. The truth regarding the eighty may never be known. The general consequences of such investigations are, however, weighty, because thousands of hours of work and many thousands of dollars were consumed; thousands of people in the service generally were demoralized —if one can believe the almost unanimous voices of those who spoke up in and out of the service; and millions of outsiders were imbued with suspicion and hostility toward Congress and the executive branch of the government.

It cannot be denied in any case that some committee chairmen have exploited their tasks and harmed the nation for the sake of winning favorable publicity. Probably the congressional committees have stimulated administrators to inspect the loyalty and security of their employees if only in order not to surrender that major power to Congress. Indeed, so fearful of congressional investigation have some administrators and their security officers become that they have committed more sins of haste and of flimsy allegation than congressmen have.

Appointment

Appointment is simply the means whereby an individual is named to office. To review the process of securing government personnel, when an administrative agency discovers that it needs employees, it notifies the Civil Service Commission of its need. The Commission now prepares an examination or group of examinations for the offices concerned, and publicizes the fact that the examination is to be held. After the examinations have been held and the papers scored, the names of the persons who have passed the test—a passing mark being customarily seventy per cent—are placed upon a register in the order of their scores, the highest score being at the top. It should be noted at this point that veterans enjoy exceptional privileges with relation to civil service examination scoring. Every veteran is entitled to have five points added to his grade; and disabled veterans, the wives of disabled veterans, and the widows of veterans, may all have ten points added to their scores, and their names placed at the top of the register irrespective of their scores. Furthermore, certain positions—mainly custodial employment such as operating elevators in government buildings —are open to veterans only. The consequence is that the vast majority of male functionaries are veterans. Few if any people will deny that the government is morally obligated to take some care of its former soldiers, especially those who have been disabled in battle. However, it is legitimate to inquire whether past military service confers extraordinary capacity upon an individual to administer a government office.

After the register has been prepared, the Civil Service Commission upon application of an administrative chief will provide the chief with the three names at the top of the list; the chief may now appoint one of these persons to the office; the names of the other two are restored to their places on the list. If the chief does not choose to name any of the three persons to the office, he returns all three names to the Commission. If he wishes more names from the register, the administrator must inform the Commission in writing why he did not name any of the three person to the post; and if the Commission finds this explanation satisfactory, it will send the next three names. On the other hand, the administrator may prefer to wait until a new register is drafted.

It is at the appointment stage that the administrator may use his discretion so far as naming the most desirable functionaries is concerned. It may very well be that the chief dislikes the party affiliations of the person highest on the register, and that he fears lest the second-highest person cannot work well with other people. Under such circumstances he may feel that appointing the third-highest person on the register will make the greatest contribution to the efficiency of his bureau or division. Too, it is possible that some person not at the head of the list has powerful support, conceivably in the form of a congressman or an important donor of party funds. The three-name system gives the administrator the leeway he needs to deal with political pressures of this type, which are very common. It should also be remembered that the appointing officer is not permanently bound by his initial choice, inasmuch as the new employee is put on probation for a period of up to six months before he achieves full civil service status.

COMPENSATION AND PERQUISITES

The compensation rate, or salary scale, of the federal civil service is based on the principle that equal work deserves equal pay. To execute this principle is one of the chief functions of the classification process. Each class in the GS and the CPC schedules has a salary rate in several steps, so that the individual may hope to see his pay raised a number of times during his career even though he may remain in the same post. The level of federal pay scales has been the subject of intense debate. At present it can be said that on the lower and intermediate levels federal employees are at least as well paid as persons in private business doing comparable work. On the upper levels, however, private business pays much more than government employment. As a result, the federal government has little difficulty in obtaining production workers and supervisors but must on occasion virtually go to its knees to procure managerial talent. The chart in Figure 66 shows the proportion of federal workers in different salary brackets. Notice that more than half of all federal employees earn between three thousand and five thousand dollars per year. Less than one per cent earn over ten thousand dollars.

Apart from compensation, the leading perquisite of federal employment is a retirement pension system. Today this system blankets the entire civil service. Employees contribute five per cent of their salaries through

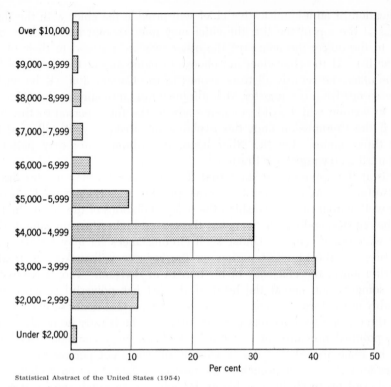

Figure 66. Percentage of Civilian Employees of the Federal Government on Different Pay Levels on June 30, 1954. (Total number of employees: 2,032,812.)

payroll deductions; and the government makes an added contribution. These sums are placed in a fund that is drawn upon after the employee retires. The amount of the pension is based upon the salary of the employee and the number of years of service; in any case it is not very large. The retirement age is seventy years; in the event the employee retires before reaching this age, he may withdraw all his contributions from the fund, plus four per cent interest.

TRAINING, DISCIPLINE, AND PROMOTION

Training

Training may be divided into two classes: pre-service and in-service. It has already been noted that the federal government does little in the way of training its employees either before or after appointment; rather, the government assumes that the employees will have acquired the bulk of their training before they are named to office. Some observers find it curious that when the government conscripts a hardware-store clerk preparatory to converting him into an Air Force pilot, it does not expect him to know how to fly an airplane; but that when it retains an administrative employee, it demands that he be trained for the position before he is appointed. Of course, it should be conceded that many of the skills needed for the armed forces have no counterpart in civilian life, but that the vast majority of civil service occupations find their parallels in private business.

There have been many projects for governmental training prior to entering the civil service. George Washington, for example, urged that Congress establish a national university for the purpose of educating administrative personnel; and the call for such a university was loudly voiced in the era of the New Nationalism after the War of 1812. The fact is that in the late eighteenth century some European universities had been erected specifically for this end; however, Congress never founded this type of school in the United States. Today in many private and State colleges and universities there are curricula designed for readying the student to hold an administrative position.

The government now does devote attention and effort to in-service training programs—that is, the training of employees after they have been admitted to the civil service. One of the most ambitious of these programs involves the junior administrative assistants, who as noted above are persons that have been selected primarily on the basis of general education. The training of these employees is aimed at procuring administrative chiefs. Probably the most intensive in-service training program is maintained by the graduate school of the Department of Agriculture; bearing in mind the vast amount of research that is conducted by this Department, one can readily understand why it would support a substantial educational program. Another important "school" is that of the Department of Justice for the training of FBI agents. Here again, as in the case of the armed forces, the personnel have to learn and master skills not found in ordinary civilian life. The State Department, Treasury Department, and Tennessee Valley Authority are other agencies that train their functionaries. Still other bodies provide a species of "apprenticeship" or of "orientation." In the main, however, these training programs are not common and have been only recently originated.

Discipline

The discipline of civil service personnel is aimed, like that of private organizations, at ensuring satisfactory performance through an appropriate balance of rewards and punishments. Adequate pay, skillful leadership, promotion, and interesting work provide the ingredients of positive discipline. Devices of negative discipline range in severity from reprimand and demerits through temporary suspension without pay (which amounts to a fine) to the ultimate of dismissal. This last device has provided a topic for intense controversy over the civil service. Many critics insist that it is so difficult to dismiss a civil service employee that inefficient workers are simply shunted from one agency to another instead of being discharged. Other commentators declare that inefficient employees are in fact removed from office.

In any event, the administrative chief must give the employee, in writing, the reasons for his dismissal. However, the chief is not obligated to hold a hearing over the dismissal; he may call such a hearing at his own discretion. The employee may take recourse to appealing the dismissal. For this purpose there are several levels of appellate bodies. By a series of appeals the employee may postpone his discharge for weeks or even months; he may even forestall it entirely, since his chief may not be able to give the time necessary for prosecuting the dismissal through the appellate procedure.

Promotion

Promotion is the process whereby an individual rises in the administrative hierarchy. It evokes two significant problems: (1) Is promotion the best means for filling superior posts? (2) What should be the basis for promotion? With respect to the best means for filling superior administrative positions, some observers insist that they should be filled only by promotion from the lower ranks. By this means, these people contend, higher posts will be staffed by persons who have had experience at the lower levels. They also argue that promotion leads toward better morale; supposedly it is demoralizing for an employee to discover that he has a new chief who has been brought in from outside the agency, and supposedly every employee may look forward to the day of his promotion. Other students of government maintain that superior officers should be appointed from outside the agency. They believe that promotion may lower the morale of those who are not promoted, and that a person who has for a long time been an employee in an office has formed relationships and interests that he cannot discard after being promoted. In recent years there has been a growing trend toward filling higher offices by promotion. This trend is one phase of the professionalization of the civil service. Perhaps the acme of this trend was attained in 1947 with the appointment of Jesse Donaldson as Postmaster General, a post to which he arose after a career as a Post Office employee.

Numerous bases for promotion have been suggested. Perhaps the oldest basis is seniority. It is easy to administer and is favored by many employees, who are assured that they will be promoted provided that they are in office long enough. However, seniority is not necessarily related to ability, and may be injurious to the morale of competent, ambitious functionaries. Another basis for promotion is examination. The most serious consideration for the administrative head is the decision as to whether the examination shall be *open* or *closed*. An open examination is one in which any person may compete; a closed examination is restricted to the personnel already in the agency. The open examination taps a far deeper well of potential candidates, but is often resented in the offices. Also, it may be difficult to construct examinations for complicated posts; how would one write an examination for the position of Minister to Guatemala? Another basis for promotion is the efficiency rating. But the failure of this basis is that demonstrated ability to perform one task is not proof that the individual can perform a more difficult task. Too, this sort of promotion may shift a very competent technician, highly skilled in dealing with ideas or things, to an administrative position where he must handle people, a duty he is quite unable to carry out.

EMPLOYEE ORGANIZATIONS

Like many employees in private business, many civil service personnel join labor unions to negotiate with the government, as their employer, concerning wages, hours and working conditions. Some unite with organizations whose members are all in government service; others unite with bodies containing persons in private as well as public employment. Which type of organization the employee chooses depends largely upon the nature of his occupation. For instance, Post Office employees may join the National Federation of Post Office Clerks or the Railway Mail Association. Virtually any civil service operative except a postal employee may enroll in the National Federation of Federal Employees. All three of these groups are linked with the AFL-CIO. The American Federation of Government Employees, by contrast, is independent. A former CIO affiliate, the United Public Workers of America, was a storm center for several years, on the ground that it was Communist-dominated; finally it was expelled from the CIO on that charge. Many federal employees join any one of the host of trade and industrial unions, such as those for various types of factory workers.

Unions have a unique relationship with the federal government as an employer, for they cannot resort to their traditional economic weapon, the strike. On the lower levels of government, civil service employees can and do strike, as the schoolteachers of Buffalo did after World War II. The national functionaries in certain European countries have struck against their governments. However, federal employees are barred from striking by the Labor-Management Relations (Taft-Hartley) Act of 1947. The Act provides that any civil service employee who strikes shall be dismissed at once, shall lose all his seniority rights, and shall be prohibited from federal employment for a period of three years. Although the unions are hampered by this prohibition, they have been able to bargain effectively for higher wages and shorter hours. Unions are expressly authorized to bring their grievances directly to Congress; in other terms, unions may lobby. The success or failure of unions in bargaining seems to depend largely upon how sympathetic they find the administrative chief with whom they are dealing.

CHARACTER OF THE SERVICE

It remains to delve into a few areas of the civil service where important problems have developed out of the conditions heretofore described: (1) the turnover of personnel; (2) problems of the merit system; (3) problems of inertia and red tape; (4) prestige and morale of the service; and (5) the political activity permitted civil service employees.

Turnover rate

The turnover rate is the rate at which present employees are separated from their positions and new employees are appointed. The turnover rate is an important index to the morale and general desirability of employment in a given enterprise; a low turnover rate suggests employee satisfaction, and a high rate indicates employee discontent. The federal civil service has a comparatively low turnover rate. In 1954, the average monthly rate of separations was 2.7 per hundred; in the same year in manufacturing industries the monthly rate averaged more than 4.0 per hundred. It is noteworthy that of the nearly 600,000 separations from government service in 1953, only 20,000, or about three per cent, were dismissals. Of the total, 372,000, or about sixty per cent, quit. By comparison, only a little more than twenty-five per cent of the separations in industry represented employees quitting; between five and ten per cent were dismissals. The greatest difference appears in the matter of lay-offs, or reductions in force; slightly more than ten per cent of civil service separations constituted reductions in force, but about one-third of the separations in private industry fell into this category. Hence actually a higher proportion of government employees than of industrial workers quit their jobs, probably to work for private enterprise. This is another illustration of the difficulties suffered by the government in holding competent and experienced administrators.

Problems of merit

The merit system has not been an unalloyed good for the government. Many people pretend, or assume, that all the ills of administration can be eradicated by the institution of a one hundred per cent merit system for non-policy-making posts. These people in a sense are the victims of a delusion. What they fail to grasp is the fact that the very term "merit system" in a way is propaganda. The determination of "merit" is subject to many disputes of goal and meaning; for example, any promotion by seniority can be easily justified as meritorious—in that experience is being rewarded, and the morale of "old-timers" is being boosted. To take a second case, an ardent political party leader might assert that merit for many kinds of jobs is best judged by an individual's fidelity to his party; consequently the spoils system in its fashion is based upon merit. Furthermore, it is not at all certain that a merit system in name is a merit system in fact. A great many people have entered the federal classified service by procedures that could scarcely be said to measure merit: they were "blanketed in" or hired after inadequate, simple testing. Often they had veterans' priorities. Moreover, of the hundreds of thousands of promotions that occur, it is likely that the greater part are made simply on the basis of seniority.

Problems of inertia and red tape

The federal civil service, like any other large organization, may be stilled by inertia and strangled with red tape. Here again the government does not have the spur of the profit motive, which often impels private business-

men to better their administrative structures. For government administrators the principal goads must be public opinion and their own pride and
morale. From time to time, however, an almost insuperable inertia will
seize a government office. It should be remembered that in public life
as in private life, habitual ways tend to be comfortable ways. Thus once
a procedure is installed, it becomes almost impossible to uproot, and finally
is invested with an aura of sanctity.

One of the most popular caricatures of the civil service employee is that
of an individual afloat on a sea of paperwork, or of one strapped in red
tape. Some truth stands behind the image. Investigating commissions
can always discover expensive leakage in a great organization. For instance,
a 1955 report of the second Hoover Commission estimated that the government could save a least a quarter of a billion dollars a year by increasing
the efficiency of its paperwork. Some twenty-six billion pieces of paper
are handled by the civil service annually. Over 750,000 employees and
more than $4 billions are devoted to paper processing. Obviously ways
to save money can always be found. Yet it is illusory to conceive that
private businesses are automatically more efficient, or more vigorous, or less
hidebound, than government offices. Most of the forces that evoke inertia
in public affairs operate also in private affairs.

Prestige and morale

Prestige is the respect with which the public views a person or institution.
Morale is the degree of zeal with which a person attacks a goal. Prestige
and morale are closely related. If the prestige of an organization is low,
the morale of its employees is apt to suffer; if the prestige is high, the
morale is likely to prosper. Thus the fact that the people regard the
Marines as a great fighting organization makes the Marines even more
intent upon deserving their reputation.

The questions of prestige and morale are highly important with regard
to the civil service. As matters stand today, the prestige of the service
is slowly but constantly rising. At one time it was commonly averred that
only a person who was a failure would seek government employment. Now,
however, especially since the public has come more and more to realize the
scope of the government, government positions are winning enhanced
respect from the public. The importance of prestige lies in the fact that
particularly with respect to the upper administrative positions it is a major
if intangible part of the compensation. In other words, the officeholder is
recompensed for his comparatively low salary rate by the prestige attached
to the post. The increase in prestige has unquestionably heightened the
morale of the federal civil service.

Political activity

The political activity of federal personnel is subject to important curbs.
In the era of the spoils system, civil service workers were often among the
most zealous party workers; however, under the merit system a number
of limitations have been placed on this activity, with the aim of making

federal employees politically neutral. At the outset the Pendleton Act forbade any executive officer save the President to solicit a financial contribution from any other executive officer for political purposes. That is, an administrative head may not ask his subordinates to give money to a political party fund. Moreover, the Act prohibited any person from asking money from a federal employee in his office. However, any private citizen may solicit funds from a federal officeholder on the street, or in his home, or at any other place not associated with government employment. The purpose of these rules is clearly to divorce party membership from offices in the classified civil service, to make tenure not contingent upon donations of money to a political party. Actually, quite within the law a party leader may solicit money from a federal employee.

Other laws further restrict the political activity of government employees. For instance, they may play only minor roles in political parties. An employee may vote and may express his political convictions in private; he may belong to a political party and attend its meetings. However, he cannot be an officer in a political party; he may not speak in political campaigns, or help manage a campaign. The net effect of these laws appears to be the protection of civil service employees from the partisanship of their superiors. Originally these limitations were imposed only upon classified service personnel. Today, however, they are incumbent upon unclassified federal personnel and even upon State and local functionaries whose offices are to some degree subsidized by the federal government. Of course, top policy-making administrators are exempt from these limitations; Department chiefs, for instance, are often found making forthrightly partisan speeches, and are expected to conduct their Departments in a manner that will aid their party.

Enforcement of these laws is the task of the Civil Service Commission. The Commission has displayed marked vigor in investigating and handling charges of partisan activity by federal employees. However, State and local employees under the provisions of these laws have been relatively unscathed. The Commission may remove from office any federal employee in the classified service found violating these laws; in the case of the classified service, the Commission notifies the agency for which the employee works. With State and local employees supported by federal funds the Commission draws the violation to the attention of officials in the government unit concerned; they are expected to dismiss the offender. If State or local authorities do not execute their prescribed duties, the federal government is empowered to withhold its funds from the agency involved.

It is certain that these laws possess a measure of virtue, in controlling what have been extreme abuses in administrative bodies. However, they perhaps detract from the morale of the service, in prohibiting officials from taking a major role in partisan politics. Indeed, this phase of the problem may be more serious than is generally realized; some persons argue that the individuals regulated by these laws have unusually strong political motivations, or they would not be civil service employees. Certainly the officers charged with enforcing these statutes have discovered that it is extremely difficult to legislate politics out of what are fundamentally political affairs. In reply to this objection it is often noted that a vast number of government positions have little if any partisan or even political flavoring; the incumbent in many cases may even be apolitical. Yet the ideals of American government that many people hold would insist that any barriers to political participation are bad; even though a man may be a clerk in the civil service and his job does not concern politics, he still is a citizen but is denied many rights of political activity while he is working for the government.

QUESTIONS AND PROBLEMS

1. Describe briefly the three periods into which the methods of recruiting the federal civil service may be divided.

2. What did the Pendleton Act provide?

3. Which of the following problems do you regard as most serious in the federal civil service: rapid turnover; seniority promotions; red tape; the ban on the right of civil servants to strike; or the ban on political activity? Explain your choice.

4. Define the classification process and give examples of its application in the federal civil service.

5. Summarize in 200 words the examining process of the federal civil service.

6. What kind of personnel security program would you regard as most desirable for eradicating communists, yet maintaining constitutionalism (300 words)?

7. Describe the types of training used for entrance and advancement in the civil service.

8. What are the major forms of discipline in the civil service?

9. What methods of promotion are possible in the civil service?

PART IX

National Finances

33. Money and Banking

Rideout and Stapp, 607, 15th St., N.W., Washington, D.C., per Federal Reserve Commission

$\mathbf{I}$N A survey made during the 1952 political campaign, 21% of a sample of all American adults declared that the Republican Party is the party of depression; by contrast 26% said that they liked the Democratic Party because it is the party of prosperity and good times. In fact, of all reasons for disliking the Republican Party and liking the Democratic Party, this was the most common. This great wave of opinion was still moving from the earthshaking depression of 1929. Most severe depressions have had great impacts upon politics, so much so that when there is a tremor of unemployment, as in the campaign of 1954, politicians of both parties become visibly agitated. Figure 67 shows how a few forms of behavior are drastically affected by economic depression. Hundreds more of such charts might be drawn; one survey listed 100 effects that a depression has on a local school system alone. Hence it is no wonder that people and politicians alike tremble at the thought of a decline in business activity.

In good times and bad, most people hold the government accountable for prosperity. The government is expected to so rule the economy that people will have jobs and will be able to provide for their families. Though

513

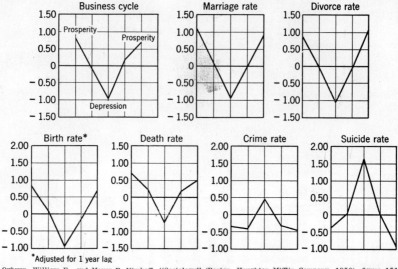

Ogburn, William F., and Meyer F. Nimkoff, "Sociology" (Boston, Houghton Mifflin Company, 1950), figure 151

Figure 67. Some Effects of Depressions upon a Society. Hardly any institution or form of behavior escapes the effects of a serious depression. Every agency of government finds its functions altered. A few general effects are shown here as they were computed from facts relating to American depressions between 1870 and 1920; averages were figured at five points, from one prosperity peak to the next peak.

perhaps not so unsophisticated in their expectations, the authors of the Constitution were intent not only upon preventing commercial stagnation, but also upon promoting business. Therefore they gave the government of the new nation ample controls over the monetary system, and enough implied powers so that subsequent financial schemes going far beyond the coinage of money might be authorized. Today the financial powers of the federal government are exercised in many places and ways. In fact, no part of the process of earning and spending money, which is pictured in Figure 68, is free from the effects of government policies. Part of the dollars earned by Americans come from government spending; the value of the dollar depends upon government practices; where and when some of the dollars go into the Treasury are questions for the government to determine. A close study of Figure 68 can be rewarding; it suggests the relations that exist among many elements of the American government to be treated in this chapter, dealing with money and banking, and in several of those that follow, discussing expenditures, taxation, income, and credit.

SOURCES OF GOVERNMENT MONETARY POWERS

The creation and management of money is one of the primary functions of the federal government. Indeed, this is a leading power of every sovereign state; it has been such for centuries. At one time the wealth of a nation was measured by its stocks of metallic money; obviously the

The Federal Reserve Building, Washington, D.C.

government must provide that its currency be sound. Since the High Middle Ages, governments have collected their revenues chiefly in money, again necessitating control over their monetary structures. The national economic systems of the twentieth century are based to a considerable extent upon money; their course is charted largely by the nature and the value of money. Governments have devised a host of new methods for controlling money in the interest of whatever group or groups may hold the tiller of the state.

Granted that national control over money is inescapable, national supervision of banks has become equally essential during the past century. Banks now create, in the form of credit, the money with which the vast bulk of the nation's business is carried on. Probably the most evident purpose of banks is to serve as custodians of deposits. Banks then combine these deposits to purchase public and private debentures. On these deposits banks also make loans to individuals and to business organizations. At one time this credit was extended in the form of bank notes printed for or by the banks. Since the Civil War, however, loans have usually been extended in the form of accounts upon which the borrowers could write checks. In this way banks actually create money, although not as coins or paper. However, several times as much business is done with this "bank money" as with currency. Consequently any effective governmental control over money must be accompanied by supervision of banking.

Many phases of the study of money and banking are difficult for a beginner to grasp. Hence this chapter will resort to rather extended historical illustrations as a means for making most clear the several important principles that are involved in national financial policies.

Control of money

Under the present Constitution the national government has exclusive power over currency. American moneys in the colonial era, during the Revolution, and under the Articles of Confederation, were chaotic and frequently almost valueless. Most of the authors of the Constitution had vested interests in a stable currency with a high purchasing power. Doubtless, too, some of them felt that an unsound money reflected poorly upon the dignity and the solvency of the new American republic. Hence the Constitution empowers Congress to "coin money" and "regulate the value thereof" (Art. I, sec. 8, cl. 5); too, it forbids the States to "coin money; emit bills of credit; make anything but gold and silver a tender in payment of debts" (Art. I, sec. 10, cl. 1). A bill of credit is a form of money issued by a State; its value in exchange is based upon the receiver's faith in the credit of the State. No State has issued a bill of credit under the present Constitution. Legal tender money is money that a creditor must accept from a debtor in payment of a debt. State banks have issued paper money whose value in exchange has depended upon popular faith in the bank's ability to redeem its notes in gold or silver coin; however, State bank notes have never been legal tender. Finally, to protect the currency, Congress is authorized "To provide for the punishment of counterfeiting the securities

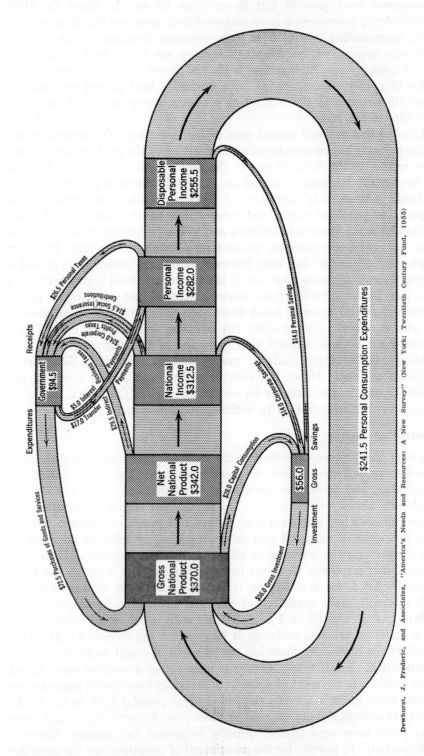

Dewhurst, J. Frederic, and Associates, "America's Needs and Resources: A New Survey" (New York; Twentieth Century Fund, 1955)

Figure 68. The Cycle of Income and Spending in the American Economy (as Predicted for 1960).

and current coin of the United States" (Art. I, sec. 8, cl. 6). Acting under these sanctions Congress in 1792 created the decimal system of dollars and cents that prevails to this day.

Control of banking

On the other hand, the federal power to charter and regulate banks is drawn solely from authority implied in the Constitution; no such power is explicitly conferred by the Constitution. Shortly after the adoption of the Constitution, Secretary of the Treasury Hamilton sought to have the government establish a Bank of the United States. After a long dispute, the first of many involving a "broad" as opposed to a "narrow" interpretation of the Constitution, Hamilton persuaded Congress and President Washington that this power was implicit in the authorization to coin money and to regulate its value. This principle was endorsed by the federal Supreme Court in the case of *McCulloch* versus *Maryland* in 1819. Thenceforth the national power to create and supervise banks was unchallenged. However, it has been exercised according to the wishes and needs of the interest group currently in command of the fiscal machinery of the national government.

DEFINITIONS OF TERMS USED IN FIGURE 68

GROSS NATIONAL PRODUCT	Gross value of all goods and services produced by business enterprises and by government agencies
CAPITAL CONSUMPTION	Value of physical capital consumed in the process of turning out goods and services
INDIRECT BUSINESS TAXES	Sales and excise taxes collected from buyers by business firms and turned over to government
CORPORATE PROFITS TAXES	Chiefly, the federal corporation income tax
SOCIAL INSURANCE CONTRIBUTIONS	Chiefly, payroll deductions for old age and survivors insurance and for unemployment compensation
PERSONAL TAXES	Personal income taxes at various levels of government
CORPORATE SAVINGS	Liquid assets of corporations, such as profits retained instead of being paid out as dividends
PERSONAL SAVINGS	Liquid assets of individuals, such as bank accounts
GROSS INVESTMENT	Primarily new construction and capital equipment; but also additions to, or subtractions from, business inventories, and foreign investment
INTEREST PAYMENTS	Payments of interest on government debts at various levels
TRANSFER PAYMENTS	Transfer of income from a government to a person without a reverse transfer of goods or services, such as old-age pensions

BIMETALLISM AND THE GOLD STANDARD

The bimetallic standard

The first money issued by the federal government was based on a bi-metallic standard of gold and silver. In this respect the United States was simply following the practice then common in Europe. The value of the two metals, for the purposes of the coinage, was set in the ratio of 15:1; that is to say, gold was to be worth fifteen times as much as silver, or, in other terms, one ounce of gold was to be worth as much as fifteen ounces of silver at the Treasury. However, this government ratio did not correspond to the market value of the two metals, since gold as bullion was worth more than fifteen times as much as silver. Hence, since gold was worth more as bullion than as coin, it virtually disappeared from circulation.[1] Under President Jackson an effort was made to restore gold to circulation by changing the ration to 16:1. Now silver was undervalued at the Treasury, for gold bullion was not worth sixteen times as much as silver bullion. Hence silver dollars disappeared; lesser silver coins continued to circulate largely because their metal was deliberately debased to keep them current. At the time the Civil War broke out, therefore, gold dollars and larger coins predominated in the coinage. Actually the bulk of the currency consisted of State bank notes; however, these were not legal tender, and fluctuated in value.

The Greenbacks

With the outbreak of the Civil War, gold coins disappeared too; they were hoarded, since their value was certain. In order to finance the war the federal government itself began to issue paper money, the so-called Greenbacks, which could not be redeemed in gold or silver but were nonetheless declared legal tender. An important outcome of the Greenback issue was monetary inflation, raising farm prices and making it easier for debtors—mainly farmers saddled with mortgages—to pay their debts. Greenbacks themselves circulated at considerably below face value with respect to gold; their value tended to rise with Union victory and fall with Union defeat. Sometimes a gold dollar would buy twice as much as a Greenback dollar. Hence after the war the debtor group insisted that the Greenbacks be kept in circulation without gold support, and organized the Greenback Party to realize their aims. However, the postwar Republican administrations were favorable to the creditors' interests, which sought deflation—that is, money with greater purchasing power.

The position of the clashing interests can be readily demonstrated. Assume that a farmer had borrowed one thousand dollars at a time when

---

[1] This process is known in economics as Gresham's Law. Another way of stating the process is to say that bad money drives good money out of circulation. Silver money at this time would be termed "bad" money because the silver in the coins was overvalued; silver coins were worth more than the silver in them would have brought as bullion.

wheat was worth one dollar a bushel. So long as the value of money remained constant, it would cost him one thousand bushels of wheat to pay the principal of his debt. To make it easier for him to pay his debt, he would campaign for inflated money, or money with a lesser purchasing power. If he were successful in his campaign, and money were so cheapened that a dollar would buy only half a bushel of wheat, he could repay his one-thousand-dollar principal with five hundred bushels of wheat.

The creditor, on the other hand, in order to make more from his loan than his simple interest, would demand deflated money, or money with a greater purchasing power. If his demands were heeded by the government, and the purchasing power of money enhanced, a dollar might buy two bushels of wheat. In this way the creditor would receive a thousand dollars that would buy two thousand bushels of wheat. Since the creditor groups after the war had the greater influence in the government, Congress in 1875 voted to establish a reserve of gold with which, starting in 1879, Greenback currency would be redeemed. Soon a Greenback dollar with this support would buy as much as a dollar in gold. The deflation of the Greenback dollars represented a major triumph for the creditor interests.

"Free silver" and the gold standard

The establishment of the gold standard in 1900 was immediately preceded by a far more strenuous and more highly emotionalized campaign than that of the Greenbackers: the campaign for "free silver." In 1873 Congress enacted a coinage law that entirely omitted the silver dollar. Actually, since this coin had for years been undervalued, it had disappeared from circulation. However, certain groups stigmatized this omission as the "Crime of '73" and began to demand, first the restoration of the silver dollar, and second the unlimited coinage of silver. Inasmuch as the silver production of the new western mines during the 1870's altered the comparative prices of gold and silver so that silver was now overvalued at the mint, unlimited coinage of silver would produce the inflation that the Greenbackers had aimed for.

The free silver movement, however, received more support, and appeared more respectable, than the Greenback Party. It was favored not only by the debtor interests but also by the silver mine owners. It appeared more respectable because silver, unlike paper, is a precious metal; moreover, inflation through silver coinage would be absolutely limited by the amount of silver that could be mined. As the dollar grew increasingly valuable, resulting in ever falling farm prices, the Greenbackers rallied to the cause of free silver. Two measures, the Bland-Allison Act of 1878 and the Sherman Silver Purchase Act of 1890, although they authorized the government to purchase more silver, actually did little to increase the amount of silver money because the Treasury bought the minimum amount allowed by law. Eventually the free silverites captured the Democratic Party through the nomination of William Jennings Bryan for the presidency in 1896; however, his defeat by McKinley sealed the fate of the free silver movement. In 1900 Congress placed the United States on the single gold standard.

The contest between the gold and the silver adherents mirrored more than a simple dispute over money. It was a contest between the debtor farming group on the one hand, and the creditor industrial and financial interests on the other, for control of the federal government. The creditor interests won the struggle; yet the inflation that the silverites had pursued was commenced before 1900 by the discovery of gold in Alaska and South Africa, inaugurating an epoch of a declining dollar and higher farm prices.

BANKS BEFORE THE FEDERAL RESERVE SYSTEM

The banks of the United States and State banks

American banking systems, like the American currency, have constantly reflected the struggles among the various financial groups in the country. In 1791 Congress created the Bank of the United States. Chartered for twenty years, this institution was designed to stabilize the currency. It was also intended to tie the financial and mercantile interests closely to the new government; the bulk of its stock was sold to the public, but only those groups could afford to purchase shares. In order to win public confidence, the Bank was empowered to issue notes based upon its holdings of gold and silver, which, although not legal tender, might circulate as money; the Bank was custodian for the funds of the federal government; and the government owned one-fifth of the stock. The Bank was so well managed that its private shareholders earned handsome dividends. Hence in 1811, when its charter expired, the Bank was not at once revived, for the government was then controlled by spokesmen for debtor interests and by advocates of State banks.

The difficulties of financing the War of 1812, and the sense of nationalism that followed the war, induced Congress to charter a second Bank of the United States. But even before its charter ran out President Jackson had begun to deposit federal revenues in State banks; in addition, the Congresses of the 1830's, like Jackson fearful of centralized banking control, refused to renew the charter (note the cartoon in Figure 69). Until the Civil War, then, the States monopolized the creation and control of American banks. This meant that many banks were weak, and that the notes they issued were sometimes unredeemable in coin. It also meant that Westerners secured credit more readily, and that the West expanded perhaps more rapidly, than might have been the case under the Bank of the United States.

Creation of the national banks

During the Civil War the supporters of a national banking system rewon control of the federal government through the Republican Party. In 1863 they pushed through Congress legislation authorizing the government to charter banks whose financial practices it could regulate. These banks were allowed to issue notes of a value up to ninety per cent of their holdings of federal bonds, which were deposited with the United States Treasury. By this device the Treasury secured additional funds to finance the war. Also, in order to give the national banks a monopoly on the issuance of bank notes, Congress levied a ten per cent tax on State bank notes, effectively driving them out of circulation.

Operation of the national banks

National banks still carry on the largest share of the nation's banking business, but they no longer issue currency. While the banks were supervised by the Treasury Department, they had no strong ties among themselves. Consequently, in the event of a sudden need for money in one section of the country, the banks in other sections were under no obligation to extend credit outside their locality. Moreover, it was often charged, and with some truth, that the banks of New York City had an unbreakable grasp upon most of the national credit facilities. Most important, experience showed that in case of a depression, when added credit might be wanted, money tended to contract rather than expand. This circumstance resulted partly from the banks' practice of selling government bonds during a depression so as to acquire ready cash. Of course, a bank that did this reduced its holding of bonds; then, since the value of the bank notes it might issue was limited to ninety per cent of its holding of bonds, the bank

Reproduced through the courtesy of the American Antiquarian Society, Worcester, Mass.

Figure 69. Andrew Jackson *versus* the Bank of the United States. Jackson's raging quarrels with the Bank led some to believe he was the victim of nightmarish delusions. Here a friend is pictured as pulling him back to bed. Indeed, beneath many a so-called economic issue of history there lie various psychological and political roots that a student may well inquire into.

was compelled to withdraw some of its notes from circulation whenever it sold some of its bonds. This difficulty was especially marked in the depression of 1907, which appears to have been little more than a bankers' panic. Subsequently a congressional investigation by the Pujo Committee in 1912 showed the weaknesses of the American banking system. In keeping with the recommendations of the Committee, Congress in 1913 passed the Glass-Owen Act, which established the Federal Reserve System.

THE FEDERAL RESERVE SYSTEM

General structure

The Federal Reserve System provides the national government a strong institution for the control of American banking. All national banks must belong to the System, and State banks that satisfy certain minimal conditions may join. Unlike the two Banks of the United States, the Federal Reserve System is regionalized. The United States is divided into twelve federal reserve districts; a Federal Reserve Bank is located in a leading city of each district, as follows: Boston, New York, Philadelphia, Cleveland, Richmond, Atlanta, Chicago, St. Louis, Minneapolis, Kansas City, Dallas, and San Francisco. The federal reserve banks are owned by the member banks of their districts, each of which must subscribe six per cent of its capital and surplus for stock in the Federal Reserve Bank. The reserve banks are each managed by a board of nine directors: three of the directors are chosen by the chief central agency of the System, the Board of Governors, which names one of its appointees chairman of the board; three directors are chosen by the member banks to represent the various economic interests of the district; and three more, also selected by the member banks, to represent the banks themselves. The terms of the directors are arranged so that one expires every year.

The chief supervisory agency of the System is the Board of Governors, which consists of seven members chosen by the President, with the advice and consent of the Senate, for overlapping fourteen-year terms. They must be selected with due consideration for the different economic groups and geographic regions of the country; no more than one may come from a single reserve district. Other central bodies are: (1) the Federal Open Market Committee, consisting of the Board of Governors and five additional members named by federal reserve banks, to manage the open market activities described below; and (2) the Federal Advisory Council, of twelve members, one from each reserve district, to furnish the System with counsel about business conditions.

Operations

Rediscounting Commercial Paper: The federal reserve banks do not carry on business with private individuals and corporations; they are "bankers' banks," for their relations are almost exclusively with member banks and with the government. Among their principal functions is the rediscounting of commercial paper held by member banks. An individual or a corporation borrowing money from a bank offers some form of security termed "commercial paper," such as a note or a mortgage, which the bank then "discounts." Before the establishment of the Federal Reserve System, a bank could lend money only to the extent of its own resources. Now, however, a bank that needs additional credit facilities may turn over to the Federal Reserve Bank of its district some of this commercial paper, along with a prescribed percentage of gold certificates (a type of paper money no longer publicly circulated, which represents gold), which the Federal Reserve Bank "rediscounts"; that is, it lends money to the member bank. This loan is given in federal reserve notes, which make up the largest part of American paper money today. In the event a federal reserve bank needs added credit facilities of its own, it may borrow from one or more of the other federal reserve banks. The consequence of this functioning is that when there is a greater demand for money, as evidenced by a larger volume of borrowing from banks, there is more money in circulation. In other words, the elasticity of credit is such that the amount of money available corresponds to the need for it.

Stabilization of Credit: Another major purpose of the Federal Reserve System is the stabilization of credit, and through it of the whole American economy. It has divers means for effecting this purpose. One is by manipulation of the rediscount rate, or rate of interest it charges on its loans to member banks. By raising the rediscount rate it can oblige member banks to raise their discount rate, thus discouraging would-be borrowers since money has become more expensive, lessening the amount of money in circulation, and bringing about a deflationary effect. By lowering the rediscount rate the System can bring about the reverse effect.

Federal reserve banks may also engage in "open-market operations" at the direction of the Open Market Committee. Such operations involve the purchase and sale of government bonds and commercial paper. For example, in the event it is desired to stimulate business activity, federal reserve banks may begin to purchase government bonds. This action, in the first place, will put more money in the hands of the public. In the second place, it will tend to lower interest rates. The demand for the bonds presumably will raise their market prices; then, since their interest rates are based on the bonds' par value, their rise in price in the face of their fixed return will constitute a lowering of the interest rate they yield. This in turn will tend to depress all other interest rates, which is considered an inflationary movement. Finally, the decline in government interest rates will encourage investment in more remunerative private undertakings. On the other hand, should it be decided that business investment ought to be curtailed, the System may begin to sell government bonds.

One other noteworthy control is the power of adjusting the percentage of reserves that banks must hold against their loans. By lowering the percentage from twenty to ten, for instance, the System can theoretically double the lending power of banks, since on reserves of $100.00 banks may now lend $1,000.00 where previously they could lend but $500.00.

Additional Services: Federal reserve banks perform numerous additional services for member banks and for the government. They hold member banks' reserves of gold and silver, and they are clearing houses for checks. The Federal Reserve System accepts deposits of government revenues; it sells government bonds, and cashes government checks and coupons. During and after World War II, through its open market operations the Federal Reserve System endeavored to keep government interest rates low by purchasing bonds whenever they threatened to drop below a specified market value, usually just above par. In this way the federal government was able to sell its short-term debentures at a lower interest rate, reducing the cost of financing the war.

Success of the Federal Reserve System

The Federal Reserve System has not succeeded in controlling the money market to the degree its creators claimed it would. Admittedly it functioned ably in the financing of World War I. However, it failed signally to cope with the depression of 1929. Raising the rediscount rate in 1929 did not stem the speculation in the stock market. In fact, since certain major parts of the economy were already depressed in 1929, this action may have been positively harmful. Furthermore, lowering the rediscount rate in the early 1930's did not noticeably stimulate recovery. After World War II the System and the Treasury Department entered a spirited dispute over the management of credit; the former wished to raise interest rates so as to curb inflation, but the latter wished to keep them low in order to make servicing of the federal debt less expensive.

This contest illustrated one important aspect of the federal government: monetary control is not concentrated, but is entrusted to these two agencies. Because the Secretary of the Treasury is directly responsible to the President, Treasury policy is apt to mirror that of the White House. Federal Reserve policies, on the other hand, are directed by a long-term Board of Governors that may have been appointed by earlier administrations with contrary fiscal policies. The clash between the two institutions may sometimes weaken the federal government; nonetheless, it does afford representation for differing monetary philosophies.

The Federal Deposit Insurance Corporation

The failure of many banks during the 1930's inspired the creation of a new federal agency to protect bank depositors, the Federal Deposit Insurance Corporation (FDIC). The FDIC is a government corporation that insures all deposits in Federal Reserve member banks, and other banks that can fill certain requirements, to the sum of $10,000 per depositor. The insurance is financed by premiums paid by the affiliated banks at the rate of one-twelfth of one per cent of their deposits. So far every depositor in a failed bank has been recompensed in full. Some bankers, however, argue that in case of a major depression the resources of the FDIC would be insufficient to deal with the needs. In some circles it is also averred that the FDIC has encouraged speculation and unsound financial practices on the part of some banks. However, since certain States already had deposit insurance corporations before 1929, it appears that public demand is apt to forbid any drastic change in the FDIC.

THE POLICY OF FLEXIBLE CURRENCY

After more than thirty years of the gold standard, the United States through a series of measures in 1933–1934 abandoned the standard and adopted a considerably revised monetary system. This change was prompted by a number of factors. In the first place, many European countries, notably Great Britain in 1931, had already discarded the gold standard. In the second place, the United States was in a serious depression, with low prices and high interest rates. Thirdly, through the election of 1932 the debtor, "easy money" interests had won domination of the federal government. Finally, there was a widespread conviction that the value of the dollar should rest, not on its gold content, but upon a price index of commodities, so that its purchasing power could be stabilized.

Steps toward a flexible currency

Among the steps bringing about this transformation in American money were the following: (1) In order to curtail the private hoarding of gold, the government required that all gold currency and bullion be surrendered to the Treasury, in exchange for paper money not based on gold. (2) An executive order authorized by the Emergency Banking Act of 1933 provided that the various kinds of currency could no longer be redeemed in gold, thus formally taking the United States off the gold standard. (3) Congress repealed the clause in public and private debentures requiring that their principal and interest be paid in gold, substituting only the obligation to pay in legal tender. (4) Empowered to do so by the Agricultural Adjustment Act of 1933, the President in 1934 reduced the value of the dollar to 59.06 cents in gold. (5) Under the Gold Reserve Act of 1934 the government began to buy domestic and foreign gold at the fixed price of $35.00 per ounce, so that by 1956 the Treasury owned almost $22 billions' worth. (6) As a gesture to the silver-mining interests and the residual "free-silver" sentiment, Congress directed the government to buy enough silver to equal one-third of the national gold stock.

The chief goal of these measures was to raise prices, especially those of farm products. Actually the resultant change in prices seems to have been far less than either the supporters or the detractors of these innovations predicted. The reason probably lies in a fact noted above, that the currency provides only a minor fraction of the money with which the nation's business is conducted. It is also evident that the supply of money is only one of several factors influencing the level of prices. But certainly these steps did give Congress and the President several new means for dealing with money.

American money today

The monetary system of the United States today is often described as "managed." This is true, at least in the sense that the value of the dollar is no longer subject only to fluctuations in the national and world price of gold. However, American money has always been "managed"; Congress ever since 1789 has been passing laws directly affecting the purchasing power of the dollar, such as the establishment of the 15:1 ratio in 1792. What is important is to determine for what group or groups American money is being "managed," and toward what ends. Management in the early years of the United States revolved primarily about the question of the ratio between gold and silver. Later it concerned the struggle between the debtor and the creditor interests. Today money management impinges upon the whole of the American economy. Furthermore, it should be remembered that until 1933, apart from the era falling roughly between Presidents Jackson and Lincoln, the national government tended to favor the creditor group. Much of the monetary control exercised under Presidents F. D. Roosevelt and Truman was at the behest of the debtor grouping. It must also be remembered that those who owe now have been joined by a mighty new force, the greatest debtor of all—the United States government.

Function of the American gold stock

Whether the gold bullion stocked by the federal government has any function is often asked. It should be recalled that American currency is still measured in terms of gold, even though it is not convertible into gold. Moreover, all federal reserve notes are based not only on commercial paper but also on at least twenty-five per cent gold certificates held by the Federal Reserve System. Too, gold is still used for payments in international trade. The bullion stock certainly has psychological power; witness the opposition to proposals occasionally emanating from the gold-mining States that the price of gold be raised, and the uneasiness resulting from sporadic reports that the USSR is exporting gold in quantity. From time to time, in fact, one still hears recommendations that the United States return to the traditional gold standard. At a minimum, gold still plays a major role in the American monetary system, but it can be safely said that a return to the traditional standard is extremely unlikely if not impossible.

QUESTIONS AND PROBLEMS

1. You are a farmer today with a $10,000 mortgage on your property. Paying that mortgage is the most important thing in your life. What action would you like to see the Federal Reserve System take? Why?

2. Under the system of national banks established in 1863, what might have been the consequences if the national debt had been entirely paid?

3. Ralph Johnson, an Ohio farmer in 1877, had a $5,000 mortgage on his property. He wanted nothing so much as to pay his mortgage. What government policies would it be logical for him to support? What policies in 1894?

4. What might be the monetary consequences if the Soviet Union should suddenly dump $20 billions' worth of gold on the market?

5. Which can be more easily inflated, paper money or coinage? Why?

6. If all the gold owned by the Treasury should suddenly vanish, what might be the results?

7. If today you held a $10,000 mortgage on a farm, and you wanted as large a profit as possible without foreclosing, what policies would you want the Federal Reserve System to follow? Why?

8. Give arguments for and against the statement that "American money has been 'managed' only since 1933."

9. What is "bank money," what is its function, and how important is it?

10. What might be the monetary consequences today if the national debt were paid in full?

THE budget of the national government is a prediction of governmental revenues and a plan for their expenditure during the coming year. The revenue phase of the budget shows where the money for spending is expected to come from. Mainly, of course, revenue comes from taxes. Often the prediction of how much money will come in is supplemented by proposals to increase, reduce, or otherwise alter the flow of revenue. The expenditures portion of the budget takes up all the activities of the numerous agencies of the government; it tells what each is intended to spend and for what purpose. The principal authors of the budget of the United States are the Bureau of the Budget, the President and his advisers, and the Departments. The task of Congress with regard to the budget is to transform it into groups of laws calling for taxes and for appropriations of money for specific activities.

The budget is chiefly a mass of figures, but the process of arriving at the figures requires deciding which activities of the government for the year ahead will be most trivial and which most important. For example, the budget will show whether the government expects to pursue intensively its investigations and prosecutions of monopoly by showing the number of people the government would like to employ in the Antitrust Division of the Department of Justice. Again, if the government is asking large increases in funds for the Air Force, a greater emphasis on air power is suggested. A government's attitude toward economy may be revealed when the budget does or does not propose a balance between revenue and expenditure; should a deficit, registering more spending than revenue, be planned, the government is in a way asserting that none of the recited activities is so unimportant that it may be cut back in order to forestall borrowing. Thus the pattern of expenditures and its balancing against revenue exposes the policy of the government.

The publication of a proposed budget is always an exciting occasion for those with a professional interest in government. A banker will be concerned because the amount of money the government will collect and spend will affect the ease or difficulty with which his customers may acquire funds, the interest rates that he gives and receives on money, and so on. Public officials read in the budget the proposed fate of their staff and plans, and they can compare their own fortune with that of other officials. The United States has a relatively open budget process; most matters in a proposed budget leak out beforehand and are publicly debated for some time after they are suggested but before they are finally decided upon. Other nations, in which the executive is in a strong position to carry out its budget proposals, as in England, keep their budgets carefully hidden from preview until the day of their announcement to the public.

Everywhere, as in America, the publication of a budget or a proposed budget attracts the attention of a discerning audience that is both domestic and foreign. For instance, when the budget of the Soviet Union is made known each year, it is pounced upon and eagerly read by a host of intelligence officers throughout the world. From it they strive to extract valuable information about the policies and intentions of the Kremlin. The expenditures planned for the army and the air force indicate changes in hostile aims, in types of armaments, and in the power of the leadership of different schools of military theory. The amount allocated to consumer goods rather than to heavy industry discloses other plans and problems of Soviet society. These are only two of the ways in which the budget of the USSR yields hints about future Soviet behavior toward the rest of the world. Americans can be sure that Soviet rulers are no less diligent in scrutinizing the American budget, for the same reasons.

The Executive Office Building, Formerly the Department of State, Washington, D.C.

FRAMING THE BUDGET

The fiscal year

It must be indicated at the outset that in money matters the national government does not adhere to the calendar. Rather, it has a so-called "fiscal year" that commences on July 1 and terminates on June 30. For purposes of enumeration, the fiscal year concludes, but does not begin, in the calendar year of its number. For instance, fiscal 1955 ran from July 1, 1954, until June 30, 1955. The body of taxes and appropriations that Congress enacts in any given year goes into effect on July 1 of that calendar year.

Agency requests

The drafting of the budget is inaugurated more than a year before the budget comes into action, by a call issued by the Bureau of the Budget to each of the different government agencies for estimates regarding the amount of money they need for their operations in the coming fiscal year. The various agencies, departmental and independent, are after all the principal spenders of federal money. More than twelve months before the inception of the fiscal year, in expectation of this call, the different agencies, starting at about the division level, have begun to ready their monetary demands for the coming year. These demands are, of course, frequently greater than the allocations of funds made during the current year; most administrative officers are convinced that the functions of their agencies should be expanded and need more money.

The division requests for funds, after being consolidated, are brought to the financial or budget office of the agency concerned. Considerable pressure may have been brought by private interests and also by congressmen upon the division, to swell its requests for money; at the same time, representatives of the Bureau of the Budget and other parts of the Executive Office of the President have impressed upon the agency chiefs the desirability of limiting their budgetary requests. The finance officers of the agency themselves appear, perhaps because of professional motivations, to constitute a restraining effect upon the monetary goals of the line officials. Eventually, after the agency chiefs have completed drafting their budgetary proposals, the draft is submitted to the Bureau of the Budget.

The Bureau of the Budget

The Bureau of the Budget, which is in the Executive Office of the President, is the most important of all the President's staff bodies. The Bureau is under the general supervision of the Director, who is appointed by the President. Significantly, the Senate has nothing to do with his appointment, at least formally; the Director serves for an indefinite term and is directly responsible to the President. Ostensibly the major function of the Bureau is to examine the requests for funds that are submitted by the different agencies; it is empowered to "assemble, correlate, revise, reduce, or increase" these requests.

However, the power of the Bureau far exceeds its purely fiscal authority, for in order to evaluate the various requests it must analyze the ends proposed for them. Thus the Bureau quite properly enters the broad field of presidential policy-making. The working of the Bureau is one of the most important indexes to the fact that the President, and not Congress, really plans the operations of the national government. One of the principal branches of the Bureau is the Office of Management and Organization, to inspect the structure and functioning of the many administrative units. The purpose of this office is to study the organization and aims of the agencies that are to spend the money they have requested. In performing this task the Office frequently counsels the President with regard to administrative problems.

Thus, once the agency proposals for money have been sent to the Bureau of the Budget, the Bureau initiates an analysis of what ends will be achieved by the money requested. Working closely with the President, the Bureau revises the budgetary proposals in terms of the general policy of the administration. It divides itself into groups for the study of different types of requests. These groups hold hearings at which the chiefs of the agencies concerned testify respecting their estimated needs for the coming year. Meanwhile, the Treasury Department transmits to the Bureau its expectations of the amount of revenue it will collect in the coming year, and a statement regarding the size of the national debt and how much interest will be due on the debt.

In any event, the President and the Bureau together compile the data given them by all the agencies, to frame the national budget. When the budget is finally assembled, it constitutes a book more than a thousand pages long, weighing several pounds. The President now prepares a message to be delivered to Congress and the nation on the occasion of his tendering the budget to Congress. Then, early in January—sometimes on the day after the State of the Union address—the President gives the budget to Congress and delivers the budget message, to introduce and explain his budgetary proposals and to urge their enactment.

The budget before Congress

In order for the national government to spend any money, Congress must appropriate the needed funds. Perhaps the most significant duty of Congress, at least so far as domestic problems are concerned, is the passing of a budget. The Constitution requires that all revenue measures begin in the House; however, appropriation bills may start in either branch of Congress. Convention dictates, however, that bills for spending money shall also commence in the House. In practice, both houses study the budget simultaneously. Once each house has received the budget, it deletes those sections referring to the acquisition of money—the revenue measures—and turns them over to the proper committee, that on Ways and Means in the House and that on Finance in the Senate. The remainder of the budget, the part that deals with expenditures—which is by far the larger portion—is submitted to the Committee on Appropriations in each house.

Each Committee on Appropriations now resolves into a number of standing subcommittees to analyze the presidential proposals, each subcommittee dealing with one broad class of expenditures. (Refer back to Figure 44, page 372.) The assignment of committee members to these subcommittees can be a powerful factor in deciding what treatment the projected budget will obtain. The principal source of information for these groups is the hearings that they conduct. The witnesses at these hearings are the chiefs of the agencies whose estimates the subcommittee is studying, and interested private persons who may either present relatively unbiased accounts, or aim frankly at swaying the subcommittee to a certain line of action. Sometimes congressmen who are not members of the Appropriations Committee but who are on the standing committee concerned with the function being examined by the subcommittee will attend these hearings, and participate in the interrogation of witnesses.

Custom directs the agency chiefs to defend the sums requested for their offices, even though these sums may not concur with the personal notions of the chiefs themselves; the chiefs, then, are advocates for the President. In practice, however, subcommittee members through questioning these chiefs may evoke statements that do not support the budgetary projects. Indeed, matters may be arranged beforehand between an agency official and a sympathetic congressman so that questioning can be aimed at bringing forth justification for large changes in the President's requests. A congressman who, for example, favors greater expenditures for a specific function than the President has recommended, who is acquainted with the agency chief, and who knows that the chief too wants to spend more money than the budget will allocate to him, may agree with the chief before the latter testifies as to what line the questioning will pursue.

After the hearings have been concluded, each subcommittee now drafts a bill for appropriating money to carry out the activities it has been studying. The bill may increase or decrease the amounts asked by the President, may completely omit some items, and may introduce items not mentioned by the President. Legally and constitutionally Congress is free to do as it wishes about the budget. Actually the presidential recommendations are very influential, especially when the President and the majority of Congress are of the same party.

However, congressmen sometimes resent the presidential suggestions, partly from a feeling that the chief executive has invaded a field of action in which Congress ought to be supreme. This sentiment is particularly noticeable in the senior members of the Appropriations Committees; they may be among the most powerful and best-informed members of Congress, men who have held office for twenty years or more. Agency chiefs often must employ great tact in presenting their cases, lest the semblance of bringing pressure upon congressmen utterly undo their projects. At the same time, as party leader the President has major extra-legal controls over Senators and Representatives who oppose him.

The individual bills one by one finally come to the floor of Congress. Only once in recent history have these bills been combined into a single grand appropriation. Subcommittees have varying amounts of work to do, and operate at different paces. As with other bills, congressmen tend to assume that the members of the subcommittee are well enough informed to have prepared a satisfactory bill; hence there is comparatively little discussion on the floor. Of course, this generalization is inapplicable in cases of highly controversial appropriations; proposed expenditures such as the Marshall Plan, to assist European economic recovery after World War II, may call forth a torrent of impassioned oratory.

Another important goal for Senators and Representatives is that one of these appropriations should arrange for an expenditure that is wished by their constituents. It is in this way that congressmen can demonstrate to their districts and States that Congress is providing for local interests. Sometimes there will be little economic justification for this type of expenditure; on such occasions, the money falls into the category known as "pork," i.e., money that is primarily a token of a congressman's work on behalf of his constituency. A fruitful source of pork is the annual appropriation for rivers and harbors under the jurisdiction of the national government; Congress has enacted many appropriations for widening rivers, "for the improvement of interstate commerce," that contain scarcely enough water to float a canoe. Senators and Representatives collaborate in their respective houses, assisting one another in enacting appropriations for pork, a practice termed "log-rolling" in which congressmen emulate the frontier settlers who helped one another to build houses.

These appropriation bills are passed in the same fashion as any other act of Congress. They are then submitted to the President for his approval or disapproval. The President only rarely vetoes an appropriation bill, for in so doing he would deprive the government of the money needed for its operations. For this reason congressmen often are able to impose expenditures upon the government that the President dislikes.

Administration of the budget

In effect, the budget is administered by the entire government, since each expenditure authorized by law comprises an act of budget administration. The leaders in this administrative process are the Bureau of the Budget and the finance and budget officers of the different agencies. The Bureau in fact supervises the operations of these officers, examines the accounting techniques of all government agencies, suggests changes in these techniques that may increase the efficiency of the agencies, and recommends to the President the changes that may improve administration. To further oversee budget administration Congress has established a major agency that is presumably outside, and independent of, the administrative branch of the government: the General Accounting Office (GAO). The chief of the GAO is the Comptroller of the United States,

who although formally independent of all other agencies is more nearly
the servant of Congress than of any other branch of the government.
The Comptroller General is appointed by the President and confirmed by
the Senate. To safeguard his independence, Congress made the term of
the Comptroller General fifteen years, and provided that he may be removed
only by Congress—by impeachment, or, if the removal is for cause, by joint
resolution.

The principal function of the Comptroller General is to examine expenditures, to see if they are authorized by law. An appropriation bill, it
should be remembered, simply empowers the Treasury Department to
grant certain sums to the various agencies, to be spent for certain purposes.
Vouchers and warrants testifying to these transactions are brought to the
GAO in freight-car loads; any disputed transaction must be studied to
determine whether the expenditure falls within the law. The Comptroller
General occupies what is potentially a policy-making office of the highest
significance, because the authority for the expenditure will depend upon
his reading of the law. The Comptroller General, then, can thwart any
program of the government by simply refusing to initial expense vouchers.
The Comptroller General during President F. D. Roosevelt's first term,
a Republican who was hostile to many New Deal undertakings, refused
to authorize many expenditures that he thought improper. This office,
then, is one more whose conduct is determined to a considerable extent by
the predispositions of the incumbent.

THE PATTERN OF FEDERAL EXPENDITURES

Federal expenditures today amount to many billions of dollars annually,
or several hundred dollars for every person in the United States. Since
1789 the total of federal government spending has increased hundreds of
times more rapidly than the population, as Figure 70 shows; the budgets
of Alexander Hamilton called for only a few millions of dollars, or about
one dollar per capita. Federal expenditures have also increased several
times as rapidly as expenditures by State and local governments. With

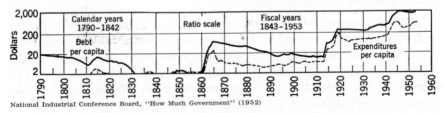

National Industrial Conference Board, "How Much Government" (1952)

Figure 70. Total Federal Government Spending, 1789 to the Present. This is a
"ratio" or logarithmic chart. That is, the increase in spending has been so great that
if the same dollar interval measure were used on the left vertical bar, the curve would
run off the page during the Civil War and during the Twentieth Century; hence,
although the natural numbers are given on the scale, the distances between 2, 20, 200
and 2000 are proportional to the logarithms of those numbers, causing a telescoping
of the measure so that it can be read at a glance.

the exception of the Civil War era, not until a century after the adoption of the Constitution did any Congress in its two-year period appropriate one billion dollars. The government did not begin to spend over a billion dollars annually until World War I. However, in the single war year 1945, Congress appropriated over one hundred billion dollars. In the first years after World War II, federal expenditures were reduced to less than forty billion dollars a year. However, to achieve the goal of defending the United States from the threat of world Communism, beginning in 1952 the federal government raised its expenditures to sixty-five billion dollars. Barring a sudden collapse of the Soviet Union, it seems that federal costs will remain this great for years to come.

What the government spends money for shows what theories of policy dominate the government, and gives some notion as to what interest groups carry the greatest weight. Figure 71 presents the government's pattern of spending in four recent years. The proportion of its funds that the government dedicates to any given task has fluctuated widely through the years. Today the largest item in the national budget is war— paying for past wars and preparing for future wars. As an illustration, in the estimates for fiscal 1957, national defense and related international costs accounted for sixty-one per cent of all expenditures; veterans' affairs, seven per cent; and interest on the national debt, which had been incurred chiefly through war, eleven per cent. All other expenditures made up only about twenty-one per cent of the total. Thus about four dollars out of every five were earmarked, directly or indirectly, for military uses. It is note- worthy that Congress and the federal court system together spend about one hundred million dollars, or around two dollars out of each thousand; all the rest is spent by the executive branch and the independent agencies.

Tremendous pressures are exerted upon Congress to restrain expendi- tures. If the government spends more than it gathers in revenues, it incurs a deficit. Government financing is not the same as personal financ- ing; a deficit does not have the same impact upon a government that it has upon an individual. However, since to many people these two forms of financing are similar, a deficit has an important effect upon national morale. For example, when the Survey Research Center in 1952 asked a national cross-section of Americans what they disliked about the Demo- cratic Party, a sizable proportion of the replies had to do with alleged uneconomic spending. When an agency does spend more money than Congress has initially awarded it, Congress must enact a so-called "de- ficiency appropriation" to give the agency the funds it needs. Deficiency appropriations generally receive little publicity, for they do not comprise an asset to the administrators for whose relief they have been passed. These appropriations can be used, and have been used, as devices for escaping from the confinement of a budget; items in a budget are some- times set so low, for political purposes, that the agency could not possibly execute its obligations with the funds given it.

Thus three types of deficit occur: (1) an overall planned deficit; (2) a deficit arising from increased agency expenditures; and (3) a deficit emerg-

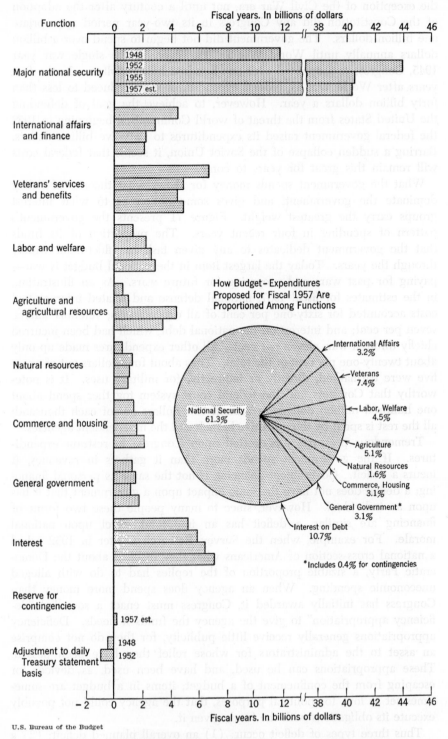

Figure 71.   The Pattern of Government Spending in Recent Years.

ing from a drop in revenues. Figure 72 pictures the relations between expenditures and receipts in recent years. It shows the amount of the deficit or surplus; and it shows the trend of appropriations. It is well to remember that appropriations, as the figure indicates, are authority for new obligations; they are *not* expenditures. It may be that an appropriation never is spent, or its spending may be delayed for years. Note should be made of the fact that beginning in 1954 more money was being spent than was being appropriated; of course, it was being spent from the appropriations of previous years. If money is appropriated for an army tank or a bomber it will not ordinarily be spent until the time of delivery, which may be months or years after the appropriation.

THE IMPACT OF GOVERNMENT SPENDING

Government spending has a significant impact upon the whole national economy. Fundamentally, the purpose of government spending is to enable the government to maintain itself and to pay for the goods and services it has undertaken to provide. In an era such as that of a century ago, the expenditures of the government amounted to relatively little more than this, save for a few special interest areas. However, in that period the total of government spending made up only a minute fraction of the entire national business; the presence or absence of government spending in a given field did not have much effect upon that field.

Today, by contrast, the government is the largest single element in the national economy. Government expenditures amount to approximately one-fourth of the total national income; that is, one dollar out of every four paid to Americans is in the form of a government check. Hence the distribution of government spending is fundamental to national wealth and prosperity. Consequently government spending is not regulated solely by the institutional requirements of the government, that is, by the need

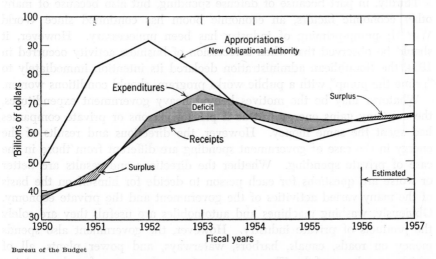

Bureau of the Budget

Figure 72. Recent Fluctuations in National Finances.

to purchase supplies and pay the salaries and wages of civil service employees. Rather, government spending is planned in terms also of the effect it will have upon the economy; by spending money, or refusing to spend money, the government may take a hand in the determination of whether the country shall have prosperity or a depression.

There are manifold ways, both deliberate and unintentional, in which government spending has an impact on the national economy. One school of thought, for example, holds that whenever a depression threatens, the government should inaugurate a major spending program, especially in the field of public works, so as to keep people at work and money circulating. This principle was applied on a large scale in the first New Deal years, in the form then known as "pump-priming." The assumption was that the national economy needed some sort of stimulus in order to revive; it was believed that once the normal circulation of money, goods, and services had been restored, the government could withdraw from the scene. As matters have evolved, the government has not to this date carried out a complete withdrawal; it appears almost certain that it will stay at least in its present relationship vis-à-vis the national economy.

The theory of "pump-priming" is nowadays an accepted part of government spending policy. However, not much is heard of it, for three reasons. In the first place, to repeat, it is accepted, and therefore it is not hotly debated as it was in the 1930's; the only questions are how, where, and when to set the process going. In the second place, World War II and the huge defense expenditures ever since have tremendously stimulated industry and employment; that is, although "pump-priming" was not the intent of the vast military programs, it was the effect, magnified ten-fold. For instance, the New Deal expenditures of fiscal 1934, when public works programs were pushed to new heights, amounted to only one-tenth of the expenditures planned for fiscal 1957, when defense spending was to be heavy.

Thirdly, in part because of defense spending, but also because of many other economic factors, an economic boom has continued since World War II; pump-priming of industry has been unnecessary. However, it should be observed that when a recession of business activity occurred in 1954, the Republican administration declared its intention immediately to "prime the pump" with a public works program, should conditions worsen.

Whatever may be the motives behind heavy government expenditures, the economy gains energy just as if private persons or private companies had spent the same money. However, the directions and results of the energy in the case of government spending are different from those in the case of private spending. Whether the directions and results are better or worse are questions for each person to decide for himself on the basis of the many varied activities of the government and the private economy. Obviously, washing machines and automobiles are useful; they are solely the products of private industry. However, the government also spends money on roads, canals, harbors, waterways, and power plants, all of which are also useful. The government spends money for the training of people in manufacturing and agriculture; private companies also spend money for training their employees. Both are useful expenditures. Most government spending is for military armaments and personnel. The nation's industry does not spend for these purposes directly, that is, businessmen do not operate private armies in modern times; yet few would say that this kind of government spending is unnecessary.

Other functions need the same examination. What does government spending for old age pensions provide? No new machines certainly; yet it fulfills an obligation to the aged that most people would acknowledge. Hence the spending is useful in that sense. Again, government spending for the conservation of natural resources such as forests and farm lands gives long-term dividends to the next generation. Is that useful spending? Most people believe that it is. Thus the purposes of government spending, even when the amounts are large, can usually be justified to a major part of the population.

QUESTIONS AND PROBLEMS

1. How does the Bureau of the Budget cope with the agency estimates?

2. What powers do the congressional Appropriations Committees have to determine the shape and size of the federal budget?

3. Describe briefly the operations of the General Accounting Office.

4. What are the ten largest categories of expenditures of the federal government?

5. Define the following in one sentence: budget; fiscal year; appropriation; deficiency appropriation; "pump-priming."

6. What are the major effects on the economy of governmental expenditures?

7. What might be the results of a fifty per cent decrease in national governmental expenditures in, for example, fiscal 1959?

Photo by Abbie Rowe. Courtesy National Park Service

BY LEVYING taxes and by borrowing money the federal government obtains most of the funds necessary for the expenditures described in the preceding chapter. The federal government does have other sources of money, but in recent years these have dwindled to the point of being almost inconsequential. However, taxation and borrowing do not have the procuring of money as their sole function. Rather, both processes are cogs in the policy-framing machinery of the government; even where employed for the end of raising money, the form they take is shaped by considerations of a non-financial kind. This chapter is concerned with the different kinds of federal taxes; the relations between taxation and policy; the national debt; and the administration of federal moneys.

THE PATTERN OF FEDERAL TAXATION

In 1789 the federal government collected about four million dollars in taxes; in 1956 it collected almost seventy billions. Thus federal taxation

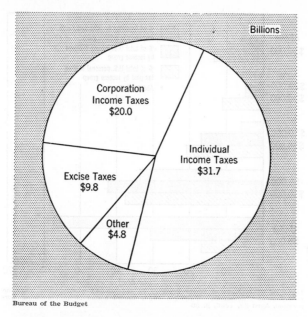

Bureau of the Budget

Figure 73. Major Sources of Federal Revenues (Fiscal 1957, Estimated).

today produces about seventeen thousand times as much money as it did in the first year of the American republic. This multiplication is not only a reflection of the vastly greater role of government in American life today; it is also a consequence of enormous changes in the pattern of taxation. Once-important sources of revenue have become almost trivial, whereas levies non-existent in 1789 have become the principal sources of revenue today. A comparison of the kinds and amount of revenues collected by the federal government is presented in Figure 73; the pattern has become fairly uniform in recent years. A discussion of each major type follows:

Income taxes

Income taxes are taxes that fall upon either the incomes of private individuals or upon the profits of business enterprise.

Individual Income Taxes: Individual income taxes today constitute the greatest source of revenue for the federal government; in 1956 they yielded over thirty-one billion dollars, or nearly half of the total. The income tax is what is known as a "progressive tax"; that is, it is levied at progressively, or proportionately, higher rates upon higher incomes. It is composed of a normal tax, which is a low percentage assessed on all taxable income, and a surtax, which incorporates the progressive feature of the tax. Normal tax and surtax combined rise from a minimum of twenty per cent on the first dollar of taxable income to a maximum of ninety-one per cent on taxable income over $200,000. Certain portions of the total income are tax-exempt, according to the number of persons dependent upon the tax-

Department of the Treasury Building, Washington, D.C.

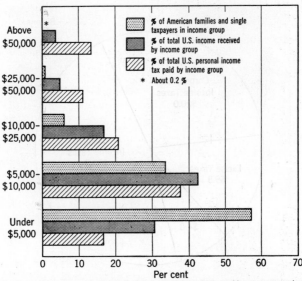

Based on "U.S. News & World Report," an independent weekly news magazine published at Washington.   Copyright 1955, United States News Publishing Corporation, April 22, 1955, p. 20

Figure 74.   Shares of American Income and of Personal Income Taxes of Different Income Groups, 1953.

payer, the age of the taxpayer, the amount of the income that has been given to charity, the amount that has been consumed for medical care, and many other factors.   Figure 74 compares entire classes of incomes of different levels and shows how numerous they are, how much of the total national income they furnish, and how much of the total tax collections they provide.

The progressive income tax enjoys excellent repute among lower income groups in the population, since it is based upon the principle of the ability to pay; that is, it operates on the assumption that the higher the individual's income, the greater is his ability to pay taxes since it is taken for granted (although it is not a fact) that one person needs no more money than another to feed, clothe, and house himself.   The income tax also has great fiscal practicality, since the amount of tax to be collected can be readily altered by simply changing the percentage of incidence.   By such manipulation, for instance, collections were raised from less than one and a half billion dollars in 1941 to more than nineteen billions in 1945, a period during which total national income rose only about eighty per cent.   The chart in Figure 75 shows how taxes on specific income levels have varied during the past forty years.

Individual income taxes must be paid annually, on or before April 15. The taxes are collected in two principal ways.   People who receive regular salaries or incomes have a portion of their incomes deducted from their paychecks by their employers, to be turned over to the government.   At the end of the year, then, such persons need pay only a small sum to make up the difference between what has been withheld from their checks and what is owed the government; indeed, it often occurs that an excess has been withheld, so that the government must refund some money. The second type of collection applies to the persons who do not receive a regular salary or wage, but whose income is derived from some other source such as stock dividends. These persons must, sometime during the calendar year, file an estimate of their annual incomes and pay installments on their tax, as computed on their estimated incomes. Then, by the April deadline, they must submit a final statement of their incomes, paying if need be an additional tax on the difference between their estimated and their actual incomes. Again, they may receive a refund in the event they have over-estimated their incomes.

The tax on individual incomes today rests upon the Sixteenth Amendment to the Constitution, adopted in 1913. This Amendment was necessitated by the constitutional provision that "No capitation, or other direct, tax shall be laid, unless in proportion to the census or enumeration herein before directed to be taken" (Art. I, sec. 9, cl. 4). A direct tax has been defined in various ways; it is generally held to be a tax whose payment cannot be transmitted to another person, such as a poll tax or a real estate

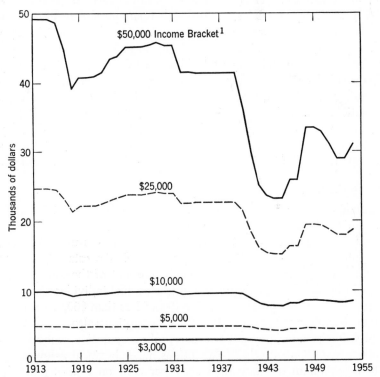

[1]Statutory net income, i.e., income less allowable deductions but before personal exemptions

Adapted from National Industrial Conference Board, Inc., "Road Maps of Industry," no. 984

Figure 75. Impact of Income Taxes on Different Income Levels, 1913–1953. The chart shows how many dollars are left to the taxpayer in five different income brackets after he pays his income tax. (It is calculated for a married couple with two children.)

tax. An indirect tax, by contrast, is a levy such as a sales tax that can be passed on to some other person. According to one school of thought, there is no such thing as a direct tax; that is, all taxes can by one means or another be passed on. For instance, the income tax of a corporation president may finally be paid by the purchaser of the commodity manufactured by the corporation.

Employment Taxes: Employment taxes are also levied upon individual incomes. However, the government does not pretend to use these assessments for current operating expenses. Rather, these taxes are imposed to finance the programs of old age and survivors insurance and of unemployment insurance. These taxes are collected from both employers and employees, as percentages of total payrolls and of individual wages and salaries. In 1956 they yielded more than $6.2 billions. These taxes will be discussed at length in the chapter on social welfare.

Corporation Income Taxes: Corporation income taxes today rank second only to personal income taxes as a source of revenue; in 1956 they yielded $18.3 billions. The corporation income tax is also progressive, although its incline is not so steep as that of the personal income tax; it rises to a maximum of fifty-two per cent. The corporation income tax has the same flexibility as the personal income tax; that is, its yield can be easily raised or lowered by an adjustment of its rates. Too, like the personal income tax it is based upon the principle of the ability to pay.

Unlike the personal income tax, however, the corporation income tax has been ruled an indirect tax. It was first levied in 1909, as a tax upon the carrying on of business, to be proportioned to the profits of each business organization. Since this tax was quite similar to the personal income tax that had been ruled unconstitutional in 1895, it was soon challenged in a federal court. However, the Supreme Court upheld the constitutionality of this tax; hence the tax is not based upon the Sixteenth Amendment.

Estate and gift taxes

The federal government imposes taxes upon both large estates and large gifts. An estate tax must be distinguished from an inheritance or legacy tax such as many States levy. An inheritance tax falls upon an heir, and is computed according to his share of an estate. An estate tax falls upon the estate of any deceased person, and is paid out of the estate. The gift tax is paid by the donor. Estate and gift taxes, like individual and corporation income taxes, are progressive. Estates of less than $60,000, and gifts of less than $3,000, are tax-exempt. Other exemptions also apply to estates and gifts; for instance, any gift to a non-profit corporation such as a university is tax-free. Outside these exemptions, taxes begin at a low rate, then rise to a maximum of more than sixty per cent on estates and fifty-five per cent on gifts. These two taxes produce far less revenue than income taxes, usually under one billion dollars together, of which the gift tax is only a small part. Like the corporation income tax, the estate tax was enacted before the adoption of the Sixteenth Amendment, was challenged, was declared to be an indirect tax, and today is not founded upon the Sixteenth Amendment.

Excise taxes

An excise tax is a tax upon a business transaction. Generally it is a sales tax that is levied upon specific items. However, the federal corporation income tax is an excise tax, levied upon the process of manufacturing. An excise tax is an indirect tax; it falls ultimately upon the consumer, for the tax is comprised in the purchase price of the item. It may be imposed either as a specific sum, in dollars and cents, or as a percentage of the retail or the manufacturer's price.

Excises fall into two broad classes: (1) retail excise taxes; and (2) manufacturers' excise taxes. Of the two, the manufacturers' tax is often regarded as unjust because of the mode of its collection; its critics hold that it works undue hardship on the consumer. The manufacturers' excise tax is a "hidden" tax. Levied at the factory, it is a tax that the manufacturer adds to his price.

Among federal excise taxes, which altogether raised $9.1 billions in 1955, those upon alcoholic beverages and tobacco products are by far the most remunerative; for they bring in about half the total. In a sense these might be termed manufacturers' excises, since the producer must pay the tax originally. However, the tax appears in the form of a stamp bearing a specific monetary value, which must be affixed to the bottle or package. Consequently the consumer pays only the cost of the stamp, and is therefore only reimbursing the manufacturer for his tax charge. There are many taxes frankly termed manufacturers' excises, such as those upon automobile tires and tubes, phonograph records, firearms, electric light bulbs, mechanical refrigerators, and the like; they have lately returned over two billion dollars annually. There are a few so-called retailers' excises, imposed upon furs, jewelry, luggage, and toilet preparations, that yield about $500 millions annually. Finally, there are a host of miscellaneous taxes, the most important of which are those on telephone and telegraph services, transportation, and entertainment; this group of taxes accounts for around $2 billions each year.

The tariff

The tariff is a tax imposed upon goods imported into the United States from another country. The tariff is different from all other taxes hitherto described, for these other taxes fall into the category known as internal revenue. The tariff, by contrast, may be termed external revenue. The tariff is one of the oldest and most important taxes in history. For many years after 1789 it was the principal source of revenue for the American national government. The solid line in Figure 76 shows what percentage the tariff has been of total national revenue throughout American history. It can be seen that for most of the time until the Civil War the tariff yielded well over eighty per cent of all national government income; the

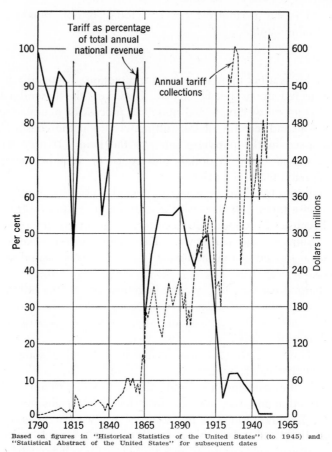

Based on figures in "Historical Statistics of the United States" (to 1945) and
"Statistical Abstract of the United States" for subsequent dates

**Figure 76. Annual Tariff Collections and Tariffs as a
Percentage of Total National Revenues, 1790–1955.**

decline in 1815 was occasioned by the War of 1812, and that about 1840
by the exceptional income from the sale of government lands. From the
time of the Civil War until the First World War, the tariff still produced
about half the entire national revenue; the extreme slump in 1865 was the
consequence of the Civil War personal income tax.

With the First World War, and the realization of the potentialities of
the personal and the corporation income tax, the tariff became a minor
factor in the tax program. Yet today it provides more than $600 millions,
whereas in 1789 it returned only $4 millions, as can be seen from the broken
line in the same figure. The tariff is a very uncertain source of revenue.
It is designed not only to gather funds for the government but also to regulate commerce. Like excises, it may be expressed either as a stipulated
sum or as a percentage *ad valorem* (to the value of the thing taxed). In
either case, if it is too low, it may displease those who seek its protection;
if it is too high, it may yield no funds. The other functions of the tariff
will be described in the following section of this chapter and in succeeding
chapters.

TAXES AND GOVERNMENT POLICY

Taxes, as stated at the outset cf this chapter, are closely associated with government policy. They not only provide the revenues for the conduct of government; they are also involved in the government regulation of money and in government management of society.

Taxes and the regulation of money

Taxes today play an important part in the governmental regulation of money. When, in 1789, all federal taxes totaled less than one per cent of the national income, federal taxation was not very influential upon money. Today, however, when the federal government collects one-fourth of the national income in taxes, these levies can have a profound effect upon money. The chief impact is upon the supply of money, or, in other terms, upon how much money is available to the public. During the Second World War, for example, many persons urged that taxes be kept high so that there would be less money in circulation, in order that inflation be restrained; some suggested that taxes be kept high in the postwar era for the same reason.

Taxes and the promotion of business

Apart from the expansion and contraction of the supply of money, numerous taxes and tax rates promote (or discourage) business enterprise. The tariff provides an important example of this feature of taxation. The operation of the tariff is simple: it promotes domestic industry that is selling its products to the domestic market by hampering foreign competition for that market. Also, the Constitution bans State tariffs (Art. I, sec. 10, cl. 2); States during the Confederation era had carried on trade wars through mutually prohibitive duties. This prohibition was designed to make the United States a free-trade area. The benefits of this principle are immediately visible to any observer; yet some States have found other devices for impeding interstate competition.

Taxes as compulsory mechanisms

Federal taxes may be imposed in order to compel persons or organizations to perform tasks demanded by federal policy. For instance, the federal government levies a tax upon payrolls, promising the employer a ninety per cent refund provided that the State in which the employer is situated enacts an unemployment insurance law satisfactory to federal authorities. Perhaps the outstanding case is the ten per cent tax that the federal government assesses on State bank notes, so as to bar their emission. This tax, incidentally, is a classic example of a tax which, if it returns any revenues, is a failure; it was created to drive these bank notes entirely out of existence.

Taxes as measures for social control

Today many taxes are instituted wholly or in part for the end of social control. For example, the personal income tax and the estate tax have been employed to equalize incomes somewhat, both because they fall more heavily upon upper-income groups and because their proceeds have been frequently applied to increasing the wealth of lower income groups through such programs as subsidies to farmers. It is asserted in many circles that present income tax levels make it impossible for individuals to invest their money in numerous fields, with the result that the government will have to undertake these once-private functions. Certainly the revenues from personal income taxes do empower the government to extend many forms of assistance to lower-income groups.

Federal taxation may express social policy also through imposing restrictions upon purchases; in this respect it can mirror economic pressures. For many years the federal government assessed a ten-cent tax on a pound of colored oleomargarine, and a one-half cent tax upon a pound of the uncolored product. Senators and Representatives from butter-producing States such as New York and Wisconsin introduced this legislation and blocked its repeal. Eventually, however, congressmen from soybean producing States (soybean oil being a prime element of oleomargarine) joined with congressmen from the less prosperous urban districts to overthrow this law on the ground that it was unfair to consumers. Also, through restricting purchases on other things, taxes may be used as deterrents to crime. For instance, the federal government today levies a per capita tax upon every employee of a gambling establishment, and it has placed a heavy sales tax on the transfer of sawed-off shotguns. These two taxes, like the tax on State bank notes, may be viewed as comparative failures if they yield a large revenue. One could cite other taxes whose incidence or whose very nature is more closely related to policy than to revenue.

Intergovernmental tax conflicts

Important political conflicts arise from the fact that the federal government and the State and local governments may impose taxes upon the same object or function. To many people the most irritating phase of this conflict emerges from the fact that more than half of the State governments today levy personal income taxes; in fact, there are even some cities, such as St. Louis, that impose taxes upon personal incomes earned in the city. Since the State of Missouri also collects a personal income tax, the individual employed in St. Louis is liable to a triple tax upon his earnings. There are many items that are subject to at least double taxation; for instance, both the federal government and the State governments tax each gallon of gasoline sold to motorists. The consequence is that one government level may vie with another in collecting taxes from an object or an operation. Federal taxes, of course, take priority over any other taxes. In return, the federal government has extended certain exemptions to relieve the burden of double taxation. For instance, the federal government allows an individual to claim a deduction for any State income tax he has paid. However, it should be pointed out, this is not the same as permitting the individual to deduct his State income tax payment from his federal income tax payment.

A number of solutions have been proposed for these overlapping tax assessments. One of the most popular has been that the national government agree with the States that each level may tax only certain objects or operations. Following this notion, only the federal government might tax personal incomes, and only the State governments might tax gasoline. Another proposal, one that is repugnant to all adherents of State sovereignty, is that the national government collect all taxes, then apportion shares among the State governments. To a limited extent this practice is already being followed, in the form of federal grants-in-aid to State and local governments. Actually, since the national government feels pinched for revenues, and since the States yet claim that they are sovereign, the current pattern of overlapping taxation is likely to continue.

NON-TAX REVENUE SOURCES

The federal government has certain other sources of revenue that are not associated with taxation. Revenue, it may be noted here, is a source of money income for the government that does not add to the debt of the government; hence the money that the government obtains through loans does not constitute revenue. The non-tax revenue sources of the federal government are not nearly so important as those of the State and local governments; their nature shows that they are much more significant in the field of policy than in that of revenue. For instance, the federal government receives some money from the lease or sale of land that it owns—land which, if not privately exploited, might remain unused, but which, when exploited, adds to the national wealth and also returns tax dividends to the national government. Federal authorities also assess fees for licenses, such as the charters of incorporation granted to national banks, from copyrights, and from patents—all stimuli to business. Besides, the federal government receives court fines for the violation of federal laws. Too, it acquires whatever profits accrue to the various service organizations it maintains, such as the Post Office (which rarely shows a profit), the Tennessee Valley Authority, and comparable bodies. These non-tax sources and others furnish the government with well over $1 billion annually.

THE NATIONAL DEBT

The national debt has arisen from the fact that the national government has had to borrow money. It has had to borrow money because it has not received sufficient revenues from taxes and non-tax sources to pay the obligations resulting from its expenditures. Taxes are among the oldest governmental phenomena on earth; so too are debts created by loans extended to rulers as individuals, in eras when state finance was identical with the king's money box. However, a national debt, incumbent upon an entire citizenry, is a comparatively modern concept. Whatever the function of the national debt is, whatever may be its role in political and economic affairs, its character in the public eye of the United States is tinctured by

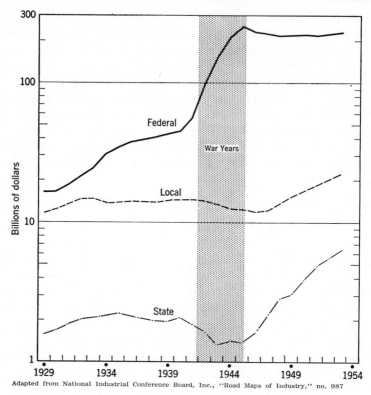

Adapted from National Industrial Conference Board, Inc., "Road Maps of Industry," no. 987

**Figure 77. Trend of Federal, State, and Local Government Debt,
1929–1953.**

centuries of conscious and unconscious rearing in a Puritan creed that
rejects personal debt, and echoes Polonius' words: "Neither a borrower
nor a lender be. . . ."

Evolution of the national debt

The national debt today amounts to about $275 billions; see the chart
in Figure 77, which also shows the increment of State and local debts.
The national debt is almost entirely the consequence of wars. The new
government in 1789 inherited a public debt of about $75 millions from the
Revolutionary War. This debt had been somewhat reduced when the
nation entered the War of 1812. After that war, thanks to high tariff
collections the debt was lowered to virtual nothingness by 1835. Thereafter, the depression of 1837, the sudden loss of revenues from the sale
of the public lands that resulted from Andrew Jackson's hard credit policies,
and the war with Mexico, created a new debt. Before the onset of the
Civil War this debt had again been reduced to less than it had been in 1789;
however, with the Civil War the debt vaulted to more than $2 billions.
Once more it was lowered, attaining a figure of less than $1 billion by
1892, and being stabilized afterward at slightly more than this sum. With
World War I it quickly rose to upwards of $25 billions. By 1930 this debt

had been reduced to $16.1 billions; and critics of the government in the 1920's contend that the debt could have been reduced even more had taxes been kept high.

With the beginning of the depression in 1929, and the determination of the government to assist the needy, the debt began once more to rise, reaching $40 billions in 1939. Commencing with this year the government began to arm itself preparatory to entering World War II; military costs soon surpassed the charges of domestic relief. After the United States declared war upon Japan, Germany, and Italy, the debt rose by leaps and bounds, reaching $269 billions in 1946. Thereafter it was somewhat reduced, chiefly through the manipulation of government cash reserves. However, the decision of the government to arm itself against possible attack by the Soviet Union, and the outbreak of war in Korea, elevated the public debt to its present status.

The form of the debt

The federal debt takes two important forms. The more obvious form so far as the public is concerned comprises federal bonds. These debentures, which are long-term and carry an interest rate greater than two per cent, actually constitute only a fraction of the debt. They are purchased not only by individuals but also by such organizations as insurance companies, since they are an investment with a certain, if small, income. Another very significant portion of the debt includes so-called short-term notes, valid for no more than one year, and sold chiefly to banks. The yield of these short-term notes is about two per cent. Most federal loans, whether as bonds or short-term paper, are sold through the Federal Reserve Banks. Savings bonds are a notable exception; they are sold by the United States Savings Bonds Division of the Treasury Department. The graph in Figure 78 shows who owns the federal debt.

The functions of the debt

The federal debt has several important functions. The most evident of these functions is to provide money for carrying on government operations, when this revenue is not available from taxes and other sources of income. This function of the debt is particularly important in modern wars, especially at their outset. Not only would it be almost impossible to finance a war entirely from taxes, but also a high tax rate at the beginning of a war might so discourage businessmen that they would not expand their industries sufficiently to cope with the added demands of the armed forces.

It might be argued that, as it stands, the federal debt affords a stabilizing or even depressing influence upon business development; however, businessmen today have more or less accepted the existence of this debt, and tend to disregard it in their calculations. The debt, particularly during wartime, may be used to soak up inflationary public buying power; that is, people may be urged, or even compelled, to buy bonds. It is noteworthy that with respect to inflation a bond sold to a private individual has an effect

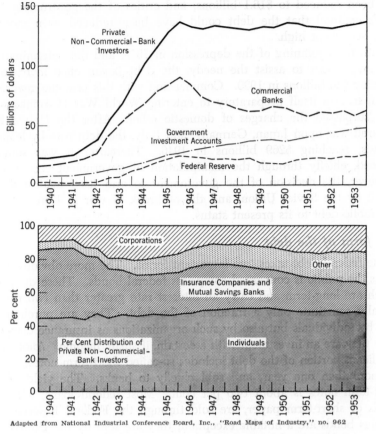

Adapted from National Industrial Conference Board, Inc., "Road Maps of Industry," no. 962

Figure 78. Ownership of the National Debt, 1940–1953.

the reverse of a bond sold to a bank. A bond sold to an individual is deflationary, since it takes a specific sum away from the individual. A bond sold to a bank is inflationary, since the bank may use the bond as the foundation for credit that it may extend. It is for this reason that during a war the government is especially interested in selling bonds to private citizens.

The federal debt in the form of interest-paying bonds provides many persons and institutions with an investment; of course, the interest payments in a way amount to a transfer of funds from one pocket to another, since they can be paid only through collecting taxes. The greatest investor is the Social Security Administration, for federal law requires that all money taken for old age and survivors insurance be used to purchase federal bonds. Hence the SSA owns about $20 billions worth of federal debentures. Finally, the public debt is a convenient weapon for those interests that seek to limit government activities favoring other interests; they can point to the debt, then invoke the horrid specter of national bankruptcy, to win a certain degree of backing from otherwise disinterested persons.

Servicing the national debt

Servicing the national debt refers simply to paying interest on the national debt. At one time the rate of interest was comparatively high, exceeding four per cent; today, however, the interest rate is little more than two per cent. At one time, the interest on the national debt concerned few persons other than those who owned federal bonds. Today, however, the federal government is the greatest debtor in the country and perhaps in the world. Hence the interest on the federal debt, and the way it is handled, have a profound influence upon the entire national economy. In effect, the rate of interest that the federal government pays determines, or at least modifies, the rate of interest paid by private concerns. By paying a low rate of interest, the government may promote low interest rates in banking circles, thus making money inexpensive to borrow and stimulating inflation. By raising its interest rates, the government may curtail, or at least strive to curtail, inflation. For many years government interest rates have been so low that the national economy has existed in a state of continuous inflation.

REVENUE AND DEBT ADMINISTRATION

Both national revenue and the national debt are administered by the Department of the Treasury, which on January 1, 1956 had 78,318 employees. This Department was one of the first created by Congress in 1789, and its Secretary ranks second only to the Secretary of State in terms of protocol. There is, however, one major finance officer in the Executive Office of the President: the Director of the Budget. The Secretary of the Treasury, then, has an important competitor for the ear of the President in drafting the budget. Whether the Director of the Budget or the Secretary of the Treasury will prevail in working upon the President is apt to be determined by the personalities of the individuals concerned.

There are two principal collection agencies for the Treasury Department: the Bureau of Internal Revenue and the Bureau of Customs. Of the two, the Bureau of Internal Revenue is by far the more important since, as seen above, it gathers many times as much money as the Bureau of Customs. There are sixty-four Bureau of Internal Revenue districts; none is greater than a single State, except that of Washington State, which includes Alaska; Florida, which includes the Canal Zone; Maryland, including the District of Columbia; and the Lower Manhattan (New York City) district, including Puerto Rico. The Bureau of Customs possesses forty-six offices situated chiefly on the Atlantic, Pacific, and Gulf coasts, and on the Canadian and Mexican land frontiers. There are, however, Bureau of Customs offices in such interior cities as Pittsburgh, Indianapolis, Denver, and Memphis, inasmuch as goods may be transported inland under seal to their final destination.

There are several other important services attached to the Department, which can trace their beginnings to the enforcement of tariff collections, but which today have vastly wider roles. For example, the Coast Guard was designed initially to prevent smuggling; today, however, it comprises a sizable adjunct to the Navy. In fact, during the Second World War it was transferred to the jurisdiction of the Navy Department; however, after the war it was restored to Treasury. The Department also houses the Bureau of Printing and Engraving, which produces federal paper money. Too, it contains the Bureau of the Mint, which coins federal metallic money. The Savings Bonds Division was noted above. One other important division is the United States Secret Service, a force that was originally created for the suppression of counterfeiting, and that now also supplies the police guard around the President.

QUESTIONS AND PROBLEMS

1. List the six major sources of federal revenue and state the total of each in fiscal 1956.

2. Describe the history of the national personal income tax. Has the tax become more or less progressive since 1932; since 1949?

3. Distinguish between an estate and an inheritance or legacy tax. What are two taxes the revenues from which are not used for general expenditures?

4. Distinguish between a direct and an indirect tax; give an example of each.

5. Would you say that both *revenue* and *policy* have been motives behind the following taxes: the tariff; the tax on State bank notes; the gambling tax; the progressive income tax; the corporation income tax? Explain your answer.

6. How in general are taxes on individuals related to inflation?

7. In what ways do federal and State tax policies conflict?

8. What groups own government bonds? What is the total indebtedness of the national government today as compared with its indebtedness in 1940?

9. What are some of the major activities of the Department of the Treasury?

PART X

Human and
Natural Resources

The national economy of the United States, like that of any other country, rests chiefly upon the composition of the population and the natural resources of the country. These two factors, coupled with the productiveness of the national economy, rank among the principal determinants of domestic and foreign policy. Their quantity and quality set absolute limits upon policy; in late years their conscious management has become an important phase of policy. This section is devoted to an analysis of the human and natural resources of the United States, and what steps the American national government has taken to preserve and protect them. This present chapter is concerned with the people themselves: their numbers and growth; other traits of the population; and how the population is enumerated.

557

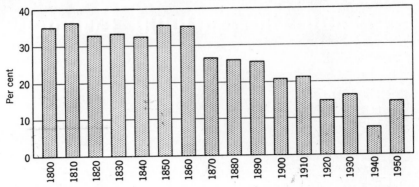

Figure 79.   Percentage of Population Increase by Decade, 1800–1950.

SIZE AND GROWTH OF THE POPULATION

On October 15, 1956, the "census clock" in the lobby of the Commerce Department building reported that there were 169 million Americans. These numbers place the United States fourth in the world in terms of total population, standing behind only China, India, and the Soviet Union, in that order. The population has risen from an estimated 1.2 millions for the thirteen colonies in 1750, to 3.9 millions in 1790, with the first decennial census under the present Constitution (an increase of more than two hundred per cent in only four decades) up to its present and ever-rising total. The graph in Figure 79 shows what percentage of expansion has been revealed at each census.

Such an increase has a profound effect upon the national economy. During the 1930's, an era suffering an economic depression as well, observers conning the low rate of population increase proclaimed that the United States had attained a stage of "economic maturity," an epoch in which the government would have to assume more and more of the activities hitherto shouldered by private citizens, because, according to these observers, the institutions of private enterprise can flourish only in a "youthful," expanding economy, one of whose hallmarks is a rapidly increasing population. The sudden rise in the population that commenced during the Second World War and that has slackened but little in the decade following the war has contributed to the birth of a new optimism that challenges the notion of American economic "stability" or "maturity," and that to some degree conflicts with the belief that the country has reached a period in its economic development that necessitates government intervention. A high rate of population increase, although it may itself create new problems demanding government regulation, certainly contributes to the expansion of the markets that are essential to an aggressive industrial economy.

Ellis Island: For Many Years a Depot for Immigrants to the United States (1890–1955).

CAUSES FOR POPULATION INCREASE

There appear to have been three major causes for the increase in the population of the United States: (1) a high birth rate; (2) a lowered mortality rate; and (3) an influx of immigrants from foreign countries.

A high birth rate

A birth rate expresses simply the proportion of children born to the size of the entire population; in the United States the ratio is stated as a certain number of births to each thousand persons. The ratio of registered births per 1,000 population in 1940 was 17.9, whereas in 1950 it was 23.6; and the birth rate appears to have risen since 1950. A high birth rate, of all the factors producing a population increase, has the greatest psychological impact upon a nation. The birth of a child, it should be remembered, tends to be a happy event in all but the most impoverished families. Large families were an asset on the frontier; each child after he was only a few years old could lend a hand with the chores. Today a high birth rate surely stimulates many phases of the national economy: first, it creates an immediate demand upon manufacturers of infants' wares; it also encourages plans for expansion by industries fabricating commodities for adults. A high birth rate also gives rise to such governmental projects as augmented educational programs and more legislation for the protection of the family. Should the national government undertake a gigantic program of federal aid to education, as has been strongly urged, this momentous step will be partly attributable to the surprising upturn in the birth rate of the past few years.

A lowered mortality rate

The mortality rate of any given area constitutes simply the ratio of deaths in that area to its entire population. The death rate in the United States has been substantially reduced since the early years of the Republic, the reduction occurring mostly since the year 1900. In 1900, the death rate for the whole American population was 17.2 per 1,000; by 1951 it had declined to 9.7 per 1,000. Like the birth rate, the death rate helps mold the national economy. However, its impact and influence are different. It does not have the psychological force of the birth rate, and it does not function in the same area of the economy. The prime effect of a lower death rate upon the population is to raise the percentage of elderly people in the country. In 1850 the median age of the American population was 18.9 years; in 1950, it was 30.2 years. In 1850, about four per cent of the population was sixty years old or more; in 1950, twelve per cent was sixty years old or more. Hence a lowered mortality rate spurs demands for social security legislation, for pensions, old age assistance, and the like. It evokes requests for new forms of recreation such as adult education. In short, it stimulates the adoption of plans for government activity in behalf of older people.

Immigration

Immigration refers to the movement of people from one region to another—in this context from other countries to the United States. Among the three factors behind the increase in the American population, immigration has been the most spectacular. It is, of course, directly or indirectly responsible for all the Caucasian and Negro population living in the United States. The movement of people from different parts of the earth into the United States during the century in which it reached its peak, from 1820 to 1920, dwarfs both relatively and absolutely any other such movement in history. Few other folk migrations begin to rival its influence; among the more important were those of the ancient Greeks to Italy and the Phoenicians to Carthage; the Germanic peoples into the Roman Empire in the first centuries of the Christian Era; the Slavs into Eastern Europe later on; the Chinese into Southeast Asia in modern times; and finally, the Europeans into South America.

By contrast with some of these other migrations that were planned, organized, and led as groups, practically all immigrants into the United States have come as individuals (although some were temporarily organized for the long journey). Only a very few immigrants came from educated or well-to-do families; however, there were such among the leaders of the New England Puritans, the Dutch colonists in New York, the French in Louisiana, the Spanish in California and in New Mexico, the various utopian colonies founded by German, Swedish, Russian, and other national bands and individuals in early Maryland, Virginia, and elsewhere. Of course, in the subsequent waves of immigration there were dissatisfied musicians, artists, and other types of intellectuals. Notably since 1930 a great many immigants have come from the higher educational and economic levels of their lands.

Causes for Immigration: Immigrants have come to the United States for various reasons. For example, many came to North America in order to escape religious persecution in Europe, among them English, French, Irish, and Jews. Many came to seek their fortunes in gold or land. Others came as an alternative to serving jail terms in the British Isles. Some were captured bodily and forced to immigrate as slaves. A few, notably Scots-Irish, migrated during the American Revolution in order to fight the English. During the early decades of the nineteenth century most immigrants were drawn by the lure of high wages in America (mentioned by Adam Smith in his *Wealth of Nations,* published in 1776) and the cheap lands in the West. After the Civil War this stream was enlarged by a growing number who came not so much on their own initiative as on the prompting of transatlantic steamship lines seeking business and of American industrial, transportation, and mining entrepreneurs desirous of low-wage and docile laborers. Practically all have come expecting to find, and indeed finding, an atmosphere of personal freedom.

Countries of Origin: Just as immigrants have differed in their primary reasons for coming to the New World, so have they differed in the countries from which they migrated. Indeed, the pattern of national origins for one decade might be far other than that for the following decade. The initial immigrants were mainly English, with some Spanish, Dutch, French, Swedes, and a scattering of others; England throughout American history has provided many settlers. The first great change in the flood of immigration did not come until the eighteenth century, when Scots-Irish and Germans began arriving in considerable numbers. Too, starting about the same time, southern planters first brought in large numbers of Negroes from Africa.

By the time of the Revolution, then, the population of the thirteen colonies comprised chiefly people of English, Scots-Irish, German, and Negro stock, with an admixture of several other nationalities—Swedes, Dutch, Portuguese, French, and Jews. These proportions were not greatly altered until the 1840's, when the southern Irish inaugurated a career of immigration that eventually halved the population of their native land. Then, in the 1850's German immigration quickly expanded vastly above its previous levels; however, in a few years it subsided to its earlier figures. About 1880 German immigration once more spurted ahead, and Scandinavia first began contributing an important fraction of immigrants.

Up to this time, as can be seen, most immigrants came from northern and western Europe. From 1880 on, by contrast, immigration from southern and eastern Europe—Italy, and the Russian and Austro-Hungarian Empires—rapidly evolved from a trickle into a torrent, so that from 1900 until the onset of World War I most immigrants came from these regions. This flow was halted by the war, but was renewed shortly thereafter. Within a few years, however, through a development to be treated below, Congress enacted restrictive legislation that cut immigration to only a memory of its one-time dimensions.

Generations of Residence: A survey of a representative sample of the population of the United States in 1952 disclosed that a majority of Americans either (a) were born abroad; (b) are descended from one or both parents born abroad; or (c) are descended from one or more grand-

TABLE 20.   RESIDENCE-TIME IN AMERICA
OF THE AMERICAN PEOPLE

Generation	Number	Per Cent[1]
First	120	7.9
Second	362	23.9
Third	328	21.6
Fourth or more (excluding Negro-Americans)	548	36.2
Fourth or more (Negro-Americans only)	157	10.4
Total	1515	100.0

[1] Source: Analysis of survey data gathered by the Survey Research Center, University of Michigan. The total is based on a probability sample of the American population over twenty-one years of age.

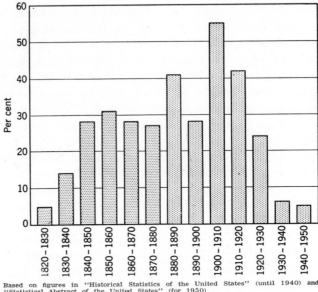

Based on figures in "Historical Statistics of the United States" (until 1940) and "Statistical Abstract of the United States" (for 1950)

Figure 80. Percentage of the Population Increase Caused by Immigration in Each Decade, 1820–1950.

parents who were born abroad. Table 20 shows the proportions of these three groupings and of the balance of the population.

Numbers of Immigrants: From 1820 until 1955 a total of 40,413,120 immigrants came to the United States.[1] This is slightly more than the total population of the United States in 1870. The decade of greatest immigration was that from 1901 to 1910, when almost 8.8 million persons moved to the United States. During this span of 125 years, Germany has sent the largest number, almost 6.5 millions; Ireland, Italy, and the nations of the old Austro-Hungarian Empire have each sent more than four millions; Russia and Great Britain have sent more than three millions apiece. The effect that immigration has had upon the increase of the American population may be judged from the graph in Figure 80, which shows what percentage the immigration in each decade has comprised of the total population gain during that decade. One must not, however, assume that these percentages represent actual gains in the population count; for during the same period, and especially after 1880, a number of persons migrated to the United States, earned considerable sums of money, then returned to their native lands with savings that amounted to modest fortunes there. Yet the number of individuals who returned to their country of origin was small by comparison with the number who remained in the New World.

Immigration Legislation: Whereas the United States once welcomed all immigrants, since about 1930 it has enforced quite restrictive legislation upon immigration. This legislation was adopted after several decades of

---

[1] Figures for periods before 1820 are unreliable. Even those for the period since 1820 are rather suspect, because of the easygoing ways of many immigration officials.

pressure upon Congress by certain interested groups. The first of such groups to demand limitations was that of working men, who had seen employers deliberately import foreign laborers who would work for lower wages than those asked by native American employees. Another group that sought restrictions included those who argued that foreign people were in some way inferior to native Americans, and that they would debase Americans' culture and physical appearance. The First World War emphasized this sentiment by exalting American nationalism. The war also brought such political chaos and economic ruin to some parts of Europe that a few American circles feared lest the United States be drowned in a tidal wave of alien mendicants. Hence during the 1920's Congress passed the laws that provide the foundation for American immigration policy today.

The Immigration and Nationality (McCarran-Walter) Act of 1952 is the statute that now regulates immigration. This law is restrictive, in that it permits only 154,657 immigrants annually (a figure that may be contrasted with the largest number of immigrants to arrive in any one year, the 1,285,349 who came in 1907). The law is also selective, in that it fixes a certain quota of immigrants for each country (except for the nations of North, Central, and South America, whose residents may freely migrate to the United States provided that they enter the country legally). The quota for principal countries is shown in Table 21.

The quota is based, through involved and necessarily uncertain calculations, upon the total number of persons originally of that national stock in the United States in 1920. Although outwardly this date has little significance, actually in the year 1920 the preponderance of Americans

TABLE 21. IMMIGRANTS UNDER THE QUOTA SYSTEM, 1955
Immigrants Entering U.S. under McCarran-Walter Act

Country	Number That Can Come in Each Year	Number Actually Admitted (Fiscal 1955)
Britain and Northern Ireland	65,361	19,267
Germany	25,814	23,430
Ireland	17,756	5,825
Scandinavia	6,834	5,000
France	3,069	2,903
Other western and northern Europe	6,331	5,882
Poland	6,488	3,657
Italy	5,645	5,398
Czechoslovakia	2,859	1,615
Soviet Union	2,697	1,283
Other eastern and southern Europe	6,813	4,666
Africa, Asia, and Pacific	4,990	3,311
Total "Quota Immigrants"	154,657	82,232
Canada and Latin-American republics	unlimited	94,274
Spouses and children of U.S. citizens	unlimited	30,882
Other "non-quota" categories	various limits	30,402
Total "Non-quota Immigrants"		155,558

stemmed from northwestern European peoples—British, Irish, and German —and only a small number came from elsewhere. This quota system was employed because northwestern European stocks were believed by many to be more easily accommodated; also the idea of proportioning new-comers according to a rough calculation of the nationalities in the country already had a strong appeal. The consequence is that the quota assigned to any one country bears little relation to the current population of that country, or to the number of people from any given country who wish to migrate to the United States. Furthermore, using the year 1920 rather than the latest census violates to a small extent the actual proportions of the population.

The three countries with the largest quotas are: Great Britain and Northern Ireland (65,361); Germany (25,814); and Ireland (17,756). Together these countries possess somewhat more than 100 million inhabitants, about four per cent of the total world population; yet they have been awarded about seventy per cent of the immigration quota for the world. Each country is given a quota of at least one hundred. It may be argued that the McCarran-Walter Act is more generous than previous legislation, since it has removed the absolute barrier to immigration by the Chinese and other Asiatic nations; however, a quota of one hundred is scant consolation to China, with its population surpassing one-half billion.

Several groups oppose the Immigration and Nationality Act of 1952. Some disapprove of the law because, like the acts it supplanted, it still discriminates in favor of Europeans, especially the nationalities of northwestern Europe. Others deplore the clauses that forbid immigration by any persons who are or ever have been anarchists, communists, or members of any "totalitarian" organization. These opponents of the law claim that this provision may block many immigrants who might become patriotic citizens and who joined the offending organization in Europe only under the pressure of circumstances.

Labor union leaders tend to be antagonistic toward the law. They are no longer so concerned with the menace of low-wage alien labor as they once were; in many industries there are agreements between factory administrators and union leaders that all employees must join the union once they are hired (union shop) or that the factory can employ only union members (closed shop). Consequently, as union members immigrants may be paid no less than any other union members. Finally, the law finds opponents among those who believe that less fortunate persons overseas should be permitted to share in the benefits of America and that America should not, and cannot afford to, offend the dignity and self-respect of most of the world's peoples by setting up their nationality as the test of whether they shall be welcome.

Immigration and Foreign Policy: During the twentieth century, American national immigration policies have had an impact upon international relations. For example, a good portion of Japanese hostility toward the United States arose from the American ban upon Japanese immigration. After the Second World War, it was recommended in some American quarters that immigration barriers be lowered somewhat so as to admit persons who had suffered exceptional hardships as a consequence of the war. Following these recommendations, Congress in 1948 passed the Displaced Persons Act, under whose terms nearly 400,000 persons were allowed to enter the United States outside the regular quota system. Subsequently Congress passed the Refugee Relief (Watkins-Graham) Act of 1953, which is specially administered by the Department of State, and which provides for admitting 214,000 "refugees, expellees, orphans, and aliens temporarily in the United States" within a three-year period. The Act set up its own quota system exclusive of that under the McCarran-Walter Act; the largest quotas were for 35,000 escapees from the Soviet Bloc in West Germany, Berlin, or Austria; 45,000 Italian refugees from Venezia Giulia (who had been displaced by the Italo-Yugoslav dispute over Trieste) or former Italian colonies; 15,000 Italians with close relatives in the United States; 15,000 Dutch refugees, and 2,000 more Dutch persons with close relatives in the United States; and 15,000 Greek refugees, along with 2,000 more Greek nationals having close relatives in the United States.

Administration of Immigration: Immigration into the United States today falls principally under the jurisdiction of the Immigation and Naturalization Service. The Service is in the Department of Justice; its administrative head is the Commissioner, who is appointed by the President with the consent of the Senate. To execute its tasks the Service maintains eleven districts. The Service determines whether or not an immigrant may be admitted to the United States, and it polices the American borders to prevent illegal immigration. Most examinations of potential immigrants are conducted not in the United States but at American consular offices overseas by agents of the Bureau of Security and Consular Affairs in the Department of State, who maintain liaison with chiefs of the Immigration Service regarding application of the law. The decision by the consular officials as to whether or not an individual shall receive a visa granting him entry to the United States as an immigrant is usually crucial; relatively few persons are denied admittance once they have passed the scrutiny of the consulate. The aim of this practice is to spare individuals the cost of transporting themselves to the United States only to be told that they cannot be admitted, and to prevent such individuals from becoming public charges.

OTHER TRAITS OF THE AMERICAN POPULATION

The westward movement

Ever since the Jamestown colony was founded, the American population has moved constantly westward. Such a movement is quite logical in view of the fact that the first settlements were on the East Coast, that the frontier was at the backs of these first settlements, and that the peopling of the country required that the frontier be pushed steadily west. However, scholars are fairly generally agreed that the frontier—that is, a clear line between populated and unpopulated territory—disappeared about the year 1890. Yet Americans have not ceased to moved westward. For

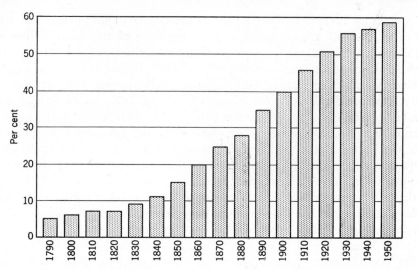

Figure 81. Proportion of the Population Living in Urban Areas, 1790–1950.

example, estimates of 1956 showed that the population of Arizona had increased 103.1% since 1940; that of California, 73.5%; that of Nevada, 100%. In the same period the population of New York State rose only 16%; that of Pennsylvania, 10.9%; that of Ohio, 24.4%; and that of Illinois, 13.7%. Vermont, Oklahoma, Arkansas, and Mississippi suffered actual declines.

This westward migration has made a deep impression upon the national economy and upon the policies of the national government. This movement has provoked calls for numerous forms of government aid, including cheap lands, protection from Indian raids, irrigation of the deserts, and low-cost electricity. The westward movement has also unearthed some of the most precious American natural resources: the soil of the Midwest; the forests of the Far West; the iron ore of Michigan and Minnesota; the gold of California; the copper of Arizona, Utah, and Montana; and many others. Finally, counter to the wishes of the Atlantic Coast States, it has brought industry definitely to the Midwest and tentatively to the Pacific Coast.

Urbanization

Since the adoption of the present Constitution, the American people have engaged in a constant process of urbanization, that is, of moving from the country to the city. The graph in Figure 81 shows the percentage of the population considered as urban residents at each census; roughly speaking, all persons living in towns of 2,500 or more or in metropolitan areas are counted as urban dwellers. The urbanization process has modified the westward movement of the American people. Stimulated particularly by World War II, farmers from the Midwest have flocked to Los Angeles, the San Francisco Bay area, and other West Coast metropolitan areas. At the same time, however, southern farmers have moved in droves to Chicago, Detroit, Cleveland, and other midwestern industrial centers where they have become factory operatives, with the result that these States have almost made up in interstate migration to their cities the rural population they have lost to the West Coast. The map in Figure 82 shows the main trend in this interstate migration.

Urbanization has been one of the most potent forces acting upon the American economy. It is inseparable from the industrialization of the country, and the conversion of the United States from a nation of farmers into one of industrial owners, managers, and workers. Thus urbanization has been conducive to more than a half-century of congressional statutes regulating such matters as industrial combinations and minimum wages for labor. Too, because unemployment and other human problems are more difficult to solve by individual and family decisions in an urban society, this movement to the cities has promoted the enactment of social insurance legislation.

The working force

According to 1956 estimates, the experienced working force of the United States included about 68 million people, about forty per cent of the population. Of these, more than 66 million were employed. Nearly thirty-three per cent of the experienced workers were women. This working force has a breadth of occupations and skills that is not surpassed by the people of any other nation.

These talents and the national economy affect each other. The national economy could not have achieved its present diversity without these myriad talents; at the same time this diversity itself constantly demands training

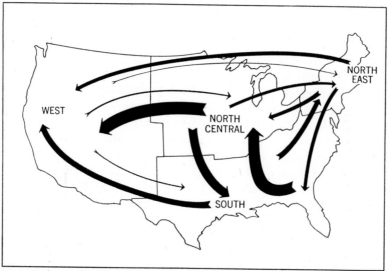

Adapted from: Henry S. Shryock, Jr., and H. T. Eldridge, "Internal Migration in Peace and War," American Sociological Review, Vol. 12 (1947), p. 28

Figure 82.   Migration Inside the United States.   Arrows indicate roughly how many people who were born in one section of the country were found living in the other sections in 1940. The pattern has not changed greatly in the last 15 years.

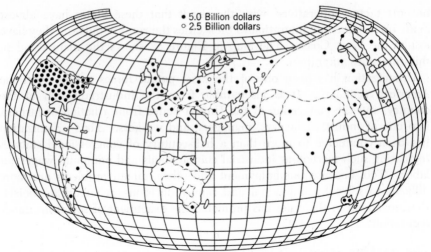

W. S. and E. S. Woytinsky, "World Population and Production" (New York, Twentieth Century Fund, 1953), p. 398

Figure 83. The Distribution of World Population and Income. On this map, continents and selected countries are drawn on the scale of their populations in 1950. Each closed dot represents about $5 billion dollars of annual income (1948) in the country where it is placed. Each open dot stands for $2.5 billions.

for, and perfection of, these occupations and skills among individual Americans. Thanks in part to all these abilities, the American people, who make up only about six per cent of the population of the world, produce about half the wealth in the world.

Income and consumption

The people of the United States have the largest per capita income of any country in the world. The map in Figure 83 shows that they earn more than one-third of the world's income. In 1955 this individual income reached $1,847. It is not evenly divided among the States, however; in that year the average per capita income in Delaware was $2,513, but in Mississippi it was $946. Of course, the income is not portioned equally among individuals. In 1953 (the latest year for which such data are available) the one per cent of the population with the greatest personal incomes received about nine per cent of the total personal income in the United States. However, this one per cent has had its share of the total diminished over past decades; in 1928, for example, this group obtained 14.9% of the total.

One result of this high income rate is that Americans are the greatest consuming public in the world. Only a handful of countries, such as New Zealand, rival the United States in the per capita consumption of food; some countries, including the Soviet Union, that approach the caloric intake of the United States, are poor in meats, which are the most expensive of staple foods. No country surpasses the United States in the consumption of mechanical devices; that is, the United States has proportionately more automobiles, telephones, electric washing machines, and the like, than any other country. The redistribution of national income in the past few years that has brought a large share to the lower income groups has doubtless lifted the consumption rate even higher. The high income rate, then, creates demand, which stimulates the development of industry. This income rate has had another important effect upon industry, that of mechanizing it. Since the wages of labor make up the principal share in the cost of almost all manufactured items, producers who seek to lower their costs so as to lower their prices or increase their profits turn first to means for lessening their labor requirements.

GOVERNMENT STATISTICAL AGENCIES

Statistics today are required by government as much as they are by industry. Since its earliest days the federal government has maintained statistics on its revenues and expenditures, as it is obliged to do by the Constitution (Art. I, sec. 9, cl. 7). The government is also required to enumerate the inhabitants of the country every ten years (Art. I, sec. 2, cl. 3). However, only in recent years have federal authorities begun the compilation of such data as personal and business incomes. These figures, of course, are essential to any organization that seeks to plan its future activities; as the government has more and more undertaken to plan the national economy, it has needed an ever increasing fund of statistics. This fund is amassed by a number of lesser units situated in different administrative agencies, and above all by the Bureau of the Census in the Department of Commerce.

Miscellaneous statistical units

Today all administrative bodies that perform services for the public possess at least one statistical unit; they must have such units in order to execute the tasks for which they were designed. For instance, in the Department of Labor there is the Bureau of Labor Statistics; in the Department of Agriculture, the Bureau of Agricultural Economics; in the Federal Deposit Insurance Corporation, the Division of Research and Statistics. Such units are concerned primarily with acquiring data for their own use in their own field or for use by immediately concerned administrators. As an illustration, the Bureau of Labor Statistics gathers figures on unemployment so as to determine what are labor-surplus areas; this information may then be taken into consideration by government agencies that plan to negotiate contracts with manufacturers, so as to place the contracts in areas having a high rate of unemployment.

The Bureau of the Census

The Bureau of the Census, in the Department of Commerce, is the most important statistical body in the United States. A census, which is an enumeration of people or property, is an ancient governmental institution. The Gospel of St. Luke makes it evident that Jesus was born in Bethlehem rather than in Nazareth, his parents' home, because Joseph and Mary had been obliged to go to Bethlehem for the Roman census; there was no room at the inn because the city was thronged with other people who had journeyed there for the same reason. A famous medieval census yielded the Domesday Book, compiled in 1085–1086 at the order of King William I of England. These early censuses were intended usually to discover either the amount of taxable property in the realm or the strength of the military forces.

As noted above, the Constitution requires that the federal government take a census every ten years, for the two purposes of apportioning membership in the House of Representatives and apportioning direct taxes among the States. Actually these two purposes now make up only a small part of the work of the Census Bureau; apportionment of House membership needs only a simple decennial polling of heads, and the government does not levy any direct taxes that are apportioned among the States according to population.

Today the Bureau of the Census gathers, through its thirty-three district offices, all sorts of data which it makes available to other agencies of the government, to private organizations, and to individuals. The Bureau is a permanent office in the Department of Commerce, with a staff of approximately 3,500 persons. As such, it may be considered as chiefly an instrument for the promotion of business. In fact, its functions reach into every part of the national economy. Its census-taking operations do not entail solely a counting of heads; they include censuses also of housing, agriculture, manufactures, and governmental units, among others.

QUESTIONS AND PROBLEMS

1. What have been the effects of the rate of increase of population in the United States since 1900? Will those effects persist after 1960?

2. What have been the motives for immigration to America since 1607?

3. Describe briefly the Immigration and Nationality Act of 1952 and the Refugee Relief Act of 1953. Are the two in any way contradictory?

4. What have been the major interstate movements of population since 1930?

5. What agencies of the federal government gather statistics on the people and the economy? Describe the operations of one of them.

6. From the *Statistical Abstract of the United States* for any year after 1950, find the following: the titles of all tables dealing with Congress; the titles of all tables treating of personal income in Illinois; the titles of all tables on the subjects of the wages and the hours of labor.

7. From the *Statistical Abstract of the United States* for any year after 1950, find an appropriate table and construct a bar chart (like Figure 81) summarizing all or part of it, on one of the following subjects: changes in the debt of the federal government since 1900; bills introduced to the Senate between 1910 and 1950; exports, types and amounts, any one year after 1948.

37. Social Security and Welfare

S OCIAL security and welfare embrace the many functions performed by the national government in its efforts to alleviate personal hardships occasioned by the lack of food, clothing, and shelter, and to promote minimum standards in such fields as education and health. These efforts, then, aim at the protection and preservation of individual men and women as units in the total of American human resources.

Every government of any consequence in the twentieth century has undertaken to execute certain forms of social security and welfare. For many years, strong interests and a considerable body of opinion in the United States resisted undertaking any steps toward what was believed to be an unwarranted extension of government functions. The ideal American individual, at least until recent years, was the self-sufficient person, the one who survived all disasters without recourse to government aid. Actually this person in many ways is as fictitious as the unicorn; a study of American history discloses that there have always been groups looking for welfare legislation from the national government. Critics of such measures today may point out that the Constitution at no point empowers Congress to legislate for the "general welfare." This term is mentioned only twice in the Constitution: first, in the Preamble—a statement of doctrine rather than law—where it is declared that the Constitution is ordained and established in order to, among other things, "promote the general welfare"; and second, in authorizing Congress to levy taxes "to . . . provide for the . . . general welfare. . . ." (Art. I, sec. 8, cl. 1). Hence, it could be argued, any law dealing with the general welfare is unconstitutional. However, the Supreme Court has often discovered grounds for upholding the constitutionality of statutes that provide for the general welfare. Sometimes the reasoning of the Court has been based upon the spending-power clause just cited; at other times clauses such as the interstate-commerce clause have provided the Court with ample justification for upholding welfare programs.

Indeed, it is almost inconceivable that there could exist a government that did not seek to enhance the general welfare. The true problem is: whose welfare shall it enhance? From its very beginnings the American government has been concerned with the welfare of some groups. When Alexander Hamilton urged the enactment of a protective tariff, he was directly promoting the welfare of American manufacturers and perhaps indirectly that of the majority of the people; when he recommended establishing a Bank of the United States, he was promoting the welfare of the creditor interests and of those wealthy enough to purchase stock in the bank. Deliberate governmental benefits to such groups were congruent with a then common theory about the national economy, according to which wealth is generated at the apex of the economic pyramid, to filter down to the levels below. In other words, if businessmen are prosperous, they will want full employment and will be able to pay the wages of labor. This viewpoint still lives in powerful and influential circles; its implementation can be seen in the Reconstruction Finance Corporation, instituted in 1932 partly to lend money to businessmen so that they could continue production.

Long before 1932, however, this theory had begun to yield ground to a different concept of the national economy, one holding that prosperity is initiated from the base of the economic pyramid, and thence rises to the apex. Otherwise phrased, this concept insists that if the low- and middle-income groups are not prosperous, their failure to have the funds with which they can demand goods and services will bring a depression to industry, commerce, and finance. Consequently social security and welfare legislation today aims at assisting those at the base of the pyramid directly and those at the apex only indirectly.

Granted that there are burdens of social security and welfare in the

Department of Health, Education, and Welfare, Washington, D.C.

1930
Total Expenditures $2,566,000,000

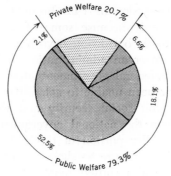

1940
Total Expenditures $6,848,000,000

1950
Total Expenditures $16,910,000,000

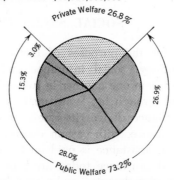

J. Frederic Dewhurst and Associates, "America's Needs and Resources: A New Survey" (New York: Twentieth Century Fund, 1955), p. 432

Figure 84. Total Public and Private Welfare Expenditures for the Last Three Decades, Excluding Public Health and Medical Services.

United States, one of the greatest problems has been the assignment of these burdens. Until about a century ago, these burdens have been assumed almost entirely by individuals, or, perhaps more exactly, by families. One must not lose sight of the fact that the United States until well into the twentieth century has suffered from a shortage of labor. Therefore unemployment has been somewhat rare; both children and grandparents could be assets to a family, for the work they could perform. With the rise of the factory system and the process of urbanization, the resultant change in the position of children and grandparents (especially the latter, since many children worked in factories), and the inability of families to support the weight of social security, a few State and local governments and many privately-supported welfare organizations tried to discharge these tasks. In passing social security and welfare statutes the State and local governments were quite within their constitutional limits; they were doing no more than to exercise their due police powers, those of legislating with respect to public morals, health, safety, and welfare, powers then supposedly denied to the federal government.

However, the depression of 1929 brought impositions that the States could not bear, if only because some of them had constitutional debt limitations that forbade borrowing beyond a fixed limit. The election of 1932 installed in power an administration and a Congress imbued with the notion that the federal government must intercede where the States had failed to act or been unable to act. Hence since the first election of Franklin D. Roosevelt social security and welfare legislation have depended largely upon the national government. Private welfare groups support a much smaller portion of the welfare programs of the nation than they once did, as Figure 84 shows, and State and local governments are active but have also shifted much of their burden to Washington. Although the constitutionality of federal legislation in this field was challenged, it was sustained by the Federal Supreme Court in 1937, and under the auspices of this decision is now unquestioned.

SOCIAL SECURITY

Social security, for the purposes of this chapter, includes two forms of government activity: social insurance and social assistance. These two activities differ from one another in two principal ways: (1) social insurance is financed through tax levies made specifically for that purpose, whereas social assistance derives its resources through general tax funds; and (2) social insurance, with certain exceptions, is paid as a matter of *right*, whereas social assistance is paid on the basis of *need*. Both social insurance and social assistance today are founded on the Social Security Act of 1935 and its amendments.

Social insurance

As will be seen in the ensuing paragraphs, there are two general forms of social insurance. One form is that of annuities, that is, pensions paid to retired workers or to their surviving dependents. The other form is that of unemployment insurance, or money paid to individuals who lose their jobs through no fault of their own.

Old Age and Survivors Insurance (OASI): Old age and survivors insurance (OASI) is the chief type of social insurance in the United States. OASI is entirely an undertaking of the federal government. Whereas originally it applied to only a limited number of kinds of employment, today it applies to virtually all working persons with the exception of physicians. It obtains its funds through contributions by both employers and employees. Beginning in 1957, owing to amendments passed in 1956, both must contribute two and one-fourth per cent of all wages and salaries up to $4,200 per annum. Self-employed persons must pay three and three-eighths per cent on all their income up to $4,200 provided that it amounts to $400 or more annually. It is true that self-employed individuals must pay a higher proportion of their incomes than clerical workers or industrial operatives; however, they have no employer to match their contributions. These sums are given to the Social Security Administration in the Department of Health, Education, and Welfare, which thereupon purchases government bonds with them. At the end of fiscal 1955 these contributions, even after deductions for expenses, made up a fund of more than $21 billions.

OASI is payable to any covered working man who retires at the age of sixty-five and any covered working woman at sixty-two. It is also payable to the widow of any employee under the system when she reaches the age of sixty-two. It is also payable to any disabled worker who is fifty years and has been covered. Finally, it is payable to a widow at any age if she has dependent minor children. However, a retired person between the ages of sixty-five and seventy-two may not earn more than $1,200 yearly if he wishes to receive the full annuity; all earnings above $1,200 are deducted from annuity payments. Persons of seventy-two years or more may earn any amount without suffering deductions. The size of the annuity depends upon the employee's average income during the years he was contributing to OASI, and the number of years he worked. As amended in 1954, the law now provides that no annuity shall be less than $30.00 per month; the largest annuity is $200.00 per month, for widows with two or more dependent children. In 1956 over eight million persons were receiving OASI benefits, at the rate of about $5 billions annually.

OASI has been criticized on several grounds, by both its supporters and its foes. One important criticism has been that OASI comprises a sort of charitable undertaking that no government should assume. However, today this argument is seldom heard; almost all political factions have accepted OASI, if only because they have discovered that promoting and perhaps expanding OASI is a political asset. Moreover, people who have reached an age at which they are unemployable might have to be supported by the government in any case.

Another significant complaint is that OASI funds, thanks to their being invested in government bonds, help the government procure revenue that Congress would not otherwise empower it to obtain. Thus, this argument

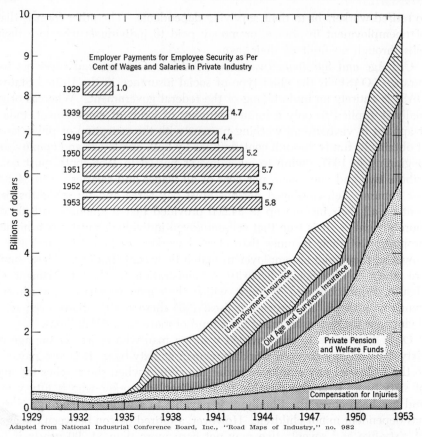

Employer Payments for Employee Security as Per
Cent of Wages and Salaries in Private Industry

1929 ////// 1.0
1939 /////////////////////// 4.7
1949 ////////////////////// 4.4
1950 ////////////////////////// 5.2
1951 //////////////////////////// 5.7
1952 //////////////////////////// 5.7
1953 ///////////////////////////// 5.8

Unemployment Insurance

Old Age and Survivors Insurance

Private Pension
and Welfare Funds

Compensation for Injuries

Adapted from National Industrial Conference Board, Inc., "Road Maps of Industry," no. 982

Figure 85.   Employer Payments for Employee Security, 1929–1953.

continues, OASI funds once they are in the possession of the government are spent in the same manner as any other funds the government may receive. Finally, this argument concludes, although the Social Security Administration in theory has many billions of dollars behind it, actually it possesses only federal bonds, or promises by the government to pay on demand. Thus ultimately the government will have to either levy additional taxes or sell more bonds in order to get this money when it is needed to pay the annuities.   Another aspect of this particular argument holds that whereas adherents of OASI state that through the purchase of government bonds the SSA is investing OASI funds, in fact such purchases do not constitute genuine investments for a government agency inasmuch as interest payments from government bonds can be made only by taxation.

Much of this criticism is valid; yet it is difficult to see precisely what the government would do with these billions of dollars if it did not purchase bonds with them.   Some critics have recommended that the fund itself be discarded entirely, and that OASI be financed from current tax revenues. This proposal has been denounced, especially by labor union leaders, who maintain that its adoption would destroy the "insurance" nature of OASI, converting it into a dole.   Since the government can and in fact does employ these funds to fulfill one function of ordinary revenues, that is, to pay government expenses, the fiscal advisers of the government are not inclined to eliminate the funds.

Since the end of World War II OASI has come to be associated with a host of private pension systems instituted by corporations for their employees. There is no doubt that OASI has stimulated this movement. Labor union officials have negotiated agreements with many large companies that officials of the company shall establish pension funds which, coupled with OASI, will assure retired employees a certain minimum annuity, usually no less than $100 per month. The management of such funds has today come to play a major role in the national economy, since these funds now contain many billions of dollars. The graph in Figure 85 shows employers' annual contributions to four different types of employee security; note how contributions to private pension and welfare funds have leapt ahead of all others, rising to almost $5 billions in 1953.

Railroad Employees' Pensions: Employees of American railroads have been placed under a pension system separate from, but similar to, OASI. This system is based on the Railroad Retirement Act of 1937. Like OASI, railroad employees' pensions are financed by contributions from both the railroads and the workers. Contributions under the Railroad Retirement Act are placed in the Railroad Retirement Account in the United States Treasury; the fund is administered by the Railroad Retirement Board. The Board consists of three persons appointed by the President and confirmed by the Senate; one represents the workers, another the railroads, and the third—the Chairman—is supposedly impartial. In 1956 there were 650,000 beneficiaries of the Railroad Retirement Act, receiving about $600 millions altogether. They received, therefore, almost $1,000 apiece; in the same year OASI beneficiaries averaged only a little more than $600, slightly more than three-fifths as much.

Civil Service Pensions: All employees of the federal government under the classified civil service, and most of those under the unclassified service, share in a pension system. Civil service employees' annuities are financed by a six per cent deduction from pay checks; if they wish a larger pension, workers may surrender up to ten per cent of their salaries. The size of the pension depends upon the salary received and the number of years worked. Retirement is compulsory at the age of seventy; those who have worked many years for the government may retire at an earlier age. In 1956 there were over 300,000 recipients of these annuities, who collected a total of about $375 millions, an average of more than $1,200 per person.

Unemployment Insurance: Unemployment insurance comprises money paid to individuals who are temporarily and unwillingly unemployed. The unemployment insurance system, unlike OASI and other government annuities, is financed and administered primarily by the State governments; however, it was adopted chiefly at the instigation of the federal government. The federal government imposes a tax of three per cent upon the payrolls of enterprises under the system, for each worker paid up to $3,000 per annum. However, the government refunds ninety per cent of such taxes to all employers in States having unemployment insurance systems that comply with certain requirements of the federal government. As noted in a previous chapter, the federal government does not *force* any State government to install such a system; however, this federal tax is of such a nature that employers would be certain to press for its adoption. Hence each State today has a system of unemployment insurance.

These State systems have certain fundamental likenesses combined with a few local distinctions. In most States the system is financed by a levy upon employers alone. Yet it is not easy to compute the true incidence of a tax, that is, the person or group that actually pays the tax. According to one line of thought, manufacturers do not pay this tax at all, but simply pass it on to consumers in the form of higher prices. Following this reasoning, it would not make much difference whether the employee did or did not contribute to unemployment insurance. These funds, although collected by the States, are entrusted to the United States Treasury, with separate accounts for each State, which may be drawn upon in the event of need.

States levy taxes up to 2.7% on employers' payrolls, this figure being equal to the ninety per cent refund of the federal government. In general, however, the States do not collect so high a percentage, inasmuch as they have sliding scales of tax rates based on the unemployment frequency of any given enterprise. The amount of insurance an unemployed person may receive is based on how long he was employed and what his wages were. States differ in the maximum available per week and the number of weeks that a person may receive checks; the range in October, 1955, was from $24 to $36 per week, with some States giving added allowances for dependents, and from sixteen to twenty-six weeks. In calendar 1955 there were about 4.6 million beneficiaries, who received about $1.4 billions of unemployment insurance payments; the average weekly payment was $25.08.

Unemployment insurance is administered through the State offices of employment; the federal government uses the ten per cent it does not refund to employers for subsidizing this administration. This method of administration is used so as to insure that beneficiaries actually are unemployed and are actively seeking employment. In most States, too, an individual is eligible only if he is unemployed through no fault of his own; those who leave their positions voluntarily, or who are discharged for misconduct, either may receive no benefits at all or else may receive them for a lessened period of time. Furthermore, the amounts paid to such persons may not be charged against the employer's account in the computation of his tax rate.

One important friendly criticism of unemployment insurance is that it does not cover enough persons; for example, it does not apply to some government workers. Another criticism of this sort is that the maximum amounts that may be paid have not been raised in proportion to the cost of living; that is, the payments available in 1939, although lower in dollars than those at hand in 1956, would purchase a great deal more.

Some observers question the ability of the system today to carry the burden of a prolonged economic depression; they note that since the system was inaugurated in 1935 the country has been relatively prosperous most of the time, so that States have collected far more money than they have expended. Actually at this time it appears rather unlikely that unemployment will in the near future reach the dimensions it attained in the 1930's, if only because the national government would take steps, or would attempt to take steps, to alleviate it. Consequently the ability of the States to support a really heavy burden of payments may never be tested. It should be pointed out here that railroad workers have their own system of unemployment insurance, just as they have their own pension system.

Social assistance

Social assistance comprises the distribution of money to persons who are suffering actual need. Social assistance is given to three important groups in the population: the aged, dependent children, and the blind. All social assistance programs, unlike OASI, are created and administered by the States. The sole function of the national government is to give money to State governments so that they can make larger payments. Again, although federal aid need not be accepted by the States, it has induced some State governments to allocate exceptional sums to the activities that are assisted by the federal government, possibly at the expense of other, equally meritorious programs that do not happen to have the support of the United States Treasury.

Old-Age Assistance: Every State today has some form of old-age assistance, or monetary relief for the aged. States differ considerably in the amounts they pay and the conditions under which they will pay anything. The State must decide whether an individual may own any property, such as a house; sometimes States make assistance contingent upon the individual's drafting a will that confers all his property on the State at his death. The federal government aids the States by giving them funds, in the form of grants-in-aid, which they may add to the total they pay. The amounts given by the federal government depend upon the size of the State allotments; hence wealthy States receive more money than impoverished States. In fiscal 1955 the States paid almost $1.5 billions in old-age assistance; they received over $900 millions from the federal government for this purpose.

The total given to any one person does not average $100 per month in any State; Connecticut, the State with the highest average, paid $89.43 in April, 1956, whereas West Virginia, the State with the lowest average, paid $28.46. However, particularly in the case of aged couples both of whom have been awarded assistance, they may receive enough money to enable them to live in their own homes independently.

Aid to Dependent Children: Aid to dependent children, like old-age assistance, is a State activity that is helped by federal grants-in-aid. It is available to families that have lost their financial support, as when a husband and father dies. The presumption is that if a woman has one or more small children she cannot leave the house to work; hence the State contributes funds for the support of the children. The amounts vary from one State to another and depend chiefly upon actual necessity; they are roughly proportionate to the number of children. In April, 1956, New York State, which made the highest payments per family per month, gave an average of $142.13 for that purpose; Connecticut, which paid the most per child per month, gave $42.04. Mississippi, which paid the least, gave $27.60 per family and $7.45 per child. The total expenditure on the dependent children program was about $550 millions, with the federal government contributing $376 millions, in fiscal 1955.

Aid to the Blind: Aid to the blind is also a State undertaking that the federal government assists with grants-in-aid. In fiscal 1954, more than 100,000 blind persons benefited from such aid. Massachusetts, which in April, 1956, granted the highest average payments, made awards of $102.24 per month; Alabama, with the lowest average, paid $33.28. The federal government allotted the States almost $36 millions in fiscal 1955 for these programs. The federal government provides one more form of assistance for blind persons: it authorizes them to deduct an additional $600 from their incomes in computing their income tax.

WELFARE

As pointed out in the introduction to this chapter, the federal government performs many functions that can be termed "welfare" activities. Scarcely any governmental activity benefits no one; also, every tax, such as the tariff and the progressive income tax, has in its incidence some measure of favoritism to some element of the public. Hence this chapter contains only a fraction of all federal welfare achievements. The functions that it does deal with may be distinguished by the fact that their principal aim is the *direct* benefit of the physical and mental well-being of large numbers of persons. They tend to fall into the category of the so-called "police powers." They are, then, fields in which the State and local governments also enact and execute laws. The work of the federal government consequently supplements that of the States and localities. There are three leading areas of national welfare legislation: health, education, and housing.

Health

For many years the federal government has taken a concern in the health of American citizens. The principal federal agency dealing with problems of health, the Public Health Service in the Department of Health, Education, and Welfare, stems from legislation enacted in 1798 authorizing the erection of hospitals for American merchant seamen. In later years, through the Social Security Act of 1935 and numerous other laws passed since then, the federal government has invaded the area of public health from many sides.

For example, the government has promoted the creation of several institutes of health for the study of particular diseases; typical of these bodies are the National Cancer Institute and the National Institute of Mental

Health. The federal government has established a system of grants-in-aid for the construction of hospitals; in 1954 these grants amounted to $90 millions. It also extended $29 millions to State and local governments for their programs of maternal and child health care, and a lesser sum for disease control and other public health projects. The government supports two large hospitals in Washington, D.C.; St. Elizabeths, for mental patients; and Freedman's, for Negroes. It maintains a number of other hospitals for civilians across the country, such as those for drug addicts at Fort Worth, Tex., and at Lexington, Ky., and the hospital for lepers at Carville, La. Of course, the government has a large group of hospitals for members of the armed forces and also for veterans of military service. The following figures show how the number of beds in federal hospitals compares with the number of beds in other types of hospitals:[1]

	Total	Federal	State and Local	Non-profit Associations and Proprietary
No. of beds	1,573,014	200,535	912,469	460,010
Per cent	100%	13%	58%	29%

One more significant health undertaking of the national government is the medical examination and, if need be, the quarantining of all immigrants. Figure 86 shows how many people were, in 1953, potentially eligible for federal medical service.

One measure that has been proposed several times but has never approached enactment is national health insurance. This measure would provide medical service and hospitalization for all Americans; it would be financed, like OASI, by compulsory deductions from pay checks. President Truman stoutly backed such legislation. Opponents of this measure have dubbed it "socialized medicine," a term that demonstrates the trend of their arguments. The contention is that this project would lower the standards of medicine and destroy the personal relations between doctor and patient. The chief antagonist of national health insurance has been the wealthy and influential American Medical Association.

In his State of the Union message in 1956, President Eisenhower did not recommend national health insurance. He did urge, however, that Congress adopt legislation that would give financial aid to private health insurance bodies. According to the President, the government should reinsure policies held by such companies; this practice would, in effect, subsidize private insurance companies to expand their operations, in that the government would share the risk on any capital that the companies used to insure people against illness. In this respect the President followed those who assert that voluntary group health plans can perform much of the task that is expected of national health insurance, without the danger of converting the medical profession into a thoroughgoing bureaucracy. Figure 87 shows the per-

[1] *Journal of the American Medical Association, The 1953 Census of Hospitals,* May 15, 1954, cited in Commission on Organization of the Executive Branch of the Government, *Task Force Report on Federal Medical Services,* February, 1955, p. 5.

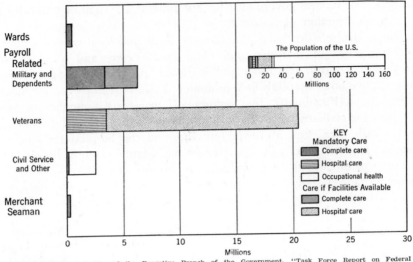

Commission on Organization of the Executive Branch of the Government, "Task Force Report on Federal Medical Services," February, 1955, p. 27

Figure 86. The Number of People Potentially Eligible for Federal Medical Service, 1953.

centage of medical expenditures that was covered by private insurance in 1952.

Education

The federal government has taken a profound interest in public education since its earliest days. In this sentiment the American national government has behaved like most other countries in the world. In the 1956 *Political Handbook of the World,* of the sixty-six countries discussed, only seven had no cabinet or council official with the word "education" in his title: Australia, Canada, Germany, El Salvador, Switzerland, Vatican City, and Yugoslavia. It is true that the United States has had such a cabinet official only since 1953; yet, inasmuch as the United States has a federal government, and inasmuch as education falls in the province of the States, each State government has had as one of its leading officials a superintendent of education, or a magistrate bearing a like title. Of the seven exceptions listed above, all but El Salvador and Vatican City are also federal states. However, there has been an Office of Education in the American government since 1867, which has been chiefly a statistical and consultative body.

Federal aid to education began even before the adoption of the present Constitution, with the Ordinance of 1785, which gave one square mile out of each thirty-six in the western lands to the States for the benefit of public education. Since that era Congress has enacted many other laws extending federal assistance to education. Yet, it must be remembered, public education lies chiefly under the authority of the State and local governments; federal laws do little more than add to State activities, furnishing States and localities with more funds for educational enterprise.

One of the most important gestures of the national government with relation to schools has been the Morrill Act of 1862, whereby the federal government gave lands to the States so that they might found public colleges emphasizing training in the mechanical and agricultural sciences. Consonant with this act, every State has established at least one such college, and some States have more than one. The government also demands that each of these schools provide military training to its students; hence all contain units of the Reserve Officers Training Corps (ROTC). Finally, each college must maintain an agricultural experiment station to conduct research on behalf of farmers. In the 1953 school year the federal government provided these colleges with more than $49 millions through regular appropriations made as grants-in-aid, and almost $120 millions additional for research projects.

The federal government has also subsidized certain kinds of education. For instance, through the Smith-Hughes Act of 1917 it helps to pay the salaries of public school teachers of agriculture and of home economics, and helps the State finance the preparation of such teachers. The federal government also contributes to vocational rehabilitation programs instituted by the States, operating once more on the theory that it is ultimately less expensive to retrain a disabled person so that he can support himself than it is to provide relief for such a person. The federal government supports Howard University for Negroes, in Washington, D.C. It provides schools for the Indian children who are the wards of the government on reservations. It furnishes free lunches to pupils of many schools, spending $83 millions on this project in 1954. Undoubtedly the most expensive educational endeavor of the government was the schooling of veterans of World War II; in the 1951 academic year alone the cost was in excess of $2.1 billions. Veterans of the Korean War were granted the same type of assistance.

It is often recommended that the federal government assume a broad policy of subsidizing schools throughout the nation. The chief justification for this policy lies in the fact that some States, being much wealthier than

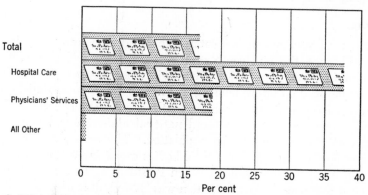

J. Frederic Dewhurst and Associates, "America's Needs and Resources: A New Survey" (New York, Twentieth Century Fund, 1955)

Figure 87. Share of Private Medical Care Expenditures Covered by Voluntary Insurance Benefits, 1952.

others, can pay higher salaries to teachers and erect more school buildings. The aim of the government, then, would be to remove some of these differences by giving poorer States more money. This type of subsidy already exists on a small scale in some States, whose governments contribute money from general funds to the less prosperous school districts. Opponents of this recommendation contend that its effect would be to place ultimate control of schools in the hands of the federal government. Certainly State governments have shown themselves capable of exploiting their grant systems to bring pressure upon school district administrators.

In rebuttal, those who support this proposal insist that localities would continue to dominate educational policies so long as the federal government made the grants without requiring States or localities to satisfy any particular conditions. Others are of the opinion that the federal government would have better school policies than the States, even if the federal authorities gained power through the move; they point out that the federal government would hasten the integration of Negro and white children in the same schools, thus carrying out more easily the unanimous decision of the Supreme Court against segregation. Not surprisingly, the southern States, where education was segregated in 1954, comprise the section of the country in which federal control is viewed with the greatest hostility.

Another problem confronting the supporters of a federal subsidy is that of dealing with private, church-controlled schools. Surely these schools would feel entitled to a share of any federal subsidy, for they have assumed part of the weight of educating the young; yet a federal subsidy to them might be interpreted as state support of religion, which is banned by the First Amendment. One other question that is not often contemplated is that of the actual relation between high teachers' salaries and the excellence of instruction. Some people take this relationship for granted. Yet more money does not solve all problems of public education, and may not solve the more important ones. The need for money, however, grows more and more acute as the flood of school-children rises (see Figure 88).

Housing

The federal government has entered the field of housing only in recent years. Through the nineteenth century it was assumed that individuals and families should supply themselves with housing; moreover, so long as most people lived on farms, housing was not an important consideration for American governments at any level. As the United States became a nation of cities, however, local, State, and national authorities all became concerned with the housing of the population. The first governmental acts regarding housing were those of local bodies exercising their police powers over such matters as sanitation. When President F. D. Roosevelt in 1933 announced that one-third of the nation was "ill-fed, ill-housed, and ill-clad," he signalized the intention of the federal government to invade the field of housing. The first steps of the government in this direction were aimed more at creating work for the unemployed than at inaugurating a major plan for razing the slums. Subsequent legislation, however, was designed frankly to improve the housing of the low- and middle-income groups.

The housing activities of the federal government today are carried out by the Housing and Home Finance Agency, an independent administrative body. The chief officer of the Agency is the Administrator, appointed by the President with the consent of the Senate. The Agency contains several important subordinate bodies. One of these is the National Housing Council, which operates more or less as a staff for the Agency. Another significant body is the Federal Housing Administration (FHA); the FHA may be regarded as primarily an insurance agency that guarantees loans made to private and public owners of housing.

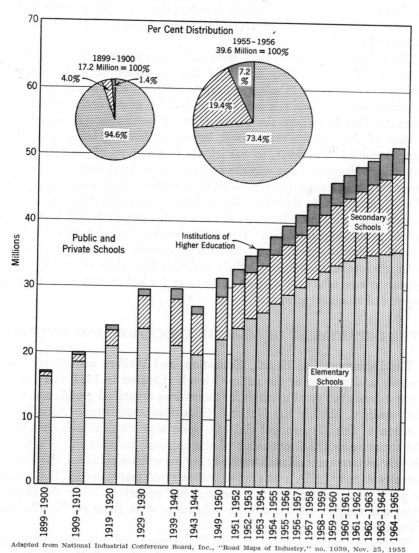

Adapted from National Industrial Conference Board, Inc., "Road Maps of Industry," no. 1039, Nov. 25, 1955

Figure 88. Actual and Predicted School Enrollment from 1899 to 1965.
Data for 1952–1953 through 1964–1965 are estimated.

A third major unit is the Public Housing Administration (PHA), which lends money to local governments that plan to build houses or apartments for low rentals. The PHA also subsidizes low-rent housing by paying local authorities the difference between the rents actually charged and the rents needed to pay for the original cost and upkeep of the buildings. A body that is independent of the Agency but that complements its work is the Federal Home Loan Bank Board. The Board is a bipartisan independent agency whose three members are appointed by the President, and confirmed by the Senate, for four-year terms. The Board supervises the Federal Home Loan Bank System, which extends credit to savings and loan associations and kindred organizations. The system includes eleven Federal Home Loan Banks in as many cities across the country; they are analogous to Federal Reserve Banks, in that their stock is entirely owned by private member banks and associations.

The federal government, then, with a few exceptions such as in defense-plant neighborhoods, does not build houses; rather, it lends money to groups that propose to erect housing, insures loans made by private organizations to individuals who plan to build a home, and executes other functions that encourage the construction of residences. A considerable portion of these endeavors aims at improving housing facilities for low-income groups. However, to participate in this type of undertaking the national government must win the cooperation of local authorities. Sometimes this cooperation is very difficult to secure. Real estate boards are almost unanimous in their hostility to housing subsidized by the national government, and these boards are among the strongest and most active groups in municipal politics. To win the cooperation of local officials the federal authorities must resort to such arguments as that slum-clearance enterprises enhance property values and that the crime rate which slums appear to engender may cost the city more for police protection than the expense of a housing project.

THE DEPARTMENT OF HEALTH, EDUCATION, AND WELFARE

The Department of Health, Education, and Welfare administers social security and welfare at the national level. Created in 1953, this Department represents a great triumph for the various organized groups concerned with welfare, notably the National Education Association. Actually the creation of this Department did not bring about exceptional changes in the structure or the functioning of the national government. There was already an important administrative organ for welfare activities, the Federal Security Agency (FSA); its growth was so rapid that it needed but a name to put it on equal terms with the other chief agencies. When the Department was created, the bulk of its obligations were those of the FSA that were transferred to it.

Hence the establishment of this Department did not mean that the national government was assuming many new burdens. Rather, the impact was psychological; the conversion of the FSA into an executive Department brought its officers into the councils of the President, since the Secretary is a member of the Cabinet. This creation also emphasized to the people the determination of the government to support welfare activities; for a cabinet post enjoys many times the publicity given to the administrator of an independent agency, an office which, regardless of its importance, is frequently quite obscure.

The Department of Health, Education, and Welfare is one of the smaller executive Departments; with 44,856 civilian employees on January 1, 1956, it was larger only than the Departments of State, Commerce, Labor, and Justice. However, it has a large budget; in fiscal 1956 it spent over $2 billions, ranking it behind only the Departments of Defense, the Treasury, and Agriculture. The principal officer is the Secretary; beneath the Secretary are an Under Secretary and two Assistant Secretaries. The chief subdivisions of the Department are the Public Health Service, the Office of Education, the Social Security Administration, the Office of Vocational Rehabilitation, and the Food and Drug Administration. There are also three institutions that are partially supported by the federal government and that are to some degree supervised by the Department: the American Printing House for the Blind, at Louisville; Gallaudet College, for the deaf, in Washington; and Howard University, also in Washington.

QUESTIONS AND PROBLEMS

1. Name and discuss the principal objections that have been made to the undertaking of social welfare and assistance programs.

2. Describe the OASI system.

3. What problems arise from the method of investing funds of the OASI? What method do you prefer? Why?

4. Could OASI be replaced by entirely voluntary means of insurance against old age and death? How? Would such means be practical? Would they be preferable to the existing system, according to your principles?

5. What are two major differences in the methods by which OASI and unemployment insurance systems are *administered?*

6. Are there any kinds or groups of American citizens who are at the present time quite unprotected with respect to youth or old age, unemployment, or medical care? If so, name them, and explain your answer.

7. What are the major reasons why a general program of federal aid to schools had not been adopted by 1957?

8. Describe briefly the several forms of federal aid to housing.

9. List all federal agencies that deal with problems of health, education, welfare (including old age and unemployment), and housing; state in each case the essential structure by which they are administered.

38. Industrial Relations and Working Conditions

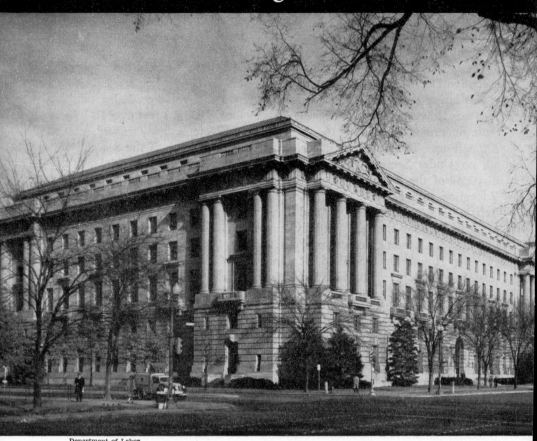

Department of Labor

THE federal government deals with labor today as a third partner in the national economy, along with business and agriculture. Federal authorities have adopted this position only in recent years; certainly until the last few decades working men have not been regarded as a separate political force. Often it was assumed either that workers had the same interests as other Americans, or that their role in life had so little dignity that their interests were unworthy of regard. About a century ago, however, there began to emerge a theory holding that labor is as essential an element in the national economy as either business or agriculture. Coupled with this theory came the recognition that although working men as a group have interests in common with both businessmen and farmers, they also have interests contrary to those of the other two groups.

There have been several important factors in the process whereby labor has attained its present stature in federal politics. One major factor has been the sentiment of humanitarianism, which has stressed the dignity and equality of all men. This sentiment is in part responsible for the fact that it is difficult to draw a logical line between federal labor legislation and federal welfare legislation. For example, old age and survivors insurance as originally designed applied only to manual and clerical workers.

Another factor has been the rise of labor organizations whose leaders can function as spokesmen for the interests of the working group. The force of these organizations, combined with the fact that an increasing number of workers had the power of voting, yielded a band of political figures who campaigned on behalf of the workers, seeking the enactment of laws favoring them. It is noteworthy that although some of these leaders stressed class-consciousness in their appeals, the working group in the main does not feel itself to be a distinct "class"; indeed, American workers are less "class-conscious" than the workers of any other industrial country in the world, often to the dismay of socialists and communists.

Finally, State governments have been incapable of dealing with strife between industries and labor unions that may both cross State lines. Such complications have evoked demands from many other groups that the federal government intercede. Under such conditions, any federal administration wishing to retain popular support has been obliged to acknowledge the power of organized labor. The upshot of these factors is that the federal government carries out two functions with regard to labor: (1) it regulates it, as in the field of industrial relations; and (2) it promotes it, as in the matter of working conditions.

THE ORGANIZATION OF LABOR

Before inspecting federal statutes dealing with labor, one should examine the organization of labor. To a considerable degree these statutes regulate organizations rather than individual workers; for example, the law concerning strikes is almost entirely a law that deals with unions on the one hand and companies on the other hand, as the two parties concerned. Even when the laws treat of subjects that impinge upon individuals instead of upon organizations, such as child-labor restrictions, they may have been enacted at the behest of organizations. Furthermore, employers in industries whose workers belong to labor organizations—and these include almost all the great industries, such as automobiles, aircraft, steel, rubber, electrical machinery, meatpacking, and the like—deal almost always with the organizations, and rarely with the individuals. Labor organizations, then, like some business and agricultural associations, are legally private but in fact governmental in nature, standing between the worker on one hand and both the employer and the federal government on the other. Hence it is necessary to see first of all what labor organizations are, what factors underlie their growth, and what are their relations with the individual workers.

The Department of Labor Building, Washington, D.C.

Labor unions today

The array of American labor unions was discussed in the chapter on interest groups. To recapitulate briefly, there were until 1955 three principal groups of American labor unions: (1) the American Federation of Labor (AFL), the largest and oldest of the three groups; (2) the Congress of Industrial Organizations (CIO), which originated in the AFL in 1935; and (3) the independent or unaffiliated unions, most important of which are the railroad brotherhoods. The AFL was based on craft or trade unions, that is, on unions of artisans possessing the same skills and working in different industries. The CIO was based on industrial unions, that is, on unions of semi-skilled and unskilled laborers working in the same type of industry. The United Brotherhood of Carpenters and Joiners of America was a characteristic AFL union; the United Steelworkers of America, a characteristic CIO body. Yet the AFL included the American Federation of Government Employees, which is not a trade or craft union; the CIO contained the Amalgamated Lithographers of America, which is not an industrial union. In 1955 such distinctions lost importance, because the AFL and the CIO merged into a single giant union organization, the AFL-CIO.

The growth of unions and its cause

Today there are approximately seventeen million union members. In 1897, the earliest date for which statistics are reliable, there were fewer than one-half million union members. In about six decades, then, union membership has multiplied more than thirty times. This increase is far greater than that of the total population, or than that of workers; in 1897 about three per cent of all employed persons belonged to unions, whereas today the percentage surpasses twenty-five. The rise in membership and in the proportion of workers in unions is shown in the graphs in Figure 89. It is remarkable that even today the ratio of union members to the total working force is barely more than one to four, so that union leaders cannot speak with assurance for the "public" or even for all workers. Yet this growth was extensive, and the causes behind it merit investigation.

There is one leading cause for the establishment of labor unions: the wish of laborers to improve working conditions for themselves. It has been pointed out many times that the nucleus of the AFL, a union of cigar makers, was born of the fear that machinery would replace hand labor. Many unions have since been founded by workers who sought higher wages, shorter hours, safer work methods, and improved surroundings for their work. The overt demands of most workers stop at this point. That union members consistently seek improvements for those not in unions, and even for members of other unions, is apt to be as much of an illusion as the contrary belief that union members have a smaller interest in the "common good" than other segments of the population. On most issues, it is fair to say that union workers share "normal" amounts of egotism and altruism.

A secondary reason for the establishment of unions is the drive of certain individuals to obtain a living by exacting union initiation fees and union dues from workers. In some large cities workers in the so-called "service trades," such as hotel employees, have been coerced into unions by elements who had no wish other than to add these assessments to their own income. A frequent procedure has been that the organizers of such unions have managed to raise the wages of the hitherto non-union employees just enough to cover union charges. Yet a third and more important reason underlying the initial organization of some of the largest and most influential unions in America has been the self-sacrificing devotion of men and women who have thought that a new and better society might spring from an enlightened labor union movement that voiced the social and political aspirations of the mass of ordinary people.

The wealth of unions

The wealth of unions today is great, and it is increasing. The Amalgamated Clothing Workers, for example, which started on borrowed money less than fifty years ago, now holds assets of $250,000,000. Only among the comparatively uninformed today can unions depict themselves as groups of impoverished workers. The fact is that union workers on the average are better paid than non-union workers. Whether this is a consequence

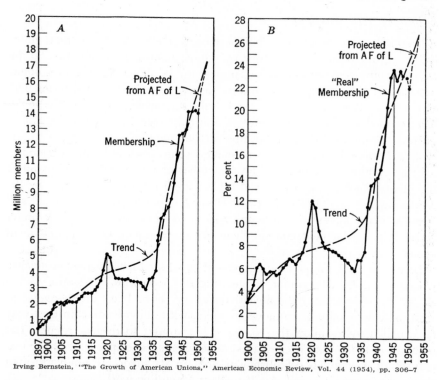

Irving Bernstein, "The Growth of American Unions," American Economic Review, Vol. 44 (1954), pp. 306–7

Figure 89. The Growth of Unions in America. A. Union Membership, 1897–1953. B. Union Membership as a Percentage of the Total Civilian Work Force, 1900–1953.

of the fact that by forming a union, workers receive better pay, or that better-paid workers create unions, would be difficult to prove. In any event, unions have large sources to tap. They derive their immediate wealth from three principal devices: dues; initiation fees; and special assessments. A study made in 1954 disclosed that union income from dues alone then amounted to more than $400 millions annually. This study asserted that it is impossible to determine the revenue from initiation fees, but indicated that it must be considerable; a few unions require $250 or more for an entry fee, although most ask only a few dollars. Special assessments ("for the burial of a beloved member") add substantially more. Today there are two more sources of union revenue that are important. First, union welfare funds are invested in remunerative enterprises, as noted in the preceding chapter. Second, a few unions have purchased income-producing businesses, such as real estate and factories.

In sum, labor unions have tremendous financial resources, so that they can easily afford to lobby in Congress for and against laws. They can also provide numerous social, recreational, and educational benefits for their members. Moreover, they can amass reserves to support their members during periods of strikes. Also they can help to elect friendly politicians, although federal law forbids their making contributions to candidates for federal office.

Relations with workers

Unions have a variety of relations with workers. So far as most union leaders are concerned, all workers should belong to a union. So far as most employers are concerned, no employees should belong to a union, unless the union is one dominated by the employer or on good terms with him. As matters stand today, unions are somewhere between the ideals of the union organizers and those of the employers. In the main, unions possess any one of four relationships with the employee:

Closed Shop: A closed shop is an enterprise in which only union members may be employed. One must be a member of the predominant union of the plant before one can be hired. The closed shop was outlawed by the Labor-Management Relations (Taft-Hartley) Act of 1947; however, it still exists in many businesses, although concealed, since employers may prefer it, for this arrangement enables them to use the union as an employment agency.

Union Shop: A union shop agreement provides that any person given a job must enroll in the union dominating the enterprise. It assures union leadership control over employees once they have been hired; again, as with the closed shop, if employees conflict with union leadership they may be expelled, whereupon the company is required to dismiss them. The union shop today may be instituted only when seventy per cent of the employees of any given establishment vote in its favor. Employers often prefer the union shop, because it tends to discipline workers.

Maintenance of Membership: Under the maintenance of membership arrangement, a worker who joins a union subsequent to being hired must remain in the union or suffer dismissal. Thanks to this sort of relationship the worker is not compelled to join the union as a condition of employment; however, should he choose to join the union he must comply with its regulations and policies.

Open Shop: In an open shop, no one needs to join a union; any person who joins a union and is thereafter expelled is not forced to suffer discharge from work on that ground. The open shop is the commonest situation for unions; it has already been shown that barely one-fourth of American workers belong to unions. However, the open shop is scarcely to be found in large industries or in industries with well-paid workers.

INDUSTRIAL RELATIONS

Industrial relations are the relations between employers and employees. Today in industry these relations are conducted almost exclusively through a process termed *collective bargaining;* that is, workers negotiate with employers not individually but as a collective organism, the union.

The weapons of industrial politics

Both employers and employees have certain traditional implements to assist and supplement their strength at collective bargaining. It should be noted from the outset that American employees have customarily used economic, not political, implements. That is, they have not combined to form a political party that might capture the government, so as to enact laws that would improve their bargaining position. What may be termed labor's greatest victory at the polls, the election of 1932, was accomplished with relatively little assistance from labor organizations, if only because they were then very weak. American workers do tend to support individual candidates who favor their position, and oppose candidates hostile to their interests; yet even in this regard, for any one of several causes workers may vote for candidates who are not friendly toward labor, or at least labor *unions.* Instead, American workers rely upon economic implements operating directly upon their employers. Most national labor laws regulate these economic implements of the unions, together with those of the employers.

The Strike: For American workers the standard implement is the strike. The graph in Figure 90 shows how many man-hours have been lost in recent years because of strikes. Note the peak in 1937, coinciding with the struggle of the CIO to create unions in the steel and automobile industries. Note also the peak in 1946, the first full year after the war, when union leaders after ceilings were removed from wages called strikes in a vast number of industries. A strike is no more than a stoppage of work; employees refuse to come to their places of business until employers meet specified conditions.

The principle underlying the strike is that if the employer does not produce goods he loses money. Unfortunately for workers, this principle is not necessarily true, especially today. Many industrialists find it profit-

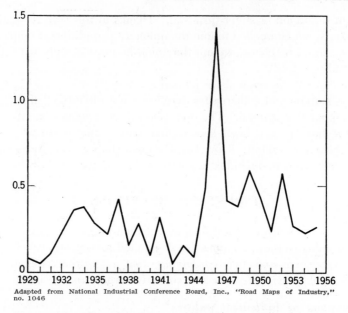

Adapted from National Industrial Conference Board, Inc., "Road Maps of Industry," no. 1046

Figure 90. Man-Days Lost in Strikes, as a Percentage of Estimated Working Time of All Workers, 1929–1955. Data for 1955 are 9-month totals.

able, because of an excess of merchandise, to cease production until a shortage develops that will enable them to market their goods more easily. Moreover, tax rebates and reductions often act to reduce the real losses of corporations from a strike. On the other hand, workers on strike cease immediately to have their regular income; rarely have they been able to save enough money to provision themselves for a strike lasting weeks or months. They are apt to be disqualified for receiving unemployment insurance. Consequently unions today build up reserves from their dues which they can draw upon and extend as a form of relief to the striking employees; in fact, on occasion another union may dip into its funds to assist the striking union. Hence employees can maintain a strike longer than their own resources would support them.

Jurisdictional Strikes: There is one other significant form of work stoppage, the jurisdictional strike, which is associated with a dispute between two or more unions as to which shall dominate an industry, a factory, or a type of work in an industry or factory. One union seeks by striking to compel an employer to deal with it, rather than with an opposing union. Jurisdictional strikes are more frequent in the period in which union representatives are seeking to install their union in a factory or industry. Jurisdictional strikes have also been outlawed by the Taft-Hartley Act.

Secondary Boycotts: Sometimes when the members of one union are on strike, the leaders of another union whose members have dealings with the same enterprise wish to demonstrate their sympathy with the strike, and perhaps add to the pressure upon the employer. These leaders call for what is termed a "secondary boycott," whereby their members do not go on strike but refuse to carry on normal business relations with the employer whose workers are striking. As an illustration, let us assume that all electricians at a General Motors Corporation plant are on strike. The leaders of the Teamsters Union desire to express their accord with the strike. They thereupon direct all truck drivers belonging to the Teamsters Union to cease delivering goods to General Motors; these drivers, however, continue to bring materials to other automotive manufacturers. Secondary boycotts likewise have been forbidden by the Taft-Hartley Act.

Picketing: One other important device used by employees is picketing. Picketing may take any one of several forms. Peaceful picketing has been upheld as a right guaranteed by the federal Constitution. Picketing that entails violence against persons or property theoretically is illegal. However, a person or group with influence over the local police can sometimes commit acts of violence against the other party with impunity, or even get police help in violating political and property rights. Thus, peaceful picketing has sometimes been violently disrupted. At other times, public officials, notably in cities such as Detroit and Chicago, where unions are politically strong, have allowed disorderly union tactics.

Employers' Tactics: Employers may resort to numerous devices to counteract the collective efforts of workers. In past years probably the commonest has been the dismissal of employees, either those who sought to organize unions or went on strike. Today federal law prohibits the discharging of any employee on the ground that he has tried to found a union. Too, companies have organized so-called "company unions," which are workers' groups created and dominated by the company. Federal law forbids a company to require any of its employees to join a company union as a condition of employment. Also, some employers have required their workers to agree not to join unions so long as they are employed by the firm in question, signing what is called a "yellow dog contract." Federal law now bans such contracts.

Yet other companies have resorted to the injunction as a means for dealing with their workers. Sometimes upon hearing rumors of an intended strike, company officials will plead in court that a strike will inflict great damages upon them and procure from the court an injunction forbidding the workers to carry out the strike. An injunction, of course, cannot in itself block a strike; however, violation of an injunction exposes the guilty person or persons to the possibility of conviction on the ground of contempt of court. On other occasions, after a strike has begun an employer may secure an injunction directing the employees to heed certain rules of behavior, such as the avoidance of loud and abusive language in the vicinity of the factory. Union leaders have sought many times to have Congress enact a law that would positively guarantee unions against injunctions. On several occasions Congress has passed a law that appeared as though it would give this guarantee. However, each time loopholes have been discovered in the law so that courts could issue injunctions in spite of the legal restraints. Today federal law authorizes the courts to issue an injunction against a union and its leaders, under specific conditions. One other device for employers is the lockout, whereby employers simply cease operations and close their factories rather than deal with employees' demands.

The government and collective bargaining

Government treatment of workers' organizations today reposes upon two major laws, the Wagner Act of 1935 and the Taft-Hartley Act of 1947. The Taft-Hartley Act is primarily an amendment to the Wagner Act; however, it introduced major changes and a new spirit into relationships between the federal government and labor organizations. Under the terms of these two laws, workers may establish unions of their own choosing. Employers may not interfere with the formation of these groups. In the event more than one such organization springs up in the same business unit, and if these organizations compete for the membership of the same workers, the workers are to conduct an election where by secret ballot they determine which organization is to prevail in their place of work. The organization that wins this election henceforth is the workers' "bargaining agent"; it represents the workers in negotiations with the company.

The National Labor Relations Board: The National Labor Relations Board (NLRB), created by the Wagner Act, supervises such elections and assures that the employers do not intercede in the formation of labor unions. Today this body has five members, who are appointed by the President and confirmed by the Senate, and who serve for overlapping five-year terms. Perhaps the most powerful official attached to the NLRB is the general counsel, a post created by the Taft-Hartley Act. In a rough fashion one may say that the counsel occupies a position analogous to that of a prosecuting attorney, whereas the NLRB performs the role of a court; hitherto the NLRB brought cases as well as tried them, so that it sometimes confused the executive and the judicial functions. On being informed (usually by a union official) that an employer is in some way preventing his workers from establishing a union, the general counsel may hale the offender before the NLRB and charge him with "unfair labor practices." Initially only employers could be charged with such practices; today, however, unions also may be charged, either by employers or by individual workers, with unfair labor practices, such as a refusal to bargain with an employer. Far more cases of charges against employers than against unions have been brought before the NLRB in the last eight years.

It is clear that the organization which secures recognition, or "certification," by the NLRB as the bargaining agent is in an extremely favorable position, for it has great power over the workers. Hence the law makes specific requirements of all organizations seeking certification. Today the most controversial of these requirements is that all officers of the organization provide the NLRB with sworn statements that they are not members of the Communist Party; any organization whose officials cannot take such an oath will be denied all services of the NLRB, which means, for example, that they cannot participate in an election to determine whether or not they shall be certified as a bargaining agent.

This requirement undoubtedly has lessened the influence of the Communist Party over some American labor unions; it has stimulated such unions into purging themselves of officers of dubious loyalty to the union and the country. On the other hand, many union leaders and union members resent being singled out for this sort of oath; they feel that the requirement casts a slur upon their loyalty. Why, they ask, are not businessmen and farmers compelled to take a similar oath; furthermore, why cannot the government locate communists by investigations of individuals?

The Taft-Hartley Act: The Taft-Hartley Act, which is the actual basis of the relations between the federal government and the labor unions today, is one of the most hotly disputed laws ever passed. It was enacted by the Eightieth Congress, the first to be dominated by the Republican Party since 1930. It was vetoed by President Truman but repassed over his veto. It reflected a great deal of the animosity that commercial, industrial, and financial circles had generated with regard to unions. Yet it also mirrored the intention of some legislators to correct what they sincerely felt was an imbalance of governmental controls in the field of industrial relations. Hence the Act outlawed the closed shop (although this portion of the Act is not strictly enforced); it instituted the oath referred to above; it provided for punishing "unfair labor practices" committed by unions; and it obliged a union to give sixty days' notice of its intention to call a strike.

The Loss of Scope by the NLRB: Since the Republican triumph at the polls in 1952, the relations between organized labor and the federal government have undergone an important if subtle transformation. In essence, the federal government has been abdicating its power over industrial relations, surrendering it to the States. It has executed this abdication by purely administrative techniques. What has occurred has been a steady increase of the requirements fixed by the NLRB for the minimum size of a plant over whose industrial relations it will assume authority. That is to say, the NLRB will not take jurisdiction over a labor dispute in any industry that is less than a certain size, usually determined by its volume of annual business and the geographic range of its activities. The NLRB has been progressively raising the minimum size.

The consequence of this process is that States are acquiring more and more authority over labor disputes. This process is quite unfavorable for labor organizations, since State governments are much more likely than the national government to be controlled, or greatly influenced, by a group of industrialists or wealthy farmers. At the present there is little that union leaders can do to overcome or retard this process, because under the law as it now stands the NLRB and its general counsel have almost unlimited power to determine what cases they shall take cognizance of. The principal hope for union officials thus is to procure the appointment of persons friendly to their interests on the Board.

The maintenance of industrial peace

The federal government has created several offices whose function is to eliminate or mitigate industrial strife. The chief agency is the Federal

Mediation and Conciliation Service. The Service comprises three members, a Director, an Associate Director, and an Assistant Director, who are appointed by the President with the consent of the Senate. The Service operates through eight regional offices located in cities across the country. It supplies mediators in the event of industrial disputes. The Service has no power of enforcement; its officers can do no more than seek to persuade the disputants to reach a compromise on issues. The Service may enter the contest either on its own initiative or at a summons by one of the parties concerned.

Special Railroad Legislation: To assure industrial peace on the railroads there are two federal agencies. A dispute between railroad employers and employees comes first before the National Mediation Board, a three-member body which, like the Federal Mediation Service, has no coercive powers. If the Mediation Board is unable to resolve the problem, it turns it over to the National Railroad Adjustment Board, which consists of thirty-six members functioning in four teams of nine persons each. If the Adjustment Board is also unable to bring about a peaceful solution, the question may now be submitted to an emergency board which the President is authorized to call. Again, such a body has no power of enforcement.

That railroad workers have a different status from that of other workers is a result partly of the fact that since railroads are engaged in interstate commerce they have always been indisputably subject to government regulation, whereas manufacturing industries were not exposed to this sort of government control until the commerce clause of the Constitution was interpreted so as to include manufacturing, in the case in which the Wagner Act was declared to be constitutional. Consequently many of the laws regulating railroad labor, particularly those limiting the hours of labor and providing means for avoiding strikes, were enacted before the laws regulating factory labor. The unusual status of railroad workers is also a consequence of the extreme importance of railroads to the country; indeed when a railroad strike looms, the federal government commonly prepares to seize the roads and operate them itself.

Laws Regarding Strikes: Federal law today holds unions to a high standard of responsibility so far as strikes are concerned. Presumably, as bargaining agent for the employees of a given factory, the union will have a written contract with the management of the factory. Often, for the duration of the contract the union leaders may not call a strike; otherwise they may be sued for breach of contract. In such cases, as the expiration date for the contract approaches, union leaders may decide to call a strike so as to win what they will deem a more advantageous contract. If they reach such a decision, they must give written notification to the managers of their position sixty days before the expiration date of the contract. They must also offer to meet with the managers to negotiate a new contract. Finally, within thirty days of this notification to the managers, the union leaders must inform both the Federal Mediation and Conciliation Service, and whatever mediation and conciliation service there is in the

State concerned, that there is a dispute between union and management. Union leaders may not call a strike until either the contract has expired or sixty days have elapsed since the notification to the managers, whichever date is later.

When it appears that workers in an industry essential to the welfare of the country may strike, such as coal miners, the managers of the enterprise may obtain from any federal court an injunction forbidding the strike for a period of eighty days. The President may now appoint a special fact-finding commission which within sixty days is to suggest to the President how the dispute may be settled. If the dispute continues, the NLRB may conduct an election to see if employees will accept the last offer made by the employers; it can be imagined that such an election may be very damaging to union leaders in the event they, and not the members, want the strike. Finally, whether or not a peaceful solution has been achieved, at the end of eighty days the injunction terminates, whereupon the leaders may call a strike if they wish.

WORKING CONDITIONS

In recent years the federal government has shown great concern over the working conditions of employees in all fields. Originally these subjects were regarded as almost entirely in the province of State legislation. The enactment of laws controlling working conditions is an exercise of police power, which supposedly is reserved to the States. However, owing to Supreme Court decisions in the past two decades the federal government now is authorized to legislate almost at will respecting the working conditions of employees for businesses that are engaged in interstate commerce; the nature of the American economy now is such that there are few large businesses whose concerns do not cross State lines. Hence the federal government has enacted a major statute, the Fair Labor Standards Act of 1938, to regulate the hours of work, minimum wages, and child labor. Through other laws it determines working conditions for particular sorts of employees.

Employment

The starting-point for federal concern about working conditions is the fact of employment. Today the federal government performs a number of tasks associated with the promotion of employment. Restrictions on immigration, for example, are designed in part to assure jobs to American citizens. In the past the government has created programs of public works aimed at making work for the unemployed; even now it is certain that if widespread unemployment should again beset the nation, the government would institute such a program anew. The various government agencies, especially the military services, are encouraged to place their contracts in areas suffering a labor surplus.

Today the federal government does not maintain an employment service to bring workers and jobs together. However, each State has such a service, and the federal government helps coordinate these services through the Bureau of Employment Security in the Labor Department. Furthermore, the federal government in part finances the operation of these services by granting them some of the money it receives through its unemployment compensation payroll tax.

The policy of the federal government today holds that full employment is essential to the prosperity of the nation; this policy is based on the conviction that if a large number of people are unemployed, their loss of purchasing power will be felt throughout the national economy. In a sense, therefore, national prosperity may be said to commence with full employment. This belief took form in the Employment Act of 1946. This Act provides that each year the President shall make an "economic report" to Congress, describing economic conditions in the country at the moment, predicting future trends, and indicating the plans of the government to cope with future economic difficulties.

The Act also establishes a Council of Economic Advisers in the Executive Office of the President, made up of three members named by the President with the consent of the Senate. The principal duties of the Council are to maintain a continuous scrutiny of American economic developments, to counsel the President regarding these developments, and to assist in the writing of the economic report. Under President Truman the members of the Council assumed a power not initially granted to them, that of bringing pressure upon Congress to enact their recommendations; in other words, the Council became a lobby for the administration, earning resentment for itself in some quarters. Finally, the Act of 1946 created a joint, fourteen-member congressional Committee on the Economic Report, to analyze the suggestions of the President in his report. Although this Act has been in effect for almost ten years, its impact on the economy cannot yet be accurately measured, if only because there has been a state of near-war during almost all of this period, with abnormal economic conditions predominating. The Act itself is a pale imitation of the original bill, which proposed actual government guarantees of employment opportunities should private enterprise falter. The defeat of this key idea, which had been strongly supported by labor leaders, made the final Act little more than a pious wish for full employment and an instrument for bringing expert opinions on the health of the economy to the attention of Congress and the President.

Hours of labor

Workers today in industrial and commercial enterprises covered by federal law have a work week of forty hours. The government does not forbid workers to toil for more than forty hours; however, it does require that employers pay workers at a rate of fifty per cent higher than their ordinary wages, or at the rate of "time-and-a-half," for all hours worked beyond forty in a given week. Some unions have negotiated agreements with employers providing for exceptional premiums for work done on holidays and Sundays, at the rate of "double time." Such arrangements, however, are private; they are not imposed by federal law. One important purpose of this requirement, which was fixed by the Fair Labor Standards Act, was to penalize employers for keeping their workers long hours, in an effort to encourage management to employ more people for fewer hours so as to distribute income and buying power.

The government has also adopted legislation controlling the hours of work in a few particular areas over which government authority can be readily found in the Constitution. For example, the government has fixed an eight-hour day for its own employees, with a seven-hour day for government clerical workers. In the interests of public safety it has placed a limit on the number of hours that any person directly connected with the operation of trains may work; in addition, through its power to regulate interstate commerce Congress in 1916 established the eight-hour day for all railroad workers. The government also restricts the hours of merchant seamen. Finally, it has fixed a maximum work week in all enterprises that are working under government contracts for $10,000 or more. All of these statutes were enacted before the Fair Labor Standards Act, since in each instance a constitutional justification was evident; by contrast, the Fair Labor Standards Act was not possible until the Supreme Court had ruled that under the commerce clause the federal government is authorized to regulate most manufacturing.

Minimum wages

The Fair Labor Standards Act provides, with its amendments, that any person whose work may be regulated by Congress must be paid no less than one dollar an hour. This law applies to only a fraction of the total national working force; for example, it does not embrace agricultural laborers. It would be hazardous to assert that this law was enacted chiefly at the urging of labor unions; indeed, unions until recently did not favor national minimum wage legislation. This law, in fact, does not have much influence over workers who are union members, since few if any earn so little money. It is principally for the benefit of workers who are not members of labor unions.

Of course, the federal government determines minimum wages for its own employees. Many years ago it established minimum rates for merchant seamen, and before passage of the Fair Labor Standards Act it set minimum wages to be paid in industry under government contract. As with other aspects of the condition of labor, the question of minimum wages is today viewed as part of the larger problem of national prosperity, that is, as a way of bringing greater purchasing power to consumers.

Child labor

The Fair Labor Standards Act provides that goods produced by industrial, commercial, mining, or transportation enterprises that employ children younger than sixteen years of age, or "hazardous" industries employing children younger than eighteen, may not be handled in interstate commerce. This law to a considerable degree has abolished child labor, at least in factories; however, it has not greatly curtailed the employment of children as farm laborers. The purpose of this part of the law was not only to keep children out of factories for the welfare of the children, but also to open more positions for adults. After all, employers paid children lower wages than they paid adults; there have been many cases in which the father of a household was unable to secure work, but was supported by his toiling children. This portion of the Act is enforced by the Bureau of Labor Standards in the Department of Labor; for example, one task of the Bureau is to declare precisely which industries are "hazardous."

Discrimination in employment

Some of the most controversial activities of the federal government in recent years have been its efforts to limit discrimination by employers against members of national, religious, and racial minorities. To date the federal government has not erected a permanent agency to investigate and prevent discrimination against such minority groups. During World War II President Roosevelt created a Fair Employment Practices Commission (FEPC) to work against this type of discrimination, which might hamper production needed for carrying on the war. However, authority for the FEPC disappeared with the end of the war and the emergency powers that Congress had given the President. Subsequent attempts to revive the FEPC as a permanent body were always thwarted by southern congressmen. Afterwards a few State governments established such commissions, and their constitutionality was upheld by the federal courts.

It is important to note that employers are not alone in the practice of discrimination against workers, on the ground of race, religion, or national origin. Government agencies and some labor unions, too, have been known to close their doors against certain minorities. The Report of the President's Committee on Civil Rights in 1947 revealed that of all the complaints received by the wartime FEPC in one year, sixty-nine per cent were against business firms, twenty-five per cent against government offices, and six per cent against labor unions. The courts tend to look severely upon such union practices. In this respect labor unions are akin to political parties; that is, although at one time they might portray themselves as private organizations with full power to determine qualifications for membership, today they play so important a part in political and economic affairs that they are obliged to accept the status of quasi-public institutions. Furthermore, wherever a closed or union shop exists, a man's livelihood might be destroyed by discrimination of some sort.

THE DEPARTMENT OF LABOR

The Department of Labor administers most of the activities of the federal government that concern labor. It is the smallest of all the civilian executive Departments, containing only 5,256 employees on January 1, 1956. The principal officer of the Department is the Secretary; immediately beneath him are an Under Secretary and four Assistant Secretaries. The duties of the Department are carried out by several important line bureaus. The Bureau of Apprenticeship supervises industrial programs for the training of skilled workers. The Bureau of Employees' Compensation administers federal workmen's compensation laws (it must be borne in mind that most compensation arrangements are at the State rather than at the federal level). The Bureau of Employment Security manages the federal side of unemployment insurance and employment services. The Bureau of Labor Standards cooperates with State authorities in improving the conditions of health and safety in industry. The Bureau of Labor Statistics has the highly publicized task today of periodically drafting an index of the cost of living; many wage scales are attached to this index, so that a rise or fall in the index may bring a corresponding rise or fall in wages. The Bureau of Veterans' Reemployment Rights assures veterans the employment rights and privileges guaranteed them by federal law. The Wage and Hour and Public Contract Divisions administer the bulk of federal laws regulating hours, wages, and child labor. Finally, the Women's Bureau works with the States to improve labor conditions for women.

QUESTIONS AND PROBLEMS

1. Explain the rise of the labor unions as major factors in American politics (additional facts may be obtained from the chapter on interest groups).

2. Define briefly the following terms: closed shop; union shop; maintenance of membership; open shop; collective bargaining; company unions; "yellow dog contracts"; lockout.

3. What policy does the national government have with respect to the closed shop? with respect to collective bargaining?

4. List all the provisions of the Taft-Hartley Act that are cited in this chapter.

5. With the aid of the *Encyclopedia Britannica Yearbook* or a similar work of the last five years, prepare a report of the history of a major strike, with especial attention to the role that the federal government played in the proceedings.

6. Reviewing related portions of Chapters 18, 28, 31, and 32, comment on the general importance and limits of the tactics of the NLRB in reducing its own jurisdiction.

7. What are the general provisions of the Fair Labor Standards Act of 1938? of the Employment Act of 1946?

8. Given the provisions of the Constitution guaranteeing rights to all American citizens, how do you explain the fact that preventing discrimination in employment requires special legislation?

Courtesy of the Oklahoma Historical Society

THE conservation of natural resources for the past half-century has been a major function of the national government. Natural resources include such raw materials as vegetable and animal life, soil, water, and minerals, any of which through manufacture or some other means of adaptation to the uses of man acquire a greatly enhanced value. The stock of these materials that a country inherits from nature is an important factor in determining how wealthy the population may become. The many conflicting opinions over how to use and increase this stock inspire many a hot political campaign and congressional debate.

Conservation coincides with, or conflicts with, many other interests. For instance, conservation of the soil and of water assist the farmer, but costs a great deal of money and helps some farmers much more than others.

Conservation of vegetable and animal life may also aid the farmer; yet simultaneously it clashes with lumbering and fishing interests. Conservation of mineral resources sometimes finds opposition from mining concerns. Conservation is practiced at the levels of both the State and the national governments; hence it plays a part in the dispute over States' rights. That is, those who would weaken conservation processes often proclaim the supremacy of the States, partly because a State government much more readily than the national government may be dominated by a single economic interest that can have its own conservation policies enacted and enforced. By contrast, those who favor tight reins on the use of natural resources urge that the federal government be charged with conservation. At the same time, some whose wish is to have a powerful national authority have in mind that the income from these resources—particularly oil—may strengthen the national government.

LAND CONSERVATION

When the white settlers first came to America they discovered a continent of nearly virgin land; the people then here, the Red Indians, were few in number, and were hunters and fishermen rather than tillers of the soil. Hence for almost three centuries there was land for those who wanted it. Farmers by the thousands cultivated one area until they had exhausted the soil, then moved westward to find new land. This practice helps to account for the fact that the center of cotton planting moved from the South Atlantic coastal States to Mississippi, Texas, and California; the soil in the old areas was depleted through constant seeding with a single crop.

Finally, however, just before 1900 American leaders began to realize that with the vanishing of the frontier an era had drawn to a close; no longer was there tillable soil available for the asking. Moreover, millions of acres of once good land had been reduced to near sterility through poor agricultural practices. Some land had been plowed that should have remained as grass; much land was badly eroded by wind or water, owing in part to the removal of the forests; vast amounts of fertile soil were swept away every year by floods, and were deposited on the floors of the oceans and of the Gulf of Mexico. American governing circles, at last alarmed at what might happen to the land of the United States—mindful, perhaps, that the northern part of what is now the Sahara had once been a principal granary of the Roman Empire—inaugurated a program of land conservation at the level of the national government.

The public lands

The public lands of the United States are the lands that are owned by the federal government. There are 1.9 billion acres of land in the United

The Oklahoma Rush for Free Land, 1893. The entry of settlers into the Cherokee Strip coincided roughly with the end of the American frontier. A new phase of American civilization was underway, one of greater social restraints and the greater employment of research, planning, conservation, and means of developing the resources at hand.

Total U.S. Land Area: 1,905 Million Acres
U.S. Average Federally Owned: 23.9%

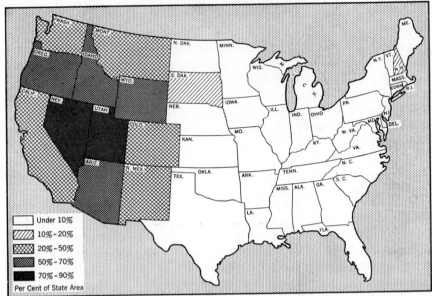

Adapted from National Industrial Conference Board, Inc., "Road Maps of Industry," no. 983

Figure 91. Federal Land Ownership. Including lands held in trust for Indians.

States; of this total, the federal government owns 405.1 million acres, about one-fifth of the entire area. Federal land holdings are not evenly distributed about the country. Most of the public lands are in the eleven westernmost States; Figure 91 shows how much of the land in each of them belongs to the federal government. The government owns about eighty-seven per cent of the land in Nevada and sixty-five per cent of that in Idaho. In the remainder of the country, only South Dakota and New Hampshire reveal federal land holdings in excess of ten per cent. The smallest federal holding in any State, 17,666 acres, is in Connecticut. These facts help explain why the center of numerous controversies over federal land policies is found in the West. The western public expects the government to settle such questions as whether public land shall be sold to private parties and, if so, how much and at what price. Westerners are often more concerned than other Americans over the use of public land and the budget of the Department of the Interior.

The federal government has acquired these lands as the country has expanded from the Atlantic to the Pacific. The first public lands were those ceded by the States to the national government after the American Revolution; each annexation of territory by the federal government, save that of Texas, has added to the public lands. At one time the federal government possessed almost 1.5 billion acres of land in the United States; however, it has given away or sold about one billion acres, largely to individuals establishing homesteads, to railroads, and to State governments. The grants to railroads were originally made to stimulate the construction of new lines. Some of the railroad land has become valuable only in recent years, with the discovery of mineral wealth. For instance, in 1954 the four million acres of land owned by the Southern Pacific Railroad Company produced an income of $2.5 millions in oil and as much more in other land uses.

The period of greatest alienation of the public lands came roughly between 1900 and 1920. However, in the 1930's the process was halted almost entirely, by government order; it was reopened only with many limitations, after World War II. Much of the land that remains has not appeared desirable enough to any person or agency to be taken over, so that it has stayed in the hands of the government.

The government has from time to time obtained—one might almost say *repossessed*—small amounts of land through purchase or condemnation, for such purposes as military bases and national parks. For example, up to June 30, 1954, the government had purchased more than 18 million acres for national forests, at a cost of $72 millions. Of the public lands today, more than half are administered by the Department of the Interior; a large amount are administered by the Department of Agriculture; most of the rest are controlled by the Department of Defense.

The government has full powers over the public lands. National authorities have not proposed to isolate these lands from the national economy; instead, recognizing that the lands may possess valuable resources, the national government leases tracts to various private interests, who are allowed to exploit these resources under strict government regulation. For instance, at the end of June, 1954, the government was leasing more than 66 million acres for the extraction of minerals; over ninety-eight per cent of this area was being exploited for oil and gas. Three States— New Mexico, Utah, and Wyoming—among them contained more than half of this leased acreage. In 1955, the government also held in trust for Indians about 56 million acres, chiefly in the West. Table 22 gives the details of other uses of federal land (leases for mineral exploitation overlap some of the other uses and are not considered in the table):

TABLE 22. THE USE OF FEDERAL LANDS[1]

Principal Use	Millions of Acres
Forests and Wildlife	186.3
Grazing	169.6
Military (except airfields)	15.2
Airfields	2.0
Parks and historic sites	15.0
Reclamation and irrigation	8.8
Flood control and navigation	3.2
Industrial uses, including atomic energy	1.8
Power development	1.5
Sites for hospitals, offices, storage, housing, other purposes	1.7
Total	405.1

[1] *U.S. News and World Report*, April 29, 1955, p. 91.

For example, the table shows that an area of about 170 million acres—slightly more than the total acreage of Texas—is reserved for the grazing of livestock. More than 20,000 owners of cattle, horses, sheep, and goats have permits or licenses to operate on these lands. These livestock owners have made vigorous efforts to win greater freedom in their employment of the range; they have found resistance not only from interested government officials but also from sportsmen, who balk at yielding their hunting grounds.

Protection of the soil

The protection of the soil today is carried out chiefly by the Department of Agriculture. The means whereby this process is executed is associated with the limitation of crops, a practice encouraged by the Department under the theory that shortages will raise farm prices, enabling farmers to profit at the market place. Under the Soil Conservation Act of 1936, farmers are urged to create soil conservation districts; by January 1, 1956, there were 2,690 such districts, under State laws, including more than 1.5 billion acres of land. The Soil Conservation Service in the Agriculture Department conducts research in matters of soil conservation, then transmits its findings to these districts. The Service also will on request prepare a plan for soil conservation for an individual farm or for a farming region.

The Service is especially concerned with the plowing techniques of farmers, the drainage systems on farms, and the types of crops planted. The Service pays farmers for raising certain kinds of crops, such as clover, which assure the farmers no immediate gain but which are soil-preserving. Farmers are not compelled to raise such crops; the government simply holds out the enticement of subsidies. Finally, the Service has attempted to establish a belt of woods and grassland in the Great Plains, partly on an area of about seven million acres of rather unproductive land which the Department has purchased, then retired from cultivation. These efforts are directed at preventing a revival of the "Dust Bowl" of the 1930's, when countless acres of soil in the Great Plains States were blown away. The Great Plains are perhaps the most critical region for American agriculture, because they are subject to cycles of rainfall, in which there may be several years of copious precipitation succeeded by several years of drought. One of the great tragedies of the 1930's was that a period of agricultural economic depression coincided with a drought era. Happily, during World War II with its exaggerated demands for food, this area was well supplied with water. In the 1950's, however, the Dust Bowl is experiencing another dry era. Whenever such a dry period occurs, political leaders from the distressed regions call upon the federal government for financial aid, especially in the form of easy loans that will tide the farmers over their hard times, and for renewed efforts at conserving the soil. The aid is usually granted, although it cannot ever be adequate to mend the damage done or prevent similar catastrophes in the future.

Land reclamation

Land reclamation is the process whereby areas whose soil is fertile enough to cultivate but which have insufficient rainfall are provided with water through irrigation. Land reclamation, then, is associated also with water conservation. Most of the irrigation in the United States is in the region made up of seventeen western States, where altogether in 1949 more than 24 million acres were irrigated by private enterprise and by State and national governments combined, with an invested capital surpassing $1.8 billions. By 1955 the federal government alone had made irrigation available to over seven million acres, of which six million were actually irrigated; and these acres yielded a harvest valued at almost one billion dollars. These projects are supervised by the Bureau of Reclamation in the Interior Department.

Land reclamation is a major undertaking that requires the construction of numerous dams to hold the water for the times at which it is needed. Usually land reclamation projects result in so-called "multi-purpose" dams that hold water not only for irrigation purposes but also to prevent floods, to assist navigation, and to supply power for hydroelectric plants. As the laws that create these projects are ordinarily phrased, however, reclamation is indicated to be the fundamental aim of these undertakings. Doubtless one reason for this phraseology is to placate the opponents of federally-owned power plants.

FORESTS

Today the national government is the custodian for much of the forests of the United States. When the first settlers came to America they found a land that was almost solidly forested, from the Atlantic Coast to beyond the Mississippi River. These forests were a hindrance to the farms that the settlers hoped to establish; moreover, they were the natural habitat of the Indians. As a result they were ruthlessly chopped down. Yet they were an immense, if unrecognized, boon to these colonists, providing them with materials for houses, barns, and fences, and with fuel; moreover, they had been instrumental in fertilizing and preserving the soil. Their significance is visible in the fact that when the settlers finally reached the limit of the forest region west of the Mississippi they did not push the frontier directly ahead into the Great Plains, but rather vaulted fifteen hundred miles to the Pacific Coast, where they discovered more forests. Americans could not populate the treeless Great Plains until, among other things, they had invented barbed wire for fencing.

Still they did not realize the value of forests; they hewed them down so rapidly that by 1900 much of the country was menaced by total deforestation. The lumbering interests, which profited immediately from the forests, exercised little if any self-control in their exploitation. In many areas the destruction of the forests led to far-reaching water erosion and flooding, because the trees that once held the water surplus in their roots had vanished. Hence about the year 1900 the federal government commenced taking what remained of the forests under its protection.

Today the federal government possesses about 180 million acres of national forests in the United States, Alaska, and Puerto Rico, an area greater than that of Texas. The government has adopted the policy that these forests should not be untouched, for in that condition the forest areas would not yield any of their potential wealth and would slowly deteriorate. Hence the federal government leases forest tracts to various undertakings, especially lumbering and paper interests, for exploitation under government supervision. It also leases these regions for grazing purposes, and keeps them open to vacationing tourists. Through these leases, the government in fiscal 1954 received over $65 millions.

The Forest Service of the Agriculture Department, which administers the national forests, carries on research in forest conservation, in seeking out such matters as destructive insect pests. It cooperates with State forest services in the protection of State forests. Finally, it participates in a reforestation program, in which trees are distributed among the States in an effort to restore certain forests. In fiscal 1955, under this program, about 475 million trees were distributed, at a cost to federal and State governments together of more than $4 millions. The principal antagonist of these federal undertakings has been the lumber industry. This industry characteristically has urged that control of the forests be returned either to the States or to private interests. Of course, it would be easier for the industry to control a State government than to control the national government; its organized pressure can be brought to bear more directly upon legislators in a small area.

FISH AND GAME

The first settlers discovered a land teeming with game, and lakes and seas abundantly supplied with fish. Three centuries of unrestricted hunting and fishing made some species extinct, others nearly extinct, and most of the remainder greatly reduced. Today the preservation of game is carried out chiefly in the interests of sportsmen, for most Americans procure their meat through stores. The preservation of fish, by contrast, is important not only for sportsmen but for the population in general, inasmuch as fish are still in the main caught as they live at large in the oceans and lakes. The consequences of uncontrolled fishing may be seen in the steadily diminished catches of mackerel and sardines on the Pacific Coast.

Matters concerning fish and game are administered by the Fish and Wildlife Service in the Interior Department. The Service has full powers over fish and game in the federal public lands. For the fish and game outside the lands, the Service performs several functions. It conducts research into conditions and objects that influence the life of fish and game. It regulates the fur-seal industry near the Pribilof Islands off Alaska. It maintains several refuges for wildlife. It supports fish hatcheries whose products it distributes in the seas, lakes, and rivers of the country; in a single year the Service will apportion several hundred million fish and fish eggs. It seeks waters prolific in fish that have not been exploited. Meanwhile it cooperates with State officials in efforts to control or to exterminate harmful animals such as wolves and harmful animal activities such as the damage inflicted by bears upon tree bark. Through international treaty the government protects migratory birds. Finally, the national government licenses hunters and fishermen who venture upon federal territory and waters.

MINERALS

The United States is one of the most bountifully endowed of all countries with regard to mineral resources. Early settlers discovered sufficient iron in New Jersey and eastern Pennsylvania to set up blast furnaces, such as that at Valley Forge, as a basis for the colonial iron industry. Later, the vast western Pennsylvania coalfields were unearthed. Some time afterward, in 1859, oil was found near Titusville, Pennsylvania, and iron ore was located in northern Michigan. Since that era the United States has become the greatest consumer and producer of iron, coal, and oil in the world. For some years now, however, there has been concern lest the United States become deficient in mineral resources. Some administrators and legislators have argued that the United States must adopt a foreign policy that includes the protection of numerous overseas areas solely because of the raw materials they can furnish to the United States. Meanwhile the federal government itself, primarily through the Interior Department, has sought to limit the use of certain minerals, and finds new sources of them.

Metals and non-metallic resources

The prime metal for present-day industry is iron ore. For many years the United States seemed to have an almost inexhaustible stock of high-grade ore in Michigan and Minnesota. However, the demands of modern industry, and the impositions of two world wars, have so reduced these mines that the end of their yield of high-quality ore is now apparent. Still, they also contain vast amounts of low-grade ore called taconite which can be used, although the cost of processing it will be high. Recently large reserves of good quality ore have been found in Venezuela and in Canada; American steel fabricators are preparing to extract this ore for use in the mills at Chicago, Pittsburgh, Youngstown, and Cleveland—traditional steel centers —and at new plants on the Delaware River near Philadelphia, strategically placed so as to combine Pennsylvania coal with Venezuela ore. The decision of the government, after decades of hesitation, to go ahead with the construction of the St. Lawrence Waterway is attributed in part to the fact that the Waterway will transport Canadian ore to the harbors on Lake Erie, whence it can be transshipped to the mills of Ohio and Pennsylvania. The Waterway as it is now planned will extend the channel for ocean-going vessels only as far as Toledo, Ohio, and not through the Detroit River; hence the steel interests in the Chicago-Gary steel basin will not benefit unless they can economically transfer the ore from boat to train at Toledo.

The United States has varying reserves of other metals and non-metallic resources. Certain metals are entirely or almost entirely lacking; among these is manganese, which is essential for the production of high-grade steel. The United States is deficient also in tin, chromium, and tungsten, among important metals. It procures its nickel from Canada. Supplies of some other metals, notably the bauxite ore which yields aluminum, seem to be decreasing.

One imponderable factor is the change in future requirements that may occur as a result of technological developments. Aluminum is one of the commonest metals on earth; cheaper means may be discovered for extracting it from clay. The oceans contain immeasurable quantities of magnesium, an extremely valuable metal for industry. In the past few years still another metal, titanium, has been found to possess almost unique qualities of hardness and heat resistance.

The principal government agency connected with the conservation of these resources is the Geological Survey in the Interior Department. The Survey among its other duties seeks new sources of raw materials and administers the conservation of known sources. For example, it is trying to produce manganese from sources in Virginia and Tennessee. The Survey also conducts research into more efficient extractive methods. It collaborates with the governments of foreign countries in its quest for mineral resources; for instance, recently it assisted investigations in Mexico, South America, the Near East, and Asia.

Another important government agency is the Bureau of Mines in the Interior Department; with respect to metals, it supports research into problems of the treatment and refinement of ore, and the recapture of metals from slag. The Bureau of Mines also assists the Atomic Energy Commission in its search for uranium and other fissionable materials. One other agency that is concerned with metals is the Bureau of Land Management in the Interior Department, which leases public lands to private individuals who wish to exploit the mineral resources of the area. The Bureau allows such exploitation only under its own rules; the fact is that so far the public lands have not been a major source of minerals.

Fuels

Coal: The leading fuel for modern industry is coal. The United States is in an extremely fortunate position respecting coal resources; it is estimated that present supplies are sufficient for perhaps one thousand more years. Actually, coal as a source of energy, although always very important, has lost its pre-eminence; the graph in Figure 106 shows how the percentage of all American energy that is contributed by coal has decreased over the last century. One leading cause for this decline has been the greatly increased cost of coal, resulting chiefly from the higher wages that the United Mine Workers union has negotiated for its members; although these wages are perhaps not high in relation to those of other workers or in view of the unpleasant work, they add to the cost of a material that is in competition with other low cost materials such as oil and natural gas. Another reason for this decline has been the gasoline-powered automobile, which provides transportation for millions of Americans today who fifty years ago would have ridden on coal-powered trains. Too, the rise in the price of coal, and certain shortcomings in steam locomotives, have induced the railroads to replace coal-driven locomotives with Diesel engines, which operate on oil.

It is quite possible that the absolute amount of coal used will drop even further, owing to more efficient means for employing it; the powdered coal turbine engine, for example, is much more efficient than the reciprocating piston engine. Also, coal will be used more and more not as a fuel but as a valuable mineral resource. Recently Admiral Lewis L. Strauss, Chairman of the Atomic Energy Commission, stated: ". . . There's more of value in coal than thermal units. What we do now is roughly analogous to burning up the books in this room in order to keep warm. You could get heat from these books, but it would be a crime to use them for heat. And so there is a great deal more in coal than just heat."[1] Coal is an essential element in the manufacture of such products as nylon and synthetic dyes.

Because the use of coal has been decreasing, and because present resources are copious, the federal government has not been especially concerned with discovering new reserves. The Bureau of Mines does interest itself in coal, but largely with an eye to the safety of the miners. One important political consequence of the decline of coal and the rise of oil has been the progressive fall in the influence of the coal States and the simultaneous rise in the influence of the oil States, notably Texas.

Oil: Today a fuel that has achieved apparent equality with coal as an energy source is oil. The United States has been generously dowered with oil; however, the reserves of oil are not nearly so great as those of coal, at least so far as is known. Precisely how much oil there is in reserve cannot be stated. From time to time observers have predicted that American oil reserves would be exhausted in a few years; yet in spite of increased production and consumption, the proved reserves of oil have been rising still more rapidly. For instance, in 1952 1.2 barrels of reserves were discovered for each barrel consumed.

It would appear that at present rates of consumption all reserves would be depleted in about twelve years; yet oil companies continue to find new reserves. In the past few years the pockets of oil lying off the shores of Texas and Louisiana in the Gulf of Mexico, and off the shores of California in the Pacific Ocean, have been the targets of considerable attention.

The Republican Eighty-third Congress, to the dismay of all those favoring national conservation agencies and a distribution of oil proceeds more equally among the forty-eight States, enacted legislation turning over to the States the ownership of oil lands out to the limit of their political sovereignty—three miles in the cases of Louisiana and California, twelve-and-one-half in that of Texas. Naturally, the strongest agitation for this measure came from the States that were best situated to enjoy the oil fields, including particularly the three just named. Texas, ordinarily quite Democratic, voted for Eisenhower in 1952 partly because he was known to be friendly to State ownership of tidelands oil rights. The "States' rights" doctrine of Jefferson received an entirely new application in the debates concerning State sovereignty over their neighboring waters. Further explo-

---

[1] *U.S. News and World Report*, December 17, 1954, p. 64.

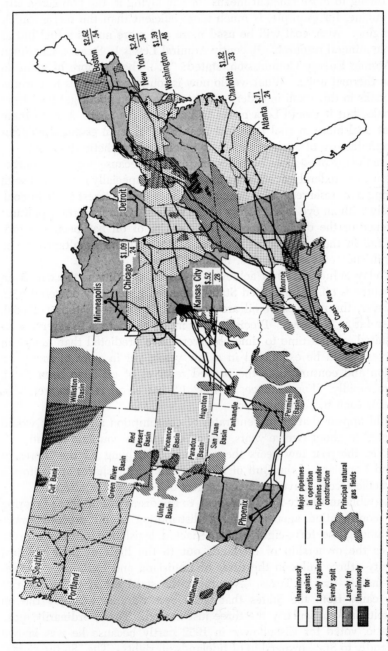

Adapted and quoted from "Life" Magazine, February 6, 1956, p. 35, with the permission of "Life" and Mr. Antonio Petruccelli

Figure 92. The Vote on Natural Gas Controls in the House, 1956. Gas rates per 1000 cubic feet are shown for seven cities: upper figures are charges to utilities by pipelines; lower figures are charges to residential consumers by utilities.

ration has disclosed that vast pools underlie the continental shelf, which reaches many miles out into the Gulf of Mexico and which is under the authority of the national government.

The Bureau of Mines again is the chief federal agency associated with the production of oil. It assists private companies in their search for oil. It also carries on important experiments in the extraction of petroleum from other sources, particularly from oil shale and from low-grade coal. The established oil companies are very hostile to these experiments, for evident reasons; in 1955 Democratic Senator Joseph O'Mahoney of Wyoming, protesting the fact that the presidential budget made no appropriations for these experiments, stated that the shales of Colorado, Utah, and Wyoming contain more oil than all the reserves of Saudi Arabia, supposedly the richest oil area known. The Bureau of Land Management also leases public lands for oil exploitation, as noted above. The fact is that most of the regulation of the petroleum industry is administered by the States; the federal government cooperates with the States as far as it is constitutionally empowered to do so.

Natural Gas: Somewhat the same relations between industry and government exist with respect to natural gas as prevail with regard to oil. Once a neglected by-product of the petroleum industry, natural gas became a huge enterprise after World War II, when the pipelines mapped in Figure 92 were built to link the producing areas with the consuming areas. In 1954, the federal Supreme Court ruled that the production of natural gas was subject to the regulatory power of the Federal Power Commission. In 1956, an intense struggle developed in Congress over a bill designed to relieve the producers from federal control. How the vote of the House of Representatives split on the issue is shown by Figure 92; in general, the delegates from consuming States opposed the bill and those from the producing States favored it. Not the least of the results of the controversy was the creation of a Senate committee to pursue charges that certain producers had sought to win votes by bribery.

ADMINISTRATION OF CONSERVATION

Department of the Interior

The Department of the Interior is the principal federal agency in the administration of conservation. On January 1, 1956, it had 46,463 employees. The expenditures of the Department in fiscal 1956 amounted to $525 millions, more than one-third of which was spent by the Bureau of Reclamation. The chief of the Department is the Secretary. Below the Secretary are an Under Secretary, who is the deputy of the Secretary; and four Assistant Secretaries, one each for Mineral Resources, Public Land Management, Water and Power Development, and administration of the Department. The Department itself is a rather uncoordinated agglomeration of several offices; those that pertain to conservation are six in number. The Bureau of Land Management administers the resources on the public lands. The Bureau of Mines is entrusted with the conservation of mineral resources.

The Bureau of Reclamation manages irrigation projects. The Fish and Wildlife Service promotes the conservation of all forms of wildlife. The Geological Survey is a research agency that prepares maps of the United States and that seeks out additional deposits of mineral resources. Lastly, the National Park Service governs 180 national parks and other recreational areas covering a total of almost 24 million acres, about the extent of the State of Indiana. Beyond these divisions the Department has others that will be described in the pertinent chapters.

Department of Agriculture

In recent years the Department of Agriculture has interested itself in problems of conservation, although not with so great a scope as the Department of the Interior. The conservation work of the Agriculture Department is under the general direction of the Assistant Secretary for Federal-States Relations. His administration includes the Agricultural Conservation Program, which gives farmers financial aid for instituting various agricultural conservation practices; the Forest Service, which controls 153 national forests and assists in the conservation of State-owned and privately owned woodlands; and the Soil Conservation Service, which works through locally established soil conservation districts to introduce programs for soil and water conservation. In these undertakings the Agriculture Department coordinates its operations with those of the Interior Department, the Federal Power Commission, and the Army Engineers Corps. The Department of Agriculture has numerous other functions connected with farmers. These functions are the subject of the next chapter.

QUESTIONS AND PROBLEMS

1. What are the tasks of conservation? Do you believe that the natural resources of the nation are being conserved enough to provide security for another century? Explain your answer.

2. It has been proposed that the government sell practically all of the public lands save those needed for the national park system. Would such a transfer to private hands result in better or worse conservation practices? Would strict legislation regulating land use prevent abuses by private owners?

3. Describe the work of the Soil Conservation Service.

4. How can a congressman consistently vote for new land reclamation and irrigation projects and also for subsidies to farmers to prevent losses from growing too much of certain staple crops?

5. How has the place of coal as a primary fuel changed over the last fifty years?

6. What new sources of industrial energy are in the offing? What effects might they have upon the American political scene?

7. List all major and minor agencies named in the chapter as having functions connected with conservation; give, in each case, a description of their function or functions.

PART XI

Commercial Interests
of the Government

40. The Government and Agriculture

USDA Photo

For many years the federal government has performed numerous services on behalf of farmers. The principal services include research into land use and into plant and animal life, the regulation of marketing, and the provision of credit facilities. These services are partly the consequence of pressure upon Congress skillfully exerted by large farmers' organizations. The services also testify to the conviction in governing circles that if farmers are not prosperous—if farmers have a limited purchasing power—the entire national economy is apt to suffer. Legislators and administrators remember that the stock market crash of 1929 and the ensuing industrial, commercial, and financial depression were preceded by a farmers' depression extending back almost to the end of World War I; they assume that the farmers' depression laid the groundwork for the nation-wide depression of the 1930's. Whenever they seem to be forgetting the notion that

TABLE 23. ATTITUDES AMONG DIFFERENT OCCUPATIONS
TO THE PRESENT EXTENT OF GOVERNMENT ACTIVITY[1]

Occupation	Should Do More	About Right	Should Do Less	More of Some Things	More of Some Things Less of Others	Less of Some Things	Don't Know or No Answer	%	Total No. of Cases
Professional & semi-professional	17%	35%	28%	9%	5%	3%	3%	100%	125
Self-employed businessmen, artisans, & officials	19	42	23	7	3	3	3	100	251
Clerical & sales, buyers, agents, and brokers	20	43	16	7	3	3	8	100	174
Skilled and semi-skilled	21	50	10	9	1	2	7	100	507
Unskilled, service workers, farm laborers	20	57	4	5	1	1	12	100	193
Farm Operators	13	51	18	4	4	2	8	100	190

[1] From author's analysis of Survey Research Center materials, Study 400, 1952.

farm prosperity underlies national prosperity, one or another of the strong farmers' interest groups, such as the Farm Bureau Federation, is certain to remind them of it.

FARMERS IN POLITICS

Many people mistakenly believe that farmers are much less likely than other parts of the public to seek government aid when they are in economic trouble. This belief is contradicted by a long history of agrarian agitations stretching back to colonial times. Table 23 gives the results of a recent survey of people's opinions regarding the need for more or less government activity on behalf of the general welfare, such as more support for public education, old age assistance, and housing. It reveals that farmers may be only a little more reluctant than other groups to expand the scope of government.

Farmers have influence and power in politics that are far greater than their proportion of either the wealth or the numbers of the country. There is no need at this point to describe the interest groups of farmers, for that topic has been discussed in a foregoing chapter. It is well to note here,

Department of Agriculture Building, Washington, D.C., Entrance on the Mall.

however, that in two ways the power that farmers enjoy is partly to be attributed to the form of the American government. In the first place, since each State regardless of population has two Senators, and since there are more farm States than industrial States, farmers have a greater voice than other occupations in the upper house of Congress. In the second place, since farmers have the same kind of dominant voice in most State legislatures, and since State legislatures draw the boundaries for congressional districts, farmers tend to be overrepresented in the House of Representatives as well. From these advantages farmers have reaped a body of favorable legislation. Their interests in Congress are managed, first by the usually sympathetic Committee on Agriculture in each house, and second by a bipartisan group known as the Farm Bloc (some of whose members are on one Agriculture Committee or the other), which can be counted upon to give a respectful hearing to any plea the farmers may utter.

Farmers do not speak with one voice, nor even with just several, but with many. There are different types of farming over the country; and each area, even each crop, has its own economic interest that lends its color to the politics of the nation. Figure 93 discloses the location of the major types of farming in the United States. The vineyardists of California probably have no more in common with the dairy farmers of Wisconsin than an aircraft manufacturer in Washington State does with a lace manufacturer in Rhode Island. Indeed, growers of the same crop may often be at odds; in 1954 the California and the southern cotton growers had a heated debate regarding the means by which quotas should be set for controlling cotton production; in California, where cotton-growing is a new operation, the growers thought that the quotas did not take into account how rapidly their production was expanding.

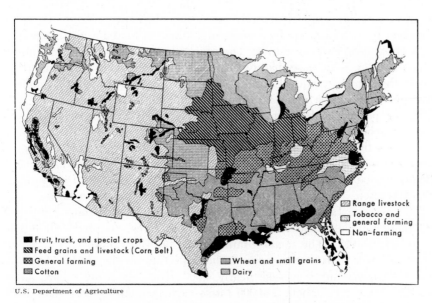

Range livestock
Tobacco and general farming
Non-farming
Fruit, truck, and special crops
Feed grains and livestock (Corn Belt)
General farming
Cotton
Wheat and small grains
Dairy

U.S. Department of Agriculture

Figure 93. Major Types of Farming in the United States.

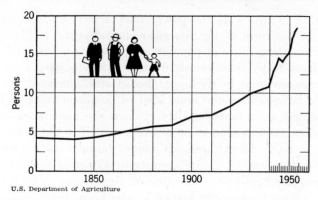

U.S. Department of Agriculture

Figure 94. Number of Persons Supported by One Farm Worker, 1820–1955. One farm worker fed four others in 1820, and 18 others in 1955. Note the rapid recent increase in the ratio, owing to the recent sharp advances in farm technology.

STRUCTURE OF AMERICAN AGRICULTURE

American agriculture is big business—indeed, it is still the biggest business in the country. American farms have greatly evolved since 1787. At one time most farmers produced only enough for their own needs, along with a small surplus to enable them to buy what they could not produce themselves. Today farmers produce only a small amount of what they consume; most of their production is aimed at the market place. One estimate, that shown in Figure 94, indicates that a great many more farm families were needed to grow food for non-farm families in 1820 than in 1955. These figures actually understate the true situation greatly. Many farmers of today produce scarcely more than their own subsistence; other farmers, by contrast, produce great quantities of food for non-farmers.

Number and Size of Farms: There are about 4.8 million farms in the United States, with more than twenty million people living on them. However, the United States Census Bureau in 1955 estimated that ninety-five per cent of the market supply of commodities is produced by only fifty-five per cent of the farms. The other forty-five per cent, from a narrow economic viewpoint, are mainly "surplus" farms. They are not needed in the larger economy of agriculture. Both farms and farmers are fewer today than they were some decades ago; yet owing to the mechanization of agriculture and to improved techniques of cultivation, farm production has risen. Thus fewer people raise more food on larger farms.

The average farm in 1954 contained 242 acres, about three-eighths of a square mile; in 1880 the average was 133 acres, and by 1920 it had risen only to 148. The smallest farms are in the East; those in New Jersey average fewer than seventy acres. The largest are in the Rocky Mountain States; Arizona farms average nearly 4,000 acres, about six square miles. In 1954 there were about 130,000 farms each containing more than 1,000 acres; although they numbered only two per cent of all the farms in the country, they included more than forty per cent of all farm land. In 1920 such farms embraced only twenty-five per cent of all farm land. Thus farms, like industrial organizations, appear to be growing larger and less numerous.

Farm Ownership: The pattern of farm ownership is very important. In 1954, 24.4% of American farms were operated by tenants, that is, by

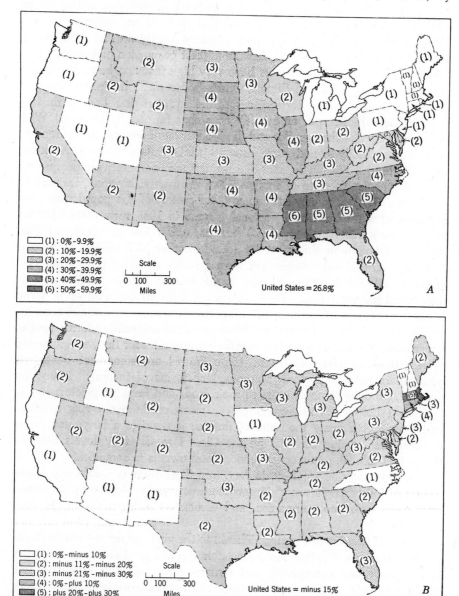

Statistical Abstract of the United States, 1954

Figure 95. Farm Tenancy in America. *A.* Proportion of Tenant Farms to All Farms, by State, 1950. *B.* Change in the Proportion of Tenant Farms in Each State, 1945 to 1950.

farmers who did not own the land but rented it, paying either cash or a share of their crops to the owner. The maps in Figure 95 show the percentage of tenants out of all farmers in each State, and how the percentage shifted between 1945 and 1950. The proportion of tenants has been steadily declining, partly because farm prosperity in recent years has enabled many tenants to purchase their own farms, and partly because many tenants have given up farming and moved to a city to work in industry or the service trades. It can be seen from the map that there is no necessary relation between farm wealth and the proportion of tenants. True, the South, where farm incomes are lowest, has the highest proportion of tenants. Too, California, a State whose farmers have very high incomes, has a low tenant proportion. Yet Iowa and Illinois, whose farmers also have high incomes, have high tenant rates. Indeed, across the entire nation, land farmed by tenants has a higher per acre value than that farmed by owners. What is important is that the number and the proportion of tenants are decreasing, so that the family-owned farm remains the standard unit of American agriculture; hence it may be said that farmers are comparatively prosperous.

Farm Income: In spite of their relative prosperity, however, farmers do not have as large a money income as other sectors of the population. For example, of a total national personal income in 1955 surpassing $303 billions, farmers received only $14.3 billions, under five per cent, for their product, although to this must be added another $5.7 billions of income from non-agricultural sources; yet farm families constituted 13.5 per cent of the population in 1955. Moreover, this income is by no means equally distributed among farms. Table 24 throws light on the number of farms in different regions of America and upon the wide range of incomes received by different groups of farms. In 1950 more than one million farms (out of fewer than six million) reported that their entire sales for the year amounted to less than $250.00. However, these figures are somewhat deceptive, for farmers have important, non-monetary forms of income. Many, for instance, produce some or most of their food; and farm proprietors live in their own houses. The owners of the more productive farms have investments worth many thousand of dollars; it requires a large sum today to enter the farming business on the Class I to Class IV levels that are shown in Table 24. As a consequence, farm owners in some States, notably in the West, may be wealthy; in fact, in a State such as California, where so-called "industrial farming" is practiced, very large farms may be owned by banks, insurance companies, and associated industries such as food processors.

Economic Position of Farmers: Thanks to the very nature of their business, farmers occupy a disadvantageous economic position. Each farmer is, after all, an individual enterpriser, and farmers rarely of their own free will combine in order to manipulate prices. Furthermore, unlike manufacturers, farmers do not often voluntarily restrict production in the face of declining prices. Indeed, when agricultural prices drop by one-half, farmers may double output in an effort to compensate for the difference.

The nature and growth of the American economy have imposed a fundamental handicap upon the farmer. The United States has for over a century been an important source of food for Europe; in other words, it has been an exporter of food. Hence the prices received by American farmers have been influenced by world food prices, since they have had to compete with the farmers from other food-exporting countries such as Canada, Australia, and Argentina. By contrast, until fairly recent times the United States has imported manufactured goods. At the behest of American manufacturers, Congress enacted tariff laws to bar competing finished goods; as a result, American industry has been more or less able to fix its own prices regardless of world prices. Therefore, since the United States has higher prices than most other countries, farmers, who have had to charge world prices for their products, have suffered by comparison with factory owners. Lately American farmers have begun to lose their export market save in time of war.

Today, then, farmers do not have much control over the prices they receive save through governmental action in their behalf. Farm prices tend to be set in the short run by the beliefs and expectations of food processors and speculators on the commodity exchanges. After World War II, for instance, the prices paid to farmers dropped, yet the prices paid for food in stores remained more or less constant, or even rose, so that the farmers received a smaller percentage of consumers' food costs. In 1946 the farmer's share of the consumer's food dollar was fifty-two cents; in 1956, it was

TABLE 24. AN ECONOMIC ANALYSIS OF AMERICAN FARMS, BY REGION[a]

Numbers of Farms in the Different Regions of the United States and the Amount of Income Earned by Groups of Differently Sized Farms

Economic Class	Class Interval (Value of Products Sold)	United States Number	United States %	North %	South %	West %
All farms: number		5,382,100		(2,268.0)	(2,652.5)	(461.7)
total %			100.0	100.0	100.0	100.0
Commercial farms						
Class I	$25,000 and over	105,500	2.0	2.0	1.1	6.9
Class II	$10,000 to $24,999	386,100	7.2	10.9	3.0	12.8
Class III	$5,000 to $9,999	725,600	13.5	21.9	5.8	16.1
Class IV	$2,500 to $4,999	882,300	16.4	21.4	12.3	15.6
Class V	$1,200 to $2,499	895,900	16.6	14.4	19.2	12.9
Class VI	$250 to $1,199[b]	707,700	13.1	7.4	19.3	5.6
Other farms						
Part-time farms	$250 to $1,199[c]	642,100	11.9	9.7	13.7	12.5
Residential farms	Under $250	1,032,400	19.2	12.2	25.5	17.4
Abnormal farms[d]		4,500	.1	0.1	0.1	0.2

Source: The Agricultural Situation, U.S. Bureau of Agricultural Economics, March 1952.

[a] Preliminary census data; totals obtained by adding state or county census releases.

[b] With the operator working off the farm less than 100 days and farm sales greater than other family income.

[c] With the operator working off the farm 100 or more days and/or other family income exceeding farm sales.

[d] Chiefly public and private institutional farms.

forty-one cents. It is true that part of the rise in the cost of foods should be ascribed to the higher wages paid laborers in the food-canning and meat-packing industries; however, another part of this rise constituted profits for distributors. This type of situation is largely responsible for farmers' demands that the national government assure them a minimum income.

PRODUCTION IMPROVEMENT

The federal government in many ways helps farmers to improve both the quantity and the quality of farm products. Most of this assistance is handled by the Agriculture Department, which has rightly been labeled "one of the greatest research institutions in the world." The operations of the government regarding soil conservation were described in the previous chapter. Beyond this activity, scientists in the various offices of the Agricultural Research Service conduct research into almost every conceivable question in the several fields of agriculture. They study means for utilizing agricultural commodities for new industrial purposes. They investigate the causes for animal diseases; for instance, they cooperated with Mexican authorities to suppress hoof-and-mouth disease in cattle. They seek means for producing superior breeds of livestock. They strive for dairy herds yielding more and richer milk. They discover new species of harmful insects, and attempt to create effective insecticides. They analyze eating habits of the American people, and devise new methods for preparing foods. They inquire into plant life, the diseases that afflict plants, the relationship between types of soil and plant growth, and the best techniques and machinery for sowing, cultivating, and harvesting plant crops. The Department maintains an Agricultural Research Center at Beltsville, Maryland, in the environs of Washington, a town that has given its name to the succulent five-pound turkeys developed by its poultry breeders.

The findings of the Department are broadcast through various media. In the first place, the Department publishes a tremendous number of books and pamphlets. Too, the Department works through the agriculture and the domestic science branches of land-grant colleges to instruct students, especially future farmers, farm wives, and teachers of home economics in the public schools. The Extension Service of the Department works through the county agents who have been appointed in nearly all rural American counties.

These agents deserve particular note; they are public officers named usually by the State agricultural extension services connected with the State land-grant colleges. They are paid ordinarily by the States, which are assisted by a federal grant-in-aid program. Occasionally, counties are required to contribute funds for the agents' salaries. However, they are frequently selected on the basis of recommendations by either the State land-grant college or the State or county farmers' organization, especially the local affiliate of the American Farm Bureau Federation. In almost every case, the Federation, too, works closely with the county agent; hence the

Federation may often depend upon the county agent as a transmission belt to the Department of Agriculture.

MARKETING

The federal government plays an important role in the marketing of agricultural products, with an eye to securing "just" prices for farmers. In this program the federal government subsidizes farmers for refraining from raising certain crops, and buys surpluses of other crops so as to remove them from the market. Some observers hold this practice to be rather absurd, since millions of people in the world are hungry. However, the needs of these millions cannot bring as much pressure upon Congress as farmers' organizations can, with their demands for prices based upon "parity," that is, prices they deem fair. It is necessary first of all to explain the nature of "parity" before going on to describe government operations in the agricultural markets.

Parity

Parity, which in the mouths of some leaders is a sacred incantation, in fact is nothing more than a ratio. It is a ratio just as one-half or fifty per cent is the ratio of two to four. The parity ratio is the ratio between the prices received by farmers (price index) and the prices paid by them for the things they need in order to live (parity index). Parity equals 100 at a time chosen as a "normal" one; at present it is the base period from 1909 until 1914, when the prices received for crops are believed to have been in a good relation to the costs of the things the farmer bought. When the system of price supports for farm goods was being worked out in the 1930's, this era was chosen deliberately as one in which farmers had exceptionally high purchasing power. The graph in Figure 96 shows how farm prices and other prices have risen and fallen between 1910 and 1955, and the status of parity during those years; the graph makes it evident that all during the 1920's farm prices were below parity; the rises in parity after 1915, 1940, and 1950 show how the two world wars and the Korean conflict were financially advantageous for farmers.

Hence the expression, "to keep prices at parity," or "to guarantee parity," means simply that the government will manipulate the prices of farm goods so that these goods will purchase as much as an equal quantity of goods would buy in the base period. For example, in 1920 the parity ratio was almost exactly 100. Both the items a farmer bought in that year and the items he sold were far more expensive than they had been in 1913; however, both had risen in the same proportion, so that the ratio was about 100 in each year. If the government is guaranteeing one hundred per cent parity prices, and if wheat, for an illustration, falls below that percentage of parity, then the government must intercede in the market so as to raise the price of wheat, or else give the farmer a parity price and take the wheat itself. It must be noted that the government acts only on a specific crop; each commodity *has its own parity price* and, of course, *its own market*

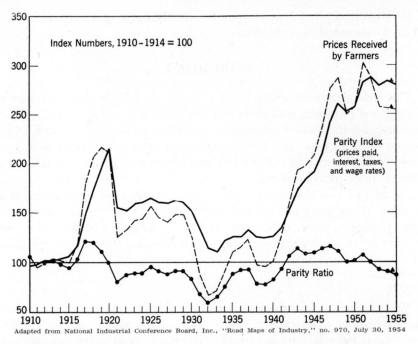

Figure 96. Prices Paid, Prices Received, and the Parity Ratio for Farm Products, 1910 to 1955.

price. That is to say, the parity index referred to in Figure 96, and above in the text, gives an average. If, for example, wheat is at seventy-five per cent of parity and hogs at 105%, the government then acts to raise the price the farmer gets for his wheat, but not the price he gets for his hogs.

Price supports

Today the government supports the prices of numerous farm goods in terms of parity. Present laws require support for the prices of corn, wheat, rice, tobacco, cotton, peanuts, wool, mohair, tung nuts, honey, and milk and butterfat. The government may support the prices of other crops as well. Support is implemented by controls over both production and marketing; that is, farmers are given acreage allotments and marketing quotas so that the country may avoid a surplus of farm products, in which case the relation of supply to demand may bring prices up to a point at which government support will be unnecessary. Both allotments and quotas are administered by the Commodity Stabilization Service (CSS) in the Agriculture Department. Each year the CSS fixes the total national acreage that shall be devoted to the crops concerned; the total is based upon calculations of the probable demand and the past productivity of farms.

In 1956, as another means for raising farm prices, and also as a method for reducing surplus production, Congress established the so-called "soil bank" program. Under this arrangement, Congress each year is to make $1.2 billions available to pay farmers for refraining from planting crops in a portion of their fields. Up to $750 millions may be paid farmers for withdrawing acreage from the production of corn, cotton, peanuts, rice, tobacco, or wheat, and allowing the land to lie fallow. Up to as much as $450 millions more will be appropriated to pay those who replace these stipulated crops with other, soil-conserving crops.

The distribution of acreage among the individual farmers (and part of the Agricultural Conservation Program as well) is executed by a descending series of farmer committees, one in each State, one in each of about 3,000 counties, and about 29,000 at the community level. The members of these committees are farmers who have been elected by other farmers. This decentralized organization has been highly praised by some administrators as a means for rooting policy in the locality. However, as Professor Reed L. Frischknecht points out, comparatively few farmers take part in the community elections, and committee members are often reelected, so that there has grown up a group of professional farmer-committee members, usually from the most ardent supporters of the plans of the Agriculture Department.[1]

In an attempt to increase farmer participation, reduce the influence of farm pressure organizations, and guarantee reliable administration of the decentralized program, the Department of Agriculture in 1953 ordered three changes: (1) No committeeman might serve for more than three annual terms; (2) no official of a general private farm organization might hold a committee post; and (3) each county and community committee would choose an office manager to carry out its work on a regular basis. Mr. John A. Baker of the National Farmers' Union in 1955 criticized these changes as actually reducing farmer participation because, he said, the important work of the committees had been turned over to hired managers; the system of decentralized administration, he wrote, "has been so weakened that farmers now have little voice in the government program with which they are most closely concerned."[2] In any case, the community committees determine the acreage allotments of the individual farmers within their jurisdiction. The farmer is not compelled to abide by his allotment; however, if he does, and if he turns the remainder of his land into pasturage, or if he plants soil conserving crops there, he is entitled to receive benefit payments under the Soil Conservation and Domestic Allotment Act of 1936.

It sometimes occurs that in spite of acreage allotments, at harvest time a surplus may be impending. Under these conditions the CSS may fix a marketing quota, limiting the amount of the crop that may be sold in interstate commerce. Any proposal for marketing quotas must be submitted to the farmers in a nation-wide referendum of those raising the crop; the quotas cannot go into effect unless the referendum passes by at least a two-thirds majority. It is noteworthy again that despite the allegations about the presumed "rugged individualism" and "economic independence" of the American farmers, they usually support the quotas in these referenda,

[1] Frischknecht, Reed L., "The Democratization of Administration: the Farmer Committee System," *American Political Science Review*, 47 (1953), pp. 704–727.

[2] Letter of May 17, 1955, to the office of the author.

by large majorities. If the farmers reject the quota proposal in the referendum, they lose also the government price support. These quotas are also allocated among farmers by the farmer committees. In cases of violations of these quotas, when farmers place more than their share into interstate commerce, they are subject to fine.

The management of farm surpluses

The government manages farm surpluses by combining them and storing them in what is known as the "ever-normal granary." The ever-normal granary is simply a device for retaining surplus harvests so that they may be used in years with small or deficient harvests. This is a very ancient institution; it has been used for centuries in China, and it is typified in the Old Testament account of how Joseph when in Egypt kept some of the harvests during the seven fat years. The American ever-normal granary is administered by the CSS and financed by the Commodity Credit Corporation (CCC).

The CCC is a federal agency whose executive is a seven-man board of directors under the chairmanship of the Secretary of Agriculture, an *ex officio* member of the board; the other six members are appointed by the President and confirmed by the Senate. The CCC also possesses a five-man advisory council. The CCC is a lending and purchasing agency; it is empowered to borrow up to $14.5 billions to carry out its duties. A farmer may borrow money from the CCC, using his harvest as collateral; the CCC then stores his crop. The CCC must lend the farmer whatever percentage of parity is at that time guaranteed on his crop. If subsequently the market price of the crop rises above this guarantee, the farmer may now sell his property to a private purchaser on the market, then repay his loan from the CCC with his returns. If, on the other hand, the market price of the crop does not reach the guaranteed percentage of parity, the farmer may simply turn his crop over to the CCC. In such a transaction, regardless of the market price of the crop the farmer owes the CCC nothing but the crop.

The CCC has had a somewhat checkered history. During World War II, when there was a tremendous demand for food and when food prices were over parity, the CCC carried little surplus and actually made money from interest payments on its loans. However, after the war, when prices fell the CCC gradually began accumulating a huge surplus. Indeed its very existence encouraged the cultivation of surpluses since farmers were guaranteed a specific percentage of parity on their harvests. On May 31, 1956, the federal government held surpluses amounting to $2.7 billions in wheat, $2.5 billions in cotton, $1.9 billions in corn, $0.2 billions in dairy products, and $1.2 billions in other items, a total of $8.5 billions altogether. At least one point may be admitted: the United States has no cause to fear a small harvest.

For the government, perhaps the most embarrassing phase of this undertaking is the disposal of the surplus commodities. After all, agricultural goods cannot be stored indefinitely; items such as butter will spoil. However, the CCC has only limited means for ridding itself of these properties. The most obvious way for disposing of them would be to give them away; however, any such idea would encounter instant opposition, since it would destroy the market for farmers. The CCC might also sell them cheaply, but this method, too, would injure the market. Occasionally the CCC tries to purvey these goods abroad, so that at least they will not compete in the domestic market. Here again the CCC must tread warily, lest it conflict with other nations such as Argentina which export food; indeed, the CCC will not sell its goods overseas at prices under those of the world market, lest it make enemies for the United States.

One means for disposition that the government does use is a free-lunch program for public school pupils; it gives some food to the schools, and participates in a grant-in-aid system with States which finance free-lunch programs. Yet even this program occasionally undergoes attacks by congressmen from food-producing States, who try to reduce the appropriations. Some stocks, especially of perishable foods, are also made available to public and private welfare organizations both in the United States and abroad.

Too, the United States has been using these foods to bolster the economies of certain foreign powers. It sells the commodities to the foreign government, receiving in exchange money that would have little if any value in the United States, but which can be spent in the purchasing country for articles that the United States may need. Sometimes, instead of spending the money, the United States lends it to the purchasing country, for the construction of roads or public buildings, thereby creating employment opportunities. Finally, the American government sometimes does give away its food, in cases of exceptional need abroad.

Various plans for eliminating these surpluses have been put forward, but each has roused such a hurricane of opposition from one side or the other that none has been wholly adopted. The Department of Agriculture even tries to dispose of surplus products through publicizing their virtues. For instance, in the spring of 1955 the Department launched a campaign to sell more milk and milk products, partly because milk is a wholesome food but also because there were huge surpluses of milk products and because the monetary support of milk and its products was very expensive to the Department. Fortunately, almost everyone agrees that milk is wholesome; the Department might promote it without encountering great public opposition. By contrast, it would be quite out of the question for the Department to promote the sale of bonded whiskey (which at this time was also in surplus supply) even thought it might thereby increase government revenues that are lost when stored whiskeys are removed for sale before the owners have to pay a tax on its bonding.

FARM CREDIT

Until recent years one of the most oppressive difficulties for farmers has been their inability to borrow as much money as they wished or needed.

Through American history the farmer traditionally has been indebted; he has found it difficult to borrow, and has supported inflationary policies that would make it easier for him to procure money. However, until the past few decades money and credit facilities in the United States have been dominated by so-called "hard-money" advocates, by groups desiring that the dollar have a high purchasing power and restricting credit so as to have fewer dollars in circulation. Moreover, lending facilities have been controlled by eastern banks, especially by those in New York, so that banks in the corn and wheat belts have had small lending capacities. This situation has produced the exaggerated dislike farmers have shown for "Wall Street." Only in the past four decades have farmers been able to win congressional sympathy respecting their credit needs. Today, as a result, the federal government contains important machinery for extending credit to farmers.

Farm Credit Administration

The Farm Credit Administration includes most of the farmers' lending agencies under the federal government. For the purposes of the Administration, the United States is divided into twelve farm credit districts—thus imitating the regional pattern set by the Federal Reserve System. The Administration itself is an independent agency. The policy-making organ of the Administration is the thirteen-member Federal Farm Credit Board; twelve members, one from each district, are chosen by the President, who usually heeds the recommendations of farm interests, and the thirteenth is named by the Secretary of Agriculture as his spokesman. The executive officer of the Administration is the Governor, who is appointed by the Board.

The Administration extends four types of services: land bank; intermediate credit bank; production credit; and cooperative bank. Each service except the intermediate credit bank has as its chief a Deputy Governor and Director chosen by the Governor. In each district there is one of each of the four main types of farm credit organizations: a federal land bank; a federal intermediate credit bank; a production credit corporation; and a bank for cooperatives. The policies for each district are set by a farm credit board of seven members who are *ex officio* members of the credit organizations in that district. The executive officer in each district is the General Agent, who serves as joint officer for the four bodies.

These four types of agencies provide a comprehensive lending service to farmers. Federal land banks, which are owned by national farm loan associations in each district, lend money to farmers who are recommended by the associations. The borrower must then purchase stock in the association, which in turn purchases stock from the land bank. After the loans are repaid, the stock is retired. In exchange, the banks accept first mortgages on farms. The loans may not be more than $200,000 nor less than $100, but in any case may not be more than sixty-five per cent of the value of the farm. Banks in the nine districts west of the Appalachian Mountains collect four per cent per annum interest; those from New England to Virginia, four-and-one-half per cent; and that from North Carolina southward, five per cent. The purposes of these loans are to enable farmers to buy land; erect buildings; purchase needed supplies, equipment, and stock; and retire their debts.

Intermediate credit banks function much like Federal Reserve Banks. They do no business directly with farmers; rather, they deal with organizations that offer credit to farmers, by lending money to, or discounting notes and commercial paper for, such agricultural financial institutions as livestock loan companies. Too, as with Federal Reserve Banks, the notes discounted by intermediate credit banks are short-term, usually no more than a year. These banks are owned by the federal government. They procure money for their own operations by selling short-term notes to the public, for which all twelve banks are jointly responsible. The purpose of these loans, then, is to endow private bodies with greater credit facilities.

Production credit corporations function through the 498 local production credit associations of farmers across the country. The corporations supervise the associations and provide them with some of their money; however, 440 of the 498 associations are now independent of government capital. Voting stock in the associations is owned by the members. The associations, although they handle the loans, do not lend government money; instead, they discount farmers' notes with the intermediate credit banks. These loans are extended for all types of farming operations; in simplest terms, their purpose is to tide farmers over between the time of sowing a crop, in which they may have invested almost all their cash, and that of harvesting the crop, which is the earliest moment at which they may expect a return. They are short-term loans guaranteed by the farmers' crops.

Banks for cooperatives lend money to responsible and eligible farmers' cooperative associations. There is a Central Bank for Cooperatives, which deals with nation-wide cooperative organizations and which makes direct loans to the district banks. The district banks in turn serve generally those bodies whose scope does not reach beyond their district. The extent of the operations of all these types of farmers' credit institutions is apparent in the fact that during the calendar year 1955 they lent farmers and farm cooperatives $2.6 billions.

Farmers Home Administration

The Farmers Home Administration, in the Department of Agriculture, is designed chiefly for the benefit of less prosperous farmers; it furnishes credit services to those who may be unable to obtain them from any other source, or can obtain them only at exorbitant interest rates. The Administration conducts its operations through county committees, made up of three persons at least two of whom must be farmers, who determine whether or not an individual may be given credit.

The Administration extends two principal forms of loans. First, it lends money for operating expenses to individuals owning small farms, and to tenant farmers. These loans are to be employed for the purchase of supplies, improvement of farms, and other relatively short-term goals. Such a loan may be no more than $7,000; it is to be repaid in from one to seven years, at five per cent yearly interest. The second type of loan provided by the Administration is for the purchase of farms. The loans are made to tenants, sharecroppers, farm laborers, veterans, and others seeking to buy a farm. Hence the Farmers Home Administration has been a factor in reducing the proportion of tenant farmers in the United States. These loans run for forty years, at four per cent annual interest.

The Administration also insures mortgages on loans made by private institutions, in much the same manner as the Federal Housing Administration deals with city dwellers. Finally, the Administration is empowered to lend money to farmers in the arid western States so that they may supply themselves with water, and to provide credit in the event of farm disaster. In fiscal 1955 the Administration made operating loans of $134 millions and farm ownership loans of $19 millions; it insured farm ownership loans supplied by private institutions to the amount of $32 millions.

Rural Electrification Administration

The Rural Electrification Administration (REA) is an agency to grant credit to organizations that furnish either electric power or telephone service to farm residents. As it has functioned, the REA has come to be actually an example of government promotion of business, and is thus considerably more than a simple farm credit body. Hence it will receive only a brief note here, with fuller treatment reserved for the chapter describing the government's promotional activities.

THE DEPARTMENT OF AGRICULTURE

The Department of Agriculture is the chief federal agency concerned with farmers. It is the oldest of what might be termed the "vocational-interest" Departments, the others being Commerce, Labor, and Health, Education, and Welfare. The Department was created in 1862, another manifestation of the victory won by the western farmers in the election of 1860. Initially the head of the Department was a Commissioner, who was not a member of the presidential cabinet; in 1889 the Commissioner was replaced by a Secretary, who took a seat in the Cabinet. Today it is one of the largest Departments; on January 1, 1956, it had 76,358 employees, a number exceeded only by the defense establishment, the Post Office, and the Treasury. In fiscal 1956 its expenditures amounted to almost $5.2 billions, more than half of which was spent by the Commodity Credit Corporation. In one way the Department has been a model for other federal agencies; it developed outstanding methods for recruiting and selecting its personnel, and it instilled in them a sense of professionalism.

The Secretary is almost always an individual who is connected with agriculture. Among the fifteen Secretaries since 1889, all but one have come from the Mississippi Valley; the one exception, Ezra Taft Benson of Utah, Secretary under President Eisenhower, was no stranger to farming. Under the Secretary are an Under Secretary, who is the deputy of the Secretary; and four Assistant Secretaries, one each for departmental administration, Federal-States Relations, Marketing and Foreign Agriculture, and Agricultural Stabilization. One of the most important institutions supervised by the Administrative Assistant Secretary is the Department of Agriculture Library, the largest agricultural research library in the world, containing about one million volumes.

Under Federal-States Relations the Department carries on the extensive work in the field of conservation that was treated in the last chapter. This branch also embraces the Agricultural Research Service, which manages such functions as the crops regulatory programs, the livestock regulatory programs, and research in crops, farm and land management, livestock, home economics, and crop utilization. The findings of this research are disseminated by the Extension Service of the Department. Under Marketing and Foreign Agriculture are the Agricultural Marketing Service, which helps farmers to sell their crops; the Commodity Exchange Authority, which regulates commodity exchanges; and the Foreign Agricultural Service, which attempts to find markets overseas for surplus American farm products. Agricultural Stabilization includes the Commodity Credit Corporation, the Commodity Stabilization Service, and the Federal Crop Insurance Corporation. This last agency strives to protect farmers from crop disasters brought about by forces beyond their control. The Corporation operates on the county level; it offers insurance in counties where at least 200 farmers, or at least one-third the farmers producing the given crop, take part in an insurance program. Insurance rates are based on losses suffered in previous years and on the amount of premiums paid in the past by the farmers in the county. Finally, the credit services of the Agriculture Department include the Farmers Home Administration and the Rural Electrification Administration.

QUESTIONS AND PROBLEMS

1. Cite several historical examples of farmer movements that have sought government aid.

2. Where is farm tenancy increasing in America and where is it declining? Where is farm tenancy most common?

3. Why are farm prices difficult to control by personal or by governmental means?

4. In what ways does the federal government assist farmers with their production problems?

5. In what ways does the federal government assist farmers with their marketing problems?

6. Define *parity*. What has been the relation between the prices received by farmers and the parity index since 1930?

7. Describe how the acreage allotments and marketing quotas system functions when farm prices fall below parity.

8. What are the problems of surplus commodities under the government crop loan system?

9. Describe briefly: the federal land banks; federal intermediate credit banks; production credit corporations; banks for cooperatives.

10. List all the principal divisions of the Department of Agriculture and describe in one sentence the major functions of each.

41. Government Promotion of Business

Since its earliest days the American government has interested itself in the promotion of business. Indeed, the very drafting of a new Constitution was stimulated by those who wished a government that would promote the business of the entire thirteen States, so as to supplant a regime that allowed each State government to promote the business of its own inhabitants at the expense of the inhabitants of the other twelve States. The Philadelphia Convention of 1787 included many men engaged in industry, trade, or finance, who, although they certainly had other intentions as well, planned to create a national government that would block the States from taxing each other's commerce to death.

The present Constitution, with its authorizations of federal control over interstate and foreign commerce, was in part the consequence of their wishes.

The government, then, is empowered to promote business in a number of ways: it may protect property, impose preferential taxes, grant subsidies, extend credit, construct facilities for commerce, and provide technical aid and information. The national government began to exercise these permissive powers from the earliest days of its existence; Alexander Hamilton's first program, recommending means for combatting inflation and the levying of a tariff, was frankly aimed at the promotion of business. Since that era the government has greatly expanded these activities. Thus it may be said that for more than a century and a half the American national government has been a "welfare state" for industry, commerce, and finance.

PROTECTION OF PROPERTY

The federal Constitution and its Amendments arrange for several ways in which the federal government is to protect property; however, it is noteworthy that the word "property" itself does not appear until the Fifth Amendment. Some of these protections, especially those related to slavery, today have no force; they have in effect been repealed by the Thirteenth Amendment. Others, which prohibit a State from passing a law that breaks a contract, and forbid both the federal and the State governments from taking property save by due process of law, have been discussed elsewhere in the text. There are certain other important protections that should be dealt with at this point.

Protection of interstate and foreign commerce

The United States government protects all interstate commerce and all peacetime foreign commerce issuing from, or aimed at, its shores. Any commodity in interstate or foreign commerce is the property of some person; by extending its shelter over such items the federal government certainly promotes business. With respect to foreign commerce, at the time the Constitution was adopted this protection could be related to the menace of piracy, which was fairly common at the time; owing to this authorization Thomas Jefferson was able to wage war against the Barbary pirates of the Mediterranean during his presidency. Today piracy is comparatively rare. Yet from this clause a basis can be found for defending American overseas trade against any sort of attack, whether or not piratical; for example, President Wilson employed this protective authority in 1917, citing German interference with American transatlantic shipping as his principal justification for asking Congress to declare war.

The Kew Gardens Interchange, New York City. The most complicated interchange in existence. In one 24-hour period, the traffic using the interchange in all directions amounted to 194,884 vehicles. Federal assistance to the interchange amounted to $6,594,000 on 26 federal-aid projects over 21 years of time.

Federal control over interstate commerce appears to have been at first designed to restrain State governments from tampering with such trade. Ultimately, thanks to this protection, the United States became the largest free-trade area in the world. This freedom of commerce has doubtless been a major factor in contributing to the wealth of the American people. Yet, in spite of the national advantages of this unrestricted trade, today a number of States place bothersome restrictions upon commerce with other States. For example, a truck going from State to State has to satisfy the special rules of each State regarding weight, height, length, number of lights, licenses, and other traits. As another instance, California even stops all private automobiles to insure that their passengers are not bringing pest-ridden vegetables and fruits across the State line. The delays and interferences act to discourage traffic in such commodities. Inasmuch as the State may claim to be only performing its reserved police power of barring insect pests, there is little that the national government can do to break down these barriers.

Patents, trade-marks, and copyrights

Patents, trade-marks, and copyrights are all tokens of property that are protected by the government. A patent is a grant of the exclusive right, for a limited time, to use a certain process or to manufacture a certain commodity. It is conferred upon the inventor or discoverer of a "useful" contrivance (perpetual-motion machines cannot be patented), production method, or variety of fruit or vegetable. Patents are administered by the Patent Office in the Department of Commerce. One seeking a patent supplies the Office with an example of his device. The Office then studies the device, primarily to determine whether or not it is in fact a new device or simply a modification of a previously patented object. If the Office decides that the object satisfies all requirements, it confers the patent upon payment of a fee by the inventor. He may permit others to use his contrivance, but possession of the patent authorizes him to charge a royalty for this use. After the lapse of seventeen years the device becomes public property, or part of the "public domain."

A trade-mark is a label that identifies the products of a specific manufacturer. It is a valuable property, since it may identify the product more readily than the name does. A trade-mark may be registered with the Patent Office, at which time the possessor obtains exclusive rights to its use for twenty years. The mark then becomes public domain. As with a patent, a trade-mark must be protected by its owner, who brings a civil suit in the event of infringement.

A copyright is the grant of an exclusive right to "an intellectual product" such as a book, magazine article, song, or photograph. Copyrights are administered by the Copyright Office in the Library of Congress. A person seeking a copyright must submit two copies of his work to this Office, which thereupon grants a copyright for the payment of a fee. The process of granting a copyright differs from that connected with a patent, in that the Copyright Office makes no investigation to determine the originality of the publication. Any person who believes that another publication has copied, or plagiarized, his work, may bring suit for damages. A copyright lasts for twenty-eight years, and may be renewed once. After fifty-six years, then, a copyrighted item must enter the public domain.

Bankruptcy laws

Bankruptcy laws establish an orderly procedure whereby creditors may regain as much as possible of their property from an individual or organization that is crushed by debt. They also set a limit to the penalties that can be inflicted on persons who become bankrupt. Whereas the States once controlled bankruptcy proceedings, the federal government now regulates them. The proceedings are administered by federal district courts. They may be initiated either by the debtors or the creditors. After a petition for bankruptcy has been filed with the appropriate court, the court appoints one or more "referees in bankruptcy," persons competetent to analyze the assets of the debtor, so as to calculate how much they will be worth if sold. These assets may then be sold, the creditors usually receiving shares in proportion to the amounts owed them.

Sometimes, however, in the case of industries the assets are not sold; instead the business continues to operate. It is under court control, however, to insure that it has a chance to pay its debts without the harassment of creditors' suits, and also that its receipts are used as much as possible to pay its creditors. In this manner federal courts manage a large number of businesses, often adding a great burden to their judicial responsibilities. The Chicago streetcar system is an example of a bankrupt company that continued in business for many years under court jurisdiction.

It is noteworthy that, when a large company is bankrupt and operated under court direction, frequently the control does not change hands; rather, there may be only a reorganization of the corporate structure, leaving most of the same people in charge of the concern. Observers of this practice find justification for it in the fact that the original directors know more about the functioning of the company than anyone else, and that they are most likely to be able to operate the company in such a fashion that it can liquidate some or all of its debts. On the other hand, they may sometimes use their advantageous position to continue their incompetent practices under the protection of the court.

It might be said that federal bankruptcy laws were designed originally to obstruct certain kinds of business, rather than to promote business. Certainly a strong reason for giving Congress the power to establish a uniform law of bankruptcy was in order to stop the tendency on the part of some State governments to let bankrupts off scot-free. Hence perhaps it is best to regard the power vested in the government as a power aimed at benefiting established and responsible businesses and at preventing States from giving special favors to debtors.

TAXATION

Taxation is often employed as a device for promoting business. It might appear that under any conditions taxation should be a hindrance rather than an aid to business. But granted that taxes are as inescapable as death itself, the ways in which taxes are levied and collected can restrain some businesses and help others. It is the incidence of taxes that makes them promotional devices.

The tariff

A tariff is a tax levied upon goods imported from another country, both in order to collect revenue and to prevent competition from goods produced overseas. In the United States, only the national government may levy tariffs; in this respect it has full power over foreign commerce. The tariff has been an extremely important tax in the United States. As has been noted before, during most of the history of the United States the tariff has been the chief source of revenue. It has also played a major role in the development of the American economy. Whereas the United States is now the greatest industrial nation in the world, it was at one time considerably behind certain European countries, especially England, in its industrial plant. A leading cause for the American Revolution was the desire of American manufacturers to be able to ward off the competition of British goods; one of the first laws passed after the adoption of the present Constitution was a tariff.

By the 1930's, however, it had become evident that American industry with few exceptions was strong enough to be able to dispense with the tariff. Furthermore, it was clear that the high American tariff was actually harmful to the United States, for since other countries could not sell their products in this country they could not buy from this country either. Hence starting in the 1930's the United States began a steady lowering of its tariffs, so that today, apart from particular items, the United States is a comparatively low-tariff country. Today, then, the tariff has acquired a third function, which operates negatively; it is an important element in the conduct of foreign relations. Indeed, this may be the chief function of the tariff now, since it yields proportionately little revenue, and since very few American industries need fear competition from other nations.

The tariff today is fixed primarily by the executive branch of the government. At one time Congress had full control over the tariff; hence the knowledge that a new tariff law was to be enacted brought lobbyists for all the affected economic interests pouring into Washington, including both the owners of industries seeking protection and the working men who feared they might be put out of work by the competition of less-expensive foreign wares produced by low-wage laborers. However, Congress about four decades ago abdicated this power and created a United States Tariff Commission which, together with the President, is authorized to establish tariff rates.

The Commission is made up of six members appointed by the President and confirmed by the Senate for six-year terms, with one term lapsing each year. The Commission maintains a continuous study of foreign trade, of foreign business conditions, and of foreign methods of production. When the Commission discovers that another country is discriminating against the goods of the United States, or that methods of production in some foreign country have changed so as to alter the competitive relations between these producers and American manufacturers, it is to notify the President, and recommend to him what changes should be made in American tariff rates. The President then is empowered to raise or lower the tariff by as much as fifty per cent. Hence the interest groups bring their pressure today upon the President and the Tariff Commission rather than upon Congress. The only circumstances under which they act upon Congress is when Congress proposes to change, not the rates, but the power of the President and the Commission over the rates.

Tariff rates may also be fixed by treaty. Under the authority of the Trade Agreements Act of 1934 and its amendments, the President may negotiate treaties with other countries providing for reciprocal changes in tariff rates. This law is intended to enable the United States and other nations to make mutually advantageous concessions to one another; it is designed to increase foreign trade. Since the enactment of the law the United States has arranged one or more of these treaties with most countries in the world. Foreign powers tend to favor these agreements, since the United States is an excellent customer.

However, both the United States and other nations concerned may misunderstand the importance of their trade with each other. Some foreign countries, especially Great Britain, are dependent upon foreign commerce for their economic survival. Furthermore, some countries may have only one principal item of export, but send most of it to the United States; this is the plight of the coffee and banana countries of Latin America. Hence

Exports to Venezuela Originate in the Towns and Cities Shown

Creole Petroleum Corporation

Figure 97. Michigan and Wisconsin Communities That Export to Venezuela.

American tariff rates may have a tremendous impact upon the domestic economies of these states. Certainly the very high Hawley-Smoot Tariff Act of 1930 helped bring about economic depression in Europe and then worsened it. For the United States, foreign trade affects the prosperity of every part of the Union. A glance at the map in Figure 97 will illustrate how the communities of only two States, Michigan and Wisconsin, rely for some measure of their output upon sales to only one foreign importer, Venezuela. Yet most American industries sell abroad only a small fraction of their goods, perhaps only one-twentieth over the nation as a whole; for this reason, American industry has not felt the urgency of a thriving foreign market as strongly as have the industries of such countries as England.

The general tax schedule

The general tax schedule of the United States as a whole tends to promote business whenever possible. For example, the tax upon business profits or gains is at a lower rate than the tax upon personal incomes. As an illustration, if a person purchases some shares of stock, and if the stock rises in value so that when the person sells his stock he nets a profit, that profit is termed a "capital gain" and is taxed at a smaller percentage than that upon personal incomes. Through this device the government seeks to encourage people to invest in business. Along the same line, the income tax law of 1954 introduced a system whereby a certain amount of the income from dividends paid on shares of stock might be deducted from tax obligations.

Also, the government permits corporations to make allowances for the depreciation of their property when computing their net income for the year. That is, a corporation may deduct a certain amount for losses it has presumably suffered through deterioration of its plant. The government has fixed a maximum that may be deducted. By raising the amount that may be deducted, the federal government makes it more attractive for an organization to build new factories, since their cost may be more rapidly charged off as depreciation. A similar, and hotly contested, promotional tax device is the so-called "depletion allowance" granted oil producers. On the assumption that the removal of oil from a well gradually empties the well, or depletes it, oil producers are allowed to deduct twenty-seven per cent from their profits before calculating their taxes, so that the value of their property is not extinguished without any allowance for creating a new oil property.

Special tax preferences

Finally, a tax may be preferential, in that it is levied upon one product so as to give an advantage, or preference, to another product. Probably the most famous preferential tax—already mentioned in another connection —was that once imposed upon colored margarine, so as to make its price closer to that of butter. This tax was passed, of course, at the instance of dairying States such as Wisconsin. Originally the soybean States (soybeans are a principal element in margarine) were not strong enough to have the law repealed. However, after the Second World War the cost of butter rose to such heights, and margarine had acquired social respectability in so many homes owing to the wartime shortage of butter, that the soybean States such as Illinois were able to have the tax overturned. As a consequence public use of margarine increased rapidly, and the Commodity Credit Corporation became the owner of huge supplies of butter. These examples illustrate how the pattern of national taxation can promote one business and depress another.

SUBSIDIES

Subsidies are grants of money, or some other form of wealth, made by the government to some person or group. It is a kind of taxation in reverse. The federal government has promoted and supported many businesses through subsidies.

Land grants

The earlier types of subsidies were made in the form of land, which the government had in abundance; that is, the federal government made outright gifts of the public domain to favored companies. The greatest beneficiaries of such land grants were the trans-Mississippi railroads during the 1860's. Altogether railroads such as the Union Pacific and the Northern Pacific were given more than 120 million acres of land, an area greater than that of California, usually as alternating square miles on each side of the right-of-way in a belt many miles wide. This land the railroads might sell, or they might exploit it for its natural wealth. Some railroads still hold part of their grants, for their mineral resources. Thanks to these gifts the railroads were able to procure money for their construction; besides, by selling some of their lands to people who would settle on them the railroads supplied themselves with customers for their services. These subsidies were so important in the financing of the railroads that the monetary embarrassment many of them have suffered in the twentieth century is partly the result of their not having had to support themselves initially from their revenues alone, as they had to do when the subsidies ceased and most of the lands had been sold.

Money

Today the subsidies of the federal government usually take the form of money. An American industry that could hardly exist without federal subsidies is the merchant marine. High American wages impose two handicaps upon the American merchant marine: American ships are costly to build, and they are costly to operate. However, it is generally accepted that the United States must have a merchant fleet, in the event of war; hence the federal government gives monetary assistance both to American shipbuilders and to the shipping lines, so that American shippers will not patronize foreign ships and so that American operators of shipping lines will not buy their ships overseas.

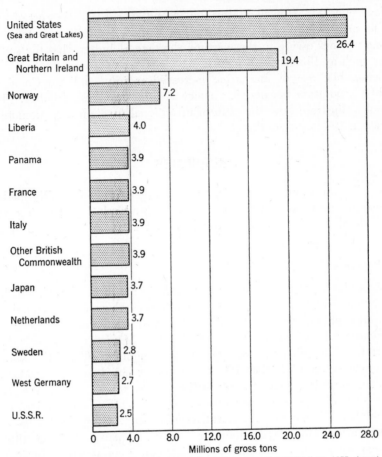

Adapted from National Industrial Conference Board, Inc., "Road Maps of Industry," no. 1057, August 6, 1954

Figure 98. Merchant Fleets of the World. Steamships and motorships over 100 tons.

This program is administered by the Maritime Administration in the Department of Commerce. This body makes a continuous study of ocean services, of the shipping lines of other countries, and of the shipping requirements of the United States. It enters into contracts with American shipbuilders whereby it undertakes to compensate the shipbuilder for the difference between the price he will charge the purchaser of a ship—a price that is governed by world prices—and the actual cost of building the vessel; in that way the Administration enables American shipbuilding concerns to compete with those of other nations. The Administration also pays shipping lines the difference between their rates and the actual cost of furnishing transportation. Within the Administration is the National Shipping Authority, whose function is to assure the United States an adequate fleet of merchant ships in case of war. The Administration also maintains the Merchant Marine Cadet Corps for the training of ships' officers. In fiscal 1956 the federal government expended $220 millions for the direct promotion of the merchant marine. It also granted a considerable indirect subsidy, in that the Post Office paid ships more than the actual cost for transporting mail. Coincidentally, the Post Office gave the same type of subsidy to domestic commercial airlines.

Yet, despite the efforts of the government the American shipping fleet is declining both relatively and absolutely. Although larger than any other (see Figure 98), the American merchant fleet in 1953 was smaller than it had been in 1948; and in June, 1954, five countries—Great Britain, Germany, the Netherlands, Sweden, and France—each had more ships under construction than the United States. It is notable, too, that the American fleet today is larger than that of Great Britain, whereas in 1939 it was smaller. This growth is only the consequence of World War II, whose demands made costs immaterial. The American merchant fleet grew enormously also during World War I; however, the interwar years saw this fleet decline, as American shipping lines could not compete with those of other countries in peacetime. It appears that the pattern is being repeated after World War II.

CREDIT

The federal government has 104 incorporated and unincorporated agencies engaged in lending money, in guaranteeing against loss the loans made by private groups, and in insuring private property. They employ all together about 40,000 persons. On June 30, 1954, the total of loans, guarantees, and insured liabilities made or covered by all these agencies amounted to $244 billions. The government had a capital of $16.9 billions invested in these agencies, and had authorization to employ another $14.1 billions for further loans and underwriting of risks. These lending, insurance, and credit agencies were not all established for the purpose of extending credit for the promotion of business, however. Most of them were concerned with veterans' life insurance, aid to foreign governments, aid to agriculture, insurance of bank deposits, and stimulation of home ownership. Yet a number of the credit agencies are directly obligated to promote the development of business enterprise. For example, the gigantic Federal Reserve System itself, described in the chapter on money and banking, uses such credit instruments as the rediscount rate in order to promote general financial prosperity. The federal government in this sense manages the whole credit structure of the nation. The agencies discussed in the following pages have the narrower purpose of making credit available to persons or groups which usually could not obtain credit from any other source.

Rural Electrification Administration

The Rural Electrification Administration (REA), whose existence was noted in the chapter on agriculture, is intended primarily to bring electric power and telephone service into rural areas. The REA is in the Agriculture Department; it is managed by an Administrator. It makes loans lasting

up to thirty-five years, with two per cent annual interest, to organizations
that propose to erect power or telephone systems. It also supplies borrowers
with technical assistance. In making these loans the REA favors public
bodies and cooperatives. By January 1, 1956, the REA had lent over $3.1
billions to nearly 1,100 borrowers, for electrical projects. At the same date
there were more than one thousand companies financed by the REA,
bringing electrical service to more than four million consumers. The REA
has only recently entered the area of telephone service; yet by March 1,
1956, it had approved $283 millions for loans to telephone companies, and
by the same date, 215 organizations had REA-financed facilities operating.
The map in Figure 99 shows where REA-assisted power systems are
located.

The REA has been harshly criticized as an example of government
participation in business; indeed, although formally the REA is no more
than a lending agency, in its functioning it does resemble a business
enterprise. However, it is difficult to deny that the REA has provided
electric power and telephone communication for people who would not
have had these facilities without the REA, since private service would
have had to operate at a loss in order to be economically attractive to the
consumer. An important indirect result of REA activities has been the
creation of a large new market for electrical appliances, inasmuch as REA
has put electricity in millions of farm homes which without it could not
have had radios, electric washing machines, electric refrigerators, or other
electrical devices.

Small Business Administration

The Small Business Administration (SBA), created only in 1953, is
designed to aid small businesses. Its executives are an Administrator and
three Deputy Administrators. Affiliated with the SBA is the Loan Policy
Board, consisting of the Administrator of the SBA, the Secretary of the
Treasury, and the Secretary of Commerce. The various functions of
the SBA include lending money to small businesses; procuring contracts
from the government for them; extending technical aid to them; and
subletting portions of prime contracts to them. The SBA is also empowered
to lend money to any business, regardless of size, in case of disaster. The
SBA is more or less the heir of the Reconstruction Finance Corporation,
the giant lending body established in 1932 that assisted American business
in recovering from the depression that began in 1929, then continued its
work as a credit agency during World War II. The life of the RFC, except
for liquidation proceedings, terminated in 1953.

Export-Import Bank of Washington

The Export-Import Bank of Washington is a credit agency that lends
money so as to increase foreign trade. It is a government corporation
headed by a five-member Board of Directors; two of the members are the
President and the First Vice President of the Bank, and the other three
are chosen by the President of the United States with the consent of the

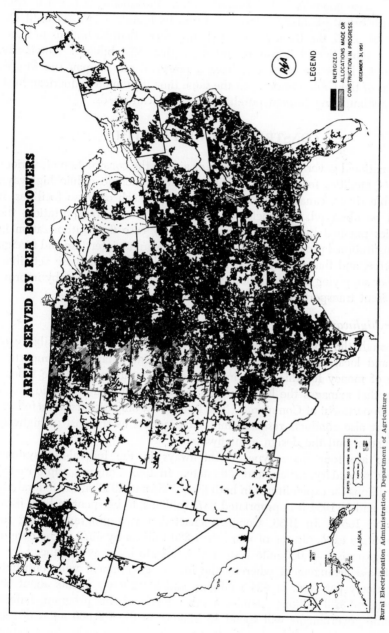

Rural Electrification Administration, Department of Agriculture

Figure 99. Areas Served by REA-Assisted Power Systems.

Senate. On January 1, 1956, the Bank had 167 employees, all in the United
States. The Bank has $1 billion worth of capital stock, all owned by the
government; it may borrow up to four times as much. The Bank lends
money to foreign countries and their business organizations, so that they
may purchase goods from the United States. Presumably it is not to compete with private banking interests. From its founding in 1934 until December 31, 1955, the Bank extended slightly more than $5 billions in loans;
over the same period it was repaid more than $2.4 billions. Obviously,
through its loans the Bank can have a powerful effect upon the foreign
relations of the United States. At the same time it promotes American business by stimulating foreign purchases of American goods.

CONSTRUCTION OF FACILITIES

The national government constructs, or aids in the construction of, various
types of facilities for business. These facilities include public highways,
navigable rivers, canals, harbors, and airports. Each of these facilities, it
should be observed, is associated with some form of transportation; the
activities pursued by the government in every case find authorization in
the constitutional provision that Congress may regulate interstate and foreign
commerce, and that it may construct post roads. Each of these activities,
by either supplying transportation where none existed before, or by improving present transportation, tends to promote business.

Public highways

Although the construction of highways is largely the responsibility of
State and local officials, the national government today is an important
source of money for this work, in the form of grants-in-aid. The federal
agency that manages the highway program is the Bureau of Public Roads
in the Department of Commerce. The Bureau not only disburses the federal
grants; it also conducts research into such matters as the cost of highway
construction and the design of highways.

There are four main types of highways in the federal-aid system:
primary, secondary, urban, and interstate. In 1952 Congress appropriated
$575 millions for expenditures in both fiscal 1954 and 1955 on the federal-aid
system; and in 1954 it appropriated $875 millions, to be spent in both fiscal
1956 and 1957. In 1956, Congress enacted a vast program calling for
federal-State expenditures of more than $30 billions by 1972. The core of
the program is a 41,000-mile system of interstate highways, financed by a
grant-in-aid arrangement whereby the federal government will contribute
about ninety per cent, or $24.8 billions, and State governments about ten
per cent, or $2.8 billions. Under another phase of this program, federal
and State governments will spend $6 billions on the 750,000 miles of sec-
ondary roads termed federal-aid highways. Some of the major construction
projects in which the federal government has participated are the Kew
Gardens Interchange, New York City (shown at the beginning of this
chapter); the Schuykill Expressway near Philadelphia; the Detroit-Toledo

Expressway; the Harbor Freeway in Los Angeles; and the relocation of Route 99 in Oregon.

These undertakings also illustrate the power that the automobile and truck industries have acquired in politics, and the slow decline of railroads as political factors. As railroads lately have each year carried less of the total of intercity freight (see Figure 100), they have become more sensitive to the threat of motor carrier competition and power. The anger of the Association of American Railroads is reflected in its lengthy series of institutional advertisements extolling railroads as the one means of transportation that "pays its own way"—of course, neglecting to mention that thousands of miles of present railroad trackage repose on lands that were outright gifts from the government in the nineteenth century.

Navigable rivers

The federal government has jurisdiction over all rivers that are navigable or that through dredging might become navigable. Owing to this authority the government is constantly engaged in numerous projects to improve rivers as channels for commerce. Most of this work is performed by the Army Engineers Corps; some of it is connected with the great multi-purpose dams. There is no coherent program for improving the navigability of rivers. Instead, a large portion of these undertakings are designed solely to placate local interests. In other words, the improvement of a supposedly navigable stream is sometimes no more than a present from a congressman

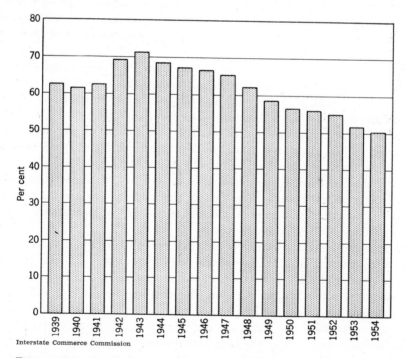

Figure 100. Percentage of Intercity Freight Carried by Railroads, 1939–1954.

to his district, to assist himself in his campaign for reelection. By contrast, some of these projects are of immense value to the community in which they are situated, and are a genuine aid to commerce and business generally. One outstanding example is the Ohio River, on which the Army Engineers Corps has built forty-six navigation locks and dams. Thus over the 981 miles from Pittsburgh to its mouth the Ohio has a nine-foot channel; in 1954 it carried 55 million short tons of freight, considerably more than the Panama Canal.

Canals

The federal government has constructed several canals that have been of great importance in the rise of American industry. The most spectacular of these canals is that through the Isthmus of Panama linking the Atlantic and Pacific Oceans. The Canal carried its first ship in 1914. The building of the Panama Canal was to a considerable degree motivated by the requirements of national defense; the American people had been greatly stirred by the two-month, fourteen-thousand-mile voyage of the battleship *Oregon*, which had had to sail around Cape Horn to get from the Pacific Coast to the Atlantic at the time of the Spanish-American War.

Initially, American coastwise shipping was to be allowed to pass toll-free; however, the British protested so loudly that Congress repealed this privilege. This action was probably necessary in order to win British support for the then hostile American policy toward Mexico; a contributing factor was the pressure brought by the transcontinental railroads, which feared competition from the Canal. In fiscal 1954 there were 8,293 transits of the Canal by vessels; they carried over forty million net tons of cargo and paid $35.1 millions in tolls.

Another canal, which is less spectacular than the Panama and which is not so clearly associated with national defense, but which is the busiest canal in the world, is that around the falls of the St. Marys River flowing from Lake Superior into Lake Huron—the Sault Sainte Marie Canal, or the "Soo." The principal function of the Soo is to furnish an exit from Lake Superior so that ships may transport iron ore from Duluth and Superior to the ore docks at Chicago, Detroit, Cleveland, Ashtabula, and Conneaut. In 1954 the Soo carried 84 million short tons of freight, almost nine-tenths of which were eastbound. The Soo is operated by the Army Engineers Corps. The federal government maintains several other canals, such as that through Cape Cod in Massachusetts.

In 1954 the federal government enacted legislation enabling it to participate with Canada in a St. Lawrence Seaway project. This undertaking will provide a channel from the Atlantic Ocean to Toledo for ships with a twenty-seven-foot draft. Certain elements in the United States had been striving for at least half a century to procure this legislation, but other interests, especially the railroads and the railroad labor organizations, hitherto had succeeded in blocking congressional action.

Success in 1954 may be attributed to several factors. One was the threat of the Canadian government to go ahead with the project, whether or not the United States cooperated. Another was the realization that the Minnesota iron mines are nearing exhaustion, and that a deeper channel would be necessary if the United States planned to bring Canadian ore down the St. Lawrence into Lake Erie. A third important factor was the presence of Secretary of the Treasury Humphrey, who in private life is a steel company official. A possible added factor is the lessened influence that the railroads, which have been the chief opponents of the Seaway, can bring to bear upon Congress. A final important factor was the willingness of the Eisenhower administration to allow some agency other than the federal government to produce hydroelectric power; thus the antagonists of federally-owned power stations were appeased.

To execute and supervise this project Congress established the St. Lawrence Seaway Development Corporation, which is empowered to issue $105 million worth of bonds to pay the share of the United States. The chiefs of the Corporation are an Administrator and a Deputy Administrator. Policy for the Corporation is to be set by a five-member Advisory Board. All these officers are named by the President with the advice and consent of the Senate. The Corporation is under the supervision and direction of the Secretary of Defense. The hydroelectric phase of this undertaking is in the hands of the Power Authority of New York State and the Hydro-Electric Power Commission of Ontario. The map in Figure 101 depicts the Seaway.

Harbors

The federal government has undertaken many projects to improve harbors. The government deepens the harbors, erects lighthouses and breakwaters, and dredges out turning basins. These tasks are performed mainly by the Army Engineers Corps. As with the operations connected with river navigation, harbor projects often are carried out not as promotions of commerce but as demonstrations by Senators and Representatives that they are doing their best for their constituents. At the same time it is undeniable that some of these projects, notably those involving ports on the Great Lakes, have so promoted business that they have been beneficial for the entire nation.

Airports and air navigation

The federal government plays an important role in the construction of airports and the installation of air navigation systems. These activities are conducted by the Civil Aeronautics Administration (CAA) in the Commerce Department. The national government, through the Federal Aid Airport Program, shares with local authorities the cost of building airports; in fiscal 1954 the federal government made grants-in-aid of $17 millions for the Program. The CAA also makes technical recommendations of various types with reference to airport construction. For air navigation control the government has established a Federal Airways System of more than 100,000 miles in length, composed of airlanes bounded by radio signals. The government is also installing electronic devices that will enable the pilot of an

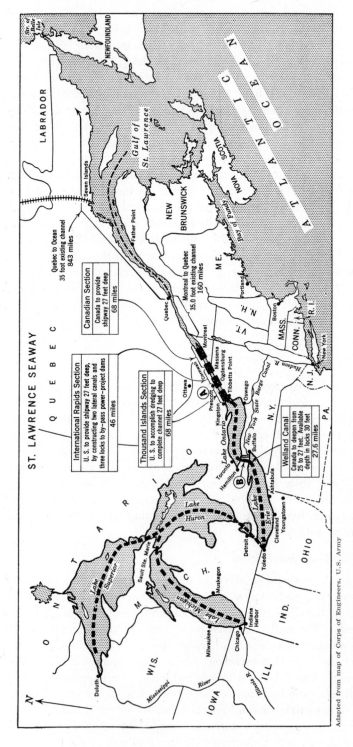

Adapted from map of Corps of Engineers, U.S. Army

Figure 101. The St. Lawrence Seaway. As contemplated under the law of May 13, 1954.

airship to land his craft by instruments alone, and to know from gages on his instrument panel his distance from a given station.

TECHNICAL AID AND INFORMATION

The federal government today provides many different sorts of technical aid and information for the business community. Most of this aid and information emanates from the Department of Commerce. Perhaps the greatest source of this type of factual data is the Bureau of the Census, which has been dealt with in Chapter 36. It suffices to remember that the Census Bureau counts the entire population every ten years; that it maintains a constant population estimation service in the period between the regular decennial censuses; that it performs many other censuses, such as those for agriculture, business, manufactures, mineral industries, and transportation; and that it carries on frequent studies of the techniques of census-taking and statistics. It should be quite evident that facts of this nature can be of enormous value to the businessman in such matters as reckoning a potential market. Another institution that assists business by supplying it with information, also described in a previous chapter (Chapter 38), is the Council of Economic Advisers. Apart from these two bodies there are several federal agencies clearly intended for the welfare of tradesmen, financiers, and manufacturers.

Business and Defense Services Administration

The Business and Defense Services Administration (BDSA) in the Department of Commerce is perhaps the outstanding illustration of the way in which the Department executes the functional representation of business in the national government. A comparatively new agency, first announced on October 1, 1953, the BDSA consolidates a number of former offices within the Department, including the Office of Technical Services, the Office of Distribution, and the Office of Industry and Commerce. One significant feature of the BDSA is the inclusion of twenty-five Industry Divisions making up a cross-section of American industry, to bring the wishes of manufacturers to the executive branch of the government. The BDSA, then, works directly with trade associations through their spokesmen.

Other portions of the BDSA are intended to convey technological information from the government to business, to assist industry in the standardization of products in the interest of economy, to help regions and localities with problems attached to their economic development, and to transmit all types of data on economic conditions to the businesses concerned. The work of the BDSA is complemented by that of the Office of Business Economics, which analyzes current business conditions, then sends its findings to enterprisers.

National Bureau of Standards

The National Bureau of Standards in the Commerce Department is an immense scientific laboratory for the establishment of weights and measurements and for research in such fields as mathematics, chemistry, physics, and engineering. The authorization for the Bureau is derived from the constitutional clause empowering Congress to ". . . fix the standard of weights and measures" (Art. I, sec. 8, cl. 5). Today the Bureau determines thousands of such standards for use in all public and private experimentation in the United States. It tests equipment and materials for the public, as well as for government purchasing. The range of Bureau concerns is evident from the titles of a few of its scientific divisions: Atomic and Radiation Physics; Building Technology; Electricity and Electronics; Mineral Products; Radio Propagation Physics. All discoveries of the Bureau save those that must be classified as solely for the use of the government are available to business interests.

The Weather Bureau

The Weather Bureau in the Department of Commerce provides important services to business, especially in the field of transportation. That the Weather Bureau aids farmers and the military forces as well can be seen from the fact that in the past it has been in both the Agriculture Department and the Army Signal Corps. The Bureau has 331 stations in the United States and its territories, and enjoys the assistance of 12,600 cooperating stations. With respect to commerce, the Weather Bureau supplies an unending stream of data respecting meteorological conditions, so that both merchant ships and commercial airliners may adapt their routes to find the areas with the least weather disturbance. Another important aid given to business by the Bureau is a river and flood forecasting system, so that industries situated along river banks, river transportation systems, and all enterprises using water power, may have sufficient warning of coming floods.

Coast and Geodetic Survey

The Coast and Geodetic Survey in the Commerce Department is largely a mapping organization. It provides important aids for seaborne commerce, by surveying and charting coastal areas, and by computing tides and ocean currents. It assists airborne trade by producing aeronautical maps. It helps both forms of transportation through its studies of the magnetism of the earth and its effect upon magnetic compasses. It also analyzes earthquakes, supplying valuable information to the construction industry. In its geodetic work (geodesy being a method of surveying that takes into account the curvature of the earth) the Survey makes it possible to draw more accurate maps and to reach more exact determinations of the elevations of the earth's surface; thus the Survey is of considerable significance to such undertakings as private hydroelectric stations. In one way the Survey appears to have invaded, probably inadvertently, the jurisdiction of the Interior Department; in its charting of the coast of the Gulf of Mexico the Survey was largely responsible for the discovery of the underseas oil resources off the coasts of Louisiana and Texas.

Bureau of Foreign Commerce

The Bureau of Foreign Commerce in the Commerce Department aims at furnishing American businessmen with data about economic conditions abroad, so as to promote the foreign trade of the United States. It has already been noted that the total amount of American overseas trade is surpassed many times by its domestic trade. Yet the quantity of American foreign commerce is important to some segments of the American economy, including certain shippers, bankers, manufacturers, and workers. The pattern of American foreign trade has passed through two major phases since 1789. In the first, which extended to the years just after the Civil War, the United States imported more than it exported; that is, as a nation it bought more than it sold. Its chief exports were foods; its leading imports were manufactured wares. Since the decade of the 1870's, by contrast, the United States has usually exported more than it imported; in other words, it has sold more than it has bought. Its principal exports are factory goods.

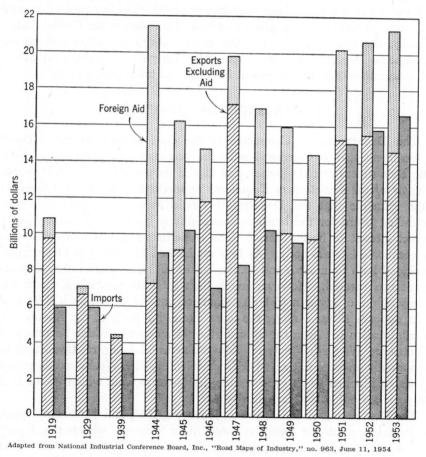

Adapted from National Industrial Conference Board, Inc., "Road Maps of Industry," no. 963, June 11, 1954

Figure 102. Exports and Imports of Goods and Services.

In the past few years, however, although its exports have continued to be greater than its imports, the surplus has sometimes been the result of foreign aid, in the guise of both military equipment and goods for civilian consumption. One of the greatest burdens the Bureau of Foreign Commerce has assumed is that of reshaping American international commerce so that its profits will result from actual sales rather than from gifts by the government. The graph in Figure 102 shows what have been the relations among imports, foreign purchases, and the total of exports.

Therefore the Bureau of Foreign Commerce has attempted in several ways to promote business that is not based upon governmental financial assistance. It provides information, on request, to American businessmen desirous of buying or selling abroad. It analyzes the domestic economic and political situation of foreign countries so as to encourage Americans to invest their money abroad. It sends technical advisers to other countries to assist them in improving and expanding their own manufacturing facilities; these endeavors will assist American trade in that they will enable foreign countries to sell more to the United States, giving them the money with which they can purchase American products. The Bureau furthermore aids foreign technicians to acquire industrial training in the United States. Finally, the Bureau carries out the functional-representation task of the Commerce Department in the area of foreign policy, speaking on behalf of American economic interests at international trade conventions.

DEPARTMENT OF COMMERCE

The Department of Commerce is the chief agency in the national government that is concerned with the promotion of business. Indeed, the Department frankly argues that this is its purpose; the 1953 *Annual Report of the Secretary of Commerce* approvingly notes the existence of "the principle that the Department should serve as a spokesman and sounding board for the business community in governmental activities of direct interest to businessmen." The Department of Commerce, then, is a vocational-interest body. As first established in 1903, the Department included both Commerce and Labor; but in 1913 a separate Labor Department was created. However much their interests may clash, there are many affairs of concern to both commerce and labor, although they may take opposite sides. Among the more interesting traits of the Eisenhower administration has been the often forthright manner in which Secretary of Commerce Weeks has entered into problems of labor relations, a field supposedly reserved to the Labor Department; in fact, Weeks and Secretary of Labor Mitchell had a considerable dispute as to what would be the best way for amending the Taft-Hartley Act.

The Department of Commerce on January 1, 1956, had 42,866 employees. It includes, under the Secretary, one Under Secretary who is the deputy of the Secretary, and a second Under Secretary, for Transportation. That the transportation administrator should have this rank rather than that of an Assistant Secretary suggests the important place that transportation has in the functioning of the Department. There are three Assistant Secretaries: for Domestic Affairs; for International Affairs; and for Administration. Among the major subordinate bodies, the Patent Office, the National Bureau of Standards, and the Coast and Geodetic Survey are supervised by the Under Secretary. The Weather Bureau, the Bureau of Public Roads, the Maritime Administration, and the Civil Aeronautics Administration are directed by the Under Secretary for Transportation. The Bureau of the Census and the BDSA are under the guidance of the Assistant Secretary for Domestic Affairs. The Bureau of Foreign Commerce is the chief concern of the Assistant Secretary for International Affairs.

QUESTIONS AND PROBLEMS

1. Define *patent*, *trade-mark*, and *copyright*. If you were to discover a new means for binding books, called it the NUBIND process, and then wrote a pamphlet describing the process, what steps would you take to protect your property rights in your work in each case?

2. How do bankruptcy laws both promote and hinder business? Do copyright laws also promote and hinder business?

3. How high does a tariff have to be in order to be obviously a device solely for the promotion of business and not for the purpose of obtaining revenue?

4. Describe the process of determining and administering the tariff schedule on goods from abroad.

5. Give an example of each of the following devices for promoting business: the capital gains tax; depletion allowances; preferential tax; monetary subsidy; non-monetary subsidy. Do any or all of these devices constitute a hindrance to business in any way?

6. How do loans for developing electric power and telephone systems promote business?

7. Describe the promotional activities of the government in the field of transportation.

8. List the agencies of the government that gather and disseminate technical aid and information, and state in one sentence their field of interest.

Tʜᴇ federal government not only promotes business; it also regulates
it. The process of regulation has several aspects; it includes limits upon
certain types of business structures, such as trusts; restrictions on business
financial practices, such as dishonest advertising of corporation stocks; and
consumers' welfare activities, such as the setting of railroad rates. In terms
of the goals of their regulation, American businesses fall into two broad
classes, the line between which often shifts. One class is ordinarily regarded
as "competitive"; that is, in this class there are apt to be two or more
business organizations vying with each other for profits. These organizations
are typically manufacturers, such as the automobile producers. In their
case, the principal task of regulation is to ensure that competition will not
be stifled. The second class of business is termed a "natural monopoly,"
that is, one in which the existence of several firms is viewed as wasteful.
This class includes the so-called "businesses vested with a public interest,"

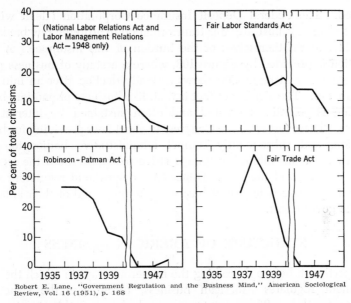

Robert E. Lane, "Government Regulation and the Business Mind," American Sociological Review, Vol. 16 (1951), p. 168

Figure 103.   Adjustment of Business Attitudes to Government Controls. Per cent of total number of criticisms of each of four laws that were made in each of several years in a journal of business.

or the "public utilities." These organizations are usually distributive, such as the railroads. Here the goal of regulation is primarily to protect the consumer from exorbitant rates.

It is sometimes difficult to separate business regulation from business promotion. In general, the government helps develop an activity when it promotes it, and restricts an activity when it regulates it. Yet the two terms simply are not clear. Hence it is necessary to understand at least what they stand for and how not to be confused by their application. Promotion in itself demands regulation; the tariff, for example, by forbidding entry to certain goods, is a regulative device with respect to those goods. By the same token, regulation may be promotional. It may promote other businesses: if railroad rates are set very high, other forms of transportation may prosper. On the other hand, regulation of a given business may promote that business: insistence by the government that a certain mode of transportation adopt safety devices is likely to increase the traffic. Frequently regulation does not directly or immediately benefit either one form of business or its competitors, but the consumer. Then again, the benefits may go only to some consumers and not to others. Few Americans buy oil corporation stocks; yet the Securities and Exchange Commission (SEC) regulates their sale.

There have been many occasions wherein a regulatory process was opposed by the business concerned when the process was established; yet later the regulation was first grudgingly, and at length enthusiastically,

The Federal Trade Commission Building, Washington, D.C.

approved. The Federal Deposit Insurance Corporation (dealt with in a previous chapter) illustrates this transformation in attitude; few banks today would like to rid themselves of the burden of this insurance. A second illustration is provided by Figure 103, wherein a study of business protests against government regulation shows a steady decline after an initial peak of resentment. The significant fact is that, like business promotion, business regulation is sometimes created and often sustained by interest group pressures. These forces oblige Congress to enact laws providing for business regulation, and subsequently compel administrative bodies to execute these laws. Meanwhile other groups strive to oppose both the legislation and the execution of the laws. Hence the composite of regulatory statutes mirrors the relative influence of business groupings and of their antagonists upon the government.

STRUCTURE OF AMERICAN BUSINESS

It is pertinent, before describing the numerous ways in which the federal government regulates American business, to analyze the structure of American business. There are two general phases to this structure: individual businesses, and combinations of businesses. Individual businesses may be subdivided into single proprietors, partnerships, and corporations; combinations may be subdivided into pools, cartels, trusts, and holding companies.

Individual businesses

Single Proprietors: The single proprietorship is the commonest form of business structure; it is typified by any of the thousands of small retail stores throughout the country. The proprietor may employ the labor of other persons. He is, however, individually responsible for all debts incurred by the business; that is, his personal property may be sold in order to satisfy the obligations of the business. The business as such dissolves at his death; whereas the properties of the business may be willed to his heirs, the business itself will acquire an entirely new legal status because of its changed ownership.

Partnerships: Partnerships legally are similar to single proprietorships; they simply provide means whereby two or more persons may unite their assets to obtain a larger monetary fund for a business. Shares in the profits are usually assigned in proportion to each partner's monetary contribution. Each partner is individually responsible for all debts of the company, regardless of his share in the financing of the business. If, for example, one partner should abscond with all the assets of the company, his partner or partners could be held liable for the obligations of the business. A partnership terminates with the death of one partner.

Corporations: The corporation is the leading structural form adopted by large businesses today. It has certain major advantages over both single proprietorships and partnerships. A corporation is a legal personality; it acquires this stature through a charter secured from any one of the

State governments. Once it has a charter, a corporation may buy and sell goods, employ laborers, incur debts (by selling bonds), and sue or be sued in court. The corporation obtains money apart from loans through selling shares of stock; the profits of the company are divided among the stockholders after the obligations of the business have been fulfilled. The stockholders are the owners of the corporation.

One of the chief advantages of the corporate structure is that the liability of the owners is limited to their holdings of stock. The corporation, therefore, possesses "limited liability," which is the meaning of the abbreviation "ltd." following the name of any British corporation. If a corporation is bankrupted, the owners lose no more than their investment in stock; the creditors may not seize the personal property of the stockholders. Thus the corporate form greatly reduces the risk associated with business, and encourages people with limited wealth to invest.

Another advantage of the corporate structure is that management can be divorced from ownership. A giant corporation such as the American Telephone and Telegraph Company may have hundreds of thousands of stockholders or "owners." In theory these owners entrust the operation of the company to a board of directors, who presumably are their employees. The fact is that corporate direction adheres to Roberto Michels' "iron law of oligarchy": the many vote but the few rule; the board of directors ordinarily governs the company much as it sees fit. Hence the owners are actually relieved of the burden of administering the company and of the responsibilities linked with administration; yet this separation may permit the management to carry out its own desires with the owners' money.

A third important advantage of the corporate form is that its existence does not terminate with the death of one or more of its owners. Conceivably the organization might be immortal; usually, however, States impose some limit to the life of the charter. In any case, both the owners and the creditors of the corporation may rely upon its surviving the death of any of its stockholders or directors. Owing to these three aspects of its structure, the corporation has appeared to be the most desirable form for a business organization. At the same time, much of the regulatory machinery that the federal government has instituted results from the abuses that can be made of these advantages.

Although corporations today number only about 300,000 out of a total of several million American businesses, they dominate the economy of the country. Moreover, corporations themselves are by no means equally wealthy and influential; rather, a few giants among them tower above the rest. The graph in Figure 104 shows that, in 1950, 200 of the 300,000 American corporations accounted for more than forty per cent of the entire output. The accompanying figures for 1935 show that the concentration of corporate strength has increased; this is pointed up by the fact that in 1935 there were only about 200,000 corporations, so that 200 corporations then were a larger percentage of the whole number than they were in 1950. This enormous concentration of money and power in 200 or, for that

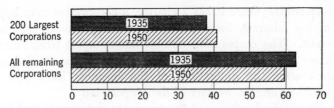

Figure 104.   Change in Concentration of Manufacturing, 1935 and 1950. Percentage of total U.S. manufactured output contributed by 200 largest corporations and percentage contributed by remaining corporations.

matter, in 1,000 or 10,000 companies, tends constantly to influence public policy; it would do so to an even larger degree were it not for government restraints.   Indeed, government regulation of business could well be termed the reaction to business regulation of government.   A balance of forces is created that shifts back and forth, somewhat like the balance between Congress and the presidency.

Business combinations

A business combination is an arrangement among two or more individual enterprises that generally aims at the restriction of competition, so as to fix prices or output, or both.   Government regulation of such combinations has the goal of restoring competition.

Pools: A pool is a business combination wherein several companies performing the same type of service or manufacturing the same type of commodity agree among themselves to restrict competition by such a device as allocating certain markets as monopolies to individual members of the pool, the other members agreeing that they will solicit no business in those markets.   In a typical pool, the members place their revenues in a common fund, or "pool"; regularly the contents of the entire fund are divided among all the contributors according to a previously established ratio which may be proportioned to the anticipated contribution of each member.   The pool often is not very satisfactory; it is only a "gentlemen's agreement" from which the members are at liberty to withdraw at any time when they feel that withdrawal may be to their advantage.

Cartels: The term "cartel" is subject to a number of definitions.   In Germany, for example, it is commonly used as a synonym for "pool." However, when used in the United States and applied to American businesses, it is apt to have the connotation of an international business agreement.   As an illustration, considerable evidence has been adduced to show that, before World War II, some of the greatest American corporations, in such fields as petroleum refining, rubber, and aluminum, had reached cartel agreements with the German dye trust (*I.G. Farben A.G.*) regarding the distribution of markets and particularly the exchange of technical information.   It seems that through these cartels the Germans were able to limit American production and the building of new productive facilities by American enterprises while expanding their own, and managed to obtain important knowledge about such matters as producing synthetic rubber from petroleum without contributing any significant data to the United States. Indeed, whereas the American firms regarded these cartels as economic arrangements, the Germans were exploiting them for political and military ends.

Trusts: A trust is a far more tightly bound combination of businesses than either a pool or a cartel. Under a trust structure, the participating companies surrender a portion of their stocks to a board of trustees, who then establish the policies of the member enterprises. Organizers of business combinations began using the trust rather than the pool after about the year 1880; and the following three decades saw the formation of the wealthiest trusts in the nation, such as the United States Steel Corporation. These groups were the targets of the antitrust legislation that Congress started to enact in 1890.

Holding Companies: A holding company is a business arrangement enabling a small group of persons with a limited monetary investment to control gigantic financial empires. The holding company itself produces nothing; it is solely a device for owning other companies. It draws its virtue from the fact that the person or group that owns as much as fifty-one per cent of the stock in a given company may direct the company; actually those who would dominate a company may need no more than five or ten per cent of its stock, since the owners of the remaining stock may be quite inactive in the management of the company. Holding companies once were pyramided one on top of the other to a height of six or eight levels, all organized by a small number of persons, so that a holding company capitalized at only a few millions of dollars might enable its chief stockholders to control an industrial realm valued at a billion dollars or more. This sort of control also enabled the directors to allocate the profits in such a way that they could enrich themselves while ruining the actual manufacturing concerns.

REGULATION OF BUSINESS ORGANIZATION

Antitrust laws

Government regulation of business organization is carried out chiefly through the antitrust laws. There are two outstanding statutes: the Sherman Act of 1890, and the Clayton Act of 1914. The Sherman Act prohibits combinations designed to restrain trade or fix prices, and declares that such acts shall be regarded as misdemeanors and be punishable by the courts. The Clayton Act outlaws specific so-called "unfair trade practices" such as prices that tend to discriminate between two purchasers; in addition, the Act bars interlocking directorates in corporations with a capital worth exceeding a stated value. It also makes corporation officials personally liable for any specified misdeeds of their organizations.

The enforcement of the Sherman and Clayton Acts has been very irregular. Like any other laws, they depend for their execution upon the determination of administrative officers to apply them. In the first decade after its enactment the Sherman Act was rarely invoked. Moreover, in one of the rare cases in which the Act was applied, in a suit against the sugar trust, the Supreme Court ruled that the Act was of no force; although admitting that the sugar trust dominated the refining of sugar in the United States, the Court held that manufacturing was only incidental to commerce, and that whereas the Constitution empowers the federal government to regulate interstate commerce it does not authorize it to control manufacturing. Therefore, the Court argued, breaking up a monopoly of sugar-refining was not a proper function of the national government. This judgment, of course, reflected the then current predisposition of the Court not to interfere in business combinations. Furthermore, the federal courts soon discovered that the Sherman Act could be employed against labor unions, which might be defined as "conspiracies in restraint of trade," forbidden by the Sherman Act. To prevent this interpretation, the Clayton Act specifically exempts labor unions from its controls.

One other blow at the regulation of trusts was the "rule of reason" that the Supreme Court handed down. According to this principle (which was no new discovery, but an old doctrine of English common law), bigness in itself is not a crime; the concentration must only avoid imposing "unreasonable" restraints upon trade. This decision saddled the courts with the burden of determining what were, and what were not, "unreasonable" restraints upon trade. So long as the courts were generously inclined toward business combinations, the Sherman Act was likely to be ineffective. One aim of the Clayton Act was to define trade practices that are "unfair"—that, in short, comprise "unreasonable" restraints on trade.

Antitrust administration

The Sherman and Clayton Acts are administered by two agencies. One of these is the Antitrust Division of the Justice Department, which enforces the Sherman Act. A case usually arises out of a complaint by a small businessman that he is being forced to contend with a monopolistic combination. Such charges are first studied by the Federal Bureau of Investigation; if it appears that there are sufficient grounds, the Justice Department files a suit against the offender, with the aim of at least compelling him to cease his monopolistic activities. At most the Division may hope to persuade the court to sentence the guilty organization to pay a fine; no one has ever gone to jail for violating the Sherman Act. The Antitrust Division is almost entirely dependent upon Congress for its success, since that body appropriates the money for its work; ordinarily Congress does not give the Division much money, as can be seen from the fact that in January of 1956 it had but 434 employees. Figure 105 shows how one trust, the American Tobacco Company, was dissolved by government action based on the Sherman Law.

The other administrative agency associated with antitrust legislation is the Federal Trade Commission (FTC), established in 1914 to carry out the Clayton Act. The Commission is an independent agency made up of five members, appointed by the President with the consent of the Senate, who serve overlapping seven-year terms. One of the chief desires of certain pressure groups, then, is to procure the nomination of commissioners favorable to their position on governmental regulation of business.

The Commission has authority over a number of different types of unfair trade practices, which are normally brought to its attention by the complaint of an affected businessman. The FTC has long been concerned with deceptive advertising; for example, it ordered one manufacturer of patent medicines to drop the word "liver" from the title of one of its products because, the FTC argued, the product had nothing to do with the liver. Parallel to this activity, the Commission has devoted considerable time to examining the animal-fur trade, since garment manufacturers have sometimes labeled furs in a manner suggesting that they came from valuable pelts when they were no better than rabbit. The FTC investigates charges that a manufacturer is selling his products to one industrial consumer for lower prices than he asks of other industrial consumers, because the manufacturer owns stock in the first consumer. The Commission also seeks to prevent one company from procuring the assets of another company, when this procurement might lessen competition.

The action of the FTC, when it finds that charges of unfair trade practices are borne out by the facts, is to issue a cease and desist order, a command that is more or less equivalent to an injunction save that it emanates from an administrative rather than a judicial body. The plaintiff may appeal such an order to a federal court of appeals and even to the Supreme Court. The Commission, finally, is empowered to supervise the execution of its orders by inspection of the businesses concerned. The scope of its work may be seen from the fact that during fiscal 1955 the FTC issued thirty-six antimonopoly complaints and eighty-two orders to cease and desist deceptive practices; and that on June 30, 1955, the FTC had 264 antimonopoly investigations pending.

Monopolies among public utilities

Government regulation of monopolistic practices by any of the public utilities is based not on the Sherman and Clayton Acts but on other laws passed especially to control the individual utilities. If it is necessary, both the Sherman and Clayton Acts can be invoked and applied. However, there are particular kinds of business restraints among utilities that are detected and prosecuted by the independent agencies that have been created to supervise the utilities. For instance, railroads are forbidden to transport any goods (with a few exceptions) in which they have an immediate financial interest; furthermore, they may not invest in, or operate, a water carrier that competes with them. Telegraph and telephone companies are prohibited from discriminating against any of their users. Commercial airlines are denied ". . . unjust discriminations, undue preferences or advantages, or unfair or destructive competitive practices." Yet it must be emphasized that these restrictions, although analogous to those fixed

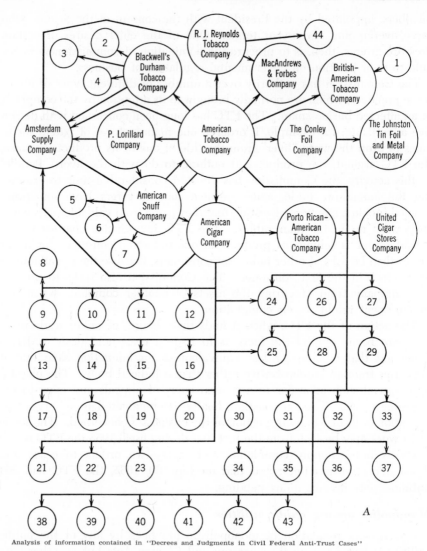

Analysis of information contained in "Decrees and Judgments in Civil Federal Anti-Trust Cases"

Figure 105. American Tobacco Company Before and After Antitrust Action.
A. Before.   B. After.

THE AMERICAN TOBACCO COMPANY
(before and after antitrust action)

(Arrows point *from* stockholding company *to* company part or all of whose stock is held.)

1. Imperial Tobacco Company
2. F. R. Penn Tobacco Company
3. Scotten-Dillon Company
4. Wells-Whitehead Tobacco Company
5. H. Bolander
6. De Voe Snuff Company
7. Standard Snuff Company
8. R. D. Burnett Cigar Company

9. American Stogie Company
10. M. Blaskower Company
11. Cliff Weil Cigar Company
12. Cuban Land and Leaf Tobacco Company
13. Havana Tobacco Company
14. Dusel, Goodloe & Co.
15. J. J. Goodrum Tobacco Company

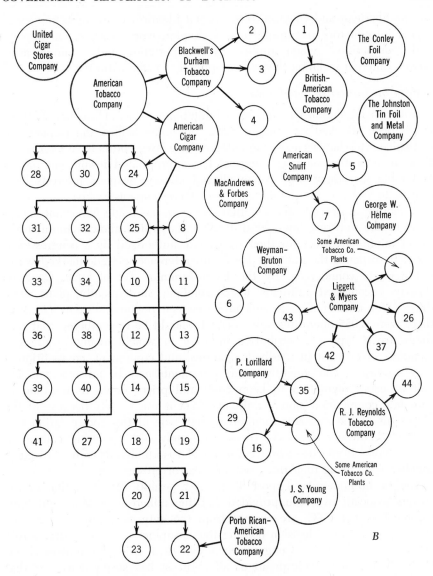

16. Federal Cigar Real Estate Company
17. Havana American Company
18. Louisiana Tobacco Company, Limited
19. Jordan, Gibson, & Baum, Incorporated
20. The J. B. Moos Company
21. Corporation J. B. Moos
22. Porto-Rican Leaf Tobacco Company
23. The Smokers' Paradise Corporation
24. The Kentucky Tobacco Product Company
25. International Cigar Machinery Company
26. The John Bollman Company
27. Jno. W. Carroll Tobacco Company
28. F. F. Adams Tobacco Company
29. S. Anargyros

30. Crescent Cigar & Tobacco Company
31. Thomas Cusack Company
32. Day and Night Tobacco Company
33. Garson Vending Machine Company
34. Golden Belt Manufacturing Company
35. Luhrman & Wilbern Tobacco Company
36. Manhattan Briar Pipe Company
37. Nall & Williams Tobacco Company
38. Mengal Box Company
39. Monopol Tobacco Works
40. Nashville Tobacco Works
41. R. A. Patterson Tobacco Company
42. Pinkerton Tobacco Company
43. Spaulding & Merrick
44. Lippert-Scales Company

by the Sherman and Clayton Acts, are not identical to them; as suggested in the introductory paragraph to this chapter, words such as "monopoly" and "competition" when applied to transportation and communication have a different meaning than when applied to manufacturing.

Limits on antitrust legislation

Antitrust legislation has numerous limitations. Since it was first adopted it has been attacked from many sides. As noted before, the Department of Justice often has been slow to enforce these laws; courts have interpreted them in a hostile manner; Congress has appropriated insufficient money to enable investigators to probe alleged abuses; business interests have striven to procure the naming of sympathetic commissioners.

It should also be pointed out that Congress has made important exceptions to the antitrust laws. Fair-trade laws, which allow manufacturers to set minimum prices for their goods, are authorized by a congressional act that suspends the antitrust laws with reference to trade-marked wares in interstate commerce. By the Esch-Cummins Act of 1920, Congress frankly encouraged railroads to consolidate; subsequently plans were drafted for uniting all railroads into nineteen regional systems (in 1920 there were 1,085 operating railways). It should be remembered that railroads are a type of distributive industry in which, owing to the tremendous investment in roadbeds, stations, and equipment, competition is very expensive; consequently, many arguments may be advanced on behalf of using regulation to keep costs and prices down rather than to stimulate competition among railroads. Yet it was largely because of the objections of the railroads themselves that little of this consolidation was realized (however, by 1952 there were only 454 operating railways). Later, thanks to the Reed-Bulwinkle Act of 1948, railroads were allowed to collaborate in fixing their rates, without fear of prosecution.

The Webb-Pomerene Export Trade Act permits the formation of exporters' associations which, provided that they adhere to certain regulations enforced by the FTC, are exempt from the antitrust laws. In the face of a Supreme Court decision holding that insurance companies play a role in interstate commerce, Congress exempted them from the antitrust laws. Certainly the most widespread of all antitrust law suspensions was that authorized by the National Industrial Recovery Act of 1933 (NIRA), which obliged enterprisers in several hundred fields to combine into trade associations for the purpose of setting prices and standards. The NIRA was declared unconstitutional in 1935.

The chief factor in the enforcement of antitrust legislation seems to be the conclusion reached by interest groups, and by the government officials over whom the groups have the strongest influence, as to whether or not a competitive situation is advantageous to themselves. In recent years it has seemed that many groups, or at least major individual enterprisers, have opposed competition, and have managed to have their will prevail in the government.

CONTROL OF FINANCIAL OPERATIONS

During the past twenty years the federal government has actively intervened into the financial operations of American businesses, especially corporations, to protect the public against improper financial behavior. The corporate structure lends itself singularly well to such behavior: ownership of a corporation is so widely diffused, and often is so isolated from its management, that the directors of a corporation have been able to manipulate company funds so as to enrich themselves while beggaring the stockholders. A classic demonstration of such a proceeding occurred during the construction of the Union Pacific Railroad from Omaha, Nebraska, to Ogden, Utah. The promoters of the railroad established as a construction firm a corporation known as the Credit Mobilier, whose stock the promoters themselves owned almost entirely, with the exception of a few shares distributed so as to blind the eyes of inquisitive government officials. Using the money invested by the public in the railroad, they paid extravagant prices to the Credit Mobilier for construction materials; the upshot was that the investors in the railroad received no dividends, whereas the owners of the Credit Mobilier harvested enormous profits.

Another favorite device of directors was to sell stock to the public, then fail to invest the monetary returns in equipment. Hence the total amount of stock in circulation far exceeded the true worth of the company; it was diluted, or "watered." Business organizers also might exaggerate the prospects of new corporations, inducing people to invest their money in undertakings that would profit only their creators. Moreover, the holding company displayed itself as a superb mechanism for fleecing investors. Wealthy individuals vied with one another in speculating upon food commodities, especially grains, regardless of the interests of smaller investors or of those who depended upon a "normal" return from commodities for their livelihood. The collapse of the stock market in 1929 convinced federal officers that such varied operations must be regulated; hence in F. D. Roosevelt's first term Congress enacted laws setting restrictions upon stock markets, holding companies, and commodity exchanges.

Stock markets

Through the Securities Act of 1933 and the Securities Exchange Act of 1934, the national government today regulates stock markets and virtually the entire procedure of selling stocks and bonds in order to obtain funds for business activities. The principal administrative agency involved in these regulative proceedings is the Securities and Exchange Commission (SEC), made up of five members appointed by the President and confirmed by the Senate to serve five-year terms, one of which ends each year. The SEC is intended to be a typical quasi-judicial body exempt from political control; no more than three of its members may belong to the same political party. The decisions of the SEC may be reviewed by a federal court of appeals. It is of course under great pressure, both from those who support government regulation and from those who deplore it.

The government makes numerous demands upon businesses in order to regulate them. Any business that plans to issue stocks for sale in interstate commerce in excess of $300,000 must register with the SEC and must provide the SEC with a sample of the information it proposes to give the public. The SEC conducts an examination to determine whether the information is true or false; however, registration with the SEC in itself is not proof that the information is true. In any case, it is unlawful to submit false statements to potential investors. The SEC does not guarantee that the business will succeed; its guiding purpose is to assure the public of some essential, financially true facts about the enterprise. Companies must also furnish the SEC with statements about their financial condition. Likewise, all persons engaged in the sale of securities must register with the SEC; the Commission seeks to prevent such persons from committing deceptions and misrepresentations in the vending process.

Furthermore, the SEC supervises investment trusts, which are companies that invest money lent or subscribed to them by individuals or by other companies. The chief justifications for an investment trust are that its officials are apt to know more about profitable stocks than the individual investor can, and that owing to its diversified holdings it can usually provide a safe return. The SEC also regulates investment counsellors, who are paid advisers to people on the worth of stocks and bonds. It is evident from these functions that the federal government intends to guarantee the small investor who may be rather innocent of stock-market wiles from the less reputable practices of some brokers and corporation directors.

Holding companies

The federal government regulates some holding companies, also through the Securities and Exchange Commission, under the terms of the Public Utility Holding Company Act of 1935. The nature and purposes of holding companies have already been dealt with. In accordance with this Act the SEC regulates the financial relationships between the companies and the public utilities they control. The law forbids the erection of holding companies above the "second level"; that is, the pyramid legally may not rise above a holding company dominating other holding companies that control public utilities. The SEC also imposes geographic limits upon holding companies by restricting their control to "physically integrated and coordinated properties." To phrase it otherwise, a holding company may not found a combination of utility companies that is united only financially; the combination must have functional unity as well.

Commodity exchanges

A commodity exchange is a market for the buying and selling of agricultural products, especially staple foods, such as corn and Irish potatoes, and textile sources, such as cotton. The Chicago Board of Trade is a commodity exchange. The particular activity on commodity exchanges that is regulated by the federal government is the trade in so-called "futures." A future is either one of two things: it may be an agreement to sell a given commodity in the future, at a price arranged in the present; on the other hand, it may be an agreement to buy a given commodity in the future, at a price arranged in the present. When legitimately employed, trading in futures by either the growers or the processors of these commodities is known as "hedging." Hedging is a method whereby a grower or a processor protects himself against either a rise or a fall in commodity prices, whichever would be disadvantageous to him. The grower, since he enters the exchange as a seller, hedges against a fall in prices; the processor, entering the exchange as a buyer, hedges against a rise. In reality most growers and processors have neither the time, money, nor ability to engage in continuous hedging operations. Rather, many persons who own not a bushel of corn nor a bale of cotton enter the exchange to buy or sell futures for the sole aim of speculating on rises or drops in prices. Such speculators perform a useful function when they compete against one another so successfully that they cause the price of a commodity to move along in a stable way. However, speculators can, through dealing in futures, effect price changes that bear no relationship to the genuine supply and demand situation of the given commodity. It is argued that the sudden drop in grain prices during 1947 and 1948 resulted largely from the doings of speculators.

In order to prevent this type of speculation the federal government has created two agencies for the supervision of commodity exchanges. One of these is the Commodity Exchange Commission, established in 1922, which has three members: the Secretary of Agriculture, the Secretary of Commerce, and the Attorney General. The other agency is the Commodity Exchange Authority, which is an office in the Department of Agriculture, under the Assistant Secretary for Marketing and Foreign Agriculture. Of the two, the Authority is the more important; this fact leads to the inference that since it is a branch of a political agency, the Agriculture Department—being in that respect quite different from the formally non-political Securities and Exchange Commission—it is designed to serve a vocational-interest group, the farmers, and not the public as a whole. In its functioning, however, the Commodity Exchange Authority often does protect the public against extreme food costs. Its principal tasks are to protect those who hedge against the market, to prevent the spreading of false information about crops that may influence prices, and to block the establishment of corners on agricultural commodities. The Commodities Exchange Commission works through the Authority. It deals with violations by commodity exchanges of the Commodity Exchange Act of 1936, and may set limits upon the amount of trading in futures.

REGULATION FOR CONSUMERS' WELFARE

The government regulation of business that aims at protecting the welfare of consumers takes one or the other of two major forms. On the one hand, the government regulates prices; or, to state the matter some-what more precisely, since the regulation is applied primarily to means of transportation and of communication, the government fixes *rates*. On the other hand, the government establishes certain standards of *quality*, whether of performance or of materials.

Rates

The Basis of Rate-Fixing: The process of rate-fixing is based primarily on a formula devised many years ago: rates must be just and reasonable, giving a fair return on the value of the property. The leading difficulty is to judge what shall be a "fair return" on the value of the property. Once one has decided what the value of the property is, one may conclude that a certain percentage of the value comprises a fair return upon it. However, there are several means for computing the value of a property. It is unnecessary here to discuss all of these means, but two may be singled out to illustrate the complexity of rate-fixing. One means for valuation employs the original cost of the property; a fair return, then, would be a percentage of what the property cost when built. A second means for valuation utilizes the replacement cost; a fair return under these circumstances would be a percentage of what it would cost to replace the property.

Now, suppose that the rates are to be fixed during an inflationary era, that is, one in which prices have gone up. The owners of the property would argue for rates based upon replacement costs, since they would yield a higher return; consumers would ask for an original cost valuation, so as to obtain lower rates. By contrast, it may be that rates are to be fixed in a deflationary era, one in which prices have dropped. Now the owners may ask for an original cost valuation, whereas the consumers will demand a replacement cost valuation.

It is evident that there will be conflict among the various groups inter-ested in the rate-fixing process; it is likely that whichever means for valua-tion is used will provide the identity of the stronger group or groups. Today even the principle of a fair return on the value of the property is being challenged. Within the past fifteen years the federal Supreme Court has ruled that a just and reasonable rate might be set even though it were insufficient to provide a fair return; this decision would hold that the leading function of a public utility is to furnish services to the consumer rather than give profits to its owners.

The Pattern of Rate-Fixing: The Interstate Commerce Commission (ICC), through various acts of Congress, today fixes the rates of most forms of transportation engaged in interstate commerce: railroads, ships, buses, trucks, pipelines (save those for natural gas and for water), ferries, express companies, and the like. The railroads were the first mode of transportation whose rates were subjected to ICC determination. From the date of its creation, in 1887, the ICC has been authorized to prohibit unjust and unreasonable rates; it was only through laws passed in 1906 and 1920 that the ICC was empowered to fix the rates directly. Even today, however, the ICC is largely dependent upon the railroads for establishing the rates.

That is, a railroad or group of railroads that believes it should earn more money files a petition with the ICC for an increase in rates, and the ICC must to some extent rely upon the data provided by railroads to attain a decision.

The federal government strives to prevent railroads from discriminating against some shippers in favor of others. For example, it prohibits railroads from giving rebates, which are the return of part of the cost of transportation to a shipper; at one time the Standard Oil Company shipped so much oil by rail that it was able, by threatening to give its business to another line, to collect rebates not only on its own shipments but also on those of other oil producers. Such rebates were a manifest discrimination against the competitors of the Standard Oil Company.

The federal government also forbids railroads to charge more for a short haul than for a long haul, seeking to ban discrimination arising out of competition between the railroads themselves. The following type of situation actually has existed in the past: Railroads A and B link Chicago and New York. Only A serves Cleveland, and only B serves Pittsburgh. Hence A and B compete for shipments between Chicago and New York; however, A has a monopoly between Chicago and Cleveland, and B has a monopoly between Chicago and Pittsburgh. Therefore in vying for the commerce between Chicago and New York, each railroad may lower its rates to the point where it is losing money; A will make up its losses by charging high, monopolistic rates between Chicago and Cleveland (and between New York and Cleveland, for that matter), and B will recoup its losses through monopolistic rates between Chicago and Pittsburgh and between New York and Pittsburgh. Even today there are railroads that charge the *same* rate for a short haul as for a long haul; this practice is not illegal. Indeed, these somewhat discriminatory rates may be aimed at competing on the long haul not with another railroad but with the airlines.

It is noteworthy that although the federal Constitution authorizes the federal government to legislate only with respect to interstate commerce, today the government has found justification for major controls over intrastate rates as well. Ordinarily railroad rates in intrastate commerce would be fixed by a commission in each State comparable to the ICC. Let us assume, however, that there are factories in Schenectady, New York, and in Toledo, Ohio, that produce an item needed by a large concern in Buffalo, New York. Toledo and Schenectady are about the same distance from Buffalo; in the one case the commerce is interstate, but in the other it is intrastate. Now, quite possibly stimulated by the Schenectady manufacturer, the public utility commission of New York State might fix a railroad rate between Buffalo and Schenectady lower than that between Buffalo and Toledo, so as to favor the Schenectady firm at the expense of the Toledo firm. However, long ago the Supreme Court ruled such an act unconstitutional, on the ground that it discriminated against interstate commerce, which is controlled by the federal government. Hence in effect the ICC establishes rates for intrastate commerce wherever that commerce competes with interstate commerce. Thus the States have almost no power over railroad rates save those on commuter passenger trains.

The federal government establishes rates collected by all other "common carriers," or means of transportation that are for hire by any person, operating in interstate commerce. Those regulated by the ICC have already been enumerated. Rates for commercial airlines today are fixed by the Civil Aeronautics Board (CAB), a typical independent administrative agency comprising five members appointed by the President with the consent of the Senate. Rates for pipelines transmitting oil are set by the ICC; on the other hand, rates for pipelines carrying natural gas are fixed by the Federal Power Commission (FPC), another independent agency, made up of five members chosen by the President and confirmed by the Senate. One of the most vigorous legislative contests in recent years has been that in Congress over a proposed statute that would exempt natural gas producers from FPC control. The federal government also controls rates charged by the telephone and telegraph companies for interstate communications; the task is specifically delegated to the Federal Communications Commission. However, although the FCC has considerable powers over the radio broadcasting industry, it does not have the power to establish the rates that radio broadcasters charge advertisers, for radio stations are not considered to be "common carriers" by Congress or the courts.

Quality

Transportation and Communication: The federal government regulates the quality of transportation and communication in several ways. In the first place, the government requires that those who would enter the fields of interstate transportation and communication obtain a license from the appropriate authority; a license is a grant of liberty to undertake an activity that is otherwise forbidden. Federal transportation and communication licenses are not issued until it can be shown that the public convenience and necessity will be served. For instance, motor truck carriers procure their licenses from the ICC; radio broadcasting stations, from the FCC; private hydroelectric power interests, from the FPC; and airlines, from the CAB.

The granting or denying of these licenses may be accompanied by considerable political maneuvering. Advocates of federally owned hydroelectric plants, for instance, will lobby against issuing a license to a private concern. In recent years one airline has managed to secure most American overseas air traffic (excepting that carried by foreign countries); it is famed for its vigilance and for the pressure it brings whenever petitions from other airlines come before the CAB. The airline also enlisted the aid of a prominent Senator, whom it retained as its lawyer, at a handsome fee.

Moreover, not only must these concerns obtain licenses from the government in order to enter business; they must also secure permission, from the appropriate agency, to discontinue service. In recent years the most important applications have been made by the railroads, which have sought leave to abandon unprofitable lines. Here the ICC has had to consider both the good of the railroads, whose financial status might be improved if they were allowed to cease operations, and of the communities involved, which might be economically damaged for lack of transportation, as well as the railroad brotherhoods, whose members might thus be deprived of employment.

The federal government also is deeply concerned with the installation of safety devices, and the adoption of safety practices, on the modes of transportation under its control. Railroads have been the particular targets of this form of regulation. A not often recognized fact is that railroading is a hazardous employment; for instance; in 1953, when forty-nine railroad passengers were killed in accidents, 343 railroad employees were killed. Hence the railroad brotherhoods have been among the most powerful forces for the adoption of safety devices; the railroads themselves, usually in the name of economy, have vigorously fought the brotherhoods and the ICC, which has decreed the use of these safety devices. Indeed, the ICC maintains a Bureau of Safety and Service, which in 1954 found more than ten per cent of all steam locomotives defective. Also, partly in order to increase the safety of passengers and wares, the federal government has set the maximum number of consecutive hours that operating employees in the various types of transportation may work. Finally, the several administrative agencies are empowered to investigate all accidents on the carriers under their jurisdiction.

Industry: Government regulations of industry are generally designed to ensure that the consumer obtains the level of quality he has paid for in making a purchase. At the same time these regulations protect the honest manufacturer against the dishonest one; for this reason the federal regulation of industrial standards is sometimes supported by reputable manufacturers.

One type of particular consumer service has already been noted, that performed by the Federal Trade Commission in controlling the labeling of animal pelts. The Federal Trade Commission is a versatile agency; it can examine correspondence courses as well as furs. Thus in April, 1955, the FTC announced that a certain musical studio had been compelled to cease its claims that "its home study courses enable people to play the piano," without "disclosing that such playing is limited to single note melodies with one hand and a simple bass chord accompaniment with the other."

Another sort of business regulation is that of the marketing service programs in the Agriculture Department, setting grades such as "U.S. Choice" for various commodities, the use of some of which is mandatory. The same Department also had compulsory inspection laws for specified farm products, fixing their requirements on such bases as the United States Cotton Standards and the United States Grain Standards. Too, the Department enforces the so-called "truth-in-labelling statutes," such as the Federal Seed Act. Perhaps the largest agency for carrying out this sort of consumers' services is the Food and Drug Administration in the Health, Education, and Welfare Department. The Administration is founded on the Food and Drugs Act of 1906, whose enactment apparently was stimulated by the revelations in Upton Sinclair's novel of the Chicago stockyards, *The Jungle*. The Administration looks into the materials used in the processing of foods, drugs, and cosmetics; the cleanliness of the manufacturing environment; the processing techniques; and the labeling of the products. The Administration is an important laboratory, carrying on research into the commodities under its jurisdiction. It is especially watchful over the distribution, prescription, and efficacy of new drugs, such as streptomycin and aureomycin.

From the nature of these variegated regulations, one might assume that the federal government would better satisfy many interest groups by direct ownership of industrial facilities. At the same time, the flexibility of the regulatory system is shown in the shifting character of the rules; sometimes they are stringent, and sometimes they are lax. Outright government ownership and management of businesses that are now closely regulated would forego such flexibility once and for all; rarely has a government-owned business been transferred back to private hands. Partly in order to keep the door open to changing beliefs, the American national government has itself undertaken relatively few businesses. This governmental participation in business is the topic of the following chapter.

QUESTIONS AND PROBLEMS

1. Why is it difficult to distinguish between government promotion and government regulation of business?

2. Define briefly the following forms of organization: corporation; pool; cartel; trust; holding company.

3. Describe the nature of the Sherman and Clayton Acts and the limitations of their meanings that have occurred up to the present time, both by the courts and by Congress.

4. Describe the work occurring in a commodity exchange. Why has the government regulated the exchanges?

5. How does politics enter the question of deciding what shall be a "fair return" on the value of property?

6. Describe the activities of the ICC in regulating rates.

7. Suppose that a railroad offered to lower its rates on shipping books and newspapers across the country, over the protests of the ICC. Might it appeal to the courts on the ground that the ICC, by demanding uniform, higher rates was interfering with liberty of speech and of the press? What arguments do you suppose could be advanced by the ICC and by the railroad?

8. What are some important types of licensing activities of federal agencies?

9. By what techniques does the FTC exercise its powers?

10. What are the functions of the SEC?

43. Government Participation in Business

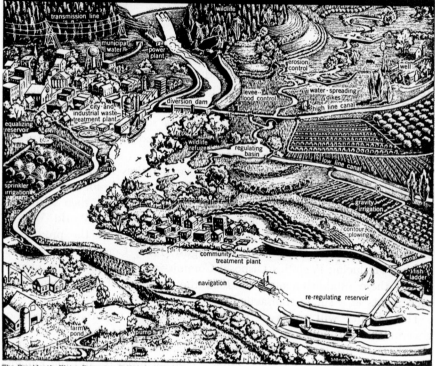

The President's Water Resources Policy Commission

THE American federal government participates directly in business. According to the Bureau of the Budget, in 1956 the government was engaged in 19,771 commercial and industrial activities producing goods and services; they represented capital assets of $11.9 billions. By comparison with most other countries of the globe, the government of the United States has title to only a small fraction of the national investment in the production and distribution of goods. In communist countries, for example, the government in one way or another owns all but the most minor sort of business undertakings. The governments in most non-communist countries, especially those of western Europe and of certain Latin-American states, own a greater share of the national economy than the American federal government does. Even American States and cities are more active commercially than the national government is. Yet the extent of federal business holdings in absolute terms is great; if the government sold its enterprises and could use the money thus obtained to buy merchant ships, it could buy every ship on the Seven Seas.

Outside the communist nations, when governments invade the realm of business ownership they usually do so in the sector of the distributive industries. For instance, both the British and the French governments own the railroads in their respective countries. Many American city governments own water systems, electric power generating companies, and public transportation networks. It is in this realm that the national government has to some extent penetrated, for its operations in the main are confined to the power industry and to transportation facilities. Apart from these undertakings the federal government also owns and operates the Post Office and the Government Printing Office. In its territorial possessions the national government manages some large and important properties. Finally, the armed forces own and operate some special manufacturing and distributive enterprises.

The government sometimes during a war acquires business properties, then sells them after the war. During World War I, for example, the government built and operated a fleet of merchant vessels, then sold them to shipping lines after the close of hostilities. During World War II the government created a number of establishments for the production of synthetic rubber; afterward, in August 1953, Congress set up the Rubber Producing Facilities Disposal Commission, an independent agency, to sell these establishments. In 1955 the government sold twenty-four such plants in a single transaction.

This chapter will endeavor to discuss the most important aspects of government participation in business that have not been dealt with elsewhere in the text. The aspects that have been previously described include national credit agencies, federal housing projects, and the Panama and Soo Canals. Save for the housing projects, they were created primarily in order to promote business. This chapter will confine itself to the Post Office, the Government Printing Office, the Tennessee Valley Authority and other electric power undertakings, the Atomic Energy Commission, such territorial enterprises as the Panama Canal Company, and the business operations of the armed forces.

THE POST OFFICE

The United States Post Office executes one of the oldest types of government functions in the world. Governments have had postal services for thousands of years; there is evidence that the Babylonian Empire had this service as early as the year 3800 B.C. The original purpose of this service appears to have been to supply the government itself with a means for carrying official messages, such as instructions from the central administration to a provincial governor, or commands from the ruler to a military leader. Government control was more common than private ownership, because the government alone had the force to protect the mails. Given the usefulness of controlling what was in the mails, the government preferred that, if the mails were to be used for

A Schematic Picture of a Multiple-Purpose River Basin Development.

anyone, they would be used for the state. Neither argument is as strong today as it once was. There was a postal service in the British colonies of North America; one of the first acts of the Confederation government was to found a post office. Today the Post Office reaches into every hamlet in the nation.

The chief executive of the Post Office Department is the Postmaster General, a member of the Cabinet, appointed by the President and confirmed by the Senate. There is a tradition that this official shall be a major political figure, often the past chairman of the administration party. This tradition may have arisen because the office supposedly is a sinecure, a post whose administration does not require any especial talents. Too, at one time many thousands of the best government positions outside the classified civil service were in the Post Office—the local postmasterships. It may have been felt that the party chairman should be named Postmaster General as the person best acquainted with the devotion of party followers. A third possibility is that since the position does in fact offer opportunities for the display of great administrative ability, it may be given to a party chieftain because he has revealed sufficient administrative ability to organize the party that has won a national election.

Under the Postmaster General are a Deputy Postmaster General and five Assistant Postmasters General, one each to head the Bureaus of Personnel, Facilities, Finance, Transportation, and Post Office Operations. The hub of Post Office activities, of course, is the individual Post Office situated in cities, towns, and villages. The Post Office is the largest civilian executive Department; on January 1, 1956, it had 509,032 employees.

Unlike any other Department, the Post Office conducts itself as a business; it is the only Department that receives a steady income for the services it performs. Indeed, the United States Post Office may be the largest business in the world, at least in non-communist countries. In 1955 there were 38,316 individual post offices (a considerable reduction from the year 1900, when there were 76,688). The Post Office handled over fifty-five billion pieces of mail, the majority of them first class. It delivered almost eleven billion pounds of mail, three-fifths of the weight being parcel post. It issued $5.8 billions worth of money orders. The Post Office in this year had a gross revenue of more than $2.3 billions, and gross expenditures of more than $2.7 billions; the annual deficit amounted to about $362 millions.

The Post Office deficit is a matter of great displeasure for persons both inside and outside the government. Actually for most of the last century the Post Office has operated at a deficit, save during two world wars of the present century. Hence each year Congress must vote a deficiency appropriation to give the Post Office enough money to perform its duties. The handling of this deficit, and its causes, have given rise to severe criticism of the Department. The deficit has also furnished opponents of federally owned enterprises with evidence that the government is not competent to participate in business. Indeed, according to its own reports the Post Office today does not show a profit on any type of mail—not even letters.

At the same time it must be realized that the Post Office carries out numerous valuable functions for business. The national economy could hardly operate unless businessmen had some means for exchanging information and for communicating with the public. In several ways the Post Office subsidizes businesses. For instance, it pays merchant ships and commercial airlines far more than their actual costs for transporting mail. It carries periodicals such as newspapers and magazines as "second-class" mail, which in fiscal 1954 yielded a loss of more than $218 millions, a sum that may be accounted a subsidy to publishing firms. The Post Office has established a category termed "third-class" mail, for circular matter, advertising, and the like, which is also a boon to private enterprise; in 1954 it yielded a loss of $147 millions, which might also be described as a subsidy.

There are few people who would suggest that the government turn the postal service over to private hands, and fewer still who would suggest that the government run the Post Office just as the States maintain highways, as a service without fees, paid for out of general tax receipts. Abandoning any of the various kinds of subsidies would bring protests from the groups affected. The only means for ending the deficit that would not bring loud protests appears to be the installation of greater economies in operations.

The Post Office also serves as a bank for individual depositors, through the Postal Savings System. At the end of fiscal 1955 the System had total deposits of more than $2 billions, with over 2.7 million depositors. These deposits draw two per cent interest, and are protected by the credit of the national government. The System is administered by a board of trustees made up of the Postmaster General, the Secretary of the Treasury, and the Attorney General, which invests the funds after they have been deposited. The funds of comparable systems in other countries are usually invested in government bonds; in the United States, by contrast, they are placed in "reputable" banks, preferably members of the Federal Reserve System.

That the Post Office should act as a savings bank has sometimes been questioned. At one time, private banks were less safe, perhaps, and did not welcome the smallest accounts; too, it was considered good policy to encourage everyone to save, even though few would recommend that the government engage itself deeply in encouraging every desirable impulse. It is unlikely that the System would be adopted today, if it were being proposed for the first time; however, it now stands firmly rooted in history.

THE GOVERNMENT PRINTING OFFICE

The United States Government Printing Office is probably the largest printing house in the world. The Office is supervised by Congress; hence it is not an administrative or executive division. The leading figure in the Office is the Public Printer, who "is required to be a practical printer, versed in the art of bookbinding." He is appointed by the President and confirmed by the Senate, but to a large degree he is responsible to the Joint Congressional Committee on Printing. The Office prints all the state papers of the federal government save those of a confidential nature. The sale of these publications is administered by the Superintendent of Documents; he also sends copies of these documents to the many libraries that are termed "depositories," which have been chosen to receive a copy of most publications. Finally, the Superintendent prepares catalogues of the materials that the Office has for sale.

Just as in the case of the Postal Savings System, an advocate of private enterprise might disagree that the government should engage in such extensive printing operations. Few would deny that the government has the elementary function of publishing congressional debates and legal documents, although the earliest of such records, here and in England, were privately printed. Yet a great part of the work of the Printing Office consists of printing, binding, advertising, and selling materials of the "how-to-do-it" character, together with a host of special studies that do not have legal force, such as analyses of the coal-mining industry. A critic may ask: "If the government wishes to publish a study it has made of the coal industry, why cannot it contract with a commercial publishing firm to print and sell the work, with or without subsidy?" Such a course of action would be more complicated and troublesome than the present arrangement, although it might promote the publishing business.

POWER

The federal government in the past two decades has entered the field of power generation, especially the areas of electric power and atomic power. These two fields in one sense are radically different; that is, the generation of electric power was practiced long before the federal government began to participate in it, but essentially the generation of atomic power was discovered under the auspices of the federal government. The sources of energy in the United States are constantly changing (see Figure 106). A century ago man-power and horse-power were major sources of energy for farms and factories. Coal then became the chief source of energy; now its use is declining. Atomic energy is now coming to the fore; probably by 1970 it will supply an important part of all energy consumed in the United States. Solar energy, obtained from the sun's rays, is also in the initial stages of practical development.

The generation of power by federal enterprise has given birth to harsh controversy; whereas there is little dispute that the postal service is a proper governmental function, heated debate occurs for and against the belief that the government should undertake power generation. For several years after its inception atomic power was a monopoly of the government, largely for reasons of national security but also because of the influence of those who professed fear that a few great corporations might establish a private monopoly if facts and materials were released

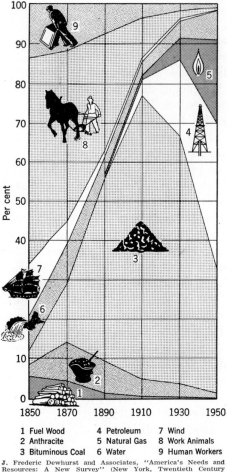

1 Fuel Wood   4 Petroleum   7 Wind
2 Anthracite   5 Natural Gas   8 Work Animals
3 Bituminous Coal 6 Water   9 Human Workers

J. Frederic Dewhurst and Associates, "America's Needs and Resources: A New Survey" (New York, Twentieth Century Fund, 1955), Figure 104

Figure 106. Percentage of Total Work Output Obtained from Different Sources of Energy in the United States, 1850–1950.

to the public. With the passage of time, it became apparent that information regarding atomic power was available to other countries; hence a government monopoly for the sake of national security had become unimportant. Furthermore, powerful industrial interests brought pressure upon the government to surrender part of its knowledge. Under the Eisenhower administration, Congress enacted legislation making it possible for private industry to obtain fissionable materials, attempting to hedge about the law with protections against monopoly.

Occasionally it is urged that the federal government sell its electric power generating plants to private business; these spokesmen have especially aimed at dissolving the Tennessee Valley Authority. At present, however, it appears that not only will the government retain these properties but also it plans to build many more such facilities. Certainly private enterprise has not despaired of erecting such facilities, nor have municipal governments; the graph in Figure 107, showing the percentage of electricity generated by federally owned utility stations, discloses that between 1945 and 1950 the federal share actually declined. The future proportions between private and public facilities will be decided by the victors in many political struggles to come; the arenas of debate can be imagined from the distribution of potential hydroelectric plants drawn in Figure 108.

Electric power

Tennessee Valley Authority: The Tennessee Valley Authority (TVA) is the outstanding example of a government electric power project in the United States. The TVA is a government corporation created in 1933 for the purposes of improving navigation on the Tennessee River and its tributaries, controlling floods in the Tennessee River basin, manufacturing fertilizer and other nitrate and phosphate products, and generating and distributing hydroelectric power. The TVA is administered by a three-member board of directors appointed by the President with the consent of the Senate. The TVA has expanded as the years have gone by, so that it has become an illustration of regional planning and general river-basin development. For instance, it concerns itself with the conservation of forests; it has linked its fertilizer production with a program of general agricultural improvement; it attends to the health and welfare of all persons living under its jurisdiction. It has great economic influence over an area of about 41,000 square miles (about the size of Ohio or of Tennessee itself) and the lives of its roughly 3.5 million residents. The map in Figure 109 shows the location and scope of the TVA region.

The foundation of TVA activities is the system of twenty dams and reservoirs on the Tennessee River and its confluents. These dams serve

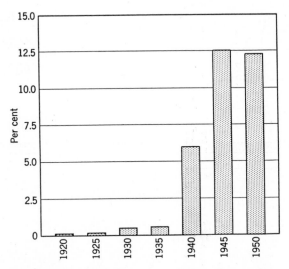

Figure 107. Percentage of Electric Power Generated by Federally Owned Plants, 1920 to 1950.

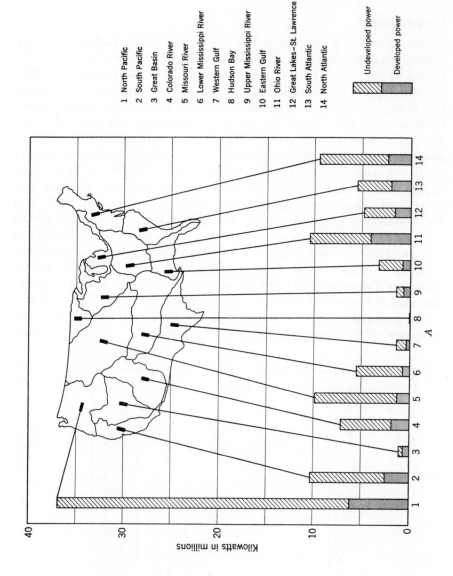

1 North Pacific
2 South Pacific
3 Great Basin
4 Colorado River
5 Missouri River
6 Lower Mississippi River
7 Western Gulf
8 Hudson Bay
9 Upper Mississippi River
10 Eastern Gulf
11 Ohio River
12 Great Lakes–St. Lawrence
13 South Atlantic
14 North Atlantic

Undeveloped power
Developed power

Kilowatts in millions

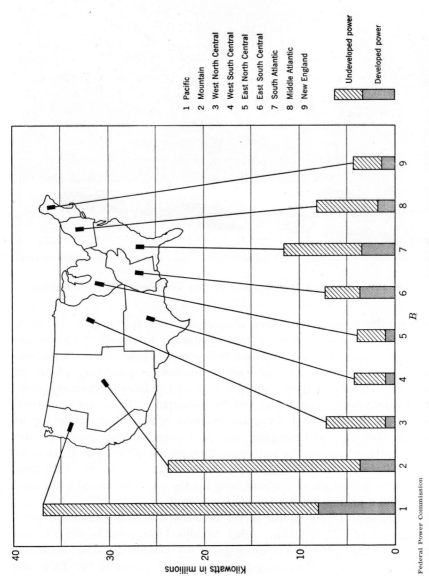

1 Pacific
2 Mountain
3 West North Central
4 West South Central
5 East North Central
6 East South Central
7 South Atlantic
8 Middle Atlantic
9 New England

Undeveloped power

Developed power

Kilowatts in millions

B

Federal Power Commission

Figure 108. Developed and Undeveloped Hydroelectric Power. *A.* By major drainages. *B.* By geographic divisions.

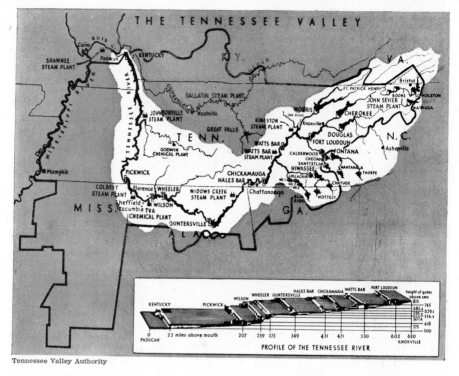

Tennessee Valley Authority

Figure 109.   Regional Development by the Tennessee Valley Authority.

to control floods, and, since they convert the river into a series of lakes, to provide a freight waterway from Paducah, Kentucky, to Knoxville, Tennessee, a distance of more than 600 miles. These are multi-purpose dams, for the government has built hydroelectric generating plants on their sites. The electricity produced here is sold to federal agencies, public and private power companies, and to industries. The most important consumer is the Atomic Energy Commission, which buys power for its plants at Oak Ridge, Tennessee, and at Paducah. This power is also retailed to the inhabitants of the region through the many local distributors that buy it from the TVA. Electric power is cheaper in the TVA area than it is in the nation as a whole; also for the past two decades the area has become a leading market for electrical appliances.

The cheapness of the power in the region is the first great merit cited on behalf of the TVA. Many other benefits have been brought to the entire region through such means as spreading information about conservation practices and good farming techniques. Advocates of the TVA also point out that the per capita use of electricity in the area is exceptionally high. They further assert that the per capita income of those living in the TVA domain has since 1929 risen proportionately more than the per capita income of the nation. This is an incontrovertible fact. However, it is also a fact that per capita income in all southern States has risen sharply since 1929, that this rise seems to be the consequence of several factors, and that the TVA is probably but one of the factors. Indeed, South Carolina, whose 310% per capita income rise between 1929 and 1955 was by far the greatest for any State in the country, is not considered a TVA State.

The TVA has been subject to some unfriendly criticisms. One important charge, based on the recent activities of the TVA, is that it has become a spearhead for government invasion of the whole power-generating field. Initially the TVA produced only hydroelectric power. Now, this type of power might be viewed as a "by-product" of the other functions of the TVA; that is, one might assume that the principal tasks of the TVA are to build dams that control floods and improve navigation, and that it has undertaken the generation of hydroelectric power simply because the dams make an excellent potential for that generation. However, in the past few years the TVA has constructed a number of huge coal-powered steam-generating plants; and the 1955 annual *Report* of the TVA disclosed that the TVA now generates more electricity at its steam plants than at its water plants.

Of course, in this respect the TVA is adapting itself to the national pattern; in 1950 only 29.1% of all electric power in public utilities was generated at hydroelectric plants, and the percentage had dropped from 40.3% in 1935. However, by no stretch of the imagination could one term steam-generated electricity a "by-product"; it is the single and direct purpose of these stations. TVA administrators contend that they must erect these plants in order to satisfy the demands for electric power in the region; future plans of the TVA call for the building of more steam-powered generators. Apparently a great demand for low-cost electricity is still developing in the region. Perhaps a final complaint may be recorded that has some relation to the costs of power. It has been alleged that the TVA buys non-union, "scab" coal for power generation, so as to keep expenditures low.

Another set of criticisms has revolved about the financing and accounting methods of the TVA. One goal of the TVA is supposedly to establish a "yardstick" of electric power rates with which privately owned utility rates may be compared. In this respect the TVA fares well; its rates are low. However, it is pointed out that the TVA has some important advantages over the private enterprises with which it competes. First, the TVA pays very low interest rates on the money lent it by the government, by contrast with the high interest rates their competitors must pay on the bonds sold to the public. Secondly, the TVA pays no taxes; however, it is now obliged to pay a certain sum to the government each year in lieu of taxes, but this sum does not equal as high a proportion of its income as the taxes paid by privately owned concerns are of their incomes.

The most severe criticism along this line is that the TVA employs deceptive accounting methods. TVA dams have three main purposes: flood control, navigation improvement, and power generation. Each of these purposes levies certain costs upon the enterprise. Only one of these purposes, that of power generation, has a monetary return, through the sale of electricity; the other purposes must be financed through government money, as shown by the fact that in fiscal 1954 Congress appropriated more than $188 millions for the TVA. The problem arises from the allocation of costs among the various functions. Hostile critics allege that the TVA manages to show an annual profit by allocating too little of its actual costs to power generation, and too much to flood control and navigation improvement. By this means, it is asserted, the cost of generating power is made to seem less than it really is. Hence, these observers say, only through bookkeeping devices can the TVA appear a "yardstick"; the fact is, they aver, that the true costs are far higher, and that the power is subsidized by appropriations which only on paper are spent for purposes other than power generation.

Whatever the validity of these criticisms, the majority of the people living in the TVA region endorse the project; industry is moving into the area so as to profit from the low power rates; national officeholders from the States concerned support the TVA; and the TVA has contributed immensely to the national security by providing the power necessary for refining fissionable materials. Looking backward to the discouraged and narrow-visioned thinking of the leadership in the area before Senator Norris and the TVA task force moved in on the economic problems of the valley, it is difficult to assure oneself that all of this development would have happened in any case.

Other Electric Power Facilities: The federal government owns and operates many other electric power generating stations in the country. Most of these have been erected in the period since the beginning of the depression in 1929; indeed, some of the earliest undertakings, such as the Hoover Dam, were intended to make work for the unemployed. Today, however, these plants are erected for the services they will yield.

The other federally owned plants differ from the TVA in that they do not embrace regional planning as well. Like those of the TVA, the other dams are multi-purpose, including such matters as flood control, navigation improvement, irrigation, and electric power generation. However, these are the sole purposes of these dams; there are no organized undertakings for the bettering of an entire river system. Moreover, these dams are not the property of a government corporation; instead, they are erected either by the Army Engineers Corps or by the Bureau of Reclamation, two agencies that often enter into spirited competition for the prestige of building one of these projects.

The merchandising of power from these stations is entrusted chiefly to three administrative agencies, all in the Department of the Interior: (1) the Bonneville Power Administration, which handles power generated in the Columbia River Valley, notably that from Bonneville, Grand Coulee, and Hungry Horse Dams, and a number of other structures across the Columbia, Willamette, Snake, Pend Oreille, and Kootenai Rivers, embracing parts of Washington, Oregon, Idaho, and Montana; (2) the Southwestern Power Administration, which sells power produced at federal dams in all of Arkansas and Louisiana and in parts of Kansas, Missouri, Oklahoma, and Texas; and (3) the Southeastern Power Administration, which markets surplus electricity generated at dams owned by the Department of the Army in Kentucky, Tennessee, Mississippi, Alabama, Florida, Georgia, South Carolina, North Carolina, Virginia, and West Virginia. These organizations are all to abide by "sound business principles," and to deal with "federal agencies, public bodies, rural electric cooperatives, and privately owned companies."

Of the three areas, that serviced by the Bonneville Power Administration appears to have enjoyed the greatest benefits. This area, too, is experiencing the gravest shortage of power, owing both to its exceptional population increase and to the movement of industry into the area. Plans have been considered for the establishment of other regional systems akin to the TVA, especially for the Missouri Valley; however, to the present no comparable agency has been created, because of both the pressure of affected interests and the reluctance of Congress.

Atomic power

Agencies Controlling Atomic Power: Atomic power in the United States until the very recent past has been entirely produced and controlled by the federal government; even today the federal government licenses all civilian users of fissionable materials. The principal agency for these operations has been the Atomic Energy Commission (AEC), sometimes termed "an island of socialism in an ocean of capitalism." The AEC was created in 1946 as a civilian group to take over what had hitherto been a military project, the Manhattan Engineer District, which had created the atomic bomb. The Commission is made up of a five-member board, named by the President and confirmed by the Senate. The Commission appoints a General Manager as the administrative chief for its activities. The Commission itself is assisted by three permanent committees, with which it frequently consults: (1) the General Advisory Committee, comprising nine civilians chosen by the President, for recommendations concerning scientific and technical affairs; (2) the Military Liaison Committee, representing the Department of Defense, for advice on matters regarding the armed forces; and (3) the Joint Committee on Atomic Energy, including nine Senators and nine Representatives, as a link with Congress.

Functioning of the AEC: The AEC is designed to encourage private research into atomic energy; to control information related to the production of atomic energy, looking forward to an era when national security will allow its publication; to carry out research for the federal government; to manage government control, use, and ownership of materials for atomic energy; and to administer affairs related to atomic energy in a manner consistent with the national requirements and international obligations of the United States. The AEC is one of the largest of the independent agencies, having 6,234 employees on January 1, 1956. In fiscal 1954 its expenditures were almost $1.9 billions; in fiscal 1955, over $1.85 billions. The AEC supervises numerous important laboratories and production facilities, among which the leading ones are those at Oak Ridge and at

Hanford, Washington; the AEC also cooperates with, and depends upon, atomic research studies at such institutions of higher learning as Iowa State College and the University of California, and at such industries as the General Electric Corporation in Schenectady. The AEC built and manages the towns of Oak Ridge and Richland; however, legislation, backed by the Republican administration, was introduced in 1955 for the purpose of ending their government ownership and management.

Today the AEC no longer exercises a monopoly over the development of power by devices using atomic materials. Legislation has been enacted permitting individual enterprises to employ these materials for the generation of power. Hence, for example, the Westinghouse Electric Corporation is erecting an atomically powered electric generating plant near Pittsburgh.

TERRITORIAL ENTERPRISES

The federal government owns and operates a number of business enterprises in its territorial possessions. These enterprises seem to have brought the territories concerned much closer than the United States to a type of socialist economy. The federal government has the power to organize such territorial businesses through the constitutional authorization given Congress ". . . to dispose of and make all needful rules and regulations respecting the territory or other property belonging to the United States. . . ." (Art. IV, sec. 3, cl. 2). It is significant, too, that there are few if any powerful interest groups in the territories that could oppose these government enterprises. Furthermore, since whatever groups there may be do not elect congressmen or cast electoral votes, they lack the essential means for expressing their opposition.

The Panama Canal Company

The Panama Canal Company is a government corporation functioning as an independent agency whose chief purpose is to operate the Panama Canal, but which also carries out many other business tasks associated with the operation of the Canal. Apart from the Canal, the Company maintains and operates ". . . a steamship line between New York and the Isthmus of Panama; a railroad across the Isthmus; the cargo docks and piers and harbor terminal facilities on the Isthmus; a coaling plant for ships; an oil handling plant; commissary stores, including cold storage plants, supplying employees and ships; a hotel; electric power, water, and telephone systems; procurement and storehouse facilities; motor transportation services, a printing plant; restaurants, theaters, bowling alleys, and miscellaneous merchandising activities; marine and general repair shops; and an employees' housing system." The Company is associated with the administration of the Canal Zone, since its chief executive, the President of the corporation, is also the Governor of the Canal Zone. The United States government is represented in the corporation by the Secretary of the Army, and he appoints the board of directors for the Company.

The Alaska Railroad

The Alaska Railroad is a government corporation in the Office of Territories in the Interior Department. It operates the only railroad in Alaska, about 500 miles long; it transports both passengers and freight. The Railroad also owns river boats and barges for use on the Yukon and Tanana Rivers, and it is part owner of the Knik Arm electric power plant. Initially the railroad was constructed to aid in the settlement and the development of agriculture and industry in Alaska; today it plays an important role in the national security program of the United States, for Alaska is recognized as a probable battle zone in the event of war between the United States and the Soviet Union.

The Virgin Islands Corporation

The Virgin Islands Corporation is a second government corporation in the Office of Territories. The Corporation is under the general supervision of the Secretary of the Interior. It is managed by a seven-man board of directors, including the Secretary of the Interior, the Secretary of Agriculture, an Assistant Secretary of the Treasury, the Governor of the Virgin Islands, and three American businessmen chosen by the President of the United States. The Corporation is intended to foster the economic welfare of the Virgin Islands. To execute this mission it performs a number of tasks. It raises sugar cane for the production of raw sugar and molasses. It generates, distributes, and sells electric power to the whole island of St. Croix; it serves a growing total of consumers, and is conducting the business at a profit. In 1952 it bought the private company that had been supplying electric power to the island of St. Thomas, and is now operating and improving these facilities. It has, however, sold its hotel there and its rum distillery. It also conducts important experiments in agricultural technology, in an especial effort to determine whether some crop besides sugar can be profitably cultivated. Finally, the Corporation makes grants for land and water conservation undertakings on St. Croix.

ARMED FORCES ENTERPRISES

The business operations of the armed forces are little known but are large and varied in character. That they are not well publicized is owing to the impression of the public that whatever is undertaken by the armed forces must be within the special and undisputed province of national defense. The Hoover Commission on Organization of the Executive Branch of Government, 1953–1955, assailed the logic of this impression on two counts: first, the Commission said that the military effort can be subjected to the same examination for efficiency as any other agency of the government; and second, that the military forces ought not extend their province freely into all the kinds of businesses that supply its needs. For example, until 1955 the Navy operated a coffee-roasting plant that it had started in 1858 because the quality and cost of commercial coffee were unacceptable. It also owned the Boston Ropewalk, a cordage factory that it had begun in 1834 because good rope was not being made or sold in America. Both kinds of business today are done by many private concerns. Hence, some argue, why maintain such irrelevant functions in the armed forces, which are already so huge as to be difficult to administer?

As pressure mounted through the Eisenhower administration and the Hoover Commission reports, more and more civilian-type businesses were terminated.. It was reported in 1955 that the Defense Department had closed down seven bakeries, nine laundries, twenty-four scrap-metal operations, four cement-mixing plants, a caustic-soda plant, four ice plants, two garden nurseries, a clothing factory, and a chain factory. The fate of 168 ice-cream plants in thirty-six States was in doubt. More work was being shifted from government shipyards to private ones, from Air Force maintenance shops to private ones, and from Army air, sea, and motor transportation to private carriers. In short, so far as the armed forces are concerned, the government is "going out of business" in a number of fields.

QUESTIONS AND PROBLEMS

1. Summarize the extent of the participation of the federal government in business, including such activities as are treated in other chapters of the text.

2. Could the Post Office be operated by private enterprise? What would be the effects, in your opinion, of a transfer of title from public to private ownership?

3. Describe the ways in which the Post Office and the TVA promote private business.

4. What have been the results of TVA in the region of its operations? Could or would these results have been achieved by private individuals or groups? Explain your opinion.

5. Name and locate several major river development plans of the federal government.

6. What reasons might explain the many business enterprises of the federal government in the Panama Canal Zone, the Virgin Islands, and Alaska?

7. What rule or principle would you suggest adopting for distinguishing between the business operations of the armed forces that are "necessary for defense" and those that are "unnecessary" and could be abandoned?

PART XII

National Security
and Foreign Affairs

44. The Makers of Foreign Policy

Department of State

$\mathbf{T}_{\text{HE}}$ federal government possesses a monopoly over the conduct of the foreign relations of the United States. The Constitution denies the States such powers as negotiating treaties, forming alliances, supporting troops, or waging war, powers without which the States cannot enter the arena of foreign relations. This is one of the principles that distinguishes a federal from a confederate government; it sets off the present Constitution from the Articles of Confederation, under which each State could and did have its own relations with other nations. Moreover, the federal courts have proclaimed that the management of foreign affairs is an inherent power of a sovereign government, and is therefore a function reserved exclusively to federal authorities. A corollary of this latter doctrine is that the federal government has unlimited power with respect to foreign relations; unlike its obligations in the matter of domestic affairs, it is not compelled to seek justification from the Constitution for much of its behavior regarding other countries.

American foreign policy is set in many ways by history and circumstances, but the actual making of the policy is done by certain persons. The makers of foreign policy must arrive at decisions; that is, they must choose between two or more alternative policies regarding another country, a group of

695

countries, or an international situation. The most important persons associated with the making of foreign policy are the President, the Secretary of State and his aides in the State Department, the members of the National Security Council, the Joint Chiefs of Staff, the members of certain other administrative agencies such as the Departments of Defense and of the Treasury, outstanding figures in Congress, and the leaders of a few pressure groups. Furthermore, public opinion in a sense to be defined later also influences the making of foreign policy.

THE PRESIDENT

The President is the focus of decision in foreign policy. His office is singularly equipped for the making of decisions, since it is the hub of all channels of communication respecting foreign affairs. It receives information concerning those phases of international relations in which the United States is interested, and today American interests extend to the entire world. Yet the President does not reach decisions regarding foreign policy solely on the ground of information brought him by government officials. He may also have made commitments to the chiefs of other countries which he is obliged to honor. He is forced to respect the opinions of the public, if only because it is the public that placed him in office. Should public opinion deviate so far from his own purposes that the execution of his policy might endanger his or his party's chances in the next election, he may endeavor to shape public opinion to his own ends. He has, of course, entered office with certain convictions regarding what is an appropriate foreign policy for the United States. These, too, guide his activities.

Finally, for any one of several reasons, different Presidents, and the same President at different times, will rely more upon one source of information and advice than upon others. For example, the President may have chosen his Secretary of State so as to placate an opposing faction in his party rather than to have an experienced diplomat in charge of foreign affairs; this President will not place much reliance upon the judgment of the Secretary, and the Secretary may cause him some trouble. Such were the relations between Woodrow Wilson and his first Secretary, William Jennings Bryan. A President who has unusual regard for military officers may turn to them in reaching final decisions about foreign policy. Such, for instance, was Harry S. Truman's attitude toward General George C. Marshall. Sometimes a private individual will have exceptional access to the President, and will have more influence over his policies than any government official. Colonel Edward M. House had this sort of association with President Wilson. It is almost impossible to enumerate all the conceivable variations.

The President of the United States is also the leader of the country in matters of national defense. He is the Commander in Chief of all military forces of the United States. He carries on, or is at least responsible for, all negotiations with foreign powers regarding American security. Whereas he

The New Department of State Building, Washington, D.C.

cannot declare war, he can so manage foreign relations, and so deploy American armed forces, that war becomes almost inevitable. The President chooses all the important figures, save congressmen, who share in making decisions concerning national security; all lines of information converge upon the presidency, and all lines of command radiate from it. Ultimately, all the threads of military and civil policy and strategy are drawn together in the office of the President.

THE SECRETARY OF STATE

The Secretary of State next to the chief executive is the most important official in making foreign policy. In the process of reaching decisions the Secretary is checked both from above and from below. That is, he may serve under a President such as either of the Roosevelts, or Truman, who will grant him slight latitude; on the other hand he may hold office under a President such as Eisenhower, who will permit him broad discretion. At the same time he must depend upon his numerous subordinates, both in the United States and abroad, for the information upon which he must base his conclusions. Thus the Secretary's subordinates, by withholding facts or by unduly stressing them, or by being ignorant of them, may help to shape American foreign policy. In the Department itself, he has a formidable legislative and publicity machine at his disposal. During the Eighty-first to Eighty-third Congresses, the Department drafted ninety-eight pieces of legislation and about 105 treaties or executive agreements, and presented its views on 4,764 bills that other interests had introduced. It dealt with at least 6,000 inquiries from congressmen and issued probably in excess of 2,000 press releases. Therefore, a determined Secretary with a loyal staff can forcefully project his ideas.

NATIONAL SECURITY COUNCIL

The National Security Council (NSC) is the principal agency in the Executive Office of the President for gathering and interpreting facts relative to national security. It is an extremely secretive organization; Anthony Leviero, writing in the *New York Times* on January 30, 1955, described it as "untouchable, unreachable, and unquotable." It consists of the President, Vice-President, Secretary of State, Secretary of Defense, and Director of the Office of Defense Mobilization (ODM). The President may name other members of the Cabinet to the NSC provided that the Senate confirms these nominations; usually the Chairman of the Atomic Energy Commission is also present at NSC meetings. The chief administrative officer of the NSC is known as the Special Assistant to the President for National Security Affairs. Under the direction of the NSC are three subordinate bodies: (1) the Planning Board, comprising officials at the rank of Assistant Secretary, from the Departments of State, Defense, and Treasury, and from the ODM, which recommends policies; (2) the Operations Coordinating Board, including the Under Secretary of State, Deputy Secretary of Defense, the

Director of the Central Intelligence Agency (CIA), the Director of the United States Information Agency, and a representative of the President, to assure that NSC policies are executed; and (3) the Secretariat, to keep the records of the NSC. Apart from these bodies, yet subordinate to the NSC, is the CIA, which assembles and correlates intelligence materials from the different government offices, then advises the NSC on the basis of its findings. In bald language, the CIA is the nucleus of the espionage activities of the United States.

The NSC evaluates the ability of the United States to perform its various obligations, such as those fixed by its military treaties, in terms of the military and industrial power of its allies. It also analyzes questions respecting national security that are of importance to other government agencies. Thereafter the NSC can reach decisions on security issues which, since the President is a member of the NSC, amount to presidential decisions. One recent conclusion ascribed to the NSC was that the United States should depend upon a policy of "massive retaliation"—that is, in the event a communist aggression should start in a country bordering upon the Soviet Union that was clearly instigated and assisted by the Soviet Union, the United States should not confine itself to a containing action as it did in Korea but should strike at the heart of the communist domains with its mightiest armaments.

THE JOINT CHIEFS OF STAFF

The Joint Chiefs of Staff (JCS) consist of the Chairman of the JCS; the Chief of Staff, United States Army; the Chief of Naval Operations; and the Chief of Staff, United States Air Force. When the JCS are considering Marine Corps affairs, the Commandant of the Marine Corps sits with the other members of the JCS as their equal. Each of these men is a high-ranking military officer who is appointed by the President. The Chairman has exceptional authority. He presides over the meetings of the JCS and directs the 200-odd men in the various specialized military committees that serve the needs of the group. He also enjoys special access to the President and to Congress, so that his voice can count more than the others in the making of decisions respecting foreign affairs. The Chairman may be from any of the military services.

Today the Joint Chiefs of Staff, who are responsible for guiding the policies of the armed forces, are of great significance in the shaping of American foreign policy. This lofty place is one that the military leaders have only recently attained; their present eminence is largely the result of the fact that American foreign policy today, much more than ever before, must be supported by large-scale and immensely complicated military forces. It has been pointed out that the role of the military leaders in achieving foreign policy decisions has undergone considerable evolution. Initially, the military leaders were called upon primarily to offer expert counsel; that is, they were asked to notify civilian chiefs what impact a particular conclusion might have upon the armed forces. Later, however, perhaps because there had arisen a practice of calling upon the military leaders for advice, their role changed to that of representing an arm of the state which had an inherent right to share in policy-forming. A revealing bit of evidence concerning the rise of military spokesmen in the realm of foreign affairs is provided by Figure 110, which shows how the Joint Chiefs have risen socially in Washington circles.

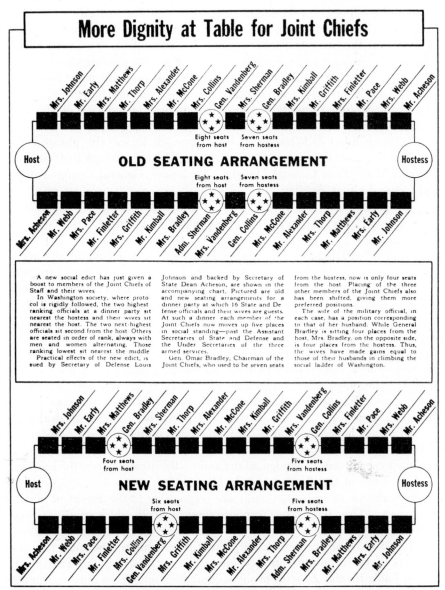

Figure 110. Etiquette Changes with Power. An alert journal catches the significance of a seating arrangement in reflecting the increased role of the military in American life as a consequence of World War II.

In some respects the JCS have more independence than the Secretary of State. That is, although they are appointed by the President, their choice is determined by few political considerations. The subordinates of the Secretary of State are mostly professional career officers, but the Secretary need not be, and indeed rarely is. By contrast, both the Joint Chiefs and their subordinates are professional soldiers. Hence the Joint Chiefs are not responsible to control by political parties, and are subject to comparatively little public criticism. Like the Secretary of State, however, they must fall back upon their subordinates for detailed information. These subordinates, like those in the State Department, may be ignorant of, or may withhold, or may overemphasize, certain data; the Yalta papers disclose that General George C. Marshall, then Army Chief of Staff, also pressed upon Roosevelt the need for assuring Soviet military assistance against Japan. To what degree the so-called "military mind" determines the policies of the JCS is difficult to establish, since there is as yet no unimpeachable definition of the "military mind." Whoever is brave enough to use the phrase must consider the vast differences among the minds, for example, of General Douglas MacArthur, General Dwight Eisenhower, General George Patton, and General Omar Bradley.

OTHER ADMINISTRATIVE AGENCIES

Several other administrative bodies contribute to the making of foreign policy; some are directly responsible to the President, and others are independent agencies. The Departments of Defense, of the Treasury, of Agriculture, and of Commerce all lend a hand in making foreign policy decisions. Their contributions, of course, are all less than, and usually inferior to, those of the State Department. On the other hand, a few of these contributions have been of great importance; for example, the Treasury Department elaborated a plan for the handling of Germany after World War II—the so-called Morgenthau Plan—which, if not put into effect literally, did help fashion American treatment of the defeated enemy. In the main, however, these offices were not primarily intended to deal with foreign policy; hence they can assist in making it only with respect to certain phases. The Secretary of the Treasury, for instance, can effectively discourage expenditures in foreign affairs and on the armed forces; the Director of the Bureau of the Budget can do likewise.

Secretaries of these Departments are responsible to the President and to their party. They have other responsibilities as well, which condition their attitudes toward foreign policy. For example, the Departments of Commerce and of Agriculture, which represent functional groups, must take the interests of those groups into account. The Secretary of the Treasury is in part liable for the solvency of the federal government; he must remember this duty while operating in a foreign policy-making role. The Secretary of Defense is occupied with achieving administrative efficiency in the armed forces; in fact, his direct contributions to foreign policy decisions may be very slight. All of these Departments, save Defense, suffer an important disability; they do not have access to the information available to the President, the Secretary of State, and the Joint Chiefs. This condition also restricts their participation in decisions.

The United States Information Agency is the most important arm of the government in foreign affairs outside of the State Department, the National Security Council, and the Department of Defense. However, to this moment the functions it has performed have been more significant than the leadership it has contributed to the making of policy. Hence it will be discussed in a subsequent chapter. The main point to grasp here is that the Director has little influence in setting the ultimate policy of the Agency; the Secretary of State is more potent in determining what the propaganda policies of the government will be.

CONGRESS

In spite of the dominance of the chief executive in the areas of foreign policy and of national security, Congress still plays an important role. Perhaps most significant of all, Congress must vote the funds needed for the national military establishment. Today, however, this power is not nearly so great as it once was. The Constitution empowers Congress to appropriate money for the support of armies, but provides that such appropriations may not last longer than two years (Art. I, sec. 8, cl. 12). The aim of the Founding Fathers was to prevent the armies from having sufficient funds to support themselves indefinitely, so that they might dispense with Congress and usurp its power over national expenditures. (Interestingly enough, this limitation was not applied to naval appropriations, perhaps because, since naval strength is on the sea, a navy is not in an advantageous position to overthrow a government.)

Until very recent times this bar to lengthy appropriations has caused little strain. Today, however, a new military weapon requires several years for the evolution from original conception through research, planning, and testing, to mass production. Hence the government must be able to negotiate contracts with industries for a period of several years, so as to procure new arms. Therefore a considerable part of the money appropriated for the armed forces remains unspent at the end of the year, and will not be spent for several years to come. In 1955 there were enough unexpended funds for the armed forces to maintain them for an entire year, even if Congress were to appropriate no money at all.

The powers of Congress in foreign affairs are also reduced by the growing demand for secrecy on all matters concerning foreign affairs. The restrictions on congressmen's obtaining information that the agencies consider vital to the security of the nation have mounted greatly. For instance, the National Security Council has stated that "Classified defense information possessed by the NSC may be made available to the Congress only under appropriate security safeguards (as authorized by the President) by member or participating agencies of the NSC which originate or receive such classified defense information."[1] Other agencies connected with national security follow the same line. The Atomic Energy Commission in fiscal 1955 twice refused information to the Joint Committee on Atomic Energy, and the Central Intelligence Agency refused information to committees on seven occasions during the same year.

Sometimes a feeling of inadequacy assails a congressman, who is supposed to represent his constituency on matters of war and peace, when he cannot learn some of the fundamental information needed for judging certain foreign policies. Moreover, Congress cannot force executive agencies to yield this information; the agencies may release it at their own discretion or by command of the President. Several committees, such as the Senate Foreign Relations Committee, are the only congressional groups that are ordinarily allowed to see some of the important materials or documents on national security and foreign affairs; members of this Committee are expected to regard these matters as confidential. In 1930, under President Hoover, the Senate Foreign Relations Committee could not, however, obtain from the Secretary of State certain confidential letters and telegrams leading up to the London Conference and London Treaty. All three Presidents since his time, and several before him, have on occasion refused to release information to the legislative branch when, using the words of President Eisenhower (May 17, 1954), "its disclosure would be incompatible with the public interest or jeopardize the safety of the Nation."

In one important respect, Congress has gained added stature in foreign affairs. Its control of taxes and appropriations allows it increasingly to play a hand in the determinations of the executive branch of the government. At one time, American foreign policies did not provide for large expenditures of money in the form of loans and grants to other nations. In later years, however, every annual budget has contained provisions for lending and spending money abroad. Congress must approve and enact these provisions if they are to be carried out. Consequently, the power of Congress in foreign affairs has been extended.

In making foreign policy, congressmen encounter public opinions different from those that administrative officials meet. Since different regions of the United States have varying attitudes toward problems involving other countries, the foreign policy that is ultimately adopted by Congress will tend to be less clear and more compromising than the policy of the State Department or of the Joint Chiefs of Staff. Moreover, inasmuch as public opinion samplings have shown the vast majority of the population to be almost utterly ignorant of the details of foreign affairs, the opinions that congressmen voice tend to echo the arguments of organized groups that are strong in their districts.

---

[1] Committee on Government Operations, *Replies from Federal Agencies to Questionnaire submitted by the Special Subcommittee on Government Information* (Washington: U.S. Government Printing Office, 1955), p. 360.

INTEREST GROUPS

A number of American interest groups take a direct concern in foreign policy. A few are organized specifically to influence foreign affairs; one example is the American Association for the United Nations, Inc. Many American cities have Foreign Policy Councils; however, these bodies more frequently incite individual interest and action in foreign affairs than take a position as organized groups. The English-Speaking Union and the America-Italy Society are examples of cultural organizations that work primarily for greater mutual appreciation between two countries. The AFL-CIO represents American views in the affairs of the International Labor Organization and often leads American policy concerning labor unions and working conditions abroad. On problems of military preparedness, the chiefs of the American Legion and of the Veterans of Foreign Wars give advice to Congress and the President, and also conduct campaigns among the public on behalf of their views.

Other interest groups move onto the foreign affairs scene when a specific piece of legislation affects them. For example, the American Farm Bureau Federation lent its support to the Marshall Plan for the reconstruction of Europe following World War II; it explained part of its support as benevolence toward the unfortunate masses abroad, but it clearly admitted a second motive of seeking foreign outlets for farm surpluses that were threatening to lower prices. The introduction of the subject of tariffs in Congress is the signal for the convergence upon Washington of a host of special representatives for different branches of industry and commerce. E. E. Schattschneider, in his study of how Congress enacted the Hawley-Smoot Tariff Act of 1930, concluded that a large number of the provisions of the law were written by spokesmen for high tariffs. Congress once sought to rid itself of some of these pressures by creating the Tariff Commission. The Commission was required to provide the government with information on trade and tariffs, and a general schedule of rates and rules for raising and lowering tariffs. But the burden had been only partially lifted from Congress, as matters turned out, and both the legislature and its administrative creation suffer the onslaughts of tariff lobbies still.

Perhaps the most simple means of illustrating the concern of different groups in foreign affairs is to list the groups appearing before a congressional committee that is studying a piece of legislation. In 1949, 105 Representatives proposed that the House of Representatives adopt a concurrent resolution (H. C. Res. 64, 81st Congress, 1st Session) to seek conversion of the United Nations into a World Federation. The House Committee on Foreign Affairs then held hearings for two days on the motion to have Congress declare "that it should be a fundamental objective of the foreign policy of the United States to support and strengthen the United Nations and to seek its development into a world federation open to all nations with defined and limited powers adequate to preserve peace and prevent aggression through the enactment, interpretation, and enforcement of world law." Fifty-seven congressmen appeared before, or gave statements on the resolution to, the Committee. The private groups submitting views to the Committee through spokesmen or in written form for inclusion in the record of the hearings were the following:

> American Association for the United Nations, Inc.
> American Federation of Hosiery Workers
> American Professional Writers
> Atlantic Union Committee
> A member of the Institute for Nuclear Studies
> General Federation of Women's Clubs
> Citizens Committee for United Nations Reform, Inc.
> International Association of Men's Y Clubs
> United World Federalists
> Steering Commission to Study the Organization of the Peace
> Chairman, President's Air Policy Commission
> National Economic Council, Inc.
> American Veterans Committee
> Brotherhood of Railroad Trainmen
> Veterans of Foreign Wars
> Kiwanis International
> Americans for Democratic Action
> National Society of the Daughters of the American Revolution
> Friends' Committee on National Legislation
> Liberal Party of New York
> American Veterans of World War II
> Norfolk Committee for the United Nations
> National Sojourners
> National Farmers' Union
> A former Supreme Court justice
> National Grange
> Florida Junior Chamber of Commerce
> Cooperative League of America

Most of these groups were friendly to the resolution; the major objection, and of course the key obstacle to all similar legislation, was that the independence of the United States would be completely submerged in such a world government. However, the point emphasized here is not the merits of the resolution, but rather the way in which interest groups close in upon a resolution dealing with foreign policy. Every proposed law or resolution, regardless of its contents, will attract the attention of groups, although each bill or resolution will have a different pattern of interested groups.

Some peculiarities of the relations between pressure groups and the government on matters of foreign affairs deserve mention. The National Security Council and the Department of Defense, which, as has been noted, are influential in determining foreign policies, are somewhat pressure-proof with respect to their foreign policy functions. By custom, by reason of their professional structure, and because of their unpublicized mode of operation, they are not beset directly or indirectly by interest groups as much as the State Department or President are.

The State Department in turn is in a weaker position to defend itself against pressures than are other Departments or agencies. The reason for this condition is a complicated one. Since there are no great pressure groups that have an immediate economic stake in its work and some control over its policies, the State Department can be strongly moved by pressure groups that work through the presidency and Congress. For example, the Departments of Labor and of Agriculture are to a degree controlled, but also and therefore promoted and protected by, respectively, several great labor and farm organizations. When the budgets and the programs of the Departments are under attack, these great pressure groups often rise to their defense.

This is not the case with the State Department. It has to give an intellectual defense of its views and needs, and intellectual arguments go only so far against the arguments of aggressive economic interests. Some of the strongest supporters of the policies of the State Department are the foreign allies of the United States; yet nothing could damage the case of the Department so badly as the use of pressure by friendly foreigners on Congress or on the President. Other State Department supporters are simply foreign affairs discussion groups here and there in the United States; these often feel no great personal stake in the policies of the Department. Consequently, no agency of the government is so likely as the Department of State to be buffeted helplessly by gusts of congressional anger.

This situation only provides one more reason for the State Department to find itself close to, and responsive to, the President. Yet this closeness has its own problems, for the President gives a cordial ear to the voices of interest groups that are well placed with respect to influencing the electoral vote of heavily populated States. When the State Department reports its soundings from abroad, it may again influence the President intellectually, but often not so effectively as he is influenced by the votes in the hands of American interests.

THE PUBLIC

Where does the public as a whole fit into the picture of the makers of foreign policy? Generally the public behaves in foreign affairs along the lines that it follows in other kinds of public affairs, a tendency described in the chapter on public opinion. That is, a tiny fraction of the adult public is informed or active in creating "mass opinion"; a great many people react to international events only at the polls; some do not react to foreign affairs at all. Professor Gabriel Almond, in *The American People and Foreign Policy*, states that the task of getting an informed attention to foreign affairs from most people is impossible. The best that can be hoped for in the way of public involvement in foreign policy, he says, is to increase somewhat the size of the tiny fraction of informed and active citizens, and to make better informed those who as leaders of interest groups and political parties are already influencing foreign policy.

An example of the development of a new public opinion group was the

Committee for a National Trade Policy, formed by a group of business-men who sought to interest their own circles in President Eisenhower's program of lowering international trade barriers. Hitherto, advocates of high tariffs had had a virtual monopoly on the attention of businessmen; suddenly, new names and powerful connections appeared in the struggle for a freer foreign trade policy. As a result, decisions about foreign trade policy could be made from richer sources of opinion and interest than were known before.

The public as a whole gives attention only to spectacular events on the international scene. Its interest goes first to the local, then national, and then international news. Only eight per cent of a sample of American adults in 1953 expressed a desire to have a greater proportion of inter-national news in the papers, that proportion being now only one to eleven according to one survey of international versus domestic content. Of course, the most exciting of all events has been war. The tedious process by which peace is sought is generally ignored. Therefore the leaders of policy must contend with public moods rather than public opinions about war and peace; they must ask themselves such questions as: "Are most people angry and excited against a foreign power? Do they trust the in-tentions of other countries? Are they firmly opposed to military action by the United States?" Then, since many people cast their votes according to their mood about world affairs, the leaders adjust their foreign goals to the limits set by this mood.

Professor Hadley Cantril, in his study *Gauging Public Opinion* (1944), used the chart in Figure 111 to show the changing moods of the public on policies connected with entering World War II. Note how much more popular was the desire to help England than was the wish to declare war on Germany, despite the fact that the two wishes were tied together in many ways. The American government could have concluded that either policy was the popular one, and followed it. Note, too, how a widely held notion about history, to wit, that it was a mistake to enter World War I, was abandoned in the face of events that seemed contradic-tory to that attitude. Note, finally, how well prepared the public was to re-ceive the notion of war with the Axis, just before the enemy struck. It is almost as if the Axis had waited to attack the United States until Ameri-can opinion was prepared for war. Perhaps, more plausibly, people had sensed the meaning of developments and were moving to an aggressive climax; meanwhile the enemy, realizing the trend, launched their assault. Although President Roosevelt from 1938 to 1941 held a clear personal position favoring drastic American intervention against the Axis, he was always held back by strong currents of opinion from making his intentions (which were of course shared by many others) the official policy.

Taking into account the various relations described in this chapter, the roles of the different "makers" of American foreign policy can be generalized in a rough way. The President and the Joint Chiefs of Staff seem to have the greatest power and initiative. The National Security Council has extraordinary significance through its functions of gathering

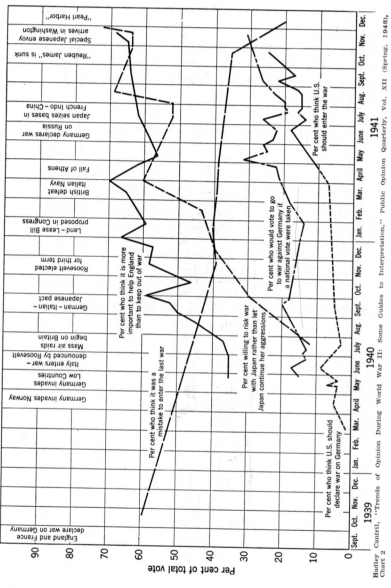

Figure 111.   Shifts of Public Opinion in the Crisis Before America Entered World War II.

and of intepreting data on foreign affairs. The Secretary of State is quite dependent upon the President, and can be powerful only with strong presidential backing; the several other chiefs of agencies dealing with foreign affairs, such as the Director of the United States Information Agency, have only minor voices; Congress, and especially the Senate, have an essentially critical and restraining role; and pressure groups operate effectively—perhaps more positively—through the President and—perhaps more critically—through Congress. Public opinion works through pressure groups, Congress, and the President; however, the active, informed public with respect to foreign affairs is very small. The moods of the public nevertheless set almost impassable limits to the desires and the abilities of the individual makers of foreign policy.

QUESTIONS AND PROBLEMS

1. What powers does the President have in foreign affairs?

2. Describe the structure and the functions of the National Security Council.

3. What changes have occurred in the role of American military leaders in the formulation of American foreign policy since 1900?

4. What powers does Congress possess in foreign affairs?

5. Every locality with a considerable population has one or more groups that have taken a stand on foreign policy. Discover one such group (usually a branch of a national organization) and interview its officers to learn and report on its activities over the past year.

6. Describe the disadvantages the State Department has in the politics of foreign policy.

7. What influence does the public have on the making of foreign policy?

45.

Military Organization and Domestic Mobilization

"Midnight Ride of Paul Revere" by Grant Wood is reproduced through the courtesy of the Metropolitan Museum of Art with the permission of the Associated American Artists. Radar outpost, painting by Ken Davies, courtesy of the Anaconda Company

THE military organization and domestic mobilization of the United States are the two essential elements for the defense of American national security. These two elements have greatly changed in the past twenty years. Before World War II the Joint Chiefs of Staff, the National Security Council, the United States Information Agency, the Civil Defense Organization, and most other defense agencies and activities did not exist. The nation had a rather simple defense structure. The President dealt directly with the Secretaries of State, of the Army, and of the Navy; on most occasions he dealt with them individually rather than in concert. During peacetime the military forces had little influence on foreign policy.

However, the character of international relations has altered so much in recent years that the United States has had to make vast changes in its organization for domestic security. Today the military, diplomatic, and

Warnings of War: Then and Now. Paul Revere could warn his townsfolk by horse after receiving a signal from a watchtower. Today they must be warned by lonely radar outposts in the farthest reaches of the Arctic wastelands.

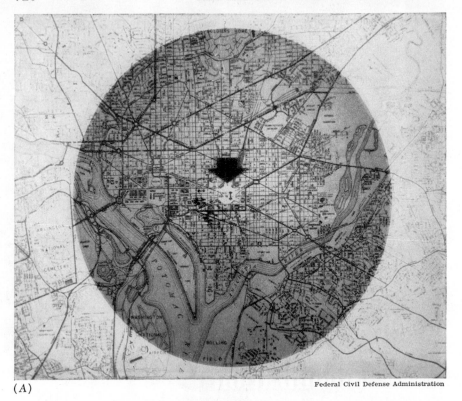

(A)   Federal Civil Defense Administration

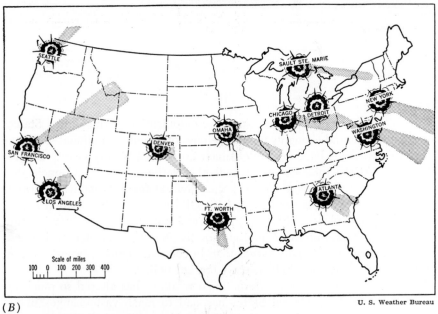

(B)   U. S. Weather Bureau

civil authorities must be constantly in touch with one another and always on the alert. The United States is engaged at a great number of different places in the world in both peaceful and warlike moves; simultaneously, it must keep its own territory and economy in a perpetual state of readiness for an absolute struggle for survival.

THE CHANGED NATURE OF WARFARE

Today the United States lives in the shadow of hostile aircraft that are expected to be carrying nuclear weapons. In spite of American interceptor planes, various types of missiles, the radar warning net, and the small army of civilian skywatchers, American military leaders admit that in case of an enemy air raid a number of the attacking craft might penetrate American defenses and succeed in dropping bombs. If they did, the industrial centers of the United States might be gravely damaged. Figure 112 maps the areas that might be destroyed or endangered by a dozen hydrogen bomb bursts on certain places.

Even supposing that the United States succeeds in avoiding war, contemporary international politics forces a degree of planning and utilization of resources not before realized. The tools of war are highly developed, so that the armed forces are continuously interested in fundamental scientific research and the fabrication of special equipment. Economic and psychological warfare have become necessary adjuncts to the armed forces and diplomacy. Resources flow out continuously along these channels; for instance, the well-being of the Indonesians and the attitudes of the Egyptians have become important to American policy, whereas at one time the diplomats and warriors of America would scarcely have conceived these to be anything but domestic problems of the peoples cited.

Beyond even these interests abroad, American forces have been engaged in "little wars" and must be prepared for more of them. Korea, the primary example, cost the nation more casualties than World War I. The Indochina crisis of 1954 almost became another little war, as did the Berlin blockade of 1948–1949, the Trieste dispute of 1945–1954, the Formosan crisis of 1955, and the seizure of the Suez Canal in 1956. No sure prediction of where a great war would begin is possible; a great war could happen as a result of any of these smaller conflicts. In these areas the soldiers and diplomats must work side by side, because no one knows which of the two will be called on for their skills from one month to the next. Today, therefore, the armed services of the United States are a vastly different organization from what they were in 1940.

Figure 112. Potential Effects of Hydrogen Bomb Raids Against the United States. (A) Potential effects of a burst over the Capitol at Washington, D.C. The shaded portion shows the three-mile radius in which destruction would be complete. The thermonuclear detonation would also cause moderate damage out to seven miles and light damage as far as ten miles. The bomb is of the type exploded in the Marshall Islands in 1952. (B) Fallout areas from simulated bombing of twelve critical locations. Based on the wind data prevailing Monday morning, September 10, 1956. The shaded areas would be made deadly by radioactive fallout from explosions over the twelve places and would have to be evacuated immediately for days or weeks. Changing daily wind patterns make most of the country a potential fallout area.

THE MILITARY ESTABLISHMENT

The military establishment of the United States consists of three services —the Army, the Navy, and the Air Force—all subject to a unifying Department of Defense. The chain of command in the Department is diagrammed in Figure 113. The leading trait of the American military establishment is that the Department of Defense itself, and each of the three services likewise, are all controlled by civilian chiefs, in every case a Secretary. There is, however, one major difference among these chiefs: the Secretary of Defense is a member of the Cabinet, but the Secretaries of the Army, of the Navy, and of the Air Force are not.

Department of Defense

The Department of Defense, which is supreme over the entire American military establishment, is largely a coordinating office, an agency that performs staff and auxiliary tasks for the three services. In spite of the powers vested in it, and the functions entrusted to it, the Defense Department proper is the smallest in the federal government, having on January 1, 1956, only 1,883 employees; indeed, it is accurately termed the "Office of the Secretary of Defense."

The Secretary of Defense is appointed by the President and confirmed by the Senate; he is a member not only of the Cabinet but also of the National Security Council and of the Defense Mobilization Board in the Office of Defense Mobilization. The law creating the office forbids the President to select any person in the armed forces; however, Congress waived this prohibition in 1950 in the case of General Marshall. The aims of this post can be seen in the choice, in 1953, of the President of the General Motors Corporation, Charles E. Wilson, as Secretary; the incumbent is expected to handle primarily the business concerns of the armed forces, and not to have a large share in deliberations regarding military operations save as they are related to such matters as supply. Beneath the Secretary, and chosen in the same manner, is the Deputy Secretary, who heads the Department in the Secretary's absence.

The principal work of the Department is carried out under the direction of nine Assistant Secretaries of Defense, all named by the President with the advice and consent of the Senate. The functions of their posts are apparent from their titles: (1) Comptroller; (2) Manpower, Personnel and Reserve; (3) Legislative and Public Affairs; (4) International Security Affairs; (5) Research and Development; (6) Applications Engineering; (7) Supply and Logistics; (8) Properties and Installations; and (9) Health and Medical. Two of these offices merit especial note. The Assistant Secretary for Legislative and Public Affairs is in essence the lobbyist for the Department; that is, he is responsible for bringing the wishes and needs of the Department to the ear of Congress, especially while the budget is being drafted. The Assistant Secretary for Supply and Logistics has one duty that illustrates an important goal sought in unifying the services. Each of the services, of course, requires thousands of different items of supply, down to nuts and bolts for the engineers. Before unification was accomplished, each service had its own supply catalog; these catalogs included numerous items with identical functions but slight differences in structure, so that distinct orders had to be made for each service. This Assistant Secretary has the task of preparing a single catalog for all three services so as to achieve the savings that will result from single large orders.

The Secretary of Defense relies upon two other bodies for counsel. One is the Joint Chiefs of Staff. The composition of the JCS was described in the preceding chapter. The JCS are the prime source of military advice for the President and the National Security Council as well as for the Secretary of Defense. Moreover, as a group they hold supreme command over the armed forces of the United States. They determine what shall be the disposition of the forces, what tasks the forces shall carry out, how supplies shall be allocated among the forces, and who shall command specific areas. The second body that advises the Secretary of Defense is the Armed Forces Policy Council. It consists of the Secretary and the Deputy Secretary of Defense; the Secretaries of the three services; the Joint Chiefs of Staff; and any other government official whom the Secretary may summon to the meetings of the Council as an interested party. It seeks to correlate policies of the three services.

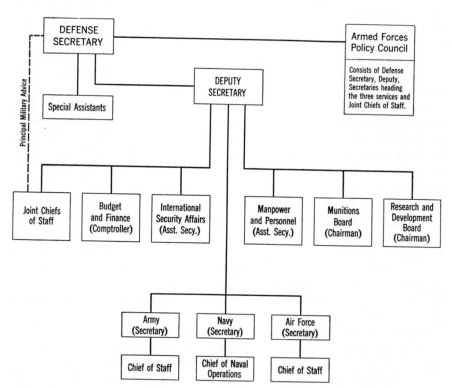

Figure 113. The Chain of Command in the Defense Department.

The unified services

Presumably today the United States has but a single military organization for national security, which might be loosely termed the armed services, operating under the direction of the Secretary of Defense and the Joint Chiefs of Staff. Actually there are three distinctive military Departments, those of the Army, the Navy, and the Air Force. Yet, largely because the Secretaries of these Departments are not in the Cabinet, and because the Secretary of Defense is in the Cabinet, the military Departments are one step removed from the eminence they formerly occupied.

Unification of the services, accomplished by acts of Congress in 1947 and 1949, aimed at preventing some of the disagreements and struggles that used to break out between the services when they had direct access to the President and to Congress, and when they had no unity of command save through the President. One area of disagreement comprised military operations themselves. During a war the conquest of a given piece of land redounds to the advantage of the conquering force, increasing its prestige and sometimes the amount of money that Congress will appropriate for its future operations. Too, being the first to employ a new type of weapon can win honor in the eyes of the public. During World War II in the Pacific there was considerable rancor between the Army and the Marine Corps respecting zones of activity. The Army and the Navy vied with one another for the use of their respective air arms. The Army Air Force won fame through being the first to drop an atomic bomb. Today, owing to the Joint Chiefs of Staff, many of these conflicts have been eliminated. Yet the Navy has refused to surrender its air force, and all three services are competing vigorously for nuclear weapons.

The second area of dispute supposedly removed by unification was that embracing congressional appropriations. Prior to unification the Secretaries of War and of the Navy, each with Cabinet status, could and did bring pressure directly upon the President, the Bureau of the Budget, and Congress, for additional funds. Presumably after unification the single Department of Defense was to handle all requests for money. Yet each service has its financial office to draft its budget, and each has a legislative representative, or lobbyist. In the first years after unification Congress tended to vote each service an approximately equal sum. However, it is unquestionable that since security plans now emanate from a unified source, the budgets submitted by the armed forces more and more reflect their proportionate shares in defending the United States. Since 1948, the proportion expended by the Air Force has greatly risen, whereas the share of the Army has declined.

The following paragraphs contain a short description of each of the military services. It should be observed how, in spite of certain differences in names, the services possess relatively parallel structures:

The Army: Under the Secretary of the Army are an Under Secretary, and Assistant Secretaries for Financial Management, for Manpower and Reserve Forces, for Civil-Military Affairs, and for Logistics, all of whom are civilians. The principal military figure in the Department is the Chief of Staff. The leading military advisory body of the Department is the Army Staff, which is the planning agency for army operations. The Army Field Forces, which are under the direction of the Staff and the Chief of Army Field Forces, make up the Army as a military arm. The Field Forces have the assistance of various technical services, such as those under the Quartermaster General (which provides food, clothing, and other equipment), the Chief Signal Officer, and the Chief of Engineers. In the United States the Army is administered through six Army Areas, with headquarters in New York, Maryland, Georgia, Texas, Illinois, and California. There are comparable offices in the District of Columbia, Hawaii, the Canal Zone, Puerto Rico, and Alaska. The principal task of the Army is to maintain the ground forces of the United States. The Army also has certain important civilian duties, most of which are executed by the Engineers Corps, such as improving the navigation of rivers, building dams, and operating such enterprises as the Sault Canal. The Army, as the map in Figure 114 discloses, has troops in numerous sectors of the globe.

The Navy: Beneath the Secretary of the Navy are an Under Secretary, and four Assistant Secretaries, one each for Material, Financial Management, Personnel and Reserve Forces, and Air, all civilians. The leading military officer is the Chief of Naval Operations; the principal advisory body is the Office of the Chief of Naval Operations. Whereas the Navy is concerned primarily with sea forces, it includes also a land force, the Marine Corps, which is headed by the Commandant of the Marine Corps. Too, during war the Navy may be joined by the Coast Guard, which is ordinarily in the Treasury Department. The Navy includes certain technical services such as the Bureaus of Aeronautics, of Medicine and Surgery, and of Ordnance. The Navy is administered through ten naval districts in the United States and four more in American possessions. The Navy today has few civilian duties; however, it does govern as a trust territory the Mariana Islands, including Saipan, that were captured from Japan during World War II.

The Air Force: Subordinate to the Secretary of the Air Force are an Under Secretary; an Assistant Secretary for Financial Management; an Assistant Secretary, Manpower, Personnel and Reserve; an Assistant Secretary for Matériel; and an Assistant Secretary, Research and Development. The foremost military personage is the Chief of Staff, who presides over the leading advisory body of the Air Force, the Air Staff. There are a Vice Chief of Staff, three Assistant Chiefs, and five Deputy Chiefs, most of whom are in charge of technical agencies. The Air Force is administered through seventeen Commands, the most notable of which are the Strategic Air Command, which handles air operations that are designed to be an end in themselves; the Tactical Air Command, which executes operations that join with ground or sea forces in achieving their goals; and the five overseas Commands—United States Air Forces in Europe, Far East Air Forces, Alaskan Air Command, Caribbean Air Com-

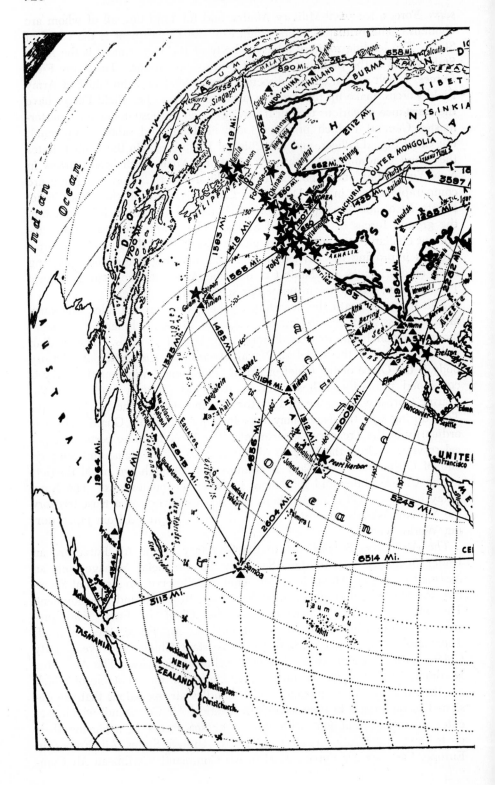

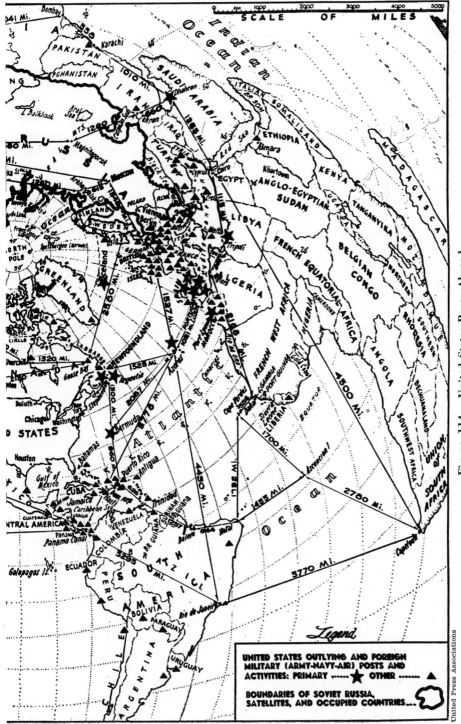

Figure 114. United States Bases Abroad.

mand, and Northeast Air Command. Because the Air Force is a newly created service, it has not been burdened with civilian obligations.

Personnel

On June 30, 1955, there were over 2.9 million personnel on active service in the armed forces of the United States; of these, about 1.1 million were in the Army; 660,000, in the Navy; 960,000, in the Air Force, and 205,000, in the Marine Corps.

In terms of command and obedience, military personnel can be divided into two broad groupings. The upper and smaller consists of commissioned officers, from generals and admirals at the top to second lieutenants and ensigns at the bottom; they hold their ranks through a commission issued by the President and confirmed by the Senate. The larger and subordinate grouping comprises the enlisted men, the upper ranks of whom are the non-commissioned officers; they receive their appointments through warrants from their superior, commissioned officers. There are two aspects of military personnel that merit particular comment: recruitment and discipline.

Recruitment: The recruitment of enlisted men differs considerably from that of commissioned officers. Military forces have two classic means for procuring enlisted men: by conscripting them, and by inducing them to volunteer. During most of its history the United States has filled its military ranks with volunteers. Such personnel are desirable in one important respect: presumably they have entered the service of their own free will, so that they will make a profession of military service and will remain in it until they have reached the age of retirement. On the other hand, volunteering does not usually provide enough recruits, especially in the United States, where until very recently enlisted men of the armed forces occupied a low social status. Furthermore, volunteering does not provide all the special skills and aptitudes that the armed forces need, and it may draw men who should remain in their civilian posts. Hence today the United States secures most of its enlisted personnel through the draft, based on the Universal Military Training and Service Act of 1948 and its amendments, which established the present Selective Service System (SSS). In this respect the United States is similar to other countries in the world. Table 25 shows the draft age and required service in other nations.

The central administration of the Selective Service System is entrusted to a Director and a Deputy Director, along with several assistants and a number of divisions. Most of the work of the SSS, however, is carried out on the State and local level. There is a headquarters for the SSS in each State, with a State director chosen by the President upon the recommendation of the Governor. The State headquarters coordinate the work of the local boards, of which there is at least one in almost every county of the nation. The local board, made up of three or more members resident within its jurisdiction, makes the initial decision as to whether an individual is liable for military service. Decisions of the local board may be carried to an appeal board, of which there is one in each federal judicial district. Decisions of these boards may be brought to what amounts to a court of last resort, the National Selective Service Appeal Board.

By law, each American male between the ages of eighteen and twenty-six must register with his local board, and he may be called to service when he has attained the age of eighteen years and six months. Deferments may be granted upon certain grounds, such as physical, mental, or moral incapacity; the economic dependence of his family upon the registrant; provable conscientious objection to war; or the fact that the registrant practices a trade or profession that makes him more valuable as a civilian. Today the armed forces administer a test to college students; those achieving a sufficiently high score are permitted to continue their studies, on the theory that their training in college may be of greater value to the country. Conscripted soldiers must serve on active duty for two years, then be in the reserves for six more years.

The recruiting of officers is solely on a volunteer basis. In peacetime the majority of officers are trained at any of the various schools designed for that purpose. The federal government itself maintains one academy for

TABLE 25.   DRAFT AGE AND TERMS OF SERVICE
IN VARIOUS COUNTRIES[1]

Country	Age (Years)	Service (Months)
Australia	18	3
Belgium	18	18
Canada	Depends on Volunteers	
China (Communist)	Unknown	Indefinite
China (Nationalist)	18	Indefinite
Denmark	20	12–18
France	19	18
Germany (West)	18	Undecided[2]
Greece	21	24
Italy	18	16
Japan	Depends on Volunteers	
Korea (North)	17	Indefinite
Korea (South)	18	Indefinite
Netherlands	18	20
Norway	19	16
Philippines	20	10
Portugal	20	4–22
Spain	20	15–18
Sweden	20	10
Switzerland	19	4
Turkey	20	24
USSR	16	24–60
United Kingdom	18	24
United States	18½	24
Yugoslavia	19	24

[1] As of July, 1954. Adapted from U.S. News and World Report, July 2, 1954, p. 28, and revised.

[2] Draft law passed in 1956 provided no term of service.

each service, where officers are educated for their tasks. Most of the students in these academies are appointed by the Senator or Representative of their State or district. There are other schools authorized to train officers, which students may attend voluntarily. Many colleges, including all land-grant schools, have Reserve Officers' Training Corps establishments. During a war, soldiers may receive commissions as officers on the field. Conscripts with unusual aptitude may be selected for preparation as officers. Individuals in particularly essential professions, such as medicine and dentistry, may usually—almost invariably in wartime—obtain a commission simply by applying for it.

Discipline: The discipline exacted by the armed forces is much more rigorous than that demanded in any phase of civilian life, with the possible exception of penitentiaries—which are under a species of military rule. Disciplinary requirements vary from one country to another—those of the Soviet Union are much more strict than those of the United States. Discipline in the American armed forces is based upon the Uniform Code of Military Justice, passed by Congress in 1950. These laws set forth what are military offenses and what their punishment shall be. Violators of military law may be arrested by the military police maintained by each service and tried by the courts-martial of their service, which are supervised by the Judge Advocate General of each service. There are three types, or levels, of courts-martial: summary, special, and general; they try cases, respectively, that are roughly analogous to civil crimes known as summary offenses, misdemeanors, and felonies.

Procedure in a court-martial is quite different from that in a civil court. There is no jury; the judge or judges hand down the decision. A general court-martial has several judges, in the same manner as the United States Supreme Court. Until recently only commissioned officers might sit on a court-martial; today, however, non-commissioned officers may participate in the trial of an enlisted man. It is a standing principle that no person is to be tried by anyone of lesser rank; hence officers are tried only by officers. The accused may have counsel, and may produce witnesses; he is entitled to hear the evidence against him.

Military personnel are not exempt from the jurisdiction of civil courts, and may be tried and sentenced by them for offenses against civilian criminal law. Indeed, since many acts are crimes under both civilian and military law, military personnel may be tried and sentenced in both civilian courts and courts-martial for the same act without undergoing double jeopardy, since they have violated the laws of two distinct jurisdictions. Convictions in courts-martial that affect a general or an admiral, or that involve a death sentence, may be appealed to the United States Court of Military Appeals, which has been described in Chapter 27.

CIVILIAN MOBILIZATION

Civil defense

Civil defense is the task of protecting the civilian population in the event of direct enemy attack upon the United States that would bring problems of mass evacuation from the cities, public panic, looting, and other disorders consequent upon the bombing of metropolitan centers. It is assumed that a considerable part of this work will be undertaken by the regular military forces. However, these forces are numerically too few to handle the population if many cities were raided simultaneously. During World War II organizations of this type in the warring European countries made significant contributions to the work of their armed forces. Such an organization also existed in the United States; however, owing to the fact that no enemy bombing planes ever reached the United States, civil defense officials then had little to do beyond enforcing "dim-out" and "black-out" regulations.

Civil defense in the United States today is a task shared by national, State, and local authorities. The chief national office is the Federal Civil Defense Administration (FCDA), an independent agency. The chief executive of the FCDA is the Administrator, who, with the Deputy Administrator, is appointed by the President and confirmed by the Senate. The FCDA carries on studies of such matters as the effects of bombing upon the individual human being, and the best form of air-raid shelter. It maintains a system of defense communication linking all parts of the nation.

In the main, however, the FCDA is an office for coordinating the work of State and local civil defense agencies. That is, civil defense in the United States is decentralized; this type of organization is not only in keeping with the federal traditions of the country, but also assures that a single bomb cannot destroy the head of civil defense throughout the country. Each State is expected to establish its own civil defense body and to inform the citizens about it; the FCDA helps to train the State leaders. It also makes financial contributions to State civil defense undertakings; however, it does not pay the salaries of State officials or buy land for their use.

In an actual emergency the FCDA acquires vast powers; for instance, it may take any property needed for civil defense purposes without regard for existing laws. It can also direct any other federal agency to surrender its resources for the necessities of civil defense. The work of the FCDA is supplemented by that of the Ground Observer Corps, made up of civilian "skywatchers" who report the approach of any aircraft in their vicinity to the district headquarters which they serve. This headquarters then determines whether the aircraft is friendly or hostile through its charts of scheduled flights in the area. Should the plane be either hostile or unknown the headquarters notifies the nearest Air Force base which then dispatches American aircraft in pursuit.

The national economy

Modern war, it has already been pointed out, demands not only valorous and well-trained soldiers but also a productive national economy. The country must have machinery, resources, transportation, and men; beyond these elements it must have an agency that brings them together at the right place and the right time. The Office of Defense Mobilization (ODM) in the Executive Office of the President is the agency that is designed to coordinate the national economy for purposes of national security. Its principal officers are the Director and the Deputy Director, each appointed by the President and confirmed by the Senate. Many of its other officers are either heads of government agencies, leaders of private organizations, or professional men.

The ODM includes four major divisions, whose aims are apparent from their titles and their personnel: (1) the Defense Mobilization Board, comprising the Director of the ODM as Chairman; the Secretaries of State, Defense, the Treasury, the Interior, Agriculture, Commerce, and Labor; the Chairman of the Federal Reserve Board of Governors; and the Administrator of the FCDA; (2) the Health Resources Advisory Committee, made up of several members of the medical profession; (3) the Science Advisory Committee, containing both practical and theoretical physical scientists; and (4) the Labor-Management Manpower Policy Committee, with representatives from both private industry and labor unions. Working through these and several other subordinate offices, the ODM aims at procuring the most efficient use of all aspects of the national economy so as to obtain the greatest possible industrial output for security needs.

Industry: The federal government encourages industrial expansion so as to cope with the demands of national security. The pattern for the expansion is established by the requirements of the Defense Department; thus the identity and interests of the Secretary of Defense may influence the outlines of this expansion. One of the most pressing issues has been the size of the industrial base for national security, that is, whether it should include many or few plants. Under the leadership of Defense Secretary Charles E. Wilson, the government adopted the policy of having comparatively few plants, that is, a narrow base, for its defense production needs. Inasmuch as modern weapons become obsolete quickly, the government has decided to keep only a relatively small amount of them in reserve to bear the shock of the first enemy assault, relying upon the ability of its arms production base to supply its needs almost from the outset of hostilities.

To lessen the fiscal burden of industry in constructing these plants, the government has authorized their owners to compute a very high depreciation rate (depreciation being deductible from corporation profit taxes) so that the plants can be speedily "written off." Too, the government has instituted a system of priorities and allocations, administered by the Business and Defense Services Administration in the Commerce Department, that enables the owners of these plants to have first call on scarce raw materials. Finally, the government has recommended that industry stockpile its machine tools, which are perhaps the most essential implements in industry since they make the machines and tools that produce the goods themselves.

Resources: The government fosters the discovery and exploitation of the great number of resources necessary for the conduct of warfare today. For example, through the Defense Minerals Exploration Administration in the Interior Department the government subsidizes projects aimed at the finding of new mineral resources. To assure the government an adequate amount of the resources needed for industrial production, the General

Services Administration, supervised by the Office of Defense Mobilization, purchases and stockpiles the minerals that may be in short supply in the United States. During the Eisenhower administration the stockpiling program was somewhat slackened in favor of one stimulating the erection of productive facilities.

Transport: The government seeks in many ways to augment and to coordinate the transportation facilities of the nation that may be necessary for defense purposes. The grants-in-aid from the Bureau of Public Roads to the State governments have been intended not only for the promotion of business but also for defense needs, especially since the railroads have discontinued service on many unprofitable lines. The Bureau of Safety and Service in the Interstate Commerce Commission makes programs regarding transport and storage and issues allocations and priorities for their use, except in the case of pipelines, aircraft, and coastal shipping. The Defense Air Transportation Administration in the Commerce Department fills this purpose with respect to aircraft. In time of war the problems of supplying adequate transportation are multiplied several times, because such materials as liquid fuels and rubber become so essential to the armed forces that their civilian use must be restricted; highway travel is then limited, so that rail and water transportation must shoulder a far greater burden of freight and passengers. It may be predicted that in case of war, although the government will not actually take over these properties, it will place them under tight controls.

Manpower: One result of the changes in military techniques during the past century has been a greatly augmented demand for manpower. Armed forces are much more numerous than they were, even in proportion to the entire population, and the material requirements of the armed forces necessitate another army made up of industrial workers. Today the principal agency for recruiting industrial manpower in the event of war is the Office of Manpower Administration in the Department of Labor. At present this office is little more than a skeleton; its regional directors, for example, are those of the Bureau of Employment Security. This duplication of function reveals, too, that one of the chief purposes of this office is to allocate defense contracts in such a manner as to relieve conditions of severe regional unemployment. In the event of a full-fledged war this Office would doubtless gain increased power, so that laborers would be under about the same number of controls as were imposed upon them during World War II.

Civil discipline and morale

One of the principal tasks for the government during a war is to convince the civilian population that it must support the national security program. The government has two general methods for achieving these ends—the stick and the carrot, or, in other terms, force and moral suasion. The American government has never been obliged to use force in dealing with the mass of the American people with respect to a war; however, it has the machinery at hand in the event it is needed: martial law. Martial law is not to be confused with military law; military law is that body of rules which controls the behavior of military personnel, whereas martial law is a group of regulations imposed by military authorities upon the civilian population.

Martial law has rarely been invoked in the United States; during World War II it was used in Hawaii, when that territory seemed in imminent danger of invasion by the Japanese. (After the end of martial rule there, the Supreme Court declared that it had been unconstitutional.) Under martial law ordinary courts are suspended, and only special military courts function. Martial law itself is not based on any code; it is derived solely from the intermittent proclamations of the commanding officer to the civilians concerned. The federal courts have shown great hostility to martial law; they have ruled that whenever there is access to civil courts martial law cannot prevail. Through ordinary civil procedure, of course, the government has less stringent methods for compelling public obedience to the requirements of national security; it can imprison a man for failing to register with selective service officials, or for raising prices above their statutory levels.

The government would far rather use moral persuasion for upholding civilian discipline and morale. It is less expensive, and incurs little resentment. After all, whereas they may disparage the government in power, practically all Americans are loyal and patriotic. The United States is not, like European countries, saddled with a national police that is devoted to ferreting out "political" crimes. Moral suasion takes the form of "selling" the war to the citizens; that is, they are shown that "justice" is on the side of the United States. During each of the recent world wars the government established agencies for persuading Americans of the rightness of the American cause; in World War II it was known as the Office of War Information (OWI). To a great degree the OWI did little more than supplement the work of the myriad unofficial and unpaid individuals who convinced other individuals that they should give further efforts in behalf of national security. Today there is no parallel to the OWI; however, should war break out, such an agency would quickly emerge.

QUESTIONS AND PROBLEMS

1. What changes in the organization and procedures of national defense have occurred principally since 1945?

2. Considering the damage that would occur were a hydrogen bomb to be exploded in New York, do you regard the civil defense system as adequate to cope with the situation? What changes would you suggest?

3. In your opinion, does the character of warfare today make distinctions between enlisted men and officers more or less necessary than they were fifty years ago?

4. What measures are taken in peace and in war to gear the economy to the needs of national security?

5. What is martial law? Do you think it advisable to place the entire nation under martial law at the very beginning of hostilities, considering the expected character of a possible future war? Explain your reasoning.

6. Is the American obligation of military service less or more onerous than that of Great Britain, France, or the Soviet Union?

46. The Civil Arm
of Foreign Policy

Department of State

T HE civil arm of American foreign policy consists of the State Department, the United States Information Agency (USIA), and a number of secondary offices and divisions in the executive Departments and the independent agencies. The State Department is by far the most important among these elements; yet it is not beyond possibility that both the propaganda and the economic forces of the government abroad, which have undergone an erratic but spectacular development in the years after World War II, will find an increasingly important place in future foreign policy administration. The inertia of the old ways of behaving in international affairs acts to repress evidence of the effectiveness of continuous economic and psychological operations; when they are constantly and systematically executed, and when they are financed merely with a fraction of the generosity accorded to military expenditures, they are effective and flexible instruments of foreign policy. Propaganda and foreign economic operations have been costing recently only about five per cent as much as military activities.

THE DEPARTMENT OF STATE

General features

Although the President is the mainstay of civilian control of foreign policy, he works in many ways through the State Department, which is the principal executive body for the conduct of foreign relations. It is the oldest of all the present Departments, having been created in 1789. During most of its history it was a small and comparatively unimportant establishment; in fact, it was even burdened with domestic responsibilities such as the custody of federal laws after they had been signed by the President. As recently as December, 1939, it had but 6,249 employees, and in fiscal 1939 it spent only $19,145,000. The Second World War and its aftermath, however, greatly enhanced the significance of the Department; it underwent several reorganizations, and was relieved of almost all tasks connected with domestic matters. On January 1, 1956, it had 29,088 employees, and in fiscal 1956 its expenditures amounted to about $138 millions. Even today it has fewer employees than any other Department save that of Labor, and its budget is smaller than that of any other Department. On the other hand, owing to the greatly increased participation by the United States in international affairs, the State Department today ranks in importance with the enormous defense Departments.

The Department of State has four major tasks: (1) It gathers information concerning all aspects of other countries, including political, economic, social, and cultural matters. (2) It assimilates and coordinates this material, and, in conjunction with other agencies such as the National Security Council, it assists the President in the making of foreign policy. (3) Through its overseas personnel, it represents the United States to the world. (4) Through these personnel, under the guidance of the President, it carries on negotiations with other nations.

The Secretary of State

The Secretary of State is the chief official of the State Department. He is appointed by the President with the advice and consent of the Senate; and, because his Department is the oldest, he enjoys precedence over all other members of the Cabinet. The nature of the persons who have been chosen Secretary of State merits note. From 1789 to 1957 there have been fifty-one Secretaries of State. Almost without exception, they have been outstanding

American Embassies: a Variety of Architectural Styles. *Left,* top to bottom: Stockholm, Sweden; Jidda, Saudi Arabia; Madrid, Spain. *Right,* top to bottom: Rio de Janeiro, Brazil; Paris, France.

political figures; that is, they have held high rank in their parties. Three of these exceptions have held the office since 1940: Edward R. Stettinius, Jr., who might best be described as a political businessman; General George C. Marshall, a career soldier; and Dean G. Acheson, a skilled lawyer who for several years was Under Secretary of State. In fact, Secretary John Foster Dulles had not been deeply engaged in politics save on the international plane. Thirty-two Secretaries have been elected to one or both houses of Congress; only six of these have held office since 1898. Twenty have been members of State legislatures, only two of them since 1895. Ten have been State Governors, only one of them since 1877. Seventeen have occupied other posts in the Cabinet, none since 1933. Nineteen may be said to have had considerable previous diplomatic experience, most of them before the Civil War. Nearly all have been lawyers.

It does appear that there have been changes in the criteria used for naming Secretaries of State. It seems improbable that another Secretary will be chosen because he represents an important faction of the party that did not capture the White House, as Wilson chose William Jennings Bryan. Actually, it now appears that unswerving attachment to the party is no longer essential; for example, Dulles lent his talents to both Democratic and Republican administrations before his choice by Eisenhower. Experience as an overseas representative of the American government has become less of a prerequisite, although prior acquaintance with the State Department itself may be demanded. All of these factors appear connected with political developments that have tended to (1) remove the State Department from partisan politics; and (2) emphasize the administrative obligations of the Department and the skills that its governing requires.

Domestic structure of the State Department

The State Department today, in spite of the small number of its employees, has an unusual number of levels of responsibility. Immediately subordinate to the Secretary is the Under Secretary of State, who is the deputy of the Secretary and is his agent during the Secretary's absence. Beneath the Under Secretary are three Deputy Under Secretaries: one for Administration, one for Political Affairs, and one for Economic Affairs.

Under these officials are twelve functionaries possessing the title or at least the rank of Assistant Secretary. Four of them possess duties that may be defined as auxiliary; that is, they are related to the upkeep of the Department. Two, the Counselor and the Legal Adviser, deal with matters involving, respectively, international law and domestic law. The Assistant Secretary for Congressional Relations maintains liaison with the legislative branch. This office is unusually important because the State Department cannot rely upon the support of pressure groups, as the Agriculture Department may count on the Farm Bureau Federation, or the Commerce Department on the NAM, to expound its program to often unsympathetic congressmen. The Assistant Secretary-Controller assists the Deputy for Under Secretary for Administration.

The remaining eight have obligations under which they either carry out the work for which the Department was intended, or afford research and advice to the chiefs of the Department. Five of these Assistant Secretaries are heads of so-called "Regional Bureaus": Inter-American Affairs; European Affairs; Far Eastern Affairs; Near Eastern, South Asian and African Affairs; and International Organization Affairs. Each of these Bureaus is subdivided into Offices; for example, in the Bureau of Far Eastern Affairs there are Offices of Chinese Affairs, Northeast Asian Affairs, and Philippines and Southeast Asian Affairs.

Offices then are broken down into "desks" for individual countries; the Office of Northeast Asian Affairs contains a desk for Korea and a desk for Japan. Heading each desk is an individual expert on that country, who performs research on all phases of activity within the country that may be of interest to the United States, then submits reports on his conclusions to his superiors. It should be apparent that the preferences of the official holding a given desk on such matters as the political organization or the distribution of wealth in the country under his scrutiny may have a large effect upon foreign policy decisions finally taken by the President.

The other three officials at this level head agencies that deal with functional problems. The Assistant Secretary for Policy Planning aids the Secretary and the Under Secretary in evaluating and formulating policy, and represents the Department on the National Security Council Planning Board. The Assistant Secretary for Public Affairs administers the public information undertakings of the Department, along with associated duties that include the maintenance of the official history of American diplomacy and the supervision of programs for the exchange of students and professional personnel with other nations. The Special Assistant for Intelligence, whose rank is equal to that of an Assistant Secretary, coordinates the information returned to the United States about other countries. A final office in the Department, with both auxiliary and line functions but not under an Assistant Secretary, is the Bureau of Security and Consular Affairs. This Bureau, which is responsible to the Deputy Under Secretary for Administration, controls the issuance both of passports to American citizens—so that they may travel overseas—and of visas to aliens—so that they may visit the United States.

The Foreign Service

The Foreign Service comprises the State Department organization in foreign countries. The State Department maintains three types of offices outside the United States: embassies, legations, and consulates. Embassies and legations deal primarily with diplomatic issues, with relations between the United States government and the governments of other countries. The principal distinction between them is that the chief of an embassy is an ambassador, and the chief of a legation is a minister. Supposedly an ambassador is the deputy of the entire government, but a minister represents only the chief of state. Inasmuch as an ambassador takes precedence over a minister, an embassy is considered more honorific than a legation. Although at one time the United States had no overseas embassies, today it sends an ambassador to virtually all countries with which it maintains diplomatic relations. The United States now has seventy-four embassies and but four legations.

A consulate handles affairs involving the relations between an American citizen and the government of a foreign country, between a citizen of a foreign country and the government of the United States, and between a private American citizen or group and a foreign citizen or group. The American government now possesses more than 160 consulates apart from the consular offices in connection with embassies and legations. The map in Figure 115 shows where these offices are situated. It is noteworthy that, because of the tensions between the United States and the Soviet Bloc, there are no American representatives in the Soviet Union outside of the Moscow embassy, no American offices at all in either Bulgaria or China, and only legations in Hungary and Romania. The offices are, of course, concentrated in western Europe and in Canada and Mexico along the borders of the United States. Foreign Service personnel on January 1, 1956, totalled 15,931.

Chiefs of Mission: The chiefs of mission are the ambassadors and ministers; they are the principal officers of the "mission," or group of representatives, that the United States government sends to foreign countries. Chiefs of mission are appointed by the President and confirmed by the Senate. They do not need to prove any experience or training for their post; frequently they do not speak the language of the country to which they are delegated. Many chiefs of mission have been appointed because they were important party figures or because they had made large campaign contributions. Under these conditions it was necessary only for the President to determine that the individual was *persona grata*—in other words, acceptable—to the country in which he was to represent the United States. In recent years, however, there has been a growing trend toward naming persons whose careers have been in the State Department, and who are prepared through training and professional experience to administer their offices. Furthermore, the political appointees have been chosen recently from among highly educated, as well as wealthy, men and women. Figure 116 provides a comparison between the political and the career chiefs of mission in the American embassies and legations.

Chiefs of mission, and all their subordinates in the field of diplomacy as well, enjoy what is known as "diplomatic immunity"; that is, they may not be arrested or prosecuted for any offense in the country to which they are accredited. Of course, it is of the utmost importance that they avoid violating any laws, lest the action strain relations between that government and the United States. Should a diplomat break a law, the government of the offended country might simply declare him *"persona non grata,"* in which case the United States would have no other recourse than to recall him. If the government of the foreign country discovered other reasons for becoming hostile toward the United States, it might ask the American government to recall its chief of mission. Should the American government

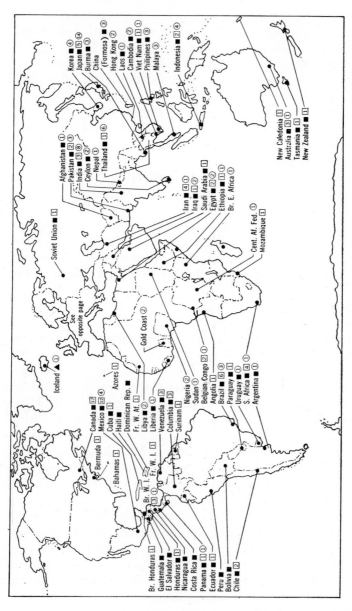

Key to Maps

■ Embassy

▲ Legation

1 Number of Consulates

① Number of U.S. Information Offices

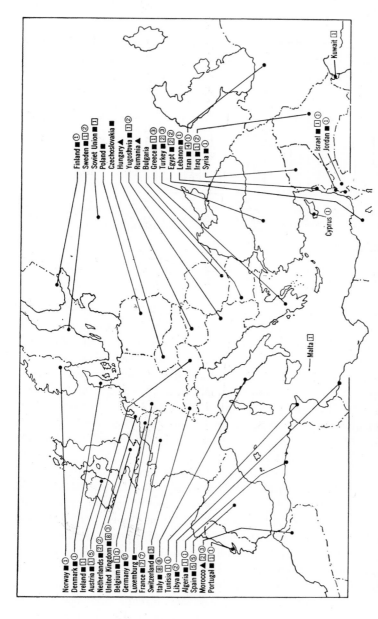

Figure 115. Locations of American Diplomatic and Information Services Abroad. These maps are based upon information available in 1954; therefore they vary in a few details from the situation today and from several later figures used in the text.

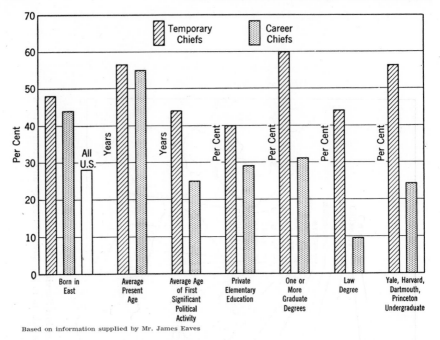

Based on information supplied by Mr. James Eaves

Figure 116.   Contrast of Temporary and Career Chiefs of Mission, 1954.

refuse, or even hesitate, the government of the nation concerned might give the diplomat his passport and dismiss him.   Usually, although not always, this is a quite serious step which may be the prelude to war.   Finally, the State Department may recall the diplomat temporarily in order to consult with him or to give him particular instructions.   Chiefs of mission are paid salaries up to $27,500 per annum, along with allowances for housing and living necessities that may add another $25,000.   Even $50,000 yearly may be insufficient to pay the costs of the social obligations connected with a diplomatic post such as London or Paris, so that frequently the incumbent must be an independently wealthy person.

Foreign Service Officers: Foreign Service officers make up most of the trained diplomatic and consular corps immediately subordinate to the chiefs of mission.   They hold such positions as counselor of embassy or of legation, diplomatic secretary, consul general, consul, and vice consul.   Foreign Service officers are recruited through a series of difficult written and oral examinations; of the several hundred that ordinarily commence these tests —which are given annually—fewer than one hundred pass.   The candidate must demonstrate a broad knowledge of history, politics, economics, and general culture; be able to use at least one foreign language; and have desirable personal traits.   He must almost certainly be a college graduate; however, an advanced degree is not necessarily advantageous.   Successful candidates after their appointment are given intensive training in Washington under the supervision of the State Department; they then may be named to a diplomatic or a consular post.   After two or three years they may be recalled to Washington for further training, then assigned to another post. A Foreign Service officer may be transferred from the diplomatic service to the consular service, and the reverse. The officer may look forward to a more or less regular series of advancements, depending upon the quality of his performance, rising to the level of consul general or of first counselor. At any point, if his superiors determine that he does not merit promotion, he may be dropped from the Service rather than allowed to superannuate at a low level because of his inefficiency.

Other Foreign Service Personnel: Apart from Foreign Service officers there are several other grades of Foreign Service employees. Foreign Service Reserve Officers are members of other government agencies who hold temporary assignments in the State Department, for no longer than four years. Foreign Service staff officers hold lower-ranking positions in American embassies and consulates; they are clerks, accountants, book-keepers, translators, and members of other trades and professions necessary for the maintenance of American overseas offices. The federal government also employs many natives of the country involved, to serve as chauffeurs, porters, and interpreters. Finally, the government designates businessmen —either American or foreign—as consular agents in cities where the United States does not have a regular embassy or consular office. All these personnel are chosen by the Secretary of State or a representative of his offices, as distinct from Foreign Service officers, who are named by the President with the advice and consent of the Senate.

THE UNITED STATES INFORMATION AGENCY

The United States Information Agency (USIA) is the office that administers American overseas information activities. In clearer terms, the USIA is the propaganda arm of the American government. It is an independent agency, whose origins are singular. It was created on August 1, 1953, by authority of the President's Reorganization Plan 8, and approved by Congress. Formerly, the main body of its personnel and work had been located in the International Information Administration of the Department of State. Other parts of the USIA came from the Technical Cooperation Administration and the Mutual Security Agency. The chief executive of the USIA, the Director, reports the activities of the Agency to the National Security Council; however, since the NSC is an advisory and not an executive group, the Director resorts to the President for immediate orders and aid. The Director receives daily guidance on United States foreign policy from the office of the Secretary of State; it is on the basis of these statements of American attitudes with respect to the questions of the day that the Agency prepares its materials for dissemination throughout the world.

On October 22, 1953, the White House issued a directive establishing the primary mission of the USIA: "to submit evidence to peoples of other nations by means of communications techniques that the objectives and policies of the United States are in harmony with and will advance their

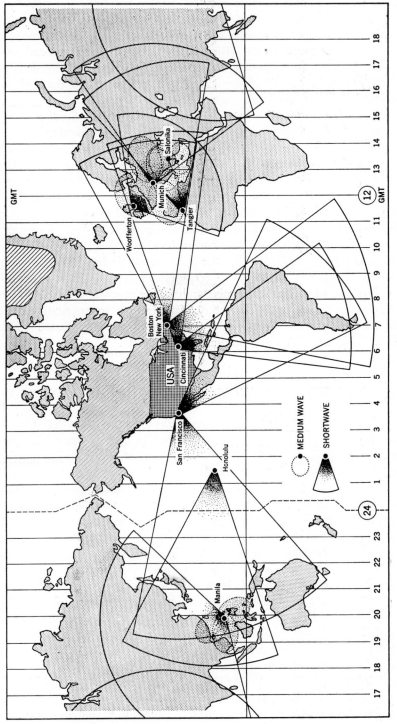

Figure 117.   Foreign Areas Reached by the Voice of America.

legitimate aspirations for freedom, progress and peace." The directive further detailed the functions of the Agency, as follows:

(1) explaining and interpreting to foreign peoples the objectives and policies of the United States Government;

(2) depicting imaginatively the correlation between U.S. policies and the legitimate aspirations of other peoples of the world;

(3) unmasking and countering hostile attempts to distort or to frustrate the objectives and policies of the United States;

(4) delineating those important aspects of the life and culture of the people of the United States which facilitate understanding of the policies and objectives of the Government of the United States.

The structure of the USIA is modeled after that of the Department of State. Its Director is appointed by the President and serves at his pleasure; the first Director, Theodore C. Streibert, had been Chairman of the Board of Directors of the Mutual Broadcasting System before assuming this post in 1953. Under the Director are seven Assistant Directors. One, for Administration, handles auxiliary tasks. A second, for Policy and Programs, administers staff functions. Four manage specific areas: American Republics; Europe; Far East; and Near East, South Asia, and Africa. The seventh Assistant Director, for Radio and Television (Broadcasting Service), is in charge of coordinating broadcasting activities.

There are 172 field offices, each known as the United States Information Service, located altogether in eighty-two countries (see Figure 115). In each country is a Public Affairs Officer, who administers the several types of local operations. He reports to, and receives policy directives from, the chief of the American mission in the country; this point is noteworthy, because, although the USIA is in structure an independent agency and is

---

The Voice of America's Global Network of Broadcasting Facilities

This visualization of the world, on Mercator's Projection, aims to show at a glance how a vast array of transmitters and relay stations carry Voice of America programs in 30 languages to listeners everywhere.

For European countries, the programs are transmitted from stations in the United States located near New York City, Boston and Cincinnati, via directional antennas with powers ranging from 50,000 to 200,000 watts.

The transmissions are beamed toward Europe, where a network of relay stations pick up and re-broadcast the programs. Shortwave relay stations are located at Munich, Germany, Tangier, North Africa, and Woofferton, England, while medium wave transmitters are located in Munich, Germany, and Salonika, Greece.

Latin American programs are transmitted from shortwave stations located near New York City, Boston, Cincinnati and San Francisco, to all countries south of the United States.

To Far Eastern countries the programs are broadcast from high-powered transmitters located near San Francisco, then relayed by shortwave transmitters at Honolulu and Manila and by a medium-wave transmitter at Manila.

The map indicates a considerable overlap of radio coverage from the various transmitters. Sometimes the overlapping areas indicate different language programs, and sometimes they indicate that a single language program is broadcast on several wavelengths, in order to give listeners a choice of the clearest signal in a locality.

Vertical lines indicate Time Zones, with GMT at 12 and the International Date Line at 24.

responsible directly to the President, it is closely tied to the State Department both in Washington and abroad.

In effect the Agency has two superiors, the Secretary of State at home and the ambassador or minister in the field. Thus there has been an incomplete severing of bonds between the child and the parent agency; this situation was not unforeseen, however, for it was considered desirable to tie the USIA closely enough to the State Department to assure that the United States was not speaking with two voices throughout the world. One may very well ask why the split was instituted at all; apparently the USIA, when it was a part of the State Department, was an uncomfortable burden upon the administrators of the Department, especially since the information services were for a time under attack by Congress, on the grounds that they were harboring a number of persons who were "security risks" and that they were incompetent in managing the propaganda campaigns of the United States abroad. The State Department, too, is a tradition-laden body that does not take easily to new and "undignified" tasks.

It has been noted that the directive establishing the USIA speaks of communication techniques as the means for carrying out its objectives. These techniques include the radio, press, pamphlets, libraries, motion pictures, and various miscellaneous means for conveying ideas and attitudes to overseas audiences. In 1956 the USIA was maintaining a number of facilities for transmitting abroad the messages of the government. It was shipping printed and filmed materials, some produced in the United States and others produced locally, to the field offices. Most USIA offices contained libraries, some of which were the best in their areas, especially for works on technology and on the American way of life. The USIA was also operating the Voice of America, a world-wide radio broadcasting system beamed particularly at the nations of the Soviet Bloc. Figure 117 indicates how the facilities of the Voice reach the peoples of the world; it should be added, however, that both the British Broadcasting Corporation and the Soviet radio transmitters have larger audiences, partly because they are on the air more hours of the day.

The operations of the USIA are administered by a staff which on January 1, 1956, numbered 10,500 employees; of this corps, 8,118, or four-fifths, were stationed abroad. The Americans of the USIA staff are under the merit system. Plans are under way also to establish a separate Information Service corps akin to the Foreign Service of the State Department; a career development system was installed in 1954 and a recruitment program launched to bring in young persons who wish to make the information program their life work.

COUNCIL ON FOREIGN ECONOMIC POLICY

The Council on Foreign Economic Policy is an agency that helps plan the direct foreign economic undertakings of the federal government. For a number of years federal authorities have been convinced that in order to assure itself of cooperative relations with certain nations the United States must bolster the economies of these nations through loans, technical advice, and outright gifts of money. American officials have concluded that one of the principal reasons for which countries resort to Communism is internal poverty; moreover, these officials believe that foreign governments will cooperate more willingly with the United States in various international ventures if they can obtain material benefits from such cooperation.

The Council on Foreign Economic Policy is the successor to a number of agencies that have dealt with this program; it was established in 1954 to coordinate the work of all the federal agencies that were concerned with American overseas economic undertakings. The Chairman of the Council, who also bears the title of Special Assistant to the President, occupies an office with Cabinet rank. It is reported that the first tenant of this post, Joseph M. Dodge, formerly Budget Director and in private life the head of the Detroit Bank, had vast powers, for supposedly he could overrule even the Secretary of State and the Secretary of the Treasury in deciding issues.[1] The Council also includes the Secretaries of State, of the Treasury, of Commerce, and of Agriculture; the Special Assistant to the President for National Security Affairs; the Administrative Assistant for Economic Affairs; and one member of the Council of Economic Advisers. The Chairman of the Council collaborates with the National Security Council and the National Advisory Council on International Monetary and Financial Problems. The Council maintains a number of economic missions abroad, supervising the expenditures of the United States on behalf of the economic development of various countries and in emergency aid for lands threatened by famine, plague, or other natural disaster.

Other Departments, too, whose link with foreign policy is not immediately visible, nonetheless include bureaus or divisions for international operations. The foreign responsibilities of the Commerce Department have been described previously; then, there is an Office of International Labor Affairs in the Department of Labor, and a Foreign Agricultural Service in the Department of Agriculture. Altogether there are several dozens of agencies in the federal government that carry on some detail of the intricate foreign relations of the United States. The fact is that events elsewhere in the world are so likely to have some effect upon the United States in one respect or another that all the major administrative bodies are almost compelled to heed the political and economic events occurring in all parts of the globe.

QUESTIONS AND PROBLEMS

1. From what kinds of backgrounds have Secretaries of State been recruited? Has there been any recent change?

2. Describe the organization of the Department of State.

3. What arguments can you offer to justify the existence of a special Foreign Service outside the general Civil Service?

---

[1] *U.S. News and World Report*, July 1, 1955, pp. 68–71.

4. Compare the backgrounds of the political and the Foreign Service occupants of ambassadorial and ministerial posts.

5. How is the USIA organized? What functions are assigned to it?

6. Explain the process by which Foreign Service officers are recruited. In your opinion, is it more or less likely than the recruitment process of the armed forces to yield officers who are capable of administering foreign policies? Explain your answer.

7. Describe the membership and functions of the Council on Foreign Economic Policy.

A FOREIGN policy is the kind of relations that a government seeks to have with other nations and the means it uses to achieve them. It is a goal, a desired condition of its affairs with a foreign country or with the world. It is also the means, such as a loan or an alliance, that it employs in order to reach the goal. Today the formation and execution of its foreign policies are generally regarded as the most critical tasks facing the American government. No other problems concern the lives, fortunes, and beliefs of the people as strongly as war and peace, international communism, and world prosperity. At the same time, the problems of foreign affairs are most complex; there are many disputes among American voters and leaders regarding what should be the goals of the nation in the world. Furthermore, the choice of means for carrying out any policies range from complete isolation from the world to total economic, diplomatic, and military intervention throughout the globe. At no given moment will one find people in unanimous agreement upon either the ends or the means of foreign policy. What one does find are persistent and widespread tendencies of

739

the American government to seek certain foreign objectives and to use certain means to these ends.

THE ESSENTIALS OF AMERICAN FOREIGN POLICY

The foreign policy of the United States is based generally upon three political goals: (1) self-defense; (2) peace; and (3) spreading the American way of life. These goals have often been concrete enough to be considered the actual leading principles of American foreign policy. They have carried substantial weight with Americans since the United States won its independence from England in 1783. Each has expanded and contracted in importance and vitality from time to time, and each has been affected by the conditions of the other two principles at any given moment.

Self-defense

Like every other country in the world, the United States is eminently concerned with its welfare, its freedom and its safety from attack by other countries. As the United States has grown from thirteen States to forty-eight, as means of transportation and communication have grown more rapid, and as weapons have become more destructive, the United States has had to modify its devices for assuring its own defense. To this time, no effective means of insuring an adequate and eternal defense have been found; the irony of the history of the desire for defense is that America, risen from a fourth-rate power in 1790 to the greatest power in the world today, has never before been so gravely concerned abouts its capacity to defend itself against a foreign enemy.

Continentalism: One historic component in the defense policy of the United States has been continentalism. The doctrine of continentalism holds that the real interests of the United States are confined to the Western Hemisphere; indeed, some interpreters would restrict American interests to the territory of the United States and its possessions. This is the oldest doctrine of American foreign policy, originating in the first days of the Republic. It obtained its classic statement in the Farewell Address of George Washington, who asserted that the United States had interests separate from those of the rest of the world and that the United States in the future must "avoid entangling alliances" with the countries of Europe. When Washington enunciated this doctrine he did so not with the expectation of establishing a permanent concept but under the prodding of contemporary events; at this epoch Europe was being rocked by the wars of the French Revolution, and the United States was split between those who would honor, and those who would disregard, the Franco-American alliance made in 1778.

However, this doctrine satisfied the needs and aims of the United States during most of the nineteenth century; even today it is a most important element in American foreign policy. It was an ideal principle for a nation strung out along a coast with a vast hinterland to exploit. Under its aegis

The Pentagon, Headquarters of the Armed Forces, just outside Washington, D.C.

the United States purchased Louisiana; fought the War of 1812 against Great Britain; annexed Florida, Texas, and the Oregon Territory; drove Mexico out of the Southwest, and bought Alaska from Russia. The notion of continentalism is shared both by those who believe that the United States should turn its back upon the world, and by those who propose many other international involvements. In the former case, continentalism is a kind of isolationism that regards the concerns of non-American nations as not being immediately associated with the security and welfare of the United States. The non-isolationists hold that continentalism comes first, but that other international relations are also vital.

The Monroe Doctrine: The Monroe Doctrine, enunciated by President James Monroe in 1823, holds that European nations must not meddle with the domestic affairs of American countries, and that they must not seek to obtain further territorial possessions in the New World. The Monroe Doctrine was also based upon contemporary circumstances, the apparent aim of France and Spain to restore Spanish rule to the former colonies in Latin America that had just achieved independence. The Doctrine is a logically consistent expansion of continentalism; its premise was that the security of the United States required that European states should not have bases in South or Central America from which they might launch attacks on the United States.

The Monroe Doctrine since its enunciation has received two major amendments. The first of these, termed the Roosevelt Corollary, was stated by President Theodore Roosevelt in 1904. Essentially, it holds that in the event some nation in the Western Hemisphere shows itself incapable of self-government, if particularly it cannot pay its international obligations, the United States has the right to intercede so as to establish a government that would comply with the rules of international morality. Subsequently, to forestall European intervention, the United States occupied, first the Dominican Republic, then Nicaragua, two countries that had been unable to pay their debts or to protect the assets of American investors; the United States reorganized their fiscal system and administered their revenues until they were again solvent.

The other important amendment to the Monroe Doctrine was the Good Neighbor Policy, proclaimed by President Franklin D. Roosevelt in 1934 but inaugurated in fact if not in name by President Hoover. The Good Neighbor Policy was designed to create better feelings among the American nations; in a fashion it was aimed at superseding the Roosevelt Corollary. Certain Latin-American powers, especially the Argentine, resented the Roosevelt Corollary as a doctrine that subjected them to the control of the United States and in effect cast a shadow over their independence. The guiding principle of the Good Neighbor Policy is that all American nations are in law equal, and that the United States shall not view other American countries as its protectorates. An important purpose of the Policy has been to unite the Americas in the face of external aggression. The Policy has taken institutional form in the Organization of American States, the successor to the Pan American Union (see Figure 121, pp. 760–1).

The Defense of Non-Communist Asia: Today the United States has committed itself to the defense of all the countries in Asia that are not now dominated by the Soviet Union. At one time American policy with respect to Asia was limited to the protection of American markets in the Orient, according to the so-called "Open Door" Policy (1899). The role of the United States in the Far East was, however, sufficiently annoying to the Japanese military and economic leaders that in 1941 they seized the initiative and launched an all-embracing attack upon Western interests in the Far East. Yet after the end of World War II, when China had been freed from Japanese control, the United States did not act decisively to prevent the communists from overrunning the country.

Finally, in 1950 the United States spearheaded the action of the United Nations to block the communist North Koreans from absorbing non-communist South Korea; and in 1953 it renewed its material support to the anti-communist, pro-American Nationalist Government of China which the communists had forced to seek asylum on the island of Formosa. As matters stand today, the Open Door Policy, an economic concept, has been supplanted by the military concept that the western defense line of the United States is made up of the Philippines, Formosa, Okinawa, and Japan —all of them together comprising a string of islands off the eastern coast of Asia. In addition, the United States in 1954 established a South East Asia Treaty Organization (SEATO) to protect these and other non-communist Asian nations from communist aggression (see Figure 121, pp. 760–1).

Anti-communism: Anti-communism has been the leading element in the foreign policy of the United States since shortly after the end of World War II. The principle of anti-communism is directed against the Soviet Union and its satellites in Europe, and against China and its satellites in Asia. It is based on the recognition that communism is a world movement aimed at the overthrow of all non-communist governments, and that the United States is the chief target of Soviet rulers. Under these conditions the tasks of the United States have been to procure allies and to help in reconstructing the world economy, so as to confront the Soviet Union and its allies on at least an equal basis.

The true extent of anti-communism in American foreign policy is impossible to determine save as events occur and the nation has to choose a position. Some Americans would define the policy to embrace a universal attack from every quarter to eliminate communism as an effective force. Others are quite content to let communism triumph everywhere save in the United States. A third very large group, which probably dominates the actual foreign operations of the government, moves back and forth from aggressive anti-communism to passive anti-communism. As a result, at one moment the American policy seems to be one of "appeasement," that is, of letting the communist nations take whatever they can short of assault upon America; then at another moment, the policy seems to be one of increasing pressures and restriction of communism by all means, including the threat of war over "the next" movement of communist forces into a non-communist foreign territory.

Between 1954 and 1956, for example, the policy of "co-existence" was being debated; England, France, and other allies of the United States were joining with Soviet Russians and Chinese in extolling the notion that the two different worlds might live side by side indefinitely. However, in America, many considered co-existence as synonymous with appeasement and a decline in American vigilance. It appeared that the American government was unwilling to define strictly its degree of anti-communism and was unable to do so because of the shifting currents of official and public opinion in America. However, one should not conclude either that other countries were immune to these difficulties—including even the Soviet Union—or that the foreign policy emerging from such uncertainty was less effective than that being pursued by the allies or the enemies of the United States.

Peace

Although often bellicose itself, the government of the United States has sought to encourage peace by setting an example of peaceful relations that other nations might well emulate. Washington emphasized fostering peace by example in his Farewell Address. One of the most remarkable phenomena in present world politics is the almost undefended three-thousand-mile frontier between Canada and the United States extending from the Atlantic to the Pacific. The United States has provided further illustrations of the peaceful settlement of disputes through its various agreements with Great Britain, especially the satisfaction of the *Alabama* claims after the American Civil War resulting from the depredations of a sea-raider, the *Alabama*, built for the Confederate States by the British.

Beginning in the twentieth century the United States has concerned itself with the maintenance of peace in Europe. For example, in 1906, under Theodore Roosevelt the United States took part in the Algeciras Conference, which was summoned to settle differences between Germany and France over Morocco. The United States also took part in the Hague Conferences of 1899 and 1907, which had gathered to seek means for resolving international disputes by methods short of war. The United States also negotiated many treaties with various countries arranging for the arbitration of international questions. After World War I the United States took a leading role in drafting the Pact of Paris, or Kellogg-Briand Pact, of 1928, whose signatories renounced war "as an instrument of national policy."

After each world war of the twentieth century the victorious powers have created an international organization for the keeping of peace: the League of Nations after World War I and the United Nations after World War II. The United States did not join the League of Nations; the Senate found several reasons for objecting to it, most prominent of which was that apparently membership in the League might compel the United States to engage in war without any action on the part of the United States government, thus taking the power of declaring war away from Congress.

By contrast, the United States has joined the United Nations; it is the seat of the United Nations, and it is very active in United Nations affairs. Since the USSR has demonstrated a unique notion of what a just peace should be, and since it has employed the United Nations as a sounding-board for its beliefs, the United States has tended to rely on other mechanisms for avoiding war, such as bilateral and multilateral alliances. The fact is that today the United States government regards only one country, the Soviet Union, as a continuous threat to peace.

America has often been viewed abroad as essentially a warlike and imperialist nation. It is known to much of the world by two things: the atomic bomb and Wall Street. Are all these people deluded? Many Americans think not, as shown by the fact that the government for many years has been under attack for aggressiveness and economic exploitation even at home. How then can it also be said that peace is a major principle of American foreign policy?

The riddle posed by these questions is not difficult to explain if one considers that the American public, as described in an early chapter, is not a single, unanimous body, but is a collection of publics, each with different interests. To begin with, one of the most persistent and profound splits in the American public is that which divides a very strong and vocal pacifist sentiment from an equally strong and brash nationalist spirit. Each wants to go its own way, and by so doing makes the task of government difficult. Both beliefs are strong; both are American; and their existence cannot be denied. Knowing these facts, one can think about the foreign policy of the United States with less confusion and doubt; many foreigners and many Americans keep running to some political oculist because they think they are seeing America double, when they would do better to become adjusted to a double America.

Spreading the American way of life

A third constant stream in American foreign policy has been the effort to spread the American way of life around the earth; this is expressed in the brash nationalism and aggressiveness just mentioned. The American people and their government have been convinced since the American Revolution that the American way of life is unique. This is undoubtedly correct. The thirteen colonies, with the assistance of several European powers, broke away from one of the greatest colonial empires of its day and a few years thereafter created an unexampled government under a written constitution. The United States under this regime was able to expand to the Pacific Ocean, to unearth and exploit a superb endowment of natural resources, and to create the highest standard of living in the world and the most comprehensive industrial system. It is little wonder that Americans ascribed much of their good fortune in international affairs to their political system of a representative government under the rule of law and an economic system permitting great latitude to individual judgment and initiative; it is also little wonder that Americans, particularly with their merchandising talents, should strive to have these principles accepted by all countries.

Spreading the American Political System: The American people, or at least certain groups in American society, have often tried to persuade other countries to adopt governmental structures akin to that of the United States.

In the 1790's, the adherents of Thomas Jefferson professed to see in the French Revolution a movement analogous to the process that had brought the American Declaration of Independence. The Monroe Doctrine was motivated partly by the wish of the American government to see republicanism triumph in Latin America. Indeed, until recent years Americans have applauded virtually every attempt by a colonial people to achieve independence; of late, however, they have sometimes hesitated to support aspirations of colonial people, as in the case of Morocco, because by so doing they might alienate an ally—in this case, France. In 1918, President Wilson refused to negotiate with the Kaiser's government, and would not discuss peace until the empire had been supplanted by a republic. After each world war the United States government exhorted all nations to install constitutional, representative polities.

Cultural Affinities: Cultural affinities have been of some consequence in the foreign policy of the United States; it has taken action sometimes for reasons of sentiment and respect for certain nations that it would not have taken for reasons of power and profit. This behavior is not unique. The Greek city-states had different rules of war for conflict among themselves than for struggles against non-Greek, "barbarian" peoples. The Crusades of Christians against "infidels," the wars between Catholic Spain and France on the one hand and Protestant England and Holland on the other, and the wars of the French Revolution against non-republican governments, were all justified by cultural concepts. Of course, many diplomats of the past, such as Catholic King Francis I of France, who formed an alliance with the Moslem Turks, and the Catholic Cardinal Richelieu, who united France with Protestant Sweden, were not impressed by cultural or ideological similarities. It is not surprising, then, that the United States should base its foreign policy partly upon cultural affinities, and yet also be to a certain extent free of their restraints.

The most important cultural affinity of the United States has been that with Great Britain. The language of each nation is English. The government in each nation, although the British is a monarchy and the American a republic, is based upon constitutionalism. Almost half the people of the United States are descended in part or wholly from British forebears. Communications between the two countries have been frequent and rich. The two governments also have a tradition of peacefully solving their disputes. The record of 1775 and of 1812 is not sufficient to undo these cultural ties. The foreign affairs leadership in the United States, save perhaps that in Congress, regards the Anglo-American alliance as almost unbreakable, in spite of the fact that American and English interests clash in various corners of the world. The British Conservative Party leadership has the same view of the tie. The United States tends to be on amicable terms with all members of the British Commonwealth whose predominant tongue is English— Canada, Australia, and New Zealand; indeed, it has replaced their mother country in some respects.

America has also a cultural affinity with France, based partly upon the influence of eighteenth-century French philosophy in the British North

American colonies, the republican structure of the French government, the revolutionary traditions of that government, and the fact that France supported the colonies in their war for independence. Correspondingly, the United States manifests great friendship for France, although French and American interests are at odds in various regions. The foreign policy of the United States is generally favorable also toward the small countries of western Europe—the Scandinavian nations, Ireland, the Low Countries, and Switzerland—partly because of their common attachment to peace, their representative governments, and their backgrounds of striving for national independence or of resisting powerful aggressors. A friendly concern is expressed for Israel because of its ideals and institutions, and because of the kinship felt for the Jews among many Americans. Moreover, especially because of the large Roman Catholic element in America, the government is inclined to assist all anti-communist forces in Italy.

Germany seems to be an exception to the general point being made. A moment of reflection will bring an explanation. Germany in the twentieth century has suffered two bellicose governments, the Kaiser's and the Nazis'. In each case, its targets were Britain and France; moreover, the Nazis' violence against other European groups, such as the Jews and Poles, made them millions of enemies in America. Hence a strong cultural regard for Germany in the United States has had to give way before other policies and friendships. Yet one notes that the United States has been generous to Germany after its defeat in both World War I and World War II. Toward most other nations in the world the foreign policy of the United States does not show any pronounced leaning that is based chiefly upon likenesses of ideas, though no doubt Europe and Latin America command generally more affection and interest in the United States than Asia does.

Spreading the American Economic System: Most of the activity connected with spreading the American economic system has occurred since the end of World War II. It has been based on the idea that this system assures a people against poverty, and that a defense against poverty is one of the surest barriers to communism. This logic contributed to the Marshall Plan and has prompted a number of other undertakings such as the Point Four Program, whereby the United States is attempting to bring industry to technologically retarded areas. (See pp. 755–6 below.) A noteworthy feature of American economic intervention in the world lately has been its softened tone of anti-socialism; most American efforts have aimed at avoiding controversy over fundamental principles and have stressed the improvement of industrial and agricultural techniques.

QUESTIONS AND PROBLEMS

1. Name and describe briefly the three major principles of American foreign policy presented in this chapter.

2. What parallels can be drawn between the process of international politics, as discussed in the last section of this book, and the domestic political process of American government? Explain your answer.

3. In what ways can the policy of self-defense conflict with the policy of peace?

4. In what ways can the policy of peace conflict with the policy of spreading the American system of government?

5. Describe the transformation of the Open Door Policy into a military policy.

6. What is meant by the American policy of anti-communism?

7. In what ways do American cultural affinities with western Europe (including England) play a part in the foreign policies of the United States?

8. What are the foreign economic interests of the United States? Which among these is or are important for military reasons?

9. Describe briefly the advantages of the geographical position of the United States.

10. What do you consider to be the condition of American morale in foreign affairs today?

48. Foreign Policy Operations

United Nations

THE foreign policy operations of the United States are simply its efforts toward accomplishing its goals in relation to other countries. Such efforts are numerous and of extremely varied character. All of them require some method of influencing one or more of the nations in the world. The United States today recognizes the sovereignty of seventy-eight different nations, by sending them either ambassadors or ministers; in addition, there are a handful of countries which the United States does not recognize as sovereign, but which nonetheless have their own political organizations. Communist China is an example of an independent government that the United States refused to recognize; instead it regards Nationalist China, holding only the island of Formosa, as the rightful representative of the Chinese nation to the outside world.

FORMAL ACTIONS

The formal actions of the government with respect to other nations are: the recognition of other governments; treaties; executive agreements with other states; and joint resolutions of Congress respecting foreign affairs.

Recognition

Recognition is the act whereby one government acknowledges the legality of another government. Recognition is the essential preliminary to all diplomatic operations; it is the indication that one government wishes to arrange diplomatic relations with another. Recognition is ordinarily followed by an exchange of representatives—ambassadors or ministers, and consuls. The withholding of recognition may be employed as a device to show dissatisfaction with a particular government. Until the twentieth century the United States usually extended recognition to any government that was actually in power, on the assumption that effective political rule merited recognition. During the present century, however, the federal government has indicated its aversion to several governments by denying them recognition. For instance, in 1913 President Wilson refused to recognize the regime of Victoriano Huerta in Mexico, on the theory that Huerta had usurped power; and this step by Wilson seems to have contributed to the subsequent fall of that government. The government of the United States did not recognize the Communist government in Russia until 1933.

Recognition is a power of the executive branch of the government, that is, of the President. Recognition may be tendered in any of several ways, the commonest being by the simple exchange of envoys. Another means for giving recognition is by a presidential proclamation. The Senate does have indirect control over recognition through its power to refuse assent to a presidential appointment of a diplomat; however, since the President may wait until the end of a congressional session before selecting an ambassador or minister, the Senate does not have assurance of being able to interfere in the recognition process. Once one government has recognized another, the two may carry on all the conventional practices of diplomacy, such as the arrangement of treaties and alliances. Governments that do not recognize each other must conduct their relationships through the envoys of a third government that each does recognize.

Treaties

Treaties are official agreements between two or more countries. They may be negotiated to deal with almost any question regarding the governments of the countries involved. Since 1789 the United States has entered into about one thousand treaties with other countries, regulating a host of problems. Most of these treaties deal with comparatively minor

General Assembly of the United Nations, New York City.

issues. Some have been designed to handle only a temporary situation; others, by contrast, have been expected to endure as long as the signatory government did.

The negotiation of treaties is also an executive function. The actual arrangements are normally drafted by the State Department, but in the event of important matters the President closely supervises the activities of the Department. Treaties may be initiated by any sovereign government; discussions may go on either in foreign embassies in Washington or in American embassies in foreign capitals. After all disputed points in the language or terms have been eliminated, representatives of the participating governments all sign the treaty.

However, in the United States a treaty does not become operative until it has secured the approval of the Senate, by an affirmative vote of two-thirds of the Senators present. Senate approval is in the main granted or denied by the Senate Committee on Foreign Relations, a powerful and influential group. The Senate has not rejected many treaties; yet some of those to which it has denied approval have been important, such as the Versailles Treaty after World War I. The Senate must accept the text as it stands; if it insists upon changing the text, the signatory powers must then give their approval to the amended version. After the Senate has approved of the treaty, it can go into effect. This may occur as soon as the President exchanges so-called "articles of ratification" with the heads of the other governments concerned. It should be emphasized that the Senate does not "ratify" a treaty; it only gives its approval.

Executive agreements

Executive agreements are arrangements negotiated by the heads of states. Unlike a treaty, an executive agreement does not require the approval of the Senate. The precise difference between the impact of an executive agreement and that of a treaty has never been established. It might appear that the agreements are binding only on the chief executive, and not on the entire government; treaties, by contrast, might be said to obligate the entire government. In practice, however, the government exhibits about the same response to an agreement as to a treaty.

In the early years of the American Republic the government did not often resort to executive agreements; but in the twentieth century the agreement has become a very common instrument of American diplomacy. So far as the President is concerned, the agreement possesses the virtue of secrecy. Of course, the Senate may deliberate a treaty behind locked doors; yet there remains the danger that some of its provisions may be revealed. In the case of the executive agreement, the President is not compelled to divulge its contents to any person in the American government. During World War II President Roosevelt often had recourse to the agreement, for handling such matters as the trade of fifty American destroyers for the right to lease air bases on certain British island colonies. The use of the agreement to bypass the Senate has aroused a great deal of resentment in congressional circles; members of the upper house contend that the President has usurped powers not rightfully his. The proposed "Bricker amendment" to the Constitution includes a clause that would deny the President the power to make such agreements.

Joint resolutions

The joint resolution is another means for settling an international problem. The resolution is simply adopted by Congress and signed by the President. Either Congress or the President may initiate the resolution; that is, the President may initiate it by submitting it to his congressional leaders, who can then bring it to the floor. A joint resolution, unlike a treaty, requires only a simple majority, but it does entail action by both houses of Congress. The joint resolution has been used many times in American history; an outstanding case of its use was the termination of World War I against Germany, after the Senate had refused its assent to the Versailles Treaty.

DIPLOMACY

With the exception of joint resolutions, the forms of action described in the previous section are initiated and developed through some of their phases by the diplomatic service of the United States (of course, in conjunction with the parallel services of other nations). Diplomats are thus agents working in behalf of principals, their governments. Because of the ease and rapidity of present means of communications, however, only rarely does the agent have full powers to negotiate and contract all phases of an accord with other nations. Indeed, the diplomats of the United States, owing to the important role of the Senate in treaty-making, have rarely possessed the initiative and responsibility given to the diplomats of most other nations in the past. Still, every encounter across national boundaries has a certain delicacy and difficulty about it, so that the standards of intelligence required even of junior Foreign Service officers must remain high.

Today more than in the past, the crucial negotiations with foreign countries are carried on by government officials at the highest level. Again, the reason lies in rapid communications. Secretary of State Dulles has been even more active than other high-ranking diplomats of the present day in conducting directly the relationships of the United States with other parts of the world; by the time he had been fifteen months in office, he had traveled 100,000 miles. If he had had to rely upon the transportation methods of 1853 in his travels, he would have been en route at some point every minute of the time and still not have completed the itinerary.

For those officers in the diplomatic service who do not achieve the highest posts, the pattern of work keeps them tied closely to one post after another, with intervening periods at Washington for advanced training and observation of the making of American foreign policy in the United States. The State Department itself defines "the assignments in Washington or abroad that a Foreign Service officer may expect to receive in the course of his career" as the following:

> Reporting on and analyzing political, economic, commercial, and labor conditions in countries abroad.
> Representing the United States in negotiations with other governments.
> Performing consular duties—issuing visas and passports, providing assistance to American shipping and seamen, protecting American citizens and property abroad, handling veterans' affairs.
> Promoting American trade.
> Distributing educational, scientific, cultural, and informational materials.
> Assisting in the exchange-of-persons program.
> Participating in the administration of Foreign Service posts or of the Department—budget, fiscal, personnel, and management work.
> Intelligence research requiring special area and language knowledge.
> Working with international organizations such as the United Nations.
> Communications and cryptography [code] work.
> Country and area "desk" work in the Department covering many or all of these activities in the day-to-day conduct of foreign affairs.

Depending, of course, upon the country and the times, this pattern of work may be pleasant, or it may be extremely tiring and discouraging. During the present state of "cold war," posts in the Soviet Bloc afford few pleasures to the American staffs. Relations with the native population are confined mostly to chill and formal encounters with officials of the government. The staff must be constantly alert so as not to provoke conflicts of any kind. Yet the work, as difficult as it may be, is highly important, for it is precisely these areas about which the United States lacks information and guidance.

ECONOMIC OPERATIONS

Today the government of the United States carries on a major part of its foreign policy through economic operations. There are many precedents for this practice, for both the United States and other nations. The Venetian navies and merchant fleets, working closely together, dominated the eastern Mediterranean for centuries. English colonies in the Orient were established, governed, and guarded by the East India Company; only in the nineteenth century did the English government take over the "political" government of India, leaving its commercial exploitation to private groups. The United States government has sometimes used force to protect the overseas commercial interests of its citizens, as when its navy defeated the pirates of Tripoli, who had been preying upon American shipping in the late eighteenth and early nineteenth centuries. Moreover, if one reconsiders the purchase of Alaska and the Virgin Islands, the seizure of the Philippines and the Spanish possessions in the Caribbean, the annexation of the Hawaiian Islands, and other similar cases, one must conclude that the United States had not, even before World War II, been innocent of the use of the economic tools of foreign policy and of the combination of money and force to open doors in the world.

Today, however, the makers of American foreign policy use economic manipulations in world affairs much more consciously and systematically. They realize that a dollar can sometimes do what a bullet or a stirring phrase cannot do. They further realize that a dollar cannot do today what it could do at one time. Consequently the methods of economic foreign policy have changed; nations today are wary of sheer commercial exploitation, so that economic policy usually has to be justified to the people on whom the policy is expected to work as well as to the Americans who must supply the money.

The several types of economic practices of American foreign policy comprise the manipulation of the tariff structure, assistance to and control over American business ventures abroad, loans and gifts of money to other countries, and technical assistance to foreign nations. The United States, as the producer of half the manufactured goods of the world, is in a better position than any other nation to use economic weapons as tools of foreign policy. The American government must, however, recognize that dollars, like words and armaments, can be wasted on useless projects that do not benefit, or even may harm, the efforts to achieve American goals overseas. This point can be seen in the following discussion.

The tariff

The tariff now has an important share in the execution of American foreign policy. Some countries are dependent for their economic survival upon their sales to the United States. If the federal government imposes a high tariff upon the products of those countries it may alienate their governments; yet if it fails to respond to the pressures of domestic groups, it may lose their assistance at election time. Today, for example, it is of the utmost importance to the Japanese government that its people be able to sell tuna fish to the United States. At the same time the tuna-fishing interests of southern California are waging a steady campaign to have the tariff on Japanese tuna raised; they assert that the Japanese tuna is unfairly competitive. Since the American government regards the health of the Japanese economy and the contentment of the Japanese people with the United States as important factors in the struggle against world Communism, it has so far kept the tariff low. It is evident that in some cases the United States levies its tariffs as much to implement its foreign policy as to protect American businessmen and workers from foreign competition. An outstanding illustration of American management of its tariff so as to implement American foreign policy is American adherence to the General Agreement on Tariffs and Trade (GATT), which thirty-five nations have signed. GATT provides means whereby governments may negotiate reciprocal tariff reductions. Nations that comply with GATT seek to avoid trade discrimination.

Promotion and regulation of American business abroad

The American government promotes and regulates American business abroad. As noted earlier in the text, American businessmen may receive advice, information, and, in some cases, subsidies for their work in expanding the export and import trade of the United States. The makers of foreign policy take care, however, to watch and control American enterprise abroad much more than once was the case. The guiding aim of such controls is to prevent any business from conflicting, through its foreign operations, with American policy. A case of the sort that occurred before World War II, when American businesses were exporting critical war materials such as scrap metal to Japan, is not likely to happen again. Indeed, American leaders watch not only American businessmen but also those of allied nations, to the same end; some of the most bitter debates in Congress from 1950 on concerned the quantity of trade that American allies had engaged in with the Soviet Bloc.

Sometimes the government takes the initiative in asking American interests to take part in foreign affairs along lines that the government cannot well undertake. The following paragraph, from a pamphlet on the Iranian Oil Agreement of 1954, published by the Standard Oil Company of New Jersey, illustrates the point:

> By then Iranian oil was no longer vital to the world's energy supply; additional refining capacity had been rapidly developed in other countries, the volume of crude oil production in Saudi Arabia and Kuwait had been greatly expanded, and Iraq production was moving up. But since a stable, prosperous Iran would be a political asset to the Western world, the companies having oil interests in other Middle East areas were urged by their respective governments to form a consortium, or association, whose purpose would be "the restoration of Iranian oil to world commerce." United States oil companies, in particular, were encouraged by their government to participate, and an opinion was rendered by the Justice Department that participation in the proposed consortium would not violate the United States anti-trust laws.

The "consortium" referred to reached an agreement with the Iranian government, and the relations of Iran with the western nations, particularly England, were stabilized on a peaceful and cooperative basis.

Loans and gifts

Today the United States government extends long-term loans, and actually gives money and materials, to foreign nations. The total assistance afforded by the United States has been considerable, amounting to some $50 billions between 1945 and 1956. Figure 118 on p. 755 presents the sums granted to the several areas of the world. Of course, assistance, chiefly of a military nature, had been going on since before the United States entered World War II; and some of the aid that had been pledged but not delivered during the war was sent after the war had ended.

Examining the American aid programs over the whole world one can perceive that beginning in 1948 the ratio between gifts for general purposes and those for military purposes started to change. In 1946 and 1947 the ratio was roughly one hundred to one; in 1948 it became less than twenty to one. In 1952 the ratio was one to one; of the slightly more than $5 billions extended in foreign aid, general purposes and military purposes accounted for approximately equal amounts. The trend continued in favor of military aid, so that the foreign aid budget of 1957 called for grants of $1.8 billions for general assistance and $2.5 billions for military aid. Much of this aid now went to Asiatic countries. However, European beneficiaries had already enjoyed so much economic improvement that they now had little need for general aid from the United States; indeed, in every case they had exceeded their prewar levels of production and living standards.

Technical assistance

"*Point Four*": "Point Four" is a program of technical assistance for countries whose agriculture and industry are underdeveloped. This program obtained its name through being the fourth of a series of "points" for com-

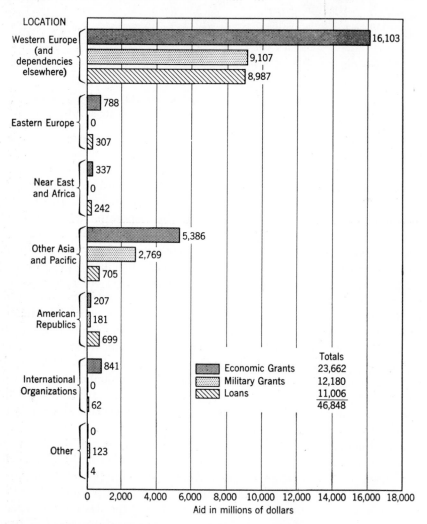

Figure 118. Total United States Aid to the World (July 1, 1945, to June 30, 1954).

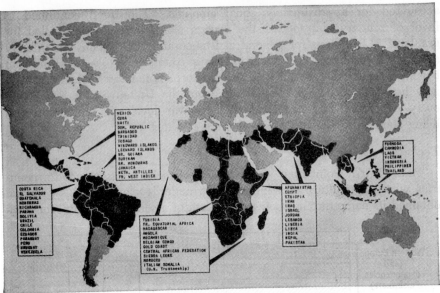

International Cooperation Administration

Figure 119. Technical Cooperation Around the World. Countries with whom the United States has separate Technical Cooperation Agreements are shown in black. The United Nations has a similar type of arrangement with some countries; such agreements are not shown here, even though the United States also contributes money and personnel to them.

batting communism that were submitted to Congress and the nation by President Truman in his Inaugural Address on January 20, 1949. The administration of this program is currently the responsibility of the International Cooperation Administration of the State Department. Its aims are to help countries such as India that lack modern farming practices to improve their agricultural techniques, to assist others such as Egypt to develop their water resources and mineral deposits, and to aid yet others to construct modern industrial facilities. Some of the technical aid goes abroad indirectly through American universities that contract with the federal government to set up an educational program under the sponsorship of the host government. The nations with which the United States has made "Point Four" agreements are designated on the map in Figure 119. It can be seen that they are countries that either have been under colonial rule in the recent past or for other reasons have lagged behind Europe and the United States in improving their agricultural and mechanical techniques during the last century.

Atomic Energy Development: A second, and newer, part of the American technical assistance programs is that of sharing with other nations American preeminence in the development of atomic energy for peaceful purposes. On December 8, 1953, in an address before the United Nations, President Eisenhower appealed for a universal plan to control the destructive aspects of atomic energy and to promote everywhere its peaceful uses. Congress, in the Atomic Energy Act of 1954, authorized the United States to participate in an international program of this sort. The United States, unable to push its plan through the United Nations because of Soviet opposition, nevertheless in 1955 began to sign agreements with other nations in an effort to create an International Atomic Energy Agency. The Agency would be a clearing house for the exchange of technical information and the negotiation of cooperative arrangements.

INFORMATION PROGRAMS

The United States Information Agency (USIA) has the difficult task of assuring the recipients of American aid that the meaning of the aid is that American foreign policy is right and Soviet foreign policy is wrong. The USIA, of course, must do the same for the military and diplomatic opera-

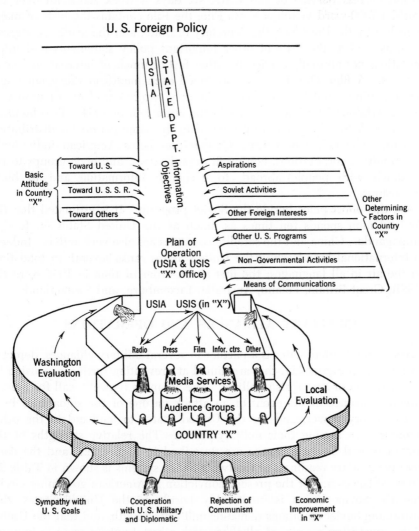

Figure 120. How United States Propaganda Is Developed.

tions of the United States. It is the grand American apologist among the peoples of the world. The elaborate apparatus for spreading the American point of view, as described in the last chapter, works according to a process that is diagrammed in Figure 120. Policy directives go into one end of the process, and, it is hoped, attitudes more favorable to the United States emerge from the other end.

The scope of the American propaganda operations is impressive. Though they change from time to time, some recent figures on the programs are worth mentioning. The Voice of America broadcasts daily in thirty-eight languages: Europe receives seventeen hours and thirty-five minutes of American broadcasts every day; the Far East, eight hours and five minutes; the Near East, Southern Asia, and Africa, four hours and a half; and South America, half an hour. The International Press Service of the USIA six days a week sends all over the world a 7000-word Wireless News File; the File contains the texts of major speeches by the President, the Secretary of State, and the leading congressmen, as well as the texts of other important policy statements and interpretations not normally carried by other fast channels of international news services. A film, *Our Times,* is produced each month in thirty languages for sixty-nine countries. The approximately two hundred information centers entertained 54 million visitors in the latter half of 1954. Two hundred eighty book translations were produced in the same period for distribution abroad. The Office of Private Cooperation helps American individuals, communities, corporations, non-profit organizations, and civic groups to get in touch with people abroad, to exchange information and to build friendships.

Yet this effort pales beside the Soviet program. It is estimated that the Soviet Union spends ten times as much as the United States on foreign propaganda. China and the satellite countries are also very active. Indeed, in international broadcasting the United States ranks seventh in total time on the air in all languages; the first six in order of time in 1954 were the USSR, Great Britain, Poland, Australia, Luxemburg, and Switzerland.

MILITARY ALLIANCES AND OPERATIONS

Today the United States is a partner in several military alliances, depicted in the map in Figure 121, that are aimed at preventing further expansion by Soviet Russia or any of its satellites. The alliances typically call for mutual armed assistance in the event of an attack on one of the signatories by a non-signatory power, and for the United States to lend aid to the other signatories in arming their military forces. The relative strengths of the American and Soviet alliances are described in Figure 122, and the comparative military readiness of the two alliance systems is shown in Table 26. These alliances mirror the present conviction in American governing circles that the Soviet Union is unalterably hostile to the United States, that restraining Soviet ambitions demands military strength, and that the United States must form a series of alliances with other countries so as to improve its position with respect to the Soviet Bloc. Too, these alliances demonstrate the belief that the United States could not survive if Soviet Russia were allowed to absorb all of the Eurasian continent. They mean that the United States has assumed military commitments all over the globe. Finally, they assure that the United States will have tremendous military budgets, and that the government will have a major role in the national economy.

The most important of the postwar alliances is the North Atlantic Treaty Organization (NATO), established by the North Atlantic Treaty of 1949. NATO includes fifteen countries in Europe and America, along the Atlantic Ocean and the Mediterranean Sea. The goal of this organization is to bar Soviet expansion into western Europe. It is administered by a North Atlantic Council, made up of the foreign ministers of the signatory powers; it also has a Council of Deputies and a number of boards and committees. Its principal military figure is the Supreme Allied Commander —Europe, a post that up to this time has always been filled by an American general.

NATO has been criticized on two grounds. The first is that the organization marks a reversion from universal collective security, as typified by the

TABLE 26. THE COMPARATIVE MILITARY READINESS OF THE UNITED STATES AND THE USSR, TOGETHER WITH THEIR ALLIES[1]

Manpower

	U.S.	USSR	NATO (except U.S.)	European Satellites	China & Satellites	TOTALS WEST	EAST
ARMY	1,300,000	2,500,000	2,300,000	1,200,000	3,500,000	3,600,000	7,200,000
AIR FORCE	960,000	800,000	400,000	90,000	80,000	1,360,000	970,000
NAVY	907,000	825,000	300,000	13,000	25,000	1,207,000	863,000
TOTALS	3,167,000	4,125,000	3,000,000	1,303,000	3,605,000	6,167,000	9,033,000

Air Forces. Combat Planes

	U.S.	USSR	NATO (except U.S.)	European Satellites	China & Satellites	TOTALS WEST	EAST
Interceptors	2,700	10,000	2,000	1,350	1,800	4,700	13,150
Fighters & Bombers	2,400	6,100	2,250	1,040	780	4,650	7,920
Strategic Bombers	1,700	1,600	None Committed	0	10	1,700	1,610
Transports	700	1,800	to NATO	110	220	700	2,130
TOTALS	7,500	19,500	4,250	2,500	2,810	11,750	24,810

Navies

	U.S.	USSR	NATO (except U.S.)	European Satellites	China & Satellites	TOTALS WEST	EAST
Battleships	15	3	9	0	0	24	3
Carriers	101	0	26	0	0	127	0
Cruisers & Destroyers	429	293	528	7	11	957	311
Submarines	200	375	132	7	0	332	382
TOTALS	745	671	695	14	11	1,440	696

[1] *Time*, May 9, 1955, p. 29.

Figure 121.   United States Collective Defense Arrangements.

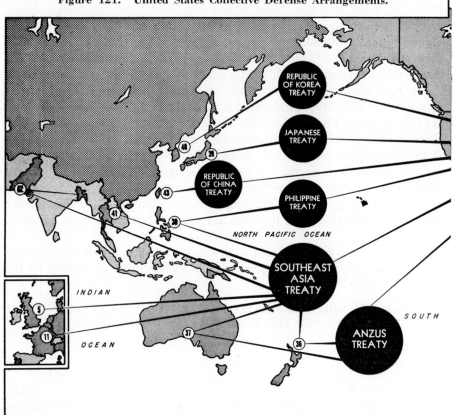

North Atlantic Treaty (15 Nations).   A treaty signed April 4, 1949, by which "the parties agree that an armed attack against one or more of them in Europe or North America shall be considered an attack against them all; and . . . each of them . . . will assist the . . . attacked by taking forthwith, individually and in concert with the other Parties, such action as it deems necessary including the use of armed force . . ."   1 United States; 2 Canada; 3 Iceland; 4 Norway; 5 United Kingdom; 6 Netherlands; 7 Denmark; 8 Belgium; 9 Luxembourg; 10 Portugal; 11 France; 12 Italy; 13 Greece; 14 Turkey; 15 Federal Republic of Germany.

Rio Treaty (21 Nations).   A treaty signed September 2, 1947, which provides that an armed attack against any American State "shall be considered as an attack against all the American States and . . . each one . . . undertakes to assist in meeting the attack . . ."   1 United States; 16 Mexico; 17 Cuba; 18 Haiti; 19 Dominican Republic; 20 Honduras; 21 Guatemala; 22 El Salvador; 23 Nicaragua; 24 Costa Rica; 25 Panama; 26 Colombia; 27 Venezuela; 28 Ecuador; 29 Peru; 30 Brazil; 31 Bolivia; 32 Paraguay; 33 Chile; 34 Argentina; 35 Uruguay.

Anzus (Australia–New Zealand–United States) Treaty (3 Nations).   A treaty signed September 1, 1951, whereby each of the parties "recognizes that an armed attack in the Pacific Area on any of the Parties would be dangerous to its own peace and safety and declares that it would act to meet the common danger in accordance with its constitutional processes."   1 United States; 36 New Zealand; 37 Australia.

Philippine Treaty (Bilateral).   A treaty signed August 30, 1951, by which the parties recognize "that an armed attack in the Pacific Area on either of the Parties would be dangerous to its own peace and safety" and each party agrees that it will act "to

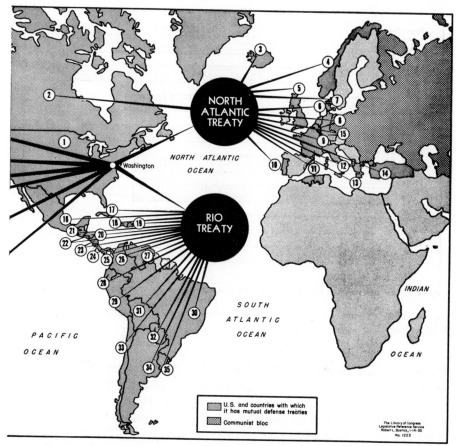

meet the common dangers in accordance with its constitutional processes." 1 United States; 38 Philippines.

Japanese Treaty (Bilateral). A treaty signed September 8, 1951, whereby Japan on a provisional basis requests, and the United States agrees, to "maintain certain of its armed forces in and about Japan . . . so as to deter armed attack upon Japan." 1 United States; 39 Japan.

Republic of Korea (South Korea) Treaty (Bilateral). A treaty signed October 1, 1953, whereby each party "recognizes that an armed attack in the Pacific area on either of the Parties . . . would be dangerous to its own peace and safety" and that each Party "would act to meet the common danger in accordance with its constitutional processes." 1 United States; 40 Republic of Korea.

Southeast Asia Treaty (8 Nations). A treaty signed September 8, 1954, whereby each Party "recognizes that aggression by means of armed attack in the treaty area against any of the Parties . . . would endanger its own peace and safety" and each will "in that event act to meet the common danger in accordance with its constitutional processes." 1 United States; 5 United Kingdom; 11 France; 36 New Zealand; 37 Australia; 38 Philippines; 41 Thailand; 42 Pakistan.

Republic of China (Formosa) Treaty (Bilateral). A treaty signed December 2, 1954, whereby each of the parties "recognizes that an armed attack in the West Pacific Area directed against the territories of either of the Parties would be dangerous to its own peace and safety," and that each "would act to meet the common danger in accordance with its constitutional processes." The territory of the Republic of China is defined as "Taiwan (Formosa) and the Pescadores." 1 United States; 43 Republic of China (Formosa).

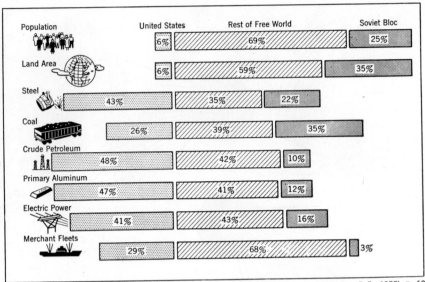

Mutual Security Administration, "The Mutual Security Program: Fiscal Year 1956" (Washington, D.C., 1955), p. 10

Figure 122. The Comparative Physical Strength of the United States and the USSR, Together with Their Allies.

United Nations, to a conventional sort of regional military alliance. The second criticism is that, because the Treaty contains the proviso that "The parties agree that an armed attack against one or more of them in Europe or North America shall be considered an attack against them all. . . ," it takes the power to declare war away from Congress. This criticism is of somewhat dubious validity, because the Treaty does not state what assistance the member countries should give to any nation that is attacked. The United States has also reached an agreement with the Spanish government whereby it maintains air bases in Spain.

The United States has negotiated alliances with several Asian countries. It has joined Australia and New Zealand to form ANZUS. It has military pacts with the Republic of the Philippines, the Republic of Korea, the Nationalist government of China, and Japan. It has contributed to the defense of South Viet Nam against the Indochinese Communists. Apart from these alliances, the United States in 1954 organized the South East Asia Treaty Organization (SEATO) for mutual defense against Communist aggression. Finally, as a co-signer of the Rio Pact of 1947, the United States has a military alliance with every nation in the Western Hemisphere.

Thus the United States has striven to make an unassailable bastion of the New World, and to girdle the Soviet Bloc with a series of military alliances. The only region in which the United States does not have such pacts is the Middle East, excepting that with Turkey. Pakistan has an agreement with the United States which is not, however, a military alliance; India and most of the Arab nations seem to favor a policy of neutrality.

PARTICIPATION IN INTERNATIONAL ORGANIZATIONS

The United States participates in many international organizations, which are devoted to a variety of tasks. Some of the bodies, such as the Universal Postal Union, are sheerly administrative; that is, they are not concerned with issues of political power. Others, such as the Committee of Control of the International Zone of Tangier, do deal with matters of political force. A number of these organizations are affiliated with the United Nations, although some, including the International Labor Organization, are older than the UN. Others, among them the Inter-American Defense Board, are limited to the Western Hemisphere. The United States may be fairly described as an enthusiastic member of these associations, and it works through a number of them to implement its foreign policy. The limitations of space forbid an extended description of the dozens of international groups that count the United States among their constituents; however, a few of the more important bodies merit particular note.

Regulatory agencies

Methods of transportation and communication have in a sense bound up the civilized world into a single community. Therefore most of the nations in this community have banded together to form agencies to regulate various kinds of activities that frequently cross international frontiers, to lessen the problems that may arise from differences in the same type of institutions situated in neighboring countries. For example, the International Civil Aviation Organization handles questions of international air traffic, promotes the adoption of safety practices and devices, supervises the operation of a fleet of weather-observation vessels in the Atlantic Ocean, and grants technical aid to retarded countries seeking to establish air routes. The International Monetary Fund is designed to stabilize the moneys of the world, to restrain member countries from inflating their currencies in an effort to encourage their export trade, and to simplify the international exchange of funds. The International Telecommunication Union drafts regulations for international telephone, telegraph, and radio services; perhaps its most important task today is the allocation of radio frequencies to broadcasters. The Universal Postal Union fixes rules for the handling of postal matter sent from one country to another, aiming especially at procuring uniform rates. Each of these bodies is an agency of the United Nations.

Promotional and welfare organizations

Just as the national government has undertaken many promotional and welfare functions on the domestic scene, so, too, the United States has joined a number of organizations dedicated to these tasks at the international level. This practice has been especially noticeable since the end of World War II, for the decade since the termination of hostilities has been marked by great American concern for the well-being of other peoples. The American government is a member of some organizations designed to improve the lot of the population in certain regions. For example, the United States, France, the Netherlands, and the United Kingdom, have formed a Caribbean Commission to elevate the living standards of the area about the Caribbean Sea; the United States has also joined with those countries, and with Australia and New Zealand as well, to establish a South Pacific Commission, to improve economic conditions in the islands of the South Pacific; finally, the United States is a member of the Pan American Sanitary Organization, to cope with problems of disease in the New World.

The United States also participates in promotional and welfare organizations that are world-wide in scope. It has joined the World Health Organization, which strives to conquer disease and emphasizes preventive medicine. It belongs to the World Meteorological Organization, which seeks to facilitate the international exchange of weather information. It is a member of the United Nations Educational, Scientific, and Cultural Organization (UNESCO), which aims at reducing international tensions and hostilities by international bartering of science, culture, and education. It has been the chief contributor to the funds of the International Bank for Reconstruction and Development, whose purposes have been to lend money for the rebuilding of economies ruined by World War II, and to make loans to technologically backward states that intend to erect new industrial facilities. It is associated with the International Labor Organization, which attempts to raise wage levels everywhere in the world. Finally, it has joined the Food and Agriculture Organization of the United Nations, which is devoted to raising levels of nutrition throughout the world. These activities typify an attitude that may be designated as "enlightened selfishness"; that is, the government appears to feel that its investments will be returned in future years in the shape of increased trade with the populations concerned. Of course, these activities also reflect the conviction among some political leaders that the alleviation of poverty is essential in order to succeed in the struggle with the Soviet Union.

Organization of American States

The Organization of American States (OAS), the successor to the Pan American Union, is a major international agency for the United States, since it in a fashion embodies one of the most important aspects of American foreign policy—the Monroe Doctrine. The OAS, a regional agency within the United Nations, comprises the twenty-one republics of the Americas. Its goal is to defend its members against outside attack. Its governing body is the Council, made up of one representative from each member nation; each nation has one vote. Its Secretariat, or administrative framework, is the Pan American Union. Among its other tasks, the OAS holds consultations regarding disputes between American countries, and is vigilant for any threat by a non-American power to an American republic. The OAS also contains several specialized agencies for managing such technical concerns as social, economic, legal, and cultural matters. The structure of the OAS, with each country having an equal voice in the Council, shows how the United States has discarded its former practices of "dollar diplomacy" and how it has concluded that it can hope for much more success in the conduct of its foreign policy if it treats the other American nations as its peers. At the same time the existence of the OAS demonstrates that American foreign policy emphasizes the protection of the Western Hemisphere.

United Nations

Structure: The United Nations is a political organization containing today eighty nations. Its principal aims are to preserve the peace and to furnish a body within which nations may cooperate in finding solutions for political, social, economic, and cultural problems. Created in 1945, the United Nations is situated on Manhattan Island, in a skyscraper reared close to the East River. Here the UN exercises certain sovereign powers, such as the issuance of stamps and the control of its own police; moreover, delegates to the UN possess diplomatic immunity. The framework of the UN is set forth in its Charter, drafted in San Francisco in 1945, which amounts to the constitution of the United Nations. This Charter provides for six major bodies and many subsidiary units, as shown in Figure 123.

1. GENERAL ASSEMBLY. The General Assembly may be termed the legislature of the United Nations. Each member country may send delegates to the General Assembly, and each country has a single vote. The Assembly names many of the other officers of the United Nations. It also keeps a watchful eye upon international politics, and brings situations that menace peace to the attention of the Security Council. It enacts the budget of the United Nations and apportions the expenses among the members. Ordinarily the Assembly meets every year; it may also be called into special session.

2. SECURITY COUNCIL. The Security Council performs the functions of a special legislature devoted to problems of peace and war. It has eleven members, each from a different country. Five of the seats are assigned permanently to the so-called "Big Five"—the United States, Great Britain, the Soviet Union, France, and China. The General Assembly elects the other six members of the Council, choosing three annually to hold office for two years. The function of the Council is to "act on behalf of the members of the United Nations in the maintenance of international peace and security." In the event of international disputes the Council is authorized by the Charter to take appropriate steps to avoid the outbreak of hostilities. In any situation calling for substantive action, at least seven members of the Council must cast affirmative votes for the action, including all five permanent members. The Council is in permanent session.

3. ECONOMIC AND SOCIAL COUNCIL. The Economic and Social Council (ECOSOC) is the principal welfare agency of the United Nations. It consists of eighteen members elected by the General Assembly for three-year terms. It is designed to investigate economic and social conditions that the United Nations may improve, and to draw up studies recommending possible improvements.

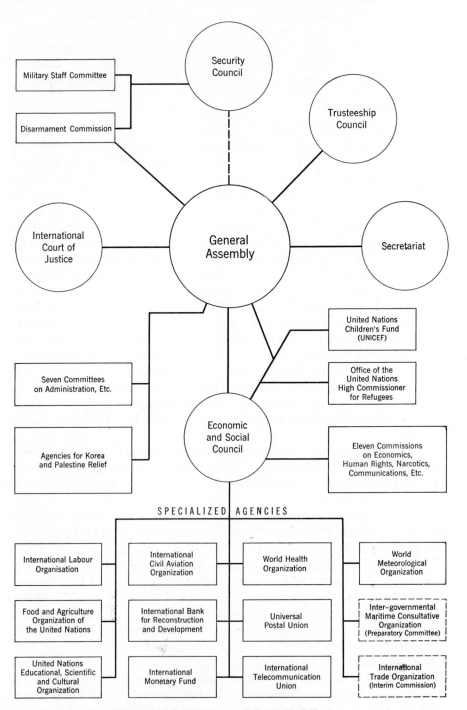

Figure 123.   Structure of the United Nations.

4. TRUSTEESHIP COUNCIL. The Trusteeship Council supervises the administration of the former colonial areas that have been placed under the International Trusteeship System. Under this arrangement, these territories are assigned to a specific country for administrative purposes; the administering government can be held responsible for its governmental practices. The areas presently under this system include mandated regions (colonies of defeated World War I powers, notably Germany and Turkey, that were assigned to the victorious nations but were under League of Nations supervision) and the territories taken from the powers defeated in World War II; provision has been made for administering colonies whose proprietors have placed them under this system, but no country has so far done so. The Council is made up of all nations that administer trust territories, and an equal number of nations that do not administer any territories; each of the Big Five must be represented on the Council. The General Assembly elects the non-administering powers. On July 1, 1956, the Council had twelve members; the administering countries were Australia, Belgium, France, New Zealand, Great Britain, and the United States.

5. THE INTERNATIONAL COURT OF JUSTICE. The International Court of Justice is the chief judicial body of the United Nations. Only governments may bring cases before the Court. All members of the United Nations are by the fact of membership authorized to appear in the Court; other countries may be admitted according to conditions set by the General Assembly. The Court is made up of a President, a Vice President, and fifteen justices chosen by the General Assembly and the Security Council, voting separately, for nine-year terms. No two justices may come from the same country. The Court handles disputes arising out of provisions of the United Nations Charter and the Statute appended to the Charter. For example, the Court will decide cases in which a treaty between nations seems to be in conflict with the Charter, which is declared to be supreme over other treaties. Like some American State courts, but unlike the federal Supreme Court, the International Court may also render advisory decisions. Its decisions are final, and binding when a case is one that a country has submitted to its jurisdiction; in the event any government fails to comply with the terms of a decision, the Court may ask the Security Council to take steps that will force compliance.

6. SECRETARIAT. The Secretariat is the administrative office of the United Nations. It consists of the Secretary General, who is appointed by the General Assembly on the recommendation of the Security Council, and whatever additional staff may be necessary. Members of the Secretariat are to comport themselves as officials of an international organization; they are not to abide by counsel given them by any sovereign government, nor are the member states to attempt to influence personnel of the Secretariat. The functions of the Secretary General are to prepare an annual report on the activities of the United Nations, for the use of the General Assembly, to draw the attention of the Security Council to any disputes among nations that imperil world peace, and to direct the operations of the Secretariat.

Activities: The United Nations has had an important role in the resolution of numerous world problems. It supported South Korea when that country was invaded by the North Koreans. It condemned Communist China as an aggressor when that country sent its troops into the Korean War. It has not admitted Communist China to membership in place of Nationalist China. In 1946 the UN helped bring pressure on the USSR to withdraw its troops from Iran. It aided the Israeli and the Arabs to sign a truce after bloody warfare over the possession of Palestine. It helped the United States and the Soviet Union to solve their dispute respecting the so-called Berlin blockade of 1948–1949. It contributed to preventing a war between India and Pakistan over Kashmir, which each claimed for its own. It has actively sought some type of international control of atomic energy. It sent an international police force into Egypt in 1956.

Apart from these endeavors in behalf of world peace, the United Nations has engaged in many efforts at achieving higher standards of welfare throughout the world. It has helped underdeveloped nations with technical assistance and information services. It has provided food and supplies to millions of refugees in Europe, Palestine, Korea, and elsewhere. It has resettled hundreds of thousands of displaced persons in new homes. It has given milk, medicine, and other care to millions of children in devastated areas. It has investigated and published reports on the atrocities of the communists in Korea and the practice of the USSR in using the slave labor of millions of people. It has been active in investigating and in fostering legislation for the control of the world commerce in narcotics. In general it has provided a world forum in which all nations could express their needs, likes, and dislikes, and could debate issues with each other.

The United Nations has been unable to accomplish some things that were predicted for it, such as becoming a federal union of the world. The creation of an effective world political organization presents almost insuperable difficulties. It is naive to draw a parallel between the thirteen American States after 1783 and the powers of the world today. Although there were important differences among the American States, their populations did speak the same tongue, shared a common legal system, had just finished a war against a common enemy, and were confronted by the possibility of attack from that enemy. More important than anything else, there was a group of respected leaders from all the States who worked together by spending money, agitating, propagandizing, and organizing, to unite the country. They would be imprisoned or executed for such activities in half the nations of the world today. Moreover, today there is not such an accomplished group of leaders who can work independently in world politics or who can work to the end of world organization without violating oaths of office.

By contrast, the modern world powers have enormous differences among themselves. They have not had the unifying experience of fighting the same enemy. It is frequently proclaimed that modern nations should unite against war, or poverty, or famine; however, the fact is that countries do not band together solely in opposition to such abstractions. Peoples today speak a multitude of languages, and have conflicting theories of government. Leaders and peoples subsist from day to day on local resources and give only academic attention to the rest of the world. To match the power and qualities of the Founding Fathers, there would have to be a conclave of men such as Nikita Khrushchev, Chou En-lai, Dwight Eisenhower, Sir Anthony Eden, Pandit Jawaharlal Nehru, Pope Pius XII, and others equally powerful and respected, conspiring and working together for a world government based on principles to which all adhered.

Most countries do not acknowledge, or are completely ignorant of, the rule of law, whose preservation was a leading cause for the writing of the present American Constitution. Perhaps only a slow acceptance of the rule of law by the other countries of the world, and a decrease in the blind submission to the doctrines of inevitable conflict that form part of the communist ideology, might ease the birth of a working international organization. The success of the American way of government may hasten the acceptance of the rule of law everywhere.

QUESTIONS AND PROBLEMS

1. How would the United States recognize Communist China should it desire to do so? What would be the practical consequences of such a recognition? Why does the United States refuse to do so?

2. How are treaties negotiated and approved?

3. Why have executive agreements grown in number in recent years?

4. Describe the work of American Foreign Service officers.

5. Compare American expenditures for diplomacy, economic aid, propaganda, military operations, and international organizations.

6. What foreign operations would you expand next year should you wish to bring greater success to American foreign policies?

7. How can propaganda operations contribute to the success of diplomatic, military, and economic activities?

8. Describe the world-wide system of American alliances.

9. Describe the structure of the United Nations, and the functions it performs.

State and Local Government

PART XIII

Foundations of State and Local Government

A CCORDING to the Bureau of the Census, in 1952 there were 116,743 governmental units in the United States. This figure was 38,000, or almost twenty-five per cent, lower than the comparable figure of ten years before. These units fall into seven broad classes. There are, of course, the national government and the State governments. There are also the chief units of rural government: the counties, and the smaller, usually rural, areas known as towns or townships. There are urban regions organized as municipalities. There are governmental units for education—the school districts. Finally, there are many so-called special districts, which are political entities that have been established usually for the conduct of a single task such as water supply, sewage disposal, mosquito abatement, or park management. The Bureau of the Census has enumerated these classes as shown in Table 27.

The most noteworthy change in this enumeration has been the disappearance of more than 40,000 school districts, which have been consolidated with other districts or absorbed as administrative agencies in county or city governments. During this period, for example, in Illinois alone almost 9,000 districts vanished, the total falling from 12,138 to 3,484. On the other hand, it is also significant that the number of special districts has mounted by nearly fifty per cent.

These units are distributed very irregularly throughout the nation; their numbers do not seem to have any predictable connection with either population or area. For instance, for each county in the United States there are about thirty-seven political units of the various lesser types. However, in Minnesota there are 104 such units per county, whereas in Virginia there are but three. The county with the greatest number of local governments is Cook (Chicago), with 422; the county with the second greatest number is Otter Tail, in Minnesota, with 334. According to the 1950 Census, Cook County was the most populous in the nation, with 4,508,792 people; Otter Tail was just about average, with 51,320. Fourteen other counties, all but three of them in either Wisconsin, Minnesota, or Nebraska, each have more than 200 governing units apiece. Yet New York City, embracing eight million people in the area once occupied by five counties, has only two governmental units.

TABLE 27. NUMBER OF GOVERNMENT UNITS IN THE UNITED STATES

	Number of Units		Per Cent Change
Type	**1952**	**1942**	**1942–1952**
All types	116,743	155,116	−24.7
U.S. Government	1	1	0.0
States	48	48	0.0
Counties	3,049	3,050	less than 0.5
Municipalities	16,778	16,220	3.4
Townships	17,202	18,919	−9.1
School districts	67,346	108,579	−38.0
Special districts	12,319	8,299	48.4

The boundaries of the various units of government in the United States have a bewildering complexity. One noteworthy trait is that these boundaries may be drawn by any one of several agencies, depending both upon the type of the unit and upon its location. The boundaries of the States admitted after 1789 were set out by the combined action of the residents of the States concerned and the United States Congress. County lines are set forth by the State governments, either through constitutional provision or by legislative enactment. City limits may be fixed by any one of several authorities, depending upon the State in which the city is located. Township lines are determined by State or county governments. The boundaries of school districts and of special districts are also established by the State governments.

Another aspect of the boundaries of local governments is that most of them are not "rational." That is, they do not usually correspond with

1313 East 60th Street, Chicago. The home, since 1938, of numerous national associations interested in government and public administration, the oldest of which, the American Public Works Association, was formed in 1894, and the youngest of which, the Interstate Clearing House on Mental Health, was established in 1953. Other groups located here are the Council of State Governments (1933), the International City Managers Association (1914), and the American Municipal Association (1924).

any social, economic, or geographic entity. For example, the southern boundaries of Ohio, Indiana, and Illinois follow the Ohio River; yet the Ohio River more nearly unites than separates the southern portion of those States with Kentucky, for the entire Ohio River valley is a "natural" economic region. Many boundaries of most types of local governing units are quite artificial; even the boundaries of the typical American city, which is often judged to be the most nearly "natural" political unit in the country, does not include all the people or territory directly associated with the city.

CREATION OF STATE AND LOCAL GOVERNMENTS

The State governments and the different types of local governments are created by a variety of means.

State governments

The creation of State governments has been partly dealt with in a previous chapter, with respect to the admission of new States. To recapitulate and point up this discussion, essentially the government of a State is created by, and receives all its powers from, the citizens of the State. That is, in doctrine, at least, representatives of the citizens meeting in convention draft a proposed constitution for the State in which they establish the organs of government and allocate powers among these organs. Furthermore, according to this doctrine, the role of the national government is limited to approving the new constitution and admitting the State to the Union. Finally, the

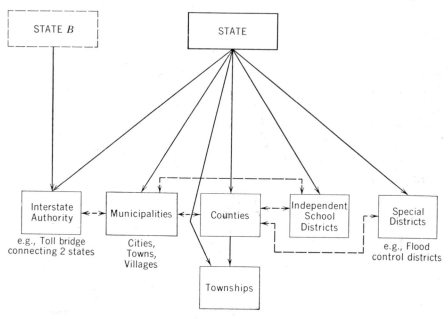

Figure 124. The State's Control over Local Governments. (A common pattern.)

citizens of the State give the State government all the powers it has, and they may give it any power not prohibited to the States by the federal Constitution.

The State is at the head of a number of different governments. Whereas the federal government stands alone, having, save for the District of Columbia and the territories, only administrative districts to manage, the State governments command a galaxy of satellite units. A simple diagram, as in Figure 124, may help remind one of the State in its capacity as a peak government. It will be noticed that none of these subordinate units of the State is superior to other units. For instance, the State rules the city and the county, but the county does not rule the city, nor does the city rule the county.

Municipal governments

All municipal governments formally are created by States. However, the establishment of a municipal government is frequently initiated by the residents of a densely populated area. A settled community actually becomes a city, town, borough, or village, with a municipal government, when it receives a charter. The charter is either drafted and enacted by the State legislature or drafted by the people of the community and approved by the State legislature. This charter enumerates the powers of the municipal government; in this respect it is a sort of constitution for the municipality. The charter also transforms the community into what is known as a "municipal corporation." That is, the municipal government becomes a legal personality, whose officers in its name can negotiate contracts, provide services, incur debts, and sue and be sued in court. A municipal charter, unlike the charter of a private corporation, is not a contract; hence a State may amend or even abolish a municipal charter as it wills.

Other local governments

The other local governments, whose chief forms are counties, townships, school districts, and special districts, have been created by the State. These governments have a fundamental difference from the governments of municipalities: they are not corporations, but "quasi-corporations" or "quasi-municipal corporations." As such, these governments are empowered to carry out many functions similar to those of municipalities, the range of their powers varying from one State to another and from one form of local government to another. However, these local governments with rare exceptions, such as the chartered counties of California, do not have charters; that is, their powers are not set forth in a single document. Rather, these governments obtain their authority from any number of general laws that the State legislature may have enacted to deal with them.

TYPES OF FUNCTIONS

The thousands of units of State and local governments of America perform a host of functions. Many of the functions are of the same character as those of the national government. For instance, the federal, State, county, and city governments all have an interest in the control of narcotics and liquor. They all are engaged in the planning and promotion of highways. All of them carry out measures to protect public health. They all own and manage parks and recreation areas. They all have some role to play in the general field of education. They all maintain libraries.

Yet even when they perform the same general type of activity, the different levels of government usually emphasize special areas of concern. Thus the federal government gives money for the building of roads, but almost all roads are actually built by the State and local governments. Also, the national and State governments manage penitentiaries, and the counties and cities operate jails. Generally speaking, the federal government does research in education, the States and some localities maintain colleges, and the local governments are in charge of elementary and secondary schools.

Moreover, a few out of the several hundreds of activities are almost the exclusive domain of one level of government: the federal government conducts foreign relations; the States regulate insurance rates; cities and special districts operate water works, public markets, and ports and harbors. For most functions, there exist parallel efforts on two or more levels of government, with considerable overlapping and numerous jurisdictional struggles. The mere fact that two overlapping governments are interested in the same kind of problem does not, in itself, demonstrate a wasteful or wrongful condition. The doctrine of federalism indeed justifies numerous parallel functions on the ground that local autonomy produces greater interest, initiative, diversity, and efficiency. The doctrine of local autonomy accords the same merits to many of the functions shared by States and localities.

INTERGOVERNMENTAL RELATIONS

Since there are several types of government in the United States, there are several possible sets of interrelations among them. Among these various sets, perhaps the two most important, and certainly the most contrasting, are national-State and State-local. The relations between the national and the State governments, which have already been discussed at length in Chapter 8, provide the essence of federalism. State-local interrelations are utterly different. A State government, like that of Great Britain or France, is a unitary government, in which all the authority of the local governing units legally stems from the central State authority. In other words, local governments exist because of the State to carry out tasks assigned to them by the State. This principle must be borne in mind throughout the remaining chapters of this text; it accounts for the logic of allocating a distinct section to treating the functions of the national government, and another section for treating State and local functions.

National-local relations

The most important among the national-local relations are those involving cities. The first sort of relation between the national government and the cities was one in which the national government simply lent or even gave funds to the cities for the purpose of relief, to be given those suffering unemployment or to lessen the hardships of the unemployable and the aged. Shortly thereafter, the national government enacted legislation whereby municipalities whose debts far exceeded their ability to repay them might plead bankruptcy in federal court; means were provided by which creditors might be satisfied to the best of the capacities of the cities. Both the Reconstruction Finance Corporation and its successor, the Small Business Administration, have been authorized to lend money to financially embarrassed local governments. Certain New Deal agencies, notably the Works Progress Administration and the Public Works Administration, reduced the burden of local public relief by supplying work for the unemployed and also gave many communities new streets and federal buildings. Even today the government is encouraged to place contracts when possible in communities with a labor surplus.

State-local relations

The most important State-local relations are those between the State and the municipal governments, if only because municipalities perform more services than any other type of local governing unit. Hence what follows is concerned principally with the relations between States and cities; some of it, however, is relevant also to counties, townships, school districts, and special districts. The problem is fundamentally that of State control over these units. States have three means for exercising this control: legislative, judicial, and administrative.

Legislative Controls: The legislative controls that State governments have over localities are perhaps most apparent with respect to the creation of the local governing units. However, they also have a part in the continued management of these units for State purposes.

With respect to the *counties* and their subdivisions, the State constitution and laws set up the counties, give them their organization and powers, and delegate to them many different administrative tasks. Thus, education, road building and maintenance, tax collection, police and fire protection, are in large part and in many States turned over to these subordinate divisions of the State. At the same time, it should be realized that the strong localism in American politics encourages the development of political power in the counties. Hence, the State government is often run by coalitions of politicians from various county strongholds.

So far as *cities* are concerned, these controls appear in the various means whereby the charter of the city is first granted, and is then amended. There are five of these means: special law, general law, classification, optional charter system, and home rule. Most States employ a combination of two or more of these means.

Under the *special law system,* the charter of each city is both granted and amended by single, particular acts of the State legislature. In certain regards, this is an admirable system, since it can offer each city a charter suited to its needs and peculiarities. However, it also means that State legislators must devote a great deal of time to affairs of local government, and that they may be the targets of great pressure from the representatives of the various cities seeking either some amendment to their charter that will be advantageous to them or some amendment to the charter of a neighboring city that will be disadvantageous to that city.

Under the *general law system*, State law provides a single form of charter that is granted to all cities in the State. Such a system does away with some of the abuses of the special law method, but it compels every city regardless of local requirements to function under the same governmental form.

In the *classification system*, which is a modification of the general law system, the cities of the State are divided into classes, usually on the basis of population; each class is then assigned its own type of charter. Classification may be carried to such lengths that it results in special legislation. For instance, each county in California occupies a separate class, so that legislation enacted for one given class affects only one county. Under this method, at least, a large city need not suffocate in the toils of a charter best adapted to a small community, and a small city need not stagger under the burden of a vast administrative system fit only for a metropolis. At the same time the classification system does allow legislators to penalize individual communities at their whim by placing them alone in a class.

Under the *optional charter system*, another modification of the general law system, the State offers any community seeking a charter its choice among two or more forms. The actual choice may be determined either by vote or by petition by the inhabitants, or by a decision of the municipal council—if the community already has a government. Under the optional charter system, then, the people of the community either directly or indirectly have some part in selecting the type of government they shall have.

In the *home rule system*, legislative control is reduced to a somewhat lower level, for in the States where home rule exists the residents of cities are empowered to draft their own charters for the governing of local affairs. Home rule may be granted in either one of two ways. In twenty-one States it is extended by the State constitution; most of these States are west of the Appalachians, and they include the majority of the great population centers —New York, Pennsylvania, Ohio, Michigan, Texas, and California. In eight other States, five of them south of the Ohio and east of the Mississippi, home rule is permitted by State legislation.

The process of adopting a home rule charter has a roughly similar pattern wherever it prevails. First, the citizens must choose a commission to draft the charter. Once the charter is drafted it is submitted to the people for approval, usually by simple majority vote. In most of the States the charter may now take effect. However, in a handful of States, it must also secure approval by some officer or organ of the State government; for instance, in California it must be adopted in a concurrent resolution by both houses of the legislature. Later amendments to the charter generally are drafted and ratified by the municipal government and the citizens; again, in California these amendments must win approval by the State legislature.

The effects of home rule have been rather important in certain areas of municipal government, and negligible in others. So far as their actual form of government is concerned, and the regulation of unquestionably local affairs, home rule cities do enjoy greater independence than those under immediate State legislative control. On the other hand, with respect to any matters in which the State may claim an interest, such as police protection, urban finances, or the management of schools, home rule cities do not appear to have much more freedom than cities without home rule.

Judicial Controls: The judicial controls of the States over local governments, particularly cities, fall into two important areas: (1) decisions as to whether a city government or an officer of a city government has committed some act that is *ultra vires,* or beyond its or his authority to commit; and (2) decisions as to whether a city government may be held financially responsible for alleged damages to a private individual or organization. Decisions as to the extent of municipal authority usually rest on the contents of the municipal charter; what is crucial is that courts have denied any "inherent" rights of municipal self-government. Decisions as to municipal responsibility generally rest upon the type of service that inflicted the alleged damages. If the service was one such as the fire department—where damages resulted when a private automobile was struck by a fire engine going to put out a fire—which is a service that the city carries out for the State, courts generally hold the city to be not responsible. However, if the service was one such as a municipally owned bus line—where damages resulted when a private automobile was struck by a bus—courts are apt to assess damages upon the city itself, since this service is one that might be performed by a private corporation.

Administrative Controls: Administrative controls of the State over local governments have become increasingly widespread in late years. This process resembles the growth of administrative mechanisms and techniques in the national government. However, the American States are still far from the arrangement in France, where the Ministry of the Interior directly supervises the majority of local government undertakings. By contrast, in the American States the typical administrative bond is between a specific State administrative office and its parallel on the local level. A few States, especially New Jersey with its Division of Local Government in the State Department of Finance and Taxation, are attempting to establish machinery for wider administrative controls, and more offices of this sort may be created in the future.

States have various means for implementing their control. They may simply require periodic reports from the local agencies and supply information and advice based upon these reports. They may give various sorts of technical aid to local authorities. States have several more or less coercive devices at their disposal. They may issue orders to local officers; depose local officers; refuse permits for certain types of activity; or withhold grants-in-aid. This last device is a principal weapon in the arsenals of the States today, because a very large proportion of the budget of the State may be devoted to subventions for school districts; by threatening to withhold a grant, the State office of education may force local school authorities to comply with State requirements even though the residents of the districts concerned may oppose the demands of the State.

Local government interrelations

Local governments of the various types have significant relations with each other. It must be stressed from the outset that local government interrelations are different from any of the other intergovernmental relations discussed above, for local governments within one State are more or less legal equals of each other—all being subordinate to the State—and local governments do not claim to possess sovereignty.

The most common sort of interrelation between or among local governments occurs where they occupy either the same or adjacent territory. For example, a county may share in the assessment of property values in cities within the county. The core city of a metropolitan district may provide some services for neighboring small municipalities and for the residents of the unincorporated rural zone. A county and its principal city may unite to erect and maintain a joint city-county public office building. Counties, cities, and school and special districts may either compete or cooperate in obtaining finances for their operations. At the same time, school and special districts look to either cities or counties, or both, to furnish them with such services as police and fire protection. Actually, since there are more than 100,000 units of local government in the United States, the total of possible interrelations is astronomical. However, the numbers of such interrelations that exist today, aiming at improving governmental services for the public, is but a minute fraction of the potential number of such combinations. Public apathy, lack of imagination or energy on the part of public officials, and groups with vested interests, contribute to forestalling the creation of innumerable other interrelations.

QUESTIONS AND PROBLEMS

1. What types of government changed in number between 1942 and 1952? How do you account for these changes?

2. What authority determines the boundaries of the different types of governments in America?

3. In what respects may it be said that urban Americans do not live within "rational" boundaries of government?

4. What is the extent of national-local relations? Explain why this situation persists?

5. What controls does the state legislature exercise over local governments?

6. In what ways do the courts restrict local governments?

7. What kinds of administrative control over local government have developed?

8. Do local governments sometimes cooperate voluntarily? Cite an example.

9. Supposing one wanted to save money and simplify the units of government so that an ordinary citizen might be less confused, what units would you recommend be kept or abolished?

10. With the aid of an encyclopedia, find the number of governments which the citizens of any foreign nation are governed by. What do you think would be the political and administrative consequences of the greater or lesser number?

IN EVERY State there is a written constitution as the formal basis for the State government. Each State constitution establishes certain organs of government for the State, vests these organs with their powers, and denies either these organs or the entire State government certain other powers. Like the federal Constitution, these written constitutions of the States do not comprise an entire "constitution" or fundamental law. That is, in addition to its documentary constitution each State government rests upon legislative enactments, executive decrees, judicial rulings, and custom and habit. There are often great differences between the constitution of one State and that of another. However, upon close inspection many of these differences turn out to be superficial. The fact is that in their principal elements, State constitutions are all similar to one another; indeed, the authors of State constitutions have not hesitated to copy each other's work.

GENERAL NATURE OF STATE CONSTITUTIONS

The powers of State governments

The general nature of State constitutions is based upon the type of powers that State governments possess and exercise. It should be remembered that according to the Tenth Amendment to the federal Constitution, "The powers not delegated to the United States by the Constitution, nor prohibited by it to the States, are reserved to the States respectively, or to the people." In other words, the federal government has only the powers specifically given it by the federal Constitution; the States and the people have all other powers. At many times and in many places this statement has been interpreted to mean that State governments possess all powers not denied them by either the federal Constitution or their own constitution. Consequently a substantial portion of a State constitution is negative, denying the State government certain powers.

Length of State constitutions

State constitutions are quite long. The shortest of all, that of Vermont, contains 8,419 words, about 2,000 more than the federal Constitution. The longest, that of Louisiana, has 184,053 words. The average of the forty-eight present constitutions is about 27,000 words, or four times as many as the federal text. It is notable that the recent constitutions tend to be longer than those written a century ago; Figure 125 shows how the length of modern State constitutions surpasses that of those a hundred years old and more. However, the New Jersey constitution, written in 1947, has but 12,500 words.

There are several causes underlying the length of State constitutions. One is the increased number of services that States have been called upon to render. In the main, these are the services that the State carries out under its police power. Another cause is that influential citizens often lack confidence in their legislatures. In principle, at least, the legislature is the ultimate repository of the reserved powers of the State; more than any other branch of the State government, it has been the one that seemed to need restraint. Too, many State legislatures have shown themselves easily corrupted or readily managed by a pressure group for the satisfaction of the particular ends of the group. Therefore, certain types of legislative activity have been banned. Also, the constitutions frequently give precise form and function to many of the administrative agencies of the State, so that the legislature—which under ordinary circumstances would create these agencies—is deprived of the power of overseeing the administration of the laws that it enacts. A final cause for the length of State constitutions is the wish of some interests to guarantee that some portion of the State government

The Capitol Building, Madison, Wisconsin. An example of traditional capitol design, much like the national Capitol in style and mood.

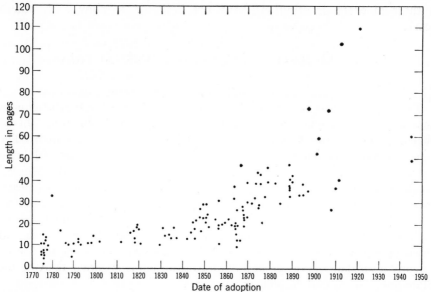

Alfred de Grazia, "State Constitutions—Are They Growing Longer?", State Government, April, 1954, p. 82

Figure 125. Increasing Length of State Constitutions. The relation between the length and date of adoption of all American State constitutions. The unit of length was set at the approximate page size in Francis N. Thorpe's collection, *The Federal and State Constitutions* . . . , Washington, 1909. (Each dot represents the date of adoption and the length of a single state's constitution.)

shall have a certain specified power. These interests take such steps as precautions against a possible ruling by a State court that the silence of the constitution regarding a power in effect denies it to the government.

THE CONTENTS OF STATE CONSTITUTIONS

State constitutions so differ from one another in particular matters that any detailed treatment of them would be far longer than necessary for this text. However, these constitutions resemble each other sufficiently in general outline that their contents may be summarized in a brief discussion. Nonetheless, it should be borne in mind that what is being described is a typical constitution, not any particular one, and that some of the following statements, although true for most State constitutions, are not true for every one.

Preamble

A State constitution usually opens with a preamble, which is a brief doctrinal foreword setting forth the presumed reasons for which the constitution was drafted and adopted, and including some mention of the Supreme Being.

Protections of rights

Every State constitution possesses a "bill of rights" or "declaration of rights." Such protections of rights have appeared necessary in spite of the federal Bill of Rights, for there are many ways in which a State may abuse its powers against which the federal Bill of Rights offers no protection. The State bills and declarations provide about the same guarantees against State governments as the federal Bill of Rights provides against federal authorities. They protect such political rights as the freedom of religion, freedom of speech and the press, and freedom of assembly. State constitutions also assure a number of protections to persons charged with a crime, such as a guarantee of a speedy and public trial before an impartial jury, a ban on *ex post facto* laws, and a prohibition on cruel and unusual punishments. Finally, State constitutions guarantee property rights by insisting on due compensation in the exercise of eminent domain and by forbidding that any person be deprived of property without due process of law. It may be noted that some States in their catalogues of protections include material that is not law but doctrine; that is, it is no more enforceable in a court than the Preamble to the federal Constitution is. For example, according to the Constitution of Maryland (Article I): "That all government of right originates from the people, is founded in compact only, and instituted solely for the good of the whole; and they have, at all times, the inalienable right to alter, reform or abolish their form of Government in such manner as they may deem expedient."

Suffrage and elections

State constitutions have considerable portions dealing with the suffrage and elections. They specify the various qualifications for the electorate, including such matters as age, residence, and citizenship. They also arrange for all sorts of elections, going so far as to set the dates for particular elections and to establish the local administrative machinery for the balloting.

Organs of government

State constitutions provide for the organs of the State government. First among these organs is the legislature; the constitution may detail the characteristics of the legislature, including not only the qualifications and terms of the members but also their salaries and the boundaries of their districts. Next, the constitution sets forth the office of the Governor, his qualifications and term of office, and sometimes his salary. It also, at this point or some other, may create the other executive offices of the State, such as the attorney general and the secretary of state, arranging for their selection and terms of office. Finally, the constitution sets up the judiciary, with its qualifications, terms of office, and means of selection. Together with the clauses establishing these organs of government, the constitution may contain other provisions endowing them with some of their powers.

Local government

State constitutions include considerable portions devoted to the establishment and regulation of the various types of local government, since the State exercises many of its powers with these governments as its agencies. This section may be very detailed, containing such specific matters as the boundaries of the individual counties and the definitions of the classes into which cities and counties will fall. This section moreover is apt to include whatever grants of constitutional home rule that the cities and counties of the State enjoy.

Taxation and debt

The State constitutions set forth the power of the State government to levy taxes and to incur debt. Sometimes the constitution forbids the State to levy certain types of taxes, and to incur a debt beyond a specified sum of money.

Powers of government

The largest part of the State constitution is devoted to an enumeration of the general powers of the State government. Often this enumeration is found partially in the section on the organs of State government and partially in a rather disorganized group of sections that deal solely with powers. At one point or the other, the constitution gives the State its vast powers over the welfare of the citizens, including such matters as public education; public health; assistance for dependent children, the blind, and the aged; the prevention and punishment of crime, along with the State prison and correctional system; and similar functions.

The constitution also empowers the State to regulate labor, with respect to such questions as the hours of work; the supervision of working conditions in mines and factories; and compensation for unemployment, industrial injuries, and illness. Another section deals with agriculture and the conservation of natural resources. One of the weightiest sections gives the State its controls over business; it deals with the chartering of private corporations and the restrictions upon both corporations chartered in the State and those chartered elsewhere. A related passage governs such State aids for business and the general population as public highways and other State enterprises. Finally, the constitution grants the State certain military powers.

AMENDMENT AND REVISION

A final portion of the State constitution provides means for amending and revising it. This part of the constitution, along with its effects upon the document and its connection with the whole political process, are so important that their discussion is reserved for a separate heading in this chapter. Like the federal Constitution, State constitutions evolve through both formal and informal means. There are three formal methods usually appearing in State constitutions whereby the constitution may be amended or revised: (1) legislative proposal; (2) popular initiative; and (3) constitutional convention. There is moreover a fourth formal means that is not specifically authorized by any State constitution but that has always been accepted by the courts: constitutional commission. Usually the first two of these methods are held to result in *amendment*, and the third and fourth in *revision*. Table 28 shows what methods the constitution in each State provides.

TABLE 28.   WAYS PROVIDED BY STATE CONSTITUTIONS FOR THEIR AMENDMENT AND REVISION[1]

State	Legislative Proposal	Popular Initiative	Constitutional Convention
Alabama	X	—	X
Arizona	X	X	X
Arkansas	X	X	—
California	X	X	X
Colorado	X	X	X
Connecticut	X	—	—
Delaware	X	—	X
Florida	X	—	X
Georgia	X	—	X
Idaho	X	—	X
Illinois	X	—	X
Indiana	X	—	—
Iowa	X	—	X
Kansas	X	—	X
Kentucky	X	—	X
Louisiana	X	—	—
Maine	X	—	X
Maryland	X	—	X
Massachusetts	X	X	—
Michigan	X	X	X
Minnesota	X	—	X
Mississippi	X	—	—
Missouri	X	X	X
Montana	X	—	X
Nebraska	X	X	X
Nevada	X	X	X
New Hampshire	—	—	X
New Jersey	X	—	—
New Mexico	X	—	X
New York	X	—	X
North Carolina	X	—	X
North Dakota	X	X	—
Ohio	X	X	X
Oklahoma	X	X	X
Oregon	X	X	X
Pennsylvania	X	—	—
Rhode Island	X	—	—
South Carolina	X	—	X
South Dakota	X	—	X
Tennessee	X	—	X
Texas	X	—	—
Utah	X	—	X
Vermont	X	—	—
Virginia	X	—	X
Washington	X	—	X
West Virginia	X	—	X
Wisconsin	X	—	X
Wyoming	X	—	X

[1] Adapted from Albert L. Sturm, *Methods of State Constitutional Reforms* (Ann Arbor: University of Michigan Press, 1954), p. 20.

Legislative proposal

Amendment by legislative proposal is inaugurated by the State legislature, which proposes an amendment to the constitution. This way of initiating constitutional amendment exists in every State save New Hampshire, where the constitution may be amended only through a convention. Ordinarily, the legislative proposal must be submitted to the people for their approval; only in Delaware may the legislature alone amend the constitution. Generally the legislature must adopt the proposal by a simple majority, a three-fifths majority, or a two-thirds majority of the elected membership. In a number of States the legislature must vote on the proposal twice, once in each of two legislative sessions; in a few of these, a legislative election must fall between the two sessions. So far as the popular vote is concerned, the constitutions of thirty-two States require only a majority of those voting on the proposal; in four more States, the courts have interpreted the constitutional provision to mean a majority of those voting on the proposal. In a few States the constitution requires that a majority of all those taking part in the election approve of the proposed amendment; inasmuch as fewer people vote on proposed amendments than on candidates, amending the constitution of one of these States is quite difficult.

Popular initiative

Amendment by popular initiative is inaugurated by the people, who through petition propose an amendment. This means of amendment exists in thirteen States, all but Massachusetts, Michigan, and Ohio being west of the Mississippi. In every State the initiative begins with the drafting of the proposed constitutional amendment by a band of interested citizens. This proposition is then placed upon petitions which are circulated among the people for their signature. The petitions must be signed either by a specified percentage of the registered voters or by a stated number of voters. In some States the signatures must be obtained from voters rather equitably distributed about the area of the State. When the stipulated percentage, or number, of voters have signed the petitions, the proposed amendment is submitted to the people at an election, for their approval or rejection. Usually a simple majority of the votes cast suffices to ratify the amendment. It is noteworthy that in the States in which amendments may be proposed by the popular initiative, more amendments are proposed by legislative action than by the initiative; furthermore, a larger proportion of those proposed by the legislature is ratified by the voters.

Constitutional conventions

Constitutional conventions are designed chiefly for bringing about major revisions in existing constitutions, or for drafting new constitutons. They are the oldest of the three formal processes in the evolution of State constitutions, dating from the eighteenth century. In thirty-six States the constitution specifically empowers the people to hold a convention; in the other twelve it has been universally acknowledged that the people have this right.

Summoning the Convention: Revision of the present constitution, or the drafting of a new constitution, by means of a constitutional convention requires a number of stages. First, in most States the legislature must submit to the people the proposal that a convention be summoned. In most States the legislature makes this proposal solely on its own initiative— formally, at least, although it may be under great extra-legal pressure from outside interests. In eight States, however, it is obliged to make this proposal periodically, at intervals ranging from every seven years in New Hampshire to every twenty years in each of five States. The majority of the legislative vote needed to submit the proposal differs from State to State, or may not even be specified in the constitution. Now the people are to vote upon the proposal; again, by majorities that vary from State to State, the voters decide whether or not a convention is to meet. If the proposal is accepted by the voters, the legislature must then enact measures to provide for the convention.

Convention Organization and Functioning: State constitutional conventions in many respects are similar to the Philadelphia Convention of 1787. Where they meet, how the delegates are chosen, how many delegates there shall be, how the convention shall be organized, and what the convention may do, are matters that are sometimes set forth in the State constitution and sometimes arranged by the legislature. For example, if it has the authority to do so, the legislature may provide that delegates to the convention shall be apportioned throughout the State in the same manner as the State legislators are; with this arrangement, the various interests of the State will be represented with about the same relative influence in the convention that they already have in the legislature. The delegates to a convention are chosen by the voters. Once their members have been elected, most conventions organize themselves much like a legislative body, with presiding officers, rules, and committees.

The purpose of a convention is either to revise the constitution or to draft a new one; yet how full its power is toward either of these ends has been a matter of frequent dispute. Sometimes the legislature, in summoning the convention, has forbidden its members to deal with certain phases of government, such as the apportionment of the legislature itself. The convention is an arena in which various interests tug and haul. Some interests will want no changes at all; others will want differing changes, their nature and extent depending upon the wants of the interests concerned. In any event, the convention proceeds until it either drafts a new constitution, prepares amendments for the current constitution, or—which is quite unlikely—adjourns without having reached a conclusion.

Popular Approval: If the convention succeeds in producing a new constitution, or major revisions for the constitution in force, the results of its work are almost certain to be offered to the people for their approval in an election. At present the constitutions of only a few States require the voters to approve the work of a convention. However, where there are no constitutional provisions, it may be assumed that any new constitution is apt to contain a provision specifying the majority of the popular vote that will be necessary to ratify it.

Constitutional commissions

The constitutional commission as an instrument for amending or revising a State constitution differs from all other instruments in that it does not repose on direct constitutional authority. In most cases the commission is a temporary body established by an act of the State legislature, to recommend changes in the constitution; hence the typical commission is an implement of the legislature. On the other hand, the legislature may assign the undertaking to a permanent body, as when in 1946 in Louisiana the State assembly instructed the Louisiana State Law Institute to prepare a draft for a new constitution. Occasionally, as in Kentucky in 1949, the commission may be established as an advisory body by the Governor alone. The constitutional commission is not authorized to submit its proposals in a formal manner directly to the electorate; they must be filtered through the legislature. On the other hand, the constitutional commission may bring substantial pressure upon the legislature if by skillful publicity work it can convince the voters that its recommendations are sound.

The typical commission is appointed by the Governor and the legislature; sometimes, however, either the Governor alone, or the legislature alone, may do the selecting. Occasionally the State judiciary shares in naming commission personnel. The size of commission membership has ranged from three to thirty-eight. Sometimes the members come solely from the legislature; sometimes they come from all three branches of the government. Generally, lawyers have made up a large proportion of the members; businessmen, laborers, and social studies specialists have constituted a small minority.

To carry on its principal tasks the commission usually subdivides itself into committees, each to handle one particular phase of the constitution. Sometimes these committees may include persons not members of the commission. Apparently committees do not often enjoy the assistance of large research staffs; generally they must rely upon regular State agencies for the bulk of their information. Eventually, when each of the committees has finished studying the topic assigned to it, the entire commission gathers and discusses, sometimes in executive sessions, the conclusions of each of the committees. From these sessions the commission drafts its final recommendations, which commonly take the form either of a proposed new constitution or suggested amendments to the present constitution. It is a rare commission that does not submit some propositions for change, since such a body is not apt to be organized unless pressure for change exists.

QUESTIONS AND PROBLEMS

1. Why are State constitutions on the average longer than the federal Constitution?

2. What are the several parts of the typical State constitution?

3. What are the formal methods of amending constitutions in use among the States?

4. How is the constitution of your home State amended and revised? Is this different from the methods used in most States?

5. What are the most frequently used methods of amending State constitutions? What method is least used?

6. Describe the purpose and operations of constitutional commissions. Do you think that their use will increase in the next generation? Why?

51. Politics and Elections

Dept. of Commerce and Industry, State of Louisiana

THE politics of State and local governments are in part identical with national politics and in part separate and different in character. That is, many politicians and active citizens are in politics at all three levels. The State government creates the party structure and generally provides a single party system for all levels of government: thus, a county committeeman of the Republican Party has duties assigned to him in connection with the national, State, and local campaigns. In the people's mind, too, the distinction among the three levels of politics is not always clear: many a local campaign has been won on the issues of international politics, and many a national office has been captured by reason of popular revulsion against local corruption.

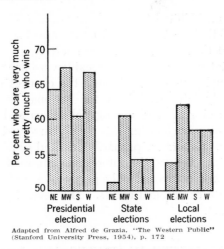

Adapted from Alfred de Grazia, "The Western Public"
(Stanford University Press, 1954), p. 172

**Figure 126.　Regional Differences in
Interest in Elections.**

However, State, local, and national politics stand distinct in other ways. Some people are more interested in one level of government than another; most politicians and interest groups have a special interest in one level of government; issues tend to be different on the three levels; election systems are changed at the various levels; a party's strength in the State and local governments may not match the vote it gives to the party's national ticket. This chapter deals with such differences one by one.

POPULAR INTEREST AND PARTICIPATION

Fewer people are interested in State and local politics than are concerned with national politics. A survey in 1952 on this subject produced the results shown in Figure 126 for the four regions of the country—Northeast, Midwest, South, and West. It will be noted there that only about two-thirds of the population expressed interest in the presidential elections. Moreover, ten to fifteen per cent fewer people were interested generally in who won State elections. Interest in local elections was midway between the national and State levels. The same figure shows that somewhat more Midwesterners take an interest in State and local elections than do Americans of other regions.

The number of people who vote in State and local elections, *when those elections are held separately,* is also usually smaller than the number who vote in national elections. For instance, in Colorado, where the Governor is elected every two years, the total vote for Governor is greater in those years when a President is being elected. More people know elected executives than know legislators. From a sample of 149 persons on the voting lists of a "middle-class" Minneapolis legislative district, one study found that 98% knew the name of the Governor, 41% the Lieutenant Governor,

---

The State Capitol, Baton Rouge, Louisiana. "Skyscraper modern" architectural design.

78% the name of one United States Senator, and 60% the other Senator, whereas 8% named their State Senator, and 7% and 4%, respectively, named one or the other of their two State representatives.

People who are interested in State or local government are not necessarily interested in national government, though the chances are good that they are at least partially informed about the national government. Among inactive and active citizens, and among politicians and interest groups as well, there are many who feel far less deeply involved in national affairs than in State affairs. Others are primarily oriented towards county, municipal, or school affairs. Hence, the interested, informed, and active public on municipal affairs is composed only partly of people who are similarly concerned with State or national affairs. The several publics overlap, but they are still distinct.

POLITICAL ISSUES IN STATES AND LOCALITIES

Popular attention varies as described partly because the State and local governments emphasize functions, problems, and issues that are unlike those of the national government. This is especially true of the municipal and county governments; their problems include sanitation, the care of roads, the maintenance of local law and order, the dispensing of aid to the poor and the aged, and the regulation of uses of business and residential areas. The State level, too, is likely to accent issues concerning highways, business licensing, liquor control, and regulation of corporations. Meanwhile, the federal government is more concerned with foreign affairs and national defense.

One might think that there would be three sets of political parties, each set dealing with the issues on one level of government; that, of course, is not the case. No matter how strained its reasoning may seem, each political party in any given locality will have a platform espousing issues on all three levels of government. For instance, the Democratic Party organization of Los Angeles may well take a stand on city, State, and national issues.

Why does this condition persist? In the first place, a person who is interested in both national and local affairs would be hard pressed to belong to two or three different political parties. In the second place, to achieve a goal on one level of government often requires the cooperation of other levels of government. Thirdly, some broad political principles, such as the desire for less government spending or the aim of protecting Negroes from discrimination in employment, can be advanced by concerted action at all levels of government.

Consequently, the political party strives to act in a coordinate manner in the town, State, and nation. It often falls far short of this goal. Ideas cannot hold together men and women who are independently chosen and not legally accountable to a party, unless the ideas are very strongly held. Hence, it is common to discover party organizations on a local level that are operated on the practical principles of a mutual benefit association, but which in their national capacity support ideological movements. Thus the national "New Deal" of Franklin D. Roosevelt rested partly upon a base of city machines in Chicago, Boston, Jersey City, and New York, and of county and State machines of conservative and even hostile leaders in the South.

Many voters, of course, appreciate the differences between their local or State politics and national politics, and in presidential elections will find cause to split their ballots. Table 29 discloses how many voters in 1952 probably split their votes on the national level and on the State and local levels. It shows that more splitting occurred at the State-local level, where, to be sure, there were more offices to be filled and therefore more opportunities to move into the other party's column.

DIFFERENT ELECTION SYSTEMS

Non-partisan ballots

A number of states have tried to separate local, and, in Minnesota and Nebraska, even State, officers from national politics by means of non-partisan elections. In such elections, candidates for office are not permitted to attach party labels to their names on the ballot. For instance, in Santa Clara County, California, the city councils and county Board of Supervisors are chosen in non-partisan elections at the same time as State and national legislators and executives are chosen in partisan elections. Non-partisanship on the ballot does not guarantee non-partisanship in fact: at the most, it is colored by the shading of party politics from the political circles in which the "non-partisan" candidates move; at the least, it is a mere omission of a word, inasmuch as the party organizations may dominate the nomination and elections of the "non-partisan" candidates. For instance, in Santa Clara County, California, the "non-partisan" county supervisors move generally in either Republican or Democratic circles, and lend some force to one or another party group even in the absence of any controlling party machine. However, in Chicago the "non-partisan" aldermen are likely to be among the most powerful party officials in their wards.

The "long ballot"

Another common distinction between national and State or local politics concerns the number of independently elected officials who are provided for by the constitutions. The federal Constitution prescribes the election only of members of Congress, a President, and a Vice President, and the latter are to be indirectly chosen. By contrast, the state constitutions usually demand the election of Governors, Lieutenant Governors, secretaries of state, treasurers, auditors, superintendents of education, and attorneys general; they also provide for numerous elective county and municipal officials. Therefore, the voter faces a long ballot in most State and local elections; most voters know nothing about the candidates for most offices but vote by party label or by an impulse of the moment. Such integration among the executives as is accomplished under the circumstances comes usually from party or factional caucuses behind the scenes; they select and back

TABLE 29. SPLIT-TICKET VOTING BY REGION AND PARTY

Allocation of Votes for All Candidates in 1952[1]	The South		All Other Regions		Entire Country		Total
	Eisenhower Voters	Stevenson Voters	Eisenhower Voters	Stevenson Voters	Eisenhower Voters	Stevenson Voters	
Voted straight ticket	26	93	65	69	59	75	66
Split away from their presidential votes:							
At national level only	8	3	2	4	3	4	3
At state or local level only	13	3	24	19	23	15	19
At both levels	53	1	9	8	15	6	12
Total	100%	100%	100%	100%	100%	100%	100%
Number of cases	164	111	583	383	687	494	1,181

[1] Those who voted a straight ticket except in the case of senator or congressman are categorized as splitting "at the national level only." Those who voted for the presidential and congressional candidates of one party, but for some or all of the state and local candidates of the other party, are shown as splitting "at state or local level only." Those who voted for the presidential candidate of one party, but for one or more candidates of the other party at both the national and local levels, are shown as "splitting at both levels." Source: Campbell, Angus; Gerald Gurin; and Warren E. Miller, *The Voter Decides* (Evanston: Row, Peterson and Company, 1954), p. 24.

certain candidates. A State or local candidate gains what is called a strong personal following when, to a roughly 50-50 division of the votes by random and party-label voting, there are added some hundreds or thousands of votes from personal acquaintances or distant admirers of his name, record, or conduct.

Initiative, referendum, and recall

The States and localities favor special types of election that are almost wholly foreign to the national government: the initiative, referendum, and recall. The recall is a special election, begun by a petition, to pass judgment of approval or rejection on an elective official before his term has expired. Sometimes the law declares that opposing candidates can run against the officer who is under attack. At other times, his name stands

TABLE 30. LAWS FOR THE RECALL OF PUBLIC OFFICERS[1,2]

State	To Whom Applicable		% of Voters' Signatures Required
	State Officers	Local Officers	
Arizona	All	All	25
Arkansas	—	Cities	35
California	All	All	12–25
Colorado	All	All	25–40
Idaho	All	All	10–35
Illinois	—	Cities	55
Iowa	—	Cities	25
Kansas	All	All	10–25
Louisiana	All	All	25–33⅓
Michigan	All	All	25
Minnesota	—	Cities	Set by municipal charter
Mississippi	—	Cities	25
Missouri	—	Cities	20
Montana	—	Cities	25
Nebraska	—	All	25–30
Nevada	All	All	25
New Jersey	—	Cities	25
New Mexico	—	Cities	15
North Carolina	—	Cities	25
North Dakota	All	All	30
Ohio	—	Cities	15
Oregon	All	All	Not over 25
South Carolina	—	Cities	20–40
South Dakota	—	Cities	15
Washington	All	All	25–35
West Virginia	—	All	20
Wisconsin	All	All	25–33⅓
Wyoming	—	All	25

[1] Source: Graves, W. Brooke, *American State Government* (4th ed., Boston: D. C. Heath and Co., 1953), p. 152.

[2] In a number of States, judges are excepted from recall elections. In several States, local recall is confined to cities possessing the commission form of city government. All current provisions for recall were adopted in the period from 1907 to 1941.

alone on the recall ballot and a special election is held, usually at the same time, to fill his post should the voters reject him. The various provisions of the law of recall in the 28 states that permit its use are charted in Table 30. Some states allow the recall for all elective officers, some states only for certain local officials. The recall is rarely used.

TABLE 31. INITIATIVE AND REFERENDUM LAWS
(FOR STATE-WIDE LEGISLATION)[1]

| | Initiative | | Referendum | | | |
| | | | Submission by | | | |
State	Voters' Signatures Necessary for Petitions	Vote Required for Enactment	Peti-tion	Legis-lative Action	Voters' Signatures Necessary for Petitions	Vote Required for Enactment
Arizona	15%	Majority	2	2	5%	Majority
Arkansas	8%	Majority	2	—	6%	Majority
California	8%	Majority	2	2	5%	Majority
Colorado	8%	Majority	2	2	5%	Majority
Idaho	10%	Majority	2	2	10%	Majority
Maine	10%	Majority	2	2	10%	Majority
Maryland	Does not use initiative system		2	—	10,000	Majority
Massachusetts	3%	Majority + 30 % of total votes cast at election	2	—	1½–2%	Majority
Michigan	8%	Majority	2	2	5%	Majority
Missouri	5%	Majority	2	2	5%	Majority
Montana	8%	Majority	2	2	5%	Majority
Nebraska	7%	Majority + 35% of total votes cast at election	2	—	5%	Majority + 35% of total votes cast at election
Nevada	10%	Majority	2	—	10%	Majority
New Mexico	Does not use initiative system		2	—	10%–25%	Majority
North Dakota	10,000	Majority	2	—	7,000	Majority
Ohio	3%	Majority	2	—	6%	Majority
Oklahoma	8%	Majority	2	2	5%	Majority
Oregon	8%	Majority	2	2	5%	Majority
South Dakota	5%	Majority	2	—	5%	Majority
Utah	10%	Majority	2	2	10%	Majority
Washington	50,000	Majority + 1/6 of total votes cast at election	2	2	30,000	Majority + 1/6 of total votes cast at election

[1] The Book of the States, 1954–55.

[2] Numerous special exceptions to requirements are not described here. A dash (−) indicates that the legislature cannot act.

Table 31 shows the different forms of initiative and referendum found among the States. The *initiative* is a means by which people can introduce legislation by petition. The *direct* type of initiative puts a measure onto the ballot for approval, without the intervention of the legislature. The *indirect* type places a measure before the legislature, where it must either be acted upon by the legislature and Governor within a specified period of time or else be referred back to the voters for approval or rejection. The *referendum* is a means of obtaining popular ratification of a measure. Often the measure is placed on the ballot by petition of a certain proportion of voters. Sometimes the legislature must refer certain kinds of measures to the voters for approval. Both devices are used liberally in many States and localities. The number of propositions referred to voters of counties, towns, and special districts in any single year amounts to some thousands. A referred bill or proposition is even less likely to be known to the voters than candidates are. Usually many fewer votes are cast on such matters than are cast for candidates, and, when an election is held solely to consider such propositions as a bond issue for a new school or a water conservation district, sometimes fewer than 20% of the registered voters participate.

Apportionment

Constitutional Provisions for Apportionment: In every State the constitution provides to a greater or lesser degree for the apportionment of the legislators. There are five general categories of methods for apportionment; as is apparent in the following discussion, most are based either upon population, area, or a combination of the two.[1] The capital letter after each heading in the outline furnishes the key to Table 32, which shows what method is used in each house of the legislature of every State.

ABSOLUTELY PROPORTIONATE TO POPULATION (A). In thirty-five of the ninety-five State legislative houses (the Nebraska legislature being unicameral, there is one fewer than twice forty-eight houses), apportionment is based absolutely on the population. That is, the population of the State is divided by the membership of the house, to fix a ratio of apportionment or representation. Now, the State may be divided into legislative districts, each with an equal number of representatives (often only one per district). On the other hand, the constituencies may be some fixed unit such as towns or counties, each of which shall be assigned one or more legislators as determined through dividing its population by the ratio.

RELATIVELY PROPORTIONATE TO POPULATION (B). In fourteen legislative houses, apportionment is relatively proportionate to population, a situation achieved by a method that is termed "weighted ratios." Although this method has several distinct forms, its invariable consequence is to favor units with smaller populations.

EQUAL REPRESENTATION FOR EACH UNIT (C). In eight legislative houses the members are apportioned on the basis of one for each unit, regardless of its population.

---

[1] The following is adapted from Jewell, Malcolm E., "Constitutional Provisions for State Legislative Apportionment," *Western Political Quarterly*, 8 (1955), 271–279.

TABLE 32.   CONSTITUTIONAL PROVISIONS FOR
LEGISLATIVE APPORTIONMENT

State	Upper House	Lower House	State	Upper House	Lower House
Alabama	D	D	Nebraska	A	(unicameral)
Arizona	C	D	Nevada	C	D
Arkansas	A	D	New Hampshire	E	B
California	D	A	New Jersey	C	D
Colorado	A	A	New Mexico	C	D
Connecticut	D	D	New York	B & D	D
Delaware	D	D	North Carolina	A	D
Florida	B	D	North Dakota	A	A
Georgia	A	D	Ohio	A	D
Idaho	C	D	Oklahoma	A	B & D
Illinois	D	A	Oregon	B	B
Indiana	A	A	Pennsylvania	B & D	B & D
Iowa	D	D	Rhode Island	D	D
Kansas	A	D	South Carolina	C	D
Kentucky	A	D	South Dakota	A	A
Louisiana	A	D	Tennessee	A	B
Maine	D	D	Texas		B
Maryland	D	B & D	Utah	A	D
Massachusetts	A	A	Vermont	D	C
Michigan	D	B	Virginia	A	A
Minnesota	A	A	Washington	A	A
Missouri	A	B & D	West Virginia	A	B
Mississippi	A	D	Wisconsin	A	A
Montana	C	A	Wyoming	D	D

BASED ON A COMBINATION OF AREA AND POPULATION FACTORS (D).   In forty-five legislative houses apportionment is based on a combination of area and population factors.   Sometimes apportionment is based upon population save that each unit is assured at least one representative.   In other States a variety of devices are employed to give units with small populations an exceptionally large representation.

BASED ON TAX PAYMENTS (E).   In a single legislative body, the New Hampshire senate, apportionment is based on the direct taxes paid by the people to the State government.

Multi-Member Districts: The State and local election systems, unlike the federal system and because of their more complicated systems of apportionment, provide many instances of multi-member districts.   In both the single-member and multi-member districts, there may be numerous candidates on the ballot; however, in the single-member districts, only one candidate can be elected, whereas in the multi-member districts, the law prescribes that two or more candidates shall be elected and each voter can cast one vote for each candidate to be elected.   A survey by Dr. Maurice Klain in 1955 reported that twelve per cent of all State senate seats and 45.4 per cent of all State assembly seats are filled from multi-member districts.   Multi-member districts are common, too, in the counties, school districts, townships, and municipalities of America (see, for example, Table 46).   In the vast majority of these districts those candidates who have received the highest numbers of votes are declared elected. For example, in an election in which four candidates are to be elected and ten candidates are running for office, the results might be as follows:

A	11,000	F	7,000
B	10,000	G	6,000
C	9,500	H	5,000
D	7,500	I	4,000
E	7,000	J	1,000

Candidates A, B, C, and D would be declared the winners.

Evidence concerning the effects of multi-member by contrast with single-member plurality districts is scanty; some say that the multi-member districts, which are generally larger, excite "better" men to run, whereas others say that single-member districts allow the full attention of the voter to fix upon the choice and behavior of one man. One important trait of multi-member districts is that a party or group which attracts no more than fifty-one per cent of the popular vote in the district can elect *all* of the members from the district.

Apportioning and Districting Agency: Apportioning and districting must be carried out by some agency. In three States—Delaware, Michigan, and New Mexico—the State constitution itself fixes apportionment and districting for either one or both houses. In certain other States, although the constitution does not precisely set forth apportionment or districting, it may have provisions that affect them fundamentally; for example, some constitutions forbid subdividing counties into districts. Hence the constitutional convention is one of the most important agencies for apportioning and districting. However, in most States the constitution empowers the State legislature to reapportion the State after each federal census. Because legislatures are often loath to act, a few State constitutions have given the task to some other body. In Ohio, for instance, reapportionment is executed by a commission made up of the Governor, the auditor, and the secretary of state, or any two of them.

The Present Status of Apportionment: At present, the actual apportionment in most States displays close connections with the strongest social groupings within the State. In general the membership of legislatures is so apportioned that it favors less densely populated, rural areas. The simple refusal of a legislature to reapportion after a census favors the countryside, since urban population is increasing, whereas rural population is diminishing. Table 33 shows the considerable discrimination against urban centers that exists in the States.

When, as in most States, the legislature is entrusted with the duty of reapportionment, there is no means for compelling it to act even when it violates a constitutional order to carry out reapportionments at fixed intervals of time. By contrast, in the few States in which a commission of executive officers is directed to reapportion one or both houses, in case these officers neglect their constitutional or legal obligations they may be constrained to perform them by a writ of *mandamus.*

TABLE 33. REPRESENTATION OF PRINCIPAL URBAN AREAS[1]

(ranging generally from most severe to least severe distortions of equality of representation)

States	Selected Urban Areas	Per Cent of State Population	Per Cent of Lower House	Per Cent of Senate
Georgia	6 largest urban counties	32	9	7
Florida	9 most urban counties	60	23	24
Delaware	Wilmington urbanized area	59	23	24
Maryland	Baltimore & 3 largest urban counties	67	44	31
Connecticut	10 largest cities	46	7	46[2]
Rhode Island	10 largest cities	77	67	34
New Jersey	8 largest urban counties	75	73	38
California	4 largest urban counties	59	59	10
New York	New York City	53	43	43
Kansas	3 largest urban counties	26	7	8
Alabama	3 largest urban counties	30	13	9
Iowa	5 largest urban counties	24	10	10
Oklahoma	2 largest urban counties	26	12	6
Texas	4 largest urban counties	29	19	13
Minnesota	2 largest urban counties	35	23	22
New Mexico	largest urban county	21	11	3
Tennessee	4 largest urban counties	38	22	20
Arizona	2 largest urban counties	62	62	7
Nevada	2 largest urban counties	62	40	12
Michigan	Wayne County	38	35	21
Missouri	St. Louis & 2 largest urban counties	45	25	41
Illinois	Chicago	42	39	31
Ohio	8 largest urban counties	54	39	54
South Carolina	3 largest urban counties	22	22	7
Vermont	entire urban population	36	6	36[2]
Idaho	4 largest urban counties	28	19	9
North Dakota	4 largest cities	17	12	10
Montana	5 largest urban counties	37	32	9
North Carolina	4 largest counties	22	16	16[2]
Mississippi	2 largest urban counties	10	4	4
Utah	3 largest urban counties	64	48	48
Indiana	6 largest urban counties	46	32	34
Washington	3 largest urban counties	52	44	48
Colorado	Denver city	31	26	23
Oregon	largest urban county	31	27	23
Nebraska	2 largest urban counties	30		23
Kentucky	3 largest urban counties	23	17	18
Louisiana	3 largest urban parishes	34	26	26
Maine	8 largest cities	27	19	27[2]
Pennsylvania	2 largest urban counties	34	32	28
Virginia	8 largest cities & 4 largest urban counties	34	28	33
West Virginia	3 largest urban counties	21	19	12
Wyoming	5 most urban counties	48	41	33
South Dakota	6 largest urban counties	30	28	23
Arkansas	3 largest urban counties	16	12	14
New Hampshire	3 largest cities	27	25	29
Wisconsin	3 largest urban counties	33	32	33
Massachusetts	All cities over 50,000 population	50	50	50[2]

[1] Baker, Gordon E., *Rural versus Urban Political Power*, Doubleday Short Studies in Political Science (New York, 1955), p. 16–17.

[2] Approximate.

One typical method for distorting legislative apportionment is relatively uncommon in the States: gerrymandering. Of course, a number of States, by prohibiting such districting techniques as the subdivision of counties, rather effectively bar the drawing of constituencies with unusual shapes. Another important factor is that in many States party lines are either unclear or even non-existent—as in the one-party States—so that gerrymandering, as it is sometimes practiced in the case of congressional district boundaries, is needless. At the same time, however, since many State constitutions guarantee thinly populated areas an extraordinary representation in one or both houses of the State legislature, disproportionate rural strength is provided without the kind of gerrymandering that is practiced with respect to the national House of Representatives.

Proportional Representation: One more distinguishing mark of State and local election systems may be mentioned. That is the occasional use of methods of proportional representation. Proportional representation is a system of voting and counting votes that grants a candidate of a minority group special advantages. These advantages consist in general of setting up a multi-member district in which the largest bloc of voters cannot elect all of the officers to be chosen and a fair-sized minority can elect at least one of its candidates. Behind the procedure rests an idea that it is unjust to give voice in the governing of a district solely to the majority or plurality of voters; instead, the minority, which may number as many as 49%, should also have representation in the council or legislature. Hence methods have been devised not only to let several candidates be elected from any given ward, city, or district, but to insure that at least one of those elected comes from the second largest party or group in the area. The Illinois House of Representatives is filled by one kind of proportional representation. In Cincinnati and some other cities the council is elected by another type of "P.R."

VARIATIONS IN PARTY STRENGTH AND CONTROL

In an earlier section of this book, it was shown in what respects the federal government does and does not have party government; the conclusion was reached that the Democrats and Republicans in Congress often cross party lines in voting on many issues but hold together as parties in organizing the Congress and in voting on many bills and motions. The same might be said of the State legislatures as a whole. However, there are forty-eight State legislatures, and they vary greatly in the degree to which party ties govern the behavior of their members.

In the first place, eleven southern States operate under a single-party system so that issues that agitate politics in and out of the legislature are espoused by two or more factions of the Democratic Party. Moreover, in two midwestern States the legislatures are elected on a non-partisan ballot, so that party government is made feeble. In twelve other States in recent years, one party has been so strong that the party bond has had little influence on the behavior of the legislatures. Wisconsin has been governed

TABLE 34.   PARTY VOTING ON ISSUES IN STATE LEGISLATURES[1]

Type of Issue	Number of Party Votes[2]	% of Party Votes[2] out of Total Roll Calls on Issue
Elections and reapportionment	65	44
Appointments	12	44
National issues	12	44
Labor	52	41
Appropriations	68	38
Legislative procedure and organization	47	37
Taxation	62	29
Veterans affairs	8	28
Welfare, health, education	79	22
Civil service	28	21
State administration	16	19
Local administration	15	14
Judicial and legal	21	11
Business regulation	14	6
Other issues	84	11
Total:	583	Average 21%

[1] Source: "Party Voting in American State Legislatures," *American Political Science Review*, XLIX (1955), 788.

[2] Party votes are those on which the parties are opposed and both have an index of cohesion of at least 80. [An index of 80 results when 90% of a party vote one way and 10% vote the other way.]

largely by a Republican and Progressive coalition and the Democrats in the legislature have adjusted their habits to the dominant faction.   Among the remaining twenty-two States, something resembling two-party government has colored the conduct of the legislative branch of government over the past twenty years.

A recent study by Dr. Malcolm E. Jewell uncovered facts concerning the degree of party government that is found in eight of these last twenty-two States at times when there is a fairly close division of the legislature between the Republicans and Democrats.   Table 34 presents the extent to which the members of each party rallied to their party's stand on different kinds of issues in one or two sessions of recent years in all of the eight States.

The unit of measure of party difference was called a "party vote."   A "party vote" was achieved on a roll-call vote in the legislature whenever 90% or more of the members of one party voted oppositely to 90% or more of the members of the other party.   Take all roll-call votes on questions concerning labor, for example; should 90% of the members of the two parties hold opposing sides on every one of such votes, there would without doubt be very strong party discipline and party government in those eight legislatures.   In point of fact, the table shows that the party members were so aligned on only 41% of all labor issue roll-calls.   The sharpest party divisions, 44% of the total roll-calls, occurred on the subjects of elections and reapportionment, confirmation of appointments, and resolutions on national issues.

TABLE 35.   EXTENT OF PARTY CONTROL IN THE STATES[1]

States According to Number of Years, 1931–1952, in which Governorship and One or Both Legislative Houses were Controlled by Opposite Parties[2]

Division of Control Number of Years	States Number	Per Cent	Names of States
0	15	32.6	Alabama, Arkansas, Florida, Georgia, Louisiana, Mississippi, North Carolina, Oklahoma, South Carolina, Tennessee, Texas, Virginia, New Hampshire, Vermont, South Dakota
2	4	8.7	Arizona, Iowa, West Virginia, Wisconsin[3]
4	6	13.0	New Mexico, Kansas, Maine, Oregon. Pennsylvania, Kentucky
6	5	10.9	California, Idaho, Illinois, Maryland, Michigan
8	3	6.5	North Dakota, Ohio, Utah
9	1	2.2	New Jersey
10	5	10.9	Colorado, Delaware, Montana, Washington, Missouri
12	4	8.7	Rhode Island, Wyoming, Indiana, New York
14	2	4.3	Massachusetts, Nevada
16	1	2.2	Connecticut[4]
Total:	46[5]	100.00	

[1] Key, V. O., Jr., and Corinne Silverman, *Party and Separation of Powers: A Panorama of Practice in the States,* reprinted from *Public Policy,* V (1954).

[2] The basic data for this table are from the New York *Legislative Manual* and George Gallup's *Political Almanac, 1952.* The computations for this table rest on a comparison of the political affiliation of legislators and Governors from the election of 1930 through that of 1950. For States holding elections in odd years, the period 1929–1949 was used except for Kentucky, for which the elections of 1931–1947 were used.

[3] Third party and independent Governors were excluded. The exclusion includes the 1930 Oregon election, the 1936 North Dakota election, and the elections of 1934, 1936, 1940, and 1942 in Wisconsin.

[4] The elections of 1934 and 1938 gave the Republicans minorities in the State Senate but by coalition with the handful of Socialists they obtained working control. These elections were considered as having resulted in Republican control. Throughout, in situations of a 50-50 division between Republicans and Democrats, the assignment of party control was determined by the party affiliation of the presiding officer and the party affiliations of committee chairmen.

[5] Minnesota and Nebraska are excluded from this tabulation, since their legislators are elected on a non-partisan ballot.

On the subject of business regulation, judicial and legal affairs, and State and local administration, party lines almost dissolved, for a party vote occurred in fewer than 20% of all roll-calls. In fact, the proportion of party votes of all roll-call votes came only to 21%. Considering that the eight legislatures are among the 22 with the greatest chance of providing party government of the 48 states, the general picture of party operations is one of weakness rather than strength. At least this is true of the legislative branches of government.

The slackness of party lines in the legislatures is both the result and the cause of weak party government in the structure of State politics as a whole. "Responsible party government" is defined as the ability of a party to control the machinery of government to the extent necessary to carry out its policies. A recent study by Dr. V. O. Key, Jr., and Corinne Silverman demonstrates that opportunities for such responsible party government are the exception rather than the rule in State politics. Even supposing that the politicians of one or the other party generally were in favor of and prepared to support a party program, they would be faced with the hard fact that many years might go by in many States without their ever being able to swing into effective action as a party government. As Table 35 reveals, in a good many States in recent years the governorship and one or both houses of the legislature were in the hands of opposing parties a large part of the time and hence the government had to be conducted according to bipartisan principles, or not conducted at all.

It is especially important to note that those States where party government was most possible in the period surveyed are States in which one party is overwhelmingly strong. By contrast, those States that have the least chance of party government are States where the two-party system is "healthiest." One concludes, therefore, that the State political systems are so constructed that they repress any tendencies of politics to develop and put into effect one or the other of two competing programs of legislation or administration. In short, the State political systems impede party government. The study of the national government has shown how the same impediments exist in national politics; but they do not exist to the same extent as in the States. The study of the structure and operations of State and local governments must therefore be conducted in full awareness of the fact that, in most States at most times, either party lines are loose within the parties or else the parties cannot control the whole government. Probably the greatest part of State politics and government can be called bipartisan or non-partisan.

QUESTIONS AND PROBLEMS

1. List the general ways in which State politics and elections differ from national politics and elections.

2. Referring back to Chapter 11 (Public Opinion and Activity), list from there the major points that pertain to, or are also true of, State and local politics.

3. What major points of Chapter 13 (Composition and Structure of Political Parties) are also true of State and local politics?

4. What major points of Chapter 14 (Party Functions) are also true of State and local politics?

5. What major points of Chapter 15 (Nominations and Elections) are also true of State and local politics?

6. Define briefly: non-partisan elections; a "long ballot"; initiative; referendum; recall; multi-member district; proportional representation.

7. What types of initiative, referendum, and recall—if any—are used in your home State? Are they typical of those used in other States? How often are they employed?

8. What mode of apportionment does your home State's law provide for? Is this typical of the States generally?

9. Does your home State have districts of equal population in both houses (except Nebraska) or are rural districts smaller? Is the situation more or less extreme than is generally the case?

10. To what extent does a two-party system govern the 48 States?

11. On what issues do the legislators of two-party States seem to divide along party lines? Can you explain the reasons for differences among the issues?

PART XIV

Structure
of State Government

New Mexico State Tourist Bureau

THE State legislature is the policy-framing organ of the State government. That is to say, the legislature enacts the laws of the State. The legislature has a number of other functions as well. As an elected body, it represents the people of the State in the government. It appropriates the money for, and supervises the workings of, the administrative agencies of the State; sometimes it also creates these agencies and sets forth their tasks. It fulfills a judicial role in conducting impeachment trials of State officials and in determining the qualifications of its own members. In general, each State legislature has about the same relation to the State government as Congress has to the national government. This chapter treats of the State legislatures in four sections. First it outlines their structure, with particular reference to their names, number, and sessions. A second section describes the traits of the legislators; a third, the organization of State legislatures; and a fourth, legislative procedure in State governments.

STRUCTURE

The structure of the legislature, as it will be dealt with here, concerns the mere framework of the organism. It involves three topics: the number of houses in the legislature; the number of legislators; and the length and frequency of the sessions of the legislature.

Bicameralism

Every State legislature except that of Nebraska is bicameral; that of Nebraska is unicameral. State legislatures as a unit, and each of the branches, have a variety of names. Table 36 lists the various names for each State. In this text the branch that is by courtesy termed the "upper house"—although there is little if any reason for such a term today—is called the *senate;* the other branch—the "lower house"—is called the *house.*

Size

The size of State legislatures varies greatly from one State to another, and seems to have little relation to the population or area of the State. The largest legislature is that of New Hampshire, with 423 members; the smallest bicameral legislature, that of Delaware, with fifty-two members. The largest senate, with sixty-seven members, is in Minnesota; the smallest, with seventeen, in both Delaware and Nevada. The largest house, comprising 399 members, is in New Hampshire; the smallest, comprising thirty-five, in Delaware. What may be considerably more suggestive is the number of people represented on the average by legislators from different States. For instance, according to the 1950 Census, each member of the national House of Representatives has on the average a district containing 345,000 people. By contrast, each member of the New Hampshire house represents about 1,300 people. At the other end of the scale among the States is the California house, each of whose eighty members represents more than 130,000 people. Table 10 also gives the membership of each house in the forty-eight State legislatures.

Sessions

In the main, State legislatures do not have as frequent regular sessions as Congress has, and the sessions are not so long. Most State legislatures gather for regular sessions only in each odd-numbered year. A few meet every even-numbered year. In only fourteen States does the legislature assemble annually; among six of these, the purpose of the meeting in every other year is to deal solely with fiscal and emergency matters. Hence in a large majority of the States the legislature does not have the opportunity to work during regular sessions that Congress has. A further restriction on the work of State legislatures is the limitation on the duration of the regular session that is imposed in many States. In Alabama, for instance, the legislature

New Mexico State Capitol. Spanish architecture and Indian architecture are adapted to modern use, style, and materials.

TABLE 36. NAMES, SIZE, TERMS, AND PAY OF
STATE LEGISLATURES

State	Name of State Legislature	Senate Size	Senate Term	House Size	House Term	Maximum Annual Pay[1] Dollars
Alabama	Legislature	35	4	106	4	360
Arizona	Legislature	28	2	80	2	480
Arkansas	General Assembly	35	4	100	2	600
California	Legislature	40	4	80	2	6,000
Colorado	General Assembly	35	4	65	2	1,800
Connecticut	General Assembly	36	2	280	2	300
Delaware	General Assembly	17	4	35	2	1,000
Florida	Legislature	38	4	95	2	1,200
Georgia	General Assembly	54	2	205	2	400
Idaho	Legislature	44	2	59	2	600
Illinois	General Assembly	58	4	177	2	5,000
Indiana	General Assembly	50	4	100	2	1,800
Iowa	General Assembly	50	4	108	2	1,000
Kansas	Legislature	40	4	125	2	450
Kentucky	General Assembly	38	4	100	2	1,500
Louisiana	Legislature	39	4	101	4	2,700
Maine	Legislature	33	2	151	2	625
Maryland	General Assembly	29	4	123	4	1,800
Massachusetts	General Court	40	2	240	2	4,500
Michigan	Legislature	34	2	110	2	4,000
Minnesota	Legislature	67	4	131	2	2,400
Mississippi	Legislature	49	4	140	4	1,000
Missouri	General Assembly	34	4	157	2	1,500
Montana	Legislative Assembly	56	4	94	2	1,200
Nebraska	Legislature (Unicameral legislature, 2-year term)					872
Nevada	Legislature	17	4	47	2	900
New Hampshire	General Court	24	2	399	2	100
New Jersey	Legislature	21	4	60	2	5,000
New Mexico	Legislature	32	4	66	2	1,200
New York	Legislature	58	2	150	2	7,500
N. Carolina	General Assembly	50	2	120	2	1,350
N. Dakota	Legislative Assembly	49	4	116	2	300
Ohio	General Assembly	33	2	136	2	5,000
Oklahoma	Legislature	44	4	121	2	1,975
Oregon	Legislative Assembly	30	4	60	2	600
Pennsylvania	General Assembly	50	4	210	2	1,500
Rhode Island	General Assembly	44	2	100	2	300
S. Carolina	General Assembly	46	4	124	2	1,000
S. Dakota	Legislature	35	2	75	2	525
Tennessee	General Assembly	33	2	99	2	750
Texas	Legislature	31	4	150	2	3,000
Utah	Legislature	25	4	64	2	500
Vermont	General Assembly	30	2	246	2	800
Virginia	General Assembly	40	4	100	2	540
Washington	Legislature	46	4	99	2	1,200
W. Virginia	Legislature	32	4	100	2	1,500
Wisconsin	Legislature	33	4	100	2	2,400
Wyoming	Legislature	27	4	56	2	480

[1] Where pay plan is calculated on days in session, the maximum days allowed is multiplied by the daily pay. Where the pay is allotted to a two-year period, one-half the total is taken.

may meet for only thirty-six legislative (as distinct from calendar) days during a session. Hence legislation in many States must be enacted in the utmost haste; the last few days of a session are apt to be a bedlam, with the rules suspended and even the clock stopped so as to maintain the fiction that the time limit has not been exceeded.

One innovation to cope with the session-ending rush is the so-called "split session." Under this arrangement the legislators meet for a few weeks at the beginning of the session, when bills are introduced and assigned to committees. The legislature then recesses for a few weeks, to enable the committees to study the proposed laws and the individual legislators to sound out their constituents. Finally the legislature reassembles, presumably to do no more than to enact laws, for supposedly the members have by this time thoroughly examined and comprehended all the bills of interest to them. New bills may now be introduced only by extraordinary majorities. In theory, then, laws may now be passed in somewhat more leisurely fashion. As this arrangement has worked out in California it has not fulfilled the promises made in its behalf. The most notable device employed to circumvent the purposes of the split session is the "skeleton bill," a rough outline of a projected law which after the recess may be so greatly amended that the total effect is little different from the introduction of a new bill.

A much more widespread consequence of the short and infrequent regular sessions is the special session. Some State legislatures may hold as many as half-a-dozen special sessions between regular sessions, each perhaps of but a few days' duration. In most States the Governor alone may summon a special session, at his own discretion. In six States he must call a special session upon receipt of a petition signed by an extraordinary majority of the legislators and in four States the legislature itself may arrange for a special session. In nearly half the States the constitutions also limit the duration of special sessions, and in about an equal proportion the constitutions empower the Governor to set the agenda of the session.

STATE LEGISLATORS

Occupations

According to a survey of State legislators in 1949, businessmen are the largest occupational group among them (see Table 37). Lawyers are the second largest group, and farmers are third largest. There are relatively few laborers and craftsmen; in the legislatures of such industrial States as New York and Michigan there are scarcely any laborers. Yet it may be that a labor lawyer can act as a far better spokesman for laborers than a laborer himself can. In the main, however, business and agriculture are far more heavily represented in State legislatures than labor is.

Qualifications

State constitutions generally set a few qualifications for members of the legislature, primarily those of age, residence, and citizenship. Sometimes

TABLE 37. OCCUPATIONS OF STATE LEGISLATORS[1]
(1949)

Occupation	Upper House	Lower House	Total
Lawyer	596	1078	1674
Farmer	358	1110	1468
Merchant	268	795	1063
Insurance	75	236	311
Banks and trusts	41	101	142
Real estate	38	174	212
Doctor	34	46	80
Teacher	33	155	188
Laborer	16	129	145
Craftsman	31	191	222
Undertaker	9	31	40
Retired	41	286	327
Other	285	1318	1604
Totals	1825	5650	7475

[1] Zeller, Belle, *American State Legislatures* (New York: Thomas Y. Crowell Company, 1954) p. 71.

the qualifications for each house are the same; sometimes those for the upper house are a trifle more stringent. A typical group of qualifications is that members of the upper house be twenty-five years old, and members of the lower house, twenty-one; that all members be citizens; and that all members have resided in the State a certain number of years. Table 38 lists these qualifications for each State. There may be numerous other unwritten "qualifications" as well, such as residence in the district, nationality, race, religion, profession, marital status, and the like.

Term and tenure

State legislators today are everywhere elected for either two-year or four-year terms (see Table 36). In a few States the four-year terms are overlapping, so that the voters name half the legislative house every two years. The tenure of most State legislators is much shorter than that of congressmen; in other words, turnover among members of State legislatures is rapid. As Figure 127 shows, in 1950 one out of four members of senates and three out of eight members of houses were serving their first terms. Professor Zeller, from whose text these data were drawn, warns that these figures apply to only one year, and declares that the amount of experience among legislators may vary considerably from one year to the next. However, it is clear that many State legislators have not served for a long enough time to have grasped the rudiments of the lawmaking process. Hence it is perhaps easier for a small group to secure dominance over a State legislature than over Congress. It is noteworthy that even in the single year concerned there were great differences from one State to another.

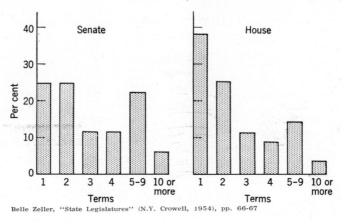

Belle Zeller, "State Legislatures" (N.Y. Crowell, 1954), pp. 66-67

Figure 127.   Tenure of State Legislators (as of 1950).

Salary

Salaries for State legislators range from a low of $200 per term in New Hampshire to a high of $7,500 per year in New York.   In general, salaries are quite low; on the average they are lower than the average salaries of councilmen in each of the thirteen largest cities in the United States.   However, in cities of this size, the councilmen are apt to have to devote most if not all of their working hours to their governmental duties, whereas State legislators contribute only a fraction of their time to the obligations of office. In many States the lawmakers are paid on a daily rather than on an annual basis.   Some State constitutions and laws employ this method of payment as an instrument for shortening legislative sessions; for instance, Georgia legislators receive $10.00 per day for a maximum of forty days.   A considerable number of States do implement legislators' salaries with allowances for travel or for expenses during sessions.   Table 36 shows what the legislators in each State are paid in the way of salary.

ORGANIZATION

The organization of the State legislature is the machinery that puts it into motion so that it can carry out its tasks.   In every State the organization consists of several or all of the following elements: the party caucuses; the presiding officer; other legislative and party officers; legislative committees and their chairmen; technical services for legislators; and agencies for planning legislation.   Outwardly, at least, the machinery is based upon the State constitution, laws, and the rules and customs of the legislative body.   Actually to a great degree it is founded upon the interrelations among political parties and interest groups in the State.   Because these interrelations differ greatly from one State to another, the relative importance of each of these elements also differs from one State to another.

TABLE 38. CONSTITUTIONAL QUALIFICATIONS FOR STATE LEGISLATORS[1] AND GOVERNORS

State	Legislators						Governors		
	Age		U.S. Citizenship	Length of State Residence		Other	Age	U.S. Citizenship	State Citizenship or Residence
	Senate	House		Senate	House				
Alabama	25	21	Yes	State 3	Same		30	10	7
Arizona	25	25	Yes	County 1	Same		25	10	4
Arkansas	25	21	Yes	State 2 / District 1	Same		30	Yes	7
California			Yes	State 3 / District 1	Same		25	5	5
Colorado	25	25	Yes	District 1	Same	Electors	30	Yes	2
Connecticut	(21)	(21)	(Yes)	Town 1	Same		30	(Yes)	(1)
Delaware	27	24	Yes	State 3	Same	Last year of residence must be in district	30	12	6
Florida	(21)	(21)	(Yes)	County 4	Same	Electors	(21)	10	5
Georgia	25	21	Yes	State 2 / District 1	S. 2 / D. 1		30	15	6
Idaho	(21)	(21)	Yes	County or District 1	Same	Electors	30	Yes	2
Illinois	25	21	Yes	State 5 / District 2	Same		30	5	5
Indiana	25	21	Yes	State 2 / District 1	Same		30	5	5
Iowa	25	21	Yes	State 1 / District 1	Same		30	2	2
Kansas	(21)	(21)	(Yes)	County or District 60 days		Electors	—	—	—
Kentucky	30	24	Yes	State 6 / District 1	S. 2 / D. 1		30	—	6
Louisiana	25	(21)	(Yes)	State 5 / District 2	Same	Electors	30	10	10

[1] Where information is enclosed by parentheses, as (21) or (Yes), it is a direct inference from the word "electors" but not an explicit qualification in the Constitution.

TABLE 38. CONSTITUTIONAL QUALIFICATIONS FOR STATE LEGISLATORS[1] AND GOVERNORS—Continued

	Legislators						Governors		
	Age		U.S. Citizen-ship	Length of State Residence		Other	Age	U.S. Citizen-ship	State Citizen-ship or Residence
State	Senate	House		Senate	House				
Maine	25	21	Yes for 5 yrs.	State 3, District	Same		30	natural born	5
Maryland	25	21	Yes	State 3, District 1, 6 mos.	Same		30	(Yes)	10
Massachusetts	—	—	—	State 5	D. 1		(21)	—	7
Michigan	(21)	(21)	Yes	District, District	Same		30	5	2
Minnesota	—	—	—	—	—	Electors. Each house shall be the judge of the election returns & eligibility of its own members	25	Yes	1
Mississippi	25	21	Yes	District 2	S. 4, D. 2		30	20	5
Missouri	30	24	Yes	County or District 1	Same	S—Qualified voters for 3 yrs. R—Qualified voters for 2 yrs.	30	15	10
Montana	24	21	Yes	District	Same		30	Yes	2
Nebraska	(21)	(21)	(Yes)	District 12 mos.		1 year in District. Electors	30	5	5
Nevada	(21)	(21)	(Yes)	District, Resident of State 7 yrs., District	Same, S. 2, C. or D.	Electors	25	(Yes)	2
New Hampshire	30	—	—	District			30	—	7
New Jersey	30	21	Yes	State 4, District 1	S. 2, D. 1		30	20	7
New Mexico	25	21	—	—	—		30	Yes	5
New York	—	—	Yes	State 5, District 1	D. 1		30	Yes	5

TABLE 38. CONSTITUTIONAL QUALIFICATIONS FOR STATE LEGISLATORS[1] AND GOVERNORS—Continued

| State | Legislators | | | | | | Governors | | |
	Age Senate	Age House	U.S. Citizenship	Residence Senate	Residence House	Other	Age	U.S. Citizenship	State Citizenship or Residence
N. Carolina	25	—	Yes	State 2, District 1	D. 1		30	5	2
N. Dakota	25	21	(Yes)	State 2	Same	Electors	30	Yes	5
Ohio	—	—	—		—	—		—	
Oklahoma	25	21	(Yes)	County or District 1		Electors	31	Yes	(10)
Oregon	21	(21)	Yes		Same		30	Yes	3
Pennsylvania	25	21	Yes	State 4, District 1	Same		30	Yes	7
Rhode Island	—	—	—	—	—	Each house shall be the judge of the electors & qualifications of its members	—	—	—
S. Carolina	25	21	(Yes)	State	—	Electors	30	5	5
S. Dakota	25	25	Yes	State 2	Same	Electors	30	Yes	2
Tennessee	30	21	Yes	State 3, District 1	Same		30	Yes	7
Texas	26	21	Yes	State 5, District 1 (last year)	S. 2, D. 1 (last year)	Electors	30	Yes	5
Utah	25	25	Yes	State 3, District 1	Same	Electors	30	(Yes)	5
Vermont	30	—	—	—	S. 2, Town 1	Senators must be freemen from county	—	—	4
Virginia	(21)	(21)	(Yes)	District	Same	Electors	30	10	5
Washington	(21)	(21)	(Yes)	—	—	Electors	(21)	Yes	(1)
W. Virginia	—	—	—	District 1	Same		30	(Yes)	5
Wisconsin	(21)	(21)	(Yes)	State 1	Same		(21)	Yes	(1)
Wyoming	25	21	Yes	District 1	Same	Electors	30	Yes	5

Party caucus

The party caucus, where it is found, is primarily an instrument that nominates the candidates of the party for legislative office. Where it exists, then, and is active, it is the root of legislative organization. A little more than two-thirds of the States have majority party caucuses; in a third of these States the caucuses are of little importance. In one-third of the States, there is no majority party caucus at all. Slightly more than half of the States have minority party caucuses.

The presiding officer

Every State legislative body has a presiding officer. In the house this officer is invariably termed the speaker; he is always a majority-party member who is elected by the other members. His position is extremely powerful, more so than that of the Speaker in the national House of Representatives. The outstanding difference between the State speakers and the national Speaker is that in almost all States the speaker names the members of the standing committees; furthermore, in many of these States the speaker chooses the standing committee chairmen. Another major power of many speakers is the unrestricted authority of assigning bills to committees. Finally, the speaker exercises the same general powers as those of the national Speaker, such as the control of parliamentary debate and the appointment of members to special and conference committees.

The various State senates have different presiding officers. In thirty-eight States there is an elected executive officer, the Lieutenant Governor, who corresponds to the Vice President of the United States; in each of these States save Massachusetts he is the presiding officer of the senate. In Massachusetts and the remaining ten States the senate elects one of its own number as president. Moreover, in every State but nine—most of the nine being among those with a president of the senate—the senate also chooses one of its members as president *pro tempore*. In many of the State senates, including almost half of those with a Lieutenant Governor, the presiding officer names the members of committees. In most States the presiding officer of the senate also refers bills to committees. In most, but not all, of the States with a Lieutenant Governor, he is empowered to vote in case of a tie vote among the senators. Senate presiding officers enjoy other powers typical of their posts, such as managing floor procedure and choosing members for special and conference committees.

Legislative and party officers

Like Congress, State legislatures have a host of legislative and party officers. Typical legislative officers include sergeants-at-arms, doorkeepers, chaplains, and an array of clerks. Many of these officers have little to do; it is argued in defense of their posts that they are essential to the maintenance of party government, since their incumbents can devote most of their time to working for their political party. Most State legislatures do not have the formidable and cohesive structure of party officers and instruments that

the national House of Representatives has. Certain party officers, notably
floor leaders, exist in somewhat more than half the States; such party organizations as steering or policy committees and committees on committees are
relatively uncommon. In many State legislatures the standing committees
are not predominating party devices, and in less than half the States are
the rules committees significant. Where these officers and agencies are important, they occupy approximately the same roles that they do in the
national House of Representatives.

The committee system

Standing committees of State legislatures, like those of Congress, are
bodies into which the legislature subdivides itself for the purpose of studying bills and of determining their importance. Members of standing committees are chosen in a variety of ways; they are most often appointed by the
presiding officer of the legislative body concerned. Among State legislatures
there are ten in which the minority party appears to have no representation
on standing committees—eight one-party States and two non-partisan States.
In three other States—Oregon, South Dakota, and Tennessee—the minority
party is not assured representation; in each of these three States one major
party has exceptional power.

Seniority is not nearly so significant in State legislatures as in Congress
for deciding the choice of committee chairmen; in fact, as the graph in
Figure 128 reveals, many State committee chairmen are serving their first
terms. (This graph, based on a questionnaire, is applicable to only forty-
five States; the respondents in Arizona, Idaho, and Ohio answered little
more than that all committee chairmen had had prior legislative experience.)
The available data for the States show that in State legislatures having a high
proportion of experienced members a large percentage of committee chairmen are apt to be experienced; for instance, in 1950 in the California senate
all six of the members who had served ten or more terms were committee
chairmen. By contrast, in the same year all fourteen chairmen in the Alabama house were in their first term, in spite of the fact that forty-five members of that body were in their second, third, or fourth term. Factors apart

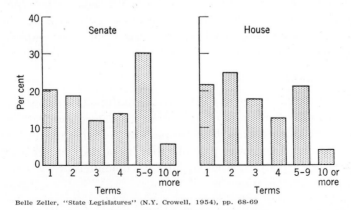

Belle Zeller, "State Legislatures" (N.Y. Crowell, 1954), pp. 68-69

Figure 128.   Experience of Standing Committee Chairmen in State Legislatures.

from seniority that may be conclusive in the selection of committee chairmen include the friendship of the presiding officer, status in the party, the influence of pressure groups, and the support of the executive branch. At the same time, State committee chairmen are apt to lack the dominance over their committees enjoyed by congressional committee chairmen; the guiding force may instead be a union of the majority party members in the committee or even of the group that controls the whole legislative body.

The number of committees shows wide differences from one State to another. Senate committees range from seven in New Mexico to forty-six in Mississippi; house committees range from eight in South Carolina to sixty-four in Missouri. The number of committees in any State legislature does not seem to have any particular connection with either the size of the legislative body or the amount of business that the body conducts. In three States—Maine, Massachusetts, and Connecticut—the number of committees has been substantially reduced and the legislative process simplified by the establishment of joint standing committees for the consideration of almost all bills and resolutions. These joint committees make it possible to have a single hearing for a bill and to send a single report to each house on a bill.

Technical services for legislators

In most State legislatures today there are a number of technical services available to the members. These services involve chiefly either research on matters concerning which the legislator may wish to propose a law, or assistance in drafting the text of a proposed law itself. Almost all of the States now have a legislative reference service which has as its primary functions the supplying of information to legislators and the comparing of laws in other States on some subject for which the legislature of the given State may be planning bills. A number of States provide legislators with bill-drafting services. Although many bills are drawn up by attorneys in private employment, legislators more and more are relying upon bill-drafting offices. These offices may be either set up by the legislatures as distinct agencies, or connected with some other group such as the legislative reference service or the office of the State attorney general. Other types of staff and research facilities, which the national government provides, but many States do not, are staff personnel for legislative committees and office space for individual legislators.

Legislative planning

Legislative planning is concerned with the drafting of a series of proposed laws which, in the opinion of one group of legislators, the State legislature would, in the coming session, find it especially desirable to consider and, if possible, to enact. Legislative planning may be carried out either by a more or less temporary body such as an interim committee or by a permanent agency such as a legislative council.

Interim Committees: Interim committees are bipartisan agencies created by a legislature out of its own membership to study proposed laws during the period between sessions—the interim—so as to assist the legislature in planning its activities for the coming session. The interim committee is a temporary body designed to handle one field of possible legislation. Ordinarily it does not have any professional research assistance or staff. In its functioning the committee is to analyze the circumstances that appear to call for legislation; examine various means for coping with these circumstances through the enactment of statutes; and finally submit a report of its findings to the entire legislature sometime before the opening of the next session, or at the very outset of the next session. Although the reports that they finally provide for the legislators are sometimes unskillfully prepared and poorly distributed, these committees do make an important contribution to the planning of legislation.

Legislative Councils: Legislative councils, like interim committees, are bipartisan groups established by State legislatures (except in Missouri, where the council is created by the constitution) to plan the lawmaking activities for the coming session. However, a legislative council is a far more intricate and comprehensive apparatus than an interim committee. Save in the case of Nebraska, it includes members from both houses. In a number of States certain members of the legislature—the speaker, for example—are ex officio members of the council. Apart from those who hold their positions ex officio, members of these councils are usually named by the presiding officers of the two legislative houses; however, in Kentucky the Governor is a member, and in Arkansas the Governor may name one member. The councils of Nebraska, Oklahoma, and South Dakota include all members of the legislature.

The legislative council is in a sense a permanent "super-interim" committee. Its primary function is to draft a legislative program for the coming session. In one or more States it has such additional functions as striving to improve the efficiency of the administrative branch of the government and to improve the relations between State and local authorities. The means given to the councils for carrying out their primary function vary from State to State. In some States the council has only advisory powers; in other States it may introduce legislation in its own name. One trait common to all legislative councils is a large research staff. Councils in many States rely upon interim committees and upon the State legislative reference service to furnish them with information about particular subjects. In some States the councils have the power to subpoena witnesses.

PROCEDURE

The lawmaking procedure in State legislatures is much like that in Congress. It includes the introduction of a bill into one house; its study by a committee; its discussion on the floor and its passage; its transmission to the second house; its discussion, study, and passage there; and finally, if need be, its revision so that it is approved by each house in identical form. As in Congress, this whole procedure is hedged about with a set of rules. However, certain phases of legislative procedure in at least some States are not the same as they are in Congress. The following discussion is designed to single out only two features in which considerable deviations from federal practice may be noted.

Rules

Every State legislature proceeds according to rules much like those of Congress. However, State legislatures differ from the national House of Representatives in that in almost all States the rules committee in each house is quite weak. It does propose amendments to the standing rules of the house. Yet, in a majority of States the calendars on which bills are placed after being reported out of committee are rather strictly adhered to, so that the calendars time the arrival of bills on the floor. Since perhaps the chief function of the Rules Committee in the national House is to schedule the debating of proposed legislation, and since in most States the calendar or calendars relieve the rules committee of this power, it is evident that most State rules committees are relatively unimportant. In a few States, by contrast, the rules committees do play a major role in the timing of legislative discussion; here they are significant agencies. In most States the rules committees are appointed by the presiding officer, at least in the house; indeed, the speaker is sometimes chairman of the house rules committee. Hence the committee tends to be subservient to the speaker.

Sources of bills

Bills that come before State legislatures, like those that appear before Congress, may have any of several sources. Every legislator, of course, is empowered to introduce a bill into his house; moreover, no one but a legislator may directly submit a bill. Individual members of legislatures, standing committees, interim committees, and legislative councils supply many bills. An even more important source is government agencies at the national, State, and local level. The judiciary, too, because its organization and proceedings are regulated if not created by the legislature, is another major source. Finally, many private individuals and organizations present bills for consideration. Table 39 shows the sources for bills submitted to the New York State legislature in 1941.

The figures on these proposals for which source information was available are especially instructive when they are reduced to percentages. Of the 1,641 proposals, 884, or fifty-three per cent, were enacted into law. Bills proposed by administrative bodies amounted to a minority, or forty-six per cent, of the total proposed; yet the total of those proposed by administrative bodies that were enacted into law made up a majority, or fifty-six per cent, of all laws enacted. In other words, sixty-five per cent of the administrative proposals became law. It is true that seventy per cent of the proposals stemming from legislative sources—119 out of 169—were enacted. However, these enactments totaled only thirteen per cent of all bills passed. The degree of influence that pressure groups have on State legislatures is partly visible in the fact that only twenty-seven per cent of the bills sponsored by formal private groups were passed. Of course, it must not be forgotten that the principal task of many pressure groups is not the enactment of laws but their prevention. It is also true that many administrative agencies work closely with private organizations, and that they often consult with these organizations when they are drafting a bill. Therefore pressure groups have had and do have a strong influence indirectly upon proposals submitted to the legislatures. In any case, it is evident that in the New York State legislature in 1941, administrative agencies were the source of more than half the bills passed. Two other notable facts are that local government agencies supplied nearly as many proposals for laws as State departments did, and

TABLE 39.   SOURCES OF BILLS BEFORE THE LEGISLATURE OF
NEW YORK STATE, 1941[1]

Sources	Number of Proposals Introduced	Number of Proposals Enacted
Administrative		
Federal agencies	14	4
State departments	376	240
Independent commissions	8	6
Local government agencies	348	241
State and local officials	23	11
Total	769	502
Judicial		
Courts and court officials	56	28
State judicial council	32	19
Total	88	47
Legislative		
Law revision commission	51	44
Temporary legislative committees and commissioners	87	47
Legislators	31	28
Total	169	119
Governmental employee associations	97	28
Non-governmental		
Organizations	395	110
Individuals or unorganized groups	123	78
Total	518	188
Total of proposals on which information is available	1,641	884
Proposals on which source information is lacking	1,199	71
Grand total	2,840	955

[1] Scott, Elizabeth McK., and Belle Zeller, "State Agencies and Lawmaking," *Public Administration Review* 2 (1942), 205–220, quoted in Lane W. Lancaster and A. C. Breckenridge, *Readings in American State Government* (New York: Rinehart & Co., Inc., 1950), p. 116.

that a higher proportion of the local proposals were enacted than of the departmental proposals.

QUESTIONS AND PROBLEMS

1. What do you think may be the reasons why unicameralism is found in only one State?

2. Describe the size of the legislature of your home State and how and when it meets. Does your home State follow a common or an unusual pattern in these practices?

3. What are the legal qualifications, terms, and salaries of the legislators of your home State? To what extent are these typical of those found in the other States?

4. Describe the differences in the organization of State legislatures and Congress.

5. Describe the sources of bills introduced into the New York legislature in 1941.

6. Compare the formal legislative procedure in the State legislatures and Congress.

Herbert Georg Studio

THE Governor is the chief executive officer of the State. He occupies a position much like that of the President of the United States; he is a major figure in his political party, and he has important ceremonial, executive, and legislative functions. However, the precise role of the Governor in any one State differs from that in any other State, so that what is said about the Governor in a specific State must be modified when it is said about the Governor in another State.

OFFICE OF THE GOVERNOR

Qualifications for office

In every State an individual must satisfy certain qualifications in order to hold the office of Governor. Some of these qualifications are constitutional (see Table 38); others are extraconstitutional. Constitutional qualifications in the main include a minimum age—commonly thirty years or thereabouts; a requirement of American citizenship; and a minimum number of years of citizenship of the State, or residence in the State, or both. The extraconstitutional qualifications may be quite weighty; their number, importance, and

TABLE 40. BACKGROUNDS OF AMERICAN GOVERNORS, 1955

Average age upon election (43)[1]	47	Lawyer	26
Education (40)		Businessman	14
High school	2	Judge	2
Some college	3	Publisher	3
College degree	13	Salesman	1
Law degree	22	Journalist	1
Married (41)	39	Farmer	2
Religion (29)		Aviator	1
Baptist	2	School teacher	2
Episcopalian	4		
Lutheran	3	Experience:	
Protestant	4	as Mayor (43)	8
Methodist	8	in other local office (42)	12
Presbyterian	3	in State legislature (44)	22
Roman Catholic	3	as State judge (43)	1
Congregationalist	1	as State administrator (43)	10
Mormon	1	as Lieutenant Governor (44)	8
Profession (46; 6 have double		as Congressman (43)	10
professions that are recorded		as other major federal office-	
twice)		holder (43)	4

[1] Number of men on whom facts are available in each category are reported in parentheses.

nature vary from one State to another. Race is sure to be a major consideration in most if not all States; religion also is apt to be important in certain States. The profession, education, and even manner of speech of an individual may play a part in his "availability." Some idea of the nature and variety of these extraconstitutional qualifications may be obtained from the survey, shown in Table 40, of the backgrounds of the forty-eight men who were Governors in the United States on January 1, 1956.

Nomination and election

The nomination and election of all State Governors follow the general pattern of nominations and elections set forth in a previous chapter. Candidates for the governorship in most States are nominated in primary elections. In a few States they are chosen in State party conventions; Republican candidates in southern States are sometimes named by the State central committee of the party. In primary elections the victor is generally the nominee who secures the largest number of votes. In most southern States, however, the victor must win an absolute majority of all votes cast. Hence it is sometimes necessary to hold a second, "run-off" primary between the two nominees receiving the largest numbers of votes in the first primary.

Official Residence of the Governor of Illinois at Springfield.

The Governor is finally chosen in a typical general election, the victor being the candidate winning the most votes in a State-wide polling. In almost all States the office of Governor is filled at the same election as certain national offices, such as those of the President and Congress. Hence the election of the Governor may be influenced by the presidential election, or, on the other hand, it may help determine which party wins the electoral vote of the State.

Structure of the Governor's office

Term and Salary: Every State Governor today serves for either a two-year or a four-year term. The tendency in past years has been to transform the two-year terms into four-year terms, so that the Governor today enjoys the longer term in a majority of the States. In most States the Governor may succeed himself, and may serve as often as he can manage to be reelected. However, in a number of States, mostly in the South, a Governor either may not succeed himself, or may hold office for a limited number of consecutive terms. These restrictions mirror the old and now widely discarded fear of strong executives, and timidity lest a Governor so entrench himself in office that he cannot be defeated in an election. Their frequency in the South is, of course, related to the predominance of the Democratic Party there, for in most southern States the official Democratic Party candidate in an election always wins. Every Governor receives an annual salary, those in 1956 ranging from a low of $9,000 in North Dakota to a high of $50,000 in New York. Over three-fourths of all Governors are paid between $10,000 and $20,000. They receive additional income in the form of expense accounts or allowances, and services attached to the office.

Removal: There are two important means for removing a Governor from office, apart from defeat at the polls. One is by impeachment, an instrument available in every State except Oregon. Impeachment proceedings in the States are much like those in the national government; the house of the State legislature functions as the prosecution, drawing up a case against the Governor and bringing the charges before the State senate, which serves as judge. In Nebraska, with its unicameral assembly, the legislature prosecutes the case and the State supreme court hears it. The size of the senate vote necessary for conviction ranges from a majority of the membership to a two-thirds majority of the membership. Only four Governors have been convicted in impeachment trials. The other important means for removing a Governor, available in eleven States, is the recall; only one Governor has been removed in this manner. Other methods for removal that exist in a few States are based on such causes as conviction of a felony.

Succession: Just as in the national government the Constitution provides that the Vice President shall succeed the President in the case of the death, removal, resignation, or incapacity of the President, in every State there is a line of succession to the Governor. In most States the immediate successor is the Lieutenant Governor. Indeed, this "stand-by" function, and the duty of presiding over meetings of the senate, are about the only tasks of the Lieutenant Governor. In any event, he does have the same qualifications for office as the Governor. Where there is no Lieutenant Governor the succession usually falls to the president of the senate or the speaker of the house. Where there is a Lieutenant Governor they may be in line after him. Others who may be named along with these three officers are such executives as the secretary of state and the attorney general.

Cabinet and Advisers: In very few States does the Governor have an effective cabinet, in the sense in which that term is ordinarily employed. That is, there are few Governors who can turn to the group of other executive officers in the State for advice and suggestions. There are specific reasons for the absence of a cabinet in most States. One is that there are so many executive officers in some States, both as single heads of departments and as members of boards and commissions, that any gathering of all of them would be far too large to make up a workable advisory body. Another leading reason is the fact that in almost every State there is at least one important executive officer in charge of an administrative agency who is elected independently (as distinct from the national government, where the only elected executives are the President and the Vice President) and who therefore does not have to obey the Governor. Consequently the Governor tends to seek advice from his personal staff (which may be considerable), from the outstanding members of the legislature, and from private citizens close to him. However, it must not be thought that Governors seek no advice from administrative chieftains; on the contrary, they may consult with heads of administrative agencies quite frequently—but *as individuals.*

Party position of the Governor

Governors today often hold an important position in their political party, at both the State and the national levels. They are generally superior to any other State officer or State party leader in the councils of the State party organization. Elected State administrative officials, although in certain constitutional respects equal to the Governor, do not occupy the rank in the public eye that the Governor does. Furthermore, the current tendency to make more and more State administrators appointive places them in a niche lower than that held by the Governor, if only because he is responsible for all acts of those whom he names to their posts. The predominance of Governors over State party leaders who are either private citizens, occupants of inferior State offices, or federal officials, is a more or less recent development. At one time many Governors were little more than puppets of a State political machine. However, machines have declined, and the process whereby the administrative role of the Governor was expanded—through such techniques as increasing his appointive power—gave more and more political power to the Governor. Thomas E. Dewey, who dominated the Republican Party of New York State while serving as Governor there, exemplified this new type of State leadership.

The only elected federal officials who might contest the Governor's rule over the State party organization are the United States Senators from that State. The fact is, however, that Governors have certain advantages over national Senators in disputes over party control. One advantage of the

Governor is that he is alone, whereas there are two Senators. Hence the Senators may compete with each other as well as with the Governor, thereby weakening their position. Another advantage for the Governor is the steady diminution of the amount of national patronage, thanks to the expansion of the classified civil service at the national level. Meanwhile the growing concentration of administrative power in the hands of the Governor made him more and more the chief dispenser of State patronage, especially since the time that Governors have been authorized to appoint the holders of the chief executive offices of the State. Finally, the adoption of the Seventeenth Amendment broke almost all ties between national Senators and State legislatures; meanwhile the increased participation of the Governors in the legislative activities of State governments has given the Governors heightened influence over State assemblymen. Thus Governors have in many cases been able to triumph over Senators in contests for dominion over State party organizations.

Governors are coming to have more and more power in national politics. One illustration of this trend is the increased power that Governors have won in national presidential nominating conventions, apparently at the expense of congressional leaders. Conventions with growing frequency are turning to Governors as presidential candidates, because, for reasons cited in a previous chapter, Governors have exceptional "availability" as presidential candidates. In certain ways, then, it may be said that the office of Governor ranks second only to that of President in its importance in national party politics.

FUNCTIONS OF THE GOVERNOR

The functions of the Governor fall into three main categories: (1) ceremonial, (2) executive, and (3) legislative.

Ceremonial functions

Like chief executives throughout the world, the Governor has many ceremonial functions. He must appear at numerous social affairs such as weddings, formal dinners, and sporting trips, that include influential people in the State. He participates in the dedication of public buildings, speaks at commencement exercises of the State university, and cheers at the baseball games of the capital city team. He welcomes distinguished visitors to the State. These ceremonial functions reach down to the host of people and groups he admits briefly into his office—labor union representatives seeking a higher minimum wage law, lawyers for industries asking preferential tax treatment, individuals wanting a job with the State government, and persons who only want to shake hands with the Governor; all typify the callers at the executive offices. These functions are among the most important means whereby the Governor conducts his public relations, assuring himself, or at least his party or faction, of the continuing good will of the voters. Their most regrettable aspect is that they require many hours that might be more profitably devoted to administration or legislation.

Executive functions

Appointments and Administration: Every State Governor has the power to appoint certain subordinate executive officials. This power is different in every State from every other, depending upon two major types of limitation: (1) the number of significant executive officials who are directly elected by the people; and (2) the degree to which the lower ranks of executive officers are recruited through a classified civil service system. The power to appoint his subordinates determines to a large degree the power of the Governor to carry out his own policies so far as the administration and enforcement of the laws enacted by the legislature are concerned. Today the appointive powers, and the administrative potential that flows from them, of almost all Governors are limited. Only in New Jersey is the Governor the sole elected executive officer. In all other States there is at least one other elected excutive officer besides the Governor. Furthermore, so far as the choice of these executive officers is concerned, the State constitutions usually impose upon the Governor (as upon the President) the requirement that his appointments obtain the approval of the State senate. In a few cases his dismissals also must have legislative confirmation; in a few other cases the dismissals must be "for cause," with written statements.

As chief executive of the State the Governor must supervise and implement the work of the lesser administrative officials. Since it is his responsibility to see that the laws are carried out, he must so direct his subordinates that they do carry out the enactments of the legislature. Usually the Governor may implement administration through rules and orders. In this function he may, in spite of legislative action, introduce his own policies either by neglecting legislative directions or by executing them in a manner not specified by the legislature.

Drafting and Administering the Budget: Drafting and administering the budget are two powers enjoyed to a greater or lesser degree by all Governors; in late years the trend has been to allot more financial responsibility to the Governor in keeping with his increased authority over administrative agencies. These financial powers, it must be noted at the outset, are legislative as well as executive; that is, they offer the Governor a means for expressing and implementing his policies. In some States, just as in the national government, the Governor submits the budget to the legislature together with a budget message explaining the aims of the budget. Also, in a few States the legislature may lower, but not raise, the appropriation figures of the Governor. The administering of the budget is a major executive function of the Governor. That is, it is his responsibility to see that the money appropriated by the legislature is spent as the legislature has directed. In this role, too, the Governor has the opportunity to bring his policies into play, if only because the legislature will find it difficult to penalize a Governor who does not administer expenditures precisely according to the legislative mandate.

Judicial: The Governor, again like other chiefs of State, is a final court of appeal in criminal cases; his powers typically are those of pardon, reprieve, commutation, and amnesty. These four judicial powers of the Governor are approximately the same as those of the President, described in a preceding chapter. As in the case of the President, the exercise of these powers might occupy all the time of the Governor; hence the actual decision is usually turned over to some other person or agency. In some States the Governor is bound by the decision of a State pardon board; such restraints have seemed desirable because some Governors have been known to grant pardons after being bribed or subjected to some form of political pressure. Finally, it must be noted that the Governor's jurisdiction extends only to crimes under State law.

Military: The Governor is the principal military officer of the State. In this position he is in command of two organizations of armed men: the State militia, or National Guard, and the agency that is termed either the State police or the highway patrol. Because the federal Constitution prohibits the States from supporting military forces in time of war, the military power of the Governor applies chiefly to the enforcement of the laws and the maintenance of the peace. He may, for instance, call out the militia to restore peace and order in the event of rioting or natural calamity. Too, he may direct the State police, or highway patrol, to perform a variety of tasks.

Legislative functions of the Governor

Like the President of the United States, the Governor not only is the chief executive officer of his government but also possesses numerous legislative functions. These functions may be divided into two broad classes: (1) obtaining the enactment of legislation, and (2) vetoing legislation. It should be noted that in some States the Governor may devote even a greater proportion of his time to legislative tasks than the President does, since many of the administrative duties are performed by elected executive officers who are not subject to the Governor's supervision.

Obtaining the Enactment of Legislation: The Governor has various means for seeking to obtain the enactment of legislation. One means is to secure political leadership in the legislature. This he may accomplish by winning the election of legislative chiefs—presiding officers and committee chairmen —who are favorable to his program. Another means is through the drafting and introduction of proposed legislation. Invariably at the beginning of a legislative session the Governor has a program that in one fashion or another he submits to the legislature. Occasionally the Governor and his advisers may draft some proposed laws after the session has commenced, owing perhaps to an unexpected popular demand. The Governor may strive to further his proposals with messages to the legislature, some of which may be intended primarily for public consumption. He may hold conferences with legislative chiefs; he may offer, or withhold, patronage for legislators, depending upon their willingness to cooperate in passing the Governor's recommendations. If the legislature refuses to act in its regular session, the Governor may call a special session. In some States he may determine what matters the legislature shall handle during a special session; with this power he may block legislators from attempting to enact laws in the special session that they could not pass in the regular session. The amount of success that Governors have in winning passage for their proposals differs from State to State.

Vetoing Legislation: In every State except North Carolina the Governor may veto laws. The extent of the veto power varies greatly from one State to another, but in all cases the procedure resembles that in the national government. In general, once a State assembly has passed a bill, the bill is sent to the Governor. If the Governor approves of the bill he may sign it, whereupon it becomes a law. If he disapproves of it he may either take no action or veto it. If he vetoes it he returns it, with a message, to the State legislature for its action. The legislature may overturn the veto by again passing the bill; depending upon the State, the vote required to overturn a veto ranges from a simple majority of those present to a two-thirds majority of the entire membership. Most Governors, like the President, also have a pocket veto; the period that must elapse between the Governor's receipt of the bill and the adjournment of the legislature differs from State to State. Usually a pocket veto is final; however, in a few States the legislature must return to a special session to deal with bills that have received a pocket veto.

Unlike the President, Governors in most States do not have to accept an entire bill; in more than three-fourths of the States, Governors may veto items in appropriation bills. In South Carolina and Washington they may veto items in any bill. With the power of imposing vetoes on items in appropriation bills Governors may block both items aimed at pleasing legislators' constituents and items devised as extortions from the Governor as the price of a legislator's support.

QUESTIONS AND PROBLEMS

1. Compare the legal qualifications of American Governors with those of the President.

2. How are Governors nominated? What differences, if any, are apt to result from these methods in contrast to the method of nominating the President?

3. In what sense do Governors have cabinets like that in the federal government?

4. What are the common patterns of salaries, causes of removal, and mode of succession of the Governors?

5. Do Governors on the average have more or less control over their parties than the President has over his?

6. What State's governorship, in your opinion, is likely to give its incumbent the best chance of becoming President? Which the least chance? Explain your answer in each case.

7. Describe briefly the executive functions of the Governor.

8. What executive powers does the President have that are seldom, or not ever, granted to Governors?

9. Describe the legislative functions of Governors. How do they differ from those of the President?

10. Are the functions of the Governors likely to increase or decrease in number, scope, and importance in the coming generation? Explain your answer.

54. The State Court Systems

George S. Flohn

STATE court systems are extremely important in the administration and enforcement of law in the United States. One authority has estimated that ninety per cent of the total number of cases at law arising during a single year are handled entirely by the State courts. A State court system has much the same relation to the Governor, the State legislature, and State administrative agencies that federal courts have to the President, Congress, and the national administrative organization. State court systems have structures, procedures, and functions similar to those of the federal system, for they both deal with patterns of laws which, although they apply to separate jurisdictions, are in many respects alike. But here the similarity ends. Each State court system is individual, differing, to a greater or lesser extent, from all other State court systems.

STRUCTURE OF STATE COURT SYSTEMS

The structure of a State court system includes all courts in the State that are not part of the federal court system. Hence, although some courts bear the title of some subordinate geographic areas, such as "municipal courts" and "county courts," they are not elements in the government of a municipality or of a county; they are State courts. The structure of a State court system, like that of the federal courts, rises through a series of grades, from the lowest and most numerous trial courts at the base, to a single appellate court at the apex that is supreme over all other courts in the State system. (In Oklahoma and Texas, however, there is a separate Court of Criminal Appeals.) In any given State the system of courts has three principal levels: (1) trial courts of limited jurisdiction, (2) trial courts of general jurisdiction, and (3) courts of appeal. Moreover, these types are often further broken down into subtypes; for example, there may be two levels of trial courts with limited jurisdiction, and two levels of courts of appeal.

Trial courts of limited jurisdiction

Justices of the Peace: The justice of the peace is the lowest court in most State systems. The office of justice of the peace is very old, having existed in England long before the founding of the first British colonies in North America. Today in the United States most justices of the peace are elected to office, although in a few States they are appointed. They are chosen from quite small areas, such as voting precincts (Alabama), districts into which counties have been divided for this purpose (Florida), townships (Michigan), or towns (Vermont).

The authority of justices of the peace extends usually to three types of cases: (1) They may try, and render decisions in, cases involving minor violations of the law; (2) justices of the peace may conduct preliminary hearings in the instance of more serious violations of the law, and "bind over" the suspect for trial in a superior court; (3) they may hear civil suits involving limited amounts of money—for example, a maximum of $100.00 in Iowa, of $200.00 in Mississippi, and of $300.00 in West Virginia. Finally, justices may conduct wedding ceremonies and, in certain southern States, are members of the board that governs a county.

The office of justice of the peace has been the target of a great deal of criticism. Seldom does either the law or constitution require that justices have any legal training or experience; in fact, only a small minority are lawyers. Decisions are often rendered with little respect for the provisions of the law. The fee system has been found objectionable, since fees usually may be assessed only when judgment has been passed against the defendant; detractors note that the initials "J.P." may represent not only "justice of the peace" but also "judgment for the plaintiff." In some States, such as New Jersey, the office has been abolished, in others its authority has been drastically curtailed, and in some the government has undertaken to instruct and closely supervise the justices. Change is difficult to accomplish, however; often it requires constitutional amendment, and it is apt to be opposed by the justices, who may be quite influential in their communities.

Police and Magistrate Courts: Police courts—or magistrate courts, as they are sometimes called—perform in the cities of some States the tasks that justices of the peace carry out in rural districts in the field of criminal offenses. That is, police courts are designed chiefly to hear cases of alleged

New York Supreme Court, Appellate Division.

violations of municipal ordinances. In a few areas police courts also have the same civil powers as justices of the peace. Sometimes police judges are ex officio justices of the peace in their county; in other places, justices of the peace are ex officio police judges in any incorporated towns in their county. Police and magistrate courts have been stigmatized even more severely than justice courts. It is said that not only is supervision lax, and legal experience uncommon, but also that corruption is rife. Actually in matters of this sort it is difficult to prove that a city is any more "impure" than a rural area.

Municipal Courts: Municipal courts are courts that certain States have authorized to handle legal matters beyond the jurisdiction of either justices of the peace or police courts. For instance, in Cleveland the municipal court has authority over civil cases involving disputes over matters whose value does not exceed $5,000. Membership in municipal courts sometimes specifically requires legal training. Generally speaking, municipal courts are highly praised by lawyers. Municipal courts are sometimes courts of record. In great metropolitan centers municipal courts may be subdivided along functional lines; in Chicago, for example, there are special courts to hear cases respecting traffic violations, juvenile offences, domestic upheavals, misdemeanors, and civil suits. In New York City, by comparison, the municipal court is subdivided on geographic lines.

County Courts: County courts are courts instituted by some States as intermediaries between justices of the peace and the courts of general jurisdiction. As in the case of municipal courts, some legal experience may be required of county court members; also, county courts are sometimes courts of record. The jurisdiction of this type of court is always restricted, but encompasses authority over cases that involve more money than justices' courts may handle. For example, in Nebraska justices of the peace may hear only those cases not involving more than $200.00, but county courts may deal with cases in which as much as $1,000.00 is at stake.

Probate Courts: Probate courts, found in a number of States, deal with the property of deceased persons. Some people leave a will or testament that declares who shall receive their property upon their death; others leave no will. Inheritance laws are very complex, and wills of rich persons are sometimes contested by those who believe they should be heirs. The functions of a probate court are to determine whether or not a will is sound; whether its provisions can be enforced; and, should a person die without leaving a will, what distribution of his estate should be made. Sometimes, when an estate is left to children, a probate court administers the estate until the recipients achieve legal maturity.

Finally, as will be seen in a following chapter, judges of probate courts are sometimes the presiding officers of county boards. It should be noted that although a probate court is a court of limited jurisdiction, the authority of the court is limited in terms of the subject of its competence, rather than in terms of how much money may be involved. For this reason the probate court stands somewhat above other courts of limited jurisdiction in the measure of its actual power and influence.

Trial courts of general jurisdiction

In every State there are trial courts of general jurisdiction, which have a variety of names. These courts have jurisdiction over all cases not in the province of the lesser, or inferior, courts. Sometimes they share jurisdiction with the lower courts over specified types of cases. They are courts of first instance for the bulk of major cases under State law. They handle almost all cases in which a person is charged with having violated a law and committed an offense that may send him, on conviction, to the State penitentiary for a term longer than one year. These trial courts also deal with civil cases—charges of torts, breaches of contract, and the like—that concern sums of money surpassing those that fall under the jurisdiction of lower courts. Another major task of the State trial courts of general jurisdiction is to serve as courts of appeal for cases that have been initiated in courts of limited jurisdiction.

Appellate courts

Inferior Appellate Courts: In thirteen States, including all of those more populous than Michigan, there are inferior appellate courts, established chiefly to lessen the burden of the State supreme courts. These courts deal with cases that have been appealed from the State trial courts of general jurisdiction, and those that have been appealed from State administrative agencies.

State Supreme Courts: State supreme courts, which are called by a different name in several of the States, are the apex of the State court system. All of them have as their primary task the hearing of cases that have been appealed from some lower State court, usually a trial court of general jurisdiction. Hearings in these courts are typically appellate, revolving about an appeal of a decision from some lower State court, whose record is sent to the supreme court for study. Occasionally State supreme courts are also courts of first instance for suits against the State government. Finally, they sometimes have the authority to issue advisory decisions, as will be noted subsequently. As in the national government, the supreme court in every State is a "collegiate" court; that is, it contains several judges, in almost all States an odd number such as three, five, seven, or nine. These justices are usually chosen at large from the State, although in eight States they are elected from particular districts.

THE STATE JUDICIARY

Selection of State judges

The method by which State judges are selected is one of the most sensitive issues concerning State court systems. Yet, despite this, State judges, at least in the chief appellate courts, are usually honest, efficient, and well-trained.

Election: In most States, judges at all levels are elected to their posts. The map in Figure 129, which shows how judges are chosen in every State, reveals the frequency of election. American politics being what they are, judges in many States run on partisan tickets and must campaign for both the primary and the general elections. This method for selecting the judiciary has been subjected to heavy criticism. The weightiest charge has been that the voters are not competent to choose men who are capable of serving them on the bench. Another attack is based on the feeling that the elected judge, obligated to the party or group that has supported him, may render a biased decision if confronted by a defendant who is associated with that party.

In a few States certain judges are appointed to office. For instance, in New Hampshire and Massachusetts all judges are appointed. Both California and Missouri have an unusual arrangement with respect to appellate judges, much like that urged by the American Bar Association. When a judicial post becomes vacant, the Governor appoints a judge to fill it, basing his appointment on the recommendation of a special group. In California this group consists of the Chief Justice of the Supreme Court, the presiding justice of the district court of appeal in the relevant district, and the State attorney general. In Missouri the group includes the Chief Justice, three private citizens named by members of the bar, and three persons selected by the Governor, one from each of the three appellate districts into which the State is divided. In these two States the Governor may appoint judges

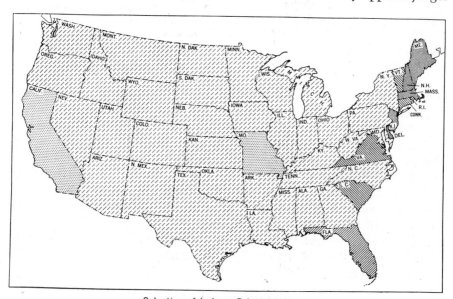

Selection of Judges—Principal Modes

Appointment by executive subject to confirmation, some minor exceptions in some states

Trial judges appointed by executive, others selected by popular or legislative vote

Modified appointment plans, applicable to appellate judiciary, others elected

Selection by legislature

Elected by popular vote, with minor exceptions in some states

A. T. Vanderbilt, "Minimum Standards of Judicial Administration" (New York: National Council of Judicial Officials, 1949), p. 7

Figure 129. Methods of Judicial Selection in the States.

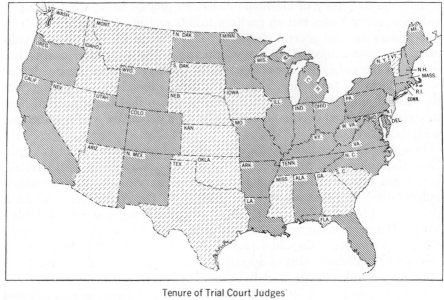

Tenure of Trial Court Judges

Life, during good behavior

Ten-year terms or longer

Life, upon reappointment, following
an initial term of seven years

Five-year terms or longer, less than ten years

Less than five-year terms

Vanderbilt, op. cit., p. 19

Figure 130.   Tenure of Office of State Judges.

only from the list presented to him by the particular group.   Then, after the
lapse of a given period of time, these judges must win the support of the
electorate.

Whether judges are elected, appointed, or chosen by a method such as
that prevailing in California and Missouri, the lawyers of the given State
may have considerable influence upon the election, or at least upon the
choice of candidates for the election.   In certain parts of Illinois and New
York, the lawyers must be consulted regarding the candidates for the bench.
In about half the remaining States the bar has an evident influence upon
the selection of judges.   In all States, however, it can be assumed that the
State bar association either formally or informally has a considerable influence upon the choice of judges.

Qualifications, term, salary, retirement

In most States either the constitution or the laws establish certain qualifications for appointment to the judiciary.   Only in New Hampshire, Massachusetts, and Connecticut, are there no constitutional or legal qualifications for members of the judiciary.   Such qualifications refer primarily to
United States citizenship, State and judicial district residence, age, education in the law, and legal experience.   Such requirements bear the stamp

of the law associations in the various States, and their pressure upon the legislatures.

Terms of State judges have a wide range, as Figure 130 discloses. The terms of appellate judges, ranging from as short a time as two years, in Vermont, to life, in Rhode Island and Massachusetts, are commonly longer than those of trial judges. In no State where judges hold office for life or during good behavior are they popularly elected to their posts. Judges may be removed from office by a variety of means. In all States except Colorado there is some method for removing an unfit judge. For instance, in twenty-two States judges may be impeached. In some other States judges may be removed by a special court. In Louisiana, for example, a judge of the State supreme court may be removed by a court of seven judges comprising members of the supreme court and the senior judges from the State court of appeals. In some States the Governor is empowered to remove a judge, and in some the legislature may do so by adopting a concurrent resolution to that effect.

Judges in all States are paid a regular annual salary, except, of course, the justices of the peace who are compensated by fees. As might be expected, in most States the judges do not receive as large a salary as that enjoyed by members of the federal bench. As an illustration, salaries of members of State supreme courts run from a low of $8,500, in Idaho, to a high of $35,000, in New York. Judges of inferior courts receive correspondingly less. In twenty States the chief justice is paid slightly more than other members of the supreme court.

THE PROSECUTING ARM

The prosecuting arm of the State court system is the group of personnel charged with conducting trials and suits to which the State is a party, in behalf of the State.

As in the federal government, so also in every State there is an important official in the administrative branch—the attorney general. In the majority of States the attorney general is an elected officer; only in a few is he appointed by the Governor. The attorney general is the principal legal officer of the State. Yet, unlike his federal counterpart, he is not likely to be in charge of the trials of persons accused of breaking the law. He does represent the State in civil suits to which the State is a party. Also, he is the chief legal advisor of the Governor. When the attorney general is of the same political party as the Governor, especially when he has been appointed to office, he may have a great deal of influence upon the Governor's policies.

Prosecution in the trial courts of general jurisdiction is entrusted to a prosecuting attorney, one of whom serves in every State judicial district. Because there is almost invariably far more business than the prosecuting attorney can manage alone, he is usually empowered to appoint one or more assistant district attorneys for his district. The prosecuting attorneys bear various official titles, among them district attorney, public prosecutor, and simply prosecuting attorney. They are ordinarily elected by the voters of their judicial districts; whatever may be the boundaries of these districts, the attorneys are officers of the State government. The principal duty of the prosecuting attorney is to bring to trial the persons accused of violating the law in his district and to secure conviction of the guilty.

The office of district attorney often has important political overtones. By winning a conviction of a person charged with committing an especially heinous crime, a prosecuting attorney catches the eye of the public and may hope to obtain popular support for a higher office. Hence, young and politically ambitious men seek election as district attorney preliminary to seeking election to Congress or the office of Governor. Thomas E. Dewey and Earl Warren are outstanding illustrations of district attorneys who have succeeded in using their post as a springboard to higher office.

PROCEEDINGS IN STATE COURTS

Proceedings in State courts, whether criminal or civil, are quite similar to those in federal courts. It is true that procedural rules vary somewhat in different States. Also, in some States, a defendant is not hedged about with as many actual protections as he can have in a federal court—although the State constitution may guarantee these protections. (Indeed, several States guarantee more procedural protection than the federal courts do, and actually fulfill those guarantees.) However, the elements of legal proceedings in each State resemble those in every other State, and in all States these proceedings resemble those in federal courts. Louisiana may be cited as a partial exception to this principle, inasmuch as a fair-sized portion of the laws of Louisiana are based on the French Napoleonic Code from the time that the State was a French colony.

Advisory opinions

An advisory opinion is an opinion rendered by a court regarding the constitutionality of a given law or the meaning of a statute, under circumstances in which there is no case before the court involving the given law. It was noted in a prior chapter that federal courts do *not* render advisory opinions; that is, a federal court will rule on the constitutionality of a statute only in hearing a genuine case in which the law is at issue. In some States, however, courts are authorized to hand down such opinions. Ordinarily they do so on the application of the Governor, the State attorney general, or some other official charged with the enforcement of the law.

The impact of an advisory opinion is not the same in all States. In some States, for instance, it is an "opinion," and nothing more. That is, it reflects the court's feelings respecting the law, but is in no way binding. In certain other States, however, an advisory opinion is equal to an opinion or ruling handed down in an actual court trial; it may be cited as a legal precedent, and is as binding on an executive official or another court as a true legal precedent.

QUESTIONS AND PROBLEMS

1. Name the three principal levels of the State court systems and describe briefly their functions. What are their precise names in your home State?

2. Compare police and magistrate courts with the courts of justices of the peace.

3. Is the probate court a trial court of general jurisdiction? Is it the same as a county court?

4. Distinguish between the State supreme courts and trial courts of general jurisdiction.

5. How are judges chosen in your home State? Are these ways typical of the methods used in other States?

6. Compare the organization of the State prosecuting systems with that of the Federal government.

PART XV

Structure
of Local Government

Mrs. Eva W. Davis, Old Cour House Museum, Vicksburg, Miss.

THE NATURE OF THE COUNTY

Counties, unlike cities, blanket the map of the United States. They are subordinate to the State. As a political unit the county has an independent governing body and enough financial power to carry out the functions that have been assigned to it by the State government. There are only a few classes of regions in the United States that do not have typical counties: (1) those such as New York City, where the county governments are dependent upon the city governments; (2) those such as San Francisco, where

843

the government is termed that of a "city-county"; (3) those such as St. Louis, which are "independent cities" outside counties; (4) those such as Armstrong County, South Dakota, which are termed counties but which have no organized government; and (5) those such as Yellowstone Park, which are federal zones.

There are 3,049 counties in the United States (those in Louisiana being called "parishes"). They range from three in Delaware to 254 in Texas. Counties also vary greatly in size; the smallest is Arlington, Virginia, with twenty-four square miles, and the largest is San Bernardino, in California, with 20,131 square miles, about half again as many as in Connecticut, Rhode Island, and Massachusetts combined. In general the counties in the far western States are larger than those elsewhere in the nation. The average county is about 1,000 square miles in area, or would make a square a little more than thirty miles on a side.

Counties also show great variations in their population; according to the 1950 census they range from 227, in Loving County, Texas, to 4,508,792, in Cook County (Chicago), Illinois. Four other counties—Los Angeles (California), Wayne (Michigan), Allegheny (Pennsylvania), and Cuyahoga (Ohio)—each contain more than one million people, and a considerable number have more than one hundred thousand. The average county, however, has a population of about fifty-five thousand, and the majority of American counties have fewer people than this number. Indeed, most counties in the United States do not contain a single city with more than ten thousand people. Thus, whereas certain American counties have large urban populations—in 1950 only nine States had more people than Cook County—most counties have fewer than 50,000 people, and are fundamentally rural in character. The predominantly rural aspect of most counties plays an important role in fashioning their political needs and activities.

The county is an important unit in little more than the political sense; in fact, its possession of other sorts of unity is founded upon its political unity in virtually every case. It is a geographic unit chiefly in the sense that it has boundaries separating it from other counties; however, these boundaries ordinarily are only surveyors' lines, so that the landscape on either side of a county line varies little. It is rarely a social unit, for in most cases the people in one county do not live differently from the people in the next county. The county may be an economic unit at least so far as local merchandising is concerned, when the county seat is the one important retailing center of the county; however, so far as production is concerned the county is unlikely to be an economic unit because neighboring counties are apt to produce the same type of commodities. In general, then, a county has a sort of unity only in relation to government.

This unity refers of course to the formal structure of government. It is also related to the structure of the major political parties: the county is an important unit in party organization. County party chairmen together

---

The Former County Court House of Warren County, Mississippi, at Vicksburg.
An expansive flowering of Ante-Bellum Southern architecture, showing the great importance of the County then (and also now) in Southern society.

often dominate the party organization of the entire State; delegates to State conventions are often apportioned by counties. The strength of political parties at the county level may be attributed to at least two of the features of county government. One is that authority is so diffused among the various offices in the county government that a strong party organization—often called the "court house gang"—may readily fill in the power vacuum in the formal structure of the government. The other is that the non-partisan examination system for filling administrative posts is perhaps weakest at the county level of government, so that a party organization may strengthen its position in county politics through the number of government offices it may have awarded to the party faithful.

THE NATURE OF COUNTY GOVERNMENT

An agent and creature of the State

The county, as noted in a previous chapter, is a creature and an agent of the State. It is established chiefly to carry out functions or policies of the State at the local level. Counties serve as geographic units for the administration of justice, the collecting of taxes, and the conduct of elections. County governments perform tasks in connection with such State activities as education, welfare, liquor control, and soil conservation. They possess only those powers that are delegated to them by the States, either by constitutional provision or by legislative enactment. Hence, except when they are based on the State constitution, these powers may be added to, subtracted from, or even abolished, at the will of the State legislature.

Functions of county governments

The functions of county governments are primarily administrative. It is true that counties do have a few legislative powers, in declaring policy respecting a limited number of fields, but by and large they administer policies that have been expressed by the State legislature. Of course, the various officials of the county government may impress their own policies, and those of the voters, upon the policies of the State government, through the methods by which, and the degrees to which, they implement State legislative enactments. That the primary functions of county governments are administrative is confused by the fact that the leading agency of most county governments is an elective board composed of several members, for usually such a body—Congress, or a State legislature—is regarded as a legislature. A related paradox is that many individual officers of the county government, such as the sheriff, the coroner, and the clerk, most or all of whose assigned duties are administrative, are also elected.

Regional variations in the importance of counties

The importance of counties in the United States varies greatly from one region to another. In New England, for example, counties are relatively unimportant. In that region the chief political unit subordinate to the State is the town; as an illustration, in some New England States the legislative districts are based not on counties but on the towns. By contrast, in the South Atlantic States the counties are very important, exercising numerous functions at the local level. It is probably significant that southern States have been among the boldest in experimenting with the structure of county government. The difference between these two extremes may be ascribed to their settlement in colonial times: New England was settled by religious groups who founded towns, but the South was settled by less solidly organized groups. In the Middle Atlantic States counties are important, but less so than in the South. West of the Appalachians the importance of counties depends to some extent upon which of the original thirteen States furnished their earliest leading groups. In Ohio, first populated by New Englanders, counties are less important than they are in Mississippi, colonized by southerners. In most States of the trans-Mississippi West, counties are rather important if only because towns are few.

THE AGENCIES OF COUNTY GOVERNMENT

The typical county government includes a bewildering array of agencies for the performance of governmental tasks. In general, no one of these agencies possesses ultimate authority in the county; rather, each of the principal agencies stands upon the same plane as all of the others. For this reason county government is often termed "headless." Moreover, there is no separation of powers among these agencies; any of them may be authorized to wield legislative, executive, and judicial powers.

The county board

Title and Composition: The most prominent agency in almost all county governments is a body composed of several members and known generally as the "county board." A tabulation published by the Census Bureau in 1947 disclosed that there were then more than twenty-five different names for the county board in various counties across the nation. According to this tabulation, in more than five-sixths of all counties this agency was called either a board of commissioners, a board of supervisors, a county court, or a commissioners court.

Apart from their titles, there are four principal types of county board, as determined by their composition: (1) a board of commissioners or of supervisors, comprising officials entrusted solely with the government of the county; (2) a board of town or township supervisors, made up of officials who manage both the governments of towns or townships and the government of the county; (3) a board of judge and commissioners, whose presiding officer also holds a judicial position but whose other members deal only with the government of the county; and (4) a board consisting of a judge and justices of the peace, all of whose members hold judicial office and share in the government of the county.

Besides these four main types there are five others, all infrequent. Table 41 shows the number of counties in which each of these types appears, the total number of members of the boards of each type, the average number per board, and the number of board members per 10,000 population under each type. It can be seen that hoards of commissioners or of supervisors are the commonest form of this agency, since they exist in two-thirds of all American counties. Of the six States whose boards consist of town or township supervisors, four—Illinois, Michigan, Nebraska, and Wisconsin—are among the North Central States; the other two—New Jersey and New York—are Middle Atlantic States. Judge-and-commissioners boards are found in some or all of the counties of Alabama, Georgia, Kentucky, Tennessee, and Texas—all southern States—and in Oregon. Judge-and-justices-of-the-peace boards prevail in Kentucky and Tennessee, and the minor types are also found chiefly in the South.

Number of Members: The number of members on county boards ranges from one, in all Arkansas and some Georgia and South Carolina counties, to eighty-two, in Dane County, Wisconsin. The commonest numbers, embracing almost three-quarters of all counties, are three and five. The size of the board is related to its composition; boards consisting of town or township supervisors are on the average more than six times as large as boards of commissioners or supervisors, and boards consisting of judges and justices of the peace are on the average more than four times as large. This fact helps to account for the exceptional size of the boards in such States as Tennessee, Illinois, and New Jersey. In each of twenty-six States all county boards are the same size.

TABLE 41. NUMBER AND CHARACTERISTICS OF COUNTY GENERAL GOVERNING BODIES[1]

Character of Membership	Number of Counties	Number of Members	Average Number of Members Per County	Number of Members Per 10,000 Inhabitants
Board of commissioners or supervisors	2,012	7,993	4.0	1.0
Board composed of town (township) supervisors	297	7,616	25.6	5.1
Judge and commissioners	350	1,666	4.8	1.8
Judge and justices of the peace	193	3,300	17.1	8.0
Single judge	86	86	1.0	2.5
Plural-member court	75	359	4.8	0.7
Single non-judicial officer	32	32	1.0	0.5
Non-judicial ex officio body	4	21	5.3	0.6
Executive and town (township) supervisors	1	7	7.0	0.2
Totals	3,050	21,080	6.9	1.8

[1] United States Department of Commerce, Bureau of the Census, *Governmental Organization No. 2. County Boards and Commissions* (Washington: Government Printing Office, 1947). One county, Nantucket (Massachusetts), has since 1952 been counted as a township; another county, East Baton Rouge Parish (Louisiana), has been combined with the city of Baton Rouge and is counted as a city. At the same time one new county, Los Alamos (New Mexico) has been created. Consequently there are now 3,049 counties, whereas in 1947 there were 3,050.

Election: Most county boards in the United States are popularly elected. However, there are several methods for choosing board members in terms of geographic representation. The usual method, one that prevails in about three counties out of ten, is to elect each member from a separate district in the county. Another common practice is to elect some members at large from the county and others from individual districts. A third way is to elect all members at large, with the requirement that candidates either reside in a specific district or be nominated by the residents of a given district. In one county out of ten, the board members are elected from towns or townships. Finally, in some counties all board members are elected at large, with no proviso concerning district representation. A few board members in Alabama, Connecticut, Georgia, and South Carolina are appointed by some other official or officials.

Terms and Presiding Officers: Terms of office for board members range from one year to eight years. In almost three-quarters of all counties, however, members serve for either two- or four-year terms, the four-year terms in many cases overlapping. In thirty-two States all county board members have terms of the same length; eight of the States in which variations exist are in the South. Each county board has a presiding officer, whose identity and means of selection ordinarily depend upon the type of the board. Boards of supervisors or commissioners generally name their own presiding officer, who serves for only one year or at the pleasure of the board. Boards composed of a judge and commissioners or a judge and justices of the peace have a judge—usually a probate judge—as presiding officer, whose term is based upon that of his judicial office.

Functions: The functions of county boards, although they differ greatly from one State to another, are primarily executive or administrative. Many boards do have certain powers that may be termed legislative. Most important among these legislative powers are those of drafting a budget, levying taxes, and appropriating money. Whereas such fiscal powers at the national and State levels are important means for declaring and executing policy, on the county level they are not so significant since they involve primarily the fulfilling of tasks assigned to the county by the State legislature. Some county boards also have a certain amount of ordinance-making power that results in the enactment of a subordinate kind of law.

One leading executive or administrative function is that of appointing other administrative officials. This power is often limited by State requirements that particular officeholders in each county must be elected by the people.

County fiscal boards

In some or all of the counties in eleven States the fiscal needs of the counties are handled not by the county board but by a separate agency. In five States—Maine, New Hampshire, Massachusetts, Connecticut (all in New England), and South Carolina, the State legislature performs these tasks. In New Hampshire these duties are assigned to the county convention, or legislative delegates from the towns, for each county; in Connecticut, to the

State representatives and senators from each county; and in Maine, Massachusetts, and South Carolina, to the entire State legislature, although in these States it may be assumed that the representatives from each county will have exceptional influence respecting the affairs of their constituencies.

In six other States, four in the South—Arkansas, Florida, Georgia, and Tennessee—and two in the Midwest—Indiana and Michigan—some or all of the counties have distinct boards at the county level for the management of their finances, to a greater or lesser degree. In Indiana, for example, the voters of every county choose a separate county council that appropriates money for county operations, fixes the tax rate, and arranges for the borrowing of money. The creation of these distinct fiscal bodies probably reflects public mistrust in county boards and the consequent decision to separate taxing and appropriating powers from spending powers.

Other county boards and commissions

In every State except Maine and New Hampshire (and, of course, Rhode Island, which has no organized county governments), the State constitution or State laws, or both, authorize the establishment of other county boards or commissions for the performance of specific tasks. These boards and commissions are not to be confused with the governing bodies of special districts; they do not have any corporate or quasi-corporate status, and are subordinate in one way or another to the county board. Members of these boards may be selected in any of a number of ways. They may be popularly elected; appointed by a related State agency, a court, the county board, or some other body; or serve ex officio. Sometimes part of the members of a given board may be chosen by one of these methods and part by another. In a handful of cases the method for choosing board members is not specified.

Such special function boards have been authorized for dealing with a host of tasks; in Illinois, for example, these tasks include airports, assessment, defense, elections, health, highways, hospitals, justice, libraries, personnel, planning, schools, veterans, and welfare. In some instances the creation of these boards is mandatory upon the counties; sometimes, it is discretionary.

Principal officials of the county

A number of the functions of county government are performed not by boards or commissions but by offices headed by individuals. The numbers and types of these offices vary from State to State and even from county to county, although in some States the constitution or the laws require that a specified office exist in each county of the State. The method for choosing these officials, their terms of office, their powers and duties, differ likewise from one county to another. Throughout the country as a whole the number of kinds of such officials is legion. However, because almost all counties perform particular tasks, certain among these officials are found in virtually every county.

The Sheriff: The sheriff is probably the most important single officeholder in the typical county government. In most counties the sheriff is chosen in a popular election, which in many instances is non-partisan. Partisan elections for the sheriff's office may be significant enough in populous counties to have an important influence upon national elections when the two coincide; it is generally agreed that the defeat of Senator Scott Lucas of Illinois, Democratic floor leader, in his campaign for reelection in 1950 was largely brought about by voters' repugnance for the Democratic candidate for sheriff in Cook County. Often a number of candidates put themselves forward for this post, despite the comparatively low salary. However, many sheriffs are also paid fees for a variety of tasks, such as serving warrants and transporting accused persons from the point of their arrest to the county jail, so that the total income may be very large.

The sheriff has three principal types of duty. In the first place, he is the head of the county police forces, obligated to maintain the peace and to protect persons and property. The sheriff exercises this duty in rural parts of the county. However, in counties that have an important metropolitan center the office of sheriff may be rather insignificant, partly because only a small portion of the county falls under his jurisdiction, and also because the city police forces are often far better equipped than he to investigate crimes. Yet, since most American counties do not have a city with as many as 10,000 people, the sheriff is still an important police official in most of the country.

The second type of duty involves the sheriff's tasks with relation to the county court. For example, he must see to it that accused persons and witnesses are present for criminal cases. In this respect he is in fact an officer of the county court, and subsequently an officer of the State government as well as of the county. Finally, the sheriff is in charge of the county jail, concerned with the maintenance of the physical plant and the needs of the prisoners.

The Coroner: Another county officer associated with the detection of crime and the punishment of criminals is the coroner, whose principal task is to investigate deaths that appear to result from other than natural causes. To carry out this task the coroner is ordinarily not very well equipped himself, for although the position really calls for a physician it is rarely occupied by one. Hence the coroner must frequently engage the assistance of a doctor in his investigations. The coroner is also empowered to summon a jury to which he submits testimony in cases of mysterious deaths. Having weighed the testimony the jury decides whether the death resulted from a crime. If such is the decision, the evidence is then turned over to the district attorney's office for prosecution.

The County Clerk: The county clerk is an official whose duties vary widely from one State to another. In most counties the clerk is elected, but in a few he is appointed by some other officer or agency. The chief tasks of the clerk revolve about the recording and custody of non-judicial public documents, especially deeds to real estate and mortgages. Beside these fundamental duties clerks may be assigned any of a great number of unrelated obligations. Clerks are often important election officials, charged with such functions as preparing the ballots. A clerk may be empowered to issue licenses for different sorts of business undertakings. Sometimes he is the secretary of the county board, keeping the minutes of the meetings and drafting agenda for board sessions; with these powers he has the opportunity of becoming the most powerful official of the county government. He may have certain financial powers such as those of examining the accounts or even of drawing up the budget. In small counties he may also serve as clerk of the county court, although this is often a separate office, with duties that are outlined below.

The Clerk of the County Court: The clerk of the county court is actually an officer of the State government, but since most State court systems are divided into districts along county lines, clerks are chosen according to counties. Most court clerks are elected; a few are named by the courts. The chief task of the court clerk is to make and preserve a record of court proceedings. This is a very important duty, if only because the records of court cases must be available for study by the judges of an appellate court in the event a case is appealed. Obviously court records must be exact. Court clerks may also have the duty of summoning prospective jurors for trials.

Finance Officers: Most counties have at least one officer concerned primarily with the finances of the county government; large counties have several such officers. The most important of such officers are the tax collector, who gathers taxes frequently not only for the county but also for State and local governments; the treasurer, who has custody of county funds; the assessor, who appraises property for tax purposes; the controller, who studies all planned expenditures to determine if they are authorized by law, and who strives for financial efficiency in the administering of the laws; the auditor, who examines expenditures after they have been made, to insure that they have been legal; and the budget director, who drafts the budget. In many instances the duties of two or more of these offices will be united in a single person because the county is not sufficiently populous to keep more than one person busy at these tasks.

Superintendent of Schools: Most counties today have a superintendent of public schools. His functions differ considerably from one State to another, depending largely upon the relations between the school system and the county government. In many cases his powers are limited to the schools in the rural districts, since the incorporated cities have their own superintendents. The county superintendent serves as an intermediary between the State board of education and the district school superintendents. He shares in the appointing of new teachers, helps select textbooks, and oversees the maintenance of academic standards. Often the county school superintendent is an elected official, although he may be chosen in a non-partisan election, or be named by the county board of education. State law generally provides certain qualifications for holding this office, mainly along the lines of a minimum amount of education and a minimum number of hours of college courses in school administration and supervision.

County reform: the county manager

In about a score of American counties, sometimes under authority extended by general law and sometimes under home-rule arrangements, the post of county manager, or chief executive officer, has been created. This post strongly resembles that of city manager: the incumbent is appointed by the county board, is presumably non-partisan and in fact "non-political," and is made administrative chief of the county government. Probably his most important task is the drafting of the budget, in consultation with agency heads. He may also function as purchasing officer for the county government, and may furthermore supervise public works. He is expected to serve as the general manager of the county government. The creation of this office is an attempt to concentrate administrative power and responsibility upon a single person. Some counties with managers, notably Los Angeles County in California, do appear to provide examples of unusually efficient government at their levels.

QUESTIONS AND PROBLEMS

1. What is the size of your home county? Are there any consequences of its size that you regard as unfortunate? What are they? Are these problems typical of many other counties?

2. List the functions commonly performed by county governments.

3. Describe the different methods of electing county supervisors.

4. Besides the county boards, are there other county-wide political and administrative bodies in one or more States?

5. Describe the present role and function of the sheriff in the United States.

6. Read the article on "sheriff" in an encyclopedia. How does the sheriff's role in America differ from that of the English sheriff of the Middle Ages?

7. List, and describe in two sentences, the functions of three other common county officers besides the sheriff.

8. Describe in a paragraph the principal governing agency of your home or college county. Is it a common type in the United States?

56. Municipalities, Townships, and Special Districts

"New York Times" and Essex Institute, Salem, Mass. (Frank Cousins' collection)

MUNICIPALITIES

A MUNICIPALITY is a public corporation that has been vested with general governing powers over a relatively small, densely populated area. As a public corporation it may sue and be sued, negotiate contracts, own land and other properties, and incur debts. The mere fact that there is a concentration of people shows the presence of common bonds; otherwise these people would not have settled in one place. Hence a municipality is more nearly a "natural" political unit than any other governmental body. However, when this population nucleus obtains a municipal government its residents acquire yet another set of common interests, those associated with a formal political organization.

Types of municipalities

In the United States there are four types of municipalities: cities, villages, towns, and boroughs. It is important to remember that the hallmark of a municipality is its corporate status. A city, at least in the United States, is always assumed to be incorporated, so that all American cities are municipalities. However, there are instances in which villages, towns, and boroughs are not incorporated, so that they sometimes cannot be classed as municipalities. For example, the term "village" is often loosely applied to any hamlet whether or not it is incorporated; the "towns" of New England, New York State, and Wisconsin are not incorporated; and the five boroughs that comprise New York City are not regarded as municipalities. The prime factor in determining what is the type of a municipality, or what is the class of a city or village, is the size of its population. That is, State law or the State constitution provides that, for example, a given municipality is a village if its population is below a stipulated number, and may be a city if its population exceeds that number; classes of cities and villages are likewise fixed by numbers of population. In Ohio, for instance, in order to have the rank of city an incorporated place must have more than 5,000 inhabitants; otherwise it has the status of a village. In Pennsylvania there are four levels or classes of cities: first class, 1,000,000 or more inhabitants; second class, 500,000 to 1,000,000; second class A, 135,000 to 500,000; and third class, fewer than 135,000.

Traits of the city

Prominence: The city is one of the most prominent features on the twentieth-century American landscape. Half of the people in the United States reside in 168 so-called "metropolitan" areas, each composed of a central city with a population of at least 50,000 and its dependent suburbs, that dot the country from coast to coast. Between forty and fifty million people reside in the fourteen metropolitan areas each containing more than one million persons. In 1950 nearly two-thirds of all Americans lived in an area having municipal government; Table 42 shows the numbers and percentages of those living in cities (and other municipalities) in various population groups. New Jersey was the most urban of all States, with 86.6 per cent of its people in municipalities. North Dakota, with 26.6 per cent, was the least urban.

Problems Created by Cities: Cities cause a host of problems not found in a rural civilization, and many of these problems call for solutions by gov-

---

The Town House of Marblehead, Mass. (1727), Where Town Meetings Were Held for over 200 Years, and the New York City Hall.

ernmental means. Indeed, as the population of a city rises, the number of problems created and of solutions demanded rises at an even faster pace. The inhabitants of cities require a multitude of services, such as public transportation, a water supply, means for disposing of wastes, and fire and police protection. Inasmuch as cities are the chief location for industry, they are the principal sufferers from the ills of industrial society, notably periodic unemployment; most cities have undertaken vast welfare programs to cope with such ills. Whereas cities are not the sinks of iniquity that rural legend pictures them to be, they do have a higher crime rate than the countryside, resulting in a demand for greater protective services. Too, whereas farm districts are not typified by exalted standards of morality, vice in cities is apt to be professional and organized. Thus municipal government deals with a host of everyday personal matters concerning numerous people, and comes much closer to the average individual than the federal government does.

Political Status of Cities: To recapitulate and reemphasize what has been said previously, cities are agents of the State, designed to govern local areas. They are created by the State and vested with their powers by the State. Often the State government treats its cities in a manner that is either unsympathetic or negligent. Although the population in more than half the States is classed as predominantly urban, State legislatures tend to be controlled by representatives from rural constituencies; these representatives are frequently hostile toward cities, denying them powers needed to satisfy certain demands of their population. As a consequence the ruling groups in many cities have turned for aid to the federal government; cities, it is true, are underrepresented also in Congress, but not to the extent that they are in State legislatures. Thanks to some effective lobbying in Congress cities have managed to secure direct financial assistance from the national Treasury, without the intercession of the State authorities. Figure 131 describes in some detail the tasks of a city lobbyist.

TABLE 42. DISTRIBUTION OF THE MUNICIPAL POPULATION AMONG CITIES OF VARIOUS SIZES [1]

| | | | 1950 | |
Population Size Group	Number of Municipalities	Per Cent of Total	Population (Thousands Omitted)	Per Cent of Total
100,000 or more	106	0.6	44,313	46.1
50,000–100,000	126	0.8	8,932	9.3
25,000–50,000	250	1.5	8,737	9.1
10,000–25,000	751	4.5	11,485	11.9
5,000–10,000	1,094	6.5	7,582	7.9
2,500–5,000	1,562	9.3	5,529	5.8
1,000–2,500	3,422	20.4	5,402	5.6
Fewer than 1,000	9,467	56.4	4,125	4.3
Total U.S.	16,778	100.0	96,106	100.0

[1] United States Department of Commerce, Bureau of the Census, *Governments in the United States in 1952* (Washington: Government Printing Office, 1953), p. 2.

Mayor Picks Col. Weed For City's Lobbyist

Mayor George Christopher named the man yesterday he wants as the city's lobbyist in Washington—Colonel Thomas J. Weed, the East Coast representative of the Port of San Francisco.

Mayor Christopher said he has asked the Board of State Harbor Commissioners to let San Francisco have half Colonel Weed's time. The Board has given its informal approval, he said.

The city would pay half of Colonel Weed's $16,000-a-year salary, the Mayor declared.

Christopher said he would ask the Board of Supervisors to approve the appointment tomorrow.

Colonel Weed, 63, has a lifetime of experience in shipping and transportation behind him and also has extensive contacts in Washington.

"He has a high personal regard for both of our Congressmen," Mayor Christopher said. "He can get along with them nicely."

"He is familiar with procedures in the General Services Administration, which has extensive properties here, and will be helpful in increasing traffic at San Francisco International Airport.

"He knows how foreign air-

COL. THOMAS WEED
He's Mayor's choice

lines make applications with the State Department for new routes."

CONFLICTS OF INTEREST

The Mayor said Colonel Weed was his choice over all other lobbyists.

"All the others have four, five or ten other clients," Christopher said. "There might be conflicts of interest.

"With Colonel Weed I am convinced there would be no conflict of interest.

"He would give us permanent representation in Washington. Before, we got perhaps one day a month at an annual cost of $30,000. Now we would have many times more service for less than one-third the cost."

EXPENSE MONEY

The Mayor said Colonel Weed would be granted—indeed, had asked for—a maximum of $1200 a year for expenses.

"Those expenses would be Continued on Page 17, Col. 1

Lobbyist Nominated: Mayor Picks Col. Weed

Continued from Page 1

based on vouchers," Christopher said, "and he believes that's all he needs.

"He doesn't believe in elaborate expenditures. He believes a proper, logical and sensible approach to legislators is more effective. They don't want to be lavishly wined and dined."

(The city's present lobbyist, ex-Supervisor Marvin E. Lewis, who retires January 31, has been under fire for allegedly "lavish, wanton and extravagant" spending habits in the Nation's capital.)

CONFERENCE HERE

Colonel Weed flew here for a conference yesterday with the Mayor, State Board of Harbor Commissioners Chairman Cyril Magnin and Henry J. Budde, a board member.

When they emerged from the Mayor's office shortly after noon, Christopher announced the terms of a contract with Colonel Weed had been "arrived at informally."

He added that under the proposed contract Colonel Weed would pay his own office expenses and "will have us listed in the telephone book and on his door. These are things that never happened before."

The ex-Army man's salary from the city would be $4000 less than Lewis received.

LIMITED WORK

He, the Mayor and Magnin agreed that his work for the Port of San Francisco would be limited to the Washington area if the contract is approved.

Mayor Christopher said the Harbor Board wants to establish another office in New York, with a full-time employee, to solicit cargoes there and in other Eastern cities.

Colonel Weed has been working for the port on the East Coast since October, and Magnin said that at least some of the increase in tonnage noted in recent months is attributable to him.

ARMY CAREER

The Board of State Harbor Commissioners hired Colonel Weed away from the Port of Stockton.

Texas-born, Colonel Weed was an Army officer for 35 years. He retired in 1952. His service began in World War I and was climaxed by his command of the Army's Port of Embarkation at Le Havre, France, following the invasion of Normandy in 1944.

"San Francisco Chronicle," January 29, 1956, p. 1

Figure 131. Tasks of a City Lobbyist.

These arrangements sometimes increase the hostility of the State legislators from rural zones. The result is that in the legislatures of such States as Illinois and Michigan, there is often as clear a division between "city" members and "downstate" or "upstate" members as there is between Republicans and Democrats.

Forms of municipal government

There are three principal forms of municipal government in the United States today: (1) mayor-council; (2) commission; and (3) council-manager. Figure 132 sketches their major structural features. The mayor-council form has two important subtypes: weak-mayor and strong-mayor.   Each type also has certain minor variations from one State to another.   Table 43 shows the number and percentage of cities with each form in several population groups.

Mayor-Council: The mayor-council form of city government possesses an executive branch—the mayor—and a legislative branch—the council. Hence it resembles the national government.   (City courts, to reiterate, are in fact State courts.)   However, although the executive and the legislative branches are distinct, there is not the degree of separation of powers that

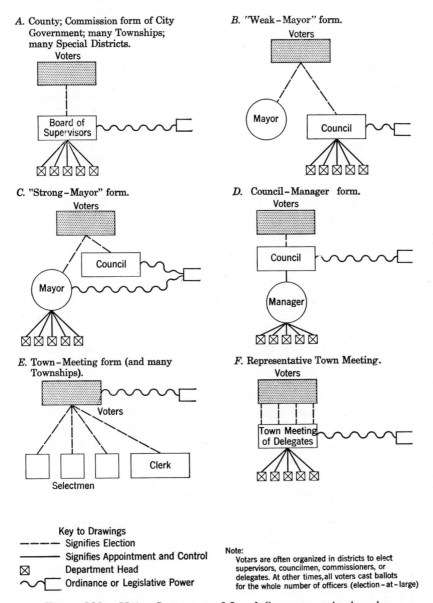

A. County; Commission form of City Government; many Townships; many Special Districts.

B. "Weak–Mayor" form.

C. "Strong–Mayor" form.

D. Council–Manager form.

E. Town–Meeting form (and many Townships).

F. Representative Town Meeting.

Key to Drawings
- – – – – Signifies Election
- ———— Signifies Appointment and Control
- ☒ Department Head
- ∿⊏ Ordinance or Legislative Power

Note:
Voters are often organized in districts to elect supervisors, councilmen, commissioners, or delegates. At other times, all voters cast ballots for the whole number of officers (election–at–large)

Figure 132.   Major Structures of Local Government in America.

TABLE 43. FORM OF GOVERNMENT IN 2,527 CITIES (WITH POPULATIONS EXCEEDING 5,000)[1]

Population Group	Number of Cities	Mayor-Council		Commission		Council-Manager	
		Number	%	Number	%	Number	%
More than 500,000	17	16	94.1	0	0.0	1	5.9
250,000–500,000	23	8	34.8	6	26.1	9	39.1
100,000–250,000	65	28	43.1	14	21.5	23	35.4
50,000–100,000	129	46	35.7	27	20.9	55	42.6
25,000–50,000	277	107	38.6	48	17.3	113	40.8
10,000–25,000	835	376	45.0	132	15.8	283	33.9
5,000–10,000	1,181	734	62.2	129	10.9	280	23.7
Total U.S.	2,527	1,315	52.0	356	14.1	764	30.3

Population Group	Town Meeting		Representative Town Meeting	
	Number	%	Number	%
50,000–100,000	0	0.0	1	0.8
25,000–50,000	3	1.1	6	2.2
10,000–25,000	24	2.9	20	2.4
5,000–10,000	27	3.1	1	0.1
Total U.S.	64	2.5	28	1.1

[1] *1955 Municipal Yearbook*, p. 57. These data include New England towns and other townships, which, being few in number, do not greatly influence either the totals or the percentages, save for those respecting town meetings and representative town meetings.

exists in the national government. For example, whereas neither the President nor any other executive officer in the national government can be forced to obey a congressional subpoena, a mayor may be obliged to surrender documents to the council on the demand of the council. In 1942 a New York State court ruled that the "theory of co-ordinate, independent branches of government has been generally held to apply to the national system and to the states but not to the government of cities."

THE MAYOR. Mayors have varying amounts and kinds of powers. In the weak-mayor form, which is gradually disappearing, the mayor may be little more than a figurehead. For instance, the office of mayor may be filled not by popular vote but by the council, which chooses one of its members to preside over council meetings. This sort of arrangement, as it happens, is much more frequent in commission and council-manager governments than in mayor-council governments. Table 44 shows how American mayors are selected.

The weak mayor typically has little appointive power; most executive offices are filled by popular election, saddling the voters with a long ballot. The weak mayor also may have a restricted veto power. The weak mayor does not have much to do with the framing of the budget. The strong mayor, by contrast, appoints a large number of executive officers, so that the people have a short ballot. He has considerable veto power; that is, his veto can be overridden only by an extraordinary majority vote of the council. (It should be observed that the mayor does not have a pocket veto, for the council usually meets at least once a week during the entire year.) He frames the budget, perhaps with the aid of a budget director. He also proposes other types of ordinances for the consideration of the council.

A survey of the mayors of the twenty-five largest American cities in 1955 shows that mayors do not appear to have much in common except that they are politically active. The vast majority of these mayors had held some other political office; they had been members of the State legislature, sat on a State judicial bench, been aldermen, or occupied some other elective post. A candidate for the office of mayor in a large city, then, is apt to be a person of demonstrated political talent. In other respects, however, these men differed widely from one another. Fewer than half were lawyers; almost an equal number had been businessmen, in such fields as insurance and automobile retailing. Their ages at the times they were first elected mayor ranged from thirty-three to fifty-seven years. Fewer than half had held office in a political party. About one-third were Catholic.

The office of mayor in a great metropolis frequently represents the culmination of a political career; mayors of small cities sometimes do advance to Congress, but men who become mayors of cities with more than half a million people rarely go higher on the political ladder. One important exception to this principle in the 1950's is Frank Lausche, who became Governor of Ohio after serving as Mayor of Cleveland, and who in 1956 was seriously considered in some circles as Democratic candidate for President. Frank Murphy, a member of the federal Supreme Court in the 1940's, had at one time been Mayor of Detroit. On the other hand, Fiorello La Guardia and Norris Poulson were both members of the national House of Representatives before becoming mayors, respectively, of New York and Los Angeles. The fact is that the office of mayor in a large city may pay better than federal office, have more prestige, and be less exhausting for the incumbent.

THE COUNCIL. The council in mayor-council governed cities ranges in size from two members to fifty; outside of the largest cities, the typical coun-

**TABLE 44. SELECTION OF MAYORS IN CITIES
OVER 5,000 POPULATION[1]**

| | | Percentage of Reporting Cities | | |
Form of Government	Cities Reporting	Direct Election	Council Election	Highest Vote in Council Election
Mayor-council	1,295	95	4	1
Commission	332	69	30	1
Council-manager	792	45	54	1
Town meeting	54	54	44	2
Representative town meeting	25	68	32	0

[1] *1956 Municipal Yearbook*, p. 58. These data include towns and townships as well as municipalities.

cil has fewer than ten members. With rare exceptions city councils are unicameral. Councilmen may be elected either from wards or at large. A few cities have attempted a variety of means for combining the two electoral systems. In some cities, such as Baltimore and Houston, most councilmen are elected by wards but a few are elected at large. In some other cities, councilmen are elected at large but nominated by wards. A few cities have experimented with proportional representation; New York City, however, discarded the system. In many cities councilmen are chosen in nonpartisan elections. Tables 45 and 46 show a few of the characteristics of councilmanic elections.

Councilmen are chosen for terms that may be as short as one year or as long as six; four years is a common term, especially in large cities. In some cities councilmen's terms overlap. Although in the largest cities a council post comes close to being a full-time position, councilmen's salaries in mayor-council cities are not high; councilmen in St. Louis, for instance, are paid only $1,800 per year. However, those in Detroit receive $12,000.

A municipal council, as a policy-framing body, operates much like any other legislative organization. As noted above, it commonly meets once each week in the year. When the council is large it may subdivide itself into a number of committees for the consideration of particular sorts of proposed ordinances. Under these circumstances councilmen, like congressmen, defer to the judgment of the committees. As American mayors have grown stronger in relation to the councils, councilmen have come more and more to depend upon the mayor's office for a program. This is especially true of the drafting of the budget, which in an important way is the key to the whole program of the municipal government in that it shows the activities for which money will be appropriated.

TABLE 45.　DISTRIBUTION OF PARTISAN AND NON-PARTISAN COUNCIL ELECTIONS[1]

Form of Government	Number of Cities	Cities Reporting	Partisan	Non-Partisan
Mayor-council	1315	1280	54.9	45.1
Commission	356	347	34.3	65.7
Council-manager	764	742	15.8	84.2
Town meeting	64	49	51.0	49.0
Rep. town meeting	28	23	26.1	73.9
Population Group				
More than 500,000	17	17	35.3	64.7
250,000–500,000	23	23	17.4	82.6
100,000–250,000	65	65	41.5	58.5
50,000–100,000	129	127	29.9	70.1
25,000–50,000	277	268	38.1	61.9
10,000–25,000	835	805	39.4	60.6
5,000–10,000	1181	1136	41.9	58.1
U.S. Totals	2527	2441	39.7	60.3

Commission: The commission form of municipal government consists primarily of a group termed a commission, made up commonly of five members. The commissioners are usually elected at large from the entire city (see Table 46). They serve as both legislators and executives. Each commissioner is the administrative head of one of the city departments; meanwhile the commission as a whole enacts ordinances for the city. In some cities the candidates for the city commission run for a particular administrative post; in other cities the candidates merely run for the commission, and are assigned to a particular administrative office after election. In this latter arrangement the administrative assignments are made by a majority vote of the commission itself; it is obvious that a considerable amount of pulling and tugging is done by commission members so that they may receive the most desirable offices. In certain municipalities the commissioners only assume responsibility for the proper operation of their administrative division; they appoint a trained administrator to do the actual work of the office. In other municipalities the commissioners themselves do the actual work.

Commission government has been credited with numerous advantages but has also been charged with many shortcomings. The principal advantage for which the commission form has been praised is that of making city government more efficient. Most criticisms of the commission form can be reduced to the simple proposition that this form does not supply leadership for the administration of the municipal government. For that reason the number of cities with the commission form is steadily dropping; for many years scarcely any city has adopted the commission form, whereas many others have abandoned it in favor of the mayor-council or council-manager form.

TABLE 46. METHODS OF ELECTING COUNCILS [1]

Type of Government	Number of Cities	Cities Reporting	At Large	By Wards	Combined
Mayor-council	1315	1273	38.2	36.6	25.2
Commission	356	340	98.8	0.9	0.3
Council-manager	764	740	74.5	14.7	10.8
Town meeting	64	45	97.8	2.2	0.0
Rep. town meeting	28	23	91.4	4.3	4.3
Population Group					
More than 500,000	17	17	29.4	41.2	29.4
250,000–500,000	23	23	60.9	13.0	26.1
100,000–250,000	65	64	62.5	15.6	21.9
50,000–100,000	129	129	60.5	17.0	22.5
25,000–50,000	277	264	54.6	22.7	22.7
10,000–25,000	835	800	60.8	21.9	17.3
5,000–10,000	1181	1124	59.7	27.0	13.3
U.S. Totals	2527	2421	59.4	24.0	16.6

[1] *1955 Municipal Yearbook,* p. 59. These data include New England towns as well as municipalities.

Council-Manager: The council-manager form consists primarily of a popularly elected council and a manager appointed by the council. The council, usually rather small, is chosen in a non-partisan election from the city at large or from wards. The council ordinarily names one of its members to serve as mayor, a post that requires little more than that the incumbent shall preside over council meetings and represent the city on ceremonial occasions. The council is chiefly a legislative body; it has the major function typical of legislative bodies, of overseeing the functioning of the administrative department.

The chief executive of the city is the city manager, appointed by the council for an indefinite term and responsible to the council. Supposedly the manager is a non-partisan, college-trained administrator whose principal duty is to supervise the execution of the ordinances enacted by the city council. One of the manager's most important duties is to draft a proposed budget for the city government; in larger cities he may have the assistance of a budget director for this task, but in smaller communities the manager may be budget director as well. The manager also frequently is in charge of the hiring of city employees under the career civil service system. These are both functions in which the policies of the manager are revealed. Finally, the manager also appoints all other principal administrative chiefs.

Presumably, so long as the manager directs affairs in a manner satisfactory to the council, he retains office; when he displeases the council, he may be dismissed. City management is an important career field. Because it is expected that the manager may come from some other city, managers may move from one city to another. Likewise, a council seeking a manager usually tries to hire one currently holding office in some other city.

Observers find much to praise, and little to censure, in the council-manager form. They assert that it improves the efficiency of the government. They concede that the council-manager form may be more expensive than the mayor-council form, but insist that it provides far more services for the money spent. They contend that the manager supplies the leadership that is absent in the commission form, and that on the other hand the manager cannot become as dictatorial as a mayor. They approve of an arrangement that separates the legislative and the executive functions, as a council-manager government does, yet makes it possible to hold some person or agency responsible for any given act of the government.

They admit that some cities have had unfortunate experiences with city managers, but maintain that the fault lay not in the system itself but in the way in which it was operated. For example, a manager may become involved in politics to the degree that he will urge the election of certain persons to the council and oppose the election of others. Under such conditions the manager is almost certain to be discharged if the candidates he opposed should be elected; such a discharge would be contrary to the theory of council-manager government since it would not be related to the administrative capabilities of the manager. Too, it is difficult for policy leadership to emerge in the council, since councilmen at least in theory are equals;

the council may in despair turn to the manager for leadership. Finally, some critics feel that the "non-political" nature of the council-manager system lessens public interest in, and awareness of, government issues which, they believe, are best brought to light and solved through partisan political debate.

If frequency of occurrence is a measure of success, the council-manager form of city government has been very successful; considerable numbers of cities adopt it every year, and few reject it. So far, however, it has been introduced almost entirely in medium-sized and smaller cities; the largest municipality ever to attempt it, Cleveland, discarded the system after a few years. The largest city with the council-manager form today is Cincinnati. It can be seen from Table 44 that the mayor-council form still predominates in the great metropolitan cities.

One important fact must be noted: the council-manager form itself is no assurance of efficiency and honesty in government. Rather, a government of this type may be as easily corrupted as any other. Where a formerly inefficient or corrupt mayor-council government has been superseded by a council-manager regime that is able and honest, it is certain that interests seeking an able and honest government have managed to secure control of the city. The council-manager form has not so much caused the change in the quality of the government as it has been the instrument through which these changes have been instituted.

Metropolitan areas

A metropolitan area may be defined as a central city and all the surrounding territory, whether suburbs or unincorporated zones, that is economically dependent upon the central city. The metropolitan area, then, is an economic unit; moreover, to a substantial degree it is also a social and a cultural unit. However, it is not a political unit; in fact, metropolitan areas may contain scores or even hundreds of different governments, including counties, municipalities, and school and other special districts. The consequence is a host of political problems, especially for the central city. These problems are accentuated today by the process termed "the flight to the suburbs," whereby millions of people, although they continue to work in the central cities, have taken up residence in the suburbs. The outlying cities and other areas have been gaining in population far more rapidly than the central cities. Between 1940 and 1950, among the fifteen largest metropolitan areas of the nation, the outlying populations increased from two to forty times more than the populations of the central cities.

There have been two important consequences, both largely financial. In the first place, as people have moved out of the central cities, property values have dropped there, compelling municipal authorities to seek other sources of revenue. In the second place, the growth of the suburban areas has made an increasing number of persons dependent upon services of the central city without paying taxes to support these services. Finally, the mere presence of numerous governments in these relatively small areas leads to confusion and waste. A number of political solutions have been attempted, or at least proposed. Special districts are dealt with under their own heading below; the most important other solutions have been as follows:

Annexation of Unincorporated Territory: Many cities have annexed adjacent unincorporated territory. In 1955, for example, 526 cities with populations greater than 5,000 carried out annexations. Annexation of course affects both the central city and the hitherto unincorporated area in varying degrees. To the central city it often brings the task of supplying services to a larger area; it also gives the city more property to tax. It does add to the tax burden of the people living in the annexed territory; on the other hand, it usually provides them with facilities they did not previously enjoy. A survey of the areas annexed in 1955 shows that less than one-half were adequately supplied with any of such fundamental services as water supply, sewage disposal, and police and fire protection. The residents of an unincorporated area that a city proposes to annex often are hostile to the suggestion. They commonly fear the higher taxes that they will have to pay, and sometimes they feel that annexation to the central city will in one way or another depreciate their neighborhood. These sentiments may be instilled or stimulated by certain public officials who are interested in having the area remain unincorporated.

Annexation in most States requires the consent of the inhabitants of the area to be annexed; hence the whole proposition ordinarily must be made attractive to them in order to succeed. In Virginia, however, a city may annex territory regardless of the wishes of the persons in the area to be annexed, by simple authorization of a three-man court. In Texas and Missouri, annexation requires only the amendment of a home-rule charter, without recourse to a popular vote.

Consolidation of the Central City and the County: Consolidation of the central city and the county may take one of a number of forms. Primarily it involves merging all or part of the two largest governments of a metropolitan area. By the elimination of duplicating offices this arrangement can achieve important savings in governmental costs; by the same token a proposal of consolidation is apt to incur the hostility of all those whose offices would be eliminated. New York City, Philadelphia, and Baton Rouge have undergone extensive consolidations of city and county functions.

Separation of the Central City and the County: Sometimes a central city will be entirely separated from the county in which it is located; what remains of the county will be established as a new county under its own government. This procedure has been followed in such cities as Baltimore, Denver, St. Louis, and San Francisco; moreover, as soon as any city in Virginia has 10,000 people, it is at once separated from its county. This sort of arrangement may be favored by the central city because the residents of the city usually not only pay for their own services but also help to pay for those of the people in the unincorporated county areas; separation from the county relieves them of these added charges.

Voluntary Cooperation: Voluntary cooperation between different governments can provide a method for solving individual problems of a metropolitan district. Sometimes two or more cities may unite to deal with a single matter of common interest, such as water supply or sewage disposal. Cities may also cooperate in dealing with a particular class of services that may concern more than one of them only occasionally, but that at that time may be much better administered by intercity cooperation; such services include police and fire protection. In still other instances, the central city may supply services to the outlying cities; some large cities, for example, sell water, either to the residents of the suburb or to the suburban government. In a fourth type of case, cities either depend upon counties to provide them with a particular service, or may cooperate with the county in furnishing a service. For instance, a county may administer a career civil service system for a small municipality; on the other hand, a county and a city may unite in carrying out planning and zoning tasks or in maintaining parks.

TOWNSHIPS

New England towns

Political Status: A New England town is a government for a given area rather than being, like a municipality, a government for a particular concentration of population; thus, it may often govern a rural area. Another frequent difference between a New England town and a municipality is that whereas a municipality is always a corporation a New England town is sometimes a chartered general corporation and at other times a quasi-corporation, which, like a county, has no charter. In either event, many New England towns have powers almost equal to those of municipalities because their government holds sway over an urban district whose population demands many services found generally in cities, such as police and fire protection, water supply, garbage and sewage disposal, welfare assistance, and public education. New England towns also serve as districts for the election of State legislators, the enforcement of State laws, and the assessment and collection of State taxes.

The Structure of Government: There are three general and interrelated types of government for New England towns. The classic type is that of the town meeting (see Figure 132E). In this type of government all the qualified voters of the town are authorized to assemble once a year, usually in the spring, to function both as the legislature and the electorate of the town. As a legislature their primary function is to enact the taxes and appropriate funds for the coming year; they also pass ordinances regulating local issues. Furthermore, the town meeting chooses the principal officers for the town.

The leading officers chosen are the selectmen, commonly three in number. They are the chief administrators of the town, obligated to execute the policies set forth by the town meeting but also in a position to impose their own policies on those of the meeting through the ways in which they enforce enactments of the meeting. Sometimes the selectmen are also empowered to appoint certain lesser administrative officers. Perhaps the most important individual elected officer is the town clerk; in many respects he actually sees to it that the selectmen execute the enactments of the meeting, he performs a great deal of simple administrative work, and he keeps the principal legal records of the community. There may be a variety of additional elected officers, such as a tax collector, an assessor, a justice of the peace, members of the school board, a constable, and others. All of these officials are directly or indirectly responsible to the meeting, which, since it is composed of the qualified voters gathered in one place, may exercise rigid control.

A second form of town government is that of the "representative" or "limited" town meeting (see Figure 132F). This type is commonest in large towns, where it may be inconvenient or virtually impossible for all voters to assemble in one place. Under these circumstances the town may be divided into a number of districts; the voters in each of these districts then choose a considerable number of representatives or delegates, who sit as the town meeting. Otherwise this type is much like that of the simple town meeting. The third type of town government is known as the "town-manager" type. In this arrangement the town meeting (or sometimes the selectmen) names a single person to function as a manager, much like the chief administrator in a council-manager city. There are hundreds of town-manager governments in New England today, being unusually common in Maine. Their popularity results from their ability to deal with problems that might baffle the uncoordinated administrative organization of the typical town meeting government.

Townships elsewhere

Outside of New England there are townships with organized governments in New York, New Jersey, Pennsylvania, eleven midwestern States, and Washington State. Like New England towns these townships are quasi-corporations. In many respects they are much more nearly subdivisions of counties, for in most of these States they are sheerly units for governing rural districts. Table 47 shows that almost two-thirds of all townships have fewer than 1,000 inhabitants. In about half of these States the townships officially are governed by a town meeting. The meeting selects officers and passes ordinances; however, it does not have so much power as a New

TABLE 47. TOWNSHIP POPULATION[1]

Population Group	Number of Townships	Per Cent of Total	1950 Population (Thousands Omitted)	Per Cent of Total
More than 50,000	36	0.2	3,569	11.3
25,000–50,000	104	0.6	3,542	11.2
10,000–25,000	335	2.0	4,923	15.6
5,000–10,000	639	3.7	4,438	14.1
2,500–5,000	1,218	7.1	4,245	13.5
1,000–2,500	3,889	22.6	5,942	18.8
Fewer than 1,000	10,981	63.8	4,894	15.5
U.S. Total	17,202	100.0	31,553	100.0

[1] United States Department of Commerce, Bureau of the Census, *Governments in the United States in 1952* (Washington: Government Printing Office, 1953), p. 3.

England town meeting, nor is it ordinarily so well attended. In other States the voters of the township name their officers in a conventional general election. The most commonly found officers are a board of supervisors or of trustees, and a clerk. In some States there are a few other officers. By contrast, in New York and Illinois there is a single chief administrative officer called the township supervisor. In some heavily populated townships in New Jersey, New York, Pennsylvania, and Wisconsin, township governments exercise powers similar to those of municipalities. In general, however, these townships have as their chief duty the maintenance of local roads and bridges, and occasionally the supervision of such facilities as libraries, cemeteries, land-use zoning, fire protection, garbage collection, and street lighting. Although township officials are a strong political force against change, it appears that townships in the Midwest may vanish in the near future, as their functions are more and more absorbed by municipal and county governments.

SPECIAL DISTRICTS

A special district is a governmental unit that has been created or authorized, usually by a State government, or by two or more State governments, to perform one specific function or a group of specific functions. Like a township, a special district is a quasi-corporation vested with sufficient powers along the line of levying taxes, incurring debts, and owning property, to carry out its functions; it is, however, solely an agent of the State. In 1952, there were, according to the Bureau of the Census, 12,319 special districts. (School districts, which resemble special districts in many ways, are not included either in this enumeration or in the discussion that follows; they are treated in the second part of Chapter 59.) There are some special districts in every State, but a few States have an exceptional concentration of these districts; the following six States contain half of all such areas in the nation:

Illinois	1,546
California	1,390
New York	968
Missouri	886
Kansas	724
Washington	644

That there are great numbers of special districts in some States, and relatively few in others, may be partly explained by the willingness of the ruling circles in some States to hand over the administration of many functions to existing units of government, and the insistence of the ruling circles in other States that these functions be administered separately. This logic helps to account for the small number of these districts in the southern States, where the county governments are very powerful. Usually a special district is governed by a board which may have some members serving ex officio. This board has little power beyond that of administering the relevant State laws.

TABLE 48.   FUNCTIONS OF SPECIAL DISTRICTS[1]

Functional Class	Number	Per Cent of Total
Fire	2,272	18.4
Highways	774	6.3
Health and hospitals	371	3.0
Sanitation	429	3.5
Non-highway transport	159	1.3
Housing	863	7.0
Drainage	2,174	17.6
Soil conservation	1,981	16.1
Irrigation, water conservation	641	5.2
Other natural resources	428	3.5
Cemeteries	911	7.4
Urban water supply	665	5.4
Other	651	5.3
U.S. Total	12,319	100.0

[1] United States Department of Commerce, Bureau of the Census, *Governments in the United States in 1952* (Washington: Government Printing Office, 1953), p. 5.

Special districts may be established to carry out any of a great number of tasks.   However, more than half have any of three functions: fire protection; land drainage; and soil conservation.   Table 48 above lists the numbers and percentages of special districts assigned to each major type of function. Many districts fill another general purpose; they serve as an additional means for handling the problems of a metropolitan region.   Such districts may be established to administer only one problem in a metropolitan area, but one that affects several municipalities and perhaps some unincorporated territory as well.   In this function the special district may be more acceptable to the suburbanites than any other arrangement, for it does not threaten them with total subordination to the government of the central city.   The special district is also apt to be supported by any group interested in special treatment for the problem, and also by reformers who may believe that establishment of a special district will remove the function from politics. Actually the special district is not immune from politics; moreover, it introduces one more governmental unit to the scene, with consequent overlapping of authority and duplication of services and personnel.

QUESTIONS AND PROBLEMS

1. Define a municipality.   What are the several types of municipalities and what distinguishes each from the others?

2. Is your home State more or less urban than the United States as a whole? Do its urban centers have equal apportionment of representation in the State legislature?

3. Describe briefly the major forms of municipal government in the United States.

4. Describe the form of government of the town in which your college is situated or, alternatively, of your home town.

5. What general conclusions can be drawn from the backgrounds of the mayors of America's twenty-five largest cities?

6. What methods of choosing city councils, if any, are not used in electing county boards, and vice versa?

7. Describe in about 150 words the council-manager form of government.

8. What are some of the political and administrative results of the growth of metropolitan suburbs?

9. What reasons compel residents of: (1) incorporated suburbs, and (2) unincorporated areas, to fight for or against annexation to a metropolis?

10. Distinguish between the form and function of the New England town and the midwestern township.

11. Who would benefit from the abolition of the township, and who would gain nothing?

12. What are special districts? Why have they developed in large numbers? In what States are they most numerous?

PART XVI

State and Local Government Functions

Photo by Hawks-Terrell, Inc., Tulsa

THE administrative organization and financial operations of State and local governments are in many ways similar to their counterparts in the national government; however, they are different in important respects. Many divergencies from national administrative practices are attributable to three fundamental conditions: the tug of war between State power and local home-rule forces; the weak position of most Governors as chief executives; and the absence of a firm separation of powers among the branches of local governments.

871

ADMINISTRATIVE ORGANIZATION

Nature

State and local administrative organization generally is chaotic. Like administrative agencies at the national level, State and local administrative bodies have sprung up piecemeal. They have arisen largely in response to demands that some level of government provide a certain sort of service for a section of the public, or for the entire public. First, the wish for this service develops; then, an interest group centered about this wish brings pressure upon the policy-framing, or lawmaking, organ of the government concerned, such as a State legislature or a city council; finally, if the pressure is effective, this organ reacts by establishing an appropriate administrative agency. Furthermore, such pressure may be applied not merely to a lawmaking organ; it may be directed toward a group that is drafting the fundamental law for the government involved, such as a State constitutional convention. Too, interest groups have contrived to have their wishes submitted to the people as initiative proposals for amendments to the fundamental law. As a result, many State and local administrative agencies are created by provisions in the fundamental law; hence these agencies are much more durable than federal administrative bodies, all of which are established by act of Congress. State and local agencies, therefore, can offer great resistance to both abolition and reform.

Another leading trait of State and local administrative organization, which results largely from the pattern of its creation, is its general incoherence and lack of plan. The heads of many departments are elected, so that they are practically uncontrolled by the chief executive. Especially at the State level, other departments have been created with appointive heads or boards; their precise relations with the elected heads have been difficult to determine. Sometimes, when a State administrative agency did not perform its tasks in accordance with the will of the legislature, the legislature has created a new agency, vesting it with the same functions as those of the existing agency. On the other hand, the legislature has occasionally assigned to a State agency certain new functions that had no bearing upon its present obligations. State agencies, all presumed to be directly responsible to the Governor, multiplied so rapidly and greatly that their number defied his efforts to control all of them. Table 49 shows how many agencies are found in some States. The consequence of this situation was that in most States the administrative machinery operated in a disorderly manner and did not provide either the government or the people with the services it was intended to carry out.

Some State and local governments have attempted to reorganize their administrative organization by a variety of means. One of the most noteworthy phenomena of the past decade has been the so-called "Little Hoover

Model of the Projected Civic Center of Tulsa. A new conception of the local community is reflected in this modern architectural design, which provides distinctive quarters for the cultural and governmental activities of the city of the future.

Commissions" modeled after the first Hoover Commission, which scrutinized federal administrative agencies in the late 1940's. Some State governments, such as that of California, have dealt with administrative reorganization as a continuing problem by creating interim legislative committees to examine administrative bodies. In spite of all these activities, however, State and local administrative organization is frequently confused; the inertia of rest, to say nothing of the pressure of both public and private interest groups, suffices in a vast number of instances to block all change.

Types of administrative agencies

Single Head: Many administrative agencies have a single head. A few of these single heads are, in the majority of States, elected: (1) the secretary of state; (2) the treasurer; (3) the attorney general; (4) the superintendent of education; and (5) the auditor. At the local level, the commission form of city government is an outstanding example of a government with elected single heads for administrative bodies. The functions of all the above State officers save the secretary of state will be described elsewhere in the text; because the secretary of state is not attached to any of the great functions of the State government, it is appropriate to discuss his office at this point. The secretary of state handles such matters as assembling and publishing

TABLE 49. NUMBER OF AGENCIES IN SELECTED STATES[1]

State	Total of State Agencies	Number of Major Departments	Number of Other Agencies
Alabama	117	26	91
Colorado	140	9	131
Connecticut	172	32	140
Delaware	76	NA	NA
Florida	87	26	61
Georgia	29	12	17
Illinois	75	15	60
Iowa	87	35	52
Kentucky	93	22	71
Louisiana	102	NA	NA
Massachusetts	56	20	36
Minnesota	101	35	66
Nevada	104	39	65
New Hampshire	84	47	37
North Dakota	75	36	39
Ohio	122	12	110
Oregon	110	78	32
Pennsylvania	49	42	7
South Dakota	64	33	31
Tennessee	87	12	75
Texas	124	54	70
Wisconsin	71	25	46
Wyoming	76	33	43

NA: Data not available.

[1] Council of State Governments, *Reorganizing State Government* (Chicago, 1950).

the laws enacted by the State legislature; he in some cases administers the election system of the State, and publishes election statistics; he keeps the official record of all acts of the Governor; he has custody of the great seal of the State, without which no action of the State government is official; and he is often assigned a variety of other, unrelated duties.

It should be noted that none of these offices, save that of superintendent of education, performs services for the people; rather, each is concerned with the maintenance of the State government. By contrast, some of the newer State offices, for example those dealing with such matters as agriculture and labor, that perform services for the people, have single heads who are appointed. At the municipal level there is a general trend toward installing types of government in which the large majority of administrative chiefs are appointed; the strong-mayor and council-manager forms exemplify this tendency. The evident advantage of the single head is that when the duties of these heads are sheerly ministerial, there can be no question as to who shall see to it that the tasks of the agency are carried out. The chief executive has a single person to direct, and the subordinates within the agency have the orders of a single person to obey.

Commissions and Boards: A considerable number of State agencies today have as their chief a number of persons constituting a commission or board (terms that for the purpose of this discussion may be viewed as synonymous). A typical commission has three characteristics: (1) it has an odd number of members; (2) its members have overlapping terms; and (3) its membership is required by law to be bipartisan. This type of structure is often defended on the ground that it allows for deliberation and consultation. This argument doubtless has some validity when it is applied to the regulation of certain private undertakings such as the production of oil and natural gas. Commissions or boards with such duties perform quasi-legislative and quasi-judicial as well as administrative tasks, for which they seem to be well adapted. They not only allow for the debating of issues, but they also supply representation to varying interests and different regions in the area concerned. Often, however, it appears that commissions and boards have been utilized to head agencies whose functions allowed little if any discretion. In such cases, many observers insist that the board or commission should be replaced by a single administrator; they hold that when the office permits little if any discretion, it is most desirable to have a single administrator in charge, so that the duties of the agency may be executed with a minimum of delay.

Combined Head: Some State and local administrative agencies have as their head a combination of a board or commission and a single administrator. This sort of arrangement appears especially suitable for an agency whose tasks call for both deliberation of policy and speed of execution; accordingly, it is commonest with bodies that deal with health, education, and welfare. For instance, a State ordinarily has both a board of education and a superintendent of education. The board, with its several members, deliberates educational policy; the superintendent executes the policy as finally decided by the board. Actually the situation is rarely so uncomplicated as this illustration suggests. For example, the superintendent is usually a professional educator, closely attached to and supported by the teachers' association of the State; the board, on the other hand, is made up of men who are not professional educators, who may be hostile to the teachers' association, and who are apt to struggle with the superintendent.

The role of private interests

As on the federal level, so too at the State and local levels, private interests strive in various ways to influence the decisions of administrative bodies, in order to achieve their desires. One frequent tactic is to bring pressure upon certain members of the agency concerned; spokesmen for the interest may testify at agency hearings, entertain agency members, represent their views as being closest to the "public interest," offer the members profitable business contracts or associations, or have recourse to any other of many possible devices. Business groups that must undergo regulation seek to place sympathetic persons on the regulating agency. To block these efforts, State laws establishing the agencies often forbid membership to any individual with an interest in the business that he is to help supervise; for instance, anyone with an interest in the liquor business is usually barred from appointment to an alcoholic beverage control commission. Notwithstanding these checks, private interests do appear to succeed rather frequently in influencing members of regulatory bodies.

In some cases, private interest groups have managed to obtain a statutory guarantee that they shall be represented on regulatory bodies. Perhaps the most numerous cases of this sort involve the licensing of trades and professions by the State government. Licensing of a trade or profession is often demanded by its practitioners, and the law that creates the licensing agency is apt to be written in accordance with their wishes, or the wishes of their association. A few illustrations will demonstrate the operation of this principle. All members of the Louisiana Board of Pharmacy must be registered pharmacists. The Vermont Public Accountants Board of Accounting consists of three practicing certified public accountants. The Massachusetts Board of Registration in Medicine comprises seven persons registered as qualified physicians who have been in active practice for at least ten years. Occasionally the members of the agency represent subordinate interests within the trade or profession. For instance, the three members of the Oregon Examining Board of Plumbers are (1) a journeyman plumber; (2) a person registered to conduct a plumbing business; and (3) a member or employee of the State Board of Health. In any event, the senior members of the profession or trade are empowered by law to determine who may enter their practice and what the qualifications for entry shall be.

Administrative personnel

Numbers: According to the Bureau of the Census, in October, 1955, there were about 4,335,000 full-time State and local employees altogether. Slightly under 1,100,000 of these were State personnel, and slightly more than 3,250,000 were local. For the entire nation there were about 273 full-time State and local employees per 10,000 population; the ratios in the States ranged from a minimum of 213 in Kentucky to a maximum of 377 in Wyoming. Hence among all the States the proportions of State and local employees combined did not have great extremes, the largest proportion being only eighty per cent greater than the smallest. These proportions seem to be connected in part with the wealth of the States and also with the number of their services.

There are, however, considerable differences among the States so far as the number of State employees and the number of local employees are concerned, when these two categories are viewed separately. For the entire country there are about sixty-eight State employees for each 10,000 population; among the States the range is from forty-nine in Texas to 180 in North Carolina. There are almost exactly 204 local government employees per 10,000 population throughout the country; here the range is from fifty-eight in North Carolina to 265 in New York. The exceptional situation in North Carolina may be ascribed to the fact that there the public school teachers, who are in all States the most numerous public employees, are employees of the State government, whereas elsewhere they are employees of some unit of local government. The proportion of State to local employees in any one State depends to a great degree upon which level of government is made responsible for the tasks to be performed. The graph in Figure 133 shows what percentage of State and local civil servants in all States were occupied in certain fundamental tasks of government.

Career Civil Service Systems: The extent to which a career civil service system has been adopted varies widely from State to State and locality to

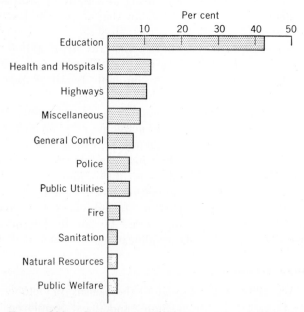

Figure 133. Percentages of State and Local Government Personnel Engaged in Major Functions (October, 1954).

locality. Owing to the influence and requirements of the federal government there are some career employees in every State and in many local governments. This situation prevails because for many years the federal government when making a grant-in-aid to a State or locality has prescribed that the employees on the given project be chosen on a non-partisan basis and according to the standards of a career system. The chief impetus of this sort came with the federal Social Security Act of 1935. The fact is, however, that in a large minority of the States and in a host of localities these are the only workers selected in this fashion.

Yet, quite apart from the stimulus furnished by the federal government, and in a number of cases before 1935, different States have erected career civil service systems, sometimes by law and sometimes by constitutional provision. Today there are comprehensive career systems in a majority of the States, and career systems for certain classes of employees in certain other States. With respect to local governments, the career system appears to be weakest at the county level. According to a recent estimate the system has been introduced into only about 200 counties, about six per cent of the national total. However, it is noteworthy that the system has been installed in such populous counties as Los Angeles and Hamilton (Cincinnati); moreover, such other populous areas as New York City, St. Louis, and San Francisco have no county government. The career system is much more widespread among cities than among counties; furthermore, large cities are more apt than small cities to have a career system of some sort. It seems, too, that where the system does not include all municipal employees, it is most likely to include the members of certain fields of employment, notably those in the police and fire departments. Finally, with respect to other units of local government, it should be stated that most public school teachers and administrators are under a career system. Here, however, officials and agencies of the State government fix standards and carry out administration.

Salary: Most State and local government employees, and all those under the career system, are paid regular annual salaries. There is a considerable range in the average salaries paid in the various States; in October, 1955, the lowest average, in Mississippi, was $209 per month, and the highest, in California, was $394. Understandably, the salaries paid in the more populous and wealthy States are higher than those in the other States. In general the salaries of State and local employees since 1950 have risen more rapidly than the cost of living. This is especially true of the salaries of public school teachers, partly because of the strength of their organization as a lobby in State legislative halls. Other groups of employees, too, have had effective pressure organizations. This rise has come about also through the wish of those who have felt that higher salaries could recruit and then hold a superior type of person as a career employee.

Personnel Agencies: In State and local governments where the career system has been installed there is usually a personnel agency analogous to the federal Civil Service Commission. In the States this body often consists of an odd number of members—three or five—who serve for overlapping terms that are longer than the term of the official who appointed them.

These boards generally are bipartisan; their members frequently are chosen by the Governor with the confirmation of the State senate. In a large city, too, there may be a civil service commission; in smaller cities with the council-manager form the city manager may function as the chief personnel officer.

These commissions supervise the recruiting, examination, appointment, and discipline of career personnel. Sometimes their authority extends beyond the usual jurisdiction of their government; in Massachusetts, for instance, the State civil service commission manages the recruiting of city employees as well as of State personnel. Governments in some areas have found that the best sort of personnel agency for their purpose is one with a combined head, a board or commission to make policy and a single director to execute it.

FINANCIAL OPERATIONS

State and local financial operations involve two chief activities: (1) spending money in order to carry out the functions of government; and (2) gathering money needed to carry out these functions. These operations in all States and in many localities include a third aspect: drafting a budget as a plan for spending and gathering the money. In all States and in most localities these operations are performed by one or more agencies especially entrusted with their conduct.

Contrasting national, State, and local financial powers

It is important first to note that in certain fundamental respects the financial activities of State and local governments differ from those of the national government. In the first place, State and local governments do not have the same freedom as the national government regarding the manner in which they gather money. A government collects the majority of its funds by a combination of two methods: levying taxes, and borrowing money (one important exception to this rule is a government unit such as a housing authority, which secures most of its funds from charges for the services it renders). So far as taxation is concerned, the federal government has virtually a free hand. By contrast, so far as their taxing powers are concerned, State and local governments are restricted by both the federal Constitution and their own organic laws. State and local governments also do not have as much power as the national government in the matter of borrowing money. A fundamental distinction is that the federal government is almost unlimited in its borrowing power whereas State and local governments in most cases have narrow formal limits.

Finally, State and local governments have different powers than the national government in the matter of spending money. Presumably the national government may spend money only for purposes enumerated in the Constitution. State governments, by contrast, may spend money for virtually any purpose not denied them by the federal Constitution or their own constitution.

The budget

Today in each State, and in most local governments, there is a person or agency that drafts the budget and a person or agency that is considered the budget-making authority. Where these agencies exist, outside of county governments they usually are either responsible to the chief executive of the government or are in the office of the chief executive. So far as the preparation of the budget is concerned, most State governments contain either a Budget Director or a Budget Commission. However, in Arkansas preparation of the budget is entrusted to the Legislative Council; in Georgia, to the head of each State agency; and in Montana, to each State Department. The budget-making authority in most States is the Governor. In four States there are either Boards or Commissions, each including the Governor as a member. In a few other States there are yet other arrangements. The one State in which the authority is not part of the executive branch is Arkansas, where it is the Legislative Council.

So far as local governments are concerned, in counties the budget is apt to be drafted by the county board, save where there is a county manager. In strong-mayor and council-manager cities, the chief executive drafts the budget; in weak-mayor and commission cities, the council, a council committee, or the commission, drafts it. In special districts it is drawn up by the executive officer or board of the district.

The budgets of State and local governments are prepared similarly to those of the national government. A State or local budget is prepared by some agency, usually executive; subsequently a legislative body enacts the budget by levying taxes and appropriating money for expenditures. The sums that are appropriated are based upon requests sent to the drafting agency by each of the various executive offices in the government. It is the task of the chief finance officers to insure that the sums appropriated will bear some relation to the amount of money that will be collected through taxes and loans, and that the appropriations will reflect the general policy of the State administration, usually personified by the Governor.

Administration of the budget includes primarily the custody of government funds and the examination of State expenditures to determine whether or not they have been authorized by law. In many jurisdictions the officials who administer the budget are elected. One important officer is the treasurer; he has custody of all government funds, and is to release them for a given function only when he receives a legislative order directing him to do so. Another major officer is the controller or comptroller (the words have identical pronunciations). The function of the controller is to "pre-audit" all expenditures. In the main, he must see to it that all expenditures planned by the executive branch have been duly authorized by the legislative branch; he is in a position to bar expenditures that are not so authorized. The auditor is an official who conducts a "post-audit" to determine both whether expenditures have been authorized and whether they have been conducted with the greatest possible administrative efficiency. Sometimes the pre-audit and the post-audit are carried out by the same person or office.

Of the three officials, the auditor is most likely to be popularly elected; he
may be chosen by this means even in council-manager cities.

Expenditures

The expenditures of State and local governments are enmeshed with the
functions of those governments. Hence the following discussion of State
and local expenditures will be brief, because there is an extended treatment
of operations in the subsequent chapters. In general it should be noted
that State and local governments, like the national government, have greatly
broadened their spending in recent years; whereas altogether State and local
governments spent but a little over one billion dollars in 1902, today they
spend more than thirty billions. It is true that the national government
spends twice this sum; however, the total cost of the civilian activities of
the national government is not so great as that of State and local governments. Too, it must be observed that the expenditures of State governments
have risen at a faster pace than those of local governments have. The expenditures of State governments today nearly equal those of local governments; in 1902 they were only one-fifth as great.

Among the various items for which State and local governments spend
money, public education by far surpasses all others. In 1955 State and local
governments spent $11.9 billions for public education; of this sum, State gov-
ernments spent $1.9 billions, city governments $1.1 billions, and school districts $8 billions. A second major item was highways, for which State and
local governments spent about $6.5 billions; the States alone expended $3.9
billions, and cities and counties each about $1.1 billions. State and local
public welfare cost $3.2 billions; public hospitals, $2.1 billions; police forces,
$1.2 billions; public utilities and liquor store expenditures, $3.9 billions; and
various State insurance trusts, $2.8 billions. It is clear that State and local
governments spend money for numerous functions that directly affect the
lives of all citizens in one way or another.

Revenue

State and local governments obtain the majority of their revenue from
taxes. However, numbers of government units obtain a considerable portion of their income from the sale of services such as public utilities. Finally,
State and local governments are receiving a growing percentage of their
income in the form of grants from some other government. This section
will deal with the most important sources of revenue for State and local
governments together, noting for which level of government each source is
most important. States and localities all have different revenue patterns;
the pattern in itself in part discloses the relative power of various interests
in the government. Figure 134 shows what proportion the major taxes contribute to the total revenue of each State. Figure 135 shows what amounts
all States collect, and have been collecting, from various major taxes.

Taxes: PROPERTY TAXES. Property taxes are taxes that are levied upon
property of various sorts. There are two broad classes of property taxes·
those on real property, and those on personal property. A tax on real prop-

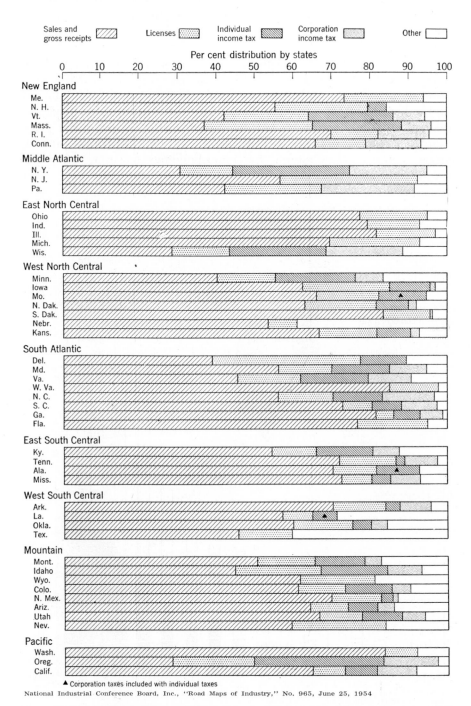

Figure 134. Different Taxes Collected by Individual State Governments in 1953.

erty is one that falls on land and buildings; it is by far the more significant. A personal property tax is one imposed on other forms of property, either tangible, as furniture or automobiles, or intangible, as shares of stock in a corporation.

The property tax, at least in theory, is quite simple in operation. It requires merely that property be listed with the government and that a value be set on it. Financial officials then need only fix a rate at which the tax shall be levied, and see to its collection. However, in spite of its appearance of simplicity, the property tax has many complications. In the first place, personal property can easily be concealed; as a result, a personal property tax rarely yields a large return. Land and buildings, however, being more or less immovable, are much more satisfactory for taxing purposes.

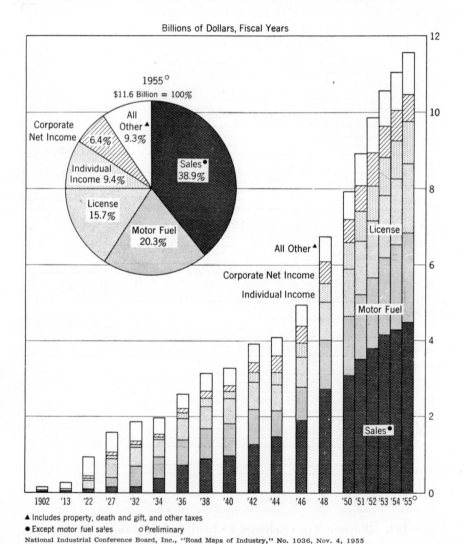

Billions of Dollars, Fiscal Years

▲ Includes property, death and gift, and other taxes
● Except motor fuel sales   ○ Preliminary
National Industrial Conference Board, Inc., "Road Maps of Industry," No. 1036, Nov. 4, 1955

Figure 135.   Total State Government Tax Collections by Type of Tax, 1902–1955.

Another shortcoming of this tax derives from the evaluating, or assessing, of the property. This task is ordinarily the duty of an official termed the *assessor*. Until recent years most assessors have had little, if any, training for their posts; frequently the office was elective. Hence property was often inaccurately assessed; different assessors might have widely varying notions of the value of the same piece of property. Lately, however, there have been important advances in the technique of assessing. There is a National Association of Assessing Officers, which has drafted a code of professional ethics and has laid the foundation for a group of in-service training schools for assessors.

The property tax is also criticized on the ground that it is a "regressive" tax, that is, a tax that falls most heavily on the low-income groups. It is true that at one time in the United States the amount of landed property a man owned was a fair index to his wealth. Today, by contrast, wealth is apt to be measured in some other way, as by the possession of corporation stocks and bonds. Too, the property tax is one that may be passed along; that is, it may be paid not by the owner of the property but by some person who rents or leases it. Despite this charge, the property tax remains one of the most fruitful in the nation. At one time it was the principal source of revenue for State governments. However, State governments today rely upon other sources for their income; it is the governments of counties, cities, and school and special districts that are the chief beneficiaries of property taxes. In 1955 local governments received slightly more than $10 billions in property taxes.

SALES AND GROSS RECEIPTS TAXES. A sales or gross receipts tax is a tax on business transactions. Every State levies some sort of sales tax, and a growing number of cities and counties do likewise. These taxes altogether furnish State governments with their largest source of income; in 1955 they rose to more than $6.8 billions, to which the tax on motor fuels contributed $2.3 billions. Besides motor fuels, two other specific items which are widely taxed are tobacco products and alcoholic beverages. Apart from these selective taxes, a general sales or gross receipts tax is collected in each of thirty-three States, based upon a percentage of the amount involved in the transaction; in 1955 these taxes yielded more than $2.5 billions. Sales and gross receipts taxes have been popular probably because of the ease with which they can be collected. However, like the property tax, they have been criticized on the ground that they are regressive; it is argued that they fall on objects that persons in the lower-income groups cannot do without. In some jurisdictions, such as Ohio and California, these taxes are not imposed upon food sold in grocery stores. One other factor contributing to the popularity of these taxes is that they can be collected from any person enjoying the services of the government, whether or not he is a resident of the area.

INDIVIDUAL AND CORPORATION INCOME TAXES. In 1955 individual income taxes were levied in thirty-one States, and corporation income taxes were levied in thirty-three. Together they yielded about $1.8 billions. Certain cities, too, have begun to impose an individual income tax; when such a tax is imposed upon the payrolls of private businesses, it can enable the city to charge the residents of suburbs who commute to work in the city for the services that the city government provides them. States levy these taxes at various rates. For instance, in 1955 the individual income tax returned $33.83 per capita in Delaware but only $1.08 per capita in Tennessee. The corporation income tax yielded $13.09 in New York, per capita, and twenty-six cents per capita in South Dakota. Rates are considerably below those of the federal government; yet they are progressive.

Licenses: A license is a permit sold by a government to a person or organization that allows the person or organization to own a certain piece of property or carry on some form of activity. A license actually has two functions: it enables the government to police its citizens, and it yields a revenue for the government. Both these considerations are apt to influence legislators and private interest groups. Licenses have been a lucrative source of revenue for both State and local governments; in 1953 they produced $1.6 billions for State governments and $500 millions for local governments. State licenses for motor vehicles and their operators returned almost $950 millions of the total revenue from licenses.

Utility and Liquor Store Revenues: Public utilities and liquor stores are two forms of economic endeavor in which both State and local governments participate and which yield a substantial income for these governments. In 1955, for instance, State governments received nearly $1 billion from the operation of State-owned liquor stores. Local governments harvested $2.7 billions from their liquor stores and utilities. It must be stressed, however, that most, if not all, of the income from these undertakings is consumed by the expense of running them. In 1953 only liquor stores returned a net profit to State and local governments. The fact is that these governments have in many cases been forced to assume ownership and management of such utilities as public transportation because these utilities are essential yet apparently cannot be operated profitably by private owners. It is noteworthy that some city governments now collect specific charges for some services that in past years were paid for out of the general fund; sewerage management and garbage collection are typical of these services.

Intergovernmental Revenue: Intergovernmental revenue, which comprises funds given one government by another government, occupies a major role in States and localities. This revenue often takes the form of grants-in-aid for some stated purpose. Federal grants to the States were described in a previous chapter; in 1954 they amounted to more than $2.65 billions, or 17.4% of all State revenue. In the same year the State governments themselves distributed over $5.67 billions to other governments, primarily local, accounting for 30.4% of all State expenditures. Figure 136 shows what governments receive different proportions of such funds and for what purposes they receive them.

Intergovernmental revenue at the State level may take the form of either a grant or a shared tax. The general principle of the grant is the same whether it is made by the federal government or a State government; it is designed to encourage local authorities to perform a certain task, is apt to

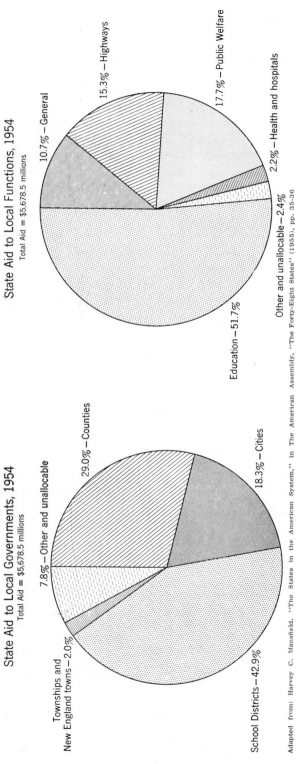

State Aid to Local Functions, 1954
Total Aid = $5,678.5 millions

15.3% – Highways

10.7% – General

17.7% – Public Welfare

2.2% – Health and hospitals

Other and unallocable – 2.4%

Education – 51.7%

State Aid to Local Governments, 1954
Total Aid = $5,678.5 millions

7.8% – Other and unallocable

29.0% – Counties

18.3% – Cities

Townships and
New England towns – 2.0%

School Districts – 42.9%

Adapted from: Harvey C. Mansfield, "The States in the American System," in The American Assembly, "The Forty-Eight States" (1955), pp. 35-36

Figure 136.   State Aid to Local Governments, 1954.   (*a*) State aid to local governments, 1954; (*b*) State aid to local functions, 1954.

be offered on the basis of need, and frequently contains specifications that must be heeded respecting standards of achievement. These grants may be awarded in an effort to enable impoverished local governments to provide services for their population that are equal to those supplied by wealthy governments.

A shared tax, by contrast, is simply a tax that one government collects entirely, then shares with another government or group of governments. A shared tax does not have the aspect of charity that some people find undesirable in grants; on the other hand, because the tax is generally shared on the basis of a fixed percentage of the total collected, it does not lessen inequalities of financial powers of local governments. The principal beneficiaries of intergovernmental revenue are public school districts, which in 1954 received more than $2.44 billions in this manner.

Borrowing

State and local governments may resort to borrowing money in the event their expenditures are greater than their revenues. It is true that most of these governments are restrained by laws or constitutions in the matter of incurring debts. Nevertheless, in 1954 the combined debts of all State governments totaled $10.2 billions, and of all local governments, $27.7 billions. In that year State and local governments sold $6.9 billions of bonds. One noteworthy aspect of these bond issues was that forty-six per cent of the total, or about $3.2 billions, were revenue bonds; a revenue bond is one whose redemption is guaranteed by the income of the facility whose construction it has been used to finance, such as the toll from a highway, tunnel, or bridge.

QUESTIONS AND PROBLEMS

1. What functions do secretaries of state perform?

2. Which level of government, in your opinion, would have the greatest attraction for persons of college education seeking civil service employment—national, State, or local? Explain your answer.

3. Compare the amounts spent by the federal government and by all the States together for six major functions.

4. Obtain from the *Municipal Yearbook* for any recent year the figures on the bonded debt of the ten largest cities in America and of ten cities of 50,000–100,000 population. Which group has the lower bonded debt per capita? Can you explain the difference or lack of difference?

5. Why has the development of State and local administration been disorderly?

6. Who will benefit in what ways from instituting: (1) a single head for an agency and (2) a commission or board as the agency head?

7. What proportions of the total revenue of your home State are supplied by the four major tax sources? Are these proportions typical of the other States?

8. What factors explain the differences in the ratio of State to local employees from one State to another?

"Palo Alto Times," March 28-29, 1956. Photos by Gene Tupper

Protective services, as the term shall be used in this chapter, comprises the activities of only two agencies of government and the bodies associated with them: police forces and fire departments. The fact is that governments carry out myriad tasks clearly "protective" by nature; as illustrations, governments block the distribution and sale of impure food, outlaw financial dishonesty on the part of businessmen, and reduce excessively high public utility rates. All these functions are obviously protective. However, the protective services that will be treated in this chapter have one distinguishing trait: they have to do chiefly with shielding people and things from overt violence and physical harm.

Police and fire protective services traditionally have formed separate departments in a government. There are, it is true, a number of jurisdictions in which the two have been combined, for administrative purposes, under a single heading such as "Department of Public Safety." Usually, however, where this situation has prevailed the department has contained two subdivisions, one of police and one of fire.

A few governments have experimented with an organization that united the two services not only administratively but also functionally. Sunnyvale, California, a city of 25,000 people, has provided a laboratory for such an experiment; there, members of the organization are trained as both policemen and firemen, and may serve as either according to the needs of the moment. A study of the performance of this system during the past few years reveals that the community in general is well satisfied with it; apparently it is possible with this arrangement to have exceptionally large numbers of either policemen or of firemen at times of crisis, and there are considerable monetary savings as well.

POLICE SERVICES

Administrative structure

Police services are supplied principally by local governments. However, federal police officers may share in the investigation of crimes under State law when asked to do so by local officials; too, on application of local officials the federal agencies provide technical information such as personal data about criminals. Also, State governments have two bodies of police forces: the National Guard, and the State police, or highway patrol. Nevertheless, the police officer with whom citizens have by far the most frequent dealings is an agent of the local government.

National Guard: The National Guard, which, as the descendant of the State militia presumably constitutes the armed forces of the individual States, is today closely tied to the armed forces of the United States. The National Guard is supported primarily by funds from the national government, and in time of war may be called into national service by the President. Thus it amounts to a trained reserve for the standing army of the United States.

In peacetime, however, the National Guard is under the authority of the State governments. The commander in chief in each State is the Governor; actual leadership is in the hands of the adjutant general, who is a military officer of high rank. Its organization is patterned after that of the United States Army, with various types of units: infantry, armored, engineer, signal, and the like. The National Guard also has an air component resembling

San Quentin, California State Prison. Over 4000 "residents" make "Q," as they call it, a little city under totalitarian rule, but with industrial and cultural activities resembling those found in communities outside.

the Air Force. The personnel of the Guard in each State are volunteers from that State, who serve a certain period during each year.

In peacetime, the National Guard is employed chiefly for quelling disorders and coping with disasters, acting under the command of the Governor in situations that he has proclaimed to be emergencies.

State Police: In every State there is a police force known most commonly as the State police but also termed highway patrol, motor patrol, and State patrol. As a State administrative agency, the State police are subordinate to the Governor. In some States the personnel are recruited and appointed through a career civil service system; in some others, appointment is based on party membership. In most States, regardless of the basis of appointment, the recruits undergo one of the most rigorous courses in police training that has been established in any American jurisdiction. The membership of State police forces in July, 1953, ranged from thirty-seven in South Dakota to 1,900 in Pennsylvania.

Authority of the State police also varies widely from State to State. In every State they are directed to enforce the laws of the highway. In twelve States this is their only function; in California and Florida they have only limited additional functions. In thirty-four States, however, officially the State police have general powers of law enforcement; in fact, only in a few States, among them New York, New Jersey, Pennsylvania, and West Virginia, do they exercise these powers.

Rural Police: The chief rural police officers are the sheriff and his deputies. The functions of the sheriff have been outlined in a previous chapter. Another rural police officer is the constable; he is usually attached to the court of a justice of the peace, is elected to office from the same jurisdiction as the justice, and has little authority beyond that of serving legal papers upon defendants and witnesses commanding them to appear in court. Generally constables are paid by fees. Because they have shown themselves to have little effectiveness in police work, constables have been stripped of most of their powers. There have been a number of suggestions that the police authority of sheriffs and constables be transferred entirely to some other police body. One has been that the State police be given full powers of law enforcement in all unincorporated districts. This recommendation is of course opposed by sheriffs in particular, who do not want to see their offices deprived of any of their powers.

Municipal Police: Municipal police forces are responsible to the chief executive officer of the city government. In a typical large city police organization, the executive chief of the police forces is either a police commissioner or police commission, chosen by the mayor or city manager. Commissioners and members of commissions are not career police officers, and are not expected to manage the technical affairs of the police department. Rather, they are expected to handle broad administrative matters and to provide liaison between the police department and the municipal executive.

The principal officer of the police department is the police chief, a career official, who is appointed by the commissioner or commission. Where there is no commissioner or commission, the police chief is usually selected by the mayor or city manager, and is directly subordinate to him. Exceptions to these general practices exist in Boston, Baltimore, Kansas City (Missouri), and St. Louis, where the chief is named by the State Governor. The personnel of the department are ranged in military fashion below the chief, from inspectors or majors through captains, lieutenants, and sergeants, to patrolmen.

Policemen today in most cities are recruited and appointed through a career civil service system; indeed, it is noteworthy that even though most employees of a city may not be career officeholders, policemen will be. Promotions in grade, too, are likely to depend upon performance in competitive tests. The salaries of policemen, although considerably larger than they once were, still seem low to many who point to the hazards policemen must face in the line of duty and the responsibilities they must assume. In 1956 the median entrance salary for policemen in cities of more than 500,000 population was $4,080; that is, equal numbers earned less than $4,080 and more than $4,080. In cities of between 10,000 and 25,000 population, the median salary was $3,450. The median maximum salary for the largest cities was $4,925; for cities between 10,000 and 25,000, $3,840.

There are comparatively more policemen in large cities than in small ones. In 1954 in all cities the ratio of police officers to population was 1.8 per 1,000. However, in cities with fewer than 10,000 people the ratio was 1.3 per 1,000, whereas in cities of more than 250,000 it was 2.3 per 1,000. One notable trend in police departments generally has been the increased employment of "civilians," that is, non-uniformed personnel. Of the more than 23,000 police employees in New York in 1956, over 1,000 were civilian technicians and clerks.

Functions

The patrol function of police departments, probably their most important task and the one demanding the largest number of police personnel, aims at both preventing crime and at the immediate detection of those who have committed a crime. The actual conduct of police patrols has greatly changed in recent years, owing largely to the development of automobiles and motorcycles. Today, it appears that the foot patrolman is vanishing, except in the largest cities.

A second important task of a police force is crime detection, which involves primarily discovering who has committed a particular crime. In large cities this task is the obligation of a specialized detective force; county police organizations that are well staffed, and State police forces, also have detective bureaus. Detectives sometimes are appointed from the ranks of uniformed policemen; on other occasions they are deliberately recruited. Crime detection today is in many respects a laboratory science. A fully equipped detective force has a large laboratory and extensive files.

The enforcement of traffic laws has become a leading function of both State and local police officers. The concern of the police with highway traffic has increased each year, as intrastate and interstate commerce by automobile, bus, and truck have become more and more important to the national economy. The enforcement of traffic laws is closely related to the problems of highway engineering and area planning. For example, the police are under clashing pressures with regard to highway speed laws, one group demanding lax enforcement so that traffic may move quickly from place to place, and another group asking strict enforcement to reduce highway accidents.

Highway law enforcement is more and more buttressed by accident prevention undertakings. One form of accident prevention has to do with highway engineering and construction; such matters as speed limits, traffic signals, the elimination of grade railroad crossings, one-way streets, and limited-access highways fall in this group. Another sort of accident prevention undertaking involves the enforcement of traffic laws. Too, automobile inspection requirements aim at keeping from the streets and highways the cars whose condition makes them a traffic menace. Moreover, the licensing of drivers is designed to keep the incompetents from the road, and the suspension and revocation of licenses to get habitual law violators from behind the wheel. In the past two decades a large number of public school systems have established courses in driver education for high-school students, some areas making these courses mandatory.

Police in all parts of the country today are showing a great concern in juvenile delinquency. Statistics on juvenile offenses do reveal an increase in juvenile crime that many people find alarming. However, such figures must be interpreted with some care; part of this rise may be attributable to such factors as superior police detection of crime, expanded police reporting of crime, the practice of terming as a crime today an act that a century ago might have been simply shrugged off as to be expected of adolescents, and the sheer increase in the number of juveniles. Even taking all these factors into consideration, however, it is true that juveniles commit large numbers of crimes of violence.

Police handling of juvenile delinquency includes both detection and prevention. Today in all cities of more than 500,000 people, and in many that are smaller, there are special juvenile officers. In 132 cities policewomen are assigned to this field as well. Many cities have special buildings for detaining juvenile offenders, so that they will not mingle with adult criminals in the city jail, and special juvenile courts. Some cities also retain psychiatrists, psychologists, sociologists, and family relations authorities, for probing juvenile delinquency. In many jurisdictions special attention is accorded the juvenile who has been found violating the law for the first time, in efforts to keep him out of difficulty in the future. Schools and recreation areas are designed in part to lessen delinquency. Many city councils have enacted curfews requiring adolescents to be off the streets at a certain hour.

Correctional institutions

Correctional institutions include all institutions where those who have been found guilty of violating the law are for a time penalized by the loss of their personal freedom. There are several principles underlying the establishment of these institutions. One is that the person who breaks the law must be punished; this is an ancient notion that is discredited in some quarters. Another principle is that offenders must be segregated from society for the protection of society. Yet a third concept, which is implicit in the term "correctional institution," is that in some way the civic training of criminals has been faulty or even entirely lacking, and that they must be rehabilitated with an eye to their finally assuming a proper role in society. This last principle is very important in the administration of these institutions today. It is associated with such practices as the indeterminate sentence and parole, two devices giving the authorities of these institutions some discretion in deciding whether or not an offender has been rehabilitated.

There are correctional institutions at all levels of government. Virtually every municipality has a jail. Municipal jails have two principal functions; they are places of detention for persons awaiting trial or transportation to a prison after being sentenced, and they house persons actually convicted of minor offenses—misdemeanors—who do not have the money to pay their fines. Most counties, too, have jails. These institutions have the same general functions as city jails, save that in counties where there is a municipality with a jail the county institution houses primarily individuals who have been convicted of misdemeanors and who serve out their terms there. In general, no one is sentenced to a county jail for more than one year, that being ordinarily the maximum term for a misdemeanor.

At the State level there are two general types of correctional institutions. Both of these are for the detention of those who have been found guilty of committing a felony, and who have been sentenced for a term of a year and a day, or more. One type, which may be termed the reformatory, is designed chiefly for adolescents and young first offenders who can take a normal place in society after a period of rehabilitation.

The second type of State correctional institution, termed the penitentiary, is designed for the imprisonment of adult offenders, particularly for those who have been convicted several times. Rehabilitation is much less emphasized in penitentiaries than it is in reformatories, because many of their inmates appear unable to adjust to the requirements of normal living. However, in some States there is a conscious program of rehabilitation in penitentiaries.

FIRE SERVICES

Fire services like police services are chiefly a function of local governments. The reason for this arrangement is in part purely physical, that is, the need to have equipment near every point where a fire may break out, so as to be able to go into action speedily. Another reason, of course, is political; local authorities who now have the power of appointing fire chiefs do not wish to yield this privilege to a larger unit of government. In recent years, however, State officials have taken increasing concern in the matter of fire prevention, and carry on a good deal of study whose results they transmit to local fire fighting agencies.

In thirty-eight States there is a fire marshal, or similar functionary, who is the chief officer in the State for handling questions of fire prevention and extinction. This office in twenty States is in the insurance department; in four States it is connected with the State police; and in four States it is in the department of public safety. The tasks of the fire marshal have to do primarily with the investigation of arson and fire prevention; the marshal is not in charge of a fire department equipped to extinguish fires.

Urban fire departments are actually the nucleus of the fire fighting organization in the United States. The fire department in some cities is under a fire commissioner or board, chosen by the chief executive of the city. In some other cities the department is administratively united with the police forces under a board of public safety. Under any of these circumstances the commissioner or board carries out solely administrative tasks. The principal functioning executive officer is the fire chief, who may be selected by the commissioner or board, or by the mayor, the city manager, or the city council. The chief is a professional fire fighter who usually has advanced to this post after years of experience in the department; sometimes, however, he is chosen from the fire department of another city.

Under the chief are ranged the various operating personnel of the department. Some of these personnel are assigned to housekeeping or research duties such as purchasing and records; others perform the actual fire fighting tasks of the department. The smallest functional unit in the department is the company, which is made up of a single piece of equipment, such as a pumper or a ladder truck, along with the firemen needed to operate it. Companies are installed singly or in groups in the various fire stations that are scattered about the city.

Organization for protection against fire in rural areas, and in small municipalities as well, may take any of several forms. Protection may be supplied by the forces of some other government. In 1955 several hundred cities were providing fire protection for adjacent unincorporated areas, half of them without charge. Those that did charge for their services did so according to numerous arrangements, either a flat rate per call, an hourly rate for men and equipment, an annual contract, or some other basis. Sometimes rural areas and small municipalities depend upon the county government to furnish this protection; the government of Los Angeles County maintains a large fire department for this purpose. Small municipalities and rural areas may combine under the authorization of the State government to establish a fire district, which, as a quasi-corporation, may own equipment and employ firemen. Finally, many rural districts are protected only by volunteer forces; however, when these districts have invested in good equipment they may enjoy excellent service.

QUESTIONS AND PROBLEMS

1. What are the several terms used to designate the State police force, and what are its roles in the several States?

2. Describe the personnel of rural law enforcement and their administrative organization.

3. Describe the mode of organization of municipal police departments and the functions that they perform.

4. What protective activities, in your opinion, require the services of different types of psychological workers?

5. Compare the salaries of police with the salaries of all American and of all national government employees (see the Index for location of this information).

59. Public Welfare, Education, and Labor

Photo by Roger Sturtevant

PUBLIC WELFARE

Public welfare includes such governmental activities as social security, public health, public housing, and the regulation of domestic relations and of alcoholic beverages. Until recent times these welfare activities have been entrusted for the most part to private hands. Indeed, even today private individuals and organizations often play important parts in the solution of these problems: private doctors, hospitals, and medical research all contribute toward improving the health of the American people; private realtors and private building companies still erect the houses and apartment buildings of the United States regardless of the ownership of these structures; there are numerous private marital counseling agencies for husbands and wives who find themselves at odds with one another.

However, both because many citizens have demanded it, and because some government officials have become interested in it, public authorities

895

have interceded more and more into the problem of welfare. Furthermore, the personnel that deal with these affairs in the name of the government have become increasingly professionalized, and their organizations have become another source of pressure for the continuation and expansion of government welfare activities. Many of these activities involve cooperation on the part of national, State, and local governments; others are entirely, or almost entirely, State and local enterprises.

Social security

Social security comprises government financial aid for persons who, owing to one reason or another, cannot fend for themselves. National social security undertakings, such as old age and survivors insurance (OASI) and grants-in-aid to State programs of assistance for the aged, have been described in a previous chapter. The one important type of social security that is financed and operated solely by State and local governments is the so-called general assistance program. General assistance constitutes aid chiefly for the needy who are ineligible for any other form of social security; however, sometimes it is also granted to those participating in other programs who cannot subsist on that type of aid alone.

General assistance is administered by about 10,000 units of local government, usually township governments in New England and county governments elsewhere in the nation. In some States it is integrated with other programs of assistance; in other States it is not. The proportion of general assistance that is paid by the State government, and that paid by local governments, varies from one State to another. In ten States the State welfare department pays all costs; in fifteen more States this department pays at least half the costs. On the other hand, in fifteen States the local governments bear all the expense. The number of persons receiving general assistance across the country is relatively small; in October, 1954, there were 310,000 persons on the relief rolls.

Public health

Public health undertakings include both remedial medicine—that is, the curing of disease—and preventive medicine—the averting of disease. Both State and local governments carry out public health measures. In a majority of States there is a department of health; in a minority, there is a health board. The governments of many large cities contain a department of health. In a rather populous county where there is no large city, public health activities may be entrusted to a county health department. In sparsely settled regions, two or more counties may be united to form a single health district. State health departments are apt to have a considerable staff and substantial amounts of technical equipment. On the local level, especially in small communities, the tasks may be assigned to a single doctor of medicine and one or more visiting nurses. On the other hand,

Modern School Design at the John Muir School in California. John Lyon Reid and Partners, Architects, San Francisco.

health departments in large and prosperous cities may resemble those of State governments.

Remedial Medicine: Remedial medicine has only in recent years been accepted as a proper subject for government concern; indeed, even today most of the curing of disease is undertaken by privately employed doctors and technicians, and in privately supported institutions. However, national, State, and local governments all together have assumed increased responsibility in this area, particularly in the construction and management of hospitals for low-income groups. One of the most important types of public hospitals, which exists at both State and local levels, is that for persons suffering from mental ailments. State and local governments also maintain clinics and institutions for the cure of such ailments as tuberculosis and venereal diseases.

Preventive Medicine: Preventive medicine has been an obligation of governments far longer than remedial medicine has been, partly because governments are in a much better position than private organizations to finance it and because public preventive medicine, unlike public remedial medicine, is not the personal concern of the patient or his doctor. Preventive medicine actually includes two broad fields of activity: (1) the prevention of specific diseases; and (2) the creation of an environment that is inhospitable to any disease. One of the oldest public methods for the prevention of a specific disease is the quarantine (from Italian *quarantina,* "forty days") of any person suffering from a contagious disease, notably such children's ailments as mumps, chicken pox, and measles. In recent years the authorities of many communities have been adding sodium fluoride to the water supply in an effort to deter tooth decay, a proceeding that has aroused a hornets' nest of disputation regarding its alleged merits and defects. Among the numerous State and local programs designed to yield a healthful environment are those seeking to guarantee that the water supplied to the public is clean, and those aiming at the most effective disposal of sewage and garbage.

Public housing

Public housing consists of government undertakings that are aimed at assuring good residential facilities for low-income groups. Under congressional enactments of 1954, amended in 1955, the national, State, and local governments, and local organizations, cooperate to raze slum areas, prevent other areas from deteriorating into slums, and erect low-rent housing structures. Figures demonstrate that in slum areas the rates of criminality, juvenile delinquency, public assistance, and disease, are higher than they are in any other part of the city. Too, assessed property valuation falls in slum districts, so that municipal income is reduced. The upshot is that a slum area demands more in city expenditures than it provides in revenues. Ultimately the emergence of a slum menaces the value of adjacent real estate. Hence slums concern many agencies of a municipal government, not merely its police, welfare, and health departments, but also its financial authorities. Finally, the eradication and prevention of slums are one portion ɔf the task of the municipal planning commission and the local department of public works.

Slum Clearance and Urban Renewal: Slum clearance and urban renewal involve the destruction or rehabilitation of slum districts. These projects are inaugurated by the local government. They are programs whereby a city government buys a slum area, razes the buildings, and then sells the cleared area to a private organization that will erect new buildings, such as a housing project, there. Many obstacles, however, confront such programs, as Figure 137 shows. First, city officials must persuade the State legislature to pass an enabling act that permits them to undertake the project. Having obtained this permission, the municipal government must get funds from State and local sources, and draft plans for rebuilding the area. Actually, most of these funds come from local sources only; State governments generally, with a few exceptions such as that of Pennsylvania, have not contributed to these undertakings. If the local officials conclude that they need federal assistance, they submit their plans to the Urban Renewal Administration in the Housing and Home Finance Agency of the federal government. If

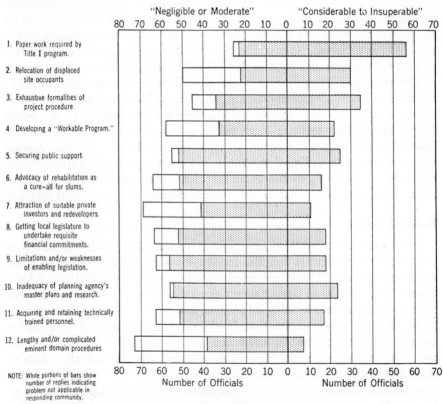

NOTE: White portions of bars show number of replies indicating problem not applicable in responding community.

Morris R. Smith, Surveying the Barriers to Local Redevelopment Progress, "The American City," Vol. 71, No. 3, March 1956, p. 155

Figure 137. Major Obstacles to Urban Redevelopment. How local redevelopment officials rated their problems in a survey. The Title I program referred to is part of the national government's statute that offers assistance to localities. Sixty-two per cent of the nation's redevelopment directors responded.

the Agency accepts these plans, it pays up to two-thirds of the difference between what the local government has paid for the area and the price it will receive for it from the private organization that has agreed to construct a housing project there. The municipal government may pay its share either in money or in some other form, such as improvements for the district.

Occasionally municipal authorities will discover that the buildings already in the district are not beyond repair; indeed, the authorities may assume ownership of a zone to forestall its becoming a slum, if there is evidence of such a trend. Under these conditions the municipal government arranges for the rehabilitation of these buildings by plastering and painting, replacing the wiring and plumbing, and installing furnaces and sanitary facilities where they are defective or totally absent. Sometimes, where a district threatens to develop into a slum, the city government will not purchase the district, but will encourage or even require the property owners to improve their buildings, and may ease their way toward obtaining loans for this purpose.

Public Housing Structures: Public housing structures are apartment buildings erected by local governments for rental to low-income groups. A public housing project is built, owned, and managed by a housing authority, which is a local, quasi-corporate agency established by State law. The authority must draft plans for a project; then, if it wishes to secure federal aid, it must submit these plans to the Public Housing Administration of the federal government. Once the Administration has approved these plans, it contracts to pay the authority the difference between the cost of erecting and operating the project, and the income the authority receives in the form of rent. Since the properties of the authority are exempt from municipal taxes, the directors of the authority must agree to pay the city government a sum in place of taxes, that amounts to ten per cent of the rental income. The directors must also fix a maximum income that any person or family residing in the project may earn, and oust those whose income surpasses the maximum. Most States have not participated in financing these projects; a few— California, Connecticut, Illinois, Massachusetts, New Hampshire, New Jersey, New York, Ohio, Pennsylvania, and Wisconsin—have. It is noteworthy that most of these States have a high urban concentration, so that there are more delegates to the State legislature from cities than in most States. Probably the unwillingness of the typical rural-dominated State legislature to aid in the construction of such projects has been the chief factor that has impelled city governments to turn to the federal government for money. By contrast, in New York State by 1955 more housing had been erected with State aid than with federal aid.

Regulation of domestic relations

State and local governments today regulate many phases of domestic relations, that is, the relations among the members of a family, that were once the concern of private secular agencies and the church. For example, local governments, as well as or instead of churches, register all births. A church ceremony now does not suffice to legalize a marriage; State governments generally demand that the man and woman obtain a marriage license from civil authorities prior to the wedding. Only a few States now recognize the validity of common-law marriages, which result from the simple fact that a man and woman have lived together for a certain period of time. Furthermore, most States require that both parties to a proposed marriage first submit to a physical examination, to determine whether either is suffering from a venereal disease. Moreover, each State provides a minimum age at which persons may enter marriage. Finally, many States fix a minimum period that must elapse between either the obtaining of the license or the taking of the physical examination, and the marriage itself. These various requirements are designed to lessen the possibility of hasty marriages and, in the case of the physical examination, to prevent the spread of disease. It is important to bear in mind that a marriage is a civil contract as well as a moral agreement and is involved in such matters as the disposition of property.

Governments are also concerned with the position of children in the home. For instance, a husband and father is obligated to support his family. However, in the recent past, one who was disappointed in his home life might desert his family, cross a State line, and escape responsibility for his dependents. Today, by contrast, it is difficult for him to flee his legal duties, because all but two States have uniform reciprocal enforcement of support laws; hence a man who has deserted his family may be arrested in all but two States and compelled to send money for the support of his family. State and local governments also seek to guarantee children a stable home; if government officials discover that for some reason the parents of a child or children are incapable of rearing them, the officials in many jurisdictions may remove the children from the home and assign them either to a public institution or to a foster home. Finally, many married couples for one reason or another are unable to have children of their own. There are many children under the immediate control of the State who are potentially available for adoption. Childless couples may seek out such children for themselves; the authorities subject these couples to a searching test to determine whether they can become desirable foster parents.

In the long run it may turn out that some couples find themselves so unsuited to one another that one or the other partner seeks a divorce, or legal dissolution of the marriage. Every State in the nation permits divorce for one or several causes. Generally the grounds for divorce are the same for men as for women, except for non-support, which is a ground for women alone in twenty-one States. Adultery is a ground for divorce in every State; the next most common grounds are cruelty, desertion, and alcoholism. There are many other grounds that appear in fewer States. Every State legislature has prescribed a minimum period that a person must reside in the State to qualify for a divorce there, ranging from six weeks in Nevada and Idaho to as much as a year or even more in some States. Courts generally at their discretion may decide whether the wife (in rare instances, the husband) shall receive alimony (Latin *alimonia,* "sustenance"), to replace the support she will lose because of the divorce.

Alcoholic beverage control

Alcoholic beverage control since the repeal of the Eighteenth Amendment to the federal Constitution has been the task of State and local governments. The federal government now has few duties with regard to alcoholic beverages. It does establish whether a whisky is "bonded," that is, whether it has a particular content of absolute alcohol. Too, because it gathers considerable revenue—$10.50 per gallon from such distilled beverages as whisky—the federal government takes great pains to seek out those who produce alcoholic beverages without paying federal taxes. Finally, the Twenty-first Amendment provides as an assurance to the States that it shall be a federal offense to bring alcoholic beverages into States or localities that have laws banning such beverages; this provision of the Amendment is rarely enforced.

State laws and local ordinances in general, where the sale of alcoholic beverages is permitted, have to do with what sort of beverage may be sold and until how late an hour the selling may go on. The laws also prescribe the minimum age at which an individual may be served alcoholic beverages; sometimes it is a criminal offense for one under age to represent himself as old enough to drink legally. In various places there are laws that forbid women to work behind bars, and laws that prohibit women from sitting at bars to drink. A number of State governments have a monopoly on the sale of beverages by the bottle at stores, so that in these States there are no private liquor stores.

One of the most important aspects of alcoholic beverage control today is the institution known as local option, a device whereby the residents of a locality may determine through an election whether alcoholic beverages

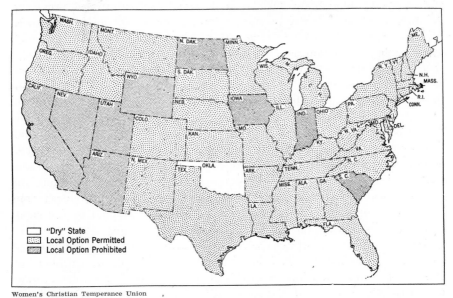

"Dry" State
Local Option Permitted
Local Option Prohibited

Women's Christian Temperance Union

Figure 138. States Providing Local Option for Control of Alcoholic Beverages.

shall be sold in their locality. In most States the citizens have one form or
another of local option; the map in Figure 138 shows in which States there
is local option. Depending upon the State, local option may apply to the
county, the city, or as small an area as the precinct. Through local option
the voters may fix the hours of sale and the type of beverage that may be
sold. Local option has been widely employed. It has been estimated that
26,000,000 people live under State and local option laws that ban the sale
of distilled beverages. (It would be foolish, of course, to assume that none
of these people drinks alcoholic beverages; "dry laws" are often badly
enforced.) Table 50 lists the percentage of people living in areas in which
the sale of alcoholic beverages has been outlawed by local option, in States
with the greatest use of local option enactments.

TABLE 50. PERCENTAGE OF STATE POPULATIONS LIVING UNDER LOCAL OPTION DRY LAWS (17 STATES)

Georgia	60	Florida	17
Tennessee	60	Virginia	11
Kentucky	55	Minnesota	11
Alabama	47	West Virginia	8
Texas	45	Wisconsin	8
North Carolina	37	New Hampshire	8
Maine	35	Ohio	8
Vermont	30	Pennsylvania	7
Michigan	23		

For the entire country it is reported that there are 865 counties dry for
spirits, 786 dry for wines, and 561 dry for beer. There are 2,336 cities and
towns dry so far as spirits are concerned, 2,334 dry for wines, and 1,974
dry for beer. One State, Oklahoma, is dry by constitutional provision;
another, Mississippi, is dry by statutory provision except for four per cent
beer, and wines. Because in large cities a single block may be a precinct,
one may find a situation such as that in Chicago, where along a main street
there may be first a "dry" block, then a "wet" one, then a "dry" one, and
so on. In addition to the foregoing "dry" areas, there are some municipalities whose charters contain "dry" provisions. This is one way of restricting
the sale of alcoholic beverages in States in which local option is not permitted. One instance of this method is found in Pacific Grove, California.

There are powerful groups that influence the enactment of liquor legislation. On the one hand is the Women's Christian Temperance Union
(WCTU), which everywhere urges the adoption of laws forbidding the
sale of alcoholic beverages. On the other hand are the various associations
of beverage producers, intent not only on assuring freedom of sale in as
many areas as possible but also on keeping their taxes low.

Governments today are also becoming concerned with an ailment that
arises in connection with alcoholic beverages—alcoholism. Neither the
causes nor even the true nature of this disease have yet been isolated; however, it is generally agreed that it is manifest in an uncontrollable desire for
any sort of liquor. Government handling of alcoholism varies. In the State

of Oregon, for instance, the authorities publish a list of individuals who have shown themselves to be suffering from alcoholism, and to whom the law forbids the sale of liquors. In a few areas the government supports an institution for alcoholic research; however, few persons reach such institutes save when they are referred to one by a court after having been arrested for common drunkenness. Indeed, owing largely to the fact that most Americans regard alcoholic addiction as a moral or criminal offense, persons who are found to be frequently under the influence of intoxicating beverages are more likely to be sent frequently to jail than to an agency that might cure them.

EDUCATION

The pattern of American public education

Public education is the largest civilian undertaking of government in the United States. There are over 25,000,000 students enrolled in public schools at all levels; there are one million teachers and supervisors. During the 1955–1956 school year, federal, State, and local governments spent more than $12 billions for public education. Public schools include primarily the eight-year elementary schools and the four-year high schools, capped in every State by one or more public colleges and universities as well as by municipal, county, and district junior colleges, colleges, and universities. In each locality the elementary and secondary schools are "articulated," so that a student completing work in the elementary school is automatically admitted to the secondary school without question of his being prepared for the higher level of schooling. Furthermore, in most jurisdictions the student who has completed secondary school can be admitted without question to a public college, provided that he has satisfactorily completed certain "college-preparatory courses" such as English grammar and mathematics.

Administrative structure

The keynote of the administrative structure of public schools is the predominance of State and local governments. Although, it is true, there is an Office of Education in the federal Department of Health, Education, and Welfare, the federal government in the main does not operate schools save on military bases or for Indians on government reservations; the Office of Education is primarily an advisory body. Public education is one of the reserved powers guaranteed the States by the Tenth Amendment to the Constitution. Besides, in most States the actual administration of the schools is performed through independent units of government termed school districts. School authorities have almost everywhere won political independence of other units of government; many members of the public have endorsed this set of relations with other governments, if only because they believe that political independence is essential for intellectual independence. The fact is that in spite of their independence, public school systems may be rife with politics and that the same group that predominates over a city or county may likewise predominate over a school system.

State Agencies: In certain respects the most important State agency connected with the public schools is the State legislature. This body establishes the school system, determines its underlying pattern and administrative structure, appropriates money for its operations, and exercises a general supervisory function over the system. In many States it grants more money to the schools than to any other agency of the State government. The chief State school agencies are the one or more education boards that exist in every State, and the chief executive officer at the State level, who is known usually as either the superintendent or the commissioner.

REGULATORY EDUCATION BOARDS. There are two general types of State education boards: regulatory or supervisory, and governing. The most significant of these boards, which is termed the *board of education* (to distinguish it from the general term *education board*) is essentially a regulatory agency. Its principal tasks are to coordinate the various school systems across the State, to set forth educational policy, to establish standards for local schools and teachers, sometimes to prepare a list of approved textbooks, to issue credentials to teachers authorizing them to teach in schools of the State, and to conduct an unending survey of local school operations.

Membership of these boards ranges from three, in Mississippi, to twenty-three, in Ohio. These members are selected by various means; depending upon the State, they are appointed by the Governor, elected by the people, elected by the legislature, serve ex officio, or, in two cases, are chosen by other methods. In seventeen States some or all of the members serve ex officio, most frequently the chief State school official and the Governor. Table 51 shows the number of members in each State and the mode of their selection.

Terms of these boards vary among the States; often they are overlapping, so as to make policy continuous. Moreover, in a number of States the members are chosen from different parts of the State, so that all portions of the State may be represented. Board of education members serve without pay, and in many States it is forbidden that the members have any professional connection with schools. The principle is that the people, and not professional educators, shall determine school policies. Actually, State teachers' associations may have considerable influence upon the choice of board members.

SUPERINTENDENTS. The office of a chief executive for the State public schools, commonly termed the superintendent or commissioner, exists in every State. His primary function is to carry out the decisions of the State board of education; in States in which there is no board, he executes the decisions of the State legislature. Superintendents and commissioners are also chosen in various ways, as shown in Table 52. Appointment by the State board of education is being installed in a growing number of States; the reasoning is that, because the chief tasks of the superintendent are to execute the directives of the board, the superintendent is responsible to the board and should be elected by it.

State law sometimes requires that the superintendent have professional training and experience in education; however, in a number of States there

TABLE 51. SIZE AND SELECTION OF STATE BOARDS OF EDUCATION

| State | Chief Method of Selection | | | | | Number | |
	Elected by People	Named by Governor	Named by Legislature	Wholly ex Officio	Miscellaneous	Total	Ex Officio
Alabama		x				11	2
Arizona					x	8	5
Arkansas		x				9	0
California		x				10	0
Colorado	x					5	0
Connecticut		x				9	0
Delaware		x				6	0
Florida				x		5	5
Georgia		x				10	0
Idaho		x				6	1
Illinois	State has no board						
Indiana		x				19	1
Iowa	x					9	0
Kansas		x				7	0
Kentucky		x				8	1
Louisiana	x					11	0
Maine		x				10	0
Maryland		x				7	0
Massachusetts		x				9	0
Michigan	State has no board						
Minnesota		x				7	0
Mississippi				x		3	3
Missouri		x				8	0
Montana		x				11	3
Nebraska	x					6	0
Nevada	x					7	2
New Hampshire		x				7	0
New Jersey		x				12	0
New Mexico		x				7	2
New York			x			13	0
North Carolina		x				13	3
North Dakota	State has no board						
Ohio	x					23	0
Oklahoma		x				7	1
Oregon		x				7	0
Pennsylvania		x				10	1
Rhode Island		x				7	0
South Carolina		x				9	2
South Dakota		x				7	0
Tennessee		x				11	2
Texas	x					21	0
Utah	x					9	0
Vermont		x				7	0
Virginia		x				7	0
Washington					x	12	0
West Virginia	x					10	1
Wisconsin	State has no board						
Wyoming					x	7	1

is no such requirement. In Ohio he may not have any connection with any textbook firm. Informally the State teachers' association has a powerful voice in the choice of the superintendent, as do the professors of education in the various State colleges and universities. Here is another reason why appointment is often by the board of education: the sway that these groups have over that body. Terms of superintendents are of various lengths, or are for an indefinite period. The office carries a rather high salary, which in some States exceeds that paid any other State executive official save the Governor.

GOVERNING EDUCATION BOARDS. In most States there are other education boards, for both supervisory and governing tasks. However, in some instances the State board of education not only regulates the public elementary and secondary schools but also governs some institutions. In California, for example, the board is the governing agency for the nine State colleges, the State school for the blind, and the three State schools for the deaf. The Louisiana State Board governs thirty-six State institutions. In a large number of States there are public schools for the blind and the deaf that are administered by the State board. Under such circumstances the board is saddled with a dual responsibility, for of course as governing body it must select the chief administrative officials and teachers of these schools.

Many State legislatures have instead created additional boards to handle the governing of State schools. In some instances a single additional board deals with all State institutions; in other States each institution has its own board. In Pennsylvania, for example, there is a State board of education, a board of trustees for the Pennsylvania State University, and a separate board for each of the seventeen State teachers' colleges, making nineteen boards in all. Members of these boards are selected in various ways; the vast majority of them are appointed by the Governor.

PROFESSIONAL STAFFS. The members of all these State boards must rely to a considerable extent upon the professional staffs that the legislature provides for them. Usually these staff members have had professional training in education. The consequence is that although State law may forbid the appointment of any person who has had any professional training or experience in education as a member of one of these boards, so as to insure popular control of the schools, professional educators have a great deal of influence over them through staff personnel. Other avenues for the influence of educators are legislative committees before which educators may testify with respect to proposed school laws, and the office of superintendent, which, even though the law does not require it, may be held by a professional educator.

Local Agencies: The chief agencies for the public schools at the local level are the local boards of education and local superintendents. Usually these agencies, and the district they administer, are independent, but sometimes they are dependent. An independent school system may be described as one that functions as, and is classed by the Bureau of the Census as, an actual unit of government that is authorized to establish its own policy and to provide for its own finances. A dependent school system,

TABLE 52. SELECTION OF CHIEF SCHOOL OFFICIAL IN EACH STATE

State	Appointed by Board	Elected by People	Appointed by Governor
Alabama		x	
Arizona		x	
Arkansas	x		
California		x	
Colorado	x		
Connecticut	x		
Delaware	x		
Florida		x	
Georgia		x	
Idaho		x	
Illinois		x	
Indiana		x	
Iowa	x		
Kansas		x	
Kentucky		x	
Louisiana		x	
Maine	x		
Maryland	x		
Massachusetts	x		
Michigan		x	
Minnesota	x		
Mississippi		x	
Missouri	x		
Montana		x	
Nebraska	x		
Nevada		x	
New Hampshire	x		
New Jersey			x
New Mexico		x	
New York	x		
North Carolina		x	
North Dakota		x	
Ohio	x		
Oklahoma		x	
Oregon		x	
Pennsylvania			x
Rhode Island	x		
South Carolina		x	
South Dakota		x	
Tennessee			x
Texas	x		
Utah	x		
Vermont	x		
Virginia			x
Washington		x	
West Virginia		x	
Wisconsin		x	
Wyoming		x	

by contrast, is one that is a department in some other government, notably that of a city or of a county. According to an enumeration made in 1952, there were then 67,346 independent school systems and 2,409 dependent systems. In five States—Maryland, Massachusetts, North Carolina, Rhode Island, and Virginia—all systems were dependent. In twenty-six other States, all systems were independent. Finally, in seventeen States there were both dependent and independent systems.

LOCAL SCHOOL BOARDS. The principal officials in local school agencies, whether independent or dependent, are a school board and a local superintendent. Usually the board in an independent system is elected by the voters of the district. Boards of dependent systems are apt to be chosen by some other means; for instance, most boards in Maryland are appointed by the Governor. Yet the dependent boards in both Massachusetts and Rhode Island are elected. The hallmark of a dependent school board is the fact that its financial structure and needs are administered by some other agency of the government.

Where school districts are independent, they provide for their monetary needs under little if any outside, formal supervision. School administrators prefer such an arrangement, for it allows them the freedom to plan for the future without having to submit to the control of other government agencies. By contrast, where the system is dependent, school officials must compete with other government departments for appropriations of money. The tasks of all boards are to set the policies for the schools, employ teachers, and often to choose textbooks.

LOCAL SUPERINTENDENTS. The chief executive official for the district is the superintendent, who ordinarily is appointed by the board. State law generally requires that he be a professional educator who has completed a minimum number of hours or courses in school administration studies and that he hold an administrator's credential issued by the State on the basis of his preparation. Presumably the superintendent is subordinate to the board. However, he often in fact leads or directs the board. He is, after all, a professional person; furthermore, he enjoys the advantage conferred by the unity of his office, whereas the board members may be divided in their opinions. Finally, a superintendent, in the case of a dispute with the board, may almost always count on the support of the association of school administrators as well as that of the teachers' association.

SIZE OF DISTRICTS. School districts vary widely in both size and population. They may contain only one school, one teacher, and a handful of students; on the other hand, they may include dozens of schools reaching from kindergartens to colleges, hundreds of teachers, and thousands of students. The New York City school system, with nearly a million students, is by far the largest single system in the country. It is noteworthy that dependent systems on the average have far more students than independent systems have; in 1952 the more than 67,000 independent systems included about twenty million students, making an average of about 300 per system, whereas the 2,400 dependent systems included more than six million students, for an average of about 2,500 per system. School administrators contend that a district with but 300 students is far too small to assure the best educational services; indeed, they feel that a single school should contain more than 300 students. Nevertheless, as Table 53 shows, five out of six independent school districts have no more than 300 students.

State governments have made strenuous efforts to reduce the number of school districts within their boundaries. One method has been to make the awarding of grants contingent upon unification of two or more districts, or upon some minimum population or school enrollment in the district. Yet at the same time many school districts are outstanding illustrations of how a government that is so small and so inefficient that it cannot provide the funds for its operations can be revived and sustained by injudicious grants from the State treasury. Without such grants, in fact, a throng of school districts would vanish. However, school boards usually oppose any plan that would abolish them; moreover, the people in a school district argue that consolidation might deny them the freedom they now have in determining education policies.

Financing

The financing of schools traditionally has been the duty of local governments, fundamentally that of the school districts themselves. However, in recent years State governments for various reasons have been playing a larger and larger role in supplying money for school systems, so that in some States the bulk of all school money comes from State funds. Yet on the average, local sources still provide most of the money used by school districts in the United States. The map in Figure 139 shows what percentage of school funds come from State sources in every State.

Local Financing: The majority of local funds for education come from the property tax. This tax is one that does not fluctuate very widely in response to business conditions; indeed, it is a quite inflexible tax. Hence

TABLE 53. NUMBERS OF SCHOOL DISTRICTS OF VARIOUS SIZES[1]

Enrollment Size Group	Number of School Districts	Per Cent of Total	Enrollment of School Districts (in Thousands)	Per Cent of Total
U.S. Total	67,346	100.0	20,241	100.0
More than 25,000	58	0.1	3,852	19.0
12,000–25,000	97	0.1	1,638	8.1
6,000–12,000	265	0.4	2,091	10.3
3,000–6,000	611	0.9	2,568	12.7
1,500–3,000	1,300	2.0	2,711	13.4
750–1,500	2,294	3.4	2,417	11.9
300–750	5,379	8.0	2,541	12.6
150–300	5,047	7.5	1,093	5.4
50–150	7,902	11.7	704	3.5
Less than 50	44,393	65.9	625	3.1

[1] United States Department of Commerce, Bureau of the Census, *Governments in the United States in 1952.* (Washington: Government Printing Office, 1953.) P. 4.

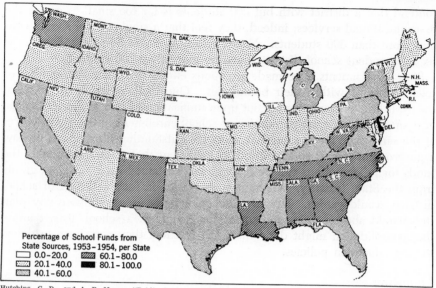

Hutchins, C. D., and A. R. Munse, "Public School Finance Programs of the United States" (Washington: Government Printing Office, 1955), p. 14

Figure 139. Percentage of School Funds Obtained from State Sources, 1953–1954 by State.

it does not react to changed conditions that demand more money for schools. As a result, local governments are turning to other sources for school money, and are awarded ever-rising grants by the State governments. So far as the other taxes are concerned, there are only five States—Indiana, Mississippi, Missouri, Pennsylvania, and Vermont—in which they supply as much as ten per cent of the total school revenues. School district officials may levy such taxes only when authorized to do so by the State legislature. Moreover, State law usually limits the rate at which the property tax may be levied; an increase above this rate is permissible generally only when supported in a referendum election. Local officials also may raise money through selling bonds. State laws or the State constitution also tend to restrict borrowing, by such means as setting a percentage of the assessed valuation of the district that the total debt of the district may not exceed. The fact is that local school administrators depend more and more upon the State governments to provide them with money.

State Financing: State financing of education for the school year 1953–1954 amounted to nearly $3.2 billions, which was 41.4% of all school revenues. Of this sum, a little more than one per cent was appropriated for the State departments of education, and between five and six per cent was appropriated for the State contributions to the educational retirement system. The remainder, ninety-two per cent in all, was expended on State aids to school districts.

GENERAL-PURPOSE AND SPECIAL-PURPOSE GRANTS. State aids fall into several classes. They may first of all be divided into general-purpose grants and special-purpose grants. A general-purpose grant is one that is made with little or no specification by the State legislature as to the purposes to which it shall be devoted. A special-purpose grant is one that the legislature makes for a stated end, such as teacher training, the education of exceptional children, vocational education, or textbooks. School administrators prefer general-purpose grants, if only because they feel that they are better qualified than the legislature to determine what shall be the use of State aid. Legislatures often prefer special-purpose grants, particularly when they have little or no faith in the discretion and wisdom of school administrators. School administrators, however, seem to have triumphed over the diffidence of legislators; in 1953–1954, general-purpose grants amounted to 78.9% of all State aid, and special-purpose to only 21.1%. In every State but Delaware there was at least one general-purpose grant, and in only four States did such grants comprise less than ten per cent of all State aid. By contrast, in eighteen States general-purpose grants totaled more than ninety per cent of all State aid; the government of Nevada made no special-purpose grants.

FLAT GRANTS AND EQUALIZING GRANTS. State aid may also be classified according to whether it takes the form of a flat grant or that of an equalizing grant. A flat grant is one that is made to all school districts on the same basis, such as population or average daily attendance—called ADA by schoolmen. An equalizing grant, on the other hand, is one that is adjusted not only according to population or ADA but also according to the wealth of the district, that is, according to its ability to support educational institutions. In 1953–1954, flat grants amounted to 54.6% of all State aids, and equalizing grants to 45.4%. In Arizona, Delaware, Maine, Nebraska, South Carolina, and South Dakota, there were only flat grants; in eight other States, flat grants made up more than ninety per cent of all aid. By contrast, in no State did all aid take the form of equalizing grants; in six States— Florida, Idaho, Indiana, Pennsylvania, Utah, and West Virginia—equalizing grants accounted for ninety per cent or more of the total.

Equalizing grants are usually administered in conjunction with a so-called "foundation program." A foundation program, which is established by State law, constitutes a statement of the minimum services that each school district shall furnish for its residents. In a State in which a foundation program has been installed, State authorities compute the ability of each school district to finance the program. They then distribute equalization funds to each district unable to carry out the program. Sometimes equalizing grants are made for general purposes; in other instances they are offered for special purposes. In any event, equalizing grants are becoming more and more common as local districts prove incapable of supplying all the educational services that State officials feel they should provide. The consequence of these grants is two-fold: in the first place, school services throughout each State are becoming uniform from one district to another regardless of the financial resources of the individual districts; in the second place, through its authority to offer or withhold such grants, the State board of education is acquiring increased influence over local school policies and conduct.

LABOR

State governments today regulate various aspects of labor. The aspects that will be discussed in the following section are (1) industrial accident compensation; (2) wages, hours, and working conditions; (3) industrial relations; and (4) fair employment practices commissions.

Industrial accident compensation

Industrial accident compensation is insurance against the medical costs that may arise from an injury that an employee suffers in the course of his work; it also guarantees that the employee will have some income while he is recovering from his injury and is unable to work. Until the fairly recent past it was quite easy for an employer to escape all responsibility in connection with an injury to a worker; the employer need merely show that the worker himself had been negligent in some way, or that some fellow-worker had been negligent, or that the injury was a reasonable expectation because the work was hazardous, to be relieved of all obligation in the matter. In short, the employee was assumed to be responsible unless the reverse could be demonstrated. Today, by contrast, in every State the law provides that in the case of injury or accidental death suffered by a worker the employer shall be presumed to be responsible.

Industrial accident compensation is the principal form of workingmen's insurance that is financed and administered exclusively by State governments. This insurance system is usually financed by a State tax on employers, based on the payroll of the particular business; in some States employers may take out policies with private insurance companies. This tax, or the cost of the insurance, is normally added to the price of the employer's goods or services, so that it is ultimately paid by the consumer; thus it may be said that accident compensation is now the burden of the entire public, which pays for it. The core of the program is the weekly payments made to the injured worker, generally some specified percentage of his average earnings, for some period of time that may be as much as ten years or more. Frequently the employer must make a lump sum settlement to the worker's survivors in the case of death. In a few States the survivors are also entitled to weekly payments for a certain time. States differ with respect to the sort of injuries that they cover; in some States compensation is paid for occupational diseases as well as for injuries.

Wages, hours, and working conditions

State governments have enacted a host of laws regulating the wages, hours, and working conditions of employees. It must be noted first of all that these State enactments apply chiefly to workers in intrastate business only; those in interstate business fall under the provisions of the national Fair Labor Standards Act of 1938 and its amendments. In general these State laws are not so exacting as federal laws; for example, State minimum wages are lower than the $1.00 per hour minimum that Congress has established for workers who are under federal jurisdiction. This circumstance is probably due largely to the great influence that agricultural and manufacturing concerns have over State governments. Both State and local authorities play an important role in supervising the conditions of work, particularly in the enforcement of safety in dangerous occupations.

States also carry out numerous functions related to woman and child labor. Every State government has fixed a minimum age at which a child may work in a factory. Moreover, State governments often require that an adolescent have a work permit before he can be employed. Too, children of school age commonly are forbidden to work during school hours. State laws sometimes ban employment of children, and of women as well, after a certain hour in the day; they may also prohibit the employment of women and children in stipulated hazardous industries. Furthermore, State laws may require that women be given a rest period after a certain time of work; commonly, State laws prescribe the maximum number of hours per day and per week that women and children may labor.

Industrial relations

State governments have passed a group of laws concerning industrial relations. Again, a considerable fraction of this task has been undertaken by the federal government through the Wagner and Taft-Hartley Acts, which relate to interstate commerce. However, some State governments have enacted statutes resembling the federal laws, to control the industrial relations of intrastate businesses. To maintain industrial peace, some State governments have established mediation and conciliation services. However, only a few State governments have installed agencies for the arbitration of industrial disputes, partly because both employers and employees tend to dislike the compulsory features of arbitration.

Some State and local governments have attempted in various ways to restrain labor organizations. For example, in about one-third of the States the legislature has enacted a so-called "right-to-work" law forbidding the union shop. These State laws specify that no person may be compelled to join any organization as a condition of employment. Most of these States are predominantly rural, so that labor unions have comparatively little political influence at the State capital. In five States—New Hampshire, Pennsylvania, Indiana, Wisconsin, and Texas—the legislature has forbidden labor unions to contribute to political campaigns. Some State and local laws that restricted unions have been overthrown by the courts; for example, the courts have ruled that a statute outlawing peaceful picketing is an unconstitutional denial of the freedom of speech and the freedom of assembly.

One other phase of industrial relations that concerns State and local governments is the fact that these governments themselves are employers on a large scale. Many employees of State and local governments belong to unions. Some belong to unions whose membership is limited to government employees, such as the American Federation of State, County, and Municipal Employees; others belong to unions open also to those in private business, such as the teamsters' union. Some small cities, particularly in the South, either forbid or discourage their civil service workers' joining unions. Table 54 shows the number and percentage of cities in each of several population groups that have at least some employees who belong to one or more unions. This table, which applies to municipal employees as of January 1, 1955, does not include those who belonged to unions that were not designed solely for government workers.

TABLE 54. UNION MEMBERSHIP AMONG MUNICIPAL EMPLOYEES

Population Group	Cities Reporting	Cities with Employees in Organizations	Percentage of Cities with Employees in Organizations
More than 500,000	18	18	100.0
250,000–500,000	23	22	95.7
100,000–250,000	65	65	100.0
50,000–100,000	113	108	95.6
25,000–50,000	231	194	83.9
10,000–25,000	535	285	53.3
Totals	985	692	70.3

State and local government employees conduct their relations with their employers much as employees of private corporations manage their relations with corporation executives. However, public employees do not have so much freedom in going on strike as private employees do. In some States and municipalities there are statutes prohibiting strikes by government employees. In other jurisdictions, whereas most employees may strike, members of the police and fire departments may not, probably because of their connection with public security.

Fair employment practices commissions

Fair employment practices commissions, which have been established by a number of State and local governments, are agencies that strive to prevent discrimination in employment on the ground of religion, race, or nationality. Those interested in outlawing discrimination have persuaded officials in about a dozen States and in several municipalities to adopt appropriate laws. In some cases, however, there is no instrument for enforcing the laws, so that they are of little if any effect. On the other hand, in some places there are commissions to investigate complaints that some person has been denied a job because of his religion, race, or nationality. Often an offender, when threatened with unfavorable publicity, will comply with the law, whether or not the government can impose a material penalty. Also, some States have fixed penalties for the violation of these laws. Some of these laws also prohibit the officials of labor unions from denying union membership to any person on these discriminatory grounds. Finally, some State and local governments have deleted all reference to race, religion, and nationality from application forms for civil service posts.

QUESTIONS AND PROBLEMS

1. What reasons are given for maintaining the "political independence" of the schools? In what ways are schools politically independent or not independent?

2. Compare the extent of unionism among the employees of the federal government with the extent among local government employees.

3. If cities had complete powers over slum clearance and removal and the erection of public housing, do you think there would be more or less of these activities? Explain your answer.

4. Describe the several major areas of State regulation of working conditions and industrial relations, distinguishing in each case whether the activity is reserved to the States, joint, or concurrent with respect to the federal government.

5. Define briefly: "board of education"; "superintendent"; "dependent school system"; "general-purpose educational grant"; "equalizing grant."

6. How are the Board of Education and chief State school official chosen in your home State? What different methods of selection are found in other States?

7. To what extent is the United States "dry" today with respect to alcoholic beverages? What several forms of "dry" legislation has the Twenty-first Amendment permitted?

8. Explain as best you can why chlorination of drinking water is not a heated political issue but fluoridation is.

9. Is your home State characterized by dependent or independent school systems? Is it typical of the nation in this respect?

10. Using the materials of this chapter and those of the related chapters on the federal government, prepare a list of public welfare activities carried on mostly by State governments, mostly by the federal government, mostly by local governments, and jointly by a combination of governments.

11. If you desired federal money for your home State school systems, but wished absolutely no federal control, what kind of grant system could you conceive, and what conditions would you seek to avoid?

12. What percentage of school funds come from State sources in your home State? Is this proportion typical of the nation as a whole? Is it typical of the States of roughly similar population and degree of urbanization?

60. Planning and Commercial Interests

National Archives

THE activities of State and local governments that are associated with planning and commercial interests involve primarily the control of land use and the various ways in which the governments concerned promote business, participate in business, and regulate business. The activities of each State and local government in these fields are the measure of its intervention in the economy of the area over which it has jurisdiction.

GOVERNMENT PLANNING

The nature of planning

Planning may be defined as the conscious process of seeking for, and reaching, a decision as to what are the most effective means for coping with a given situation. Governments and their officials are not alone in planning. For instance, private individuals may regulate land use. An individual may plan to raise a garden, buy the vacant lot next to his home, then plant a garden there instead of erecting a house on it; he has regulated the use of that lot. Families plan vacations; manufacturers plan production quotas; labor-union leaders plan negotiations for higher wages; gangsters plan bank robberies. Virtually every private individual and organization not only plans, but *must* plan.

Governments do not necessarily plan in terms of the "general good" (even sometimes when their officials may think they are doing so). Rather, government planning almost invariably reflects the wishes of the interest group, or combination of interest groups, that controls the government. Furthermore, the majority of the persons in this interest group, or these interest groups, are private citizens. Because control of the government in a large country today usually reposes in a combination of interests, the plans of the government will ordinarily represent a compromise among the goals of the several interests. The important facts to recognize are that the decision by a government to adopt a given plan is rarely motivated by the desire to please or help *everyone*, and that this decision has been strongly influenced by some group or groups most of whose members are *not* government officials.

The agencies of government planning

Government planning is carried on by a host of agencies at the national, State, and local levels. Furthermore, at all levels of government there are several types of planning agency. First, there are general budget offices such as the national Bureau of the Budget and the budget boards and commissions in many States. A budget office is concerned with planning all sorts of government activities. True, this budget planning is conducted in terms of finances; nonetheless, it is one of the principal determinants as to what the activities of the government shall be. Second, there are budget bureaus or divisions in many government administrative departments; these departmental budget agencies influence both the behavior of their departments and the final decisions of the central budget office. Third, there are advisory or counseling bureaus attached to many departments, to provide administrative chiefs with technical planning facilities. Finally, there are the more or less independent and unified planning agencies proper, which, without especial regard for monetary questions, draft programs for many sorts of government undertakings.

What is particularly noteworthy is that there is a great deal of competition among these planning agencies, both among agencies at different levels of government and among agencies of different types at the same level of government. As an illustration, the States and the federal government disputed for many years the authority to regulate the extraction of oil from wells off the seacoast; Congress in 1954 resolved the issue by turning this power over to the States. The conclusion of any dispute of this sort is founded not simply on law but also on many kinds of political pressure that the interests concerned can bring upon significant government bodies.

Unified and more or less independent planning agencies exist only in State and local governments; the planning functions of the national government are dispersed among many agencies. In 1955 there were planning, or development, agencies in forty-six States. A survey made in 1953 disclosed that then there were planning boards or commissions in several hundred counties. Of the 174 "urban" counties each containing more than 100,000 persons, eighty-nine, or 51.2%, were the seats of planning bodies. With respect to

---

Local Industries, a mural painting by John R. Ballator, at the Post Office of St. Johns, Oregon.

cities, of the 835 each with a population exceeding 10,000 that responded to a survey in 1954, 716 replied that there was a planning agency in their government. This survey also showed that large cities are more likely than small ones to have a planning group.

Planning agencies may take any one of three primary forms. One is that of a single director; another, of a commission or board; and the third, of a board or commission united with a director. As between a commission alone and a director alone, most students of public administration favor the director, if only because a single official can much more readily reach decisions than a multi-member board or commission can. On the other hand, the commission form allows for deliberation, and provides the different and sometimes clashing interests of the area with representation on the planning body. The combined form, with the board to deliberate and the director to execute, in many respects appears a satisfactory compromise. In cities where there is a planning director, he may be chosen by either the planning commission, the city manager, the mayor, or the council. In cities without a full-time director, some other official may hold this post on a part-time basis; he may be the city manager, the city engineer, the chairman of the planning commission, the mayor, or the building inspector.

Planning agencies have various degrees of power. Sometimes their power is solely consultative; that is, they may do no more than draft plans and programs, then submit them to the legislative body where perhaps they may be allowed to defend them at public hearings. On the other hand, the power of a planning agency may extend to an actual share in policy-making; for instance, some municipal planning commissions have the authority to veto enactments of the city council that are related to planning. There are many informal arrangements that modify the actual power of a planning commission. One of the most important is the support it has from the predominant interests of the community. Another may be the personnel of the commission itself; for instance, if there is no full-time director, and if the mayor serves as a part-time planning director, because of his other powers he may have much more power as planning director than a full-time director has. Yet, simply because of his many other tasks, he may be able to afford little time for planning.

The conduct of government planning

The conduct of government planning refers to the fundamental steps through which the planning agency achieves its decisions as to what activities the government should undertake or emphasize. These decisions in an organized and durable form are called the *master plan*. Briefly, to commence its work the planning agency must analyze the present situation. If it is planning for a city it must acquire exhaustive data on such matters as the number of people in the area; their type of residence; their economic and social status and structure; the street pattern of the city; the water, electricity, sewerage, and public transit facilities; the park and recreation services; the distribution of industrial, commercial, and residential areas; the physical characteristics of the region; and the tax base.

Next, the agency must determine its objectives. It must learn, perhaps best of all through public hearings, what the various interests of the city want. Having discovered which features of the city the different groups want changed, which features they want unchanged, what should be the degree of change, and which changes should take precedence, the agency may arrive at a conclusion as to what its objectives are. This conclusion, naturally, will be affected by the influence that some segments of the population may be able to bring upon the agency, by the predispositions of the agency members themselves, and by the influence that some agency members may have over others.

A third step consists of analysis of the data unearthed by the research of the agency, and synthesis of this data with the objectives determined by the agency. It must, for example, compare the number of parking spaces in the downtown section with the average number of persons who drive to work downtown every day; it must then set these figures beside the demands of local merchants that the city government create more parking space for shoppers; it must also take into consideration the amount of land in the downtown area available for municipal parking lots, and the public transit facilities. It may then reach a decision as to whether the government should arrange for municipal parking lots and, if so, how many and how large.

The last step is the drafting of the master plan on a single map with accompanying explanatory material. Since the master plan is intended to project the development of the community for years to come, it will probably gain wider public acceptance if it is exposed to public hearings before it is transmitted to the city council for final adoption. The master plan is essentially a statement of how the land in the community is to be used during the years to come. A master plan has been typified as comprehensive, longrange, and general. Because future growth and needs cannot invariably be predicted, the master plan probably should be flexible as well.

LAND USE REGULATION

The regulation of land use has one broad meaning for State governments and another broad meaning for local governments. So far as State governments are concerned, land-use regulation has to do chiefly with the conservation of natural resources; so far as local governments are concerned, it has to do primarily with the zoning of certain areas for especial purposes. However, at certain points State and local goals and regulations overlap.

Zoning

Zoning is largely an undertaking of city and of county governments. It comprises an enactment of the local legislative body that divides the area into sections or "zones," declares the use to which the land in the zone shall be put, and prescribes the major dimensions of the buildings in the zone: their height and the portion of the lot they may occupy. There are three chief forms of land use in cities: residential, commercial, and industrial.

The zoning ordinance may, and often does, establish subsections in each of these three forms; as an illustration, some residential areas are apt to be set aside for single dwellings and others for multiple dwellings or apartments. In recent years county governments, too, have been enacting zoning ordinances.

Presumably one of the most important functions of a zoning ordinance is to prevent the building of a factory in a residential neighborhood, since it would lessen the desirability of the neighborhood as a residence and therefore lower property values. However, zoning of unsettled areas so as to reserve some of them for industry is also important. For example, areas close to railroads are especially attractive to manufacturers because of the shipping facilities. When such zoning is not specially provided, residential subdivisions may spring up in these areas; an official of the Western Pacific Railroad, which links Salt Lake City with Oakland and San Jose, reported in 1954 that his corporation had spent over $6,000,000 after World War II buying land to keep it from residential use. Where zoning ordinances have not been in command, housing subdivisions have encroached on land necessary for airports, notably in California; the result has been that airport authorities have been unable to extend runways to handle faster and larger aircraft. Another purpose of zoning laws is to keep buildings back from street curbs, so that city or county authorities may widen streets and roads to accommodate more traffic. Failure to have such regulations may compel the city to spend vast sums for condemning these structures. Zoning ordinances also set forth where schools and public buildings shall be erected, and where parks and other recreational areas shall be situated.

Today most large cities and many small ones have a zoning code. Several hundred county boards, too, have enacted zoning regulations; for instance, California law requires all California county boards to do so. Sixty-seven of the 174 urban counties have zoning ordinances. The fact is that most interests in any given locality find a code profitable, in that it stabilizes the value of their property, and may even raise it; disputes are not nearly so often as to whether or not there shall be a code as they are over what shall be the contents of the code.

State land-use activities

State governments carry out many activities in conjunction with regulating land use. It should be noted that many of these activities involve both the national government and local governments as well. A number of them have already been touched on at other points in this text. For example, national, State, and local governments cooperate in urban redevelopment and public housing projects. The task of the State government may be no more than to enact a law permitting a local government to accept and use national funds. Another cooperative project is soil conservation, in which the State government may do no more than pass legislation enabling local groups to establish soil conservation districts. On the other hand, there are certain activities which, although they parallel undertakings of the federal government, are exclusively in the province of the State governments.

Forests: Today there are several million acres of wooded lands in State forests. Moreover, there are county and municipal forests as well. State and local forests together cover twenty-six million acres, more than half of which are in four States: Minnesota, Michigan, Wisconsin, and Pennsylvania. The functions of the State government are much like those of the national government relative to national forests; that is, the State may lease some of the area to lumber companies, supervising the removal of the trees. State governments distribute seedling trees to private forest owners, and plant trees in State forests. Perhaps the most extensive activity of States with regard to forests is in the matter of fire prevention. Local governments manage their forests in much the same way; indeed, there are instances of municipal forests that are so well managed that they bring a considerable annual sum to the municipal treasury, enabling the city government to keep its taxes low.

Minerals: Like the national government, State governments display great concern for the mineral wealth beneath their soil. They regulate the amount of mineral resources that may be extracted; the government of Oklahoma, for instance, limits the amount of oil that may be brought from the ground, and restricts the digging of oil wells. State governments also conduct research to discover new sources of minerals. Finally, some States impose a "severance" tax, which is a tax on the removal of minerals; the government of Texas obtains more revenue from its severance tax than from any other tax.

Fish and Game: State governments protect the wildlife within their jurisdiction. They limit the number of fish that may be caught and the number of wild animals and birds that may be shot or trapped; they confine hunting and fishing to certain seasons. Too, they maintain hatcheries for the propagation of fish, and try to keep their lakes and streams well stocked. Also, they license hunters and fishermen, generally imposing a higher tax on non-residents than on residents.

Recreational Areas: State governments establish parks for the recreation of their citizens and their visitors. In 1954 there were more than 1,950 State parks and similar recreation areas, covering a total area greater than five million acres. Some States have many small parks along the highways, equipped with picnic tables and running water whose purity is tested and guaranteed by the State government. State governments also seek out scenic points, as in mountainous areas, where they provide parking areas. Finally, State governments set up markers at historic spots, sometimes including a brief account of the episode that makes the spot remarkable.

PROMOTION OF BUSINESS

Encouragement of immigration of industries

In recent years many States have turned increased attention to encouraging the immigration of industries. For example, many State governments buy advertising space in periodicals so that they may extol their low taxes, low costs, generous incorporation laws, abundant and skilled labor, and

THE WALL STREET JOURNAL, Thursday, January 5, 1956   11

GOVERNOR ORVAL E. FAUBUS *of the State of Arkansas*

cordially invites your use of the new

ARKANSAS INDUSTRIAL DEVELOPMENT COMMISSION

WINTHROP ROCKEFELLER, CHAIRMAN

and takes great pleasure in announcing

WILLIAM P. ROCK, EXECUTIVE DIRECTOR *and*

WILLIAM R. EWALD JR., CHIEF OF DEVELOPMENT

State Capitol, Little Rock .

January, 1956

"Wall Street Journal," Jan. 5, 1956, p. 11

Figure 140.   A State Advertisement Inviting New Industry.

other features that may appeal to manufacturers. (See, for example, Figure 140.) Interstate competition for industrial development may have considerable effect upon the tax structure of a State; States may vie with one another to make their taxing systems attractive to industrialists. Furthermore, local industrialists may contrive, through pressure on State legislators, to obtain laws that discriminate against out-of-State products.

States also provide financial aid for manufacturers seeking to erect new plants within their borders; the governments of some States allow cities to issue revenue bonds for assistance to private industry. The government of Maine has established an organization that has served as a model for all other New England States: The Development Credit Corporation. This is a body chartered by the State government and endowed with enough State funds to organize itself; it is expected to secure most of its money from private sources such as banks and insurance companies, but enjoy the prestige of the State. These funds the Corporation may lend to private companies planning to enter Maine. Local governments, too, compete for new industries; moreover, private companies, especially railroads and electric power generating and distributing concerns, invite the building of new factories. In the main, however, both local governments and private companies must rely upon State governments to create the atmosphere that industry will find most healthful.

Public works

Public works embrace a number of construction activities of governments. They are the capital investments of government. All, of course, are associated with planning; they also promote business. Because some of these undertakings, notably schools, hospitals, and correctional institutions, are related to other functions of government, they are discussed in the pertinent chapters.

Streets and Highways: The building of streets and highways is one of the most important functions of government in the United States. There are in the United States today about 3,400,000 miles of urban and rural highways (see Table 55). About 300,000 miles are city streets; over 3,000,000 miles are rural highways. Hard-surfaced roads amount to 1,800,000; the remainder are not hard-surfaced. State governments control over 600,000 miles; local governments administer the rest. The ratio of State to local highways varies greatly from one State to another. There are no roads under local control in either Delaware or North Carolina, and scarcely any in Virginia or West Virginia. By contrast, in Iowa, Kansas, Michigan, and the Dakotas, fewer than ten per cent of the roads are under State control. There are actually fewer than 100,000 miles of federal roads in the United States; the States with the greatest mileages are California and Oregon, in each of which the federal roads amount to more than ten per cent of all roads.

One of the most notable trends in connection with highway administration in late years has been the transfer of their control to larger and larger units of government. It is true that in many areas the counties and townships are still the primary agencies for highway construction and maintenance. However, many of these local units simply do not have the financial resources needed for modern highways. The number of automobiles and trucks has become so large, and the cost of building roads so high, that State governments have been compelled to at least help local governments with financial grants, if not to assume the entire burden. Automobile owners' groups, and truckers' associations, have become mighty pressure groups that can make their influence felt in State capitals. Furthermore, they are extending their influence over Congress, so that today the national government aids both States and localities in constructing streets and highways. Associations have succeeded in having State legislatures earmark the revenue from automobile registrations and operators' licenses for highway purposes.

Municipal Parking Lots: One innovation with respect to automobiles is the municipal parking lot. Several circumstances have united to bring the

TABLE 55. STATE AND LOCAL ROADS AND STREETS (SEGREGATED ACCORDING TO FEDERAL-AID SYSTEMS AND NON-FEDERAL-AID MILEAGE)[1]

State or Local Road System	Federal-Aid Primary Highway System		Federal-Aid Secondary Highway System	Not on Federal-Aid Systems	Total
	Rural	Urban			
State primary highway system:					
Rural	197,766	1,882	147,406	32,009	379,063
Municipal, 5,000 pop. and over	—	12,049	1,643	4,137	17,829
Municipal under 5,000	9,638	753	5,089	1,473	16,953
State secondary highway system:					
Rural	433	43	45,976	42,930	89,382
Municipal, 5,000 pop. and over	—	27	244	818	1,089
Municipal under 5,000	16	99	940	1,917	2,972
Local roads under State control:					
Rural	38	—	39,852	88,750	128,640
Municipal, 5,000 pop. and over	—	26	96	296	418
Municipal under 5,000	4	3	506	1,097	1,610
County roads	1,172	92	237,350	1,487,910	1,726,524
Town and township roads	244	35	4,951	612,083	617,313
City streets	25	1,534	3,411	306,367	311,337
Roads not overlapping State, County, or other local systems:					
State park, forest, and reservation roads	12	179	16	8,196	8,403
National park, forest, and reservation roads	204	1	104	91,354	91,663
Toll and other roads	352	48	—	904	1,304
Municipal parks	—	—	—	61	61
Total existing mileage	209,904[2]	16,771[2]	487,584[2]	2,680,302	3,394,561

[1] U.S. Department of Commerce, Bureau of Public Roads, *Highway Statistics, 1954* (1955), page 116.

[2] These totals do not include mileage of approved new routes not yet constructed, as follows: Federal-aid primary highway system, rural 4,216 miles; urban 1,813 miles; and Federal-aid secondary system 2,940 miles.

pressure that has resulted in these lots. The most obvious circumstance is the growing practice of people to drive into the downtown area rather than use public transit, a practice adopted both by people who work in this section and by those who shop there. Another circumstance is the demand of merchants who fear lest people refuse to shop downtown if they believe they may be unable to park their cars, and will instead patronize suburban shopping districts. Yet another circumstance is the desire of municipal authorities to keep the downtown section economically vigorous, so that its property can be assessed at a high rate and provide a sturdy tax base for the city government. Under these conditions, hundreds of cities today have established municipal parking lots. Out of 1,137 cities of more than 10,000 people reporting in a 1955 survey, 675 have such lots. Yet it appears that these lots do not supply a final solution for the traffic problems of large cities; indeed, they may add to them since they encourage more people to drive into the city.

Airports: Both State and local governments are quite active in building and managing airport facilities. These undertakings have been stimulated in late years by grants-in-aid from the federal government. The fact is that with the rise in air travel, cities today compete as vigorously for airline service as they did a century ago for railroads. One of the most persuasive arguments is, of course, a well-equipped airport with long, paved runways that can accommodate the largest aircraft. As can be seen from Table 56 on page 926, in 1955 there were 525 cities with over 5,000 population, 21.1% of all cities of this size, that reported owning and operating airports. Many counties, too, own airports. State governments also pay some attention to air traffic: there are aeronautics commissions in forty-three States. These commissions provide some air navigation facilities, although most work of this sort is carried on by the Civil Aeronautics Administration of the federal government. State commissions do mark routes and cities for aircraft.

Harbors: A number of American city governments own and operate harbor facilities; in 1955, sixty-six cities of more than 5,000 population, or 2.7% of all such cities, reported such enterprises. In spite of the competition of automobiles and airplanes, to say nothing of railroads, water transportation for freight remains extremely important, since it is still the cheapest means for conveying large amounts of goods in bulk, such as grain or iron ore, over long distances where speed is of little concern. It may be noted that the percentage of cities owning harbor facilities is much smaller than that operating airports; of course, only a small minority of American cities are located on navigable waterways, whereas all are open to the air. Interest in municipally owned harbor facilities is especially keen in the Great Lakes area today, because of the increased trade that the opening of the St. Lawrence Seaway is expected to bring.

Participation in business: public utilities

Public utilities may be owned by either a government or a private organization. All public utilities are closely connected with one or more governments; however, in the case of privately owned utilities, this connection

TABLE 56. OWNERSHIP AND OPERATION OF UTILITIES IN CITIES OF OVER 5,000 POPULATION [1]

Type of Utility	All Cities over 5,000		Over 500,000	250,000–500,000	100,000–250,000	50,000–100,000	25,000–50,000	10,000–25,000	5,000–10,000
	Number	Per Cent of Reporting Cities							
Auditorium	413	16.6	8	17	25	33	47	137	146
Bus or trolley bus	33	1.3	3	1	1	4	8	12	4
Electricity generating and distributing	280	11.2	2	3	6	12	30	87	140
Electricity distributing only	224	9.0	0	1	3	3	16	68	133
Gas manufacturing and distributing	41	1.6	2	3	3	2	6	17	8
Gas distributing only	85	3.4	0	1	1	2	6	23	52
Incinerator	430	17.3	14	10	38	48	77	131	112
Port facilities	66	2.7	10	8	12	5	15	7	9
Street railway	6	0.2	3	1	0	0	1	1	0
Sewage treatment plant	1261	50.7	12	16	36	55	141	417	584
Water supply and distributing	1678	67.4	16	20	55	99	184	533	771
Water distributing only	159	6.4	0	0	3	9	22	50	75
Airport	525	21.1	12	15	46	51	74	151	175
Cities with none of above	319	12.8	1	0	2	6	28	111	171
Cities not reporting	70	2.8	0	0	0	0	3	25	42

[1] 1956 Municipal Yearbook, p. 64. For number of cities in each population group, see Table 46.

takes the form of regulation and supervision. This section is concerned only with governmentally owned utilities, which are a type of government participation in business.

In general, State governments do not own public utilities. They do, however, create a large number of special districts that own and operate utilities. Also, few counties own utilities; of the 174 urban counties cited above, in 1954 one reported owning gas manufacturing and distributing facilities; seven, harbor facilities, one jointly with a city; twenty-five, sewerage systems; eighteen, sewage treatment plants; nine, water supply and distribution systems; and six, water distribution services. Eighty-one reported owning no major utilities. It is at the municipal level that one finds the greatest number of governmentally owned utilities; Table 56 shows how many cities own different types of utilities, and divides the cities into population groups. From this table it can be seen that cities are most likely to own and operate the sewage treatment plant and the water supply and distribution system.

Public transportation in cities is one of the most troublesome aspects of the utilities problem. Public transportation systems almost without exception either lose money or else earn very little, whether owned by a government or not; there are few cities like Cleveland, whose publicly owned Transit System is both debt-free and unsubsidized. Solving the issue of whether or not to subsidize a transit system requires solving the issue as to who benefits from the system—the whole community, or the riders alone. If one decides that only the riders benefit from the system, one might then hold that all transit revenue should come from operating income. If, on the other hand, one maintains that the entire community is the beneficiary, one might argue in behalf of a nominal fare coupled with a generous subsidy. What conclusion will be reached is apt to depend, however, not on the acceptance of one or the other theory as "true" but upon the ability of the property-owners' organizations to veto any proposed subsidy—for the subsidy would have to come out of the property tax they pay.

BUSINESS REGULATION

Licensing of trades and professions

All State governments, and some local governments, license the members of certain trades and professions; thanks to this authority, State and local officials may determine who shall be allowed to practice these trades and professions. Which trades and professions are licensed varies from State to State and locality to locality. The following persons must be licensed in all States: accountants, architects, attorneys, chiropodists, dentists, dental hygienists, embalmers, engineers, nurses, optometrists, osteopaths, pharmacists, physicians, teachers in public elementary and secondary schools, and veterinarians. Table 57 lists the members of some other trades and professions that must be licensed in some, but not all, States.

The licensing of a trade or profession is frequently administered by a board established for that field alone, independent of the Governor, to carry out the general policies of the legislature by decrees and rulings. In about

TABLE 57.   EXTENT OF STATE LICENSING
OF SELECTED TRADES AND PROFESSIONS

Trade or Profession	Number of States
Barbers	46
Beauticians	45
Chiropractors	44
Contractors	19
Funeral directors	40
Insurance brokers	26
Midwives	15
Miners and inspectors	13
Practical nurses	37
Physical therapists	15
Plumbers	17
Real estate brokers	40
Surveyors	33

Source: *Book of the States, 1954–1955*, p. 414.

one-third of the States, however, a single board has been created to regulate a number of vocations. Any given State has no obligation to admit a person licensed in another State to practice in its jurisdiction. A number of States, however, have drawn up reciprocity agreements so that, for example, a realtor licensed in State A may go into business in State B, and a realtor licensed in State B may go into business in State A.

Chartering of corporations

State governments have broad powers over corporations in general. Foremost among these powers is the actual creation of corporations; that is, apart from the relatively few corporations that are organized under federal law, corporations receive charters from State governments. These charters, as noted in a previous chapter, establish the corporation as a legal personality that is empowered to negotiate contracts, own property, borrow money, and sue and be sued. State law generally sets forth such matters as the minimum number of stockholders a corporation may have, the minimum amount of stock it may issue, and similar features. Corporation charters ordinarily are issued under general State laws, which are administered by an industrial commission or comparable body.

Each State has the authority to charter corporations; however, because corporation laws in some States such as Delaware are very generous, many corporations are chartered there even though they may do no business east of the Mississippi River. Yet the fact that a corporation has been chartered in one State does not automatically authorize it to go into business in each of the other States; in fact, every State has a considerable body of law regulating "foreign" corporations, that is, corporations that have been chartered in another State.

Controls over banks and other financial institutions

State and local governments pay exceptional attention to the operations of banks and of other financial institutions, notably insurance companies and small loan companies. Banks are chartered corporations like many other types of businesses. However, not all banks are supervised by State governments. There are first of all several thousands of national banks, that is, banks that received their charters from Congress; these banks are subject to the control of the federal government. Moreover, there are several thousand State banks, or banks that have received their charters from State governments, that are members of the Federal Reserve System and the Federal Deposit Insurance Corporation; these banks are in part regulated by the national government. Furthermore, the banks in these two classes make up by far the largest institutions in the country. Yet there are thousands of small State banks that are subject chiefly to the authority of the State governments. Each State government includes an administrative office to supervise banking; there is a department of banking in more than half the States, and in a few others there is a department of banking and commerce.

Perhaps the most important function of the State in this administrative area is to examine banks; that is, usually one bank examiner or more each year calls on every bank under State control, to inspect its accounts. State governments are especially concerned with the type of loans that banks make, what percentage of their deposits and reserves they lend, and what forms their investments take; these are cardinal factors in determining whether or not a bank can satisfy a sudden demand by its depositors that their savings be returned to them. State officials generally are empowered to close a bank whose operations are so unsatisfactory that they threaten the bank with insolvency.

State governments also, at least on paper, regulate insurance companies very strictly. They are particularly concerned with how insurance companies distribute their money in investments, so that persons who have bought insurance will be safeguarded. State governments also must approve the premium rates that insurance concerns charge. Too, State governments regulate lending by insurance companies to their clients, including the interest rates that they charge. Finally, when State governments grant insurance firms their charters of incorporation they carefully examine the structure of the proposed company. These undertakings by State governments indicate why insurance companies endeavor to install a powerful lobby in the State capital.

State governments also supervise the interest rates that are collected by small loan companies and by pawnbrokers. The attention of the State authorities has been stimulated by the fact that often the patrons of such enterprises are not very well informed about the operation of interest rates and may sometimes be cajoled or coerced into paying extremely high amounts. One may recall the character in William Faulkner's novel *The Hamlet* who would lend sharecroppers five dollars on condition that they pay him ten cents a week interest, and who was highly regarded in some circles because he might go on for as long as two years without saying anything to the debtor about the five dollars provided he received his interest payments. It should be noted that local police officials often keep a watchful eye on pawnbrokers' establishments, since individuals in possession of stolen goods frequently dispose of them, or seek to dispose of them, in pawnshops.

Public utility regulation

State and local governments share in the regulation of privately owned public utilities. A public utility, it has been noted before, is a business with peculiar traits: it supplies some service essential to the community, and is apt to be a monopoly. Besides, a utility may be a semi-public institution, in that it may have the power of eminent domain. Owing to the facts that a utility carries out functions that are necessary for the community, and that it rarely meets competition, utility officials have exceptional opportunities for providing bad service and for charging high rates. Of course, if a utility is owned by some unit of government, supposedly it will be operated for purposes other than profit, and will strive to furnish good services to the public; otherwise the voters may hold government officials responsible for the shortcomings of the utility. By contrast, if a utility is owned by a private group, it can be effectively regulated only by a government agency.

State and local regulation of privately owned utilities, therefore, is concerned chiefly with guaranteeing adequate service and with fixing, or at least controlling, rates. The quality of service is a technical question that does not need discussion here. It suffices to say that changes in service are commonly initiated by the utility, which then submits them to the appropriate government agency for its approval; the reaction of the agency will depend somewhat upon the weight of the pressure that the utility involved can bring upon the agency. Sometimes, it is true, the agency, impelled by a third group, may direct the utility to make some changes in its services; subsequently the utility and the other group, usually comprised of discontented patrons, must vie with one another to determine which has the greater influence over the agency.

It would be well to comment briefly on some details relative to the fixing of rates, so as to demonstrate the complexity of utility regulation. Today it is assumed that any utility is entitled to a fair return on the value of its property; six per cent has been widely accepted as a "fair return." The chief problem arises in deciding what is the value of the property. Some persons hold that the value should be based on the original cost of the utility assets, with adjustments for depreciation of the property and for additional investments. However, because prices have been generally rising ever since about the year 1900, utility owners oppose this method of valuation. Another means for setting the value is on the "reproduction costs," or what it would cost to replace the present assets of the utility; owing to the general rise in prices, consumers tend to reject this method, although the courts have often used it.

A third method, growing in popularity today, is a modified form of the original cost method that determines the value according to the "prudent investment" theory. Following this notion, those who are evaluating the property must estimate what a prudent investor would have paid for the assets originally, what he would have paid for any later additions, and what are "reasonable" deductions for depreciation. Supporters argue that this method is preferable both because only a "prudent" investment is entitled to a "fair return" and because "true" value can be most easily computed by this method in a time when the value of money is changing rapidly. It is clear that the decision as to which method, or combination of methods, will be used is apt to be subject to pressure from interests on all sides.

Utility regulation today is carried out chiefly by State officials. In forty-six States there is a public utility commission, set up by the legislature and vested by it with broad powers. In general these commissions have from three to seven members. In twenty-nine States the commissioners are named by the Governor; in fifteen, they are elected by the people; and in two, they are chosen by the legislature. In Oregon there is a single Commissioner, and in Rhode Island there is a single Administrator; each is selected by the Governor. State commissions not only examine the quality and the cost of the services but also supervise utility financing and the merger of utility companies. Cities in some instances still give utilities their franchises, which set forth the powers of the utilities and the nature of the services they are to provide. City governments play one more role in the management of utilities: they may also send spokesmen to urge State commissioners to lower utility rates.

Fair trade laws

A fair trade law is an act of a State legislature permitting manufacturers to set minimum retail prices in the given State for any of their products that carry trade marks or brand names. Hence a fair trade law is an exception to federal anti-trust legislation. Such State laws were authorized by the Miller-Tydings Act, which was a rider to the District of Columbia Appropriation Act of 1937. When the federal Supreme Court later ruled this law unconstitutional, Congress in 1952 reacted by passing the McGuire Act, which satisfied the objections of the Court. In most States the law provides that a manufacturer need negotiate a price-fixing agreement in regard to a particular commodity with only one retailer in order to compel all other retailers to adopt the same price.

By 1956 the future of fair trade laws had become doubtful. Many important manufacturers were expressing discontent with the laws; the Westinghouse Electric Corporation had ceased price-fixing on its smaller appliances, and the W. A. Sheaffer Pen Company had discarded it on all its products. Yet some of the competitors of these firms persisted in their agreements with retailers. Further weakening the general principle of these laws, during 1955 the high courts of Arkansas, Georgia, Florida, Michigan, and Nebraska all declared these laws unconstitutional in their States. In Massachusetts the court ruled that it would not enforce the law in a case brought by one manufacturer against a retailer because, the court said, the manufacturer had not sufficiently enforced its contracts with retailers. Too, by 1956 there had emerged considerable pressure on Congress to repeal the Miller-Tydings and McGuire Acts. Yet a number of State courts have ruled in favor of these laws in pertinent cases before them. The only safe conclusion is that these laws will stand or fall depending upon whether the groups favoring them, or the groups opposing them, are the more successful in influencing the governments and the officials concerned.

QUESTIONS AND PROBLEMS

1. What issues plague the setting of rates for public utility services?

2. What must a municipal master plan take into account?

3. What kinds of utilities are owned and operated in the class to which your home city belongs?   How common is such ownership?   (If your home community has fewer than 5,000 people, use the 5,000 population category.)

4. Why is the national government very active in chartering banking corporations but not other business corporations?

5. What special planning agencies are found in the national, State, and local governments of the United States?

6. What are the primary concerns of the States in the fields of the development and conservation of resources?

7. Define "fair trade laws."   Do they promote monopoly?

8. What means can you suggest for insuring that planning of a county takes favorably into account the interests of a maximum number of the population?

9. What trades and professions are most commonly licensed by the States? How is the licensing typically administered?

10. How would you divide planning and zoning authority between the county and city governments of a county with a total population of 200,000 and three separate cities with 40,000 each within it?   What would your goals be?

THIS study has aimed at introducing its readers to the American way of government, and at increasing their self-confidence in matters of state. It may thereby promote their personal civic participation.

There is a chronic shortage of players in the civic arena. Conditions are no better elsewhere in the world and may actually be much worse. Yet it is painful to reflect that there may be as many active criminals in America as there are active citizens. American government needs a larger public; the task of representative government would be greatly eased if just one additional person in a hundred were to accept a modest, disinterested, and general role in politics and civic affairs. All of the formal invitations are given an American at birth: they are the Declaration of Independence, the Constitution, and the words of innumerable distinguished leaders. The knowledge gained even by this single course on American government is enough training in the rules, customs, and etiquette of the playing field.

The remaining question may well be: By which gate do I enter the field? The least crowded gate is the main gate—the entrance to the body of generally active citizens, the people who attend regularly to the full range of public affairs and encourage governmental action that takes into consideration the interests of all people. Almost everyone will concede that this sense of the commonweal and this activity directed at the commonweal creates the main force behind a stable and progressive nation—no matter what its form of government. The representative form of government is particularly emphatic in demanding a large active public. Hence, whether it come through the medium of political parties, the printed word, or dedication to a range of civic obligations, this general public activity must be forthcoming.

Other gates open up to the practice of government, too. They are more specialized; some of them are more secure financially. They include teaching, the practice of law and public relations, the representation of special interests, government service, participation in various kinds of civic groups, business, party organization, and general or special programs and personalities. A paragraph or two on each of these fields of governmental practice will show how they supply necessary elements and energy to public affairs and public policy.

Several thousands of Americans teach political science in colleges and universities. Many more thousands teach American government in elementary schools and high schools, even though their work is not always labeled as such. In addition, a large part of all educators are concerned with the political and social problems of school systems. Indeed, as Plato pointed out over two thousand years ago, education is a rehearsal of statecraft. A society's government is mirrored in the curriculum and school environment of its children. Hence the affairs of government are inherent in school programs, and impinge upon the school systems from the outside in the form of laws, rules, controls, and plans.

A sizable fraction of the American public thus consists of teachers, educators, and professors. True, most of them tend to be specially concerned with the relations between education and politics, but a great many of them are also interested in politics generally, within the limits of their positions. Since educators often hold no public office, their influence is frequently underestimated. It can be very great. Take, for example, the case of an instructor of American government at a large State university in a State of a million people; he has for twenty-five years been lecturing to about three hundred students annually. About 7,500 adults, most of them now living in the State, have acquired information and insights into government from him. Those ex-students are likely to be much more active and influential than the average citizen. Therefore, his influence must be measured not only by the large number of students who have worked with him but also be weighed by the unusual activity and influence of those ex-students in the government of society. His ideas live on and spread far and wide. Few persons in the State and community can compete with the teacher's short- and long-term impact upon opinion and action. Also, should one examine the biographies contained in the Directory of the American Political Science Association, he would discover a hundred examples of direct academic action. The list of past presidents of the Association includes a President of the United States, diplomats, agency chiefs, and advisers of officials of all sorts from the highest to the most humble offices of the land.

The practice of law and public relations offers another entrance into the political life of the community. Among those who have achieved emi-

The Drive to Get Out the Vote. It is part of every American election campaign, as is attested by this striking emblem of a century ago.

nence in the specialized functions of the law in politics are many judges—
such as Felix Frankfurter, Oliver Wendell Holmes, and Louis Brandeis.
Abraham Lincoln, John Foster Dulles, and Wendell Willkie are examples
of lawyers engaging in politics of the broadest type. The lawyer, even if
narrowly trained, has several distinct advantages in contributing his energy
to public affairs; he is versed in the body of laws that govern human relations
here and now; his vocational success requires clients, and political activity
generates acquaintances who may directly or indirectly provide him with
clients; he is more apt to be skilled at public speaking and bargaining than
are members of other occupations; and he has an easier task than most people
in adjusting his time schedule to the demands of politics. Hence, there is
every reason to expect and encourage a full participation in public life among
attorneys-at-law.

Public relations is a young and growing profession. Closely akin to advertising, it emphasizes individual contacts more than the advertising profession
does. Its distinct advantages in providing ingress to politics and government
lie in the skills of persuasion and promotion that it demands, and also in the
flexible time schedules it allows. Examples of personal successes scored by
public relations advisers in politics include William Benton, former Senator
from Connecticut, and Chester Bowles, former Governor of Connecticut and
former Ambassador to India.

More political campaigns today are being waged by public relations
experts than ever before; this is partly due to the decline of political patronage and the consequent inability of candidates to depend upon professional
party workers. One outstanding firm specializing in political campaigns
is Whitaker and Baxter, the California husband-and-wife team that worked
for Governor Earl Warren and many other California politicians. Political
journalists should not be overlooked; they commonly hold important posts
in politics and government; James Hagerty, Press Secretary to President
Eisenhower, and Henry Cabot Lodge, Jr., American delegate to the United
Nations, came into politics through newspaper work.

Special interests abound in America and hundreds of men and women
find their vocations or avocations in representing them before the legislatures
or agencies of government. Some of such advocates acquire their influence
by means that are not respected, but many of them display talents and
energies that excite general admiration. Of course, the leaders of great
interest groups, such as Walter Reuther of the CIO, or Walter White, former
head of the NAACP, are important political leaders. But thousands of
individuals of less fame represent professionally these groups and hundreds
of others.

Frequently, special interest representatives move into their work from
positions in the industry they will serve; others have backgrounds of government work, membership in legislatures, law, or public relations. But there
is a special skill involved in such representation, and a number of men and
women pursue lengthy careers at it. Occasionally, the chance is afforded
and accepted to engage in general political activity after gaining experience
in pressure group politics. For instance, the Democratic candidate for Gov-

ernor of California in 1954, Richard P. Graves, had many years of experience in representing the California cities' interests before the State legislature. Governor George Craig of Indiana was at one time head of the American Legion.

The civil service is, of course, a continual source of influence upon politics and public policy. Annually, thousands of American college graduates enter into careers with the national, State, and local governments. Indeed, public administration is the ultimate destination of more students who take graduate courses in political science than is any other occupation. The income, prestige, and security of civil service on all levels of government have been steadily increasing in the past two generations and now compare favorably in the large middle-level group with similar posts outside of government.

Responsibilities vary greatly, of course, with the tasks assigned one in the service, but the opportunities for leadership in an important special segment of American society and economy are numerous; furthermore, to an increasing extent, persons with successful backgrounds in government work are called upon for broader political tasks, such as assistants to leading political figures, standing for election to public office, or representing the Government in broad-gaged political negotiations with other nations or groups of domestic interests. Numerous ambassadors of the career service, such as George Kennan, come to mind, as do men like David Lilienthal, former head of the TVA, and even Dwight D. Eisenhower, career military officer.

Civic groups include organizations such as the League of Women Voters, the Community Chest, the Y.M.C.A., charitable groups, local improvement associations, and many other kinds of voluntary activities that are not tied directly to a person's economic interests but excite him and inspire him to realize his ideals regarding how the community should be designed and ordered. The chances for engaging in such groups or movements are many. Every locality includes a number of them. They invite recruits and have jobs for everyone who seeks to aid their efforts. They form a kind of civic action (which is often not called political) that is typically American. On many occasions they provide a training ground for persons who wish to engage in more general political activity, including running for office. They allow one the exercise of his skills at public speaking, organizing, managing finances, advertising, and promoting a cause among the public, and for acquiring civic judgment that is useful for making many kinds of public policy. The gratitude people have earned for their work in civic groups and the reputation for skill and judgment they have acquired in them, have often propelled them into the higher fields of general politics.

Formerly, it was commonly believed that business was quite separate from politics and that a dedication to one's productive interests forbade his concerning himself with the public good. However, business today is affected by politics in many ways. The public relations aspects of business have acquired greater importance, and despite certain difficulties and conflicts, an increasing number of businessmen have been openly concerned with governmental affairs in recent years. It is true that business has always had an eye on public policy although in the past this interest was frequently in ill-repute, like that of the old-time lobby. Today, broader education is being offered in business training and, although the line between permissible "non-political" and non-permissible "political" activity still exists, the tendency in business is to promote participation of employees in civic affairs. Famous examples of businessmen lately active in politics and public affairs include Paul Hoffman, President of the Studebaker Corporation, Charles E. Wilson of General Electric Company, Charles E. Wilson of General Motors Corporation, Clint Murchison, Texas oil and industrial promoter, and Bernard Baruch, financier.

Unlike the law and some other vocations, business generally demands an everyday devotion to tasks; consequently, employees and even the heads of businesses cannot afford the easy scheduling of hours that would enable them to work most effectively in politics. Therefore, much of the participation of businessmen in politics is still carried on via the route of special business representation or the presentation of special grievances or requests to politicians. In any community, only a handful of men with long careers in established businesses engage in general political activities over a long period of time.

Work in party organizations used to be a common mode of expressing one's general political interests. James Farley in New York, Edward Kelly in Chicago, and many other leaders worked their way to general political influence through dedication to party tasks. Carmine De Sapio of New York is a current leader who has labored in the party organization to achieve general eminence. Also, of course, a great many leaders have lent part of their energies and resources to keeping their parties alive. Yet opportunities to be a professional politician have been severely limited by civil service laws that require political neutrality. Hence the number of positions available to people who desire to be professional politicians and who have to earn a living is numbered only in several thousands in the federal government and similarly small proportions in the many States and localities. Whereas at one time a person might make politics a career and a living, even though he might never hold elective office, today very few individuals can build a career in politics in the pay of a party or of the government. Some well-to-do men and women do, however, undertake civic and political work as a career.

Finally, in addition to the avenues of political participation already described, it cannot be gainsaid that participation, at least on a modest scale, is open to every American who has some spare time. The parties invite, and, where they do not invite, cannot withstand, the active desire of citizens of all walks of life to make their influence felt. Moreover, in fact, many distinguished careers in American politics are founded upon an early and intense desire to influence public affairs, notwithstanding the lack of any clear occupational avenue. Among such men would be included very different types: Franklin Roosevelt, Hubert Humphrey, Joseph McCarthy and Averell Harriman. A person with a mission or a calling to public affairs may well discard all the statements that are made to show the advantages of one or another avenue to political participation, for his or her great asset is the will to participate. Such a will, conveyed by a set of ideals of a special or general kind, or by a personality that attracts support in its own right, may feed upon itself and require no security or inducements or ready-prepared stage and audience.

Therefore, the American public, although it needs many thousands of recruits, is accessible by more gates than the beginner may know. The idea that participation is restricted to a clique, a pressure group, or a type of character, is based upon false information. The gates to the public are wide open. Those who wish the practice of representative government to continue must enter and take part.

Appendix

Supplementary Readings

(arranged according to the several sections of the book)

$\mathbf{T}$HE BOOKS AND ARTICLES that are cited in this reading list have been chosen with three points in mind. The first is that there be provided in each section at least one general and comprehensive survey of the material dealt with in the section. The second aim is to suggest titles that would be suitable for additional reading and that lend themselves well to book reviews by students who are not advanced. The third is a consideration respecting the availability of books in most college libraries.

Before listing the supplementary readings by section, however, it may be well to recall to the student a number of books, magazines, newspapers, and documents that contain current materials on American government or that tell him where to find such materials:

A. Sources of current materials

1. *The New York Times*, published daily and Sunday, covers national government affairs scrupulously and well. It is also indexed by subject and name in a pamphlet that appears twice each month. At the end of each year these pamphlets are combined into a single annual index that appears several months after the end of the year.

2. *The United States Government Organization Manual* is published annually by the United States Government Printing Office. It comprises an inventory of the names, addresses, organization, and functions of all national agencies, at the beginning of the fiscal year.

3. *The Book of the States*, published every two years by the Council of State Governments, 1313 East 60th Street, Chicago 37, Illinois, contains a great deal of comparative information about State governments, State-federal relations, and interstate relations.

4. *The Statistical Abstract of the United States*, published annually by the United States Government Printing Office, is a valuable collection of all manner of statistics concerning the American economy, the people, and government operations.

5. *The Statesman's Year-Book*, published annually by The Macmillan Company, affords concise accounts of the organization, expenditures, press, and economics of the nations of the world.

6. Several encyclopedias publish annual supplements in the form of Yearbooks. One such work is the *Encyclopedia Britannica Yearbook*, which contains articles on many features of government.

7. *The World Almanac*, published each year by the *New York World Telegram and Sun*, and usually available in February, is one of the earliest published summaries of the events and the statistics of the previous year.

8. *The Encyclopedia of the Social Sciences* includes articles on such subjects as constitutionalism, representation, the state, capitalism, and federalism.

9. The *Congressional Directory*, published every March by the United States Government Printing Office, gives information about Congress and congressmen.

10. The *Congressional Quarterly*, a privately published weekly periodical, is the most compact and regular account and analysis of the work and personnel of Congress. At the end of each year the most important data in the weekly reports are published in the *Congressional Quarterly Almanac*.

B. Sources of titles (bibliographies)

1. *Reader's Guide to Periodical Literature*
2. *Book Review Digest*
3. *International Index to Periodical Literature*
4. *Public Affairs Information Service*
5. *The American Political Science Review* publishes a relatively complete bibliography of books and articles on American government and politics in each issue, which appears quarterly.

I. THE ROOTS OF AMERICAN GOVERNMENT

Adams, R. G., *The Political Ideas of the American Revolution* (1922).

Beals, Ralph, and Hoijer, Harry, *Introduction to Anthropology* (1953).

Beard, C. A., and M. R. Beard, *The Rise of American Civilization* (1933).

Becker, Carl, *The Declaration of Independence* (1942).

Brant, Irving, *James Madison: Father of the Constitution, 1787–1800* (1941).

Commager, H. S. (ed.), *Documents of American History* (1949).

de Grazia, Alfred, *Elements of Political Science* (1952).

————, *Public and Republic* (1951).

Farrand, Max, *The Fathers of the Constitution* (1921).

————, *The Framing of the Constitution* (1936).

————, *The Records of the Federal Convention* (1937).

Haas, W. H., *The American Empire* (1940).

Jensen, Merrill, *The Articles of Confederation* (1940).

Koppers, Wilhelm, "Primitive Man, State, and Society," *Diogenes*, 3 (Winter, 1954), 69–76.

Lasswell, H. D., *Politics: Who Gets What, When, How* (1936).

MacDonald, William (ed.), *Select Charters and Other Documents Illustrative of American History, 1606–1775* (1910).

McIlwain, C. H., *The American Revolution: A Constitutional Interpretation* (1923).

McIver, Robert, *The Web of Government* (1947).

McLaughlin, A. C., "The Background of American Federalism," *American Political Science Review*, 12 (1918), 215–40.

————, "Social Compact and Constitutional Construction," *American Historical Review*, 5 (1900), 467–90.

Mason, A. T., *Free Government in the Making* (1949).

Merriam, C. E., *American Political Ideas* (1929).

Michels, Roberto, *First Lectures in Political Sociology* (1949).

Rossiter, Clinton, *Seedtime of the Republic* (1953).

Schachner, Nathan, *The Founding Fathers* (1954).

Swisher, C. B., *American Constitutional Development* (1954).

————, *The Growth of Constitutional Power in the United States* (1946).

Thorpe, F. N., *The Federal and State Constitutions, Colonial Charters, and Other Organic Laws* (1909).

Tocqueville, Alexis de, *Democracy in America* (several editions since 1836).

Van Doren, Carl, *The Great Rehearsal: the Story of the Making and Ratifying of the Constitution of the United States* (1948).

Van Tyne, C. H., *The Causes of the War of Independence* (1922).

II. THE FEDERAL SYSTEM

Benson, George, *The New Centralization: A Study of Intergovernmental Relationships in the United States* (1941).
Bowie, R. R., and others, *Studies in Federalism* (1945).
Christensen, A. N., and E. M. Kirkpatrick (eds.), *The People, Politics, and the Politician* (1950).
Clark, J. P., *Rise of a New Federalism* (1938).
U.S. Commission on Intergovernmental Relations, *Report to the President* (1955).
Corwin, E. S., *The Constitution and What It Means Today* (1954).
————, *Constitutional Revolution* (1941).
Council of State Governments, *Federal Grants-in-Aid* (1949).
Dauer, M. J., *The Adams Federalists* (1955).- *Unio Fla hd PolSci dpr*
Friedrich, C. J., *Constitutional Government and Democracy* (1950).
Graves, W. B., *American State Government* (1953).
Haines, C. G., *The Role of the Supreme Court in American Government and Politics,* 1789–1835 (1944).
Hamilton, Alexander, James Madison, and John Jay, *The Federalist* (many eds.).
Holcombe, A. N., *Our More Perfect Union* (1950).
Jensen, Merrill (ed.), *Regionalism in America* (1951).
Latham, Earl (ed.), *The Declaration of Independence and the Constitution* (1949).
McBain, H. L., *The Living Constitution* (1928).
Merriam, C. E., *The Written Constitution and the Unwritten Attitude* (1931).
Musmanno, M. A., *Proposed Amendments to the Constitution* (1929).
Myers, D. P., *The Process of Constitutional Amendment* (1941).
Orfield, L. B., *The Amending of the Federal Constitution* (1942).
Read, Conyers (ed.), *The Constitution Reconsidered* (1938).
Swisher, C. B., *American Constitutional Development* (1954).
Wheare, K. C., *Federal Government* (1947).
White, L. D., *The State and the Nation* (1953).

III. THE PUBLIC

Ashmore, H. S., *The Negro and the Schools* (1954).
Bailey, S. K., *Congress makes a Law; The Story behind the Employment Act of 1946* (1950).
Becker, Carl, *Freedom and Responsibility in the American Way of Life* (1945).
Becker, Carl, and others, *Safeguarding Civil Liberty Today* (1944).
Bentley, A. F., *The Process of Government* (1949).
Berelson, Bernard, and Morris Janowitz (eds.), *Reader in Public Opinion and Communication* (1953).
Berelson, Bernard, P. F. Lazarsfeld, and W. N. McPhee, *Voting: A Study of Opinion Formation in a Presidential Campaign* (1954).
Bishop, H. M., and Samuel Hendel (eds.), *Basic Issues of American Democracy* (1951).
Blaisdell, D. C., *Government under Pressure* (1942).
Bose, H. A., *American Politics and the Party System* (1955).
Burnham, James, *The Web of Subversion* (1954).
Carr, R. K., *Federal Protection of Civil Rights: Quest for a Sword* (1947).
————, *The House Committee on Un-American Activities, 1945–1950* (1952).
Chafee, Zechariah, *Free Speech in the United States* (1946).
————, *How Human Rights Got into the Constitution* (1952).
Chase, Harold, *Security and Liberty; 1947–1955* (1955).
Chase, Stuart, *Democracy under Pressure: Special Interests versus the Public Welfare* (1945).

Commager, H. S., *Freedom, Loyalty, and Dissent* (1954).

Commission on Freedom of the Press, *A Free and Responsible Press: A General Report on Mass Communications* (1947).

Cook, T. I., *Democratic Rights versus Communist Activity* (1954).

Corwin, E. S., *Liberty against Government: The Rise, Flowering, and Decline of a Famous Judicial Concept* (1948).

Crawford, K. G., *The Pressure Boys* (1939).

Dabney, Virginius, *Dry Messiah: The Life of Bishop Cannon* (1949).

Davis, Elmer, *But We Were Born Free* (1954).

Dewey, John, *The Public and Its Problems* (1927).

Ebersole, Luke, *Church Lobbying in the Nation's Capitol* (1951).

Emerson, T. I., and D. Haber, *Political and Civil Rights in the United States* (1952).

Eysenck, H. J., *The Psychology of Politics* (1955).

Fraenkel, O. K., *Our Civil Liberties* (1944).

Garceau, Oliver, *The Political Life of the American Medical Association* (1941).

Gosnell, H. F., *Democracy: Threshold of Freedom* (1948).

Grodzins, Morton, *Americans Betrayed* (1949). - VERY GOOD

Hardin, C. M., *The Politics of Agriculture: Soil Conservation and the Struggle for Power in Rural America* (1952).

Herring, E. P., *The Politics of Democracy* (1940).

Irion, F. C., *Public Opinion and Propaganda* (1950).

Katz, Daniel, and others (eds.), *Public Opinion and Propaganda* (1954).

Kesselman, L. C., *The Social Politics of FEPC* (1948).

Key, V. O., Jr., *Politics, Parties, and Pressure Groups* (1952).

Kile, O. M., *The Farm Bureau through Three Decades* (1948).

Lasswell, H. D., *National Security and Individual Freedom* (1950).

Leonard, N. H., *Political Science and Political Goals* (1955).

Lippmann, Walter, *Public Opinion* (1922).

Luthin, R. H., *American Demagogues: Twentieth Century* (1954).

McDonald, Neil, *Public Opinion in the United States, 1954* (1955).

McKean, D. D., *Party and Pressure Politics* (1949).

Meiklejohn, Alexander, *Free Speech and Its Relations to Self-Government* (1948).

Miller, J. C., *Crisis in Freedom: The Alien and Sedition Acts* (1951).

Myrdal, Gunnar, *An American Dilemma* (1944).

Odegard, P. H., *Pressure Politics: The Story of the Anti-Saloon League* (1928).

————, and E. A. Helms, *American Politics* (1947).

Ogle, M. B., *Public Opinion and Political Dynamics* (1950).

Penniman, H. R., *Sait's American Parties and Elections* (1952).

Porter, K. H., *A History of the Suffrage in the United States* (1918).

Pritchett, C. H., *Civil Liberties and the Vinson Court* (1954).

Schattschneider, E. E., *Politics, Pressures and the Tariff* (1935).

Seldes, George, *One Thousand Americans* (1948).

Smith, T. V., *The Promise of American Politics* (1936).

Truman, D. B., *The Governmental Process: Political Interests and Public Opinion* (1951).

United States President's Commission on Immigration and Naturalization, *Whom We Shall Welcome* (1953)

United States President's Committee on Civil Rights, *To Secure These Rights* (1947).

Williams, R. M., Jr., and M. W. Ryan (eds.), *Schools in Transition: Community Experiences in Desegregation* (1954).

Zeller, Belle, *Pressure Politics in New York* (1937).

IV. THE PARTY PROCESS

Albright, S. D., *The American Ballot* (1942).

Binkley, W. E., *American Political Parties: Their Natural History* (1945).

Burnham, W. D., *Presidential Ballots, 1836–1892* (1955).

Charlesworth, J. C. (ed.), "Meaning of the 1952 Presidential Election," *The Annals*, 283 (1952).

Christensen, A. N., and E. M. Kirkpatrick (eds.), *The People, Politics, and the Politician* (1950).

Cresap, D. R., *Party Politics in the Golden State* (1954).

de Grazia, Alfred, *The Western Public, 1952 and Beyond* (1954).

David, P. T., Malcolm Moos, and R. M. Goldman (eds.), *Presidential Nominating Politics in 1952* (1954).

Farley, J. A., *Behind the Ballots* (1938).

Flynn, E. J., *You're the Boss* (1947).

Heard, Alexander, *A Two-Party South?* (1952).

Key, V. O., Jr., *Politics, Parties, and Pressure Groups* (1952).

—————, *Southern Politics in State and Nation* (1949).

"Legislative Reapportionment," *Law and Contemporary Problems*, 17 (1952), no 2.

Logan, E. B. (ed.), *The American Political Scene* (1938).

Lubell, Samuel, *The Future of American Politics* (1952).

McKean, D. D., *The Boss* (1940).

—————, *Party and Pressure Politics* (1949).

Moley, Raymond, *Twenty-Seven Masters of Politics* (1949).

Moos, Malcolm, *Politics, Presidents, and Coattails* (1955).

Moscow, Warren, *Politics in the Empire State* (1948).

Odegard, P. H., and E. A. Helms, *American Politics* (1947).

Overacker, Louise, *Money in Elections* (1932).

—————, *Presidential Campaign Funds* (1946).

Penniman, H. R., *Sait's American Parties and Elections* (1952).

Riordan, W. L., *Plunkitt of Tammany Hall* (with an introduction by R. V. Peel, 1948).

Salter, J. T., *Boss Rule* (1935).

—————, *The Pattern of Politics* (1940).

————— (ed.), *Public Men in and out of Office* (1946).

Schattschneider, E. E., *Party Government* (1942).

Taylor, L. R., *Party Politics in the Age of Caesar* (1955).

Truman, D. B., *The Governmental Process: Political Interest and Public Opinion* (1951).

V. THE PRESIDENCY

Bell, H. C. F., *Woodrow Wilson and the People* (1945).

Binkley, W. E., *The President and Congress* (1947).

Brownlow, Louis, *The President and the Presidency* (1949).

Carman, H. J., and R. H. Luthin, *Lincoln and the Patronage* (1943).

Corwin, E. S., *The President: Office and Powers* (1948).

Herring, E. P., *Presidential Leadership* (1940).

Hyman, Sidney, *The American President* (1954).

Ickes, Harold, *Secret Diary* (1953).

Koenig, L. W., *The Presidency and the Crisis: Powers of the Office from the Invasion of Poland to Pearl Harbor* (1944).

Laski, H. J., *The American Presidency* (1940).

Learned, H. B., *The President's Cabinet* (1912).

MacLean, J. C., *President and Congress: The Conflict of Powers* (1955).

Marz, Carl, *Presidential Commissions* (1944).

Milton, G. F., *The Use of Presidential Power, 1789–1943* (1944).

Morstein Marx, Fritz, *The President and his Staff Services* (1947).

Nevins, Allan, *Grover Cleveland: A Study in Courage* (1934).

Patterson, C. P., *Presidential Government in the United States: The Unwritten Constitution* (1949).

Perkins, Frances, *The Roosevelt I Knew* (1946).

Pollard, J. E., *The Presidents and the Press* (1947).

Pringle, H. F., *The Life and Times of William Howard Taft* (1939).

————, *Theodore Roosevelt* (1931).

Rankin, R. S., *The Presidency in Transition* (1949).

Rich, B. M., *The Presidents and Civil Disorder* (1941).

Rossiter, C. L., *Constitutional Dictatorship* (1948).

Sherwood, R. E., *Roosevelt and Hopkins* (1948).

Smith, W. H., *History of the Cabinet of the United States* (1925).

White, W. A., *A Puritan in Babylon: The Story of Calvin Coolidge* (1938).

VI. CONGRESS

Bailey, S. K., and H. D. Samuel, *Congress at Work* (1952).

Burdette, F. L., *Filibustering in the Senate* (1940).

Burns, J. W., *Congress on Trial* (1949).

Busbey, L. W., *Uncle Joe Cannon* (1927).

Chamberlain, L. H., *The President, Congress, and Legislation* (1946).

Dennison, E. E., *The Senate Foreign Relations Committee* (1942).

Dimock, M. E., *Congressional Investigating Committees* (1929).

Finletter, T. K., *Can Representative Government Do the Job?* (1945).

Galloway, G. B., *The Legislative Process in Congress* (1953).

Griffith, E. S., *Congress: Its Contemporary Role* (1951).

Gross, Bertram, *The Legislative Struggle* (1953).

Haynes, G. H., *The Senate of the United States* (1938).

Heller, Robert, *Strengthening the Congress* (1945).

Johnson, J. E., *Investigating Powers of Congress* (1951).

Kefauver, Estes, and Jack Levin, *A Twentieth-Century Congress* (1947).

Larsen, J. A. O., *Representative Government in Greek and Roman History* (1955).

McCune, Wesley, *The Farm Bloc* (1943).

Matthews, Donald, *United States Senators* (1955).

Ogden, A. R., *The Dies Committee* (1943).

Riddick, F. M., *The United States Congress: Organization and Procedure* (1949).

Rogers, L., *The American Senate* (1926).

Simpson, Alexander, *A Treatise on Federal Impeachments* (1916).

Smith, T. V., *The Legislative Way of Life* (1940).

Steiner, G. Y., *The Congressional Conference Committee* (1950).

Voorhis, Jerry, *Confessions of a Congressman* (1947).

Walker, Harvey, *The Legislative Process* (1948).

Westphal, A. C. F., *The House Committee on Foreign Affairs* (1942).

Wilson, H. J., *Congress, Corruption, and Compromise* (1951).

Wilson, Woodrow, *Congressional Government: A Study in American Politics* (1885).

Young, Roland, *This Is Congress* (1946).

VII. THE JUDICIAL BRANCH

Beard, C. A., *The Supreme Court and the Constitution* (1938).

Berger, Morroe, *Equality by Statute* (1952).

Beveridge, A. J., *Life of John Marshall* (1919).

Blaustein, A. P., and C. O. Porter, *The American Lawyer* (1954).

Boudin, L. B., *Government by Judiciary* (1932).

Bowen, C. D., *Yankee from Olympus* (1944).

Cahill, F. V., *Judicial Legislation, a Study in American Legal Theory* (1952).

Cardozo, Benjamin, *The Nature of the Judicial Process* (1921).

Carr, R. K., *Democracy and the Supreme Court* (1936).

Corwin, E. S., *Constitutional Revolution, Ltd.* (1941).

Cummings, H. S., and C. McFarland, *Federal Justice* (1937).

Cushman, R. E. (ed.), *Leading Constitutional Decisions* (1955).

Dickinson, E. D., *Law and Peace* (1951).

Doob, L. W., *The Plans of Men* (1940).

Frank, Jerome, *Courts on Trial* (1949).

Frankfurter, Felix, *Law and Politics* (1939).

Freund, P. A., *On Understanding the Supreme Court* (1949).

Harris, R. J., *The Judicial Power of the United States* (1940).

Heller, F. H., *The Sixth Amendment* (1951).

Hendel, Samuel, *Charles Evans Hughes and the Supreme Court* (1951).

Johnson, A. W., and F. H. Yost, *Separation of Church and State in the United States* (1948).

Lowenthal, Max, *The Federal Bureau of Investigation* (1950).

MacKenzie, Findlay (ed.), *Planned Society* (1937).

Mason, A. T., and W. B. Beaney, *American Constitutional Law* (1954).

Matthews, J. M., *The American Constitutional System* (1940).

Morris, R. B., *Fair Trial* (1952).

Peltason, Jack, *Federal Courts in the Political Process* (1955).

Pound, Roscoe, *The Organization of Courts* (1940).

Pritchett, C. H., *Civil Liberties and the Vinson Court* (1954).

————, *The Roosevelt Court* (1948).

Rodell, Fred, *Nine Men* (1955).

Twiss, B. R., *Lawyers and the Constitution* (1942).

Umbreit, Kenneth, *Our Eleven Chief Justices* (1938).

Warren, Charles, *Congress, the Constitution, and the Supreme Court* (1935).

Wendell, Mitchell, *Relations between the Federal and State Courts* (1949).

Wright, B. F., Jr., *The Contract Clause of the Constitution* (1938).

VIII. PUBLIC POLICY AND ITS ADMINISTRATION

American Assembly, The (Columbia University), *The Federal Government Service: Its Character, Prestige and Problems* (1955).

Appleby, P. H., *Big Democracy* (1945).

————, *Federal Regulatory Action and Control* (1940).

————, *Morality and Administration in Democratic Government* (1952).

Bortecou, Eleanor, *The Federal Loyalty-Security Program* (1953).

Charlesworth, J. C., *Governmental Administration* (1951).

Coker, F .W., *Democracy, Liberty, and Property* (1942).

Corson, J. J., *Executives for the Federal Service* (1952).

Fainsod, Merle, and Lincoln Gordon, *Government and the American Economy* (1948).

Fesler, J. W., *Area and Administration* (1949).

Finer, Herman, *The Road to Reaction* (1945).

Frankfurter, Felix, *The Public and Its Government* (1930).

Friedrich, C. J., and others, *Problems of the American Public Service* (1935).

Glueck, Sheldon (ed.), *The Welfare State and the National Welfare* (1952).

Graves, W. B., *Public Administration in a Democratic Society* (1950).

Hayek, F. A., *The Road to Serfdom* (1944).

Herring, E. P., *Public Administration and the Public Interest* (1936).

Hyneman, C. S., *Bureaucracy in a Democracy* (1950).

Millett, J. D., *Management in the Public Service* (1954).

Millspaugh, A. C., *Toward Efficient Democracy* (1949).

Mises, Ludwig von, *Omnipotent Government* (1944).

Natt, Milton, *Employee Training in Public Service* (1941).

Pfiffner, J. M., and R. V. Presthus, *Public Administration* (1953).

Redford, E. S., *Administration of National Economic Control* (1952).

Reeves, F. W., and P. T. David, *Personnel Administration in the Federal Government* (1937).

Spero, Sterling, *Government as Employer* (1948).

Toner, Joseph, *Educational Preparation for Public Administration* (1948).
Wallace, Schuyler, *Federal Departmentalization* (1941).
White, L. D., *Civil Service in Wartime* (1945).
————, *Introduction to the Study of Public Administration* (1956).

IX. NATIONAL FINANCES

Abbott, C. C., *The Federal Debt* (1953).
Allen, E. D., and O. H. Brownlee, *Economics of Public Finance* (1947).
Anshen, Melvin, and F. D. Wormuth, *Private Enterprise and Public Policy* (1954).
Berle, A. A., Jr., *The 20th Century Capitalist Revolution* (1954).
Colm, Gerard, *Essays in Public Finance and Fiscal Policy* (1955).
Council of Economic Advisers, *Report to the President* (annual).
Crockett, Joseph P., *The Federal Tax System of the United States: A Survey of Law and Administration* (1955).
Dimock, M. E., *Business and Government* (1949).
Douglas, P. H., *Economy in the National Government* (1952).
Foster, M. B., and R. Roger, *Money and Banking* (1947).
Groves, H. M., *Financing Government* (1954).
Hansen, A. H., *Monetary Theory and Fiscal Policy* (1949).
Kaplan, A. D. H., *Big Enterprise in a Competitive System* (1954).
Murad, Anatol, *Private Credit and Public Debt* (1954).
Nourse, E. G., *Economics in the Public Service* (1953).
Paul, R. E., *Taxation in the United States* (1954).
Smith, H. D., *The Management of Your Government* (1945).
United States Bureau of the Budget, *The Federal Budget in Brief* (annual).
Wector, Dixon, *The Age of the Great Depression, 1929–1941* (1948).

X. HUMAN AND NATURAL RESOURCES

Baker, Gladys, *The County Agent* (1939).
Bernstein, Irving, *Arbitration of Wages* (1954).
Duffus, R. L., and C. Krutch, *The Valley and Its People: A Portrait of the T.V.A.* (1944).
Fesler, J. W. (ed.), "Government and Water Resources," *American Political Science Review*, 44 (1950), 575–649.
Finer, Herman, *The T.V.A.: Lessons for International Application* (1944).
Gagliardo, Domenico, *American Social Insurance* (1949).
Ginzberg, Eli, *The Labor Leader* (1948).
Gulick, L. H., *American Forest Policy: A Study of Government Administration and Economic Control* (1951).
Gustafson, A. F., and others, *Conservation in the United States* (1949).
Handlin, Oscar, *The American People in the 20th Century* (1954).
Hopkins, W. S., *Labor in the American Economy* (1948).
Hutt, W. H., *The Theory of Collective Bargaining* (1954).
Lauterbach, Albert, *Man, Motives, and Money: Psychological Frontiers of Economics* (1954).
Leek, J. H., *Government and Labor in the United States* (1952).
Lilienthal, David, *T.V.A.—Democracy on the March* (1944).
Lindblom, C. E., *Unions and Capitalism* (1949).
Maas, A., *Muddy Waters: The Army Engineers and the Nation's Rivers* (1951).
McKinley, Charles, *Uncle Sam in the Pacific Northwest* (1952).
McLendon, S. G., *History of the Public Domain of Georgia* (1924).
McNaughton, W. L., and Joseph Lazar, *Industrial Relations and the Government* (1954).
Means, J. H., *Doctors, People, and Government* (1953).
Metz, H. W., *Labor Policy of the Federal Government* (1945).

Mills, C. W., *The New Men of Power* (1948).

Osborn, Fairfield, *Our Plundered Planet* (1948).

Pinchot, Gifford, *Breaking New Ground* (1947).

Potter, D. M., *People of Plenty: Economic Abundance and the American Character* (1954).

Pritchett, C. H., *The Tennessee Valley Authority* (1943).

Reynolds, L. G., *Labor Economics and Labor Relations* (1954).

Robbins, R. M., *Our Landed Heritage: The Public Domain, 1776–1936* (1942).

Sears, P. B., *Deserts on the March* (1947).

Selznick, Philip, *TVA and the Grass Roots* (1949).

Sufrin, S. C., and R. C. Sedgwick, *Labor Law* (1954).

Taft, Philip, *The Structure and Government of Labor Unions* (1954).

Timmons, J. F., and W. G. Murray (eds.), *Land Problems and Policies* (1950).

Warner, C. E., and others, *Labor in Postwar America* (1949).

Wengert, Norman, *Natural Resources and the Political Struggle* (1955).

Windmuller, J. P., *American Labor and the International Labor Movement, 1940 to 1953* (1954).

XI. COMMERCIAL INTERESTS OF THE GOVERNMENT

Adams, Walter, and Horace M. Gray, *Monopoly in America* (1955).

Anshen, Melvin, and F. D. Wormuth, *Private Enterprise and Public Policy* (1954).

Baker, Gladys, *The County Agent* (1939).

Bernstein, Marver H., *Regulating Business by Independent Commission* (1955).

Black, J. D., *Introduction to Economics for Agriculture* (1953).

Clapp, Gordon R., *The TVA: An Approach to the Development of a Region* (1955).

Commission on Foreign Economic Policy, *Report to the President* (1954).

Corwin, E. S., *The Commerce Power versus State's Rights* (1936).

Dewhurst, J. F., and Associates, *America's Needs and Resources: A New Survey* (1955).

Dirlam, J. B., and A. E. Kahn, *Fair Competition* (1954).

Galbraith, J. K., *American Capitalism* (1952).

Gaus, John, and Leon Wolcott, *Public Administration and the United States Department of Agriculture* (1941).

Hardin, Charles, *The Politics of Agriculture* (1952).

Isard, Walter, and Vincent Whitney, *Atomic Power: An Economic and Social Analysis* (1955).

Kaplan, A. D. H., *Big Enterprise in a Competitive System* (1954).

Latham, Earl, *The Group Basis of Politics, a Study in Basing-Point Legislation* (1952).

Lilienthal, David, *Big Business, A New Era* (1953).

Lindblom, Charles, *Unions and Capitalism* (1949).

Locklin, D. P., *Economics of Transportation* (1954).

McConnell, Grant, *The Decline of Agrarian Democracy* (1953).

Millis, Harry, and Royal Montgomery, *Organized Labor* (1954).

Papandreou, A. G., and J. T. Wheeler, *Competition and Its Regulation* (1954).

Redford, E. S., *Administration of National Economic Control* (1952).

Schultz, T. W., *Agriculture in an Unstable Economy* (1945).

Steiner, G. A., *Government's Role in Economic Life* (1953).

Wilcox, Clair, *Public Policies toward Business* (1955).

Wilson, G. L., and L. A. Bryan, *Air Transportation* (1949).

XII. NATIONAL SECURITY AND FOREIGN AFFAIRS

Allen, H. C., *Great Britain and the United States: A History of Anglo-American Relations (1783–1952)* (1954).

Aycock, W. B., and S. W. Wurfel, *Military Law under the Uniform Code of Military Justice* (1955).

Bailey, T. A., *A Diplomatic History of the American People* (1950).

Barker, A. W., *Foreign Policies of the United States* (1954).

Beanler, W. L., *Career Ambassador* (1951).

Bingham, J. B., *Shirt-Sleeve Diplomacy: Point Four in Action* (1954).

Bowles, Chester, *Ambassador's Report* (1954).

Brinton, Crane, *From Many One* (1948).

Brookings Institution, *Governmental Mechanism for the Conduct of U.S. Foreign Relations* (1949).

Brown, W. A., and R. Opie, *American Foreign Assistance* (1953).

Cheever, D. S., and H. F. Haviland, *Organizing for Peace* (1954).

Childs, J. R., *American Foreign Service* (1948).

Commission to Frame a World Constitution, *Preliminary Draft of a World Constitution* (1953).

Corwin, E. S., *Total War and the Constitution* (1947).

Dangerfield, R. J., *In Defense of the Senate, A Study in Treaty Making* (1933).

Dunn, F. S., and others, *The Absolute Weapon: Atomic Power and World Order* (1946).

Finletter, T. K., *Power and Policy* (1954).

Guerrant, E. O., *Roosevelt's Good Neighbor Policy* (1950).

————, *Modern American Diplomacy* (1954).

Harris, J. P., *The Advice and Consent of the Senate* (1953).

Hart, A. G., *Defense and the Dollar: Federal Credit and Monetary Policies* (1953).

Hull, Cordell, *Memoirs* (1948).

Huszar, G. B. de, and Associates, *Soviet Power and Policy* (1955).

Huzar, Elias, *The Purse and the Sword; Control of the Army by Congress through Military Appropriations, 1933–1950* (1950).

Jennings, D. H., Eugene Clark, and B. E. Grimes, *Goals of American Foreign Policy* (1955).

Jessup, Philip, *Elihu Root* (1938).

Kelsen, Hans, *The Law of the United Nations* (1950).

Kennan, G. F., *American Diplomacy, 1900–1950* (1951).

————, *Realities of American Foreign Policy* (1954).

Kerwin, J. G. (ed.), *Civil Military Relationships in American Life* (1948).

Lasswell, H. D., *National Security and Individual Freedom* (1950).

Levi, Werner, *Fundamentals of World Organization* (1950).

Liddell Hart, B. H., *Strategy* (1954).

Lincoln, G. A., W. S. Stone, and T. H. Harvey (eds.), *Economics of National Security* (1950).

Lissitzyn, O. T., *The International Court of Justice* (1951).

London, Kurt, *How Foreign Policy Is Made* (1950).

McCamy, J. L., *The Administration of American Foreign Affairs* (1950).

McKinley, S. B., *Democracy and Military Power* (1934).

Mangione, G. J., *A Short History of International Organization* (1954).

Marshall, C. B., *The Limits of Foreign Policy* (1954).

Osgood, R. E., *Ideals and Self-Interest in America's Foreign Relations* (1953).

Perkins, Dexter, *The American Approach to Foreign Policy* (1952).

Potter, E. B., and J. R. Fredland (eds.), *The United States and World Sea Power* (1955).

Pratt, J. W., *A History of United States Foreign Policy* (1955).

Price, H. B., *The Marshall Plan and Its Meaning* (1955).

Randall, C. B., *A Foreign Economic Policy for the United States* (1954).

Rostow, W. W., and R. W. Hatch, *An American Policy in Asia* (1955).

Schleicher, C. P., *Introduction to International Relations* (1954).

Schuman, F. L., *The Commonwealth of Man: An Inquiry into Power Politics and World Government* (1952).

————, *International Politics* (1953).

Scott, John, *Political Warfare* (1955).

Smith, Louis, *American Democracy and Military Power* (1951).

Snyder, R. C., and E. S. Furniss, Jr., *An Introduction to American Foreign Policy* (1955).

Staley, Eugene, *The Future of Underdeveloped Countries* (1954).

Stimson, H. L., and McGeorge Bundy, *On Active Service in Peace and War* (1947).

Strausz-Hupé, Robert, and Stefan Possony, *International Relations* (1954).

Stuart, G. H., *The Department of State* (1949).

Van Alstyne, R. W., *American Diplomacy in Action* (1947).

Wallace, Donald, *Economic Controls and Defense* (1953).

Walters, F. P., *A History of the League of Nations* (1952).

Westerfield, H. B., *Foreign Policy and Party Politics: Pearl Harbor to Korea* (1955).

Wright, Quincy, *The Control of American Foreign Relations* (1922).

————, *A Study of War* (1942).

————, *The World Community* (1948).

XIII. FOUNDATIONS OF STATE AND LOCAL GOVERNMENT

American Assembly, The, *The Forty-Eight States* (1955).

Anderson, William, *The Nation and the States, Rivals or Partners?* (1955).

Beals, Carleton, *The Story of Huey P. Long* (1935).

Bebout, John, *The Making of the New Jersey Constitution* (1945).

Bowie, Robert R., and Carl Friedrich, *Studies in Federalism* (1954).

Council of State Governments, *Federal Grants-in-Aid* (1949).

————, *State-Local Relations* (1946).

Fordham, Jefferson B., *A Larger Concept of Community* (1956).

Kallenbach, Joseph E., *Federal Cooperation with the States under the Commerce Clause* (1942).

Key, V. O., Jr., *Southern Politics in State and Nation* (1949).

MacMahon, Arthur W. (ed.), *Federalism, Mature and Emergent* (1955).

McKean, Dayton D., *Pressures on the Legislature of New Jersey* (1938).

Morlan, Robert (ed.), *Capitol, Courthouse and City Hall: Readings in American State and Local Government* (1954).

Moscow, Warren, *Politics in the Empire State* (1948).

New York State Constitutional Convention Committee, *Report: Problems Relating to Home Rule and Local Government* (1938).

O'Rourke, Vernon A., and Douglas W. Campbell, *Constitution-Making in a Democracy* (1943).

Peel, Roy V., *State Government Today* (1948).

Phillips, J. C., *State and Local Government in America* (1954).

Shambaugh, B. F., *The Constitution of Iowa* (1934).

Sikes, P. S. and J. E. Stoner, *Bates and Field's State Government* (1954).

Sturm, A. L., *Methods of State Constitutional Reform* (1954).

United States Senate, *Federal, State, and Local Government Fiscal Relations,* Senate Document No. 69, 78th Cong., 1st Sess. (1943).

Warren, Roland L., *Studying Your Community* (1955).

Zeller, Belle, *Pressure Politics in New York* (1937).

Zink, Harold, *City Bosses in the United States; a Study of Twenty Municipal Bosses* (1930).

XIV. STRUCTURE OF STATE GOVERNMENT

Borchard, Edwin M., *Declaratory Judgments* (1941).

Buehler, Ezra C. (ed.), *Unicameral Legislatures* (1937).

Council of State Governments, *Our State Legislatures* (1948).

Crouch, Winston W., *The Initiative and Referendum in California* (1950).

————, and Dean E. McHenry, *California Government: Politics and Administration* (1949).

Dodd, Walter F., and Sue H. Dodd, *Government in Illinois* (1923).

Donnelly, Thomas C., *The Government of New Mexico* (1947).

Farmer, Hallie, *The Legislative Process in Alabama: Legislative Apportionment* (1944).

————, *Local and Private Legislation* (1944).

————, *Standing Committees* (1945).

————, *Recess and Interim Committees* (1946).

————, *Legislative Costs* (1947).

Garst, Doris S., *The Story of Wyoming and its Constitution and Government* (1938).

Graves, W. Brooke, *American State Government* (1953).

Gray, Robert A., and Florence R. Tryon, *The Government of Florida* (1941).

Hannan, W. E., and M. B. Csontos, *State Court Systems* (1940).

Holloway, W. W., and C. W. Smith, Jr., *Government and Politics in Alabama* (1941)

Irwin, Leonard B., *New Jersey; the State and Its Government* (1948).

Johnson, Samuel A., *Missouri; the State and Its Government* (1943).

Kalijarvi, Thorsten V., and Chamberlin, William C., *The Government of New Hampshire* (1939).

Kise, Joseph, and George B. Sjoselius, *Minnesota; the State and Its Government* (1951).

Lepawsky, Albert, *Judicial Systems of Metropolitan Chicago* (1932).

Lipson, Leslie, *The American Governor* (1939).

MacDonald, Austin F., *American State Government and Administration* (1955).

Neuberger, Richard, *Adventures in Politics: We Go to the Legislature* (1954).

Patterson, C. P., and others, *State and Local Government in Texas* (1948).

Patterson, R. F., *The Office of Lieutenant Governor in the United States* (1944).

Peel, Roy V., *State Government Today* (1948).

Perkins, John A., *The Role of the Governor of Michigan in the Enactment of Appropriations* (1943).

Pigeon, Helen D., *Probation and Parole in Theory and Practice* (1942).

Plaisted, John W., *Legislative Procedure in the General Court of Massachusetts* (1948).

Pound, Roscoe, *Criminal Justice in America* (1930).

Ransone, Coleman B., Jr., *The Office of Governor in the South* (1951).

Ruscowski, Casimir W., *The Constitutional Governor* (1943).

Sanders, Wiley B., *The Juvenile Courts of North Carolina* (1948).

Scace, Homer E., *The Organization of the Executive Office of the Governor* (1950).

Sikes, Pressly, *Indiana State and Local Government* (1946).

Talbott, Forrest, *Intergovernmental Relations and the Courts* (1950).

United States Department of Health, Education and Welfare, *Standards for Specialized Courts Dealing with Children* (1954).

Vanderbilt, Arthur T. (ed.), *Minimum Standards of Judicial Administration* (1949).

Walker, R. A., and Floyd Cave, *How California is Governed* (1953).

Warren, George, *Traffic Courts* (1942).

Winfield, Charles H., *The Grand Jury* (1928).

Zeller, Belle (ed.), *American State Legislatures* (1954).

XV. STRUCTURE OF LOCAL GOVERNMENT

Adrian, Charles R., *Governing Urban America: Structure, Politics, and Administration* (1955).

Allen, Robert S. (ed.), *Our Fair City* (1947).

Anderson, William, and E. W. Weidner, *American City Government* (1950).

Barclay, Thomas S., *The Movement for Municipal Home Rule in St. Louis* (1943).

Bromage, Arthur W., *Introduction to Municipal Government and Administration* (1950).

Council of State Governments, *The States and the Metropolitan Problem* (1956).

Griffith, Ernest S., *History of American City Government* (1938).

Hughes, Melvin C., *County Government in Georgia* (1944).

Jones, Victor, *Metropolitan Government* (1942).

Kneier, Charles M., *City Government in the United States* (1947).

Lancaster, Lane W., *Government in Rural America* (1952).

MacCorkle, Stu...

—, State Fina. READINGS

—, and Wilfred L. *ican Municipal Government and Administration* (1948).
MacDonald, Austin F., *.. over Cities in Texas* (1937).
Mott, Rodney L., *Home Rul...ms of Local Government* (1948).
Mumford, Lewis, *The Culture o,.. Government and Administration* (1956).
Pontius, Dale, *State Supervision o) 's Cities* (1949).
(1942).
Robson, W. A., *Great Cities of the World*.
Schulz, Ernst B., *American City Government...ment; Its Development in Massachusetts*
Shaw, Frederick, *The History of the New York c.*
Snider, Clyde F., *County Government in Illinois*
Spicer, G. W., *Ten Years of County Manager Govern..*
Wager, Paul W. (ed.), *County Government Across th* (1954).
Wallace, Schuyler, *State Administrative Supervision Over*
(1928).   *a* (1945).
Woodbury, Coleman (ed.), *The Future of Cities and Urban Re...*).
—, *Urban Redevelopment; Problems and Practices* (1953).   *United States*
Works, George A., and Simon O. Lesser, *Rural America Today* (1942).
Zink, Harold, *Government of Cities in the United States* (1948).   '953).

XVI. STATE AND LOCAL GOVERNMENT FUNCTIONS

Ball, Carleton R., *Federal, State and Local Administrative Relationships in Agriculture* (1938).
Baum, Robert D., *The Federal Power Commission and State Utility Regulation* (1942).
Beach, Fred F., *The Functions of State Departments of Education* (1950).
Beckwith, Edmund R., and others, *Lawful Action of State Military Forces* (1944).
Bird, Frederick L., *A Study of the Port of New York Authority* (1949).
Blakey, Roy G., and Violet Johnson, *Sales Taxes and Other Excises* (1945).
Bollens, John C., *Administrative Organization of State Government in Michigan, Bulletin No. 5* (1936).
Buck, A. E., *The Reorganization of State Governments in the United States* (1938).
Buehler, Alfred G., *Public Finance* (1948).
Carpenter, W. S., *The Unfinished Business of Civil Service Reform* (1952).
Council of State Governments, *Securities Regulation in the Forty-eight States* (1942).
—, *The Forty-eight State School Systems* (1949).
—, *Reorganizing State Government* (1950).
—, *Higher Education in the Forty-eight States* (1952).
—, *Public Authorities in the States* (1953).
Crouch, Winston W., *State Aid to Local Government in California* (1939).
Fesler, J. W., *The Independence of State Regulatory Agencies* (1942).
Gagliardo, Domenico, *American Social Insurance* (1949).
Greene, Lee S., and others, *Rescued Earth: A Study of the Administration of Natural Resources in Tennessee* (1948).
Hardin, C. M., *Freedom in Agricultural Education* (1955).
Hiscock, I. V., *Community Health Organization* (1950).
International City Managers' Association, *Municipal Finance Administration* (1949).
Keesecker, Ward W., *State Boards of Education and Chief State School Officers* (1950).
Killingsworth, Charles C., *State Labor Relations Acts* (1948).
Kilpatrick, Wylie, *State Supervision of Local Budgeting* (1939).
—, *State Supervision of Local Finance* (1941).
Martin, Roscoe C., *The Growth of State Administration in Alabama* (1942).
Meriam, Lewis, *Relief and Social Security* (1946).
Monroe, Davd G., *State and Provincial Police* (1941).
Mustard, H. S., *Government in Public Health* (1945).

Owen, Wilfred, *Automotive Transportation* (1949).   ᴇ *Merit System in Illinois*
Paul, Randolph E., *Taxation in the United States* (19ᴦ
Pois, Joseph, Edward M. Martin, and Lyman ᶜ
    (1935).   ᴛᴏry *of Public Welfare in New York*
Porter, Kirk H., *State Administration* (193�
Schneider, David M., and Albert Deᵥ' ˢnd Alvin Blocksom Biscoe, *State Grants-in-
    State* (1938–1941).   ᴄ ᴠme *Tax* (1955).
Shavely, Tipton Ray, Duncan ᴀstration *in the United States* (1947).
    Aid in Virginia (193�Ꞓᴇ *United States* (1949).
Sigafoos, Robert A., *Theᴄ Services by Government—Local, State and Federal* (1946).
Smillie, W. G., *Publiᴄ Alice MacDonald, *State and Local Public Welfare Agencies*
Smith, Bruce, *Polᴊ
Stern, Bernhᵃᶜecent *Trends in State Grants-in-Aid and Shared Taxes* (1948).
Stevensonᴊᴊner, *Budgetary Methods in National and State Governments* (1938).
    ᴊon, Inc., *Constitutional Debt Control in the States* (1954).
Stoᴠᴜgust, *The Criminal* (1949).
    ᶜ and A. E. Parker, *Crime and the State Police* (1935).
ᴊgner, Paul, and Donald B. Hayman, *Resource Management in North Carolina* (1947).
Wilson, Orlando W., *Police Administration* (1950).

Author's note: This index carries the more frequently mentioned or more important things, places, people, and ideas of the text, and omits particulars that are only briefly mentioned or are of less importance.